T0180747

Lecture Notes in Computer Science 12491

More information about this subseries at http://www.springer.com/series/7410

Shiho Moriai · Huaxiong Wang (Eds.)

Advances in Cryptology – ASIACRYPT 2020

26th International Conference on the Theory
and Application of Cryptology and Information Security
Daejeon, South Korea, December 7–11, 2020
Proceedings, Part I

Springer

Editors
Shiho Moriai
Network Security Research Institute (NICT)
Tokyo, Japan

Huaxiong Wang [iD]
Nanyang Technological University
Singapore, Singapore

ISSN 0302-9743   ISSN 1611-3349   (electronic)
Lecture Notes in Computer Science
ISBN 978-3-030-64836-7   ISBN 978-3-030-64837-4   (eBook)
https://doi.org/10.1007/978-3-030-64837-4

LNCS Sublibrary: SL4 – Security and Cryptology

This Springer imprint is published by the registered company Springer Nature Switzerland AG
The registered company address is: Gewerbestrasse 11, 6330 Cham, Switzerland

Preface

The 26th Annual International Conference on Theory and Application of Cryptology and Information Security (ASIACRYPT 2020), was originally planned to be held in Daejeon, South Korea, during December 7–11, 2020. Due to the COVID-19 pandemic, it was shifted to an online-only virtual conference.

The conference focused on all technical aspects of cryptology, and was sponsored by the International Association for Cryptologic Research (IACR).

We received a total of 316 submissions from all over the world, the Program Committee (PC) selected 85 papers for publication in the proceedings of the conference. The two program chairs were supported by a PC consisting of 66 leading experts in aspects of cryptology. Each submission was reviewed by at least three PC members (or their sub-reviewers) and five PC members were assigned to submissions co-authored by PC members. The strong conflict of interest rules imposed by the IACR ensure that papers are not handled by PC members with a close working relationship with authors. The two program chairs were not allowed to submit a paper, and PC members were limited to two submissions each. There were approximately 390 external reviewers, whose input was critical to the selection of papers.

The review process was conducted using double-blind peer review. The conference operated a two-round review system with a rebuttal phase. After the reviews and first-round discussions, the PC selected 205 submissions to proceed to the second round, including 1 submission with early acceptance. The authors of 204 papers were then invited to provide a short rebuttal in response to the referee reports. The second round involved extensive discussions by the PC members.

The three volumes of the conference proceedings contain the revised versions of the 85 papers that were selected, together with the abstracts of 2 invited talks. The final revised versions of papers were not reviewed again and the authors are responsible for their contents.

The program of ASIACRYPT 2020 featured two excellent invited talks by Shweta Agrawal and Jung Hee Cheon. The conference also featured a rump session which contained short presentations on the latest research results of the field.

The PC selected three papers to receive the Best Paper Award, via a voting-based process that took into account conflicts of interest, which were solicited to submit the full versions to the *Journal of Cryptology*: "Finding Collisions in a Quantum World: Quantum Black-Box Separation of Collision-Resistance and One-Wayness" by Akinori Hosoyamada and Takashi Yamakawa; "New results on Gimli: full-permutation distinguishers and improved collisions" by Antonio Flórez Gutiérrez, Gaëtan Leurent, María Naya-Plasencia, Léo Perrin, André Schrottenloher, and Ferdinand Sibleyras; and "SQISign: Compact Post-Quantum signatures from Quaternions and Isogenies" by Luca De Feo, David Kohel, Antonin Leroux, Christophe Petit, and Benjamin Wesolowski.

Many people contributed to the success of ASIACRYPT 2020. We would like to thank the authors for submitting their research results to the conference. We are very grateful to the PC members and external reviewers for contributing their knowledge and expertise, and for the tremendous amount of work that was done with reading papers and contributing to the discussions. We are greatly indebted to Kwangjo Kim, the general chair, for his efforts and overall organization. We thank Michel Abdalla, McCurley, Kay McKelly, and members of the IACR's emergency pandemic team for their work in designing and running the virtual format. We thank Steve Galbraith, Joo Young Lee, and Yu Sasaki for expertly organizing and chairing the rump session. We are extremely grateful to Zhenzhen Bao for checking all the latex files and for assembling the files for submission to Springer. Finally, we thank Shai Halevi and the IACR for setting up and maintaining the Web Submission and Review software, used by IACR conferences for the paper submission and review process. We also thank Alfred Hofmann, Anna Kramer, and their colleagues at Springer for handling the publication of these conference proceedings.

December 2020
Shiho Moriai
Huaxiong Wang

Organization

General Chair

Kwangjo Kim — Korea Advanced Institute of Science and Technology (KAIST), South Korea

Program Chairs

Shiho Moriai — Network Security Research Institute (NICT), Japan
Huaxiong Wang — Nanyang Technological University, Singapore

Program Committee

Shweta Agrawal — IIT Madras, India
Gorjan Alagic — University of Maryland, USA
Shi Bai — Florida Atlantic University, USA
Zhenzhen Bao — Nanyang Technological University, Singapore
Paulo Barreto — University of Washington Tacoma, USA
Lejla Batina — Radboud University, The Netherlands
Amos Beimel — Ben-Gurion University, Israel
Sonia Belaïd — CryptoExperts, France
Olivier Blazy — University of Limoges, France
Jie Chen — East China Normal University, China
Yilei Chen — Visa Research, USA
Chen-Mou Cheng — Osaka University, Japan
Jun Furukawa — NEC Israel Research Center, Israel
David Galindo — University of Birmingham, Fetch.AI, UK
Jian Guo — Nanyang Technological University, Singapore
Swee-Huay Heng — Multimedia University, Malaysia
Xinyi Huang — Fujian Normal University, China
Andreas Hülsing — TU Eindhoven, The Netherlands
Takanori Isobe — University of Hyogo, Japan
David Jao — University of Waterloo, evolutionQ, Inc., Canada
Jérémy Jean — ANSSI, France
Zhengfeng Ji — University of Technology Sydney, Australia
Hyung Tae Lee — Jeonbuk National University, South Korea
Jooyoung Lee — KAIST, South Korea
Benoît Libert — CNRS, ENS, France
Dongdai Lin — Chinese Academy of Sciences, China
Helger Lipmaa — University of Tartu, Estonia, and Simula UiB, Norway
Feng-Hao Liu — Florida Atlantic University, USA

Giorgia Azzurra Marson	University of Bern, Switzerland, and NEC Laboratories Europe, Germany
Daniel Masny	Visa Research, USA
Takahiro Matsuda	AIST, Japan
Brice Minaud	Inria, ENS, France
Shiho Moriai	NICT, Japan
Kartik Nayak	Duke University, VMware Research, USA
Khoa Nguyen	Nanyang Technological University, Singapore
Svetla Nikova	KU Leuven, Belgium
Carles Padró	UPC, Spain
Jiaxin Pan	NTNU, Norway
Arpita Patra	Indian Institute of Science, India
Thomas Peters	UCL, Belgium
Duong Hieu Phan	University of Limoges, France
Raphael C.-W. Phan	Monash University, Malaysia
Josef Pieprzyk	CSIRO, Australia, and Institute of Computer Science, Polish Academy of Sciences, Poland
Ling Ren	VMware Research, University of Illinois at Urbana-Champaign, USA
Carla Ràfols	Universitat Pompeu Fabra, Spain
Rei Safavi-Naini	University of Calgary, Canada
Yu Sasaki	NTT laboratories, Japan
Jae Hong Seo	Hanyang University, South Korea
Ron Steinfeld	Monash University, Australia
Willy Susilo	University of Wollongong, Australia
Qiang Tang	New Jersey Institute of Technology, USA
Mehdi Tibouchi	NTT laboratories, Japan
Huaxiong Wang	Nanyang Technological University, Singapore
Xiaoyun Wang	Tsinghua University, China
Yongge Wang	The University of North Carolina at Charlotte, USA
Chaoping Xing	Shanghai Jiao Tong University, China, and NTU, Singapore
Yu Yu	Shanghai Jiao Tong University, China
Mark Zhandry	Princeton University, NTT Research, USA

External Reviewers

Behzad Abdolmaleki	Marcel Armour	Saikrishna Badrinarayanan
Parhat Abla	Gilad Asharov	
Mamun Akand	Man Ho Au	Mir Ali Rezazadeh Baee
Orestis Alpos	Benedikt Auerbach	Joonsang Baek
Hiroaki Anada	Khin Mi Mi Aung	Karim Baghery
Benny Applebaum	Sepideh Avizheh	Gustavo Banegas
Diego F. Aranha	Christian Badertscher	Laasya Bangalore

Subhadeep Banik
James Bartusek
Carsten Baum
Rouzbeh Behnia
Aner Ben-Efraim
Fabrice Benhamouda
Francesco Berti
Luk Bettale
Tim Beyne
Shivam Bhasin
Nina Bindel
Nir Bitansky
Xavier Bonnetain
Katharina Boudgoust
Florian Bourse
Zvika Brakerski
Jaqueline Brendel
Olivier Bronchain
Benedikt Bunz
Seyit Camtepe
Ignacio Cascudo
Gaëtan Cassiers
Suvradip Chakraborty
Jorge Chávez Saab
Hao Chen
Hua Chen
Long Chen
Rongmao Chen
Yu Chen
Yuan Chen
Ding-Yuan Cheng
Ji-Jian Chin
Seongbong Choi
Wonseok Choi
Ashish Choudhury
Sherman S. M. Chow
Heewon Chung
Michele Ciampi
Benoît Cogliati
Craig Costello
Nicholas Courtois
Geoffroy Couteau
Alain Couvreur
Daniele Cozzo
Hongrui Cui
Edouard Cuvelier

Jan Czajkowski
João Paulo da Silva
Jan-Pieter D'anvers
Joan Daemen
Ricardo Dahab
Nilanjan Datta
Bernardo David
Gareth Davies
Yi Deng
Amit Deo
Patrick Derbez
Siemen Dhooghe
Hang Dinh
Christoph Dobraunig
Javad Doliskani
Jelle Don
Xiaoyang Dong
Dung Duong
Betül Durak
Avijit Dutta
Sabyasachi Dutta
Sébastien Duval
Ted Eaton
Keita Emura
Muhammed F. Esgin
Thomas Espitau
Xiong Fan
Antonio Faonio
Prastudy Fauzi
Hanwen Feng
Shengyuan Feng
Tamara Finogina
Apostolos Fournaris
Ashley Fraser
Philippe Gaborit
Steven Galbraith
Pierre Galissant
Chaya Ganesh
Romain Gay
Chunpeng Ge
Kai Gellert
Nicholas Genise
Alexandru Gheorghiu
Hossein Ghodosi
Satrajit Ghosh
Benedikt Gierlichs

Kristian Gjøsteen
Aarushi Goel
Huijing Gong
Junqing Gong
Zheng Gong
Alonso González
Rishab Goyal
Benjamin Grégoire
Jiaxin Guan
Cyprien de Saint Guilhem
Aldo Gunsing
Chun Guo
Fuchun Guo
Qian Guo
Felix Günther
Ariel Hamlin
Ben Hamlin
Jinguang Han
Kyoohyung Han
Keisuke Hara
Debiao He
Chloé Hébant
Javier Herranz
Shoichi Hirose
Deukjo Hong
Akinori Hosoyamada
Hector Hougaard
Qiong Huang
Shih-Han Hung
Kathrin Hövelmanns
Akiko Inoue
Tetsu Iwata
Ashwin Jha
Dingding Jia
Shaoquan Jiang
Chanyang Ju
Eliran Kachlon
Saqib A. Kakvi
Ghassan Karame
Sabyasachi Karati
Angshuman Karmakar
Shuichi Katsumata
Marcel Keller
Dongwoo Kim
Jihye Kim
Jinsu Kim

Jiseung Kim
Jongkil Kim
Minkyu Kim
Myungsun Kim
Seongkwang Kim
Taechan Kim
Elena Kirshanova
Fuyuki Kitagawa
Susumu Kiyoshima
Michael Kloss
François Koeune
Lisa Kohl
Markulf Kohlweiss
Chelsea Komlo
Yashvanth Kondi
Nishat Koti
Toomas Krips
Veronika Kuchta
Thijs Laarhoven
Jianchang Lai
Qiqi Lai
Huy Quoc Le
Byeonghak Lee
Changmin Lee
Moon Sung Lee
Liang Li
Shuaishuai Li
Shun Li
Xiangxue Li
Xinyu Li
Ya-Nan Li
Zhe Li
Bei Liang
Cheng-Jun Lin
Fuchun Lin
Wei-Kai Lin
Dongxi Liu
Fukang Liu
Guozhen Liu
Jia Liu
Joseph K. Liu
Meicheng Liu
Qipeng Liu
Shengli Liu
Yunwen Liu
Zhen Liu

Julian Loss
Yuan Lu
Zhenliang Lu
Lin Lyu
Fermi Ma
Hui Ma
Xuecheng Ma
Bernardo Magri
Monosij Maitra
Christian Majenz
Nathan Manohar
Ange Martinelli
Zdenek Martinasek
Ramiro Martínez
Pedro Maat C. Massolino
Loïc Masure
Bart Mennink
Lauren De Meyer
Peihan Miao
Kazuhiko Minematsu
Rafael Misoczki
Tarik Moataz
Tal Moran
Tomoyuki Morimae
Hiraku Morita
Travis Morrison
Pratyay Mukherjee
Sayantan Mukherjee
Pierrick Méaux
Helen Möllering
Michael Naehrig
Yusuke Naito
Maria Naya-Plasencia
Ngoc Khanh Nguyen
Jianting Ning
Ryo Nishimaki
Ariel Nof
Kazuma Ohara
Daniel Esteban Escudero
    Ospina
Giorgos Panagiotakos
Bo Pang
Lorenz Panny
Anna Pappa
Anat Paskin-Cherniavsky
Alain Passelègue

Shravani Patil
Sikhar Patranabis
Kateryna Pavlyk
Alice Pellet-Mary
Geovandro Pereira
Thomas Peyrin
Phuong Pham
Stjepan Picek
Zaira Pindado
Rafael del Pino
Rachel Player
Geong Sen Poh
David Pointcheval
Yuriy Polyakov
Ali Poostindouz
Frédéric de Portzamparc
Chen Qian
Tian Qiu
Sai Rahul Rachuri
Adrian Ranea
Divya Ravi
Jean-René Reinhard
Peter Rindal
Francisco
    Rodríguez-Henríquez
Mélissa Rossi
Partha Sarathy Roy
Ajith S.
Yusuke Sakai
Kosei Sakamoto
Amin Sakzad
Simona Samardjiska
Olivier Sanders
Partik Sarkar
Santanu Sarkar
John Schanck
André Schrottenloher
Jacob Schuldt
Mahdi Sedaghat
Ignacio Amores Sesar
Siamak Shahandashti
Setareh Sharifian
Yaobin Shen
Sina Shiehian
Kazumasa Shinagawa
Janno Siim

Javier Silva
Ricardo Dahab
Siang Meng Sim
Leonie Simpson
Daniel Slamanig
Daniel Smith-Tone
Fang Song
Yongcheng Song
Florian Speelman
Akshayaram Srinivasan
Jun Xu
Igors Stepanovs
Ling Sun
Shi-Feng Sun
Akira Takahashi
Katsuyuki Takashima
Benjamin Hong
    Meng Tan
Syh-Yuan Tan
Titouan Tanguy
Adrian Thillard
Miaomiao Tian
Ivan Tjuawinata
Yosuke Todo
Alin Tomescu
Junichi Tomida
Ni Trieu
Viet Cuong Trinh
Ida Tucker
Aleksei Udovenko
Bogdan Ursu
Damien Vergnaud
Fernando Virdia

Srinivas Vivek
Misha Volkhov
Quoc Huy Vu
Alexandre Wallet
Ming Wan
Chenyu Wang
Han Wang
Junwei Wang
Lei Wang
Luping Wang
Qingju Wang
Weijia Wang
Wenhao Wang
Yang Wang
Yuyu Wang
Zhedong Wang
Gaven Watson
Florian Weber
Man Wei
Weiqiang Wen
Thom Wiggers
Zac Williamson
Lennert Wouters
Qianhong Wu
Keita Xagawa
Zejun Xiang
Hanshen Xiao
Xiang Xie
Yanhong Xu
Haiyang Xue
Shota Yamada
Takashi Yamakawa
Sravya Yandamuri

Jianhua Yan
Zhenbin Yan
Bo-Yin Yang
Guomin Yang
Kang Yang
Rupeng Yang
Shao-Jun Yang
Wei-Chuen Yau
Kisoon Yoon
Yong Yu
Zuoxia Yu
Chen Yuan
Tsz Hon Yuen
Aaram Yun
Alexandros Zacharakis
Michal Zajac
Luca Zanolini
Arantxa Zapico
Ming Zeng
Bin Zhang
Bingsheng Zhang
Cong Zhang
Hailong Zhang
Jiang Zhang
Liang Feng Zhang
Xue Zhang
Zhenfei Zhang
Zhifang Zhang
Changan Zhao
Yongjun Zhao
Zhongxiang Zheng
Yihong Zhu
Arne Tobias Ødegaard

Abstracts of Invited Talks

Unlikely Friendships: The Fruitful Interplay of Cryptographic Assumptions

Shweta Agrawal[1]

IIT Madras, India
shweta.a@cse.iitm.ac.in

Abstract. The security of cryptographic protocols is based on the conjectured intractability of some mathematical problem, typically a *single* problem. However, in some cases, novel constructions emerge out of the surprising interplay of seemingly disparate mathematical structures and conjectured hard problems on these. Though unusual, this cooperation between assumptions, when it happens, can lead to progress on important open problems. This sometimes paves the way for subsequent improvements, which may even eliminate the multiplicity and reduce security to a single assumption.

In this talk, we will examine some interesting examples of the above phenomenon. An early example can be found in the primitive of fully homomorphic encryption (**FHE**), where Gentry and Halevi (FOCS, 2011) provided a beautiful construction that eliminated the "squashing" step from Gentry's original **FHE** blueprint (STOC, 2009) by designing a hybrid of "somewhat homomorphic encryption" based on Learning with Errors (**LWE**), and "multiplicatively homomorphic encryption", based on Decision Diffie Hellman (**DDH**). More recently, Agrawal and Yamada (EUROCRYPT 2020) provided the first construction of optimal broadcast encryption from standard assumptions, by leveraging a serendipitous interplay of **LWE** and assumptions based on bilinear maps. Lastly, we will examine some very recent constructions of indistinguishability obfuscation which rely on such interaction – the construction by Brakerski *et al* (EUROCRYPT 2020) and subsequent improvement by Gay and Pass (Eprint 2020), based on **LWE** and the Decisional Composite Residues (**DCR**) problem, and the construction by Jain, Lin and Sahai (Eprint 2020) which is based on **LWE**, Symmetric eXternal Diffie Hellman (**SXDH**). Learning Parity with Noise (**LPN**) and the existence of Boolean **PRG** with polynomial stretch in NC_0.

We will conclude with a discussion about future directions.

---

[1] Supported by the Swarnajayanti fellowship and an Indo-French Cefipra grant.

Approximate Computation on Encrypted Data

Jung Hee Cheon

Department of Math and RIM, Seoul National University, Korea

Abstract. Homomorphic encryption (HE) has been in the limelight as a perfect tool for privacy since 1978. Not only the theoretic depth and beauty, but also the plenty of applications beyond the classical ones make this primitive so attractive. Privacy preserving machine learning is not a dream anymore with homomorphic encryption, not to mention private AIs. In this invited talk, we will briefly review the 40+ years of homomorphic encryptions and several important steps toward secure and practical HE. We then proceed to survey on a variety of applications of HE, especially focusing on the recent development of approximate HE and approximate computation on encrypted data. Interestingly, it rekindled our interest in the old mathematical problem of polynomial approximation of an arbitrary function from different aspects and suggests us a new research area. We conclude with several real-world applications, ongoing standardization activities and some possible future directions.

Contents – Part I

Post-quantum Cryptography

Cryptanalysis

Symmetric Key Cryptography

Message Authentication Codes

Side-Channel Analysis

Contents – Part II

Isogeny-Based Cryptography

Quantum Algorithms

Authenticated Key Exchange

Contents – Part III

Zero Knowledge

Blockchains and Contact Tracing

Best Paper Awards

Finding Collisions in a Quantum World: Quantum Black-Box Separation of Collision-Resistance and One-Wayness

Akinori Hosoyamada[1,2]([✉]) and Takashi Yamakawa[1]

[1] NTT Secure Platform Laboratories, Tokyo, Japan
{akinori.hosoyamada.bh,takashi.yamakawa.ga}@hco.ntt.co.jp
[2] Nagoya University, Nagoya, Japan
hosoyamada.akinori@nagoya-u.jp

Abstract. Since the celebrated work of Impagliazzo and Rudich (STOC 1989), a number of black-box impossibility results have been established. However, these works only ruled out classical black-box reductions among cryptographic primitives. Therefore it may be possible to overcome these impossibility results by using quantum reductions. To exclude such a possibility, we have to extend these impossibility results to the quantum setting. In this paper, we study black-box impossibility in the quantum setting.

We first formalize a quantum counterpart of fully-black-box reduction following the formalization by Reingold, Trevisan and Vadhan (TCC 2004). Then we prove that there is no quantum fully-black-box reduction from collision-resistant hash functions to one-way permutations (or even trapdoor permutations). We take both of classical and quantum implementations of primitives into account. This is an extension to the quantum setting of the work of Simon (Eurocrypt 1998) who showed a similar result in the classical setting.

Keywords: Post-quantum cryptography · One-way permutation · One-way trapdoor permutation · Collision resistant hash function · Fully black-box reduction · Quantum reduction · Impossibility

1 Introduction

1.1 Background

Black-Box Impossibility. Reductions among cryptographic primitives are fundamental in cryptography. For example, we know reductions from pseudorandom generators, pseudorandom functions, symmetric key encryptions, and digital signatures to one-way functions (OWF). On the other hand, there are some important cryptographic primitives including collision-resistant hash functions (CRH), key-exchanges, public key encryption (PKE), oblivious transfer, and non-interactive zero-knowledge proofs, for which there are no known reductions to OWF. Given this situation, we want to ask if it is impossible to reduce

© International Association for Cryptologic Research 2020
S. Moriai and H. Wang (Eds.): ASIACRYPT 2020, LNCS 12491, pp. 3–32, 2020.
https://doi.org/10.1007/978-3-030-64837-4_1

these primitives to OWF. We remark that under the widely believed assumption that these primitives exist, OWF "imply" these primitives (i.e., these primitives are "reduced" to OWF) in a trivial sense. Therefore to make the question meaningful, we have to somehow restrict types of reductions.

For this purpose, Impagliazzo and Rudich [IR89] introduced the notion of *black-box reductions*. Roughly speaking, a black-box reduction is a reduction that uses an underlying primitive and an adversary in a black-box manner (i.e., use them just as oracles).[1] They proved that there does not exist a black-box reduction from key-exchange protocols (and especially PKE) to one-way permutations (OWP). They also observed that most existing reductions between cryptographic primitives are black-box. Thus their result can be interpreted as an evidence that we cannot construct key-exchange protocols based on OWP with commonly used techniques. After their seminal work, there have been numerous impossibility results of black-box reductions (See Sect. 1.4 for details).

Post-quantum and Quantum Cryptography. In 1994. Shor [Sho94] showed that we can efficiently compute integer factorization and discrete logarithm, whose hardness are the basis of widely used cryptographic systems, by using a quantum computer. After that, post-quantum cryptography, which treats classically computable cryptographic schemes that resist quantum attacks, has been intensively studied (e.g., [McE78, Ajt96, Reg05, JF11]). Indeed, NIST has recently started a standardization of post-quantum cryptography [NIS16]. We refer more detailed survey of post-quantum cryptography to [BL17].

As another direction to use quantum computer in cryptography, there have been study of quantum cryptography, in which even honest algorithms also use quantum computers. They include quantum key distribution [BB84], quantum encryption [ABF+16, AGM18], quantum (fully) homomorphic encryption [BJ15, Mah18, Bra18], quantum copy-protection [Aar09], quantum digital signatures [GC01], quantum money [Wie83, AC12, Zha19], etc. We refer more detailed survey of quantum cryptography to [BS16].

Our Motivation: Black-Box Impossibility in a Quantum World. In this paper, we consider black-box impossibility in a quantum setting where primitives and adversaries are quantum, and a reduction has quantum access to them.

Quantum reductions are sometimes more powerful than classical reductions. For example, Regev [Reg05] gave a quantum reduction from the learning with errors (LWE) problem to the decision version of the shortest vector problem (GapSVP) or the shortest independent vectors problem (SIVP). We note that there are some follow-up works that give classical reduction between these problems in some parameter settings [Pei09, BLP+13], but we still do not know any

---

[1] This is an explanation for *fully-black-box reduction* using the terminology of Reingold, Trevisan, and Vadhan [RTV04]. Since we only consider fully-black-box reductions in this paper, in this introduction, we just say black-box reduction to mean fully-black-box reduction.

classical reduction that works in the same parameter setting as the quantum one by Regev. This example illustrates that quantum reductions are sometimes more powerful than classical reductions even if all problem instances (e.g., implementations of primitives, adversaries, and reduction algorithms) are classical. Therefore it may be possible to overcome black-box impossibility results shown in the classical setting by using quantum reductions.

Since quantum computers may also be used to implement cryptographic primitives in the near future, it is of much interest to study how the classical impossibility results change in the quantum setting. In particular, it is theoretically very important to study whether the impossibility of black-box reductions from CRH to OWP shown by Simon [Sim98], which is one of the most fundamental results on impossibility and revisited in many follow-up works [HR04, HHRS07, AS15], can be overcome in the quantum setting. Despite the importance of the problem, the (im)possibility of the quantum reductions has not been studied.

1.2 Our Results

This paper shows that the impossibility of black-box reductions from CRH to OWP cannot be overcome in the quantum setting. First, we formally define the notion of quantum black-box reduction based on the work by Reingold, Trevisan and Vadhan [RTV04], which gave a formal framework for the notion of black-box reductions in the classical setting. Then we prove the following theorem.

Theorem 1 (informal). *There does not exist a quantum black-box reduction from CRH to OWP.*

We note that though we do not know any candidate of OWP that resists quantum attacks, the above theorem is still meaningful since it also rules out quantum black-box reductions from CRH to OWF (since OWP is also OWF) and there exist many candidates of post-quantum OWF. This theorem is stated with OWP instead of OWF just because this makes the theorem stronger.

We also extend the result to obtain the following theorem.

Theorem 2 (informal). *There does not exist a quantum black-box reduction from CRH to trapdoor permutations (TDP).*

Note that our results do not require any unproven assumptions nor the existence of any oracles. Some oracles are introduced in our proofs, but they are just technical tools.

Remark 1. In this paper, by quantum black-box reduction we denote reductions that have quantum black-box oracle accesses to primitives. We always consider security of primitives against quantum adversaries, and do not discuss primitives that are only secure against classical adversaries. In addition, since our main goal is to show the impossibility of reductions from CRH to OWP and CRH to TDP, and when we consider primitives with interactions in the quantum setting we have some subtle issues that do not matter in the classical setting (e.g., rewinding is sometimes hard in the quantum setting [ARU14]), we treat only primitives such that both of the primitives themselves and security games are non-interactive.

1.3   Technical Overview

Here, we give a brief technical overview of our results. We focus on the proof of Theorem 1 since Theorem 2 can be proven by a natural (yet non-trivial) extension of that of Theorem 1. We remark that we omit many details and often rely on non-rigorous arguments for intuitive explanations in this subsection.

First, we recall the *two-oracle technique*, which is a technique to rule out black-box reductions among cryptographic primitives in the classical setting introduced by Hsiao and Reyzin [HR04]. Roughly speaking, they showed that a black-box reduction from a primitive $\mathcal{P}$ to another primitive $\mathcal{Q}$ does not exist if there exist oracles Φ and Ψ^Φ such that $\mathcal{Q}$ exists and $\mathcal{P}$ does not exist relative to these oracles. As our first contribution, we show that a similar argument carries over to the quantum setting if we appropriately define primitives and black-box reductions in the quantum setting.

For proving the separation between CRH and OWP, we consider oracles $\Phi = f$, which is a random permutation over $\{0,1\}^n$, and $\Psi^\Phi = \mathsf{ColFinder}^f$, which is an oracle that finds a collision of any function described by an oracle-aided quantum circuit C that accesses f as an oracle by brute-force similarly to the previous works in the classical setting [Sim98, HHRS07, AS15]. CRH does not exist relative to f and $\mathsf{ColFinder}^f$ since we can compute a collision for any (efficiently computable length-decreasing) function C^f by querying C to $\mathsf{ColFinder}^f$. Thus, what is left is to prove that a random permutation f is hard to invert even if an adversary is given an additional oracle access to $\mathsf{ColFinder}^f$.

We first recall how this was done in the classical setting based on the proof in [AS15].[2] The underlying idea behind the proof is a very simple information theoretic fact often referred to as the "compression argument," which dates back to the work of Gennaro and Trevisan [GT00]: if we can encode a truth table of a random permutation into an encoding that can be decoded to the original truth table with high probability, then the size of the encoding should be almost as large as that of the truth table. Based on this, the strategy of the proof is to encode a truth table of f into an encoding that consists of a "partial truth table" of f that specifies values of $f(x)$ for all $x \in \{0,1\}^n \backslash G$ for an appropriately chosen subset G so that one can decode the encoding to the original truth table by recovering "forgotten values" of $f(x)$ on $x \in G$ by using the power of an adversary $\mathcal{A}$ that inverts the permutation f with oracle accesses to f and $\mathsf{ColFinder}^f$. What is non-trivial in the proof is that the decoding procedure has to simulate oracles f and $\mathsf{ColFinder}^f$ for $\mathcal{A}$ whereas the encoding only contains

---

[2]   Though the basic idea is similar to the proof of Simon [Sim98], we explain the description in [AS15] since this is more suitable for explaining how we extend the proof to the quantum setting.

a partial truth table of f. To overcome this issue, they demonstrated a very clever way of choosing the subset G such that the simulation of oracles f and $\mathsf{ColFinder}^f$ does not require values of f on G. Especially, they showed that the larger $\mathcal{A}$'s success probability is, the larger the subset G is, i.e., the smaller the encoding size is. By using the lower bound of the encoding size obtained by the compression argument, they upper bound $\mathcal{A}$'s success probability by a negligible function in n.

Unfortunately, their proof cannot be directly extended to the quantum setting since the choice of the subset G crucially relies on the fact that queries by $\mathcal{A}$ are classical. Indeed, $\mathcal{A}$ may query a uniform superposition of all inputs to the oracle f, in which case it is impossible to perfectly simulate the oracle f with a partial truth table. Thus, instead of directly generalizing their proof to the quantum setting, we start from another work by Nayebi et al. [NABT15], which showed that it is hard to invert a random permutation f with a quantum oracle access to f.[3] The proof strategy of their work is similar to the above, and they also rely on the compression argument, but a crucial difference is that they choose the subset G in a randomized way.[4] Specifically, they first choose a random subset $R \subset \{0,1\}^n$ of a certain size, and define G as the set of x such that (1): $x \in R$, (2): $\mathcal{A}$ succeeds in inverting $f(x)$ with high probability, and (3): query magnitudes of $\mathcal{A}$ on any element in $R \backslash \{x\}$ is sufficiently small. The condition (3) implies that $\mathcal{A}$ is still likely to succeed in inverting $f(x)$ even if the function (oracle) f is replaced with any function f' that agrees with f on $\{0,1\}^n \backslash (R \backslash \{x\})$.[5] Especially, a decoder can use the function h_y that agrees with f on $\{0,1\}^n \backslash G$ and returns y on G instead of the original oracle f when it runs $\mathcal{A}$ on an input $y \in f(G)$. Since the function h_y can be implemented by the partial truth table of f on $\{0,1\}^n \backslash G$, the decoder can simulate the oracle for $\mathcal{A}$ to correctly invert y in f for each $y \in f(G)$, which implies that the decoder can recover the original truth table of f from the partial truth table. Finally, they showed that an appropriate choice of parameters gives a lower bound of the size of G, which in turn gives an upper bound of $\mathcal{A}$'s success probability based on the compression argument.

For our purpose, we have to prove that a random permutation is hard to invert for a quantum adversary $\mathcal{A}$ even if it is given a quantum access to the additional oracle $\mathsf{ColFinder}^f$. Here, we make a simplifying assumption that the oracle $\mathsf{ColFinder}^f$ is only classically accessible since this case conveys our essential idea and can be readily generalized to the quantumly accessible case. For generalizing the proof of [NABT15] to our case, we have to find a way to simulate $\mathsf{ColFinder}^f$ by using the partial truth table of f on $\{0,1\}^n \backslash G$.

Before describing our strategy about how to simulate $\mathsf{ColFinder}^f$, here we give its more detailed definition: At the beginning of each game before $\mathcal{A}$ runs

---

[3] Actually, they showed that a random permutation is hard to invert even given a classical advice string.

[4] Such a randomized encoder was also used in some works in the classical setting, e.g., [DTT10].

[5] Formally, this is proven by using the swapping lemma shown by Vazirani [Vaz98, Lem. 3.1].

relative to $\mathsf{ColFinder}^f$, two permutations $\pi_C^{(1)}, \pi_C^{(2)} \in \mathsf{Perm}(\{0,1\}^m)$ are chosen uniformly at random for each circuit C ($\{0,1\}^m$ is the domain of the function C^f). On each input C, $\mathsf{ColFinder}^f$ runs the following procedures:

1. Set $w^{(1)} \leftarrow \pi_C^{(1)}(0^m)$.
2. Compute $u = C^f(w^{(1)})$ by running the circuit C relative to f on $w^{(1)}$.
3. Find the minimum t such that $C^f(\pi_C^{(2)}(t)) = u$ by running the circuit C relative to f on the input $\pi_C^{(2)}(i)$ and checking whether $C^f(\pi_C^{(2)}(i)) = u$ holds for $i = 0, 1, 2 \ldots$, sequentially. Set $w^{(2)} \leftarrow \pi_C^{(2)}(t)$.
4. Return $(w^{(1)}, w^{(2)}, u)$.

Next, we explain our strategy to simulate $\mathsf{ColFinder}^f$. Given a query (circuit) C and an (appropriately produced) partial truth table of f, the simulator works similarly to $\mathsf{ColFinder}$ except that it uses the partial truth table instead of f to simulate outputs of C. For making sure that this results in a correct simulation of $\mathsf{ColFinder}^f$, we require the following two properties:

P1. Given $w^{(1)}$ and $w^{(2)} = \pi_C^{(2)}(t)$, the simulator computes the value $C^f(w^{(1)}) = C^f(w^{(2)}) = u$ correctly.

P2. For $i < t$, the simulator does not misjudges that "the value $C^f(\pi_C^{(2)}(i))$ is equal to u".

The first property P1 is obviously necessary to simulate $\mathsf{ColFinder}^f$. The second property P2 is also indispensable since, if it is not satisfied, there is a possibility that the simulator responds with a wrong answer $(w^{(1)}, \pi_C(i), u)$. We have to make sure that the properties P1 and P2 will hold as well when we design our encoder (or, equivalently, how to choose $G \subset \{0,1\}^n$).

Let us explain how to encode the truth table of each permutation f into its partial table. We choose another random subset $R' \subset \{0,1\}^n$ of a certain size and require two additional conditions for x to be in G: (4): $x \in R'$ and (5): All oracle-aided quantum circuits C queried by $\mathcal{A}$ when it runs on input $f(x)$ are "good" w.r.t. (R', x) in the following sense.[6] We say that C is good w.r.t. (R', x) if query magnitudes of C on any element of $R' \backslash \{x\}$ is "small" when C runs on input $w^{(1)}$ or $w^{(2)}$ relative to f, where $(w^{(1)}, w^{(2)})$ is the collision found by $\mathsf{ColFinder}^f$. Finally, we encode f into the partial truth table that specifies the value of $f(x)$ if and only if $x \in \{0,1\}^n \backslash G$.

Intuitively, the condition (5) implies that a collision $(w^{(1)}, w^{(2)})$ found by $\mathsf{ColFinder}^f$ for any $\mathcal{A}$'s query C is not likely to change even if its oracle f is replaced with any function f' that just agrees with f on $\{0,1\}^n \backslash (R' \backslash \{x\})$, which implies that the property P1 is satisfied. In our proof, suitable permutations $\pi_C^{(1)}$ and $\pi_C^{(2)}$ are fixed and the decoder have the truth table of them. In particular, the decoder knows the correct $w^{(1)} = \pi_C^{(1)}(0^m)$ for each C, and can compute the correct $u = C^f(w^{(1)})$ since the outputs of $C^{f'}(w^{(1)})$ is likely to be the same

---

[6] The definition of "good" given here corresponds to the negation of "bad" defined in the main body.

value as $C^f(w^{(1)})$ if f' agrees with f on $\{0,1\}^n \setminus (R' \setminus \{x\})$ due to the definition of goodness of C.

Thus, in this case, the oracle $\mathsf{ColFinder}^f$ seems to be simulatable with the partial truth table of f on $\{0,1\}^n \setminus G$. However, there is an issue: It is not trivial how to ensure that the property P2 holds. Note that the property P2 holds and the issue is resolved if we can ensure that the simulator judges "I cannot compute the correct value $C^f(\pi_C^{(2)}(i))$" (instead of misjudging "the value $C^f(\pi_C^{(2)}(i))$ is u" for some $i < t$) when the given partial table of f does not contain enough information to compute the value $C^f(\pi_C^{(2)}(i))$. We can easily ensure it in the classical setting by measuring the queries made by C and judging that "the information is not enough" if the value $f(x)$ is not defined in the partial table for a query x made by C. However, it is highly non-trivial how to ensure it in the quantum setting since measuring queries may disturb C's computations significantly, and $\mathsf{ColFinder}^f$ runs C on $\pi_C^{(2)}(i)$ for (possibly exponentially) many i until it finds the minimum t such that $C^f(\pi_C^{(2)}(t)) = u$, in which case its total query magnitude on $R' \setminus \{x\}$ is not always small.[7]

We overcome the issue by introducing a new technique. Specifically, whenever the simulation algorithm picks i, it checks whether the partial truth table contains enough information to compute the correct value of $C^f(\pi_C^{(2)}(i))$ by running C on the input $\pi_C^{(2)}(i)$ relative to f' for all possible permutations f' that are consistent with the given partial truth table of f on $\{0,1\}^n \setminus (R' \setminus \{x\})$, and judges that "the partial truth table contains enough information to compute the correct value of $C^f(\pi_C^{(2)}(i))$" only if the outputs of $C^{f'}(\pi_C^{(2)}(i))$ are the same value for all possible oracles f'. (Otherwise, it judges that "The partial truth table does not contain enough information to compute the correct value of $C^f(\pi_C^{(2)}(i))$" and do the same again for the next index $(i+1)$.) This procedure prevents the simulation algorithm from outputting a "wrong" collision $(w^{(1)}, \pi_C^{(2)}(i))$ that is different from $(w^{(1)}, w^{(2)})$ and the property P2 is satisfied since the actual function f is one of the candidates of f' with which the validity of the collision is checked. On the other hand, the correct collision $(w^{(1)}, w^{(2)})$ cannot be judged to be a wrong one since the outputs of $C^{f'}(w^{(2)})$ are likely to be the same value for all f' due to the definition of goodness of C.

In this way, we can simulate both oracles f and $\mathsf{ColFinder}^f$ by using the partial truth table of f on $\{0,1\}^n \setminus G$. Similarly to the proof in [NABT15], an appropriate choice of parameters enables us to upper bound $\mathcal{A}$'s success probability by a negligible function in n. This implies that OWP exists relative to oracles f and $\mathsf{ColFinder}^f$, and thus there does not exist a black-box reduction from CRH to OWP.

We believe that our new technique can be used in more and more applications when we want to apply compression arguments with some complex oracles (such as $\mathsf{ColFinder}$) in the quantum setting.

---

[7] Note that we consider information theoretic encoder and decoder, and we do not care whether they run efficiently.

1.4 Related Work

Rotem and Segev [RS18] showed a limitation of black-box impossibility by giving an example that overcomes the black-box impossibility result by Rudich [Rud88] by using a non-black-box reduction. Nonetheless, black-box impossibility results are still meaningful since we know very limited number of non-black-box techniques. Indeed, they left it as an open problem to overcome the black-box separation of CRH and OWP shown by Simon [Sim98].

Bitansky and Degwekar [BD19] gave a new proof for the black-box separation of CRH from OWP in the classical setting, which is conceptually different from previous ones [Sim98, HHRS07, AS15]. However, it is unclear if their proof extends to the quantum setting.

Holmgren and Lombardi [HL18] gave a construction of CRH based on a stronger variant of OWF which they call one-way product functions (OWPF). However, since they do not give a construction of OWPF from OWF (or OWP) even with exponential security, their result does not overcome the impossibility result by Simon [Sim98].

Chia, Hallgren and Song [CHS18] considered the problem of separating OWP from NP hardness in the quantum setting. They ruled out a special type of quantum reductions called locally random reductions under a certain complexity theoretic assumption. We note that in our work, we do not put any restriction on a type of a reduction as long as it is quantum fully-black-box, and we do not assume any unproven assumption. Also, they focus on the separation of OWP from NP hardness, and do not give a general definition of black-box reduction in the quantum setting. Thus their work is incomparable to ours.

Hhan et al. [HXY19] also used the compression technique in the quantum setting to analyze the quantum random oracle model in the presence of auxiliary information. A crucial difference between their work and this work is that they consider a setting where an adversary is given an auxiliary information which is fixed at the beginning of a security game whereas we consider a setting where an adversary can adaptively make a query to the quantum oracle ColFinder during the game. Thus, our results are incomparable to theirs.

See Sect. 1.4 of this paper's full version [HY18] for more about related works.

1.5 Paper Organization

Section 2 describes notations, definitions, and fundamental technical lemmas that are used throughout the paper. Section 3 gives formalizations of quantum primitives and quantum fully-black-box reductions. Section 4 shows the impossibility of quantum fully-black-box reductions from CRH to OWP. Section 5 shows the impossibility of quantum fully-black-box reductions from CRH to TDP.

2 Preliminaries

A classical algorithm is a classical Turing machine, and an efficient classical algorithm is a probabilistic efficient Turing machine. We denote the set of positive integers by $\mathbb{N}$. We write A instead of $A \otimes I$ for short, for any linear operator A. For sets

X and Y, let $\mathsf{Func}(X, Y)$ denote the set of functions from X to Y, and $\mathsf{Perm}(X)$ denote the set of permutations on X. Let $\Delta(f, g)$ denote the set $\{x \in X | f(x) \neq g(x)\}$ for any functions $f, g \in \mathsf{Func}(X, Y)$. Let $\{0, 1\}^*$ denote the set $\cup_{n \geq 1} \{0, 1\}^n$, and by abuse of notation we let $\mathsf{Perm}(\{0, 1\}^*)$ denote the set of permutations $\{P : \{0, 1\}^* \to \{0, 1\}^* | P(\{0, 1\}^n) = \{0, 1\}^n \text{ for each } n \geq 1\}$. When we say that $f : \{0, 1\}^* \to \{0, 1\}^*$ is a permutation, we assume that $f(\{0, 1\}^n) = \{0, 1\}^n$ holds for each n, and thus f is in $\mathsf{Perm}(\{0, 1\}^*)$ (i.e., in this paper we do not treat permutations such that there exist $n \neq n'$ and $x \in \{0, 1\}^n$ such that $f(x) \in \{0, 1\}^{n'}$). We say that a function $f : \mathbb{N} \to \mathbb{R}$ is negligible if, for any positive integer c, $f(n) \leq n^{-c}$ holds for all sufficiently large n, and we write $f(n) \leq \mathsf{negl}(n)$.

2.1   Quantum Algorithms

We refer basics of quantum computation to [NC10, KSVV02]. In this paper, we use the computational model of quantum circuits. Let $\mathcal{Q}$ be the standard basis of quantum circuits [KSVV02]. We assume that quantum circuits (without oracle) are constructed over the standard basis $\mathcal{Q}$, and define the size of a quantum circuit as the total number of elements in $\mathcal{Q}$ used to construct it. Let $|C|$ denote the size of each quantum circuit C. An oracle-aided quantum circuit is a quantum circuit with oracle gates. When an oracle-aided quantum circuit is implemented relative to an oracle O represented by a unitary operator, the oracle gates are replaced by the unitary operator. When there are multiple oracles, each oracle gate should specify an index of an oracle. In this paper, we assume that all oracles are stateless, that is, the behavior of the oracle is independent from a previous history and the same for all queries. For a stateless quantum oracle O, we often identify the oracle and a unitary operator that represents the oracle, and use the same notation O for both of them. Note that each classical algorithm can be regarded as a quantum algorithm. We fix an encoding $\mathcal{E}$ of (oracle-aided) quantum circuits to bit strings, and we identify $\mathcal{E}(C)$ with C. For a quantum circuit C, we will denote the event that we measure an output z when we run C on an input x and measure the final state by $C(x) = z$.

First, we define quantum algorithms. We note that we only consider classical-input-output quantum algorithms.

Definition 1 (Quantum algorithms). *A quantum algorithm $\mathcal{A}$ is a family of quantum circuits $\{\mathcal{A}_n\}_{n \in \mathbb{N}}$ that acts on a quantum system $\mathcal{H}_n = \mathcal{H}_{n,in} \otimes \mathcal{H}_{n,out} \otimes \mathcal{H}_{n,work}$ for each n. When we feed $\mathcal{A}$ with an input $x \in \{0, 1\}^n$, $\mathcal{A}$ runs the circuit $\mathcal{A}_n$ on the initial state $|x\rangle |0\rangle |0\rangle$, measures the final state with the computational basis, and outputs the measurement result of the register which corresponds to $\mathcal{H}_{n,out}$. We say that $\mathcal{A}$ is an efficient quantum algorithm if it is a family of polynomial-size quantum circuits, i.e., there is a polynomial $\lambda(n)$ such that $|\mathcal{A}_n| \leq \lambda(n)$ for all sufficiently large n.*

Remark 2. Though we use a Turing machine for a computational model of classical computation, we use a quantum circuit for a computational model of quantum computation. This is just because quantum circuits are better studied than quantum Turing machines [Yao93], and are easier to treat. We remark that we do not intend to rule out reductions with full non-uniform techniques as was done in [CLMP13].

Next, we define oracle-aided quantum algorithms, which are quantum algorithms that can access to oracles.

Definition 2 (Oracle-aided quantum algorithms). *An oracle-aided quantum algorithm* $\mathcal{A}$ *is a family of oracle aided quantum circuits* $\{\mathcal{A}_n\}_{n \in \mathbb{N}}$ *that acts on a quantum system* $\mathcal{H}_n = \mathcal{H}_{n,in} \otimes \mathcal{H}_{n,out} \otimes \mathcal{H}_{n,work}$ *for each* n. *Let* $O_1 = \{O_{1,i}\}_{i \in \mathbb{N}}, ..., O_t = \{O_{t,i}\}_{i \in \mathbb{N}}$ *be families of quantum oracle gates. When we feed* $\mathcal{A}$ *with an input* $x \in \{0,1\}^n$ *relative to oracles* $(O_1, ..., O_t)$, $\mathcal{A}$ *runs the circuit* $\mathcal{A}_n^{O_{1,n}, ..., O_{t,n}}$ *on the initial state* $|x\rangle|0\rangle|0\rangle$, *measures the final state with the computational basis, and outputs the measurement result of the register which corresponds to* $\mathcal{H}_{n,out}$.[8] *We note that an oracle-aided quantum circuit* $\mathcal{A}_n^{O_{1,n}, ..., O_{t,n}}$ *that makes* q *queries can be described by a unitary operator*

$$\mathcal{A}_n^{O_{1,n}, ..., O_{t,n}} = \left(\prod_{j=1}^{q(n)} (U_{j,t,n} O_{t,n} \ldots U_{j,1,n} O_{1,n}) \right) U_{0,n}, \tag{1}$$

where $(U_{0,n}, \{U_{j,1,n}, \ldots, U_{j,t,n}\}_{j \in [q]})$ *are some unitary operators.*

Remark 3. We also often consider an oracle access to a quantum algorithm. This is interpreted as an oracle access to a unitary operator that represents $\mathcal{A}$.

Next, we define *randomized quantum oracles*, which are quantum oracles that flip classical random coins before algorithms start.

Definition 3 (Randomized quantum oracles). *Let* R_n *be a finite set for each* n, *and* $R := \prod_{n=1}^{\infty} R_n$ *(note that each element* $r \in R$ *is an infinite sequence* $(r_1, r_2, \cdots)$). *A randomized quantum oracle* $O := \{O_r\}_{r \in R}$ *is a family of quantum oracles such that* $O_{r,n} = O_{r',n}$ *if* $r_n = r'_n$. *When we feed* $\mathcal{A}$ *with an input* $x \in \{0,1\}^n$ *relative to* O, *first* r_n *is randomly chosen from the finite set* R_n *(according to some distribution), and then* $\mathcal{A}$ *runs the circuit* $\mathcal{A}_n^{O_{r,n}}$ *on the initial state* $|x\rangle|0\rangle|0\rangle$. *We denote* $O_{r,n}$ *by* O_{r_n} *and* $\{O_{r_n}\}_{r_n \in R_n}$ *by* O_n, *respectively, and identify* O *with* $\{O_n\}_{n \in \mathbb{N}}$.[9]

---

[8] We assume that the queries are always performed in a sequential order (e.g., before each query to O_2, the adversary always makes a query to O_1), but there is no reason for an adversary to fix the order. We assume this only for an ease of notation. There are multiple ways to fix it, but changes of the order does not essentially affect (im)possibility of reductions.

[9] Note that the meaning of the symbol O_X changes depending on the set that the index X belongs to. R_n is the set of random coins for the security parameter n, and each coin $r_n \in R_n$ corresponds to one fixed unitary operator O_{r_n}. O_r is an infinite family $\{O_{r_1}, O_{r_2}, \dots\}$ for each fixed $r = (r_1, r_2, \dots) \in R$, and O_n is the finite family $\{O_{r_n}\}_{r_n \in R_n}$ for each fixed n. Each of O_r and O_n can be regarded as a subset of O. In addition, $O_{r,n}$ denotes "the n-th element of O_r" for each fixed r, which is the same as O_{r_n}.

Similarly, when $\mathcal{A}$ is given oracle access to multiple randomized oracles $(O_1, \ldots, O_t)$, we consider that an oracle gate is randomly chosen and fixed for each of the t oracles before $\mathcal{A}$ starts. The distributions of $O_1, \ldots, O_t$ can be highly dependent.

Remark 4 Later we consider the situation that a quantum algorithm $\mathcal{A}$ has access to a randomized quantum oracle O, and another quantum algorithm $\mathcal{B}$ has access to $\mathcal{A}^O$. This is interpreted as follows: Before $\mathcal{B}$ starts, $r_n \in R_n$ is chosen uniformly at random, and $\mathcal{B}$ is given an oracle access to the unitary operator that represents $\mathcal{A}_n^{O_{r_n}}$. In particular we do not change r_n while $\mathcal{B}$ is running.

Next, we define what "a quantum algorithm computes a function" means.

Definition 4 (Functions computed by quantum algorithms). *A quantum algorithm $\mathcal{A}$ computes a function $f : \{0,1\}^* \rightarrow \{0,1\}^*$ if we have $\Pr[\mathcal{A}(x) = f(x)] > 2/3^{10}$ for all $n \in \mathbb{N}$ and $x \in \{0,1\}^n$. An oracle-aided quantum algorithm $\mathcal{A}$ computes a function $f : \{0,1\}^* \rightarrow \{0,1\}^*$ relative to an oracle Γ if we have $\Pr[\mathcal{A}^\Gamma(x) = f(x)] > 2/3$ for all $n \in \mathbb{N}$ and $x \in \{0,1\}^n$.*

2.2 Technical Lemmas

This section introduces some technical lemmas for later use. First, we use the following basic lemma as a fact. See textbooks on quantum computation and quantum information (e.g., [NC10]) for a proof.

Lemma 1. $\mathsf{trD}(|\psi_1\rangle\langle\psi_1|, |\psi_2\rangle\langle\psi_2|) \leq \||\psi_1\rangle - |\psi_2\rangle\|$ *holds for any pure states $|\psi_1\rangle$ and $|\psi_2\rangle$, where trD denotes the trace distance function.*

By applying the above claim, we can show the following lemma.

Lemma 2. *Let $\Gamma = (f_1, \ldots, f_t), \Gamma' = (f_1', \ldots, f_t')$ be sequences of oracles, and assume that $\mathcal{A}$ is given oracle access to either Γ or Γ'. Then,*

$$\left| \Pr\left[\mathcal{A}^\Gamma(x) = z\right] - \Pr\left[\mathcal{A}^{\Gamma'}(x) = z\right] \right| \leq \left\| \mathcal{A}_n^\Gamma |x, 0, 0\rangle - \mathcal{A}_n^{\Gamma'} |x, 0, 0\rangle \right\| \quad (2)$$

holds for any input $x \in \{0,1\}^n$ and output z.

It is straightforward to show the lemma. See this paper's full version [HY18] for a complete proof.

---

[10] Here we are using the value $2/3$ for the threshold, but it does not make any essential difference even if we use another constant c such that instead of $2/3$, as long as $1/2 < c < 1$.

Swapping Lemma for Multiple Oracles. Next we introduce a generalized version of the *swapping lemma* [Vaz98, Lem. 3.1] for multiple oracles. The original swapping lemma formalizes our intuition that the measurement outcome of oracle-aided algorithm will not be changed so much even if the output values of the oracles are changed on a small fraction of inputs. Since this paper considers the situation that multiple oracles are available to adversaries, we extend the original lemma to a generalized one so that we can treat multiple oracles. To simplify notation, below we often omit the parameter n when it is clear from context (e.g., we write just q instead of $q(n)$). Here we introduce an important notion called *query magnitude*.

Query Magnitude. Let $\Gamma = (f_1, \ldots, f_t)$ be a sequence of quantum oracles, where each f_i is a fixed oracle and not randomized. Let $\mathcal{A}$ be a q-query oracle-aided quantum algorithm relative to the oracle Γ.[11]

Fix an input x, and let $|\phi_j^{f_i}\rangle$ be the quantum state of $\mathcal{A}^\Gamma$ on input $x \in \{0,1\}^n$ just before the j-th query to f_i. Without loss of generality, we consider that the unitary operator O_{f_i} acts on the first $(m_i(n)+\ell_i(n))$-qubits of the quantum system. (Here we assume that f_i is a function from $\{0,1\}^{m_i(n)}$ to $\{0,1\}^{\ell_i(n)}$.) Then $|\phi_j^{f_i}\rangle = \sum_{z \in \{0,1\}^{m_i(n)}} \alpha_z |z\rangle \otimes |\psi_z\rangle$ holds for some complex numbers α_z and quantum states $|\psi_z\rangle$. If we measure the first $m_i(n)$ qubits of the state $|\phi_j^{f_i}\rangle$ with the computational basis, we obtain z with probability $|\alpha_z|^2$. Intuitively, this probability corresponds to the "probability" that z is sent to f_i as the j-th quantum query by $\mathcal{A}$.

Definition 5 (Query magnitude to f_i)

1. The query magnitude of the j-th quantum query of $\mathcal{A}$ to f_i at z on input $x \in \{0,1\}^n$ is defined by

$$\mu_{z,j}^{\mathcal{A},f_i}(x) := |\alpha_z|^2. \tag{3}$$

2. The (total) query magnitude of $\mathcal{A}$ to f_i at z on input $x \in \{0,1\}^n$ is defined by

$$\mu_z^{\mathcal{A},f_i}(x) := \sum_j \mu_{z,j}^{\mathcal{A},f_i}(x). \tag{4}$$

The following lemma can be proven in the same way as the original swapping lemma [Vaz98, Lem. 3.1], using the hybrid argument introduced by Bennet et al. [BBBV97].[12] See the proof for Lemma 3 of this paper's full version [HY18] for a complete proof.

Lemma 3 (Swapping lemma with multiple oracles). *Let $\Gamma = (f_1, \ldots, f_t)$, $\Gamma' = (f_1', \ldots, f_t')$ be sequences of oracles, where each f_i and f_i' are fixed oracles and not randomized. Assume that $\mathcal{A}$ is given oracle access to either Γ or Γ'. Then*

$$\left\| \mathcal{A}_n^\Gamma |x, 0, 0\rangle - \mathcal{A}_n^{\Gamma'} |x, 0, 0\rangle \right\| \leq 2 \sum_{1 \leq i \leq t} \sqrt{q(n) \sum_{z \in \Delta(f_i, f_i')} \mu_z^{\mathcal{A},f_i}(x)} \tag{5}$$

holds for all $x \in \{0,1\}^n$.

---

[11] We sometimes call a sequence of oracles just "oracle".

[12] The original swapping lemma is the special case of Lemma 3 such that $t = 1$.

3   Quantum Primitives and Black-Box Quantum Reductions

Here, we define quantum primitives, which is a quantum counterpart of a primitive, in addition to the notion of fully-black-box reduction in quantum regime (see Def. 2.1 and Def. 2.3 in [RTV04] for classical definitions). Note that we consider reductions that have quantum black-box oracle accesses to primitives. We always consider security of primitives against quantum adversaries, and do not discuss primitives that are only secure against classical adversaries. When we consider primitives with interactions in the quantum setting we have some subtle issues that do not matter in the classical setting (e.g., rewinding is sometimes hard in the quantum setting [ARU14]). Thus we treat only primitives such that both of the primitives themselves and security games are non-interactive.

Definition 6 (Quantum primitives). *A quantum primitive* $\mathcal{P}$ *is a pair* $\langle F_\mathcal{P}, R_\mathcal{P} \rangle$*, where* $F_\mathcal{P}$ *is a set of quantum algorithms* $\mathcal{I}$*, and* $R_\mathcal{P}$ *is a relation over pairs* $\langle \mathcal{I}, \mathcal{A} \rangle$ *of quantum algorithms* $\mathcal{I} \in F_\mathcal{P}$ *and* $\mathcal{A}$*. A quantum algorithm* $\mathcal{I}$ *implements* $\mathcal{P}$ *or is an implementation of* $\mathcal{P}$ *if* $\mathcal{I} \in F_\mathcal{P}$*. If* $\mathcal{I} \in F_\mathcal{P}$ *is efficient, then* $\mathcal{I}$ *is an efficient implementation of* $\mathcal{P}$*. A quantum algorithm* $\mathcal{A}$ $\mathcal{P}$*-breaks* $\mathcal{I} \in F_\mathcal{P}$ *if* $\langle \mathcal{I}, \mathcal{A} \rangle \in R_\mathcal{P}$*. A secure implementation of* $\mathcal{P}$ *is an implementation* $\mathcal{I}$ *of* $\mathcal{P}$ *such that no efficient quantum algorithm* $\mathcal{P}$*-breaks* $\mathcal{I}$*. The primitive* $\mathcal{P}$ *quantumly exists if there exists an efficient and secure implementation of* $\mathcal{P}$*.*

Definition 7 (Quantum primitives relative to oracle). *Let* $\mathcal{P} = \langle F_\mathcal{P}, R_\mathcal{P} \rangle$ *be a quantum primitive, and* $\Gamma = (O_1, \ldots, O_t)$ *be a family of (possibly randomized) quantum oracles. An oracle-aided quantum algorithm* $\mathcal{I}$ *implements* $\mathcal{P}$ *relative to* Γ *or is an implementation of* $\mathcal{P}$ *relative to* Γ *if* $\mathcal{I}^\Gamma \in F_\mathcal{P}$*. If* $\mathcal{I}^\Gamma \in F_\mathcal{P}$ *is efficient, then* $\mathcal{I}$ *is an efficient implementation of* $\mathcal{P}$ *relative to* Γ*. A quantum algorithm* $\mathcal{A}$ $\mathcal{P}$*-breaks* $\mathcal{I} \in F_\mathcal{P}$ *relative to* Γ *if* $\langle \mathcal{I}^\Gamma, \mathcal{A}^\Gamma \rangle \in R_\mathcal{P}$*. A secure implementation of* $\mathcal{P}$ *is an implementation* $\mathcal{I}$ *of* $\mathcal{P}$ *relative to* Γ *such that no efficient quantum algorithm* $\mathcal{P}$*-breaks* $\mathcal{I}$ *relative to* Γ*. The primitive* $\mathcal{P}$ *quantumly exists relative to* Γ *if there exists an efficient and secure implementation of* $\mathcal{P}$ *relative to* Γ*.*

Remark 5. In the above definition, $\mathcal{I}^\Gamma$ and $\mathcal{A}^\Gamma$ are considered to be quantum algorithms (rather than oracle-aided quantum algorithms) once an oracle Γ is fixed so that $\mathcal{I}^\Gamma \in F_\mathcal{P}$ and $\langle \mathcal{I}^\Gamma, \mathcal{A}^\Gamma \rangle \in R_\mathcal{P}$ are well-defined. This is possible since we assume that an oracle Γ is stateless. (If Γ is randomized, we regard the randomness of Γ as a part of the randomness of the quantum algorithms $\mathcal{I}^\Gamma$ and $\mathcal{A}^\Gamma$. See also Remark 4.)

Next we define quantum fully-black-box reductions, which is a quantum counterpart of fully-black-box reductions [RTV04, Def. 2.3].

Definition 8 (Quantum fully-black-box reductions). *A pair (G, S) of efficient oracle-aided quantum algorithms is a quantum fully-black-box reduction from a quantum primitive $\mathcal{P} = \langle F_\mathcal{P}, R_\mathcal{P} \rangle$ to a quantum primitive $\mathcal{Q} = \langle F_\mathcal{Q}, R_\mathcal{Q} \rangle$ if the following two conditions are satisfied:*

1. *(Correctness.) For every implementation $\mathcal{I} \in F_\mathcal{Q}$, we have $G^\mathcal{I} \in F_\mathcal{P}$.*
2. *(Security.) For every implementation $\mathcal{I} \in F_\mathcal{Q}$ and every quantum algorithm $\mathcal{A}$, if $\mathcal{A}$ $\mathcal{P}$-breaks $G^\mathcal{I}$, then $S^{\mathcal{A},\mathcal{I}}$ $\mathcal{Q}$-breaks $\mathcal{I}$.*

Hsiao and Reyzin showed that if there exists an oracle (family) that separates primitives $\mathcal{P}$ and $\mathcal{Q}$, then there is no fully-black-box reduction from $\mathcal{P}$ to $\mathcal{Q}$ [HR04, Prop. 1]. The following lemma guarantees that a similar claim holds in the quantum setting. Although we need no arguments which is specific to the quantum setting, we give a proof for completeness.

Lemma 4 (Two oracle technique). *There exists no quantum fully-black-box reduction from $\mathcal{P}$ to $\mathcal{Q}$ if there exist families of quantum oracles Γ_1 and $\Gamma_2 = \{\Psi_\lambda^\Phi\}_{\Phi \in \Gamma^1, \lambda \in \Lambda}$, where Λ is a non-empty set, and the following two conditions hold.*

1. Existence of $\mathcal{Q}$. *There exists an efficient oracle-aided quantum algorithm $\mathcal{J}_0$ that satisfies the following conditions:*

1. *$\mathcal{J}_0^\Phi \in F_\mathcal{Q}$ holds for any $\Phi \in \Gamma_1$.*
2. *For any efficient oracle-aided algorithm $\mathcal{B}$ and any $\lambda \in \Lambda$, there exists $\Phi \in \Gamma_1$ such that $\mathcal{B}^{\Phi, \Psi_\lambda^\Phi}$ does not $\mathcal{Q}$-break $\mathcal{J}_0^\Phi$.*

2. Non-Existence of $\mathcal{P}$. *For any efficient oracle-aided quantum algorithm $\mathcal{I}$ such that $\mathcal{I}^\Phi \in F_\mathcal{P}$ holds for any $\Phi \in \Gamma_1$, there exists an efficient oracle-aided quantum algorithm $\mathcal{A}_\mathcal{I}$ and $\lambda \in \Lambda$ such that $\mathcal{A}_\mathcal{I}^{\Psi_\lambda^\Phi}$ $\mathcal{P}$-breaks $\mathcal{I}^\Phi$ for any $\Phi \in \Gamma_1$.*

Proof. We prove the claim by contradiction. Suppose that there exists a quantum fully-black-box reduction (G, S) from $\mathcal{P} = \langle F_\mathcal{P}, R_\mathcal{P} \rangle$ to $\mathcal{Q} = \langle F_\mathcal{Q}, R_\mathcal{Q} \rangle$. Let $\mathcal{J}_0$ be an algorithm that satisfies the conditions on existence of $\mathcal{Q}$ in Lemma 4. Then $\mathcal{J}_0^\Phi \in F_\mathcal{Q}$ holds for arbitrary $\Phi \in \Gamma_1$. Hence, from the correctness of the quantum fully-black-box reductions (in Definition 8), it follows that $G^{\mathcal{J}_0^\Phi} \in F_\mathcal{P}$ holds for arbitrary $\Phi \in \Gamma_1$. Thus, if we set $\mathcal{I}_0 := G^{\mathcal{J}_0}$, from the second condition of Lemma 4, it follows that there exists an efficient oracle-aided quantum algorithm $\mathcal{A}_{\mathcal{I}_0}$ and $\lambda \in \Lambda$ such that $\mathcal{A}_{\mathcal{I}_0}^{\Psi_\lambda^\Phi}$ $\mathcal{P}$-breaks $\mathcal{I}_0^\Phi$ for any $\Phi \in \Gamma_1$. Therefore, from the second property of quantum fully-black-box reduction ("security" in Definition 8), it follows that $S^{\mathcal{A}_{\mathcal{I}_0}^{\Psi_\lambda^\Phi}, \mathcal{J}_0^\Phi}$ $\mathcal{Q}$-breaks $\mathcal{J}_0^\Phi$ for any $\Phi \in \Gamma_1$. Since $G, \mathcal{A}_{\mathcal{I}_0}$, and $\mathcal{J}_0$ are all efficient, there exists an efficient oracle-aided quantum algorithm $\mathcal{B}$ such that $\mathcal{B}^{\Phi, \Psi_\lambda^\Phi} = S^{\mathcal{A}_{\mathcal{I}_0}^{\Psi_\lambda^\Phi}, \mathcal{J}_0^\Phi}$. Now we have that there exists an efficient oracle-aided algorithm $\mathcal{B}$ and $\lambda \in \Lambda$ such that $\mathcal{B}^{\Phi, \Psi_\lambda^\Phi}$ $\mathcal{Q}$-breaks $\mathcal{J}_0^\Phi$ for any $\Phi \in \Gamma_1$. However, it contradicts the second part of the first condition of Lemma 4, which completes the proof. □

Note that, due to Lemma 4, if we want to show that there *does not exist any quantum fully-black-box reductions* from a quantum primitive $\mathcal{P}$ to another quantum primitive $\mathcal{Q}$, it suffices to show that there exists *at least one pair* of quantum oracles (Γ_1, Γ_2) that satisfies the two conditions.

Remark 6. Remember that each fixed (resp., randomized) quantum oracle O is an infinite family of unitary gates $\{O_n\}_{n \in \mathbb{N}}$ (resp., $O = \{O_n\}_{n \in \mathbb{N}}$ and $O_n = \{O_{r_n}\}_{r_n \in R_n}$, where R_n is the set of random coins), where O_n is used when an oracle-aided algorithm runs relative to O on an input in $\{0, 1\}^n$. For example, (the quantum oracle of) a permutation $f \in \mathsf{Perm}(\{0,1\}^*)$ is represented as a family $\{f_n\}_{n \in \mathbb{N}}$, where $f_n = f|_{\{0,1\}^n}$. We implicitly assume that $\Psi_{\lambda,n}^{\Phi}$ depends only on Φ_n and is independent of Φ_m for $m \neq n$.

Later, to prove impossibility of quantum fully-black-box reductions from collision resistant hash functions to one-way permutations, we will apply this lemma with the condition that Λ is the set of all polynomials in n, $\Gamma_1 = \mathsf{Perm}(\{0,1\}^*)$, and $\Gamma_2 = \{\mathsf{ColFinder}_\lambda^f\}_{f \in \Gamma_1, \lambda \in \Lambda}$. Here, $\mathsf{ColFinder}_\lambda^f$ is a randomized oracle that takes, as inputs, oracle-aided quantum circuits that computes functions, and returns collision of the functions. The number $\lambda(n)$ denotes the maximum size of circuits that $\mathsf{ColFinder}_{\lambda,n}^f$ takes as inputs for each $n \in \mathbb{N}$.

3.1 Concrete Primitives

In this section, we define one-way permutations, trapdoor permutations, and collision-resistant hash functions.

We define two quantum counterparts for each classical primitive. One is the *classical-computable* primitive that can be implemented on classical computers, and the other is the *quantum-computable* primitive that can be implemented on quantum computers but may not be implemented on classical computers. Here we note that, in this paper, all adversaries are quantum algorithms for both of classical-computable and quantum-computable primitives.

Definition 9 (One-way permutation). *Quantum-computable (resp., classical-computable) quantum-secure one-way permutation* QC-qOWP *(resp.,* CC-qOWP*) is a quantum primitive defined as follows: Implementation of* QC-qOWP *(resp.,* CC-qOWP*) is an efficient quantum (resp., classical) algorithm* Eval *that computes a function* $f : \{0,1\}^* \rightarrow \{0,1\}^*$ *such that* $f_n := f|_{\{0,1\}^n}$ *is a permutation over* $\{0,1\}^n$*. For an implementation* $\mathcal{I}$ *of* QC-qOWP *(resp.,* CC-qOWP*) that computes* f *and a quantum algorithm* $\mathcal{A}$*, we say that* $\mathcal{A}$ QC-qOWP-*breaks* $\mathcal{I}$ *(resp.,* CC-qOWP-*breaks* $\mathcal{I}$*) if and only if*

$$\Pr\left[x \xleftarrow{\$} \{0,1\}^n; y \leftarrow f_n(x); x' \leftarrow \mathcal{A}(y) : x' = x\right] \tag{6}$$

is non-negligible.

Remark 7. Since there is no function generation algorithm Gen in the above definition, this captures "public-coin" one-way permutations. This makes the definition of one-way permutations stronger, and thus makes our negative result stronger.

Definition 10 (Trapdoor permutation). *Quantum-computable (resp., classical-computable) quantum-secure trapdoor permutation* QC-qTDP*(resp., CC-QTDP) is a quantum primitive defined as follows: Implementation of* QC-qTDP *(resp., CC-qTDP) is a triplet of efficient quantum (resp., classical) algorithms* (Gen, Eval, Inv). *In addition, we require* (Gen, Eval, Inv) *to satisfy the following:*

1. *For any* (pk, td) *generated by* Gen(1^n), Eval(pk, ·) *computes a permutation* $f_{pk,n}\{0,1\}^n \to \{0,1\}^n$.
2. *For any* (pk, td) *generated by* Gen(1^n) *and any* $x \in \{0,1\}^n$, *we have that the inequality* $\Pr[\mathsf{Inv}(\mathsf{td}, f_{pk,n}(x)) = x] > 2/3$ *holds (i.e.,* Inv(td, ·) *computes* $f_{pk,n}^{-1}(\cdot)$*).*

For an implementation $\mathcal{I} = $ (Gen, Eval, Inv) *of* QC-qTDP *(resp., CC-qTDP) and a quantum algorithm* $\mathcal{A}$, *we say that* $\mathcal{A}$ QC-qTDP*-breaks* $\mathcal{I}$ *(resp.,* CC-qTDP*-breaks* $\mathcal{I}$*) if and only if*

$$\Pr\left[(\mathsf{pk}, \mathsf{td}) \leftarrow \mathsf{Gen}(1^n); x \xleftarrow{\$} \{0,1\}^n; y \leftarrow f_{pk,n}(x); x' \leftarrow \mathcal{A}(\mathsf{pk}, y) : x' = x\right] \quad (7)$$

is non-negligible.

Definition 11 (Collision-resistant hash function). *Quantum-computable (resp., classical-computable) quantum-collision-resistant hash function* QC-qCRH *(resp., CC-qCRH) is a quantum primitive defined as follows: Implementation of* QC-qCRH *(resp., CC-qCRH) is a pair of efficient quantum (resp., classical) algorithms* (Gen, Eval).

Gen(1^n): *This algorithm is given* 1^n *as input, and outputs a function index.*
Eval(σ, x): *This algorithm is given a function index* $\sigma \in \{0,1\}^{s(n)}$ *and* $x \in \{0,1\}^{m(n)}$ *as input, and outputs* $y \in \{0,1\}^{\ell(n)}$.

In addition, we require (Gen, Eval) *to satisfy the following:*

1. *We have* $m(n) > \ell(n)$ *for all sufficiently large* $n \in \mathbb{N}$.
2. Eval(·, ·) *computes a function* $H(\cdot, \cdot) : \{0,1\}^{s(n)} \times \{0,1\}^{m(n)} \to \{0,1\}^{\ell(n)}$.

For an implementation $\mathcal{I} = $ (Gen, Eval) *of* QC-qCRH *(resp., CC-qCRH) and a quantum algorithm* $\mathcal{A}$, *we say that* $\mathcal{A}$ QC-qCRH*-breaks* $\mathcal{I}$ *(resp.,* CC-qCRH*-breaks* $\mathcal{I}$*) if and only if*

$$\Pr\left[\sigma \leftarrow \mathsf{Gen}(1^n); (x, x') \leftarrow \mathcal{A}(\sigma) : H(\sigma, x) = H(\sigma, x')\right] \quad (8)$$

is non-negligible.

Remark 8. If we replace "quantum algorithm" with "probabilistic Turing machine" verbatim, Definition 11 completely matches the classical definition [HR04].

Remark 9. Though trapdoor permutations and collision-resistant hash functions are defined to be a tuple of algorithms, we can capture them as quantum primitives as defined in Definition 6 by considering a unified quantum algorithm that runs either of these algorithms depending on prefix of its input. We also remark that any classical algorithm can be seen as a special case of quantum computation, and thus classical-computable variants are also captured as quantum primitives.

4 Impossibility of Reduction from QC-qCRH to CC-qOWP

The goal of this section is to show the following theorem.

Theorem 3. *There exists no quantum fully-black-box reduction from* QC-qCRH *to* CC-qOWP.

To show this theorem, we define two (families of) oracles that separate QC-qCRH from CC-qOWP. That is, we define an oracle that implements CC-qOWP, in addition to an oracle that finds collisions of functions, and then apply the two oracle technique (Lemma 4). Our oracles are quantum analogues of those in previous works on impossibility results [Sim98, HHRS07, AS15] in the classical setting. Roughly speaking, we simply use random permutations f to implement one-way permutations. As for an oracle that finds collisions of functions, we use a randomized oracle ColFinder.

Remark 10. The statement of Theorem 3 is the strongest result among possible quantum (fully-black-box) separations of CRH from OWP, since it also excludes reductions from CC-qCRH to CC-qOWP, reductions from QC-qCRH to QC-qOWP, and reductions from CC-qCRH to QC-qOWP.[13]

Oracle ColFinder.

Intuitive Idea. Intuitively, our oracle ColFinder^f works as follows for each fixed permutation f. As an input, ColFinder^f takes an oracle-aided quantum circuit C. We say that C is a *valid* input if it computes a function $F_C^{f'} : \{0,1\}^m \to \{0,1\}^\ell$ relative to the oracle f', for arbitrary permutation f' (here we assume that m and ℓ are independent of the permutation f'). We say that C is *invalid* if it is not valid. Given the input C, first ColFinder^f checks whether C is invalid, and return $\perp$ if it is. Second, ColFinder^f chooses $w_{Cf}^{(1)} \in \{0,1\}^m$ uniformly at random, and computes $u = F_C^f(w_{Cf}^{(1)})$ by running the circuit C on input $w_{Cf}^{(1)}$ relative to f. Third, ColFinder^f chooses $w_{Cf}^{(2)}$ from $(F_C^f)^{-1}(u)$ uniformly at random. Finally ColFinder^f returns $(w_{Cf}^{(1)}, w_{Cf}^{(2)}, u)$. If F_C^f has many collisions (for example, if $m > \ell$), ColFinder^f

---

[13] Note that it also excludes possible quantum (fully-black-box) reductions from collapsing hash functions to one-way permutations, since the notion of collapsing is stronger than collision-resistance.

returns a collision of F_C^f with a high probability. The idea of the above oracle ColFinder originally comes from the seminal work by Simon [Sim98]. Below we give a formal description of ColFinder, following the formalization of Asharov and Segev [AS15].

Formal Description. Here we give a formal description of ColFinder. Let valid and invalid denote the set of valid and invalid circuits, respectively. Let $\lambda : \mathbb{N} \to \mathbb{R}_{\geq 0}$ be a function, and $\mathsf{Circ}(\lambda(n))$ denote the set of oracle-aided quantum circuits C of which size is less than or equal to $\lambda(n)$. Note that $\mathsf{Circ}(\lambda(n))$ is a finite set for each n. Let $\Pi_n = \{\pi_C^{(1)}, \pi_C^{(2)}\}_{C \in \mathsf{Circ}(\lambda(n)) \cap \mathsf{valid}}$ be a set of permutations, where $\pi_C^{(1)}, \pi_C^{(2)}$ are permutations over $\{0,1\}^m$, which is the domain of F_C that the circuit C computes. Let $R_{\lambda,n}$ be the set of all possible such assignments Π_n, and R_λ be the product set $\prod_{n=1}^{\infty} R_{\lambda,n}$.

For each fixed permutation f and a function λ, we define a randomized quantum oracle $\mathsf{ColFinder}_\lambda^f = \{\mathsf{ColFinder}_{\lambda,\Pi}^f\}_{\Pi \leftarrow R_\lambda}$. Here, by $\Pi \leftarrow R_\lambda$ we ambiguously denote the procedure that Π is chosen uniformly at random before adversaries make queries to $\mathsf{ColFinder}_\lambda^f$, and $\mathsf{ColFinder}_{\lambda,\Pi}^f = \{\mathsf{ColFinder}_{\lambda,\Pi,n}^f\}_{n \in \mathbb{N}}$ is a fixed quantum oracle for each Π. When we feed an algorithm $\mathcal{A}$ with an input $x \in \{0,1\}^n$ relative to $\mathsf{ColFinder}_\lambda^f$, first $\Pi_n \in R_{\lambda,n}$ is chosen uniformly at random (i.e., two permutations $\pi_C^{(1)}, \pi_C^{(2)}$ are chosen uniformly at random for each oracle-aided quantum circuit $C \in \mathsf{Circ}(\lambda(n)) \cap \mathsf{valid}$), and then $\mathcal{A}$ runs the circuit $\mathcal{A}_n^{\mathsf{ColFinder}_{\lambda,\Pi,n}^f}$ on the initial state $|x\rangle|0\rangle|0\rangle$. For each fixed n and Π_n, the deterministic function $\mathsf{ColFinder}_{\lambda,\Pi,n}^f$ is defined by the following procedures:

1. Take an input C, where C is an oracle-aided quantum circuit of which size is less than or equal to $\lambda(n)$.
2. Check if C is a valid input by checking whether the following condition is satisfied: For arbitrary $f_n' \in \mathsf{Perm}(\{0,1\}^n)$ and $x \in \{0,1\}^m$, there exists $y \in \{0,1\}^\ell$ such that $\Pr[C^{f_n'}(x) = y] > 2/3$. If C is an invalid input, return $\perp$.
3. Compute $w_{Cf}^{(1)} := \pi_C^{(1)}(0^m)$.
4. Compute $F_C^f(w_C^{(1)})$. That is, compute the output distribution of C^f on input $w_{Cf}^{(1)}$, find the element y such that $\Pr[C^f(w_{Cf}^{(1)}) = y] > 2/3$, and set $u \leftarrow y$.
5. Search for the minimum $t \in \{0,1\}^m$ such that $F_C^f(\pi_C^{(2)}(t)) = u$ by checking whether
$$\Pr\left[C^f\left(\pi_C^{(2)}(i)\right) = u\right] > 2/3$$
holds for $i = 0, 1, 2, \ldots$ in a sequential order, and set $w_{Cf}^2 := \pi_C^{(2)}(t)$ (note that such t always exists since $F_C^f(w_{Cf}^{(1)}) = u$).
6. Return $(w_{Cf}^{(1)}, w_{Cf}^{(2)}, u)$.

Later we will apply Lemma 4 (the two oracle technique) with $\Gamma_1 := \mathsf{Perm}(\{0,1\}^*)$ and $\Gamma_2 := \{\mathsf{ColFinder}_\lambda^f\}_{f \in \Gamma_1, \lambda \in \Lambda}$, where Λ is the set of polynomials in n.

4.1   The Technically Hardest Part

The technically hardest part of proving Theorem 3 is to show the following proposition, which states that the random permutation f is hard to invert even if the additional oracle ColFinder^f is available for adversaries. Note that the oracle gate ColFinder$^f_{\lambda,\Pi,n}$ is (and thus the circuit $\mathcal{A}_n^{f_n,\mathsf{ColFinder}^f_{\lambda,\Pi,n}}$ is) fixed once f_n and Π_n are fixed, since the output values of ColFinder$^f_{\lambda,\Pi,n}$ are independent of f_m and Π_m for $m \neq n$.

Proposition 1. *Let λ, q, ϵ be functions such that $1 \leq \lambda(n), q(n)$ and $0 < \epsilon(n) \leq 1$. Let $\mathcal{A}$ be a q-query oracle-aided quantum algorithm. Suppose that there is a function $\eta(n) \leq \lambda(n)$ such that, for each circuit C that $\mathcal{A}_n$ queries to ColFinder, C makes at most $\eta(n)$ queries. If*

$$\Pr_{\substack{f_n,\Pi_n \\ y \leftarrow \{0,1\}^n}} \left[x \leftarrow \mathcal{A}_n^{f_n,\mathsf{ColFinder}^f_{\lambda,\Pi,n}}(y) : f_n(x) = y \right] \geq \epsilon(n) \qquad (9)$$

holds for infinitely many n, then there exists a constant const *such that*

$$\max\{q(n), \eta(n)\} \geq \mathsf{const} \cdot \epsilon(n) \cdot 2^{n/7} \qquad (10)$$

holds for infinitely many n.

Below we prove Proposition 1. See Sect. 1.3 for an intuitive overview of our proof idea. We begin with describing some technical preparations.

Preparations. We construct another algorithm $\hat{\mathcal{A}}$ that iteratively runs $\mathcal{A}$ to increase the success probability, and then apply the encoding technique to $\hat{\mathcal{A}}$.

Let c be a positive integer. Let $\mathcal{B}_c$ be an oracle-aided quantum algorithm that runs as follows, relative to the oracles f and ColFinder$^f_\lambda$.[14]

1. Take an input y. Set guess $\leftarrow \bot$.
2. For $i = 1, \ldots, c\lceil 1/\epsilon(n) \rceil$ do:
3.   Run $\mathcal{A}^{f,\mathsf{ColFinder}^f_\lambda}$ on the input y. Let x denote the output.
4.   Query x to f. If $f(x) = y$, then set guess $\leftarrow x$.
5. End For
6. Return guess.

Let $Q(n) := c\lceil 1/\epsilon(n) \rceil (\max\{q(n), \eta(n)\} + 1)$. Then $\mathcal{B}_c$ can be regarded as a Q-query algorithm, and for each quantum circuit C that $\mathcal{B}_c$ queries to ColFinder$^f_{\lambda,n}$, C makes at most $Q(n)$ queries[15].

---

[14] Later, we will set $\hat{\mathcal{A}} := \mathcal{B}_c$ for a constant c.

[15] We introduced Q here just for convenience. Q is an upper bound of both of i) The number of queries made by $\mathcal{B}_c$ to f and ColFinder, and ii) The number of queries to f made by quantum circuits that are queried by $\mathcal{B}_c$ to ColFinder. Because the notations in later proofs become simpler when i) and ii) are the same (i.e., $q = \eta$), we introduced Q here.

Remark 11. The randomness Π_n of $\mathsf{ColFinder}^f_\lambda$ is chosen before $\mathcal{B}_c$ starts, and unchanged while $\mathcal{B}_c$ is running (see Remark 4).

Lemma 5. *Let* p_1, p_2 *be any positive constant values such that* $0 < p_1, p_2 < 1$. *For a sufficiently large integer* c, *the following condition is satisfied for infinitely many* n:

Condition. *There exist* $X \subset \mathsf{Perm}(\{0,1\}^n)$ *and* Π_n *such that* $|X| \geq p_1 \cdot |\mathsf{Perm}(\{0,1\}^n)|$ *and*

$$\Pr_{y \leftarrow \{0,1\}^n}\left[\Pr\left[x \leftarrow \mathcal{B}^{f_n, \mathsf{ColFinder}^f_{\lambda, \Pi, n}}_{c,n}(y) : f_n(x) = y\right] \geq 2/3\right] \geq p_2 \qquad (11)$$

for all $f_n \in X$.

This lemma can be shown by simple averaging arguments. See the proof for Lemma 5 of this paper's full version [HY18] for a complete proof.

In what follows, we fix constants p_1, p_2 such that $0 < p_1, p_2 < 1$ arbitrarily. Then, from the above lemma, it follows that there exists a constant c that satisfies the condition in Lemma 5 for infinitely many n. Let us denote $\mathcal{B}_c$ by $\hat{A}$. We use the encoding technique to this Q-query algorithm $\hat{A}$, here $Q(n) = c\lceil 1/\epsilon(n)\rceil (\max\{q(n), \eta(n)\} + 1)$. Below we fix a sufficiently large n in addition to Π_n and X such that the condition in Lemma 5 is satisfied. For simplicity, we write Q, q, ϵ, η, f, and $\mathsf{ColFinder}^f$ instead of $Q(n)$, $q(n)$, $\epsilon(n)$, $\eta(n)$, f_n, and $\mathsf{ColFinder}^f_{\lambda, \Pi, n}$ respectively, for simplicity.

Information Theoretic Property of Randomized Compression Scheme. Here we introduce an information theoretic property of a randomized compression scheme $(E_r : X \rightarrow Y \cup \{\bot\}, D_r : Y \rightarrow X \cup \{\bot\})$, where r is chosen according to a distribution $\mathcal{R}$. Generally, if encoding and subsequent decoding succeed with a constant probability p, then $|Y|$ cannot be much smaller than $|X|$:

Lemma 6 ([DTT10], **Fact 10.1**). *If there exists a constant* $0 \leq p \leq 1$ *such that* $\Pr_{r \sim \mathcal{R}}[D_r(E_r(x)) = x] \geq p$ *holds for all* $x \in X$, *then* $|Y| \geq p \cdot |X|$ *holds.*

Below we formally define an encoder E and a decoder D that compress elements (truth tables of permutations) in X. In the encoder E, random coin r is chosen according to a distribution $\mathcal{R}$. On the other hand, we consider that D is deterministic rather than randomized, and regard r as a part of inputs to D. Note that we do not care whether encoding and decoding can be efficiently done, since Lemma 6 describes a purely information theoretic property.

Encoder E. Let δ be a sufficiently small constant ($\delta = (1/8)^4$ suffices). When we feed E with $f \in X$ as an input, E first chooses subsets $R, R' \subset \{0,1\}^n$ by the following sampling: For each $x \in \{0,1\}^n$, x is added to R with probability

$\delta^{3/2}/Q^2$, and independently added to R' with probability $\delta^{5/2}/Q^4$. (The pair (R, R') is the random coin of E.)

According to the choice of R', "bad" inputs (oracle-aided quantum circuits) to $\mathsf{ColFinder}^f$ are defined for each $x \in \{0,1\}^n$ as follows. Note that now $\pi_C^{(1)}$ and $\pi_C^{(2)}$ have been fixed for each oracle-aided quantum circuit $C \in \mathsf{Circ}(\lambda(n)) \cap$ valid, and thus the output $\mathsf{ColFinder}^f(C) = (w_{Cf}^{(1)}, w_{Cf}^{(2)}, F_C^f(w_{Cf}^{(1)}))$ is uniquely determined. Since C is an oracle-aided quantum circuit, we can define the query magnitude of C to f on input $w_{Cf}^{(1)}$ and $w_{Cf}^{(2)}$ at $z \in \{0,1\}^n$ (see Definition 5). We say that a quantum circuit $C \in \mathsf{Circ}(\lambda(n)) \cap$ valid is *bad* relative to x if $\sum_{z \in R' \setminus \{x\}} \mu_z^{C,f}(w_{Cf}^{(1)}) > \delta/Q$ or $\sum_{z \in R' \setminus \{x\}} \mu_z^{C,f}(w_{Cf}^{(2)}) > \delta/Q$ hold, and otherwise we say that C is *good* relative to x. Let $\mathsf{badC}(R', x)$ denote the set of bad circuits relative to x, for each $R' \subset \{0,1\}^n$.

Next, E constructs a set $G \subset \{0,1\}^n$ depending on the input f. Let $I \subset \{0,1\}^n$ be the set of elements x such that $\hat{\mathcal{A}}$ successfully inverts $f(x)$, i.e., $I := \{x \mid \Pr[x' \leftarrow \hat{\mathcal{A}}^{f,\mathsf{ColFinder}^f}(f(x)) : x' = x] \geq 2/3\}$. Then $|I| \geq p_2 \cdot 2^n$ holds by definition of X (Remember that X is chosen in such a way as to satisfy the condition in Lemma 5). Now, a set G is defined to be the set of elements $x \in I$ that satisfies the following conditions:

Conditions for G

(Cond. 1) $x \in R \cap R'$.

(Cond. 2) $\sum_{z \in R \setminus \{x\}} \mu_z^{\hat{\mathcal{A}}, f}(f(x)) \leq \delta/Q$.

(Cond. 3) $\sum_{C \in \mathsf{badC}(R', x)} \mu_C^{\hat{\mathcal{A}}, \mathsf{ColFinder}^f}(f(x)) \leq \delta/Q$.

Finally, E encodes f into $(f|_{\{0,1\}^n \setminus G}, f(G))$ if $|G| \geq \theta$, where $\theta = (1 - 60\sqrt{\delta})\delta^4 p_2 2^n / 2Q^6$. Otherwise E encodes f into $\perp$.

In addition, here we formally define the set Y (the range of E) as

$$Y := \{(f|_{\{0,1\}^n \setminus G}, f(G)) \mid f \in \mathsf{Perm}(\{0,1\}^n), G \subset \{0,1\}^n, |G| \geq \theta\}. \qquad (12)$$

In fact $E((R, R'), f) \in Y \cup \{\perp\}$ holds for any choice of (R, R') and any permutation $f \in X$.

Decoder D. D takes $(\tilde{f}, \tilde{G})$ as an input in addition to (R, R'), where $\tilde{G} \subset \{0,1\}^n$ and $\tilde{f}$ is a bijection from a subset of $\{0,1\}^n$ onto $\{0,1\}^n \setminus \tilde{G}$, and R, R' are subsets of $\{0,1\}^n$. If $\{0,1\}^n \setminus (\text{the domain of } \tilde{f}) \not\subset R \cap R'$ holds, then D outputs $\perp$. Otherwise, D decodes $(\tilde{f}, \tilde{G})$ and reconstructs the truth table of a permutation $f \in \mathsf{Perm}(\{0,1\}^n)$ as follows.

For each x in the domain of $\tilde{f}$, D infers the value $f(x)$ as $f(x) := \tilde{f}(x)$. For other elements $x \in \{0,1\}^n$ which is not contained in the domain of $\tilde{f}$, what D now knows is only that $f(x)$ is contained in $\tilde{G}$. To determine the remaining part of the truth table of f, D tries to recover the value $f^{-1}(y)$ for each $y \in \tilde{G}$ by using $\hat{\mathcal{A}}$.

For each fixed $y \in \tilde{G}$, D could succeed to recover the value $f^{-1}(y)$ if D were able to determine the output distribution of $\hat{\mathcal{A}}$ on input y relative to oracles f

and ColFinder^f. However, D cannot determine the distribution even though D has no limitation on its running time, since f itself is the permutation of which D wants to reconstruct the truth table, and the behavior of ColFinder^f depends on f. Thus D instead prepares oracles h_y and SimCF^{h_y} which approximates f and ColFinder^f, respectively, and computes the output distribution of $\hat{\mathcal{A}}^{h_y,\text{SimCF}^{h_y}}$ on input y. SimCF^{h_y} uses a subroutine CalC$_y$ that takes (C, w) as an input (C is a valid oracle-aided circuit that may make queries to f and computes a function F_C^f, and w is an element of the domain of F_C^f) and simulates the evaluation of $F_C^f(w)$. D finally infers that $f^{-1}(y)$ is the element which $\hat{\mathcal{A}}^{h_y,\text{SimCF}^{h_y}}$ outputs with probability greater than $1/2$. (If there does not exist such an element, then D outputs $\perp$.) Below we describe h_y, CalC$_y$, and SimCF^{h_y}.

Oracle h_y. The oracle (function) $h_y : \{0,1\}^n \to \{0,1\}^n$ is defined by

$$h_y(z) = \begin{cases} \tilde{f}(z) & \text{ifz} \notin R \cap R', \\ y & \text{otherwise.} \end{cases} \tag{13}$$

Subroutine CalC$_y$. Let $P_{\text{candidate}} := \{h' \in \text{Perm}(\{0,1\}^n)) \mid \Delta(h', h_y) \subset R \cap R'\}$. CalC$_y$ is defined as the following procedures.

1. Take an input (C, w), where C is an oracle-aided circuit and w is an element of the domain of the function F_C.
2. Compute the output distribution of the quantum circuit $C^{h'}$ on input w for each $h' \in P_{\text{candidate}}$, and find $u(C, w, h') \in \{0,1\}^\ell$ such that $\Pr[C^{h'}(w) = u(C, w, h')] > 1/2$. If there is no such value $u(C, w, h')$ for a fixed h', set $u(C, w, h') := \perp$.
3. If $u(C, w, h') = u(C, w, h'') \neq \perp$ for all $h', h'' \in P_{\text{candidate}}$, return the value $u(C, w, h')$. Otherwise return $\perp$.

Oracle SimCF^{h_y}. SimCF^{h_y} is defined as the following procedures:

1. Take an input C, where C is an oracle-aided quantum circuit of which size is less than or equal to $\lambda(n)$.
2. Check if C is a valid input by checking whether the following condition is satisfied: For arbitrary $f'_n \in \text{Perm}(\{0,1\}^n)$ and $x \in \{0,1\}^m$, there exists $y \in \{0,1\}^\ell$ such that $\Pr[C^{f'_n}(x) = y] > 2/3$. If C is an invalid input, return $\perp$.
3. Compute $\tilde{w}_{Cf}^{(1)} := \pi_C^{(1)}(0^m)$.
4. If CalC$_y(C, \tilde{w}_{Cf}^{(1)}) = \perp$, return $\perp$.
5. Otherwise, search the minimum $t \in \{0,1\}^m$ such that CalC$_y(C, \tilde{w}_{Cf}^{(1)}) = $ CalC$_y(C, \pi_C^{(2)}(t))$ by checking whether CalC$_y(C, \tilde{w}_{Cf}^{(1)}) = $ CalC$_y(C, \pi_C^{(2)}(i))$ holds for $i = 0, 1, 2, \ldots$ in a sequential order, and set $\tilde{w}_{Cf}^{(2)} := \pi_C^{(2)}(t)$.
6. Return $(\tilde{w}_{Cf}^{(1)}, \tilde{w}_{Cf}^{(2)}, \text{CalC}_y(C, \tilde{w}_{Cf}^{(1)}))$.

Note that D is an information theoretic decoder, and we do not care whether CalC$_y$ and SimCF^{h_y} run efficiently.

Analysis. Here we provide a formal analysis of encoding scheme's success probability. See Sect. 1.3 for an intuitive overview. The following lemma shows that h_y, CalC_y, and SimCF^{h_y} satisfy some suitable properties. Here we consider the situation that D takes an input $(\tilde{f}, \tilde{G})$ such that $(\tilde{f}, \tilde{G}) = E((R, R'), f)$ for some subsets $R, R' \subset \{0,1\}^n$ and a permutation $f \in \mathsf{Perm}(\{0,1\}^n)$, and tries to recover the value $f^{-1}(y)$ for some $y \in \tilde{G}$.

Lemma 7. h_y, CalC_y, and SimCF_{h_y} satisfy the following properties.

1. $\Delta(h_y, f) = R \cap R' \backslash \{f^{-1}(y)\}$ holds.
2. $\mathsf{CalC}_y(C, w) = F_C^f(w)$ or $\perp$ holds for any $C \in \mathsf{Circ}(\lambda(n)) \cap$ valid and w.
3. $\mathsf{CalC}_y(C, w_{Cf}^{(1)}) = F_C^f(w_{Cf}^{(1)})$ and $\mathsf{CalC}_y(C, w_{Cf}^{(2)}) = F_C^f(w_{Cf}^{(2)})$ hold for each circuit $C \in \mathsf{Circ}(\lambda(n)) \cap$ valid which is good relative to $f^{-1}(y)$.
4. $\mathsf{SimCF}^{h_y}(C) = \mathsf{ColFinder}^f(C)$ holds for each circuit $C \in \mathsf{Circ}(\lambda(n)) \cap$ valid which is good relative to $f^{-1}(y)$. In particular, $\Delta(\mathsf{ColFinder}^f, \mathsf{SimCF}^{h_y}) \subset \mathsf{badC}(R', f^{-1}(y))$ holds.

Proof. The first property is obviously satisfied by definition of h_y.

For the second property, since $f \in P_{\text{candidate}}$, if $\mathsf{CalC}_y(C, w) \neq \perp$ then we have $\mathsf{CalC}_y(C, w) = u(C, w, f) \neq \perp$ by definition of CalC_y, and $u(C, w, f) = F_C^f(w)$ always holds. Hence the second property holds.

For the third property, for each $h' \in P_{\text{candidate}}$, from Lemma 2 we have

$$\Pr\left[C^{h'}(w_{Cf}^{(1)}) = F_C^f(w_{Cf}^{(1)})\right] \geq \Pr\left[C^f(w_{Cf}^{(1)}) = F_C^f(w_{Cf}^{(1)})\right]$$
$$- \left\| C^f | w_{Cf}^{(1)}, 0, 0\rangle - C^{h'} | w_{Cf}^{(1)}, 0, 0\rangle \right\|. \quad (14)$$

From the swapping lemma (Lemma 3) it follows that

$$\left\| C^f | w_{Cf}^{(1)}, 0, 0\rangle - C^{h'} | w_{Cf}^{(1)}, 0, 0\rangle \right\| \leq 2\sqrt{Q \sum_{z \in \Delta(f, h')} \mu_z^{C, f}(w_{Cf}^{(1)})}. \quad (15)$$

Since $\Delta(f, h') \subset R \cap R' \backslash \{f^{-1}(y)\} \subset R' \backslash \{f^{-1}(y)\}$ holds for all $h' \in P_{\text{candidate}}$, and C is a good circuit relative to $f^{-1}(y)$, the right hand side of the above inequality is upper bounded by $2\sqrt{\delta}$. Thus, for a sufficiently small δ we have

$$\Pr\left[C^{h'}(w_{Cf}^{(1)}) = F_C^f(w_{Cf}^{(1)})\right] \geq \frac{2}{3} - 2\sqrt{\delta} > \frac{1}{2}, \quad (16)$$

which implies that $u(C, w_{Cf}^{(1)}, h') = F_C^f(w_{Cf}^{(1)})$ holds for every $h' \in P_{\text{candidate}}$. Thus $\mathsf{CalC}_y(C, w_{Cf}^{(1)}) = F_C^f(w_{Cf}^{(1)})$ holds if C is good relative to $f^{-1}(y)$. The equality $\mathsf{CalC}_y(C, w_{Cf}^{(2)}) = F_C^f(w_{Cf}^{(2)})$ can be shown in the same way.

The fourth property follows from the definition of SimCF^{h_y}, the second property, and the third property. □

The following lemma shows that the decoding always succeeds if the encoding succeeds.

Lemma 8. *If* $E((R, R'), f) \neq \perp$, *then* $D((R, R'), E((R, R'), f)) = f$ *holds.*

Proof (of Lemma 8). Let $\tilde{f} := f|_{\{0,1\}^n \setminus G}$ and $\tilde{G} := f(G)$. We show that D can correctly recover $x = f^{-1}(y)$ for each $y \in \tilde{G}$.

We apply the swapping lemma (Lemma 3) to the oracle pairs $(f, \mathsf{ColFinder}^f)$ and $(h_y, \mathsf{SimCF}^{h_y})$. Then we have

$$\left\| \hat{\mathcal{A}}_n^{f, \mathsf{ColFinder}^f} |f(x), 0, 0\rangle - \hat{\mathcal{A}}_n^{h_y, \mathsf{SimCF}^{h_y}} |f(x), 0, 0\rangle \right\|$$
$$\leq 2 \sqrt{Q \sum_{z \in \Delta(f, h_y)} \mu_z^{\hat{\mathcal{A}}, f}(f(x))} + 2 \sqrt{Q \sum_{C \in \Delta(\mathsf{ColFinder}^f, \mathsf{SimCF}^{h_y})} \mu_C^{\hat{\mathcal{A}}, \mathsf{ColFinder}^f}(f(x))}.$$
$$(17)$$

Since $\Delta(f, h_y) = R \cap R' \setminus \{f^{-1}(y)\} \subset R \setminus \{f^{-1}(y)\} = R \setminus \{x\}$ and $\Delta(\mathsf{ColFinder}^f, \mathsf{SimCF}^{h_y}) \subset \mathsf{badC}(R', f^{-1}(y)) = \mathsf{badC}(R', x)$ from Lemma 7, the right hand side of inequality (17) is upper bounded by

$$2 \sqrt{Q \sum_{z \in R \setminus \{x\}} \mu_z^{\hat{\mathcal{A}}, f}(f(x))} + 2 \sqrt{Q \sum_{C \in \mathsf{badC}(R', x)} \mu_C^{\hat{\mathcal{A}}, \mathsf{ColFinder}^f}(f(x))}. \quad (18)$$

Due to the conditions (Cond. 2) and (Cond. 3) (see p. 21), each term of the above expression is upper bounded by $2\sqrt{\delta}$. Thus, eventually we have

$$\left\| \hat{\mathcal{A}}_n^{f, \mathsf{ColFinder}^f} |f(x), 0, 0\rangle - \hat{\mathcal{A}}_n^{h_y, \mathsf{SimCF}^{h_y}} |f(x), 0, 0\rangle \right\| \leq 4\sqrt{\delta} \quad (19)$$

Finally, from Lemma 2, for sufficiently small δ it follows that

$$\Pr \left[\hat{\mathcal{A}}^{h_y, \mathsf{SimCF}^{h_y}}(f(x)) = x \right]$$
$$\geq \Pr \left[\hat{\mathcal{A}}^{f, \mathsf{ColFinder}^f}(f(x)) = x \right]$$
$$- \left\| \hat{\mathcal{A}}_n^{f, \mathsf{ColFinder}^f} |f(x), 0, 0\rangle - \mathcal{A}_n^{h_y, \mathsf{ColFinder}^h} |f(x), 0, 0\rangle \right\|$$
$$\geq 2/3 - 4\sqrt{\delta} > 1/2, \quad (20)$$

which implies that D correctly recovers $x = f^{-1}(y)$. $\quad\square$

The following lemma is a generalization of a claim showed by Nayebi et al. [NABT15, Claim 8], which shows that our E and D work well with a constant probability. See the proof for Lemma 9 of this paper's full version [HY18] for a complete proof.

Lemma 9. *If* $Q^6 \leq \delta^4 p_2 2^n / 32$,

$$\Pr_{(R, R')} [D((R, R'), E((R, R'), f) = f] \geq 0.7 \quad (21)$$

holds for each $f \in X$.

Finally, we show that Proposition 1 follows from the above lemmas.

Proof (of Proposition 1). First, remember that the set Y is defined as

$$Y := \left\{ (f|_{\{0,1\}^n \setminus G}, f(G)) \mid f \in \mathsf{Perm}(\{0,1\}^n), G \subset \{0,1\}^n, |G| \geq \theta \right\}. \quad (22)$$

For each fixed positive integer $\theta \leq M \leq 2^n$, the cardinality of the set

$$Y_M := \left\{ (f|_{\{0,1\}^n \setminus G}, f(G)) \mid f \in \mathsf{Perm}(\{0,1\}^n), G \subset \{0,1\}^n, |G| = M \right\} \quad (23)$$

is equal to $(2^n - M)! \cdot \binom{2^n}{M} = (2^n)!/M!$. Thus $|Y|$ is upper bounded as

$$|Y| = \sum_{M=\lceil \theta \rceil}^{2^n} \frac{(2^n)!}{M!} \leq 2^n \cdot \frac{(2^n)!}{(\lceil \theta \rceil)!} \quad (24)$$

for sufficiently large n. Here we show the following claim.

Claim. If $Q^6 \leq \delta^4 p_2 2^n / 32$, there exists a constant const_1 such that $Q^6 \geq \mathsf{const}_1 \cdot 2^n/n$ holds. We can choose const_1 independently of n.

Proof (of Claim). By definition of X, $|X| \geq p_1(2^n)!$ holds. In addition, from inequality (24), we have $|Y| \leq 2^n \cdot \frac{(2^n)!}{(\lceil \theta \rceil)!}$. Moreover, since now we are assuming that $Q^6 \leq \delta^4 p_2 2^n / 32$ holds, it follows that $|Y| \geq 0.7|X|$ from Lemma 6 and Lemma 9. Hence we have $2^n \cdot \frac{(2^n)!}{(\lceil \theta \rceil)!} \geq 0.7 \cdot p_1(2^n)!$, which is equivalent to $\frac{2^n}{0.7p_1} \geq \lceil \theta \rceil!$.

Since p_1 is a constant and $n! \geq 2^n$ holds for $n \geq 4$, there exists a constant const_2, which can be taken independently of n, such that $\lceil \mathsf{const}_2 \cdot n \rceil! \geq 2^n/(0.7p_1)$ holds. Now we have $\lceil \mathsf{const}_2 \cdot n \rceil \geq \lceil \theta \rceil$, which implies that $\mathsf{const}_2 \cdot n + 1 \geq \theta = \delta^4 \left(1 - 60\sqrt{\delta}\right) \frac{p_2 2^n}{2Q^6}$ holds. Moreover, since δ and p_2 are also constants, there exists a constant const_1 that is independent of n and $Q^6 \geq \mathsf{const}_1 \cdot 2^n/n$ holds, which completes the proof of the claim. □

Let $\mathsf{const}_3 := \min\{\delta^4 p_2/32, \mathsf{const}_1\}$. Then, from the the above claim, it follows that $Q^6 \geq \mathsf{const}_3 \cdot 2^n/n$ holds. Since $Q = c \lceil \frac{1}{\epsilon} \rceil (\max\{q, \eta\} + 1)$ by definition of Q, we have $c^6 \lceil \frac{1}{\epsilon} \rceil^6 (\max\{q, \eta\} + 1)^6 \geq \mathsf{const}_3 \cdot 2^n/n$. Hence there exists a constant const such that $\max\{q, \eta\} \geq \mathsf{const} \cdot \epsilon \cdot 2^{n/6}/n^{1/6} \geq \mathsf{const} \cdot \epsilon \cdot 2^{n/7}$ holds for all sufficiently large n, which completes the proof. □

4.2 Proof of Theorem 3

This section shows that Theorem 3 follows from Proposition 1. First, we can show that the following lemma follows from Proposition 1.

Lemma 10. *For any efficient oracle-aided quantum algorithm $\mathcal{B}$ and for any polynomial λ, there exists a permutation $f : \{0,1\}^* \to \{0,1\}^*$ such that*

$$\Pr_{y \leftarrow \{0,1\}^n} \left[x \leftarrow \mathcal{B}^{f, \mathsf{ColFinder}_\lambda^f}(y) : f(x) = y \right] < 2^{-n/8} \quad (25)$$

holds for all sufficiently large n.

The proof of the lemma is straightforward. See the proof of Lemma 10 in this paper's full version [HY18] for a complete proof.

Proof (of Theorem 3). Let $\Gamma_1 := \mathsf{Perm}(\{0,1\}^*)$ and $\Gamma_2 := \{\mathsf{ColFinder}_\lambda^f\}_{f \in \Gamma_1, \lambda \in \Lambda}$, where Λ is the set of all polynomials in n. (If $\lambda(n) \leq 0$ for some n, we assume that $\mathsf{ColFinder}_{\lambda,n}^f$ does not take any inputs.) Below we show that the two conditions of Lemma 4 are satisfied.

For the first condition of Lemma 4, we define an oracle-aided quantum algorithm $\mathcal{J}_0$ as follows: When we feed $\mathcal{J}_0$ with an input x relative to a permutation f, $\mathcal{J}_0$ queries x to f and obtains the output $f(x)$. Then $\mathcal{J}_0$ returns $f(x)$ as its output. We show that this algorithm $\mathcal{J}_0$ satisfies the first condition of Lemma 4 (existence of CC-qOWP). It is obvious that $\mathcal{J}_0^f \in F_{\mathsf{CC\text{-}qOWP}}$ for any permutation f, by definition of $\mathcal{J}_0$. Let $\mathcal{B}$ be an efficient oracle-aided quantum algorithm, and λ be a polynomial in n.

From Lemma 10, it follows that, for any efficient oracle-aided quantum algorithm $\mathcal{B}$ and any $\lambda \in \Lambda$, there exists a permutation f such that

$$\Pr_{y \leftarrow \{0,1\}^n} \left[x \leftarrow \mathcal{B}^{f, \mathsf{ColFinder}_\lambda^f}(y) : f(x) = y \right] < \mathsf{negl}(n) \tag{26}$$

holds, which implies that $\mathcal{B}^{f, \mathsf{ColFinder}_\lambda^f}$ does not CC-qOWP-break $\mathcal{J}_0^f$ relative to $(f, \mathsf{ColFinder}_\lambda^f)$. Hence the first condition (existence of CC-qOWP) of Lemma 4 is satisfied.

Next, we show that the second condition (non-existence of QC-qCRH) of Lemma 4 is satisfied. For any efficient oracle-aided quantum algorithm $\mathcal{I} = (\mathsf{Gen}, \mathsf{Eval})$ such that $\mathcal{I}^f \in F_{\mathsf{CC\text{-}qCRH}}$ holds for any permutation f, let λ be a polynomial such that $\lambda(n) > |\mathcal{I}_n|$ for all n. We define a family of oracle-aided quantum algorithms $\mathcal{A}_\mathcal{I}$ as follows: Given an input σ, $\mathcal{A}_\mathcal{I}$ queries the oracle-aided quantum circuit $\mathsf{Eval}_n(\sigma, \cdot)$ to $\mathsf{ColFinder}_\lambda^f$, obtains an answer $(w^{(1)}, w^{(2)}, H^f(\sigma, w^{(1)}))$[16], and finally outputs $(w^{(1)}, w^{(2)})$. When $\mathcal{A}_\mathcal{I}^{\mathsf{ColFinder}_\lambda^f}$ is given an input σ, the output will be $(w^{(1)}, w^{(2)})$, where $w^{(1)}$ is uniformly distributed over the domain of $H^f(\sigma, \cdot) : \{0,1\}^{m(n)} \to \{0,1\}^{\ell(n)}$ and $w^{(2)}$ is uniformly distributed over the set $(H^f(\sigma, \cdot))^{-1}(H^f(\sigma, w^{(1)}))$. Since $m(n) > \ell(n)$ holds by definition of implementations of QC-qCRH, the probability that $w^{(1)} \neq w^{(2)}$, which implies that $(w^{(1)}, w^{(2)})$ is a collision of $H^f(\sigma, \cdot)$, is at least $1/4$. Thus it follows that there exists $\mathcal{A}_\mathcal{I}$ and $\lambda \in \Lambda$ such that $\mathcal{A}_\mathcal{I}^{\mathsf{ColFinder}_\lambda^f}$ CC-qCRH-breaks $\mathcal{I}^f$ for any permutation f. Hence the second condition of Lemma 4 is satisfied. $\square$

---

[16] Since $\mathcal{I}^{f'} \in F_{\mathsf{CC\text{-}qCRH}}$ for any permutation f', $\mathsf{Eval}_n^{f'}(\cdot, \cdot)$ computes a function $H^{f'}(\cdot, \cdot)$ for any permutation f' by definition of QC-qCRH. In particular, even when σ is generated by $\mathsf{Gen}^f(1^n)$ and $f' \neq f$, $\mathsf{Eval}_n^{f'}(\sigma, \cdot)$ computes the function $H^{f'}(\sigma, \cdot)$. Hence $\mathsf{ColFinder}_\lambda^f$ does not return $\perp$ on the input $\mathsf{Eval}_n(\sigma, \cdot)$.

5   Impossibility of Reduction from QC-qCRHto CC-qTDP

As well as the impossibility of reduction from QC-qCRH to CC-qOWP, we can show the following theorem.

Theorem 4. *There exists no quantum fully-black-box reduction from* QC-qCRHto CC-qTDP.

Remark 12. The statement of Theorem 4 is the strongest result among possible quantum (fully-black-box) separations of CRH from TDP, since it also excludes reductions from CC-qCRH to CC-qTDP, reductions from QC-qCRH to QC-qTDP, and reductions from CC-qCRH to QC-qTDP.[17]

Here we give only a proof intuition. See Sect. 5 of this paper's full version [HY18] for a complete proof.

Proof Intuition. To show this theorem, again we define two oracles that separate QC-qCRH from CC-qTDP. That is, we define an oracle (g, f, f^{inv}) that implements random trapdoor permutations, in addition to an oracle ColFinder$^{g,f,f^{\mathrm{inv}}}$ that finds collisions of functions, and then apply Lemma 4 (the two oracle technique). Here, $g : \{0,1\}^n \to \{0,1\}^n$ is a random permutation and $f : \{0,1\}^n \times \{0,1\}^n \to \{0,1\}^n$ is a family of random permutations $(f(z, \cdot) : \{0,1\}^n \to \{0,1\}^n$ is a random permutation for each $z \in \{0,1\}^n)$. f^{inv} is the inverse of f defined by $f^{\mathrm{inv}}(z, \cdot) := (f(g(z), \cdot))^{-1}$. At the beginning of each game, a trapdoor td $\in \{0,1\}^n$ is chosen randomly, and a public key pk is set as pk $:= g(\mathsf{td}) \in \{0,1\}^n$. We consider the situation that each adversary $\mathcal{A}$ is given the public key pk and a randomly chosen target y to invert, in addition to oracle accesses to (g, f, f^{inv}) and ColFinder$^{g,f,f^{\mathrm{inv}}}$, and $\mathcal{A}$ tries to find x such that $f(\mathsf{pk}, x) = y$.

Recall that the most technically difficult part of the proof in Sect. 4 was to show that, if $\mathcal{A}$ inverts a random permutation with a high probability, it has to make exponentially many queries. Similarly the most technically difficult part to prove Theorem 4 is to show that, if $\mathcal{A}$ inverts y in $f(\mathsf{pk}, \cdot)$ (with a high probability), $\mathcal{A}$ has to make exponentially many queries.

We consider three separate cases: The first case is the one that $\mathcal{A}$'s query magnitude on the trapdoor td to f^{inv} is large (we denote this event by TDHIT$_1$). The second case is the one that $\mathcal{A}$'s query magnitude on a quantum circuit C to ColFinder$^{g,f,f^{\mathrm{inv}}}$ that queries the trapdoor td to f^{inv} is large (we denote this event by TDHIT$_2$). The third case is the one that both of TDHIT$_1$ and TDHIT$_2$ do not occur.

In the first and second cases, by using $\mathcal{A}$ we can construct another algorithm $\mathcal{B}$ that makes almost as much queries as $\mathcal{A}$ and inverts pk $= g(\mathsf{td})$ in g (with a

---

[17] Note that it also excludes possible quantum (fully-black-box) reductions from collapsing hash functions to trapdoor permutations, since the notion of collapsing is stronger than collision-resistance.

high probability). Since g is just a random permutation, from the results shown in Sect. 4 it follows that $\mathcal{B}$ has to make exponentially many queries, which implies that $\mathcal{A}$ has to make exponentially many queries. In the third case, intuitively, we can construct a randomized compression scheme that compresses the truth table of the random permutation $f(\mathsf{pk}, \cdot)$ without the inverse oracle $f^{\mathrm{inv}}(\mathsf{td}, \cdot)$ since the query magnitude to $f^{\mathrm{inv}}(\mathsf{td}, \cdot)$ is always small if $\neg(\mathsf{TDHIT}_1 \vee \mathsf{TDHIT}_2)$ occurs.

Acknowledgments. We thank anonymous reviewers for their insightful comments. Especially, we thank reviewers of STOC 2019 and CRYPTO 2020 who pointed out technical errors in previous versions of this paper.

References

[Aar09] Aaronson, S.: Quantum copy-protection and quantum money. In: CCC 2009, Proceedings, pp. 229–242 (2009)

[ABF+16] Alagic, G., Broadbent, A., Fefferman, B., Gagliardoni, T., Schaffner, C., St. Jules, M.: Computational security of quantum encryption. In: Nascimento, A.C.A., Barreto, P. (eds.) ICITS 2016. LNCS, vol. 10015, pp. 47–71. Springer, Cham (2016). https://doi.org/10.1007/978-3-319-49175-2_3

[AC12] Aaronson, S., Christiano, P.: Quantum money from hidden subspaces. In: Karloff, H.J., Pitassi, T. (eds.) 44th ACM STOC, pp. 41–60. ACM Press (May 2012)

[AGM18] Alagic, G., Gagliardoni, T., Majenz, C.: Unforgeable quantum encryption. In: Nielsen, J.B., Rijmen, V. (eds.) EUROCRYPT 2018. LNCS, vol. 10822, pp. 489–519. Springer, Cham (2018). https://doi.org/10.1007/978-3-319-78372-7_16

[Ajt96] Ajtai, M.: Generating hard instances of lattice problems (extended abstract). In: 28th ACM STOC, pp. 99–108. ACM Press (May 1996)

[ARU14] Ambainis, A., Rosmanis, A., Unruh, D.: Quantum attacks on classical proof systems: the hardness of quantum rewinding. In: 55th FOCS, pp. 474–483. IEEE Computer Society Press (October 2014)

[AS15] Asharov, G., Segev, G.: Limits on the power of indistinguishability obfuscation and functional encryption. In: Guruswami, V. (ed.) 56th FOCS, pp. 191–209. IEEE Computer Society Press (October 2015)

[BB84] Bennett, C.H., Brassard, G.: Quantum cryptography: public key distribution and coin tossing. In: Proceedings of IEEE International Conference on Computers, Systems, and Signal Processing, India, pp. 175–179 (1984)

[BBBV97] Bennett, C.H., Bernstein, E., Brassard, G., Vazirani, U.: Strengths and weaknesses of quantum computing. SIAM J. Comput. **26**(5), 1510–1523 (1997)

[BD19] Bitansky, N., Degwekar, A.: On the complexity of collision resistant hash functions: new and old black-box separations. In: Hofheinz, D., Rosen, A. (eds.) TCC 2019. LNCS, vol. 11891, pp. 422–450. Springer, Cham (2019). https://doi.org/10.1007/978-3-030-36030-6_17

[BJ15] Broadbent, A., Jeffery, S.: Quantum homomorphic encryption for circuits of low T-gate complexity. In: Gennaro, R., Robshaw, M. (eds.) CRYPTO 2015. LNCS, vol. 9216, pp. 609–629. Springer, Heidelberg (2015). https://doi.org/10.1007/978-3-662-48000-7_30

[BL17]   Bernstein, D.J., Lange, T.: Post-quantum cryptography. Nature **549**, 188–194 (2017)

[BLP+13] Brakerski, Z., Langlois, A., Peikert, C., Regev, O., Stehlé, D.: Classical hardness of learning with errors. In: Boneh, D., Roughgarden, T., Feigenbaum, J. (eds.) 45th ACM STOC, pp. 575–584. ACM Press (June 2013)

[Bra18]   Brakerski, Z.: Quantum FHE (almost) as secure as classical. In: Shacham, H., Boldyreva, A. (eds.) CRYPTO 2018. LNCS, vol. 10993, pp. 67–95. Springer, Cham (2018). https://doi.org/10.1007/978-3-319-96878-0_3

[BS16]   Broadbent, A., Schaffner, C.: Quantum cryptography beyond quantum key distribution. Des. Codes Cryptogr. **78**(1), 351–382 (2016)

[CHS18]   Chia, N.-H., Hallgren, S., Song, F.: On basing one-way permutations on NP-hard problems under quantum reductions. CoRR arxiv:1804.10309 (2018)

[CLMP13] Chung, K.-M., Lin, H., Mahmoody, M., Pass, R.: On the power of nonuniformity in proofs of security. In: Kleinberg, R.D. (ed.) ITCS 2013, pp. 389–400. ACM (January 2013)

[DTT10]   De, A., Trevisan, L., Tulsiani, M.: Time space tradeoffs for attacks against one-way functions and PRGs. In: Rabin, T. (ed.) CRYPTO 2010. LNCS, vol. 6223, pp. 649–665. Springer, Heidelberg (2010). https://doi.org/10.1007/978-3-642-14623-7_35

[GC01]   Gottesman, D., Chuang, I.: Quantum digital signatures. CoRR, abs/quant-ph/0105032 (2001)

[GT00]   Gennaro, R., Trevisan, L.: Lower bounds on the efficiency of generic cryptographic constructions. In: 41st FOCS, pp. 305–313. IEEE Computer Society Press (November 2000)

[HHRS07] Haitner, I., Hoch, J.J., Reingold, O., Segev, G.: Finding collisions in interactive protocols - a tight lower bound on the round complexity of statistically-hiding commitments. In: 48th FOCS, pp. 669–679. IEEE Computer Society Press (October 2007)

[HL18]   Holmgren, J., Lombardi, A.: Cryptographic hashing from strong one-way functions (or: one-way product functions and their applications). In: Thorup, M. (ed.) 59th FOCS, pp. 850–858. IEEE Computer Society Press (October 2018)

[HR04]   Hsiao, C.-Y., Reyzin, L.: Finding collisions on a public road, or do secure hash functions need secret coins? In: Franklin, M. (ed.) CRYPTO 2004. LNCS, vol. 3152, pp. 92–105. Springer, Heidelberg (2004). https://doi.org/10.1007/978-3-540-28628-8_6

[HXY19]   Hhan, M., Xagawa, K., Yamakawa, T.: Quantum random oracle model with auxiliary input. In: Galbraith, S.D., Moriai, S. (eds.) ASIACRYPT 2019. LNCS, vol. 11921, pp. 584–614. Springer, Cham (2019). https://doi.org/10.1007/978-3-030-34578-5_21

[HY18]   Hosoyamada, A., Yamakawa, T.: Finding collisions in a quantum world: quantum black-box separation of collision-resistance and one-wayness. IACR Cryptology ePrint Archive: Report 2018/1066 (2018)

[IR89]   Impagliazzo, R., Rudich, S.: Limits on the provable consequences of one-way permutations. In: 21st ACM STOC, pp. 44–61. ACM Press (May 1989)

[JF11]   Jao, D., De Feo, L.: Towards quantum-resistant cryptosystems from supersingular elliptic curve isogenies. In: Yang, B.-Y. (ed.) PQCrypto 2011. LNCS, vol. 7071, pp. 19–34. Springer, Heidelberg (2011). https://doi.org/10.1007/978-3-642-25405-5_2

[KSVV02] Kitaev, A.Y., Shen, A., Vyalyi, M.N., Vyalyi, M.N.: Classical and Quantum Computation, vol. 47. American Mathematical Society, Calgary (2002)

[Mah18] Mahadev, U.: Classical homomorphic encryption for quantum circuits. In: Thorup, M. (ed.) 59th FOCS, pp. 332–338. IEEE Computer Society Press (October 2018)

[McE78] McEliece, R.J.: A public-key cryptosystem based on algebraic coding theory. DSN Prog. Rep. **44**, 114–116 (1978)

[NABT15] Nayebi, A., Aaronson, S., Belovs, A., Trevisan, L.: Quantum lower bound for inverting a permutation with advice. Quantum Inf. Comput. **15**(11&12), 901–913 (2015)

[NC10] Nielsen, M.A., Chuang, I.L.: Quantum Computation and Quantum Information: 10th, Anniversary edn. Cambridge University Press (2010)

[NIS16] NIST: Post-quantum cryptography standardization (2016). https://csrc. nist.gov/Projects/Post-Quantum-Cryptography

[Pei09] Peikert, C.: Public-key cryptosystems from the worst-case shortest vector problem: extended abstract. In: Mitzenmacher, M. (ed.) 41st ACM STOC, pp. 333–342. ACM Press, May/June 2009

[Reg05] Regev, O.: On lattices, learning with errors, random linear codes, and cryptography. In: Gabow, H.N., Fagin, R. (eds.) 37th ACM STOC, pp. 84–93. ACM Press (May 2005)

[RS18] Rotem, L., Segev, G.: Injective trapdoor functions via derandomization: how strong is Rudich's black-box barrier? In: Beimel, A., Dziembowski, S. (eds.) TCC 2018. LNCS, vol. 11239, pp. 421–447. Springer, Cham (2018). https://doi.org/10.1007/978-3-030-03807-6_16

[RTV04] Reingold, O., Trevisan, L., Vadhan, S.: Notions of reducibility between cryptographic primitives. In: Naor, M. (ed.) TCC 2004. LNCS, vol. 2951, pp. 1–20. Springer, Heidelberg (2004). https://doi.org/10.1007/978-3-540-24638-1_1

[Rud88] Rudich, S.: Limits on the provable consequences of one-way functions. Ph.D. thesis, University of California, Berkeley (1988)

[Sho94] Shor, P.W.: Algorithms for quantum computation: discrete logarithms and factoring. In: 35th FOCS, pp. 124–134. IEEE Computer Society Press (November 1994)

[Sim98] Simon, D.R.: Finding collisions on a one-way street: can secure hash functions be based on general assumptions? In: Nyberg, K. (ed.) EUROCRYPT 1998. LNCS, vol. 1403, pp. 334–345. Springer, Heidelberg (1998). https://doi.org/10.1007/BFb0054137

[Vaz98] Vazirani, U.: On the power of quantum computation. Philos. Trans.-R. Soc. Lond. Ser. A Math. Phys. Eng. Sci. **356**, 1759–1767 (1998)

[Wie83] Wiesner, S.: Conjugate coding. SIGACT News **15**(1), 78–88 (1983)

[Yao93] Yao, A.C.-C.: Quantum circuit complexity. In: 34th Annual Symposium on Foundations of Computer Science, Palo Alto, California, USA, 3–5 November, 1993, pp. 352–361 (1993)

[Zha19] Zhandry, M.: Quantum lightning never strikes the same state twice. In: Ishai, Y., Rijmen, V. (eds.) EUROCRYPT 2019. LNCS, vol. 11478, pp. 408–438. Springer, Cham (2019). https://doi.org/10.1007/978-3-030-17659-4_14

New Results on **Gimli**: Full-Permutation Distinguishers and Improved Collisions

Antonio Flórez Gutiérrez[✉], Gaëtan Leurent, María Naya-Plasencia,
Léo Perrin, André Schrottenloher, and Ferdinand Sibleyras

Inria, Paris, France
{antonio.florez-gutierrez,gaetan.leurent,maria.naya_plasencia,
leo.perrin,andre.schrottenloher,ferdinand.sibleyras}@inria.fr

Abstract. Gimli is a family of cryptographic primitives (both a hash function and an AEAD scheme) that has been selected for the second round of the NIST competition for standardizing new lightweight designs. The candidate Gimli is based on the permutation Gimli, which was presented at CHES 2017. In this paper, we study the security of both the permutation and the constructions that are based on it. We exploit the slow diffusion in Gimli and its internal symmetries to build, for the first time, a distinguisher on the full permutation of complexity 2^{64}. We also provide a practical distinguisher on 23 out of the full 24 rounds of Gimli that has been implemented.

Next, we give (full state) collision and semi-free-start collision attacks on Gimli-Hash, reaching respectively up to 12 and 18 rounds. On the practical side, we compute a collision on 8-round Gimli-Hash. In the quantum setting, these attacks reach 2 more rounds. Finally, we perform the first study of linear trails in the permutation, and we propose differential-linear cryptanalysis that reach up to 17 rounds of Gimli.

Keywords: Gimli · Symmetries · Symmetric cryptanalysis · Full-round distinguisher · Collision attacks · Linear approximations

1 Introduction

Gimli is a cryptographic permutation that was published at CHES 2017 [5]. It is also the core primitive of a submission to the NIST lightweight cryptography project [6] which is part of the 32 candidates that made it to the second round. It is intended to run well on a vast variety of platforms and contexts, from powerful processors supporting vector instructions to side-channel protected hardware.

A cryptographic permutation is a versatile primitive which is easily used to construct a hash function (as originally intended for this type of object [7]). It was later shown that they can also be used to build authenticated ciphers [10], pseudo-random number generators [9], etc. In all such structures, the security of the cryptographic function relies on the properties of the permutation. In particular, it is assumed in the underlying security proofs that the permutation

© International Association for Cryptologic Research 2020
S. Moriai and H. Wang (Eds.): ASIACRYPT 2020, LNCS 12491, pp. 33–63, 2020.
https://doi.org/10.1007/978-3-030-64837-4_2

used behaves like a permutation picked uniformly at random—apart of course from the existence of a compact implementation, a property which should not be expected from a random object.

By definition, a cryptographic permutation does not have a key. Thus, we cannot define its security level using a game that relies on distinguishing a random permutation from a keyed instance with a random key. Still, since it should behave like a permutation picked uniformly at random, we can assess its security level by trying to identify properties that hold for the permutation studied but which should not be expected for one picked uniformly at random. In this context, cryptanalysts can re-use approaches originally intended for block cipher cryptanalysis (e.g. differential attacks [11]). In fact, given that no key material is involved, we can also borrow techniques from hash function cryptanalysis such as rebound attacks [24].

The aim is usually then to obtain inputs of the permutation satisfying a certain property using an algorithm which is more efficient than the generic one, i.e. the one that would work on a random permutation.

Our Contributions. In this paper, we complete the original security analysis of the designers of Gimli by targeting both the permutation on its own, and the NIST candidate Gimli-Hash. Our results on the permutation are summarized in Fig. 1 (plain lines). In order to account for the different costs of the generic attacks, we divided the logarithm of the time complexity of our distinguishers by the logarithm of the time complexity of the corresponding generic distinguisher. In Fig. 1, a distinguisher is valid if the ratio is under 1.0. Previous attacks from the literature are represented with dotted lines. The complexities of all our attacks (included those against the hash function) are given in Table 1, along with all the results from the literature we are aware of.

Our main result is a distinguisher of the full 24-round permutation with a cost of 2^{64}, while a similar generic distinguisher has a cost of 2^{96}. We also propose a distinguisher on 23 rounds that is practical, with a cost of 2^{32}, and has been successfully implemented. These distinguishers exploit internal symmetries that are encouraged by the round function. The 23-round distinguisher could be extended by 1 round for free if the rounds were shifted[1].

Using similar guess-and-determine ideas, we increase to 12 the number of rounds susceptible to collision attacks on Gimli-Hash. A reduced-round version of this attack has been implemented. In the quantum setting, we obtain collisions up to 14 rounds. We also build semi-free start collisions, i.e. we show how to find one internal state value and two different messages (thus not affecting the capacity part) that provide a collision on the capacity after applying the permutation. This attack is more efficient than a generic one for 18 rounds classically, and up to 20 quantumly. As a side note, these results provide a new example where quantum attacks reach more rounds than classical ones, much like in [21].

In addition, we provide the first extensive study of the linear properties of the round function of Gimli, and use them to perform differential-linear distinguishers

---

[1] This behaviour appears because the linear layer of Gimli is round dependent.

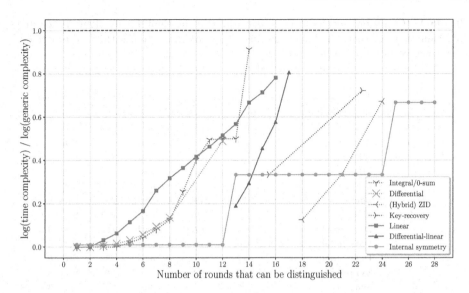

Fig. 1. Comparison of various cryptanalysis techniques. Note that we may consider "shifted" variants of Gimli that do not start at round 24. Dotted lines correspond to results from the literature.

up to 17 rounds. While this distinguisher is less efficient than the one based on internal symmetries, it is the most efficient statistical distinguisher in terms of rounds covered.

Our implementations (23-round distinguisher, reduced-round collision attack, search for linear trails) are available at this URL[2].

Organization of the Paper. The organization of the paper is as follows. In Sect. 2 we provide the description of the Gimli permutation and primitive, as well as previous known results. Section 3 provides the new distinguishers exploiting the internal symmetries that allow to distinguish the full permutation, and to build practical distinguishers up to 23 rounds. Section 4 presents improved collision and semi-free start collision attacks, and Sect. 5 their quantum counterpart. Section 6 presents our new results regarding statistical distinguishers, with optimal linear trails and new differential-linear attacks. We conclude the paper in Sect. 7 with a summary, a discussion on the impact of our results and a proposal of tweak that would mitigate their reach.

2   Preliminaries

In this section we describe the Gimli permutation and we provide an overview of previous cryptanalysis results. The Gimli-Hash function is described directly in Sect. 4.

---

[2] https://project.inria.fr/quasymodo/files/2020/05/gimli_cryptanalysis_eprint.tar.gz.

Table 1. (Quantum) results against algorithms of the Gimli family. Time is counted in evaluations of Gimli, and memory in 128-bit blocks. Attacks that were actually implemented are written in **bold**. ϵ is a term that we only estimated experimentally ($\epsilon \approx 10$, see Sect. 4). In rounds attacked, $r_1 \rightarrow r_2$ means rounds r_1 to r_2 included.

	Technique	Rounds	Time	Memory	Generic	Reference
Distinguishers	Key-recovery on Gimli-PRF	$25 \rightarrow 2.5$	138.5	128	192	[20]
on the		15.5	64	64	192	[20]
permutation	Zero-sum	14	351	negl.	384	[14]
(real rounds:	ZID	18	2	negl.	4	[29]
$24 \rightarrow 1$)	ZID	21	65	negl.	192	[29]
	ZID	24	129	negl.	192	[29]
	Linear	12	198	negl.	384	Sect. 6.1
	Linear	16	300	negl.	384	Sect. 6.1
	Differential-Linear	15	87.4	negl.	192	Sect. 6.2
	Differential-Linear	16	110.8	negl.	192	Sect. 6.2
	Differential-Linear	17	154.8	negl.	192	Sect. 6.2
	Symmetry	$\mathbf{23 \rightarrow 0}$	**32**	**negl.**	**96**	Sect. 3
	Symmetry	$27 \rightarrow 0$	64	negl.	96	Sect. 3
Preimages on	Divide-and- conquer	2	42.4	32	128	[29]
Gimli-Hash		5	96	65.6	128	[29]
Preimages on		9	104	70	128	[29]
Gimli-XOF-128						
Collisions on	Divide-and- conquer	5	65	–	128	[27]
Gimli-Hash		**3**	**Practical**	–	**128**	[27]
		6	64	64	128	[28]
	Symmetry	$\mathbf{21 \rightarrow 14}$	$\mathbf{32 + \epsilon}$	**negl.**	**128**	**Sect. 4**
	Symmetry	12	$96 + \epsilon$	negl.	128	Sect. 4
	Quantum	14	$64 + \epsilon$	negl.	85.3	Sect. 4
Semi-free start	Symmetry	8	64	negl.	128	[28]
collisions on	Symmetry	12	$32 + \epsilon$	negl.	128	Sect. 4
Gimli-Hash	Symmetry	16	$96 + \epsilon$	negl.	128	Sect. 4
	Symmetry	18	$96 + \epsilon$	64	128	Sect. 4
	Quantum	20	$64 + \epsilon$	64	85.3	Sect. 4

We adopt the following notations in this paper: $\ll, \gg, \lll, \ggg$ represent respectively shift left, shift right, *rotate left* and rotate right operations. x, y, z will denote elements of $\mathbb{F}_2^{32}$. SP is the 96-bit SP-Box. We denote x_i the $(i \bmod 32)^{th}$ bit of x ($x_{33} = x_1$) with x_0 least significant (right-most). We denote the output of the SP box as $SP(x, y, z) = (x', y', z')$ and $SP^2(x, y, z) = (x'', y'', z'')$.

2.1   The Gimli Permutation

State Structure. We denote by S the 384-bit Gimli state, which is the concatenation of 4 *columns* of 96-bit, that we denote A, B, C, D, where A is column number 0, and D is column number 3. Each column is cut into three 32-bit *words* x, y, z which are denoted *e.g.* A_x, A_y, A_z. Thus, the state is a $4 \times 3 \times 32$ parallelepiped. We will speak of the x *lane* to denote the sequence or concatenation of words A_x, B_x, C_x, D_x.

Algorithm 1. The full Gimli permutation.

   Input: State $S = A, B, C, D$
   Output: Gimli(S)
1: **for** $r = 24$ downto 1 inclusive **do**
2:     $A, B, C, D \leftarrow SP(A), SP(B), SP(C), SP(D)$ ▷ SP-Box layer
3:     **if** $r \mod 4 = 0$ **then**
4:        Swap A_x and B_x, swap C_x and D_x ▷ small swap
5:        $A_x \leftarrow A_x \oplus \mathsf{rc}_r$ ▷ Constant addition
6:     **else if** $r \mod 2 = 0$ **then**
7:        Swap A_x and C_x, swap B_x and D_x ▷ big swap
8:     **end if**
9: **end for**
   Return S

SP-Box. The only non-linear operation in Gimli is the SP-Box, which is applied columnwise. On input x, y, z, it updates the three words as follows:

1. Rotate x and y: $x \leftarrow x \lll 24, y \leftarrow y \lll 9$.
2. Perform the following non-linear operations in parallel (shifts are used rather than rotations):
$$x \leftarrow x \oplus (z \ll 1) \oplus ((y \wedge z) \ll 2),$$
$$y \leftarrow y \oplus x \oplus ((x \vee z) \ll 1),$$
$$z \leftarrow z \oplus y \oplus ((x \wedge y) \ll 3).$$
3. Swap x and z: $(x, z) \leftarrow (z, x)$.

Rounds. Gimli applies a sequence of 24 rounds numbered from 24 downto 1 inclusively. Each round applies an SP-Box layer, then performs a *swap* (every two rounds, either a "big swap" or a small "small swap" as shown in Algorithm 1) and a constant addition (every four rounds). The constant at round i, if there is one, will be denoted rc_i in what follows. In Gimli we have: $\mathsf{rc}_i = \text{0x9e377900} \oplus i$. Note that all the attacks studied in this paper are independent of the choice of round constants.

An algorithmic depiction of full Gimli is given in Algorithm 1

Boolean Description of the SP-Box. Now we give a full description of the SP box using Boolean functions:

– for x':

$$\begin{cases} x_0' = y_{23} + z_0 \\ x_1' = y_{24} + z_1 \\ x_2' = y_{25} + z_2 \\ x_i' = y_{i-9} + z_i + x_{i+5}y_{i-12}, \quad 3 \le i \le 32, \end{cases} \tag{1}$$

– for y':

$$\begin{cases} y_0' = x_8 + y_{23} \\ y_i' = x_{i+8} + y_{i-9} + x_{i+7} + z_{i-1} + x_{i+7}z_{i-1}, \quad 1 \le i \le 32, \end{cases} \tag{2}$$

– and for z':

$$\begin{cases} z_0' = x_8 \\ z_1' = x_9 + z_0 \\ z_i' = x_{i+8} + z_{i-1} + y_{i-11}z_{i-2}, \quad 2 \le i \le 32. \end{cases} \tag{3}$$

Description of the SP^2 Box. If $x_0' = y_{23} + z_0$ as in Eq. (1) then it naturally holds that $x_0'' = y_{23}' + z_0'$ and thus we can use Eqs. (2) and (3) to get the full formula. Here we write some of them:

$$x'' \begin{cases} x_0'' = x_8 + x_{30} + x_{31} + y_{14} + z_{22} + x_{30}z_{22} \\ x_1'' = x_9 + x_{31} + x_0 + y_{15} + z_0 + z_{23} + x_{31}z_{23} \\ x_2'' = x_{10} + x_0 + x_1 + y_{16} + z_1 + z_{24} + y_{23}z_0 + x_0z_{24} \\ x_i'' = x_{i-2} + x_{i-1} + x_{i+8} + y_{i-18} + z_{i-10} + z_{i-1} + x_{i-2}z_{i-10} + y_{i-11}z_{i-2} \\ \quad + x_{i-4}y_{i-4} + x_{i-4}z_{i+5} + y_{i-4}y_{i+11} + y_{i+11}z_{i+5} + x_{i-5}z_{i+5} + x_{i-5}y_{i-4} \\ \quad + y_{i-4}z_{i-13} + z_{i-13}z_{i+5} + x_{i-4}x_{i+10}y_{i-7} + x_{i+10}y_{i-7}y_{i+11} \\ \quad + x_{i-5}y_{i-4}z_{i-13} + x_{i-5}z_{i-13}z_{i+5} + x_{i-5}x_{i+10}y_{i-7} + x_{i+10}y_{i-7}z_{i-13} \\ \quad + x_{i-5}x_{i+10}y_{i-7}z_{i-13}, \; i \ne 0, 1, 2, 9, 12, 27, 28, 29 \mod 32 \end{cases} \tag{4}$$

$$y'' \begin{cases} y_0'' = x_{30} + x_{31} + y_{14} + y_{31} + z_8 + z_{22} + x_{13}y_{28} + x_{30}z_{22} \end{cases} \tag{5}$$

$$z'' \begin{cases} z_0'' = y_{31} + z_8 + x_{13}y_{28} \\ z_1'' = x_8 + y_0 + z_9 + x_{14}y_{29} \end{cases} \tag{6}$$

The 2-round probability 1 linear relation $x_0'' + y_0'' + z_0'' = x_8$ follows.

2.2 Previous Work

We provide here a brief overview of the main previous third-party results of cryptanalysis against either the permutation or the NIST candidate Gimli. Notice that all the cryptanalysis previously considered were classical attacks, while in this paper, we will also give quantum attacks on reduced-round Gimli-Hash. Let us point out that no search of linear trails was done prior to our work.

Zero-Sum Permutation Distinguishers on 14 Rounds. In [14], Cai, Wei, Zhang, Sun and Hu present a zero-sum distinguisher on 14 rounds of Gimli. This distinguisher uses the inside-out technique and improves by one round the integral distinguishers given by the designers.

Structural Permutation Distinguisher on 22.5 Rounds. In [20], Hamburg proposed the first third-party cryptanalysis of the Gimli permutation, providing distinguishers on reduced-round versions of the permutation. This analysis does not depend on the details of the SP-Box, and is based only on the slow diffusion of Gimli. Thus, it follows a similar path as the distinguishers of Sect. 3. In his work, Hamburg defines a PRF with 192-bit input x and 192-bit key k that computes $F(k,x) = \text{trunc}_{192}(\text{Gimli}(k\|x))$. He gives a distinguishing attack in time 2^{64} for 15.5 rounds (omitting the final swap), and a key-recovery attack on F when using 22.5 rounds of Gimli, precisely rounds 25 to 2.5 (omitting again the final swap). This attack runs in time $2^{138.5}$ with a memory requirement of 2^{129}, which is faster than the expected 2^{192}, and thus shows that 22.5-round Gimli behaves differently than what could be expected from a random permutation.

Hamburg's attacks are based on a meet-in-the-middle approach, exploiting the slow diffusion by tabulating some of the values that are passed from an SP-Box to another. The 15.5-round distinguisher relies on a table of size 2^{64}, and the 22.5-round attack on a table of size 2^{128}. None of these attacks are practical.

ZID Permutation Distinguishers. In an independent and simultaneous work posted very recently on ePrint [29], Liu, Isobe, and Meier present a "hybrid zero-internal differential" (ZID) distinguisher on full Gimli, which extends a ZID distinguisher of previous unpublished work. The basic ZID distinguisher happens to be what we call an *internal symmetry distinguisher*, where states with symmetries are produced in the input and in the output of a reduced-round variant of Gimli. A "hybrid" one adds a limited birthday-like property (which is absent from our distinguishers). The steps that they take are however different from ours, as this distinguisher only spans 14 rounds. Compared with our analysis in Sect. 3, they will actually start from a much more constrained middle state, which limits the number of rounds by which one can extend the distinguisher afterwards (or significantly increases the complexity). In contrast, we complete the middle state in multiple successive steps, each step ensuring that more rounds will be later covered.

Collisions and Preimages on Gimli-Hash. In [32], Zong, Dong and Wang study Gimli among other candidates of the competition. They present a 6-round collision attack on Gimli-Hash of complexity 2^{113}, using a 6-round differential characteristic where the input and output differences are active only in the rate. This differential characteristic was invalidated in [28].

In [27,29] and [28] Liu, Isobe and Meier give collision and preimage attacks on reduced-round Gimli-Hash. Their attacks rely on divide-and-conquer methods, exploiting the lack of diffusion between the columns, as did Hamburg, but they also rely on SP-Box equations in order to attack the hash function itself. These equations are different from those that we will solve in Sect. 4, and they mostly relate the input and outputs of a single SP-Box, whereas we study directly two SP-Boxes. Their analysis is also much more precise, since they prove running times of solving these equations.

After giving a meet-in-the-middle generic preimage attack of time and memory complexity 2^{128}, which sets a bound against the sponge construction used in Gimli-Hash, they give practical preimage attacks on 2-round Gimli-Hash and practical collision attacks on 3-round Gimli-Hash. They give a collision attack on 5-round Gimli-Hash with a time complexity 2^{65} and a second preimage attack with time complexity 2^{96}. They give in [29] a preimage attack on 5-round Gimli-Hash. In [28], they give a semi-free start collision attack on 8 rounds and a state-recovery attack on the AE scheme for 9 rounds.

3   Internal Symmetry Distinguishers Against Gimli

In this section we present new distinguishers on the Gimli permutation. Our distinguishers improve upon the best previously known ones, reaching the full 24-round permutation. They are practical on 23 rounds and have been implemented. The results presented in this section do not exploit the specifics of the SP-Box: they would work equally well if the SP-Box was replaced with a permutation picked uniformly at random. Like all the other analyses presented in this paper, they do not depend on the values of the round constants.

Our distinguishers rely on internal symmetries. The general idea consists in identifying a specific form of symmetry (formally, a vector space) that is preserved by the round function under some circumstances, and then trying to craft an input for the permutation such that this symmetry traverses all the rounds so that the output has the same type of property.

In our case, we formalize the symmetry using the notion of *2-identical* states.

Definition 1 (2-identical states). *A state S is* 2-identical *if $B = D$, if $A = C$, or if one of these properties holds up to a swap and a constant addition.*

Our *internal symmetries distinguisher* aims at finding a 2-identical input that is mapped to a 2-identical output. Since there are 96 bits of constraint, a generic algorithm returning such an input should run in time 2^{96} by evaluating the permutation on a set of inputs satisfying the property until the output matches it by chance. Our aim is to find more efficient algorithms in the case of Gimli.

This definition is similar to the one used in [15]. In fact, an internal symmetry distinguisher can be seen as a stronger variant of a *limited birthday distinguisher* of the type used in [15]. Indeed, we can build a limited birthday pair using our distinguisher: by producing a pair of inputs S, S' satisfying the internal symmetry property, we obtain $S \oplus S' \in V_{in}$ and $\Pi(S) \oplus \Pi(S') \in V_{out}$. Further, since the converse is not true, an internal symmetry distinguisher is *strictly* stronger.

From now on, S^i denotes the Gimli state before round i.

3.1 23-Round Practical Distinguisher

We design an internal symmetry distinguisher on 23 rounds of Gimli, that is represented in Fig. 2, running in time equivalent to 2^{32} evaluations of Gimli on average. Algorithm 2 starts from a symmetric state in the middle and completes the state S^{11} in three steps. Each step assigns a value to more words of the state, and ensures that the 2-identical symmetry property traverses more rounds.

Algorithm 2. 23-round internal symmetry distinguisher.

Output: a 2-identical state S such that $\mathsf{Gimli}(23,1)(S)$ is 2-identical
We start from the middle. We will be interested in the state S^{11}.

1. Select $A_x^{15}, A_y^{15}, A_z^{15}$ and $C_x^{15} = A_x^{15} \oplus \mathsf{rc}_{16}$, $C_y^{15} = A_y^{15}$, $C_z^{15} = A_z^{15}$ such that $B_x^{11} = D_x^{11}$.
   Notice that due to the small swap operation, the values B_x^{11} and D_x^{11} actually come from A and C and depend only on A^{15} and C^{15}. At this point, we have ensured that for any values of $B^{15} = D^{15}$:
   - S^{23} is 2-identical: indeed, A and C will remain identical from rounds 16 to 19 backwards. Then, the small swap backwards injects the same value in A and C since B and D are also identical. Thus, $A^{23} = C^{23}$.
   - S^7 is 2-identical: indeed, since $B_x^{11} = D_x^{11}$, B and D remain equal until the SP-Box layer of round 8, and the 2-identical property remains after the small swap of round 8.
   Once good values have been found, we can compute part of the state S^{11}: $A_{y,z}^{11}$, $C_{y,z}^{11}$, and $B_x^{11} = D_x^{11}$ are fixed. The rest remains free.
2. Select $A_x^{11} = C_x^{11} \oplus \mathsf{rc}_{12}$ such that $B_x^7 = C_x^7$. At this point, the two-identicality of the output state is preserved through 4 more rounds (until round 4 included): S^3 is 2-identical.
   In the state S^{11}, $B_{y,z}^{11} = D_{y,z}^{11}$ remain free.
3. Select $B_{y,z}^{11} = D_{y,z}^{11}$ such that $B_x^3 = C_x^3$. Thus, the output S^0 is 2-identical.

Each step of Algorithm 2 requires to evaluate a few SP-Boxes 2^{32} times (we do not even need to evaluate the inverse SP-Box). The total amount of computations is smaller than 2^{32} evaluations of 23-round Gimli. Notice also that the algorithm uses only a small amount of memory. Our implementation of Algorithm 2 ran in less than one hour on a regular laptop.

The time complexity of the algorithm can be computed as follows: 8×2^{32} SP-Box evaluations for the first step, 8×2^{32} for the second and 16×2^{32} for the third, meaning a total of $8 \times 2^{32} + 8 \times 2^{32} + 16 \times 2^{32} = 40 \times 2^{32}$ which is less than 2^{32} evaluations of 23-round Gimli (each of them consisting essentially of 92 SP-Box evaluations). This complexity is to be compared to that of the generic algorithm for obtaining our internal symmetry property, which costs 2^{96}.

Below, we provide an example of input-output pair that we obtained, with a 2-identical input S that remains 2-identical after Gimli$(23, 1)$:

	7f9fcf70	6aedf7e6	7f9fcf70	cb2f0e6a
Input:	0ba2f1f9	f339b619	0ba2f1f9	f70cf15c
	b2ee8259	df0b4801	b2ee8259	3856106d
	a8ef848d	8c17b743	9615b3bc	8c17b743
Output:	541122c5	30530879	8d9d5d30	30530879
	74b6dbe6	18885a6e	744b55c1	18885a6e

3.2   Distinguisher on Full Gimli and Extensions

Here we will describe how to extend the 23-round distinguisher to the full Gimli permutation, and even to more rounds. All these results are summarized in Fig. 1 from Sect. 1. An extension of our distinguisher to the full Gimli is a trivial matter. Indeed, after running Algorithm 2, we obtain a 2-identical input state $S^{23} = A^{23}, B^{23}, C^{23}, D^{23}$ with $A^{23} = C^{23}$. Then, if $B_x^{23} = D_x^{23}$, which is a 32-bit condition, the state remains 2-identical after the inverse round 24. By repeating the previous procedure 2^{32} times, we should find an input value that verifies the output property. The generic complexity of finding a 2-identical input that generates a 2-identical output is still 2^{96}. Thus, full Gimli can be distinguished in time less than $2^{32+32} = 2^{64}$ full Gimli evaluations, and constant memory.

An interesting question is: how many rounds of a Gimli-like permutation can we target? The distinguisher works mainly because the diffusion in Gimli is somewhat slow. Thus, a possible fix would be to increase the number of swaps, for example by having one in each round instead of every two rounds. An attack exploiting this behaviour that worked previously for r rounds would now a priori work for $r/2$ rounds only. Of course, the details of the SP-box could allow further improvement of these results given that a single iteration would now separate the swaps rather than a double.

Extending to 28 Rounds. It is trivial to adapt this distinguisher to an extended version of Gimli with more rounds. The 2-identicality of S^0 is preserved after one round since the next round would apply only an SP-Box layer and a small swap. Similarly, the 2-identicality of S^{24} is preserved after 3 more inverse rounds since the next swap operation is a big swap which exchanges data between A and C only. Thus, our practical distinguisher works against Gimli$(23, 0)$ (a 24-round version of Gimli shifted by one round), and our extended distinguisher works against Gimli$(27, 0)$ (a 28-round version of Gimli).

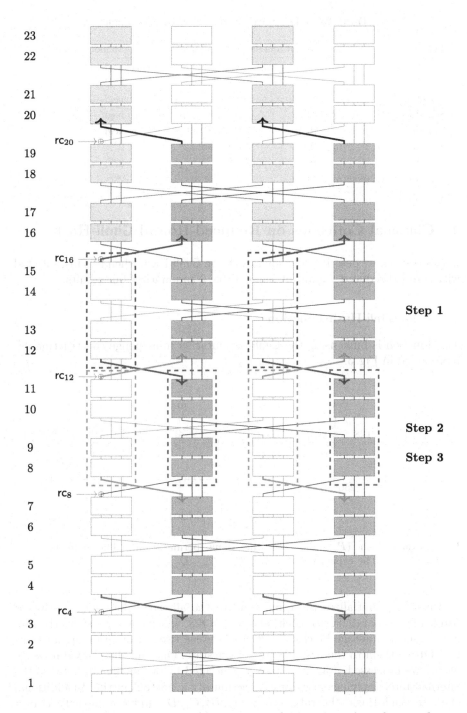

Fig. 2. Distinguisher on 23 rounds. The same color for symmetric branches or columns at a given round means that they are equal.

Table 2. Collision attacks on round-reduced Gimli

Type	Nbr of rounds	Time complexity	Memory complexity
Standard	8	$8 \times 2^{32} \times t_e$ (practical)	negl.
Standard	12	$8 \times 2^{96} \times t_e$	negl.
Quantum	14	$\simeq 8 \times 2^{64} \times t_e$	negl.
Semi-free start	12	$10 \times 2^{32} \times t_e$	negl.
Semi-free start	16	$10 \times 2^{96} \times t_e$	negl.
Semi-free start	18	$7 \times 2^{96} \times t_e$	2^{64}
Semi-free start	18	2^{96}	2^{96}
Semi-free start, quantum	20	$\simeq 2^{64} \times 10 \times t_e$	2^{64}

4 Classical Collisions on Reduced-Round **Gimli**-Hash

In this section, we describe collision attacks on Gimli-Hash when it is instantiated with a round-reduced variant of Gimli. Table 2 summarizes our results.

4.1 The **Gimli**-Hash Function

This function is built using the Gimli permutation in a sponge construction [8], represented in Fig. 3.

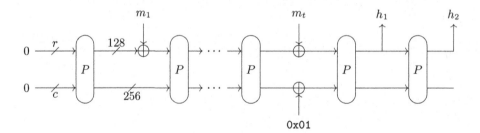

Fig. 3. Gimli-Hash (P stands for the Gimli permutation). The rate is $r = A_x, B_x, C_x, D_x$. The capacity is $c = A_{y,z}, B_{y,z}, C_{y,z}, D_{y,z}$.

Gimli-Hash initializes the Gimli state to the all-zero value. The message is padded and separated into blocks of size $r = 128$, which corresponds to the rate r, introducing message blocks of 128 bits between two permutation applications by XORing them to the first 128 bits of the state. Once all the padded message blocks are processed, a 32-byte hash is generated by outputting 16 bytes of the internal state, applying once more the permutation, and outputting 16 additional ones. In Gimli-Hash, the rate is $r = A_x, B_x, C_x, D_x$ and the capacity is $c = A_{y,z}, B_{y,z}, C_{y,z}, D_{y,z}$.

We will consider two kinds of collision attacks:

- Full-state collision attacks: we will build pairs of two-block messages M_0, M_1 and M_0, M_1' such that the state after absorbing these pairs becomes again equal. Thus, one can append any sequence of message blocks after this and obtain the same hash.
- Semi-freestart collision attacks: we will build pairs of (384-bit) states S, S' such that S differs from S' only in a single x, and after r rounds of Gimli, $\pi(S)$ and $\pi(S')$ differ only in a single x as well. This does not yield a collision on the hash function as we would need to choose the value of the same initial state; however, it represents a vulnerability that may be used in the context of the Gimli modes of operation. For example, in Gimli-cipher, the initial state contains a key of 256 bits and a nonce of 128 bits which is put in the x values. Then each block of plaintext is handled in the same way as Gimli-hash. Thus, by XORing the right values before and after π, one can create a key, a nonce and a pair of messages which yield the same tags.

4.2 SP-Box Equations and How to Solve Them

All collision attacks in this section exploit the slow diffusion of Gimli and the simplicity of the SP-Box (contrary to the distinguishers on the permutation, which worked regardless of the SP-Box used). In this section, we describe a series of "double SP-Box equations"; solving them will be the main building block of our attacks. We define the following equations.

$$\text{Given } y, z, \text{ find } x \neq x' \text{ such that } SP^2(x, y, z)_x = SP^2(x', y, z)_x. \tag{7}$$

$$\text{Given } y, z, y', z', \text{ find } x \text{ such that } SP^2(x, y, z)_x = SP^2(x, y', z')_x. \tag{8}$$

$$\text{Given } y, z, y', z', \text{ find } x \text{ such that } SP^2(x, y, z)_z = SP^2(x, y', z')_z. \tag{9}$$

$$\text{Given } y, z, x', \text{ find } x \text{ such that } SP^2(x, y, z)_x = x'. \tag{10}$$

Number of Solutions. Except Eq. (7), all these equations have *on average*, when the inputs are drawn uniformly at random, a single solution. However, the variance on the number of solutions depends on the equation considered. For example, only approx. 6.2% of inputs to Eq. (8) have a solution, and they have on average 82.4 solutions each. Equation (10) gives a little more than 1.5 solutions. This variance is not a problem for us, as long as we can produce efficiently all solutions of the equations, which remains the case. In order to simplify our presentation, we will do as if Eqs. (8), (9) and (10) always gave exactly a single solution for each input.

Solving the Equations. We use an off-the-shelf SAT solver [31]. In some cases, more time seems spent building the SAT instance rather than solving it, and we believe that our current implementation is highly unoptimized.

The solver allows us to retrieve all solutions of a given equation (we treat Eq. (7) differently because it has on average 2^{32} of them). Let us consider the average time to produce a solution when random inputs are given. On a standard laptop, this time varies between approximately 0.1 ms (Eq. (8)) and 1 ms

(Eq. (10)). This difference mainly stems from the fact that Eq. (8) often has no solutions, and that the solver quickly finds a counterexample, while Eq. (10) practically always has solutions that must be found.

On the same computer, an evaluation of the full Gimli permutation (not reduced-round) takes about 1 μs, so there is approximately a factor 1000 between computing Gimli and solving a double SP-Box equation.

We consider that all equations have approximately the same complexity and introduce a factor t_e that expresses the time taken to solve them in number of evaluations of Gimli or a reduced-round version (depending on the studied case).

4.3 Practical 8-Round Collision Attack

We consider 8 rounds of Gimli, *e.g.* rounds 21 to 14 included, and name Gimli(21, 14) this reduced-round permutation. We omit the last swap, because it has no incidence (it only swaps x values). The situation is represented on Fig. 4. As before, we name S^i the partial state immediately before round i.

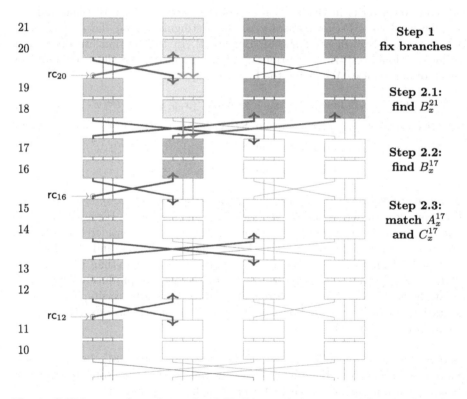

Fig. 4. Collision attack on 8 rounds of Gimli, extended to 12 rounds. The first step fixes the branches in red, which have equal values for the two inputs $A_x^{21}, A_x'^{21}$. Then we find values of $B_x^{21}, C_x^{21}, D_x^{21}$ that will conform to these branches. Then, the whole states are deduced. The branches A_x^{13} and A_x^{11} remain to match. (Color figure online)

Algorithm 3. 8-round collision attack.

Input: an input state $A^{21}, B^{21}, C^{21}, D^{21}$.
Output: values $A_x^{21}, A_x'^{21}, B_x^{21}, C_x^{21}, D_x^{21}$ such that by putting $A_x^{21}, B_x^{21}, C_x^{21}, D_x^{21}$ and $A_x'^{21}, B_x^{21}, C_x^{21}, D_x^{21}$ respectively in the rate, after Gimli$(21, 14)$ (without the last swap), the state differs only on A_x.
Complexity: $7 \times 2^{32} \times t_e$ time and 2^{32} memory *or* $8 \times 2^{32} \times t_e$ and negligible memory.

The attack runs in two main steps, both of which must solve 2^{32} times a sequence of SP-Box equations.

Step 1: find good $A_x^{21}, A_x'^{21}$.

1. Find all pairs $A_x^{21}, A_x'^{21}$ such that the branch B_x^{19} collides (there are 2^{32} such pairs, that can be found in time 2^{32}).
2. For each pair, compute $A_y^{19}, A_z^{19}, A_y'^{19}, A_z'^{19}$ and solve the SP-Box Eq. (8): find A_x^{19} such that the branch C_x^{17} collides (there is on average one solution)
3. Given this value, compute $A_y^{17}, A_z^{17}, A_y'^{17}, A_z'^{17}$ and solve the SP-Box Eq. (8) again: find A_x^{17} such that the branch B_x^{15} collides (there is on average one solution)
4. Given these values, compute $A_y^{15}, A_z^{15}, A_y'^{15}, A_z'^{15}$ and solve Eq. (9): find A_x^{15} such that A_z^{13} and $A_z'^{13}$ collide.

Since we do that 2^{32} times, we expect on average a single solution such that A_y^{13} and $A_y'^{13}$ also collide.

Now that we have found $A_x^{21}, A_x'^{21}$, it remains to find $B_x^{21}, C_x^{21}, D_x^{21}$ that give the wanted $A_x^{19}, A_x^{17}, A_x^{15}$ (in red on Fig. 4). We expect on average a single solution, and little variation on the number of solutions, as only Eq. (10) is involved.

Step 2: find $B_x^{21}, C_x^{21}, D_x^{21}$.

1. Find B_x^{21} by solving Eq. (10), given the input y and z, and the output x wanted. Deduce the values of B_y^{17}, B_z^{17}
2. Given B_y^{17}, B_z^{17}, and A_x^{15}, solve Eq. (10) again to get B_x^{17}.
3. Now find C_x^{21}, D_x^{21} that lead to the wanted A_x^{17}, B_x^{17}. First guess the value of C_x^{21}, deduce C_y^{19}, C_z^{19} and with $C_y^{19}, C_z^{19}, A_x^{17}$, solve Eq. (10) to obtain C_x^{19}. Next, given D_y^{21}, D_z^{21} and C_x^{19}, solve Eq. (10) to obtain D_x^{21}. Deduce a value for B_x^{17} and check if it matches what we want; we expect to find a match after trying all 2^{32} guesses for C_x^{21}.

Algorithm 3 finds on average a single solution, with any input state. There is some variance on the number of solutions, that is induced by the SP-Box equations, but it is small in practice. Furthermore, we can eliminate the memory requirement by solving Eq. (7) for many input random states. Starting from a given state, it suffices to apply one more Gimli permutation with a random message block, in order to re-randomize the input.

Remark that if we omit the second step then we already have a semi-free-start collision attack, because we can reconstruct the inputs C^{21} and D^{21} immediately from the middle.

Practical Application: First Step. In our practical computations, we considered rounds 21 to 14 included. We solved step 1, starting from $0, 0, 0, 0$ and using a random message $m_1, 0, 0, 0$ to randomize the first block. We also solved at the same time the two Eqs. (10) that enabled us to go back to A_x^{17}, B_x^{17}.

We had to produce $15582838652 \simeq 2^{33.86}$ solutions for Eq. (7) until we found a solution for Step 1 *and* for both equations. We verified experimentally that each solution for Eq. (7) yielded on average a solution for the final equation. We obtained in total 5 solutions (Table 3). There are two different solutions for $A_x^{15} \oplus rc_{16}$, which yield two and three solutions respectively for B_x^{17}. The total computation ran in less than 5000 core-hours. It was easy to run on many concurrent processes as this algorithm is trivial to parallelize.

Practical Application: Second Step. We solved step 2, that is, looking for C_x^{21}, D_x^{21} that lead to one of the pairs A_x^{17}, B_x^{17}. This step was much faster than the previous one, although it ought to have the same complexity: this is because we paid in step 1 the probability to find a solution (twice) in Eq. (10), while in step 2 we benefited from having 5 different possible solutions. We found two solutions: $C_x^{21}, D_x^{21} = $ 819b1392, 9f4d3233 and $C_x^{21}, D_x^{21} = $ aa9f6f2d, 3a6e613a.

Table 3. Results of the first step

m_1	A_x^{21}	$A_x'^{21}$	$A_x^{19} \oplus rc_{20}$	A_x^{17}	B_x^{21}
dc84bf38	bbdb41f3	1b1da6e4	07f25303	f793fb5f	aae48b72

$A_x^{15} \oplus rc_{16}$	B_x^{17}	$A_x^{15} \oplus rc_{16}$	B_x^{17}
ddfbc88b	92f536b6	ddfbc803	f72044db
ddfbc88b	0d9605fe	ddfbc803	b1c91a60
		ddfbc803	55d2252a

Putting both Steps Together. With these solutions, we built two collisions on 8-round Gimli(21, 14). We start from $m_1, 0, 0, 0$, then after one round, we inject the values $A_x^{21}, B_x^{21}, C_x^{21}, D_x^{21}$ and $A_x'^{21}, B_x^{21}, C_x^{21}, D_x^{21}$ respectively in the rate; then we obtain two states that differ only on the x-coordinate of the third column (not the first, due to a big swap), and we inject two different blocks to cancel out this difference, obtaining the same state. The full state then collides, and we can append any message block that we want. The two collisions are given in Table 4.

Table 4. Two 8-round collisions on Gimli-Hash

Starting state (first message block)		
dc84bf38 00000000 00000000 00000000‖dc84bf38 00000000 00000000 00000000		
Second message block		
bbdb41f3 4333192c bc17e444 8a9d06c7‖1b1da6e4 4333192c bc17e444 8a9d06c7		
Third message block		
00000000 00000000 00000000 00000000‖00000000 00000000 afad801e 00000000		
Starting state (first message block)		
dc84bf38 00000000 00000000 00000000‖dc84bf38 00000000 00000000 00000000		
Second message block		
bbdb41f3 4333192c 971398fb 2fbe55ce‖1b1da6e4 4333192c 971398fb 2fbe55ce		
Third message block		
00000000 00000000 00000000 00000000‖00000000 00000000 afad801e 00000000		

Extending the Attack. Remark that the first step can be extended to span any number of SP^2-boxes. However, each time we add two more rounds, there is one more branch coming from the B, C, D states which has to match an expected value, so we add a factor 2^{32} in complexity. Since $t_e \ll 2^{32}$, we can do that twice before meeting the bound 2^{128}. Thus, a collision on 12-round Gimli-Hash can be built in time $2^{96} \times 4 \times t_e$.

4.4 Semi-free Start Collisions on Reduced-Round Gimli

We will now design semi-free start collision attacks based on the same principle. This time, our goal is to obtain two input states S, S' that differ only in the rate (in practice, only in A_x) and such that after applying a reduced-round Gimli, the output states differ only in the rate (the x values). They can also be seen as finding one state and two pairs of 2-block messages such that after inserting both messages we obtain a collision. The previous "first step" remains the same, with an extension to whichever number of rounds we are targeting. The "second step" is changed, because we can now choose completely the columns B, C, D, *e.g.* by starting from the middle instead of having to choose only the input rate.

Doing this allows us to reach 4 rounds more for the same cost as before, as outlined on Fig. 5 and Algorithm 4. We can then append new rounds as before, reaching 16 rounds classically in time $2^{96} \times 10 \times t_e$.

Another Improvement using Precomputations. We are going to win a factor 2^{32} using $2^{64} \times t_e$ precomputations and a table of size 2^{64}. This way, we can attack two more rounds. Indeed, once we have computed the first step, the two branches C_x^{17} and A_x^{13} contain arbitrary fixed values. Then, when we try to find the right C, we could have a table that for all C_y^{15}, C_z^{15}, gives all input-output values for C^{17} and C^{14}, and we could directly use this table to match the values C_x^{15} and D_x^{15} that come from D (instead of having to make a guess of C_z^{15}).

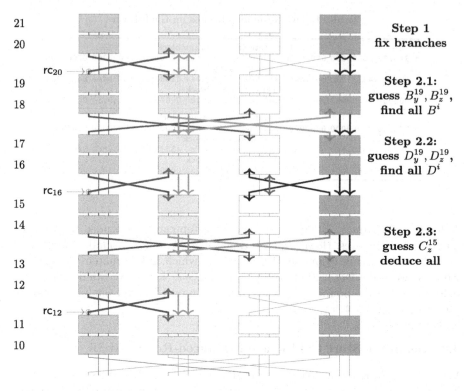

21
20
rc$_{20}$
19
18
17
16
rc$_{16}$
15
14
13
12
rc$_{12}$
11
10

Step 1
fix branches

Step 2.1:
guess B_y^{19}, B_z^{19},
find all B^i

Step 2.2:
guess D_y^{19}, D_z^{19},
find all D^i

Step 2.3:
guess C_z^{15}
deduce all

Fig. 5. Semi-free start collision attack on 12 rounds of Gimli (see Algorithm 4). (Color figure online)

Let us fix $C_x^{17} = A_x^{13} = 0$. Thus, we repeat step 1 in Algorithm 4 a total of 2^{64} times in order to have $C_x^{17} = A_x^{13} = 0$. Step 1 now costs $2^{96} \times t_e$.

The table that we precompute shall contain: for each x', x'', all values (on average 1) of y', z' such that $SP^2(0, *, *) = x', y', z'$ and $SP^2(x'', y', z') = 0, *, *$.

Now, in Algorithm 4, for each guess of $B_{y,z}^{19}$, and for each guess of $D_{y,z}^{19}$, we can find the value of C that matches all the fixed branches in time 1, using this table. Thus, we can repeat this 2^{96} times, extending the attack by 6 rounds.

- Step 1 costs $2 \times 2^{96} \times t_e$ (we solve only 2 equations most of the time, before aborting if the wanted "0" do not appear).
- The table costs $2^{64} \times t_e$, which is negligible
- Step 2 costs $2^{96} \times 5 \times t_e$, since it is the same as before, and we only need forwards computation of SP-Boxes to check if the full path is correct.

Algorithm 4. 12-round semi-free start collision attack (see Fig. 5).

Input: an initial A (can be given)
Output A_x, A'_x, B, C, D such that after $\mathsf{Gimli}(21, 10)$, only the rate differs.
As before, we don't write the last swapping step.

Step 1: Same step as in Algorithm 3, extended to 12 rounds. It gives a total of 10 32-bit branches (input values) that are required, that are represented in red on Fig. 5.

Step 2: we will start from the middle.

1. We take an arbitrary value for $B^{19}_{y,z}$. This guess enables to deduce all values of the column B, from B^{21} to B^{10}, either by simply computing the SP-Box, or by solving Eq. (10) (given two input branches y, z, given the output x, deduce the input x). From this, we deduce the value in all branches that go from B to D on the figure, hence 4 branches. They are represented in orange on Fig. 5.

2. We take an arbitrary value for $D^{19}_{y,z}$. Again, this enables to deduce the whole sequence of states from D^{20} to D^{10}, either by computing the SP-Box when possible, or by finding the input x value corresponding to a given output. We also obtain the values of branches that are transmitted from D to C.

3. We now guess C^{15}_z. Given this, and C^{15}_x, and the output A^{13}_x that must be met, we obtain the whole state by solving another simple SP-Box equation (which is not Eq. (10), but has a similar form).

4. Having deduced C^{15}, we have only 2^{-32} chances of obtaining the right C^{17}_x, so we have to repeat all of this 2^{32} times.

In total, we have to solve 5 SP-Box equations, 2^{32} times, in both steps, so the time complexity is $2^{32} \times 10 \times t_e$.

Note that we can get rid of the term t_e if we use a memory of size 2^{96} to store the solutions of the SP-Box equations. In that case, the overall time complexity is slightly below 2^{96} evaluations of Gimli, since fewer SP-Boxes are evaluated in each step than in the full primitive.

5   Better Quantum Collision Attacks

In this section, we explain how our attacks can be extended in the quantum setting, where even more rounds can be broken. We want to emphasize that, as our goal is simply to determine a security margin, we will not go into the details of the implementation of these attacks as quantum algorithms. We will only show how to use well-known building blocks of quantum computing in order to build these new attacks, and show why they perform better than the corresponding generic quantum attacks. At this point, we assume that the reader is familiar with the basics of quantum computing that are covered in textbooks such as [30]. We define quantum algorithms in the *quantum circuit model*. The circuit starts with a set of qubits (elementary quantum systems) initialized to a basis state and applies quantum operations. The state of the system lies in a Hilbert space of dimension 2^n if there are n qubits. Quantum operations are linear operators of this space, and a quantum circuit is built from such elementary operators coined *quantum gates*. The result of a quantum computation is accessed through *measurement* of the qubits, which destroys their state.

The cryptanalytic algorithms that we consider in this section do not require any form of query to a black-box, since we want only to build a collision on the hash function. Thus, they do not require any more specific model (*e.g.* the Q2 model used in some works in quantum cryptanalysis).

5.1   Tools, Model and Complexity Estimates

Most of the collision attacks presented in this section rely on an exhaustive search. For example, consider the 8-round attack of Algorithm 3. Both steps are exhaustive searches in spaces of size 2^{32} that contain on average a single solution:

- In the first step, we find A_x^{21} such that, after solving a sequence of SP-Box equations, a 32-bit condition is met: the first equation finds $A_x'^{21}$ such that there is a collision in x after two SP-Boxes, the second equation finds A_x^{19} such that there is a collision in x after two SP-Boxes, *etc.*, and the final 32-bit condition is that $A_z'^{13}$ and A_z^{13} must collide.
- In the second step, we find the good C_x^{21} by guessing it and trying to match with a 32-bit condition.

Quantumly, Grover's algorithm [19] speeds up exhaustive search quadratically. Amplitude Amplification [12] is a powerful generalization which applies to any pair $\mathcal{A}, \chi$ such that:

- $\mathcal{A}$ is a quantum algorithm without measurements (a unitary and reversible operation), that takes no input and produces an output $x \in X$.
- $\chi : X \to \{0, 1\}$ is a function that decides whether $x \in X$ is a "good" output of $\mathcal{A}$ ($\chi(x) = 1$) or a "failure" of $\mathcal{A}$, such that χ can also be implemented as a quantum algorithm.

Theorem 1 (Amplitude Amplification [12], informal). *Let $\mathcal{A}$ be a quantum algorithm without measurements that succeeds with probability p and O_χ be a quantum algorithm that tests whether an output of $\mathcal{A}$ is a failure or not. Then there exists a quantum algorithm that finds a good output of $\mathcal{A}$ using $O(\sqrt{1/p})$ calls to $\mathcal{A}$ and O_χ.*

Quantum Embeddings. Any classical algorithm admits a *quantum embedding*, that is, a quantum algorithm that returns the same results. Note that this is not a trivial fact, because a quantum algorithm without measurement is reversible.

Definition 2. *Let $\mathcal{A}$ be a randomized algorithm with no input. A* quantum embedding *for $\mathcal{A}$ is a quantum algorithm $\mathcal{A}'$ that has no input, and the distribution over the possible outcomes of $\mathcal{A}'$ (after measurement) is the same as the distribution over possible outcomes of $\mathcal{A}$.*

This quantum embedding admits similar time and space complexities, where classical elementary operations (logic gates) are replaced by quantum gates and classical bits by qubits. Generic time-space trade-offs have been studied in [4, 23, 26], but precise optimizations are required in practice, where the bulk of the work comes from making the computation reversible. As we just want to compare costs with quantum generic attacks, the following fact will be useful.

Remark 1. The ratio in time complexities is approximately preserved when embedding classical algorithms into quantum algorithms.

For example, if a classical algorithm has a time complexity equivalent to 1000 evaluations of Gimli, we can consider that the corresponding quantum embedding has a time complexity equivalent to 1000 quantum evaluations of Gimli. In all quantum attacks, we will give quantum time complexities relatively to quantumly evaluating Gimli. In order to use Amplitude Amplification (Theorem 1 above), we simply need to define classical randomized algorithms for $\mathcal{A}$ and O_χ.

5.2   Example

We take the example of the classical 8-round collision attack. Both steps run in classical time $2^{32} \times 4 \times t_e$ by running 2^{32} iterates of a randomized algorithm of time complexity $4 \times t_e$. Using Amplitude Amplification, we obtain a corresponding quantum algorithm with time complexity *approximately* $2^{16} \times 4 \times t_{qe}$, where t_{qe} is the time to solve quantumly an SP-Box equation, relative to the cost of a quantum implementation of Gimli. As we remarked above, we can approximate $t_{qe} \simeq t_e$.

This approximation comes from different factors:

- a small constant factor $\frac{\pi}{2}$ which is inherent to quantum search.
- the trade-offs between time and space in the detailed implementations of the primitive and its components. Let us simply notice that Gimli, compared to other primitives that have been studied in this setting, *e.g.* AES [22], seems fairly easy to implement using basic quantum computing operations. In the example of AES, the most costly component is the S-Box [22], and Gimli does not have such.

We are mainly interested in the security margin, and these approximations will be sufficient for us to determine whether a given algorithm runs faster or slower than the corresponding quantum generic attack. Thus, we will write that the quantum 8-round attack on Gimli-Hash runs in time $\simeq 2^{16} \times 4 \times t_e$.

5.3   Quantum Collision Bounds and Quantum Attacks

The best quantum generic attack for finding collisions depends on the computational model, more precisely, on the cost assigned to quantum-accessible memory. Different choices are possible, which are detailed *e.g.* in [21]. In short, the overall cost of quantum collision search depends on the cost that is assigned to quantum hardware.

In this paper, we will simply consider the most conservative setting, where quantum memory is free. Note that this actually makes our attacks overall *less* efficient, since the generic algorithm is the most efficient possible (and they'll also work in the other settings). In this situation, the best collision search algorithm is by Brassard, Høyer and Tapp [13]. It will find a collision on Gimli-Hash in approximately $2^{256/3} \simeq 2^{85.3}$ quantum evaluations of Gimli, using a quantum-accessible memory of size $2^{85.3}$.

Quantum Collision Attacks Reaching more Rounds than Classical Ones. In [21], Hosoyamada and Sasaki initiated the study of *dedicated quantum* attacks on hash functions. They remarked that quantum collision search does not benefit from a square-root speedup (it goes from roughly $2^{n/2}$ to $2^{n/3}$ with the BHT algorithm, and the gain is even smaller in more constrained models of quantum hardware), while some collision-finding procedures may have a better speedup, say, quadratic. Thus:

- there may exist quantum collision attacks such that the corresponding classical algorithm is *not* an attack (it gets worse than the generic bound);
- the *quantum* security margin of hash functions for collision attacks is likely to be smaller than the *classical* one.

Hosoyamada and Sasaki studied differential trails in the hash functions AES-MMO and Whirlpool. Although our attacks are based on a different framework, we show that similar findings apply for Gimli.

5.4 Quantum Collision Attacks on Gimli

We assume that $t_e < 2^{20}$, hence solving an equation costs less than evaluating reduced-round Gimli 2^{20} times, which is suggested by our computations, and should hold in the quantum setting as well.

Full-State Collisions. By adding another 32-bit condition in the classical 12-round collision attack, we obtain a procedure which runs classically in time $4 \times 2^{128} \times t_e$, which is too high. However, using Amplitude Amplification, we obtain a procedure that runs in quantum time $\simeq 4 \times 2^{64} \times t_e$ and reaches 14 rounds, with less complexity than the quantum collision bound.

Semi-free Start Collisions. We can extend the 18-round semi-free start collision attack in the same way. Building the table will still cost a time 2^{64}. This table must be stored in a classical memory with quantum random access. The first step goes from $2 \times 2^{96} \times t_e$ classically to approximately $2 \times 2^{48} \times t_e$ quantumly. The second step does as well. Thus, adding a 32-bit condition enables us to attack 20 rounds in quantum time $2^{64} \times 4 \times t_e$.

6 Statistical Analyses of **Gimli**

6.1 Linear Cryptanalysis

This section aims to provide the first analysis of the linear properties of the Gimli permutation and its components. We use a Mixed Integer Linear Programming (MILP) modelization of the operations constructed according to [1], and then solve it with the SCIP software [17,18] to search for linear trails with optimal correlation.

Linear Trails of the (Double) SP-Box. We begin by studying the linear trails of the SP-Box. Since the Gimli permutation mainly uses the composition of the SP-Box with itself, we focus on the "double" SP-Box SP^2.

Let us consider that we apply the double SP-box to $A = (x, y, z)$ to obtain $A'' = (x'', y'', z'') = SP^2(x, y, z)$. We are interested in correlated linear approximations, that is, masks $\alpha = (\alpha_x, \alpha_y, \alpha_z)$ and $\beta = (\beta_x, \beta_y, \beta_z)$ for which

$$c(SP^2, \alpha, \beta) = 2^{-96} \Big(\big| \{A : \alpha \cdot A \oplus \beta \cdot A'' = 0\} \big| - \big| \{A : \alpha \cdot A \oplus \beta \cdot A'' = 1\} \big| \Big)$$

is as large (in absolute value) as possible. From Sect. 2.1 we already know that the relationship $x_8 + x_0'' + y_0'' + z_0'' = 0$ always holds. This is a linear trail of the double SP-box with correlation 1, and it is unique.

An automated MILP-based search for linear trails of correlation 2^{-1} and 2^{-2} shows that there exist at least 41 trails of the former kind and 572 of the latter, but this is not an exhaustive count. Although these approximations probably only account for a very small fraction of the possible ones, a more thorough study of the distribution of the different correlation values among all the trails would be of interest.

We have found no signs of significant linear-hull effects within the double SP-box, although since we have not considered every linear trail, they might still exist.

Some Linear Trails of Round-Reduced Gimli. In order to provide some linear trails for reduced-round Gimli, we first focus on trails with only one active SP-Box in each round, or more specifically, with masks which only cover one column in each round. They do not provide an upper bound on the correlation of more general trails, but we still think they could be of interest, and this restriction greatly limits the search space.

More specifically, we consider linear trails on powers of the SP-box such that the mask for the x word is zero every two rounds. This means that the mask is unaffected by the big and small swaps, and these trails easily translate into trails for the reduced-round Gimli construction with the same correlation.

We first look at iterative linear trails for the double SP-box so that both the input and output masks have the x word set to zero. We find that the optimal correlation is 2^{-26}, and this is the (maybe not unique) associated trail:

$$\Gamma_1 : \begin{array}{c} 00000000 \\ 0a064e03 \\ 0c08e406 \end{array} \xrightarrow{2^{-14}} \begin{array}{c} 0c8b0507 \\ 01040322 \\ 00054302 \end{array} \xrightarrow{2^{-12}} \begin{array}{c} 00000000 \\ 0a064e03 \\ 0c08e406 \end{array}.$$

Since this trail is iterative, we can construct $2l$-round trails with correlation 2^{-26l}. Next, we provide a similar iterative trail for four rounds with correlation 2^{-47}, though other trails with larger correlation might exist with the same restrictions:

$$\Gamma_2 : \begin{array}{c} 00000000 \\ 02060000 \\ 00020541 \end{array} \xrightarrow{2^{-19}} \begin{array}{c} 06422511 \\ 088a8131 \\ 08828111 \end{array} \xrightarrow{2^{-11}} \begin{array}{c} 00000000 \\ 15024215 \\ 0405003a \end{array} \xrightarrow{2^{-10}} \begin{array}{c} 04054102 \\ 00010280 \\ 000182a0 \end{array} \xrightarrow{2^{-7}} \begin{array}{c} 00000000 \\ 02060000 \\ 00020541 \end{array}.$$

With this, we can construct trails of $4l$ rounds with correlation 2^{-47l}. At this point the search for iterative trails becomes computationally expensive so we search for non-iterative trails. We find an optimal four-round trail with correlation 2^{-16}:

$$\Gamma_3 : \begin{array}{c} 00000000 \\ 90002000 \\ 00400110 \end{array} \xrightarrow{2^{-3}} \begin{array}{c} 00400100 \\ 00000020 \\ 00000000 \end{array} \xrightarrow{2^{-1}} \begin{array}{c} 00000000 \\ 00004000 \\ 00000001 \end{array} \xrightarrow{2^{-2}} \begin{array}{c} 00000001 \\ 00800001 \\ 00800001 \end{array} \xrightarrow{2^{-10}} \begin{array}{c} 00000000 \\ 000002aa \\ 010002aa \end{array}.$$

Next, we attempt to extend this trail at the end. We find the following four-round trail with correlation 2^{-48} which has the output mask of the previous one as its input mask:

$$\Gamma_4 : \begin{array}{c} 00000000 \\ 000002aa \\ 010002aa \end{array} \xrightarrow{2^{-18}} \begin{array}{c} 01448312 \\ 01094200 \\ 0101f260 \end{array} \xrightarrow{2^{-11}} \begin{array}{c} 00000000 \\ 18040003 \\ 0a054480 \end{array} \xrightarrow{2^{-12}} \begin{array}{c} 0a040580 \\ 02450200 \\ 02050200 \end{array} \xrightarrow{2^{-7}} \begin{array}{c} 00000000 \\ 88040004 \\ 080c0401 \end{array}.$$

Combining both trails, we obtain an eight-round trail of correlation 2^{-64}. There are no approximations for the double SP-box for which the output mask is the input mask of Γ_3 and so that the input mask has the x word set to zero. However, by removing the last condition we can add two rounds with a 2^{-16} correlation:

$$\Gamma_5 : \begin{array}{c} 68009800 \\ 40202088 \\ 403510d4 \end{array} \xrightarrow{2^{-10}} \begin{array}{c} 40211090 \\ 00480010 \\ 00200088 \end{array} \xrightarrow{2^{-6}} \begin{array}{c} 00000000 \\ 90002000 \\ 00400110 \end{array}.$$

In the same way, we can add two additional rounds at the end of Γ_4 with correlation 2^{-19}:

$$\Gamma_6 : \begin{array}{c} 88040004 \\ 40202088 \\ 080c0401 \end{array} \xrightarrow{2^{-10}} \begin{array}{c} 080a0281 \\ 000c0901 \\ 000c0901 \end{array} \xrightarrow{2^{-9}} \begin{array}{c} 48000800 \\ 70100a00 \\ e0180002 \end{array}.$$

By combining these four trails, we obtain a twelve-round linear trail for Gimli with correlation 2^{-99}. Then, by combining several trails in a similar manner we obtain the following 14-round trail with correlation 2^{-128}:

$\Gamma_7:$
$$
\begin{array}{c}
00408000 \\
20e04060 \\
e0c1c000
\end{array}
\xrightarrow{2^{-19}}
\begin{array}{c}
e0e9e078 \\
206c202e \\
206060a0
\end{array}
\xrightarrow{2^{-12}}
\begin{array}{c}
00000000 \\
f8606840 \\
80808180
\end{array}
\xrightarrow{2^{-7}}
\begin{array}{c}
80808180 \\
40400060 \\
40400040
\end{array}
\xrightarrow{2^{-4}}
\begin{array}{c}
00000000 \\
80008080 \\
00800001
\end{array}
\xrightarrow{2^{-6}}
$$

$$
\begin{array}{c}
00000001 \\
01010101 \\
01010101
\end{array}
\xrightarrow{2^{-8}}
\begin{array}{c}
00000000 \\
02020202 \\
03020202
\end{array}
\xrightarrow{2^{-8}}
\begin{array}{c}
00000000 \\
04040404 \\
04040404
\end{array}
\xrightarrow{2^{-8}}
\begin{array}{c}
00000000 \\
08080808 \\
08080808
\end{array}
\xrightarrow{2^{-8}}
\begin{array}{c}
00000000 \\
10101010 \\
10101010
\end{array}
\xrightarrow{2^{-8}} \cdot
$$

$$
\begin{array}{c}
00000000 \\
20202020 \\
20202020
\end{array}
\xrightarrow{2^{-8}}
\begin{array}{c}
00000000 \\
40404040 \\
40404040
\end{array}
\xrightarrow{2^{-10}}
\begin{array}{c}
00000000 \\
80c08080 \\
80e08080
\end{array}
\xrightarrow{2^{-10}}
\begin{array}{c}
80110000 \\
01800101 \\
01c20101
\end{array}
\xrightarrow{2^{-8}}
\begin{array}{c}
01020800 \\
01000802 \\
01801c02
\end{array}
$$

Table 5. Linear trails for reduced-round Gimli. Some of them apply to shifted versions of the algorithm starting with two consecutive SP-box substitutions instead of one.

# Rounds	Correlation	Construction	Shift
1	1	Probability 1 trail from 2.1	No
2	1	Probability 1 trail from 2.1	Yes
3	2^{-6}	First three rounds of Γ_3	Yes
4	2^{-12}	Last round of Γ_5, first three rounds of Γ_3	No
5	2^{-22}	Last round of Γ_5, Γ_3	No
6	2^{-32}	Γ_5, Γ_3	Yes
7	2^{-50}	Γ_5, Γ_3, first round of Γ_4	Yes
8	2^{-61}	Γ_5, Γ_3, first two rounds of Γ_4	Yes
9	2^{-70}	Last round of Γ_5, Γ_3, Γ_4	No
10	2^{-80}	Last round of Γ_5, Γ_3, Γ_4, first round of Γ_6	No
11	2^{-89}	Last round of Γ_5, Γ_3, Γ_4, Γ_6	No
12	2^{-99}	Γ_5, Γ_3, Γ_4, Γ_6	Yes
13	2^{-109}	Last thirteen rounds of Γ_7	No
14	2^{-128}	Γ_7	Yes
15	2^{-137}	Last rounds of Γ_8 and Γ_9,Γ_7	No
16	2^{-150}	Γ_8,Γ_9,Γ_7	Yes

Finally, this trail can be extended at the top by adding the following two-round trails (they now have two active SP-Boxes in each round because of a swap):

$\Gamma_8:$
$$
\begin{array}{c}
48f00060 \\
6818cc18 \\
21a404c8
\end{array}
\xrightarrow{2^{-9}}
\begin{array}{c}
018060c0 \\
20085810 \\
40408000
\end{array}
\xrightarrow{2^{-11}}
\begin{array}{c}
00000000 \\
20e04060 \\
e0c1c000
\end{array}
$$

$\Gamma_9:$
$$
\begin{array}{c}
40a04000 \\
20000008 \\
00204000
\end{array}
\xrightarrow{2^{-4}}
\begin{array}{c}
00000000 \\
00002040 \\
00408000
\end{array}
\xrightarrow{2^{-2}}
\begin{array}{c}
00408000 \\
00000000 \\
00000000
\end{array}
$$

Using these, we obtain a 16-round trail with correlation 2^{-150}. In general, by combining these trails in different ways, we provide the linear trails for up to 16 round of Gimli shown in Table 5.

These are just some linear trails of Gimli which belong to a very specific sub-family, and for more than four rounds we have not proven optimality even within that family, so it is quite possible that better linear trails exist. We have also searched for any significant linear trails which share the same input and output masks to see if there is a noticeable linear hull effect for these approximations, but we have found no additional trails of large correlation.

All these trails can be used to mount distinguishing attacks on the Gimli permutation with a data complexity proportional to the inverse of the square of the correlation, which also works for the block cipher built with the Even-Mansour construction from the Gimli permutation. It is possible to reduce the complexity slightly by using multiple linear cryptanalysis. By considering the same trail but in the four columns we can increase the capacity by a factor of four. By shifting the iterative trail by two rounds we can obtain an additional factor two in the 16-round attack.

6.2 Differential-Linear Cryptanalysis

We now consider differential-linear cryptanalysis, a technique that combines a differential trail and a linear trail built independently.

We use the approach of Leurent [25] where we actually split the cipher in three parts $E = E_\perp \circ E_\perp \circ E_\top$, with a differential trail in $E_\top$, a linear trail in $E_\perp$, and an experimental evaluation of the bias in E_I. This gives a more accurate evaluation of the complexity. More precisely, we consider

- a differential trail $\delta_{\text{in}} \to \delta_{\text{out}}$ for $E_\top$ with probability $p = \Pr_X \left(E_\top(X) \oplus E_\top(X \oplus \delta_{\text{in}}) = \delta_{\text{out}} \right)$.
- an experimental bias b from δ_{out} to β for E_I:

$$b = c(\alpha \cdot E_I(W), \alpha \cdot E_I(W \oplus \delta_{\text{out}}))$$
$$= 2 \Pr_W(\alpha \cdot E_I(W) = \alpha \cdot E_I(W \oplus \delta_{\text{out}})) - 1$$

- a linear trail $\alpha \to \beta$ for $E_\perp$ with correlation $c = 2 \Pr_Y(\alpha \cdot Y = \beta \cdot E_\perp(Y)) - 1$.

If the three parts are independent then we can estimate the bias of the differential-linear distinguisher as:

$$c(\beta \cdot E(X), \beta \cdot E(X \oplus \delta_{\text{in}})) = 2 \Pr_X(\beta \cdot E(X) = \beta \cdot E(X \oplus \delta_{\text{in}})) - 1 \approx pbc^2$$

Therefore, the complexity of the distinguisher is about $2/p^2 b^2 c^4$.

In Gimli, there are no keys, so the assumption of independence does not hold, but experiments show that the computed bias is close to the reality. In practice, the best results are obtained when δ_{out} and α have a low hamming weight [25].

Differential Trail. We start by picking a trail that mainly follows the one given by the designers [5] with slight changes to optimize it for our number of rounds. We chose a trail with a difference pattern δ_{out} with two active bits. A differential trail over 5 rounds with probability $p = 2^{-28}$ is given in Table 6. We considered trade-offs between the different phases, and it never seems to be worth it to propagate the trail any further.

Experimental Bias. Starting from the target difference pattern δ_{out} at round 19, we experimentally evaluate the bias after a few rounds with all possible masks α with a single active bit. Concretely, we choose the state at random, build the second state by adding δ_{out} and observe the bias a few rounds later.

The most useful results are on the least significant bit z_0 of the last word, where the probability of having a difference is smaller than $1/2$. After computing 8 round, the probability of having an active difference on this bit in round 12 is $\frac{1}{2} - 2^{-6.2}$, a correlation of $b = -2^{-5.2}$. After 9 rounds, at the end of round 11, there is a correlation of $b = -2^{-16.9}$. These probabilities are large enough to be experimentally significant after the 2^{40} trials we have made.

Table 6. A 5-round differential trail.

δ_{in}	40418080	02010000	00000000	00000000
	40400010	00000000	00000000	00000000
	80002080	80010080	00000000	00000000
Round 24	80010080	00000000	00000000	00000000
$p = 2^{-18}$	00402000	00000000	00000000	00000000
	80400080	00000000	00000000	00000000
Round 23	00000080	00000000	00000000	00000000
$p = 2^{-8}$	00400000	00000000	00000000	00000000
	80000000	00000000	00000000	00000000
Round 22	00000000	00000000	00000000	00000000
$p = 1$	00000000	00000000	00000000	00000000
	80000000	00000000	00000000	00000000
Round 21	80000000	00000000	00000000	00000000
$p = 1$	00000000	00000000	00000000	00000000
	00000000	00000000	00000000	00000000
δ_{out}	00000000	00000000	00000000	00000000
Round 20	00800000	00000000	00000000	00000000
$p = 2^{-2}$	00800000	00000000	00000000	00000000

Linear Trail. We use assisted tools to find good linear trails, starting from the mask corresponding to z_0. The diffusion is not the same depending whether we start after round 12 or 11 so we show the best 3 rounds linear approximation for both case. We find a correlation c of 2^{-17} and 2^{-16} respectively, see Tables 7 and 8.

Table 7. Diffusion of z_0 starting at the end of round 12.

Round 12	00000000	00000000	00000000	00000000
	00000000	00000000	00000000	00000000
	00000000	00000000	00000000	00000001
Round 11	00000000	00000000	00000000	00000001
corr $= 2^{-0}$	00000000	00000000	00000000	00000001
	00000000	00000000	00000000	00000001
Round 10	00000000	00800001	00000000	00000000
corr $= 2^{-5}$	00000000	00000000	00000000	00800201
	00000000	00000000	00000000	01c00201
Round 9	00000000	00880000	00000000	01000201
corr $= 2^{-12}$	00000000	00f10000	00000000	01040000
	00000000	01e00000	00000000	01840000

Complexity of the Distinguishers. We can combine the trails in different way to obtain distinguishers on 15, 16 or 17 rounds (starting from round 24).

Table 8. Diffusion of z_0 starting at the end of round 11.

Round 11	00000000	00000000	00000000	00000000
	00000000	00000000	00000000	00000000
	00000001	00000000	00000000	00000000
Round 10	00000000	00000000	00000001	00000000
corr $= 2^{-0}$	00000001	00000000	00000000	00000000
	00000001	00000000	00000000	00000000
Round 9	00000001	00000000	00800000	00000000
corr $= 2^{-5}$	00000201	00000000	00800000	00000000
	00000201	00000000	01c00000	00000000
Round 8	00000000	00200201	00000000	01004000
corr $= 2^{-11}$	00000001	00000000	01004001	00000000
	01000001	00000000	0180e001	00000000

15 Rounds. We use 5 rounds for $E_\top$, 8 rounds for E_I, 2 rounds for $E_\perp$. The corresponding complexity is $2/pbc^2 = 2 \times 2^{2 \times 28} \times 2^{2 \times 5.2} \times 2^{4 \times 5} = 2^{87.4}$.
16 Rounds. We use 5 rounds for $E_\top$, 9 rounds for E_I, 2 rounds for $E_\perp$. The corresponding complexity is $2/pbc^2 = 2 \times 2^{2 \times 28} \times 2^{2 \times 16.9} \times 2^{4 \times 5} = 2^{110.8}$.
17 Rounds. We use 5 rounds for $E_\top$, 9 rounds for E_I, 3 rounds for $E_\perp$. The corresponding complexity is $2/pbc^2 = 2 \times 2^{2 \times 28} \times 2^{2 \times 16.9} \times 2^{4 \times 16} = 2^{154.8}$.

Those distinguishers can be used when the Gimli permutation is used to build a block cipher with the Even-Mansour construction. Such a cipher should ensure a birthday bound security of up to 2^{192} query, which is less efficient than our differential-linear distinguisher if the number of rounds Gimli is reduced to 17 (or fewer). Further improvement should be possible with the partitioning technique of [25], but we leave this to future work.

7 Conclusion

A common point of the results presented in this paper is that they exploit the relatively slow diffusion between the columns of the Gimli state. This issue has trivial causes: swaps are effectively the identity for 256 out of the 384 bits of the internal state, and occur only every second round. Thus, the Gimli SP-Box is always applied twice, except at the first and last rounds. This means that the permutation can be viewed as an SPN with only 12 rounds, and with very simple linear layers. Meanwhile, the double SP-Box is a rather simple function, and some of our attacks rely crucially on solving efficiently equations that relate its inputs and outputs.

Though our results do not pose a direct threat to the Gimli NIST candidate, low-complexity full-round distinguishers on the permutation or reduced-round attacks for a high proportion of the rounds (specially when not predicted by the designers) have been considered in some cases as an issue worth countering by proposing a tweak, as can be seen for instance in the modification [3] recently proposed by the SPOOK team [2] to protect against the cryptanalysis results from [15].

In addition, Gimli designers studied other linear layers instead of the swaps, like using an MDS or the linear transformation from SPARX [16], and they found some advantages in proving security against various types of attacks. On the other hand, they also found it unclear whether these advantages would outweight the costs. We believe our results show some light in this direction: the other variants that were considered seem a priori to be stronger regarding our analysis, though an extensive study should be performed.

We believe the distinguishers might still be improved by exploiting the properties of the SP-Box, which we have not done yet.

In order to mitigate the attacks based on internal symmetries and guess-and-determine methods (including our distinguishers on the permutation) a simple fix would be to perform a swap at each round instead of every second round. This would however imply a renewed cryptanalysis effort.

Acknowledgments. The authors would like to thank all the members of the *cryptanalysis party* meetings, for many useful comments and discussions, in particular many thanks to Anne Canteaut, Virginie Lallemand and Thomas Fuhr for many interesting discussions over previous versions of this work. Thanks to Donghoon Chang for finding some mistakes and inaccuracies, including an error in a 32-round version of our distinguisher. This project has received funding from the European Research Council (ERC) under the European Union's Horizon 2020 research and innovation programme (grant agreement no. 714294 - acronym QUASYModo).

References

1. Abdelkhalek, A., Sasaki, Y., Todo, Y., Tolba, M., Youssef, A.M.: MILP modeling for (large) s-boxes to optimize probability of differential characteristics. IACR Trans. Symmetric Cryptol. **2017**(4), 99–129 (2017)

2. Bellizia, D., et al.: Spook: sponge-based leakage-resilient authenticated encryption with a masked tweakable block cipher. Submission to the NIST Lightweight Cryptography project (2019). https://csrc.nist.gov/CSRC/media/Projects/lightweight-cryptography/documents/round-2/spec-doc-rnd2/Spook-spec-round2.pdf
3. Bellizia, D., et al.: Spook: sponge-based leakage-resilient authenticated encryption with a masked tweakable block cipher. IACR Trans. Symmetric Cryptol. **2020**, 295–349 (2020). (Special Issue on NIST Lightweight)
4. Bennett, C.H.: Time/space trade-offs for reversible computation. SIAM J. Comput. **18**(4), 766–776 (1989)
5. Bernstein, D.J., et al.: GIMLI: a cross-platform permutation. In: Fischer, W., Homma, N. (eds.) CHES 2017. LNCS, vol. 10529, pp. 299–320. Springer, Cham (2017). https://doi.org/10.1007/978-3-319-66787-4_15
6. Bernstein, D.J., et al.: Gimli. Submission to the NIST Lightweight Cryptography Project (2019). https://csrc.nist.gov/CSRC/media/Projects/Lightweight-Cryptography/documents/round-1/spec-doc/gimli-spec.pdf
7. Bertoni, G., Daemen, J., Peeters, M., Van Assche, G.: Sponge functions. In: ECRYPT Hash Workshop (2007)
8. Bertoni, G., Daemen, J., Peeters, M., Van Assche, G.: On the indifferentiability of the sponge construction. In: Smart, N.P. (ed.) EUROCRYPT 2008. LNCS, vol. 4965, pp. 181–197. Springer, Heidelberg (2008). https://doi.org/10.1007/978-3-540-78967-3_11
9. Bertoni, G., Daemen, J., Peeters, M., Van Assche, G.: Sponge-based pseudorandom number generators. In: Mangard, S., Standaert, F.X. (eds.) CHES 2010. LNCS, vol. 6225, pp. 33–47. Springer, Heidelberg (2010). https://doi.org/10.1007/978-3-642-15031-9_3
10. Bertoni, G., Daemen, J., Peeters, M., Van Assche, G.: Duplexing the sponge: single-pass authenticated encryption and other applications. In: Miri, A., Vaudenay, S. (eds.) SAC 2011. LNCS, vol. 7118, pp. 320–337. Springer, Heidelberg (2012). https://doi.org/10.1007/978-3-642-28496-0_19
11. Biham, E., Shamir, A.: Differential cryptanalysis of DES-like cryptosystems. J. Cryptol. **4**(1), 3–72 (1991). https://doi.org/10.1007/BF00630563
12. Brassard, G., Hoyer, P., Mosca, M., Tapp, A.: Quantum amplitude amplification and estimation. Contemp. Math. **305**, 53–74 (2002)
13. Brassard, G., Høyer, P., Tapp, A.: Quantum cryptanalysis of hash and claw-free functions. In: Lucchesi, C.L., Moura, A.V. (eds.) LATIN 1998. LNCS, vol. 1380, pp. 163–169. Springer, Heidelberg (1998). https://doi.org/10.1007/BFb0054319
14. Cai, J., Wei, Z., Zhang, Y., Sun, S., Hu, L.: Zero-sum distinguishers for round-reduced GIMLI permutation. In: Mori, P., Furnell, S., Camp, O. (eds.) Proceedings of the 5th International Conference on Information Systems Security and Privacy, ICISSP 2019, Prague, Czech Republic, February 23–25, 2019, pp. 38–43. SciTePress (2019)
15. Derbez, P., Huynh, P., Lallemand, V., Naya-Plasencia, M., Perrin, L., Schrottenloher, A.: Cryptanalysis results on spook. Cryptology ePrint Archive, Report 2020/309 (2020). https://eprint.iacr.org/2020/309
16. Dinu, D., Perrin, L., Udovenko, A., Velichkov, V., Großschädl, J., Biryukov, A.: Design strategies for ARX with provable bounds: SPARX and LAX. In: Cheon, J.H., Takagi, T. (eds.) ASIACRYPT 2016. LNCS, vol. 10031, pp. 484–513. Springer, Heidelberg (2016). https://doi.org/10.1007/978-3-662-53887-6_18
17. Gleixner, A., et al.: The SCIP optimization suite 6.0. Technical report, Optimization Online (July 2018). http://www.optimization-online.org/DB_HTML/2018/07/6692.html

18. Gleixner, A., et al.: The SCIP optimization suite 6.0. ZIB-Report 18–26, Zuse Institute Berlin (July 2018). http://nbn-resolving.de/urn:nbn:de:0297-zib-69361
19. Grover, L.K.: A fast quantum mechanical algorithm for database search. In: 28th ACM STOC, pp. 212–219. ACM Press (May 1996)
20. Hamburg, M.: Cryptanalysis of 22 1/2 rounds of Gimli. Cryptology ePrint Archive, Report 2017/743 (2017). http://eprint.iacr.org/2017/743
21. Hosoyamada, A., Sasaki, Y.: Finding hash collisions with quantum computers by using differential trails with smaller probability than birthday bound. In: Canteaut, A., Ishai, Y. (eds.) EUROCRYPT 2020. LNCS, vol. 12106, pp. 249–279. Springer, Cham (2020). https://doi.org/10.1007/978-3-030-45724-2_9
22. Jaques, S., Naehrig, M., Roetteler, M., Virdia, F.: Implementing Grover oracles for quantum key search on AES and LowMC. In: Canteaut, A., Ishai, Y. (eds.) EURO-CRYPT 2020. LNCS, vol. 12106, pp. 280–310. Springer, Cham (2020). https://doi.org/10.1007/978-3-030-45724-2_10
23. Knill, E.: An analysis of Bennett's pebble game. CoRR abs/math/9508218 (1995)
24. Lamberger, M., Mendel, F., Schläffer, M., Rechberger, C., Rijmen, V.: The rebound attack and subspace distinguishers: application to Whirlpool. J. Cryptol. **28**(2), 257–296 (2015)
25. Leurent, G.: Improved differential-linear cryptanalysis of 7-round Chaskey with partitioning. In: Fischlin, M., Coron, J.S. (eds.) EUROCRYPT 2016. LNCS, vol. 9665, pp. 344–371. Springer, Heidelberg (2016). https://doi.org/10.1007/978-3-662-49890-3_14
26. Levin, R.Y., Sherman, A.T.: A note on Bennett's time-space tradeoff for reversible computation. SIAM J. Comput. **19**(4), 673–677 (1990)
27. Liu, F., Isobe, T., Meier, W.: Preimages and collisions for up to 5-round Gimli-hash using divide-and-conquer methods. Cryptology ePrint Archive, Report 2019/1080 (2019). https://eprint.iacr.org/2019/1080
28. Liu, F., Isobe, T., Meier, W.: Automatic verification of differential characteristics: application to reduced Gimli. CRYPTO 2020 (2020). https://eprint.iacr.org/2020/591, to appear
29. Liu, F., Isobe, T., Meier, W.: Exploiting weak diffusion of Gimli: a full-round distinguisher and reduced-round preimage attacks. Cryptology ePrint Archive, Report 2020/561 (2020). https://eprint.iacr.org/2020/561
30. Nielsen, M.A., Chuang, I.L.: Quantum information and quantum computation. Cambridge: Cambridge Univ. Press **2**(8), 23 (2000)
31. Soos, M., Nohl, K., Castelluccia, C.: Extending SAT solvers to cryptographic problems. In: Kullmann, O. (ed.) SAT 2009. LNCS, vol. 5584, pp. 244–257. Springer, Heidelberg (2009). https://doi.org/10.1007/978-3-642-02777-2_24
32. Zong, R., Dong, X., Wang, X.: Collision attacks on round-reduced Gimli-Hash/Ascon-Xof/Ascon-Hash. Cryptology ePrint Archive, Report 2019/1115 (2019). https://eprint.iacr.org/2019/1115

SQISign: Compact Post-quantum Signatures from Quaternions and Isogenies

Luca De Feo[1,7,8], David Kohel[2], Antonin Leroux[3,7,8], Christophe Petit[4,9], and Benjamin Wesolowski[5,6]

[1] IBM Research, Zürich, Switzerland
[2] Aix Marseille University, CNRS, Centrale Marseille, I2M, Marseille, France
[3] DGA, Paris, France
[4] University of Birmingham, Birmingham, UK
[5] Univ. Bordeaux, CNRS, Bordeaux INP, IMB, UMR 5251, F-33400 Talence, France
[6] INRIA, IMB, UMR 5251, F-33400 Talence, France
[7] LIX, CNRS, Ecole Polytechnique, Institut Polytechnique de Paris, Paris, France
antonin.leroux@polytechnique.org
[8] INRIA, Rocquencourt, France
[9] Université libre de Bruxelles, Brussels, Belgium

Abstract. We introduce a new signature scheme, *SQISign*, (for *Short Quaternion and Isogeny Signature*) from isogeny graphs of supersingular elliptic curves. The signature scheme is derived from a new one-round, high soundness, interactive identification protocol. Targeting the post-quantum NIST-1 level of security, our implementation results in signatures of 204 bytes, secret keys of 16 bytes and public keys of 64 bytes. In particular, the signature and public key sizes combined are an order of magnitude smaller than all other post-quantum signature schemes. On a modern workstation, our implementation in C takes 0.6 s for key generation, 2.5 s for signing, and 50 ms for verification.

While the soundness of the identification protocol follows from classical assumptions, the zero-knowledge property relies on the second main contribution of this paper. We introduce a new algorithm to find an isogeny path connecting two given supersingular elliptic curves of known endomorphism rings. A previous algorithm to solve this problem, due to Kohel, Lauter, Petit and Tignol, systematically reveals paths from the input curves to a 'special' curve. This leakage would break the zero-knowledge property of the protocol. Our algorithm does not directly reveal such a path, and subject to a new computational assumption, we prove that the resulting identification protocol is zero-knowledge.

Keywords: Post-quantum · Signatures · Isogenies

1 Introduction

Isogeny-based cryptography has existed since at least the work of Couveignes in 1997 [9] and has developed significantly in the last decade due to increasing

© International Association for Cryptologic Research 2020
S. Moriai and H. Wang (Eds.): ASIACRYPT 2020, LNCS 12491, pp. 64–93, 2020.
https://doi.org/10.1007/978-3-030-64837-4_3

interest in post-quantum cryptography. The CGL hash function of [6] and the SIDH key exchange proposed in [20] have put isogenies between supersingular elliptic curves at the center of attention. The security of these schemes relies on the hardness of finding a path in the ℓ-isogeny supersingular graph between two given vertices. This problem is believed to be hard for both classical and quantum computers. This assumption was studied by Kohel, Lauter, Petit and Tignol, who in [22] introduced a new algorithm (often called KLPT in the literature) that solves the quaternion analog of the ℓ-isogeny path problem under the Deuring correspondence. This algorithm revealed its full potential in [17], leading to several reductions between computational problems related to isogenies between supersingular curves, most notably a heuristic security reduction between the ℓ-isogeny path problem and the endomorphism ring computation.

In parallel to these cryptanalytic efforts, isogeny-based cryptography has continued to develop with several new proposals. We can mention CSIDH [5], an efficient reinterpretation of Couveignes' idea using supersingular elliptic curves defined over $\mathbb{F}_p$. Another active area of research has been isogeny-based signature schemes, see for instance [3,12,14,19,33].

Galbraith, Petit and Silva's signature scheme [19] (also known as GPS) was the first constructive cryptographic application of the KLPT algorithm. However, their work remains mainly theoretical and, to this day, we are not aware of any implementation of their scheme. We follow in the footsteps of GPS by introducing a new signature scheme based on the quaternion ℓ-isogeny path problem. Indeed, GPS relies on the KLPT algorithm for so-called "special" maximal orders (the main focus of [22]), whereas our protocol requires a new variant of KLPT working for arbitrary maximal orders, which we introduce here.

The contributions of this paper can be summarized as follows:

- A new interactive identification protocol and the resulting signature scheme based on a generic algorithm for the quaternion ℓ-isogeny path problem.
- A new generic KLPT algorithm, suited for our signature scheme, which produces a smaller output than the existing algorithm of [22].
- A proof of the interpretation of Eichler orders and their class sets under the Deuring correspondence, and its application to the analysis of the output of our algorithm. This leads us to a natural security assumption from which we prove zero-knowledge of the identification scheme, and consequently unforgeability of the signature scheme.
- New algorithms for the efficient instantiation of the protocol, along with parameters targeting the NIST-1 level of post-quantum security, and a complete implementation of our signature scheme in C.

The remainder of this paper is organized as follows. Section 2 contains preliminaries on elliptic curves and quaternion algebras. Section 3 sketches our new protocols along with some proofs. Section 4 lays out the mathematical background on Eichler orders necessary for the rest of the paper. Section 5 gives a generic description of our new Generalized KLPT algorithm. Section 6 provides the generic variant used in our protocols. Section 7 studies the zero knowledge property of the identification scheme. Finally, Sect. 8 provides algorithms for efficient implementation of the schemes.

2 Preliminaries

A negligible function $f : \mathbb{Z}_{>0} \to \mathbb{R}_{>0}$ is a function whose growth is bounded by $O(x^{-n})$ for all $n > 0$. In the analysis of a probabilistic algorithm, we say that an event happens with *overwhelming probability* if its probability of failure is a negligible function of the length of the input. We say that a distinguishing problem is hard when any probabilistic polynomial-time distinguisher has a negligible advantage with respect to the length of the instance. Two distributions are computationally indistinguishable if their associated distinguishing problem is hard.

Throughout this work, p is a prime number and $\mathbb{F}_q$ a finite field of characteristic p. We are interested in supersingular elliptic curves over $\mathbb{F}_q = \mathbb{F}_{p^2}$, in an isogeny class such that the full endomorphism ring is defined over $\mathbb{F}_q$, and is isomorphic to a maximal order in a quaternion algebra. The extended version of this work [13] contains more background on elliptic curves and their endomorphism rings; other useful references are [10,21,29,31].

2.1 The Deuring Correspondence

In [15], Deuring made the link between the geometric world of elliptic curves and the arithmetic world of quaternion algebras over $\mathbb{Q}$ by showing that the endomorphism ring of a supersingular elliptic curve E defined over $\mathbb{F}_{p^2}$ is isomorphic to a maximal order in the quaternion algebra $\mathcal{B}_{p,\infty}$ ramified at p and infinity. This correspondence is in fact an equivalence of categories [21] between supersingular elliptic curves and left ideals for a maximal order $\mathcal{O}$ of $\mathcal{B}_{p,\infty}$, inducing a bijection between conjugacy classes of supersingular j-invariants and maximal orders (up to equivalence). Given a supersingular curve E_0, this lets us associate each pair (E_1, φ), where E_1 is another supersingular elliptic curve and $\varphi : E_0 \to E_1$ is an isogeny, to a left integral $\mathcal{O}_0$-ideal (with $\mathrm{End}(E_0) \simeq \mathcal{O}_0$), and every such ideal arises in this way. In this case $\mathrm{End}(E_1)$ is isomorphic to the right order of this ideal. The explicit correspondence between isogenies and ideals is given through kernel ideals as defined in [32]. Given I an integral left-$\mathcal{O}_0$-ideal we define the set $E_0[I] = \{P \in E_0(\overline{\mathbb{F}}_{p^2}) : \alpha(P) = 0 \text{ for all } \alpha \in I\}$ as the kernel of I. To I, we associate the isogeny φ_I of kernel $E_0[I]$ defined by $\varphi_I : E_0 \to E_0/E_0[I]$. Conversely given an isogeny φ, the corresponding kernel ideal is defined as $I_\varphi = \{\alpha \in \mathcal{O}_0 : \alpha(P) = 0 \text{ for all } P \in \ker(\varphi)\}$.

Remark 1. In the definitions above we identify $\alpha \in \mathcal{O}_0$ with the related endomorphism in $\mathrm{End}(E_0)$, implicitly assuming a fixed isomorphism between $\mathcal{O}_0$ and $\mathrm{End}(E_0)$. This is a simplification that we will reiterate throughout this paper to lighten notations. In fact, we will sometimes go further and also write α for the principal ideal $\mathcal{O}_0\alpha$. It is easily verified that this ideal corresponds to the kernel ideal I_α, and conversely any principal ideal corresponds to an endomorphism $\varphi_{\mathcal{O}_0\alpha}$.

We summarize the main properties of this correspondence in Table 1.

Table 1. The Deuring correspondence, a summary.

Supersingular j-invariants over $\mathbb{F}_{p^2}$	Maximal orders in $\mathcal{B}_{p,\infty}$
$j(E)$ (up to galois conjugacy)	$\mathcal{O} \cong \mathrm{End}(E)$ (up to isomorpshim)
(E_1, φ) with $\varphi : E \to E_1$	I_φ integral left $\mathcal{O}$-ideal and right $\mathcal{O}_1$-ideal
$\theta \in End(E_0)$	Principal ideal $\mathcal{O}\theta$
$\deg(\varphi)$	$n(I_\varphi)$
$\hat{\varphi}$	$\overline{I_\varphi}$
$\varphi : E \to E_1, \psi : E \to E_1$	Equivalent ideals $I_\varphi \sim I_\psi$
Supersingular j-invariants over $\mathbb{F}_{p^2}$	$Cl(\mathcal{O})$
$\tau \circ \rho : E \to E_1 \to E_2$	$I_{\tau \circ \rho} = I_\rho \cdot I_\tau$

2.2   Algorithmic Building Blocks

In this section we introduce some sub-algorithms that will be used in the remaining of the paper. These algorithms are either classical or inherited from recent works [19,22] in the literature.

We will write $\mathsf{CRT}_{M,N}(x,y)$ for the Chinese Remainder algorithm, that takes $x \in \mathbb{Z}/M\mathbb{Z}$, $y \in \mathbb{Z}/N\mathbb{Z}$ and returns $z \in \mathbb{Z}/MN\mathbb{Z}$ with $z = x \bmod M$ and $z = y \bmod N$.

KLPT Algorithm. A significant part of the present work is spent on providing a new generalization of the KLPT algorithm [22] (see Algorithm 3). This algorithm takes an integral ideal I as input and finds an equivalent ideal $J \sim I$ of given norm. For instance, the norm can be required to be ℓ^e for some $e \in \mathbb{N}$. In general, in the rest of this paper when an output of an algorithm is required to be a power of ℓ, we write $\ell^\bullet$.

We start by introducing a few notations taken from [22], before introducing several sub-algorithms that we will use. Finally we describe a short version of KLPT in Algorithm 1 built from these sub-algorithms.

An important notion introduced in [22] is that of *special extremal* orders, i.e., maximal orders $\mathcal{O}_0$ containing a suborder admitting an orthogonal decomposition $R + jR$ where $R = \mathbb{Z}[\omega] \subset \mathbb{Q}[i]$ is a quadratic order of minimal discriminant (or equivalently such that ω has smallest norm in $\mathcal{O}_0$). By orthogonal decomposition we mean that $R \subset (jR)^\perp$. The order $\mathcal{O}_0 = \mathbb{Z}\langle\sqrt{-1}, \sqrt{-p}\rangle$, corresponding to the elliptic curve of j-invariant 1728 when $p = 3 \bmod 4$, is one of the simplest examples of such special extremal orders, as it contains the suborder $\mathbb{Z}[\sqrt{-1}] + (\sqrt{-p})\mathbb{Z}[\sqrt{-1}]$. For the rest of this paper, we fix these notations for j, R, ω. The method of resolution resulting in Algorithm 1 is inspired by [22, Lemma 5]. We introduce here a reformulation of this lemma using notations that we will keep for the rest of this article.

Lemma 1. *For any integral ideal I, the map $\chi_I(\alpha) = I\overline{\alpha}/n(I)$ is a surjection from $I \smallsetminus \{0\}$ to the set of ideals J equivalent to I. For $\alpha \neq \beta$, we have $\chi_I(\alpha) = \chi_I(\beta)$ if and only if $\alpha = \beta\delta$ where $\delta \in \mathcal{O}_R(I)^{\times}$.*

Proof. This map is well-defined as proved in [22]. We see that it is a surjection by identifying $\overline{I} \cdot J$ with a principal ideal $\mathcal{O}_R(I)\overline{\beta}$. Then, it is clear that $\beta \in I$ and $J = \chi_I(\beta)$. Finally, one can verify that $\mathcal{O}_R(I)\beta_1 = \mathcal{O}_R(I)\beta_2$ if and only if $\beta_1 = \delta\beta_2$ where $\delta \in \mathcal{O}_R(I)^{\times}$.

With $n(\chi_I(\alpha)) = n(\alpha)/n(I)$, we see that finding $J \sim I$ of given norm N is equivalent to finding some $\alpha \in I$ of norm $n(I)N$. This observation underlies the solution of [22] for Algorithm 1.

Remark 2. In what follows will often define a projective point $(C_0 : D_0) \in \mathbb{P}^1(\mathbb{Z}/N\mathbb{Z})$ for some prime N and then, by an abuse of notation, define an element $C_0 + \omega D_0$ inside our maximal order.

Below we list sub-algorithms introduced in [22] as part of KLPT; see [13, 22, 25] for detailed descriptions of each.

- EquivalentPrimeIdeal(I) Given a left $\mathcal{O}_0$-ideal I, find an equivalent left $\mathcal{O}_0$-ideal of prime norm.
- RepresentInteger$_{\mathcal{O}_0}(M)$ Given $M \in \mathbb{N}$ with $M > p$, find $\gamma \in \mathcal{O}_0$ of norm M.
- IdealModConstraint(I, γ) Given an ideal I of norm N, and $\gamma \in \mathcal{O}_0$ of norm Nn, find $(C_0 : D_0) \in \mathbb{P}^1(\mathbb{Z}/N\mathbb{Z})$ such that $\mu_0 = j(C_0 + \omega D_0)$ verifies $\gamma\mu_0 \in I$.
- StrongApproximation$_\mathsf{F}(N, C_0, D_0)$ Given a prime N and $C_0, D_0 \in \mathbb{Z}$, find $\mu = \lambda\mu_0 + N\mu_1 \in \mathcal{O}_0$ of norm dividing F, with $\mu_0 = j(C_0 + \omega D_0)$. We write StrongApproximation$_{\ell\bullet}$ when the expected norm is a power of ℓ.

Remark 3. For our scheme, we will need to turn KLPT into a deterministic algorithm. The sub-routine EquivalentPrimeIdeal can be made deterministic if we look for the ideal of smallest norm satisfying the desired condition. Since we are looking at lattices of dimension at most 4, finding an ordered set of smallest vectors can be done efficiently. StrongApproximation can also be made deterministic, as the method in [25] involves solving a closest vector problem in some lattice. The sub-routine IdealModConstraint is deterministic as was shown in [22]. For RepresentInteger$_{\mathcal{O}_0}$, this is less natural as there are several solutions for a given input M. Still, if we want, we can find an ordering for the tuple (x, y, z, t) of coordinates over $\mathbb{Z}\langle\omega, j\rangle$ and search for the smallest solution with respect to that ordering.

With these sub-routines we are able to give a compact description of the KLPT algorithm. There are several versions of this algorithm depending on the norm sought for the output: we will write KLPT$_{\ell\bullet}$ when the algorithm produces an output of norm a power of ℓ; KLPT$_T$ when the norm is a divisor of $T \in \mathbb{Z}$. The changes between the two variants are minimal; for simplicity, we describe only KLPT$_{\ell\bullet}$ in Algorithm 1.

Remark 4. A result of [19] shows that the outputs of EquivalentPrimeIdeal and KLPT only depend on the equivalence class of the input (in fact this is only true with a minor tweak to the original algorithm of [22]). Hence, we will sometimes abuse notations and use both as if they took inputs in $\mathrm{Cl}(\mathcal{O}_0)$.

Algorithm 1. $\mathsf{KLPT}_{\ell^\bullet}(I)$

Require: I a left $\mathcal{O}_0$-ideal.
Ensure: $J \sim I$ of norm ℓ^e.
 1: Compute $L = \mathsf{EquivalentPrimeIdeal}(I)$, $L = \chi_I(\delta)$ for $\delta \in I$ with $N = n(L)$.
 2: Compute $\gamma = \mathsf{RepresentInteger}_{\mathcal{O}_0}(N\ell^{e_0})$ for $e_0 \in \mathbb{N}$.
 3: Compute $(C_0 : D_0) = \mathsf{IdealModConstraint}(L, \gamma)$.
 4: Compute $\nu = \mathsf{StrongApproximation}_{\ell^\bullet}(N, C_0, D_0))$ and set $\beta = \gamma\nu$ and e such that $n(\beta) = N\ell^e$.
 5: **return** $J = \chi_L(\beta)$.

---

3   New Identification Protocol and Signature Scheme

3.1   An Identification Protocol

Let λ be a security parameter. We start by describing an interactive identification protocol based on supersingular isogeny problems.

setup : $\lambda \mapsto$ param Pick a prime number p and a supersingular elliptic curve E_0 defined over $\mathbb{F}_p$ with known special extremal endomorphism ring $\mathcal{O}_0$. Select an odd smooth number D_c of λ bits and $D = 2^e$ where e is above the diameter of the supersingular 2-isogeny graph.

keygen : param $\mapsto$ (pk $= E_A$, sk $= \tau$) Pick a random isogeny walk $\tau : E_0 \to E_A$, leading to a random elliptic curve E_A. The public key is E_A, and the secret key is the isogeny τ.

To prove knowledge of the secret τ, the prover engages in the following Σ-protocol with the verifier.

Commitment. The prover generates a random (secret) isogeny walk $\psi : E_0 \to E_1$, and sends E_1 to the verifier.

Challenge. The verifier sends the description of a cyclic isogeny $\varphi : E_1 \to E_2$ of degree D_c to the prover.

Response. From the isogeny $\varphi \circ \psi \circ \hat{\tau} : E_A \to E_2$, the prover constructs a new isogeny $\sigma : E_A \to E_2$ of degree D such that $\hat{\varphi} \circ \sigma$ is cyclic, and sends σ to the verifier.

Verification. The verifier accepts if σ is an isogeny of degree D from E_A to E_2 and $\hat{\varphi} \circ \sigma$ is cyclic. They reject otherwise.

We summarize the protocol in Fig. 1. Completeness follows from the correctness of Algorithm 3, allowing a honest prover to construct $\sigma : E_A \to E_2$

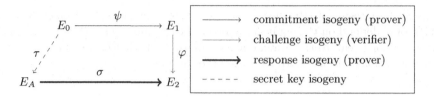

Fig. 1. A picture of the identification protocol

such that $\hat{\varphi} \circ \sigma$ is cyclic. Soundness is analysed in Subsect. 3.2, and follows from the difficulty of the Smooth Endomorphism Problem—a problem heuristically equivalent to the classic Endomorphism Ring Problem. Zero-knowledge is more difficult to prove, as we argue in Subsect. 3.3, and we defer its analysis to Sect. 7.

3.2 Soundness

Problem 1 (Supersingular Smooth Endomorphism Problem). Given a prime p and a supersingular elliptic curve E over $\mathbb{F}_{p^2}$, find a cyclic endomorphism of E of smooth degree.

Remark 5. Note that under heuristics similar to those used in [17], the above problem is equivalent to the Endomorphism Ring Problem (given $E/\mathbb{F}_{p^2}$, compute endomorphisms forming a $\mathbb{Z}$-basis of $End(E)$).

Theorem 1 (Soundness). *If there is an adversary that breaks the soundness of the protocol with probability w and expected running time r for the public key E_A, then there is an algorithm for the Supersingular Smooth Endomorphism Problem on E_A with expected running time $O(r/(w - 1/c))$, where c is the size of the challenge space.*

The theorem is a consequence of the following lemma.

Lemma 2. *Given two accepting conversations (E_1, φ, σ) and (E_1, φ', σ') where $\varphi \neq \varphi'$, the composition $\hat{\sigma}' \circ \varphi' \circ \hat{\varphi} \circ \sigma$ is a non-scalar endomorphism of E_A of smooth degree.*

Proof. By construction, $\hat{\sigma}' \circ \varphi' \circ \hat{\varphi} \circ \sigma$ is an endomorphism of E_A of degree $(DD_c)^2$. This shows that the degree is smooth. It remains to prove that it is not a scalar. Suppose by contradiction that $\hat{\sigma}' \circ \varphi' \circ \hat{\varphi} \circ \sigma = [DD_c]$. The compositions $\hat{\varphi} \circ \sigma$ and $\hat{\varphi}' \circ \sigma'$ are two cyclic isogenies from E_A to E_1 of same degree. Therefore $\hat{\sigma}' \circ \varphi'$ is the dual of $\hat{\varphi} \circ \sigma$. We deduce that $\hat{\varphi} \circ \sigma = \hat{\varphi}' \circ \sigma'$, a contradiction.

Proof of Theorem 1. The endomorphism $\hat{\sigma}' \circ \varphi' \circ \hat{\varphi} \circ \sigma$ in Lemma 2 corresponds to a (possibly backtracking) sequence of isogenies, and removing the backtracking subsequences, we obtain a solution to the Supersingular Smooth Endomorphism Problem of E_A. Therefore the protocol has *special soundness* for the relation R defined as

$$(E_A, \alpha) \in R \iff \alpha \text{ is a cyclic smooth degree endomorphism of } E_A.$$

It is therefore a proof of knowledge for R with knowledge error $1/c$—see for instance [11, Theorem 1]. In other words, an adversarial prover with success probability w and running time r can be turned into a knowledge extractor for R of expected running time $O(r/(w - 1/c))$.   □

3.3 Zero-Knowledge: Two Insecure Approaches

The sketch given in Subsect. 3.1 is incomplete, as it does not specify a method to compute the response isogeny σ. Zero-knowledge of the scheme clearly depends upon this method, and it turns out that the only known solutions so far are insecure. Indeed the trivial approach of setting $\sigma = \varphi \circ \psi \circ \hat{\tau}$ immediately reveals the secret, while using the algorithm from [22] instead (like in [19]) ends up revealing some path from E_A to E_0, which is equivalent to revealing τ thanks to the reductions in [17].

In Sects. 5 and 6 we will introduce a new variant of the KLPT algorithm that conjecturally does not suffer from the same leakages. Then, we will prove zero-knowledge in Sect. 7, under a new conjecturally hard computational problem.

3.4 The Signature Scheme

The new signature scheme is simply a Fiat-Shamir transformation of the identification protocol introduced in Subsect. 3.1. Following the construction of [6] extended in [28] for smooth degrees, if $D_c = \prod_{i=1}^n \ell_i^{e_i}$, we write $\mu(D_c) = \prod_{i=1}^n \ell_i^{e_i-1}(\ell_i + 1)$ and we define an arbitrary function $\Phi_{D_c}(E, s)$, mapping integers $s \in [1, \mu(D_c)]$ to non-backtracking sequences of isogenies of total degree D_c starting at E. Let $H : \{0, 1\}^* \to [1, \mu(D_c)]$ be a cryptographically secure hash function.

The signature scheme is as follows.

sign : $(\mathsf{sk}, m) \mapsto \Sigma$ Pick a random (secret) isogeny $\psi : E_0 \to E_1$. Let $s = H(j(E_1), m)$, and build the isogeny $\Phi_{D_c}(E_1, s) = \varphi : E_1 \to E_2$. From the knowledge of $\mathcal{O}_A$, and of the isogeny $\varphi \circ \psi : E_0 \to E_2$, construct an isogeny $\sigma : E_A \to E_2$ of degree D such that $\hat{\varphi} \circ \sigma$ is cyclic. The signature is the pair (E_1, σ).

verify : $(\mathsf{pk}, m, \Sigma) \mapsto$ true or false Parse Σ as (E_1, σ). From $s = H(j(E_1), m)$, recover the isogeny $\Phi_{D_c}(E_1, s) = \varphi : E_1 \to E_2$. Check that σ is an isogeny from E_A to E_2 and that $\hat{\varphi} \circ \sigma$ is cyclic.

Theorem 2. *The signature described above is secure against chosen-message attacks in the random oracle model assuming the hardness of Problems 1 and 2.*

4 Eichler Orders and the Deuring Correspondence

We recall here the notion of Eichler orders and we interpret them under the Deuring correspondence. As the results of this section are well known, we only state the main theorems without proof here; for a detailed treatment see the extended version of this work [13], or [16, 26, 31].

An *Eichler order* is the intersection of two maximal orders inside $\mathcal{B}_{p,\infty}$. In all this section we will consider the case of the Eichler order $\mathfrak{O} = \mathcal{O}_0 \cap \mathcal{O}$ where $\mathcal{O}_0$ and $\mathcal{O}$ are maximal orders connected through an ideal I of norm $n(I)$ such that $I \not\subseteq n\mathcal{O}_L(I)$ for any $n > 1$. This setting corresponds to curves E_0, E connected by an isogeny φ_I of cyclic kernel and degree $n(I)$ with $End(E_0) \cong \mathcal{O}_0$ and $End(E) \cong \mathcal{O}$.

Proposition 1. $\mathfrak{O} := \mathcal{O}_0 \cap \mathcal{O} = \mathcal{O}_L(I) \cap \mathcal{O}_R(I) = \mathbb{Z} + I$.

One goal of this section is to interpret the elements in $\mathfrak{O}$ under the Deuring correspondence.

The decomposition $\mathbb{Z} + I$ allows us to interpret the elements of $\mathfrak{O}$. In fact, we can separate elements in $\mathfrak{O}$ according to whether their norm is coprime to $n(I)$ or not. Given that $n(I)\mathbb{Z} \subset I$, it is easily verified that this partition can be written as $\mathfrak{O} = (I \cup \bar{I}) \bigcup (\mathbb{Z} \setminus n(I)\mathbb{Z} + I)$. It is well-known that $I = Hom(E, E_0)\varphi_I$. Hence, the elements in I correspond to the endomorphisms $\psi \circ \varphi_I$ for any isogeny $\psi : E \to E_0$. The same analysis proves $\bar{I} = Hom(E_0, E)\hat{\varphi}_I$. The elements of $\bar{I}$ correspond to the same endomorphisms as those of I, but decomposed as $\hat{\psi} \circ \hat{\varphi}_I$ in $End(E)$.

4.1 Commutative Isogeny Diagrams

We define commutative diagrams of isogenies using the classical notations of *pushforward* and *pullback* maps. Let us take 3 curves E_0, E_1, E_2 and two separable isogenies $\varphi_1 : E_0 \to E_1$ and $\varphi_2 : E_0 \to E_2$ of coprime degrees, N_1 and N_2. Then, there is a fourth curve E_3 and two *pushforward isogenies* $[\varphi_1]_*\varphi_2$ and $[\varphi_2]_*\varphi_1$ going from E_1 and E_2 toward E_3, verifying $\deg([\varphi_1]_*\varphi_2) = N_2$ and $\deg([\varphi_2]_*\varphi_1) = N_1$.

The isogenies $[\varphi_2]_*\varphi_1$ and $[\varphi_1]_*\varphi_2$ are defined as the separable isogenies of respective kernels $\varphi_2(\ker(\varphi_1))$ and $\varphi_1(\ker(\varphi_2))$. We will sometimes refer to $[\varphi_2]_*\varphi_1$ as *the image of* φ_1 through φ_2. The two sides of the diagram can be seen as two decompositions of the same isogeny $\psi = [\varphi_2]_*\varphi_1 \circ \varphi_2 = [\varphi_1]_*\varphi_2 \circ \varphi_1$.

There is a dual notion of *pullback isogeny*: given $\varphi_1 : E_0 \to E_1$ and $\rho_2 : E_1 \to E_3$, of coprime degrees, we can define the pullback of ρ_2 by φ_1 as $[\varphi_1]^*\rho_2 = [\hat{\varphi}_1]_*\rho_2$. With this definition it is easy to see that $\varphi_2 = [\varphi_1]^*[\varphi_1]_*\varphi_2$.

For simplicity, when the isogenies have not been defined we will implicitly write $[I]_*J$ for the ideal $I_{[\varphi_J]_*\varphi_I}$ corresponding to the pushforward of φ_J by φ_I. The same holds for $[I]^*J$. With this convention, we extend the terms *pushforward* and *pullback* to ideals.

4.2 The Endomorphism Ring $\mathfrak{O}$

The next proposition states that the image through φ of the endomorphism corresponding to any element in $\mathfrak{O} \subset \mathcal{O}_0$ (which is neither in I nor in $\bar{I}$) is an endomorphism of E.

Proposition 2. *Let $\beta \in \mathcal{O}_0$ of norm coprime with N, then $[\mathcal{O}_0\beta]_*I = I$ if and only if $\beta \in \mathfrak{O} \setminus (I \cup \overline{I})$. In particular, $[I]_*\mathcal{O}_0\beta$ is a principal $\mathcal{O}$-ideal equal to $\mathcal{O}\beta$.*

Said otherwise, the endomorphisms in $\mathfrak{O} \setminus (I \cup \overline{I})$ leave φ_I stable. Equivalently, the endomorphisms of $\mathfrak{O}$ remain endomorphisms after being pushed forward by φ_I, and thus belong to both $End(E_0)$ and $End(E)$.

From Proposition 2, we deduce the following result which will underlie Algorithm 3; it is a reformulation using the map χ of Lemma 1.

Corollary 1. *Let J_1, J_2 be $\mathcal{O}_0$-ideals, with $J_1 \sim J_2$ and $\gcd(n(J_1)n(J_2), n(I)) = 1$. Suppose that $J_1 = \chi_{J_2}(\beta)$ with $\beta \in J_2 \cap \mathfrak{O}$. Then $[I]_*J_1 \sim [I]_*J_2$ and $[I]_*J_1 = \chi_{[I]_*J_2}(\beta)$.*

4.3   Ideal Class Sets of Eichler Orders

In this section, we write again $\mathfrak{O} = \mathcal{O}_0 \cap \mathcal{O}$. We write I for the ideal connecting $\mathcal{O}_0$ and $\mathcal{O}$ and we assume in this section that its norm N is prime.

Class sets of ideals play an important role through the Deuring correspondence. When $\mathcal{O}$ is a maximal order we can put $Cl(\mathcal{O})$ in bijection with the set of supersingular curves (see Table 1). This motivates studying Eichler orders, and indeed isogeny graphs were first constructed through class sets of quaternion orders by [27], and only later reinterpreted as isogeny graphs in [6]. Eichler [16] proved a formula for the class number $h(\mathfrak{O}) = |Cl(\mathfrak{O})|$. When N is prime it gives

$$h(\mathfrak{O}) = \frac{(p+1)(N+1)}{12} + \varepsilon_{N,p}$$

where $\varepsilon_{N,p}$ is a small value depending on N and p modulo 12. This, combined with $h(\mathcal{O}_0) = p/12 + \varepsilon_p$, ($\varepsilon_p$ depends on the value $p \mod 12$) suggests that there is a $(N+1)$-to-1 correspondence between $Cl(\mathfrak{O})$ and $Cl(\mathcal{O}_0)$, which we are now going to exhibit.

Let us write $\mathcal{I}_N(\mathcal{O})$ for the set of left integral $\mathcal{O}$-ideals of norm coprime to N for any order $\mathcal{O}$. We start by showing a connection between $\mathcal{I}_N(\mathcal{O}_0)$ and $\mathcal{I}_N(\mathfrak{O})$.

Lemma 3. *The map*

$$\Psi : \mathcal{I}_N(\mathcal{O}_0) \longrightarrow \mathcal{I}_N(\mathfrak{O})$$
$$J \longmapsto J \cap \mathfrak{O}$$

is a well-defined bijection between the set of integral $\mathcal{O}_0$-ideals and $\mathfrak{O}$-ideals of norm coprime with N. Its inverse is given by : $\Psi^{-1} : \mathfrak{J} \mapsto \mathcal{O}_0\mathfrak{J}$.

From the fact that any ideal class of $Cl(\mathfrak{O})$ or $Cl(\mathcal{O}_0)$ has a representative of norm coprime with N, we can easily identify the equivalence classes of $\mathcal{I}_N(\mathcal{O}_0)$ and $\mathcal{I}_N(\mathfrak{O})$ to the ones of $\mathcal{O}_0$ and $\mathfrak{O}$ respectively.

The bijection of Lemma 3 suggests defining the following equivalence relation $\sim_\mathfrak{O}$ on left $\mathcal{O}_0$-ideals of norm coprime with N. We say that $J \sim_\mathfrak{O} K$ if and only if $\Psi(J) \sim \Psi(K)$ as $\mathfrak{O}$-ideals (here $\sim$ is the classical equivalence relation between ideals having the same left order). The bijection Ψ transports the structure of $\sim$ to $\sim_\mathfrak{O}$ and this implies that we have defined an equivalence relation.

Definition 1. *We write $Cl_{\mathfrak{O}}(\mathcal{O}_0)$ for the set of equivalence classes of $\mathcal{I}_N(\mathcal{O}_0)$ under $\sim_{\mathfrak{O}}$.*

From the definition, we have that $Cl_{\mathfrak{O}}(\mathcal{O}_0)$ is in bijection with $Cl(\mathfrak{O})$ through Ψ. In the next proposition we show that we can obtain an explicit correspondence between ideals of norm N and $Cl_{\mathfrak{O}}(\mathcal{O}_0)$ using pushforward ideals.

Proposition 3. *$J \sim_{\mathfrak{O}} K$ if and only if there exists $\beta \in \mathfrak{O}$ such that $K = \chi_J(\beta)$ and $\beta^{-1}[K]_*I\beta = [J]_*I$.*

An interesting question is how the new equivalence relation $\sim_{\mathfrak{O}}$ relates to the classical one $\sim$. In fact, $\sim_{\mathfrak{O}}$ is compatible with $\sim$ in the sense that $J \sim_{\mathfrak{O}} K$ implies $J \sim K$, as is easily verified from Corollary 1. This suggests partitioning $Cl_{\mathfrak{O}}(\mathcal{O}_0)$ in subsets indexed by the elements of $Cl(\mathcal{O}_0)$. Hence, we write $Cl_{\mathfrak{O}}(\mathcal{O}_0) = \bigcup_{\mathcal{C} \in Cl(\mathcal{O}_0)} Cl_{\mathfrak{O}}(\mathcal{C})$ where $Cl_{\mathfrak{O}}(\mathcal{C})$ is the set of classes in $Cl_{\mathfrak{O}}(\mathcal{O}_0)$ contained in $\mathcal{C}$. The respective sizes of $Cl(\mathcal{O}_0)$ and $Cl(\mathfrak{O})$ suggest that the partition above provides an $(N+1)$-to-1 correspondence between $Cl(\mathcal{O}_0)$ and $Cl(\mathfrak{O})$. This correspondence only fails for a small number of classes, as the following proposition shows.

Proposition 4. *For $\mathcal{C} \in Cl(\mathcal{O}_0)$, let us take $L \in \mathcal{C}$ and define $\mathcal{O}_{\mathcal{C}} := \mathcal{O}_R(L)$. If $\mathcal{O}_{\mathcal{C}}^{\times} = \langle \pm 1 \rangle$, then for any $\gamma \in L \setminus N\mathcal{O}_0$ and quadratic order $S = \mathbb{Z}[\omega_s]$ of discriminant Δ_S inside $\mathcal{O}_0$ in which N is inert, the map:*

$$\Theta : \mathbb{P}^1(\mathbb{Z}/N\mathbb{Z}) \longrightarrow Cl_{\mathfrak{O}}(\mathcal{C})$$
$$(C : D) \longmapsto \chi_L((C + \omega_s D)\gamma)$$

is a bijection. In particular, $|Cl_{\mathfrak{O}}(\mathcal{C})| = N + 1$.

5   New Generalized **KLPT** Algorithm

We introduce in this section a new algorithm to perform the computation of the response in our identification protocol. We aim at solving the issues raised in Subsect. 3.3 with the original KLPT algorithm [22].

The existence of the suborder $\mathfrak{O} = \mathbb{Z}\langle \omega, j \rangle = R + Rj$ introduced in Subsect. 2.2 is what makes special extremal orders good candidates for applying the KLPT algorithm. Here, $R = \mathbb{Z}[\omega]$ is a quadratic order of small discriminant generated by ω, an element of small norm. The norm equation $f(x, y) = M$ over R has a good probability of being solvable for any M and as a consequence, solving norm equations over $\mathfrak{O}$ is easy.

To extend the KLPT algorithm to arbitrary orders, our approach is to find an appropriate Eichler suborder in which we know how to solve norm equations. More precisely, let us take $\mathcal{O}_0$ a special extremal order and $\mathcal{O}$ an arbitrary maximal order, our goal is to extend the KLPT algorithm to left $\mathcal{O}$-ideals. Then, the Eichler order $\mathfrak{O} = \mathcal{O} \cap \mathcal{O}_0$ is a suborder of $\mathcal{O}_0$, thus we can apply the techniques developed in [22] for special extremal orders.

5.1   The Generic Algorithm

We now use our observations of Sect. 4 to design a new GeneralizedKLPT algorithm. As already mentioned, there are several possible variants of this algorithm depending on the kind of norm we need to obtain. For simplicity, we present the case $\ell^\bullet$ where we look for an equivalent ideal of norm ℓ^e. Any other variant is easily derived from this.

For the rest of this paper, let $\mathcal{O}_0$ and $\mathcal{O}$ be two maximal orders, with $\mathcal{O}_0$ being special extremal. These maximal orders are respectively isomorphic to the endomorphism rings of two supersingular curves E_0 and E. From now on, we write I_τ (instead of I in the previous section) for the ideal connecting $\mathcal{O}_0$ with $\mathcal{O}$, and we denote its norm by N_τ. This notation is motivated by the fact that, in the signature context, I_τ will be the ideal corresponding to the secret isogeny τ of degree N_τ. Up to replacing $\mathcal{O}$ with an isomorphic representative, we can assume that N_τ is prime and inert in R (we explain in Subsect. 6.2, the reasons behind this last condition). We consider the Eichler order $\mathfrak{O} = \mathcal{O} \cap \mathcal{O}_0$ of level N_τ.

Let I be a left integral $\mathcal{O}$-ideal, given as input. Our purpose is to find $e \in \mathbb{N}$ and $J \sim I$ of norm ℓ^e upon input I. As a consequence of Lemma 1, this problem is equivalent to finding $\beta \in I$ of norm $n(I)\ell^e$ and setting $J = \chi_I(\beta)$. From Corollary 1, we see that if $\beta \in I \cap \mathfrak{O}$ we have $[I_\tau]^* J = \chi_{[I_\tau]^* I}(\beta)$. In particular, $\beta \in \mathfrak{O} \cap [I_\tau]^* I$ and so we can search for β inside $([I_\tau]^* I) \cap \mathfrak{O}$ instead. The ideal $K' := [I_\tau]^* I$ is a left $\mathcal{O}_0$-ideal and this is a situation close to KLPT$_{\ell^\bullet}$. The fact that we look for a solution inside $K' \cap \mathfrak{O}$ instead of just K' will add an additional constraint. Proposition 1 allows us to write $\mathfrak{O} = \mathbb{Z} + I_\tau$, and intuitively this decomposition tells us that the algorithm for integral ideals used in [22] will be applicable to Eichler orders with small changes.

This suggests the method detailed in Algorithm 2, which can be seen as an adaptation of the KLPT$_{\ell^\bullet}$ algorithm (Algorithm 1), replacing the input I by $I \cap \mathfrak{O}$. In KLPT$_{\ell^\bullet}$ we satisfy the constraint that the desired element is in I using the sub-algorithm IdealModConstraint. We proceed similarly in Step 4 to ensure that the solution is in $\mathfrak{O}$ as well. Combining the two constraints ensures that the solution is in their intersection. An algorithm to perform Step 4 will be described in Subsect. 6.2; its description is not needed to convey the principle of Algorithm 2. We omit the extension of StrongApproximation to the case where N is not prime; the interested reader will find it in the extended paper [13].

Lemma 4. *Algorithm 2 is correct and returns $J \sim I$ of norm ℓ^e.*

Proof. We assume here that the algorithm terminates without failure and do not consider its complexity for now. First, Lemma 1 and the conservation of the norm through pushforward ideals shows that J has norm ℓ^e. Then Corollary 1 applied to $\chi_L(\beta) = \chi_{K'}\left(\frac{\beta\delta}{n(L)}\right)$ implies that $[I_\tau]_* \chi_L(\beta) \sim [I_\tau]_* K$ since $\beta\delta \in \mathfrak{O}$. This proves $J \sim I$. □

Remark 6. As pointed out in Remark 3, KLPT is essentially deterministic when one looks for the smallest possible solution with this method. Given that the only major difference in Algorithm 2 is the additional Step 4 (for which there is only one solution as we will see in Subsect. 6.2) it is not difficult to argue that Algorithm 2 can be made deterministic.

Algorithm 2. GeneralizedKLPT$_{\ell^\bullet}(I, I_\tau)$

Require: I, a left $\mathcal{O}$-ideal, and I_τ, a left $\mathcal{O}_0$-ideal and right $\mathcal{O}$-ideal of norm N_τ.
Ensure: $J \sim I$ of norm ℓ^e.
1: Compute $K' = [I_\tau]^* I$ and set $L = $ EquivalentPrimeIdeal(K'), $L = \chi_{K'}(\delta)$ for $\delta \in K'$
   with $N = n(L)$.
2: Compute $\gamma = $ RepresentInteger$_{\mathcal{O}_0}(N\ell^{e_0})$.
3: Compute $(C_0 : D_0) = $ IdealModConstraint(L, γ).
4: Find $(C_1 : D_1) \in \mathbb{P}^1(\mathbb{Z}/N_\tau\mathbb{Z})$ such that $\gamma j (C_1 + \omega D_1)\delta \in \mathbb{Z} + I_\tau$.
5: Compute $C = $ CRT$_{N_\tau, N}(C_0, C_1)$ and $D = $ CRT$_{N_\tau, N}(D_0, D_1)$.
6: Compute $\mu = $ StrongApproximation$_{\ell^\bullet}(NN_\tau, C, D)$ of norm ℓ^{e_1}
7: Set $\beta = \gamma\mu$ and $e = e_0 + e_1$ such that $n(\beta) = N\ell^e$.
8: **return** $J = [I_\tau]_* \chi_L(\beta)$.

5.2 On the Length of the Solution

The length of the output of Algorithm 2 can be derived from the one of KLPT$_{\ell^\bullet}$. Indeed, in terms of norm, the only real difference is the fact that the Strong-Approximation is performed on NN_τ instead of just N. From the analysis provided in [22] and [25], we see that this implies $e = e_0 + e_1 \sim \frac{9}{2}\log_\ell(p)$ (instead of $e \sim 3\log_\ell(p)$ for KLPT$_{\ell^\bullet}$). This estimate is obtained by considering the plausible approximation $N_\tau \sim \sqrt{p}$. We will argue in Subsect. 7.1 that it might be acceptable to consider cases where N_τ is significantly smaller than this average estimate. This allows us to decrease the size of the solution. We give in Subsect. 6.3 a more proper statement for the approximations introduced above.

In our signature scheme, we will use a variant of Algorithm 2, called Signing-KLPT, suited for our application. The purpose of Sect. 6 is to detail this algorithm and to fill in the gaps left in the description of Algorithm 2.

6 Application to the Signature Scheme: The **SigningKLPT** Algorithm

In this section, we describe the SigningKLPT procedure used in our signature scheme. This procedure, described in Algorithm 3, is a variant of Algorithm 2. Most of its building blocks are common to Algorithm 1 and were introduced in [22]. The rest of this section fills in the remaining gaps as follows. In Subsect. 6.1, we introduce the EquivalentRandomEichlerIdeal used in Step 1. In Subsect. 6.2, we describe the EichlerModConstraint algorithm to perform Step 5 of Algorithm 3 (or Step 44 in Algorithm 2). The parameter e is fixed (and it only depends on

p). To ensure this, we will need to adapt the exponent e_0 and e_1 to the values $N = n(L)$ and N_τ. That is why we will write $e_0(N)$. In Subsect. 6.3 we justify that this is possible. We establish the termination, correctness and complexity of our algorithm in Subsect. 6.4.

Algorithm 3. SigningKLPT(I, I_τ)

Require: I_τ a left $\mathcal{O}_0$-ideal and right $\mathcal{O}$-ideal of norm N_τ, and I, a left O-ideal.
Ensure: $J \sim I$ of norm ℓ^e, where e is fixed.
1: Compute $K = $ EquivalentRandomEichlerIdeal(I, N_τ)
2: Compute $K' = [I_\tau]^* K$ and set $L = $ EquivalentPrimeIdeal(K'), $L = \chi_{K'}(\delta)$ for $\delta \in K'$ with $N = n(L)$. Set $e_0 = e_0(N)$ and $e_1 = e - e_0$.
3: Compute $\gamma = $ RepresentInteger$_{\mathcal{O}_0}(N\ell^{e_0})$.
4: Compute $(C_0 : D_0) = $ IdealModConstraint(L, γ).
5: Compute $(C_1 : D_1) = $ EichlerModConstraint$(\mathbb{Z} + I_\tau, \gamma, \delta)$.
6: Compute $C = $ CRT$_{N_\tau, N}(C_0, C_1)$ and $D = $ CRT$_{N_\tau, N}(D_0, D_1)$. If $\ell^e p(C^2 + D^2)$ is not a quadratic residue, go back to Step 3.
7: Compute $\mu = $ StrongApproximation$_{\ell^\bullet}(NN_\tau, C, D)$ of norm ℓ^{e_1}
8: Set $\beta = \gamma\mu$.
9: **return** $J = [I_\tau]_* \chi_L(\beta)$.

6.1   The Randomization Procedure

The purpose of Step 1 is to perform a randomization step which we will use to argue the security of our signature. This addition has two interesting consequences for us. First, the output of Algorithm 3 only depends on the equivalence class of the input I. Second, it randomizes the execution as otherwise the algorithm would be essentially deterministic as noted in Remark 6.

The EquivalentRandomEichlerIdeal algorithm receives an ideal I as input and returns an equivalent random ideal. In this context equivalent random ideal means that if we write $\mathcal{C}$ the class of I in $Cl(\mathcal{O})$, we want an output ideal equivalent to I and lying in a uniformly random class of $Cl_{\mathfrak{D}}(\mathcal{C})$ (see Definition 1). This condition might seem a bit arbitrary at first; however Proposition 5 will justify that this is exactly the kind of randomness we need.

To reach this goal, we use the classical technique of finding some well-chosen $\beta \in I$ and output $\chi_I(\beta)$. The method to choose the β is inspired by the results of Subsect. 4.3. The idea is to use the bijection from Proposition 4 in order to sample a class uniformly. Note that Proposition 4 does not hold for some special cases of maximal orders $\mathcal{O}$, but we may assume that this is not the case here (in the worst case there are two such types of maximal orders among $O(p)$ possibilities).

We start by showing that Algorithm 4 terminates and that the output distribution is correct.

Lemma 5. *Algorithm 4 terminates in polynomial time and outputs an ideal equivalent to I and uniformly distributed among the $N_\tau + 1$ possible classes of $Cl_{\mathfrak{D}}(\mathcal{O})$.*

Algorithm 4. EquivalentRandomEichlerIdeal(I, N_τ)

Require: I a left $\mathcal{O}$-ideal.
Ensure: $K \sim I$ of norm coprime with N_τ.
 1: Sample a random element ω_S in $\mathcal{O}$ until N_τ is inert in $\mathbb{Z}[\omega_S]$.
 2: Sample γ a random element in I such that $n(\gamma)/n(I)$ is coprime with N_τ.
 3: Select a random class $(C : D) \in \mathbb{P}^1(\mathbb{Z}/N_\tau\mathbb{Z})$.
 4: Set $\beta = (C + \omega_S D)\gamma$.
 5: **return** $K = \chi_I(\beta)$

Proof. We can find in $O(\log(p))$ attempts a quadratic suborder $\mathbb{Z}[\omega_S] \subset \mathcal{O}$ in which N_τ is inert. Then, it is clear that taking a random element in I will verify that $n(\gamma)/n(I)$ is coprime with N_τ with overwhelming probability. Thus, the algorithm terminates in polynomial time.

The algorithm concretely instantiates the map Θ from Proposition 4. This map is bijective and we choose $(C : D)$ uniformly at random inside $\mathbb{P}^1(\mathbb{Z}/N_\tau\mathbb{Z})$ so the output is uniformly distributed.

Consequently, the output of EquivalentRandomEichlerIdeal only depends on the class (inside $Cl(\mathcal{O})$) of the ideal in input. The call to EquivalentRandomEichlerIdeal in Step 1 of Algorithm 3 thus implies the following lemma that will prove useful in Sect. 7.

Lemma 6. *For any I_τ, the output distributions of* SigningKLPT(I, I_τ) *and* SigningKLPT(J, I_τ) *are the same for any $I \sim J$. Said otherwise, for fixed I_τ, the output distribution of Algorithm 3 only depends on the equivalence class of the ideal I in input.*

Next, we describe how the distribution of L (as defined in Step 2 of Algorithm 3) is determined by the output distribution of EquivalentRandom EichlerIdeal. This is what motivates the current formulation of Algorithm 4.

Proposition 5. *The set $\mathcal{G}_I = \{L, L = $ EquivalentPrimeIdeal$([I_\tau]^*K)$ for $K \sim I\}$ has size at most $N_\tau + 1$ and for every $L \in \mathcal{G}_I$ there exists an output $K = $ EquivalentRandomEichlerIdeal(I) such that $L = $ EquivalentPrimeIdeal$([I_\tau]^*K)$. When $\#\mathcal{G}_I = N_\tau + 1$, the ideal L is uniformly distributed inside this set.*

Proof. As we mentioned already, there are exactly $N_\tau + 1$ classes for $K \sim I$ in $Cl_{\mathfrak{O}}(\mathcal{O})$. By Corollary 1[1], the class of K in $Cl_{\mathfrak{O}}(\mathcal{O})$ uniquely determines the class of $[I_\tau]^*K$ in $Cl(\mathcal{O}_0)$. As noted in Subsect. 2.2, the output of EquivalentPrimeIdeal is well-defined and deterministic on $Cl(\mathcal{O}_0)$. The result is proved if we combine the above remark with Lemma 5.

---

[1] Corollary 1 uses pushforwards rather than pullbacks, but we obtain the desired result by replacing I with $\overline{I}$.

6.2   Eichler Modular Constraint

Step 5 in Algorithm 3 (or Step 4 of Algorithm 2) is essential to find a solution that lies in $\mathfrak{O} = \mathcal{O} \cap \mathcal{O}_0$. More precisely for given γ, δ of norm coprime with N_τ we need to find $\mu_1 \in jR$ such that $\gamma\mu_1\delta \in \mathfrak{O}$. In fact, this can be done for any γ, δ of norm coprime with N_τ. This is stated and proved in Proposition 6 below, following a reasoning similar to the one used in [22] for IdealModConstraint.

The method of resolution is also strongly inspired by IdealModConstraint. Namely, we use an explicit isomorphism $\mathcal{O}_0/N_\tau\mathcal{O}_0 \cong \mathbb{M}_2(\mathbb{Z}/N_\tau\mathbb{Z})$ and a correspondence between the set of proper nonzero left ideals in $\mathbb{M}_2(\mathbb{Z}/N_\tau\mathbb{Z})$ and $\mathbb{P}^1(\mathbb{Z}/N_\tau\mathbb{Z})$ to translate the condition $\gamma\mu_1\delta \in \mathbb{Z} + I_\tau$ as a system of linear equations $\bmod N_\tau$. We write EichlerModConstraint$(\mathfrak{O}, \gamma, \delta)$ for this. It outputs $(C_1 : D_1) \in \mathbb{P}^1(\mathbb{Z}/N_\tau\mathbb{Z})$ such that $\gamma j(C_1 + \omega D_1)\delta \in \mathfrak{O}$.

We remind the reader that we consider N_τ inert in R (where R is defined, like in Subsect. 2.2, as the quadratic suborder of minimal discriminant inside $\mathcal{O}_0$). If N_τ is split, the method is very likely to work as well but there may be some cases where it fails. Since the constraint that N_τ is inert in R is quite easy to satisfy (see Subsect. 8.3) we may assume that it holds.

Proposition 6. *The sub-routine* EichlerModConstraint *on any input* $\mathfrak{O}, \gamma, \delta$ *returns* $(C_1 : D_1) \in \mathbb{P}^1(\mathbb{Z}/N_\tau\mathbb{Z})$ *such that* $\gamma\mu\delta \in \mathfrak{O}$ *with* $\mu = (C_1 + \omega D_1)j$.

Proof. In Algorithm 3, we want to find μ such that $\beta = \gamma\mu$ verifies $\beta\delta \in \mathfrak{O}$ to ensure that $[I_\tau]_*\chi_L(\beta) \sim I$. In Subsect. 4.3, we showed that this was equivalent to $\chi_L(\beta)$ lying in the correct equivalence class of $Cl(\mathfrak{O})$. To prove that a solution can always be found it suffices to show that the map $\Theta' : \mathbb{P}^1(\mathbb{Z}/N_\tau\mathbb{Z}) \to Cl(\mathfrak{O})$ sending $(C : D)$ to $\gamma(C + \omega D)$ is surjective. In fact, this map is almost the one from Proposition 4 and is bijective (thus surjective) for the same reasons.

Hence we see that there always exists a solution μ such that $\chi_L(\gamma\mu)$ lies in the correct class in $Cl_\mathfrak{O}(\mathcal{O}_0) \equiv Cl(\mathfrak{O})$ and this proves the result.

We deduce a useful corollary, which shows that EichlerModConstraint is independent of the choice of δ.

Corollary 2. *Taking* δ, δ' *as above, for any given* $\gamma \in \mathcal{O}_0$ *of norm coprime with* N_τ, EichlerModConstraint$(\mathfrak{O}, \gamma, \delta) = $ EichlerModConstraint$(\mathfrak{O}, \gamma, \delta')$.

Proof. In the proof of Proposition 6, we showed that the map $(C_1 : D_1) \to \gamma j(C_1 + \omega D_1)$ is injective for any γ of norm coprime with N_τ. This justifies that there is only one solution in $\mathbb{P}^1(\mathbb{Z}/N_\tau\mathbb{Z})$ giving a β lying in the correct class inside $L/\sim_\mathfrak{O}$ (and thus with $\chi_L(\beta)$ in the correct class of $Cl_\mathfrak{O}(\mathcal{O}_0)$). Hence, EichlerModConstraint$(\mathfrak{O}, \gamma, \delta)$ and EichlerModConstraint$(\mathfrak{O}, \gamma, \delta')$ are both equal to this unique solution.

6.3   Suitable Values for e_0 and e_1

For security (specifically zero-knowledge) it is important that our output has fixed norm so that the size of the output does not reveal any information on the input. In this section, we justify that it is possible to find a parameter e such that finding an output of exact size ℓ^e is possible for almost every input. The exponent e is the sum of two exponents $e_0(N)$ and $e_1(N, N_\tau)$ whose individual values depend on N and N_τ but whose sum can be fixed. In fact, we will pick e following the approximations of [22] presented in Subsect. 5.2 as they appear to be quite tight in practice. To simplify notations we write log instead of $\log_\ell$ in the rest of this section. Let us refine the statements of Subsect. 5.2. For KLPT, the most important parameter is the size of N. We state in Lemma 7 that N cannot be a lot bigger than $\sqrt{p}$. This result holds under an assumption on the norms of elements in a Minkowski basis of an integral ideal, and heuristic assumptions on the distribution of primes represented by some quadratic forms (see [22]). We stress that this approximation is quite tight in practice as illustrated in the experimental results of [22] and it seems to hold by taking $\varepsilon = \log\log(p)$.

Lemma 7. *There exists $\varepsilon = O(\log\log(p))$ such that for a random class $\mathcal{C} \in Cl(\mathcal{O}_0)$, the norm N of EquivalentPrimeIdeal($\mathcal{C}$) verifies $\log(N) < \log(p)/2 + \varepsilon$ with overwhelming probability.*

This approximation is valid for both N and N_τ, and we will assume that it holds for both values for the rest of this section. As we will not be able to provide a tight lower bound on $\log(N), \log(N_\tau)$, we need to adjust the exponents e_0 and e_1 and that is why we write $e_0(N)$ and $e_1(N, N_\tau)$ for the lower bounds of Lemmas 8 and 9. We recall our assumption that the failure probability in the quadratic residuosity condition of Step 6 is $3/4$ on average for a given γ and δ.

In Lemmas 8 and 9, we assume that we are in an execution of Algorithm 3 that led to an ideal L of norm N. We keep the notation ε from Lemma 7.

Lemma 8. *For any $\kappa \in \mathbb{N}$, there exists $\eta_0 = O(\log\log(p) + \log(\kappa))$ such that for any $e_0 \geq e_0(N) = \log(p) - \log(N) + \varepsilon + \eta_0$, the probability that there exists a solution $\gamma = $ RepresentInteger$_{\mathcal{O}_0}(N\ell^{e_0})$ that will lead to a correct execution of Algorithm 3 is higher than $1 - 2^{-\kappa}$.*

Remark 7. We note that taking $\kappa \sim \log(p)$ ensures that the success probability in Lemma 8 is overwhelming. In the case of (very unlikely) failure where one of the assumptions above does not hold, we simply abort and start the computation again.

We conclude this section by evaluating the size of the exponent e_1 in the output of StrongApproximation. The algorithm for StrongApproximation($N, \cdot$) in [25] computes close vectors in some lattice of discriminant $\tilde{O}(N^3 p)$.

Lemma 9. *There exists $\eta_1 = O(\log\log(p))$ such that if $e_1 \geq e_1(N, N_\tau) \log p + 3\log(N) + 3\log(N_\tau) + \eta_1$, Step 7 of Algorithm 3 succeeds in finding a solution μ of norm ℓ^{e_1} with overwhelming probability.*

6.4   Termination, Correctness and Complexity

We are now ready to state the following proposition. As noted in Remark 7, we take $\kappa \sim \log(p)$ for Lemma 8.

Proposition 7. *Algorithm 3 terminates in heuristic probabilistic polynomial time. It returns an ideal $J \sim I$ of fixed norm ℓ^e for any input I with overwhelming probability if $e \geq 9/2 \log(p) + 6\varepsilon + \eta_0 + \eta_1$ where $\varepsilon, \eta_0, \eta_1$ are defined as in Lemma 7 to 9.*

Proof. The proof of correctness follows almost directly from Lemma 4, replacing I by an equivalent K. Since the correctness of Algorithm 2 holds for any input and $K \sim I$, we see that Algorithm 3 is correct. Combining Lemmas 8 and 9 we see that we need to pick e_0, e_1 above the bounds $e_0(N), e_1(N, N_\tau)$ for the computation to succeed with overwhelming probability. We obtain $e_0 + e_1 \geq 2 \log(p) + 2 \log(N) + 3 \log(N_\tau) + \eta_0 + \eta_1 + \epsilon$. Taking the upper bound of Lemma 7 for both N and N_τ we obtain $e \geq 9/2 \log(p) + 6\varepsilon + \eta_0 + \eta_1$. Given that the probability of failure is $3/4$, the number of different values γ that we need to choose before finding a fitting choice is logarithmic in p. This proves termination. The complexity statement follows directly from the heuristic polynomial-time complexities argued in [22]. From the description in Subsect. 6.2, it is clear that the complexity of EichlerModConstraint is the same as IdealModConstraint and it is also polynomial in $\log(p)$. $\qquad\square$

7 Zero-Knowledge

In Sect. 3 we left open the question of proving zero-knowledge of the identification scheme, and consequently unforgeability of the signature scheme. Unlike other identification schemes based on isogenies [3,12], SQISign does not achieve perfect zero-knowledge, but necessitates an *ad hoc* computational assumption instead. As usual, we need to prove that there exists a simulator that outputs transcripts indistinguishable from real interactions between prover and verifier, and it is easy to see that this boils down to proving that the distribution of the response isogenies σ for a given secret τ can be simulated without knowledge of τ. Of course, the distribution of σ depends on the variant of KLPT employed, and we already argued in Subsect. 3.3 that the variants known prior to this work provide no security at all. In this section we shall state the security assumption and sketch the associated security reduction for algorithm SigningKLPT. Due to space constraints all proofs are omitted here; they can be found in [13].

7.1 On the Distribution of Signatures

We want to understand the distribution of the isogenies σ obtained from $J =$ SigningKLPT(I, I_τ) for some secret τ. It turns out any such σ is the image under τ of some other isogeny ι, whose properties are precisely stated in the following lemma.

Lemma 10. *Let $L \subset \mathcal{O}$ and $\beta \in L$ be as in Steps 2, 8 respectively of Algorithm 3. The isogeny σ corresponding to the output J of Algorithm 3 is equal to $\sigma = [\tau]_* \iota$, where ι is an isogeny of degree ℓ^e verifying $\beta = \hat{\iota} \circ \varphi_L$.*

We will argue that there exists a set $\mathcal{P}_{N_\tau}$, depending only on the degree N_τ, such that $\iota \in \mathcal{P}_{N_\tau}$ if and only if $\sigma = [\tau]_* \iota$ for some output σ of Algorithm 3. $L \subset \mathcal{O}$ being defined as in Lemma 10, it is clear that the codomain of ι is determined by the class of L in $Cl(\mathcal{O}_0)$. Suppose we have chosen a class for L among the $N_\tau + 1$ candidates, we want to determine how the rest of the computation follows from this initial choice. During Step 3 we compute a value γ, and it is clear that $N = n(L)$ uniquely determines the distribution of outputs for $\mathsf{RepresentInteger}_{\mathcal{O}_0}(N\ell^{e_0(N)})$. Then, the projective pair $(C_0 : D_0)$ only depends on L and γ. We have proved in Corollary 2 that the projective pair $(C_1 : D_1)$ did not depend on the actual value of δ, so it is also uniquely determined by the choice of class for K (and thus of L) and γ. The rest of the computation is deterministic from there (up to failures that imply picking another γ). We are now ready to characterize the set of all possible outputs of our algorithm SigningKLPT.

Let us take the value $e_0(N)$ and $e_1(N, N_\tau)$ as defined in Subsect. 6.3 for Algorithm 3. For a given L of norm N, we consider $\mathcal{U}_{L,N_\tau}$ as the set of all isogenies ι computed as in Lemma 10 from elements $\beta = \gamma\mu \in L$ where γ is a random output of $\mathsf{RepresentInteger}_{\mathcal{O}_0}(N\ell^{e_0(N)})$ and $\mu = (C + \omega D)j$ where $p(C^2 + D^2)\ell^{e_1(N,N_\tau)}$ is a quadratic residue $\mathrm{mod} N N_\tau$ and is defined as $C = \mathsf{CRT}_{N,N_\tau}(C_0, C_1)$, $D = \mathsf{CRT}_{N,N_\tau}(D_0, D_1)$ where $(C_0 : D_0) = \mathsf{IdealModConstraint}(L, \gamma)$ and $(C_1 : D_1)$ is a random element of $\mathbb{P}^1(\mathbb{Z}/N_\tau\mathbb{Z})$. For an equivalence class $\mathcal{C}$ in $Cl(\mathcal{O}_0)$ we write $\mathcal{U}_{\mathcal{C},N_\tau}$ for $\mathcal{U}_{L,N_\tau}$ where $L = \mathsf{EquivalentPrimeIdeal}(\mathcal{C})$.

Definition 2. $\mathcal{P}_{N_\tau} = \bigcup_{\mathcal{C} \in Cl(\mathcal{O}_0)} \mathcal{U}_{\mathcal{C},N_\tau}$

Proposition 8. *The set $\mathcal{P}_{N_\tau}$ from Definition 2 can be computed from the sole knowledge of N_τ. The set $\{J, J = [I_\tau]_* I_\iota, \iota \in \mathcal{P}_{N_\tau}\}$ is exactly the set of outputs* SigningKLPT(I, I_τ) *for I ranging over all the non-trivial classes in $Cl(\mathcal{O})$.*

7.2 Hardness Assumption for Zero-Knowledge

We are now ready to formulate a computational assumption which zero-knowledge reduces to. For $D \in \mathbb{N}$ and a supersingular curve E, we define $\mathrm{Iso}_{D,j(E)}$ as the set of cyclic isogenies of degree D, whose domain is a curve inside the isomorphism class of E. When $\mathcal{P}$ is a subset of $\mathrm{Iso}_{D,j(E)}$ and $\tau : E \to E'$ is an isogeny with $\gcd(\deg \tau, D) = 1$, we write $[\tau]_* \mathcal{P}$ for the subset $\{[\tau]_* \phi \mid \phi \in \mathcal{P}\}$ of $\mathrm{Iso}_{D,j(E')}$. Finally, we denote by $\mathcal{K}$ a probability distribution on the set of cyclic isogenies whose domain is E_0, representing the distribution of SQISign private keys.

Problem 2. Let p be a prime, and D a smooth integer. Let $\tau : E_0 \to E_A$ be a random isogeny drawn from $\mathcal{K}$, and let N_τ be its degree. Let $\mathcal{P}_{N_\tau} \subset \mathrm{Iso}_{D,j_0}$ as in Definition 2, and let O_τ be an oracle sampling random elements in $[\tau]_* \mathcal{P}_{N_\tau}$. Let $\sigma : E_A \to \star$ of degree D where either

1. σ is uniformly random in $\mathrm{Iso}_{D,j(E_A)}$;
2. σ is uniformly random in $[\tau]_* \mathcal{P}_{N_\tau}$.

The problem is, given $p, D, \mathcal{K}, E_A, \sigma$, to distinguish between the two cases with a polynomial number of queries to O_τ.

We assume that Problem 2 cannot be solved with non-negligible advantage by any polynomial time adversary. In [13] we briefly discuss several potential attack strategies; however, given current knowledge, no strategy seems to be better than a direct key recovery, computing τ from the knowledge of E_A only.

In order to state the security reduction, we also need some additional heuristic assumptions which are plausibly true.

Assumption 1. *Under the heuristic assumptions used in Subsect. 6.3, we can fix a given degree $D = \ell^e$ with e depending only on p, such that Algorithm 3 succeeds in finding an output of norm D for any input with overwhelming probability.*

Assumption 2. *The distribution of classes obtained by taking the classes of the ideals I_ι corresponding to $\iota \in \mathcal{P}_{N_\tau}$ is statistically close to the uniform distribution on $Cl_{\mathfrak{O}}(\mathcal{O}_0)$.*

We can finally state the main result of this section.

Proposition 9. *Let E_A be a SQISign public key. When SQISign is instantiated with Algorithm 3, distinguishing between the distribution $\mathcal{D}(E_A)$ of isogenies σ output by SQISign, and the uniform distribution of D-isogenies starting from E_A, reduces to Problem 2, under the heuristic assumptions listed above.*

8   Efficiency

In this section, we describe a concrete instantiation of our scheme. This includes a precise description of the protocols outlined in Subsect. 3.1, along with all the missing sub-algorithms, concrete parameters and various ideas to improve the overall efficiency. The resulting signature reaches 128-bit of classical security and the post-quantum NIST level 1 and is very compact as highlighted in Table 2. We also provide a proof-of-concept implementation of the protocol.

The algorithm SigningKLPT was extensively studied in Sects. 5 and 6, and we will see in Subsect. 8.6 that it is reasonably efficient. The efficiency bottleneck of our signature scheme turns out to be the translation of the input and output ideals of Algorithm 3 from and to isogenies. Specifically, we seek to define two families of algorithms:

- IdealToIsogeny: Given a left $\mathcal{O}$-ideal I of smooth norm D, compute the corresponding isogeny φ_I as a sequence of prime-degree isogenies.
- IsogenyToIdeal: Given an isogeny from E of smooth degree D, compute the corresponding left $\mathcal{O}$-ideal.

Algorithms for these tasks in the case where $\mathcal{O}$ and E are special extremal were already introduced in [19]. They are very general, but not really efficient, owing to their use of D-torsion points defined in algebraic extensions of $\mathbb{F}_{p^2}$. A classical solution would be to choose a special prime p such that the D-torsion is $\mathbb{F}_{p^2}$-rational. However in our case D is a power of 2 and, following the estimates of Subsect. 5.2, we need $D \approx p^{9/2}$ (or at best $D \approx p^{15/4}$ using the idea of Subsect. 8.3). With these requirements finding such a prime is not feasible, we thus devise new solutions to the two problems.

This section is organized as follows. We first present our version of IdealTo-Isogeny in Subsect. 8.1. We then introduce a set of concrete parameters in Subsect. 8.2, and we analyze two possible key spaces in Subsect. 8.3. Following up, we give a detailed description of our identification scheme in Subsect. 8.4. Size and time performances of the resulting signature scheme are presented in Subsect. 8.6.

8.1   Translating Ideals to Isogenies

Let I be a left $\mathcal{O}_0$-ideal of smooth norm D where $\mathcal{O}_0$ is a special extremal maximal order, and let E_0 be a curve such that $\mathcal{O}_0$ is isomorphic to $End(E_0)$. In this section we assume that we know an explicit representation of $\mathcal{O}_0$, meaning that we know an explicit isomorphism between $End(E_0)$ and $\mathcal{O}_0$, allowing us to efficiently evaluate endomorphisms of E_0. We want to find the isogeny φ_I of degree D and domain E_0 corresponding to I. We will describe φ_I as the composition of several prime degree isogenies represented by their kernels. Most of the ideas presented in this section are adaptations of algorithms introduced in [17,19]; below we first recall these algorithms then describe our improvements.

Algorithm in [17]. As each primary factor of D can be treated separately let us for simplicity assume that $D = \ell^e$. The idea is to divide φ_I into g isogenies of smaller degrees ℓ^f where the ℓ^f-torsion is defined over a reasonably small field extension. Following [17], to write $\varphi_I = \varphi_g \circ \ldots \varphi_2 \circ \varphi_1$ under the ideal filtration $I = I_1 \cdot I_2 \cdots I_g$, we need an explicit representation of $\mathcal{O}_i = \mathcal{O}_R(I_i)$ in order to compute the action of $End(E_i)$ on $E_i[\ell^f]$, where E_i is the codomain of φ_i. A formula is introduced in [17] providing such a representation from an ideal connecting $\mathcal{O}_i$ to $\mathcal{O}_0$ (equivalently an isogeny connecting E_i with E_0). However this formula involves division by the norm N_i of this ideal. In particular if e_i is the ℓ-adic valuation of N_i, we would need to compute the ℓ^{f+e_i}-torsion points. It thus appears that having N_i coprime to ℓ is essential for efficiency. We will therefore not be able to use $I_1 \cdots I_i$ as the connecting ideal, but we will instead use an equivalent ideal J_i of coprime degree. Fortunately, this can be found with KLPT. This idea underlies all the algorithms introduced in this section.

The discussion above motivates the introduction of a smooth integer T representing the torsion coprime with ℓ that is *accessible* (i.e., defined over small extensions of $\mathbb{F}_{p^2}$), we refer to Subsect. 8.2 for concrete parameters illustrating what we mean by "accessible" and "small". Ideally, we would like to have J_i of norm dividing T (obtained by execution of the variant KLPT$_T$) so that the translations into the corresponding isogenies are efficient. However, once again we are hindered by the size of KLPT's outputs, which have norm around p^3. We now describe two tricks to reduce the torsion requirements.

Computing Half of the Isogeny from the Image Curve. Let us assume that our ideal corresponds to $\psi : E_1 \to E_2$ where ψ has degree $D_1 D_2$ (with D_1 and D_2 not necessarily coprime). Instead of trying to express ψ from E_1 and using the $E_1[D_1 D_2]$ torsion, we can try and split ψ as $\hat{\psi}_2 \circ \psi_1$ where $\deg \psi_i = D_i$, $i = 1, 2$. We compute ψ_1 from $E_1[D_1]$ and ψ_2 from $E_2[D_2]$. We apply this idea in Algorithm 5 to translate an ideal of norm dividing T^2 (instead of T previously) to the corresponding isogeny. This means we now only need $T \sim p^{\frac{3}{2}}$ instead of $T \sim p^3$. We will see in Subsect. 8.2 that this is indeed possible.

Meet-in-the-Middle. Let us now assume that $D = D_1 D_2 D'$, where D' is a reasonably small integer (in our application, D, D_1, D_2, D' are all ℓ-powers). We can write an isogeny ψ of degree D as $\hat{\psi}_2 \circ \theta \circ \psi_1$ where $\deg \psi_1 = D_1$, $\deg \theta = D'$ and $\deg \psi_2 = D_2$. The two isogenies $\psi_1, \hat{\psi}_2$ can be computed using $E_1[D_1]$ and $E_2[D_2]$ as before. Writing E_3 and E_4 for their codomains we know that there is $\theta : E_3 \to E_4$ of degree D'. If D' is small and smooth, a meet-in-the-middle search allows us to recover θ efficiently. This idea, combined with that of Subsect. 8.1, underlies Algorithm 6 $\mathsf{IdealToIsogeny}_{\ell^{2f}+\Delta}$, that is illustrated in Fig. 2. In our implementation, this trick decreases the number of T-isogeny computations, which currently are the efficiency bottleneck.

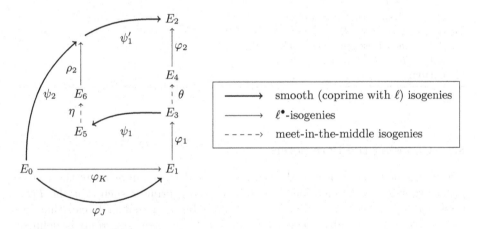

Fig. 2. Graphical representation of the ideal to isogeny translation of Algorithm 6

Ideal to Isogeny: Our Optimized Solution. We are now ready to present the algorithm $\mathsf{IdealToIsogeny}_{\ell^\bullet}$ used in our implementation. The algorithm translates an $\mathcal{O}$-ideal in the corresponding isogeny for any maximal order $\mathcal{O}$. It requires K a left $\mathcal{O}_0$-ideal and right $\mathcal{O}$-ideal of degree $\ell^\bullet$ along with the corresponding isogeny $\varphi_K : E_0 \to E$ where $\mathcal{O} \cong End(E)$. As before we write ℓ^f for the accessible $\ell^\bullet$-torsion and T for the accessible smooth torsion coprime to ℓ. We write Δ for a meet-in-the-middle parameter $\ell^\Delta = D'$ (see Subsect. 8.1). The algorithm uses the following subroutines.

- SpecialIdealToIsogeny(J, I, φ_I): described in Algorithm 5, it takes I, J two left $\mathcal{O}_0$-ideals of norm $n(I) = \ell^\bullet$ and $n(J)$ dividing T^2 along with the isogeny $\varphi_I : E_0 \to E$ and outputs φ_J.
- IdealToIsogeny$_{\ell^{2f+\Delta}}(I, J, K, \varphi_J, \varphi_K)$: described in Algorithm 6, it takes I a left $\mathcal{O}_0$-ideal of norm dividing $T^2\ell^{2f+\Delta}$, J containing I of norm dividing T^2 and $K \sim J$ of norm $\ell^\bullet$ along with φ_J, φ_K and outputs φ of degree $\ell^{2f+\Delta}$ such that $\varphi_I = \varphi \circ \varphi_J$.

The algorithm IdealToIsogeny$_{\ell^\bullet}(I, K, \varphi_K)$ is described in Algorithm 7. Note that we do not provide any proof of correctness and termination for Algorithms 55 to 7. This is because these algorithms already existed in essence in [17,19] and were only improved with the ideas of Subsect. 8.1 and Subsect. 8.1 for efficiency.

Algorithm 5. SpecialIdealToIsogeny(J, I, φ_I)

Require: Two equivalent left ideals I, J of $\mathcal{O}_0$, with J of norm dividing T^2 and I of norm $\ell^\bullet$, and the corresponding isogeny $\varphi_I : E_0 \to E$.

Ensure: φ_J.

1: $H_1 \leftarrow J + T\mathcal{O}_0$.
2: Let $\alpha \in I$ such that $J = \chi_I(\alpha)$.
3: $H_2 \leftarrow \langle \alpha, (n(J)/n(H_1)) \rangle$.
4: $\varphi_{H_i} \leftarrow$ IdealToIsogeny$_T(H_i) : E_0 \to E_i$.
5: Let $\psi : E \to E/\varphi_I(\ker \varphi_{H_2}) = E_1$.
6: **return** $\hat{\psi} \circ \varphi_{H_1}$.

8.2   Choosing the Parameters

We discuss now the choice of the parameters and most importantly the prime p that we will use. As mentioned above, we need a prime p such that the $T\ell^f$-torsion is accessible for $T \simeq p^{3/2}$ and f is as big as possible. Recall that by "accessible" we generally mean that the full $T\ell^f$-torsion subgroup is defined over a small extension of $\mathbb{F}_{p^2}$. We can strengthen this by asking that $T\ell^f \mid (p^2 - 1)$, which implies that the full $T\ell^f$-torsion is generated by four points with x-coordinates in $\mathbb{F}_{p^2}$, or equivalently by two $\mathbb{F}_{p^2}$-rational points on the curve with Frobenius trace $-2p$ and two other $\mathbb{F}_{p^2}$-rational points on its twist. Similar primes were recently considered for use in B-SIDH [7], an adaptation of SIDH with smaller (uncompressed) public keys.

Algorithm 6. IdealToIsogeny$_{\ell^{2f+\Delta}}(I, J, K, \varphi_J, \varphi_K)$

Require: I a left $\mathcal{O}_0$-ideal of norm dividing $T^2\ell^{2f+\Delta}$, an $\mathcal{O}_0$-ideal in J containing I of norm dividing T^2, and an ideal $K \sim J$ of norm a power of ℓ, as well as φ_J and φ_K.

Ensure: $\varphi = \varphi_2 \circ \theta \circ \varphi_1 : E_1 \to E_2$ of degree $\ell^{2f+\Delta}$ such that $\varphi_I = \varphi \circ \varphi_J$, $L \sim I$ of norm dividing T^2 and φ_L.

0: Write $\varphi_J, \varphi_K : E_0 \to E_1$.
1: Let $I_1 = I + \ell^f \mathcal{O}_0$.
2: Let $\varphi_1' = \mathsf{IdealToIsogeny}_{\ell^f}(I_1)$.
3: Let $\varphi_1 = [\varphi_J]_* \varphi_1' : E_1 \to E_3$.
4: Let $L = \mathsf{KLPT}_T(I)$.
5: Let $\alpha \in K$ such that $J = \chi_K(\alpha)$.
6: Let $\beta \in I$ such that $L = \chi_I(\beta)$.
7: Let $\gamma = \beta\alpha/n(J)$. We have $\gamma \in K$, $\bar{\gamma} \in L$, and $n(\gamma) = T^2\ell^{2f+\Delta}n(K)$.
8: Let $H_1 = \langle \gamma, n(K)\ell^f T \rangle$. We have $\varphi_{H_1} = \psi_1 \circ \varphi_1 \circ \varphi_K : E_0 \to E_5$, where ψ_1 has degree T.
9: Let $H_2 = \langle \bar{\gamma}, \ell^f T \rangle$. We have $\varphi_{H_2} = \rho_2 \circ \psi_2 : E_0 \to E_6$, where ψ_2 has degree T and φ_2 has degree ℓ^f.
10: Find $\eta : E_5 \to E_6$ of degree ℓ^Δ with meet-in-the-middle.
11: Let $\varphi_2 \circ \theta = [\hat{\psi}_1]_* \hat{\rho}_2 \circ \eta : E_3 \to E_2$ and $\psi_1' = [\hat{\varphi}_2 \circ \eta]_* \hat{\psi}_1$
12: **return** $\varphi = \varphi_2\theta \circ \varphi_1$, L and $\psi_1' \circ \psi_2$.

Algorithm 7. IdealToIsogeny$_{\ell^\bullet}(I, K, \varphi_K)$

Require: A left $\mathcal{O}$-ideal I of norm a power of ℓ, K a left $\mathcal{O}_0$-ideal and right $\mathcal{O}$-ideal of norm $\ell^\bullet$, the corresponding φ_K.

Ensure: φ_I.

1: Write $I = I_n \subset \cdots \subset I_1 \subset I_0 = \mathcal{O}$ where $n(I_i)/n(I_{i-1}) \leq \ell^{2f+\Delta}$.
2: $J \leftarrow \mathsf{KLPT}_T(K)$.
3: $\varphi_J \leftarrow \mathsf{SpecialIdealToIsogeny}(J, K, \varphi_K)$.
4: **for** $i = 1, \ldots, n$ **do**
5:     $\varphi_i, J, \varphi_J \leftarrow \mathsf{IdealToIsogeny}_{\ell^{2f+\Delta}}(J \cdot I_i, J, K, \varphi_J, \varphi_K)$.
6:     $K \leftarrow K \cdot I_i$.
7:     $\varphi_K \leftarrow \varphi_i \circ \varphi_K$.
8: **end for**
9: **return** $\varphi_n \circ \cdots \circ \varphi_1$.

For λ bits of classical security, we need a prime of 2λ bits. In the implementation described in Subsect. 8.6, we used the 256-bits prime p such that

$$p + 1 = 2^{33} \cdot 5^{21} \cdot 7^2 \cdot 11 \cdot 31 \cdot 83 \cdot 107 \cdot 137 \cdot 751 \cdot 827 \cdot 3691 \cdot 4019 \cdot 6983$$
$$\cdot 517434778561 \cdot 26602537156291,$$
$$p - 1 = 2 \cdot 3^{53} \cdot 43 \cdot 103 \cdot 109 \cdot 199 \cdot 227 \cdot 419 \cdot 491 \cdot 569 \cdot 631 \cdot 677 \cdot 857 \cdot 859$$
$$\cdot 883 \cdot 1019 \cdot 2713 \cdot 4283.$$

This prime verifies that $p^2 - 1$ is a multiple of $2^{33}T$ where T is a 395-bit 2^{13}-smooth number. We give more details on the search for such primes in [13].

Algorithm 7 requires numerous evaluations of T-isogenies, and this will prove to be the bottleneck of our scheme. The recent work of [2] provided a square root speedup to compute and evaluate an isogeny of degree d. Their method appears to be faster than the naive method for $d \geq 100$ approximately and our scheme's implementation also benefits from this improvement.

8.3   Defining the Key Space

For statistical security, the secret isogeny should be of degree sufficiently large, so to ensure a nearly uniform distribution of the public key E_A in the set of supersingular curves. However, a larger degree results in a bigger output for Algorithm 3, hence poorer performance. In this section we discuss an alternative key sampling method which trades off statistical security for efficiency. The key idea is to sample the degree of the secret isogeny as a secret big prime (instead of a public smooth number). Choosing the degree not smooth thwarts meet-in-the-middle attacks, while keeping it secret enlarges the search space. Together, these two facts allow us to pick a degree N_τ of size $\log(N_\tau) = \lambda/2$ for λ bits of security. The key sampling method is described in Subsect. 8.4. A more detailed security analysis can be found in the longer version [13].

This improvement produces a shorter and more efficient signature for the same level of security, as it reduces the output size of Algorithm 3 from $\frac{9}{2} \log_\ell(p)$ to $\frac{15}{4} \log_\ell(p)$. We use it for the implementations presented in Subsect. 8.6.

8.4   The Concrete Protocol

Now that we have all the preliminary algorithms, we can provide a concrete description of our identification scheme. Let us assume that we have found a prime p as described above in Subsect. 8.2. We recall that $T \approx p^{3/2}$ is the smooth torsion defined over $\mathbb{F}_{p^2}$ for supersingular elliptic curves. For the challenge and the commitment we divide T as $D_c \cdot T'$ where D_c is a λ-bit integer and T' a 2λ-bit integer. In the protocol presented below we decided to use $D = \ell^\bullet$.

Building τ (keygen). We use the efficiency improvement from Subsect. 8.3 hence fix $B_\tau = \frac{1}{2}\lambda$. The degree N_τ is a prime number inert in R and smaller than B_τ, chosen uniformly at random among such numbers.

Since N_τ is a large prime number, we never compute concretely the isogeny τ as this would be too inefficient. Instead we use the corresponding ideal I_τ. This is enough to apply SigningKLPT but it does not give us the public key E_A. For this, we compute another isogeny $\tau' : E_0 \to E_A$ of degree $\ell^\bullet$. This can be done with KLPT. We briefly summarize the description above for keygen:

1. Select a prime $N_\tau \leq B_\tau$ that is inert in R uniformly at random.
2. Select a left $\mathcal{O}_0$-ideal I_τ of norm N_τ, uniformly at random among the $N_\tau + 1$ possibilities.
3. Compute $J_\tau = \mathsf{KLPT}_{\ell^\bullet}(I_\tau)$
4. Compute $\tau' = \mathsf{IdealToIsogeny}_{\ell^\bullet}(J_\tau, \mathcal{O}_0, [1]_{E_0})$ and set $\mathsf{pk} = E_A$ the codomain of τ'.

Building ψ (commitment). There are several options for building the commitment (and incidentally the challenge); we present the most efficient option here. We note that for security reasons, ψ must be as hard to recover as the secret. This suggests taking a smooth isogeny of degree about p (here we do not gain anything by using the same idea as in Subsect. 8.3). Given the factorization $T = D_c \cdot T'$, we choose ψ as a random isogeny of degree T' from E_0. With this choice, computing the isogeny and converting it to an ideal is efficient. Let $I_\psi := \mathsf{IsogenyToIdeal}_{T'}(\psi)$.

Building φ (challenge). The previous choice of commitment generation was motivated by the fact that we want an efficient way to translate the challenge into its corresponding ideal. For λ-bit soundness security we need a challenge space of size $2^\lambda = O(\sqrt{p})$, so the challenge isogeny needs to be of degree $O(\sqrt{p})$. Let $\varphi : E_1 \to E_2$ be a random cyclic isogeny of degree D_c. Since the $T = T'D_c$-torsion is accessible, computing the corresponding ideal will be efficient for the prover.

Building σ (response). The response is computed as follows:

1. Compute $I_\varphi = [I_\psi]_* \left(\mathsf{IsogenyToIdeal}_{D_c}([\psi]^*\varphi) \right)$.
2. Set $I = \overline{I_\tau} \cdot I_\psi \cdot I_\varphi$ and compute $J = \mathsf{SigningKLPT}(I, I_\tau)$.
3. Compute $\sigma = \mathsf{IdealToIsogeny}_{\ell^\bullet}(J, J_\tau, \tau')$.

8.5 Response and Verification

In this section we discuss the verification part of the protocol. We remind the reader that upon receiving σ, the verifier needs to check that it is an isogeny of degree D between E_A and E_2 such that the composition with the challenge φ is cyclic (this last part is trivial when D and D_c are coprime). All this can be done by computing the chain of isogenies associated with σ. We decompose σ of degree $D = \ell^e$ as $\sigma_g \circ \cdots \circ \sigma_1$ where each of the σ_j has degree at most ℓ^f ($f = 33$ in our case). The main problem is to find a compact and efficient representation of σ that can be sent to the verifier. A wide array of solutions already exist in the literature for SIDH/SIKE [1,8,23,24,34] most of which can be applied to our setting. In the longer version [13], we describe two compress, decompress algorithms well-suited to our application.

8.6 The Concrete Instantiation

We discuss below the performance features of our implementation.

Signature Size and Comparison with Existing Schemes. For λ bit of classical security, we take a prime $p \approx 2^{2\lambda}$. The public key is the j-invariant of the curve E_A and it is of size $2\log_2(p) = 4\lambda$. The secret can be seen as a pair N_τ, I_τ. The integer N_τ is a $\log(p)/4$-bit prime, and we can represent I_τ as a number in $[1, N_\tau + 1]$, so another $\log(p)/4$-bit integer. In total the secret key has size λ. The signature is made of E_1 and σ, where σ is compressed as described in Subsect. 8.5. As argued there, we can either use a full compression of exactly e bits, or allow for a few additional bits to accelerate the verification time. With the second method the size is $e + 4(\lceil e/f \rceil - 1)$. We recall that, using for keys as in Subsect. 8.3, $e = 15/4 \log(p) + O(\log(\lambda))$. Representing the commitment curve E_1 requires $2 \log_2(p) = 4\lambda$ additional bits. We summarize these values in Table 2 when $\lambda = 128$, for our concrete instantiation we have $\log_2(p) = 256$, $f = 33$ and $e = 1000$.

Table 2. Size of SQISign keys and signature for the NIST-1 level of security.

Secret key (bytes)	Public key (bytes)	Signature (bytes)
16	64	204

These sizes make SQISign the most compact post-quantum digital signature targeting NIST-1 level of security, in terms of combined public key and signature size. With respect to round 2 candidates, it is more than 5 times more compact than Falcon [18] in terms of combined size, and only trails GeMSS [4] in terms of signature size. Signatures are more compact than RSA, and about three times larger than ECDSA, for a comparable level of classical security.

Performance. We implemented SQISign in C, on top of the `libpari` library of PARI/GP 2.11.4 [30], and a port of the isogeny evaluation code published in [2]. Our code is available at https://github.com/SQISign/sqisign. We ran experiments on a 3.40GHz Intel Core i7-6700 (Skylake) CPU with Turbo Boost disabled. The code was compiled using `clang-6.0 -O3 -Os -march=native -mtune=native -Wall -Wextra -std=gnu99 -pedantic`.

The results are summarized in Table 3. We empirically chose the parameter $\Delta = 14$. For key generation we generated 100 random keys. For signature we generated 10 random keys and signed 10 random messages under each key. For verification we generated 5 random keys, we signed 5 random messages under each key, and we ran verification 10 times. We stress that we did not attempt at producing a constant-time implementation, which appears to be an intensive task owing to the complexity of the algorithms involved.

Table 3. Performance of SQISign in millions of cycles and in milliseconds. Statistics over 100 runs for key generation and signature, and over 250 runs for verification.

		Keygen	Sign	Verify
Mcycles	1st quartile	1,922	7,687	140
	Median	1,959	7,767	142
	3rd quartile	2,000	7,909	148
Ms	1st quartile	564	2,256	41
	Median	575	2,279	42
	3rd quartile	587	2,321	43

9 Conclusion

We introduced a new signature scheme along with a concrete instantiation and implementation. Our implementation proves that our signature is quite efficient compared to other isogeny-based candidates. The associated identification scheme is sound under classical isogeny assumptions, while its zero-knowledge relies on hardness of a new *ad hoc* problem. We briefly justified that this new problem bears some resemblance with existing hard problems, lending some credibility to its conjectured hardness.

More work on understanding the output distribution of our generalized KLPT algorithm is needed to gain confidence in the security of SQISign. It would be interesting, for example, to reduce the zero-knowledge property to more classical assumptions. Such a result would probably come at a cost in terms of efficiency as this would mean using a different generalization of KLPT. Indeed, from our analysis in Sect. 7 it appears unlikely to prove security under classical assumptions with the current algorithm.

The second direction for improvement is efficiency. The scheme is complex and there is a lot of potential for optimizations. A search for better parameters could allow one to obtain a more efficient signature, and algorithmic progress in any aspect of isogeny computations and evaluations would probably impact the performance. The main bottleneck remains the translation from ideals to isogenies, new techniques for which could greatly benefit our protocol. For instance, finding a more direct algorithm that does not rely as heavily on rational torsion points could yield a more efficient translation. Finally, any improvement to KLPT producing ideals of smaller norm in reasonable time would improve every single step of the translation, thus greatly reducing the signature time.

References

1. Azarderakhsh, R., Jao, D., Kalach, K., Koziel, B., Leonardi, C.: Key compression for isogeny-based cryptosystems. In: Proceedings of the 3rd ACM International Workshop on ASIA Public-Key Cryptography, pp. 1–10. ACM (2016)
2. Bernstein, D.J., De Feo, L., Leroux, A., Smith, B.: Faster computation of isogenies of large prime degree. ANTS XIV (2020)
3. Beullens, W., Kleinjung, T., Vercauteren, F.: CSI-FiSh: efficient isogeny based signatures through class group computations. In: Galbraith, S.D., Moriai, S. (eds.) ASIACRYPT 2019. LNCS, vol. 11921, pp. 227–247. Springer, Cham (2019). https://doi.org/10.1007/978-3-030-34578-5_9
4. Casanova, A., Faugere, J.C., Macario-Rat, G., Patarin, J., Perret, L., Ryckeghem, J.: GeMSS: a great multivariate short signature. NIST Post-Quantum Cryptography Standardization (2019). https://www-polsys.lip6.fr/Links/NIST/GeMSS.html
5. Castryck, W., Lange, T., Martindale, C., Panny, L., Renes, J.: CSIDH: an efficient post-quantum commutative group action. In: Peyrin, T., Galbraith, S. (eds.) ASIACRYPT 2018. LNCS, vol. 11274, pp. 395–427. Springer, Cham (2018). https://doi.org/10.1007/978-3-030-03332-3_15

6. Charles, D.X., Lauter, K.E., Goren, E.Z.: Cryptographic hash functions from expander graphs. J. Cryptology **22**(1), 93–113 (2009). https://doi.org/10.1007/s00145-007-9002-x
7. Costello, C.: B-SIDH: supersingular isogeny Diffie-Hellman using twisted torsion. In: ASIACRYPT 2020 (2019)
8. Costello, C., Jao, D., Longa, P., Naehrig, M., Renes, J., Urbanik, D.: Efficient compression of SIDH public keys. In: Coron, J.-S., Nielsen, J.B. (eds.) EUROCRYPT 2017. LNCS, vol. 10210, pp. 679–706. Springer, Cham (2017). https://doi.org/10.1007/978-3-319-56620-7_24
9. Couveignes, J.M.: Hard homogeneous spaces. IACR Cryptology ePrint Archive, Report 2006/291 (2006)
10. Cox, D.: From fermat to Gauss. In: Primes of the Form $x^2 + ny^2$, pp. 7–85. John Wiley and Sons, Ltd. (2013). https://doi.org/10.1002/9781118400722.ch1
11. Damgård: On Σ protocols (2010). http://www.cs.au.dk/%7eivan/Sigma.pdf
12. De Feo, L., Galbraith, S.D.: SeaSign: compact isogeny signatures from class group actions. In: Ishai, Y., Rijmen, V. (eds.) EUROCRYPT 2019. LNCS, vol. 11478, pp. 759–789. Springer, Cham (2019). https://doi.org/10.1007/978-3-030-17659-4_26
13. De Feo, L., Kohel, D., Leroux, A., Petit, C., Wesolowski, B.: SQISign: compact post-quantum signatures from quaternions and isogenies. Cryptology ePrint Archive, Report 2020/1240 (2020). https://eprint.iacr.org/2020/1240
14. Decru, T., Panny, L., Vercauteren, F.: Faster SeaSign signatures through improved rejection sampling. In: Ding, J., Steinwandt, R. (eds.) PQCrypto 2019. LNCS, vol. 11505, pp. 271–285. Springer, Cham (2019). https://doi.org/10.1007/978-3-030-25510-7_15
15. Deuring, M.: Die Typen der Multiplikatorenringe elliptischer Funktionenkörper. Abhandlungen aus dem Mathematischen Seminar der Universität Hamburg **14**(1), 197–272 (1941)
16. Eichler, M.: Über die Idealklassenzahl total definiter Quaternionenalgebren. Math. Z. **43**(1), 102–109 (1938)
17. Eisenträger, K., Hallgren, S., Lauter, K., Morrison, T., Petit, C.: Supersingular isogeny graphs and endomorphism rings: reductions and solutions. In: Nielsen, J.B., Rijmen, V. (eds.) EUROCRYPT 2018. LNCS, vol. 10822, pp. 329–368. Springer, Cham (2018). https://doi.org/10.1007/978-3-319-78372-7_11
18. Fouque, P.A., et al.: Falcon: fast-fourier lattice-based compact signatures over NTRU. NIST Post-Quantum Cryptography Standardization (2019). https://falcon-sign.info/
19. Galbraith, S.D., Petit, C., Silva, J.: Identification protocols and signature schemes based on supersingular isogeny problems. In: ASIACRYPT (2017)
20. Jao, D., De Feo, L.: Towards quantum-resistant cryptosystems from supersingular elliptic curve isogenies. In: Yang, B.-Y. (ed.) PQCrypto 2011. LNCS, vol. 7071, pp. 19–34. Springer, Heidelberg (2011). https://doi.org/10.1007/978-3-642-25405-5_2
21. Kohel, D.: Endomorphism rings of elliptic curves over finite fields. Ph.D. thesis, University of California, Berkeley (1996)
22. Kohel, D., Lauter, K.E., Petit, C., Tignol, J.P.: On the quaternion ℓ-isogeny path problem. IACR Cryptology ePrint Archive, Report 2014/505 (2014)
23. Naehrig, M., Renes, J.: Dual isogenies and their application to public-key compression for isogeny-based cryptography. In: Galbraith, S.D., Moriai, S. (eds.) ASIACRYPT 2019. LNCS, vol. 11922, pp. 243–272. Springer, Cham (2019). https://doi.org/10.1007/978-3-030-34621-8_9

24. Pereira, G.C.C.F., Doliskani, J., Jao, D.: X-Only point addition formula and faster torsion basis generation in compressed sike. Cryptology ePrint Archive, Report 2020/431 (2020). https://eprint.iacr.org/2020/431
25. Petit, C., Smith, S.: An improvement to the quaternion analogue of the l-isogeny path problem (2018). Conference talk at MathCrypt
26. Pizer, A.: An algorithm for computing modular forms on $\gamma_0(n)$. Journal of Algebra **64**, 340–390 (1980). https://doi.org/10.1016/0021-8693(80)90151-9
27. Pizer, A.K.: Ramanujan graphs and Hecke operators. Bull. Am. Math. Soc. **23**(1), 127–137 (1990)
28. de Saint Guilhem, C.D., Kutas, P., Petit, C., Silva, J.: Séta: Supersingular encryption from torsion attacks. Technical report, Cryptology ePrint Archive, Report 2019/1291 (2019). https://eprint.iacr.org/2019/1291
29. Silverman, J.H.: The Arithmetic of Elliptic Curves. Gradute Texts in Mathematics, vol. 106. Springer-Verlag, New York (1986)
30. The PARI Group: Université de Bordeaux: PARI/GP version 2.11.4 (2020). http://pari.math.u-bordeaux.fr/
31. Voight, J.: Quaternion Algebras. Graduate Texts in Mathematics Series. Springer, Cham (2018)
32. Waterhouse, W.C.: Abelian varieties over finite fields. Annales scientifiques de l'École Normale Supérieure **2**(4), 521–560 (1969)
33. Yoo, Y., Azarderakhsh, R., Jalali, A., Jao, D., Soukharev, V.: A post-quantum digital signature scheme based on supersingular isogenies. In: Kiayias, A. (ed.) FC 2017. LNCS, vol. 10322, pp. 163–181. Springer, Cham (2017). https://doi.org/10.1007/978-3-319-70972-7_9
34. Zanon, G.H.M., Simplicio, M.A., Pereira, G.C.C.F., Doliskani, J., Barreto, P.S.L.M.: Faster isogeny-based compressed key agreement. In: Lange, T., Steinwandt, R. (eds.) PQCrypto 2018. LNCS, vol. 10786, pp. 248–268. Springer, Cham (2018). https://doi.org/10.1007/978-3-319-79063-3_12

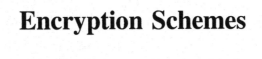

Encryption Schemes

Public-Key Generation with Verifiable Randomness

Olivier Blazy[1], Patrick Towa[2,3]($\boxtimes$), and Damien Vergnaud[4,5]

[1] Universite de Limoges, Limoges, France
[2] IBM Research – Zurich, Rüschlikon, Switzerland
`patrick.towa@gmail.com`
[3] DIENS, École Normale Supérieure, CNRS, PSL University, Paris, France
[4] Sorbonne Université, CNRS, LIP6, 75005 Paris, France
[5] Institut Universitaire de France, Paris, France

Abstract. We revisit the problem of proving that a user algorithm selected and correctly used a truly random seed in the generation of her cryptographic key. A first approach was proposed in 2002 by Juels and Guajardo for the validation of RSA secret keys. We present a new security model and general tools to efficiently prove that a private key was generated at random according to a prescribed process, without revealing any further information about the private key.

We give a generic protocol for all key-generation algorithms based on probabilistic circuits and prove its security. We also propose a new protocol for factoring-based cryptography that we prove secure in the aforementioned model. This latter relies on a new efficient zero-knowledge argument for the double discrete logarithm problem that achieves an exponential improvement in communication complexity compared to the state of the art, and is of independent interest.

1 Introduction

Cryptographic protocols are commonly designed under the assumption that the protocol parties have access to perfect (i.e., uniform) randomness. However, random sources used in practical implementations rarely meet this assumption and provide only a stream of bits with a certain "level of randomness". The quality of the random numbers directly determines the security strength of the systems that use them. Following preliminary work by Juels and Guajardo [22] and Corrigan-Gibbs, Mu, Boneh and Ford [15], we revisit the problem of proving that a cryptographic user algorithm has selected and correctly used a truly random seed in the generation of her cryptographic public-secret key pair.

Related Work. A prominent example that the use of randomness in public-key cryptography (and especially in key-generation protocols) is error-prone is the recent randomness failure known as the *ROCA vulnerability* [25]. This weakness allows a private key to be recovered efficiently from the public key only (in factoring-based cryptography). The flawed key-generation algorithm selects specific prime numbers as part of the private key instead of generating uniformly

© International Association for Cryptologic Research 2020
S. Moriai and H. Wang (Eds.): ASIACRYPT 2020, LNCS 12491, pp. 97–127, 2020.
https://doi.org/10.1007/978-3-030-64837-4_4

random primes and many certified devices were shown vulnerable. This kind of weaknesses is not new as in 2012, Lenstra, Hughes, Augier, Bos, Kleinjung and Wachter [23] did a sanity check of factoring-based public keys collected on the web. They showed that a significant percentage of public keys (0.5%) share a common prime factor, and this fact was explained [21] by the generation of these low entropy keys during booting. Since cryptographic failures due to weak randomness can be dire [21,23,25], designers should build schemes that can withstand deviations of the random sources from perfect randomness.

Following seminal works by Simmons on the threat of covert channels (also called subliminal channels) in cryptography [29], the concept of *kleptography* was proposed by Young and Yung [32]. It models the fact that an adversary may subvert cryptographic algorithms by modifying their implementations in order to leak secrets using for instance covert channels present in the randomized algorithms. Several sources have recently revealed that cryptographic algorithms have effectively been subverted to undermine the security of users. This raises the concern of guaranteeing a user's security even when she may be using a compromised machine or algorithm.

For factoring-based public-key cryptography, in light of the known shortcomings of implemented key generators, a line of research has focused on proving that RSA moduli satisfy certain properties [1,11,18], or on attesting that RSA prime factors were generated with a specified prime generator [5]. This line of work is only concerned with the structure of the keys, not with the fact that they are generated with enough entropy. Juels and Guajardo [22] suggested as early as in 2002 an approach for users to prove to another party (which is typically a trusted certificate authority or CA) that her public-secret key pair was generated honestly using proper randomness. In their setting, the CA provides an additional source of randomness in an interactive process, and the user algorithm proves that it has not weakened, whether intentionally or unintentionally, the key-generation procedure. The security goal of such a primitive is threefold.

1. **Maintain User Privacy:** if the user uses a randomness source with high entropy, then an adversary (possibly the CA himself) has no additional information on the secret-key compared to a key generated by the real key-generation algorithm on uniform randomness.
2. **Improve Randomness Quality:** if the user *or* the CA use a randomness source with high entropy, then, an adversary (other than the CA) has no additional information on the secret-key compared to a key generated by the real key-generation algorithm on uniform randomness.
3. **Resist Information Exfiltration:** the generated public key leaks no information whatsoever to the outer world. In particular, a faulty user algorithm cannot use it to convey any information. In this sense, the CA certifies to the end user, that she can securely use to the generated key.

A malicious user can obviously publish her secret key, but the problem we tackle is different: we want the CA to only certify keys that he knows to have been generated with high-entropy randomness and without covert channels.

Juels and Guajardo proposed a formal security model for *verifiable random key generation* with the goal to achieve these three security objectives. Their model is unfortunately not strong enough to capture real-world threats since

- it is restricted to public-key cryptosystems where a given public key corresponds to a *unique* secret key (and cannot be used for many recent schemes);
- it considers only a stand-alone or independent key-generation instances (and therefore does not prevent attacks such as the one considered in [21,23] where several public-keys are generated with correlated randomness sources);
- it only bounds the distance that a dishonest user algorithm can generate a key to that of an honest algorithm executing the key generation protocol.

As a simple example, consider the problem of generating an ElGamal public key g^x in a group $\mathbb{G} = \langle g \rangle$ of prime order p. Juels and Guajardo outlined a protocol for generating such a key with verifiable randomness. The natural idea to generate a public-key g^x in this (illusorily) simple setting is to share the secret key x as $x = x_U + x_{CA} \bmod p$ where x_U denotes the user randomness and x_{CA} denotes the CA randomness. However, this protocol fails to achieve (3) as the user algorithm can choose x_U to match a specify value after seeing x_{CA}. To overcome this issue, a simple idea would be to make the user first commit to x_U and then prove its knowledge. However, the hiding and zero-knowledge properties of commitment schemes and proof systems inherently rely on perfect randomness, which the user algorithm is assumed not to have at its disposal.

Juels and Guajardo also proposed a protocol for the generation of RSA keys where the distance in (3) increases by a factor which is polynomial in the security parameter λ (assuming some number-theoretic conjecture). Therefore, their protocol does not rule out the existence of covert channels with $O(\log \lambda)$ bit capacity. Their model was reconsidered by Corrigan-Gibbs, Mu, Boneh and Ford [15] in a weaker setting that guarantees (1) and (2) but not (3), and does not even prevent a malicious user algorithm from generating malformed keys.

Contributions. We revisit the verifiable key-generation primitive and provide the first strong security models and efficient, provably secure constructions.

Game-Based Security Model. We propose a game-based model that covers concurrent protocol executions with different instances of protocol algorithms. It is inspired by the Bellare-Pointcheval-Rogaway (BPR) model for authenticated key exchange [4]. The communication between the user and the CA is assumed to be carried over an insecure channel. Messages can be tapped and modified by an adversary, and the communication between the user and the CA is asynchronous. The adversary is split into two algorithms: (1) the *sampler* which provides the randomness sources to the user and the CA (for multiple instances of the protocol) and (2) the *distinguisher* which tries to gain information from the generated public key. The protocol is deemed secure if the distinguisher is unable to do so assuming that the entropy of either random source is high enough.

The main difficulty to define the security model for this primitive is to formalize the third security objective. A dishonest user algorithm can indeed always execute several instances of the protocol with the CA until she obtains a public-key which has some specific property which allows to exfiltrate information. This is similar to the "halting attack" subliminal channel [16] and cannot be avoided We manage to take this *narrow-band* subliminal channel into consideration in our security model while capturing the fact that in a secure protocol, this should be the only possible covert channel for a dishonest user algorithm. In practical applications, this covert channel can be prevented easily if the CA charges an important fee for a user that performs too many key generation procedures, or if an increasing time-gating mechanism for repeating queries is introduced.

This model does not suffer from the shortcomings of the model proposed in [22] as it allows for multiple dependent runs of the protocol and captures the resistance to exfiltration of information (with only the narrow-band subliminal channel from the "halting attack"). It guarantees security with concurrent sessions (and is thus much stronger than security considered in the similar notion of cryptographic reverse firewalls [24]) but not composition.

Providing a universal-composability definition seems natural in this setting, but the main hurdle in doing so comes from the fact that the sampler cannot communicate at all with the distinguisher since it would otherwise allow for covert channels (and break property (3)) as further explained in Sect. 3.2. As a consequence, a universal-composability definition would need functionalities with local adversaries, which would change the target of the paper.

Generic Protocol for Probabilistic Circuits. We then present a generic approach for key generation based on (families of) probabilistic circuits and we prove its security in our stringent security model. It relies on two-source randomness extractors, pseudo-random-function families and extractable commitments with associated zero-knowledge proofs. Since two-party computation (2PC) protocols rely on perfect randomness, a generic 2PC protocol cannot be used in this setting; moreover such a protocol guarantees privacy and correctness, but it does not guarantee that a user cannot influence the result (and thus requirement (3)).

Efficient Protocol for RSA Keys. We also propose a new generic protocol for factoring-based cryptography and prove it secure in our model. It relies on classical cryptographic tools (namely commitments, pseudo-random functions (PRFs) and zero-knowledge proofs). We provide an instantiation based on the Dodis-Yampolskiy PRF [17] in the group of quadratic residue modulo a safe prime which outputs group elements. The main technical difficulty is to convert the outputs of this PRF into integers while proving that the RSA prime factors are outputs of the PRF. In the process, we propose a new efficient zero-knowledge proof system for the so-called *double discrete logarithm problem* (in groups of public order). A double discrete logarithm of an element $y \neq 1_{\mathbb{G}}$ in a cyclic group $\mathbb{G}$ of prime order p with respect to bases $g \in \mathbb{G}$ and $h \in \mathbb{Z}_p^*$ (generators of $\mathbb{G}$ and $\mathbb{Z}_p^*$ respectively) is an integer $x \in \{0, \ldots, p-1\}$ such that $y = g^{h^x}$. Stadler introduced this computational problem for verifiable secret-sharing [30] and it was used to design numerous cryptographic protocols (e.g. group signatures [12], e-cash systems [13] and credential systems [14]). All these constructions rely on a proof system proposed by Stadler which has $\Omega(\log p)$ computational and communication complexity (in terms of group elements). Our new proof system outputs proofs with only $O(\log \log p)$ group elements and permits an efficient instantiation of our generic protocol for factoring-based cryptography. As a by-product, our new protocol can be used directly in all the aforementioned applications in a public-order setting to exponentially reduce their communication complexity.

2 Preliminaries

Notation. For $n \in \mathbb{N}$, the set of n-bit strings is denoted by $\{0,1\}^n$ and the set of integers $\{1, \ldots, n\}$ is denoted $[\![n]\!]$. The set of prime numbers is denoted $\mathbb{P}$. The security parameter is denoted λ, and input lengths are always assumed to be bounded by some polynomial in λ. A Probabilistic algorithm is said to run in Polynomial-Time (it is said to be a PPT algorithm) if it runs in time that is polynomial in λ. A function μ is negligible if $\mu(\lambda) = \lambda^{-\omega(1)}$.

The random variable defined by the value returned by a PPT algorithm $\mathcal{A}$ on input x is denoted $\mathcal{A}(x)$. The value returned by $\mathcal{A}$ on input x and random string r is denoted $\mathcal{A}(x; r)$. Given a probability distribution S, a PPT algorithm that samples a random element according to S is denoted by $x \leftarrow_\$ S$. For a finite set X, $x \leftarrow_\$ X$ denotes a PPT algorithm that samples an element uniformly at random from X. Given a group $\mathbb{G}$ with neutral element $1_\mathbb{G}$, $\mathbb{G}^*$ denotes $\mathbb{G} \backslash \{1_\mathbb{G}\}$. For any two sets X and $\mathcal{Y}$, denote by $\mathcal{Y}^X$ the set of functions from X to $\mathcal{Y}$.

Vectors are denoted in bold font. For two vectors $\boldsymbol{a}$ and $\boldsymbol{b}$ in R^n where R is a ring and n a positive integer, $\boldsymbol{a} \circ \boldsymbol{b}$ denotes the Hadamard product of $\boldsymbol{a}$ and $\boldsymbol{b}$, i.e., $\boldsymbol{a} \circ \boldsymbol{b} := [a_1 b_1 \cdots a_n b_n]$.

Group Families. A *group-family generator* G is a PPT algorithm which takes as input a security parameter λ and returns a tuple $(\mathbb{G}, \ell, g)$, with $\mathbb{G}$ a cyclic multiplicative group of prime order ℓ, and $g \in \mathbb{G}$ a generator of $\mathbb{G}$ (i.e. $g \in \mathbb{G}^*$).

Randomness Sources and Min-entropy. Imperfect randomness is modeled as arbitrary probability distributions with a certain amount of *entropy*. The *min-entropy* notion is used to measure the randomness in such an imperfect random source. A source is said to have k bits of min-entropy if its distribution has the property that each outcome occurs with probability at most 2^{-k}.

Pseudo-Random Functions. A Pseudo-Random Function (PRF) [20] is an efficiently computable function of which the values are computationally indistinguishable from uniformly random values.

Formally, a function PRF: $\mathcal{K}(\lambda) \times X(\lambda) \rightarrow \mathcal{Y}(\lambda)$ is a (T, q, ε)-secure PRF with key space $\mathcal{K}$, input space X and range $\mathcal{Y}$ (all assumed to be finite) if the advantage

$$\left| \Pr\left[1 \leftarrow \mathcal{A}^{\mathsf{PRF}(K, \cdot)} : K \leftarrow_\$ \mathcal{K} \right] - \Pr\left[1 \leftarrow \mathcal{A}^{f(\cdot)} : f \leftarrow_\$ \mathcal{Y}^X \right] \right|$$

of every adversary $\mathcal{A}$ that runs in time at most $T(\lambda)$ is at most $\varepsilon(\lambda)$.

Dodis-Yampolskiy Pseudo-Random Function. Let G be a group family generator. The Dodis-Yampolskiy pseudo-random function [17] in an ℓ-order group $(\mathbb{G}, \ell, g) \leftarrow_{\$} \mathsf{G}$ is the map $F : (K, x) \in \mathcal{K} \times \mathcal{X} \mapsto g^{1/(K+x)} \in \mathbb{G}^*$, with $\mathcal{K} = \mathbb{Z}_\ell^*$ and $\mathcal{X} \subset \mathbb{Z}_\ell^*$. This PRF is $\left(T / \left(q \lambda^{O(1)}\right), q, \varepsilon q\right)$-secure under the (T, q, ε)-Decisional Diffie-Hellman Inversion (DDHI) assumption [6,7] for G, where $q(\lambda) = O(\log \lambda)$ is an upper-bound on the bit-size of $\mathcal{X}$ for all λ [17, § 4.2].

3   Model

This section formalizes key-generation protocols for arbitrary, predetermined key-generation algorithms. Such a protocol is executed between a *user* $\mathcal{U}$ and a *certification authority* $C\mathcal{A}$. At the end of the protocol, $\mathcal{U}$ obtains a pair of public-secret keys that $C\mathcal{A}$ certifies to be indistinguishable from keys generated by a fixed algorithm KeyGen, and to have been generated with proper randomness. These requirements are formally captured by a model for randomness verifiability given below. The security definition of the model ensures that a protocol satisfying its conditions fulfills the following properties:

1. $C\mathcal{A}$ can infer no more information about the secret key than it would from a public key generated by KeyGen if $\mathcal{U}$'s randomness source has high entropy
2. no external attacker can distinguish a public key generated via the protocol from a public key generation with KeyGen if the randomness source of either $\mathcal{U}$ or $C\mathcal{A}$ has high entropy
3. $\mathcal{U}$ cannot bias the generation of the keys if the randomness source of $C\mathcal{A}$ has high entropy. In particular, $\mathcal{U}$ cannot use the public key as a subliminal channel to convey information.

3.1   Syntax

An interactive asymmetric-key-generation protocol is a triple $\mathsf{IKG} = (\mathsf{Setup}, \mathsf{U}, \mathsf{CA})$ of algorithms such that $\mathsf{Setup}\left(1^\lambda\right) \rightarrow pp$ is a probabilistic algorithm which returns public parameters and $\langle \mathsf{U}(pp; r_\mathcal{U}) \rightleftharpoons \mathsf{CA}(pp; r_{C\mathcal{A}}) \rangle \rightarrow \langle (pk_\mathcal{U}, sk), pk_{C\mathcal{A}} \rangle$ are interactive algorithms. At the end of the protocol, the user key-generation algorithm U returns a pair of public-secret keys, and the certificate-authority key-generation algorithm CA returns a public key.

Algorithm Setup may require some randomness, but the parameters it generates can be fixed once for all and used across multi sessions and by several users and authorities. Once parameters are fixed, high-entropy randomness is still needed to securely generate keys, and this is formalized in Sect. 3.2.

Definition 3.1 (Correctness). In the O-oracle model, a key-generation protocol IKG is δ-correct w.r.t. a class $\mathscr{A}$ of algorithms if for all $\lambda \in \mathbb{N}$, for every $\mathcal{A} \in \mathscr{A}$,

$$\Pr \left[pk_\mathcal{U} = pk_{C\mathcal{A}} \neq \bot : \begin{array}{l} pp \leftarrow_{\$} \mathsf{Setup}\left(1^\lambda\right) \\ (\mathcal{D}_\mathcal{U}, \mathcal{D}_C \mathcal{A}) \leftarrow_{\$} \mathcal{A}^{O(\cdot)}(pp) \\ r_\mathcal{U} \leftarrow_{\$} \mathcal{D}_\mathcal{U}, r_{C\mathcal{A}} \leftarrow_{\$} \mathcal{D}_C \mathcal{A} \\ \langle (pk_\mathcal{U}, sk), pk_{C\mathcal{A}} \rangle \leftarrow \langle \mathsf{U}(pp; r_\mathcal{U}) \rightleftharpoons \mathsf{CA}(pp; r_{C\mathcal{A}}) \rangle \end{array} \right] \geq \delta.$$

Note that the last line of the probability event implicitly implies that U and CA *must terminate*.

The above definition is given in model in which $\mathcal{A}$ has oracle access to O. This latter is used to "distinguish" different models: it may be a random oracle, but it could also simply be an oracle which returns a fixed value (i.e., the common-reference-string model) or no value at all (the standard model). The reason for this distinction is that if a component of the protocol (e.g. a randomized primality-testing algorithm) is not perfectly correct, then its correctness probability is only defined for perfect randomness although the parties only have access to imperfect randomness. However, in the random-oracle model for instance, this imperfect randomness chosen by the algorithm in the definition may depend on the random-oracle queries made by this latter.

3.2 Security

This section gives a game-based security model for key-generation protocols with verifiable randomness. It covers concurrent protocol executions with different instances of protocol algorithms. It is inspired by the BPR model for authenticated key exchange [4] but with key differences.

Protocol Participants. A set of user identities U and a set of certificate-authority identities CA are assumed to be fixed. The union of the those sets form the overall identity space ID. For readability, it is implicitly assumed that during protocol executions, the messages exchanged are always prepended with the instance identifier of the receiving party. Note that several instances of the same algorithm may concurrently run during the game.

Adversaries. The game features a two-stage adversary $(\mathcal{A}_1, \mathcal{A}_2)$. Adversaries $\mathcal{A}_1$ and $\mathcal{A}_2$ may agree on a common strategy before the beginning of the game. That is to say, the strategy may be part of their code, and it may dictate which queries to make (possibly depending on the oracle answers), the order of the queries and so forth. All but the challenge query can only be made by $\mathcal{A}_1$. The role of $\mathcal{A}_2$ is essentially only to guess whether a public key was generated with KeyGen or with the protocol, while $\mathcal{A}_1$ can make arbitrary queries according to the pre-established strategy.

However, $\mathcal{A}_1$ and $\mathcal{A}_2$ cannot communicate after the beginning of the game. It reflects the fact that in practice, an implementer may distribute its key generator, but does not necessarily wiretap the execution of the key-generation protocol for a particular user. From a technical viewpoint, the reason is that in a key-generation protocol, a user has to prove to the authority that she correctly performed her computation. However, the randomness used in these proofs can be used as a subliminal channel to convey information about the secret key. For instance, an engineer could in practice implement a bogus key generator which only terminates the protocol if the first bits of the proof and secret key match. The proof then serves as subliminal channel to leak information about the secret key. Later on, when a user wants to generate a certified public key, if the

$\mathsf{Init}\left(1^\lambda, U, CA, I\right)$	$h \leftarrow_\$ \Omega;\ pp \leftarrow_\$ \mathsf{Setup}\left(1^\lambda\right)$
	$ID \leftarrow U \cup CA$
	for $i \in \llbracket I \rrbracket$ and $id \in ID$ do
	$\quad st^i_{id} \leftarrow r^i_{id} \leftarrow \bot$
	$\quad used^i_{id} \leftarrow \text{FALSE}$
	$\quad acc^i_{id} \leftarrow term^i_{id} \leftarrow flag^i_{id} \leftarrow \text{FALSE}$
	$\quad sid^i_{id} \leftarrow pid^i_{id} \leftarrow \bot$
	$\quad sk^i_{id} \leftarrow pk^i_{id} \leftarrow \bot$
	$Q_{\mathsf{Reveal}} \leftarrow Q_{\mathsf{Corrupt}} \leftarrow \emptyset$
	return (pin, sin)
$\mathsf{Oracle}(M)$	return $h(M)$
$\mathsf{Dist}\left(id, i, \mathcal{D}^i_{id}\right)$	$r^i_{id} \leftarrow_\$ \mathcal{D}^i_{id}$ // r^i_{id} is simply generated and *not* returned to $\mathcal{A}_1$
$\mathsf{Exec}(\mathcal{U}, i, C\mathcal{A}, j)$	if $\left(\mathcal{U} \notin U \text{ or } C\mathcal{A} \notin CA \text{ or } used^i_{\mathcal{U}} \text{ or } used^j_{C\mathcal{A}}\right)$ return $\bot$
	if $r^i_{\mathcal{U}} \neq \bot$ and $r^j_{C\mathcal{A}} \neq \bot$
	$\quad$ return $\left\langle \mathsf{U}_i\left(pp, r^i_{\mathcal{U}}\right), \mathsf{CA}_j\left(pp, r^j_{C\mathcal{A}}\right)\right\rangle$
	return $\bot$ // $\mathcal{A}_1$ must specify distributions beforehand
$\mathsf{Send}(id, i, M)$	if $r^i_{id} = \bot$ return $\bot$ // $\mathcal{A}_1$ must specify a distribution beforehand
	if $term^i_{id}$ return $\bot$
	$used^i_{id} \leftarrow \text{TRUE}$
	$\left\langle m_{out}, acc, term, sid, pid, pk, sk, st^i_{id}\right\rangle \leftarrow \left\langle \mathsf{IKG}\left(id, st^i_{id}, M; r^i_{id}\right)\right\rangle$
	if acc and $\neg acc^i_{id}$
	$\quad sid^i_{id} \leftarrow sid;\ pid^i_{id} \leftarrow pid$
	$\quad acc^i_{id} \leftarrow acc$
	if $term$ and $\neg term^i_{id}$ // Set keys only after termination
	$\quad pk^i_{id} \leftarrow pk;\ sk^i_{id} \leftarrow sk$
	return $\left(m_{out}, sid, pid, pk, sk, acc, term^i_{id}\right)$
$\mathsf{Reveal}(id, i)$	$Q_{\mathsf{Reveal}} \leftarrow Q_{\mathsf{Reveal}} \cup \{(id, i)\}$
	return $\left(pk^i_{id}, sk^i_{id}\right)$
$\mathsf{Corrupt}(id)$	$Q_{\mathsf{Corrupt}} \leftarrow Q_{\mathsf{Corrupt}} \cup \{id\}$
	for $i \in \llbracket I \rrbracket \{$if $\neg acc^i_{id}$ then $flag^i_{id} \leftarrow \text{TRUE}\}$
	return $\{st^i_{id}\}_{i\in\llbracket I\rrbracket}$
$\mathsf{Test}_b(id^*, i^*)$	if $\left(\exists(id_0, id_1, i, j)\colon pid^i_{id_0} = id_1 \text{ and } pid^j_{id_1} = id_0 \text{ and } acc^i_{id_0}\right.$
	$\quad$ and $\left. \neg term^j_{id_1}\right)$ return $\bot$
	// Once an instance accepts, its partner must eventually terminate
	if $\neg term^{i^*}_{id^*}$ return $\bot$
	if $flag^{i^*}_{id^*}$ return $\bot$
	// Reject if id^* was corrupt before (id^*, i^*) accepted
	if $(id^*, i^*) \in Q_{\mathsf{Reveal}}$ or $\left(\exists(id', j)\colon pid^{i^*}_{id^*} = id' \text{ and } pid^j_{id'} = id^*\right.$
	$\quad$ and $\left. (id', j) \in Q_{\mathsf{Reveal}}\right)$
	$\quad\quad$ return $\bot$
	// Reject if the key of (id^*, i^*) or of its partner has been revealed
	if $pk^{i^*}_{id^*} \neq \bot$
	$\quad$ if $b = 0$
	$\quad\quad (pk, sk) \leftarrow_\$ \mathsf{KeyGen}\left(1^\lambda\right)$
	$\quad\quad$ return pk
	$\quad$ return $pk^{i^*}_{id^*}$
	return $\bot$ // Reject if (id^*, i^*) does not have a key

Fig. 1. Oracles for the Key-Generation Indistinguishability Experiment.

engineer could wiretap the protocol execution, he could infer some information about her secret key through the proof of correct computation. It is the reason why communication between the adversaries cannot be allowed.

The restriction that $\mathcal{A}_1$ and $\mathcal{A}_2$ cannot communicate after the beginning of the game means that the attacks in which the protocol executions are listened to are excluded, but as explained above, it seems to be a minimal requirement.

Game Overview. At the beginning of the game, the challenger first runs an initialization algorithm. After that, $\mathcal{A}_1$ can make several queries to the algorithm instances. It can in particular

- specify distributions from which randomness is drawn and given as an input to the instances,
- ask for the protocol to be executed between different instances of the protocol algorithms without its intervention, i.e., perform passive attacks,
- perform active attacks by sending messages to algorithm instances,
- later on reveal the keys that were generated by a particular instance,
- corrupt a party (user or certificate authority), and thereby gain access to the state of all its algorithm instances.

As for $\mathcal{A}_2$, it can reveal keys or make a test query that returns either (with probability $1/2$ each) keys freshly generated by the key-generation algorithm or keys generated by instances of its choice via queries made by $\mathcal{A}_1$. Adversary $\mathcal{A}_2$ must eventually return a guess for the origin of the keys it was returned, and $(\mathcal{A}_1, \mathcal{A}_2)$ wins the game if the guess of $\mathcal{A}_2$ is correct.

Initialization and Game Variables. During the initialization phase, game variables are declared for every instance of the protocol algorithms. Assume that there are at most $I = I(\lambda)$ instances of any participant id. Each instance $i \in I$ of a participant id maintains a state st_{id}^i. A session identity sid_{id}^i and a partner identity pid_{id}^i allow to match instances together in protocol executions. It is assumed that for each sid_{id}^i there can be at most one partner instance, i.e., one pair (id', j) such that $pid_{id}^i = id'$ and $sid_{id}^i := \left(id, i, id', j, sid_{id}^{i'}\right)$.

Public/secret-key variables (denoted pk_{id}^i and sk_{id}^i) hold the keys that were output, if any, by the ith instance of the algorithm of party id at that step of the computation. For certificate authorities, the secret keys are always set to $\perp$.

A variable $used_{id}^i$ indicates whether the adversary has performed an active attack on the ith algorithm instance of participant id.

Variables acc_{id}^i and $term_{id}^i$ respectively indicate whether the algorithm of the ith instance of participant id has accepted and terminated. As in the BPR model [4], termination and acceptance are distinguished. When an instance terminates, it does not output any further message. However, it may accept at a certain point of the computation, and terminate later. In the present context, it may for instance occur when an instance expects no further random input from its partner instance, and the rest of its computation is purely deterministic. It may then only terminate after finishing its computation. This distinction is crucial for the security definition. It is important to exclude the trivial case in which, although every computation was honestly performed, a user discards the public key if it does not follow a certain pattern, thereby influencing the distribution of the output public key (i.e., perform rejection sampling), and possibly using it as subliminal channel to convey information about the secret key.

Another variable flag^i_{id} (new compared to the BPR model) indicates whether party id was corrupted before its ith instance had accepted. Recall that acceptance intuitively means that an instance expects no further random input from its partner instance. As long as flag^i_{id} is set to FALSE, the only information the adversary has about r^i_{id} is its distribution and therefore, if this distribution has high min-entropy, the adversary cannot bias the generation of the keys.

A variable r^i_{id} holds the random string to be used the ith instance of the algorithm of id.

The challenger maintains a set (initially empty) Q_{Reveal} of identity-instance pairs of which the keys were revealed. It also maintains a set (initially empty) Q_{Corrupt} of corrupt identities.

At the end of the initialization phase, the public parameters, the sets of participants and the user public keys are returned in a public input pin, and the rest is set in a secret input sin. That is, $pin \leftarrow (pp, U, CA, I, (pk_{id})_{id})$ and $sin \leftarrow \left(pin, (sk_{id})_{id}, \left(st^i_{id}, sid^i_{id}, pid^i_{id}, acc^i_{id}, term^i_{id}, used^i_{id}\right)_{i,id}, Q_{\mathsf{Corrupt}}, Q_{\mathsf{Reveal}}\right)$. The secret input sin is later made available to all oracles.

Oracles. Throughout the game, adversary $\mathcal{A}_1$ is given access to the oracles summarized below and defined in Fig. 1. It can query them *one at a time*.

- Oracle : gives access to a function h chosen uniformly at random from a probability space Ω. The adversary and the protocol may depend on h. The probability space Ω specifies the model in which the protocol is considered. If it is empty, then it is the standard model. If it is a space of random functions, then it is the random oracle model. As for the Common-Reference String (CRS) model, Ω is a space of constant functions.
- Dist : via this oracle, the adversary specifies the distribution $\mathcal{D}^i_{id}$ from which the randomness of the ith instance of id is drawn. These distributions are always assumed to be independent of oracle Oracle. However, the distributions specified by the adversary for different instances *can be correlated in any way*. Oracle Dist then generates a bit string r^i_{id} according to the input distribution and does *not* return it to the adversary. Whenever oracle Exec or oracle Send is queried on (id, i), it uses randomness r^i_{id} for its computation. This new (compared to the BPR model) oracle is essential to express requirements on the minimal entropy used by the instances, and also to express reasonable winning conditions. It allows to properly capture properties like the fact that (1) the authority cannot infer any information about the secret key if the randomness of the user algorithm has high entropy, (2) that the output keys are indistinguishable from keys generated with the key-generation algorithm if the randomness used by the algorithm of either of the parties has

high entropy, or (3) that a potentially malicious user algorithm cannot bias the distribution of the output keys if the randomness of the authority algorithm has high entropy. That is first because the test query later made by $\mathcal{A}_2$ requires the min-entropy of the randomness of either the challenge instance or of its partner to be high. It is also due to the fact that the adversary cannot corrupt the challenge instance (thus learning its randomness) before the partner randomness necessary to generate the challenge key is committed, which is monitored by the flags. It for instance means that if the CA is the target of the test and the adversary plays the role of a user algorithm (in which case the partner randomness is considered to have nil entropy) and possibly deviates from the protocol, then the test CA must be given high-entropy randomness and the definition ensures that the resulting key is indistinguishable from keys generated with KeyGen.

- Exec : returns the transcript of an honest (i.e., without the interference of the adversary) protocol execution between the ith instance of U and the jth instance of CA. The protocol is executed with the random strings generated for these instances by oracle Dist on the input of adversarial distributions. The notations U_i and CA_j mean that algorithms U and CA are executed using the state of the ith instance of U and the jth instance of CA respectively. It is implicitly assumed that the states $acc_{\mathcal{U}}^i$, $term_{\mathcal{U}}^i$, $acc_{C}^j\mathcal{A}$ and $term_{C}^j\mathcal{A}$ are set to TRUE after an honest protocol execution. Moreover, if the termination variable of either party is set to TRUE, the protocol is not executed and $\bot$ is returned. In essence, by querying oracle Exec, adversary $\mathcal{A}_1$ performs a passive eavesdropping attack.

- Send : adversary $\mathcal{A}_1$ can perform active attacks via this oracle. $\mathcal{A}_1$ can send any message to an instance of its choice, e.g., the ith instance of a user algorithm, which runs the honest protocol algorithm of the corresponding party on the input of the message chosen by the adversary.

  To prompt the ith instance of id to initiate a protocol execution with the jth instance of id', adversary $\mathcal{A}_1$ can make a Send query on $\big(id, i, (id', j)\big)$.

  IKG($id, *$) denotes the IKG algorithm of party id, i.e., either U or CA. The algorithm is executed using the randomness generated by oracle Dist for that instance. (Note that the input random string may be used only at certain steps of the computation.) The oracle then returns the output of the instance to the adversary. It also specifies if this instance accepted and/or terminated, and returns the session identifier and the identity of its partner in the protocol execution, as well as the public and secret keys returned by this instance, if any. Note that if the instance is that of a certificate-authority algorithm, the secret key is always set to $\bot$.

- Reveal : on input (id, i), returns the keys held by the ith instance of the algorithm of id. The couple (id, i) is added to the set Q_{Reveal} of revealed keys.

- Corrupt : on input id, returns the states of all the instances of the algorithm of id. The identity id is added to the set Q_{Corrupt} of corrupt identities. Besides, for any instance i of id, if it has not yet accepted, $flag_{id}^i$ is set to TRUE.

Remark 3.1. The first main difference with the BPR model is the new oracle Dist. It allows to capture an adversary running several instances of the protocol with correlated randomness. In the new model, it is also important to express winning conditions that exclude the trivial (and unavoidable) rejection-sampling attack. Another difference is that the variable $flag_{id}^i$ is set to TRUE if $\mathcal{A}_1$ corrupts id before its ith instance has accepted. It is to say that for instance, if an adversary (e.g., a malicious user algorithm) knows the randomness of the other party (by corrupting the CA) before it has "committed" to its randomness, then that party can influence the resulting key and break property (3).

As for adversary $\mathcal{A}_2$, it is given access to oracles Oracle, Reveal and to oracle

- Test_b : on input (id^*, i^*), it returns the public key $pk_{id^*}^{i^*}$ generated via IKG (with an Exec query or Send queries) if $b = 0$ or a fresh public key generated via KeyGen if $b = 1$.

  An important restriction on this query is that the following condition must be satisfied: for any instance i of the algorithm of a party id_0, once it has accepted, i.e., once $acc_{id_0}^i$ is set to TRUE, the partner instance algorithm, say the jth instance of id_1, must eventually terminate, i.e., $term_{id_1}^j$ must have been set to TRUE as well by the time of query Test. It prevents $\mathcal{A}_1$ from biasing the distribution of the keys by prematurely aborting the protocol although it was followed, if the resulting key does not follow a certain pattern, and which would allow $\mathcal{A}_2$ to guess b with a non-negligible advantage. The other restrictions are simply that i^*-th instance of id^* must have terminated, that id^* was not corrupt before (id^*, i^*) had accepted[1], that neither the key of the i^*th instance of id^* nor of its partner instance has been revealed, and that the i^*th instance of id^* must already hold a key.

  Note that $\mathcal{A}_2$ can query Test only once. A definition with multiple queries would be asymptotically equivalent via a standard hybrid argument.

Adversary $\mathcal{A}_2$ must eventually return a bit b' as a guess for the origin (i.e., either IKG or KeyGen) of the key returned by oracle Test_b.

To achieve any form of indistinguishability from a key-generation algorithm, it is clear that either the distribution $\mathcal{D}_{id^*}^{i^*}$ or the distributions $\mathcal{D}_{id'}^j$ for the partner instance (j, id') of (i^*, id^*) must have high entropy. Indeed, if distributions with low entropy were allowed, $\mathcal{A}_1$ and $\mathcal{A}_2$ could agree on these identities, instances and distributions beforehand. Adversary $\mathcal{A}_2$ could then simply return

---

[1] To understand why it is necessary for id^* not to be corrupt before (id^*, i^*) accepts even though $\mathcal{A}_1$ and $\mathcal{A}_2$ do not communicate, suppose that this condition were not imposed and consider the following strategy which allows $(\mathcal{A}_1, \mathcal{A}_2)$ to trivially win: $\mathcal{A}_1$ and $\mathcal{A}_2$ agree on (id^*, i^*) and on a distribution $\mathcal{D}_{id^*}^{i^*}$. Adversary $\mathcal{A}_1$ prompts (id^*, i^*) to initiate a protocol execution by making a Send query. It then corrupts id^* and obtains $st_{id^*}^{i^*}$, from which it can read $r_{id^*}^{i^*}$. Adversary $\mathcal{A}_1$ could then play the role of its partner and adapt the messages it sends to make sure that the resulting public key follows a certain pattern known to $\mathcal{A}_2$. This latter would then be able to win the game with a non-negligible advantage.

1 if and only if the challenge key is the most likely key w.r.t. $\mathcal{D}_{id^*}^{i^*}$ and $\mathcal{D}_{id'}^{j}$, and thereby win the game with a non-negligible advantage.

A parameter κ for the maximal min-entropy of $\mathcal{D}_{id^*}^{i^*}$ and $\mathcal{D}_{id'}^{j}$ specified by $\mathcal{A}_1$ is therefore introduced. If the adversary modified any message from the partner (j, id') of (id^*, i^*) before (id^*, i^*) accepts, then $\mathcal{D}_{id'}^{j}$ is set to be the Dirac mass at the zero bit-string by convention (and it thus has no entropy). The underlying idea is that as long as at least one of the two parties has a randomness source with high entropy, the key returned at the end of the protocol should be indistinguishable from a key generated by the KeyGen algorithm. The security of a key-generation protocol is then defined for adversaries that specify challenge distributions with min-entropy at least κ.

Definition 3.2 (Indistinguishability). An interactive key-generation protocol IKG is $(T, q_{\mathsf{Oracle}}, q_{\mathsf{Dist}}, q_{\mathsf{Exec}}, q_{\mathsf{Send}}, q_{\mathsf{Reveal}}, q_{\mathsf{Corrupt}}, \kappa, \varepsilon)$-indistinguishable from a key-generation algorithm KeyGen (running on uniform randomness) if for all $\lambda \in \mathbb{N}$, for every adversary $(\mathcal{A}_1, \mathcal{A}_2)$ that runs in time at most $T(\lambda)$ and makes at most q_O queries to $O \in \{\mathsf{Oracle}, \mathsf{Dist}, \mathsf{Exec}, \mathsf{Send}, \mathsf{Reveal}, \mathsf{Corrupt}\}$, and such that $\max\left(H_\infty\left(\mathcal{D}_{id^*}^{i^*}\right), H_\infty\left(\mathcal{D}_{id'}^{j}\right)\right) \geq \kappa$ for query Test, the advantage (function of λ)

$$\left| \Pr\left[b = b' : \begin{array}{l} (pin, sin) \leftarrow \mathsf{Init}\left(1^\lambda, U, CA, I\right) \\ O_1 \leftarrow \{\mathsf{Oracle}, \mathsf{Dist}, \mathsf{Exec}, \mathsf{Send}, \mathsf{Reveal}, \mathsf{Corrupt}\} \\ \mathcal{A}_1^{O_1(sin, \cdot)}(pin) \\ b \leftarrow_\$ \{0, 1\} \\ O_2 \leftarrow \{\mathsf{Oracle}, \mathsf{Reveal}, \mathsf{Test}_b\} \\ b' \leftarrow \mathcal{A}_2^{O_2(sin, \cdot)}(pin) \\ \text{return } (b, b') \end{array} \right] - 1/2 \right|$$

of $(\mathcal{A}_1, \mathcal{A}_2)$ is at most $\varepsilon(\lambda)$.

From a practical perspective, this definition (which implies requirement 3 as it enforces indistinguishability from keys generated by IKG) means that keys generated via a protocol satisfying the definition above are not subject to randomness vulnerabilities such as the ROCA vulnerabilities [25] and those [21,23] in which several public keys are generated with correlated randomness sources.

4   Generic Constructions

This section presents a protocol that covers a wide class of key-generation algorithms, namely those that can be represented as probabilistic circuits, and another protocol specific to the generation of RSA keys. The first protocol is of theoretical interest and shows that randomness verifiability can be achieved for wide class of key-generation algorithms, whereas the second protocol is a solution that can actually be used in practice.

4.1 Key-Generation Protocol with Verifiable Randomness for Probabilistic Circuits

This section gives a key-generation protocol with verifiable randomness for a large class of key-generation algorithms. The focus is here on the class of key-generation algorithms that can be modeled as *probabilistic circuits*.

The advantage of probabilistic circuits compared to general Turing Machines for this purpose is that the running time of a probabilistic circuit is independent of the random inputs. In a key-generation protocol with verifiable randomness, the user has to prove to the authority that she correctly performed her computation. Having a constant running time then ensures that no one can infer any information about the secret key from the statement proved by the user or the proof itself. It prevents malicious user algorithms from using the proofs as subliminal channels to pass information about the secret key.

To understand why it is important for the running time to be constant, consider the following artificial random number generator. To generate a k-bit string $t = (t_0, \ldots, t_{k-1})$, it consists in flipping a random coin s several times for each bit t_i and to set this bit to the parity of the number of flipped coins to obtain the first "Head". It produces a k-bit string uniformly distributed within expected time complexity $O(k)$ and it could be used as a secret-key generation algorithm (and the public key would then be a deterministic function of the generated secret key). See the full version [6] for a formal description of the algorithm. For a user to prove that she correctly generated the random bit string t, she would have to commit to the t_i values and compute a proof on the successive s values. However, each t_i is simply the parity of the number of trials before $s = 0$. Therefore, from the number of s values for which the user has to perform a proof, the authority can infer t_i. For example, if the user generated two s values for t_1, the authority knows that $t_1 = 0$. In other words, the statement of the proof itself reveals some information about the secret key to the certification authority; and the issue is here that the running time changes from one random run of the algorithm to the other. Restricting to probabilistic circuits eliminates this issue.

The restriction to circuits comes at a cost though. It for instance excludes the class of algorithms for which there is no known circuit that can represent them. It is for instance the case of algorithms that must efficiently generate primes during the process. Indeed, there is no known circuit that can efficiently generate prime numbers. On this ground, the generic protocol for probabilistic circuits of Sect. 4.1 does not apply to the RSA-key generation for instance[2]. See rather Sect. 4.2 for the specific case of RSA-key generation with verifiable randomness for arbitrary properties that the keys must satisfy.

Before describing our protocol, we first formally define probabilistic circuits.

---

[2] One can construct families of probabilistic "circuits" which output an RSA key but *only* with overwhelming probability (and not probability 1) by relying on the prime number theorem and Chernoff's bound. However, such constructions would have large gate complexity and randomness complexity and applying our generic construction to such circuits family would result in schemes with prohibitive efficiency.

Probabilistic Circuits. A probabilistic circuit is essentially a deterministic circuit augmented with uniformly random gates. The random gates produce independent and uniform random bits that are sent along their output wires.

We equivalently define a probabilistic circuit as a uniform random variable over a finite collection of deterministic boolean circuits. These boolean circuits are restricted to have the same amount n of input variables, and r fixed inputs. The number r of fixed inputs depends on the security parameter 1^λ. Denote such a circuit as $\Gamma_{b_1 \cdots b_r}(x_1, \ldots, x_n)$, with $x_1, \ldots, x_n$ the input variables and $b_1, \ldots, b_r$ the fixed inputs. To each element in $\{0,1\}^r$ corresponds a circuit in the collection with the bit string as fixed inputs, so that there are 2^r circuits in the collection. However, these circuits are not required to form a uniform family (i.e., they are not required to be output by a single Turing machine); the circuit families here considered can be non-uniform.

A probabilistic circuit Γ is then defined as a uniform random variable over the set (of circuits) $\{\Gamma_b\}_{b \in \{0,1\}^r}$. Namely, for input variables $x_1, \ldots, x_n$, the evaluation $\Gamma(x_1, \ldots, x_n)$ is a uniform random variable over the set (of values) $\{\Gamma_b(x_1, \ldots, x_n)\}_{b \in \{0,1\}^r}$. If $\omega \in \{0,1\}^r$ denotes the random input to the probabilistic circuit Γ, the evaluation $\Gamma(x_1, \ldots, x_n; \omega)$ is then $\Gamma_\omega(x_1, \ldots, x_n)$.

The advantage of this second definition is that randomness is invoked only once instead of invoking it for each of the r random gates. To generate keys, PRFs are often used to provide random bit strings from small secret seeds. As the goal is to build a key-generation protocol which allows the CA to certify that the keys are generated with high-entropy randomness, the user will have to prove that she correctly performed the pseudo-random evaluations. Invoking randomness only once then allows to invoke the PRF only once in the protocol.

Generic Protocol. We now give a two-party protocol in the CRS model to generate, with verifiable randomness, keys computed by probabilistic circuits. Requiring that keys are generated with verifiable randomness here means that the random inputs to the circuits must be uniformly generated in a verifiable manner. The deterministic inputs can simply be considered as public parameters.

Building Blocks. The protocol involves (see the full version [6] for definitions)

- a function family $\mathcal{H} = \{H_{hk}\}_{hk \in \{0,1\}^{d(\lambda)}}$ which is a universal computational extractor w.r.t. unpredictable sources
- a two-source extractor Ext with key space $\{0,1\}^{\delta(\lambda)}$
- an extractable commitment scheme $\mathscr{C} = (\mathsf{Setup}, \mathsf{Com}, \mathsf{ComVf}, \mathsf{TSetup}, \mathsf{ExtCom})$ for the user algorithm to commit to its random string *before receiving any input from the CA*, thereby preventing it from biasing the distribution of the keys. The parameters returned by Setup are implicit inputs to the other algorithms of $\mathscr{C}$
- a non-interactive, extractable, zero-knowledge proof system Π with $\Pi = \left(\mathsf{Setup}, \mathsf{Prove}, \mathsf{Verf}, \mathsf{TSetup}^{zk}, \mathsf{Sim}, \mathsf{TSetup}^{ext}, \mathsf{Ext}\right)$ for the relation

$$\mathcal{R}_\Pi := \{((x_i)_i, k, C, r_{\mathcal{CA}}, pk; r'_{\mathcal{U}}, d, sk) : \mathsf{ComVf}\,(C, r'_{\mathcal{U}}, d) = 1$$
$$\wedge (pk, sk) = \Gamma\,(x_1, \ldots, x_n; \mathsf{Ext}_k\,(r'_{\mathcal{U}}, r_{\mathcal{CA}}))\},$$

- a pseudo-random function PRF to generate the randomness for Π.Prove.

Parameters. Given a circuit Γ with deterministic inputs $x_1, \ldots, x_n$, to generate public parameters for the protocol on the input a security parameter 1^λ, run $pp_{\mathscr{C}} \leftarrow \mathscr{C}.\mathsf{Setup}\left(1^\lambda\right)$ ($pp_{\mathscr{C}}$ is a tacit input to the algorithms of $\mathscr{C}$), $crs \leftarrow \Pi.\mathsf{Setup}\left(1^\lambda\right)$, and generate $hk \leftarrow_{\$} \{0,1\}^{d(\lambda)}$ and $k \leftarrow_{\$} \{0,1\}^{\delta(\lambda)}$. Return $pp \leftarrow (crs, pp_{\mathscr{C}}, hk, k, x_1, \ldots, x_n)$.

Formal Description. Consider the interactive protocol IKG_Γ on Fig. 2 between a user $\mathcal{U}$ and a certification authority $\mathcal{CA}$. Each algorithm maintains acceptance and termination variables acc_{id} and $term_{id}$, for $id \in \{\mathcal{U}, \mathcal{CA}\}$, initially set to FALSE. On the input of pp and of their respective random strings $r_\mathcal{U}$ and $r_{\mathcal{CA}}$, the party algorithms proceed as follows:

1. U separates the domain of H_{hk} in two and applies it to its randomness. It commits to the first output with the second output as randomness, and sends the resulting commitment C to $\mathcal{CA}$
2. CA, upon receiving the commitment from $\mathcal{U}$, sets $acc_{\mathcal{CA}} \leftarrow$ TRUE and sends its random string $r_{\mathcal{CA}}$ to $\mathcal{U}$
3. U, upon receiving $r_{\mathcal{CA}}$ from $\mathcal{CA}$, sets $acc_\mathcal{U} \leftarrow$ TRUE. Next, it extracts a seed s with Ext from the joint randomness. It evaluates Γ on $x_1, \ldots, x_n$ and s, and obtains a key pair (pk, sk). It generates another seed s' with H_{hk}. Algorithm U then evaluates PRF mode on s' to generate the randomness necessary to compute Π.Prove since U has no other random string than $r_\mathcal{U}$ available, i.e., it computes $r_\Pi \leftarrow \mathsf{PRF}(s', 0)$. Algorithm U then proves that it followed the protocol and correctly evaluated Γ at $x_1, \ldots, x_n$, i.e., it computes a proof $\pi \leftarrow \Pi.\mathsf{Prove}\left(crs, ((x_i)_i, k, C, r_{\mathcal{CA}}, pk), (r'_\mathcal{U}, d, sk); r_\Pi\right)$. After that, it erases all variables but pk, sk, π, sends pk and π to $\mathcal{CA}$, returns (pk, sk) and sets $term_\mathcal{U} \leftarrow$ TRUE
4. CA, upon receiving (pk, π) from $\mathcal{U}$, verifies the proof. If the proof is valid, it returns pk, otherwise it returns $\bot$. It then sets $term_{\mathcal{CA}} \leftarrow$ TRUE.

Correctness and Indistinguishability. In the full version [6], we show that IKG_Γ is 1-correct w.r.t. all algorithms if $\mathscr{C}$ is correct and if Π is complete. Moreover, it is indistinguishable from Γ in the CRS model for sources with min-entropy at least $\kappa = \max(\kappa_\mathcal{H}, \kappa_{\mathsf{Ext}})$ if Ext is a $(\kappa_{\mathsf{Ext}}, \varepsilon_{\mathsf{Ext}})$-extractor for $\kappa_{\mathsf{Ext}} \leq \min(|r'_\mathcal{U}|, |r_{\mathcal{CA}}|)$, if $\mathcal{H}$ is UCE-secure w.r.t. simply unpredictable sources of min-entropy at least $\kappa_\mathcal{H}$, if $\mathscr{C}$ extractable and hiding, if Π is extractable and composable zero-knowledge, and if PRF is a secure PRF.

Discrete-Logarithm Keys. The full version of the paper [6] presents a simple illustration of this generic protocol (but rather in the random-oracle model for better efficiency) applied to discrete-logarithm keys.

$$\mathsf{U}\left(crs, pp_{\mathscr{C}}, hk, k, x_1, \ldots, x_n; r_{\mathcal{U}}\right) \qquad\qquad \mathsf{CA}\left(crs, pp_{\mathscr{C}}, hk, k, x_1, \ldots, x_n; r_{C\mathcal{A}}\right)$$

$$r'_{\mathcal{U}} \leftarrow H_{hk}\left(0\|r_{\mathcal{U}}, 1^{|r'_{\mathcal{U}}|}\right)$$

$$\rho_{\mathcal{U}} \leftarrow H_{hk}\left(1\|r_{\mathcal{U}}, 1^{|\rho_{\mathcal{U}}|}\right)$$

$$(C, d) \leftarrow \mathsf{Com}\left(r'_{\mathcal{U}}; \rho_U\right)$$

$$\xrightarrow{\;\;C\;\;}$$
$$\xleftarrow{\;r_{C\mathcal{A}}\;}$$

$$s \leftarrow \mathsf{Ext}_k\left(r'_{\mathcal{U}}, r_{C\mathcal{A}}\right)$$

$$(pk, sk) \leftarrow \Gamma(x_1, \ldots, x_n; s)$$

$$s' \leftarrow H_{hk}\left(2\|r_{\mathcal{U}}, 1^{|s'|}\right)$$

$\pi \leftarrow \Pi$ proof of correct computation
with random string $\mathsf{PRF}\left(s', 0\right)$

Erase all variables but pk, sk, π $\qquad \xrightarrow{\;\;pk, \pi\;\;}\qquad \Pi.\mathsf{Verf}\left(crs, ((x_i)_i, k, C, r_{C\mathcal{A}}, pk), \pi\right) \overset{?}{=} 1$

return (pk, sk) $\qquad\qquad\qquad\qquad\qquad\qquad\qquad\qquad\qquad$ return pk

Fig. 2. Key-generation protocol with verifiable randomness for probabilistic circuits.

4.2 RSA-Key Generation Protocol with Verifiable Randomness

This section gives a two-party protocol for RSA-key generation with verifiable randomness between a user $\mathcal{U}$ and a certification authority $C\mathcal{A}$. The resulting keys can be used in any RSA cryptosystem. The protocol attests that the resulting keys were generated with high-entropy randomness and that they satisfy (fixed) arbitrary properties. These properties are captured by a relation

$$\mathcal{R}_W := \{(N, e \in \mathbb{Z}; p, q \in W \subseteq \mathbb{P}): p \neq q \land N = pq \land \gcd(e, \varphi(N)) = 1\}$$

to which the keys generated should belong, where W is a set that defines the predicates p and q must satisfy, e.g., $p = q = 3 \mod 4$ or p and q are safe primes. Its relative language is denoted $\mathcal{R}_W$. Efficient proof systems for such properties exist [1,11,31], though none of them aims at proving that the keys were generated with proper randomness.

In comparison, the protocol by Juels and Guajardo [22] only guarantees the first two properties, and does *not* ensure that the user algorithm cannot bias the distribution of the keys. Without the third property, an interactive key-generation protocol is only beneficial if the user does not have high-entropy randomness locally whereas the CA does, otherwise it is only a burden for the user. On the other hand, the third property additionally guarantees the end user that if the CA has high-entropy randomness, her keys are not faulty.

As for the attestation scheme of Benhamouda et al. [5], it allows to prove that the RSA primes were generated with an arbitrary generator; and the protocols of Camenisch and Michels [11], of Auerbach and Poettering [1], and of Goldberg et al. [19], only allow to prove that RSA primes satisfy certain properties, not that they were generated with high entropy. In a sense, our goal is complementary to that of proving that RSA moduli satisfy certain properties without proving that the keys were generated with high-entropy randomness.

RSA Key-Generation Algorithm. The NIST standard [26] for the RSA [28] key-generation algorithm, further denoted $\mathsf{KeyGen}_{\mathrm{RSA}}$, is the following:

- choose at random two distinct large primes p and q
- compute $N \leftarrow pq$ and $\varphi(N) \leftarrow (p-1)(q-1)$
- choose an integer $2^{16} < e < 2^{256}$ such that $\gcd(e, \varphi(N)) = 1$ (e may be chosen deterministically or at random); compute $d \leftarrow e^{-1} \mod \varphi(N)$
- Return $pk \leftarrow (N, e)$ and $sk \leftarrow (N, d)$.

Equivalently, the secret key sk can be set to (p, q, e) instead of (N, d) as one can compute (N, d) from (p, q, e) and vice-versa. It is this variant that is hereafter considered. To formally capture the requirement on p and q to be large, a parameter $b = b(\lambda)$ that specifies the bit-length of p and q is introduced.

Interpretation. There is some ambiguity as to how p and q are generated. The interpretation (which follows how the algorithm would implemented in practice) of $\mathsf{KeyGen}_{\mathrm{RSA}}$ in the rest of the paper is first that there exists a PPT primality-test algorithm $\mathsf{PrimeTest}_W (\lambda, b, e, p) \to \zeta \in \{0, 1\}$ (parameter λ is further omitted from its syntax) which tests whether an integer p is in W, b-bit long and such that $\gcd(e, (p-1)) = 1$. Algorithm $\mathsf{KeyGen}_{\mathrm{RSA}}$ then generates, uniformly at random, integers in $[\![2^{b-1}, 2^b - 1]\!]$ until it finds an integer p such that $\mathsf{PrimeTest}_W (b, e, p) = 1$, and continues until it finds a second one $q \neq p$ such that $\mathsf{PrimeTest}_W (b, e, q) = 1$. If no such two integers are found in a specified number of iterations $T_{\mathrm{RSA}}(\lambda)$, the algorithm aborts and returns an invalid pair, e.g., $(0, 0)$. The random variable with values in $\{0, 1, 2\}$ that counts the number of distinct primes found in at most $T_{\mathrm{RSA}}(\lambda)$ iterations is further denoted ctr_{RSA}.

Protocol. We now describe our protocol, further denoted $\mathsf{IKG}_{\mathrm{RSA}}$, to generate RSA keys with verifiable randomness. The protocol is given in the random-oracle model to allow for practical efficiency.

Building Blocks. The protocol builds on

- the same primality-test algorithm $\mathsf{PrimeTest}_W$ as the one run by $\mathsf{KeyGen}_{\mathrm{RSA}}$. It is said to be δ-*correct* if with probability at most $1 - \delta$, $\mathsf{PrimeTest}_W (b, e, p) = 0$ for $p \in W \cap [\![2^{b-1}, 2^b - 1]\!]$ such that $\gcd(e, (p-1)) = 1$, or $\mathsf{PrimeTest}_W (b, e, p) = 1$ for $p \notin W \cap [\![2^{b-1}, 2^b - 1]\!]$ or such that $\gcd(e, (p-1)) > 1$ (i.e., it is an upper-bound on the probability that it returns a false negative or a false positive)
- a random oracle of which the domain is separated to obtain pairwise independent random oracles $\mathcal{H}$, $\mathcal{H}_C$, $\mathcal{H}_\Pi$ and $\mathcal{H}_{\Pi_W}$
- a commitment scheme $\mathscr{C} = (\mathsf{Setup}, \mathsf{Com}, \mathsf{ComVf})$ for the user algorithm to commit to its random string *before* receiving any input from the CA. The parameters returned by Setup are tacit inputs to $\mathscr{C}$ other algorithms.

- a pseudo-random function PRF with range (non-empty) $R_{\mathsf{PRF}} \subseteq \mathbb{N}$ for $\mathcal{U}$ to generate the RSA primes from the seed extracted with $\mathcal{H}$
- an extractable non-interactive zero-knowledge (NIZK) argument system $\Pi_C = (\mathsf{Setup}, \mathsf{Prove}, \mathsf{Verf}, \mathsf{Sim}, \mathsf{Ext})$ for the relation $\{(C; r'_{\mathcal{U}}, d) : \mathsf{ComVf}(C, r'_{\mathcal{U}}, d) = 1\}$ with random oracle $\mathcal{H}_C$, i.e., for the user to prove knowledge of an opening to her committed randomness
- an extractable NIZK argument system $\Pi = (\mathsf{Setup}, \mathsf{Prove}, \mathsf{Verf}, \mathsf{Sim}, \mathsf{Ext})$ with random oracle $\mathcal{H}_\Pi$ for the relation

$$\{(C, r_{C\mathcal{A}}, N, (a_\gamma)_{\gamma \neq i,j}; r'_{\mathcal{U}}, d, a_i, a_j) : \mathsf{ComVf}\,(C, r'_{\mathcal{U}}, d) = 1,\ s = r'_{\mathcal{U}} \oplus \mathcal{H}(r_{C\mathcal{A}}),$$
$$\forall \gamma \in \llbracket j \rrbracket\ a_\gamma = \mathsf{PRF}(s, \gamma),\ 2^{b(\lambda)-1} \leq a_i, a_j \leq 2^{b(\lambda)} - 1, N = a_i a_j \text{ in } \mathbb{N} \},$$

i.e., for the user to prove the RSA primes are really the *first two primes* generated with the seed derived from the committed randomness and the randomness of the CA. This relation is further denoted $\mathcal{R}_\Pi$
- a NIZK argument system $\Pi_W = (\mathsf{Setup}, \mathsf{Prove}, \mathsf{Verf}, \mathsf{Sim})$ with random oracle $\mathcal{H}_{\Pi_W}$ for relation $\mathcal{R}_W$
- another pseudo-random function PRF' with variable output length (encoding in unary as last input) for $\mathcal{U}$ to generate the randomness necessary to compute $\Pi_C.\mathsf{Prove}$, $\mathsf{PrimeTest}_W$, $\Pi.\mathsf{Prove}$ and $\Pi_W.\mathsf{Prove}$, as the only available randomness to the parties are their input random bit strings.

Throughout the protocol, e is assumed (without loss of generality) to be a fixed[3], hard-coded value in U. For the sake of simplicity, e is further assumed to be prime, e.g., $e = 65537$ (it is a value commonly used in practice).

Parameters. Given a security parameter 1^λ and a function $T : \mathbb{N} \to \mathbb{N}_{>1}$ that gives an upper bound on the number of iterations in Algorithm 1 (and thus the running time of U), to generate parameters for $\mathsf{IKG}_{\mathrm{RSA}}$, run $pp_{\mathscr{C}} \leftarrow \mathscr{C}.\mathsf{Setup}\,(1^\lambda)$, $pp_{\Pi_C} \leftarrow \Pi_C.\mathsf{Setup}\,(1^\lambda)$, $pp_\Pi \leftarrow \Pi.\mathsf{Setup}\,(1^\lambda)$ and $pp_{\Pi_W} \leftarrow \Pi_W.\mathsf{Setup}\,(1^\lambda)$. Set and return $pp \leftarrow \big(b(\lambda), T(\lambda), pp_{\mathscr{C}}, pp_{\Pi_C}, pp_\Pi, pp_{\Pi_W}\big)$.

Formal Description. Consider the interactive protocol on Fig. 3 between a user $\mathcal{U}$ and a certification authority $C\mathcal{A}$. Each algorithm maintains acceptance and termination variables acc_{id} and $term_{id}$ for $id \in \{\mathcal{U}, C\mathcal{A}\}$ initially set to FALSE. The party algorithms proceed as follows:

1. U applies the random oracle $\mathcal{H}$ twice to its randomness $r_{\mathcal{U}}$ to compute $r'_{\mathcal{U}} \leftarrow \mathcal{H}(0\|r_{\mathcal{U}})$ and $\rho_U \leftarrow \mathcal{H}(1\|r_{\mathcal{U}})$, commits to $r'_{\mathcal{U}}$ with ρ_U as random string. Next, a seed $s' \leftarrow \mathcal{H}(2\|r_{\mathcal{U}})$ from which it derives the randomness necessary to compute $\Pi_C.\mathsf{Prove}$, and computes of proof of knowledge of an opening to the commitment. U sends the commitment and the proof to $C\mathcal{A}$

---

[3] Alternatively, in the protocol on Fig. 3, after N is computed, U could continue to generate pseudo-random values until it finds one that is coprime with $\varphi(N)$ and then sets it as e. Algorithm U would then also have to reveal the values that did not satisfy this property and prove that they did not, and also to prove that the chosen e and $\varphi(N)$ are coprime. Assuming e to be fixed in advance avoids this complication.

2. CA, upon receiving the commitment and the proof from $\mathcal{U}$, sets $acc_C\mathcal{A} \leftarrow$ TRUE. It verifies the proof and if it holds, sends its randomness to $\mathcal{U}$, and otherwise returns $\perp$ and sets $term_C\mathcal{A} \leftarrow$ TRUE

3. U, upon receiving $r_{C\mathcal{A}}$ from $C\mathcal{A}$, sets $acc_{\mathcal{U}} \leftarrow$ TRUE. It extracts a seed s with $\mathcal{H}$ from the joint randomness. It continues by generating by running $\left((a_\gamma)_{\gamma=1}^j, i \right) \leftarrow$ Algorithm 1.

Algorithm 1

Require: PrimeTest$_W$, integers T, b, e, pseudo-random function PRF, seed s.
Ensure: Pseudo-random numbers a_γ and integer i.
1: $ctr, i, j \leftarrow 0$
2: **while** $ctr < 2$ and $j < T$ **do**
3:     $j \leftarrow j + 1$; $a_j \leftarrow$ PRF(s, j)
4:     **if** PrimeTest$_W$ $(b, e, a_j;$ PRF$(s, j))$ **then**
5:         **if** $ctr = 0$ **then**
6:             $i \leftarrow j$
7:         **end if**
8:         $ctr \leftarrow ctr + 1$
9:     **end if**
10: **end while**
11: **if** $ctr < 2$ **then**
12:     **return** $\left((a_\gamma)_{\gamma=1}^j, \perp \right)$
13: **else**
14:     **return** $\left((a_\gamma)_{\gamma=1}^j, i \right)$
15: **end if**

(a) if $i = \perp$ (i.e., Algorithm 1 did not find 2 primes such that PrimeTest$_W(b, e, a_j;$ PRF$(s, j)) = 1$ in T iterations; this case is not depicted on Fig. 3), U sends $\left(r_{\mathcal{U}}, (a_\gamma)_{\gamma=1}^j \right)$ to $C\mathcal{A}$, returns $(0, 0)$ and sets $term_{\mathcal{U}} \leftarrow$ TRUE

(b) if $i \neq \perp$, U computes a proof π that it correctly performed its computation with Π, and a proof π_W that the RSA public key is in $\mathcal{L}_W$ with Π_W. After computing the proofs, U erases all variables but N, e, p, q, i, π, π_W and $(a_\gamma)_{\gamma \neq i,j}$. It sends these latter to $C\mathcal{A}$, except p and q, returns $(pk_{\mathcal{U}} \leftarrow (N, e), sk \leftarrow (p, q, e))$, and sets $term_{\mathcal{U}} \leftarrow$ TRUE

4a. CA, upon receiving $\left(r_{\mathcal{U}}, (a_\gamma)_{\gamma=1}^j \right)$ from $\mathcal{U}$, computes $r'_{\mathcal{U}}, \rho_{\mathcal{U}}$ and s as U, computes $(C', d') \leftarrow$ Com $(r'_{\mathcal{U}}, \rho_{\mathcal{U}})$, and verifies that $C' = C$ and that PRF$(s, \gamma) = a_\gamma$ for all $\gamma \in [\![j]\!]$. If all verifications succeed, CA returns 0, otherwise it returns $\perp$. It sets $term_C\mathcal{A} \leftarrow$ TRUE

4b. CA, upon receiving $(N, e, \pi, \pi_W, i, (a_\gamma)_{\gamma \neq i,j})$ from $\mathcal{U}$, generates a seed s'' with $\mathcal{H}$ from its randomness, and uses it to generate the randomness necessary to compute PrimeTest$_W$. The resulting random string is denoted r'_W. It verifies that for all $\gamma \in [\![j-1]\!] \setminus \{i\}$, PrimeTest$_W$ $(b, e, a_\gamma; r'_W) = 0$, and that π and π_W are valid. If one of the verifications did not succeed, CA returns $\perp$, otherwise it returns $pk_C\mathcal{A} \leftarrow (N, e)$. It sets $term_C\mathcal{A} \leftarrow$ TRUE.

$U(pp, e; r_U)$	$CA(pp; r_{CA})$

$r'_U \leftarrow \mathcal{H}(0\|r_U); \rho_U \leftarrow \mathcal{H}(1\|r_U)$

$(C, d) \leftarrow \mathsf{Com}\left(r'_U; \rho_U\right)$

$s' \leftarrow \mathcal{H}(2\|r_U); r_{\Pi_C} \leftarrow \mathsf{PRF}'\left(s', 0, 1^{|r_{\Pi_C}|}\right)$

$\pi_C \leftarrow \Pi_C.\mathsf{Prove}\left(pp_{\Pi_C}, C, \left(r'_U, d\right); r_{\Pi_C}\right)$

$\xrightarrow{C, \pi_C}$

$\Pi_C.\mathsf{Verf}\left(pp_{\Pi_C}, C, \pi_C\right) \overset{?}{=} 1$

$\xleftarrow{r_{CA}}$

$s \leftarrow r'_U \oplus \mathcal{H}(r_{CA})$

$\left(\left(a_\gamma\right)_{\gamma=1}^j, i\right) \leftarrow \text{Alg.1 with random string}$

$\quad \mathsf{PRF}'\left(s', \gamma, 1^{|r_W|}\right)$ for $\mathsf{PrimeTest}_W$

$p \leftarrow a_i, \ q \leftarrow a_j, \ N \leftarrow pq$

$\pi \leftarrow \Pi$ proof of correct computation with

$\quad$ random string $\mathsf{PRF}'\left(s', j+1, 1^{|r_\Pi|}\right)$

$\pi_W \leftarrow \Pi_W$ proof that $(N, e) \in \mathcal{L}_W$ with

$\quad$ random string $\mathsf{PRF}'\left(s', j+2, 1^{|r_{\Pi_W}|}\right)$

Erase all variables but N, e, i, p, q

$\quad (a_\gamma)_{\gamma \neq i, j}, \pi$ and π_W

$s'' \leftarrow \mathcal{H}(r_{CA})$

$\xrightarrow{(N,e), \pi, \pi_W}$

$r'_W \leftarrow \mathsf{PRF}'(s'', 0)$

$\xrightarrow{i, (a_\gamma)_{\gamma \neq i, j}}$

$\forall \gamma \neq i, j, \ \mathsf{PrimeTest}_W\left(b, e, a_\gamma; r'_W\right) \overset{?}{=} 0$

$\Pi.\mathsf{Verf}\left(pp_\Pi, \left(C, r_{CA}, N, (a_\gamma)_{\gamma \neq i, j}\right), \pi\right) \overset{?}{=} 1$

$\Pi_W.\mathsf{Verf}\left(pp_{\Pi_W}, (N, e), \pi_W\right) \overset{?}{=} 1$

return $((N, e), (p, q, e))$

return (N, e)

Fig. 3. RSA-Key Generation Protocol with Verifiable Randomness for an Arbitrary Relation $\mathcal{R}_W$.

Discussion. U proves among other things that p and q are really the first two random primes in W such that $\gcd(e, p-1) = \gcd(e, q-1) = 1$, and therefore cannot have chosen primes with additional conditions to these. It is a subtle but crucial aspect of the protocol which ensures that U cannot bias the distribution of the keys; and not doing so is precisely what allowed for the ROCA vulnerabilities [25] in which specific primes where chosen by the user algorithm.

Correctness and Indistinguishability. Let j be the number of iterations of Algorithm 1. In the full version [6], we show that, if $\mathsf{PrimeTest}_W$ is δ-correct and if PRF' is a secure PRF, $\mathsf{IKG}_{\mathrm{RSA}}$ is approximately $(1 - j(1 - \delta))$-correct in the random-oracle model w.r.t. the class of algorithms that make few oracle queries compared to the min-entropy of the distributions they provide. Moreover, $\mathsf{IKG}_{\mathrm{RSA}}$ is indistinguishable from $\mathsf{KeyGen}_{\mathrm{RSA}}$ in the random oracle if $\mathscr{C}$ is hiding and binding, if Π_C and Π are zero-knowledge and extractable, if Π_W is zero-knowledge and sound, if PRF and PRF$'$ are secure PRFs, if the probability that Algorithm 1 fails although $\mathsf{IKG}_{\mathrm{RSA}}$ does not is small, and if the adversary makes few random-oracle queries compared to the min-entropy of the test distributions. Lastly, in [6], we also show that by tuning the running time of Algorithm 1 depending on the number of primes in the range of PRF that satisfy the conditions on p and q, the probability that Algorithm 1 fails although $\mathsf{IKG}_{\mathrm{RSA}}$ does not is small.

5   Instantiation of the RSA-Key Generation Protocol

In this section, we instantiate the protocol of Sect. 4.2 for RSA key-generation with verifiable randomness. To do so, we provide efficient instantiations for each of the building blocks.

Recently, several important advancements have been made on the efficiency of the commit-and-prove paradigm on committed values which combine algebraic and non-algebraic statements [2,10,14]. These improvements for *cross-domains* statements allow to prove efficiently for instance that some committed value corresponds to a pre-image of some value of a given hash function such as SHA-256 or that some value is the output of some non-algebraic PRF (i.e. HMAC-SHA-256 or AES) using some committed key. To generate an RSA modulus of 3072 bits (for 128-bit security) using the generic protocol from Sect. 4.2, the PRF must return 1536-bit integers and the use of non-algebraic PRF with the technique from [2,10,14] would result in prohibitive schemes.

On this account, we present an instantiation based on an algebraic PRF, namely the Dodis-Yampolskiy PRF, and use techniques [10] due to Bünz, Bootle, Boneh, Poelstra, Wuille and Maxwell for range proofs and arithmetic-circuit satisfiability to obtain short proofs of correct computation (i.e., Π in Sect. 4.2).

In the process, we give the first logarithmic-size (in the bit-length of the group order) argument of knowledge of double discrete logarithms, and argument of equality of a discrete logarithm in a group and a double discrete logarithm in another related group. In contrast, the protocol of Camenisch and Stadler [12] for the first relation, and the protocol of Chase et al. [14] for the second are linear in the security parameter.

Parameters. We consider two related group-family generators $\mathsf{GroupGen}_1$ and $\mathsf{GroupGen}_2$. Given a security parameter λ, to generate an RSA modulus which is the product of two $b(\lambda)$-bit prime numbers, let ℓ be the smallest prime of binary length equal to $b(\lambda)$ such that $2\ell + 1$ is also a prime number (i.e., ℓ is a Sophie Germain prime number, or equivalently $2\ell + 1$ is a $b(\lambda) + 1$-bit *safe prime*). $\mathsf{GroupGen}_2$ returns, on input λ, the group $\mathbb{G}_2$ of quadratic residues modulo $2\ell+1$ (which is of prime order ℓ). The group-family generator $\mathsf{GroupGen}_1$ returns on input λ some group $\mathbb{G}_1$ of prime order Λ such that ℓ divides $\Lambda - 1$

and $\Lambda > (2\ell + 1)^2$. In practice[4], $\mathbb{G}_1$ can be taken as a prime order subgroup Λ of $\mathbb{Z}_r^*$ for some prime number r such that Λ divides $r - 1$.

The restriction to quadratic residues is necessary for assumptions like the q-DDHI assumptions to hold over $\mathbb{G}_2$. However, it introduces a bias by design (not from the user algorithm) in the RSA keys generated: p and q are necessarily quadratic residues modulo $2\ell + 1$. The reason is that the values returned by the DY PRF are not actually integers but $\mathbb{G}_2$ elements. Nonetheless, it is already the case for $1/4$ of all RSA moduli since the factors p and q returned by $\mathsf{KeyGen}_{\mathsf{RSA}}$.

Commitment Scheme. Scheme $\mathscr{C}$ is the Pedersen commitment scheme [27] in $\mathbb{G}_2$ for the user to commit to her randomness and to the secret p and q.

Pseudo-Random Functions. PRF is the Dodis-Yampolskiy (DY) PRF (see Sect. 2) in the group $\mathbb{G}_2 = QR_{2\ell+1}$ of quadratic residues modulo $2\ell + 1$. It is used to generate the secret RSA primes p and q. Since $2\ell + 1$ is $b(\lambda) + 1$ bits long, p and q are $b(\lambda)$ bits long with probability close to $1/2$. The reason $2\ell + 1$ is chosen to be one bit larger than p and q is to ensure that *all* primes of $b(\lambda)$ bits can be returned by the PRF so as not to introduce a bias. As for $\mathsf{PRF'}$, it can be any efficient pseudo-random function, e.g., HMAC [3].

Argument for R_W. The argument system Π_W depends on the properties that the prime factors of N must satisfy, e.g., they must be congruent to 3 modulo 4 or be safe primes. To prove that $p = q = 3 \mod 4$, one can prove that N is of the form $p^r q^s$ with $p = q = 3 \mod 4$ using the protocol of van de Graaf and Peralta [31], and run in parallel the protocol of Boyar et al. [9] to prove that N is square-free. To prove that p and q are safe primes, there exist proof systems in the literature such as Camenisch and Michel's [11].

Besides, Goldberg et al. [19] recently built a protocol to prove that $\gcd(e, \phi(N)) = 1$.

Argument of Correct Computation. The last component is an extractable zero-knowledge argument system Π in the random-oracle model for the user algorithm to prove that it correctly performed its computation, i.e., an argument system for $\mathcal{R}_\Pi$. Section 5.1 presents a perfectly honest-verifier zero-knowledge interactive protocol for $\mathcal{R}_\Pi$ that is also extractable in the random-oracle model.

5.1 Zero-Knowledge Argument with the Dodis-Yampolskiy PRF

This section gives a zero-knowledge argument Π in the case of the DY PRF in $\mathbb{G}_2 = QR_{2\ell+1}$. Formally, let $2\ell+1$ be a $b(\lambda)+1$-bit (i.e., $b(\lambda)+1 = \lfloor \log(2\ell+1) \rfloor + 1$) safe prime (i.e., ℓ is a Sophie Germain prime) and let Λ be a prime integer such that ℓ divides $\Lambda - 1$ and $\Lambda > (2\ell + 1)^2$. Consider $\mathbb{G}_1 = \langle G_1 \rangle$ a group of prime order Λ (in which p and q will be committed) and $\mathbb{G}_2 = \langle G_2 \rangle = QR_{2\ell+1}$ the group of quadratic residues modulo $2\ell + 1$, which is a cyclic group of order ℓ. Recall that the DY PRF is defined as the map $(K, x) \mapsto G_2^{1/(K+x)}$.

---

[4] To generate RSA moduli which are products of two 1536-bit primes, one possible instantiation for the Dodis-Yampolskiy PRF is to use $\ell = 2^{1535} + 554415$ which is a Sophie Germain prime, $\Lambda = (4\ell + 18)\ell + 1$ and $r = 1572 \cdot \Lambda + 1$.

Proof Strategy. To prove knowledge of a witness for the membership of $(C, r_{C\mathcal{A}}, N, (a_\gamma)_{\gamma \neq i,j})$ to the language relative to $\mathcal{R}_\Pi$, the user algorithm commits to $p = a_i$ and $q = a_j$ in $\mathbb{G}_1$ with the Pedersen commitment scheme and respective randomness r_p and r_q. The commitments are denoted P and Q.

The user algorithm then proves knowledge of a witness for $\mathcal{R}_0 \cap \mathcal{R}_1$, with

$$\mathcal{R}_0 := \{(C, r_{C\mathcal{A}}, N, P, Q, (a_\gamma)_{\gamma \neq i,j}; r'_{\mathcal{U}}, \rho_u, a_i, a_j, r_p, r_q):$$
$$\mathsf{ComVf}(C, r'_{\mathcal{U}}, \rho_u) = 1, \; s = r'_{\mathcal{U}} + \mathcal{H}(r_{C\mathcal{A}}) \bmod \ell$$
$$\forall \gamma \in [\![j]\!], a_\gamma = \mathsf{PRF}(s, \gamma), \mathsf{ComVf}(P, a_i, r_p) = \mathsf{ComVf}(Q, a_j, r_q) = 1\}$$

and

$$\mathcal{R}_1 := \{(C, r_{C\mathcal{A}}, N, P, Q, (a_\gamma)_{\gamma \neq i,j}; r'_{\mathcal{U}}, \rho_u, a_i, a_j, r_p, r_q): \mathsf{ComVf}(P, a_i, r_p) = 1$$
$$\mathsf{ComVf}(Q, a_j, r_q) = 1, 2^{b(\lambda)-1} \leq a_i, a_j \leq 2^{b(\lambda)} - 1, N = a_i a_j \text{ in } \mathbb{N}\}.$$

To prove knowledge of a witness for relation $\mathcal{R}$, it then suffices to prove in parallel knowledge of a witness for $\mathcal{R}_0$ and of a witness for $\mathcal{R}_1$ on the same public inputs. Note that the binding property of the Pedersen commitment scheme in $\mathbb{G}_1$ (relying on the DLOG assumption) guarantees that the a_i and a_j values used in both proofs are the same (up to a relabeling).

Relation $\mathcal{R}_0$. We start by giving two preliminary protocols:

- a logarithmic-size zero-knowledge argument of knowledge of a double-discrete logarithm (Sect. 5.2) using Bulletproof techniques [10]. The resulting proofs are of size logarithmic in the bit-length of the group order. In comparison, the protocol of Camenisch and Stadler [12] has proofs of size linear in the security parameter
- a logarithmic-size argument of equality of a discrete logarithm in a group and a double discrete logarithm in another related group (Sect. 5.2). In contrast, the protocol of Chase et al. [14, Section 4.3] for this relation uses the techniques of Camenisch and Stadler and therefore has proofs of size linear in the security parameter.

We then combine the latter proof with the proof in Sect. 5.3 to obtain a proof for relation $\mathcal{R}_0$.

Relation $\mathcal{R}_1$. The aggregated logarithmic range proof of Bünz et al. [10, Section 4.2] is sufficient to prove that the values committed in P and Q modulo Λ are in $[\![2^{b-1}, 2^b - 1]\!]$ (which is equivalent to proving that the values committed in $PG_1^{-2^{b-1}}$ and $QG_1^{-2^{b-1}}$ are in $\{0, \ldots, 2^{b-1} - 1\}$). With the hypotheses on the parameters Λ and ℓ, the verifier is convinced that the equation $N = a_i a_j$ holds in $\mathbb{N}$. Indeed, the equation $N = a_i a_j \bmod \Lambda$ implies that there exists $m \in \mathbb{Z}$ such that $N = a_i a_j + m\Lambda$. Integer m cannot be strictly positive as otherwise N would be strictly greater than Λ. Besides, m cannot be strictly negative since $\Lambda > (2\ell + 1)^2 > a_i a_j$; it is therefore nil and the equation $N = a_i a_j$ holds in $\mathbb{N}$.

5.2   Logarithmic-Size Argument of Double Discrete Logarithm

This section gives a zero-knowledge argument with logarithmic communication size for proving knowledge of a double discrete logarithm. It uses as a sub-argument the logarithmic-size inner-product argument for arithmetic-circuit satisfiability of Bünz et al. [10, § 5.2], which is complete, perfectly honest-verifier zero-knowledge, and satisfies witness-extended emulation.

Following the ideas of Bootle et al. [8], Bünz et al. convert any arithmetic circuit with n multiplications gates into a Hadamard product $\mathbf{a}_L \circ \mathbf{a}_R = \mathbf{a}_O$ and $Q \leq 2n$ linear constraints of the form

$$\langle \mathbf{w}_{L,q}, \mathbf{a}_L \rangle + \langle \mathbf{w}_{R,q}, \mathbf{a}_R \rangle + \langle \mathbf{w}_{O,q}, \mathbf{a}_O \rangle = c_q$$

for $q \in [\![Q]\!]$, with $\mathbf{w}_{L,q}, \mathbf{w}_{R,q}, \mathbf{w}_{O,q} \in \mathbb{Z}_p^n$ and $c_q \in \mathbb{Z}_p$. The vectors $\mathbf{a}_L$, $\mathbf{a}_R$ respectively denote the vectors of left and right inputs to the multiplications gates, and $\mathbf{a}_O$ the vector of outputs. The linear constraints ensure the consistency between the outputs and the inputs of two consecutive depth levels of the circuit. Bootle et al. [8, App. A] give a general method to find such linear constraints, though it may not always result in the most compact ones for a specific circuit.

Bünz et al. actually give an argument for a more general relation which includes Pedersen commitments of which the openings are included in the linear consistency constraints. Concretely, given a group $\mathbb{G}$ of prime order p and positive integers n, m and Q, Bünz et al. give a zero-knowledge argument for the relation

$$\{(g, \quad h \in \mathbb{G}, \mathbf{g}, \mathbf{h} \in \mathbb{G}^n, \mathbf{V} \in \mathbb{G}^m, \mathbf{W}_L, \mathbf{W}_R, \mathbf{W}_O \in \mathbb{Z}_p^{Q \times n}, \mathbf{W}_V \in \mathbb{Z}_p^{Q \times m},$$

$$\mathbf{c} \in \mathbb{Z}_p^Q; \mathbf{a}_L, \mathbf{a}_R, \mathbf{a}_O \in \mathbb{Z}_p^n, \mathbf{v}, \gamma \in \mathbb{Z}_p^m) : V_j = g^{v_j} h^{\gamma_j} \forall j \in [\![m]\!]$$

$$\wedge \mathbf{a}_L \circ \mathbf{a}_R = \mathbf{a}_O \wedge \mathbf{W}_L \mathbf{a}_L + \mathbf{W}_R \mathbf{a}_R + \mathbf{W}_O \mathbf{a}_O = \mathbf{W}_V \mathbf{v} + \mathbf{c}\}.$$

Its soundness relies on the discrete-logarithm assumption over the generator of $\mathbb{G}$ and the prover sends $2\lceil \log_2 n \rceil + 8$ group elements and $5 \mathbb{Z}_p$ elements.

The main difficulty in the case of a proof of a double discrete logarithm relation is to re-write the problem in a way that is suitable to apply the proof for arithmetic circuits. The goal is to give a zero-knowledge argument for:

$$\mathcal{R}_{\text{2DLOG}} := \left\{ (G_1, H_1, G_2, Y; x \in \mathbb{Z}_\ell, r \in \mathbb{Z}_\Lambda) : Y = G_1^{G_2^x} H_1^r \right\}.$$

First, let $n(\lambda) + 1 := b(\lambda)$ be the bit-length of ℓ. Given the bit representation $(x_i)_{i=0}^n$ of x, $G_2^x = G_2^{\sum_{i=0}^n x_i 2^i} = \prod_i \left(G_2^{2^i} \right)^{x_i}$. An important observation is that for $x_i \in \{0, 1\}$, $\left(G_2^{2^i} \right)^{x_i} = x_i G_2^{2^i} + (1 - x_i) = x_i \left(G_2^{2^i} - 1 \right) + 1$. The addition here is over $\mathbb{Z}_\Lambda$, although the notation is purely formal since $x_i \in \{0, 1\}$. It thus follows that an argument for $\mathcal{R}_{\text{2DLOG}}$ is equivalent to an argument for:

$$\left\{ (G_1, H_1, G_2, Y; (x_i)_{i=0}^n \in \{0,1\}^n, r \in \mathbb{Z}_\Lambda) : Y = G_1^{\prod_i \left(x_i \left(G_2^{2^i} - 1 \right) + 1 \right)} H_1^r \right\},$$

which is also equivalent to an argument for:

$$\left\{ (G_1, H_1, G_2, Y; (a_i)_{i=0}^n, r \in \mathbb{Z}_\Lambda) : Y = G_1^{\prod_i a_i} H_1^r \wedge a_i \in \left\{ 1, G_2^{2^i} \right\} \right\}.$$

To this end, consider the following array

$$
\begin{array}{ccccc}
a_0 & a_1 & a_2 & \cdots & a_n \\
1 & a_0 & a_0 a_1 & \cdots a_0 a_1 \cdots a_{n-1} \\
a_0 & a_0 a_1 & a_0 a_1 a_2 & \cdots & a_0 \cdots a_n.
\end{array}
$$

Notice that its third row is the product of the first two. In other words, if $\mathbf{a} \leftarrow (a_0, a_1, \ldots, a_n) \in \mathbb{Z}_\Lambda^{n+1}$ and $\mathbf{b} \leftarrow (b_0 = a_0, b_1 = a_0 a_1, \ldots, b_{n-1} = a_0 a_1 \cdots a_{n-1}) \in \mathbb{Z}_\Lambda^n$, then $\mathbf{a} \circ (1 \quad \mathbf{b}) = (\mathbf{b} \quad y)$ for $y := G_2^x$.

Moreover, for $\mathbf{a}_L := \begin{bmatrix} \mathbf{a} & \mathbf{a} - 1^{n+1} \end{bmatrix}^T$, $\mathbf{a}_R := \begin{bmatrix} 1 & \mathbf{b} & \mathbf{a} - \mathbf{G}_2^{2^{n+1}} \end{bmatrix}^T$ and $\mathbf{a}_O := \begin{bmatrix} \mathbf{b} & y & 0^{n+1} \end{bmatrix}^T \in \mathbb{Z}_\Lambda^{2(n+1)}$ where $\mathbf{G}_2^{2^{n+1}}$ denotes the vector $\left(G_2, G_2^2, G_2^{2^2}, \ldots, G_2^{2^n} \right)$, one has $\mathbf{a}_L \circ \mathbf{a}_R = \mathbf{a}_O$. If one can prove knowledge of scalars $y, r \in \mathbb{Z}_\Lambda$ and of vectors $\mathbf{a}_L$, $\mathbf{a}_R$ and $\mathbf{a}_O$ such that $Y = G_1^y H_1^r$ and $\mathbf{a}_L \circ \mathbf{a}_R = \mathbf{a}_O$, and such that the vectors are of the form above, then one can prove knowledge of $(a_i)_{i=0}^n \in \prod_i \left\{ 1, G_2^{2^i} \right\}$ and $(b_i)_{i=0}^{n-1}$ such that $y = a_n b_{n-1} = a_n a_{n-1} b_{n-2} = \cdots = a_n a_{n-1} \cdots a_1 b_0 = a_n \cdots a_0$ and $Y = G_1^y H_1^r$. That is to say, one can prove knowledge of a double discrete logarithm.

To prove such a relation, one can use the argument of Bünz et al. [10] for arithmetic circuits with the right linear constraints to ensure that the vectors are of the appropriate form. To express these constraints, consider matrices $\mathbf{W}_L$, $\mathbf{W}_R$, $\mathbf{W}_O$ and $\mathbf{W}_V$ from Fig. 4 and vectors $\mathbf{v}^T := \begin{bmatrix} 1 & y \end{bmatrix}$, $\mathbf{c}^T := \begin{bmatrix} 0_{1 \times (n+2)} & 1^{n+1} & \mathbf{G}_2^{2^{n+1}} & 0_{1 \times (n+1)} \end{bmatrix}$.

Three vectors $\mathbf{a}_L$, $\mathbf{a}_R$ and $\mathbf{a}_O \in \mathbb{Z}_\Lambda^{2(n+1)}$ satisfy the equation $\mathbf{W}_L \mathbf{a}_L + \mathbf{W}_R \mathbf{a}_R + \mathbf{W}_O \mathbf{a}_O = \mathbf{W}_V \mathbf{v} + \mathbf{c}$ if and only if there exists $\mathbf{a} \in \mathbb{Z}_\Lambda^{n+1}$ and $\mathbf{b} \in \mathbb{Z}_\Lambda^n$ such that $\mathbf{a}_L^T := \begin{bmatrix} \mathbf{a} & \mathbf{a} - 1^{n+1} \end{bmatrix}$, $\mathbf{a}_R^T := \begin{bmatrix} 1 & \mathbf{b} & \mathbf{a} - \mathbf{G}_2^{2^{n+1}} \end{bmatrix}$ and $\mathbf{a}_O^T := \begin{bmatrix} \mathbf{b} & y & 0^{n+1} \end{bmatrix} \in \mathbb{Z}_\Lambda^{2(n+1)}$ (see [6]).

The argument of Bünz et al. is therefore sufficient to prove in zero-knowledge knowledge of a double discrete logarithm. The soundness of the proof relies on the discrete-logarithm assumption over $\mathbb{G}_1$.

Regarding the proof size, the prover sends $(2\lceil \log_2 2(n+1) \rceil + 8)\mathbb{G}_1$ elements and $5\mathbb{Z}_\Lambda$ elements. Notice that the argument of Bünz et al. requires $4(n+1)$ elements of $\mathbb{G}_1^*$ in addition to G_1 and H_1. To guarantee its soundness, no discrete logarithm relation between these elements, G_1 and H_1 must be known to the prover. They can then be choosen uniformly at random during set-up.

Logarithmic-Size Argument of Discrete Logarithm and Double Discrete Logarithm Equality. Building on the argument of double discrete logarithm of Sect. 5.2, we present in [6] a a zero-knowledge argument for the relation

$$
\underbrace{\begin{bmatrix} 0_{(n+2)\times 2(n+1)} \\ I_{n+1} \quad -I_{n+1} \\ I_{n+1}\ 0_{(n+1)\times(n+1)} \\ 0_{(n+1)\times 2(n+1)} \end{bmatrix}}_{\mathbf{W}_L}
\underbrace{\begin{bmatrix} U_{n+1}\ 0_{(n+1)\times(n+1)} \\ E_{1\times 2(n+1)}(1,1) \\ 0_{(n+1)\times 2(n+1)} \\ 0_{(n+1)\times(n+1)}\ -I_{n+1} \\ 0_{(n+1)\times 2(n+1)} \end{bmatrix}}_{\mathbf{W}_R}
\underbrace{\begin{bmatrix} -I_n\ 0_{n\times(n+2)} \\ E_{2\times 2(n+1)}(1,n+1) \\ 0_{2(n+1)\times 2(n+1)} \\ 0_{(n+1)\times(n+1)}\ I_{n+1} \end{bmatrix}}_{\mathbf{W}_O}
\underbrace{\begin{bmatrix} 0_{n\times 2} \\ 0\ 1 \\ 1\ 0 \\ 0_{3(n+1)\times 2} \end{bmatrix}}_{\mathbf{W}_V}
$$

Fig. 4. Matrices $\mathbf{W}_L$, $\mathbf{W}_R$, $\mathbf{W}_O$ and $\mathbf{W}_V$ for the proof of double discrete logarithm. U_{n+1} denotes the square $n+1$-matrix with 1 on the upper diagonal. $E_{n\times m}(i,j)$ denotes the $n \times m$ matrix with 1 at position (i,j) and 0 elsewhere.

$\mathcal{R}_{\mathrm{DLOG-2}} := \{(G_1, H_1, G_2, H_2, Y, X; x \in \mathbb{Z}_\ell, r_1, r_2 \in \mathbb{Z}_\Lambda): Y = G_1^{G_2^x} H_1^{r_1}, X = G_2^x H_2^{r_2}\}$. In total, the prover sends $2\lceil \log_2 4(n+1)\rceil + 8\mathbb{G}_1$ elements and $5\mathbb{Z}_\Lambda$ elements.

5.3 An Intermediate Protocol in $\mathbb{G}_2$

This section gives an perfect honest verifier zero-knowledge protocol for relation

$$
\mathcal{R}'_0 := \{(G_2, H_2, X_p, X_q, U, K_u, (K_\gamma)_{\gamma \neq i,j}, (a_\gamma)_\gamma; x_p, x_q, r_p, r_q, u, \rho_u):
$$
$$
\forall \pi \in \{p,q\}, X_\pi = G_2^{x_\pi} H_2^{r_\pi}, U = G_2^u H_2^{\rho_u},
$$
$$
\forall \gamma, a_\gamma = G_2^{x_\gamma}, x_\pi(u + K_\pi) = x_\gamma(u + K_\gamma) = 1 \mod \ell\}.
$$

Note that for $\pi \in \{p,q\}$, $\left(UG_2^{K_\pi}\right)^{x_\pi} H_2^{-x_\pi \rho_u} = G_2$, and that $\forall \gamma, a_\gamma^u = G_2 a_\gamma^{-K_\gamma}$, i.e., the discrete logarithms of $G_2 a_\gamma^{-K_\gamma}$ in base a_γ for all γ are the same.

The protocol is given on Fig. 5). As the proof system is public-coin, it can be made non-interactive in the random-oracle model via the Fiat-Shamir heuristic by computing c as $\mathcal{H}(G_2, H_2, (X_\pi), U, (K_\pi), (K_\gamma)_\gamma, (a_\gamma)_\gamma, (Y_\pi), V, (H_\pi), (A_\gamma))$ for a random oracle $\mathcal{H}$ with $\mathbb{Z}_\ell$ as range. The proof then consists of $(c, (z_\pi, t_\pi)_{\pi\in\{p,q\}}, w, \tau_u, (\tau_\pi)_\pi)$, i.e., $9\mathbb{Z}_\ell$ elements.

The protocol is complete, perfectly honest-verifier zero-knowledge, and satisfies witness-extended emulation under the discrete logarithm assumption over $\mathbb{G}_2$. The protocol completeness and its zero-knowledge property are straightforward.

See the full version [6] for the proof of the witness-extended-emulation.

5.4 Protocol for $\mathcal{R}_0$

To prove knowledge of a witness for $\mathcal{R}_0$, the prover starts setting by setting $K_p := \mathcal{H}(r_{\mathcal{CA}}) + i$, $K_q := \mathcal{H}(r_{\mathcal{CA}}) + j$, and $u := r'_{\mathcal{U}}$. It then

- computes two commitments $X_p = G_2^{x_p} H_2^{r_p}$ and $X_q = G_2^{x_q} H_2^{r_q}$, for $x_p = (u + K_p)^{-1} \mod \ell$ and $x_q = (u + K_q)^{-1} \mod \ell$
- computes a proof $\pi_{\mathrm{DLOG-2},p}$ that the double discrete-logarithm of P is the discrete logarithm of X_p, and similarly a proof $\pi_{\mathrm{DLOG-2},q}$ for Q and X_q

$$\mathscr{P}(\cdots ; (x_\pi)_{\pi \in \{p,q\}}, (r_\pi), u, \rho_u) \qquad\qquad \mathscr{V}\left(G_2, H_2, (X_\pi), U, (K_\pi), (K_\gamma)_\gamma, (a_\gamma)_\gamma\right)$$

$$y_\pi, s_\pi, v, \sigma_u, \sigma \xleftarrow{\$} \mathbb{Z}_\ell$$
$$Y_\pi \leftarrow G_2^{y_\pi} H_2^{s_\pi}$$
$$V \leftarrow G_2^{v} H_2^{\sigma_u}$$
$$H_\pi \leftarrow \left(U G_2^{K_u}\right)^{y_\pi} H_2^{\sigma_\pi}$$
$$A_\gamma \leftarrow (a_\gamma)^{v}$$

$$\xrightarrow{(Y_\pi)_\pi, V, (H_\pi)_\pi, (A_\gamma)_\gamma}$$

$$c \xleftarrow{\$} \mathbb{Z}_\ell$$

$$\xleftarrow{\quad c \quad}$$

$$z_\pi \leftarrow y_\pi - c x_\pi, t_\pi \leftarrow s_\pi - c r_\pi$$
$$w \leftarrow v - c u, \tau_u \leftarrow \sigma_u - c \rho_u \qquad \xrightarrow{\;\;(z_\pi, t_\pi)_\pi\;\;}_{w, \tau_u, (\tau_\pi)_\pi}$$
$$\tau_\pi \leftarrow \sigma_\pi + c x_\pi \rho_u$$

$$G_2^{z_\pi} H_2^{t_\pi} X_\pi^c \overset{?}{=} Y_\pi$$
$$G_2^{w} H_2^{\tau_u} U^c \overset{?}{=} V$$
$$\left(U G_2^{K_u}\right)^{z_\pi} H_2^{\tau_\pi} G_2^c \overset{?}{=} H_\pi$$
$$a_\gamma^{w} \left(G_2 a_\gamma^{-K_\gamma}\right)^c \overset{?}{=} A_\gamma$$

Fig. 5. Honest-verifier zero-knowledge protocol for relation $\mathcal{R}_1$.

– computes a proof π' for relation $\mathcal{R}'_0$ with X_p and X_q.

The final proof π_0 for $\mathcal{R}_0$ consists of $(X_p, X_q, \pi_{\text{DLOG-2},p}, \pi_{\text{DLOG-2},q}, \pi'_0)$.

Security. It is important to note that the security of the generated key is weakened compared to an RSA-key of the same size since the CA can recover seed s (and thus the prime factors) by solving a discrete logarithm problem in $\mathbb{G}_2$. For 3072-bit RSA moduli, this protocol therefore only provides 96 bits of security (with respect to the CA) instead of the expected 128-bit security level. To avoid this issue, one can increase the bit size of the prime numbers to 3072 bits (but at the cost of generating RSA moduli of twice this size). Another possibility is to use other groups for $\mathbb{G}_2$ with (alleged) harder discrete logarithm problem, e.g., the group of points of an elliptic curve over $\mathbb{F}_p$ or an algebraic torus defined over $\mathbb{F}_{p^2}$ (with compact representation of group elements in $\mathbb{F}_p$) for a 1536-bit prime p. This may however introduce a new bias for the generated primes and require to adapt the zero-knowledge proofs.

Efficiency. The asymptotic complexity of the communication size depends on the number of trials to obtain two primes in W since the prover has to send $(a_\gamma)_{\gamma \neq i,j}$. However, even though the communication is asymptotically linear in the number of trials, the overhead incurred by the proof of correct computation should in practice be small.

	$\mathbb{Z}_\ell$	$\mathbb{Z}_N$	$\mathbb{Z}_\Lambda$	$\mathbb{G}_1$	$\mathbb{G}_2$	Total (kB)
$\mathcal{R}_0$	9	0	10	$4\lceil \log_2 4b \rceil + 16$	2	346
$\mathcal{R}_1$	0	0	5	$2\lceil \log_2 2(b-1) \rceil + 4$	0	142

Fig. 6. Size of the arguments (for a 96-bit security level and 3072-bit RSA moduli).

Total Proof Size. As discussed in Sect. 5.2, proofs $\pi_{\text{DLOG}-2,p}$ and $\pi_{\text{DLOG}-2,q}$ both consists of $2\lceil \log_2 4(n+1) \rceil + 8\mathbb{G}_1$ elements and $5\mathbb{Z}_\Lambda$ elements.

Proof π' consists of $9\mathbb{Z}_\ell$ elements (see Sect. 5.3). Proof π_0 for $\mathcal{R}_0$ therefore consists of $2\mathbb{G}_2$ elements, $4\lceil \log_2 4(n+1) \rceil + 16\mathbb{G}_1$ elements, $10\mathbb{Z}_\Lambda$ elements and $9\mathbb{Z}_\ell$ elements. As for the proof for $\mathcal{R}_1$, the aggregated proof that 2 values committed in $\mathbb{G}_1$ are in $[\![0, 2^{b-1}-1]\!]$ consists of $2\lceil \log_2 2(b-1) \rceil + 4\mathbb{G}_1$ elements (recall that $n+1 = b$) and $5\mathbb{Z}_\Lambda$ elements.

Running Time. An important question about the protocol is the number of necessary PRF trials to obtain two primes that satisfy the conditions required for the factors of N (captured by $W \subseteq \mathbb{P}$). We estimate the number j of necessary trials in the case $W = \mathbb{P} \cap [\![2^{b-1}, 2^b - 1]\!]$, i.e., when $\mathcal{U}$ simply has to prove that p and q are prime of $b(\lambda)$ bits.

The full version [6] shows (using a number-theoretic heuristic) that the number of trials exceeds $17b(\lambda) = O(\log \lambda)$ (so the DY PRF remains secure), and that the probability that it is larger than that decreases exponentially fast.

Overall Communication Size. In the last flow of the protocol, the prover then sends an integer N, two commitments in $\mathbb{G}_1$, $17b(\lambda) - 2$ integers in $[\![0, 2\ell]\!]$ with high probability, i.e., the $(a_\gamma)_{\gamma \neq i,j}$ values which are integers returned by the PRF and not in W, and the proof of correct computation of which the size is summarized in Table 6.

Acknowledgements. The authors thank Jonathan Bootle for fruitful discussions. This work was supported by the French ANR ALAMBIC Project (ANR-16-CE39-0006), the CHIST-ERA USEIT project and the EU H2020 Research and Innovation Program under Grant Agreement No. 786725 (OLYMPUS).

References

1. Auerbach, B., Poettering, B.: Hashing solutions instead of generating problems: on the interactive certification of RSA moduli. In: Abdalla, M., Dahab, R. (eds.) PKC 2018. LNCS, vol. 10770, pp. 403–430. Springer, Cham (2018). https://doi.org/10.1007/978-3-319-76581-5_14

2. Backes, M., Hanzlik, L., Herzberg, A., Kate, A., Pryvalov, I.: Efficient non-interactive zero-knowledge proofs in cross-domains without trusted setup. In: Lin, D., Sako, K. (eds.) PKC 2019. LNCS, vol. 11442, pp. 286–313. Springer, Cham (2019). https://doi.org/10.1007/978-3-030-17253-4_10

3. Bellare, M., Canetti, R., Krawczyk, H.: Keying hash functions for message authentication. In: Koblitz, N. (ed.) CRYPTO 1996. LNCS, vol. 1109, pp. 1–15. Springer, Heidelberg (1996). https://doi.org/10.1007/3-540-68697-5_1

4. Bellare, M., Pointcheval, D., Rogaway, P.: Authenticated key exchange secure against dictionary attacks. In: Preneel, B. (ed.) EUROCRYPT 2000. LNCS, vol. 1807, pp. 139–155. Springer, Heidelberg (2000). https://doi.org/10.1007/3-540-45539-6_11

5. Benhamouda, F., Ferradi, H., Géraud, R., Naccache, D.: Non-interactive provably secure attestations for arbitrary RSA prime generation algorithms. In: Foley, S.N., Gollmann, D., Snekkenes, E. (eds.) ESORICS 2017. LNCS, vol. 10492, pp. 206–223. Springer, Cham (2017). https://doi.org/10.1007/978-3-319-66402-6_13

6. Blazy, O., Towa, P., Vergnaud, D.: Public-key generation with verifiable randomness. Cryptology ePrint Archive, Report 2020/294 (2020)
7. Boneh, D., Boyen, X.: Short signatures without random oracles. In: Cachin, C., Camenisch, J.L. (eds.) EUROCRYPT 2004. LNCS, vol. 3027, pp. 56–73. Springer, Heidelberg (2004). https://doi.org/10.1007/978-3-540-24676-3_4
8. Bootle, J., Cerulli, A., Chaidos, P., Groth, J., Petit, C.: Efficient zero-knowledge arguments for arithmetic circuits in the discrete log setting. In: Fischlin, M., Coron, J.-S. (eds.) EUROCRYPT 2016. LNCS, vol. 9666, pp. 327–357. Springer, Heidelberg (2016). https://doi.org/10.1007/978-3-662-49896-5_12
9. Boyar, J., Friedl, K., Lund, C.: Practical zero-knowledge proofs: giving hints and using deficiencies. In: Quisquater, J.-J., Vandewalle, J. (eds.) EUROCRYPT 1989. LNCS, vol. 434, pp. 155–172. Springer, Heidelberg (1990). https://doi.org/10.1007/3-540-46885-4_18
10. Bünz, B., Bootle, J., Boneh, D., Poelstra, A., Wuille, P., Maxwell, G.: Bulletproofs: short proofs for confidential transactions and more. In: 2018 IEEE Symposium on Security and Privacy, pp. 315–334. IEEE Computer Society Press (2018)
11. Camenisch, J., Michels, M.: Proving in zero-knowledge that a number is the product of two safe primes. In: Stern, J. (ed.) EUROCRYPT 1999. LNCS, vol. 1592, pp. 107–122. Springer, Heidelberg (1999). https://doi.org/10.1007/3-540-48910-X_8
12. Camenisch, J., Stadler, M.: Efficient group signature schemes for large groups. In: Kaliski, B.S. (ed.) CRYPTO 1997. LNCS, vol. 1294, pp. 410–424. Springer, Heidelberg (1997). https://doi.org/10.1007/BFb0052252
13. Canard, S., Gouget, A.: Divisible e-cash systems can be truly anonymous. In: Naor, M. (ed.) EUROCRYPT 2007. LNCS, vol. 4515, pp. 482–497. Springer, Heidelberg (2007). https://doi.org/10.1007/978-3-540-72540-4_28
14. Chase, M., Ganesh, C., Mohassel, P.: Efficient zero-knowledge proof of algebraic and non-algebraic statements with applications to privacy preserving credentials. In: Robshaw, M., Katz, J. (eds.) CRYPTO 2016. LNCS, vol. 9816, pp. 499–530. Springer, Heidelberg (2016). https://doi.org/10.1007/978-3-662-53015-3_18
15. Corrigan-Gibbs, H., Mu, W., Boneh, D., Ford, B.: Ensuring high-quality randomness in cryptographic key generation. In: Sadeghi, A.R., Gligor, V.D., Yung, M. (eds.) ACM CCS 2013, pp. 685–696. ACM Press (2013)
16. Desmedt, Y.: Simmons' protocol is not free of subliminal channels. In: Ninth IEEE Computer Security Foundations Workshop, March 10–12, 1996, Dromquinna Manor, Kenmare, County Kerry, Ireland, pp. 170–175 (1996)
17. Dodis, Y., Yampolskiy, A.: A verifiable random function with short proofs and keys. In: Vaudenay, S. (ed.) PKC 2005. LNCS, vol. 3386, pp. 416–431. Springer, Heidelberg (2005). https://doi.org/10.1007/978-3-540-30580-4_28
18. Gennaro, R., Micciancio, D., Rabin, T.: An efficient non-interactive statistical zero-knowledge proof system for quasi-safe prime products. In: Gong, L., Reiter, M.K. (eds.) ACM CCS 1998, pp. 67–72. ACM Press (1998)
19. Goldberg, S., Reyzin, L., Sagga, O., Baldimtsi, F.: Efficient noninteractive certification of RSA moduli and beyond. In: Galbraith, S.D., Moriai, S. (eds.) ASIACRYPT 2019. LNCS, vol. 11923, pp. 700–727. Springer, Cham (2019). https://doi.org/10.1007/978-3-030-34618-8_24
20. Goldreich, O., Goldwasser, S., Micali, S.: How to construct random functions (extended abstract). In: 25th FOCS, pp. 464–479. IEEE Computer Society (1984)
21. Heninger, N., Durumeric, Z., Wustrow, E., Halderman, J.A.: Mining your PS and QS: detection of widespread weak keys in network devices. In: Kohno, T. (ed.) USENIX Security 2012, pp. 205–220. USENIX Association (2012)

22. Juels, A., Guajardo, J.: RSA key generation with verifiable randomness. In: Naccache, D., Paillier, P. (eds.) PKC 2002. LNCS, vol. 2274, pp. 357–374. Springer, Heidelberg (2002). https://doi.org/10.1007/3-540-45664-3_26
23. Lenstra, A.K., Hughes, J.P., Augier, M., Bos, J.W., Kleinjung, T., Wachter, C.: Public keys. In: Safavi-Naini, R., Canetti, R. (eds.) CRYPTO 2012. LNCS, vol. 7417, pp. 626–642. Springer, Heidelberg (2012). https://doi.org/10.1007/978-3-642-32009-5_37
24. Mironov, I., Stephens-Davidowitz, N.: Cryptographic reverse firewalls. In: Oswald, E., Fischlin, M. (eds.) EUROCRYPT 2015. LNCS, vol. 9057, pp. 657–686. Springer, Heidelberg (2015). https://doi.org/10.1007/978-3-662-46803-6_22
25. Nemec, M., Sýs, M., Svenda, P., Klinec, D., Matyas, V.: The return of coppersmith's attack: practical factorization of widely used RSA moduli. In: Thuraisingham, B.M., Evans, D., Malkin, T., Xu, D. (eds.) ACM CCS 2017, pp. 1631–1648. ACM Press, October/November 2017
26. NIST: National Institute of Standards and Technology - Digital signature standard (DSS) (2013). https://csrc.nist.gov/publications/detail/fips/186/4/final
27. Pedersen, T.P.: Non-interactive and information-theoretic secure verifiable secret sharing. In: Feigenbaum, J. (ed.) CRYPTO 1991. LNCS, vol. 576, pp. 129–140. Springer, Heidelberg (1992). https://doi.org/10.1007/3-540-46766-1_9
28. Rivest, R.L., Shamir, A., Adleman, L.M.: A method for obtaining digital signatures and public-key cryptosystems. Commun. Assoc. Comput. Mach. 21(2), 120–126 (1978)
29. Simmons, G.J.: The prisoners' problem and the subliminal channel. In: Chaum, D. (ed.) CRYPTO 1983, pp. 51–67. Plenum Press, New York, USA (1983)
30. Stadler, M.: Publicly verifiable secret sharing. In: Maurer, U. (ed.) EUROCRYPT 1996. LNCS, vol. 1070, pp. 190–199. Springer, Heidelberg (1996). https://doi.org/10.1007/3-540-68339-9_17
31. van de Graaf, J., Peralta, R.: A simple and secure way to show the validity of your public key. In: Pomerance, C. (ed.) CRYPTO 1987. LNCS, vol. 293, pp. 128–134. Springer, Heidelberg (1988). https://doi.org/10.1007/3-540-48184-2_9
32. Young, A., Yung, M.: Kleptography: using cryptography against cryptography. In: Fumy, W. (ed.) EUROCRYPT 1997. LNCS, vol. 1233, pp. 62–74. Springer, Heidelberg (1997). https://doi.org/10.1007/3-540-69053-0_6

Simulation-Sound Arguments for LWE and Applications to KDM-CCA2 Security

Benoît Libert[1,2]([⊠]), Khoa Nguyen[3], Alain Passelègue[2,4], and Radu Titiu[2,5]

[1] CNRS, Laboratoire LIP, Lyon, France
benoit.libert@ens-lyon.fr
[2] ENS de Lyon, Laboratoire LIP (U. Lyon, CNRS, ENSL, Inria, UCBL),
Lyon, France
[3] Nanyang Technological University, SPMS, Singapore, Singapore
[4] Inria, Lyon, France
[5] Bitdefender, Bucharest, Romania

Abstract. The Naor-Yung paradigm is a well-known technique that constructs IND-CCA2-secure encryption schemes by means of non-interactive zero-knowledge proofs satisfying a notion of simulation-soundness. Until recently, it was an open problem to instantiate it under the sole Learning-With-Errors (LWE) assumption without relying on random oracles. While the recent results of Canetti *et al.* (STOC'19) and Peikert-Shiehian (Crypto'19) provide a solution to this problem by applying the Fiat-Shamir transform in the standard model, the resulting constructions are extremely inefficient as they proceed via a reduction to an NP-complete problem. In this paper, we give a direct, non-generic method for instantiating Naor-Yung under the LWE assumption outside the random oracle model. Specifically, we give a direct construction of an unbounded simulation-sound NIZK argument system which, for carefully chosen parameters, makes it possible to express the equality of plaintexts encrypted under different keys in Regev's cryptosystem. We also give a variant of our argument that provides tight security. As an application, we obtain an LWE-based public-key encryption scheme for which we can prove (tight) key-dependent message security under chosen-ciphertext attacks in the standard model.

Keywords: LWE · Standard model · Naor-Yung · NIZK arguments · Simulation-soundness · KDM-CCA2 security · Tight security.

1 Introduction

The Fiat-Shamir transformation [43] is a well-known technique that turns any 3-move honest-verifier zero-knowledge proof system (a.k.a. Σ-protocol [36]) into a non-interactive zero-knowledge proof (NIZK) by replacing the verifier's challenge by a hash value of the transcript so far. Bellare and Rogaway [11] showed that this approach is secure if the underlying hash function is modeled as a random oracle. Since then, the Fiat-Shamir heuristic has been used in the design of

© International Association for Cryptologic Research 2020
S. Moriai and H. Wang (Eds.): ASIACRYPT 2020, LNCS 12491, pp. 128–158, 2020.
https://doi.org/10.1007/978-3-030-64837-4_5

countless cryptographic schemes, including digital signatures [78] and chosen-ciphertext-secure public-key encryption schemes [44]. In the standard model, however, counter-examples [49] showed that it may fail to guarantee soundness. Until recently, it was not known to be securely instantiable without random oracles under any standard assumption. This situation drastically changed with the works of Canetti *et al.* [26] and Peikert and Shiehian [76], which imply the existence of Fiat-Shamir-based NIZK proofs for all NP languages under the sole Learning-With-Errors (LWE) assumption [79]. Their results followed a line of research [25,27,82] showing that Fiat-Shamir can provide soundness in the standard model if the underlying hash function is *correlation intractable* (CI). In short, correlation intractability for a relation R captures the infeasibility of finding an x such that $(x, H_k(x)) \in R$ given a random hashing key k. Intuitively, the reason why this property provides soundness is that a cheating prover's first message cannot be hashed into a verifier message admitting an accepting transcript, except with negligible probability.

While [26,76] resolve the challenging problem of realizing NIZK proofs for all NP under standard lattice assumptions, they leave open the question of building more efficient instantiations of Fiat-Shamir for specific languages, such as those arising in the context of chosen-ciphertext security [44,75,80].

In order to instantiate the Naor-Yung paradigm of CCA2-secure encryption [75] in the lattice setting, the only known solution is to proceed via a general NP reduction to graph Hamiltonicity and apply the Σ-protocol of Feige, Lapidot and Shamir [42] with the modifications suggested by Canetti *et al.* [26,30]. In addition, a direct application of [26,30,76] to CCA2 security requires to apply the generic compiler of [39] that turns any NIZK proof system into simulation-sound [80] proofs. Here, we consider the problem of more efficiently instantiating Naor-Yung in the standard model under lattice assumptions. Using correlation intractable hash functions, our goal is to directly construct simulation-sound arguments of plaintext equality without using generic techniques.

1.1   Our Contributions

We describe the most efficient post-quantum realization of the Naor-Yung paradigm so far and its first non-trivial instantiation under lattice assumptions. As an application, we obtain the most efficient public-key encryption scheme providing key-dependent message security under chosen-ciphertext attacks (or KDM-CCA2 security for short) under the standard Learning-With-Errors (LWE) assumption [79]. Our scheme is *not* the result of merely combining generic NIZK techniques [39,80] with the results [26,30,76] on NIZK proofs based on correlation intractable hash functions. In particular, we bypass the use of a Karp reduction to the graph Hamiltonicity language [26,30,42]. Instead, as a key building block, we directly build a simulation-sound NIZK proof system showing that two dual Regev ciphertexts [46] are encryptions of the same plaintext.

As a result of independent interest, we also obtain a multi-theorem NIZK argument system without using the Feige-Lapidot-Shamir (FLS) transformation [42]. Recall that the FLS compiler constructs a multi-theorem NIZK proof system for an NP language from a single-theorem NIZK proof system by using the latter to prove OR statements of the form "either element x is in the language OR some CRS component is in the range of a pseudorandom generator". Unlike FLS, our multi-theorem NIZK argument avoids the non-black-box use of a PRG. Another advantage is that it provides multi-theorem statistical NIZK in the common *random* string model while proving soundness under the LWE assumption. In contrast, achieving statistical multi-theorem NIZK by applying FLS to [30,76] requires a common reference string sampled from a non-uniform distribution.

We further show that our argument system provides *unbounded* (as opposed to one-time [80]) simulation-soundness (USS) [39], meaning that the adversary remains unable to prove a false statement, even after having seen simulated arguments for polynomially many (possibly false) statements. This makes our argument system suitable to prove KDM-CCA2 security by applying the Naor-Yung technique to the KDM-CPA system of Applebaum, Cash, Peikert, and Sahai (ACPS) [6], which is known to provide key-dependent message security for affine functions. In addition, we provide a variant of our USS argument that can be proved tightly secure, meaning that the reduction's advantage is not affected by the number of simulated proofs obtained by the adversary. The simulation-soundness property is indeed tightly related to the security of the underlying pseudorandom function. By exploiting a result of Lai *et al.* [64], it can be combined with a tightly secure lattice-based PRF so as to instantiate our scheme with a polynomial modulus.

Our first simulation-sound NIZK argument implies a public-key encryption (PKE) scheme providing KDM-CCA2 security under the LWE assumption with polynomial approximation factors. Our second NIZK argument yields an instantiation that enjoys *tight* KDM-CCA2 security. Until recently, this was only possible under an LWE assumption with large approximation factors for lack of a tightly secure low-depth lattice-based PRF based on an LWE assumption with polynomial inverse-error rate. Lai *et al.* [64] recently showed that many tightly secure LWE-based schemes (e.g., [17,18,67]) can actually be obtained using a PRF outside NC1 without going through Barrington's theorem [9]. Their technique [64] applies to our setting and ensure that any (possibly sequential) PRF with a tight security reduction from LWE with polynomial modulus and inverse-error rate allows instantiating the scheme under a similarly standard assumption.

Recall that KDM security is formalized by an experiment where the adversary obtains N public keys. On polynomially many occasions, it sends encryption queries (i, f), for functions $f \in \mathcal{F}$ belonging to some family, and expects to receive an encryption of $f(SK_1, \ldots, SK_N)$ under PK_i. Security requires the adversary to be unable to distinguish the real encryption oracle from an oracle that always returns an encryption of 0. Our KDM-CCA2 construction supports the same function family (namely, affine functions) as the KDM-CPA system it builds on. However, like previous LWE-based realizations [4,6], it can be bootstrapped using Applebaum's technique [5] so as to retain KDM security for arbitrary functions that are computable in a priori bounded polynomial time.

We believe our LWE-based instantiation of Naor-Yung to be of interest beyond KDM security. For example, it makes possible to publicly recognize ciphertexts that correctly decrypt, which is a rare feature among LWE-based schemes and comes in handy in the threshold decryption setting (see, e.g., [44]). It can also be used to obtain chosen-ciphertext security in settings – such as inner product functional encryption [1,3] or receiver selective-opening security [54] – for which we do not know how to apply the Canetti-Halevi-Katz technique [29].

1.2 Technical Overview

Our starting point is a trapdoor Σ-protocol [26,30] allowing to prove the well-formed of ciphertexts in the KDM-CPA system of Applebaum $et\ al.$ [6]. Namely, it allows proving that a given vector $\mathbf{c} = (\mathbf{u}, u) \in \mathbb{Z}_q^{n+1}$ is of the form $(\mathbf{u}, \mathbf{u}^\top \mathbf{s} + \mu \lfloor q/p \rfloor + \mathsf{noise})$, where $\mu \in \mathbb{Z}_p$ is the message, $\mathbf{s} \in \mathbb{Z}^n$ is the secret key and the public key is $(\mathbf{A}, \mathbf{b} = \mathbf{A}^\top \mathbf{s} + \mathsf{noise}) \in \mathbb{Z}_q^{n \times m} \times \mathbb{Z}_q^m$ for some $m = \Omega(n \cdot \log q)$. Recall that a standard Σ-protocol [35,36] is a 3-move protocol with transcripts of the form $(\mathbf{a}, \mathsf{Chall}, \mathbf{z})$ where Chall is the verifier's challenge and messages $\mathbf{a}$ and $\mathbf{z}$ are sent by the prover. In the common reference string model, a trapdoor Σ-protocol [26,30] has the property that, for any statement x outside the language $\mathcal{L}$ and any first message $\mathbf{a}$ sent by the prover, a trapdoor makes it possible to determine the unique challenge Chall for which a valid response $\mathbf{z}$ exists. There is an efficiently computable function $\mathsf{BadChallenge}$ that takes as input a trapdoor τ, a false statement $x \notin \mathcal{L}$, and a first prover message $\mathbf{a}$, and computes the unique Chall such that there exists an accepting transcript $(\mathbf{a}, \mathsf{Chall}, \mathbf{z})$ (that is, there is no accepting transcript of the form $(\mathbf{a}, \mathsf{Chall}', \mathbf{z})$ for any $\mathsf{Chall}' \neq \mathsf{Chall}$).

Our first observation is that, in order to preserve the soundness of Fiat-Shamir, it suffices for a trapdoor Σ-protocol to have a $\mathsf{BadChallenge}$ function that outputs "if there is a bad challenge at all for $\mathbf{a}$, it can only be Chall". Indeed, false positives do not hurt soundness as we only need the CI hash function to sidestep the bad challenge whenever it exists. Based on this observation, we can build a trapdoor Σ-protocol showing that a Regev ciphertext $\mathbf{c} \in \mathbb{Z}_q^{n+1}$ encrypts 0. Letting $\bar{\mathbf{A}} = [\mathbf{A}^\top \mid \mathbf{b}]^\top \in \mathbb{Z}_q^{(n+1) \times m}$, this can be done using by showing knowledge of a short $\mathbf{r} \in \mathbb{Z}^m$ such that $\mathbf{c} = \bar{\mathbf{A}} \cdot \mathbf{r}$. In Σ-protocols like [70,71], the verifier accepts transcripts $(\mathbf{a}, \mathsf{Chall}, \mathbf{z})$ such that $\mathbf{a} + \mathsf{Chall} \cdot \mathbf{c} = \bar{\mathbf{A}} \cdot \mathbf{z}$ if $\mathbf{z} \in \mathbb{Z}^m$ is short enough. Since the right-hand side member of the verification equation is an encryption of 0, the $\mathsf{BadChallenge}$ function can use the decryption key $\mathbf{s}$ to infer that no valid response exists for the challenge $\mathsf{Chall} = b$ when $\mathbf{a} + b \cdot \mathbf{c}$ does not decrypt to 0.

The next step is to argue that $\mathbf{c}$ encrypts an arbitrary $\mu \in \mathbb{Z}_p$. To this end, we exploit the fact the KDM-CPA scheme of [6] uses a square modulus $q = p^2$ when we compute part of the response $z_\mu = r_u + \mathsf{Chall} \cdot \mu \bmod p$ over $\mathbb{Z}_p$, while using a uniform mask $r_u \in \mathbb{Z}_p$ to hide $\mu \in \mathbb{Z}_p$ as in standard Schnorr-like protocols [81]. Now, the $\mathsf{BadChallenge}$ function can output $\mathsf{Chall} = 1 - b$ if it detects that $\mathbf{a} + b \cdot \mathbf{c}$ is not of the form $(\mathbf{u}, \mathbf{u}^\top \mathbf{s} + z_\mu \cdot p + \mathsf{noise})$, for some

$z_\mu \in \mathbb{Z}_p$. Indeed, this rules out the existence of a short enough $\mathbf{z} \in \mathbb{Z}^m$ such that $\mathbf{a} + b \cdot \mathbf{c} = \bar{\mathbf{A}} \cdot \mathbf{z} + z_\mu \cdot [\mathbf{0}^{n\top}|p]^\top$ with $z_\mu \in \mathbb{Z}_p$. The above technique extends into a trapdoor Σ-protocol for proving plaintext equalities in the ACPS cryptosystem [6]. Our instantiation of Naor-Yung thus requires to work with LWE over a composite modulus q and we leave it as an open problem to extend it to prime moduli.

The main difficulty, however, is to turn the aforementioned trapdoor Σ-protocol into a non-interactive proof system with unbounded simulation-soundness. This problem is non-trivial since the Canetti *et al.* protocol [26,30] is not known to satisfy this security notion[1]. The NIZK simulator of [26,30] generates simulated proofs by "programming" the CI hash function from which the verifier's challenge is derived. In the context of unbounded simulation-soundness [39,80], we cannot proceed in the same way since the simulator would have to program the hash function for each simulated proof (and thus for each challenge ciphertext in the proof of KDM-CCA2 security). Since the number of simulated proofs is not a priori bounded, it is not clear how to do that using a hashing key of length independent of the number of adversarial queries.

Our solution to this problem is inspired by the modification introduced by Canetti *et al.* [26,30] in the Feige-Lapidot-Shamir protocol [42]. In [30, Section 5.2], the first prover message $\mathbf{a}$ is computed using a lossy encryption scheme [10] instead of an ordinary commitment. Recall that, depending on the distribution of the public key PK, a lossy encryption scheme behaves either as an extractable non-interactive commitment or a statistically-hiding commitment. The extractable mode is used to prove the soundness property (by using the secret key SK corresponding to PK to compute the BadChallenge function) while the statistically hiding mode allows proving zero-knowledge. Our unbounded simulation-sound proof system exploits the observation made by Bellare *et al.* [10] that specific lossy encryption schemes admit an efficient opening algorithm. Namely, ciphertexts encrypted under a lossy public key can be equivocated in the same way as a trapdoor commitment using the lossy secret key SK. This suggests that, if the protocol of Canetti *et al.* [26,30] is instantiated using a lossy encryption scheme with efficient opening, we can use a strategy introduced by Damgård [38] to simulate NIZK proofs without programming the CI hash function. Namely, the simulator can generate the first prover message as a lossy encryption of 0. When receiving the verifier's challenge Chall, it can run the HVZK simulator to obtain $(\mathbf{a}, \mathbf{z})$ before using the lossy secret key SK to explain the lossy ciphertext as an encryption of the simulated $\mathbf{a}$. By doing this, we also obtain a multi-theorem NIZK argument without using the FLS transformation [42] and without using any primitive in a non-black-box way. The language of the underlying trapdoor Σ-protocol is exactly the same as that of the multi-theorem NIZK argument, so that, if the former is efficient, so is the latter.

---

[1] It can be generically achieved using NIZK for general NP relations [39] but our goal is to obtain a more efficient solution than generic NIZK techniques. In fact, even one-time simulation-soundness is not proven in [26,30].

However, standard lossy encryption schemes with efficient opening do not suffice to prove unbounded simulation-soundness: We do not only need to equivocate lossy ciphertexts in all simulated proofs, but we should also make sure that the adversary's fake proof is generated for a statistically binding (and even extractable) commitment. For this reason, we rely on a lossy encryption flavor, called $\mathcal{R}$-lossy encryption by Boyle *et al.* [19], where a tag determines whether a ciphertext is lossy or injective. The public key is generated for a computationally hidden initialization value $K \in \mathcal{K}$ and ciphertexts are encrypted under a tag $t \in \mathcal{T}$. If $\mathcal{R} \subset \mathcal{K} \times \mathcal{T}$ is a binary relation, the syntax of $\mathcal{R}$-lossy encryption [19] is that a ciphertext encrypted for a tag $t \in \mathcal{T}$ is injective if $\mathcal{R}(K, t) = 1$ and lossy otherwise. For our purposes, we need to enrich the syntax of $\mathcal{R}$-lossy encryption in two aspects. First, we require lossy ciphertexts to be efficiently equivocable (i.e., the secret key SK should make it possible to find random coins that explain a lossy ciphertext as an encryption of any target plaintext). Second, in order to simplify the description of our NIZK simulator, we need the syntax to support lossy/injective tags *and* lossy/injective keys. When the public key PK is lossy, all ciphertexts are lossy, no matter which tag is used to encrypt. In contrast, injective public keys lead to injective ciphertexts whenever $\mathcal{R}(K, t) = 1$. Our NIZK simulator actually uses lossy public keys while injective keys only show up in the proof of simulation-soundness.

We then construct an $\mathcal{R}$-lossy encryption scheme for the bit-matching relation (i.e., $\mathcal{R}_{\mathsf{BM}}(K, t) = 1$ if and only if K and t agree in all positions where K does not contain a "don't care entry") under the LWE assumption. The scheme can be viewed as a combination of the primal Regev cryptosystem [79] – which is known [77] to be a lossy PKE scheme and is easily seen to support efficient openings as defined in [10] – with the lattice trapdoors of Micciancio and Peikert [74]. An injective public key consists of a matrix $\mathbf{A} \in \mathbb{Z}_q^{n \times m}$ with short vectors in its row space. In order to encrypt $\boldsymbol{\mu} \in \{0, 1\}^{n_0}$ under a tag t, we sample a short Gaussian $\mathbf{r} \in \mathbb{Z}^{2m}$ and compute $\mathbf{c} = [\mathbf{A} \mid \mathbf{A} \cdot \mathbf{R}_t + (1 - \mathcal{R}(K, t)) \cdot \mathbf{G}] \cdot \mathbf{r} + [\mathbf{0} \mid \boldsymbol{\mu} \cdot \lfloor q/2 \rfloor]^\top$, for some small-norm $\mathbf{R}_t \in \mathbb{Z}^{m \times m}$, where $\mathbf{G} \in \mathbb{Z}_q^{n \times m}$ is the gadget matrix of [74]. In each lossy tag, we have $\mathcal{R}(K, t) = 0$, in which case the matrix $\mathbf{R}_t$ can be used as a trapdoor (using the techniques of [2,74]) to sample a Gaussian $\mathbf{r} \in \mathbb{Z}^{2m}$ that explains $\mathbf{c}$ as an encryption of any arbitrary $\boldsymbol{\mu} \in \{0, 1\}^{n_0}$. In injective tags, we have $\mathcal{R}(K, t) = 1$, so that the gadget matrix vanishes from the matrix $\mathbf{A}_t = [\mathbf{A} \mid \mathbf{A} \cdot \mathbf{R}_t + (1 - \mathcal{R}(K, t)) \cdot \mathbf{G}]$. Since $\mathbf{A}$ has short vectors in its row space, so does $\mathbf{A}_t$ and we can thus use these short vectors to recover $\boldsymbol{\mu}$ from $\mathbf{c}$ exactly as in the primal Regev cryptosystem. When the public key PK is lossy, the matrix $\mathbf{A}$ is replaced by a statistically uniform matrix over $\mathbb{Z}_q^{n \times m}$. We can then use a trapdoor for $\Lambda^\perp(\mathbf{A})$ to equivocate lossy ciphertexts for any arbitrary tag.

Our USS argument system uses our $\mathcal{R}$-lossy encryption scheme – with the standard trick of using the verification key of a one-time signature as a tag – to compute the first prover message $\mathbf{a}$ by encrypting the first message $\mathbf{a}'$ of a basic trapdoor Σ-protocol. In the security proof, we have a noticeable probability that: (i) For all adversarially-chosen statements, proofs can be simulated by equivocating lossy ciphertexts; (ii) When the adversary comes up with a proof of its own, the underlying commitment is an injective ciphertext. If these conditions are fulfilled, we can annihilate the adversary's chance of proving a false statement by using a hash function which is statistically CI for the relation that evaluates the BadChallenge function on input of the decryption of an $\mathcal{R}$-lossy ciphertext.

At a high-level, our simulation-sound proof system bears similarities with interactive proof systems described by MacKenzie and Yang [72]. Our extension of $\mathcal{R}$-lossy encryption resembles their notion of simulation-sound trapdoor commitments. The difference is that, while [72] only requires commitments to be computationally binding for tags that have never been equivocated, we need adversarially-chosen tags to be extractable.

Our first USS argument system does not provide tight security because it relies on admissible hash functions [14] to partition the tag space of the $\mathcal{R}$-lossy PKE scheme into two disjoint subspaces (which contain equivocable and extractable tags, respectively). In order to obtain tight simulation-soundness, our second USS argument partitions the tag space of an $\mathcal{R}$-lossy PKE scheme using a pseudorandom function instead of an admissible hash function. For this purpose, we build an $\mathcal{R}$-lossy PKE scheme for a relation $\mathcal{R}_{\mathsf{PRF}}$ induced by a PRF family. Analogously to [55], we consider tags $t = (t_c, t_a)$ consisting of an auxiliary component t_a (which can be an arbitrary string) and core component t_c. The PRF-induced relation $\mathcal{R}_{\mathsf{PRF}}$ is then defined as $\mathcal{R}_{\mathsf{PRF}}(K, (t_c, t_a)) = 1$ if and only if $t_c \neq \mathsf{PRF}_K(t_a)$, where K is the PRF secret key. Our $\mathcal{R}_{\mathsf{PRF}}$-lossy PKE then proceeds as in [67] and uses a public key containing Gentry-Sahai-Waters encryptions [47] $\mathbf{A}_i = \mathbf{A} \cdot \mathbf{R}_i + k_i \cdot \mathbf{G}$ of the bits of K. To encrypt $\boldsymbol{\mu} \in \{0,1\}^{n_0}$ under a tag $t = (t_c, t_a)$, the encryptor first homomorphically computes $\mathbf{A}_{F,t} = \mathbf{A} \cdot \mathbf{R}_t + (1 - \mathcal{R}_{\mathsf{PRF}}(K, t)) \cdot \mathbf{G}$ before sampling a short Gaussian $\mathbf{r} \in \mathbb{Z}^{2m}$ and computing $\mathbf{c} = [\mathbf{A} \mid \mathbf{A}_{F,t}] \cdot \mathbf{r} + [\mathbf{0} \mid \boldsymbol{\mu} \cdot \lfloor q/2 \rfloor]^\top$. In the proof of simulation-soundness, the reduction simulates all arguments by "adaptively programming" all tags $t = (\mathsf{PRF}_K(t_a), t_a)$ to ensure equivocability. At the same time, the adversary can only output an argument on an extractable tag $t^\star = (t_c^\star, t_a^\star)$, where $\mathcal{R}_{\mathsf{PRF}}(K, t^\star) = 1$, unless it can predict $t_c^\star = \mathsf{PRF}_K(t_a^\star)$.

1.3   Related Work

FIAT-SHAMIR IN THE STANDARD MODEL. The Fiat-Shamir methodology was shown [49] not to be sound in the standard model in general. Known negative results (see [12,49] and references therein) nevertheless left open the existence of secure instantiations of the paradigm when specific protocols are transformed using concrete hash functions. Of particular interest is the notion of *correlation intractable* hash function [28], which rules out specific relations between an input and its hash value. It was actually shown [52] that correlation intractability for all sparse relations[2] suffices to ensure soundness as long as the underlying

---

[2] A relation $R \subset \mathcal{X} \times \mathcal{Y}$ is sparse if, for a given $x \in \mathcal{X}$, the fraction of $y \in \mathcal{Y}$ for which $(x, y) \in R$ is negligible.

protocol is statistically sound. A recent line of work [25,27,58,82] focused on the design of correlation intractable hash functions leading to sound instantiation of Fiat-Shamir in the standard model. Canetti *et al.* [26] showed that it is actually sufficient to obtain correlation intractable hash families for *efficiently searchable* relations (i.e., where each x has at most one corresponding y, which is computable within some polynomial time bound). This opened the way to CI hash candidates based on more established assumptions like the circular security of fully homomorphic encryption (FHE) schemes [30]. Peikert and Shiehian [76] recently gave an elegant FHE-based solution relying on the hardness of the LWE problem [79] with polynomial approximation factors. While specific to the Gentry-Sahai-Waters (GSW) FHE [47], their construction does not require any non-standard circular security assumption. Together with the techniques of [26,30], it implies NIZK for all NP languages.

In [26,30], Canetti *et al.* showed that, besides the language of Hamiltonian graphs considered in [42], trapdoor Σ-protocols also exist for other languages like that of quadratic residues modulo a composite integer [48]. Using the CI hash function of [76], they thus obtained a NIZK proof for the Quadratic Residuosity language under the LWE assumption. Choudhuri *et al.* [32] showed that the hash families of [26] make the transformation sound for the sumcheck protocol.

MULTI-THEOREM NIZK. Several multi-theorem NIZK constructions are available in the literature (see, e.g., [31,40,42,50]). Under the LWE assumption, all solutions so far either rely on the FLS transformation [34,76] – thus incurring proofs of OR statements via non-black-box techniques – or restrict themselves to the designated verifier setting [34,68]. While the meta-proof approach of De Santis and Yung [40] provides an alternative to FLS, it makes non-black-box use of a single-theorem proof system for an NP-complete language. Our construction uses a single-theorem argument for the same language as the one for which we need a multi-theorem argument. Hence, if the former is efficient, so is the latter.

KDM SECURITY. This security notion was first formalized by Black, Rogaway and Shrimpton [13] and motivated by applications in anonymous credentials [23] or in disk encryption (e.g., in the BitLocker encryption utility [16]), where the key may be stored on the disk being encrypted. The first examples of KDM-secure secret-key encryption were given by Black *et al.* [13] in the random oracle model.

In the standard model, Boneh *et al.* [16] designed the first public-key scheme with provable KDM-CPA security w.r.t. all affine functions under the decisional Diffie-Hellman (DDH) assumption. Applebaum *et al.* [6] showed that a variant of Regev's system [79] is KDM-secure for all affine functions under the LWE assumption. They also gave a secret-key construction based on the hardness of the Learning Parity with Noise (LPN) problem for which Döttling gave a public-key variant [41]. Under the Quadratic Residuosity (QR) and Decisional Composite Residuosity (DCR) assumptions, Brakerski and Goldwasser [20] gave alternative constructions that additionally provide security under key leakage. Alperin-Sheriff and Peikert [4] showed that a variant of the identity-based encryption scheme of Agrawal *et al.* [2] provides KDM security for a bounded number of challenge ciphertexts.

Brakerski *et al.* [21] and Barak *et al.* [8] came up with different techniques to prove KDM security for richer function families. Malkin *et al.* [73] suggested a much more efficient scheme with ciphertexts of $O(d)$ group elements for function families containing degree d polynomials. Applebaum [5] put forth a generic technique that turns any PKE scheme with KDM security for projection functions – where each output bit only depends on a single input bit – into a scheme providing KDM security for any circuit of a priori bounded polynomial size.

KDM-CCA SECURITY. The first PKE scheme with KDM-CCA2 security in the standard model appeared in the work of Camenisch, Chandran, and Shoup [24]. They gave a generic construction based on the Naor-Yung paradigm that combines a KDM-CPA system, a standard CPA-secure encryption scheme, and a simulation-sound NIZK proof system. For their purposes, they crucially need *unbounded* simulation-soundness since the KDM setting inherently involves many challenge ciphertexts and single-challenge security is not known to imply multi-challenge security. They instantiated their construction using the DDH-based KDM-CPA system of Boneh *et al* [16] and Groth-Sahai proofs [51]. Our scheme is an instantiation of the generic construction of [24] in the lattice setting, where we cannot simply use Groth-Sahai proofs. Hofheinz [56] subsequently obtained chosen-ciphertext circular security (i.e., for selection functions where $f(SK_1, \ldots, SK_N) = SK_i$ for some $i \in [N]$) with shorter ciphertexts.

A first attempt of KDM-CCA security without pairings was made by Lu *et al.* [69]. Han *et al.* [53] identified a bug in [69] and gave a patch using the same methodology. They obtained KDM-CCA security for bounded-degree polynomial functions under the DDH and DCR assumptions. Kitigawa and Tanaka [63] described a framework for the design of KDM-CCA systems under a single number theoretic assumption (i.e., DDH, QR, or DCR). Their results were extended by Kitigawa *et al.* [62] so as to prove tight KDM-CCA2 security under the DCR assumption. Since the framework of [63] relies on hash proof systems [37], it is not known to provide LWE-based realizations (indeed, hash proof systems do not readily enable chosen-ciphertext security from LWE), let alone with tight security. To our knowledge, our scheme is thus the first explicit solution with tight KDM-CCA2 security under the LWE assumption. Before [62], the only pathway to tight KDM-CCA security was to instantiate the construction of Camenisch *et al.* [24] using a tightly secure USS proof/argument (e.g., [57]), which tends to incur very large ciphertexts. Our system also follows this approach with the difference that ciphertexts are not much longer than in its non-tight variant.

Kitigawa and Matsuda [61] generically obtained KDM-CCA security for bounded-size circuits from any system providing KDM-CPA security for projection functions. While their result shows the equivalence between KDM-CPA and KDM-CCA security, our scheme is conceptually simpler and significantly more efficient than an LWE-based instantiation of the construction in [61]. In particular, such an instantiation requires both garbling schemes and $\Omega(\lambda)$ designated-verifier proofs of plaintext equalities with negligible soundness error. While these proofs seem realizable by applying the techniques of [68] to specific Σ-protocols, each of them would cost $\Omega(\lambda^2)$ public-key encryptions. Our scheme is much simpler and only requires one argument of plaintext equality, thus compressing ciphertexts by a factor at least $\Omega(\lambda)$.

1.4 Organization

Section 2 first recalls the the building blocks of our constructions. Our first simulation-sound argument is presented in Sect. 3 together with the underlying $\mathcal{R}$-lossy PKE scheme. Its tightly secure variant is described in Sect. 4. In Sect. 5, we give a trapdoor Σ-protocol allowing to apply the Naor-Yung transformation to the ACPS cryptosystem. The resulting (tightly secure) KDM-CCA2 system is then detailed in the full version of the paper [65]. As written, our security proof only shows tightness in the number of challenge ciphertexts, but not in the number of users. In the full version of the paper, we also explain how to also obtain tightness w.r.t. the number of users.

2 Background

We recall the main tools involved in our constructions. Additional standard tools, such as NIZK proofs, are defined in the full version of the paper.

2.1 Lattices

For any $q \geq 2$, $\mathbb{Z}_q$ denotes the ring of integers with addition and multiplication modulo q. If $\mathbf{x} \in \mathbb{R}^n$ is a vector, $\|\mathbf{x}\| = \sqrt{\sum_{i=1}^n x_i^2}$ denotes its Euclidean norm and $\|\mathbf{x}\|_\infty = \max_i |x_i|$ its infinity norm. If $\mathbf{M}$ is a matrix over $\mathbb{R}$, then $\|\mathbf{M}\| := \sup_{\mathbf{x} \neq 0} \frac{\|\mathbf{M}\mathbf{x}\|}{\|\mathbf{x}\|}$ and $\|\mathbf{M}\|_\infty := \sup_{\mathbf{x} \neq 0} \frac{\|\mathbf{M}\mathbf{x}\|_\infty}{\|\mathbf{x}\|_\infty}$ denote its induced norms. For a finite set S, $U(S)$ stands for the uniform distribution over S. If X and Y are distributions over the same domain, $\Delta(X, Y)$ denotes their statistical distance.

Let $\boldsymbol{\Sigma} \in \mathbb{R}^{n \times n}$ be a symmetric positive-definite matrix, and $\mathbf{c} \in \mathbb{R}^n$. We define the Gaussian function on $\mathbb{R}^n$ by $\rho_{\boldsymbol{\Sigma}, \mathbf{c}}(\mathbf{x}) = \exp(-\pi(\mathbf{x} - \mathbf{c})^\top \boldsymbol{\Sigma}^{-1}(\mathbf{x} - \mathbf{c}))$ and if $\boldsymbol{\Sigma} = \sigma^2 \cdot \mathbf{I}_n$ and $\mathbf{c} = \mathbf{0}$ we denote it by ρ_σ. For an n dimensional lattice $\Lambda \subset \mathbb{R}^n$ and for any lattice vector $\mathbf{x} \in \Lambda$ the discrete Gaussian is defined by $\rho_{\Lambda, \boldsymbol{\Sigma}, \mathbf{c}}(\mathbf{x}) = \frac{\rho_{\boldsymbol{\Sigma}, \mathbf{c}}}{\rho_{\boldsymbol{\Sigma}, \mathbf{c}}(\Lambda)}$.

For an n-dimensional lattice Λ, we define $\eta_\varepsilon(\Lambda)$ as the smallest $r > 0$ such that $\rho_{1/r}(\widehat{\Lambda} \setminus \mathbf{0}) \leq \varepsilon$ with $\widehat{\Lambda}$ denoting the dual of Λ, for any $\varepsilon \in (0, 1)$.

For a matrix $\mathbf{A} \in \mathbb{Z}_q^{n \times m}$, we define $\Lambda^\perp(\mathbf{A}) = \{\mathbf{x} \in \mathbb{Z}^m : \mathbf{A} \cdot \mathbf{x} = \mathbf{0} \bmod q\}$ and $\Lambda(\mathbf{A}) = \mathbf{A}^\top \cdot \mathbb{Z}^n + q\mathbb{Z}^m$. For an arbitrary vector $\mathbf{u} \in \mathbb{Z}_q^n$, we also define the shifted lattice $\Lambda^\mathbf{u}(\mathbf{A}) = \{\mathbf{x} \in \mathbb{Z}^m : \mathbf{A} \cdot \mathbf{x} = \mathbf{u} \bmod q\}$.

Definition 2.1 (LWE). *Let $m \geq n \geq 1$, $q \geq 2$ and $\alpha \in (0, 1)$ be functions of a security parameter λ. The LWE problem consists in distinguishing between the distributions $(\mathbf{A}, \mathbf{A}\mathbf{s} + \mathbf{e})$ and $U(\mathbb{Z}_q^{m \times n} \times \mathbb{Z}_q^m)$, where $\mathbf{A} \sim U(\mathbb{Z}_q^{m \times n})$, $\mathbf{s} \sim U(\mathbb{Z}_q^n)$ and $\mathbf{e} \sim D_{\mathbb{Z}^m, \alpha q}$. For an algorithm $\mathcal{A} : \mathbb{Z}_q^{m \times n} \times \mathbb{Z}_q^m \to \{0, 1\}$, we define:*

$$\mathbf{Adv}_{q,m,n,\alpha}^{\mathsf{LWE}}(\lambda) = |\Pr[\mathcal{A}(\mathbf{A}, \mathbf{A}\mathbf{s} + \mathbf{e}) = 1] - \Pr[\mathcal{A}(\mathbf{A}, \mathbf{u}) = 1| \ ,$$

where the probabilities are over $\mathbf{A} \sim U(\mathbb{Z}_q^{m \times n})$, $\mathbf{s} \sim U(\mathbb{Z}_q^n)$, $\mathbf{u} \sim U(\mathbb{Z}_q^m)$ and $\mathbf{e} \sim D_{\mathbb{Z}^m, \alpha q}$ and the internal randomness of $\mathcal{A}$. We say that $\mathsf{LWE}_{q,m,n,\alpha}$ is hard if, for any PPT algorithm $\mathcal{A}$, the advantage $\mathbf{Adv}_{q,m,n,\alpha}^{\mathsf{LWE}}(\mathcal{A})$ is negligible.

Micciancio and Peikert [74] described a trapdoor mechanism for LWE. Their technique uses a "gadget" matrix $\mathbf{G} \in \mathbb{Z}_q^{n \times w}$, with $w = n \log q$, for which anyone can publicly sample short vectors $\mathbf{x} \in \mathbb{Z}^w$ such that $\mathbf{G} \cdot \mathbf{x} = \mathbf{0}$.

Lemma 2.2 ([74, Section 5]). *Assume that $\bar{m} \geq n \log q + O(\lambda)$ and $m = \bar{m} + n\lceil \log q \rceil$. There exists a probabilistic polynomial time (PPT) algorithm GenTrap that takes as inputs matrices $\bar{\mathbf{A}} \in \mathbb{Z}_q^{n \times \bar{m}}$, $\mathbf{H} \in \mathbb{Z}_q^{n \times n}$ and outputs matrices $\mathbf{R} \in \{-1, 1\}^{\bar{m} \times n \cdot \lceil \log q \rceil}$ and $\mathbf{A} = [\bar{\mathbf{A}} \mid \bar{\mathbf{A}} \mathbf{R} + \mathbf{H} \cdot \mathbf{G}] \in \mathbb{Z}_q^{n \times m}$ such that if $\mathbf{H} \in \mathbb{Z}_q^{n \times n}$ is invertible, then $\mathbf{R}$ is a $\mathbf{G}$-trapdoor for $\mathbf{A}$ with tag $\mathbf{H}$; and if $\mathbf{H} = \mathbf{0}$, then $\mathbf{R}$ is a punctured trapdoor.*

Further, in case of a $\mathbf{G}$-trapdoor, one can efficiently compute from $\mathbf{A}, \mathbf{R}$ and $\mathbf{H}$ a basis $(\mathbf{t}_i)_{i \leq m}$ of $\Lambda^\perp(\mathbf{A})$ such that $\max_i \|\mathbf{t}_i\| \leq O(m^{3/2})$.

Lemma 2.3 ([46, Theorem 4.1]). *There is a PPT algorithm that, given a basis $\mathbf{B}$ of an n-dimensional $\Lambda = \Lambda(\mathbf{B})$, a parameter $s > \|\tilde{\mathbf{B}}\| \cdot \omega(\sqrt{\log n})$, and a center $\mathbf{c} \in \mathbb{R}^n$, outputs a sample from a distribution statistically close to $D_{\Lambda, s, \mathbf{c}}$.*

2.2 Correlation Intractable Hash Functions

We consider unique-output searchable binary relations [26]. These are binary relations such that, for every x, there is at most one y such that $R(x, y) = 1$ and y is efficiently computable from x.

Definition 2.4 *A relation $R \subseteq \mathcal{X} \times \mathcal{Y}$ is **searchable** in time T if there exists a function $f : \mathcal{X} \to \mathcal{Y}$ which is computable in time T and such that, if there exists y such that $(x, y) \in R$, then $f(x) = y$.*

Letting $\lambda \in \mathbb{N}$ denote a security parameter, a hash family with input length $n(\lambda)$ and output length $m(\lambda)$ is a collection $\mathcal{H} = \{h_\lambda : \{0, 1\}^{s(\lambda)} \times \{0, 1\}^{n(\lambda)} \to \{0, 1\}^{m(\lambda)}\}$ of keyed hash functions implemented by efficient algorithms (Gen, Hash), where $\mathsf{Gen}(1^\lambda)$ outputs a key $k \in \{0, 1\}^{s(\lambda)}$ and $\mathsf{Hash}(k, x)$ computes a hash value $h_\lambda(k, x) \in \{0, 1\}^{m(\lambda)}$.

Definition 2.5 *For a relation ensemble $\{R_\lambda \subseteq \{0, 1\}^{n(\lambda)} \times \{0, 1\}^{m(\lambda)}\}$, a hash function family $\mathcal{H} = \{h_\lambda : \{0, 1\}^{s(\lambda)} \times \{0, 1\}^{n(\lambda)} \to \{0, 1\}^{m(\lambda)}\}$ is R-**correlation intractable** if, for any probabilistic polynomial time (PPT) adversary $\mathcal{A}$, we have $\Pr[k \leftarrow \mathsf{Gen}(1^\lambda)), x \leftarrow \mathcal{A}(k) : (x, h_\lambda(k, x)) \in R] = \mathsf{negl}(\lambda)$.*

Peikert and Shiehian [76] described a correlation-intractable hash family for any searchable relation (in the sense of Definition 2.4) defined by functions f of bounded depth. Their construction relies on the standard Short Integer Solution assumption (which is implied by LWE) with polynomial approximation factors.

2.3 Admissible Hash Functions

Admissible hash functions were introduced in [14] as a combinatorial tool for partitioning-based security proofs. A simplified definition was given in [45].

Definition 2.6 ([14,45]). *Let $\ell(\lambda), L(\lambda) \in \mathbb{N}$ be functions of $\lambda \in \mathbb{N}$. Let an efficiently computable function* $\mathsf{AHF} : \{0,1\}^\ell \to \{0,1\}^L$. *For each $K \in \{0,1,\bot\}^L$, let the partitioning function* $F_{\mathsf{ADH}}(K, \cdot) : \{0,1\}^\ell \to \{0,1\}$ *such that*

$$F_{\mathsf{ADH}}(K, X) := \begin{cases} 0 & \text{if} \quad \forall i \in [L] \quad (\mathsf{AHF}(X)_i = K_i) \vee (K_i = \bot) \\ 1 & \text{otherwise} \end{cases}$$

We say that AHF *is an* **admissible hash function** *if there exists an efficient algorithm* $\mathsf{AdmSmp}(1^\lambda, Q, \delta)$ *that takes as input $Q \in \mathsf{poly}(\lambda)$ and a non-negligible $\delta(\lambda) \in (0,1]$ and outputs a key $K \in \{0,1,\bot\}^L$ such that, for all $X^{(1)}, \ldots, X^{(Q)}, X^\star \in \{0,1\}^\ell$ such that $X^\star \notin \{X^{(1)}, \ldots, X^{(Q)}\}$, we have*

$$\Pr_K\left[F_{\mathsf{ADH}}(K, X^{(1)}) = \cdots = F_{\mathsf{ADH}}(K, X^{(Q)}) = 1 \wedge F_{\mathsf{ADH}}(K, X^\star) = 0\right] \geq \delta(Q(\lambda)) .$$

It is known that admissible hash functions exist for $\ell, L = \Theta(\lambda)$.

Theorem 2.7 ([59, Theorem 1]). *Let $(C_\ell)_{\ell \in \mathbb{N}}$ be a family of codes $C_\ell : \{0,1\}^\ell \to \{0,1\}^L$ with minimal distance $c \cdot L$ for some constant $c \in (0, 1/2)$. Then, $(C_\ell)_{\ell \in \mathbb{N}}$ is a family of admissible hash functions. Furthermore, $\mathsf{AdmSmp}(1^\lambda, Q, \delta)$ outputs a key $K \in \{0,1,\bot\}^L$ for which $\eta = O(\log \lambda)$ components are not $\bot$ and $\delta(Q(\lambda))$ is a non-negligible function of λ.*

Jager proved [59] Theorem 2.7 for *balanced* admissible hash functions, which provide both a lower bound and a close upper bound for the probability in Definition 2.6. Here, we only need the standard definition of admissible hash functions since we use them in a game where the adversary aims at outputting a hard-to-compute result (instead of breaking an indistinguishability property). However, the result of Theorem 2.7 applies to standard admissible hash functions.

2.4 Trapdoor Σ-protocols

Canetti *et al.* [30] considered a definition of Σ-protocols that slightly differs from the usual formulation [35,36].

Definition 2.8 (Adapted from [7,30]). *Let a language $\mathcal{L} = (\mathcal{L}_{\mathsf{zk}}, \mathcal{L}_{\mathsf{sound}})$ associated with two NP relations $R_{\mathsf{zk}}, R_{\mathsf{sound}}$. A 3-move interactive proof system $\Pi = (\mathsf{Gen}_{\mathsf{par}}, \mathsf{Gen}_\mathcal{L}, \mathsf{P}, \mathsf{V})$ in the common reference string model is a Gap Σ-protocol for $\mathcal{L}$ if it satisfies the following conditions:*

- **3-Move Form:** *The prover and the verifier both take as input* $\mathsf{crs} = (\mathsf{par}, \mathsf{crs}_\mathcal{L})$, *with* $\mathsf{par} \leftarrow \mathsf{Gen}_{\mathsf{par}}(1^\lambda)$ *and* $\mathsf{crs}_\mathcal{L} \leftarrow \mathsf{Gen}_\mathcal{L}(\mathsf{par}, \mathcal{L})$, *and a statement x and proceed as follows: (i) P takes in $w \in R_{\mathsf{zk}}(x)$, computes $(\mathbf{a}, st) \leftarrow \mathsf{P}(\mathsf{crs}, x, w)$ and sends $\mathbf{a}$ to the verifier; (ii) V sends back a random challenge Chall from the challenge space $\mathcal{C}$; (iii) P finally sends a response $\mathbf{z} = \mathsf{P}(\mathsf{crs}, x, w, \mathbf{a}, \mathsf{Chall}, st)$ to V; (iv) On input of $(\mathbf{a}, \mathsf{Chall}, \mathbf{z})$, V outputs 1 or 0.*

- **Completeness:** *If* $(x, w) \in R_{zk}$ *and* P *honestly computes* $(\mathbf{a}, \mathbf{z})$ *for a challenge* Chall, $V(crs, x, (\mathbf{a}, Chall, \mathbf{z}))$ *outputs* 1 *with probability* $1 - \mathsf{negl}(\lambda)$.
- **Special zero-knowledge:** *There is a PPT simulator* ZKSim *that, on input of* crs, $x \in \mathcal{L}_{zk}$ *and a challenge* Chall $\in \mathcal{C}$, *outputs* $(\mathbf{a}, \mathbf{z}) \leftarrow$ ZKSim$(crs, x, Chall)$ *such that* $(\mathbf{a}, Chall, \mathbf{z})$ *is computationally indistinguishable from a real transcript with challenge* Chall *(for* $w \in R_{zk}(x)$).
- **Special soundness:** *For any CRS* crs $= (par, crs_{\mathcal{L}})$ *obtained as* par $\leftarrow$ Gen$_{par}(1^\lambda)$, crs$_{\mathcal{L}} \leftarrow$ Gen$_{\mathcal{L}}(par, \mathcal{L})$, *any* $x \notin \mathcal{L}_{sound}$, *and any first message* $\mathbf{a}$ *sent by* P, *there is at most one challenge* Chall $= f(crs, x, \mathbf{a})$ *for which an accepting transcript* $(crs, x, \mathbf{a}, Chall, \mathbf{z})$ *exists for some third message* $\mathbf{z}$. *The function* f *is called the "bad challenge function" of* Π. *That is, if* $x \notin \mathcal{L}_{sound}$ *and the challenge differs from the bad challenge, the verifier never accepts.*

Definition 2.8 is taken from [7,30] and relaxes the standard special soundness property in that extractability is not required. Instead, it considers a bad challenge function f, which may not be efficiently computable. Canetti *et al.* [30] define *trapdoor* Σ-*protocols* as Σ-protocols where the bad challenge function is efficiently computable using a trapdoor. They also define instance-dependent trapdoor Σ-protocol where the trapdoor τ_Σ should be generated as a function of some instance $x \notin \mathcal{L}_{sound}$. Here, we use a definition where x need not be known in advance (which is not possible in applications to chosen-ciphertext security, where x is determined by a decryption query) and the trapdoor does not depend on a specific x. However, the common reference string and the trapdoor may depend on the language (which is determined by the public key in our application).

The common reference string crs $= (par, crs_{\mathcal{L}})$ consists of a fixed part par and a language-dependent part crs$_{\mathcal{L}}$ which is generated as a function of par and a language parameter $\mathcal{L} = (\mathcal{L}_{zk}, \mathcal{L}_{sound})$.

Definition 2.9 (Adapted from [30]). *A* Σ-*protocol* $\Pi = (\mathsf{Gen}_{par}, \mathsf{Gen}_{\mathcal{L}}, \mathsf{P}, \mathsf{V})$ *with bad challenge function* f *for a trapdoor language* $\mathcal{L} = (\mathcal{L}_{zk}, \mathcal{L}_{sound})$ *is a* **trapdoor** Σ-**protocol** *if it satisfies the properties of Definition 2.8 and there exist PPT algorithms* $(\mathsf{TrapGen}, \mathsf{BadChallenge})$ *with the following properties.*

- Gen_{par} *inputs* $\lambda \in \mathbb{N}$ *and outputs public parameters* par $\leftarrow \mathsf{Gen}_{par}(1^\lambda)$.
- $\mathsf{Gen}_{\mathcal{L}}$ *is a randomized algorithm that, on input of public parameters* par, *outputs the language-dependent part* crs$_{\mathcal{L}} \leftarrow \mathsf{Gen}_{\mathcal{L}}(par, \mathcal{L})$ *of* crs $= (par, crs_{\mathcal{L}})$.
- $\mathsf{TrapGen}(par, \mathcal{L}, \tau_{\mathcal{L}})$ *takes as input public parameters* par *and a membership-testing trapdoor* $\tau_{\mathcal{L}}$ *for the language* $\mathcal{L}_{sound}$. *It outputs a common reference string* crs$_{\mathcal{L}}$ *and a trapdoor* $\tau_\Sigma \in \{0, 1\}^{\ell_\tau}$, *for some* $\ell_\tau(\lambda)$.
- $\mathsf{BadChallenge}(\tau_\Sigma, crs, x, \mathbf{a})$ *takes in a trapdoor* τ_Σ, *a CRS* crs $= (par, crs_{\mathcal{L}})$, *an instance* x, *and a first prover message* $\mathbf{a}$. *It outputs a challenge* Chall.

In addition, the following properties are required.

- **CRS indistinguishability:** *For any* par $\leftarrow \mathsf{Gen}_{par}(1^\lambda)$, *and any trapdoor* $\tau_{\mathcal{L}}$ *for the language* $\mathcal{L}$, *an honestly generated* crs$_{\mathcal{L}}$ *is computationally indistinguishable from a CRS produced by* $\mathsf{TrapGen}(par, \mathcal{L}, \tau_{\mathcal{L}})$. *Namely, for any* aux *and any PPT distinguisher* $\mathcal{A}$, *we have*

$$\mathbf{Adv}_{\mathcal{A}}^{\text{indist-}\Sigma}(\lambda) := |\Pr[\text{crs}_{\mathcal{L}} \leftarrow \text{Gen}_{\mathcal{L}}(\text{par}, \mathcal{L}) : \mathcal{A}(\text{par}, \text{crs}_{\mathcal{L}}) = 1]$$
$$- \Pr[(\text{crs}_{\mathcal{L}}, \tau_{\Sigma}) \leftarrow \text{TrapGen}(\text{par}, \mathcal{L}, \tau_{\mathcal{L}}) : \mathcal{A}(\text{par}, \text{crs}_{\mathcal{L}}) = 1]| \leq \text{negl}(\lambda).$$

- **Correctness:** *There exists a language-specific trapdoor $\tau_{\mathcal{L}}$ such that, for any instance $x \notin \mathcal{L}_{\text{sound}}$ and all pairs $(\text{crs}_{\mathcal{L}}, \tau_{\Sigma}) \leftarrow \text{TrapGen}(\text{par}, \mathcal{L}, \tau_{\mathcal{L}})$, we have* $\text{BadChallenge}(\tau_{\Sigma}, \text{crs}, x, \mathbf{a}) = f(\text{crs}, x, \mathbf{a})$.

Note that the TrapGen algorithm does not take a specific statement x as input, but only a trapdoor $\tau_{\mathcal{L}}$ allowing to recognize elements of $\mathcal{L}_{\text{sound}}$.

2.5 $\mathcal{R}$-Lossy Public-Key Encryption With Efficient Opening

We generalize the notion of $\mathcal{R}$-lossy public-key encryption introduced by Boyle *et al.* [19]. As defined in [19], it is a tag-based encryption scheme [60] where the tag space $\mathcal{T}$ is partitioned into a set of *injective* tags and a set of *lossy* tags. When ciphertexts are generated for an injective tag, the decryption algorithm correctly recovers the underlying plaintext. When messages are encrypted under lossy tags, the ciphertext is statistically independent of the plaintext. In $\mathcal{R}$-lossy PKE schemes, the tag space is partitioned according to a binary relation $\mathcal{R} \subseteq \mathcal{K} \times \mathcal{T}$. The key generation algorithm takes as input an initialization value $K \in \mathcal{K}$ and partitions $\mathcal{T}$ in such a way that injective tags $t \in \mathcal{T}$ are exactly those for which $(K, t) \in \mathcal{R}$ (i.e., all tags t for which $(K, t) \notin \mathcal{R}$ are lossy).

From a security standpoint, the definitions of [19] require the initialization value K to be computationally hidden by the public key. For our purposes, we need to introduce additional requirements.

First, we require the existence of a lossy key generation algorithm LKeygen which outputs public keys with respect to which all tags t are lossy (in contrast with injective keys where the only lossy tags are those for which $(K, t) \notin \mathcal{R}$). Second, we also ask that the secret key makes it possible to equivocate lossy ciphertexts (a property called *efficient opening* by Bellare *et al.* [10]) using an algorithm called Opener. Finally, we use two distinct opening algorithms Opener and LOpener. The former operates over (lossy and injective) public keys for lossy tags while the latter can equivocate ciphertexts encrypted under lossy keys for any tag.

Definition 2.10. *Let $\mathcal{R} \subseteq \mathcal{K}_{\lambda} \times \mathcal{T}_{\lambda}$ be an efficiently computable binary relation. An $\mathcal{R}$-lossy PKE scheme with efficient opening is a 7-uple of PPT algorithms (Par-Gen, Keygen, LKeygen, Encrypt, Decrypt, Opener, LOpener) such that:*

Parameter generation: *On input a security parameter λ, Par-Gen(1^{λ}) outputs public parameters Γ.*

Key generation: *For an initialization value $K \in \mathcal{K}_{\lambda}$ and public parameters Γ, algorithm Keygen(Γ, K) outputs an injective public key $pk \in \mathcal{PK}$, a decryption key $sk \in \mathcal{SK}$ and a trapdoor key $tk \in \mathcal{TK}$. The public key specifies a ciphertext space CtSp and a randomness space R^{LPKE}.*

Lossy Key generation: *Given an initialization value $K \in \mathcal{K}_\lambda$ and public parameters Γ, the lossy key generation algorithm* LKeygen(Γ, K) *outputs a lossy public key $pk \in \mathcal{PK}$, a lossy secret key $sk \in \mathcal{SK}$ and a trapdoor key $tk \in \mathcal{TK}$.*

Decryption under injective tags: *For any initialization value $K \in \mathcal{K}$, any tag $t \in \mathcal{T}$ such that $(K, t) \in \mathcal{R}$, and any message* Msg $\in$ MsgSp, *we have*

$$\Pr\left[\exists r \in R^{\mathsf{LPKE}} : \mathsf{Decrypt}\big(sk, t, \mathsf{Encrypt}(pk, t, \mathsf{Msg}; r)\big) \neq \mathsf{Msg}\right] < \nu(\lambda) \ ,$$

for some negligible function $\nu(\lambda)$, where $(pk, sk, tk) \leftarrow$ Keygen(Γ, K) and the probability is taken over the randomness of Keygen.

Indistinguishability: *Algorithms* LKeygen *and* Keygen *satisfy the following:*

(i) For any $K \in \mathcal{K}_\lambda$, the distributions $D_{\mathsf{inj}} = \{(pk, tk) \mid (pk, sk, tk) \leftarrow$ Keygen$(\Gamma, K)\}$ and $D_{\mathsf{loss}} = \{(pk, tk) \mid (pk, sk, tk) \leftarrow$ LKeygen$(\Gamma, K)\}$ are computationally indistinguishable. Namely, for any PPT adversary $\mathcal{A}$, we have $\mathbf{Adv}_{\mathcal{A}}^{\mathsf{indist\text{-}LPKE\text{-}1}}(\lambda) \leq \mathsf{negl}(\lambda)$, where

$$\mathbf{Adv}_{\mathcal{A}}^{\mathsf{indist\text{-}LPKE\text{-}1}}(\lambda) := |\Pr[(pk, tk) \hookleftarrow D_{\mathsf{inj}} : \mathcal{A}(pk, tk) = 1]$$
$$- \Pr[(pk, tk) \hookleftarrow D_{\mathsf{loss}} : \mathcal{A}(pk, tk) = 1]| \ .$$

(ii) For any distinct initialization values $K, K' \in \mathcal{K}_\lambda$, the two distributions $\{pk \mid (pk, sk, tk) \leftarrow$ LKeygen$(\Gamma, K)\}$ and $\{pk \mid (pk, sk, tk) \leftarrow$ LKeygen$(\Gamma, K')\}$ are statistically indistinguishable. We require them to be $2^{-\Omega(\lambda)}$-close in terms of statistical distance.

Lossiness: *For any initialization value $K \in \mathcal{K}_\lambda$ and tag $t \in \mathcal{T}_\lambda$ such that $(K, t) \notin \mathcal{R}$, any $(pk, sk, tk) \leftarrow$ Keygen(Γ, K), and any* Msg$_0$, Msg$_1 \in$ MsgSp, *the following distributions are statistically close:*

$$\{C \mid C \leftarrow \mathsf{Encrypt}(pk, t, \mathsf{Msg}_0)\} \quad \approx_s \quad \{C \mid C \leftarrow \mathsf{Encrypt}(pk, t, \mathsf{Msg}_1)\}.$$

For any $(pk, sk, tk) \leftarrow$ LKeygen(Γ, K), the above holds for any tag t (and not only those for which $(K, t) \notin \mathcal{R}$).

Efficient opening under lossy tags: *Let D_R denote the distribution, defined over the randomness space R^{LPKE}, from which the random coins used by* Encrypt *are sampled. For any message* Msg $\in$ MsgSp *and ciphertext C, let $D_{PK,\mathsf{Msg},C,t}$ denote the probability distribution on R^{LPKE} with support*

$$S_{PK,\mathsf{Msg},C,t} = \{\bar{r} \in R^{\mathsf{LPKE}} \mid \mathsf{Encrypt}(pk, t, \mathsf{Msg}, \bar{r}) = C\} \ ,$$

and such that, for each $\bar{r} \in S_{PK,\mathsf{Msg},C,t}$, we have

$$D_{PK,\mathsf{Msg},C,t}(\bar{r}) = \Pr_{r' \hookleftarrow D_R}[r' = \bar{r} \mid \mathsf{Encrypt}(pk, t, \mathsf{Msg}, r') = C] \ .$$

There exists a PPT algorithm Opener *such that, for any $K \in \mathcal{K}_\lambda$, any keys $(pk, sk, tk) \leftarrow$ Keygen(Γ, K) and $(pk, sk, tk) \leftarrow$ LKeygen(Γ, K), any random* *coins* $r \hookleftarrow D_R$, *any tag* $t \in \mathcal{T}_\lambda$ *such that* $(K,t) \notin \mathcal{R}$, *and any messages* $\mathsf{Msg}_0, \mathsf{Msg}_1 \in \mathsf{MsgSp}$, *takes as inputs* $pk, C = \mathsf{Encrypt}(pk, t, \mathsf{Msg}_0, r)$, t, *and* tk. *It outputs a sample* $\bar{r}$ *from a distribution statistically close to* $D_{PK,\mathsf{Msg}_1,C,t}$.

Efficient opening under lossy keys: *There exists a PPT sampling algorithm* $\mathsf{LOpener}$ *such that, for any* $K \in \mathcal{K}_\lambda$, *any keys* $(pk, sk, tk) \leftarrow \mathsf{LKeygen}(\Gamma, K)$, *any random coins* $r \hookleftarrow D_R$, *any tag* $t \in \mathcal{T}_\lambda$, *and any distinct messages* $\mathsf{Msg}_0, \mathsf{Msg}_1 \in \mathsf{MsgSp}$, *takes as input* $C = \mathsf{Encrypt}(pk, t, \mathsf{Msg}_0, r)$, t *and* sk. *It outputs a sample* $\bar{r}$ *from a distribution statistically close to* $D_{PK,\mathsf{Msg}_1,C,t}$.

In Definition 2.10, some of the first four properties were defined in [19, Definition 4.1]. The last two properties are a natural extension of the definition of efficient opening introduced by Bellare *et al.* [10]. We note that property of decryption under injective tags does not assume that random coins are honestly sampled, but only that they belong to some pre-defined set R^{LPKE}.

For our applications to simulation-sound proofs, it would be sufficient to have algorithms ($\mathsf{Opener}, \mathsf{LOpener}$) that have access to the initial messages Msg_0 *and* the random coins r_0 of the ciphertext to be equivocated (as was the case in the opening algorithms of [10]). In our LWE-based construction, however, the initial messages and random coins are not needed.

3 Direct Construction of Unbounded Simulation-Sound NIZK Arguments

We provide a method that directly compiles any trapdoor Σ-protocol into an unbounded simulation-sound NIZK argument using an $\mathcal{R}$-lossy encryption scheme for the bit-matching relation $\mathcal{R}_{\mathsf{BM}}$ and a correlation intractable hash function.

Definition 3.1. *Let* $\mathcal{K} = \{0, 1, \bot\}^L$ *and* $\mathcal{T} = \{0,1\}^\ell$, *for some* $\ell, L \in \mathsf{poly}(\lambda)$ *such that* $\ell < L$. *Let* F_{ADH} *the partitioning function defined by* $\mathsf{AHF} : \{0,1\}^\ell \to \{0,1\}^L$ *in Definition 2.6. The* **bit-matching relation** $\mathcal{R}_{\mathsf{BM}} : \mathcal{K} \times \mathcal{T} \to \{0,1\}$ *for* AHF *is the relation where* $\mathcal{R}_{\mathsf{BM}}(K,t) = 1$ *if and only if* $K = K_1 \ldots K_L$ *and* $t = t_1 \ldots t_\ell$ *satisfy* $F_{\mathsf{ADH}}(K,t) = 0$ *(namely,* $\bigwedge_{i=1}^{L} (K_i = \bot) \vee (K_i = \mathsf{AHF}(t)_i))$.

3.1 An $\mathcal{R}_{\mathsf{BM}}$-Lossy PKE Scheme from LWE

We describe an $\mathcal{R}_{\mathsf{BM}}$-lossy PKE scheme below. Our scheme builds on a variant of the primal Regev cryptosystem [79] suggested in [46].

Let $\mathsf{AHF} : \{0,1\}^\ell \to \{0,1\}^L$ an admissible hash function with key space $\mathcal{K} = \{0, 1, \bot\}^L$ and let $\mathcal{R}_{\mathsf{BM}} \subset \mathcal{K} \times \{0,1\}^\ell$ the corresponding bit-matching relation. We construct an $\mathcal{R}_{\mathsf{BM}}$-lossy PKE scheme in the following way.

$\mathsf{Par\text{-}Gen}(1^\lambda)$: Given a security parameter $\lambda \in \mathbb{N}$, let $n_0 = \mathsf{poly}(\lambda)$ the length of messages. Choose a prime modulus $q = \mathsf{poly}(\lambda)$; dimensions $n = n_0 + \Omega(\lambda)$ and $m = 2n\lceil \log q \rceil + O(\lambda)$. Define the tag space as $\mathcal{T} = \{0,1\}^\ell$ where $\ell = \Theta(\lambda)$.

Define the initialization value space $\mathcal{K} = \{0, 1, \perp\}^L$ and Gaussian parameters $\sigma = O(m) \cdot L$ and $\alpha \in (0, 1)$ such that $m\alpha q \cdot (L+1) \cdot \sigma\sqrt{2m} < q/4$. Define public parameters as $\Gamma = (\ell, L, n_0, q, n, m, \alpha, \sigma)$.

Keygen(Γ, K): On input of public parameters Γ and an initialization value $K \in \{0, 1, \perp\}^L$, generate a key pair as follows.

1. Sample random matrices $\bar{\mathbf{B}} \hookleftarrow U(\mathbb{Z}_q^{(n-n_0) \times m})$, $\mathbf{S} \hookleftarrow U(\mathbb{Z}_q^{(n-n_0) \times n_0})$ and a small-norm $\mathbf{E} \hookleftarrow \chi^{m \times n_0}$ to compute

$$\mathbf{A} = \left[\frac{\bar{\mathbf{B}}}{\mathbf{S}^\top \cdot \bar{\mathbf{B}} + \mathbf{E}^\top} \right] \in \mathbb{Z}_q^{n \times m}.$$

2. Parse K as $K_1 \ldots K_L \in \{0, 1, \perp\}^L$. Letting $\mathbf{G} \in \mathbb{Z}_q^{n \times m}$ denote the gadget matrix, for each $i \in [L]$ and $b \in \{0, 1\}$, compute matrices $\mathbf{A}_{i,b} \in \mathbb{Z}_q^{n \times m}$ as

$$\mathbf{A}_{i,b} = \begin{cases} \mathbf{A} \cdot \mathbf{R}_{i,b} + \mathbf{G} & \text{if } (K_i \neq \perp) \wedge (b = 1 - K_i) \\ \mathbf{A} \cdot \mathbf{R}_{i,b} & \text{if } (K_i = \perp) \vee (b = K_i). \end{cases} \tag{1}$$

where $\mathbf{R}_{i,b} \hookleftarrow U(\{-1, 1\}^{m \times m})$ for all $i \in [L]$ and $b \in \{0, 1\}$.

Define $R^{\mathsf{LPKE}} = \{\mathbf{r} \in \mathbb{Z}^{2m} \mid \|\mathbf{r}\| \leq \sigma\sqrt{2m}\}$ and output $sk = (K, \mathbf{S})$ as well as

$$pk := \left(\mathbf{A}, \ \{\mathbf{A}_{i,b}\}_{(i,b) \in [L] \times \{0,1\}} \right), \qquad tk = (K, \{\mathbf{R}_{i,b}\}_{(i,b) \in [L] \times \{0,1\}}).$$

LKeygen(Γ, K): This algorithm proceeds identically to Keygen except that steps 1 and 2 are modified in the following way.

1. Run $(\mathbf{A}, \mathbf{T_A}) \leftarrow \mathsf{GenTrap}(1^\lambda, 1^n, 1^m, q)$ so as to obtain a statistically uniform matrix $\mathbf{A} \sim U(\mathbb{Z}_q^{n \times m})$ with a trapdoor for the lattice $\Lambda^\perp(\mathbf{A})$.
2. Define matrices $\{\mathbf{A}_{i,b} \in \mathbb{Z}_q^{n \times m}\}_{(i,b) \in [L] \times \{0,1\}}$ as in (1).

Define R^{LPKE} as in Keygen and output

$$pk := \left(\mathbf{A}, \ \{\mathbf{A}_{i,b}\}_{(i,b) \in [L] \times \{0,1\}} \right), \quad sk = \mathbf{T_A}, \quad tk = (K, \{\mathbf{R}_{i,b}\}_{(i,b) \in [L] \times \{0,1\}}).$$

Encrypt(pk, t, Msg): To encrypt $\mathsf{Msg} \in \{0, 1\}^{n_0}$ for the tag $t = t_1 \ldots t_\ell \in \{0, 1\}^\ell$, conduct the following steps.

1. Encode the tag t as $t' = t'_1 \ldots t'_L = \mathsf{AHF}(t) \in \{0, 1\}^L$ and compute $\mathbf{A}_{F,t} = \sum_{i=1}^{L} \mathbf{A}_{i,t'_i} \in \mathbb{Z}_q^{n \times m}$. Note that $\mathbf{A}_{F,t} = \mathbf{A} \cdot \mathbf{R}_{F,t} + d_t \cdot \mathbf{G}$ for some $\mathbf{R}_{F,t} \in \mathbb{Z}^{m \times m}$ of norm $\|\mathbf{R}_{F,t}\|_\infty \leq L$ and where $d_t \in \{0, \ldots, L\}$ is the number of non-$\perp$ entries of K for which $K_i \neq t'_i$.
2. Choose $\mathbf{r} \hookleftarrow D_{\mathbb{Z}^{2m}, \sigma}$ and output $\perp$ if $\mathbf{r} \notin R^{\mathsf{LPKE}}$. Otherwise, output

$$\mathbf{c} = [\mathbf{A} \mid \mathbf{A}_{F,t}] \cdot \mathbf{r} + \left[\frac{\mathbf{0}^{n-n_0}}{\mathsf{Msg} \cdot \lfloor q/2 \rfloor} \right] \in \mathbb{Z}_q^n. \tag{2}$$

Decrypt($sk, t, \mathbf{c}$): Given $sk = (K, \mathbf{S})$ and the tag $t \in \{0,1\}^\ell$, compute $t' = t'_1 \ldots t'_L = \mathsf{AHF}(t) \in \{0,1\}^L$ and return $\perp$ if $R_{\mathsf{BM}}(K, t') = 0$. Otherwise, compute $\mathbf{w} = [-\mathbf{S}^\top \mid \mathbf{I}_{n_0}] \cdot \mathbf{c} \in \mathbb{Z}_q^{n_0}$. For each $i \in [n_0]$, do the following:

1. If neither $\mathbf{w}[i]$ nor $|\mathbf{w}[i] - \lfloor q/2 \rfloor|$ is close to 0, halt and return $\perp$.
2. Otherwise, set $\mathsf{Msg}[i] \in \{0,1\}$ so as to minimize $|\mathbf{w}[i] - \mathsf{Msg}[i] \cdot \lfloor q/2 \rfloor|$.

Return $\mathsf{Msg} = \mathsf{Msg}[1] \ldots \mathsf{Msg}[n_0]$.

Opener($pk, tk, t, \mathbf{c}, \mathsf{Msg}_1$): Given $tk = (K, \{\mathbf{R}_{i,b}\}_{i,b})$ and $t \in \{0,1\}^\ell$, compute $t' = t'_1 \ldots t'_L = \mathsf{AHF}(t) \in \{0,1\}^L$ and return $\perp$ if $R_{\mathsf{BM}}(K, t') = 1$. Otherwise,

1. Compute the small-norm matrix $\mathbf{R}_{F,t} = \sum_{i=1}^L \mathbf{R}_{i,t'_i} \in \mathbb{Z}^{m \times m}$ such that $\mathbf{A}_{F,t} = \mathbf{A} \cdot \mathbf{R}_{F,t} + d_t \cdot \mathbf{G}$ and $\|\mathbf{R}_{F,t}\|_\infty \leq L$ with $d_t \in [L]$.
2. Use $\mathbf{R}_{F,t} \in \mathbb{Z}^{m \times m}$ as a trapdoor for the matrix

$$\bar{\mathbf{A}}_{F,t} = [\mathbf{A} \mid \mathbf{A}_{F,t}] = [\mathbf{A} \mid \mathbf{A} \cdot \mathbf{R}_{F,t} + d_t \cdot \mathbf{G}] \in \mathbb{Z}_q^{n \times 2m}$$

to sample a Gaussian vector $\bar{\mathbf{r}} \in \mathbb{Z}^{2m}$ such that

$$\bar{\mathbf{A}}_{F,t} \cdot \bar{\mathbf{r}} = \mathbf{c} - \begin{bmatrix} \mathbf{0}^{n-n_0} \\ \hline \mathsf{Msg}_1 \cdot \lfloor q/2 \rfloor \end{bmatrix} . \tag{3}$$

Namely, defining $\mathbf{c}_{\mathsf{Msg}_1} = \mathbf{c} - [(\mathbf{0}^{n-n_0})^\top \mid \mathsf{Msg}_1^\top \cdot \lfloor q/2 \rfloor]^\top$, sample and output fake random coins $\bar{\mathbf{r}} \hookleftarrow D_{\Lambda_q^{\mathbf{c}_{\mathsf{Msg}_1}}(\bar{\mathbf{A}}_{F,t}), \sigma}$.

LOpener($sk, t, \mathbf{c}, \mathsf{Msg}_1$): Given $sk = \mathbf{T_A}$ and $t \in \{0,1\}^\ell$, use $\mathbf{T_A}$ to derive a trapdoor $\mathbf{T}_{\mathbf{A},t}$ for the lattice $\Lambda_q^\perp(\bar{\mathbf{A}}_{F,t})$ and use $\mathbf{T}_{\mathbf{A},t}$ to sample a Gaussian vector $\bar{\mathbf{r}} \hookleftarrow D_{\Lambda_q^{\mathbf{c}_{\mathsf{Msg}_1}}(\bar{\mathbf{A}}_{F,t}), \sigma}$ satisfying (3).

The above construction requires $2L = \Theta(\lambda)$ matrices in the public key but allows for a relatively small modulus $q = \Theta(m^{5/2} n^{1/2} L^2)$. A technique suggested by Yamada [83] can be used to reduce the number of public matrices to $O(\log^2 \lambda)$ at the expense of a larger (but still polynomial) modulus. Since our application to Naor-Yung requires a public key containing a large correlation-intractable hashing key anyway, we chose to minimize the modulus size.

Theorem 3.2 states that the construction has the required properties under the LWE assumption. The proof is given in the full version of the paper [65].

Theorem 3.2. *The above construction is an $\mathcal{R}_{\mathsf{BM}}$-lossy public-key encryption scheme with efficient opening under the LWE assumption.*

3.2 A Generic Construction from Trapdoor Σ-Protocols and $\mathcal{R}_{\mathsf{BM}}$-lossy PKE

We construct unbounded simulation-sound NIZK proofs by combining trapdoor Σ-protocols and $\mathcal{R}$-lossy public-key encryption schemes. Our proof system is inspired by ideas from [72] and relies on the following ingredients:

- A trapdoor Σ-protocol $\Pi' = (\mathsf{Gen}'_{\mathsf{par}}, \mathsf{Gen}'_{\mathcal{L}}, \mathsf{P}', \mathsf{V}')$ with challenge space $\mathcal{C}$, for the same language $\mathcal{L} = (\mathcal{L}_{\mathsf{zk}}, \mathcal{L}_{\mathsf{sound}})$ and which satisfies the properties of Definition 2.9. In addition, $\mathsf{BadChallenge}(\tau_\Sigma, \mathsf{crs}, x, \mathbf{a})$ should be computable within time $T \in \mathsf{poly}(\lambda)$ for any input $(\tau, \mathsf{crs}, x, \mathbf{a})$.
- A strongly unforgeable one-time signature scheme $\mathsf{OTS} = (\mathcal{G}, \mathcal{S}, \mathcal{V})$ with verification keys of length $\ell \in \mathsf{poly}(\lambda)$.
- An admissible hash function $\mathsf{AHF} : \{0,1\}^\ell \to \{0,1\}^L$, for some $L \in \mathsf{poly}(\lambda)$ with $L > \ell$, which induces the relation $\mathcal{R}_{\mathsf{BM}} : \{0,1,\bot\}^L \times \{0,1\}^\ell \to \{0,1\}$.
- An $\mathcal{R}$-lossy PKE scheme $\mathcal{R}\text{-LPKE} = (\mathsf{Par\text{-}Gen}, \mathsf{Keygen}, \mathsf{LKeygen}, \mathsf{Encrypt}, \mathsf{Decrypt}, \mathsf{Opener}, \mathsf{LOpener})$ for the relation $\mathcal{R}_{\mathsf{BM}} : \{0,1,\bot\}^L \times \{0,1\}^\ell \to \{0,1\}$ with public (resp. secret) key space $\mathcal{PK}$ (resp. $\mathcal{SK}$). We assume that $\mathsf{Decrypt}$ is computable within time T. We denote the message (resp. ciphertext) space by MsgSp (resp. CtSp) and the randomness space by R^{LPKE}. Let also D_R^{LPKE} denote the distribution from which the random coins of $\mathsf{Encrypt}$ are sampled.
- A correlation intractable hash family $\mathcal{H} = (\mathsf{Gen}, \mathsf{Hash})$ for the class $\mathcal{R}_{\mathsf{CI}}$ of relations that are efficiently searchable within time T.

We also assume that these ingredients are compatible in the sense that P' outputs a first prover message $\mathbf{a}$ that fits in the message space MsgSp of $\mathcal{R}\text{-LPKE}$.

Our argument system $\Pi^{\mathsf{uss}} = (\mathsf{Gen}_{\mathsf{par}}, \mathsf{Gen}_{\mathcal{L}}, \mathsf{P}, \mathsf{V})$ allows P and V to input a label lbl consisting of public data. While this label will be the empty string in our KDM-CCA scheme of Section, it may be useful when several non-interactive arguments have to be bound together. The construction goes as follows.

$\mathsf{Gen}_{\mathsf{par}}(1^\lambda)$: Run $\mathsf{par} \leftarrow \mathsf{Gen}'_{\mathsf{par}}(1^\lambda)$ and output par.

$\mathsf{Gen}_{\mathcal{L}}(\mathsf{par}, \mathcal{L})$: Given public parameters par and a language $\mathcal{L} \subset \{0,1\}^N$, let $\mathcal{K} = \{0,1,\bot\}^L$ and $\mathcal{T} = \{0,1\}^\ell$. The CRS is generated as follows.

1. Generate a CRS $\mathsf{crs}'_{\mathcal{L}} \leftarrow \mathsf{Gen}'_{\mathcal{L}}(\mathsf{par}, \mathcal{L})$ for the trapdoor Σ-protocol Π'.
2. Generate public parameters $\Gamma \hookleftarrow \mathsf{Par\text{-}Gen}(1^\lambda)$ for the $\mathcal{R}_{\mathsf{BM}}$-lossy PKE scheme where the relation $\mathcal{R}_{\mathsf{BM}} : \mathcal{K} \times \mathcal{T} \to \{0,1\}$ is defined by an admissible hash function $\mathsf{AHF} : \{0,1\}^\ell \to \{0,1\}^L$. Choose a random initialization value $K \leftarrow \mathcal{K}$ and generate lossy keys $(pk, sk, tk) \leftarrow \mathsf{LKeygen}(\Gamma, K)$.
3. Generate a key $k \leftarrow \mathsf{Gen}(1^\lambda)$ for a correlation intractable hash function with output length $\kappa = \Theta(\lambda)$.

Output the language-dependent $\mathsf{crs}_{\mathcal{L}} := (\mathsf{crs}'_{\mathcal{L}}, k)$ and the simulation trapdoor $\tau_{\mathsf{zk}} := sk$, which is the lossy secret key of $\mathcal{R}\text{-LPKE}$. The global common reference string consists of $\mathsf{crs} = (\mathsf{par}, \mathsf{crs}_{\mathcal{L}}, pk, \mathsf{AHF}, \mathsf{OTS})$.

$\mathsf{P}(\mathsf{crs}, x, w, \mathsf{lbl})$: To prove a statement x for a label $\mathsf{lbl} \in \{0,1\}^*$ using $w \in R_{\mathsf{zk}}(x)$, generate a one-time signature key pair $(\mathsf{VK}, \mathsf{SK}) \leftarrow \mathcal{G}(1^\lambda)$. Then,

1. Compute $(\mathbf{a}' = (\mathbf{a}'_1, \ldots, \mathbf{a}'_\kappa), st') \leftarrow \mathsf{P}'(\mathsf{crs}'_{\mathcal{L}}, x, w)$ via κ invocations of the prover for Π'. Then, for each $i \in [\kappa]$, compute $\mathbf{a}_i \leftarrow \mathsf{Encrypt}(pk, \mathsf{VK}, \mathbf{a}'_i; \mathbf{r}_i)$ using random coins $\mathbf{r}_i \hookleftarrow D_R^{\mathsf{LPKE}}$. Let $\mathbf{a} = (\mathbf{a}_1, \ldots, \mathbf{a}_\kappa)$ and $\mathbf{r} = (\mathbf{r}_1, \ldots, \mathbf{r}_\kappa)$.
2. Compute $\mathsf{Chall} = \mathsf{Hash}(k, (x, \mathbf{a}, \mathsf{VK})) \in \{0,1\}^\kappa$.

3. Compute $\mathbf{z}' = (\mathbf{z}'_1, \ldots, \mathbf{z}'_\kappa) = \mathsf{P}'(\mathsf{crs}'_\mathcal{L}, x, w, \mathbf{a}', \mathsf{Chall}, st')$ via κ executions of the prover of Π'. Define $\mathbf{z} = (\mathbf{z}', \mathbf{a}', \mathbf{r})$.
4. Generate $sig \leftarrow \mathcal{S}(\mathsf{SK}, (x, \mathbf{a}, \mathbf{z}, \mathsf{lbl}))$ and output $\boldsymbol{\pi} = (\mathsf{VK}, (\mathbf{a}, \mathbf{z}), sig)$.

$\mathsf{V}(\mathsf{crs}, x, \boldsymbol{\pi}, \mathsf{lbl})$: Given a statement x, a label lbl as well as a purported proof $\boldsymbol{\pi} = (\mathsf{VK}, (\mathbf{a}, \mathbf{z}), sig)$, return 0 if $\mathcal{V}(\mathsf{VK}, (x, \mathbf{a}, \mathbf{z}, \mathsf{lbl}), sig) = 0$. Otherwise,

1. Write $\mathbf{z}$ as $\mathbf{z} = ((\mathbf{z}'_1, \ldots, \mathbf{z}'_\kappa), (\mathbf{a}'_1, \ldots, \mathbf{a}'_\kappa), (\mathbf{r}_1, \ldots, \mathbf{r}_\kappa))$ and return 0 if it does not parse properly. Return 0 if there exists $i \in [\kappa]$ such that $\mathbf{a}_i \neq \mathsf{Encrypt}(pk, \mathsf{VK}, \mathbf{a}'_i; \mathbf{r}_i)$ or $\mathbf{r}_i \notin R^{\mathsf{LPKE}}$.
2. Let $\mathsf{Chall} = \mathsf{Hash}(k, (x, (\mathbf{a}_1, \ldots, \mathbf{a}_\kappa), \mathsf{VK}))$. If $\mathsf{V}'(\mathsf{crs}'_\mathcal{L}, x, (\mathbf{a}'_i, \mathsf{Chall}[i], \mathbf{z}'_i)) = 1$ for each $i \in [\kappa]$, return 1. Otherwise, return 0.

Our NIZK simulator uses a technique due to Damgård [38], which uses a trapdoor commitment scheme to achieve a straight-line simulation of 3-move zero-knowledge proofs in the common reference string model.

Theorem 3.3. *The above argument system is multi-theorem zero-knowledge assuming that the trapdoor Σ-protocol Π' is special zero-knowledge.*

Proof (Sketch). We describe a simulator $(\mathsf{Sim}_0, \mathsf{Sim}_1)$ which uses the lossy secret key $\tau_{\mathsf{zk}} = sk$ of $\mathcal{R}$-LPKE to simulate transcripts $(\mathbf{a}, \mathsf{Chall}, \mathbf{z})$ without using the witnesses. Namely, on input of $\mathsf{par} \leftarrow \mathsf{Gen}_{\mathsf{par}}(1^\lambda)$, Sim_0 generates $\mathsf{crs}_\mathcal{L}$ by proceeding identically to $\mathsf{Gen}_\mathcal{L}$ while Sim_1 is described hereunder.

$\mathsf{Sim}_1(\mathsf{crs}, \tau_{\mathsf{zk}}, x, \mathsf{lbl})$: On input a statement $x \in \{0, 1\}^N$, a label lbl and the simulation trapdoor $\tau_{\mathsf{zk}} = sk$, algorithm Sim_1 proceeds as follows.

1. Generate a one-time signature key pair $(\mathsf{VK}, \mathsf{SK}) \leftarrow \mathcal{G}(1^\lambda)$. Let $\mathbf{0}^{|\mathbf{a}'|}$ the all-zeroes string of length $|\mathbf{a}'|$. Sample random coins $\mathbf{r}_0 \hookleftarrow D_R^{\mathsf{LPKE}}$ from the distribution D_R^{LPKE} and compute $\mathbf{a} \leftarrow \mathsf{Encrypt}(pk, \mathsf{VK}, \mathbf{0}^{|\mathbf{a}'|}; \mathbf{r}_0)$.
2. Compute $\mathsf{Chall} = \mathsf{Hash}(k, (x, \mathbf{a}, \mathsf{VK}))$.
3. Run the special ZK simulator $(\mathbf{a}', \mathbf{z}') \leftarrow \mathsf{ZKSim}(\mathsf{crs}'_\mathcal{L}, x, \mathsf{Chall})$ of Π' to obtain a simulated transcript $(\mathbf{a}', \mathsf{Chall}, \mathbf{z}')$ of Π' for the challenge Chall.
4. Using the lossy secret key sk of $\mathcal{R}$-LPKE, compute random coins $\mathbf{r} \leftarrow \mathsf{LOpener}(sk, \mathsf{VK}, \mathbf{a}, \mathbf{a}')$ which explain $\mathbf{a}$ as an encryption of $(x, \mathbf{a}')$ under the tag VK. Then, define $\mathbf{z} = (\mathbf{z}', \mathbf{a}', \mathbf{r})$
5. Compute $sig \leftarrow \mathcal{S}(\mathsf{SK}, (x, \mathbf{a}, \mathbf{z}, \mathsf{lbl}))$ and output $\boldsymbol{\pi} = (\mathsf{VK}, (\mathbf{a}, \mathbf{z}), sig)$.

In the full version of the paper, we show that the simulation is statistically indistinguishable from proofs generated by the real prover. $\qquad\square$

If we just target multi-theorem NIZK without simulation-soundness, the construction can be simplified as shown in the full version of the paper, where we explain how it can provide statistical zero-knowledge in the common random string (instead of the common reference string) model.

Going back to simulation-soundness, our proof builds on techniques used in [38,72]. The interactive proof systems of [72] rely on commitment schemes where the adversary cannot break the computational binding property of the commitment for some tag after having seen equivocations of commitments for different tags. Here, in order to use a correlation-intractable hash function, we need a commitment scheme which is equivocable on some tags but (with noticeable probability) becomes statistically binding on an adversarially-chosen tag. For this purpose, we exploit the observation that an $\mathcal{R}$-lossy PKE scheme can be used as a commitment scheme with these properties. Namely, it can serve as a trapdoor commitment to equivocate lossy encryptions of the first prover message in Π' while forcing the adversary to create a fake proof on a statistically binding (and even extractable) commitment.

At a high level, the proof also bears similarities with [66] in that they also use a commitment scheme that is statistically hiding in adversarial queries but becomes statistically binding in the adversary's output. The difference is that we need to equivocate the statistically-hiding commitment in simulated proofs here.

Theorem 3.4. *The above argument system provides unbounded simulation-soundness if: (i)* OTS *is a strongly unforgeable one-time signature; (ii)* $\mathcal{R}$-LPKE *is an* $\mathcal{R}_{\mathsf{BM}}$*-lossy PKE scheme; (iii) The hash family* $\mathcal{H}$ *is somewhere correlation-intractable for all relations that are searchable within time* T*, where* T *denotes the maximal running time of algorithms* BadChallenge$(\cdot, \cdot, \cdot, \cdot)$ *and* Decrypt$(\cdot, \cdot, \cdot)$*. (The proof is given in the full version of the paper.)*

The work of Peikert and Shiehian [76] implies a correlation intractable hash function for the relation R_{bad} defined in the proof of Theorem 3.4. Their bootstrapping theorem actually implies the existence of such a hash family under the LWE assumption with polynomial approximation factors.

4   Tightly Secure Simulation-Sound Arguments

To achieve tight simulation-soundness, we describe an $\mathcal{R}$-lossy PKE scheme for a relation induced by a pseudorandom function family. In Definition 4.1, we assume that the tag space $\mathcal{T}$ has a special structure. Namely, each tag $t = (t_c, t_a) \in \mathcal{T}$ consists of a core component $t_c \in \{0,1\}^\lambda$ and an auxiliary component $t_a \in \{0,1\}^\ell$.

Definition 4.1. *Let a pseudorandom function* PRF $: \mathcal{K} \times \{0,1\}^\ell \to \{0,1\}^\lambda$ *with key space* $\mathcal{K} = \{0,1\}^\lambda$ *and input space* $\{0,1\}^\ell$*. Let* $\mathcal{T} = \{0,1\}^\lambda \times \{0,1\}^\ell$*, for some* $\ell \in \mathsf{poly}(\lambda)$*. We define the PRF relation* $\mathcal{R}_{\mathsf{PRF}} : \mathcal{K} \times \mathcal{T} \to \{0,1\}$ *as* $\mathcal{R}_{\mathsf{PRF}}(K, (t_c, t_a)) = 1$ *if and only if* $t_c \neq$ PRF(K, t_a)*.*

We rely on the idea (previously used in [17,67]) of homomorphically evaluating the circuit of a PRF using the GSW FHE [47]. As observed in [22], when the circuit is in NC1, it is advantageous to convert it into a branching program using Barrington's theorem. This enables the use of a polynomial modulus q.

Lemma 4.2 (Adapted from [15,47]). *Let $C : \{0,1\}^L \to \{0,1\}$ be a NAND Boolean circuit of depth d. Let $\mathbf{A}_i = \mathbf{A} \cdot \mathbf{R}_i + k_i \cdot \mathbf{G} \in \mathbb{Z}_q^{n \times m}$ with $\mathbf{A} \in \mathbb{Z}_q^{n \times m}$, $\mathbf{R}_i \in \{-1,1\}^{m \times m}$ and $k_i \in \{0,1\}$, for $i \leq L$. There exist deterministic algorithms $\mathsf{Eval}_{\mathsf{BP}}^{\mathsf{pub}}$ and $\mathsf{Eval}_{\mathsf{BP}}^{\mathsf{priv}}$ with running time $\mathsf{poly}(4^d, L, m, n, \log q)$ that satisfy:* $\mathsf{Eval}_{\mathsf{BP}}^{\mathsf{pub}}(C, (\mathbf{A}_i)_i) = \mathbf{A} \cdot \mathsf{Eval}_{\mathsf{BP}}^{\mathsf{priv}}(C, ((\mathbf{R}_i, k_i))_i) + C(k_1, \ldots, k_L) \cdot \mathbf{G}$, *and* $\|\mathsf{Eval}_{\mathsf{BP}}^{\mathsf{priv}}(C, (\mathbf{R}_i, k_i)_i)\| \leq 4^d \cdot O(m^{3/2})$.

4.1 An $\mathcal{R}_{\mathsf{PRF}}$-Lossy PKE Scheme

We describe an $\mathcal{R}$-lossy PKE scheme for the relation $\mathcal{R}_{\mathsf{PRF}}$ of Definition 4.1.

Let $\mathsf{PRF} : \mathcal{K} \times \{0,1\}^\ell \to \{0,1\}^\lambda$ with key space $\mathcal{K} = \{0,1\}^\lambda$ and input space $\{0,1\}^\ell$ and let $\mathcal{R}_{\mathsf{PRF}} \subset \mathcal{K} \times \mathcal{T}$ the corresponding relation. We construct an $\mathcal{R}_{\mathsf{PRF}}$-lossy PKE scheme in the following way.

$\mathsf{Par\text{-}Gen}(1^\lambda)$: Given a security parameter $\lambda \in \mathbb{N}$, let $n_0 = \mathsf{poly}(\lambda)$ the length of messages. Choose a prime modulus $q = \mathsf{poly}(\lambda)$; dimensions $n = n_0 + \Omega(\lambda)$ and $m = 2n\lceil \log q\rceil + O(\lambda)$. Define the tag space as $\mathcal{T} = \{0,1\}^\lambda \times \{0,1\}^\ell$ where $\ell = \Theta(\lambda)$. Define the initialization value space $\mathcal{K} = \{0,1\}^\lambda$ and Gaussian parameters $\sigma = 4^d \cdot O(m^2)$ and $\alpha \in (0,1)$ such that $4^d m^{3.5} \alpha \cdot \sigma < q$. Define public parameters as $\Gamma = (\ell, L, n_0, q, n, m, u, \alpha, \sigma)$.

$\mathsf{Keygen}(\Gamma, K)$ On input of public parameters Γ and an initialization value $K \in \{0,1\}^\lambda$, generate a key pair as follows.

1. Sample random matrices $\bar{\mathbf{B}} \hookleftarrow U(\mathbb{Z}_q^{(n-n_0) \times m})$, $\mathbf{S} \hookleftarrow U(\mathbb{Z}_q^{(n-n_0) \times n_0})$ and a small-norm $\mathbf{E} \hookleftarrow \chi^{m \times n_0}$ to compute $\mathbf{A} = [\bar{\mathbf{B}}^\top \mid \bar{\mathbf{B}}^\top \mathbf{S} + \mathbf{E}]^\top \in \mathbb{Z}_q^{n \times m}$.
2. Parse K as $k_1 \ldots k_\lambda \in \{0,1\}^\lambda$. For each $i \in [L]$, compute matrices $\mathbf{A}_i = \mathbf{A} \cdot \mathbf{R}_i + k_i \cdot \mathbf{G}$, where $\mathbf{R}_i \hookleftarrow U(\{-1,1\}^{m \times m})$, for all $i \in [\lambda]$.

Define $R^{\mathsf{LPKE}} = \{\mathbf{r} \in \mathbb{Z}^{2m} \mid \|\mathbf{r}\| \leq \sigma\sqrt{2m}\}$ and output $sk = (K, \mathbf{S})$ as well as

$$pk := \left(\mathbf{A}, \ \{\mathbf{A}_i\}_{i \in [\lambda]} \right), \qquad tk = (K, \{\mathbf{R}_i\}_{i \in [\lambda]}).$$

$\mathsf{LKeygen}(\Gamma, K)$: This algorithm proceeds identically to Keygen except that steps 1 and 2 are modified in the following way.

1. Run $(\mathbf{A}, \mathbf{T}_\mathbf{A}) \leftarrow \mathsf{GenTrap}(1^\lambda, 1^n, 1^m, q)$ to obtain a statistically uniform $\mathbf{A} \sim U(\mathbb{Z}_q^{n \times m})$ with a trapdoor for $\Lambda^\perp(\mathbf{A})$.
2. Define matrices $\{\mathbf{A}_i \in \mathbb{Z}_q^{n \times m}\}_{i \in [\lambda]}$ as in Keygen.

Output $pk := \left(\mathbf{A}, \ \{\mathbf{A}_i\}_{i \in [\lambda]} \right)$, $sk = \mathbf{T}_\mathbf{A}$, and $tk = (K, \{\mathbf{R}_i\}_{i \in [\lambda]})$.

$\mathsf{Encrypt}(pk, t, \mathsf{Msg})$: To encrypt a message $\mathsf{Msg} \in \{0,1\}^{n_0}$ for the structured tag $t = (t_c, t_a) \in \mathcal{T} = \{0,1\}^\lambda \times \{0,1\}^\ell$, conduct the following steps.

1. Let $C_{\mathsf{PRF},t} : \{0,1\}^\lambda \to \{0,1\}$ the circuit, where $t = (t_c, t_a)$ is hard-wired, which inputs a λ-bit key $K = k_1 \ldots k_\lambda \in \{0,1\}^\lambda$ and outputs $C_{\mathsf{PRF},t}(K)$ such that $C_{\mathsf{PRF},t}(K) = 1 \Leftrightarrow t_c = \mathsf{PRF}_K(t_a) \Leftrightarrow \mathcal{R}_{\mathsf{PRF}}(K,t) = 0$. Compute $\mathbf{A}_{F,t} \leftarrow \mathsf{Eval}_{\mathsf{BP}}^{\mathsf{pub}}(C_{\mathsf{PRF}}, (\mathbf{A}_i)_i) \in \mathbb{Z}_q^{n \times m}$ such that

$$\mathbf{A}_{F,t} = \mathbf{A} \cdot \mathbf{R}_t + C_{\mathsf{PRF},t}(K) \cdot \mathbf{G},$$

where $\mathbf{R}_t = \mathsf{Eval}_{\mathsf{BP}}^{\mathsf{priv}}(C_{\mathsf{PRF},t}, (\mathbf{R}_i, k_i)_i) \in \mathbb{Z}^{m \times m}$ s.t. $\|\mathbf{R}_t\| \leq 4^d \cdot O(m^{3/2})$.

2. Choose $\mathbf{r} \hookleftarrow D_{\mathbb{Z}^{2m}, \sigma}$ and output $\perp$ if $\mathbf{r} \notin R^{\mathsf{LPKE}}$. Otherwise, output

$$\mathbf{c} = [\mathbf{A} \mid \mathbf{A}_{F,t}] \cdot \mathbf{r} + [\mathbf{0}^{n-n_0}{}^\top \mid \mathsf{Msg} \cdot \lfloor q/2 \rfloor]^\top \in \mathbb{Z}_q^n .$$

$\mathsf{Decrypt}(sk, t, \mathbf{c})$: Given the secret key $sk = (K, \mathbf{S})$ and the tag $t = (t_c, t_a) \in \mathcal{T}$, compute $C_{\mathsf{PRF},t}(K) \in \{0,1\}$ and return $\perp$ if $C_{\mathsf{PRF},t}(K) = 1$. Otherwise, Compute and return $\mathsf{Msg} = \mathsf{Msg}[1] \ldots \mathsf{Msg}[n_0]$ exactly as in Sect. 3.1.

$\mathsf{Opener}(pk, tk, t, \mathbf{c}, \mathsf{Msg}_1)$: Given $tk = (K, \{\mathbf{R}_i\}_i)$ and $t = (t_c, t_a) \in \mathcal{T}$, compute $C_{\mathsf{PRF},t}(K) \in \{0,1\}$ and return $\perp$ if $C_{\mathsf{PRF},t}(K) = 0$. Otherwise,

1. Compute the matrix $\mathbf{R}_t = \mathsf{Eval}_{\mathsf{BP}}^{\mathsf{priv}}(C_{\mathsf{PRF},t}, (\mathbf{R}_i, k_i)_i) \in \mathbb{Z}^{m \times m}$ such that $\mathbf{A}_{F,t} = \mathbf{A} \cdot \mathbf{R}_t + \mathbf{G}$ and $\|\mathbf{R}_t\| \leq 4^d \cdot O(m^{3/2})$.

2. Use $\mathbf{R}_t \in \mathbb{Z}^{m \times m}$ as a trapdoor for $\bar{\mathbf{A}}_{F,t} = [\mathbf{A} \mid \mathbf{A}_{F,t}] = [\mathbf{A} \mid \mathbf{A} \cdot \mathbf{R}_t + \mathbf{G}]$ to sample $\bar{\mathbf{r}} \in \mathbb{Z}^{2m}$ such that $\bar{\mathbf{A}}_{F,t} \cdot \bar{\mathbf{r}} = \mathbf{c} - [\mathbf{0}^{n-n_0}{}^\top \mid \mathsf{Msg}_1 \cdot \lfloor q/2 \rfloor]^\top$. Namely, defining $\mathbf{c}_{\mathsf{Msg}_1} = \mathbf{c} - [(\mathbf{0}^{n-n_0})^\top \mid \mathsf{Msg}_1^\top \cdot \lfloor q/2 \rfloor]^\top$, sample and output fake random coins $\bar{\mathbf{r}} \hookleftarrow D_{\Lambda_q^{\mathbf{c}_{\mathsf{Msg}_1}}(\bar{\mathbf{A}}_{F,t}), \sigma}$.

$\mathsf{LOpener}(sk, t, \mathbf{c}, \mathsf{Msg}_1)$: Given $sk = \mathbf{T}_\mathbf{A}$ and $t = (t_c, t_a) \in \mathcal{T}$, use $\mathbf{T}_\mathbf{A}$ to derive a trapdoor $\mathbf{T}_{\mathbf{A},t}$ for the lattice $\Lambda_q^\perp(\bar{\mathbf{A}}_{F,t})$ and use $\mathbf{T}_{\mathbf{A},t}$ to sample a Gaussian vector $\bar{\mathbf{r}} \hookleftarrow D_{\Lambda_q^{\mathbf{c}_{\mathsf{Msg}_1}}(\bar{\mathbf{A}}_{F,t}), \sigma}$ in the same coset of $\Lambda_q^\perp(\bar{\mathbf{A}}_{F,t})$ as in Opener.

The proof of Theorem 4.3 is identical to that of Theorem 3.2 and omitted.

Theorem 4.3. *The above construction is an $\mathcal{R}_{\mathsf{PRF}}$-lossy public-key encryption scheme with efficient opening under the LWE assumption.*

4.2 Unbounded Simulation-Sound Argument

We construct a tightly secure USS argument from the following ingredients:

- A pseudorandom function family $\mathsf{PRF} : \mathcal{K} \times \{0,1\}^\ell \to \{0,1\}^\lambda$ with key space $\mathcal{K} = \{0,1\}^\lambda$ and input space $\{0,1\}^\ell$, which induces the relation $\mathcal{R}_{\mathsf{PRF}} : \mathcal{K} \times \mathcal{T} \to \{0,1\}$ of Definition 4.1.
- An $\mathcal{R}_{\mathsf{PRF}}$-lossy PKE scheme $\mathcal{R}$-LPKE $= (\mathsf{Par\text{-}Gen}, \mathsf{Keygen}, \mathsf{LKeygen}, \mathsf{Encrypt}, \mathsf{Decrypt}, \mathsf{Opener}, \mathsf{LOpener})$ for the relation $\mathcal{R}_{\mathsf{PRF}} : \mathcal{K} \times \mathcal{T} \to \{0,1\}$ with public (resp. secret) key space $\mathcal{PK}$ (resp. $\mathcal{SK}$). We assume that $\mathsf{Decrypt}$ is computable within time T. We denote the message (resp. ciphertext) space by MsgSp (resp. CtSp) and the randomness space by R^{LPKE}. Let also D_R^{LPKE} denote the distribution of the random coins of $\mathsf{Encrypt}$.

- A trapdoor Σ-protocol $\Pi' = (\mathsf{Gen}'_{\mathsf{par}}, \mathsf{Gen}'_{\mathcal{L}}, \mathsf{P}', \mathsf{V}')$, a one-time signature scheme $\mathsf{OTS} = (\mathcal{G}, \mathcal{S}, \mathcal{V})$ and a correlation intractable hash family $\mathcal{H} = (\mathsf{Gen}, \mathsf{Hash})$ that satisfy the same conditions as in Sect. 3.2.

Our construction $\Pi^{\mathsf{uss}} = (\mathsf{Gen}_{\mathsf{par}}, \mathsf{Gen}_{\mathcal{L}}, \mathsf{P}, \mathsf{V})$ goes as follows.

$\mathsf{Gen}_{\mathsf{par}}(1^\lambda)$: Run $\mathsf{par} \leftarrow \mathsf{Gen}'_{\mathsf{par}}(1^\lambda)$ and output par.

$\mathsf{Gen}_{\mathcal{L}}(\mathsf{par}, \mathcal{L})$: Given public parameters par and a language $\mathcal{L} \subset \{0,1\}^N$, let $\mathcal{K} = \{0,1\}^\lambda$ and $\mathcal{T} = \{0,1\}^\ell$. The CRS is generated as follows.

1. Generate a CRS $\mathsf{crs}'_{\mathcal{L}} \leftarrow \mathsf{Gen}'_{\mathcal{L}}(\mathsf{par}, \mathcal{L})$ for the trapdoor Σ-protocol Π'.
2. Generate public parameters $\Gamma \hookleftarrow \mathsf{Par\text{-}Gen}(1^\lambda)$ for the $\mathcal{R}_{\mathsf{PRF}}$-lossy PKE scheme where the relation $\mathcal{R}_{\mathsf{PRF}} : \mathcal{K} \times \mathcal{T} \to \{0,1\}$ is defined by a PRF family $\mathsf{PRF} : \mathcal{K} \times \{0,1\}^\ell \to \{0,1\}^\lambda$. Generate lossy keys $(pk, sk, tk) \leftarrow \mathsf{LKeygen}(\Gamma, \mathbf{0}^\lambda)$, where the initialization value is the all-zeroes string $\mathbf{0}^\lambda$.
3. Generate a key $k \leftarrow \mathsf{Gen}(1^\lambda)$ for a correlation intractable hash function with output length $\kappa = \Theta(\lambda)$.

Output the language-dependent $\mathsf{crs}_{\mathcal{L}} := (\mathsf{crs}'_{\mathcal{L}}, k)$ and the simulation trapdoor $\tau_{\mathsf{zk}} := sk$. The global CRS consists of $\mathsf{crs} = (\mathsf{par}, \mathsf{crs}_{\mathcal{L}}, pk, \mathsf{PRF}, \mathsf{OTS})$.

$\mathsf{P}(\mathsf{crs}, x, w, \mathsf{lbl})$: To prove x with respect to a label lbl using $w \in R_{\mathsf{zk}}(x)$, generate a one-time signature key pair $(\mathsf{VK}, \mathsf{SK}) \leftarrow \mathcal{G}(1^\lambda)$. Then, choose a random core tag component $t_c \hookleftarrow U(\{0,1\}^\lambda)$ and do the following.

1. Compute $(\mathbf{a}' = (\mathbf{a}'_1, \ldots, \mathbf{a}'_\kappa), st') \leftarrow \mathsf{P}'(\mathsf{crs}'_{\mathcal{L}}, x, w)$ via κ invocations of the prover for Π'. For each $i \in [\kappa]$, compute $\mathbf{a}_i \leftarrow \mathsf{Encrypt}(pk, (t_c, \mathsf{VK}), \mathbf{a}'_i; \mathbf{r}_i)$ using random coins $\mathbf{r}_i \hookleftarrow D_R^{\mathsf{LPKE}}$. Let $\mathbf{a} = (\mathbf{a}_1, \ldots, \mathbf{a}_\kappa)$ and $\mathbf{r} = (\mathbf{r}_1, \ldots, \mathbf{r}_\kappa)$.
2. Compute $\mathsf{Chall} = \mathsf{Hash}(k, (x, \mathbf{a}, t_c, \mathsf{VK})) \in \{0,1\}^\kappa$.
3. Compute $\mathbf{z}' = (\mathbf{z}'_1, \ldots, \mathbf{z}'_\kappa) = \mathsf{P}'(\mathsf{crs}'_{\mathcal{L}}, x, w, \mathbf{a}', \mathsf{Chall}, st')$ via κ executions of the prover of Π'. Define $\mathbf{z} = (\mathbf{z}', \mathbf{a}', \mathbf{r})$.
4. Generate a one-time signature $sig \leftarrow \mathcal{S}(\mathsf{SK}, (x, t_c, \mathbf{a}, \mathbf{z}, \mathsf{lbl}))$ and output the proof $\pi = ((t_c, \mathsf{VK}), (\mathbf{a}, \mathbf{z}), sig)$.

$\mathsf{V}(\mathsf{crs}, x, \pi, \mathsf{lbl})$: Given a statement x, a label lbl and a candidate proof $\pi = ((t_c, \mathsf{VK}), (\mathbf{a}, \mathbf{z}), sig)$, return 0 if $\mathcal{V}(\mathsf{VK}, (x, t_c, \mathbf{a}, \mathbf{z}, \mathsf{lbl}), sig) = 0$. Otherwise,

1. Write $\mathbf{z}$ as $\mathbf{z} = ((\mathbf{z}'_1, \ldots, \mathbf{z}'_\kappa), (\mathbf{a}'_1, \ldots, \mathbf{a}'_\kappa), (\mathbf{r}_1, \ldots, \mathbf{r}_\kappa))$. Return 0 if there exists $i \in [\kappa]$ such that $\mathbf{a}_i \neq \mathsf{Encrypt}(pk, (t_c, \mathsf{VK}), \mathbf{a}'_i; \mathbf{r}_i)$ or $\mathbf{r}_i \notin R^{\mathsf{LPKE}}$.
2. Let $\mathsf{Chall} = \mathsf{Hash}(k, (x, (\mathbf{a}_1, \ldots, \mathbf{a}_\kappa), t_c, \mathsf{VK}))$. If there exists $i \in [\kappa]$ such that $\mathsf{V}'(\mathsf{crs}'_{\mathcal{L}}, x, (\mathbf{a}'_i, \mathsf{Chall}[i], \mathbf{z}'_i)) = 0$, return 0. Otherwise, return 1.

In the full version of the paper, we show that the unbounded simulation-soundness of the above argument system is tightly related to the security of its underlying building blocks, which are all instantiable (with tight security reductions) from LWE.

5   Trapdoor Σ-Protocols for ACPS Ciphertexts

The KDM-CPA system of Applebaum $et\ al.$ [6] uses a modulus $q = p^2$, for some prime p. Its public key $(\mathbf{A}, \mathbf{b}) \in \mathbb{Z}_q^{n \times m} \times \mathbb{Z}_q^m$ contains a random matrix $\mathbf{A} \sim U(\mathbb{Z}_q^{n \times m})$ and a vector $\mathbf{b} = \mathbf{A}^\top \cdot \mathbf{s} + \mathbf{e}$, for some $\mathbf{s} \sim D_{\mathbb{Z}^n, \alpha q}$, $\mathbf{e} \sim D_{\mathbb{Z}^m, \alpha q}$. Its encryption algorithm proceeds analogously to the primal Regev cryptosystem [79] and computes $\mathbf{c} = (\bar{\mathbf{c}}, c) = (\mathbf{A} \cdot \mathbf{r}, \mathbf{b}^\top \mathbf{r} + \mu \cdot p + \chi) \in \mathbb{Z}_q^{n+1}$, where $\mathbf{r} \sim D_{\mathbb{Z}^m, r}$ is a Gaussian vector and $\chi \sim D_{\mathbb{Z}, r'}$ is sampled from a Gaussian with a slightly larger standard deviation. Decryption proceeds by rounding $c - \mathbf{s}^\top \cdot \bar{\mathbf{c}} \mod q$ to the nearest multiple of p.

In this section, we describe a trapdoor Σ-protocol allowing to prove that two ACPS ciphertexts $\mathbf{c}_0 = (\bar{\mathbf{c}}_0, c_0)$, $\mathbf{c}_1 = (\bar{\mathbf{c}}_1, c_1)$ are both encryptions of the same $\mu \in \mathbb{Z}_p$. This protocol is obtained by extending a simpler protocol (described in the full version of the paper), which argues that a given vector $\mathbf{c} \in \mathbb{Z}_q^{n+1}$ is an ACPS encryption of some plaintext $\mu \in \mathbb{Z}_p$.

We note that Ciampi $et\ al.$ [33] recently gave a construction of trapdoor Σ-protocol from any Σ-protocol. The Σ-protocol described hereunder is natively trapdoor without applying the transformation of [33].

PROVING PLAINTEXT EQUALITIES IN ACPS CIPHERTEXTS. Let $q = p^2$, for some prime p, and a matrix $\mathbf{A}$ which is used to set up two Regev public keys $(\mathbf{A}, \mathbf{b}_0) \in \mathbb{Z}_q^{n \times m} \times \mathbb{Z}_q^m$ and $(\mathbf{A}, \mathbf{b}_1) \in \mathbb{Z}_q^{n \times m} \times \mathbb{Z}_q^m$, where $\mathbf{b}_0 = \mathbf{A}^\top \cdot \mathbf{s}_0 + \mathbf{e}_0$ and $\mathbf{b}_1 = \mathbf{A}^\top \cdot \mathbf{s}_1 + \mathbf{e}_1$ for some $\mathbf{s}_0, \mathbf{s}_1 \sim D_{\mathbb{Z}^n, \alpha q}$, $\mathbf{e}_0, \mathbf{e}_1 \sim D_{\mathbb{Z}^m, \alpha q}$. Let also the matrix

$$
\mathbf{A}_{\mathsf{eq}} = \left[\begin{array}{cc|cc} \mathbf{A} & & & \\ \mathbf{b}_0^\top & 1 & & \\ \hline & & \mathbf{A} & \\ & & \mathbf{b}_1^\top & 1 \end{array} \right] \in \mathbb{Z}_q^{2(n+1) \times 2(m+1)}, \tag{4}
$$

We give a trapdoor Σ-protocol for the language $\mathcal{L}^{\mathsf{eq}} = (\mathcal{L}_{\mathsf{zk}}^{\mathsf{eq}}, \mathcal{L}_{\mathsf{sound}}^{\mathsf{eq}})$, where

$$
\mathcal{L}_{\mathsf{zk}}^{\mathsf{eq}} := \Big\{ (\mathbf{c}_0, \mathbf{c}_1) \in (\mathbb{Z}_q^{n+1})^2 \mid \exists \mathbf{r}_0, \mathbf{r}_1 \in \mathbb{Z}^m, \ \chi_0, \chi_1 \in \mathbb{Z}, \ \mu \in \mathbb{Z}_p :
$$
$$
\|\mathbf{r}_b\| \le B_r, \ |\chi_b| \le B_\chi \quad \forall b \in \{0,1\}
$$
$$
\wedge \quad \mathbf{c}_b = \bar{\mathbf{A}}_b \cdot [\mathbf{r}_b^\top \mid \chi_b]^\top + \mu \cdot [\mathbf{0}^{n\top} \mid p]^\top \mod q \Big\},
$$
$$
\mathcal{L}_{\mathsf{sound}}^{\mathsf{eq}} := \Big\{ (\mathbf{c}_0, \mathbf{c}_1) \in (\mathbb{Z}_q^{n+1})^2 \mid \exists \ \bar{\mathbf{c}}_0, \bar{\mathbf{c}}_1 \in \mathbb{Z}_q^n, \ v_0, v_1 \in [-B^*, B^*], \ \mu \in \mathbb{Z}_p
$$
$$
\wedge \quad \mathbf{c}_b = \left[\begin{array}{c} \bar{\mathbf{c}}_b \\ \hline \mathbf{s}_b^\top \cdot \bar{\mathbf{c}}_b + p \cdot \mu + v_b \end{array} \right] \quad \forall b \in \{0,1\} \Big\},
$$

where

$$
\bar{\mathbf{A}}_b = \left[\begin{array}{c|c} \mathbf{A} & \\ \hline \mathbf{b}_b^\top & 1 \end{array} \right] \in \mathbb{Z}_q^{(n+1) \times (m+1)} \qquad\qquad \forall b \in \{0,1\}.
$$

We note that $\mathcal{L}_{zk}^{eq} \subseteq \mathcal{L}_{sound}^{eq}$ when $B_r \alpha q \sqrt{m} + B_\chi < B^* \ll p$. Also, $\mathcal{L}_{sound}^{eq}$ is equivalently defined as the language of pairs $(\mathbf{c}_0, \mathbf{c}_1)$ such that such that

$$\left[\begin{array}{c|c|c|c} -\mathbf{s}_0^\top & 1 & & \\ \hline & & -\mathbf{s}_1^\top & 1 \end{array}\right] \cdot \begin{bmatrix} \mathbf{c}_0 \\ \mathbf{c}_1 \end{bmatrix} \bmod q = \begin{bmatrix} v_0 \\ v_1 \end{bmatrix} + \mu \cdot \begin{bmatrix} p \\ p \end{bmatrix}$$

for some $\mu \in \mathbb{Z}_p$, $v_0, v_1 \in [-B^*, B^*]$.

$\mathsf{Gen}_{par}(1^\lambda)$: On input of a security parameter $\lambda \in \mathbb{N}$, choose moduli q, p with $q = p^2$, dimensions n, m, and error rate $\alpha > 0$ and a Gaussian parameter $\sigma_{eq} \geq \log(2m + 2) \cdot \sqrt{B_r^2 + B_\chi^2}$. Define public parameters $\mathsf{par} = \{\lambda, q, p, n, m, \alpha, \sigma_{eq}\}$.

$\mathsf{Gen}_{\mathcal{L}}(\mathsf{par}, \mathcal{L}^{eq})$: Takes in global parameters par and the description of a language $\mathcal{L}^{eq} = (\mathcal{L}_{zk}^{eq}, \mathcal{L}_{sound}^{eq})$ specifying real numbers $B^*, B_r, B_\chi > 0$ such that $B_r \alpha q \sqrt{m} + B_\chi < B^* \ll p$, and a matrix $\mathbf{A}_{eq}$ from the distribution (4). It defines the language-dependent $\mathsf{crs}_{\mathcal{L}} = \{\bar{\mathbf{A}}, B^*, B_r, B_\chi\}$. The global CRS is

$$\mathsf{crs} = \left(\{\lambda, q, p, n, m, \alpha, \sigma_{eq}\}, \{\mathbf{A}_{eq}, B^*, B_r, B_\chi\}\right).$$

$\mathsf{TrapGen}(\mathsf{par}, \mathcal{L}, \tau_{\mathcal{L}})$: Given par and a language description $\mathcal{L}^{eq}$ that specifies $B^*, B_r, B_\chi > 0$ satisfying the same constraints as in $\mathsf{Gen}_{\mathcal{L}}$, a matrix $\mathbf{A}_{eq}$ sampled from the distribution (4), as well as a membership-testing trapdoor $\tau_{\mathcal{L}} = (\mathbf{s}_0, \mathbf{s}_1) \sim (D_{\mathbb{Z}^n, \alpha q})^2$ for $\mathcal{L}_{sound}^{eq}$, output $\mathsf{crs}_{\mathcal{L}} = \{\bar{\mathbf{A}}, B^*, B_r, B_\chi\}$. The global CRS is $\mathsf{crs} = \left(\{\lambda, q, p, n, m, \alpha, \sigma_{eq}\}, \{\mathbf{A}_{eq}, B^*, B_r, B_\chi\}\right)$ and the trapdoor $\tau_\Sigma = (\mathbf{s}_0, \mathbf{s}_1) \in \mathbb{Z}^n \times \mathbb{Z}^n$.

$\mathsf{P}\left(\mathsf{crs}, (\mathbf{c}_0, \mathbf{c}_1), (\mu, \mathbf{w})\right) \leftrightarrow \mathsf{V}(\mathsf{crs}, \mathbf{x})$: Given crs and a statement

$$\begin{bmatrix} \mathbf{c}_0 \\ \mathbf{c}_1 \end{bmatrix} = \mathbf{A}_{eq} \cdot [\mathbf{r}_0^\top \mid \chi_0 \mid \mathbf{r}_1^\top \mid \chi_1]^\top + \mu \cdot [\mathbf{0}^{n\top} \mid p \mid \mathbf{0}^{n\top} \mid p]^\top \in \mathbb{Z}_q^{2(n+1)},$$

the prover P (who has $\mathbf{w} = [\mathbf{r}_0^\top \mid \chi_0 \mid \mathbf{r}_1^\top \mid \chi_1]^\top \in \mathbb{Z}^{2(m+1)}$ and $\mu \in \mathbb{Z}_p$) and the verifier V interact as follows.

1. The prover P samples a uniform scalar $r_\mu \hookleftarrow U(\mathbb{Z}_p)$ and Gaussian vector $\mathbf{r}_w \hookleftarrow D_{\mathbb{Z}^{2(m+1)}, \sigma_{eq}}$. It computes the following which is sent to V:

$$\mathbf{a} = \mathbf{A}_{eq} \cdot \mathbf{r}_w + r_\mu \cdot [\mathbf{0}^{n\top} \mid p \mid \mathbf{0}^{n\top} \mid p]^\top \in \mathbb{Z}_q^{2(n+1)}.$$

2. V sends a random challenge $\mathsf{Chall} \in \{0, 1\}$ to P.
3. P computes $\mathbf{z} = \mathbf{r}_w + \mathsf{Chall} \cdot \mathbf{w} \in \mathbb{Z}^{2(m+1)}$, $z_\mu = r_\mu + \mathsf{Chall} \cdot \mu \bmod p$. It sends $(\mathbf{z}, z_\mu)$ to V with probability $\theta = \min\left(\frac{D_{\mathbb{Z}^{2(m+1)}, \sigma_{eq}}(\mathbf{z})}{M \cdot D_{\mathbb{Z}^{2(m+1)}, \sigma_{eq}, \mathsf{Chall} \cdot \mathbf{w}}(\mathbf{z})}, 1\right)$, where $M = e^{12/\log(2(m+1)) + 1/(2\log^2(2(m+1)))}$. With probability $1 - \theta$, P aborts.
4. Given $(\mathbf{z}, z_\mu) \in \mathbb{Z}^{2(m+1)} \times \mathbb{Z}_p$, V checks if $\|\mathbf{z}\| \leq \sigma_{eq}\sqrt{2(m+1)}$ and

$$\mathbf{a} + \mathsf{Chall} \cdot \begin{bmatrix} \mathbf{c}_0 \\ \mathbf{c}_1 \end{bmatrix} = \mathbf{A}_{eq} \cdot \mathbf{z} + z_\mu \cdot [\mathbf{0}^{n\top} \mid p \mid \mathbf{0}^{n\top} \mid p]^\top \bmod q. \qquad (5)$$

If these conditions do not both hold, V halts and returns $\perp$.

BadChallenge$(par, \tau_\Sigma, crs, (c_0, c_1), a)$: Given $\tau_\Sigma = (s_0, s_1) \in \mathbb{Z}^n \times \mathbb{Z}^n$, parse the first prover message as $a = (a_0^\top \mid a_1^\top)^\top \in \mathbb{Z}_q^{2(n+1)}$. If there exists $d \in \{0,1\}$ such that no pair $(\mu'_d, v_d) \in [-(p-1)/2, (p-1)/2] \times [-B^*/2, B^*/2]^2$ satisfies

$$\left[\begin{array}{c|c|c|c} -s_0^\top & 1 & & \\ \hline & & -s_1^\top & 1 \end{array} \right] \cdot (a + d \cdot c) \bmod q = v_d + \mu'_d \cdot \begin{bmatrix} p \\ p \end{bmatrix} \tag{6}$$

over $\mathbb{Z}$, then return Chall $= 1 - d$. Otherwise, return Chall $= \perp$.

The completeness of the protocol crucially uses the fact that p divides q to ensure that the response $z_\mu = r_\mu + $ Chall $\cdot \mu \bmod p$ satisfies (5).

The intuition of BadChallenge is that, for a false statement $(c_0, c_1) \notin \mathcal{L}_{\text{sound}}^{\text{eq}}$, there exists $d \in \{0,1\}$ such that no pair (μ'_d, v_d) satisfies (6) for a small enough $v_d \in \mathbb{Z}^2$. Moreover, for this challenge Chall $= d$, no valid response can exist, as shown in the proof of Lemma 5.1. We note that BadChallenge may output a bit even when there is no bad challenge at all for a given a. These "false positives" are not a problem since, in order to soundly instantiate Fiat-Shamir, we only need the somewhere CI hash function to avoid the bad challenge when it exists.

Lemma 5.1. *The above construction is a trapdoor Σ-protocol for $\mathcal{L}^{\text{eq}}$ if we set $\sigma_{\text{eq}} \geq \log(2m + 2) \cdot \sqrt{B_r^2 + B_\chi^2}$ and*

$$B^* > \max(2\sigma_{\text{eq}}\sqrt{2m + 2} \cdot (\alpha q\sqrt{m} + 1), B_r\alpha q\sqrt{m} + B_\chi).$$

(The proof is given in the full version of the paper.)

PARALLEL REPETITIONS. To achieve negligible soundness error, the protocol is repeated $\kappa = \Theta(\lambda)$ times in parallel by first computing $(a_1, \ldots, a_\kappa)$ before obtaining Chall $=$ Chall$[1] \ldots$ Chall$[\kappa]$ and computing the response $\bar{z} = (z_1, \ldots, z_\kappa)$, $(z_{\mu,1}, \ldots, z_{\mu,\kappa})$. We then handle $\bar{z}$ as an integer vector in $\mathbb{Z}^{\kappa \cdot (m+1)}$ and reject it with probability $\theta = \min\left(1, D_{\mathbb{Z}^{2\kappa \cdot (m+1)}, \sigma_{\text{eq}}}(z)/M \cdot D_{\mathbb{Z}^{2\kappa \cdot (m+1)}, \sigma_{\text{eq}}, \text{Chall} \cdot (1^\kappa \otimes w)}(z)\right)$, where $M = e^{12/\log(2\kappa \cdot (m+1)) + 1/(2\log^2(2\kappa \cdot (m+1)))}$. Then, we need to slightly increase σ_{eq} and set $\sigma_{\text{eq}} \geq \log(2\kappa(m+1)) \cdot \sqrt{\kappa(B_r^2 + B_\chi^2)}$.

Acknowledgments. Part of this research was funded by the French ANR ALAMBIC project (ANR-16-CE39-0006). This work was also supported in part by the European Union PROMETHEUS project (Horizon 2020 Research and Innovation Program, grant 780701). Khoa Nguyen was supported in part by the Gopalakrishnan - NTU PPF 2018, by A * STAR, Singapore under research grant SERC A19E3b0099, and by Vietnam National University HoChiMinh City (VNU-HCM) under grant number NCM2019-18-01.

References

1. Abdalla, M., Bourse, F., De Caro, A., Pointcheval, D.: Simple functional encryption schemes for inner products. In: PKC (2015)
2. Agrawal, S., Boneh, D., Boyen, X.: Efficient lattice (H)IBE in the standard model. In: Eurocrypt (2010)

3. Agrawal, S., Libert, B., Stehlé, D.: Fully secure functional encryption for inner products from standard assumptions. In: Crypto (2016)
4. Alperin-Sheriff, J., Peikert, C.: Circular and KDM security for identity-based encryption. In: PKC (2012)
5. Applebaum, B.: Key-dependent message security: Generic amplification and completeness theorems. J. Cryptol. **27**(3), 53 (2013)
6. Applebaum, B., Cash, C. Peikert, D., Sahai, A.: Fast cryptographic primitives and circular-secure encryption based on hard learning problems. In: Crypto (2009)
7. Asharov, G, Jain, A., Wichs, D.: Multiparty computation with low communication, computation and interaction via threshold FHE. Cryptology ePrint Archive: Report 2011/613 (2012)
8. Barak, B., Haitner, I., Hofheinz, D., Ishai, Y.: Bounded key-dependent message security. In: Eurocrypt (2010)
9. Barrington, D.: Bounded-width polynomial-size branching programs recognize exactly those languages in nc1. In STOC, (1986)
10. Bellare, M., Hofheinz, D., Yilek, S.: Possibility and impossibility results for encryption and commitment secure under selective opening. In: Eurocrypt (2009)
11. Bellare, M., Rogaway, P.: Random oracles are practical: a paradigm for designing efficient protocols. In: ACM-CCS (1993)
12. Bitansky, N., et al.: Why "Fiat-Shamir for proof" lacks a proof. In: TCC (2013)
13. Black, J., Rogaway, P. Shrimpton, T.: Encryption-scheme security in the presence of key-dependent messages. In: SAC (2002)
14. Boneh, D., Boyen, X.: Secure identity based encryption without random oracles. In: Crypto (2004)
15. Boneh, D., et al.: Fully key-homomorphic encryption, arithmetic circuit ABE and compact garbled circuits. In: Eurocrypt (2014)
16. Boneh, D., Halevi, S., Hamburg, M., Ostrovsky, R.: Circular-secure encryption from Decision Diffie-Hellman. In: Crypto (2008)
17. Boyen, X., Li, Q.: Towards tightly secure lattice short signature and ID-based encryption. In: Asiacrypt (2016)
18. Boyen, X., Li, Q.: Almost tight multi-instance multi-ciphertext identity-based encryption on lattices. In: ACNS (2018)
19. Boyle, E., Segev, G., Wichs, D.: Fully leakage-resilient signatures. In: Eurocrypt (2011)
20. Brakerski, Z., Goldwasser, S.: Circular and leakage resilient public-key encryption under subgroup indistinguishability (or: Quadratic residuosity strikes back). In: Crypto (2010)
21. Brakerski, Z., Goldwasser, S., Tauman Kalai, Y.: Black-box circular-secure encryption beyond affine functions. In :TCC (2011)
22. Brakerski, Z., Vaikuntanathan, V.: Lattice-based FHE as secure as PKE. In: ITCS (2014)
23. Camenisch, J., Lysyanskaya, A.: An efficient system for non-transferable anonymous credentials with optional anonymity revocation. In: Eurocrypt (2001)
24. J. Camensich, N. Chandran, and V. Shoup. A public key encryption scheme secure against key dependent chosen plaintext and adaptive chosen ciphertext attacks. In Eurocrypt, 2009
25. Canetti, R., Chen, Y., Holmgren, J., Lombardi, A., Rothblum, G., Rothblum, R.: Fiat-Shamir from simpler assumptions. Cryptology ePrint Archive: Report 2018/1004
26. Canetti, R., et al.: Fiat-Shamir: from practice to theory. In: STOC (2019)

27. Canetti, R., Chen, Y., Reyzin, L., Rothblum, R.: Fiat-Shamir and correlation intractability from strong KDM-secure encryption. In: Eurocrypt (2018)
28. Canetti, R., Goldreich, O., Halevi, S.: The random oracle methodology, revisted. J. ACM **51**(4) (2004)
29. Canetti, R., Halevi, S., Katz, J.: Chosen-ciphertext security from identity-based encryption. In: Eurocrypt (2004)
30. Canetti, R., Lombardi, A., Wichs, D.: Fiat-Shamir: From Practice to Theory, Part II (NIZK and Correlation Intractability from Circular-Secure FHE). Cryptology ePrint Archive: Report 2018/1248
31. Chase, M., Lysyanskaya, A.: Simulatable VRFs with applications to multi-theorem NIZK. In: Crypto (2007)
32. Choudhuri, A., Hubacek, P., Pietrzak, K., Rosen, A., Rothblum, G.: Finding a Nash equilibrium is no easier than breaking Fiat-Shamir. In: STOC (2019)
33. Ciampi, M., Parisella, R., Ventury, D.: On adaptive security of delayed-input sigma protocols and Fiat-Shamir NIZKs. In: SCN (2020)
34. Couteau, G., Hofheinz, D.: Designated-verifier pseudorandom generators, and their applications. In: Eurocrypt (2019)
35. Cramer, R.: Modular design of secure, yet practical cryptographic protocols. Ph.D. thesis, University of Amsterdam (1996)
36. Cramer, R., Damgård, I., Schoenmaekers, B.: Proofs of partial knowledge and simplified design of witness hiding protocols. In: Crypto (1994)
37. Cramer, R., Shoup, V.: Universal hash proofs and a paradigm for adaptive chosen ciphertext secure public-key encryption. In: Eurocrypt (2002)
38. Damgård, I.: Efficient concurrent zero-knowledge in the auxiliary string model. In: Eurocrypt (2000)
39. De Santis, A., Di Crescenzo, G., Ostrovsky, R., Persiano, G., Sahai, A.: Robust non-interactive zero-knowledge. In: Crypto (2001)
40. De Santis, A., Yung, M.: Cryptograpic applications of the non-interactive metaproof and many-prover systems. In: Crypto (1990)
41. Döttling, N.: Low-noise LPN: KDM secure public key encryption and sample amplification. In: PKC (2015)
42. Feige, U., Lapidot, D., Shamir,A.: Multiple non-interactive zero-knowledge under general assumptions. SIAM J. Comput. **29**(1) (1999)
43. Fiat, A., Shamir, A.: How to prove yourself: practical solutions to identification and signature problems. In: Crypto (1986)
44. Fouque, P.-A., Pointcheval, D.: Threshold cryptosystems secure against chosen-ciphertext attacks. In: Asiacrypt (2001)
45. Freire, E., Hofheinz, D., Paterson, K., Striecks, C.: Programmable hash functions in the multilinear setting. In: Crypto (2013)
46. Gentry, C., Peikert, C., Vaikuntanathan, V.: Trapdoors for hard lattices and new cryptographic constructions. In: STOC (2008)
47. Gentry, C., Sahai, A., Waters, B.: Homomorphic encryption from learning with errors: conceptually-simpler, asymptotically-faster, attribute-based. In: Crypto (2013)
48. Goldwasser, S., Micali, S., Rackoff, C.: The knowledge complexity of interactive proof systems. SIAM Journal on Computing (1989)
49. Goldwasser, S., Tauman Kalai, Y.: On the (in)security of the Fiat-Shamir paradigm. In: FOCS (2003)
50. Groth, J., Ostrovsky, R., Sahai, A.: New techniques for noninteractive zero-knowledge. J. ACM (2012)

51. Groth, J., Sahai, A.: Efficient non-interactive proof systems for bilinear groups. In: Eurocrypt (2008)
52. Halevi, S. Myers, S., Rackoff, C.: On seed-incompressible functions. In: TCC (2008)
53. Han, S., Liu, S., Lyu, L.: Efficient KDM-CCA secure public-key encryption for polynomial functions. In: Asiacrypt (2016)
54. Hara, K., Matsuda, T., Hanaoka, G., Tanaka, K.: Simulation-based receiver selective opening CCA secure PKE from standard computational assumptions. In: SCN (2018)
55. Hofheinz, D.. All-but-many lossy trapdoor functions. In: Eurocrypt (2012)
56. Hofheinz, D.: Circular chosen-ciphertext security with compact ciphertexts. In: Eurocrypt (2013)
57. Hofheinz, D., Jager, T.: Tightly secure signatures and public-key encryption. In: Crypto (2012)
58. Holmgren, J., Lombardi, A.: Cryptographic hashing from strong one-way functions (or: One-way product functions and their applications). In: FOCS (2018)
59. Jager, T.: Verifiable random functions from weaker assumptions. In: TCC (2015)
60. Kiltz, E.: Chosen-ciphertext security from tag-based encryption. In: TCC (2006)
61. Kitagawa, F., Matsuda, T.: CPA-to-CCA transformation for KDM security. In: TCC (2019)
62. Kitagawa, F., Matsuda, V, Tanaka, K.: Simple and efficient KDM-CCA secure public key encryption. In: Asiacrypt (2019)
63. Kitagawa, F., Tanaka, K.: A framework for achieving KDM-CCA secure public-key encryption. In: Asiacrypt (2018)
64. Lai, Q., Liu, F., Wang, Z.: Almost tight security in lattices with polynomial moduli - PRF, IBE, all-but-many LTF, and more. In: PKC (2020)
65. Libert, B., Nguyen, K., Passelègue, A., Titiu, R.: Simulation-sound arguments for LWE and applications to KDM-CCA2 security. Cryptology ePrint Archive, Report 2019/908 (2020). https://eprint.iacr.org/2019/908
66. Libert, B., Peters, T., Joye, M., Yung, M.: Non-malleability from malleability: simulation-sound quasi-adaptive NIZK proofs and CCA2-secure encryption from homomorphic signatures. In: Eurocrypt (2014)
67. Libert, B., Sakzad, A., Stehlé, D., Steinfeld, R.: All-but-many lossy trapdoor functions and selective opening chosen-ciphertext security from LWE. In: Crypto (2017)
68. Lombardi, A., Quach, W., Rothblum, R., Wichs, D., Wu, D.: New constructions of reusable designated-verifier NIZKs. In: Crypto (2019)
69. Lu, X., Li, B., Jia, D.: KDM-CCA security from RKA secure authenticated encryption. In: Eurocrypt (2015)
70. Lyubashevsky, V.: Lattice-Based Identification Schemes Secure Under Active Attacks. In: PKC (2008)
71. Lyubashevsky, V.: Fiat-Shamir with aborts: applications to lattice and factoring-based signatures. In: Asiacrypt (2009)
72. MacKenzie, P., Yang, K.: On simulation-sound trapdoor commitments. In: Eurocrypt (2004)
73. Malkin, T., Teranishi, I., Yung, M.: Efficient circuit-size independent public key encryption with KDM security. In: Eurocrypt (2012)
74. Micciancio,D., Peikert, C.: Trapdoors for lattices: simpler, tighter, faster, smaller. In: Eurocrypt (2012)
75. Naor, M., Yung, M.: Public-key cryptosystems provably secure against chosen ciphertext attacks. In: STOC (1990)
76. Peikert, C., Shiehian, S.: Non-interactive zero knowledge for NP from (plain) learning with errors. In: Crypto (2019)

77. Peikert, C., Vaikuntanathan, V., Waters, B.: A framework for efficient and composable oblivious transfer. In: Crypto (2008)
78. Pointcheval, D., Stern, J.: Security arguments for digital signatures and blind signatures. J. Cryptol. **13**(3) (2000)
79. Regev, O.: On lattices, learning with errors, random linear codes, and cryptography. In: STOC (2005)
80. Sahai, A.: Non-malleable non-interactive zero-knowledge and adaptive chosen-ciphertext security. In: FOCS (1999)
81. Schnorr, C.-P.: Efficient identification and signatures for smart cards. In: Crypto (1989)
82. Tauman Kalai, Y., Rothblum, G., Rothblum, R.: From obfuscation to the security of Fiat-Shamir for proofs. In: Crypto (2017)
83. Yamada, S.: Asymptotically compact adaptively secure lattice IBEs and verifiable random functions via generalized partitioning techniques. In: Crypto (2017)

CCA-Secure (Puncturable) KEMs from Encryption with Non-Negligible Decryption Errors

Valerio Cini[✉], Sebastian Ramacher, Daniel Slamanig, and Christoph Striecks

AIT Austrian Institute of Technology, Vienna, Austria
{valerio.cini,sebastian.ramacher,daniel.slamanig,
christoph.striecks}@ait.ac.at

Abstract. Public-key encryption (PKE) schemes or key-encapsulation mechanisms (KEMs) are fundamental cryptographic building blocks to realize secure communication protocols. There are several known transformations that generically turn weakly secure schemes into strongly (i.e., IND-CCA) secure ones. While most of these transformations require the weakly secure scheme to provide perfect correctness, Hofheinz, Hövelmanns, and Kiltz (HHK) (TCC 2017) have recently shown that variants of the Fujisaki-Okamoto (FO) transform can work with schemes that have negligible correctness error in the (quantum) random oracle model (QROM). Many recent schemes in the NIST post-quantum competition (PQC) use variants of these transformations. Some of their CPA-secure versions even have a non-negligible correctness error and so the techniques of HHK cannot be applied.

In this work, we study the setting of generically transforming PKE schemes with potentially large, i.e., non-negligible, correctness error to ones having negligible correctness error. While there have been previous treatments in an asymptotic setting by Dwork et al. (EUROCRYPT 2004), our goal is to come up with practically efficient compilers in a concrete setting and apply them in two different contexts: firstly, we show how to generically transform weakly secure deterministic or randomized PKEs into CCA-secure KEMs in the (Q)ROM using variants of HHK. This applies to essentially all candidates to the NIST PQC based on lattices and codes with non-negligible error, for which we provide an extensive analysis. We thereby show that it improves some of the code-based candidates. Secondly, we study puncturable KEMs in terms of the Bloom Filter KEM (BFKEM) proposed by Derler et al. (EUROCRYPT 2018) which inherently have a non-negligible correctness error. BFKEMs are a building block to construct fully forward-secret zero round-trip time (0-RTT) key-exchange protocols. In particular, we show how to achieve the first post-quantum secure BFKEM generically from lattices and codes by applying our techniques to identity-based encryption (IBE) schemes with (non-)negligible correctness error.

Keywords: CPA-to-CCA transformations · Fujisaki-Okamoto transform · Non-negligible correctness error · Puncturable encryption

© International Association for Cryptologic Research 2020
S. Moriai and H. Wang (Eds.): ASIACRYPT 2020, LNCS 12491, pp. 159–190, 2020.
https://doi.org/10.1007/978-3-030-64837-4_6

1   Introduction

Public-key encryption (PKE) schemes or key-encapsulation mechanisms (KEM) are fundamental cryptographic building blocks to realize secure communication protocols. The security property considered standard nowadays is security against chosen-ciphertext attacks (IND-CCA security). This is important to avoid pitfalls and attacks in the practical deployments of such schemes, e.g., padding oracle attacks as demonstrated by Bleichenbacher [12] and still showing up very frequently [5,14,46,57]. Also, for key exchange protocols that achieve the desirable forward secrecy property, formal analysis shows that security against active attacks is required (cf. [22,45,50,56]). This equally holds for recent proposals for fully forward-secret zero round-trip time (0-RTT) key-exchange protocols from puncturable KEMs [20,21,34] and even for ephemeral KEM keys for a post-quantum secure TLS handshake without signatures [61].

In the literature, various different ways of obtaining CCA security generically from weaker encryption schemes providing only chosen-plaintext (IND-CPA) or one-way (OW-CPA) security are known. These can be in the standard model using the double-encryption paradigm due to Naor and Yung [54], the compiler from selectively secure identity-based encryption (IBE) due to Canetti, Halevi and Katz [18], or the more recent works due to Koppula and Waters [49] based on so called hinting pseudo-random generators and Hohenberger, Koppula, and Waters [42] from injective trapdoor functions. In the random oracle model (ROM), CCA security can be generically obtained via the well-known and widely-used Fujisaki-Okamoto (FO) transform [27,28] yielding particularly practical efficiency.

Perfect Correctness and (Non-)Negligible Correctness Error. A property common to many compilers is the requirement for the underlying encryption schemes to provide perfect correctness, i.e., there are no valid ciphertexts where the decryption algorithm fails when used with honestly generated keys. Recently, Hofheinz, Hövelmanns and Kiltz (HHK) [40] investigated different variants of the FO transform also in a setting where the underlying encryption scheme has non-perfect correctness and in particular decryption errors may occur with a negligible probability in the security parameter. This is interesting since many PKE or KEM schemes based on conjectured quantum safe assumptions and in particular assumptions on lattices and codes do not provide perfect correctness. Even worse, some of the candidates submitted to the NIST post-quantum competition (PQC) suffer from a *non-negligible* correctness error and so the FO transforms of HHK cannot be applied. Ad-hoc approaches to overcome this problem that are usually chosen by existing constructions in practice—if the problem is considered at all—is to increase the parameters to obtain a suitably small decryption error, applying an error correcting code on top or implementing more complex decoders. In practice, these ad-hoc methods come with drawbacks. Notably, LAC which is a Learning With Errors (LWE) based IND-CCA secure KEM in the 2nd round of the NIST PQC that applies an error correcting code is susceptible to a key recovery attack recently proposed by Guo et al. [37]. Also, code-based schemes have a history of attacks [26,36,59] due to decoding errors. Recently, Bindel and Schanck [10] proposed a failure boosting attack for lattice-based schemes with a non-zero correctness error. For some code-based schemes, the analysis of the decoding error is a non-trivial task as it specifically depends on the decoder. For instance, the analysis of BIKE's decoder, another 2nd round NIST PQC candidate, has recently been updated [62].

Consequently, it would be interesting to have rigorous and simple approaches to remove decryption errors (to a certain degree) from PKE and KEM schemes.

Immunizing Encryption Schemes. The study of "immunizing" encryption schemes from decryption errors is not new. Goldreich, Goldwasser, and Halevi [32] studied the reduction or removal of decryption errors in the Ajtai-Dwork encryption scheme as well as Howgrave-Graham et al. [44] in context of NTRU. The first comprehensive and formal treatment has been given by Dwork, Naor, and Reingold [25] who study different amplification techniques in the standard and random oracle model to achieve non-malleable (IND-CCA secure) schemes. One very intuitive compiler is the direct product compiler $\mathsf{Enc}^{\otimes \ell}$ which encrypts a message M under a PKE $\Pi = (\mathsf{KGen}, \mathsf{Enc}, \mathsf{Dec})$ with a certain decryption error δ under ℓ independent public-keys from KGen, i.e., $\mathsf{pk}' := (\mathsf{pk}_1, \ldots, \mathsf{pk}_\ell)$ as $\mathsf{Enc}'(\mathsf{pk}', M) := (\mathsf{Enc}(\mathsf{pk}_1, M), \ldots, \mathsf{Enc}(\mathsf{pk}_\ell, M))$. Dec', given $C' = (C_1, \ldots, C_\ell)$ tries to decrypt C_i, $1 \leq i \leq \ell$, and returns the result of a majority vote among all decrypted messages, yielding an encryption scheme with some error $\delta' \leq \delta$. Their asymptotic analysis, however, and limitation to PKEs with a binary message space does not make it immediate what this would mean in a concrete setting and in particular how to choose ℓ for practically interesting values of δ and δ'. For turning a so-obtained amplified scheme with negligible correctness error into a CCA-secure one in the ROM, they provide a transform using similar ideas, but more involved than the FO transform. Bitansky and Vaikuntanathan [11] go a step further and turn encryption schemes with a correctness error into perfectly correct ones, whereas they even consider getting completely rid of bad keys (if they exist) and, thus, completely immunize encryption schemes. They build upon the direct product compiler of Dwork et al. and then apply reverse randomization [53] and Nisan-Wigderson style derandomization [55]. Thereby, they partition the randomness space into good and bad randomness, and ensure that only good randomness is used for encryption and key generation.

Our Goals. In this work, we are specifically interested in transformations that lift weaker schemes with non-negligible correctness error into CCA-secure ones with negligible error. Thereby, our focus is on modular ways of achieving this and can be seen as a concrete treatment of ideas that have also be discussed by Dwork et al. [25], who, however, treat their approaches in an asymptotic setting only. We show that the direct product compiler can be used with variants of the standard FO transform considered by HHK [40] (in the ROM) as well as Bindel et al. [9] and Jiang et al. [48] (in the quantum ROM (QROM) [15]). They are used by many candidates of the NIST PQC, when starting from PKE schemes having non-negligible correctness error generically. As we are particularly interested in *practical compilers* in a *concrete setting* to obtain CCA security for KEMs in the (Q)ROM, we analyze the concrete overhead of this compiler and its use with widely used variants of the transforms from HHK. Moreover, we provide a rigorous treatment of non-black-box applications of these ideas and show that they yield better concrete results than the direct application of the direct product compiler. Importantly, it gives a generic way to deal with the error from weaker schemes (e.g., IND-CPA secure ones with non-negligible error) which are easier to design. An interesting question that we will study is how does increasing from one to ℓ ciphertexts compare to increasing the parameters at comparable resulting decryption errors for existing round-two submissions in the NIST PQC. As it turns out, our approach performs well in context of code-based schemes but gives less advantage for lattice-based schemes.

We also study our approach beyond conventional PKEs and KEMs. In particular, a class of KEMs that have recently found interest especially in context of full forward-secrecy for zero round-trip time (0-RTT) key-exchange (KE) protocols are so-called *puncturable KEMs* [21,33,34,63] and, in particular, Bloom Filter KEMs (BFKEMs) [20,21]. BFKEMs schemes are CCA-secure KEMs that inherently have non-negligible correctness error. Interestingly, however, the non-negligible correctness error comes from the Bloom filter layer and the underlying IBE scheme (specifically, the Boneh-Franklin [16] instantiation in [21]) is required to provide perfect correctness. Thus, as all post-quantum IBEs have at least negligible correctness error, there are no known post-quantum BFKEMs.

1.1 Contribution

Our contributions on a more technical level can be summarized as follows:

Generic Transform. We revisit the ideas of the direct product compiler of Dwork et al. [25] (dubbed $C_{p,r}$ and $C_{p,d}$ for randomized and deterministic PKEs respectively) in the context of the modular framework of HHK [40]. In particular, we present a generic transform dubbed $T^\star$ that, given any randomized PKE scheme with non-negligible correctness error, produces a derandomized PKE scheme with negligible correctness error. We analyze the transform both in the ROM and QROM and give a tight reduction in the ROM and compare it to a generic application of the direct product compiler. The transform naturally fits into the modular framework of HHK [40], and, thus, by applying the $U^{\not\perp}$ transform, gives rise to an IND-CCA-secure KEM. For the analysis in the QROM, we follow the work of Bindel et al. [9]. We show that the $T^\star$ transform also fits into their framework. Hence, given the additional injectivity assumption, we also obtain a tight proof for $U^{\not\perp}$. But even if this assumption does not hold, the non-tight proofs of Jiang et al. [48] and Hövelmanns et al. [43] still apply. Compared to the analysis of the T transform that is used in the modular frameworks, our reductions lose a factor of ℓ, i.e., the number of parallel ciphertexts required to reach a negligible correctness error, in the ROM and a factor of ℓ^2 in the QROM. For concrete schemes this number is small (e.g., ≤ 5) and thus does not impose a significant loss. An overview of the transformations and how our transform fits into the modular frameworks is given in Fig. 1 (ROM) and Fig. 2

(QROM). Furthermore, using ideas similar to T*, we discuss a modified version of the deterministic direct product compiler $C_{p,d}$ which we denote by $C^*_{p,d}$, that compared to the original one allows to reduce the number of parallel repetitions needed to achieve negligible correctness error.

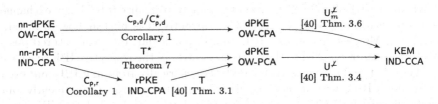

Fig. 1. Overview of the transformations in the ROM with the results related to T* highlighted in blue. rPKE denotes a randomized PKE. dPKE denotes a deterministic PKE. The prefix nn indicates encryption schemes with non-negligible correctness error. (Color figure online)

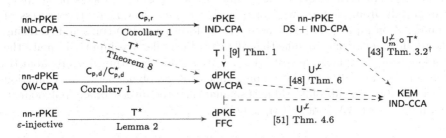

Fig. 2. Overview of the transformations in the QROM using the notation from Fig. 1. A dashed arrow denotes a non-tight reduction. DS denotes disjoint simulatability. †: Obtained by applying the modifications from Theorems 2 and 3 to [43, Thm 3.2].

Evaluation. We evaluate T* based on its application to code- and lattice-based second-round candidates in the NIST PQC. In particular, we focus on schemes that offer IND-CPA secure versions with non-negligible correctness error such as ROLLO [4], BIKE [3] and Round5 [30]. We compare their IND-CCA variants with our transform applied to the IND-CPA schemes. In particular, for the code-based schemes such as ROLLO we can observe improvements in the combined size of public keys and ciphertexts, a metric important when used in protocols such as TLS, as well as its runtime efficiency. We also argue the ease of implementing our so-obtained schemes which can rely on simpler decoders. For lattice-based constructions, we find that the use of the transform results in an increase in the sum of ciphertext and public-key size of 30% even in the best case scenario, i.e., for an IND-CPA version of KEM Round5 [30]. Nevertheless, it offers easier

constant-time implementations and the opportunity of decreasing the correctness
error without changing the underlying parameter set and, thus, the possibility
to focus on analyzing and implementing one parameter set for both, IND-CPA
and IND-CCA security.

Bloom Filter KEMs. Finally, we revisit puncturable KEMs from Bloom filter KEMs (BFKEMs) [20, 21], a recent primitive to realize 0-RTT key exchange
protocols with full forward-secrecy [34]. Currently, it is unclear how to instantiate BFKEMs generically from IBE and, in particular, from conjectured post-
quantum assumptions due to the correctness error of the respective IBE schemes.
We show that one can construct BFKEMs generically from any IBE and even
base it upon IBEs with a (non-)negligible correctness error. Consequently, our
results allow BFKEMs to be instantiated from lattice- and code-based IBEs and,
thereby, we obtain the first post-quantum CCA-secure BFKEM.

2   Preliminaries

Notation. For $n \in \mathbb{N}$, let $[n] := \{1, \ldots, n\}$, and let $\lambda \in \mathbb{N}$ be the security
parameter. For a finite set $\mathcal{S}$, we denote by $s \leftarrow_\$ \mathcal{S}$ the process of sampling
s uniformly from $\mathcal{S}$. For an algorithm A, let $y \leftarrow A(\lambda, x)$ be the process of
running A on input (λ, x) with access to uniformly random coins and assigning
the result to y (we may assume that all algorithms take λ as input). To make the
random coins r explicit, we write $A(x; r)$. We say an algorithm A is probabilistic
polynomial time (PPT) if the running time of A is polynomial in λ. A function
f is negligible if its absolute value is smaller than the inverse of any polynomial,
i.e., if $\forall c \; \exists k_0$ s.t. $\forall \lambda \geq k_0 : |f(\lambda)| < 1/\lambda^c$.

2.1   Public-Key Encryption and Key-Encapsulation Mechanisms

Public-key Encryption. A public-key encryption (PKE) scheme Π with message space $\mathcal{M}$ consists of the three PPT algorithms (KGen, Enc, Dec): KGen(λ), on
input security parameter λ, outputs public and secret keys (pk, sk). Enc(pk, M),
on input pk and message $M \in \mathcal{M}$, outputs a ciphertext C. Dec(sk, C), on input
sk and C, outputs $M \in \mathcal{M} \cup \{\bot\}$. We may assume that pk is implicitly available
in Dec.

Correctness. We recall the definition of δ-correctness of [40]. A PKE Π is
δ-correct if

$$E\left[\max_{M \in \mathcal{M}} \Pr\left[c \leftarrow \mathsf{Enc}(\mathsf{pk}, M) : \mathsf{Dec}(\mathsf{sk}, C) \neq M\right]\right] \leq \delta,$$

where the expected value is taken over all (pk, sk) $\leftarrow$ KGen(λ).

PKE-IND-CPA, PKE-OW-CPA, and PKE-OW-PCA Security. We say
a PKE Π is PKE-IND-CPA-secure if and only if any PPT adversary A has

Exp. $\mathsf{Exp}_{\Pi,A}^{\text{pke-ind-cpa}}(\lambda)$	**Exp.** $\mathsf{Exp}_{\Pi,A}^{\text{pke-ow-cpa}}(\lambda)$	**Exp.** $\mathsf{Exp}_{\Pi,A}^{\text{pke-ow-pca}}(\lambda)$
$(\mathsf{pk},\mathsf{sk}) \leftarrow \mathsf{KGen}(\lambda)$	$(\mathsf{pk},\mathsf{sk}) \leftarrow \mathsf{KGen}(\lambda)$	$(\mathsf{pk},\mathsf{sk}) \leftarrow \mathsf{KGen}(\lambda)$
$(M_0, M_1) \leftarrow A(\mathsf{pk})$	$M \leftarrow_\$ \mathcal{M}$	$M \leftarrow_\$ \mathcal{M}$
$b \leftarrow_\$ \{0,1\}$	$C^* \leftarrow \mathsf{Enc}(\mathsf{pk}, M)$	$C^* \leftarrow \mathsf{Enc}(\mathsf{pk}, M)$
$C^* \leftarrow \mathsf{Enc}(\mathsf{pk}, M_b)$	$M' \leftarrow A(\mathsf{pk}, C^*)$	$M' \leftarrow A^{\mathrm{Pco}(\cdot,\cdot)}(\mathsf{pk}, C^*)$
$b' \leftarrow A(C^*)$	if $M = M'$ then **return**	if $M = M'$ then **return** 1
if $b = b'$ then **return** 1	1 **else return** 0	**else return** 0
else return 0		

Fig. 3. PKE-x-y security with $\mathsf{x} \in \{OW, IND\}$, $\mathsf{y} \in \{CPA, PCA\}$ for Π.

only negligible advantage in the following security experiment. First, A gets an honestly generated public key pk. A outputs equal-length messages (M_0, M_1) and, in return, gets $C_b^* \leftarrow \mathsf{Enc}(\mathsf{pk}, M_b)$, for $b \leftarrow_\$ \{0,1\}$. Eventually, A outputs a guess b'. If $b = b'$, then the experiment outputs 1. For PKE-OW-CPA security, A does not receive a ciphertext for A-chosen messages, but only a ciphertext $C^* \leftarrow \mathsf{Enc}(\mathsf{pk}, M)$ for $M \leftarrow_\$ \mathcal{M}$ and outputs M'; if $M = M'$, then the experiment outputs 1. For PKE-OW-PCA security, A additionally has access to a plaintext checking oracle $\mathrm{Pco}(M, C)$ returning 1 if $M = \mathsf{Dec}(\mathsf{sk}, C)$ and 0 otherwise.

Definition 1. *For any PPT adversary A the advantage function*

$$\mathsf{Adv}_{\Pi,A}^{\text{pke-ind-cpa}}(\lambda) := \left| \Pr\left[\mathsf{Exp}_{\Pi,A}^{\text{pke-ind-cpa}}(\lambda) = 1 \right] - \frac{1}{2} \right|,$$

is negligible in λ, where the experiment $\mathsf{Exp}_{\Pi,A}^{\text{pke-ind-cpa}}(\lambda)$ is given in Fig. 3 and Π is a PKE as above.

Definition 2. *For any PPT adversary A, and $\mathsf{y} \in \{CPA, PCA\}$ the advantage function*

$$\mathsf{Exp}_{\Pi,A}^{\text{pke-OW-y}}(\lambda) := \Pr\left[\mathsf{Exp}_{\Pi,A}^{\text{pke-OW-y}}(\lambda) = 1 \right],$$

is negligible in λ, where the experiments $\mathsf{Exp}_{\Pi,A}^{\text{pke-ow-cpa}}(\lambda)$ and $\mathsf{Exp}_{\Pi,A}^{\text{pke-ow-pca}}(\lambda)$ are given in Fig. 3 and Π is a PKE as above.

We recall a well known lemma below:

Lemma 1. *For any adversary B there exists an adversary A with the same running time as that of B such that*

$$\mathsf{Adv}_{\Pi,B}^{\text{pke-ow-cpa}}(\lambda) \leq \mathsf{Adv}_{\Pi,A}^{\text{pke-ind-cpa}}(\lambda) + \frac{1}{|\mathcal{M}|}.$$

We note that Lemma 1 equivalently holds for the ℓ-IND-CPA notion below.

Multi-challenge Setting. We recall some basic observations from [8] regarding the multi-challenge security of PKE schemes. In particular, for our construction

---

Exp. $\mathsf{Exp}_{\Pi,A}^{\mathsf{pke\text{-}ffc}}(\lambda)$

  $(\mathsf{pk},\mathsf{sk}) \leftarrow \mathsf{KGen}(\lambda)$

  $L \leftarrow A(\mathsf{pk})$

  if exists $C \in L$ with $M \in \mathcal{M}$ such that $\mathsf{Enc}(\mathsf{pk}, M) = C$ and $\mathsf{Dec}(\mathsf{sk}, C) \neq M$

  then return 1 **else return** 0

Fig. 4. Finding-failing-ciphertext experiment for Π.

we need the relation between OW-CPA/IND-CPA security in the conventional single-challenge and single-user setting and n-OW-CPA/n-IND-CPA respectively, which represents the multi-challenge and multi-user setting. In particular, latter means that the adversary is allowed to obtain multiple challenges under multiple different public keys.

Theorem 1. (Th. 4.1 [8]). *Let $\Pi = (\mathsf{KGen}, \mathsf{Enc}, \mathsf{Dec})$ be a PKE scheme that provides x-CPA security with $\mathsf{x} \in \{\mathsf{OW}, \mathsf{IND}\}$. Then, it holds that:*

$$\mathsf{Adv}_{\Pi,A}^{\mathsf{pke\text{-}x\text{-}cpa}}(\lambda) \geq \frac{1}{q \cdot n} \cdot \mathsf{Adv}_{\Pi,A}^{\mathsf{n\text{-}pke\text{-}x\text{-}cpa}}(\lambda),$$

where n is the number of public keys and A makes at most q queries to any of its n challenge oracles.

Although the loss imposed by the reduction in Theorem 1 can be significant when used in a general multi-challenge and multi-user setting, in our application we only have cases where $n = 1$ and small q ($q = 5$ at most), or vice versa (i.e., $q = 1$ and $n = 5$ at most) thus tightness in a concrete setting is preserved.

Finding Failing Ciphertexts and Injectivity. For the QROM security proof we will need the following two definitions from [9].

Definition 3. (ε-injectivity). *A PKE Π is called ε-injective if*

– *Π is deterministic and*

$$\Pr\left[(\mathsf{pk}, \mathsf{sk}) \leftarrow \mathsf{KGen}(\lambda) : M \mapsto \mathsf{Enc}(\mathsf{pk}, M) \text{ is not injective}\right] \leq \varepsilon.$$

– *Π is non-deterministic with randomness space $\mathcal{R}$ and*

$$\Pr\left[\begin{array}{l} (\mathsf{pk}, \mathsf{sk}) \leftarrow \mathsf{KGen}(\lambda), \\ M, M' \leftarrow_\$ \mathcal{M}, r, r' \leftarrow_\$ \mathcal{R} \end{array} : \mathsf{Enc}(\mathsf{pk}, M; r) = \mathsf{Enc}(\mathsf{pk}, M'; r')\right] \leq \varepsilon.$$

Definition 4 (Finding failing ciphertexts). *For a deterministic PKE, the FFC-advantage of an adversary A is defined as*

$$\mathsf{Adv}_{\Pi,A}^{\mathsf{pke\text{-}ffc}}(\lambda) := \Pr\left[\mathsf{Exp}_{\Pi,A}^{\mathsf{pke\text{-}ffc}}(\lambda) = 1\right],$$

where the experiment $\mathsf{Exp}_{\Pi,A}^{\mathsf{pke\text{-}ffc}}$ is given in Fig. 4.

Key-Encapsulation Mechanism. A key-encapsulation mechanism (KEM) scheme KEM with key space $\mathcal{K}$ consists of the three PPT algorithms (KGen, Encaps, Decaps): KGen(λ), on input security parameter λ, outputs public and secret keys (pk, sk). Encaps(pk), on input pk, outputs a ciphertext C and key k. Decaps(sk, C), on input sk and C, outputs k or $\{\bot\}$.

Correctness of KEM. We call a KEM δ-correct if for all $\lambda \in \mathbb{N}$, for all (pk, sk) $\leftarrow$ KGen(λ), for all $(C, k) \leftarrow$ Enc(pk), we have that

$$\Pr\left[\mathsf{Dec}(\mathsf{sk}, C) \neq \mathsf{k}\right] \leq \delta.$$

KEM-IND-CCA Security. We say a KEM KEM is KEM-IND-CCA-secure if and only if any PPT adversary A has only negligible advantage in the following security experiment. First, A gets an honestly generated public key pk as well as a ciphertext-key pair (C^*, k_b), for $(C^*, \mathsf{k}_0) \leftarrow$ Encaps(pk), for $\mathsf{k}_1 \leftarrow_\$ \mathcal{K}$, and for $b \leftarrow_\$ \{0, 1\}$. A has access to a decapsulation oracle Dec(sk, $\cdot$) and we require that A never queries Decaps(sk, C^*). Eventually, A outputs a guess b'. Finally, if $b = b'$, then the experiment outputs 1.

Exp. $\mathsf{Exp}_{\mathsf{KEM},A}^{\mathsf{kem\text{-}ind\text{-}cca}}(\lambda)$

(pk, sk) $\leftarrow$ KGen(λ)
$(C^*, \mathsf{k}_0) \leftarrow$ Encaps(pk), $\mathsf{k}_1 \leftarrow_\$ \mathcal{K}$
$b \leftarrow_\$ \{0, 1\}$
$b' \leftarrow A^{\mathsf{Decaps}(\mathsf{sk}, \cdot)}(\mathsf{pk}, C^*, \mathsf{k}_b)$
if $b = b'$ **then return** 1 **else return** 0

Fig. 5. KEM-IND-CCA security experiment for KEM.

Definition 5. *For any PPT adversary A, the advantage functions*

$$\mathsf{Adv}_{\mathsf{KEM},A}^{\mathsf{kem\text{-}ind\text{-}cca}}(\lambda) := \left| \Pr\left[\mathsf{Exp}_{\mathsf{KEM},A}^{\mathsf{kem\text{-}ind\text{-}cca}}(\lambda) = 1\right] - \frac{1}{2} \right|,$$

is negligible in λ, where the experiment $\mathsf{Exp}_{\mathsf{KEM},A}^{\mathsf{kem\text{-}ind\text{-}cca}}(\lambda)$ is given in Fig. 5 and KEM is a KEM as above.

2.2 Identity-Based Encryption

An identity-based encryption (IBE) scheme IBE with identity space $\mathcal{ID}$ and message space $\mathcal{M}$ consists of the five PPT algorithms (KGen, Ext, Enc, Dec): KGen(λ) on input security parameter λ, outputs master public and secret keys (mpk, msk). Ext(msk, id) on input identity $id \in \mathcal{ID}$, outputs a user secret key usk_{id}. Enc(mpk, id, M) on input $mpk, id \in \mathcal{ID}$, and message $M \in \mathcal{M}$, outputs a ciphertext C. Dec(usk_{id}, C) on input usk_{id} and C, outputs $M \in \mathcal{M} \cup \{\bot\}$.

Correctness of IBE. Analogous to [40] we define δ-correctness of an IBE IBE for any $id \in \mathcal{ID}$ as

$$E\left[\max_{M \in \mathcal{M}} \Pr\left[C \leftarrow \mathsf{Enc}(mpk, id, M) : \mathsf{Dec}(usk_{id}, C) \neq M\right]\right] \leq \delta(\lambda),$$

where the expected value is taken over all $(mpk, msk) \leftarrow \mathsf{KGen}(\lambda)$ and $usk_{id} \leftarrow \mathsf{Ext}(msk, id)$.

We recall the formal definitions of IBE-sIND-CPA security in the full version.

3 CCA Security from Non-Negligible Correctness Errors

In this section, we present our approaches to generically achieve CCA secure KEMs in the (Q)ROM with negligible correctness error when starting from an OW-CPA or IND-CPA secure PKE with non-negligible correctness error. We start by discussing the definitions of correctness errors of PKE and KEMs. Then, we present a generic transform based on the direct product compiler of Dwork et al. [25] and revisit certain FO transformation variants from [40] (in particular the T and U transformations), their considerations in the QROM [9] and their application with the direct product compiler. As a better alternative, we analyze the non-black-box use of the previous technique yielding transformation $\mathsf{T}^\star$, that combines the direct product compiler with the T transformation. Finally, we provide a comprehensive comparison of the two approaches.

3.1 On the Correctness Error

In this work, we use the δ-correctness for PKEs given by HHK in [40]. With this definition, particularly bad keys in terms of correctness error only contribute a fraction to the overall correctness error as it averages the error probability over all key pairs: if there are negligible many keys with a higher correctness error, then those keys do not really contribute to the overall correctness error. At the same time this definition is tailored, via maxing over all possible messages, to the security proofs of the FO-transforms where an adversary could actively search for the worst possible message, in order to trigger decryption failure. As also done by Dwork et al. [25], we explicitly write the correctness error as a function in the security parameter:

Definition 6. *A* PKE Π *is* $\delta(\cdot)$*-correct if*

$$E\left[\max_{M \in \mathcal{M}} \Pr\left[C \leftarrow \mathsf{Enc}(\mathsf{pk}, M) : \mathsf{Dec}(\mathsf{sk}, C) \neq M\right]\right] \leq \delta(\lambda),$$

where the expected value is taken over all $(\mathsf{pk}, \mathsf{sk}) \leftarrow \mathsf{KGen}(\lambda)$.

It will be important for our transform to make explicit that the correctness error depends on the security level, as this allows us to chose a function $\ell(\cdot)$ such that $\delta(\lambda)^{\ell(\lambda)} \leq 2^{-\lambda}$. We will often just write $\delta = \delta(\lambda)$ and $\ell = \ell(\lambda)$ for simplicity.

An alternative but equivalent definition, as used in [40], can be given in the following form: a PKE Π is called $\delta(\cdot)$-correct if we have for all (possibly unbounded) adversaries A that

$$\mathsf{Adv}^{\mathsf{cor}}_{\Pi,A}(\lambda) = \Pr\left[\mathsf{Exp}^{\mathsf{cor}}_{\Pi,A}(\lambda) = 1\right] \le \delta(\lambda),$$

where the experiment is given in Fig. 6. If Π is defined relative to a random oracle H, then the adversary is given access to the random oracle and δ is additionally a function in the number of queries q_{H}, i.e., the bound is given by $\le \delta(\lambda, q_{\mathsf{H}})$. We note that in [10] an alternative definition of correctness was proposed, where the adversary does not get access to sk and the adversary's runtime is bounded. With this change, it can be run as part of the IND-CCA experiment which does not change the power of the IND-CCA adversary and additionaly removes a factor q_{H} from the correctness error and advantage analysis. In particular, one can obtain an upper bound for IND-CCA security of a scheme via the correctness error.

Exp. $\mathsf{Exp}^{\mathsf{cor}}_{\Pi,A}(\lambda)$

$(\mathsf{pk}, \mathsf{sk}) \leftarrow \mathsf{KGen}(\lambda)$
$M \leftarrow A(\mathsf{pk}, \mathsf{sk})$
if $M \ne \mathsf{Dec}(\mathsf{sk}, \mathsf{Enc}(\mathsf{pk}, M))$ **then return 1 else return 0**

Fig. 6. Correctness experiment for PKE.

We recall, for completeness, the definition of correctness error, here denoted as DNR-δ-correctness (from Dwork-Naor-Reingold), used by Dwork et al.:

Definition 7. (Def. 2, Def. 3 [25]). *A PKE Π is*

– *DNR-$\delta(\cdot)$-correct if we have that*

$$\Pr\left[\mathsf{Dec}(\mathsf{sk}, \mathsf{Enc}(\mathsf{pk}, M)) \ne M\right] \le \delta(\lambda),$$

where the probability is taken over the choice of key pairs $(\mathsf{pk}, \mathsf{sk}) \leftarrow \mathsf{KGen}(\lambda)$, $M \in \mathcal{M}$ *and over the random coins of* Enc *and* Dec.
– *DNR-(almost-)all-keys $\delta(\cdot)$-correct if for all (but negligible many) keys* $(\mathsf{pk}, \mathsf{sk}) \leftarrow \mathsf{KGen}(\lambda)$, *we have that*

$$\Pr\left[\mathsf{Dec}(\mathsf{sk}, \mathsf{Enc}(\mathsf{pk}, M)) \ne M\right] \le \delta(\lambda),$$

where the probability is taken over the choice of $M \in \mathcal{M}$ *and over the random coins of* Enc *and* Dec.

Correctness error in this sense still allows bad key pairs that potentially have an even worse error but it is not suited for our security proofs as the probability is also taken over $M \leftarrow_\$ \mathcal{M}$. Recently Drucker et al. [23] introduced the notion of message agnostic PKE and showed that all the versions of BIKE, a 2nd round candidate in the NIST PQC, are message-agnostic: in such a PKE, the probability that, given (sk, pk), the encryption of a message $M \in \mathcal{M}$ correctly decrypts is independent of the message $M \in \mathcal{M}$ itself. For such PKEs the definitions of δ-correctness and DNR-δ-correctness coincide (Cor. 1 [23]).

3.2 Compiler for Immunizing Decryption Errors

Now we present two variants of a compiler C_p denoted $C_{p,d}$ (for deterministic schemes) and $C_{p,r}$ (for randomized schemes) which is based on the direct product compiler by Dwork et al. [25]. We recall that the idea is to take a PKE scheme $\Pi = (\mathsf{KGen}, \mathsf{Enc}, \mathsf{Dec})$ with non-negligible correctness error δ (and randomness space $\mathcal{R}$ in case of randomized schemes) and output a PKE scheme $\Pi' = (\mathsf{KGen}', \mathsf{Enc}', \mathsf{Dec}')$ with negligible correctness error δ' (and randomness space $\mathcal{R}' := \mathcal{R}^\ell$, for some $\ell \in \mathbb{N}$, in case of a randomized schemes). We present a precise description of the compilers in Fig. 7. Note that in Dec', the message that is returned most often by Dec is returned. If two or more messages are tied, one of them is returned arbitrarily and we denote this operation as $\mathsf{maj}(M')$.

$\Pi'.\mathsf{KGen}'(\lambda, \ell)$	$\Pi'.\mathsf{Enc}'(\mathsf{pk}, M)$	$\Pi'.\mathsf{Dec}'(\mathsf{sk}, C)$

// if $C_{p,r}$
 return $\Pi.\mathsf{KGen}(\lambda)$
 // if $C_{p,d}$
 for $i \in [\ell]$
 $\quad (\mathsf{pk}_i, \mathsf{sk}_i) \leftarrow \Pi.\mathsf{KGen}(\lambda)$
 $\mathsf{pk} := (\mathsf{pk}_1, \ldots, \mathsf{pk}_\ell)$
 $\mathsf{sk} := (\mathsf{sk}_1, \ldots, \mathsf{sk}_\ell)$
 return $(\mathsf{pk}, \mathsf{sk})$
	for $i \in [\ell]$
	 // if $C_{p,r}$
	 $\quad r_i \leftarrow_\$ \Pi.\mathcal{R}$
	 $\quad C_i \leftarrow \Pi.\mathsf{Enc}(\mathsf{pk}, M; r_i)$
	 // if $C_{p,d}$
	 $\quad C_i \leftarrow \Pi.\mathsf{Enc}(\mathsf{pk}_i, M)$
	 $C := (C_1 \ldots, C_\ell)$
	 return C
		$C := (C_1 \ldots, C_\ell)$
		 for $i \in [\ell]$
		 // if $C_{p,r}$
		 $\quad M_i' := \Pi.\mathsf{Dec}(\mathsf{sk}, C_i)$
		 // if $C_{p,d}$
		 $\quad M_i' := \Pi.\mathsf{Dec}(\mathsf{sk}_i, C_i)$
		 return $\mathsf{maj}(M_1', \ldots, M_\ell')$

Fig. 7. Compilers $C_{p,d}$ and $C_{p,r}$.

Analyzing Correctness. Dwork et al. in [25] explicitly discuss the amplification of the correctness for encryption schemes with a binary message space $\mathcal{M} = \{0,1\}$ and obtain that to achieve DNR-δ'-correctness $\ell > c/(1-\delta)^2 \cdot \log 1/\delta'$ when starting from a scheme with DNR-δ-correctness. As c is some constant that is never made explicit, the formula is more of theoretical interest and for concrete instances it is hard to estimate the number of required ciphertexts. We can however analyze the probabilities that the majority vote in Dec' returns the correct result. As far as the correctness notion used in this work is concerned, in order to prove an acceptable good lower bound for the δ-correctness of the direct product compiler, it suffices to find an event, in which the decryption procedure fails, that happens with a large enough probability. The following reasoning applies to both its deterministic and randomized versions, $C_{p,d}$ and $C_{p,r}$ respectively. One such case is the following: only 1 ciphertext correctly decrypts and all other $\ell - 1$ ciphertexts decrypt to $\ell - 1$ distinct wrong messages. During the maj operation, one of the "wrong" messages is then returned. The probability of this event is

$$\frac{\ell-1}{\ell}\binom{\ell}{\ell-1}\delta^{\ell-1}(1-\delta)\frac{M-1}{M-1}\frac{M-2}{M-1}\cdots\frac{M-(\ell-1)}{M-1}.$$

Looking ahead to our compiler T^* presented in Sect. 3.4, if the message space is sufficiently large, this probability is bigger than $\delta^{\ell-1}(1-\delta)$, which gives that at least one more ciphertext is needed to achieve the same decryption error as with our compiler T^*. The results are shown in Table 1. One can compute the exact probability of decryption error by listing all cases in which the decryption fails and summing up all these probabilities to obtain the overall decryption failure of the direct product compiler. This computation is not going to give a significantly different result from the lower bound that we have just computed.

We note that using 2 parallel ciphertexts does not improve the correctness error, so the direct product compiler only becomes interesting for $\ell \geq 3$: indeed for $\ell = 2$, we have 3 possible outcomes in which the decryption algorithm can fail: 1) the first ciphertext decrypts and the second does not, 2) vice versa, 3) both fail to decrypt. In 1), 2), half the time the wrong plaintext is returned. Summing these probabilities gives exactly δ.

Table 1. Estimation of the correctness error for the direct product compilers. $\delta'(\ell)$ denotes the correctness error for ℓ ciphertexts.

δ	$\delta'(2)$	$\delta'(3)$	$\delta'(4)$
2^{-32}	$\approx 2^{-32}$	$\approx 2^{-63}$	$\approx 2^{-94}$
2^{-64}	$\approx 2^{-64}$	$\approx 2^{-127}$	$\approx 2^{-190}$
2^{-96}	$\approx 2^{-96}$	$\approx 2^{-191}$	$\approx 2^{-284}$

Remark 1. As far as the deterministic direct product compiler $C_{p,d}$ is concerned, the correctness error can be improved by modifying the decryption: instead of relying on the maj operation, we can re-encrypt the plaintexts obtained during decryption with the respective keys and compare them to the original ciphertexts. Only if this check passes, the plaintext is returned. If this is done, then decryption fails iff no ciphertext decrypts correctly, i.e., with probability δ^ℓ, and thereby the number of parallel repetition necessary to achieve negligible correctness-error is reduced at the cost of a computational overhead in the decryption. We denote this version of the deterministic direct product compiler by $C_{p,d}^*$.

Their security follows by applying Theorem 1 with $q = 1$ and $n = \ell$ in the deterministic case, for both $C_{p,d}$ and $C_{p,d}^*$, or vice versa with $q = \ell$ and $n = 1$ in the randomized case:

Corollary 1. *For any* x-CPA *adversary* B *against* Π' *obtained via applying* $C_{p,y}$ *to* Π, *there exists an* x-CPA *adversary* A *such that:*

$$\mathsf{Adv}_{\Pi',B}^{\mathsf{pke\text{-}x\text{-}cpa}}(\lambda) \leq \ell \cdot \mathsf{Adv}_{\Pi,A}^{\mathsf{pke\text{-}x\text{-}cpa}}(\lambda),$$

where y = d *if* x = OW *and* y = r *if* x = IND.

As the analysis above suggests, ℓ will be a small constant, so the loss in ℓ does not pose a problem regarding tightness.

3.3   Transformations T and U$^{\not\perp}$

Subsequently, we discuss basic transformations from [41] to first transform an IND-CPA secure PKE into an OW-PCA secure PKE (transformation T in [41]) and then to convert an OW-PCA secure PKE into an IND-CCA secure KEM with implicit rejection (transformation U$^{\not\perp}$ in [41]) and we discuss alternative transformations later. We stress that these transformations either work for perfectly correct schemes or schemes with a negligible correctness error.

T : IND-CPA $\implies$ OW-PCA(**ROM**)/OW-CPA(**QROM**). The transform T is a simple de-randomization of a PKE by deriving the randomness r used by the algorithm Enc via evaluating a random oracle (RO) on the message to be encrypted. More precisely, let $\Pi = (\mathsf{KGen}, \mathsf{Enc}, \mathsf{Dec})$ be a PKE with message space $\mathcal{M}$ and randomness space $\mathcal{R}$ and G: $\mathcal{M} \to \mathcal{R}$ be a RO. We denote the PKE Π' obtained by applying transformation T depicted in Fig. 8 as $\Pi' = \mathsf{T}[\Pi, \mathsf{G}]$, where $\Pi'.\mathsf{KGen} = \Pi.\mathsf{KGen}$ and is thus omitted.

$\Pi'.\mathsf{Enc}(\mathsf{pk}, M)$	$\Pi'.\mathsf{Dec}(\mathsf{sk}, C)$
$C := \Pi.\mathsf{Enc}(\mathsf{pk}, M; \mathsf{G}(M))$ **return** C	$M' := \Pi.\mathsf{Dec}(\mathsf{sk}, C)$ **if** $M' = \bot$ **or** $C \neq \Pi.\mathsf{Enc}(\mathsf{pk}, M'; \mathsf{G}(M'))$ **return** $\bot$ **else return** M'

Fig. 8. $OW\text{-}PCA$-secure scheme $\Pi' = \mathsf{T}[\Pi, \mathsf{G}]$ with deterministic encryption.

For the ROM, we recall the following theorem:

Theorem 2 (Thm. 3.2 [41] (Π IND-CPA $\implies$ Π' OW-PCA)). *Assume Π to be δ-correct. Then, Π' is $\delta_1(q_\mathsf{G}) = q_\mathsf{G} \cdot \delta$ correct and for any OW-PCA adversary B that issues at most q_G queries to the RO G and q_P queries to a plaintext checking oracle Pco, there exists an IND-CPA adversary A running in about the same time as B such that*

$$\mathsf{Adv}^{\mathsf{pke\text{-}ow\text{-}pca}}_{\Pi', B}(\lambda) \leq q_\mathsf{G} \cdot \delta + \frac{2q_\mathsf{G} + 1}{|\mathcal{M}|} + 3 \cdot \mathsf{Adv}^{\mathsf{pke\text{-}ind\text{-}cpa}}_{\Pi, A}(\lambda).$$

And for the QROM, we recall the following theorem:

Theorem 3 (Thm. 1 [9] (Π IND-CPA $\implies$ Π' OW-CPA)). *If A is an OW-CPA-adversary against $\Pi' = \mathsf{T}[\Pi, \mathsf{G}]$ issuing at most q_G queries to the quantum-accessible RO G of at most depth d, then there exists an IND-CPA adversary B against Π running in about the same time as A such that*

$$\mathsf{Adv}^{\mathsf{pke\text{-}ow\text{-}cpa}}_{\Pi', A}(\lambda) \leq (d+1)\left(\mathsf{Adv}^{\mathsf{pke\text{-}ind\text{-}cpa}}_{\Pi, B}(\lambda) + \frac{8(q_\mathsf{G} + 1)}{|\mathcal{M}|}\right).$$

$\underline{U^{\not\perp} : \text{OW-PCA}} \implies \underline{\text{IND-CCA}}.$ The transformation $U^{\not\perp}$ transforms any OW-PCA secure PKE Π' into an IND-CCA secure KEM in the (Q)ROM. The basic idea is that one encrypts a random message M from the message space $\mathcal{M}$ of Π' and the encapsulated key is the RO evaluated on the message M and the corresponding ciphertext C under Π'. This transformation uses implicit rejection and on decryption failure does not return $\perp$, but an evaluation of the RO on the ciphertext and a random message $s \in \mathcal{M}$, being part of sk of the resulting KEM, as a "wrong" encapsulation key. It is depicted in Fig. 9.

KEM.KGen(λ)	KEM.Encaps(pk)	KEM.Decaps (sk,C)
$(\text{pk}', \text{sk}') \leftarrow \Pi'.\text{KGen}(\lambda)$	$M \leftarrow_\$ \mathcal{M}$	Parse sk $= (\text{sk}', s)$
$s \leftarrow_\$ \mathcal{M}$	$C \leftarrow \Pi'.\text{Enc}(\text{pk}, M)$	$M' := \Pi'.\text{Dec}(\text{sk}', C)$
sk $:= (\text{sk}', s)$	$K := \text{H}(M, C)$	if $M' \neq \perp$
return (pk', sk)	return (K, C)	return $K := \text{H}(M', C)$
		else return $K := \text{H}(s, C)$

Fig. 9. IND-CCA-secure KEM scheme $\text{KEM} = U^{\not\perp}[\Pi', \text{H}]$.

In the ROM, we have the following result:

Theorem 4 (Thm. 3.4 [41] (Π' OW-PCA $\implies$ KEM IND-CCA)). *If Π' is δ_1-correct, then KEM is δ_1-correct in the random oracle model. For any IND-CCA adversary B against KEM, issuing at most q_H queries to the random oracle H, there exists an OW-PCA adversary A against Π' running in about the same time as B that makes at most q_H queries to the PCO oracle such that*

$$\text{Adv}_{\text{KEM},B}^{\text{kem-ind-cca}}(\lambda) \leq \frac{q_\text{H}}{|\mathcal{M}|} + \text{Adv}_{\Pi',A}^{\text{pke-ow-pca}}(\lambda).$$

For the QROM, we have the following non-tight result:

Theorem 5 (Thm. 6 [48] (Π' OW-PCA $\implies$ KEM IND-CCA)). *Let Π' be a deterministic PKE scheme which is independent of H. Let B be an IND-CCA adversary against the KEM $U^{\not\perp}[\Pi', \text{H}]$, and suppose that A makes at most q_d (classical) decryption queries and q_H queries to quantum-accessible random oracle H of depth at most d, then there exists and adversary B against Π' such that*

$$\text{Adv}_{U^{\not\perp}[\Pi',\text{H}],A}^{\text{kem-ind-cca}}(\lambda) \leq \frac{2 \cdot q_\text{H}}{\sqrt{|\mathcal{M}|}} + 2 \cdot \sqrt{(q_\text{H} + 1)(2 \cdot \delta + \text{Adv}_{\Pi',B}^{\text{pke-ow-cpa}}(\lambda))}.$$

If we assume ε-injectivity and FFC, respectively, we have tighter bounds:

Theorem 6 (Thm. 4.6 [51] (Π' OW-CPA $+$ FFC $\implies$ KEM IND-CCA)). *Let Π' be an ε-injective deterministic PKE scheme which is independent of H. Suppose that A is an IND-CCA adversary against the KEM $U^{\not\perp}[\Pi', \text{H}]$, and suppose that A makes at most q_d (classical) decryption queries and q_H queries to quantum-accessible random oracle H of depth at most d, then there exist two adversaries running in about the same time as A:*

 − *an* OW-CPA-*adversary* B_1 *against* Π' *and*
 − *a* FFC-*adversary* B_2 *against* Π' *returning a list of at most* q_d *ciphertexts,*

such that

$$\mathsf{Adv}^{\mathsf{kem\text{-}ind\text{-}cca}}_{\mathsf{U}^{\not\perp}[\Pi',\mathsf{H}],A}(\lambda) \leq 4d \cdot \mathsf{Adv}^{\mathsf{pke\text{-}ow\text{-}cpa}}_{\Pi',B_1}(\lambda) + 6\mathsf{Adv}^{\mathsf{pke\text{-}ffc}}_{\Pi',B_2}(\lambda) + (4d+6) \cdot \varepsilon.$$

$\mathsf{FO}^{\not\perp}[\Pi, \mathsf{G}, \mathsf{H}]$. By combining transformation T with $\mathsf{U}^{\not\perp}$ one consequently obtains an IND-CCA secure KEM KEM from an IND-CPA secure PKE Π. Note that the security reduction of the $\mathsf{FO}^{\not\perp} := \mathsf{U}^{\not\perp} \circ \mathsf{T}$ variant of the FO is tight in the random oracle model and works even if Π has negligible correctness error instead of perfect correctness.

$\mathsf{FO}^{\not\perp}[\Pi, \mathsf{G}, \mathsf{H}]$ **in the QROM.** Hofheinz et al. in [41] also provide variants of the FO transform that are secure in the QROM, but they are (highly) non-tight. Bindel et al. [9] presented a tighter proof for $\mathsf{U}^{\not\perp}$ under an additional assumption of ε-injectivity. This result was recently improved by Kuchta et al. [51]. Additionally, Jiang et al. [48] provided tighter proofs for the general case.

$\mathsf{U}^{\perp}, \mathsf{U}^{\perp}_m, \mathsf{U}^{\not\perp}_m$ **and Other Approaches.** Besides the transform with implicit rejection, $\mathsf{U}^{\not\perp}$, one can also consider explicit rejection, $\mathsf{U}^{\perp}$ and versions of both where the derived session key depends on the ciphertext, $\mathsf{U}^{\not\perp}_m$ and $\mathsf{U}^{\perp}_m$, respectively. Bindel et al. [9] show that security of implicit rejection implies security with explicit rejection. The opposite direction also holds if the scheme with explicit rejection also employs key confirmation. Moreover, they show that the security is independent of including the ciphertext in the session key derivation.

A different approach was proposed by Saito et al. [58], where they start from a deterministic disjoint simulatable PKE and apply $\mathsf{U}^{\not\perp}_m$ with an additional re-encryption step in the decryption algorithm. While the original construction relied on a perfectly correct PKE, Jiang et al. gave non-tight reductions for schemes with negligible correctness error in [47]. Hövelmanns et al. [43] improve over this approach by giving a different modularization of Saito et al.'s TPunc.

Black-Box Use of the Compiler $\mathsf{C}_{p,d}/\mathsf{C}_{p,d}{}^*/\mathsf{C}_{p,r}$. Using $\mathsf{C}_{p,d}$, $\mathsf{C}_{p,d}{}^*$ or $\mathsf{C}_{p,r}$ from Sect. 3.2, we can transform any deterministic or randomized PKE with non-negligible correctness error into one with negligible correctness error. Consequently, Theorem 1 as a result yields a scheme that is compatible with all the results on the T and variants of the U transformations in this section. Note that in particular this gives us a general way to apply these variants of the FO transform to PKE schemes with non-negligible correctness error.

3.4 Non Black-Box Use: The Transformation T^*

Since the direct product compiler is rather complicated to analyze, we alternatively investigate to start from an IND-CPA secure PKE Π with non-negligible correctness error δ and introduce a variant of the transform T to de-randomize a PKE, denoted T^*. The idea is that we compute ℓ independent encryptions of the same message M under the same public key pk using randomness $G(M, i)$, $i \in [\ell]$, where G is a RO (see Fig. 10 for a compact description). The resulting de-randomized PKE Π' has then correctness error $\delta' := \delta^\ell$, where ℓ is chosen in a way that δ^ℓ is negligible. To the resulting PKE Π' we can then directly apply the transformation $U^{\perp}$ to obtain an IND-CCA secure KEM KEM with negligible correctness error in the (Q)ROM.

Note that as we directly integrate the product compiler into the T transform, the correctness of the message can be checked via the de-randomization. Hence, we can get rid of the majority vote in the direct product compiler. With this change the analysis of the concrete choice of ℓ becomes simpler and, more importantly, allows us to choose smaller ℓ than in the black-box use of the compiler.

$\Pi'.\mathsf{Enc}(\mathsf{pk}, M)$	$\Pi'.\mathsf{Dec}(\mathsf{sk}, C)$
for $i = 1, \ldots, \ell$ **do**	$\mathbf{res} \leftarrow \perp, \mathbf{check} \leftarrow \perp$
$\quad C_i := \Pi.\mathsf{Enc}(\mathsf{pk}, M; G(M, i))$	**for** $i = 1, \ldots, \ell$ **do**
$C := (C_1, \ldots, C_\ell)$	$\quad \mathbf{res}[i] := \Pi.\mathsf{Dec}(\mathsf{sk}, C_i)$
return C	**for** $i \in [\ell]$ s.t. $\mathbf{res}[i] \neq \perp$ **do**
	$\quad$ **if** $\forall j \in [\ell] : C_j = \Pi.\mathsf{Enc}(\mathsf{pk}, \mathbf{res}[i], G(\mathbf{res}[i], j))$
	$\quad\quad \mathbf{check} \leftarrow i$
	if $\mathbf{check} \neq \perp$
	$\quad$ **return** $\mathbf{res}[\mathbf{check}]$
	return $\perp$

Fig. 10. OW-PCA-secure scheme $\Pi' = T^*[\Pi, G]$ with deterministic encryption and correctness error δ^ℓ from IND-CPA secure scheme Π with correctness error δ.

Remark 2. Note that in Fig. 10 we explicitly consider the case where Dec of the PKE scheme Π may return something arbitrary on failed decryption. For the simpler case where we have a PKE scheme Π which always returns $\perp$ on failed decryption, we can easily adapt the approach in Fig. 10. Namely, we would decrypt all ℓ ciphertexts C_i, $i \in [\ell]$. Let $h \in [\ell]$ be the minimum index such that $\mathbf{res}[h] \neq \perp$. Then for every element $j \in [\ell]$ run $C'_j := \Pi.\mathsf{Enc}(\mathsf{pk}, \mathbf{res}[h]; G(\mathbf{res}[h], j))$. If for all $j \in [\ell]$ we have $C'_j = C_j$ we return $\mathbf{res}[h]$. If this is not the case we return $\perp$. Note that all ℓ C'_j have to be re-encrypted and checked against C_j, as otherwise IND-CCA-security is not achieved. The difference is, that only ℓ encryptions instead of ℓ^2 are required.

We now show the following theorem.

Theorem 7 (Π IND-CPA $\implies \Pi'$ OW-PCA). *Assume Π to be δ-correct. Then, Π' is $\delta_1(q_G, \ell) \leq \dfrac{q_G}{\ell} \cdot \delta^\ell$ correct and for any OW-PCA adversary B that issues at most q_G queries to the random oracle G and q_P queries to a plaintext checking oracle PCO, there exists an IND-CPA adversary A running in about the same time as B such that*

$$\mathsf{Adv}_{\varPi',B}^{\mathsf{pke\text{-}ow\text{-}pca}}(\lambda) \leq \frac{q_{\mathsf{G}}}{\ell} \cdot \delta^{\ell} + \frac{2q_{\mathsf{G}}+1}{|\mathcal{M}|} + 3\ell \cdot \mathsf{Adv}_{\varPi,A}^{\mathsf{pke\text{-}ind\text{-}cpa}}(\lambda).$$

We provide the proof which closely follows the proof of [41, Thm 3.2] in the full version. Note that we lose an additional factor of ℓ. Additionally, when using the bounded δ-correctness notion from Bindel. et al. [10], the factor of q_{G} disappears.

We now have an $\mathsf{OW\text{-}PCA}$ secure PKE $\varPi'$ with negligible correctness error and can thus directly use $\mathsf{U}^{\not\perp}$ and by invoking Theorem 4 obtain an $\mathsf{IND\text{-}CCA}$ secure KEM KEM. Note that all steps in the reduction are tight. For the security in the QROM, we can directly conclude from Theorem 1 that the generic framework of Bindel et al. [9] can be applied to $\mathsf{C_{p,d}}$ and $\mathsf{C_{p,r}}$ with the additional constraint of ε-injectivity and FFC, respectively. Without these additional constraints, the results of Jiang et al. [48] or Hövelmanns et al. [43][1] apply without the tighter reductions that the Bindel et al.'s and Kuchta et al.'s results offer.

The security of the $\mathsf{T}^{\star}$ transform in the QROM follows in a similar vein. To highlight how ℓ influences the advantages, we follow the proof strategy of Bindel et al. [9]. Therefore, we first show that a randomized $\mathsf{IND\text{-}CPA}$-secure PKE scheme with a non-negligible correctness error is transformed to $\mathsf{OW\text{-}CPA}$-secure deterministic PKE scheme with negligible correctness error. Second, we prove that if the $\mathsf{T}^{\star}$-transformed version is also ε-injective, then it provides FFC. With these two results in place, we can apply Theorem 6 to obtain an $\mathsf{IND\text{-}CCA}$-secure KEM.

In the following theorem, we prove $\mathsf{OW\text{-}CPA}$ security of the $\mathsf{T}^{\star}$ transform in the QROM (see the full version). We follow the strategy of the proof of [9, Thm. 1] and adapt it to our transform. Compared to the T transform, we lose a factor of ℓ^2. Once the loss is incurred by Theorem 1 and once by the semi-classical one-way to hiding Theorem [2].

Theorem 8 ($\varPi$ IND$-$CPA $\implies$ $\varPi'$OW$-$CPA). *Let $\varPi$ be a non-deterministic PKE with randomness space $\mathcal{R}$ and decryption error δ. Let $\ell \in \mathbb{N}$ such that δ^{ℓ} is negligible in the security parameter λ. Let $\mathsf{G}\colon \mathcal{M} \times [\ell] \to \mathcal{R}$ be a quantum-accessible random oracle and let q_{G} the number queries with depth at most d. If A is an $\mathsf{OW\text{-}CPA}$-adversary against $\mathsf{T}^{\star}[\varPi, \mathsf{G}, \ell]$, then there exists an $\mathsf{IND\text{-}CPA}$ adversary B against $\varPi$, running in about same time as A, such that*

$$\mathsf{Adv}_{\mathsf{T}^{*}[\varPi,\mathsf{G},\ell],A}^{\mathsf{pke\text{-}ow\text{-}cpa}}(\lambda) \leq (d+\ell+1)\left(\ell \cdot \mathsf{Adv}_{\varPi,B}^{\mathsf{pke\text{-}ind\text{-}cpa}}(\lambda) + \frac{8(q_{\mathsf{G}}+1)}{|\mathcal{M}|}\right).$$

We refer to the full version for the proof. Next, we show that the transform provides the FFC property (cf. [9, Lemma 6]).

Lemma 2. *If $\varPi$ is a δ-correct non-deterministic PKE with randomness space $\mathcal{R}$, $\ell \in \mathbb{N}$ such that δ^{ℓ} is negligible in the security parameter λ, $\mathsf{G}\colon \mathcal{M} \times [\ell] \to \mathcal{R}$ is a random oracle so that $\varPi' = \mathsf{T}^{\star}[\varPi, \mathsf{G}, \ell]$ is ε-injective, then the advantage for*

---

[1] Without restating [43, Thm 3.2], note that we can adopt it the same way we highlight in Theorems 7 and 8. So, we start with their Punc to obtain disjoint simutability and then apply $\mathsf{T}^{\star}$ and $\mathsf{U}_m^{\not\perp}$.

any FFC-*adversary* A *against* Π' *which makes at most* q_G *queries at depth d to* G *and which returns a list of at most* q_L *ciphertexts is bounded by*

$$\mathsf{Adv}^{\mathsf{pke\text{-}ffc}}_{\Pi',A}(\lambda) \leq \left((4d+1)\delta^\ell + \sqrt{3\varepsilon}\right)(q_G + q_L) + \varepsilon.$$

For the proof we refer to the full version.

3.5   Comparison of the Two Approaches

The major difference between the generic approach using the direct product compiler $\mathsf{C}_{\mathsf{p,y}}, \mathsf{y} \in \{\mathsf{r,d}\}$, and $\mathsf{T}^\star$ (or the modified deterministic direct product compiler $\mathsf{C}_{\mathsf{p,d}}{}^\star$) is the number of ciphertexts required to reach a negligible correctness error. As observed in Sect. 3.2, the analysis of the overall decryption error is rather complicated and $\mathsf{C}_{\mathsf{p,y}}$ requires at least $\ell \geq 3$. With $\mathsf{T}^\star/\mathsf{C}_{\mathsf{p,d}}{}^\star$ however, the situation is simpler. As soon as one ciphertext decrypts correctly, the overall correctness of the decryption can be guaranteed. Also, for the cases analysed in Table 1, $\mathsf{C}_{\mathsf{p,y}}$ requires at least one ciphertext more than $\mathsf{T}^\star$ and $\mathsf{C}_{\mathsf{p,d}}{}^\star$. For the correctness error, we have a loss in the number of random oracle queries in both cases. For the comparison of the runtime and bandwidth overheads, we refer to Table 2. Note that if the Dec of the underlying PKE Π reports decryption failures with $\bot$, then the overhead of $\mathsf{T}^\star$ for Dec is only a factor ℓ (cf. Remark 2).

Table 2. Comparison of the runtime and bandwidth overheads of $\mathsf{C}_{\mathsf{p,y}}$, $\mathsf{y} \in \{\mathsf{r,d}\}$, with ℓ ciphertexts and $\mathsf{T}^\star$ and $\mathsf{C}^\star_{\mathsf{p,d}}$ with ℓ' ciphertexts such that $\ell \geq \ell' + 1$.

	$|\mathsf{pk}|$	$|C|$	KGen	Enc	Dec
$\mathsf{C}_{\mathsf{p,y}}$	1 (r) / ℓ (d)	ℓ	1 (r) / ℓ (d)	ℓ	ℓ
$\mathsf{C}^\star_{\mathsf{p,d}}$	ℓ'	ℓ'	ℓ'	ℓ'	ℓ'
$\mathsf{T}^\star$	1	ℓ'	1	ℓ'	ℓ'^2 / ℓ' ($\bot$)

4   Our Transform in Practice

The most obvious use-case for IND-CCA secure KEMs in practice is when considering static long-term keys. Systems supporting such a setting are for example RSA-based key exchange for SSH [39] or similarly in TLS up to version 1.2. But since the use of long-term keys precludes forward-secrecy guarantees, using static keys is not desirable. For ephemeral keys such as used in the ephemeral Diffie-Hellman key exchange, an IND-CPA secure KEM might seem sufficient. Yet, in the post-quantum setting accidental re-use of an ephemeral key leads to a wide range of attacks [7]. But also from a theoretical viewpoint it is unclear whether CPA security actually would be enough. Security analysis of the TLS handshake protocol suggests that in the case of version 1.2 an only passively secure version is insufficient [45,50] (cf. also [56]). Also, security analysis of the version 1.3 handshake requires IND-CCA security [22]. Thus, even in the case of ephemeral key exchanges, using a IND-CCA secure KEM is actually desirable and often even necessary as highlighted by Schwabe et al. [61].

For comparing KEMs in this context, the interesting metric is hence not the ciphertext size alone, but the combined public key and ciphertext size. Both parts influence the communication cost of the protocols. Additionally, the combined runtime of the key generation, encapsulation and decapsulation is also an interesting metric. All three operations are performed in a typical ephemeral key exchange and hence give a lower bound for the overall runtime of the protocol.

In the following comparison, we assume that the underlying PKE never returns $\perp$ on failure, but an incorrect message instead. Thereby we obtain an upper bound for the runtime of the Decaps algorithm. For specific cases where Decaps explicitly returns $\perp$ on failure, the runtime figures would get better since the overhead to check the ciphertexts is reduced to a factor of ℓ (cf. Remark 2).

4.1   Code-Based KEMs

KEMs based on error correcting codes can be parametrized such that the decoding failure rate (DFR) is non-negligible, negligible, or 0. Interestingly, the DFR rate is also influenced by the actual decoder. Even for the same choice of code and the exact same instance of the code, a decoder might have a non-negligible DFR, whereas another (usually more complex) decoder obtains a negligible DFR. For the submissions in the NIST PQC we can observe all three choices. The candidates providing IND-CPA-secure variants with non-negligible DFR include: BIKE [3], ROLLO [4], and LEDAcrypt [6]. We discuss the application of our transform to those schemes below. For the comparison in Table 3, we consider the DFR as upper bound for correctness error.

In Table 3, we present an overview of the comparison (see the full version for the full comparison). First we consider ROLLO, and in particular ROLLO-I, where we obtain the best results: public key and ciphertext size combined is always smaller than for ROLLO-II and the parallel implementation is faster even in case of a ℓ^2 overhead. For both BIKE (using $\mathsf{T}^\star$) and LEDAcrypt (using $\mathsf{C}^\star_{\mathsf{p,d}}$ since it starts from a deterministic PKE), we observe a trade-off between bandwidth and runtime.

4.2   Lattice-Based KEMs

For lattice-based primitives the decryption error depends both on the modulus q and the error distribution used. As discussed in [60], an important decision that designers have to make is whether to allow decryption failures or choose parameters that not only have a negligible, but a zero chance of failure. Having a perfectly correct encryption makes transforms to obtain IND-CCA security and security proofs easier, but with the disadvantage that this means either decreasing security against attacks targeting the underlying lattice problem or decreasing

Table 3. Sizes (in bytes) and runtimes (in ms and millions of cycles for BIKE), where O denotes the transformed scheme. The LEDAcrypt instances with postfix NN refer to those with non-negligible DFR. Runtimes are taken from the respective submission documents and are only intra-scheme comparable.

KEM	δ	pk	C	$\sum$	KGen	Encaps	Decaps
O[ROLLO-I-L1,5]	2^{-150}	**465**	2325	**2790**	**0.10**	**0.02/0.10**	**0.26/1.30**
ROLLO-II-L1	2^{-128}	1546	1674	3220	0.69	0.08	0.53
O[ROLLO-I-L3,4]	2^{-128}	**590**	2360	**2950**	**0.13**	**0.02/0.08**	**0.42/1.68**
ROLLO-II-L3	2^{-128}	2020	2148	4168	0.83	0.09	0.69
O[ROLLO-I-L5,4]	2^{-168}	**947**	7576	**8523**	**0.20**	**0.03/0.12**	**0.78/3.12**
ROLLO-II-L5	2^{-128}	2493	2621	5114	0.79	0.10	0.84
O[BIKE-2-L1,3]	2^{-147}	**10163**	30489	40652	**4.79**	**0.14/0.42**	**3.29/9.88**
BIKE-2-CCA-L1	2^{-128}	11779	12035	23814	6.32	0.20	4.12
O[LEDAcrypt-L5-NN,2]	2^{-128}	22272	22272	44544	5.04	**0.14/0.29**	**1.55/3.11**
LEDAcrypt-L5	2^{-128}	19040	19040	38080	4.25	0.84	2.28

performance. The only NIST PQC submissions based on lattices which provide parameter sets achieving both negligible and non-negligible decryption failure are ThreeBears [38] and Round5 [30]. The IND-CCA-secure version of ThreeBears is obtained by tweaking the error distribution, hence, our approach does not yield any improvements. For Round5 we achieve a trade-off between bandwidth and runtime. We also considered FrodoKEM [52], comparing its version [17] precedent to the NIST PQC, which only achieved non-negligible failure probability, to the ones in the second round of the above competition, but we do not observe any improvements for this scheme. For the full comparison we refer to the full version. It would be interesting to understand the reasons why the compiler does not perform well on lattice-based scheme compared to the code-based ones and whether this is due to the particular schemes analysed or due to some intrinsic difference between code- and lattice-based constructions.

4.3 Implementation Aspects

One of the strengths of $\mathsf{T}^\star$ compared to the black-box use of $\mathsf{C}_{p,y}$, $y \in \{r, d\}$ (and $\mathsf{C}_{p,d}{}^\star$), is that besides the initial generation of the encapsulated key, all the random oracle calls can be evaluated independently. Therefore, the encryptions of the underlying PKE do not depend on each other. Thus, the encapsulation algorithms are easily parallelizable – both in software and hardware. The same applies to the decapsulation algorithm. While in this case only one successful run of the algorithm is required, doing all of them in parallel helps to obtain a constant-time implementation. Then, after all ciphertexts have been processed, the first valid one can be used to re-compute the ciphertexts, which can be done again in parallel. For software implementations on multi-core CPUs as seen on today's desktops, servers, and smartphones with 4 or more cores, the overhead compared to the IND-CPA secure version is thus insignificant as long as the error is below 2^{-32}. If not implemented in a parallel fashion, providing a constant-time implementation of the decapsulation algorithms is more costly. In that case, all of the ciphertexts have to be dealt with not leak the index of invalid ciphertexts. Note that a constant-time implementation of the transform is important to avoid key-recovery attacks [35].

The $\mathsf{T}^\star$ transform also avoids new attack vectors such as [37] that are introduced via different techniques to decrease the correctness error, e.g., by applying an error-correcting code on top. Furthermore, since the same parameter sets are used for the IND-CPA and IND-CCA secure version when applying our transforms, the implementations of proposals with different parameter sets can be simplified. Thus, more focus can be put on analysing one of the parameter sets and also on optimizing the implementation of one of them.

5   Application to Bloom Filter KEMs

A Bloom Filter Key Encapsulation Mechanism (BFKEM) [20,21] is a specific type of a puncturable encryption scheme [21,33,34,63] where one associates a Bloom Filter (BF) [13] to its public-secret key pair. The initial (i.e., non-punctured) secret key is associated to an empty BF where all bits are set to 0. Encapsulation, depending on an element s in the universe of the BF, takes the public key and returns a ciphertext and an encapsulation key k corresponding to the evaluation of $BF(s)$, i.e., k hash evaluations on s yielding indexes in the size m of the BF. Puncturing, on input a ciphertext C (associated to s) and a secret key sk', punctures sk' on C and returns the resulting secret key. Decapsulation, on input a ciphertext C (with an associated tag s) and secret key sk' is able to decapsulate the ciphertext to k if sk' was not punctured on C. We want to mention, as in [20], we solely focus on KEMs since a Bloom Filter Encryption (BFE) scheme (which encrypts a message from some message space) can be generically derived from a BFKEM (cf. [27]).

The basic instantiation of a BFKEM in [20,21] is non-black box and based on the pairing-based Boneh-Franklin IBE (BF-IBE) scheme [16], where sk contains an IBE secret key for every identity $i \in [m]$ of the BF bits and puncturing amounts to inserting s in the BF and deleting the IBE secret keys for the corresponding bits. Although the BFKEM is defined with respect to a non-negligible correctness error, the underlying BF-IBE has perfect correctness. So the non-negligible error in the BFKEM is only introduced on an abstraction (at the level of the BF) above the FO transform applied to the k BF-IBE ciphertexts (so the application of the FO can be done as usual for perfectly correct encryption schemes).

However, if one targets instantiations of BFE where the underlying IBE does not have perfect correctness (e.g., lattice- or code-based IBEs), it is not obvious whether the security proof using the BF-IBE as presented in [20,21] can easily be adapted to this setting.[2]

---

[2] Note that we want the size of the BFKEM public key to be independent of the BF parameters for practical reasons (besides the descriptions of the hash functions).

We first recall necessary definitions and then show a generic construction of BFKEM from any IBE scheme with (non-)negligible correctness error.

Due to space constraints, we present the definition of Bloom filters with its formal properties in the full version.

Bloom Filter Key Encapsulation Mechanism. We recap the Bloom Filter Key Encapsulation Mechanism (BFKEM) and its formal properties from [20] that tolerates a non-negligible correctness error and the key generation takes parameters m and k as input which specify this correctness error. A BFKEM BFKEM with key space $\mathcal{K}$ consists of the PPT algorithms (KGen, Encaps, Punc, Decaps).

KGen(λ, m, k): Key generation, on input security parameter λ and BF parameters m, k, outputs public and secret keys (pk, sk$_0$).
Encaps(pk): Encapsulation, on input pk, outputs a ciphertext C and key k.
Punc(sk, C): Secret-key puncturing, on input sk and C, outputs an updated secret key sk$'$.
Decaps(sk, C): Decapsulation, on input sk and C, outputs k or $\{\perp\}$.

Definition 8 (Correctness). *For all $\lambda, m, k, n \in \mathbb{N}$ and any (pk, sk$_0$) $\leftarrow$ KGen(λ, m, k), we require the following. For any (arbitrary interleaved) sequence of invocations of sk$_{j+1}$ $\leftarrow$ Punc(sk$_j, C_j$), where $j \in \{0, \ldots, n\}$, and (C_j, k_j) $\leftarrow$ Encaps(pk), it holds that*

$$\Pr\left[\mathsf{Decaps}(\mathsf{sk}_{n+1}, C^*) \neq \mathsf{k}^*\right] \leq \left(1 - e^{-\frac{(n+1/2)k}{m-1}}\right)^k + \varepsilon(\lambda),$$

where $(C^*, \mathsf{k}^*) \leftarrow$ Encaps(pk) and $\varepsilon(\cdot)$ is a negligible function in λ.

Definition 9 (Extended Correctness). *For all $\lambda, m, k, n \in \mathbb{N}$ and (pk, sk$_0$) $\leftarrow$ KGen(λ, m, k), we require that for any (arbitrary interleaved) sequence of invocations of sk$_i$ $\leftarrow$ Punc(sk$_{i-1}, C_{i-1}$), where $i \in [n]$ and $(C_{i-1}, \mathsf{k}_{i-1}) \leftarrow$ Encaps(pk), it holds that:*

(a) Impossibility of false-negatives: Decaps(sk$_n, C_{j-1}$) $= \perp$, *for all $j \in [n]$.*
(b) Correctness of the initial secret key: $\Pr\left[\mathsf{Decaps}(\mathsf{sk}_0, C) \neq \mathsf{k}\right] \leq \varepsilon(\lambda)$, *for all $(C, \mathsf{k}) \leftarrow$ Encaps(pk) and ε is a negligible function in λ.*
(c) Semi-correctness of punctured secret keys: if Decaps(sk$_j, C$) $\neq \perp$ *then*

$$\Pr\left[\mathsf{Decaps}(\mathsf{sk}_j, C) \neq \mathsf{Decaps}(\mathsf{sk}_0, C)\right] \leq \varepsilon(\lambda),$$

for all $j \in [n]$, any C, and ε is a negligible function in λ.

All probabilities are taken over the random coins of KGen, Punc, *and* Encaps.

All probabilities are taken over the random coins of KGen, Punc, and Encaps. We recall additional properties (i.e., separable randomness, publicly-checkable puncturing, and γ-spreadness) and formal definitions of BFKEM-IND-CPA and BFKEM-IND-CCA security in the full version.

Right now, we only can guarantee this with IBE schemes as such schemes allow for exponentially many secret keys with a short master public key and, hence, we consider IBE schemes as a main building block of our BFKEM constructions.

5.1   IBE with Negligible from Non-Negligible Correctness Error

We follow the approach for randomized PKE schemes in Sect. 3.2 adapted for the IBE case (cf. Fig. 11).[3] Let IBE = (KGen, Ext, Enc, Dec) be an IBE scheme with identity, message spaces, and randomness spaces $\mathcal{ID}$, $\mathcal{M}$, and $\mathcal{R}$, respectively, with *non-negligible correctness error* $\delta(\lambda)$, we construct an IBE scheme IBE$'$ = (KGen$'$, Ext$'$, Enc$'$, Dec$'$) with identity and message spaces $\mathcal{ID}' := \mathcal{ID}$ and $\mathcal{M}' := \mathcal{M}$, respectively, with *negligible correctness error* $\delta'(\lambda)$. The construction is as follows. Set KGen$'$:= KGen and Ext$'$:= Ext while Enc$'$ and Dec$'$ are given in Fig. 11. See that $\ell = \ell(\lambda)$ can be chosen appropriately to accommodate a negligible correctness error $\delta'(\lambda)$.

Enc$'(mpk, id, M)$	Dec$'(usk_{id}, C)$
for $i \in [\ell]$	$C =: (C_1, \ldots, C_\ell)$
$\quad r_i \leftarrow_\$ \mathcal{R}$	**for** $i \in [\ell]$
$\quad C_i \leftarrow \mathsf{Enc}(mpk, id, M; r_i)$	$\quad M_i' := \mathsf{Dec}(usk_{id}, C_i)$
return $(C_1, \ldots, C_\ell)$	**return** $\mathsf{maj}(M_1', \ldots, M_\ell')$

Fig. 11. Compiler for Enc$'$ and Dec$'$ for constructing IBE with negligible correctness error from IBE with non-negligible correctness error.

As for randomized PKE schemes, by an analogue of Theorem 1 for IBEs with $q = \ell$ and $n = 1$, the security claim follows.

Corollary 2. *For any IBE-sIND-CPA adversary B against* IBE$'$ *obtained via applying the above transformation to* IBE, *there exists an IBE-sIND-CPA adversary A such that:*

$$\mathsf{Adv}^{\text{ibe-sind-cpa}}_{\text{IBE}', B}(\lambda) \leq \ell \cdot \mathsf{Adv}^{\text{ibe-sind-cpa}}_{\text{IBE}, A}(\lambda).$$

The correctness error analysis is again equivalent to the one in the PKE scenario. We refer to Sect. 3.2 for a more in depth discussion.

5.2   BFKEM from IBE with Negligible Correctness Error

The intuition for our generic construction from any IBE with negligible correctness error is as follows. We associate "user-secret keys" of IBE with the indexes $i \in [m]$ of the Bloom filter BF and annotate sk_0' as a special key for "fixed identity" 0. We consider the encapsulation key as $k_0 \oplus k_1$ where one share is encrypted under "identity" 0 (yielding C_0) while the other share is encrypted under the

---

[3] We explicitly mention that we are only concerned with randomized IBEs. Adopting $\mathsf{C}_{p,d}$ for deterministic IBEs will work as well. Though in the latter case, one can further optimize the compiler depending on whether the IBE has deterministic or randomized key extraction Ext.

"identities" $(i_j)_j$ of indexes of the BF that are determined by C_0. Put differently, C_0 acts as a tag of the overall ciphertext while the other IBE-ciphertexts $(C_{i_j})_j$ are utilized for correct decryption. The secret key is punctured on "tag" C_0. Note that the secret key sk_0' is not affected by the puncturing mechanism and one can always at least decrypt C_0. However, one additionally needs the encapsulation-key share from the other ciphertexts $(C_{i_j})_j$; those ciphertexts can only be decrypted if at least one secret key sk_{i*}' is available which can be checked with BFCheck.

Let IBE $=$ (IBE.KGen, IBE.Ext, IBE.Enc, IBE.Dec) be an IBE-sIND-CPA-secure IBE scheme with identity and message spaces $\mathcal{ID} = [m] \cup \{0\}$ and $\mathcal{M} = \{0,1\}^\lambda$, respectively, with negligible correctness error $\delta = \delta(\lambda)$, and BF $=$ (BFGen, BFUpdate, BFCheck) a BF with universe $\mathcal{U}$, we construct a BFKEM-IND-CPA-secure BFKEM scheme BFKEM $=$ (KGen, Encaps, Punc, Decaps) with key space $\mathcal{K} := \mathcal{M} = \{0,1\}^\lambda$ as a stepping stone towards a BFKEM-IND-CCA-secure BFKEM as follows.

KGen(λ, m, k): on input security parameter λ and BF parameters m, k, compute $(mpk, msk) \leftarrow$ IBE.KGen(λ), $\mathsf{sk}_{id}' \leftarrow$ IBE.Ext(msk, id), for all $id \in [m] \cup \{0\}$, and $(H, T_0) \leftarrow$ BFGen(m, k). Return pk $:= (mpk, H)$ and sk $:= (T_0, (\mathsf{sk}_{id}')_{id})$ (we assume that pk is available to Punc and Decaps implicitly).

Encaps(pk): on input $(mpk, H) :=$ pk, sample $\mathsf{k}_0, \mathsf{k}_1 \leftarrow_\$ \mathcal{K}$ and compute $C_0 \leftarrow$ Enc($mpk, 0, \mathsf{k}_0$). For $id_j := H_j(C_0)$ with $(H_j)_j := H$ and all $j \in [k]$, compute $C_{id_j} \leftarrow$ Enc(mpk, id_j, k_1) and output

$$((C_0, (C_{id_j})_j), \mathsf{k}_0 \oplus \mathsf{k}_1).$$

Punc(sk, C): on input $(T, \mathsf{sk}_0', (\mathsf{sk}_{id}')_{id \in [m]}) :=$ sk and $(C_0, \dots) := C$, compute $T' :=$ BFUpdate(H, T, C_0) and set

$$\mathsf{sk}_{id}'' := \begin{cases} \mathsf{sk}_{id}' & \text{if } T'[id] = 0, \\ \bot & \text{if } T'[id] = 1, \end{cases}$$

for $T'[id]$ the id-th bit of T'. Return $(T', \mathsf{sk}_0', (\mathsf{sk}_{id}'')_{id \in [m]})$.

Decaps(sk, C): on input $(T, (\mathsf{sk}_{id}')_{id \in [m] \cup \{0\}}) :=$ sk and $(C_0, (C_{id_j})_{j \in [k]}) := C$, output $\bot$ if BFCheck(H, T, C_0) $= 1$. Otherwise, there exists a smallest $id^* \in [m]$ such that $\mathsf{sk}_{id^*}' \neq \bot$, compute $\mathsf{k}_0 :=$ Dec(sk_0', C_0) and $\mathsf{k}_1 :=$ Dec($\mathsf{sk}_{id^*}', C_{id^*}$), and output $\mathsf{k}_0 \oplus \mathsf{k}_1$.

We prove the correctness (Definition 8), extended correctness (Definition 9), separable randomness, publicly-checkable puncturing, and γ-spreadness properties of BFKEM in the full version.

BFKEM-IND-CPA Security of BFKEM. We start by showing the BFKEM-IND-CPA security of BFKEM $=$ (KGen, Encaps, Punc, Decaps).

Theorem 9. *If* IBE *is IBE-sIND-CPA-secure, then* BFKEM *is BFKEM-IND-CPA-secure. Concretely, for any PPT adversary A there is a distinguisher D for the IBE-sIND-CPA security experiment such that*

$$\mathsf{Adv}_{\mathsf{BFKEM}, A}^{\mathsf{bfkem\text{-}ind\text{-}cpa}}(\lambda, m, k) \leq k \cdot m \cdot \mathsf{Adv}_{\mathsf{IBE}, D}^{\mathsf{ibe\text{-}sind\text{-}cpa}}(\lambda). \tag{1}$$

Proof. We show the BFKEM-IND-CPA-security of BFKEM for any valid PPT adversary A in series of games where:

Game 0. Game 0 is the BFKEM-IND-CPA-experiment.

Game i. Game i is defined as Game $i - 1$ except that the i-th challenge-ciphertext element C_{id_i} in C^* is independent of the challenge bit, for $i \in [k]$.

Game $k + 1$. Game $k + 1$ is defined as Game k except that the encapsulation key in the challenge ciphertext is independent of b'.

We denote the event of the adversary winning Game i as S_i. In Game $k + 1$, A has no advantage (i.e., success probability of $\Pr[S_{k+1}] = 1/2$) in the sense of BFKEM-IND-CPA. We argue in hybrids that the Games $i \in [k + 1]$ are computationally indistinguishable from Game 0.

Hybrids Between Games 0 and $k + 1$. Each hybrid between Games $i - 1$ and i, $i \in [k]$, is constructed as follows: on input m and k, D samples $(H, T_0) \leftarrow$ BFGen(m, k), for $H =: (H_j)_{j \in [k]}$ and sets $T_0 = 0^m$. Next, D samples $id^* \leftarrow_\$ [m]$ and sends id^* to its IBE-sIND-CPA-challenger. D retrieves mpk in return and sets pk $:= (mpk, H)$.

Furthermore, for all $id \in ([m] \cup \{0\}) \setminus \{id^*\}$, D retrieves $\mathsf{sk}_0 := (usk_{id})_{id}$ from its Ext-oracle. (Note that D does not have a secret key for id^* and A has to query the challenge ciphertext to the Punc'-oracle in order to receive secret keys via the Cor-oracle, which results in "deleting" the secret key for id^* if there were any. Particularly, all Cor-queries can be answered correctly.)

Furthermore, D sends $\mathsf{k}_1^{(0)}, \mathsf{k}_1^{(1)} \leftarrow_\$ \mathcal{M} = \{0,1\}^\lambda$ to its IBE-sIND-CPA-challenger and retrieves $C_{id^*}^* \leftarrow \mathsf{Enc}(mpk, id^*, \mathsf{k}^{(b)})$, for some $b \leftarrow_\$ \{0,1\}$.

D samples $b' \leftarrow_\$ \{0,1\}$, computes $C_0 \leftarrow \mathsf{Enc}(mpk, 0, \mathsf{k}_0)$, for $\mathsf{k}_0 \leftarrow \mathcal{M}$, and sets $(id_j)_j := (H_j(C_0))_{j \in [k]}$. If $id_i \neq id^*$, abort. (See that this happens with probability $(m-1)/m$.) Otherwise, D computes $C_{id_j} \leftarrow \mathsf{Enc}(mpk, id_j, \mathsf{k}_1^{(b')})$, for all $(id_j)_{j \in [k] \setminus [i]}$, and $C_{id_j} \leftarrow \mathsf{Enc}(mpk, id_j, \mathsf{k}_1')$, for all $(id_j)_{j \in [i-1]}$, for $\mathsf{k}_1' \leftarrow_\$ \mathcal{M}$.

D sets $C_{id_i} := C_{id^*}^*$ and sends $(\mathsf{pk}, C^* := (C_0, (C_{id_j})_j), \mathsf{k}^{(b')})$ to A, for $\mathsf{k}^{(b')} := \mathsf{k}_1^{(b')} \oplus \mathsf{k}_0$.

A has access to a Punc'(C)-oracle which runs $\mathsf{sk}_{i+1} \leftarrow \mathsf{Punc}(\mathsf{sk}_i, C)$ for each invocation $i = 0, 1, \ldots, q$ and sets $\mathcal{L} := \mathcal{L} \cup \{C\}$ for initially empty set $\mathcal{L}$. The Cor-oracle returns sk_{i+1} iff $C^* \in \mathcal{L}$. Eventually, A outputs a guess b^* which D forwards as $b^* \oplus b'$ to its IBE-sIND-CPA-challenger.

In the hybrid between Games k and $k + 1$: proceed as in Game k, but send $(\mathsf{pk}, C^* := (C_0, (C_{id_j})_j), \mathsf{k}')$, for uniform $\mathsf{k}' \leftarrow \mathcal{M}$ to A.

Analysis. In the hybrids between the Games $j - 1$ and j, for $j \in [k]$, we have that if $b' = b = 0$ or $b' = b = 1$, then the distribution of the challenge ciphertext is correct and a successful A should output $b^* = 0$ where D forwards $b^* \oplus b' = b$ as guess to its challenger which yields a successful IBE-sIND-CPA distinguisher D. If $b' \neq b$, then A is used to distinguish the j-th challenge-ciphertext component, i.e., a successful A should output $b^* = 1$ where D forwards $b^* \oplus b' = b$ as guess to its challenger which, again, yields a successful IBE-sIND-CPA distinguisher D.

In the hybrid between the Games k and $k+1$, the change is information-theoretic, i.e., the challenge ciphertext encapsulates uniformly random key-elements (independent of b') and the encapsulation key is sampled uniformly at random which yields $\Pr[S_{k+1}] = 1/2$. In each hybrid, we have that $\Pr[id_i = id^*] = 1/m$. Putting things together, for $k + 1$ hybrids, Eq. (1) holds. □

BFKEM-IND-CCA Security of BFKEM′. We construct a slight variant of our BFKEM scheme above, dubbed BFKEM′, via the FO transform [27] along the lines of [21]. We want to mention that the FO transform does not work generically for any BFKEM and no generic framework as in the case of KEMs exists. Hence, we consider the direct product compiler in Sect. 5.1 and, in the vein of [21], to prove BFKEM-IND-CCA security of our BFKEM, we introduce further properties (i.e., separable randomness, publicly-checkable puncturing, and γ-spreadness) . Furthermore, [21] requires perfect correctness for unpunctured keys which our BFKEM definition cannot guarantee. Hence, we have to reprove the BFKEM-IND-CCA-security for BFKEM′, although the proof techniques are almost the same as presented in [21]. We construct a BFKEM-IND-CCA-secure BFKEM as follows. Let BFKEM $=$ (KGen, Encaps, Punc, Decaps) be a randomness-separable BFKEM-IND-CPA-secure BFKEM scheme with key space $\mathcal{K} = \{0,1\}^\lambda$ and correctness error $\delta = \delta(\lambda)$, we construct a BFKEM-IND-CCA-secure BFKEM scheme BFKEM′ $=$ (KGen′, Encaps′, Punc′, Decaps′) with key space $\mathcal{K}' = \mathcal{K}$ using a variant of the FO transform as follows. Let G: $\mathcal{K}' \rightarrow \{0,1\}^{\rho+\lambda}$ be a hash function modeled as random oracle (RO) in the security proof.

KGen′(λ, m, k): same as KGen(λ, m, k).
Encaps′(pk): on input pk, sample $k' \leftarrow_\$ \mathcal{K}'$, compute $(r, k) := G(k') \in \{0,1\}^{\rho+\lambda}$ and $(C, k') \leftarrow$ Encaps(pk; (r, k')), and return (C, k). Punc′(sk, C): same as Punc(sk, C).
Decaps′(sk, C): on input secret key sk and ciphertext C, compute $k' \leftarrow$ Decaps(sk, C) and return $\perp$ if $k' = \perp$. Otherwise, compute $(r, k) := G(k')$ and return k if $(C, k') =$ Encaps(pk; (r, k')), else output $\perp$.

We prove the correctness (Definition 8), extended correctness (Definition 9), separable randomness, publicly-checkable puncturing, and γ-spreadness properties of BFKEM′ in the full version.

Theorem 10. *If a BFKEM BFKEM is BFKEM-IND-CPA-secure with the separable randomness, publicly-checkable puncturing, and γ-spreadness properties, and negligible correctness error probability $\delta = \delta(\lambda)$, then BFKEM′ is BFKEM-IND-CCA-secure. Concretely, for any PPT adversary A making at most $q_G = q_G(\lambda)$ queries to the random oracle G there is a distinguisher D in the BFKEM-IND-CPA-security experiment such that*

$$\mathsf{Adv}^{\mathsf{bfkem\text{-}ind\text{-}cca}}_{\mathsf{BFKEM}',A}(\lambda, m, k) \leq \mathsf{Adv}^{\mathsf{bfkem\text{-}ind\text{-}cpa}}_{\mathsf{BFKEM},D}(\lambda, m, k) + 2\delta + \frac{q_G}{2^\gamma}. \tag{2}$$

Due to space constraints, we show the proof in the full version.

5.3   Comparison of BFKEM Instantiations

To instantiate BFKEM$'$ from post-quantum IBE schemes, we investigating instantiations based on a selectively IND-CPA secure lattice-based or code-based IBEs. As far as lattices are concerned, the first such construction was [31] after which numerous others followed [1,19,24,64]. To compute the dimension of a lattice-based BFKEM, we start from the GVP-IBE instantiation of [24], for which an implementation and concrete dimensions were given for 80 and 192-bit quantum security. We set the parameter of the BFKEM as in [21], i.e., targeting the maximum number of allowed punctures to $n = 2^{20}$, which amounts to adding 2^{12} elements per day to the BF for a year, and allowing for a false-positive probability of 10^{-3}, we obtain $m = 1.5 \cdot 10^7$ and $k = 10$. A similar procedure can be applied to the code-based IBE of Gaborit et al. (GHPT) [29] achieving 128-bit quantum security. We note though that with recent advances in the cryptanalysis, these instances may provide less security. Table 4 provides an overview including the pairing-based BFKEM from [21]. For the latter, we assume the use of the pairing-friendly BLS12-381 curve with 120-bit classical security.

Table 4. Sizes of BFKEM when instantiated with GVP or GHPT.

IBE	Assumption	sk	pk	C
GVP-80	Lattice-based	19.21 GB	1.62 KB	17.46 KB
GVP-192	Lattice-based	47.15 GB	3.78 KB	40.28 KB
GHPT-128	Code-based	643.73 GB	252 KB	215.79 MB
Boneh-Franklin [21]	Pairing-based	717.18 MB	95.5 B	255.5 B

Acknowledgements. We would like to thank the anonymous reviewers for their helpful comments. This project has received funding from the European Union's Horizon 2020 research and innovation programme under grant agreement n°783119 (SECREDAS), n°826610 (COMP4DRONES), n°871473 (KRAKEN) and by the Austrian Science Fund (FWF) and netidee SCIENCE grant P31621-N38 (PROFET).

References

1. Agrawal, S., Boneh, D., Boyen, X.: Efficient lattice (H)IBE in the standard model. In: Gilbert, H. (ed.) EUROCRYPT 2010. LNCS, vol. 6110, pp. 553–572. Springer, Heidelberg (2010). https://doi.org/10.1007/978-3-642-13190-5_28
2. Ambainis, A., Hamburg, M., Unruh, D.: Quantum security proofs using semi-classical oracles. In: Boldyreva, A., Micciancio, D. (eds.) CRYPTO 2019. LNCS, vol. 11693, pp. 269–295. Springer, Cham (2019). https://doi.org/10.1007/978-3-030-26951-7_10
3. Aragon, N., et al.: BIKE. Technical report, National Institute of Standards and Technology (2019)

4. Aragon, N., et al.: ROLLO. Technical report, National Institute of Standards and Technology (2019)
5. Aviram, N., et al.: DROWN: Breaking TLS using SSLv2. In: USENIX Security (2016)
6. Baldi, M., Barenghi, A., Chiaraluce, F., Pelosi, G., Santini, P.: LEDAcrypt. Technical report, National Institute of Standards and Technology (2019)
7. Bauer, A., Gilbert, H., Renault, G., Rossi, M.: Assessment of the key-reuse resilience of NewHope. In: Matsui, M. (ed.) CT-RSA 2019. LNCS, vol. 11405, pp. 272–292. Springer, Cham (2019). https://doi.org/10.1007/978-3-030-12612-4_14
8. Bellare, M., Boldyreva, A., Micali, S.: Public-key encryption in a multi-user setting: security proofs and improvements. In: Preneel, B. (ed.) EUROCRYPT 2000. LNCS, vol. 1807, pp. 259–274. Springer, Heidelberg (2000). https://doi.org/10.1007/3-540-45539-6_18
9. Bindel, N., Hamburg, M., Hövelmanns, K., Hülsing, A., Persichetti, E.: Tighter proofs of CCA security in the quantum random oracle model. In: Hofheinz, D., Rosen, A. (eds.) TCC 2019, Part II. LNCS, vol. 11892, pp. 61–90. Springer, Cham (2019). https://doi.org/10.1007/978-3-030-36033-7_3
10. Bindel, N., Schanck, J.M.: Decryption failure is more likely after success. In: Ding, J., Tillich, J.-P. (eds.) PQCrypto 2020. LNCS, vol. 12100, pp. 206–225. Springer, Cham (2020). https://doi.org/10.1007/978-3-030-44223-1_12
11. Bitansky, N., Vaikuntanathan, V.: A note on perfect correctness by derandomization. In: Coron, J.-S., Nielsen, J.B. (eds.) EUROCRYPT 2017, Part II. LNCS, vol. 10211, pp. 592–606. Springer, Cham (2017). https://doi.org/10.1007/978-3-319-56614-6_20
12. Bleichenbacher, D.: Chosen ciphertext attacks against protocols based on the RSA encryption standard PKCS #1. In: Krawczyk, H. (ed.) CRYPTO 1998. LNCS, vol. 1462, pp. 1–12. Springer, Heidelberg (1998). https://doi.org/10.1007/BFb0055716
13. Bloom, B.H.: Space/time trade-offs in hash coding with allowable errors. Commun. ACM **13**, 422–426 (1970)
14. Böck, H., Somorovsky, J., Young, C.: Return of bleichenbacher's oracle threat (ROBOT). In: USENIX Security 2018 (2018)
15. Boneh, D., Dagdelen, Ö., Fischlin, M., Lehmann, A., Schaffner, C., Zhandry, M.: Random oracles in a quantum world. In: Lee, D.H., Wang, X. (eds.) ASIACRYPT 2011. LNCS, vol. 7073, pp. 41–69. Springer, Heidelberg (2011). https://doi.org/10.1007/978-3-642-25385-0_3
16. Boneh, D., Franklin, M.: Identity-based encryption from the Weil pairing. In: Kilian, J. (ed.) CRYPTO 2001. LNCS, vol. 2139, pp. 213–229. Springer, Heidelberg (2001). https://doi.org/10.1007/3-540-44647-8_13
17. Bos, J.W., et al.: Frodo: take off the ring! Practical, quantum-secure key exchange from LWE. In: ACM CCS (2016)
18. Canetti, R., Halevi, S., Katz, J.: Chosen-ciphertext security from identity-based encryption. In: Cachin, C., Camenisch, J.L. (eds.) EUROCRYPT 2004. LNCS, vol. 3027, pp. 207–222. Springer, Heidelberg (2004). https://doi.org/10.1007/978-3-540-24676-3_13
19. Cash, D., Hofheinz, D., Kiltz, E., Peikert, C.: Bonsai trees, or how to delegate a lattice basis. In: Gilbert, H. (ed.) EUROCRYPT 2010. LNCS, vol. 6110, pp. 523–552. Springer, Heidelberg (2010). https://doi.org/10.1007/978-3-642-13190-5_27
20. Derler, D., Gellert, K., Jager, T., Slamanig, D., Striecks, C.: Bloom filter encryption and applications to efficient forward-secret 0-RTT key exchange. IACR Cryptol. ePrint Arch. (To appear in Journal of Cryptology)

21. Derler, D., Jager, T., Slamanig, D., Striecks, C.: Bloom filter encryption and applications to efficient forward-secret 0-RTT key exchange. In: Nielsen, J.B., Rijmen, V. (eds.) EUROCRYPT 2018, Part III. LNCS, vol. 10822, pp. 425–455. Springer, Cham (2018). https://doi.org/10.1007/978-3-319-78372-7_14

22. Dowling, B., Fischlin, M., Günther, F., Stebila, D.: A cryptographic analysis of the TLS 1.3 handshake protocol candidates. In: ACM CCS (2015)

23. Drucker, N., Gueron, S., Kostic, D., Persichetti, E.: On the applicability of the Fujisaki-Okamoto transformation to the BIKE KEM. IACR ePrint 2020/510 (2020)

24. Ducas, L., Lyubashevsky, V., Prest, T.: Efficient identity-based encryption over NTRU lattices. In: Sarkar, P., Iwata, T. (eds.) ASIACRYPT 2014, Part II. LNCS, vol. 8874, pp. 22–41. Springer, Heidelberg (2014). https://doi.org/10.1007/978-3-662-45608-8_2

25. Dwork, C., Naor, M., Reingold, O.: Immunizing encryption schemes from decryption errors. In: Cachin, C., Camenisch, J.L. (eds.) EUROCRYPT 2004. LNCS, vol. 3027, pp. 342–360. Springer, Heidelberg (2004). https://doi.org/10.1007/978-3-540-24676-3_21

26. Fabšič, T., Hromada, V., Stankovski, P., Zajac, P., Guo, Q., Johansson, T.: A reaction attack on the QC-LDPC McEliece cryptosystem. In: Lange, T., Takagi, T. (eds.) PQCrypto 2017. LNCS, vol. 10346, pp. 51–68. Springer, Cham (2017). https://doi.org/10.1007/978-3-319-59879-6_4

27. Fujisaki, E., Okamoto, T.: Secure integration of asymmetric and symmetric encryption schemes. In: Wiener, M. (ed.) CRYPTO 1999. LNCS, vol. 1666, pp. 537–554. Springer, Heidelberg (1999). https://doi.org/10.1007/3-540-48405-1_34

28. Fujisaki, E., Okamoto, T.: Secure integration of asymmetric and symmetric encryption schemes. J. Cryptol. 26(1), 80–101 (2013). https://doi.org/10.1007/s00145-011-9114-1

29. Gaborit, P., Hauteville, A., Phan, D.H., Tillich, J.-P.: Identity-based encryption from codes with rank metric. In: Katz, J., Shacham, H. (eds.) CRYPTO 2017, Part III. LNCS, vol. 10403, pp. 194–224. Springer, Cham (2017). https://doi.org/10.1007/978-3-319-63697-9_7

30. Garcia-Morchon, O., et al.: Round5. Technical report, National Institute of Standards and Technology (2019)

31. Gentry, C., Peikert, C., Vaikuntanathan, V.: Trapdoors for hard lattices and new cryptographic constructions. In: 40th ACM STOC (2008)

32. Goldreich, O., Goldwasser, S., Halevi, S.: Eliminating decryption errors in the Ajtai-Dwork cryptosystem. In: Kaliski, B.S. (ed.) CRYPTO 1997. LNCS, vol. 1294, pp. 105–111. Springer, Heidelberg (1997). https://doi.org/10.1007/BFb0052230

33. Green, M.D., Miers, I.: Forward secure asynchronous messaging from puncturable encryption. In: 2015 IEEE Symposium on Security and Privacy (2015)

34. Günther, F., Hale, B., Jager, T., Lauer, S.: 0-RTT key exchange with full forward secrecy. In: Coron, J.-S., Nielsen, J.B. (eds.) EUROCRYPT 2017, Part III. LNCS, vol. 10212, pp. 519–548. Springer, Cham (2017). https://doi.org/10.1007/978-3-319-56617-7_18

35. Guo, Q., Johansson, T., Nilsson, A.: A key-recovery timing attack on post-quantum primitives using the fujisaki-okamoto transformation and its application on FrodoKEM. In: Micciancio, D., Ristenpart, T. (eds.) CRYPTO 2020, Part II. LNCS, vol. 12171, pp. 359–386. Springer, Cham (2020). https://doi.org/10.1007/978-3-030-56880-1_13

36. Guo, Q., Johansson, T., Stankovski, P.: A key recovery attack on MDPC with CCA security using decoding errors. In: Cheon, J.H., Takagi, T. (eds.) ASIACRYPT 2016, Part I. LNCS, vol. 10031, pp. 789–815. Springer, Heidelberg (2016). https://doi.org/10.1007/978-3-662-53887-6_29

37. Guo, Q., Johansson, T., Yang, J.: A novel CCA attack using decryption errors against LAC. In: Galbraith, S.D., Moriai, S. (eds.) ASIACRYPT 2019, Part I. LNCS, vol. 11921, pp. 82–111. Springer, Cham (2019). https://doi.org/10.1007/978-3-030-34578-5_4

38. Hamburg, M.: Three bears. Technical report, National Institute of Standards and Technology (2019)

39. Harris, B.: RSA key exchange for the secure shell (SSH) transport layer protocol. RFC (2006)

40. Hofheinz, D., Hövelmanns, K., Kiltz, E.: A modular analysis of the Fujisaki-Okamoto transformation. In: Kalai, Y., Reyzin, L. (eds.) TCC 2017. LNCS, vol. 10677, pp. 341–371. Springer, Cham (2017). https://doi.org/10.1007/978-3-319-70500-2_12

41. Hofheinz, D., Hövelmanns, K., Kiltz, E.: A modular analysis of the Fujisaki-Okamoto transformation. Cryptology ePrint Archive, Report 2017/604

42. Hohenberger, S., Koppula, V., Waters, B.: Chosen ciphertext security from injective trapdoor functions. In: Micciancio, D., Ristenpart, T. (eds.) CRYPTO 2020. LNCS, vol. 12170, pp. 836–866. Springer, Cham (2020). https://doi.org/10.1007/978-3-030-56784-2_28

43. Hövelmanns, K., Kiltz, E., Schäge, S., Unruh, D.: Generic authenticated key exchange in the quantum random oracle model. In: Kiayias, A., Kohlweiss, M., Wallden, P., Zikas, V. (eds.) PKC 2020. LNCS, vol. 12111, pp. 389–422. Springer, Cham (2020). https://doi.org/10.1007/978-3-030-45388-6_14

44. Howgrave-Graham, N., et al.: The impact of decryption failures on the security of NTRU encryption. In: Boneh, D. (ed.) CRYPTO 2003. LNCS, vol. 2729, pp. 226–246. Springer, Heidelberg (2003). https://doi.org/10.1007/978-3-540-45146-4_14

45. Jager, T., Kohlar, F., Schäge, S., Schwenk, J.: On the security of TLS-DHE in the standard model. In: Safavi-Naini, R., Canetti, R. (eds.) CRYPTO 2012. LNCS, vol. 7417, pp. 273–293. Springer, Heidelberg (2012). https://doi.org/10.1007/978-3-642-32009-5_17

46. Jager, T., Schinzel, S., Somorovsky, J.: Bleichenbacher's attack strikes again: breaking PKCS#1 v1.5 in XML encryption. In: Foresti, S., Yung, M., Martinelli, F. (eds.) ESORICS 2012. LNCS, vol. 7459, pp. 752–769. Springer, Heidelberg (2012). https://doi.org/10.1007/978-3-642-33167-1_43

47. Jiang, H., Zhang, Z., Chen, L., Wang, H., Ma, Z.: IND-CCA-secure key encapsulation mechanism in the quantum random oracle model, revisited. In: Shacham, H., Boldyreva, A. (eds.) CRYPTO 2018. LNCS, vol. 10993, pp. 96–125. Springer, Cham (2018). https://doi.org/10.1007/978-3-319-96878-0_4

48. Jiang, H., Zhang, Z., Ma, Z.: Tighter security proofs for generic key encapsulation mechanism in the quantum random oracle model. In: Ding, J., Steinwandt, R. (eds.) PQCrypto 2019. LNCS, vol. 11505, pp. 227–248. Springer, Cham (2019). https://doi.org/10.1007/978-3-030-25510-7_13

49. Koppula, V., Waters, B.: Realizing chosen ciphertext security generically in attribute-based encryption and predicate encryption. In: Boldyreva, A., Micciancio, D. (eds.) CRYPTO 2019. LNCS, vol. 11693, pp. 671–700. Springer, Cham (2019). https://doi.org/10.1007/978-3-030-26951-7_23

50. Krawczyk, H., Paterson, K.G., Wee, H.: On the security of the TLS protocol: a systematic analysis. In: Canetti, R., Garay, J.A. (eds.) CRYPTO 2013. LNCS, vol. 8042, pp. 429–448. Springer, Heidelberg (2013). https://doi.org/10.1007/978-3-642-40041-4_24

51. Kuchta, V., Sakzad, A., Stehlé, D., Steinfeld, R., Sun, S.-F.: Measure-rewind-measure: tighter quantum random oracle model proofs for one-way to hiding and CCA security. In: Canteaut, A., Ishai, Y. (eds.) EUROCRYPT 2020. LNCS, vol. 12107, pp. 703–728. Springer, Cham (2020). https://doi.org/10.1007/978-3-030-45727-3_24

52. Naehrig, M., et al.: FrodoKEM. Technical report, National Institute of Standards and Technology (2019)

53. Naor, M.: Bit commitment using pseudo-randomness. In: Brassard, G. (ed.) CRYPTO 1989. LNCS, vol. 435, pp. 128–136. Springer, New York (1990). https://doi.org/10.1007/0-387-34805-0_13

54. Naor, M., Yung, M.: Public-key cryptosystems provably secure against chosen ciphertext attacks. In: 22nd ACM STOC (1990)

55. Nisan, N., Wigderson, A.: Hardness vs randomness. J. Comput. Syst. Sci **49**, 149–167 (1994)

56. Paquin, C., Stebila, D., Tamvada, G.: Benchmarking post-quantum cryptography in TLS. In: Ding, J., Tillich, J.-P. (eds.) PQCrypto 2020. LNCS, vol. 12100, pp. 72–91. Springer, Cham (2020). https://doi.org/10.1007/978-3-030-44223-1_5

57. Ronen, E., Gillham, R., Genkin, D., Shamir, A., Wong, D., Yarom, Y.: The 9 lives of bleichenbacher's CAT: new cache ATtacks on TLS implementations. In: 2019 IEEE Symposium on Security and Privacy (2019)

58. Saito, T., Xagawa, K., Yamakawa, T.: Tightly-secure key-encapsulation mechanism in the quantum random oracle model. In: Nielsen, J.B., Rijmen, V. (eds.) EUROCRYPT 2018. LNCS, vol. 10822, pp. 520–551. Springer, Cham (2018). https://doi.org/10.1007/978-3-319-78372-7_17

59. Samardjiska, S., Santini, P., Persichetti, E., Banegas, G.: A reaction attack against cryptosystems based on LRPC codes. In: Schwabe, P., Thériault, N. (eds.) LAT-INCRYPT 2019. LNCS, vol. 11774, pp. 197–216. Springer, Cham (2019). https://doi.org/10.1007/978-3-030-30530-7_10

60. Schwabe, P., et al.: CRYSTALS-KYBER. Technical report, National Institute of Standards and Technology (2019)

61. Schwabe, P., Stebila, D., Wiggers, T.: Post-quantum TLS without handshake signatures. Cryptology ePrint Archive, Report 2020/534

62. Sendrier, N., Vasseur, V.: On the decoding failure rate of QC-MDPC bit-flipping decoders. In: Ding, J., Steinwandt, R. (eds.) PQCrypto 2019. LNCS, vol. 11505, pp. 404–416. Springer, Cham (2019). https://doi.org/10.1007/978-3-030-25510-7_22

63. Sun, S.-F., Sakzad, A., Steinfeld, R., Liu, J.K., Gu, D.: Public-key puncturable encryption: modular and compact constructions. In: Kiayias, A., Kohlweiss, M., Wallden, P., Zikas, V. (eds.) PKC 2020. LNCS, vol. 12110, pp. 309–338. Springer, Cham (2020). https://doi.org/10.1007/978-3-030-45374-9_11

64. Zhang, J., Chen, Yu., Zhang, Z.: Programmable hash functions from lattices: short signatures and IBEs with small key sizes. In: Robshaw, M., Katz, J. (eds.) CRYPTO 2016. LNCS, vol. 9816, pp. 303–332. Springer, Heidelberg (2016). https://doi.org/10.1007/978-3-662-53015-3_11

Possibility and Impossibility Results for Receiver Selective Opening Secure PKE in the Multi-challenge Setting

Rupeng Yang[1]($\boxtimes$), Junzuo Lai[2]($\boxtimes$), Zhengan Huang[3]($\boxtimes$), Man Ho Au[1], Qiuliang Xu[4], and Willy Susilo[5]

[1] Department of Computer Science, The University of Hong Kong, Hong Kong, China
orbbyrp@gmail.com, allenau@cs.hku.hk
[2] College of Information Science and Technology,
Jinan University, Guangzhou, China
laijunzuo@gmail.com
[3] Peng Cheng Laboratory, Shenzhen, China
zhahuang.sjtu@gmail.com
[4] School of Software, Shandong University, Jinan, China
xql@sdu.edu.cn
[5] Institute of Cybersecurity and Cryptology, School of Computing and Information
Technology, University of Wollongong, Wollongong NSW, Australia
wsusilo@uow.edu.au

Abstract. Public key encryption (PKE) schemes are usually deployed in an open system with numerous users. In practice, it is common that some users are corrupted. A PKE scheme is said to be receiver selective opening (RSO) secure if it can still protect messages transmitted to uncorrupted receivers after the adversary corrupts some receivers and learns their secret keys. This is usually defined by requiring the existence of a simulator that can simulate the view of the adversary given only the opened messages. Existing works construct RSO secure PKE schemes in a single-challenge setting, where the adversary can only obtain one challenge ciphertext for each public key. However, in practice, it is preferable to have a PKE scheme with RSO security in the multi-challenge setting, where public keys can be used to encrypt multiple messages. In this work, we explore the possibility of achieving PKE schemes with receiver selective opening security in the multi-challenge setting. Our contributions are threefold. First, we demonstrate that PKE schemes with RSO security in the single-challenge setting are not necessarily RSO secure in the multi-challenge setting. Then, we show that it is impossible to achieve RSO security for PKE schemes if the number of challenge ciphertexts under each public key is a priori unbounded. In particular, we prove that no PKE scheme can be RSO secure in the k-challenge setting (i.e., the adversary can obtain k challenge ciphertexts for each public key) if its secret key contains less than k bits. On the positive side, we give a concrete construction of PKE scheme with RSO security in the k-challenge setting, where the ratio of the secret key length to k approaches the lower bound 1.

© International Association for Cryptologic Research 2020
S. Moriai and H. Wang (Eds.): ASIACRYPT 2020, LNCS 12491, pp. 191–220, 2020.
https://doi.org/10.1007/978-3-030-64837-4_7

1   Introduction

The standard notion of security for public key encryption (PKE) schemes is indistinguishability of 1-ciphertext (denoted as IND-CPA security). That is to say, given one challenge ciphertext to an adversary, which encrypts a message from a set of two messages chosen by the adversary, it could not distinguish which message is encrypted. Such a simple security notion in fact implies semantic security with multiple challenge ciphertexts, which prevents the adversary from learning any information about the encrypted messages after viewing a priori unbounded number of ciphertexts.

In many real world scenarios, the adversary may have the capability to learn internal states of partial users via corrupting their devices. Such attacks are called selective opening attacks [DNRS99]. A PKE scheme is said to be secure against selective opening attacks if it can still protect messages transmitted between uncorrupted users. Surprisingly, standard security does not imply security against selective opening attacks immediately [BDWY12, HR14, HRW16].

The formal study of selective opening secure PKE was initialized by Bellare et al. in [BHY09]. They consider two types of selective opening attacks, namely, sender selective opening (SSO) attacks, where the attacker corrupts senders and obtains the randomness used for encrypting messages, and receiver selective opening (RSO) attacks, where the attacker corrupts receivers and obtains their secret keys. Also, for each attack, security can be defined by either an indistinguishability-based definition, which extends the standard IND-CPA security to the selective opening setting, or a simulation-based definition, which defines semantic security against selective opening attackers. In all definitions, the adversary first gets some challenge ciphertexts, then it "opens" some of them via corrupting the related users. An indistinguishability-based definition ensures that the adversary is not able to distinguish encrypted messages in unopened ciphertexts, while in a simulation-based definition, there should exist a simulator that can simulate the view of the adversary given only the opened messages.

Since selective opening security can be defined in different manners, it is important to clarify relations between different definitions. As shown in [HPW15], indistinguishability-based selective opening security is not sufficient to imply simulation-based selective opening security in both the SSO setting and the RSO setting. Thus, for selective opening security, it is desirable to consider simulation-based definitions.[1]

It is also interesting to explore whether selective opening security in the single-challenge setting, i.e., each public key is only used once to produce a single challenge ciphertext, is enough for achieving selective opening security in the multi-challenge setting, where each public key can be reused to encrypt multiple

---

[1] In addition, we prefer simulation-based definitions because indistinguishability-based selective opening security are usually defined for *efficiently conditionally re-samplable* message distributions [BHY09] only. A definition without such restriction (called full IND-SO security [BHK12, ORV14]) needs an inefficient security experiment and seems not achievable.

challenge messages. This question is particularly important for the RSO setting, because all previous works in this area only consider how to construct encryption schemes secure in the single-challenge setting and it is unknown whether they are still secure in the more realistic multi-challenge setting.

1.1 Our Results

In this work, we initiate the study of RSO security in the multi-challenge setting. In particular, we consider an adversary that can obtain k challenge ciphertexts for each public key, and denote security in this setting as RSO_k security.[2] We focus on simulation-based definitions and define security against both the chosen-plaintext adversary (SIM-RSO_k-CPA) and the chosen-ciphertext adversary (SIM-RSO_k-CCA). In summary, our contributions are as follows:

- We show that RSO security in the single-challenge setting is not enough to guarantee RSO security in the multi-challenge setting. We demonstrate this by providing a PKE scheme that is SIM-RSO_k-CCA secure, but is not SIM-RSO_{k+1}-CPA secure for any polynomial k (recall that RSO security in the single-challenge setting can be denoted as RSO_1 security). The PKE schemes build on an IND-CPA secure PKE scheme and a simulation-sound non-interactive zero-knowledge (NIZK) proof, thus, this also provides the first positive result for achieving RSO security in the multi-challenge setting.
- We prove that it is impossible to achieve SIM-RSO security in the multi-challenge setting if we do not bound the number of challenge ciphertexts for each public key. In particular, we provide a lower bound on the secret key length for any PKE scheme with RSO_k security in the non-programmable random oracle model, which indicates that the size of the secret key must be as large as the total number of message bits ever encrypted. For example, for any PKE with RSO_k security, assuming its message space is $\{0,1\}^m$ and the secret key space is $\{0,1\}^l$, then we have $l \geq mk$.
- We construct a concrete SIM-RSO_k-CPA secure PKE scheme from the DDH assumption, where the message space is $\{0,1\}$, the public key is a group element and the secret key only contains a number in $\mathbb{Z}_q$ and k bits.[3] This is nearly optimal in an asymptotic sense as the ratio of secret key length to k is $1 + \frac{\log q}{k}$, which approaches the lower bound 1 as the messages number k increases.
- We prove that the well-known Naor-Yung paradigm [NY90, Sah99] still works for SIM-RSO security and give a generic construction of SIM-RSO_k-CCA secure PKE scheme from a SIM-RSO_k-CPA secure PKE scheme, an IND-CPA secure PKE scheme, and a simulation-sound NIZK proof. The construction preserves the key length of the underlying SIM-RSO_k-CPA secure scheme. Thus, combining our (nearly) optimal SIM-RSO_k-CPA secure scheme with the generic construction, we obtain a (nearly) optimal SIM-RSO_k-CCA secure PKE scheme.

---

[2] Previous definitions in the single-challenge setting are specific cases of this new definition and can be denoted as RSO_1 security.

[3] Here, q is the group order and is fixed by the security parameter.

1.2   Technical Overview

In this section, we give a brief overview of how to achieve our negative and positive results. In a high-level, we first observe that a large enough secret key space (conditioned on some public information) is needed to achieve RSO_k security, and employ this observation to lower bound the secret key length for any RSO_k secure PKE scheme. Then we apply the observation to some concrete constructions and provide counterexamples separating RSO_k security and RSO_{k+1} security. Finally, we construct (nearly) optimal RSO_k secure PKE scheme, whose secret key length approaches the above lower bound in an asymptotic sense.

Next, we describe the ideas in more detail.

On Lower Bounding Key Length of RSO_k Secure PKE scheme. We start by showing that a RSO_k secure PKE scheme must have a long enough secret key. For simplicity of discussion, here we assume that the message space of the scheme is $\{0,1\}$ and explain why it cannot be RSO_k secure if its secret key length contains at most $k-1$ bits.

Intuitively, this is because the number of possible secret keys are not enough to explain k messages. In more detail, to simulate an adversary's output, a RSO_k simulator[4] should generate challenge ciphertexts and send them to the adversary first. Then in the opening phase, on input the opened messages, the simulator needs to generate secret keys that can map each ciphertext to corresponding message. Remember that it needs to map k fixed ciphertexts to a vector of k 1-bit messages using each secret key. Thus, the number of candidate secret keys should be at least 2^k to guarantee that the simulator is able to choose the correct secret key for every possible messages vector. However, if the secret key length of the scheme does not exceed $k-1$, then the number of possible secret keys will not exceed 2^{k-1}. That is to say, for at least half of the possible messages vectors, the simulator is not able to create a correct secret key to explain them. So, with probability $1/2$ (assuming messages are sampled uniformly), the simulation will fail.

To formalize this intuition, we use ideas in previous works [Nie02, BSW11, BDWY12, BO13] that argue impossibility to achieve simulation-based security against a key-revealing attacker.[5] In a nutshell, given a hash function, which is modeled as a non-programmable random oracle, we define a RSO_k adversary as follows. In the first phase, on receiving a set of n public keys $\boldsymbol{PK} = (pk_i)_{i \in [n]}$, it returns a uniform distribution; then in the second phase, on receiving a set of challenge ciphertexts $\boldsymbol{CT}$, it returns a set of indices $\mathcal{I} \subseteq [n]$, which is the hash of $(\boldsymbol{PK}, \boldsymbol{CT})$; finally, on receiving the opened secret keys $\boldsymbol{SK}_{\mathcal{I}}$ and messages $\boldsymbol{M}_{\mathcal{I}}$[6], it outputs $(\boldsymbol{PK}, \boldsymbol{CT}, \boldsymbol{SK}_{\mathcal{I}})$. Note that a simulator who would like to simulate

---

[4] We refer the readers to Sect. 2.2 for the formal definition of a RSO_k simulator in either the CPA setting and the CCA setting.

[5] We remark that similar lower bounds on key length are achieved in these works, but these results do not imply lower bound for SIM-RSO secure PKE scheme directly.

[6] We use $\boldsymbol{SK}_{\mathcal{I}}$ and $\boldsymbol{M}_{\mathcal{I}}$ to denote the set of secret keys for $(pk_i)_{i \in \mathcal{I}}$ and messages encrypted under $(pk_i)_{i \in \mathcal{I}}$ respectively.

the adversary's view should generate PK and CT before viewing the opened messages, since otherwise, it has to invert the random oracle, which is infeasible. Thus, if we feed the simulator with different messages, it should create secret keys conditioned on fixed PK and CT. As the number of possible messages is much larger than the number of possible secret keys[7], such simulator does not exist.

On Separating RSO_{k+1} Security and RSO_k Security. Next, we explain how to construct a scheme that is SIM-RSO_k-CCA secure, but is not even SIM-RSO_{k+1}-CPA secure. Our starting point is an encryption scheme Π_1 from the well-known Naor-Yung paradigm [NY90,Sah99], which is proved to be SIM-RSO_1-CCA secure for 1-bit message in [HKM+18]. We first recall the scheme briefly and show that it is not SIM-RSO_2-CPA secure. Then we explain how to upgrade it to a scheme that is SIM-RSO_k-CCA secure, but is not SIM-RSO_{k+1}-CPA secure.

<u>A brief review of Π_1.</u> The scheme Π_1 relies on a normal PKE scheme E and a simulation-sound NIZK proof system. Its public key $PK = (pk_0, pk_1)$ is a pair of public keys of E and its secret key is $SK = (s, sk_s)$, where s is a bit and sk_s is the secret key corresponding to pk_s. The encryption of a bit m includes an encryption of m under pk_0, an encryption of m under pk_1 and a proof indicating that the two ciphertexts encrypt the same message. To decrypt a ciphertext, the decryption algorithm first checks the validity of the proof attached and decrypts the ciphertext under pk_s using sk_s.

The SIM-RSO_1-CCA security of Π_1 comes from the fact that given a malformed ciphertext, which encrypts a random bit b under pk_0 and encrypts $1-b$ under pk_1, one can open it to any message $m \in \{0,1\}$. In particular, if $m = b$, then the returned secret key is $(0, sk_0)$ and otherwise, the returned secret key is $(1, sk_1)$. In this way, to simulate the view of a SIM-RSO_1-CCA adversary the simulator can generate such malformed ciphertext in the beginning and answer the opening query according to the opened messages. Indistinguishability between malformed ciphertexts and well-formed ciphertexts comes from security of E and zero-knowledge property of the underlying NIZK. Also, determining the secret keys until the opening stage will not affect answers to decryption oracle queries since the adversary is only allowed to submit a well-formed ciphertext, which are identically decrypted under sk_0 and sk_1.

<u>Π_1 is Not SIM-RSO_2-CPA Secure.</u> Next, we show that if for each public key of E, there exists at most one valid secret key for it and it is easy to check if a public key/secret key pair is valid[8], Π_1 will not be SIM-RSO_2-CPA secure.

Our key observation is that in this case, while the number of possible secret keys is very large, the number of possible secret keys for a fixed public key is not enough to explain 2 messages. Recall that to prove SIM-RSO_2-CPA security of Π_1, we need a simulator that is forced to produce challenge ciphertexts before

---

[7] If $|\mathcal{I}| = 1$, then the number of possible messages is 2^k while the number of possible secret keys is no more than 2^{k-1}.

[8] Concretely, we may view E as ElGamal encryption scheme.

seeing the opened messages and is required to create the correct secret keys that maps the challenge ciphertexts to the opened messages. For a public key $PK = (pk_0, pk_1)$, the best possible strategy for the simulator to generate the challenge ciphertext seems to set the first ciphertext $CT_1 = (\mathsf{E.Enc}(pk_0, b_1), \mathsf{E.Enc}(pk_1, 1 - b_1))$ and set the second ciphertext $CT_2 = (\mathsf{E.Enc}(pk_0, b_2), \mathsf{E.Enc}(pk_1, 1 - b_2))$, where b_1 and b_2 are random bits. Then, in the opening phase, the simulator can return a secret key, which is either $(0, sk_0)$ or $(1, sk_1)$, to the adversary, where sk_0, sk_1 are the unique valid secret keys for pk_0 and pk_1 respectively. The secret key $(0, sk_0)$ can decrypt the challenger ciphertexts to (b_1, b_2) and the secret key $(1, sk_1)$ can decrypt the challenger ciphertexts to $(1 - b_1, 1 - b_2)$. But if the opened messages are $(b_1, 1 - b_2)$ or $(1 - b_1, b_2)$, no secret key can map challenge ciphertexts to them. So, with probability $1/2$ (assuming messages are sampled uniformly), the simulation will fail. Therefore, we can exploit the techniques for lower bounding secret key length of RSO_k secure PKE schemes to compromise the RSO_2 security of Π_1.

Upgrading Π_1. Next, we explain how to upgrade Π_1 to a RSO_k-secure but RSO_{k+1}-insecure scheme. Our main idea is to use k pairs of public keys of E to encrypt messages. More precisely, to encrypt a bit m under a public key $PK = (pk_{1,0}, pk_{1,1}, \ldots, pk_{k,0}, pk_{k,1})$, the encryption algorithm first samples a k-bit string $(p_1, \ldots, p_k)$ that $p_1 \oplus \ldots \oplus p_k = m$, and then encrypts p_i with $(pk_{i,0}, pk_{i,1})$. Then it generates a NIZK proof proving the correctness of all k pairs of ciphertexts. The final ciphertext includes all $2k$ ciphertexts of E and the proof.

Now, to simulate the view of an adversary in a SIM-RSO_k experiment, or alternatively, to generate k ciphertexts and open them to any k-bit string, the simulator generates the ciphertexts as follows:

$(pk_{1,0}, pk_{1,1})$	$(p_{1,1}, 1 - p_{1,1})$	$(p_{2,1}, p_{2,1})$	$\cdots$	$(p_{k,1}, p_{k,1})$
$(pk_{2,0}, pk_{2,1})$	$(p_{1,2}, p_{1,2})$	$(p_{2,2}, 1 - p_{2,2})$	$\cdots$	$(p_{k,2}, p_{k,2})$
$\vdots$	$\vdots$	$\vdots$	$\ddots$	$\vdots$
$(pk_{k,0}, pk_{k,1})$	$(p_{1,k}, p_{1,k})$	$(p_{2,k}, p_{2,k})$	$\cdots$	$(p_{k,k}, 1 - p_{k,k})$
	CT_1	CT_2	$\cdots$	CT_k

where each $p_{i,j} \xleftarrow{\$} \{0,1\}$, and CT_i consists of encryption of $(p_{i,j}, p_{i,j})$ (or $(p_{i,i}, 1 - p_{i,i})$) under public key $(pk_{j,0}, pk_{j,1})$ and a fake proof generated by the NIZK simulator.

Note that, for each public key pair $(pk_{i,0}, pk_{i,1})$, the simulator is only required to cheat on one ciphertext (the ones in a dashed box), thus it can succeed in finding the correct secret key.

The reason that the new scheme is not SIM-RSO_{k+1}-CPA secure is the same as that why Π_1 is not SIM-RSO_2-CPA secure. Note that in the new scheme, the number of valid secret keys for a public key $PK = (pk_{1,0}, pk_{1,1}, \ldots, pk_{k,0}, pk_{k,1})$ is 2^k, which is much less than the number of possible opening messages (2^{k+1}).

Thus, we can use a similar strategy to show that no simulator is able to simulate the adversary's view in a SIM-RSO$_{k+1}$-CPA experiment.

On Constructing RSO$_k$ Secure PKE Scheme with (Nearly) Optimal Secret Key Length. Now, we demonstrate how to achieve SIM-RSO$_k$-CCA secure PKE scheme with (nearly) optimal secret key length. Note that standard techniques for shortening secret keys of PKE schemes (e.g., deriving secret keys from a shorter seed via a pseudorandom generator) do not work here since in the receiver selective opening setting, the simulator needs to generate secret keys satisfying some conditions and using these techniques may lead to an inefficient simulator (e.g., the simulator may have to invert a pseudorandom generator).

Our starting point is the celebrated Cramer-Shoup encryption scheme [CS98], which was shown to be SIM-RSO$_1$-CCA secure in [HKM+18, HLC+19]. Here, we will use its variant with CPA security ($\Pi_{\text{CS-CPA}}$). We first reduce the key length of the scheme. Then, we upgrade it to be SIM-RSO$_k$-CPA secure via merely adding $k-1$ bits to the secret key. Finally, we transform the scheme into a SIM-RSO$_k$-CCA secure one by employing the well-known Naor-Yung double encryption paradigm [NY90, Sah99], where a normal IND-CPA secure PKE scheme and a simulation-sound NIZK proof is additionally used. In our construction, we fix the secret key of the new scheme to be the secret key of the underlying SIM-RSO$_k$-CPA secure scheme. Also, we need to tweak the security proof to fit the definition of SIM-RSO-CPA/CCA security.

Next, we first recall $\Pi_{\text{CS-CPA}}$ and explain why it is SIM-RSO$_1$-CPA secure. Then we provide a more detailed description on how to reduce its key length and how to upgrade the scheme to achieve SIM-RSO$_k$-CPA security.

A brief review of $\Pi_{\text{CS-CPA}}$. The scheme $\Pi_{\text{CS-CPA}}$ works in a cyclic group $\mathbb{G}$ of prime order q with generator g. Let $g_0 = g^{a_0}, g_1 = g^{a_1}, h = g^b$, then the secret key of the scheme is $(s_0, s_1) \in \mathbb{Z}_q^2$ and the public key is $pk = g_0^{s_0} g_1^{s_1}$. To encrypt a bit $m \in \{0,1\}$, the encryption algorithm samples $w \xleftarrow{\$} \mathbb{Z}_q$, and computes the ciphertext $CT = (x_0, x_1, C) = (g_0^w, g_1^w, pk^w \cdot h^m)$. The decryption algorithm tests if $x_0^{s_0} x_1^{s_1} = C$ and outputs 0 if this is the case.

To simulate the view of a SIM-RSO$_1$-CPA adversary, the simulator can first sample $(s_0', s_1') \xleftarrow{\$} \mathbb{Z}_q^2$, compute $pk = g_0^{s_0'} g_1^{s_1'}$ and generate a malformed ciphertext $CT = (x_0, x_1, C) = (g_0^{w_0}, g_1^{w_1}, x_0^{s_0'} x_1^{s_1'})$ for each receiver. Here, w_0, w_1 are distinct random elements in $\mathbb{Z}_q$ and the malformed ciphertext is indistinguishable from an honestly generated one due to the DDH assumption. Then, for each corrupted receiver, assuming the opened message is m, the simulator creates the secret key (s_0, s_1) compatible with the current view by solving the following equations:

$$\begin{cases} g_0^{s_0} g_1^{s_1} = g_0^{s_0'} g_1^{s_1'} \\ x_0^{s_0} x_1^{s_1} \cdot h^m = x_0^{s_0'} x_1^{s_1'} \end{cases} \tag{1}$$

which can be transformed into

$$\begin{cases} a_0 s_0 + a_1 s_1 = a_0 s_0' + a_1 s_1' \\ a_0 w_0 s_0 + a_1 w_1 s_1 + bm = a_0 w_0 s_0' + a_1 w_1 s_1' \end{cases}$$

The equation has a solution since $w_0 \neq w_1$. Thus, the simulator can succeed in simulating the view of a SIM-RSO$_1$-CPA adversary.

Reducing the Key Length. It is worth noting that in the scheme $\Pi_{\text{CS-CPA}}$, some bits of the secret key are wasted. In particular, the simulator is able to simulate the view of the adversary if Equation (1) has solutions in both the case $m = 0$ and that $m = 1$. Thus, it is appealing to see if the equations still always have solutions in some smaller solution space.

We observe that, if we change the strategy of the simulator, then it is possible to reduce the secret key space to $\mathbb{Z}_q \times \{0, 1\}$. In more detail, for each receiver, the simulator samples $(s'_0, s'_1) \xleftarrow{\$} \mathbb{Z}_q \times \{0, 1\}$, computes $pk = g_0^{s'_0} g_1^{s'_1}$ and changes the format of malformed ciphertext into $CT = (x_0, x_1, C) = (g_0^w, g_1^w \cdot h^\alpha, x_0^{s'_0} x_1^{s'_1})$. Here $\alpha = 1$ if $s'_1 = 1$ and $\alpha = -1$ if $s'_1 = 0$, and the malformed ciphertext is still indistinguishable from an honestly generated one due to the DDH assumption. Now, the secret key (s_0, s_1) needs to satisfy the following equation:

$$
\begin{cases}
a_0 s_0 + a_1 s_1 = a_0 s'_0 + a_1 s'_1 \\
a_0 w s_0 + a_1 w s_1 + b \alpha s_1 + b m = a_0 w s'_0 + a_1 w s'_1 + b \alpha s'_1
\end{cases}
$$

It is easy to see that if $m = 0$, then $s_1 = s'_1$ and thus $s_1 \in \{0, 1\}$; if $m = 1$, then $1 = \alpha \cdot (s'_1 - s_1)$, which implies that 1) if $s'_1 = 1$, then $s_1 = 0$ and 2) if $s'_1 = 0$, then $s_1 = 1$. Therefore, the scheme is still secure if we reduce the secret key length to $\lceil \log q \rceil + 1$.

Achieving RSO$_k$ Security. Next, we show how to upgrade the revised scheme to achieving SIM-RSO$_k$-CPA security. Our first attempt is to use the idea in upgrading the counterexample Π_1, i.e., secret sharing the message into k bits and using k independent instances of the scheme to encrypt each bit. However, this will lead to a scheme with key length $k \cdot (\lceil \log q \rceil + 1)$, which is far from optimal.

To solve this problem, our key observation is that, when generating the k public key/secret key pairs, s_0 and the public key can be reused. More precisely, let $g_0 = g^{a_0}, g_1 = g^{a_1}, \ldots, g_k = g^{a_k}, h = g^b$, then we set the secret key to be $(s_0, s_1, \ldots, s_k) \xleftarrow{\$} \mathbb{Z}_q \times \{0, 1\}^k$ and set the public key to be $pk = g_0^{s_0} g_1^{s_1} \ldots g_k^{s_k}$. Note that the secret key only contains $\lceil \log q \rceil + k$ bits. Then, to encrypt a bit $m \in \{0, 1\}$, the encryption algorithm samples $w \xleftarrow{\$} \mathbb{Z}_q$, and computes the ciphertext $CT = (x_0, x_1, \ldots, x_k, C) = (g_0^w, g_1^w, \ldots, g_k^w, pk^w \cdot h^m)$. The decryption algorithm tests if $x_0^{s_0} x_1^{s_1} \ldots x_k^{s_k} = C$ and outputs 0 if this is the case.

Next, we illustrate why the above scheme is SIM-RSO$_k$-CPA secure. For each receiver, the simulator samples $(s'_0, s'_1, \ldots, s'_k) \xleftarrow{\$} \mathbb{Z}_q \times \{0, 1\}^k$ and computes $pk = g_0^{s'_0} g_1^{s'_1} \ldots g_k^{s'_k}$. Also, it generates k malformed ciphertexts, where for the i-th ciphertext, x_i is dishonestly created. That is, $CT_i = (x_{i,0}, x_{i,1}, \ldots, x_{i,i}, \ldots x_{i,k}, C) = (g_0^{w_i}, g_1^{w_i}, \ldots, g_i^{w_i} \cdot h^{\alpha_i}, \ldots, g_k^{w_i}, x_{i,0}^{s'_0} x_{i,1}^{s'_1} \ldots x_{i,k}^{s'_k})$. Here $\alpha_i = 1$ if $s'_i = 1$ and $\alpha_i = -1$ if $s'_i = 0$. Then, for each corrupted receiver, assuming the k opened messages are $m_1, \ldots, m_k$, the simulator creates the secret key $(s_0, s_1, \ldots, s_k)$ compatible with the current view by solving the following equations:

$$
\begin{cases}
\prod_{j=0}^{k} g_j^{s_j} = \prod_{j=0}^{k} g_j^{s_j'} \\
(\prod_{j=0}^{k} x_{1,j}^{s_j}) \cdot h^{m_1} = \prod_{j=0}^{k} x_{1,j}^{s_j'} \\
\quad \vdots \\
(\prod_{j=0}^{k} x_{k,j}^{s_j}) \cdot h^{m_k} = \prod_{j=0}^{k} x_{k,j}^{s_j'}
\end{cases}
$$

This is equivalent to the following equation:

$$
\begin{cases}
\sum_{j=0}^{k} a_j s_j = \sum_{j=0}^{k} a_j s_j' \\
(\sum_{j=0}^{k} a_j w_1 s_j) + b\alpha_1 s_1 + bm_1 = (\sum_{j=0}^{k} a_j w_1 s_j') + b\alpha_1 s_1' \\
\quad \vdots \\
(\sum_{j=0}^{k} a_j w_k s_j) + b\alpha_k s_k + bm_k = (\sum_{j=0}^{k} a_j w_k s_j') + b\alpha_k s_k'
\end{cases}
$$

which can be transformed into

$$
\begin{cases}
\sum_{j=0}^{k} a_j s_j = \sum_{j=0}^{k} a_j s_j' \\
m_1 = \alpha_1(s_1' - s_1) \\
\quad \vdots \\
m_k = \alpha_k(s_k' - s_k)
\end{cases}
$$

Note that, for $i \in [1, k]$, we can set $s_i = s_i'$ if $m_i = 0$ and set $s_i = 1 - s_i'$ if $m_i = 1$. Therefore, the simulator is able to produce a simulated secret key $(s_0, s_1, \ldots, s_k) \in \mathbb{Z}_q \times \{0, 1\}^k$ and thus can simulate the view of the SIM-RSO$_k$-CPA adversary.

1.3   Related Works

Since first proposed in [BHY09], PKE with selective opening security has been extensively studied. Numerous constructions of SSO secure PKE have been proposed based on various assumptions in previous works (see [FHKW10, HLOV11, Hof12, HLQ13, LP15, HJKS15, HP16, LSSS17, BL17, LLHG18] and references therein for more details).

In contrast, the setting of RSO security is less studied. It is folklore that (receiver) non-committing encryption schemes [CFGN96, Nie02, DN00, CHK05, CDSMW09] imply RSO secure PKE schemes. Then, in [HPW15], Hazay et al. show that RSO security is achievable from a variety of well-established cryptographic primitives and construct RSO secure PKE schemes from various assumptions. In subsequent works [JLL16, JLL17, HKM+18, HLC+19], chosen-ciphertext attacks (CCA) are also considered in the RSO setting and PKE schemes with RSO-CCA security are provided. Moreover, in [KT18], RSO-secure identity-based encryption scheme is constructed. However, in all these works, the proposed encryption schemes are only proved to have RSO security in the single-challenge setting.

1.4 Roadmap

We recall some preliminaries and define RSO_k security in Sect. 2. Then in Sect. 3, we provide the lower bound for RSO_k secure PKE scheme. Next, we show our counterexamples separating RSO_k security and RSO_{k+1} security in Sect. 4. Then, we construct (nearly) optimal PKE schemes with SIM-RSO_k-CPA security and SIM-RSO_k-CCA security in Sect. 5. Finally, in Sect. 6, we conclude our work with a few possible future works.

2   Preliminaries

Notations. For any positive integer n, we use $[n]$ to denote the set $\{1, 2, \cdots, n\}$. For positive integers n_1, n_2 s.t. $n_1 < n_2$, we use $[n_1, n_2]$ to denote the set $\{n_1, n_1 + 1, \cdots, n_2 - 1, n_2\}$. We use boldface to denote vectors, e.g., $\boldsymbol{x}$. We use $\boldsymbol{x}[i]$ to denote the i-th component of $\boldsymbol{x}$. Also, for a string $s \in \{0, 1\}^*$, we use $s[i]$ to denote the i-th bit of s.

For a finite set $\mathcal{S}$, we use $|\mathcal{S}|$ to denote the size of $\mathcal{S}$ and use $s \xleftarrow{\$} \mathcal{S}$ to denote the process of sampling s uniformly from $\mathcal{S}$. For a distribution $\mathcal{D}$, we use $x \leftarrow \mathcal{D}$ to denote the process of sampling x from $\mathcal{D}$. For a positive integer n, we use $\mathcal{U}_n$ to denote the uniform distribution over $\{0, 1\}^n$.

For a probabilistic algorithm A, we use $A(x; r)$ to denote the process of running A on input x and inner randomness r. We write PPT for probabilistic polynomial-time. We use $\mathtt{negl}(\lambda)$ to denote a negligible function.

2.1 Assumptions and Cryptographic Primitives

The DDH Assumption. First, we recall the DDH assumption. Let $\mathbb{G}$ be a cyclic group of prime order q with a generator g. The DDH assumption requires that it is hard to distinguish (g^a, g^b, g^c) and (g^a, g^b, g^{ab}), where $a, b, c \xleftarrow{\$} \mathbb{Z}_q$.

Unbounded Simulation-Sound NIZK Proofs. The notion of NIZK proof was proposed by Blum et al. in [BFM88]. As shown in [Sah99], an unbounded simulation-sound NIZK proof for every language in NP exists assuming the existence of (doubly-enhanced) trapdoor permutations.

Let R be an efficiently computable binary relation. A NIZK proof for a language $\mathcal{L} = \{x : \exists w, (x, w) \in R\}$ consists of three PPT algorithms:

- Gen. On input the security parameter λ, the common reference string generation algorithm outputs a common reference string crs.
- Prove. On input a common reference string crs, a statement $x \in \mathcal{L}$ and a witness w for x, the proving algorithm outputs a proof π.
- Verify. On input a common reference string crs, a statement x and a proof π, the verification algorithm outputs a bit indicating whether the proof is valid.

Also, it satisfies the following conditions:

- **Completeness.** For any $(x, w) \in R$, let crs $\leftarrow$ Gen(1^λ) and $\pi \leftarrow$ Prove(crs, x, w), then we have Verify(crs, x, π) = 1.

- **Unbounded Zero-Knowledge.** There exists a PPT simulator (S_1, S_2) that for any PPT adversary $\mathcal{A}$, we have

$$\left| \Pr \left[\begin{array}{l} \mathsf{crs} \leftarrow \mathsf{Gen}(1^\lambda); \\ \mathcal{A}^{\mathsf{P}(\mathsf{crs}, \cdot, \cdot)}(\mathsf{crs}) = 0 \end{array} \right] - \Pr \left[\begin{array}{l} (\mathsf{crs}, \mathsf{td}) \leftarrow S_1(1^\lambda); \\ \mathcal{A}^{\mathsf{S}(\mathsf{crs}, \mathsf{td}, \cdot, \cdot)}(\mathsf{crs}) = 0 \end{array} \right] \right| \leq \mathsf{negl}(\lambda)$$

where $\mathsf{P}(\mathsf{crs}, x, w)$ outputs $\mathsf{Prove}(\mathsf{crs}, x, w)$ if $(x, w) \in \mathsf{R}$ and outputs $\perp$ otherwise; $\mathsf{S}(\mathsf{crs}, \mathsf{td}, x, w)$ outputs $S_2(\mathsf{crs}, \mathsf{td}, x)$ if $(x, w) \in \mathsf{R}$ and outputs $\perp$ otherwise.

- **Unbounded Simulation-Soundness.** Let (S_1, S_2) be a PPT simulator for the zero-knowledge property of the NIZK proof. For any unbounded adversary $\mathcal{A}$, we have

$$\Pr \left[\begin{array}{l} (\mathsf{crs}, \mathsf{td}) \leftarrow S_1(1^\lambda); \\ (x, \pi) \leftarrow \mathcal{A}^{\mathsf{S}(\mathsf{crs}, \mathsf{td}, \cdot)}(\mathsf{crs}); \\ \text{Let } Q \text{ be list of input/output} \\ \text{pairs for the oracle S} \end{array} \; : \; \begin{array}{l} (x, \pi) \notin Q \wedge x \notin \mathcal{L} \\ \wedge \, \mathsf{Verify}(\mathsf{crs}, x, \pi) = 1 \end{array} \right] \leq \mathsf{negl}(\lambda)$$

where $\mathsf{S}(\mathsf{crs}, \mathsf{td}, x)$ outputs $S_2(\mathsf{crs}, \mathsf{td}, x)$.

2.2 PKE with RSO$_k$ Security

A public key encryption scheme $\mathsf{PKE} = (\mathsf{Setup}, \mathsf{Gen}, \mathsf{Enc}, \mathsf{Dec})$ consists of four PPT algorithms:

- **Setup.** On input the security parameter 1^λ, the setup algorithm outputs the public parameter pp.
- **Gen.** On input the public parameter pp, the key generation algorithm outputs a public key pk and a secret key sk.
- **Enc.** On input the public parameter pp, the public key pk and a message m, the encryption algorithm outputs a ciphertext ct.
- **Dec.** On input the public parameter pp, the public key pk, the secret key sk and a ciphertext ct, the decryption algorithm outputs a message m.

Correctness of PKE requires that $\Pr[\mathsf{Dec}(\mathsf{pp}, pk, sk, ct) \neq m] \leq \mathsf{negl}(\lambda)$ for any message m, where $\mathsf{pp} \leftarrow \mathsf{Setup}(1^\lambda), (pk, sk) \leftarrow \mathsf{Gen}(\mathsf{pp}), ct \leftarrow \mathsf{Enc}(\mathsf{pp}, pk, m)$.

The basic security requirement of PKE schemes is IND-CPA security:

Definition 2.1 (IND-CPA Security). *We say that a PKE scheme* $\mathsf{PKE} = (\mathsf{Setup}, \mathsf{Gen}, \mathsf{Enc}, \mathsf{Dec})$ *is IND-CPA secure if for any PPT adversary* $\mathcal{A} = (\mathcal{A}_1, \mathcal{A}_2)$,

$$Pr[\mathsf{pp} \leftarrow \mathsf{Setup}(1^\lambda), (pk, sk) \leftarrow \mathsf{Gen}(\mathsf{pp}), (state, m_0^*, m_1^*) \leftarrow \mathcal{A}_1(pp, pk),$$

$$b \xleftarrow{\$} \{0, 1\}, ct^* \leftarrow \mathsf{Enc}(\mathsf{pp}, pk, m_b^*) : \quad \mathcal{A}_2(state, ct^*) = b] \leq 1/2 + \mathsf{negl}(\lambda)$$

In this work, we also consider the stronger receiver selective opening security for PKE schemes. Next, we provide definitions of RSO_k security, which are adapted from previous works [HPW15, HKM+18, HLC+19]. Our definitions consider chosen-plaintext attackers and chosen-ciphertext attackers respectively and in both cases, we will define security in a simulation-based sense.

Definition 2.2 (SIM-RSO$_k$-CPA Security). *We say that a PKE scheme* PKE = (Setup, Gen, Enc, Dec) *is SIM-RSO$_k$-CPA secure, if for any polynomially bounded function $n > 0$, any PPT adversary $\mathcal{A} = (\mathcal{A}_1, \mathcal{A}_2, \mathcal{A}_3)$, there exists a PPT simulator $\mathcal{S} = (\mathcal{S}_1, \mathcal{S}_2, \mathcal{S}_3)$, such that for any PPT distinguisher $\mathcal{D}$,*

$$|Pr[\mathcal{D}(\text{Exp}_{\text{PKE},\mathcal{A},n}^{RSO_k-\text{CPA-real}}(\lambda)) = 1] - Pr[\mathcal{D}(\text{Exp}_{\text{PKE},\mathcal{S},n}^{RSO_k-\text{CPA-ideal}}(\lambda)) = 1]| \leq \text{negl}(\lambda)$$

where $\text{Exp}_{\text{PKE},\mathcal{A},n}^{RSO_k-\text{CPA-real}}$ *and* $\text{Exp}_{\text{PKE},\mathcal{S},n}^{RSO_k-\text{CPA-ideal}}$ *are defined in Fig. 1.*

Definition 2.3 (SIM-RSO$_k$-CCA Security). *We say that a PKE scheme* PKE = (Setup, Gen, Enc, Dec) *is SIM-RSO$_k$-CCA secure, if for any polynomially bounded function $n > 0$, any PPT adversary $\mathcal{A} = (\mathcal{A}_1, \mathcal{A}_2, \mathcal{A}_3)$, there exists a PPT simulator $\mathcal{S} = (\mathcal{S}_1, \mathcal{S}_2, \mathcal{S}_3)$, such that for any PPT distinguisher $\mathcal{D}$,*

$$|Pr[\mathcal{D}(\text{Exp}_{\text{PKE},\mathcal{A},n}^{RSO_k-\text{CCA-real}}(\lambda)) = 1] - Pr[\mathcal{D}(\text{Exp}_{\text{PKE},\mathcal{S},n}^{RSO_k-\text{CCA-ideal}}(\lambda)) = 1]| \leq \text{negl}(\lambda)$$

where $\text{Exp}_{\text{PKE},\mathcal{A},n}^{RSO_k-\text{CCA-real}}$ *and* $\text{Exp}_{\text{PKE},\mathcal{S},n}^{RSO_k-\text{CCA-ideal}}$ *are defined in Fig. 1.*

3   Lower Bound for PKE with RSO$_k$ Security

In this section, we establish a lower bound on the secret key size of a PKE scheme with RSO_k security. Roughly, we show that a PKE scheme cannot be SIM-RSO$_k$-CPA secure (this also implies that it is not SIM-RSO$_k$-CCA secure) if the length of its secret key is not k times larger than the length of message. Formally, we have:

Theorem 3.1. *Let $\Pi = (\text{Setup}, \text{Gen}, \text{Enc}, \text{Dec})$ be a PKE scheme with secret key space $\mathcal{SK}$ and message space $\mathcal{M}$ (w.l.o.g, we assume $\mathcal{SK} = \{0,1\}^l$ and $\mathcal{M} = \{0,1\}^m$). If $l \leq mk - 1$, then Π is not SIM-RSO$_k$-CPA secure in the non-programmable random oracle model.*

Proof. Let $H : \{0,1\}^* \to \{0,1\}^h$ be a hash function, which is modeled as a non-programmable random oracle. Let $\mathcal{PP}$, $\mathcal{PK}$ and $\mathcal{C}$ be the public parameters set, the public key space and the ciphertext space of Π respectively. Also, let $a = \lceil \log |\mathcal{PP}| \rceil$, $b = \lceil \log |\mathcal{PK}| \rceil$, $c = \lceil \log |\mathcal{C}| \rceil$ and let $\kappa = a + b + ck + 2$. Let $n = h + 1$, $\epsilon = 1/(4\kappa)$.

Consider the concrete adversary $\mathcal{A} = (\mathcal{A}_1, \mathcal{A}_2, \mathcal{A}_3)$ and distinguisher $\mathcal{D}$ defined in Fig. 2. Next, we show that for any PPT simulator $\mathcal{S} = (\mathcal{S}_1, \mathcal{S}_2, \mathcal{S}_3)$:

$$|\Pr[\mathcal{D}(\text{Exp}_{\Pi,\mathcal{A},n}^{RSO_k-\text{CPA-real}}(\lambda)) = 1] - \Pr[\mathcal{D}(\text{Exp}_{\Pi,\mathcal{S},n}^{RSO_k-\text{CPA-ideal}}(\lambda)) = 1]| > \epsilon$$

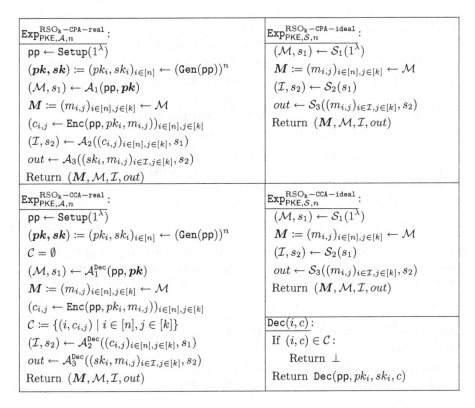

Fig. 1. Experiments for defining SIM-RSO$_k$-CPA security and SIM-RSO$_k$-CCA security. Let $\mathcal{M}$ be the message space of PKE, then in all experiments, $\mathcal{M}$ is a distribution over $\mathcal{M}^{n \times k}$ and $\mathcal{I} \subseteq [n]$.

First, by the correctness of Π, we have

$$\Pr[\mathcal{D}(\mathrm{Exp}_{\Pi,\mathcal{A},n}^{\mathrm{RSO}_k\text{-}\mathrm{CPA-real}}(\lambda)) = 1] \leq \mathtt{negl}(\lambda)$$

Next, fixing any PPT simulator $\mathcal{S} = (\mathcal{S}_1, \mathcal{S}_2, \mathcal{S}_3)$[9], let

$$\delta = \Pr[\mathcal{D}(\mathrm{Exp}_{\Pi,\mathcal{S},n}^{\mathrm{RSO}_k\text{-}\mathrm{CPA-ideal}}(\lambda)) = 1]$$

Then, it is sufficient to show that δ is notably larger than ϵ. Concretely, we will argue that $\delta \geq 1/(2\kappa)$ in the remaining part of the proof.

To lower bound δ, we consider an auxiliary experiment $\mathrm{Exp}_{\Pi,\mathcal{S},\mathcal{D},n,k,\kappa}$ defined in Fig. 3 and analyze the distribution of its output. Here, we use $\mathcal{R}_D$ to denote the distribution of the randomness for the distinguisher $\mathcal{D}$ (the randomness is used in the decryption algorithm of Π) and use $\mathcal{D}(\cdot, \cdot, \cdot, \cdot; R)$ to denote running the distinguisher $\mathcal{D}$ with randomness R.

---

[9] Here, w.l.o.g., we assume that $\mathcal{S}_2$ and $\mathcal{S}_3$ are deterministic. This will not restrict the power of $\mathcal{S}$ since we can feed coins for $\mathcal{S}_2$ and $\mathcal{S}_3$ to $\mathcal{S}_1$ and require $\mathcal{S}_1$ (resp. $\mathcal{S}_2$) to put coins for $\mathcal{S}_2$ and $\mathcal{S}_3$ (resp. $\mathcal{S}_3$) in its outputted state s_1 (resp. s_2).

$\mathcal{A}_1(\mathsf{PP},(PK_i)_{i\in[n]})$:	$\mathcal{D}((m_{i,j})_{i\in[n],j\in[k]},\mathcal{M},\mathcal{I},out)$:
$\mathcal{M}=\mathcal{U}_{mnk}$	If $\mathcal{M}\neq\mathcal{U}_{mnk}$: **Output 1**
$s_1=(\mathsf{PP},(PK_i)_{i\in[n]})$	$(\mathsf{PP},(PK_i,C_{i,j})_{i\in[n],j\in[k]},(SK_i)_{i\in\mathcal{I}})=out$
Output $(\mathcal{M},s_1)$	$t=H(\mathsf{PP},(PK_i,C_{i,j})_{i\in[n],j\in[k]})$
$\mathcal{A}_2((C_{i,j})_{i\in[n],j\in[k]},s_1)$:	$\mathcal{I}'=\{i\mid i\in[h]\wedge t[i]=1\}\cup\{n\}$
$t=H(\mathsf{PP},(PK_i,C_{i,j})_{i\in[n],j\in[k]})$	If $\mathcal{I}\neq\mathcal{I}'$: **Output 1**
$\mathcal{I}=\{i\mid i\in[h]\wedge t[i]=1\}\cup\{n\}$	$(m'_{i,j}\leftarrow\mathsf{Dec}(\mathsf{PP},PK_i,SK_i,C_{i,j}))_{i\in\mathcal{I},j\in[k]}$
$s_2=(s_1,(C_{i,j})_{i\in[n],j\in[k]})$	For $i\in\mathcal{I},j\in[k]$:
Output $(\mathcal{I},s_2)$	If $m_{i,j}\neq m'_{i,j}$: **Output 1**
$\mathcal{A}_3((SK_i,m_{i,j})_{i\in\mathcal{I},j\in[k]},s_2)$:	**Output 0**
$out=(s_2,(SK_i)_{i\in\mathcal{I}})$	
Output out	

Fig. 2. The adversary $\mathcal{A}$ and $\mathcal{D}$ in attacking SIM-RSO$_k$-CPA security of Π. Here, we abuse the notation of $\mathcal{U}_{mnk}$ to denote the description of an algorithm that outputs uniform mnk-bit string and assume that this description is hardwired in $\mathcal{A}$ and $\mathcal{D}$.

$\mathsf{Exp}_{\Pi,\mathcal{S},\mathcal{D},n,k,\kappa}$:
$(\mathcal{M},s_1)\leftarrow\mathcal{S}_1(1^\lambda)$; $(\mathcal{I},s_2)=\mathcal{S}_2(s_1)$; $R\leftarrow\mathcal{R}_\mathcal{D}$;
For $\iota\in[1,\kappa]$:
  $(m^\iota_{i,j})_{i\in[n],j\in[k]}\leftarrow\mathcal{M}$; $out^\iota=\mathcal{S}_3((m^\iota_{i,j})_{i\in\mathcal{I},j\in[k]},s_2)$
  If $\mathcal{D}((m^\iota_{i,j})_{i\in[n],j\in[k]},\mathcal{M},\mathcal{I},out^\iota;R)=1$: **Output 1**
For $\iota\in[2,\kappa]$:
  Parse $out^\iota=(\mathsf{PP}^\iota,(PK^\iota_i,C^\iota_{i,j})_{i\in[n],j\in[k]},(SK^\iota_i)_{i\in\mathcal{I}})$
  If $(\mathsf{PP}^{\iota-1},(PK^{\iota-1}_i,C^{\iota-1}_{i,j})_{i\in[n],j\in[k]})\neq(\mathsf{PP}^\iota,(PK^\iota_i,C^\iota_{i,j})_{i\in[n],j\in[k]})$:
    Output 2
Output 0

Fig. 3. The auxiliary experiment $\mathsf{Exp}_{\Pi,\mathcal{S},\mathcal{D},n,k,\kappa}$.

Lemma 3.1. $\Pr[\mathsf{Exp}_{\Pi,\mathcal{S},\mathcal{D},n,k,\kappa}=0]\leq 1/4$.

Proof. Assume the experiment outputs 0. First, we have $\mathcal{M}=\mathcal{U}_{mnk}$, thus, for each $\iota\in[\kappa],i\in[n],j\in[k]$, $m^\iota_{i,j}$ is sampled uniformly at random from $\{0,1\}^m$. Also, we know that $n\in\mathcal{I}$ and for $\iota\in[\kappa]$ and $j\in[k]$, we set $PK^\iota=PK^\iota_n$, $C^\iota_j=C^\iota_{n,j}$, $SK^\iota=SK^\iota_n$, and $m^\iota_j=m^\iota_{n,j}$. Moreover, we have $(\mathsf{PP}^{\iota-1},(PK^{\iota-1},C^{\iota-1}_j)_{j\in[k]})=(\mathsf{PP}^\iota,(PK^\iota,C^\iota_j)_{j\in[k]})$ for all $\iota\in[n]$ and thus we can write PP^ι as PP, PK^ι as PK and C^ι_j as C_j. Finally, for all $\iota\in[\kappa]$ and $j\in[k]$, we have $m^\iota_j=\mathsf{Dec}(\mathsf{PP},PK,SK^\iota,C_j;r^\iota_j)$, where r^ι_j is the randomness for Dec derived deterministically from R.

Next, for any randomness R (which determines $(r^\iota_j)_{\iota\in[\kappa],j\in[k]}$), we analyze the probability that all above requirements are satisfied.

First, fix any tuple $(\mathsf{PP}, PK, \boldsymbol{C} = (C_1, \ldots, C_k), \boldsymbol{SK} = (SK^1, \ldots, SK^\kappa))$ in $\{0,1\}^{a+b+ck+l\kappa}$, which is *not* necessary the output of the simulator, then we have

$$\Pr[\forall \iota \in [\kappa], j \in [k], m_j^\iota = \mathsf{Dec}(\mathsf{PP}, PK, SK^\iota, C_j; r_j^\iota)] = \frac{1}{2^{mk\kappa}}$$

where the probability is taken over the random choice of each m_j^ι.

As the total possible ways to choose PP, PK, $\boldsymbol{C} = (C_1, \ldots, C_k)$, and $\boldsymbol{SK} = (SK^1, \ldots, SK^\kappa)$ does not exceed $2^{a+b+ck+l\kappa} = 2^{(l+1)\kappa-2}$, we have

$$\Pr[\exists \mathsf{PP}, PK, \boldsymbol{C}, \boldsymbol{SK} : \forall \iota \in [\kappa], j \in [k],$$
$$m_j^\iota = \mathsf{Dec}(\mathsf{PP}, PK, SK^\iota, C_j; r_j^\iota)] \leq \frac{2^{(l+1)\kappa-2}}{2^{mk\kappa}} \leq \frac{2^{mk\kappa-2}}{2^{mk\kappa}} = \frac{1}{4}$$

Therefore, the probability that the auxiliary experiment $\mathsf{Exp}_{\Pi,\mathcal{S},\mathcal{D},n,k,\kappa}$ outputs 0 does not exceed $1/4$. $\square$

Lemma 3.2. $\Pr[\mathsf{Exp}_{\Pi,\mathcal{S},\mathcal{D},n,k,\kappa} = 1] \leq \kappa \cdot \delta.$

Proof. First, note that randomness of the experiment $\mathsf{Exp}_{\Pi,\mathcal{S},\mathcal{D},n,k,\kappa}$ comes from three parts, namely, R, randomness of the simulator $\mathcal{S}$ (denoted as ρ here) and randomness used in sampling $m_{i,j}^\iota$. Let $\mathcal{R}_\mathcal{S}$ be the distribution of the randomness for the simulator $\mathcal{S}$. Let

$$f(R, \rho) = \Pr \left[\begin{array}{l} (\mathcal{M}, s_1) = \mathcal{S}_1(1^\lambda; \rho); \\ (\mathcal{I}, s_2) = \mathcal{S}_2(s_1); \\ \boldsymbol{M} := (m_{i,j})_{i \in [n], j \in [k]} \leftarrow \mathcal{M}; \\ out = \mathcal{S}_3((m_{i,j})_{i \in \mathcal{I}, j \in [k]}, s_2); \end{array} \; : \; \mathcal{D}(\boldsymbol{M}, \mathcal{M}, \mathcal{I}, out; R) = 1 \right]$$

where the probability is taken over the random choice of each $\boldsymbol{M}$. Then, we have

$$\Pr[\mathsf{Exp}_{\Pi,\mathcal{S},\mathcal{D},n,k,\kappa} = 1]$$
$$= \mathbb{E}_{R \leftarrow \mathcal{R}_D, \rho \leftarrow \mathcal{R}_S} (1 - (1 - f(R, \rho))^\kappa)$$
$$\leq \mathbb{E}_{R \leftarrow \mathcal{R}_D, \rho \leftarrow \mathcal{R}_S} (\kappa \cdot f(R, \rho))$$
$$= \kappa \cdot \mathbb{E}_{R \leftarrow \mathcal{R}_D, \rho \leftarrow \mathcal{R}_S} f(R, \rho)$$
$$= \kappa \cdot \delta$$

where the second inequality comes from the Bernoulli's inequality. $\square$

Lemma 3.3. $\Pr[\mathsf{Exp}_{\Pi,\mathcal{S},\mathcal{D},n,k,\kappa} = 2] \leq 1/4.$

Proof. This comes from the collision resistant property of the non-programmable random oracle, which is a random function whose output is not controlled by the simulator.

Assuming that H has been queried (either by the adversary, the distinguisher or the simulator) Q times, where Q is a polynomial. Then the probability that there exists two distinct queries x_1, x_2 s.t. $H(x_1) = H(x_2)$ does not exceed $\frac{Q^2}{2^h}$, which is negligible.

However, if the experiment outputs 2 with a non-negligible probability (e.g., 1/4), then, via running the experiment, one can find $\iota \in [\kappa]$ that

1) $(\mathsf{PP}^{\iota-1}, (PK_i^{\iota-1}, C_{i,j}^{\iota-1})_{i \in [n], j \in [k]}) \neq (\mathsf{PP}^\iota, (PK_i^\iota, C_{i,j}^\iota)_{i \in [n], j \in [k]})$
2) $H(\mathsf{PP}^{\iota-1}, (PK_i^{\iota-1}, C_{i,j}^{\iota-1})_{i \in [n], j \in [k]}) = H(\mathsf{PP}^\iota, (PK_i^\iota, C_{i,j}^\iota)_{i \in [n], j \in [k]}) = (t[1], \dots, t[h])$, where $t[i] = 1$ iff $i \in \mathcal{I}$ (otherwise, the experiment will output 1)

with a non-negligible probability, which makes a contradiction. □

Finally, combining Lemma 3.1 to Lemma 3.3, we have

$$1 \leq 1/4 + \kappa \cdot \delta + 1/4$$

which implies $\delta \geq \frac{1}{2\kappa}$ and this completes the proof. □

Remark 3.1. Theorem 3.1 claims that if the key length of a PKE scheme is not large enough, then it is impossible to prove its SIM-RSO$_k$-CPA security even in the non-programmable random oracle model. At first glance, this also rules out standard model achievability of RSO$_k$ security for PKE schemes with short keys. However, as stated in [BO13], impossibility result in non-programmable random oracle model does not extend to that in standard model naturally, since the adversary in the non-programmable random oracle model is also able to access the random oracle and thus is stronger than a standard model adversary.

Nonetheless, We can adapt the proof for Theorem 3.1 to achieve the same lower bound (i.e. $l > mk - 1$) in the standard model. More precisely, the revised proof is identical to proof of Theorem 3.1, except that we use a collision resistant hash function to replace the use of non-programmable random oracle. But the proof only works in the auxiliary input model, where all participants, including the adversary, the distinguisher, and the simulator, are given some common auxiliary input in the beginning. Here, the auxiliary input is a random key for the underlying collision resistant hash function.

4   RSO$_k$ Security $\not\Rightarrow$ RSO$_{k+1}$ Security

We present counterexamples that separate the RSO$_k$ security and the RSO$_{k+1}$ security in this section. More precisely, for any polynomial k, we construct a PKE scheme Π that is SIM-RSO$_k$-CCA secure in the standard model but is not SIM-RSO$_{k+1}$-CPA secure in the non-programmable random oracle model.

Let λ be the security parameter and let k be a positive integer that is polynomial in λ.

Let $E = (E.Setup, E.Gen, E.Enc, E.Dec)$ be a CPA Secure PKE scheme with a deterministic decryption algorithm and an additional verification algorithm Ver. The algorithm Ver takes as input a public parameter pp and a public key/secret key pair (pk, sk), and outputs a bit indicating if (pk, sk) is a valid key pair. Also, we require that E has the following two properties:

- **Verification Correctness.** Let $pp \leftarrow E.Setup(1^\lambda)$, $(pk, sk) \leftarrow E.Gen(pp)$, then $\Pr[E.Ver(pp, pk, sk) = 1] = 1$.
- **Key Uniqueness.** For any pp and for any pk, $|\{sk \mid E.Ver(pp, pk, sk) = 1\}| \leq 1$.

It is easy to see that the well-known ElGamal encryption scheme satisfies this property.

Let $NIZK = (NIZK.Gen, NIZK.Prove, NIZK.Verify)$ be an unbounded simulation-sound NIZK proof system for NP. In particular, we will use it to prove the following language:

$$\{(pp, (pk_{i,j}, c_{i,j})_{i \in [k], j \in \{0,1\}}) : \exists ((p_i, r_{i,j})_{i \in [k], j \in \{0,1\}}),$$
$$(c_{i,j} = E.Enc(pp, pk_{i,j}, p_i; r_{i,j}))_{i \in [k], j \in \{0,1\}}\}$$

The PKE scheme $\Pi = (Setup, Gen, Enc, Dec)$ works as follows:

- **Setup.** On input a security parameter λ, the setup algorithm computes $pp \leftarrow E.Setup(1^\lambda)$ and $crs \leftarrow NIZK.Gen(1^\lambda)$. The public parameter for Π is $PP = (pp, crs)$.
- **Gen.** On input a public parameter $PP = (pp, crs)$, the key generation algorithm first computes $(pk_{i,j}, sk_{i,j}) \leftarrow E.Gen(pp)$ for $i \in [k]$ and $j \in \{0,1\}$. Then it samples $s_1, \ldots, s_k \overset{\$}{\leftarrow} \{0,1\}$. The public key $PK = (pk_{i,j})_{i \in [k], j \in \{0,1\}}$ and the secret key $SK = (s_i, sk_{i,s_i})_{i \in [k]}$.
- **Enc.** On input a public parameter $PP = (pp, crs)$, a public key $PK = (pk_{i,j})_{i \in [k], j \in \{0,1\}}$ and a message $m \in \{0,1\}$, the encryption algorithm first samples $p_1, \ldots, p_k$ uniformly at random from $\{0,1\}$ s.t. $m = p_1 \oplus p_2 \oplus \ldots \oplus p_k$. Then for $i \in [k], j \in \{0,1\}$, it samples $r_{i,j}$ randomly from the randomness space of E and computes $c_{i,j} = E.Enc(pp, pk_{i,j}, p_i; r_{i,j})$. Finally, it computes $\pi \leftarrow NIZK.Prove(crs, (pp, (pk_{i,j}, c_{i,j})_{i \in [k], j \in \{0,1\}}), ((p_i, r_{i,j})_{i \in [k], j \in \{0,1\}}))$. The ciphertext is $C = ((c_{i,j})_{i \in [k], j \in \{0,1\}}, \pi)$.
- **Dec.** On input a public parameter $PP = (pp, crs)$, a public key $PK = (pk_{i,j})_{i \in [k], j \in \{0,1\}}$, a secret key $SK = (s_i, sk_{i,s_i})_{i \in [k]}$ and a ciphertext $C = ((c_{i,j})_{i \in [k], j \in \{0,1\}}, \pi)$, the decryption algorithm first checks if π is valid and aborts with a decryption failure symbol $\bot$ if it is not the case. Otherwise, it computes $p_i = E.Dec(pp, pk_{i,s_i}, sk_{i,s_i}, c_{i,s_i})$ and outputs $m = p_1 \oplus \ldots \oplus p_k$.

Theorem 4.1. *If E is an CPA secure PKE scheme and $NIZK$ is a simulation-sound NIZK proof system, then Π is SIM-RSO$_k$-CCA secure in the standard model.*

Theorem 4.2. *If E is a PKE scheme with deterministic decryption algorithm, verification correctness and key uniqueness, then Π is not SIM-RSO$_{k+1}$-CPA secure in the non-programmable random oracle model.*

Proofs of Theorem 4.1 and Theorem 4.2 are provided in the full version.

Note that we can also prove that Π is not SIM-RSO$_{k+1}$-CPA secure in the standard model, but similar to the setting discussed in Remark 3.1, we need to assume that all participants, including the adversary, the distinguisher, and the simulator, are given some common auxiliary input in the beginning.

5   RSO$_k$ Secure PKE with (Nearly) Optimal Secret Key Length

In this section, we construct RSO$_k$ secure PKE schemes with secret key length $l = k + O(\lambda)$. Here the ratio of secret key length to the messages number k is $\frac{l}{k} = 1 + o(1)$. As shown in Sect. 3, no PKE scheme can achieve RSO$_k$ security if $l \leq k - 1$ (i.e., $\frac{l}{k} < 1$). Thus, our schemes are optimal in an asymptotic sense.

Next, in Sect. 5.1, we first construct an optimal SIM-RSO$_k$-CPA secure scheme from the DDH assumption. Then in Sect. 5.2, we upgrade the scheme to achieve SIM-RSO$_k$-CCA security by using a NIZK proof system.

5.1   SIM-RSO$_k$-CPA Secure PKE with (Nearly) Optimal Secret Key Length

Let λ be the security parameter and let k be a positive integer that is polynomial in λ. Let $\mathcal{G}$ be a group generator algorithm that takes as input a security parameter λ and outputs a multiplicative cyclic group $\mathbb{G}$ of prime order q and a generator g of $\mathbb{G}$.

The PKE scheme $\Pi = (\mathsf{Setup}, \mathsf{Gen}, \mathsf{Enc}, \mathsf{Dec})$ works as follows:

- Setup. On input a security parameter λ, the setup algorithm first generates $(\mathbb{G}, q, g) \leftarrow \mathcal{G}(1^\lambda)$ and samples $a_0, a_1, \ldots a_k, b \xleftarrow{\$} \mathbb{Z}_q$. Then it computes $g_i = g^{a_i}$ for $i \in [0, k]$ and $h = g^b$. The public parameter for Π is $\mathsf{PP} = (\mathbb{G}, q, g, g_0, g_1, \ldots, g_k, h)$.
- Gen. On input a public parameter $\mathsf{PP} = (\mathbb{G}, q, g, g_0, g_1, \ldots, g_k, h)$, the key generation algorithm first samples $s_0 \xleftarrow{\$} \mathbb{Z}_q$ and $s_1, \ldots s_k \xleftarrow{\$} \{0, 1\}$ and sets the secret key $sk = (s_0, s_1, \ldots, s_k)$. Then it computes the public key $pk = \prod_{i \in [0,k]} g_i^{s_i}$.
- Enc. On input a public parameter $\mathsf{PP} = (\mathbb{G}, q, g, g_0, g_1, \ldots, g_k, h)$, a public key pk and a message $m \in \{0, 1\}$, the encryption algorithm first samples $w \xleftarrow{\$} \mathbb{Z}_q$. Then it computes $\boldsymbol{x} = (x_0, x_1, \ldots, x_k) = (g_0^w, g_1^w, \ldots, g_k^w)$, $K = pk^w$ and $C = K \cdot h^m$. The ciphertext $CT = (\boldsymbol{x}, C)$.
- Dec. On input a public parameter $\mathsf{PP} = (\mathbb{G}, q, g, g_0, g_1, \ldots, g_k, h)$, a secret key $sk = (s_0, s_1, \ldots, s_k)$ and a ciphertext $CT = (x_0, x_1, \ldots, x_k, C)$, the decryption algorithm first computes $K' = \prod_{i \in [0,k]} x_i^{s_i}$. Then it outputs 0 if $C = K'$ and outputs 1 if $C = K' \cdot h$. Otherwise, it outputs a decryption failure symbol $\perp$.

Security. Security of Π is guaranteed by the following theorem. We put the proof of Theorem 5.1 in Sect. 5.3.

Theorem 5.1. *Assuming the DDH assumption holds in group* $\mathbb{G}$, Π *is a PKE scheme with SIM-RSO$_k$-CPA security.*

Key Length. The secret key length of Π is $k + \log q$, where $\log q$ is determined by the security parameter λ and is independent of the parameter k. For example, if we instantiate the scheme with an elliptic curve group and hope to achieve a 80-bit security, then we can fix $\log q = 160$. In this case, the ratio of key length to messages number k is $\frac{k+\log q}{k} = 1 + \frac{160}{k} = 1 + o(1)$.

5.2 SIM-RSO$_k$-CCA Secure PKE with (Nearly) Optimal Secret Key Length

Let λ be the security parameter and let k be a positive integer that is polynomial in λ. Let $\Pi' = (\Pi'.\mathsf{Setup}, \Pi'.\mathsf{Gen}, \Pi'.\mathsf{Enc}, \Pi'.\mathsf{Dec})$ be a SIM-RSO$_k$-CPA secure PKE scheme. Let $\mathsf{E} = (\mathsf{E.Setup}, \mathsf{E.Gen}, \mathsf{E.Enc}, \mathsf{E.Dec})$ be a CPA-secure PKE scheme. Let $\mathsf{NIZK} = (\mathsf{NIZK.Gen}, \mathsf{NIZK.Prove}, \mathsf{NIZK.Verify})$ be a an unbounded simulation-sound NIZK proof for NP. In particular, we will use it to prove the following language:

$$\{(\mathsf{pp}_1, pk_1, c_1, \mathsf{pp}_2, pk_2, c_2) : \exists (m, r_1, r_2),$$
$$c_1 = \Pi'.\mathsf{Enc}(\mathsf{pp}_1, pk_1, m; r_1) \wedge c_2 = \mathsf{E.Enc}(\mathsf{pp}_2, pk_2, m; r_2)\}$$

The PKE scheme $\Pi = (\mathsf{Setup}, \mathsf{Gen}, \mathsf{Enc}, \mathsf{Dec})$ works as follows:

- **Setup.** On input a security parameter λ, the setup algorithm computes $\mathsf{pp} \leftarrow \Pi'.\mathsf{Setup}(1^\lambda)$, $\tilde{\mathsf{pp}} \leftarrow \mathsf{E.Setup}(1^\lambda)$ and $\mathsf{crs} \leftarrow \mathsf{NIZK.Gen}(1^\lambda)$. Also, it generates $(\tilde{pk}, \tilde{sk}) \leftarrow \mathsf{E.Gen}(\tilde{\mathsf{pp}})$. The public parameter for Π is $\mathsf{PP} = (\mathsf{pp}, \mathsf{crs}, \tilde{\mathsf{pp}}, \tilde{pk})$.
- **Gen.** On input a public parameter $\mathsf{PP} = (\mathsf{pp}, \mathsf{crs}, \tilde{\mathsf{pp}}, \tilde{pk})$, the key generation algorithm computes $(pk, sk) \leftarrow \Pi'.\mathsf{Gen}(\mathsf{pp})$. The public key $PK = pk$ and the secret key $SK = sk$.
- **Enc.** On input a public parameter $\mathsf{PP} = (\mathsf{pp}, \mathsf{crs}, \tilde{\mathsf{pp}}, \tilde{pk})$, a public key $PK = pk$ and a message m, the encryption algorithm first samples $r, \tilde{r}$ randomly from the encryption randomness space of Π' and E respectively. Then it computes $c = \Pi'.\mathsf{Enc}(\mathsf{pp}, pk, m; r)$, $\tilde{c} = \mathsf{E.Enc}(\tilde{\mathsf{pp}}, \tilde{pk}, m; \tilde{r})$ and $\pi \leftarrow \mathsf{NIZK.Prove}(\mathsf{crs}, (\mathsf{pp}, pk, c, \tilde{\mathsf{pp}}, \tilde{pk}, \tilde{c}), (m, r, \tilde{r}))$. The ciphertext is $C = (c, \tilde{c}, \pi)$.
- **Dec.** On input a public parameter $\mathsf{PP} = (\mathsf{pp}, \mathsf{crs}, \tilde{\mathsf{pp}}, \tilde{pk})$, a public key $PK = pk$, a secret key $SK = sk$ and a ciphertext $C = (c, \tilde{c}, \pi)$, the decryption algorithm first checks if π is valid and aborts with a decryption failure symbol $\perp$ if it is not the case. Otherwise, it outputs $m \leftarrow \Pi'.\mathsf{Dec}(\mathsf{pp}, pk, sk, c)$.

Security. Security of Π is guaranteed by the following theorem. We put the proof of Theorem 5.2 in Sect. 5.4.

Theorem 5.2. *If Π' is a SIM-RSO$_k$-CPA secure PKE scheme, E is a CPA-secure PKE scheme and NIZK is an unbounded simulation-sound NIZK proof, then Π is a PKE scheme with SIM-RSO$_k$-CCA security.*

Key Length. If we instantiate the underlying SIM-RSO$_k$-CPA secure PKE scheme Π' with the one we constructed in Sect. 5.1, then we can obtain a SIM-RSO$_k$-CCA secure PKE scheme Π, where the ratio of key length to messages number k is also $\frac{k+\log q}{k} = 1 + o(1)$.

5.3   Proof of Theorem 5.1

Proof. We provide the proof of Theorem 5.1 in this section.

Let K and K' be the random variables used in generating and decrypting the same ciphertext $(x_0, x_1, \ldots, x_k, C)$ respectively. It is easy to see that the decryption algorithm can recover the correct message iff $K = K'$. As we have

$$K = pk^w = (\prod_{i \in [0,k]} g_i^{s_i})^w = \prod_{i \in [0,k]} g_i^{w \cdot s_i} = \prod_{i \in [0,k]} (g_i^w)^{s_i} = \prod_{i \in [0,k]} x_i^{s_i} = K'$$

the correctness holds.

Next, we focus on the SIM-RSO$_k$-CPA security of Π. First, for any polynomial n, any adversary $\mathcal{A} = (\mathcal{A}_1, \mathcal{A}_2, \mathcal{A}_3)$, and any distinguisher $\mathcal{D}$, we design the simulator $\mathcal{S}$ for $\mathcal{A}$, which works as in Fig. 4.

Next, we prove that output of the simulator $\mathcal{S}$ is indistinguishable from output of the adversary $\mathcal{A}$ in a real game. We argue this via defining the following games:

- **Game 0.** This is the real experiment $\text{Exp}_{\Pi,\mathcal{A},n}^{\text{RSO}_k-\text{CPA}-\text{real}}$. In particular, the challenger interacts with the adversary as follows:

  1. On input a security parameter, the challenger first generates $(\mathbb{G}, q, g) \leftarrow \mathcal{G}(1^\lambda)$ and samples $a_0, a_1, \ldots a_k, b \xleftarrow{\$} \mathbb{Z}_q$. Then it computes $g_i = g^{a_i}$ for $i \in [0, k]$, $h = g^b$, and sets $\mathsf{PP} = (\mathbb{G}, q, g, g_0, g_1, \ldots, g_k, h)$.

  2. Then, for $i \in [n]$, it samples $s_{i,0} \xleftarrow{\$} \mathbb{Z}_q$, $s_{i,1}, \ldots s_{i,k} \xleftarrow{\$} \{0,1\}$ and computes the public key $pk_i = \prod_{i \in [0,k]} g_i^{s_{i,i}}$.

  3. Next, the challenger sends $\mathsf{PP}, (pk_i)_{i \in [n]}$ to $\mathcal{A}$ and receives a distribution $\mathcal{M}$ from the adversary.

  4. Then, the challenger samples a matrix of messages $\boldsymbol{M} := (m_{i,j})_{i \in [n], j \in [k]} \leftarrow \mathcal{M}$ and for each $(i,j) \in [n] \times [k]$, it generates a challenge ciphertext for $m_{i,j}$ as follows:

     (a) Samples $w_{i,j} \xleftarrow{\$} \mathbb{Z}_q$.
     (b) Computes $\boldsymbol{x}_{i,j} = (x_{i,j,0}, x_{i,j,1}, \ldots, x_{i,j,k}) = (g_0^{w_{i,j}}, g_1^{w_{i,j}}, \ldots, g_k^{w_{i,j}})$.
     (c) Computes $C_{i,j} = pk_i^{w_{i,j}} \cdot h^{m_{i,j}}$.
     (d) Sets $CT_{i,j} = (\boldsymbol{x}_{i,j}, C_{i,j})$.

  5. Next, the challenger sends all challenge ciphertexts to $\mathcal{A}$ and receives a set $\mathcal{I} \subseteq [n]$ from the adversary.

  6. Then, the challenger sets $sk_i = (s_{i,0}, s_{i,1}, \ldots, s_{i,k})$ for $i \in \mathcal{I}$ and sends $(sk_i, m_{i,j})_{i \in \mathcal{I}, j \in [k]}$ to $\mathcal{A}$.

  7. Finally, on receiving $\mathcal{A}$'s output out, the challenger outputs $(\boldsymbol{M}, \mathcal{M}, \mathcal{I}, out)$.

$\mathcal{S}_1(1^\lambda)$:	$\mathcal{S}_2(\mathfrak{s}_1)$:
$(\mathbb{G}, q, g) \leftarrow \mathcal{G}(1^\lambda)$	For $i \in [n], j \in [k]$:
For $\iota \in [0, k]$:	$\quad w_{i,j} \xleftarrow{\$} \mathbb{Z}_q$
$\quad a_\iota \xleftarrow{\$} \mathbb{Z}_q$	$\quad$ If $s'_{i,j} = 1: \alpha_{i,j} = 1$
$\quad g_\iota = g^{a_\iota}$	$\quad$ Otherwise : $\alpha_{i,j} = -1$
$b \xleftarrow{\$} \mathbb{Z}_q$	$\quad$ For $\iota \in [0,k] \wedge \iota \neq j: x_{i,j,\iota} = g_\iota^{w_{i,j}}$
$h = g^b$	$\quad x_{i,j,j} = g_j^{w_{i,j}} \cdot h^{\alpha_{i,j}}$
$\mathsf{PP} = (\mathbb{G}, q, g, g_0, g_1, \dots, g_k, h)$	$\quad \boldsymbol{x}_{i,j} = (x_{i,j,0}, \dots, x_{i,j,k})$
For $i \in [n]$:	$\quad C_{i,j} = \prod_{\iota \in [0,k]} x_{i,j,\iota}^{s'_{i,\iota}}$
$\quad s'_{i,0} \xleftarrow{\$} \mathbb{Z}_q$	$\quad CT_{i,j} = (\boldsymbol{x}_{i,j}, C_{i,j})$
$\quad$ For $\iota \in [k]$:	$(\mathcal{I}, \mathfrak{s}'_2) \leftarrow \mathcal{A}_2((CT_{i,j})_{i \in [n], j \in [k]}, \mathfrak{s}_1)$
$\quad\quad s'_{i,\iota} \xleftarrow{\$} \{0, 1\}$	$\mathfrak{s}_2 = (\mathfrak{s}_1, \mathfrak{s}'_2)$
$\quad pk_i = \prod_{\iota \in [0,k]} g_\iota^{s'_{i,\iota}}$	Output $(\mathcal{I}, \mathfrak{s}_2)$
$(\mathcal{M}, \mathfrak{s}'_1) \leftarrow \mathcal{A}_1(\mathsf{PP}, (pk_i)_{i \in [n]})$	
$\mathfrak{s} = ((a_\iota)_{\iota \in [0,k]}, b, (s'_{i,\iota})_{i \in [n], \iota \in [0,k]})$	$\mathcal{S}_3((m_{i,j})_{i \in \mathcal{I}, j \in [k]}, \mathfrak{s}_2)$:
$\mathfrak{s}_1 = (\mathfrak{s}'_1, \mathsf{PP}, (pk_i)_{i \in [n]}, \mathfrak{s})$	For $i \in \mathcal{I}$:
Output $(\mathcal{M}, \mathfrak{s}_1)$	$\quad$ For $j \in [k]$:
	$\quad\quad$ If $m_{i,j} = 0 : s_{i,j} = s'_{i,j}$
	$\quad\quad$ Otherwise: $s_{i,j} = 1 - s'_{i,j}$
	$\quad s_{i,0} = s'_{i,0} + a_0^{-1} \sum_{\iota \in [k]} (a_\iota \cdot (s'_{i,\iota} - s_{i,\iota}))$
	$\quad sk_i = (s_{i,\iota})_{\iota \in [0,k]}$
	$out \leftarrow \mathcal{A}_3((sk_i, m_{i,j})_{i \in \mathcal{I}, j \in [k]}, \mathfrak{s}_2)$
	Output out

Fig. 4. The simulator $\mathcal{S}$ for $\mathcal{A}$ in proving SIM-RSO$_k$-CPA security of Π.

- **Game 1.** This is identical to Game 0 except that in step 4, the challenger computes new variables $(s'_{i,j}, \alpha_{i,j})_{i \in [n], j \in [k]}$. More precisely, for $i \in [n], j \in [k]$, it sets $s'_{i,j} = s_{i,j}$ if $m_{i,j} = 0$ and sets $s'_{i,j} = 1 - s_{i,j}$ otherwise. Besides, it sets $\alpha_{i,j} = 1$ if $s'_{i,j} = 1$ and sets $\alpha_{i,j} = -1$ otherwise.
- **Game 2.** This is identical to Game 1 except that the challenger changes the way to generate $C_{i,j}$. More precisely, for each $i \in [n], j \in [k]$, the challenger computes $C_{i,j} = (\prod_{\iota \in [0,k]} x_{i,j,\iota}^{s_{i,\iota}}) \cdot h^{m_{i,j}}$.
- **Game 3.** This is identical to Game 2 except that the j-th element in $\boldsymbol{x}_{i,j}$ (i.e., $x_{i,j,j}$) is generated dishonestly. More precisely, for each $i \in [n], j \in [k]$, it samples $x_{i,j,j} \xleftarrow{\$} \mathbb{G}$.
- **Game 4.** This is identical to Game 3 except that the challenger changes the way to generate $x_{i,j,j}$. More precisely, for each $i \in [n], j \in [k]$, it samples $x'_{i,j,j} \xleftarrow{\$} \mathbb{G}$ and computes $x_{i,j,j} = x'_{i,j,j} \cdot h^{\alpha_{i,j}}$.
- **Game 5.** This is identical to Game 4 except that the challenger changes the way to generate $x_{i,j,j}$. More precisely, for each $i \in [n], j \in [k]$, it computes $x'_{i,j,j} = g_j^{w_{i,j}}$ and $x_{i,j,j} = x'_{i,j,j} \cdot h^{\alpha_{i,j}}$.

- **Game 6.** This is identical to Game 5 except that the challenger changes the way to generate $C_{i,j}$. More precisely, in step 4, the challenger sets $s'_{i,0} = s_{i,0} + a_0^{-1} \sum_{i \in [k]} (a_i \cdot (s_{i,i} - s'_{i,i}))$ and for each $i \in [n], j \in [k]$, it computes $C_{i,j} = \prod_{i \in [0,k]} x_{i,j,i}^{s'_{i,i}}$.

- **Game 7.** This is identical to Game 6 except that the challenger changes the order in generating $s'_{i,j}$ and $s_{i,j}$:

  - In step 2, it samples $s'_{i,0} \xleftarrow{\$} \mathbb{Z}_q$ and $s'_{i,i} \xleftarrow{\$} \{0,1\}$ for $i \in [n], i \in [k]$ and computes $pk_i = \prod_{i \in [0,k]} g_i^{s'_{i,i}}$ for $i \in [n]$.

  - In step 4, for $i \in [n], j \in [k]$, it sets $s_{i,j} = s'_{i,j}$ if $m_{i,j} = 0$ and sets $s_{i,j} = 1 - s'_{i,j}$ otherwise. Also, it sets $s_{i,0} = s'_{i,0} + a_0^{-1} \sum_{i \in [k]} (a_i \cdot (s'_{i,i} - s_{i,i}))$ for $i \in [n]$.

Let $\mathfrak{p}_\iota$ be the probability that $\mathcal{D}$ outputs 1 when taking the output of Game ι as input, then we have $\mathfrak{p}_0 = \Pr[\mathcal{D}(\mathrm{Exp}_{\Pi,\mathcal{A},n}^{\mathrm{RSO}_k - \mathrm{CPA-real}}(\lambda)) = 1]$. Also, it is easy to see that output of Game 7 is exactly the output of the ideal experiment, so, we have $\mathfrak{p}_7 = \Pr[\mathcal{D}(\mathrm{Exp}_{\Pi,\mathcal{S},n}^{\mathrm{RSO}_k - \mathrm{CPA-ideal}}(\lambda)) = 1]$. Next, we prove that $\mathfrak{p}_0 - \mathfrak{p}_7$ is negligible via showing that $\mathfrak{p}_\iota - \mathfrak{p}_{\iota+1}$ is negligible for all $\iota \in [0,6]$.

Lemma 5.1. $|\mathfrak{p}_0 - \mathfrak{p}_1| = 0$.

Proof. Game 0 and Game 1 are identical except that in Game 1, the challenger generates some variables that are not used in this game. This will not affect the output of the game. □

Lemma 5.2. $|\mathfrak{p}_1 - \mathfrak{p}_2| = 0$.

Proof. In Game 1 and Game 2, each $C_{i,j}$ is computed in different ways. But as

$$pk_i^{w_{i,j}} = (\prod_{i \in [0,k]} g_i^{s_{i,i}})^{w_{i,j}} = \prod_{i \in [0,k]} g_i^{s_{i,i} \cdot w_{i,j}} = \prod_{i \in [0,k]} (g_i^{w_{i,j}})^{s_{i,i}} = \prod_{i \in [0,k]} x_{i,j,i}^{s_{i,i}}$$

the computation results are identical and thus outputs of these two games are identically distributed. □

Lemma 5.3. $|\mathfrak{p}_2 - \mathfrak{p}_3| \leq \mathtt{negl}(\lambda)$.

Proof. Indistinguishability between Game 2 and Game 3 comes from the DDH assumption by a standard hybrid argument.

In particular, for some fixed $i, j \in [n] \times [k]$, to show that $x_{i,j,j}$ is sampled from two computationally indistinguishable distributions in Game 2 and Game 3, we consider a DDH challenge $(g, \mathfrak{g}_1, \mathfrak{g}_2, \mathfrak{g}_3) = (g, g^x, g^y, g^z)$, where $z = xy$ or $z \xleftarrow{\$} \mathbb{Z}_q$. The reduction sets $g_j = \mathfrak{g}_1$, $g^{w_{i,j}} = \mathfrak{g}_2$, $x_{i,j,j} = \mathfrak{g}_3$ Then, it simulates the view for $\mathcal{A}$ (as in Game 2 and Game 3) with them. Note that the exact value of x and y is not needed in the simulation since 1) the challenger does not use a_j in both Game 2 and Game 3 and 2) without $w_{i,j}$, the challenger can compute $x_{i,j,i} = \mathfrak{g}_2^{a_i}$ for $i \in [0,k] \setminus \{j\}$. It is easy to see that if $z = xy$, then $x_{i,j,j} = g_j^{w_{i,j}}$ as in Game

2, and if $z \xleftarrow{\$} \mathbb{Z}_q$, then $x_{i,j,j} \xleftarrow{\$} \mathbb{Z}_q$ as in Game 3. Therefore, indistinguishability between Game 2 and Game 3 is guaranteed assuming the hardness of the DDH assumption. $\qquad\square$

Lemma 5.4. $|\mathfrak{p}_3 - \mathfrak{p}_4| = 0.$

Proof. Since in Game 3, $x_{i,j,j} \xleftarrow{\$} \mathbb{G}$, it will not change its distribution if we additionally multiply it with $h^{\alpha_{i,j}}$. Therefore, outputs of these two games are identically distributed. $\qquad\square$

Lemma 5.5. $|\mathfrak{p}_4 - \mathfrak{p}_5| \leq \mathtt{negl}(\lambda).$

Proof. Similar to the proof of Lemma 5.3, indistinguishability between Game 4 and Game 5 comes from the DDH assumption by a standard hybrid argument. $\square$

Lemma 5.6. $|\mathfrak{p}_5 - \mathfrak{p}_6| = 0.$

Proof. In Game 5 and Game 6, each $C_{i,j}$ is computed in different ways. But as

$$(\prod_{\imath \in [0,k]} x_{i,j,\imath}^{s_{i,\imath}}) \cdot h^{m_{i,j}}$$

$$= (\prod_{\imath \in [0,k]} g_\imath^{w_{i,j} \cdot s_{i,\imath}}) \cdot h^{\alpha_{i,j} \cdot s_{i,j}} \cdot h^{m_{i,j}}$$

$$= (g^{w_{i,j} \cdot (\sum_{\imath \in [0,k]} a_\imath \cdot s_{i,\imath})}) \cdot h^{\alpha_{i,j} \cdot s_{i,j} + m_{i,j}}$$

$$= (g^{w_{i,j} \cdot (\sum_{\imath \in [0,k]} a_\imath \cdot s'_{i,\imath})}) \cdot h^{\alpha_{i,j} \cdot s_{i,j} + m_{i,j}}$$

$$= (g^{w_{i,j} \cdot (\sum_{\imath \in [0,k]} a_\imath \cdot s'_{i,\imath})}) \cdot h^{\alpha_{i,j} \cdot s'_{i,j}}$$

$$= (\prod_{\imath \in [0,k]} g_\imath^{w_{i,j} \cdot s'_{i,\imath}}) \cdot h^{\alpha_{i,j} \cdot s'_{i,j}}$$

$$= \prod_{\imath \in [0,k]} x_{i,j,\imath}^{s'_{i,\imath}}$$

the computation results are identical and thus outputs of these two games are identically distributed.

Here, the first and the last equalities come from the fact that $x_{i,j,\imath} = g_\imath^{w_{i,j}}$ for $\imath \neq j$ and that $x_{i,j,j} = g_j^{w_{i,j}} \cdot h^{\alpha_{i,j}}$. Also, the third equality comes from the fact that $s'_{i,0} = s_{i,0} + a_0^{-1} \sum_{\imath \in [k]} (a_\imath \cdot (s_{i,\imath} - s'_{i,\imath}))$, which implies that $\sum_{\imath \in [0,k]} (a_\imath \cdot s'_{i,\imath}) = \sum_{\imath \in [0,k]} (a_\imath \cdot s_{i,\imath})$. For the fourth equality, if $m_{i,j} = 0$, then $s_{i,j} = s'_{i,j}$ and thus $\alpha_{i,j} \cdot s_{i,j} + 0 = \alpha_{i,j} \cdot s'_{i,j}$; if $m_{i,j} = 1$, then either $s_{i,j} = 1, s'_{i,j} = 0$ or $s_{i,j} = 0, s'_{i,j} = 1$, and in both cases, $\alpha_{i,j} \cdot (s'_{i,j} - s_{i,j}) = 1$, which implies that $\alpha_{i,j} \cdot s_{i,j} + 1 = \alpha_{i,j} \cdot s'_{i,j}$. $\qquad\square$

Lemma 5.7. $|\mathfrak{p}_6 - \mathfrak{p}_7| = 0.$

Proof. First, in both Game 6 and Game 7, each pk_i is a random element in $\mathbb{G}$, thus the adversary's views are identical in both games until step 4, where $(s_{i,\imath}, s'_{i,\imath})_{i \in [n], \imath \in [0,k]}$ are sampled in different ways.

In step 4, fixing the challenge messages $m_{i,j}$, then in both games the random variables $(s_{i,\imath}, s'_{i,\imath})_{i \in [n], \imath \in [0,k]}$ are randomly distributed in $\mathbb{Z}_q \times \mathbb{Z}_q \times \{0,1\}^{2k}$ with the restriction that for any $i \in [n]$:

$$\begin{cases} \sum_{\imath \in [0,k]} (a_\imath \cdot s'_{i,\imath}) = \sum_{\imath \in [0,k]} (a_\imath \cdot s_{i,\imath}) = \log_g pk_i \\ \forall \imath \in [k], s_{i,\imath} + s'_{i,\imath} = m_{i,j} \end{cases}$$

Therefore, they are identically distributed and that completes the proof of Lemma 5.7.

Combining Lemma 5.1 to Lemma 5.7, we have $\mathfrak{p}_0 - \mathfrak{p}_7$ negligible and this completes the proof.   □

5.4   Proof of Theorem 5.2

Proof. We provide the proof of Theorem 5.2 in this section.

Correctness of Π comes from correctness of Π' and completeness of NIZK directly.

Next, we focus on the SIM-RSO$_k$-CCA security of Π. First, for any polynomial n, any adversary $\mathcal{A} = (\mathcal{A}_1, \mathcal{A}_2, \mathcal{A}_3)$, we define an auxiliary adversary $\mathcal{B}$ for Π' as in Fig. 5. Since Π' is a SIM-RSO$_k$-CPA secure PKE scheme, there exists a simulator $\mathcal{S}' = (\mathcal{S}'_1, \mathcal{S}'_2, \mathcal{S}'_3)$ for $\mathcal{B}$ such that the output of $\mathcal{S}'$ is indistinguishable from the output of $\mathcal{B}$ in a real RSO$_k$-CPA game. Then we define the simulator $\mathcal{S}$ for $\mathcal{A}$ as $\mathcal{S} = \mathcal{S}' = (\mathcal{S}'_1, \mathcal{S}'_2, \mathcal{S}'_3)$.

Next, we prove that output of the simulator $\mathcal{S}$ is indistinguishable from output of the adversary $\mathcal{A}$ in a real RSO$_k$-CCA game. We argue this via defining the following games:

- **Game 0.** This is the real experiment $\text{Exp}_{\Pi,\mathcal{A},n}^{\text{RSO}_k\text{-CCA-real}}$. In particular, the challenger interacts with the adversary as follows:
  1. On input a security parameter, the challenger first computes $\text{pp} \leftarrow \Pi'.\text{Setup}(1^\lambda)$, $\tilde{\text{pp}} \leftarrow \text{E.Setup}(1^\lambda)$ and $\text{crs} \leftarrow \text{NIZK.Gen}(1^\lambda)$. Also, it generates $(\tilde{pk}, \tilde{sk}) \leftarrow \text{E.Gen}(\tilde{\text{pp}})$. Then, it sets the public parameter $\text{PP} = (\text{pp}, \text{crs}, \tilde{\text{pp}}, \tilde{pk})$.
  2. Then, for $i \in [n]$, it computes $(pk_i, sk_i) \leftarrow \Pi'.\text{Gen}(\text{pp})$.
  3. Next, the challenger sends $\text{PP}, (pk_i)_{i \in [n]}$ to $\mathcal{A}$ and answers $\mathcal{A}$'s decryption oracle queries as follows:
     (a) On input a pair (i, C), where $C = (c, \tilde{c}, \pi)$, the challenger first checks if π is valid and returns an error symbol $\perp$ if π is not valid.
     (b) Otherwise, it computes $m \leftarrow \Pi'.\text{Dec}(\text{pp}, pk_i, sk_i, c)$.
     (c) Finally, it returns m to $\mathcal{A}$.
  4. The adversary will send a distribution $\mathcal{M}$ to the challenger after querying the decryption oracle a few times. Then, the challenger samples a matrix of messages $\boldsymbol{M} := (m_{i,j})_{i \in [n], j \in [k]} \leftarrow \mathcal{M}$ and for each $(i,j) \in [n] \times [k]$, it generates a challenge ciphertext for $m_{i,j}$ as follows:

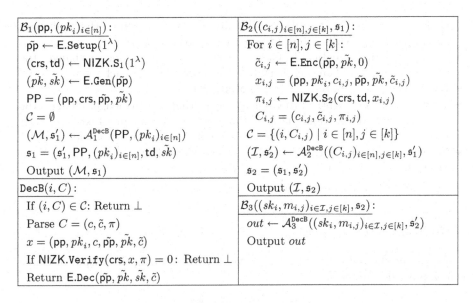

Fig. 5. The adversary $\mathcal{B}$ for Π'.

    (a) Samples $r_{i,j}, \tilde{r}_{i,j}$ randomly from the encryption randomness space of Π' and E respectively.

    (b) Computes $c_{i,j} = \Pi'.\mathsf{Enc}(\mathsf{pp}, pk_i, m_{i,j}; r_{i,j})$.

    (c) Computes $\tilde{c}_{i,j} = \mathsf{E.Enc}(\tilde{\mathsf{pp}}, \tilde{pk}, m_{i,j}; \tilde{r}_{i,j})$.

    (d) Computes
$$\pi_{i,j} \leftarrow \mathsf{NIZK.Prove}(\mathsf{crs}, (\mathsf{pp}, pk_i, c_{i,j}, \tilde{\mathsf{pp}}, \tilde{pk}, \tilde{c}_{i,j}), (m_{i,j}, r_{i,j}, \tilde{r}_{i,j})).$$

    (e) Sets $C_{i,j} = (c_{i,j}, \tilde{c}_{i,j}, \pi_{i,j})$.

5. Next, the challenger sends all challenge ciphertexts to $\mathcal{A}$ and answers $\mathcal{A}$'s decryption oracle queries as follows:

    (a) On input a pair (i, C), the challenger first checks if $C = C_{i,j}$ for some $j \in [k]$. It returns $\perp$ if this is the case.

    (b) Otherwise, the challenger parses $C = (c, \tilde{c}, \pi)$ and checks if π is valid. It returns an error symbol $\perp$ if π is not valid.

    (c) Otherwise, it computes $m \leftarrow \Pi'.\mathsf{Dec}(\mathsf{pp}, pk_i, sk_i, c)$.

    (d) Finally, it returns m to $\mathcal{A}$.

6. The adversary will send a set $\mathcal{I} \subseteq [n]$ to the challenger after querying the decryption oracle a few times. Then, the challenger sends $(sk_i, m_{i,j})_{i \in \mathcal{I}, j \in [k]}$ to $\mathcal{A}$. The challenger will answer $\mathcal{A}$'s decryption queries exactly as in step 5.

7. Finally, on receiving $\mathcal{A}$'s output out, the challenger outputs $(M, \mathcal{M}, \mathcal{I}, out)$.

- **Game 1.** This is identical to Game 0 except that when generating the common reference string and proofs, the challenger uses the simulator of NIZK instead of generating them honestly. More precisely, in the first step, the challenger computes $(\mathsf{crs}, \mathsf{td}) \leftarrow \mathsf{NIZK.S_1}(1^\lambda)$ and in step 4, the challenger computes $\pi_{i,j} \leftarrow \mathsf{NIZK.S_2}(\mathsf{crs}, \mathsf{td}, (\mathsf{pp}, pk_i, c_{i,j}, \tilde{\mathsf{pp}}, \tilde{pk}, \tilde{c}_{i,j}))$.

- **Game 2.** This is identical to Game 1 except that the challenger changes the way to generate challenge ciphertexts. More precisely, for each $i \in [n], j \in [k]$, the challenger computes $\tilde{c}_{i,j} \leftarrow \mathsf{E.Enc}(\tilde{\mathsf{pp}}, \tilde{pk}, 0)$.

- **Game 3.** This is identical to Game 2 except that the challenger changes the way to answer decryption queries. More precisely, for a ciphertext $(c, \tilde{c}, \pi)$, it returns $\mathsf{E.Dec}(\tilde{\mathsf{pp}}, \tilde{pk}, \tilde{sk}, \tilde{c})$ in the last step of the decryption oracle.

- **Game 4.** In Game 4, the challenger proceeds as follows:
  1. $(\mathcal{M}, s_1) \leftarrow \mathcal{S}_1'(1^\lambda)$
  2. $\boldsymbol{M} := (m_{i,j})_{i \in [n], j \in [k]} \leftarrow \mathcal{M}$
  3. $(\mathcal{I}, s_2) \leftarrow \mathcal{S}_2'(s_1)$
  4. $out \leftarrow \mathcal{S}_3'((m_{i,j})_{i \in \mathcal{I}, j \in [k]}, s_2)$
  5. Return $(\boldsymbol{M}, \mathcal{M}, \mathcal{I}, out)$

Let $\mathfrak{p}_\alpha$ be the probability that $\mathcal{D}$ outputs 1 when taking the output of Game α as input, then we have

$$\mathfrak{p}_0 = \Pr[\mathcal{D}(\mathrm{Exp}_{\Pi, \mathcal{A}, n}^{\mathrm{RSO_k-CCA-real}}(\lambda)) = 1]$$

Besides, we can view Game 4 as the ideal experiment $\mathrm{Exp}_{\Pi, \mathcal{S}, n}^{\mathrm{RSO_k-CCA-ideal}}$ (recall that $\mathcal{S} = \mathcal{S}' = (\mathcal{S}_1', \mathcal{S}_2', \mathcal{S}_3')$), so we have

$$\mathfrak{p}_4 = \Pr[\mathcal{D}(\mathrm{Exp}_{\Pi, \mathcal{S}, n}^{\mathrm{RSO_k-CCA-ideal}}(\lambda)) = 1]$$

Next, we prove that $\mathfrak{p}_0 - \mathfrak{p}_4$ is negligible via showing that $\mathfrak{p}_\alpha - \mathfrak{p}_{\alpha+1}$ is negligible for all $\alpha \in [0, 3]$.

Lemma 5.8. $|\mathfrak{p}_0 - \mathfrak{p}_1| \leq \mathtt{negl}(\lambda)$.

Proof. This comes from the unbounded zero-knowledge property of NIZK directly. □

Lemma 5.9. $|\mathfrak{p}_1 - \mathfrak{p}_2| \leq \mathtt{negl}(\lambda)$.

Proof. This comes from the CPA-security of E directly. □

Lemma 5.10. $|\mathfrak{p}_2 - \mathfrak{p}_3| \leq \mathtt{negl}(\lambda)$.

Proof. This comes from the fact that for any ciphertext $(c, \tilde{c}, \pi)$ with a valid π, $\mathsf{E.Dec}(\tilde{\mathsf{pp}}, \tilde{pk}, \tilde{sk}, \tilde{c}) = \Pi'.\mathsf{Dec}(\mathsf{pp}, pk_i, sk_i, c)$ with all but negligible probability, which is guaranteed by the unbounded simulation-soundness of NIZK and correctness of Π' and E. □

Lemma 5.11. $|\mathfrak{p}_3 - \mathfrak{p}_4| \leq \mathtt{negl}(\lambda)$.

Proof. It is easy to see that output of Game 3 is exactly the output of experiment $\mathrm{Exp}_{\Pi',\mathcal{B},n}^{\mathrm{RSO}_k-\mathrm{CPA-real}}$ (since $\mathcal{A}$'s view in Game 3 is identical to its view in the experiment $\mathrm{Exp}_{\Pi',\mathcal{B},n}^{\mathrm{RSO}_k-\mathrm{CPA-real}}$ when invoked by $\mathcal{B}$), thus we have

$$\mathfrak{p}_3 = \Pr[\mathcal{D}(\mathrm{Exp}_{\Pi',\mathcal{B},n}^{\mathrm{RSO}_k-\mathrm{CPA-real}}(\lambda)) = 1]$$

Also, we can view Game 4 as the ideal experiment $\mathrm{Exp}_{\Pi',\mathcal{S}',n}^{\mathrm{RSO}_k-\mathrm{CPA-ideal}}$, so we have

$$\mathfrak{p}_4 = \Pr[\mathcal{D}(\mathrm{Exp}_{\Pi',\mathcal{S}',n}^{\mathrm{RSO}_k-\mathrm{CPA-ideal}}(\lambda)) = 1]$$

Therefore, Lemma 5.11 comes from the SIM-RSO$_k$-CPA security of Π' directly.

Combining Lemma 5.8 to Lemma 5.11, we have $\mathfrak{p}_0 - \mathfrak{p}_4$ negligible and this completes the proof. □

6   Conclusion

In this work, we initiate the study of receiver selective opening security for PKE schemes in the multi-challenge setting. Several interesting open questions remain.

First, our impossibility results only work in either the non-programmable random oracle model or the auxiliary input model. It is interesting to see if we can achieve the impossibility results in the standard model without auxiliary input. Another interesting direction is to explore the relation between PKE scheme with RSO$_k$ security and some related notions, e.g., (receiver) non-committing encryption, hash proof system, etc. Besides, one may note that in our constructions of RSO$_k$ secure PKE schemes, the ciphertexts sizes grow linearly with k. It will be an interesting future work to construct a RSO$_k$ secure PKE scheme with constant-size ciphertexts. Finally, in this work, we mainly focus on the feasibility of achieving RSO$_k$ secure PKE schemes and it will also be interesting to construct practical PKE schemes with RSO$_k$ security.

Acknowledgement. We appreciate the anonymous reviewers for their valuable comments. Part of this work was supported by the National Natural Science Foundation of China (Grant No. 61922036, 61702125, 61802078, 61972332, U1636205, 61632020), the Research Grant Council of Hong Kong (Grant No. 25206317), and the Major Innovation Project of Science and Technology of Shandong Province (Grant No. 2018CXGC0702).

References

[BDWY12] Bellare, M., Dowsley, R., Waters, B., Yilek, S.: Standard security does not imply security against selective-opening. In: Pointcheval, D., Johansson, T. (eds.) EUROCRYPT 2012. LNCS, vol. 7237, pp. 645–662. Springer, Heidelberg (2012). https://doi.org/10.1007/978-3-642-29011-4_38

[BFM88] Blum, M., Feldman, P., Micali, S.: Non-interactive zero-knowledge and its applications. In: STOC, pp. 103–112. ACM (1988)

[BHK12]   Böhl, F., Hofheinz, D., Kraschewski, D.: On definitions of selective opening security. In: Fischlin, M., Buchmann, J., Manulis, M. (eds.) PKC 2012. LNCS, vol. 7293, pp. 522–539. Springer, Heidelberg (2012). https:// doi.org/10.1007/978-3-642-30057-8_31

[BHY09]   Bellare, M., Hofheinz, D., Yilek, S.: Possibility and impossibility results for encryption and commitment secure under selective opening. In: Joux, A. (ed.) EUROCRYPT 2009. LNCS, vol. 5479, pp. 1–35. Springer, Heidelberg (2009). https://doi.org/10.1007/978-3-642-01001-9_1

[BL17]   Boyen, X., Li, Q.: All-but-many lossy trapdoor functions from lattices and applications. In: Katz, J., Shacham, H. (eds.) CRYPTO 2017. LNCS, vol. 10403, pp. 298–331. Springer, Cham (2017). https://doi.org/10. 1007/978-3-319-63697-9_11

[BO13]   Bellare, M., O'Neill, A.: Semantically-secure functional encryption: possibility results, impossibility results and the quest for a general definition. In: Abdalla, M., Nita-Rotaru, C., Dahab, R. (eds.) CANS 2013. LNCS, vol. 8257, pp. 218–234. Springer, Cham (2013). https://doi.org/10.1007/ 978-3-319-02937-5_12

[BSW11]   Boneh, D., Sahai, A., Waters, B.: Functional encryption: definitions and challenges. In: Ishai, Y. (ed.) TCC 2011. LNCS, vol. 6597, pp. 253–273. Springer, Heidelberg (2011). https://doi.org/10.1007/978-3-642-19571-6_16

[CDSMW09] Choi, S.G., Dachman-Soled, D., Malkin, T., Wee, H.: Improved noncommitting encryption with applications to adaptively secure protocols. In: Matsui, M. (ed.) ASIACRYPT 2009. LNCS, vol. 5912, pp. 287–302. Springer, Heidelberg (2009). https://doi.org/10.1007/978-3-642-10366-7_17

[CFGN96] Canetti, R., Feige, U., Goldreich, O., Naor, M.: Adaptively secure multiparty computation. In: STOC, pp. 639–648 (1996)

[CHK05]   Canetti, R., Halevi, S., Katz, J.: Adaptively-secure, non-interactive public-key encryption. In: Kilian, J. (ed.) TCC 2005. LNCS, vol. 3378, pp. 150–168. Springer, Heidelberg (2005). https://doi.org/10.1007/978-3-540-30576-7_9

[CS98]   Cramer, R., Shoup, V.: A practical public key cryptosystem provably secure against adaptive chosen ciphertext attack. In: Krawczyk, H. (ed.) CRYPTO 1998. LNCS, vol. 1462, pp. 13–25. Springer, Heidelberg (1998). https://doi.org/10.1007/BFb0055717

[DN00]   Damgård, I., Nielsen, J.B.: Improved non-committing encryption schemes based on a general complexity assumption. In: Bellare, M. (ed.) CRYPTO 2000. LNCS, vol. 1880, pp. 432–450. Springer, Heidelberg (2000). https://doi.org/10.1007/3-540-44598-6_27

[DNRS99] Dwork, C., Naor, M., Reingold, O., Stockmeyer, L.: Magic functions. In: FOCS, pp. 523–534. IEEE (1999)

[FHKW10] Fehr, S., Hofheinz, D., Kiltz, E., Wee, H.: Encryption schemes secure against chosen-ciphertext selective opening attacks. In: Gilbert, H. (ed.) EUROCRYPT 2010. LNCS, vol. 6110, pp. 381–402. Springer, Heidelberg (2010). https://doi.org/10.1007/978-3-642-13190-5_20

[HJKS15] Heuer, F., Jager, T., Kiltz, E., Schäge, S.: On the selective opening security of practical public-key encryption schemes. In: Katz, J. (ed.) PKC 2015. LNCS, vol. 9020, pp. 27–51. Springer, Heidelberg (2015). https:// doi.org/10.1007/978-3-662-46447-2_2

[HKM+18] Hara, K., Kitagawa, F., Matsuda, T., Hanaoka, G., Tanaka, K.: Simulation-based receiver selective opening CCA secure PKE from standard computational assumptions. In: Catalano, D., De Prisco, R. (eds.) SCN 2018. LNCS, vol. 11035, pp. 140–159. Springer, Cham (2018). https://doi.org/10.1007/978-3-319-98113-0_8

[HLC+19] Huang, Z., Lai, J., Chen, W., Au, M.H., Peng, Z., Li, J.: Simulation-based selective opening security for receivers under chosen-ciphertext attacks. DCC **87**(6), 1345–1371 (2019)

[HLOV11] Hemenway, B., Libert, B., Ostrovsky, R., Vergnaud, D.: Lossy encryption: constructions from general assumptions and efficient selective opening chosen ciphertext security. In: Lee, D.H., Wang, X. (eds.) ASIACRYPT 2011. LNCS, vol. 7073, pp. 70–88. Springer, Heidelberg (2011). https://doi.org/10.1007/978-3-642-25385-0_4

[HLQ13] Huang, Z., Liu, S., Qin, B.: Sender-equivocable encryption schemes secure against chosen-ciphertext attacks revisited. In: Kurosawa, K., Hanaoka, G. (eds.) PKC 2013. LNCS, vol. 7778, pp. 369–385. Springer, Heidelberg (2013). https://doi.org/10.1007/978-3-642-36362-7_23

[Hof12] Hofheinz, D.: All-but-many lossy trapdoor functions. In: Pointcheval, D., Johansson, T. (eds.) EUROCRYPT 2012. LNCS, vol. 7237, pp. 209–227. Springer, Heidelberg (2012). https://doi.org/10.1007/978-3-642-29011-4_14

[HP16] Heuer, F., Poettering, B.: Selective opening security from simulatable data encapsulation. In: Cheon, J.H., Takagi, T. (eds.) ASIACRYPT 2016. LNCS, vol. 10032, pp. 248–277. Springer, Heidelberg (2016). https://doi.org/10.1007/978-3-662-53890-6_9

[HPW15] Hazay, C., Patra, A., Warinschi, B.: Selective opening security for receivers. In: Iwata, T., Cheon, J.H. (eds.) ASIACRYPT 2015. LNCS, vol. 9452, pp. 443–469. Springer, Heidelberg (2015). https://doi.org/10.1007/978-3-662-48797-6_19

[HR14] Hofheinz, D., Rupp, A.: Standard versus selective opening security: separation and equivalence results. In: Lindell, Y. (ed.) TCC 2014. LNCS, vol. 8349, pp. 591–615. Springer, Heidelberg (2014). https://doi.org/10.1007/978-3-642-54242-8_25

[HRW16] Hofheinz, D., Rao, V., Wichs, D.: Standard security does not imply indistinguishability under selective opening. In: Hirt, M., Smith, A. (eds.) TCC 2016. LNCS, vol. 9986, pp. 121–145. Springer, Heidelberg (2016). https://doi.org/10.1007/978-3-662-53644-5_5

[JLL16] Jia, D., Lu, X., Li, B.: Receiver selective opening security from indistinguishability obfuscation. In: Dunkelman, O., Sanadhya, S.K. (eds.) INDOCRYPT 2016. LNCS, vol. 10095, pp. 393–410. Springer, Cham (2016). https://doi.org/10.1007/978-3-319-49890-4_22

[JLL17] Jia, D., Lu, X., Li, B.: Constructions secure against receiver selective opening and chosen ciphertext attacks. In: Handschuh, H. (ed.) CT-RSA 2017. LNCS, vol. 10159, pp. 417–431. Springer, Cham (2017). https://doi.org/10.1007/978-3-319-52153-4_24

[KT18] Kitagawa, F., Tanaka, K.: Key dependent message security and receiver selective opening security for identity-based encryption. In: Abdalla, M., Dahab, R. (eds.) PKC 2018. LNCS, vol. 10769, pp. 32–61. Springer, Cham (2018). https://doi.org/10.1007/978-3-319-76578-5_2

[LLHG18] Lyu, L., Liu, S., Han, S., Gu, D.: Tightly SIM-SO-CCA secure public key encryption from standard assumptions. In: Abdalla, M., Dahab, R. (eds.) PKC 2018. LNCS, vol. 10769, pp. 62–92. Springer, Cham (2018). https://doi.org/10.1007/978-3-319-76578-5_3

[LP15] Liu, S., Paterson, K.G.: Simulation-based selective opening CCA security for PKE from key encapsulation mechanisms. In: Katz, J. (ed.) PKC 2015. LNCS, vol. 9020, pp. 3–26. Springer, Heidelberg (2015). https://doi.org/10.1007/978-3-662-46447-2_1

[LSSS17] Libert, B., Sakzad, A., Stehlé, D., Steinfeld, R.: All-but-many lossy trapdoor functions and selective opening chosen-ciphertext security from LWE. In: Katz, J., Shacham, H. (eds.) CRYPTO 2017. LNCS, vol. 10403, pp. 332–364. Springer, Cham (2017). https://doi.org/10.1007/978-3-319-63697-9_12

[Nie02] Nielsen, J.B.: Separating random oracle proofs from complexity theoretic proofs: the non-committing encryption case. In: Yung, M. (ed.) CRYPTO 2002. LNCS, vol. 2442, pp. 111–126. Springer, Heidelberg (2002). https://doi.org/10.1007/3-540-45708-9_8

[NY90] Naor, M., Yung, M.: Public-key cryptosystems provably secure against chosen ciphertext attacks. In: STOC, pp. 427–437. ACM (1990)

[ORV14] Ostrovsky, R., Rao, V., Visconti, I.: On selective-opening attacks against encryption schemes. In: Abdalla, M., De Prisco, R. (eds.) SCN 2014. LNCS, vol. 8642, pp. 578–597. Springer, Cham (2014). https://doi.org/10.1007/978-3-319-10879-7_33

[Sah99] Sahai, A.: Non-malleable non-interactive zero knowledge and adaptive chosen-ciphertext security. In: FOCS, pp. 543–553. IEEE (1999)

Security Reductions for White-Box Key-Storage in Mobile Payments

Estuardo Alpirez Bock[1]([✉]), Chris Brzuska[1], Marc Fischlin[2], Christian Janson[2], and Wil Michiels[3,4]

[1] Aalto University, Helsinki, Finland
{estuardo.alpirezbock,chris.brzuska}@aalto.fi
[2] Technische Universität Darmstadt, Darmstadt, Germany
{marc.fischlin,christian.janson}@cryptoplexity.de
[3] Technische Universiteit Eindhoven, Eindhoven, The Netherlands
[4] NXP Semiconductors, Eindhoven, The Netherlands
wil.michiels@nxp.com

Abstract. The goal of white-box cryptography is to provide security even when the cryptographic implementation is executed in adversarially controlled environments. White-box implementations nowadays appear in commercial products such as mobile payment applications, e.g., those certified by Mastercard. Interestingly, there, white-box cryptography is championed as a tool for secure storage of payment tokens, and importantly, the white-boxed storage functionality is bound to a hardware functionality to prevent code-lifting attacks.

In this paper, we show that the approach of using hardware-binding and obfuscation for secure storage is conceptually sound. Following security specifications by Mastercard and also EMVCo, we first define security for a *white-box key derivation functions* (WKDF) that is bound to a hardware functionality. WKDFs with hardware-binding model a secure storage functionality, as the WKDFs in turn can be used to derive encryption keys for secure storage. We then provide a proof-of-concept construction of WKDFs based on pseudorandom functions (PRF) and obfuscation. To show that our use of cryptographic primitives is sound, we perform a cryptographic analysis and reduce the security of our WKDF to the cryptographic assumptions of indistinguishability obfuscation and PRF-security. The hardware-functionality that our WKDF is bound to is a PRF-like functionality. Obfuscation helps us to hide the secret key used for the verification, essentially emulating a signature functionality as is provided by the Android key store.

We rigorously define the required security properties of a *hardware-bound white-box payment application* (WPAY) for generating and encrypting valid payment requests. We construct a WPAY, which uses a WKDF as a secure building block. We thereby show that a WKDF can be securely combined with *any* secure symmetric encryption scheme, including those based on standard ciphers such as AES.

Keywords: White-box cryptography · Key derivation function · Hardware-binding · Payment application

© International Association for Cryptologic Research 2020
S. Moriai and H. Wang (Eds.): ASIACRYPT 2020, LNCS 12491, pp. 221–252, 2020.
https://doi.org/10.1007/978-3-030-64837-4_8

1   Introduction

Near-field communication (NFC) protocols have opened up new possibilities for mobile payment applications, such as those offered by Mastercard, Visa, or Google wallet [37]. Traditionally, the NFC traffic was processed by a secure hardware component in mobile devices, that performed cryptographic operations. In 2015, Android 4.4 introduced Host Card Emulation (HCE), which allows the application processor of a mobile device to use the NFC communication, too. In this case, the cryptographic functions of mobile applications are implemented *software-only*, increasing flexibility and device coverage of the applications since no secure hardware element is required. However, implementing cryptographic functions in software leads to new attack vectors.

White-Box Cryptography. One of the core cryptographic protection technologies for HCE (as listed by the Smart Card Alliance Mobile & NFC Council [37]) is the use of *white-box cryptography*. Cryptography in the white-box attack model was introduced by Chow, Eisen, Johnson, and van Oorschot in 2002 (CEJO [18,19]). In the white-box attack scenario, an adversary has access to the program code and the complete execution environment of a cryptographic implementation, and the goal of white-box cryptography is to remain secure despite such strong attack capabilities. Unlike in the Digital Rights Management scenario considered by CEJO where the user is considered as an adversary, in an HCE context, the goal of white-box cryptography is protect an honest user against attacks performed on their device, e.g., by malware that can observe program code and executions.

Commercial Payment Applications. Payment applications need to store secret information such as transaction tokens that are decrypted when a transaction is performed. In the absence of a secure element, the tokens are stored in insecure memory and likewise, the decryption operations are performed by an insecure CPU. Thus, to protect against adversaries that use their access to the storage/CPU to extract secret information and perform payment transactions on their own, over the past years, white-box cryptography has been broadly adopted by those offering commercial payment applications. The Mastercard security guidelines for payment applications, e.g., make the use of white-box cryptography *mandatory* for implementing storage protection in order to achieve an advanced security level (see *Local Database Encryption*, Chap. 5 in [31]). Similarly, EMVCo suggests the use of white-box cryptography in their requirements documentation [24] for EMV mobile payment.

For a successful payment, the user's device needs to be close to an NFC reader. An attacker on a user's device can thus only alter a payment a user aims to make, but cannot make payments independently at readers of their choice,[1] unless the attacker gains independence from the user's device. The attacker could gain independence by (a) extracting the key, or (b) performing a code-lifting attack [38]. Thus, white-box cryptography in commercial payment applications

---

[1] We discuss relay attacks later.

needs to achieve *hardware-binding* (also see [8,20,36] for discussions of usefulness). As a consequence, commercial applications implement white-box cryptography with a hardware anchor, essentially reaching a middle-ground between software-only and hardware-only security for cryptographic implementations.

In [14] Alpirez Bock, Amadori, Brzuska and Michiels (AABM) discuss extensively the usefulness of hardware-binding for white-box programs. They explain that hardware-binding seems to be the right mitigation technique against code-lifting attacks for white-box programs deployed on real-life applications. The authors propose to focus on hardware-binding as opposed to other techniques which are popular in the white-box literature, but seem rather theoretical or unrelated to the security of payment applications. In particular, they define a security notion for white-box encryption programs with hardware-binding.

Hardware-Binding on Android. The Mastercard guidelines (see Chap. 5 in [31]) recommend, to the very least, to use a unique device fingerprint for device identification. The EMVCo documentation [24] recommends to use hardware features to bind the operation of software on a particular device. For instance, Android allows to perform checks on identifiers such as the hardware serial number, the ESN (electronic serial number) or IMEI (international mobile equipment identity) of the device via its `Build` and `TelephonyManager` classes [3,5]. This technique helps to mitigate code-lifting attacks as long as the value remains secret and/or interception of this value between hardware and software can actually be prevented. For an advanced security level, however, the guidelines suggest the use of the functionalities of the Android Key Store. The Android Key Store, e.g., implements RSA signatures, and relies on whatever secure hardware features the Android device provides. Signatures are a more useful binding functionality than single identifier values, since for each new input, they provide a different output.

Conceptual Validation. In this paper, we show that the wide-spread practical approach for building secure payment applications based on white-box cryptography is conceptually sound. We split our study into two parts:

- a hardware-bound white-box key derivation function (WKDF) which provides (1) hardware-binding and (2) secure storage;
- a secure payment application that performs (3) symmetric encryption of data on top of the WKDF.

Note that the Mastercard guidelines merely specify best practices but omit a design blueprint. Our goal is to explicate how exactly a sound design shall proceed, and what security properties the underlying primitives should obey.

Hardware-Bound White-Box Key Derivation Function (WKDF). Our WKDF notion builds on top of a standard (black-box) key derivation function (KDF). We here consider a lightweight notion for the KDF that takes uniformly random keys and a second, non-random value as input, and returns pseudorandom keys of fixed length. We therefore use the terms KDF and pseudorandom function (PRF) interchangeably, abstracting away additional KDF features such as varying output lengths (cf. Krawczyk [29]). We introduce the IND-WKDF security notion for WKDFs that models the previously discussed white-box attack scenario. I.e., the adversary is given full access to the white-box implementation of the WKDF as well as limited access to the hardware. If the adversary uses its hardware access, the adversary is able to evaluate the WKDF, but if the adversary has no access to the relevant hardware values, e.g., carrying out a code-lifting attack, then the adversary learns nothing about the WKDF values, which is modeled by a real-or-random oracle for derived keys.

Existing Security Notions for White-Box Cryptography. Outside of payment applications, Delerablée, Lepoint, Paillier, and Rivain (DLPR [22]) defined the meanwhile popular notion of *incompressibility* (for constructions and definitional refinements see [11,13,15,16,22,25,30]). Here, an adversary shall not be able to compress a cryptographic program without losing part of its functionality. Incompressibility seems unrelated to achieving the goal of real-or-random key indistinguishability for derived keys, as we aim for the WKDF in our application. Additionally, DLPR define *traceability* which is a security notion intended to trace malicious users (typically in a DRM setting) if they illegally share their white-box program with others. Traceability is a helpful to mitigate code-lifting and re-distribution attacks in the case of malicious users, but not helpful to protect honest users from adversaries copying and misusing their software.

Finally, DPLR also discuss one-wayness and security against key extraction, a baseline security property for white-box cryptography, which are both implied by our IND-WKDF notion for WKDF. Namely, if an adversary can extract the key, then the adversary can evaluate the KDF on all points itself and thereby distinguish derived keys from random keys. Similarly, an adversary can use an inversion algorithm to distinguish real derived keys from random values. Thus, a IND-WKDF-secure WKDF also resists key extraction and inversion attacks.

Secure Payment Application. We introduce a secure hardware-bound payment application scheme (WPAY). Its basic functionality is to encrypt and to authenticate valid payment requests to a server. We model validity by a predicate that acts as filter function. E.g., the filter could only allow for certain date ranges or limits the upper bound on the payment, while the server generically accepts payments of arbitrary amounts and ranges.

Our security notion IND-WPAY gives the adversary the white-box payment application WPAY. The adversary can query a hardware oracle that provides them with the necessary hardware values to generate a request using WPAY. This models that the adversary can observe (and interfere with) honest user evaluations. As soon as the adversary loses access to the hardware, confidentiality and integrity of the user requests should hold. IND-WPAY models both properties via an indistinguishability game. Note that IND-WPAY captures code-lifting attacks. Namely, the adversary has access to WPAY throughout the experiment, but only limited access to the hardware. IND-WPAY models that in the absence of the hardware, no valid requests can be generated, even given WPAY.

Constructions. To instantiate our approach for building a WKDF, we first need to specify a hardware functionality. One idea could be to rely on a signature functionality as provided for example by the Android Key Store. I.e., WKDF would send a request to the hardware, the hardware signs it, and WKDF then verifies the signature with the public verification key. But we need to (1) hide the software-related key of our WKDF and (2) make it inseparable from the verification algorithm that checks hardware values, which are both achieved by applying indistinguishability obfuscation techniques. This, in turn, forces us to use puncturable primitives for the security reduction to work. One option could thus be to use the puncturable signature scheme by Bellare, Stepanovs and Waters [10] which, notably, itself is based on indistinguishability obfuscation. To avoid this double form of obfuscation for the construction, one layer for the puncturable signature scheme and one for the hiding and binding of our KDF key, we instead use a faster symmetric-key primitive in form of a (puncturable) PRF (essentially as a message authentication code). This puncturable PRF is obfuscated once within the hardware-linked KDF construction to ensure the required security.

Hence, we build a WKDF and prove its IND-WKDF security, following techniques by Sahai and Waters [35]. This construction assumes puncturable PRFs (which are equivalent to one-way functions) and indistinguishability obfuscation. Given and IND-WKDF-secure WKDF we then prove that another layer of indistinguishability obfuscation can be used to bind the WKDF to an arbitrary secure symmetric encryption scheme and a filter function to obtain an IND-WPAY-secure white-box payment application WPAY.

Discussion and Limitations. Note that our constructions are conceptual validations and not practically efficient due to the tremendous inefficiency of indistinguishability obfuscation (see [6]). In practice, the obfuscation needs to be implemented by a mix of efficient obfuscation techniques, combined with practical white-box techniques, e.g. [27]. Thus, our work does not allow to immediately bypass the difficulty of building white-box implementations—as apparent in the past white-box competitions [21,23], where only three design candidates submitted towards the end of the second competition remained unbroken—in practice. However, our theoretical feasibility result allows us to conclude that secure white-box implementations based on strong cryptographic assumptions—indistinguishability obfuscation is not yet a mature cryptographic primitive—are indeed possible. Our results not only affirm that building secure white-box cryptography is possible, but they also explain *how* such a secure white-box implementation can be designed.

As efficiency of indistinguishability obfuscation has not yet reached reasonable levels, let us now discuss security and efficiency of current practical white-box implementations. E.g., the winner of the first white-box competition [23] had a binary size of 17 MB and needed 0.37 s for an encryption which is reasonably close to practical needs. It was broken eventually, but resisted key extraction attacks for up to 28 days [32]. This temporary robustness turns out to be useful. Namely, in practice, the goal is to maintain a complexity gap between the effort of the attacker and the effort of the designer. As software can be updated in a regular interval, one can achieve a reasonable practical security level by replace a white-box implementation, in each update, by a newer generation.

Two considerations are important to be taken into account: (1) The white-box implementation should not be susceptible to (variants of) automated attacks, since these can be implemented with little effort, see [1]. (2) Reverse-engineering efforts against previous generations of white-box implementations shall not help the attacker against the new generation of the white-box implementation. I.e., the designer needs to come up with a paradigm that allows to systematically inject a certain amount of creativity into the system that needs to be reverse-engineered anew each time. For example, if security requires bootstrapping security from white-boxing another cryptographic primitive such as a PRF, then one can use a different PRF each time, harvesting the large cryptographic research of PRF constructions. In our model, we bind each payment application to a fresh hardware sub key, derived from a main hardware key, and we allow the adversary to see other derived hardware keys. This models that potentially, earlier construction might have been broken and might have revealed the derived hardware key in use. An alternative is to directly bind to a signature functionality so that revealing the verification algorithm does not constitute an attack vector.

Note that our models do not consider plain relay attacks [26,28] where the adversary forwards the intended communication without altering it. These attacks need to be prevented by other means, e.g., via distance-bounding protocols [7], or at least mitigated via heuristics such as location correlation between phone and NFC reader [12]. Note however that we of course capture attacks where, say, the adversary modifies user requests or tries to create new requests by himself.

Finally, we remark that in our models we consider an adversary who attacks the application of an honest user. The adversary either tries to break security by extracting secret information from the application, or by code-lifting it and running it on a separate device. Our security notions model an adversary who obtains the white-box program but, if the program is securely implemented, the adversary can only run the program when using an oracle simulating part of the hardware of the user. We recall that when considering DRM applications on the other hand, the white-box definitions model an adversary who gets full access to a cryptographic program and to the device running that program (this being the adversary's own device) [18, 19].

2 Preliminaries and Notation

By $a \leftarrow A(x)$, we denote the execution of a deterministic algorithm A on input x and the assignment of the output to a, while $a \leftarrow_\$ A(x)$ denotes the execution of a randomized algorithm and the assignment of the output to a. We denote by $:=$ the process of initializing a set, e.g. $X := \emptyset$. By $x \leftarrow_\$ X$ we denote the process of randomly and uniformly sampling an element x from a given set X. Slightly abusing notation, we also use $x \leftarrow_\$ X$ to denote the sampling of x according to probability distribution X. We then denote the probability that the event $E(x)$ happens by $\Pr_{x \leftarrow_\$ X} E(x)$ or sometimes simply $\Pr[E(x)]$. We write oracles as superscript to the adversary $\mathcal{A}^O$. In cases when an adversary is granted access to a larger number of oracles, we write oracles also as subscript to the adversary $\mathcal{A}^{O_1,O_2}_{O_3,O_4}$. PPT denotes probabilistic polynomial-time and $\texttt{poly}(n)$ is an unspecified polynomial in the security parameter. Note that all algorithms receive the security parameter 1^n in unary notation as input implicitly. We write it explicitly only occasionally for clarity.

We now review useful definitions, starting with nonce-based encryption, see Rogaway [34].

Definition 1 (Symmetric Encryption). *A nonce-based symmetric encryption scheme* SE *consists of a pair of deterministic polynomial-time algorithms* (Enc, Dec) *with the syntax* $c \leftarrow \text{Enc}(k, m, nc)$ *and* $m/\perp \leftarrow \text{Dec}(k, c, nc)$. *The algorithm* Enc *takes as input a randomly generated key* k *of length* n, *a nonce* nc, *a message* m, *and outputs a ciphertext* c. Dec *takes as input a randomly generated key* k *of length* n, *a nonce* nc, *a ciphertext* c, *and outputs either a message* m *or an error symbol* $\perp$. *Moreover, the encryption scheme* SE *satisfies correctness, if for all nonces* $nc \in \{0,1\}^n$ *and for all messages* $m \in \{0,1\}^*$,

$$Pr[\text{Dec}(k_{\text{SE}}, \text{Enc}(k_{\text{SE}}, m, nc), nc) = m] = 1$$

where the probability is over sampling k.

$\text{Exp}^{\text{AE}}_{\text{SE},\mathcal{A}}(1^n)$	$\text{OENC}(m_0, m_1)$	$\text{ODEC}(nc, c)$
$b \leftarrow_\$ \{0,1\}$	**assert** $\|m_0\| = \|m_1\|$	**assert** $c \notin C$
$k_{\text{SE}} \leftarrow_\$ \{0,1\}^n$	$nc \leftarrow_\$ \{0,1\}^n$	**if** $b = 1$ **then**
$b' \leftarrow_\$ \mathcal{A}^{\text{OENC,ODEC}}(1^n)$	$c \leftarrow \text{Enc}(k_{\text{SE}}, m_b, nc)$	**return** $\perp$
return $(b' = b)$	$C := C \cup \{c\}$	**else**
	return (nc, c)	**return** $m \leftarrow \text{Dec}(k_{\text{SE}}, c, nc)$

Fig. 1. The $\text{Exp}^{\text{AE}}_{\text{SE},\mathcal{A}}(1^n)$ security game.

Definition 2 and Fig. 1 specify the security of an *authenticated encryption scheme* [9,33]. Here, the adversary is provided with a left-or-right encryption oracle and a decryption oracle where it can submit arbitrary ciphertexts except for challenge ciphertexts obtained from the encryption oracle. If $b = 0$, the decryption oracle is functional. If $b = 1$, the decryption oracle always returns $\perp$ which models ciphertext integrity. In the security game, we use **assert** as a shorthand to say that if the **assert** condition is violated, then the oracle returns an error symbol $\perp$.

Definition 2 (Authenticated Encryption). *A nonce-based symmetric encryption scheme* $\mathsf{SE} = (\mathsf{Enc}, \mathsf{Dec})$ *is called an* authenticated encryption scheme *or* AE-*secure if all PPT adversaries* $\mathcal{A}$ *have negligible distinguishing advantage in the game* $\mathsf{Exp}_{\mathsf{SE},\mathcal{A}}^{\mathsf{AE}}(1^n)$, *specified in Fig. 1.*

Note that we demand the authenticated encryption scheme to be deterministic because we will later execute the algorithm in an untrusted environment and cannot count on strong randomness. This, in turn, implies that we cannot allow the adversary to re-use any of the previous queries (m, nc), or else it would be easy to determine b from two queries (m_0, m_1, nc) and (m_0, m_1', nc).

We provide a formal definition of a key derivation function that produces pseudorandom keys. Note that our definition corresponds to a PRF, i.e., it is highly simplified compared to the framework of Krawczyk [29]. In our definition a key derivation function takes as input a key k_{kdf}, a context string e as well as the security parameter 1^n. In comparison to Krawczyk's definition, we simplify the presentation and omit the details of the smoothing step turning raw key material into random strings, the salting, and the length parameter, assuming that the key k_{kdf} is already appropriate and the length of the returned key is equal to $|k_{\mathsf{kdf}}|$.

Definition 3 (Key Derivation Function). *A* KDF *scheme consists of a randomized key generation algorithm* Kgen *and a key derivation function* KDF *that is a deterministic algorithm that takes as input a key* $k_{\mathsf{kdf}} \leftarrow_{\$} \mathsf{Kgen}(1^n)$ *and a context string* e. *The* KDF *returns a key* $\hat{k}$ *of length* $|k_{\mathsf{kdf}}|$.

Definition 4 (IND-KDF-security). *A key derivation function* KDF *is said to be* IND-KDF-*secure if all PPT adversaries* $\mathcal{A}$ *have negligible distinguishing advantage in game* $\mathsf{Exp}_{\mathsf{KDF},\mathcal{A}}^{\mathsf{IND\text{-}KDF}}(1^n)$, *specified in Fig. 2.*

Next we present the definition of a length-doubling pseudorandom generator.

Definition 5 (Pseudorandom Generator). *A deterministic, polynomial-time computable function* $\mathsf{PRG} : \{0,1\}^* \to \{0,1\}^*$ *is a pseudorandom generator if:*

- **Length-expansion:** *For all* $x \in \{0,1\}^*$, $|\mathsf{PRG}(x)| = 2|x|$.

– **Pseudorandomness:** *For all PPT* $\mathcal{A}$, $\mathrm{Adv}_{\mathrm{PRG},\mathcal{A}}(n) :=$

$$|\mathrm{Pr}_{x \leftarrow_\$ \{0,1\}^n}[\mathcal{A}(\mathrm{PRG}(x)) = 1] - \mathrm{Pr}_{z \leftarrow_\$ \{0,1\}^{2n}}[\mathcal{A}(z) = 1]|$$

is negligible in n.

We define pseudorandom functions with identical input, output and key length.

Definition 6 (Pseudorandom Function). *A deterministic, polynomial-time computable function* PRF, *such that* PRF : $\{0,1\}^n \times \{0,1\}^n \to \{0,1\}^n$ *for all* $n \in \mathbb{N}$, *is a pseudorandom function if for all PPT* $\mathcal{A}$, $\mathrm{Adv}_{\mathcal{A},\mathrm{PRF}}(n) :=$

$$|\mathrm{Pr}_{k \leftarrow_\$ \{0,1\}^n}[\mathcal{A}^{\mathrm{PRF}(k,\cdot)}(1^n) = 1] - \mathrm{Pr}_{F \leftarrow_\$ \{G:\{0,1\}^n \to \{0,1\}^n\}}[\mathcal{A}^{F(\cdot)}(1^n) = 1]|$$

is negligible in n.

Puncturable PRFs (PPRF) were introduced by Boneh and Waters [17]. PPRFs have a punctured key which allows to evaluate the PPRF on all inputs, except for one where the function still looks random.

Definition 7 (PPRF). *A puncturable pseudorandom function scheme* PPRF *consists of a triple* (PPRF, Punct, Eval), *which are defined as follows:*

- PPRF(k, x) : *This is a standard PRF evaluation algorithm. As before, this deterministic polynomial-time algorithm takes as input a key* k *and input* x, *both of length* n *and returns a value* y *of length* n.
- Punct(k, z) : *This PPT algorithm takes as input a key* $k \in \{0,1\}^n$ *and an input value* $z \in \{0,1\}^n$. *It outputs a punctured key* $k_z \leftarrow_\$ $ Punct(k, z).
- Eval(k_z, x) : *This* deterministic polynomial-time *algorithm takes as input a punctured key* k_z *and some input* $x \in \{0,1\}^n$ *and returns* $\perp$ *if* $x = z$, *and a value* $y \in \{0,1\}^n$ *otherwise.*

A puncturable PRF *is said to be* correct, *if for all security parameter* n, *all* $k \in \{0,1\}^n$, *every value* $z \in \{0,1\}^n$ *and all* $x \in \{0,1\}^n$, $x \neq z$, *it holds that*

$$\mathrm{Pr}[\mathtt{Eval}(\mathtt{Punct}(k, z), x) = \mathtt{PPRF}(k, x)] = 1.$$

$\mathrm{Exp}_{\mathrm{KDF},\mathcal{A}}^{\mathsf{IND\text{-}KDF}}(1^n)$	$\mathrm{OKDF}(e)$
$b \leftarrow_\$ \{0,1\}$	if $e \notin \mathcal{Q}$
$\mathcal{Q} := \emptyset$	$\mathcal{Q} := \mathcal{Q} \cup \{e\}$
$k_{\mathrm{kdf}} \leftarrow_\$ \mathrm{Kgen}(1^n)$	if $b = 1$
$b' \leftarrow_\$ \mathcal{A}^{\mathrm{OKDF}}(1^n)$	$\hat{k} \leftarrow \mathrm{KDF}(k_{\mathrm{kdf}}, e)$
if $b' = b$	else
$\quad$ return 1	$\hat{k} \leftarrow_\$ \{0,1\}^n$
else	return $\hat{k}$
$\quad$ return 0	else
	return $\bot$

$\mathrm{Exp}_{\mathsf{PPRF},\mathcal{A}}^{\mathsf{IND\text{-}PPRF}}(1^n)$
$b \leftarrow_\$ \{0,1\}$
$k \leftarrow_\$ \{0,1\}^n$
$(z, \mathsf{state}) \leftarrow_\$ \mathcal{A}(1^n)$
$k_z \leftarrow_\$ \mathrm{Punct}(k, z)$
if $b = 1$ then
$\quad y \leftarrow \mathrm{PPRF}(k, z)$
else $y \leftarrow_\$ \{0,1\}^n$
$b' \leftarrow_\$ \mathcal{A}(k_z, y, \mathsf{state})$
return $(b' = b)$

Fig. 2. $\mathrm{Exp}_{\mathsf{KDF},\mathcal{A}}^{\mathsf{IND\text{-}KDF}}(1^n)$ security game   **Fig. 3.** IND-PPRF security game

PPRF security requires that the PPRF value on k and z is indistinguishable from random, even when given the punctured key k_z. Note that for our purposes, we only rely on security for *random* inputs rather than adversarially chosen ones, i.e., we use a less powerful assumption which makes our result stronger.

Definition 8 (IND-PPRF-security). *A* PPRF *scheme is said to be* IND-PPRF-secure *if all probabilistic polynomial-time adversaries $\mathcal{A}$ have negligible distinguishing advantage in the* IND-PPRF *game defined in Fig. 3.*

An indistinguishability obfuscator (iO) ensures that the obfuscation of any two functionally equivalent programs (i.e. circuits) are computationally indistinguishable. In the following definition, a distinguisher $\mathcal{D}$ is an adversary that aims at identifying which of the two programs has been obfuscated.

Definition 9 (Admissible Circuit Sampler). *Let p be a polynomial. A PPT algorithm $\mathcal{S}$ is called a p-admissible circuit sampler if*

$$1 - \Pr_{(\mathsf{C}_0, \mathsf{C}_1) \leftarrow_\$ \mathcal{S}(1^n)}[\forall x \in \{0,1\}^n \ \mathsf{C}_0(x) = \mathsf{C}_1(x)]$$

is negligible in n and for all $n \in \mathbb{N}$ and all pairs $(\mathsf{C}_0, \mathsf{C}_1)$ in the range of $\mathcal{A}(1^n)$, it holds that the size of C_0 and the size of C_1 is upper bounded by $p(n)$.

Definition 10 (Indistinguishability Obfuscator). *A PPT algorithm iO, parameterized by a polynomial p, is called an* indistinguishability obfuscator *if for any p-admissible circuit sampler $\mathcal{S}$ the following conditions are satisfied:*

Correctness. *For all circuits C and for all inputs x to the circuit,*

$$\Pr[\mathsf{C}'(x) = \mathsf{C}(x) : \mathsf{C}' \leftarrow_\$ \mathsf{iO}(\mathsf{C})] = 1,$$

where the probability is over the randomness of iO.

Security. *For all p-admissible $\mathcal{S}$ and any PPT distinguisher $\mathcal{D}$, the following distinguishing advantage is negligible:*

$$|\mathrm{Pr}_{(C_0C_1)\leftarrow_\$\mathcal{S}}[\mathcal{D}(\mathrm{iO}(C_0)) = 1] - \mathrm{Pr}_{(C_0C_1)\leftarrow_\$\mathcal{S}}[\mathcal{D}(\mathrm{iO}(C_1)) = 1]| \leq negl(n),$$

where the probabilities are over the randomness of the algorithms.

When obfuscating cryptographic algorithms with keys it is often convenient to use the notation $C[k](x)$ to denote the circuit with fixed encoded key(s) k and variable input x.

3   Hardware-Bound White-Box Key Derivation Function

In this section, we first introduce our notion of a hardware module and explain how we instantiate it in our setting. Then, we provide the syntax and security notion for a hardware-bound key derivation function, present our construction and provide a security reduction to indistinguishability obfuscation and PPRFs.

3.1   Hardware Module

A schematic overview over the hardware module functionalities executed on the secure hardware is given in Fig. 4. Namely, a hardware module comes with a key generation algorithm that generates the hardware main key k_{HWm}.

This key generation algorithm is run at the manufacturer of the hardware and thus not depicted in Fig. 4. The secure hardware allows to export a sub-key via querying the secure hardware with a *label*. The hardware then runs the *sub-key generation algorithm* $\mathsf{SubKgen}_{HW}$ on k_{HWm} and *label* and returns the resulting sub-key k_{HWs}. In addition, the secure hardware can be queried with a pair $(x, label)$. The hardware, then, uses the algorithm Resp_{HW} to generate

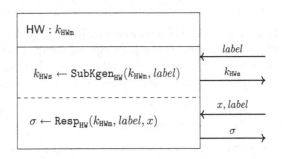

Fig. 4. Functionalities of the hardware module performed in the hardware. The **Check** operation is performed by the software program corresponding to the *label*.

a PRF/MAC value σ for x under k_{HWm}. In order to avoid storing k_{HWs} for all values *label*, the hardware re-derives k_{HWs} anew each time Resp_{HW} is called. The PRF/MAC value can be checked outside of the secure hardware by running Check_{SW} on k_{HWs} and the pair (x, σ).

Remarks. In this paper, we assume that the hardware module is secure and, as the only part of the device, not subject to white-box attacks. Even more, we assume that the hardware looks like a secure black-box to the white-box adversary and is not subject to side-channel attacks.

With regard to the white-box program, it is important that the verification key k_{HWs} is not stored in plain since, otherwise, one might derive PRF/MAC values using k_{HWs} rather than querying the hardware. Thus, the $\texttt{Check}_{SW}$ functionality will need to be white-boxed (and will later be bound to another functionality such as our white-box KDF), essentially making it asymmetric. Note that the syntax and correctness of our hardware module also allows to be directly implemented by a (standard, asymmetric) signature scheme such as provided by the Android Keystore [4]. In that case, the verification key does not need additional protection. We chose to implement the hardware with a symmetric primitive for efficiency and simplicity of the proof. Note that regardless of whether one uses MACs or signature schemes as a hardware functionality, the verification functionality needs to be cryptographically *bound to a software program* to be useful; else the software program can be code-lifted and run without performing the verification check.

Regardless of efficiency, both approaches, using signature schemes directly or making MAC verification asymmetric, are sound approaches. Importantly, in both cases, the soundness of the approach relies on *domain separation*, i.e., signatures/MAC for one *label* should not be mixed up with signatures/MACs for a different *label*. Finally, recall that fixed device identifiers (that do not depend on the input x) tend to provide very weak hardware-binding guarantees only, since once intercepted, they can be emulated for a code-lifted software program. We now give the syntax for our hardware-module.

Definition 11. (Hardware Module HWM). *A hardware module HWM consists of four algorithms* $(\texttt{Kgen}_{HW}, \texttt{SubKgen}_{HW}, \texttt{Resp}_{HW}, \texttt{Check}_{SW})$*, where* $\texttt{Kgen}_{HW}$ *is a PPT algorithm, and the algorithms* $\texttt{SubKgen}_{HW}$*,* $\texttt{Resp}_{HW}$ *and* $\texttt{Check}_{SW}$ *are deterministic algorithms with the following syntax:*

$$k_{HWm} \leftarrow_\$ \texttt{Kgen}_{HW}(1^n) \qquad\qquad \sigma \leftarrow \texttt{Resp}_{HW}(k_{HWm}, label, x)$$
$$k_{HWs} \leftarrow \texttt{SubKgen}_{HW}(k_{HWm}, label) \qquad b \leftarrow \texttt{Check}_{SW}(k_{HWs}, x, \sigma),$$

Correctness requires that for all security parameters $n \in \mathbb{N}$*,*

$$\Pr[\texttt{Check}_{SW}(\texttt{SubKgen}_{HW}(k_{HWm}, label), x, \texttt{Resp}_{HW}(k_{HWm}, label, x)) = 1] = 1,$$

where the probability is over the sampling of $k_{HWm} \leftarrow_\$ \texttt{Kgen}_{HW}(1^n)$*.*

We do not define or prove security of the hardware module as a standalone primitive, since we will later prove security of our white-box KDF directly based on the puncturable PRFs used in the hardware module construction. Note that a standalone security definition for a hardware module could not capture MACs/PRFs and signature security simultaneously. In our hardware module construction below, key generation samples a random key, sub-key generation applies a PRF to it to derive a sub-key, and $\texttt{Resp}_{HW}$ and $\texttt{Check}_{SW}$ essentially implement a PRF-based MAC. Note that the additional PRG evaluation in $\texttt{Check}_{SW}$ is merely used to enable the proof technique by Sahai and Waters [35].

Construction 1. *Let* PRG *be a pseudorandom generator,* PRF *be a pseudorandom function and* PPRF *be a puncturable pseudorandom function. We construct a hardware module* HWM *as follows:*

$\underline{\text{Kgen}_{\text{HW}}(1^n)}$

1 : $k_{\text{HWm}} \leftarrow_\$ \{0,1\}^n$

2 :   **return** k_{HWm}

$\underline{\text{SubKgen}_{\text{HW}}(k_{\text{HWm}}, label)}$

1 : $k_{\text{HWs}} \leftarrow \text{PRF}(k_{\text{HWm}}, label)$

2 :   **return** k_{HWs}

$\underline{\text{Resp}_{\text{HW}}(k_{\text{HWm}}, label, x)}$

1 : $\sigma \leftarrow \text{PPRF}(\text{PRF}(k_{\text{HWm}}, label), x)$

2 :   **return** σ

$\underline{\text{Check}_{\text{SW}}(k_{\text{HWs}}, x, \sigma)}$

1 :   **if** $\text{PRG}(\sigma) = \text{PRG}(\text{PPRF}(k_{\text{HWs}}, x))$

2 :   **return** 1 **else return** 0

Hardware-Bound White-Box Key Derivation Function. We now define and construct a hardware-bound white-box key derivation function WKDF. We here build on the previously introduced hardware module and a traditional KDF. In the compiling phase, a compiler Comp takes as input the KDF key k_{kdf} and the sub-key k_{HWs} for Check$_{\text{SW}}$. The compiler generates a program WKDF which takes as input a pair (e, σ) and, intuitively, first checks whether σ is valid for e under k_{HWs} and, if so, evaluates the KDF on k_{kdf} and e. The role of the compiler, conceptually, is to return a program where the KDF operation is *bound* to the verification operation, i.e., the two functionalities cannot be separated from each other and the (outcome of the) verification cannot be manipulated.

Definition 12. (WKDF**).** *A* white-box key derivation scheme with hardware binding WKDF *consists of a* hardware module HWM, *a* key derivation function KDF, *and a PPT compiling algorithm* Comp:

$$\text{WKDF} \leftarrow_\$ \text{Comp}(k_{\text{kdf}}, k_{\text{HWs}}).$$

For all genuine k_{HWm}, *for all* k_{kdf}, *for all* label, *for all* e, *for all* $k_{\text{HWs}} = \text{SubKgen}_{\text{HW}}(k_{\text{HWm}}, label)$ *and* $\sigma = \text{Resp}_{\text{HW}}(k_{\text{HWm}}, label, e)$, *we have*

$$\Pr[\text{KDF}(k_{\text{kdf}}, e) = \text{WKDF}(e, \sigma)] = 1$$

where the probability is taken over compiling $\text{WKDF} \leftarrow_\$ \text{Comp}(k_{\text{kdf}}, k_{\text{HWs}})$.

Security Model. We now define security for a WKDF via the IND-WKDF security game, illustrated in Fig. 5. We want to capture the pseudorandomness of keys derived from the WKDF, i.e., an adversary should not be able to distinguish between a key produced from the WKDF and an equally long key sampled at random. As a white-box adversary, the game provides the adversary with the capability of inspecting the WKDF itself (i.e. its circuit or implementation code). Recall that additionally, we want to capture the notion of hardware-binding:

$\mathsf{Exp}_{\mathsf{WKDF},\mathcal{A}}^{\mathsf{IND\text{-}WKDF}}(1^n)$	$\mathsf{OKDF}()$
$b \leftarrow_\$ \{0,1\}$	$e \leftarrow_\$ \{0,1\}^n$
$\mathcal{Q} := \emptyset$	$\mathcal{Q} := \mathcal{Q} \cup \{e\}$
$label \leftarrow_\$ \mathcal{A}(1^n)$	if $b = 0$
$k_{\mathsf{kdf}} \leftarrow_\$ \mathsf{Kgen}(1^n)$	$\quad \hat{k} \leftarrow \mathsf{KDF}(k_{\mathsf{kdf}}, e)$
$k_{\mathsf{HWm}} \leftarrow_\$ \mathsf{Kgen}_{\mathsf{HW}}(1^n)$	else
$k_{\mathsf{HWs}} \leftarrow \mathsf{SubKgen}_{\mathsf{HW}}(k_{\mathsf{HWm}}, label)$	$\quad \hat{k} \leftarrow_\$ \{0,1\}^n$
$\mathsf{WKDF} \leftarrow_\$ \mathsf{Comp}(k_{\mathsf{kdf}}, k_{\mathsf{HWs}})$	return $(e, \hat{k})$
$b' \leftarrow_\$ \mathcal{A}_{\mathsf{OSubKgen}_{\mathsf{HW}}}^{\mathsf{OResp},\mathsf{OKDF}}(\mathsf{WKDF})$	
return b'	

$\mathsf{OResp}(e)$	$\mathsf{OSubKgen}(label')$
assert $e \notin \mathcal{Q}$	assert $label' \neq label$
$\mathcal{Q} := \mathcal{Q} \cup \{e\}$	$k'_{\mathsf{HWs}} \leftarrow \mathsf{SubKgen}_{\mathsf{HW}}(k_{\mathsf{HWm}}, label')$
$\sigma \leftarrow \mathsf{Resp}_{\mathsf{HW}}(k_{\mathsf{HWm}}, label, e)$	return k'_{HWs}
return σ	

Fig. 5. The $\mathsf{Exp}_{\mathsf{WKDF},\mathcal{A}}^{\mathsf{IND\text{-}WKDF}}(1^n)$ security game.

if the adversary tries to run the WKDF without having access to its designated hardware, the WKDF should not be executable anymore.

We model this by giving the adversary hardware access via a OResp oracle, which the adversary queries by providing a context value e and which the adversary can query a polynomial number of times. With the reply σ from the hardware component, the adversary is able to run WKDF on the context value e used for querying OResp. Additionally, we grant the adversary access to an oracle OSubKgen. This oracle produces hardware sub-keys which might be used to generate new hardware-bound white-box key derivation functions. To avoid trivial attacks, the adversary is not allowed to request a sub-key under the same *label* that was used to generate the initial WKDF. To capture the pseudorandomness of derived keys, the adversary has access to a real-or-random oracle OKDF. The oracle OKDF first samples a new context value e and then, depending on a random bit b, it either returns the output of the KDF (under key k_{kdf}) or a random string of equal length. To avoid trivial attacks, the adversary is not allowed to query the OResp oracle with the same context value that was sampled by the challenger. Finally, $\mathcal{A}$ outputs a bit b' and wins if $b' = b$.

Definition 13 (IND-WKDF). *We say that a hardware-bound white-box key derivation scheme* WKDF *is* IND-WKDF-*secure if all PPT adversaries $\mathcal{A}$ have a negligible distinguishing advantage in game* $\mathsf{Exp}_{\mathsf{WKDF},\mathcal{A}}^{\mathsf{IND\text{-}WKDF}}(1^n)$, *see Fig. 5.*

Note that one could also provide the adversary with a recompilation oracle [22] so that the adversary can request several (independent) copies of the WKDF based on the same key. We refrain from including this feature into our model, but note that our construction can be shown to achieve also this stronger notion, as indistinguishability obfuscation makes recompilation adversarially simulatable.

3.2   Construction of a WKDF

We now construct a WKDF, based on a traditional KDF and the previously introduced hardware module HWM. As discussed before, the compiler Comp, on input the KDF key k_{kdf} and the hardware sub-key k_{HWs} binds the hardware Check_{SW} procedure to the KDF evaluation. Concretely, the compiler constructs a circuit $C[k_{\text{kdf}}, k_{\text{HWs}}]$ and obfuscates it using indistinguishability obfuscation. The circuit $C[k_{\text{kdf}}, k_{\text{HWs}}]$, on input (e, σ) first checks whether $\text{Check}_{\text{SW}}(k_{\text{HWs}}, e, \sigma)$ equals 1. If yes, it returns the output of $\text{KDF}(k_{\text{kdf}}, e)$. Else, it returns the all-zero string. The reason that the construction is secure, is, intuitively, that the obfuscation of $C[k_{\text{kdf}}, k_{\text{HWs}}]$ achieves the desired binding property. We now first give the KDF construction and then the WKDF construction directly below.

Construction 2. *Let* PPRF *be a puncturable pseudorandom function scheme, then we construct our* KDF *as follows:*

$\text{Kgen}_{\text{kdf}}(1^n)$	$\text{KDF}(k_{\text{kdf}}, e)$
$1:\quad k_{\text{kdf}} \leftarrow\!\!{\scriptstyle\$}\, \{0,1\}^n$	$1:\quad \hat{k} \leftarrow \text{PPRF}(k_{\text{kdf}}, e)$
$2:\quad \textbf{return } k_{\text{kdf}}$	$2:\quad \textbf{return } \hat{k}$

Construction 3. *Let* iO *be an indistinguishability obfuscator. Based on the hardware module* HWM *given in Construction 1 and the key derivation scheme* KDF *given in Construction 2, we construct* WKDF *by defining the following compiler* Comp:

$C[k_{\text{kdf}}, k_{\text{HWs}}](e, \sigma)$	$\text{Comp}(k_{\text{kdf}}, k_{\text{HWs}})$
$1:\quad v \leftarrow \text{Check}_{\text{SW}}(k_{\text{HWs}}, e, \sigma)$	$1:\quad \text{WKDF} \leftarrow\!\!{\scriptstyle\$}\, \text{iO}(C[k_{\text{kdf}}, k_{\text{HWs}}])$
$2:\quad \textbf{if } v = \bot \textbf{ return } 0^n$	$2:\quad \textbf{return } \text{WKDF}$
$3:\quad \textbf{else}$	
$4:\quad\quad \hat{k} \leftarrow \text{KDF}(k_{\text{kdf}}, e)$	
$5:\quad\quad \textbf{return } \hat{k}$	

Theorem 1. *Let* PRG *be a pseudorandom generator, let* PRF *be a pseudorandom function, let* PPRF *be a puncturable PRF, and* iO *be an indistinguishability obfuscator for appropriate p-admissible samplers. Then Construction 3 is a secure white-box KDF scheme* WKDF.

Proof. Let $\mathcal{A}$ be a PPT adversary. Let $\mathsf{Exp}_{\mathcal{A},b}^{\text{IND-WKDF}}$ denote the IND-WKDF game with a value $b \in \{0,1\}$ hardcoded. We show that

$$\mathsf{Exp}_{\mathcal{A},0}^{\text{IND-WKDF}}(1^n) \approx \mathsf{Exp}_{\mathcal{A},1}^{\text{IND-WKDF}}(1^n).$$

Overview: The proof is a hybrid argument over the number of queries q that $\mathcal{A}$ makes to the OKDF oracle which either evaluates a puncturable PRF and returns its output or a random string of the same length. Our hybrid games maintain a counter j that increases by 1 whenever the adversary queries the OKDF oracle. The i-th hybrid game Game_1^i returns a random string whenever the counter $j > i$, otherwise it returns the evaluation of the PPRF. In other words, whenever we move to the next hybrid, the oracle returns an additional random string such that we sequentially replace PPRF values by random strings of appropriate size. After at most polynomial steps we have replaced all OKDF outputs by random values and obtain $\mathsf{Exp}_{\mathcal{A},1}^{\text{IND-WKDF}}(1^n)$.

Detailed Proof: Let $q(n)$ be a polynomial which is a strict upper bound on the number of queries that $\mathcal{A}$ makes to oracle OKDF. We define a sequence of adversary-dependent hybrid games Game_1^0 to $\mathsf{Game}_1^{q(n)}$ such that

$$\mathsf{Exp}_{\mathcal{A},0}^{\text{IND-WKDF}} \approx \mathsf{Game}_1^0 \tag{1}$$

$$\mathsf{Exp}_{\mathcal{A},1}^{\text{IND-WKDF}} \approx \mathsf{Game}_1^{q(n)}. \tag{2}$$

Using 18 game hops we show that for $0 \le i \le q(n) - 1$:

$$\mathsf{Game}_1^i \approx \mathsf{Game}_{18}^i \tag{3}$$

$$\mathsf{Game}_{18}^i \approx \mathsf{Game}_1^{i+1}. \tag{4}$$

Indistinguishability of Game_1^0 and $\mathsf{Game}_1^{q(n)}$ then follows by a standard hybrid argument, guessing the hybrid index at random. We define the games and specify the game-hops below and the required circuit definitions are depicted on the right-hand side of this page. Equation 4 follows by inspection of the definitions of Game_{18}^i and Game_1^{i+1}. We now turn to showing Eq. 3 which is the technical heart of the theorem.

$\underline{\mathsf{C}_1[k_{\text{kdf}}, k_{\text{HWs}}](e,\sigma)}$

if $\mathsf{PRG}(\sigma) = \mathsf{PRG}(\mathsf{PPRF}(k_{\text{HWs}}, e))$

$\quad \hat{k} \leftarrow \mathsf{PPRF}(k_{\text{kdf}}, e)$

$\quad$ **return** $\hat{k}$

else return 0^n

$\underline{\mathsf{C}_2[k_{\text{kdf}}, z, k_z, \tau](e,\sigma)}$

if $e = z$ and $\mathsf{PRG}(\sigma) = \mathsf{PRG}(\tau)$

or if $\mathsf{PRG}(\sigma) = \mathsf{PRG}(\mathsf{Eval}(k_z, e))$

$\quad \hat{k} \leftarrow \mathsf{PPRF}(k_{\text{kdf}}, e)$

$\quad$ **return** $\hat{k}$

else return 0^n

$\underline{\mathsf{C}_3[k_{\text{kdf}}, z, k_z, y](e,\sigma)}$

if $e = z$ and $\mathsf{PRG}(\sigma) = y$

or if $\mathsf{PRG}(\sigma) = \mathsf{PRG}(\mathsf{Eval}(k_z, e))$

$\quad \hat{k} \leftarrow \mathsf{PPRF}(k_{\text{kdf}}, e)$

$\quad$ **return** $\hat{k}$

else return 0^n

$\underline{\mathsf{C}_4[k_{\text{kdf}}^z, z, k_z, y, k](e,\sigma)}$

if $e = z$ and $\mathsf{PRG}(\sigma) = y$

$\quad$ **return** k

if $\mathsf{PRG}(\sigma) = \mathsf{PRG}(\mathsf{Eval}(k_z, e))$

$\quad \hat{k} \leftarrow \mathsf{Eval}(k_{\text{kdf}}^z, e)$

$\quad$ **return** $\hat{k}$

else return 0^n

$\underline{\mathsf{C}_5[k_{\text{kdf}}^z, z, k_z, y](e,\sigma)}$

if $e = z$ and $\mathsf{PRG}(\sigma) = y$

$\quad$ **return** 0^n

if $\mathsf{PRG}(\sigma) = \mathsf{PRG}(\mathsf{Eval}(k_z, e))$

$\quad \hat{k} \leftarrow \mathsf{Eval}(k_{\text{kdf}}^z, e)$

$\quad$ **return** $\hat{k}$

else return 0^n

$\text{Game}_{18}^i(1^n)$	$\xleftarrow{\text{PRF security}}$	$\text{Game}_{17}^i(1^n)$	$\xleftarrow{\text{iO security}}$	$\text{Game}_{16}^i(1^n)$

$\text{Game}_1^i(1^n) \xrightarrow{\text{PRF security}} \text{Game}_2^i(1^n) \xrightarrow{\text{iO security}} \text{Game}_3^i(1^n) \xrightarrow{\text{PPRF sec.}}$

1 :	$z \leftarrow_\$ \{0,1\}^n, \mathcal{Q} := \{z\}$	$z \leftarrow_\$ \{0,1\}^n, \mathcal{Q} := \{z\}$	$z \leftarrow_\$ \{0,1\}^n, \mathcal{Q} := \{z\}$
2 :	$j \leftarrow 0$	$j \leftarrow 0$	$j \leftarrow 0$
3 :	$label \leftarrow_\$ \mathcal{A}(1^n)$	$label \leftarrow_\$ \mathcal{A}(1^n)$	$label \leftarrow_\$ \mathcal{A}(1^n)$
4 :	$k_{\text{kdf}} \leftarrow_\$ \{0,1\}^n$	$k_{\text{kdf}} \leftarrow_\$ \{0,1\}^n$	$k_{\text{kdf}} \leftarrow_\$ \{0,1\}^n$
5 :			
6 :	$k \leftarrow \text{PPRF}(k_{\text{kdf}}, z)$	$k \leftarrow \text{PPRF}(k_{\text{kdf}}, z)$	$k \leftarrow \text{PPRF}(k_{\text{kdf}}, z)$
7 :	$k_{\text{HWm}} \leftarrow_\$ \{0,1\}^n$	$k_{\text{HWm}} \leftarrow_\$ \{0,1\}^n$	$k_{\text{HWm}} \leftarrow_\$ \{0,1\}^n$
8 :	$k_{\text{HWs}} \leftarrow_\$ \text{PRF}(k_{\text{HWm}}, label)$	$k_{\text{HWs}} \leftarrow_\$ \{0,1\}^n$	$k_{\text{HWs}} \leftarrow_\$ \{0,1\}^n$
9 :			$k_z \leftarrow_\$ \text{Punct}(k_{\text{HWs}}, z)$
10 :			$\tau \leftarrow \text{PPRF}(k_{\text{HWs}}, z)$
11 :	$C \leftarrow C_1[k_{\text{kdf}}, k_{\text{HWs}}]$	$C \leftarrow C_1[k_{\text{kdf}}, k_{\text{HWs}}]$	$C \leftarrow C_2[k_{\text{kdf}}, z, k_z, \tau]$
12 :	$\text{WKDF} \leftarrow_\$ \text{iO}(C, 1^n)$	$\text{WKDF} \leftarrow_\$ \text{iO}(C, 1^n)$	$\text{WKDF} \leftarrow_\$ \text{iO}(C, 1^n)$
13 :	$b' \leftarrow_\$ \mathcal{A}_{\text{OSubKgen}}^{\text{Resp}_{\text{HW}}, \text{OKDF}}(\text{WKDF})$	$b' \leftarrow_\$ \mathcal{A}_{\text{OSubKgen}}^{\text{Resp}_{\text{HW}}, \text{OKDF}}(\text{WKDF})$	$b' \leftarrow_\$ \mathcal{A}_{\text{OSubKgen}}^{\text{Resp}_{\text{HW}}, \text{OKDF}}(\text{WKDF})$
14 :	**return** b'	**return** b'	**return** b'

$\text{OResp}(e)$		$\text{OResp}(e)$		$\text{OResp}(e)$
1 :	**assert** $e \notin \mathcal{Q}$	**assert** $e \notin \mathcal{Q}$		**assert** $e \notin \mathcal{Q}$
2 :	$\mathcal{Q} := \mathcal{Q} \cup \{e\}$	$\mathcal{Q} := \mathcal{Q} \cup \{e\}$		$\mathcal{Q} := \mathcal{Q} \cup \{e\}$
3 :	$y \leftarrow \text{PPRF}(k_{\text{HWs}}, e, 1^n)$	$y \leftarrow \text{PPRF}(k_{\text{HWs}}, e, 1^n)$		$y \leftarrow \text{Eval}(k_z, e, 1^n)$
4 :	**return** y	**return** y		**return** y

$\text{OKDF}()$		$\text{OKDF}()$		$\text{OKDF}()$
1 :	$j \leftarrow j + 1$	$j \leftarrow j + 1$		$j \leftarrow j + 1$
2 :	**if** $i = j$ $\boxed{k' \leftarrow_\$ \{0,1\}^n}$	**if** $i = j$ $\boxed{k' \leftarrow_\$ \{0,1\}^n}$		**if** $i = j$ $\boxed{k' \leftarrow_\$ \{0,1\}^n}$
3 :	**return** (z, k) $\boxed{(z, k')}$	**return** (z, k) $\boxed{(z, k')}$		**return** (z, k) $\boxed{(z, k')}$
4 :	**else** $e \leftarrow_\$ \{0,1\}^n$	**else** $e \leftarrow_\$ \{0,1\}^n$		**else** $e \leftarrow_\$ \{0,1\}^n$
5 :	$\mathcal{Q} := \mathcal{Q} \cup \{e\}$	$\mathcal{Q} := \mathcal{Q} \cup \{e\}$		$\mathcal{Q} := \mathcal{Q} \cup \{e\}$
6 :	**if** $j > i$	**if** $j > i$		**if** $j > i$
7 :	$\hat{k} \leftarrow \text{PPRF}(k_{\text{kdf}}, e)$	$\hat{k} \leftarrow \text{PPRF}(k_{\text{kdf}}, e)$		$\hat{k} \leftarrow \text{PPRF}(k_{\text{kdf}}, e)$
8 :	**else** $\hat{k} \leftarrow_\$ \{0,1\}^n$	**else** $\hat{k} \leftarrow_\$ \{0,1\}^n$		**else** $\hat{k} \leftarrow_\$ \{0,1\}^n$
9 :	**return** $(e, \hat{k})$	**return** $(e, \hat{k})$		**return** $(e, \hat{k})$

$\text{OSubKgen}_{\text{HW}}(label')$		$\text{OSubKgen}_{\text{HW}}(label')$		$\text{OSubKgen}_{\text{HW}}(label')$
1 :	**assert** $label' \neq label$	**assert** $label' \neq label$		**assert** $label' \neq label$
2 :	$k'_{\text{HWs}} \leftarrow \text{PRF}(k_{\text{HWm}}, label')$	$k'_{\text{HWs}} \leftarrow \text{PRF}(k_{\text{HWm}}, label')$		$k'_{\text{HWs}} \leftarrow \text{PRF}(k_{\text{HWm}}, label')$
3 :	**return** k'_{HWs}	**return** k'_{HWs}		**return** k'_{HWs}

$$\boxed{\text{Game}^i_{15}(1^n)} \xleftarrow{\text{iO sec.}} \boxed{\text{Game}^i_{14}(1^n)} \xleftarrow{\text{PRG sec.}} \boxed{\text{Game}^i_{13}(1^n)}$$

$$\text{Game}^i_4(1^n) \xrightarrow{\text{iO sec.}} \text{Game}^i_5(1^n) \xrightarrow{\text{PRG sec.}} \text{Game}^i_6(1^n) \xrightarrow{\text{iO sec.}}$$

1 : $z \leftarrow_\$ \{0,1\}^n,\ \mathcal{Q} := \{z\}$	$z \leftarrow_\$ \{0,1\}^n,\ \mathcal{Q} := \{z\}$	$z \leftarrow_\$ \{0,1\}^n,\ \mathcal{Q} := \{z\}$
2 : $j \leftarrow 0$	$j \leftarrow 0$	$j \leftarrow 0$
3 : $label \leftarrow_\$ \mathcal{A}(1^n)$	$label \leftarrow_\$ \mathcal{A}(1^n)$	$label \leftarrow_\$ \mathcal{A}(1^n)$
4 : $k_{\text{kdf}} \leftarrow_\$ \{0,1\}^n$	$k_{\text{kdf}} \leftarrow_\$ \{0,1\}^n$	$k_{\text{kdf}} \leftarrow_\$ \{0,1\}^n$
5 :		
6 : $k \leftarrow \text{PPRF}(k_{\text{kdf}}, z)$	$k \leftarrow \text{PPRF}(k_{\text{kdf}}, z)$	$k \leftarrow \text{PPRF}(k_{\text{kdf}}, z)$
7 : $k_{\text{HWm}} \leftarrow_\$ \{0,1\}^n$	$k_{\text{HWm}} \leftarrow_\$ \{0,1\}^n$	$k_{\text{HWm}} \leftarrow_\$ \{0,1\}^n$
8 : $k_{\text{HWs}} \leftarrow_\$ \{0,1\}^n$	$k_{\text{HWs}} \leftarrow_\$ \{0,1\}^n$	$k_{\text{HWs}} \leftarrow_\$ \{0,1\}^n$
9 : $k_z \leftarrow_\$ \text{Punct}(k_{\text{HWs}}, z)$	$k_z \leftarrow_\$ \text{Punct}(k_{\text{HWs}}, z)$	$k_z \leftarrow_\$ \text{Punct}(k_{\text{HWs}}, z)$
10 : $\tau \leftarrow_\$ \{0,1\}^n$	$\tau \leftarrow_\$ \{0,1\}^n;\ y \leftarrow \text{PRG}(\tau)$	$y \leftarrow_\$ \{0,1\}^{2n}$
11 : $C \leftarrow C_2[k_{\text{kdf}}, z, k_z, \tau]$	$C \leftarrow C_3[k_{\text{kdf}}, z, k_z, y]$	$C \leftarrow C_3[k_{\text{kdf}}, z, k_z, y]$
12 : $\text{WKDF} \leftarrow_\$ \text{iO}(C, 1^n)$	$\text{WKDF} \leftarrow_\$ \text{iO}(C, 1^n)$	$\text{WKDF} \leftarrow_\$ \text{iO}(C, 1^n)$
13 : $b' \leftarrow_\$ \mathcal{A}^{\text{Resp}_{\text{HW}}, \text{OKDF}}_{\text{OSubKgen}}(\text{WKDF})$	$b' \leftarrow_\$ \mathcal{A}^{\text{Resp}_{\text{HW}}, \text{OKDF}}_{\text{OSubKgen}}(\text{WKDF})$	$b' \leftarrow_\$ \mathcal{A}^{\text{Resp}_{\text{HW}}, \text{OKDF}}_{\text{OSubKgen}}(\text{WKDF})$
14 : $\textbf{return } b'$	$\textbf{return } b'$	$\textbf{return } b'$

OResp(e)	OResp(e)	OResp(e)
1 : $\textbf{assert } e \notin \mathcal{Q}$	$\textbf{assert } e \notin \mathcal{Q}$	$\textbf{assert } e \notin \mathcal{Q}$
2 : $\mathcal{Q} := \mathcal{Q} \cup \{e\}$	$\mathcal{Q} := \mathcal{Q} \cup \{e\}$	$\mathcal{Q} := \mathcal{Q} \cup \{e\}$
3 : $y \leftarrow \text{Eval}(k_z, e, 1^n)$	$y \leftarrow \text{Eval}(k_z, e, 1^n)$	$y \leftarrow \text{Eval}(k_z, e, 1^n)$
4 : $\textbf{return } y$	$\textbf{return } y$	$\textbf{return } y$

OKDF()	OKDF()	OKDF()
1 : $j \leftarrow j+1$	$j \leftarrow j+1$	$j \leftarrow j+1$
2 : $\textbf{if } i = j\ \boxed{k' \leftarrow_\$ \{0,1\}^n}$	$\textbf{if } i = j\ \boxed{k' \leftarrow_\$ \{0,1\}^n}$	$\textbf{if } i = j\ \boxed{k' \leftarrow_\$ \{0,1\}^n}$
3 : $\textbf{return } (z, k)\ \boxed{(z, k')}$	$\textbf{return } (z, k)\ \boxed{(z, k')}$	$\textbf{return } (z, k)\ \boxed{(z, k')}$
4 : $\textbf{else } e \leftarrow_\$ \{0,1\}^n$	$\textbf{else } e \leftarrow_\$ \{0,1\}^n$	$\textbf{else } e \leftarrow_\$ \{0,1\}^n$
5 : $\mathcal{Q} := \mathcal{Q} \cup \{e\}$	$\mathcal{Q} := \mathcal{Q} \cup \{e\}$	$\mathcal{Q} := \mathcal{Q} \cup \{e\}$
6 : $\textbf{if } j > i$	$\textbf{if } j > i$	$\textbf{if } j > i$
7 : $\hat{k} \leftarrow \text{PPRF}(k_{\text{kdf}}, e)$	$\hat{k} \leftarrow \text{PPRF}(k_{\text{kdf}}, e)$	$\hat{k} \leftarrow \text{PPRF}(k_{\text{kdf}}, e)$
8 : $\textbf{else } \hat{k} \leftarrow_\$ \{0,1\}^n$	$\textbf{else } \hat{k} \leftarrow_\$ \{0,1\}^n$	$\textbf{else } \hat{k} \leftarrow_\$ \{0,1\}^n$
9 : $\textbf{return } (e, \hat{k})$	$\textbf{return } (e, \hat{k})$	$\textbf{return } (e, \hat{k})$

OSubKgen$_{\text{HW}}$($label'$)	OSubKgen$_{\text{HW}}$($label'$)	OSubKgen$_{\text{HW}}$($label'$)
1 : $\textbf{assert } label' \neq label$	$\textbf{assert } label' \neq label$	$\textbf{assert } label' \neq label$
2 : $k'_{\text{HWs}} \leftarrow \text{PRF}(k_{\text{HWm}}, label')$	$k'_{\text{HWs}} \leftarrow \text{PRF}(k_{\text{HWm}}, label')$	$k'_{\text{HWs}} \leftarrow \text{PRF}(k_{\text{HWm}}, label')$
3 : $\textbf{return } k'_{\text{HWs}}$	$\textbf{return } k'_{\text{HWs}}$	$\textbf{return } k'_{\text{HWs}}$

$\mathsf{Game}_{12}^i(1^n)$ ← PPRF security ← $\mathsf{Game}_{11}^i(1^n)$ ← iO/stat. gap ← $\mathsf{Game}_{10}^i(1^n)$ ←

$\mathsf{Game}_{7}^i(1^n)$ — PPRF security → $\mathsf{Game}_{8}^i(1^n)$ — iO/stat. gap → $\mathsf{Game}_{9}^i(1^n)$ → perfect

	$\mathsf{Game}_7^i(1^n)$	$\mathsf{Game}_8^i(1^n)$	$\mathsf{Game}_9^i(1^n)$
1:	$z \leftarrow_\$ \{0,1\}^n,\ \mathcal{Q} := \{z\}$	$z \leftarrow_\$ \{0,1\}^n,\ \mathcal{Q} := \{z\}$	$z \leftarrow_\$ \{0,1\}^n,\ \mathcal{Q} := \{z\}$
2:	$j \leftarrow 0$	$j \leftarrow 0$	$j \leftarrow 0$
3:	$label \leftarrow_\$ \mathcal{A}(1^n)$	$label \leftarrow_\$ \mathcal{A}(1^n)$	$label \leftarrow_\$ \mathcal{A}(1^n)$
4:	$k_{\mathrm{kdf}} \leftarrow_\$ \{0,1\}^n$	$k_{\mathrm{kdf}} \leftarrow_\$ \{0,1\}^n$	$k_{\mathrm{kdf}} \leftarrow_\$ \{0,1\}^n$
5:	$\boxed{k_{\mathrm{kdf}}^z \leftarrow_\$ \mathsf{Punct}(k_{\mathrm{kdf}}, z)}$	$k_{\mathrm{kdf}}^z \leftarrow_\$ \mathsf{Punct}(k_{\mathrm{kdf}}, z)$	$k_{\mathrm{kdf}}^z \leftarrow_\$ \mathsf{Punct}(k_{\mathrm{kdf}}, z)$
6:	$k \leftarrow \mathsf{PPRF}(k_{\mathrm{kdf}}, z)$	$\boxed{k \leftarrow \{0,1\}^n}$	$k \leftarrow_\$ \{0,1\}^n$
7:	$k_{\mathrm{HWm}} \leftarrow_\$ \{0,1\}^n$	$k_{\mathrm{HWm}} \leftarrow_\$ \{0,1\}^n$	$k_{\mathrm{HWm}} \leftarrow_\$ \{0,1\}^n$
8:	$k_{\mathrm{HWs}} \leftarrow_\$ \{0,1\}^n$	$k_{\mathrm{HWs}} \leftarrow_\$ \{0,1\}^n$	$k_{\mathrm{HWs}} \leftarrow_\$ \{0,1\}^n$
9:	$k_z \leftarrow_\$ \mathsf{Punct}(k_{\mathrm{HWs}}, z)$	$k_z \leftarrow_\$ \mathsf{Punct}(k_{\mathrm{HWs}}, z)$	$k_z \leftarrow_\$ \mathsf{Punct}(k_{\mathrm{HWs}}, z)$
10:	$y \leftarrow_\$ \{0,1\}^{2n}$	$y \leftarrow_\$ \{0,1\}^{2n}$	$y \leftarrow_\$ \{0,1\}^{2n}$
11:	$\mathsf{C} \leftarrow \mathsf{C}_4[k_{\mathrm{kdf}}^z, z, k_z, y, k]$	$\mathsf{C} \leftarrow \mathsf{C}_4[k_{\mathrm{kdf}}^z, z, k_z, y, k]$	$\boxed{\mathsf{C} \leftarrow \mathsf{C}_5[k_{\mathrm{kdf}}^z, z, k_z, y]}$
12:	$\mathsf{WKDF} \leftarrow_\$ \mathsf{iO}(\mathsf{C}, 1^n)$	$\mathsf{WKDF} \leftarrow_\$ \mathsf{iO}(\mathsf{C}, 1^n)$	$\mathsf{WKDF} \leftarrow_\$ \mathsf{iO}(\mathsf{C}, 1^n)$
13:	$b' \leftarrow_\$ \mathcal{A}_{\mathsf{OSubKgen}}^{\mathsf{Resp}_{\mathrm{HW}}, \mathsf{OKDF}}(\mathsf{WKDF})$	$b' \leftarrow_\$ \mathcal{A}_{\mathsf{OSubKgen}}^{\mathsf{Resp}_{\mathrm{HW}}, \mathsf{OKDF}}(\mathsf{WKDF})$	$b' \leftarrow_\$ \mathcal{A}_{\mathsf{OSubKgen}}^{\mathsf{Resp}_{\mathrm{HW}}, \mathsf{OKDF}}(\mathsf{WKDF})$
14:	**return** b'	**return** b'	**return** b'

	$\mathsf{OResp}(e)$	$\mathsf{OResp}(e)$	$\mathsf{OResp}(e)$
1:	**assert** $e \notin \mathcal{Q}$	**assert** $e \notin \mathcal{Q}$	**assert** $e \notin \mathcal{Q}$
2:	$\mathcal{Q} := \mathcal{Q} \cup \{e\}$	$\mathcal{Q} := \mathcal{Q} \cup \{e\}$	$\mathcal{Q} := \mathcal{Q} \cup \{e\}$
3:	$y \leftarrow \mathsf{Eval}(k_z, e, 1^n)$	$y \leftarrow \mathsf{Eval}(k_z, e, 1^n)$	$y \leftarrow \mathsf{Eval}(k_z, e, 1^n)$
4:	**return** y	**return** y	**return** y

	$\mathsf{OKDF}()$	$\mathsf{OKDF}()$	$\mathsf{OKDF}()$
1:	$j \leftarrow j+1$	$j \leftarrow j+1$	$j \leftarrow j+1$
2:	**if** $i = j$ $\boxed{k' \leftarrow_\$ \{0,1\}^n}$	**if** $i = j$ $\boxed{k' \leftarrow_\$ \{0,1\}^n}$	**if** $i = j$ $\boxed{k' \leftarrow_\$ \{0,1\}^n}$
3:	**return** (z, k) $\boxed{(z, k')}$	**return** (z, k) $\boxed{(z, k')}$	**return** (z, k) $\boxed{(z, k')}$
4:	**else** $e \leftarrow_\$ \{0,1\}^n$	**else** $e \leftarrow_\$ \{0,1\}^n$	**else** $e \leftarrow_\$ \{0,1\}^n$
5:	$\mathcal{Q} := \mathcal{Q} \cup \{e\}$	$\mathcal{Q} := \mathcal{Q} \cup \{e\}$	$\mathcal{Q} := \mathcal{Q} \cup \{e\}$
6:	**if** $j > i$	**if** $j > i$	**if** $j > i$
7:	$\boxed{\hat{k} \leftarrow \mathsf{Eval}(k_{\mathrm{kdf}}^z, e)}$	$\hat{k} \leftarrow \mathsf{Eval}(k_{\mathrm{kdf}}^z, e)$	$\hat{k} \leftarrow \mathsf{Eval}(k_{\mathrm{kdf}}^z, e)$
8:	**else** $\hat{k} \leftarrow_\$ \{0,1\}^n$	**else** $\hat{k} \leftarrow_\$ \{0,1\}^n$	**else** $\hat{k} \leftarrow_\$ \{0,1\}^n$
9:	**return** $(e, \hat{k})$	**return** $(e, \hat{k})$	**return** $(e, \hat{k})$

	$\mathsf{OSubKgen}_{\mathrm{HW}}(label')$	$\mathsf{OSubKgen}_{\mathrm{HW}}(label')$	$\mathsf{OSubKgen}_{\mathrm{HW}}(label')$
1:	**assert** $label' \neq label$	**assert** $label' \neq label$	**assert** $label' \neq label$
2:	$k'_{\mathrm{HWs}} \leftarrow \mathsf{PRF}(k_{\mathrm{HWm}}, label')$	$k'_{\mathrm{HWs}} \leftarrow \mathsf{PRF}(k_{\mathrm{HWm}}, label')$	$k'_{\mathrm{HWs}} \leftarrow \mathsf{PRF}(k_{\mathrm{HWm}}, label')$
3:	**return** k'_{HWs}	**return** k'_{HWs}	**return** k'_{HWs}

We now reduce each game-hop to the underlying assumption. We omit boiler-plate code for simulations and focus instead on describing the conceptual argument that underlies the reduction. We discuss the game-hops in the forward direction. The reductions for the backward direction proceed analogously.

Game 1 to Game 2. This game hop reduces to the PRF security of the PRF keyed with $k_{\texttt{HWm}}$. We here rely on the fact that $\mathsf{OSubKgen}_{\texttt{HW}}(label')$ does not allow to query $\mathsf{PRF}(k_{\texttt{HWm}}, \cdot)$ on $label$.

Game 2 to Game 3. This game hop reduces to iO security and relies on the correctness of the PPRF. The correctness of the PPRF implies that the first two lines of C_1 and C_2 are equivalent, which allows to apply iO security. Note that the oracle OResp cannot be queried on z since z is added to $\mathcal{Q}$ in the very beginning of the game. Therefore, it suffices to use the punctured key k_z in OResp.

Game 3 to Game 4. This game hop reduces to the IND-PPRF security of PPRF keyed with $k_{\texttt{HWs}}$ and punctured at z. For the reduction, it is important to note that throughout the game, only punctured versions k_z of $k_{\texttt{HWs}}$ are used, except for calculating τ.

Game 4 to Game 5. This game hop replaces $C_2[k_{\texttt{kdf}}, z, k_z, \tau]$ by $C_3[k_{\texttt{kdf}}, z, k_z, y]$ and relies on iO security. Instead of hardcoding τ into C_2 and computing y as $\mathsf{PRG}(\tau)$ within circuit C_2, the value $y = \mathsf{PRG}(\tau)$ is directly hardcoded into circuit C_3. As the two circuits are functionally equivalent, the game hop reduces to iO security.

Game 5 to Game 6. This game hop replaces $y = \mathsf{PRG}(\tau)$ by a randomly sampled value y. This game hop reduces to PRG security, since the variable τ that is sampled in $\mathsf{Game}_5^i(1^n)$ is not used anywhere else in the game(s).

Game 6 to Game 7. This game hop reduces to iO security with an additional negligible statistical loss. In detail, the uniformity of the sampling of z from $\{0,1\}^n$ ensures that, with overwhelming probability, the oracle OKDF does not return $(e, *)$ for a different than the ith query of $\mathcal{A}$ to the OKDF oracle, i.e., the change to OKDF yields a negligible statistical difference between $\mathsf{Game}_6^i(1^n)$ and $\mathsf{Game}_7^i(1^n)$. The more important change is the use of $k_{\texttt{kdf}}^z$ in C_4. Due to the correctness of the puncturable PRF, the circuits C_3 and C_4 are functionally equivalent and thus, this game hop can be reduced to iO security.

Game 7 to Game 8. This game hop reduces to the IND-PPRF security of PPRF, keyed with $k_{\texttt{kdf}}$ and punctured at z. For the reduction, it is important to note that throughout the game, only the punctured version $k_{\texttt{kdf}}^z$ of $k_{\texttt{kdf}}$ is used, except for calculating k.

Game 8 to Game 9. Note that with overwhelming probability, y is not in the image of the PRG, since the image of the PRG is of size 2^n only, whereas y is sampled from a set of size 2^{2n}. Therefore, y is most likely outside the image of the PRG. If it is, then the circuits C_4 and C_5 are functionally equivalent as the **if** condition in the first line of C_4 cannot be satisfied by any input. Thus, this game hop reduces to iO security.

Game 9 to Game 10. Importantly, C_5 does not depend on k anymore and thus, it is perfectly indistinguishable for the adversary whether the OKDF uses k or an independently drawn value k' that OKDF samples in the moment of the ith query.

Game 10 to Game 18. These game hops are analogous in the backward direction. Note that k is not used in OKDF anymore in the game hops from Game 10 to Game 18.

Connecting the Hybrids. We now show that Eq. 4 holds, which we recall is

$$\text{Game}_{18}^{i} \approx \text{Game}_{1}^{i+1}$$

On a high-level, Game_{18}^{i} and Game_{1}^{i+1} are identical since they both sample the first $i + 1$ keys in the OKDF oracle at random and compute the remaining keys using the PPRF. Note that Game_{18}^{i} and Game_{1}^{i+1} are only identical up to a negligible statistical difference since the pre-sampled value z is consumed at query i to the OKDF oracle in Game_{18}^{i} and only in query $i+1$ in Game_{1}^{i+1}. However, as z is sampled uniformly at random from $\{0,1\}^n$, z remains statistically hidden from the adversary until it is returned as an output from the OKDF oracle. Thus, it is infeasible to determine when the pre-sampled value z was returned. We omit a detailed code-comparison, since it is quite simple.

Connecting the Hybrids to the Original Game. Finally, we show Eq. 1 and Eq. 2. We start with the former which we recall is

$$\text{Exp}_{\mathcal{A},0}^{\text{IND-WKDF}} \approx \text{Game}_{1}^{0}.$$

On a high-level, $\text{Exp}_{\mathcal{A},0}^{\text{IND-WKDF}}$ and Game_{1}^{0} are identical since they both compute all keys in the OKDF oracle using the PPRF. Moreover, due to the correctness of the hardware module, it is functionally equivalent to use $\text{PPRF}(k_{\text{HWs}}, e, 1^n)$ and $\text{PPRF}(\text{PRF}(k_{\text{HWm}}, e, 1^n))$ in oracle OResp. However, there is a negligible statistical difference between $\text{Exp}_{\mathcal{A},0}^{\text{IND-WKDF}}$ and Game_{1}^{0}, since Game_{1}^{0} pre-samples a uniformly random value z from $\{0,1\}^n$, while $\text{Exp}_{\mathcal{A},0}^{\text{IND-WKDF}}$ does not. However, as z is sampled uniformly at random, it remains statistically hidden from the adversary until it is returned as an output from the OKDF oracle. We omit a detailed code-comparison, since it is quite simple. The reasoning for Eq. 2 is analogous, which concludes the proof of Theorem 1.   □

4   Secure Payment Application

In this section we build a secure payment scheme, assuming an IND-WKDF-secure WKDF, as constructed in the previous section. As mentioned before, the main idea of the construction of the payment application is to bind a symmetric encryption scheme (that is only known to provide black-box security) on top of the WKDF via a layer of indistinguishability obfuscation and thereby bootstrap the security of the WKDF to the security of the symmetric encryption scheme and the entire payment application.

We start with describing the process flow of an abstract payment application, illustrated in Fig. 6. Note that this abstract payment application might also be implementable differently than assuming a WKDF. A payment application relies on a hardware module (see Definition 11), which we recall has a main hardware key k_{HWm}, allows to derive sub-keys $k_{HWs} \leftarrow \mathtt{SubKgen}(k_{HWm}, label)$ from the main hardware key and allows to obtain MAC/PRF values $\sigma \leftarrow \mathtt{Resp}_{HW}(k_{HWm}, label, x)$ that can be verified outside of the hardware via the algorithm $\mathtt{Check}_{SW}(k_{HWs}, x, \sigma)$ that returns 0 or 1.

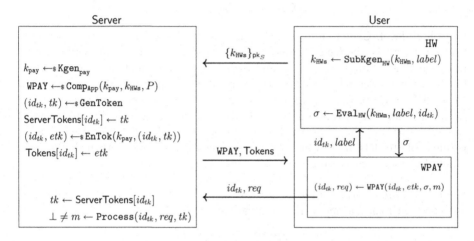

Fig. 6. Diagram of our payment scheme. The hardware calculates the value σ via the $\mathtt{Eval}_{HW}$ function on input id_{tk}, the label and the master key. WPAY executes the $\mathtt{Check}_{SW}$ function on input σ and on the sub-key and id_{tk}.

As the payment application is bound to a hardware module, the user starts by deriving a hardware sub-key $k_{HWs} \leftarrow \mathtt{SubKgen}(k_{HWm}, label)$ in their hardware and transmit it securely to the server. In Fig. 6, we hint at this secure transmission of k_{HWs} via an encryption under the server's public-key $\mathtt{pk}_S$. In our model, we later refrain from modeling this off-band transmission of k_{HWs} and simply assume that it is implemented securely.

The server then draws a symmetric key k_{pay} for the user and binds it to the user's hardware sub-key k_{HWs} via the compilation algorithm $\mathtt{Comp}_{App}$:

$$\mathtt{WPAY} \leftarrow_\$ \mathtt{Comp}_{App}(k_{pay}, k_{HWs}, P).$$

The predicate function P restricts the set of valid messages that can be encrypted via WPAY. An example for useful restrictions are limits on the amount of the payment or hardcoding of the user's payment data. Note that potentially, P can also contain cryptographic functionalities (which we do not model).

As we consider a tokenized payment scheme, in addition to WPAY the server also generates several tokens, encrypts them under k_{pay} and stores the encrypted tokens in an array Tokens that is indexed by token identifiers. It then transmits WPAY to the user, together with the array Tokens, see Fig. 6.

Now, the user can use WPAY to generate requests to the server. To do so, WPAY takes as input a message m as well as a pair of a token identifier id_{tk} and its corresponding encrypted token etk. Conceptually, the goal of WPAY is to return a request req to the server that contains an encryption of m under the unencrypted token contained in etk. To facilitate verification on the server's side, the user's WPAY will also return the token identifier id_{tk}:

$$(id_{tk}, req) \leftarrow \text{WPAY}(id_{tk}, etk, \sigma, m)$$

Importantly, in addition to the aforementioned inputs, WPAY also takes as input σ, which is a hardware value obtained from making an Resp_{HW} query to the hardware for $(label, id_{tk})$. To ensure the hardware-binding, conceptually, WPAY needs to evaluate the algorithm $\text{Check}_{\text{SW}}(k_{\text{HWs}}, id_{tk}, \sigma)$ internally and only perform the desired operations based on this check succeeding. Intuitively, the Check_{SW} operation also needs to be bound to all further operations of WPAY.

Finally, upon receiving (id_{tk}, req), the server retrieves the token tk corresponding to id_{tk} and processes the request req via the algorithm Process. If the request is accepted, Process returns the message m that the client encrypted. Else, Process returns an error symbol $\bot$.

Note that we require the server to know the secret key k_{pay} to encrypt the tokens under k_{pay} before sending it to the user. The advantage of this design is that the values of the tokens are not exposed before being stored. Note that we consider the server to be a trusted and secure party which is a necessary assumption: As the server is in charge of generating the tokens, the server knows the token values anyway. Thus, the server additionally knowing the value of the secret key k_{kdf} of the user does not compromise the security of the mobile payment application from the perspective of the user.

Definition 14 (Hardware-Bound White-Box Payment Scheme). *A hardware-bound white-box payment scheme* WPAY *is parameterized with a message length parameter $\ell(n)$ and consists of a hardware module* HWM *and the following algorithms:*

- $k_{\text{pay}} \leftarrow_{\$} \text{Kgen}_{\text{pay}}(1^n)$: *This randomized algorithm takes as input the security parameter and outputs the secret payment key k_{pay};*
- $(id_{tk}, tk) \leftarrow_{\$} \text{GenToken}(1^n)$: *This randomized algorithm takes as input the security parameter and returns a token tk and a token identifier id_{tk}, where we assume that identifiers are unique with overwhelming probability;*
- $(id_{tk}, etk) \leftarrow_{\$} \text{EnTok}(k_{\text{pay}}, (id_{tk}, tk))$: *This randomized algorithm takes as input a token tk together with its corresponding identifier id_{tk} and outputs an encrypted token etk, together with its corresponding token identifier id_{tk};*
- $\text{WPAY} \leftarrow_{\$} \text{Comp}_{\text{App}}(k_{\text{pay}}, k_{\text{HWs}}, P)$: *This randomized algorithm takes as input a payment key k_{pay}, a hardware-binding key k_{HWs} and a message filtering predicate $P : \{0,1\}^{\ell(n)} \rightarrow \{0,1\}$. It outputs a white-box payment application* WPAY *with syntax $(id_{tk}, req) \leftarrow \text{WPAY}(id_{tk}, etk, \sigma, m)$, where σ denotes a hardware*

value σ, $m \in \{0,1\}^{\ell(n)}$ denotes a payment message, and req constitutes a payment request;

- $m \leftarrow$ Process(id_{tk}, req, tk) : This deterministic algorithm takes as input a token identifier id_{tk}, a token value tk and a a request req. It outputs a message m or $\perp$.

Moreover, we require that the following correctness property holds: For all keys k_{pay}, for all main hardware keys k_{HWm}, for all pairs of tokens and token identifier (id_{tk}, tk), for all predicates P, for all messages $m \in \{0,1\}^{\ell(n)}$ such that $P(m) = 1$, for $\sigma = \text{Resp}_{HW}(k_{HWm}, label, id_{tk})$, it holds that

$$\Pr[\text{Process}(\text{WPAY}(id_{tk}, etk, \sigma, m), tk) = m] = 1,$$

where the probability is taken over compiling $\text{WPAY} \leftarrow_\$ \text{Comp}_{App}(k_{pay}, k_{HWs}, P)$ and encrypting the token $(id_{tk}, etk) \leftarrow_\$ \text{EnTok}(k_{pay}, (id_{tk}, tk))$.

4.1   Security of White-Box Payment Applications

We now specify security of a white-box payment application scheme WPAY. Correctness of WPAY ensures that when having access to the hardware, the application WPAY is useful to generate payment requests. In turn, hardware-binding security ensures that when not having access to the hardware, then the application becomes useless. In other words, in absence of the hardware, the adversary cannot generate new requests and does not learn anything about the content of the requests sent to the server. Thus, the desired security properties in the absence of the hardware are the following:

(1) Integrity of the requests transmitted from user to server.
(2) Confidentiality of the messages contained in the requests transmitted from user to server.

We capture both properties via the IND-WPAY security game, depicted in Fig. 7. IND-WPAY starts with a setup phase where the relevant keys are sampled, first for the hardware (line 3 and 4) and then for the payment application (line 5). Then, WPAY is compiled (line 6). Note that we allow the adversary to choose the filter function P, modeling that security should hold for all possible filter functions. We also allow the adversary to choose the hardware label. In practice, neither P nor label are adversarially chosen, but giving this ability to the adversary in the setup phase only makes our model stronger. Note that we consider our adversary as stateful, i.e., the adversary in the setup phase (line 2) shares state with the adversary that accesses oracles (line 7) in order to find out the secret bit b. As the adversary is a white-box adversary, it receives the compiled WPAY as input (line 7). We now turn to the explanation of the oracles.

Oracles OResp and OSubKgen model the adversary's hardware access. Upon querying OResp, a pair of token and its respective identifier are sampled at random. The value of the token identifier is used for generating the hardware value σ, and the oracle returns all three values. The adversary is thus able to

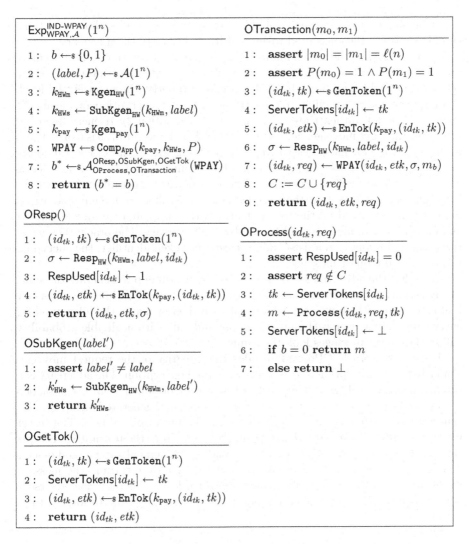

Fig. 7. $\mathsf{Exp}_{\mathsf{WPAY},\mathcal{A}}^{\mathsf{IND\text{-}WPAY}}(1^n)$ game capturing integrity and confidentiality.

run their own WPAY to generate a request message for that specific token, token id and hardware value.

OSubKgen lets the adversary observe hardware sub-key values. Such values could be values used by different applications or values from older versions of a payment application. To avoid trivial attacks, the adversary is not allowed to obtain the sub-key k_{HWs} that was used for compiling the white-box application WPAY (line 6 in the main $\mathsf{Exp}_{\mathsf{WPAY},\mathcal{A}}^{\mathsf{IND\text{-}WPAY}}$ procedure).

Oracle OGetTok models generation and encryption of the tokens on the server's side and storing them in a list. We recall that a white-box adversary might be able to access the encrypted tokens stored on a user's phone and thus, OGetTok returns the encrypted token and its identifier to the adversary.

We now turn to the two remaining oracles that encode the desired security properties of confidentiality and integrity. We start with the transaction oracle OTransaction, which encodes the confidentiality property. On a conceptual level, OTransaction plays a similar role as the left-or-right encryption oracle in the security game for authenticated encryption (cf. Definition 2): It encrypts either the left or the right message, depending on whether the secret bit b is 0 or 1. Upon submitting the two messages to the OTransaction oracle, the oracle randomly samples a pair of a token and its respective identifier and the token value is encrypted via the EnTok algorithm. The oracle then generates the necessary hardware value σ based on the sampled token identifier, and then generates a request message based on the token identifier, the encrypted token, the value σ and one of the two messages submitted by the adversary. The oracle then saves the generated request on a list C and returns the token identifier, the encrypted token and the request message.

Note that the adversary is not able to use their own app to generate the same request message received by the transaction oracle. Namely, while the adversary is able to choose which message to encrypt with their own app, the token used for encrypting the message is chosen at random and only with negligible probability will both request messages look the same.

The process oracle OProcess encodes the integrity of the request messages similarly to the decryption oracle in authenticated encryption. The adversary can submit arbitrary values as long as those were not obtained from OTransaction (check if they are in the set C) or if they were not generated using an id_{tk} generated by the OResp oracle for generating the hardware value σ. The server retrieves (line 3) the token tk corresponding to id_{tk} from the token list, decrypts (line 4) the request req with id_{tk} and tk using the Process algorithm and deletes tk from the token list. Authenticity is modeled by only returning the message to the adversary if $b = 0$ and returning an error if $b = 1$. Thereby, the adversary is able to learn the secret bit b whenever the adversary is able to forge a fresh request.

Remark. Note that many useful properties are implied by our security definition. For instance, IND-WPAY security implies that the token values remain secret, unless the adversary queries the hardware on id_{tk}.

Definition 15 (IND-WPAY Security). *A hardware-bound white-box payment application scheme* WPAY *is said to be* IND-WPAY*-secure if all PPT adversaries $\mathcal{A}$ have negligible distinguishing advantage in the game* $\mathsf{Exp}_{\mathsf{WPAY},\mathcal{A}}^{\mathsf{IND\text{-}WPAY}}(1^n)$ *as specified in Fig. 7.*

4.2 Construction of White-Box Payment Scheme

We now construct a white-box payment scheme WPAY, which is IND-WPAY-secure (see Fig. 7), assuming the IND-WKDF-security of a white-box key derivation function WKDF (see Fig. 5). We first give an overview of the algorithms of our construction. First, Kgen_{pay} randomly samples a payment key k_{pay} and the GenToken algorithm randomly samples a token tk and its respective identifier id_{tk}. EnTok encrypts a token tk in the following way: For each token with the identifier id_{tk}, it generates a key $\hat{k} \leftarrow \text{KDF}(k_{\text{pay}}, id_{tk})$, and uses an authenticated encryption scheme to encrypt the token using $\hat{k}$. That is, each token is encrypted using a different key. Note that each key is generated based on the same key k_{pay}, but based on a different context value id_{tk} since each token has a unique identifier.

$\underline{\text{Kgen}_{\text{pay}}(1^n)}$

1 : $k_{\text{kdf}} \leftarrow_{\$} \text{Kgen}(1^n)$

2 : $k_{\text{pay}} \leftarrow k_{\text{kdf}}$

3 : **return** k_{pay}

$\underline{\text{Comp}_{\text{App}}(k_{\text{pay}}, k_{\text{HWs}}, P)}$

1 : $\text{WKDF} \leftarrow_{\$} \text{Comp}(k_{\text{pay}}, k_{\text{HWs}})$

2 : $\text{WPAY} \leftarrow_{\$} \text{iO}(\text{C}[\text{WKDF}, P])$

3 : **return** WPAY

$\underline{\text{Process}(id_{tk}, req, tk)}$

1 : $nc \leftarrow id_{tk}$

2 : $c_2 \leftarrow req$

3 : $m' \leftarrow \text{Dec}_2(tk, c_2, nc)$

4 : **return** m'

$\underline{\text{GenToken}(1^n)}$

1 : $tk \leftarrow_{\$} \{0,1\}^n$

2 : $id_{tk} \leftarrow_{\$} \{0,1\}^n$

3 : **return** (id_{tk}, tk)

$\underline{\text{EnTok}(k_{\text{pay}}, (id_{tk}, tk))}$

1 : $nc \leftarrow id_{tk}$

2 : $e \leftarrow id_{tk}$

3 : $\hat{k} \leftarrow \text{KDF}(k_{\text{pay}}, e)$

4 : $c_1 \leftarrow \text{Enc}_1(\hat{k}, tk, nc)$

5 : $etk \leftarrow c_1$

6 : **return** (id_{tk}, etk)

$\underline{\text{C}[\text{WKDF}, P](id_{tk}, etk, \sigma, m)}$

1 : $e \leftarrow id_{tk}$

2 : $nc \leftarrow id_{tk}$

3 : $c_1 \leftarrow etk$

4 : $\hat{k} \leftarrow \text{WKDF}(e, \sigma)$

5 : $tk \leftarrow \text{Dec}_1(\hat{k}, c_1, nc)$

6 : **if** $|m| = \ell(n)$ **and** $P(m) = 1$

7 : $\quad c_2 \leftarrow \text{Enc}_2(tk, m, nc)$

8 : $\quad req \leftarrow c_2$

9 : **else** $req \leftarrow \bot$

10 : **return** (id_{tk}, req)

Fig. 8. Construction of a WPAY scheme

The compilation algorithm Comp_{App} of the payment scheme takes as input a payment key k_{pay}, a sub-key value k_{HWs} as well as a message filtering predicate P. It uses the compilation algorithm Comp of the WKDF and runs it on $(k_{\text{pay}}, k_{\text{HWs}})$ to obtain a hardware-bound white-box program WKDF. It then runs indistinguishability obfuscation on a circuit $\text{C}[\text{WKDF}, P]$ and returns the output of the obfuscation as WPAY. The circuit $\text{C}[\text{WKDF}, P]$ and WPAY provide the same functionality, but in WPAY, due to the layer of obfuscation, one should not be able to separate the different operations from each other (see the discussion below). $\text{C}[\text{WKDF}, P]$ takes as input a pair (id_{tk}, etk) of an encrypted token and its token identifier as well as a hardware value σ and a message m. It first runs WKDF on (id_{tk}, σ) to obtain an output $\hat{k}$, and recall that the security of WKDF ensures that $\hat{k}$ is only a KDF (and not an error value) if σ is the correct hardware value that yields $\text{Check}_{\text{SW}}(k_{\text{HWs}}, id_{tk}, \sigma) = 1$. Thus, the hardware-binding of WPAY is directly inherited from the hardware-binding of WKDF. Now, $\text{C}[\text{WKDF}, P]$ uses $\hat{k}$ to decrypt the etk (line 5), checks whether $P(m) = 1$ (line 6) and, if so, encrypts the message m using the token tk as key (line 7–8) and returns the resulting ciphertext as a request message *req* along with the token identifier (line 10). Note that in the construction, we need to avoid the use of randomness, since we cannot rely on the randomness being honestly generated. Thus, we use a nonce-based encryption scheme, and the nonce *nc* used for encryption of the token is not only retrieved (line 2) for decryption of the token (line 5), but also re-used for encrypting the request (line 7). Note that the nonce in *etk* is not malleable since we encrypt the tokens with an authenticated encryption scheme which provides ciphertext integrity.

Recall that WPAY returns not only *req* but also the token identifier id_{tk} of the token that was used to encrypt m. This is because the use of *tk* authenticates the user towards the server which, on its side, retrieves the token *tk* corresponding to id_{tk}, and runs the Process algorithm on (req, tk) which decrypts *req* with *tk* and returns the result.

Construction 4. *Based on two authenticated encryption schemes* $(\mathrm{Enc}_1, \mathrm{Dec}_1)$, $(\mathrm{Enc}_2, \mathrm{Dec}_2)$ *and the* WKDF *in Construction 3, we construct a* white-box payment scheme with hardware-binding WPAY = $(\mathrm{Kgen}_{\mathrm{pay}}, \mathrm{GenToken}, \mathrm{EnTok},$ $\mathrm{Comp}_{\mathrm{App}}, \mathrm{Process})$ *as detailed in Fig. 8.*

On the use of iO. As mentioned above, the compiler of the payment application in our construction applies indistinguishability obfuscation to the circuit describing the application (see line 2 of $\mathrm{Comp}_{\mathrm{App}}$ in Fig. 8). We obfuscate WPAY with the following purposes. First we may wish to ensure the confidentiality of internal variables, such as the outputs of the WKDF and the raw value of the tokens. Second, by obfuscating the program we can also ensure that no operation can be separated from the rest, achieving thus a form of application binding. We note however that in the security proof provided for the theorem below, we do not prove any of these properties. Namely our IND-WPAY security model does not capture any form of application binding for the WPAY and only captures confidentiality for tokens and other internal variables for the cases that an adversary does not have access to the determined hardware.

Thus, our construction directly derives its security from the WKDF and could also be proven secure even without using any form of obfuscation. However we choose to obfuscate WPAY still, given that in practice, one would usually apply one layer of obfuscation to the application in order to increase its robustness. We note however that our model could be extended in order to capture some type of application binding property, which could then be achieved by using iO on our construction, as long as the relevant primitives used within the applications are puncturable. For instance, one could challenge the adversary with providing the output $\hat{k}$ of the WKDF for a given context value e. Here, we could puncture the WKDF (which is itself constructed from puncturable PRFs) and also puncture the decryption algorithm as follows. For one ciphertext c^*, hardcode its corresponding token value tk^* and output tk^* every time c^* is provided as input. For all other ciphertexts, perform a normal decryption. Note that hardcoding the corresponding token value of a given ciphertext is possible, since the tokens are generated and encrypted in advance (see the GenToken and EnTok processes).

Given both, the puncturable WKDF and the puncturable decryption program, we can effectively apply indistinguishability obfuscation and ensure that an adversary cannot separate the WKDF from the decryption and cannot extract any value $\hat{k}$.

Theorem 2. *Let* $(\mathsf{Enc}_1, \mathsf{Dec}_1)$ *and* $(\mathsf{Enc}_2, \mathsf{Dec}_2)$ *be two* AE-*secure symmetric encryption schemes, let* WKDF *be a* IND-WKDF-*secure white-box key derivation scheme, and let* iO *be an indistinguishability obfuscator for appropriate p-admissible samplers. Then the white-box payment scheme* WPAY *in Construction 4 is* IND-WPAY-*secure.*

In the following we provide a short sketch of the proof. The full details can be found on the full version of this paper [2].

Proof Sketch. Let $\mathcal{A}$ be a PPT adversary. Let $\mathsf{Exp}_{\mathcal{A},0}^{\mathsf{IND\text{-}WPAY}}$ denote the IND-WPAY game with $b = 0$ hardcoded and let $\mathsf{Exp}_{\mathcal{A},1}^{\mathsf{IND\text{-}WPAY}}$ denote the IND-WPAY game with $b = 1$ hardcoded. We need to show that $\mathcal{A}$ has negligible distinguishing advantage, i.e., that the probability that $\mathcal{A}$ returns 1 in $\mathsf{Exp}_{\mathcal{A},0}^{\mathsf{IND\text{-}WPAY}}$ differs from the probability that $\mathcal{A}$ returns 1 in $\mathsf{Exp}_{\mathcal{A},1}^{\mathsf{IND\text{-}WPAY}}$ at most by a negligible amount.

On a high-level, the security proof proceeds as follows. (1) We replace all keys generated by the WKDF with random keys in OTransaction and OGetTok and reduce this game hop to the security of the WKDF. (2) In the OTransaction and OGetTok oracles, instead of encrypting the tokens tk with SE_1, we encrypt $0^{|tk|}$. To do so, we make a hybrid argument over the number of queries that the adversary makes to OTransaction and OGetTok and for each such query make a reduction to the AE security of SE_1. (3) In the OTransaction oracle, instead of encrypting m_0, we now encrypt m_1. At the same time, in the OProcess oracle, we do not perform decryptions anymore but rather answer all adversarial queries by $\perp$. This proof again proceeds via a hybrid argument over the number of queries to OTransaction and OGetTok, since one token value is generated in each of these calls and we need to reduce to the security to each of them. (4) We now de-idealize SE_1 again and encrypt the real token values. (5) We de-idealize the WKDF. The full technical details appear in the full version of the paper.

Acknowledgments. Marc Fischlin has been [co-]funded by the Deutsche Forschungsgemeinschaft (DFG, German Research Foundation) – 251805230/GRK 2050. Christian Janson has been [co-]funded by the Deutsche Forschungsgemeinschaft (DFG) – SFB 1119 – 236615297.

References

1. Alpirez Bock, E., et al.: White-box cryptography: don't forget about grey-box attacks. J. Cryptol. February 2019
2. Alpirez Bock, E., Brzuska, C., Fischlin, M., Janson, C., Michiels, W.: Security reductions for white-box key-storage in mobile payments. Cryptology ePrint Archive, Report 2019/1014 (2019). https://eprint.iacr.org/2019/1014

3. Android Developers. Build. Class Documentation, Last retrieved: October 2018. https://developer.android.com/reference/android/os/Build
4. Android Developers. Keystore. Class Documentation, Last retrieved: October 2018. https://developer.android.com/reference/java/security/KeyStore
5. Android Developers. Telephony manager. Class Documentation, Last retrieved: October 2018. https://developer.android.com/reference/android/telephony/TelephonyManager
6. Apon, D. Huang, Y., Katz, J., Malozemoff, A.J.: Implementing cryptographic program obfuscation. Cryptology ePrint Archive, Report 2014/779 (2014). http://eprint.iacr.org/2014/779
7. Avoine, G., et al.: Security of distance-bounding: a survey. ACM Comput. Surv. **51**(5), 94:1–94:33 (2019)
8. Banik, S., Bogdanov, A., Isobe, T., Jepsen, M.B.: Analysis of software countermeasures for whitebox encryption. IACR Trans. Symm. Cryptol. **2017**(1), 307–328 (2017)
9. Bellare, M., Namprempre, C.: Authenticated encryption: relations among notions and analysis of the generic composition paradigm. In: Okamoto, T. (ed.) ASIACRYPT 2000. LNCS, vol. 1976, pp. 531–545. Springer, Heidelberg (2000). https://doi.org/10.1007/3-540-44448-3_41
10. Bellare, M., Stepanovs, I., Waters, B.: New negative results on differing-inputs obfuscation. In: Fischlin, M., Coron, J.-S. (eds.) EUROCRYPT 2016. LNCS, vol. 9666, pp. 792–821. Springer, Heidelberg (2016). https://doi.org/10.1007/978-3-662-49896-5_28
11. Biryukov, A., Bouillaguet, C., Khovratovich, D.: Cryptographic schemes based on the ASASA structure: black-box, white-box, and public-key (extended abstract). In: Sarkar, P., Iwata, T. (eds.) ASIACRYPT 2014. Part I, volume 8873 of LNCS, pp. 63–84. Springer, Heidelberg (2014)
12. Bocek, T., Killer, C., Tsiaras, C., Stiller, B.: An nfc relay attack with off-the-shelf hardware and software. In: Badonnel, R., Koch, R., Pras, A., Drašar, M., Stiller, B. (eds.) Management and Security in the Age of Hyperconnectivity. pp, pp. 71–83. Springer, Cham (2016)
13. Alpirez Bock, E., Amadori, A., Bos, J.W., Brzuska, C., Michiels, W.: Doubly half-injective prgs for incompressible white-box cryptography. In: Matsui, M. (ed.) CT-RSA 2019. LNCS, vol. 11405, pp. 189–209. Springer, Cham (2019). https://doi.org/10.1007/978-3-030-12612-4_10
14. Bock, E.A., Amadori, A., Brzuska, C., Michiels, W.: On the security goals of white-box cryptography. IACR TCHES, **2020**(2), 327–357 (2020). https://tches.iacr.org/index.php/TCHES/article/view/8554
15. Bogdanov, A., Isobe, T.: White-box cryptography revisited: space-hard ciphers. In: Ray, I., Li, N., Kruegel, C. (eds.) ACM CCS 2015, pp. 1058–1069. ACM Press, Oct. (2015)
16. Bogdanov, A., Isobe, T., Tischhauser, E.: Towards practical whitebox cryptography: optimizing efficiency and space hardness. In: Cheon, J.H., Takagi, T. (eds.) ASIACRYPT 2016. LNCS, vol. 10031, pp. 126–158. Springer, Heidelberg (2016). https://doi.org/10.1007/978-3-662-53887-6_5
17. Boneh, D., Waters, B.: Constrained pseudorandom functions and their applications. In: Sako, K., Sarkar, P. (eds.) ASIACRYPT 2013. LNCS, vol. 8270, pp. 280–300. Springer, Heidelberg (2013). https://doi.org/10.1007/978-3-642-42045-0_15

18. Chow, S., Eisen, P.A., Johnson, H., van Oorschot, P.C.: White-box cryptography and an AES implementation. In: Nyberg, K., Heys, H.M. (eds.) SAC 2002. LNCS, vol. 2595, pp. 250–270. Springer, Heidelberg (2003)
19. Chow, S., et al.: A white-box DES implementation for DRM applications. In: Feigenbaum, J. (ed.) Security and Privacy in Digital Rights Management, ACM CCS-9 Workshop, DRM 2002, vol. 2696, LNCS, pp. 1–15. Springer (2003)
20. Cooijmans, T., de Ruiter, J., Poll, E.: Analysis of secure key storage solutions on android. In Proceedings of the 4th ACM Workshop on Security and Privacy in Smartphones & #38; Mobile Devices, SPSM 2014, pp. 11–20. ACM (2014)
21. cybercrypt. Ches 2019 capture the flag challenge - the whibox contest - edition 2 (2019). https://www.cyber-crypt.com/whibox-contest/
22. Delerablée, C., Lepoint, T., Paillier, P., Rivain, M.: White-box security notions for symmetric encryption schemes. In: Lange, T., Lauter, K., Lisoněk, P. (eds.) SAC 2013. LNCS, vol. 8282, pp. 247–264. Springer, Heidelberg (2014). https://doi.org/10.1007/978-3-662-43414-7_13
23. ECRYPT. Ches 2017 capture the flag challenge - the whibox contest (2017). https://whibox.cr.yp.to/
24. EMVCo. Emv mobile payment: Software-based mobile payment security requirements (2019). https://www.emvco.com/wp-content/uploads/documents/EMVCo-SBMP-16-G01-V1.2_SBMP_Security_Requirements.pdf
25. Fouque, P.-A., Karpman, P., Kirchner, P., Minaud, B.: Efficient and provable white-box primitives. In: Cheon, J.H., Takagi, T. (eds.) ASIACRYPT 2016. LNCS, vol. 10031, pp. 159–188. Springer, Heidelberg (2016). https://doi.org/10.1007/978-3-662-53887-6_6
26. Francis, L., Hancke, G., Mayes, K., Markantonakis, K.: Practical relay attack on contactless transactions by using NFC mobile phones. Cryptology ePrint Archive, Report 2011/618 (2011). http://eprint.iacr.org/2011/618
27. Goubin, L., Paillier, P., Rivain, M., Wang, J.: How to reveal the secrets of an obscure white-box implementation. J. Cryptographic Eng. 10(1), 49–66 (2019). https://doi.org/10.1007/s13389-019-00207-5
28. Hancke, G.: A practical relay attack on ISO 14443 proximity cards. Technical report (2005)
29. Krawczyk, H.: Cryptographic extraction and key derivation: the HKDF scheme. In: Rabin, T. (ed.) CRYPTO 2010. LNCS, vol. 6223, pp. 631–648. Springer, Heidelberg (2010). https://doi.org/10.1007/978-3-642-14623-7_34
30. Kwon, J., Lee, B., Lee, J., Moon, D.: FPL: white-box secure block cipher using parallel table look-ups. In: Jarecki, S. (ed.) CT-RSA 2020. LNCS, vol. 12006, pp. 106–128. Springer, Heidelberg (2020)
31. Mastercard. Mastercard mobile payment sdk (2017). https://developer.mastercard.com/media/32/b3/b6a8b4134e50bfe53590c128085e/mastercard-mobile-payment-sdk-security-guide-v2.0.pdf
32. Rivain, M.: White-box cryptography. Presentation CARDIS 2017 (2017). http://www.matthieurivain.com/files/slides-cardis17.pdf
33. Rogaway, P.: Authenticated-encryption with associated-data. In: Atluri, V. (ed.) ACM CCS 2002, pp. 98–107. ACM Press, New York (2002)
34. Rogaway, P.: Nonce-based symmetric encryption. In: Roy, B., Meier, W. (eds.) FSE 2004. LNCS, vol. 3017, pp. 348–358. Springer, Heidelberg (2004). https://doi.org/10.1007/978-3-540-25937-4_22
35. Sahai, A., Waters, B.: How to use indistinguishability obfuscation: deniable encryption, and more. In: Shmoys, D.B. (ed.) 46th ACM STOC, pp. 475–484. ACM Press, New York (2014)

36. Sanfelix, E., de Haas, J., Mune, C.: Unboxing the white-box: Practical attacks against obfuscated ciphers. Presentation at BlackHat Europe 2015, (2015). https://www.blackhat.com/eu-15/briefings.html

37. Smart Card Alliance Mobile and NFC Council. Host card emulation 101. white paper (2014). http://www.smartcardalliance.org/downloads/HCE-101-WP-FINAL-081114-clean.pdf

38. Wyseur, B.: White-box cryptography: Hiding keys in software (2012). http://www.whiteboxcrypto.com/research.php

Circular Security Is Complete
for KDM Security

Fuyuki Kitagawa[1(✉)] and Takahiro Matsuda[2(✉)]

[1] NTT Secure Platform Laboratories, Tokyo, Japan
`fuyuki.kitagawa.yh@hco.ntt.co.jp`
[2] National Institute of Advanced Industrial Science and Technology (AIST),
Tokyo, Japan
`t-matsuda@aist.go.jp`

Abstract. Circular security is the most elementary form of key-dependent message (KDM) security, which allows us to securely encrypt only a copy of secret key bits. In this work, we show that circular security is *complete* for KDM security in the sense that an encryption scheme satisfying this security notion can be transformed into one satisfying KDM security with respect to all functions computable by a-priori bounded-size circuits (bounded-KDM security). This result holds in the presence of any number of keys and in any of secret-key/public-key and CPA/CCA settings. Such a completeness result was previously shown by Applebaum (EUROCRYPT 2011) for KDM security with respect to projection functions (projection-KDM security) that allows us to securely encrypt both a copy and a negation of secret key bits. Besides amplifying the strength of KDM security, our transformation in fact can start from an encryption scheme satisfying circular security against *CPA* attacks and results in one satisfying bounded-KDM security against *CCA* attacks. This result improves the recent result by Kitagawa and Matsuda (TCC 2019) showing a CPA-to-CCA transformation for KDM secure public-key encryption schemes.

Keywords: Key-dependent message security · Circular security · Chosen ciphertext security

1 Introduction

1.1 Background

Key-dependent message (KDM) security, introduced by Black, Rogaway, and Shrimpton [7], guarantees confidentiality of communication even if an adversary can get a ciphertext of secret keys. This notion was formulated in order to capture situations where there could be correlations between secret keys and messages to be encrypted. Although it seems that such situations only arise from bugs or errors, it turned out that they naturally occur in natural usage scenarios of encryption schemes such as hard-disc encryption [8], anonymous credentials [10],

© International Association for Cryptologic Research 2020
S. Moriai and H. Wang (Eds.): ASIACRYPT 2020, LNCS 12491, pp. 253–285, 2020.
https://doi.org/10.1007/978-3-030-64837-4_9

and formal methods [2]. Moreover, until today, a number of works have shown that KDM security is useful when constructing various cryptographic primitives including fully homomorphic encryption (FHE) [15], non-interactive zero-knowledge (NIZK) proofs/arguments [11,12,22,25], homomorphic secret sharing [9], and chosen ciphertext secure encryption schemes and trapdoor functions [19,23].

KDM security is defined with respect to a function family $\mathcal{F}$. Informally, a public-key encryption (PKE) scheme is said to be $\mathcal{F}$-KDM$^{(n)}$ secure if confidentiality of messages is protected even when an adversary can see a ciphertext of $f(\mathsf{sk}_1, \cdots, \mathsf{sk}_n)$ under the s-th public key for any $f \in \mathcal{F}$ and $s \in \{1, \cdots, n\}$, where n denotes the number of keys. Also, KDM security is considered in both the chosen plaintext attack (CPA) and chosen ciphertext attack (CCA) settings.

Completeness of Projection-KDM Security. KDM security with respect to the family of projection functions (projection-KDM security) is one of the most widely studied notions. A projection function is an elementary function in which each output bit depends on at most a single bit of an input. Therefore, roughly speaking, projection-KDM security only guarantees that an encryption scheme can securely encrypt a copy and a negation of secret key bits.

Although this security notion looks somewhat weak at first glance, Applebaum [3] showed that it is *complete* for KDM security in the sense that we can construct an encryption scheme satisfying KDM security with respect to all functions computable by a-priori bounded-size circuits (bounded-KDM security) based on one satisfying projection-KDM security. The completeness of projection-KDM security in [3] has generality in the sense that it is insensitive to the exact setting of KDM security. More specifically, a projection-KDM secure encryption scheme can be transformed into a bounded-KDM secure one for any number of keys and in any of secret-key/public-key and CPA/CCA settings.

Moreover, recent works [22,23,25] also showed the power and usefulness of projection-KDM secure encryption schemes for achieving other security notions and constructing other primitives. Specifically, Kitagawa, Matsuda, and Tanaka [23] showed that projection-KDM secure PKE implies IND-CCA secure PKE, and Kitagawa and Matsuda [22] and Lombardi, Quach, Rothblum, Wichs, and Wu [25] independently showed that it implies a reusable designated-verifier NIZK argument system for any NP language.

Completeness of Circular Security? The focus in this work is on *circular security*, which is another elementary form of KDM security that has been widely studied from both the positive side [10,11,15,19] and the negative side [1,13,17,20,24, 28]. Circular security is a weaker security notion compared to even projection-KDM security since circular security allows us to securely encrypt only a copy of secret key bits.[1] In this work, we clarify whether this most elementary form of KDM security is also complete in the above sense or not.

---

[1] Note that the phrase "circular security" is sometimes used to mean a (similar but) different notion, such as security when encrypting key cycles.

Let us explain the motivations for studying the completeness of circular security for KDM security. From the practical aspect, although it is an elementally form of KDM security, it is known to be sufficient for many practical applications of KDM security such as anonymous credentials, formal methods, and FHE listed above. Thus, studying circular security is expected to give us insights on these applications. From the theoretical aspect, it has impacts on the study of public-key cryptography since several recent works [22,23,25] showed that a projection-KDM secure encryption scheme is useful as a building block for constructing two important and central primitives of IND-CCA secure PKE and reusable designated-verifier NIZK argument systems, among which we will expand explanations on the former in the paragraph below. Furthermore, studying whether the ability to securely encrypt only a copy of secret key bits has a similar power to that to securely encrypt both a copy and a negation of secret key bits at the same time, is well-motivated from the viewpoint of "negation-complexity" of cryptographic primitives [16,18]. For example, Goldreich and Izsak [16] showed that a one-way function can be computed by a monotone circuit and yet a pseudorandom generator cannot. It is interesting to investigate whether such a barrier exists in the context of KDM security.

Implications to the Study of CPA vs CCA. The question whether an IND-CCA secure PKE scheme can be constructed from an IND-CPA secure one has been standing as a major open question in cryptography. The completeness of circular security for KDM security also has a deep connection to this question: Hajiabadi and Kapron [19] tackled the above question, and they built an IND-CCA secure PKE scheme based on a PKE scheme satisfying circular security and a randomness re-usability property called reproducibility [6]. Also, Kitagawa et al. [23] showed that an IND-CCA secure PKE scheme can be constructed from a projection KDM secure PKE scheme.

The above two results surely made a progress on the study of CCA security versus CPA security by showing that an IND-CCA secure PKE scheme can be constructed from a PKE scheme satisfying only security notions against "CPA" (i.e. no decryption queries). Here, the above results are incomparable since the former result requires a structural property while the latter requires projection-KDM security that is stronger than circular security for the building block scheme. It is an open question whether we can construct an IND-CCA secure PKE scheme based on a PKE scheme satisfying only circular security without requiring any structural property for the building block scheme. We see that this question is solved affirmatively if we can prove the completeness of circular security for KDM security by combining it with the previous results [22,23,25].

1.2   Our Results

In this work, we show that circular security is complete in the sense that an encryption scheme satisfying this security notion can be transformed into a bounded-KDM secure one. In this work, unless stated otherwise, circular security indicates a security notion that guarantees that an encryption scheme can securely encrypt a copy of each of secret key bits separately. We show that this result has the same level of generality as the completeness of projection-KDM security shown by Applebaum [3]. Namely, we obtain the following theorem. Below, we denote circular security against CPA under n key pairs as $CIRC^{(n)}$ security.

Theorem 1 (Informal). *If there exists a $CIRC^{(n)}$ secure PKE (resp. SKE) scheme, then there exists a bounded-$KDM^{(n)}$-CCA secure PKE (resp. SKE) scheme for any number of keys n.*

Note that the above theorem implies the completeness of circular security in both the CPA and CCA settings at the same time since we start with a scheme satisfying circular security against *CPA* and obtain a scheme satisfying bounded-KDM security against *CCA*. We obtain Theorem 1 in the following way.

How to Obtain Completeness in the Public-Key Setting. We first focus on the case where there is only a single key pair. In Sect. 4, as our main technical result, we show that an encryption primitive called *targeted encryption (TE)*, formalized by Barak, Haitner, Hofheinz, and Ishai [5], can be constructed from the combination of a $CIRC^{(1)}$ secure SKE scheme and an IND-CPA secure PKE scheme. Since both of the building blocks are implied by $CIRC^{(1)}$ secure PKE, and a TE scheme in turn can be transformed into a bounded-$KDM^{(1)}$-CPA secure PKE scheme as shown by Barak et al. [5], this result implies that a $CIRC^{(1)}$ secure PKE scheme can be transformed into a bounded-$KDM^{(1)}$-CPA secure PKE scheme. Once we construct a bounded-$KDM^{(1)}$-CPA secure PKE scheme, by combining with the result by Kitagawa and Matsuda [22], we can transform it into a bounded-$KDM^{(1)}$-CCA secure PKE scheme, which is stated in Sect. 5.

We then turn our attention to the case where there are multiple key pairs. Similarly to the above, we can construct a bounded-$KDM^{(n)}$-CPA secure PKE scheme based on a $CIRC^{(n)}$ secure one for any n through a primitive called augmented TE [5] that is an extension of TE. However, in the case of multiple key pairs, there is no transformation from a KDM-CPA secure PKE scheme to a KDM-CCA secure one regardless of the function family with respect to which we consider KDM security. Thus, in this case, we cannot easily carry the result in the CPA setting to that in the CCA setting.

To overcome the above problem, in Sect. 6, we first introduce a primitive that we call *conformed TE (CTE)*. CTE is an extension of TE (with several similarities to augmented TE of Barak et al. [5]) that is conformed to the construction of a KDM-CCA secure PKE scheme in the presence of multiple key pairs. We then construct a CTE scheme based on a $CIRC^{(n)}$ secure SKE scheme and an IND-CPA secure PKE scheme. Finally, in Sect. 7, we construct a bounded-$KDM^{(n)}$-CCA secure PKE scheme from a CTE scheme, a garbling scheme, an IND-CCA secure PKE scheme, and a (reusable) DV-NIZK argument system.

The last two components are implied by a circular secure PKE scheme from our result in the case of a single key pair and the results by Kitagawa and Matsuda [22] and Lombardi et al. [25]. This implies that circular security is complete in both the CPA and CCA settings even when there are multiple key pairs. Note that this result improves that of Kitagawa and Matsuda [22] in the following two aspects: Not only our construction can start from a circular secure PKE scheme, but also it works in the case of multiple key pairs.

How to Obtain Completeness in the Secret-Key Setting. From the result shown by Backes, Pfitzmann, and Scedrov [4], we can transform a bounded-KDM$^{(n)}$-CPA secure SKE scheme into a bounded-KDM$^{(n)}$-CCA secure one for any n. Thus, in the secret-key setting, all we have to do is to construct a bounded-KDM$^{(n)}$-CPA secure SKE scheme based on a CIRC$^{(n)}$ secure one. Similarly to the public-key setting, this is possible via the secret-key version of TE for the case of a single key pair and via the secret-key version of augmented TE for the case of multiple key pairs. These constructions are almost the same as the public-key counterparts, and thus we omit their formal descriptions in the paper. (In Sect. 2, this construction is outlined since we explain a technical overview of our results using the secret-key version of TE.)

Implications of Our Completeness Result. We obtain the following additional results: We show that the construction of the bounded-KDM$^{(1)}$-CPA secure PKE scheme mentioned above, is in fact a fully black-box construction [27] if we restrict the function family to projection functions. Thus, by combining this fact with the result by Kitagawa et al. [23], we obtain a fully black-box construction of an IND-CCA secure PKE scheme from a circular secure one.[2] Moreover, by simply combining Theorem 1 with the result independently achieved by Kitagawa and Matsuda [22] and Lombardi et al. [25], we see that a reusable DV-NIZK argument system can also be constructed from a circular secure PKE scheme.

1.3 Paper Organization

The rest of the paper is organized as follows: In Sect. 2, we give a technical overview of our results. In Sect. 3, we review definitions of cryptographic primitives. In Sect. 4, we present our construction of TE. In Sect. 5, we show several implications of our TE scheme, and in particular the completeness of circular security for the single-key setting. In Sect. 6, we introduce CTE and present its construction. Finally, in Sect. 7, we present the completeness of circular security in the multi-key setting using CTE.

---

[2] Note that this result does not simply follow from Theorem 1 since the construction of KDM-CCA secure PKE used to show it is non-black-box due to the use of a DV-NIZK argument.

2   Technical Overview

In this section, we provide a technical overview of our results. Our main technical contribution is to show that we can realize TE (and conformed TE) based only on a circular secure encryption scheme in a completely generic way. Thus, in this overview, we mainly focus on this part after briefly explaining how to construct a bounded-KDM secure scheme based on TE. For simplicity, we explain our ideas in this part by showing how to construct the secret-key version of a TE scheme based only on a $\mathsf{CIRC}^{(1)}$ secure SKE scheme. In the following, for a natural number n, we let $[n]$ denote the set $\{1, \ldots, n\}$.

2.1   Secret-Key TE

We first introduce the secret-key version of TE [5]. A secret-key TE scheme consists of the three algorithms TKG, TEnc, and TDec.[3] Similarly to an ordinary SKE scheme, TKG is given a security parameter and outputs a secret key sk. We let ℓ_{sk} denote the secret key length. On the other hand, TEnc and TDec have a functionality of a somewhat special form. As we will soon see below, they are optimized for encrypting labels of garbled circuits [29]. In addition to the secret key sk, TEnc is given an index $i \in [\ell_{\mathsf{sk}}]$ and a pair of messages (X_0, X_1), and outputs a ciphertext as $\mathsf{ct} \leftarrow \mathsf{TEnc}(\mathsf{sk}, i, X_0, X_1)$. Correspondingly, given the secret key sk, the index $i \in [\ell_{\mathsf{sk}}]$, and the ciphertext ct, TDec outputs (only) $X_{\mathsf{sk}[i]}$, where $\mathsf{sk}[i]$ denotes the i-th bit of sk. (Thus, it is similar to an oblivious transfer.) For TE, we consider two security notions: *security against the receiver* and *security against outsiders*. Security against the receiver ensures that ct hides the information of $X_{1 \oplus \mathsf{sk}[i]}$ even against the receiver who holds sk. Security against outsiders ensures that ct hides both X_0 and X_1 against adversaries who do not hold sk.[4]

Bounded-$\mathsf{KDM}^{(1)}$-*CPA Security via TE.* As shown by Barak et al. [5], we can construct a bounded-$\mathsf{KDM}^{(1)}$-CPA secure SKE scheme based on a secret-key TE scheme by using garbled circuits.[5] The construction is fairly simple. The secret key of the resulting SKE scheme is that of the underlying secret-key TE scheme itself. When encrypting a message m, we first garble an ℓ_{sk}-bit-input constant function $\mathsf{C_m}$ that outputs m for any input. This results in a single garbled circuit $\widetilde{\mathsf{C}}$ and $2\ell_{\mathsf{sk}}$ labels $(\mathsf{lab}_{i,v})_{i \in [\ell_{\mathsf{sk}}], v \in \{0,1\}}$. Then, for every index $i \in [\ell_{\mathsf{sk}}]$, we encrypt the pair of labels $(\mathsf{lab}_{i,0}, \mathsf{lab}_{i,1})$ under the index i into ct_i using TEnc. The resulting ciphertext for the SKE scheme consists of $\widetilde{\mathsf{C}}$ and

---

[3] Here, we adopt the syntax that is slightly different from the one we use in the subsequent sections, in that the latter allows to encrypt X_v for each $v \in \{0,1\}$ separately. The syntax used here makes the following explanations easier and cleaner. For the formal definition, see Sect. 3.3.

[4] Hereafter, we refer to adversaries that do not hold the secret key as outsiders.

[5] Note that the actual transformation shown by Barak et al. is in the public-key setting. Also, the following explanations assume that the reader is familiar with a garbling scheme. See the full version for its formal definition.

$(\mathsf{ct}_i)_{i\in[\ell_{\mathsf{sk}}]}$. When decrypting this ciphertext, we first obtain $(\mathsf{lab}_{i,\mathsf{sk}[i]})_{i\in[\ell_{\mathsf{sk}}]}$ from $(\mathsf{ct}_i)_{i\in[\ell_{\mathsf{sk}}]}$ by using TDec with sk. Then, we evaluate the garbled circuit $\widetilde{C}$ with these labels. This results in m from the correctness of the garbling scheme.

We can prove that the above construction is bounded-$\mathrm{KDM}^{(1)}$-CPA secure. In a high level, we can generate a simulated encryption of $f(\mathsf{sk})$ without using sk itself that is indistinguishable from a real ciphertext based on the security against the receiver of the underlying secret-key TE scheme and the security of the underlying garbling scheme, where f is a function queried by an adversary as a KDM-encryption query. We then finish the security proof by relying on the security against outsiders of the secret-key TE scheme. For more details, see [5].

2.2   Secret-Key TE Based on Circular Secure SKE

Below, we explain how to construct a secret-key TE scheme based on a $\mathrm{CIRC}^{(1)}$ secure SKE scheme. We first show that a secret-key TE scheme can be naturally realized from a projection-$\mathrm{KDM}^{(1)}$ secure SKE scheme. We then show how to weaken the starting point to a $\mathrm{CIRC}^{(1)}$ secure SKE scheme.

Secret-Key TE Based on Projection-KDM Secure SKE. Consider the following naive way to realize a secret-key TE scheme based on an SKE scheme SKE. A secret key sk of SKE is used as that of the secret-key TE scheme. When encrypting (X_0, X_1) under an index $i \in [\ell_{\mathsf{sk}}]$, we just encrypt $X_{\mathsf{sk}[i]}$ into ct by using the encryption algorithm Enc of SKE with the secret key sk. We call this naive realization Naive. Naive clearly satisfies security against the receiver since ct is independent of $X_{1\oplus\mathsf{sk}[i]}$. However, it is not clear whether we can prove the security against outsiders of Naive if we only assume that SKE satisfies IND-CPA security. This is because the encrypted message $X_{\mathsf{sk}[i]}$ is dependent on the secret key sk. On the other hand, we can prove the security against outsiders of Naive if SKE satisfies projection-$\mathrm{KDM}^{(1)}$-CPA security which allows us to securely encrypt both *a copy and a negation* of $\mathsf{sk}[i]$.

To see this in detail, we suppose that $X_{\mathsf{sk}[i]}$ is encrypted by SKE in a bit-by-bit manner, and its length is μ. We denote the j-th bit of X_0 (resp. X_1) by $X_0[j]$ (resp. $X_1[j]$). We can classify the indices in $[\mu]$ into the following four types:

Type 1: $j \in [\mu]$ such that $X_0[j] = X_1[j] = 0$.
Type 2: $j \in [\mu]$ such that $X_0[j] = X_1[j] = 1$.
Type 3: $j \in [\mu]$ such that $X_0[j] = 0$ and $X_1[j] = 1$.
Type 4: $j \in [\mu]$ such that $X_0[j] = 1$ and $X_1[j] = 0$.

We have to generate the following ciphertexts of SKE for each type to encrypt $X_{\mathsf{sk}[i]}$:

– For j of Type 1, we have to generate $\mathsf{Enc}(\mathsf{sk}, 0)$ regardless of the value of $\mathsf{sk}[i]$.
– For j of Type 2, we have to generate $\mathsf{Enc}(\mathsf{sk}, 1)$ regardless of the value of $\mathsf{sk}[i]$.
– For j of Type 3, we have to generate $\mathsf{Enc}(\mathsf{sk}, \mathsf{sk}[i])$, that is, an encryption of a *copy* of $\mathsf{sk}[i]$.

- For j of Type 4, we have to generate $\mathsf{Enc}(\mathsf{sk}, 1 \oplus \mathsf{sk}[i])$, that is, an encryption of a *negation* of $\mathsf{sk}[i]$.

Namely, when some bit of X_0 is 0 and the corresponding bit of X_1 is 1, we have to generate an encryption of a copy of $\mathsf{sk}[i]$. Similarly, when some bit of X_0 is 1 and the corresponding bit of X_1 is 0, we have to generate an encryption of a negation of $\mathsf{sk}[i]$. However, if SKE is projection-KDM$^{(1)}$-CPA secure, then $X_{\mathsf{sk}[i]}$ is hidden from outsiders. Since $X_{1 \oplus \mathsf{sk}[i]}$ is completely hidden (even against the legitimate receiver), Naive satisfies security against outsiders based on the projection-KDM$^{(1)}$-CPA security of SKE.

Replacing Projection-KDM-CPA Secure SKE with Circular Secure SKE. We now try to realize a secret-key TE scheme based on a circular secure (CIRC$^{(1)}$ secure) SKE scheme. Recall that CIRC$^{(1)}$ security allows us to securely encrypt only a copy of secret key bits. Thus, as the first attempt to avoid encrypting negations of secret key bits, we modify the above construction Naive into the following construction that we call Naive^*.

In Naive^*, when encrypting (X_0, X_1) under an index $i \in [\ell_{\mathsf{sk}}]$, we basically encrypt $X_{\mathsf{sk}[i]}$ in a bit-by-bit manner in the same way as Naive. However, for indices $j \in [\mu]$ of Type 4, we replace the ciphertext of SKE with the special symbol $\mathtt{flip}$. When receiving the symbol $\mathtt{flip}$ instead of the j-th ciphertext, the receiver sets the value of $X_{\mathsf{sk}[i]}[j]$ as $1 \oplus \mathsf{sk}[i]$. This is possible since the receiver has sk and knows the value of $\mathsf{sk}[i]$. Thus, if we modify the construction in this way, the receiver holding sk can obtain the entire bits of $X_{\mathsf{sk}[i]}$ similarly to Naive.

In Naive^*, we now need to generate encryptions of only a copy of $\mathsf{sk}[i]$ and not those of a negation of $\mathsf{sk}[i]$. However, we cannot prove that Naive^* satisfies the two security notions of TE (security against the receiver/outsiders) based on the CIRC$^{(1)}$ security of SKE. For example, considering security against outsiders, X_0 and X_1 are partially leaked to outsiders because of the use of the symbol $\mathtt{flip}$. Concretely, outsiders can know that $X_0[j] = 1$ and $X_1[j] = 0$ for the indices j of Type 4. A similar problem lies in the argument on security against the receiver. Concretely, the receiver holding sk can know $X_{1 \oplus \mathsf{sk}[i]}[j]$ for the indices j of Type 4 and either one of Type 1 or 2 depending on the value of $\mathsf{sk}[i]$. The reason why $X_{1 \oplus \mathsf{sk}[i]}[j]$ for the indices j of Type 4 are leaked to the receiver is clear. The reason why those for the indices j of Type 1 or 2 are leaked to the receiver is as follows. For example, when $\mathsf{sk}[i] = 0$, the receiver finds that the value of $X_{1 \oplus \mathsf{sk}[i]}[j]$ is 1 for j of Type 2 from the fact that the decrypted message from the j-th ciphertext is 1 but the symbol $\mathtt{flip}$ was not sent for this j.

To summarize, if SKE is CIRC$^{(1)}$ secure, the following properties hold for Naive^*: $X_0[j]$ and $X_1[j]$ for the indices j of Type 1, 2, and 3 are hidden but those for the indices j of Type 4 are leaked to outsiders. Also, $X_{1 \oplus \mathsf{sk}[i]}[j]$ for the indices j of Type 3 and either one of Type 1 or 2 are hidden but the remaining parts are leaked to the receiver holding sk.

Transforming into a Full-Fledged Secret-Key TE Scheme. A natural question here is whether the above Naive^* is useful or not. We show that by using a *leakage-resilient* SKE scheme lrSKE, we can transform Naive* into an ordinary secret-key TE scheme sTE. As we will explain later, the type of leakage-resilience that lrSKE should satisfy is weak, and any IND-CPA secure SKE scheme can be transformed into one satisfying it. Thanks to this transformation, we can realize a secret-key TE scheme based only on a $\mathrm{CIRC}^{(1)}$ secure SKE scheme.

The description of sTE is as follows. The secret key sk of sTE is that of Naive* itself. When encrypting (X_0, X_1) under the index $i \in [\ell_{sk}]$, we first generate two keys lrk_0 and lrk_1 of lrSKE. Then, we encrypt X_0 and X_1 into lrct_0 and lrct_1 by using lrSKE with the keys lrk_0 and lrk_1, respectively. Moreover, we encrypt $(\mathsf{lrk}_0, \mathsf{lrk}_1)$ into ct by using Naive* with the key sk. The resulting ciphertext of sTE is $(\mathsf{lrct}_0, \mathsf{lrct}_1, \mathsf{ct})$. When decrypting this ciphertext, we first obtain $\mathsf{lrk}_{sk[i]}$ from ct by using Naive* with the key sk. We then obtain $X_{sk[i]}$ by decrypting $\mathsf{ct}_{sk[i]}$ using lrSKE with the key $\mathsf{lrk}_{sk[i]}$.

We now argue that sTE satisfies (full-fledged) security against the receiver and that for outsiders. Without loss of generality, we assume that lrk_0 and lrk_1 are uniformly random n-bit strings. We define Type 1, 2, 3, and 4 for indices in $[n]$ as before using lrk_0 and lrk_1 instead of X_0 and X_1. Since lrk_0 and lrk_1 are chosen uniformly at random, these four types appear equally likely. In this case, ct hides expectedly a $1/2$-fraction of bits of $\mathsf{lrk}_{1 \oplus sk[i]}$ against the receiver holding sk. Also, ct hides expectedly a $3/4$-fraction of bits of each of lrk_0 and lrk_1 against outsiders. Thus, if lrSKE is resilient against both forms of secret key leakage, sTE satisfies both security against the receiver and security against outsiders.

Fortunately, the leakage-resilience that lrSKE should satisfy in the above argument is weak. The amount of leakage is (expectedly) only a constant fraction. In addition, more importantly, which bits of the secret key are leaked is determined completely at random from the fact that Type 1, 2, 3, and 4 appear uniformly at random, out of the control of adversaries. Leakage-resilience against such secret key leakage is weak, and we can transform any IND-CPA secure SKE scheme into one satisfying it by using the leftover hash lemma [14, 21]. From this fact, sTE can be realized from a $\mathrm{CIRC}^{(1)}$ secure SKE scheme.

2.3   Towards the Completeness in the Public-Key Setting

As we mentioned earlier, in the actual technical sections, we deal with the public-key setting. Namely, we prove Theorem 1 in the PKE setting. We finally explain how to prove it with the techniques explained so for.

Single-Key Setting. We first construct a (public-key) TE scheme based on a $\mathrm{CIRC}^{(1)}$ secure SKE scheme and an IND-CPA secure PKE scheme both of which are implied by a $\mathrm{CIRC}^{(1)}$ secure PKE scheme. This construction is almost the same as that of sTE above except that we use a leakage-resilient PKE scheme instead of a leakage-resilient SKE scheme. By combining this transformation with the previous results [5, 22], we can obtain Theorem 1 in the PKE setting for the number of key pairs $n = 1$.

Multi-key Setting. We then move on to the case of multiple key pairs. As mentioned before, for achieving the completeness in this setting, we introduce an extended version of TE that we call conformed TE (CTE). CTE is conformed to construct $KDM^{(n)}$-CCA secure PKE schemes for $n > 1$. Roughly, CTE is TE that satisfies the following two additional properties.

- When generating a public/secret key pair, it additionally generates a trapdoor that enables us to recover both a "0-side" message X_0 and a "1-side" message X_1 from a ciphertext encrypting (X_0, X_1). (Recall that in ordinary TE, the receiver can recover only one of them even having the secret key.)
- A CTE scheme has additional (untargeted and secret-key) encryption and decryption algorithms, and a ciphertext generated by the additional encryption algorithm is indistinguishable even under the existence of the above trapdoor and encryptions of a "key cycle" generated by the additional encryption algorithm. Encryptions of a key cycle are ciphertexts such that the s-th ciphertext is an encryption of the $(s \bmod n) + 1$-th secret key under the s-th secret key when there are n keys. We call this property *special weak circular security*.

We remark that a TE scheme satisfying only the second property is almost the same as augmented TE introduced by Barak et al. [5] to construct a bounded-$KDM^{(n)}$-CPA secure PKE scheme for $n > 1$. Roughly speaking, when constructing a KDM-CCA secure PKE scheme, the first property mainly plays its role to deal with decryption queries, and the second property plays its role to deal with multiple key pairs. For the details of the formalization of CTE as well as its relation to augmented TE, see Sect. 6.

We construct a CTE scheme based on a $CIRC^{(n)}$ secure SKE scheme and an IND-CPA secure PKE scheme. Basically, this construction is again an extension of sTE in which a leakage-resilient PKE scheme is used instead of a leakage-resilient SKE scheme. The trapdoor of the construction consists of secret keys of the leakage-resilient PKE scheme. Also, the special weak circular security of it is proved based on the $CIRC^{(n)}$ security of the underlying SKE scheme.

We finish the proof of Theorem 1 in the public-key setting for $n > 1$ by constructing a bounded-$KDM^{(n)}$-CCA secure PKE scheme from the combination of the following four building blocks: (1) a CTE scheme, (2) an IND-CCA secure PKE scheme, (3) a garbling scheme for circuits, and (4) a reusable DV-NIZK argument system for NP languages. As we already explained, by Theorem 1 for $n = 1$ and results by [22,25], an IND-CCA secure PKE scheme and a reusable DV-NIZK argument system can be constructed from the combination of an IND-CPA secure PKE scheme and a $CIRC^{(1)}$ secure SKE scheme. Also, a garbling scheme for circuits can be constructed from a one-way function. Thus, all the building blocks can be based on the combination of an IND-CPA secure PKE scheme and a $CIRC^{(n)}$ secure SKE scheme. This completes the proof of Theorem 1 in the PKE setting for $n > 1$.

Our construction of bounded-KDM-CCA secure PKE in the multi-key setting can be seen as combining the construction ideas from the two existing constructions: the construction of KDM-CPA secure PKE in the multi-key setting based on an augmented TE scheme by Barak et al. [5], and the construction of KDM-CCA secure PKE in the single key setting based on an IND-CPA secure PKE scheme and a projection-KDM secure SKE scheme by Kitagawa and Matsuda [22]. However, a simple combination of each of the techniques from [5,22] as it is is not sufficient. We bridge the gap with the properties of the CTE scheme. For the details, see Sect. 7.

3 Preliminaries

In this section, we review the basic notation, and the definitions as well as existing results for cryptographic primitives treated in this paper.

3.1 Basic Notation and Notions

For $n \in \mathbb{N}$, we define $[n] := \{1, \ldots, n\}$. For strings x and y, "$|x|$" denotes the bit-length of x, "$x[i]$" (with $i \in [|x|]$) denotes the i-th bit of x, and "$(x \overset{?}{=} y)$" is the operation that returns 1 if $x = y$ and 0 otherwise. For a discrete finite set S, "$|S|$" denotes its size, and "$x \overset{r}{\leftarrow} S$" denotes choosing an element x uniformly at random from S. For a (probabilistic) algorithm A, "$y \leftarrow \mathsf{A}(x)$" denotes assigning to y the output of $\mathcal{A}$ on input x, and if we need to specify a randomness r used in A, we write "$y \leftarrow \mathsf{A}(x; r)$". If furthermore $\mathcal{O}$ is a function or an algorithm, then "$\mathsf{A}^{\mathcal{O}}$" means that A has oracle access to $\mathcal{O}$. A function $\epsilon(\lambda) : \mathbb{N} \to [0, 1]$ is said to be *negligible* if $\epsilon(\lambda) = \lambda^{-\omega(1)}$. We write $\epsilon(\lambda) = \mathsf{negl}(\lambda)$ to mean ϵ being negligible. The character "λ" always denotes a security parameter. "PPT" stands for *probabilistic polynomial time*. For a distribution $\mathcal{X}$, the *min-entropy of* $\mathcal{X}$ is defined by $\mathbf{H}_\infty(\mathcal{X}) := -\log_2(\max_x \Pr[\mathcal{X} = x])$. For distributions $\mathcal{X}$ and $\mathcal{Y}$ (forming a joint distribution), the *average min-entropy of* $\mathcal{X}$ given $\mathcal{Y}$ is defined by $\widetilde{\mathbf{H}}_\infty(\mathcal{X}|\mathcal{Y}) := -\log_2(\mathbf{E}_{y \leftarrow \mathcal{Y}}[\max_x \Pr[\mathcal{X} = x | \mathcal{Y} = y]])$.

3.2 Public-Key and Secret-Key Encryption

Here, we recall the definitions for public-key and secret-key encryption schemes. We first introduce the definitions for PKE, and then briefly mention how to recover those for SKE.

Syntax of Public-Key Encryption. A PKE scheme PKE consists of the three PPT algorithms (KG, Enc, Dec):[6]

- KG is the key generation algorithm that takes 1^λ as input, and outputs a public/secret key pair (pk, sk).
- Enc is the encryption algorithm that takes a public key pk and a message m as input, and outputs a ciphertext ct.

---

[6] In this paper, we only consider (public-key/secret-key) encryption schemes in which secret keys and messages are bit strings, whose lengths are determined by the security parameter λ.

$$\mathsf{Expt}^{\mathsf{wlr}}_{\mathsf{PKE},\mathcal{A},L}(\lambda):$$
$$(f,\mathsf{st}) \leftarrow \mathcal{A}_0(1^\lambda)$$
$$(\mathsf{pk},\mathsf{sk}) \leftarrow \mathsf{KG}(1^\lambda)$$
$$b \xleftarrow{r} \{0,1\}$$
$$b' \leftarrow \mathcal{A}_1^{\mathcal{O}_{\mathsf{Enc}}(\cdot,\cdot)}(\mathsf{pk}, f(\mathsf{sk}), \mathsf{st})$$
$$\text{Return } (b' \overset{?}{=} b).$$

$$\mathcal{O}_{\mathsf{Enc}}(\mathsf{m}_0, \mathsf{m}_1): \quad // |\mathsf{m}_0| = |\mathsf{m}_1|$$
$$\text{Return } \mathsf{ct} \leftarrow \mathsf{Enc}(\mathsf{pk}, \mathsf{m}_b).$$

Fig. 1. The weak noisy-leakage-resilience experiment for PKE. In the experiment, it is required that $L \geq \mathbf{H}_\infty(\mathsf{sk}) - \widetilde{\mathbf{H}}_\infty(\mathsf{sk}|f(\mathsf{sk}), \mathsf{st})$.

– Dec is the (deterministic) decryption algorithm that takes a public key pk, a secret key sk, and a ciphertext ct as input, and outputs a message m or the invalid symbol $\perp$.

A PKE scheme PKE = (KG, Enc, Dec) is said to be *correct* if for all $\lambda \in \mathbb{N}$, $(\mathsf{pk},\mathsf{sk}) \leftarrow \mathsf{KG}(1^\lambda)$, and m, we have $\mathsf{Dec}(\mathsf{pk},\mathsf{sk},\mathsf{Enc}(\mathsf{pk},\mathsf{m})) = \mathsf{m}$.

We refer to a PKE scheme whose message space is 1-bit as a *bit-PKE* scheme.

Simple Key Generation. We say that a PKE scheme has *simple key generation* if its key generation algorithm KG first picks a secret key sk uniformly at random (from some prescribed secret key space) and then computes a public key pk from sk. For PKE with simple key generation, we slightly abuse the notation and simply write $\mathsf{pk} \leftarrow \mathsf{KG}(\mathsf{sk})$ to denote this computation. Any IND-CPA/IND-CCA secure PKE scheme can be viewed as one with simple key generation by just regarding a randomness used in the key generation algorithm as sk.

Weak Noisy-Leakage-Resilience. We will use a PKE scheme that satisfies *weak noisy-leakage-resilience* (against CPA), formalized by Naor and Segev [26]. In the weak "noisy" leakage setting, an adversary's leakage function f must be chosen before seeing pk, and must satisfy the condition that the average min-entropy of sk given $f(\mathsf{sk})$ is greater than a pre-determined lower bound.

Formally, for a PKE scheme PKE = (KG, Enc, Dec), a polynomial $L = L(\lambda)$, and an adversary $\mathcal{A} = (\mathcal{A}_0, \mathcal{A}_1)$, consider the experiment described in Fig. 1. In the experiment, $\mathcal{A}$ is required to be *L-noisy-leakage-respecting*, which requires that $L \geq \mathbf{H}_\infty(\mathsf{sk}) - \widetilde{\mathbf{H}}_\infty(\mathsf{sk}|f(\mathsf{sk}), \mathsf{st})$ hold.

Definition 1 (Weak Noisy-Leakage-Resilience). *Let $L = L(\lambda)$ be a polynomial. We say that a PKE scheme PKE is* weakly *L-noisy-leakage-resilient if for all PPT L-noisy-leakage-respecting adversaries $\mathcal{A} = (\mathcal{A}_0, \mathcal{A}_1)$, we have* $\mathsf{Adv}^{\mathsf{wlr}}_{\mathsf{PKE},\mathcal{A},L}(\lambda) := 2 \cdot |\Pr[\mathsf{Expt}^{\mathsf{wlr}}_{\mathsf{PKE},\mathcal{A},L}(\lambda) = 1] - 1/2| = \mathsf{negl}(\lambda)$.

Any IND-CPA secure PKE scheme can be straightforwardly converted into a weakly noisy-leakage-resilient one by using the leftover hash lemma [14,21]. In fact, Naor and Segev [26] showed this fact for the case of weak "bounded" leakage-resilience (where the output-length of a leakage function is bounded), and it is easy to see that their proof carries over to the case of weak noisy-leakage-resilience. Furthermore, this conversion is fully black-box and preserves

$$
\begin{array}{ll}
\mathsf{Expt}_{\mathsf{PKE},\mathcal{F},\mathcal{A},n}^{\mathsf{kdmcca}}(\lambda): & \mathcal{O}_{\mathsf{kdm}}(\alpha, f_0, f_1): \quad // \ \alpha \in [n], \ f_0, f_1 \in \mathcal{F} \\
\quad L_{\mathsf{kdm}} \leftarrow \emptyset & \quad \mathsf{m} \leftarrow f_b((\mathsf{sk}^s)_{s \in [n]}) \\
\quad \forall s \in [n] : (\mathsf{pk}^s, \mathsf{sk}^s) \leftarrow \mathsf{KG}(1^\lambda) & \quad \mathsf{ct} \leftarrow \mathsf{Enc}(\mathsf{pk}^\alpha, \mathsf{m}) \\
\quad b \xleftarrow{\mathsf{r}} \{0,1\} & \quad L_{\mathsf{kdm}} \leftarrow L_{\mathsf{kdm}} \cup \{(\alpha, \mathsf{ct})\} \\
\quad b' \leftarrow \mathcal{A}^{\mathcal{O}_{\mathsf{kdm}}(\cdot,\cdot,\cdot), \mathcal{O}_{\mathsf{dec}}(\cdot,\cdot)}((\mathsf{pk}^s)_{s \in [n]}) & \quad \text{Return ct.} \\
\quad \text{Return } (b' \overset{?}{=} b). & \mathcal{O}_{\mathsf{dec}}(\alpha, \mathsf{ct}): \quad\quad\quad // \ \alpha \in [n] \\
& \quad \text{If } (\alpha, \mathsf{ct}) \in L_{\mathsf{kdm}} \text{ then return } \perp. \\
& \quad \text{Return } \mathsf{Dec}(\mathsf{pk}^\alpha, \mathsf{sk}^\alpha, \mathsf{ct}).
\end{array}
$$

Fig. 2. The KDM-CCA experiment for PKE.

the simple key generation property. (It works for SKE as well.) Since we will use this fact in Sect. 5, we state it formally, whose formal proof is given in the full version.

Lemma 1. *Assume that there exists an IND-CPA secure PKE scheme with simple key generation whose secret key length is $\ell_{\mathsf{sk}} = \ell_{\mathsf{sk}}(\lambda)$. Then, for any polynomials $L = L(\lambda)$ and $\ell'_{\mathsf{sk}} = \ell'_{\mathsf{sk}}(\lambda)$ satisfying $\ell'_{\mathsf{sk}} - (L + \ell_{\mathsf{sk}}) = \omega(\log \lambda)$, there exists a weakly L-noisy-leakage-resilient PKE scheme with simple key generation whose secret key length is ℓ'_{sk}. Furthermore, the construction is fully black-box.*[7]

For example, from an IND-CPA secure PKE scheme with simple key generation with secret key length ℓ_{sk}, for any constant $\beta \in [0,1)$, we can construct a scheme whose secret key length is ℓ'_{sk} and satisfies weak $(\beta \ell'_{\mathsf{sk}})$-noisy-leakage-resilience by setting the term $\omega(\log \lambda)$ simply as λ and setting $\ell'_{\mathsf{sk}} := \frac{\ell_{\mathsf{sk}} + \lambda}{1 - \beta}$.

KDM-CCA/CPA Security. We recall KDM-CCA/CPA security for PKE.

Definition 2 (KDM-CCA/CPA Security). *Let $\mathsf{PKE} = (\mathsf{KG}, \mathsf{Enc}, \mathsf{Dec})$ be a PKE scheme whose secret key length and message length are ℓ_{sk} and μ, respectively. Let $n = n(\lambda)$ be a polynomial, and $\mathcal{F}$ be a family of functions with domain $(\{0,1\}^{\ell_{\mathsf{sk}}})^n$ and range $\{0,1\}^\mu$. We say that PKE is KDM-CCA secure with respect to $\mathcal{F}$ in the n-key setting ($\mathcal{F}$-KDM$^{(n)}$-CCA secure) if for all PPT adversaries $\mathcal{A}$, we have $\mathsf{Adv}_{\mathsf{PKE},\mathcal{F},\mathcal{A},n}^{\mathsf{kdmcca}}(\lambda) := 2 \cdot |\Pr[\mathsf{Expt}_{\mathsf{PKE},\mathcal{F},\mathcal{A},n}^{\mathsf{kdmcca}}(\lambda) = 1] - 1/2| = \mathsf{negl}(\lambda)$, where the experiment $\mathsf{Expt}_{\mathsf{PKE},\mathcal{F},\mathcal{A},n}^{\mathsf{kdmcca}}(\lambda)$ is described in Fig. 2.*

KDM-CPA security with respect to $\mathcal{F}$ in the n-key setting ($\mathcal{F}$-KDM$^{(n)}$-CPA security) is defined analogously, except that $\mathcal{A}$ is disallowed to use $\mathcal{O}_{\mathsf{dec}}$.

Function Families for KDM Security. In this paper, the function families for KDM security that we will specifically treat are as follows.

---

[7] A fully black-box construction of a primitive Q from another primitive P means that (1) the construction of Q treats an instance of P as an oracle, and (2) the reduction algorithm (for proving the security of the construction of Q) treats the adversary attacking the construction of Q and the instance of P as oracles. (See [27] for the formal treatment.).

$\mathsf{Expt}^{\mathsf{circ}}_{\mathsf{PKE},\mathcal{A},n}(\lambda):$

$\quad \forall s \in [n] : (\mathsf{pk}^s, \mathsf{sk}^s) \leftarrow \mathsf{KG}(1^\lambda)$

$\quad b \xleftarrow{r} \{0,1\}$

$\quad b' \leftarrow \mathcal{A}^{\mathcal{O}_{\mathsf{circ}}(\cdot,\cdot)}((\mathsf{pk}^s)_{s\in[n]})$

$\quad$ Return $(b' \overset{?}{=} b)$.

$\mathcal{O}_{\mathsf{circ}}(\alpha, \mathsf{cmd}):$ // $\alpha \in [n]$,

$\qquad$ // $\mathsf{cmd} \in ([n] \times [\ell_{\mathsf{sk}}]) \cup \{\mathbf{zero}, \mathbf{one}\}$

$$\mathsf{m}_1 \leftarrow \begin{cases} \mathsf{sk}^\beta[i] & \text{if } \mathsf{cmd} = (\beta, i) \in [n] \times [\ell_{\mathsf{sk}}] \\ 0 & \text{if } \mathsf{cmd} = \mathbf{zero} \\ 1 & \text{if } \mathsf{cmd} = \mathbf{one} \end{cases}$$

$\qquad \mathsf{m}_0 \leftarrow 0$

$\qquad$ Return $\mathsf{ct} \leftarrow \mathsf{Enc}(\mathsf{pk}^\alpha, \mathsf{m}_b)$

Fig. 3. The circular security experiment for bit-PKE.

- $\mathcal{P}$ (Projection functions): A function is said to be a projection function if each of its output bits depends on at most a single bit of its input. We denote by $\mathcal{P}$ the family of projection functions.
- $\mathcal{B}_{\mathsf{size}}$ (Circuits of a-priori bounded size size): We denote by $\mathcal{B}_{\mathsf{size}}$, where $\mathsf{size} = \mathsf{size}(\lambda)$ is a polynomial, the function family each of whose members can be described by a circuit of size size.

Circular Security. In this paper, we also treat circular security (against CPA), which we consider for bit-encryption schemes. Although it is a special case of KDM security, it is convenient for us to introduce a separate definition in the form we use in this paper.

Definition 3 (Circular Security for Bit-PKE). *Let $n = n(\lambda)$ be a polynomial. Let $\mathsf{PKE} = (\mathsf{KG}, \mathsf{Enc}, \mathsf{Dec})$ be a bit-PKE scheme with the secret key length ℓ_{sk}. We say that PKE is circular secure in the n-key setting ($\mathrm{CIRC}^{(n)}$ secure) if for all PPT adversaries $\mathcal{A}$, we have $\mathsf{Adv}^{\mathsf{circ}}_{\mathsf{PKE},\mathcal{A},n}(\lambda) := 2 \cdot |\Pr[\mathsf{Expt}^{\mathsf{circ}}_{\mathsf{PKE},\mathcal{A},n}(\lambda) = 1] - 1/2| = \mathsf{negl}(\lambda)$, where the experiment $\mathsf{Expt}^{\mathsf{circ}}_{\mathsf{PKE},\mathcal{A},n}(\lambda)$ is described in Fig. 3.*

Our definition here follows the definition called "circular security with respect to indistinguishability of oracles" formalized by Rothblum [28], with a slight modification to the interface of the oracle: In addition to capturing the multi-key setting, the circular-encryption oracle $\mathcal{O}_{\mathsf{circ}}$ in our definition accepts the special commands "**zero**" and "**one**" (returning an encryption of 0 and that of 1, respectively, in the case $b = 1$) to explicitly capture ordinary IND-CPA security. This is for convenience and clarity: A bit-encryption scheme satisfies our definition if and only if it simultaneously satisfies the original definition in [28] (without the augmentation of the oracle interface) and IND-CPA security.

Secret-Key Encryption. An SKE scheme SKE consists of the three PPT algorithms $(\mathsf{K}, \mathsf{E}, \mathsf{D})$:

- K is the key generation algorithm that takes 1^λ as input, and outputs a secret key sk.
- E is the encryption algorithm that takes a secret key sk and a message m as input, and outputs a ciphertext ct.

- D is the (deterministic) decryption algorithm that takes a secret key sk and a ciphertext ct as input, and outputs a message m or the invalid symbol $\perp$.

An SKE scheme $\mathsf{SKE} = (\mathsf{K}, \mathsf{E}, \mathsf{D})$ is said to be *correct* if for all $\lambda \in \mathbb{N}$, $\mathsf{sk} \leftarrow \mathsf{K}(1^\lambda)$ and m, we have $\mathsf{D}(\mathsf{sk}, \mathsf{E}(\mathsf{sk}, \mathsf{m})) = \mathsf{m}$.

We refer to an SKE scheme whose message space is 1-bit as a *bit-SKE* scheme.

Weak noisy-leakage-resilience, KDM security, and circular security for (bit-)SKE are defined analogously to those defined for (bit-)PKE, with the following natural adaptions in the security experiments:

- All of $(\mathsf{pk}, \mathsf{sk}) \leftarrow \mathsf{KG}(1^\lambda)$, $\mathsf{Enc}(\mathsf{pk}, \cdot)$, and $\mathsf{Dec}(\mathsf{pk}, \mathsf{sk}, \cdot)$ in the experiments for PKE are replaced with $\mathsf{sk} \leftarrow \mathsf{K}(1^\lambda)$, $\mathsf{E}(\mathsf{sk}, \cdot)$, and $\mathsf{D}(\mathsf{sk}, \cdot)$ in the experiments for SKE, respectively. We do the same treatment for those with the superscripts $s, \alpha \in [n]$.
- All the public keys pk and pk^s $(s \in [n])$ given as input to an adversary in the experiments for PKE are replaced with 1^λ in the experiments for SKE.

Results from [22,23]. We recall the results on IND-CCA/KDM-CCA secure PKE from [22,23], which we will use in Sect. 5.

Theorem 2 ([23]). *If there exist an IND-CPA secure PKE scheme and a $\mathcal{P}$-KDM$^{(1)}$-CPA secure SKE scheme, then there exists an IND-CCA secure PKE scheme. Furthermore, the construction is fully black-box.*

Theorem 3 ([22]). *If there exist an IND-CPA secure PKE scheme and a $\mathcal{P}$-KDM$^{(1)}$-CPA secure SKE scheme, then for any polynomial $\mathsf{size} = \mathsf{size}(\lambda)$, there exists a $\mathcal{B}_{\mathsf{size}}$-KDM$^{(1)}$-CCA secure PKE scheme.*

We note that [22] also showed a construction of a multi-key-KDM-CCA secure PKE scheme by additionally assuming (passive) *RKA-KDM security* with respect to projection functions for the underlying SKE scheme. We do not formally recall it here since it is not known if it follows from the multi-key version of ordinary $\mathcal{P}$-KDM security and our result in Sect. 7 improves it in terms of the strength of assumptions.

3.3 Targeted Encryption

Here, we recall targeted encryption (TE) [5]. A TE scheme TE consists of the three PPT algorithms $(\mathsf{TKG}, \mathsf{TEnc}, \mathsf{TDec})$:

- TKG is the key generation algorithm that takes 1^λ as input, and outputs a public/secret key pair (pk, sk), where $|\mathsf{sk}| =: \ell_{\mathsf{sk}}$.
- TEnc is the encryption algorithm that takes a public key pk, an index $i \in [\ell_{\mathsf{sk}}]$, a bit $v \in \{0, 1\}$, and a message m as input, and outputs a ciphertext ct.
- TDec is the (deterministic) decryption algorithm that takes a public key pk, a secret key $\mathsf{sk} \in \{0, 1\}^{\ell_{\mathsf{sk}}}$, an index $i \in [\ell_{\mathsf{sk}}]$, and a ciphertext ct as input, and outputs a message m or the invalid symbol $\perp$.

$$\mathsf{Expt}_{\mathsf{TE},\mathcal{A}}^{\mathsf{receiver}}(\lambda):$$
$\quad (i^* \in [\ell_{\mathsf{sk}}], \mathsf{st}) \leftarrow \mathcal{A}_0(1^\lambda)$
$\quad (\mathsf{pk}, \mathsf{sk}) \leftarrow \mathsf{TKG}(1^\lambda)$
$\quad b \xleftarrow{r} \{0, 1\}$
$\quad b' \leftarrow \mathcal{A}_1^{\mathcal{O}_{\mathsf{TEnc}}(\cdot, \cdot)}(\mathsf{pk}, \mathsf{sk}, \mathsf{st})$
$\quad$ Return $(b' \overset{?}{=} b)$.

$\mathcal{O}_{\mathsf{TEnc}}(\mathsf{m}_0, \mathsf{m}_1): \quad // \ |\mathsf{m}_0| = |\mathsf{m}_1|$
$\quad \mathsf{ct} \leftarrow \mathsf{TEnc}(\mathsf{pk}, i^*, 1 \oplus \mathsf{sk}[i^*], \mathsf{m}_b)$
$\quad$ Return ct.

$$\mathsf{Expt}_{\mathsf{TE},\mathcal{A}}^{\mathsf{outsider}}(\lambda):$$
$\quad (i^* \in [\ell_{\mathsf{sk}}], v^* \in \{0, 1\}, \mathsf{st}) \leftarrow \mathcal{A}_0(1^\lambda)$
$\quad (\mathsf{pk}, \mathsf{sk}) \leftarrow \mathsf{TKG}(1^\lambda)$
$\quad b \xleftarrow{r} \{0, 1\}$
$\quad b' \leftarrow \mathcal{A}_1^{\mathcal{O}_{\mathsf{TEnc}}(\cdot, \cdot)}(\mathsf{pk}, \mathsf{st})$
$\quad$ Return $(b' \overset{?}{=} b)$.

$\mathcal{O}_{\mathsf{TEnc}}(\mathsf{m}_0, \mathsf{m}_1): \quad // \ |\mathsf{m}_0| = |\mathsf{m}_1|$
$\quad \mathsf{ct} \leftarrow \mathsf{TEnc}(\mathsf{pk}, i^*, v^*, \mathsf{m}_b)$
$\quad$ Return ct.

Fig. 4. The experiments for TE: Security against the receiver (left) and security against outsiders (right).

As the correctness for a TE scheme, we require that for all $\lambda \in \mathbb{N}$, $(\mathsf{pk}, \mathsf{sk}) \leftarrow \mathsf{TKG}(1^\lambda)$, $i \in [\ell_{\mathsf{sk}}]$, and m, we have $\mathsf{TDec}(\mathsf{pk}, \mathsf{sk}, i, \mathsf{TEnc}(\mathsf{pk}, i, \mathsf{sk}[i], \mathsf{m})) = \mathsf{m}$.

Barak et al. [5] defined two kinds of security notions for TE: *security against the receiver* and *security against outsiders*. We recall them here.

Security Against the Receiver. As the name suggests, this is a security notion against a receiver who holds a secret key. More specifically, this security notion ensures that for every $i \in [\ell_{\mathsf{sk}}]$, if a message is encrypted under the position $(i, 1 \oplus \mathsf{sk}[i])$, its information does not leak to the receiver of the ciphertext who holds a secret key sk. For convenience, we introduce the multi-challenge version of this security notion, which can be shown to be equivalent to the single-challenge version defined in [5] via a query-wise hybrid argument.

Formally, for a TE scheme $\mathsf{TE} = (\mathsf{TKG}, \mathsf{TEnc}, \mathsf{TDec})$ and an adversary $\mathcal{A} = (\mathcal{A}_0, \mathcal{A}_1)$, consider the experiment $\mathsf{Expt}_{\mathsf{TE},\mathcal{A}}^{\mathsf{receiver}}(\lambda)$ described in Fig. 4 (left). We emphasize again that since this security is considered against a receiver, an adversary is given a secret key sk as input.[8]

Definition 4 (Security against the Receiver). *We say that a TE scheme* TE *satisfies security against the receiver if for all PPT adversaries $\mathcal{A}$, we have* $\mathsf{Adv}_{\mathsf{TE},\mathcal{A}}^{\mathsf{receiver}}(\lambda) := 2 \cdot |\Pr[\mathsf{Expt}_{\mathsf{TE},\mathcal{A}}^{\mathsf{receiver}}(\lambda) = 1] - 1/2| = \mathsf{negl}(\lambda)$.

Security Against Outsiders. This security notion simply ensures that ciphertexts generated under any pair $(i, v) \in [\ell_{\mathsf{sk}}] \times \{0, 1\}$ do not leak the information of encrypted messages. Again, we introduce the multi-challenge version for this security notion, which is equivalent to the single-challenge version formalized in [5].

Formally, for a TE scheme $\mathsf{TE} = (\mathsf{TKG}, \mathsf{TEnc}, \mathsf{TDec})$ and an adversary $\mathcal{A} = (\mathcal{A}_0, \mathcal{A}_1)$, consider the experiment $\mathsf{Expt}_{\mathsf{TE},\mathcal{A}}^{\mathsf{outsider}}(\lambda)$ described in Fig. 4 (right).

---

[8] The original definition by Barak et al. [5] considered statistical security (i.e. security against computationally unbounded adversaries), but it was remarked there that computational security suffices for their construction of KDM-CPA secure PKE.

Definition 5 (Security against Outsiders). *We say that a TE scheme* TE *satisfies* security against outsiders *if for all PPT adversaries* $\mathcal{A}$, *we have* $\mathsf{Adv}_{\mathsf{TE},\mathcal{A}}^{\mathsf{outsider}}(\lambda) := 2 \cdot | \Pr[\mathsf{Expt}_{\mathsf{TE},\mathcal{A}}^{\mathsf{outsider}}(\lambda) = 1] - 1/2| = \mathsf{negl}(\lambda)$.

Result from [5]. Barak et al. [5] showed the following result, which we will use in Sect. 5.

Theorem 4 ([5]). *If there exists a TE scheme satisfying security against the receiver and security against outsiders, then for any polynomial* $\mathsf{size} = \mathsf{size}(\lambda)$, *there exists a* $\mathcal{B}_{\mathsf{size}}$-$KDM^{(1)}$-*CPA secure PKE scheme. Furthermore, there is a fully black-box construction of a* $\mathcal{P}$-$KDM^{(1)}$-*CPA secure PKE scheme from a TE scheme satisfying the two security notions.*

We remark that the result on the fully black-box construction can be extended to any function family such that a canonical description of a circuit computing any function in the family can be learned and reconstructed (with overwhelming probability) by just making polynomially many oracle queries to the function. (This is because in the security proof in [5], what is garbled is a function queried as a KDM-encryption query.) We only state it for $\mathcal{P}$-KDM security since it is sufficient for our purpose.

We also remark that [5] also showed that their construction achieves KDM-CPA security in the multi-key setting by additionally assuming that the underlying TE scheme is an *augmented TE* scheme satisfying circular security in the multi-key setting. We do not recall this result and the formal definition of augmented TE since we do not use them directly. In Sect. 6, we introduce conformed TE, which is also an extension of TE in a similar manner to augmented TE but has several differences. For the details, see the explanation there.

3.4 Additional Primitives

Here, we briefly recall the syntax of a DV-NIZK argument system and a garbling scheme used in Sect. 7. Due to the space limitation, we omit the formal security definitions in the proceedings version. See the full version for them.

Designated-Verifier Non-interactive Zero-Knowledge Arguments. Let L be an NP language associated with the corresponding NP relation R. A DV-NIZK argument system DVNIZK for L consists of the three PPT algorithms (DVKG, P, V): DVKG is the key generation algorithm that takes 1^λ as input, and outputs a public proving key pk and a secret verification key sk; P is the proving algorithm that takes a public proving key pk, a statement x, and a witness w as input, and outputs a proof π; V is the (deterministic) verification algorithm that takes a secret verification key sk, a statement x, and a proof π as input, and outputs either accept or reject.

For correctness, we require that for all $\lambda \in \mathbb{N}$, $(\mathsf{pk}, \mathsf{sk}) \leftarrow \mathsf{DVKG}(1^\lambda)$, and $(x, w) \in R$, we have $\mathsf{V}(\mathsf{sk}, x, \mathsf{P}(\mathsf{pk}, x, w)) = \mathsf{accept}$.

We require that a DV-NIZK argument system satisfy *(adaptive) soundness* and *(adaptive) zero-knowledge*. As in [22,25], we consider the *reusable* setting, where the security experiment for soundness (resp. zero-knowledge) allows an adversary to make multiple verification (resp. proving) queries. A DV-NIZK argument system satisfying these versions of soundness and zero-knowledge is called *reusable*. The formal definitions are given in the full version.

Garbling. Let $\mathcal{C} = \{\mathcal{C}_n\}_{n\in\mathbb{N}}$ be a family of circuits, where the input length of each member in $\mathcal{C}_n$ is n. A garbling scheme GC for $\mathcal{C}$ consists of the three PPT algorithms (Garble, Eval, Sim): Garble is the garbling algorithm that takes as input 1^λ and (the description of) a circuit $\mathsf{C} \in \mathcal{C}_n$, where $n = n(\lambda)$ is a polynomial. Then, it outputs a garbled circuit $\widetilde{\mathsf{C}}$ and $2n$ labels $(\mathsf{lab}_{i,v})_{i\in[n],v\in\{0,1\}}$; Eval is the (deterministic) evaluation algorithm that takes a garbled circuit $\widetilde{\mathsf{C}}$ and n labels $(\mathsf{lab}_i)_{i\in[n]}$ as input, and outputs an evaluation result y; Sim is the simulator algorithm that takes 1^λ, the size parameter size (where size $=$ size(λ) is a polynomial), and a string y as input, and outputs a simulated garbled circuit $\widetilde{\mathsf{C}}$ and n simulated labels $(\mathsf{lab}_i)_{i\in[n]}$.

For correctness, we require that for all $\lambda, n \in \mathbb{N}$, $\mathsf{x} \in \{0,1\}^n$, and $\mathsf{C} \in \mathcal{C}_n$, the following two conditions hold: (1) $\mathsf{Eval}(\widetilde{\mathsf{C}}, (\mathsf{lab}_{i,\mathsf{x}[i]})_{i\in[n]}) = \mathsf{C}(\mathsf{x})$ holds for all $(\widetilde{\mathsf{C}}, (\mathsf{lab}_{i,v})_{i\in[n],v\in\{0,1\}})$ output by $\mathsf{Garble}(1^\lambda, \mathsf{C})$, and (2) $\mathsf{Eval}(\widetilde{\mathsf{C}}, (\mathsf{lab}_i)_{i\in[n]}) = \mathsf{C}(\mathsf{x})$ holds for all $(\widetilde{\mathsf{C}}, (\mathsf{lab}_i)_{i\in[n]})$ output by $\mathsf{Sim}(1^\lambda, |\mathsf{C}|, \mathsf{C}(\mathsf{x}))$, where $|\mathsf{C}|$ denotes the size of C.

4   Targeted Encryption from Circular Security and Leakage-Resilience

In this section, as our main technical result, we show how to construct a TE scheme from the combination of a circular secure bit-SKE scheme (in the single-key setting) and a weakly noisy-leakage-resilient PKE scheme.

Construction. Our construction uses the following building blocks:

- Let $\mathsf{SKE} = (\mathsf{K}, \mathsf{E}, \mathsf{D})$ be a $\mathrm{CIRC}^{(1)}$ secure bit-SKE scheme with the secret-key length ℓ_k for some polynomial $\ell_\mathsf{k} = \ell_\mathsf{k}(\lambda)$. We assume that there exists a special symbol `flip` that is perfectly distinguishable from possible outputs of E.
- Let $\mathsf{PKE} = (\mathsf{KG}, \mathsf{Enc}, \mathsf{Dec})$ be a weakly L-noisy-leakage-resilient PKE scheme with simple key generation whose secret-key length is ℓ_sk for some polynomial $\ell_\mathsf{sk} = \ell_\mathsf{sk}(\lambda)$. We assume $L = 0.6\ell_\mathsf{sk}$.

Using these building blocks, we construct a TE scheme $\mathsf{TE} = (\mathsf{TKG}, \mathsf{TEnc}, \mathsf{TDec})$, whose secret key length is ℓ_k, as described in Fig. 5.

Correctness. The correctness of TE follows from that of the building blocks SKE and PKE. Specifically, since $\mathsf{TEnc}(\mathsf{PK}, i, \mathsf{SK}[i] = \mathsf{k}[i], \mathsf{m})$ just computes $\mathsf{Enc}(\mathsf{pk}_{i,\mathsf{k}[i]}, \mathsf{m})$ and $\mathsf{TDec}(\mathsf{PK}, \mathsf{SK}, i, \mathsf{ct})$ computes $\mathsf{Dec}(\mathsf{pk}_{i,\mathsf{k}[i]}, \mathsf{sk}', \mathsf{ct})$ in its last step, it suffices to see that sk' computed in TDec always equals to $\mathsf{sk}_{i,\mathsf{k}[i]}$ for any $i \in [\ell_\mathsf{k}]$. Indeed, for every $j \in [\ell_\mathsf{sk}]$, we have

$$\begin{array}{|l|}
\hline
\mathsf{TKG}(1^\lambda): \\
\quad \mathsf{k} \leftarrow \mathsf{K}(1^\lambda) \\
\quad \forall i \in [\ell_\mathsf{k}]: \\
\quad\quad \forall v \in \{0,1\}: \ \mathsf{sk}_{i,v} \xleftarrow{r} \{0,1\}^{\ell_\mathsf{sk}}; \ \ \mathsf{pk}_{i,v} \leftarrow \mathsf{KG}(\mathsf{sk}_{i,v}) \\
\quad\quad \forall j \in [\ell_\mathsf{sk}]: \\
\quad\quad\quad \mathsf{e}_{i,j} \leftarrow \begin{cases} \mathtt{flip} & \text{if } (\mathsf{sk}_{i,0}[j],\mathsf{sk}_{i,1}[j]) = (1,0) \\ \mathsf{E}(\mathsf{k},\mathsf{sk}_{i,\mathsf{k}[i]}[j]) & \text{otherwise} \end{cases} \\
\quad \mathsf{PK} \leftarrow (\mathsf{pk}_{i,0},\mathsf{pk}_{i,1},\mathsf{e}_{i,1},\ldots,\mathsf{e}_{i,\ell_\mathsf{sk}})_{i \in [\ell_\mathsf{k}]}; \ \ \mathsf{SK} \leftarrow \mathsf{k} \\
\quad \text{Return } (\mathsf{PK},\mathsf{SK}). \\
\hline
\end{array}$$

$\mathsf{TEnc}(\mathsf{PK}, i, v, \mathsf{m}):$	$\mathsf{TDec}(\mathsf{PK}, \mathsf{SK} = \mathsf{k}, i, \mathsf{ct}):$
$(\mathsf{pk}_{i,0},\mathsf{pk}_{i,1},\mathsf{e}_{i,1},\ldots,\mathsf{e}_{i,\ell_\mathsf{sk}})_{i \in [\ell_\mathsf{k}]} \leftarrow \mathsf{PK}$	$(\mathsf{pk}_{i,0},\mathsf{pk}_{i,1},\mathsf{e}_{i,1},\ldots,\mathsf{e}_{i,\ell_\mathsf{sk}})_{i \in [\ell_\mathsf{k}]} \leftarrow \mathsf{PK}$
Return $\mathsf{ct} \leftarrow \mathsf{Enc}(\mathsf{pk}_{i,v},\mathsf{m}).$	$\forall j \in [\ell_\mathsf{sk}]:$
	$\quad \mathsf{sk}'[j] \leftarrow \begin{cases} 1 \oplus \mathsf{k}[i] & \text{if } \mathsf{e}_{i,j} = \mathtt{flip} \\ \mathsf{D}(\mathsf{k},\mathsf{e}_{i,j}) & \text{otherwise} \end{cases}$
	Return $\mathsf{m} \leftarrow \mathsf{Dec}(\mathsf{pk}_{i,\mathsf{k}[i]},\mathsf{sk}',\mathsf{ct}).$

Fig. 5. The construction of a TE scheme TE from a circular secure bit-SKE scheme SKE and a weakly noisy-leakage-resilient PKE scheme PKE.

- If $(\mathsf{sk}_{i,0}[j],\mathsf{sk}_{i,1}[j]) = (1,0)$, then note that this case implies $\mathsf{sk}_{i,\mathsf{k}[i]}[j] = 1 \oplus \mathsf{k}[i]$. On the other hand, $\mathsf{e}_{i,j} = \mathtt{flip}$ holds by the design of TKG. Hence, TDec sets $\mathsf{sk}'[j] \leftarrow 1 \oplus \mathsf{k}[i] = \mathsf{sk}_{i,\mathsf{k}[i]}[j]$.
- Otherwise (i.e. $(\mathsf{sk}_{i,0}[j],\mathsf{sk}_{i,1}[j]) \neq (1,0)$), $\mathsf{e}_{i,j}$ is just an encryption of $\mathsf{sk}_{i,\mathsf{k}[i]}[j]$. Thus, TDec decrypts it as $\mathsf{sk}'[j] = \mathsf{D}(\mathsf{k},\mathsf{e}_{i,j}) = \mathsf{sk}_{i,\mathsf{k}[i]}[j]$.

Hence, we have $\mathsf{sk}'[j] = \mathsf{sk}_{i,\mathsf{k}[i]}[j]$ for every $j \in [\ell_\mathsf{sk}]$, namely, $\mathsf{sk}' = \mathsf{sk}_{i,\mathsf{k}[i]}$ holds. Thus, TE satisfies correctness.

Security. We now show that TE satisfies the two security notions for TE.

Theorem 5. *If* PKE *is weakly* $(0.6\ell_\mathsf{sk})$-*noisy-leakage-resilient, then* TE *satisfies security against the receiver.*

Proof of Theorem 5. Let $\mathcal{A} = (\mathcal{A}_0, \mathcal{A}_1)$ be any PPT adversary that attacks the security against the receiver of TE. We show that for $\mathcal{A}$, there exists a PPT $(0.6\ell_\mathsf{sk})$-noisy-leakage-respecting adversary $\mathcal{B}$ such that $\mathsf{Adv}^{\mathsf{receiver}}_{\mathsf{TE},\mathcal{A}}(\lambda) = \mathsf{Adv}^{\mathsf{wlr}}_{\mathsf{PKE},\mathcal{B},0.6\ell_\mathsf{sk}}(\lambda)$, which implies the theorem. The description of $\mathcal{B} = (\mathcal{B}_0, \mathcal{B}_1)$ is as follows.

$\mathcal{B}_0(1^\lambda)$: $\mathcal{B}_0$ first runs $(i^*, \mathsf{st}) \leftarrow \mathcal{A}_0(1^\lambda)$. Next, $\mathcal{B}_0$ computes $\mathsf{k} \leftarrow \mathsf{K}(1^\lambda)$, and picks $\mathsf{sk}_{i^*,\mathsf{k}[i^*]} \xleftarrow{r} \{0,1\}^{\ell_\mathsf{sk}}$. Let $P := \{j \in [\ell_\mathsf{sk}] \mid \mathsf{sk}_{i^*,\mathsf{k}[i^*]}[j] = 1 \oplus \mathsf{k}[i^*]\}$ and $\ell := |P|$, and suppose P is $\{p_1,\ldots,p_\ell\}$ such that $1 \leq p_1 < \cdots < p_\ell \leq \ell_\mathsf{sk}$. $\mathcal{B}_0$ defines the leakage function $f_P : \{0,1\}^{\ell_\mathsf{sk}} \to \{0,1\}^\ell$ by

$$f_P(\mathsf{z}) := (\mathsf{z}[p_1],\ldots,\mathsf{z}[p_\ell]) \in \{0,1\}^\ell.$$

Then, $\mathcal{B}_0$ sets $\mathsf{st}_\mathcal{B}$ as all the information known to $\mathcal{B}_0$, and terminates with output $(f_P, \mathsf{st}_\mathcal{B})$.

$\mathcal{B}_1^{\mathcal{O}_{\mathsf{Enc}}(\cdot,\cdot)}(\mathsf{pk}', f_P(\mathsf{sk}') = (\mathsf{sk}'[p_1], \ldots, \mathsf{sk}'[p_\ell]) \in \{0,1\}^\ell, \mathsf{st}_\mathcal{B})$: (where $(\mathsf{pk}', \mathsf{sk}')$ denotes the key pair generated in $\mathcal{B}$'s experiment) $\mathcal{B}_1$ first computes $\mathsf{pk}_{i^*, \mathsf{k}[i^*]} \leftarrow \mathsf{KG}(\mathsf{sk}_{i^*, \mathsf{k}[i^*]})$, and regards pk' as $\mathsf{pk}_{i^*, 1 \oplus \mathsf{k}[i^*]}$ (correspondingly, implicitly regards sk' as $\mathsf{sk}_{i^*, 1 \oplus \mathsf{k}[i^*]} \in \{0,1\}^{\ell_{\mathsf{sk}}}$). Then, for every $j \in [\ell_{\mathsf{sk}}]$, $\mathcal{B}_1$ generates $\mathsf{e}_{i^*, j}$ by

$$\mathsf{e}_{i^*, j} \leftarrow \begin{cases} \texttt{flip} & \text{if } j \in P \wedge \mathsf{sk}'[j] = \mathsf{k}[i^*] \\ \mathsf{E}(\mathsf{k}, \mathsf{sk}_{i^*, \mathsf{k}[i^*]}[j]) & \text{otherwise} \end{cases}.$$

Note that by the definition of P, we have $\mathsf{sk}_{i^*, \mathsf{k}[i^*]}[j] = 1 \oplus \mathsf{k}[i^*]$ if and only if $j \in P$. Furthermore, by the definition of the leakage function $f_P(\cdot)$, we have $\mathsf{sk}'[j] = \mathsf{sk}_{i^*, 1 \oplus \mathsf{k}[i^*]}[j]$ for all $j \in P$. Hence, we have

$$j \in P \wedge \mathsf{sk}'[j] = \mathsf{k}[i^*] \iff (\mathsf{sk}_{i^*, \mathsf{k}[i^*]}[j], \mathsf{sk}_{i^*, 1 \oplus \mathsf{k}[i^*]}[j]) = (1 \oplus \mathsf{k}[i^*], \mathsf{k}[i^*])$$
$$\iff (\mathsf{sk}_{i^*, 0}[j], \mathsf{sk}_{i^*, 1}[j]) = (1, 0).$$

Hence, the generation of $\mathsf{e}_{i^*, j}$ is in fact exactly the same as in $\mathsf{Expt}_{\mathsf{TE}, \mathcal{A}}^{\mathsf{receiver}}(\lambda)$. Then, $\mathcal{B}_1$ generates the remaining components in $\mathsf{PK} = (\mathsf{pk}_{i,0}, \mathsf{pk}_{i,1}, \mathsf{e}_{i,1}, \ldots, \mathsf{e}_{i,\ell_{\mathsf{sk}}})_{i \in [\ell_{\mathsf{k}}]}$ (i.e. the components for the positions $i \in [\ell_{\mathsf{k}}] \setminus \{i^*\}$) by itself exactly as $\mathsf{TKG}(1^\lambda)$ does.

Now, $\mathcal{B}_1$ runs $\mathcal{A}_1(\mathsf{PK}, \mathsf{SK} = \mathsf{k}, \mathsf{st})$. When $\mathcal{A}_1$ submits an encryption query $(\mathsf{m}_0, \mathsf{m}_1)$, $\mathcal{B}_1$ just forwards it to its own encryption oracle $\mathcal{O}_{\mathsf{Enc}}(\cdot, \cdot)$, and returns whatever returned from the oracle to $\mathcal{A}_1$.

When $\mathcal{A}_1$ terminates with output b', $\mathcal{B}_1$ terminates with output b'.

The above completes the description of $\mathcal{B}$. As mentioned above, $\mathcal{B}$ generates the key pair $(\mathsf{PK}, \mathsf{SK})$ with exactly the same distribution as that in the actual experiment for security against the receiver. Since $\mathcal{B}$ embeds its instance pk' to the position $(i^*, 1 \oplus \mathsf{k}[i^*])$, it is straightforward to see that $\mathcal{B}$ perfectly simulates the security experiment for $\mathcal{A}$ so that $\mathcal{A}$'s the challenge bit is that of $\mathcal{B}$'s, and thus $\mathcal{B}$'s advantage is exactly the same as that of $\mathcal{A}$'s.

It remains to confirm that $\mathcal{B}$ is a $(0.6\ell_{\mathsf{sk}})$-noisy-leakage-respecting adversary, namely, $0.6\ell_{\mathsf{sk}} \geq \mathbf{H}_\infty(\mathsf{sk}') - \widetilde{\mathbf{H}}_\infty(\mathsf{sk}'|f_P(\mathsf{sk}'), \mathsf{st}_\mathcal{B}) = \ell_{\mathsf{sk}} - \widetilde{\mathbf{H}}_\infty(\mathsf{sk}'|f_P(\mathsf{sk}'), \mathsf{st}_\mathcal{B})$ or equivalently $2^{-\widetilde{\mathbf{H}}_\infty(\mathsf{sk}'|f_P(\mathsf{sk}'), \mathsf{st}_\mathcal{B})} \leq 2^{-0.4\ell_{\mathsf{sk}}}$ holds. To see this, firstly note that $\mathsf{st}_\mathcal{B}$ output by $\mathcal{B}_0$ is independent of the choice of $\mathsf{sk}' \xleftarrow{\mathsf{r}} \{0,1\}^{\ell_{\mathsf{sk}}}$, and thus we have $\widetilde{\mathbf{H}}_\infty(\mathsf{sk}'|f_P(\mathsf{sk}'), \mathsf{st}_\mathcal{B}) = \widetilde{\mathbf{H}}_\infty(\mathsf{sk}'|f_P(\mathsf{sk}'))$. Thus, it is sufficient to show $2^{-\widetilde{\mathbf{H}}_\infty(\mathsf{sk}'|f_P(\mathsf{sk}'))} \leq 2^{-0.4\ell_{\mathsf{sk}}}$. Next, notice that P is distributed uniformly over $2^{[\ell_{\mathsf{sk}}]}$ (i.e. all the subsets of $[\ell_{\mathsf{sk}}]$), since P is determined by the random choice of $\mathsf{sk}_{i^*, \mathsf{k}[i^*]} \xleftarrow{\mathsf{r}} \{0,1\}^{\ell_{\mathsf{sk}}}$. Thus, we have

$$2^{-\widetilde{\mathbf{H}}_\infty(\mathsf{sk}'|f_P(\mathsf{sk}'))} = \mathop{\mathbf{E}}_{P \xleftarrow{\mathsf{r}} 2^{[\ell_{\mathsf{sk}}]}, \ y \xleftarrow{\mathsf{r}} \{0,1\}^{|P|}} \left[\max_{x^*} \Pr_{\mathsf{sk}' \xleftarrow{\mathsf{r}} \{0,1\}^{\ell_{\mathsf{sk}}}} [\mathsf{sk}' = x^* | f_P(\mathsf{sk}') = y] \right]$$

$$= \mathop{\mathbf{E}}_{P \xleftarrow{\mathsf{r}} 2^{[\ell_{\mathsf{sk}}]}} \left[2^{-\ell_{\mathsf{sk}} + |P|} \right] = 2^{-2\ell_{\mathsf{sk}}} \cdot \sum_{P' \subseteq [\ell_{\mathsf{sk}}]} 2^{|P'|} = 2^{-2\ell_{\mathsf{sk}}} \cdot \sum_{k=0}^{\ell_{\mathsf{sk}}} \binom{\ell_{\mathsf{sk}}}{k} \cdot 2^k$$

$$\overset{(*)}{=} 2^{-2\ell_{\mathsf{sk}}} \cdot 3^{\ell_{\mathsf{sk}}} = 2^{-(2 - \log_2 3)\ell_{\mathsf{sk}}} \overset{(\dagger)}{<} 2^{-0.4\ell_{\mathsf{sk}}},$$

where the equality (*) uses $\sum_{k=0}^{n} \binom{n}{k} x^k = (1+x)^n$, and the inequality (†) uses $\log_2 3 < 1.6$. Hence, $\mathcal{B}$ is $(0.6\ell_{sk})$-noisy-leakage-respecting. ☐ (**Theorem 5**)

Theorem 6. *If* SKE *is* $CIRC^{(1)}$ *secure and* PKE *is* $(0.6\ell_{sk})$-*noisy-leakage-resilient, then* TE *satisfies security against outsiders.*

Proof of Theorem 6. Let $\mathcal{A} = (\mathcal{A}_0, \mathcal{A}_1)$ be any PPT adversary that attacks the security against outsiders of TE. We show that there exist PPT adversaries $\mathcal{B}_c$ and $\mathcal{B}_w$ (where the latter is $(0.6\ell_{sk})$-noisy-leakage-respecting) satisfying

$$\mathsf{Adv}_{\mathsf{TE},\mathcal{A}}^{\mathsf{outsider}}(\lambda) \leq 2 \cdot \mathsf{Adv}_{\mathsf{SKE},\mathcal{B}_c,1}^{\mathsf{circ}}(\lambda) + \mathsf{Adv}_{\mathsf{PKE},\mathcal{B}_w,0.6\ell_{sk}}^{\mathsf{wlr}}(\lambda), \tag{1}$$

which implies the theorem.

To this end, we consider the following two games Game 1 and Game 2.

Game 1: This is the experiment for security against outsiders $\mathsf{Expt}_{\mathsf{TE},\mathcal{A}}^{\mathsf{outsider}}(\lambda)$.

Game 2: Same as Game 1, except that every invocation of $\mathsf{E}(k, \cdot)$ during the generation of PK is replaced with $\mathsf{E}(k, 0)$.

For $t \in \{1, 2\}$, let SUC_t be the event that $\mathcal{A}$ succeeds in guessing the challenge bit (i.e. $b' = b$ occurs) in Game t. By the definitions of the games and events and the triangle inequality, we have

$$\mathsf{Adv}_{\mathsf{TE},\mathcal{A}}^{\mathsf{outsider}}(\lambda) = 2 \cdot \left| \Pr[\mathsf{SUC}_1] - \frac{1}{2} \right| \leq 2 \cdot \left| \Pr[\mathsf{SUC}_1] - \Pr[\mathsf{SUC}_2] \right| + 2 \cdot \left| \Pr[\mathsf{SUC}_2] - \frac{1}{2} \right|. \tag{2}$$

In the following, we show how the terms appearing in Eq. 2 are bounded.

Lemma 2. *There exists a PPT adversary* $\mathcal{B}_c$ *such that* $\mathsf{Adv}_{\mathsf{SKE},\mathcal{B}_c,1}^{\mathsf{circ}}(\lambda) = |\Pr[\mathsf{SUC}_1] - \Pr[\mathsf{SUC}_2]|.$

Proof of Lemma 2. The description of $\mathcal{B}_c$ is as follows. Below, k and β denote the secret key and the challenge bit, respectively, chosen in $\mathcal{B}_c$'s experiment. Furthermore, since there is only a single key in the experiment of $\mathcal{B}_c$, we simplify the interface of the circular-encryption oracle $\mathcal{O}_{\mathsf{circ}}$ to take just $\mathsf{cmd} \in [\ell_k] \cup \{\mathsf{zero}, \mathsf{one}\}$ as input.

$\mathcal{B}_c^{\mathcal{O}_{\mathsf{circ}}(\cdot)}(1^\lambda)$: $\mathcal{B}_c$ first runs $(i^*, v^*, \mathsf{st}) \leftarrow \mathcal{A}_0(1^\lambda)$. Next, for every $i \in [\ell_k]$, $\mathcal{B}_c$ does the following:

1. For both $v \in \{0, 1\}$, pick $\mathsf{sk}_{i,v} \xleftarrow{r} \{0, 1\}^{\ell_{sk}}$ and compute $\mathsf{pk}_{i,v} \leftarrow \mathsf{KG}(\mathsf{sk}_{i,v})$.
2. For the positions $j \in [\ell_{sk}]$ for which $(\mathsf{sk}_{i,0}[j], \mathsf{sk}_{i,1}[j]) = (1, 0)$ holds, set $\mathsf{e}_{i,j} \leftarrow \mathsf{flip}$.
3. For the remaining positions $j \in [\ell_{sk}]$ with $(\mathsf{sk}_{i,0}[j], \mathsf{sk}_{i,1}[j]) \neq (1, 0)$, set

$$\mathsf{cmd}_j \leftarrow \begin{cases} \mathsf{zero} & \text{if } (\mathsf{sk}_{i,0}[j], \mathsf{sk}_{i,1}[j]) = (0, 0) \\ \mathsf{one} & \text{if } (\mathsf{sk}_{i,0}[j], \mathsf{sk}_{i,1}[j]) = (1, 1) \,, \\ i & \text{if } (\mathsf{sk}_{i,0}[j], \mathsf{sk}_{i,1}[j]) = (0, 1) \end{cases}$$

submit cmd_j to $\mathcal{B}_c$'s oracle $\mathcal{O}_{\mathsf{circ}}(\cdot)$, and receive $\mathsf{e}_{i,j}$ as the answer from $\mathcal{O}_{\mathsf{circ}}$.

Note that if $(\mathsf{sk}_{i,0}[j], \mathsf{sk}_{i,1}[j]) = (0,1)$ then $\mathsf{sk}_{i,\mathsf{k}[i]}[j] = \mathsf{k}[i]$ holds, and the latter is trivially true for the cases $(\mathsf{sk}_{i,0}[j], \mathsf{sk}_{i,1}[j]) \in \{(0,0),(1,1)\}$. Thus, $\mathcal{O}_{\mathsf{circ}}$ computes $\mathsf{e}_{i,j}$ as follows:

$$\mathsf{e}_{i,j} \leftarrow \begin{cases} \mathsf{E}(\mathsf{k}, \mathsf{sk}_{i,\mathsf{k}[i]}[j]) & \text{if } \beta = 1 \\ \mathsf{E}(\mathsf{k}, 0) & \text{if } \beta = 0 \end{cases}.$$

Therefore, if $\beta = 1$ (resp. $\beta = 0$), then $\mathsf{e}_{i,j}$ for every $j \in [\ell_{\mathsf{sk}}]$ is computed exactly as in Game 1 (resp. Game 2).

Then, $\mathcal{B}_{\mathsf{c}}$ sets $\mathsf{PK} \leftarrow (\mathsf{pk}_{i,0}, \mathsf{pk}_{i,1}, \mathsf{e}_{i,1}, \ldots, \mathsf{e}_{i,\ell_{\mathsf{sk}}})_{i \in [\ell_{\mathsf{k}}]}$, picks $b \xleftarrow{\mathsf{r}} \{0,1\}$, and runs $\mathcal{A}_1(\mathsf{PK}, \mathsf{st})$.

$\mathcal{B}_{\mathsf{c}}$ answers encryption queries $(\mathsf{m}_0, \mathsf{m}_1)$ from $\mathcal{A}_1$ by returning $\mathsf{ct} \leftarrow \mathsf{Enc}(\mathsf{pk}_{i^*,v^*}, \mathsf{m}_b)$ to $\mathcal{A}_1$.

When $\mathcal{A}_1$ terminates with output b', $\mathcal{B}_{\mathsf{c}}$ terminates with output $\beta' \leftarrow (b' \overset{?}{=} b)$.

The above completes the description of $\mathcal{B}_{\mathsf{c}}$. It is straightforward to see that if $\beta = 1$ (resp. $\beta = 0$), then $\mathcal{B}_{\mathsf{c}}$ simulates Game 1 (resp. Game 2) perfectly for $\mathcal{A}$. Since $\mathcal{B}_{\mathsf{c}}$ outputs $\beta' = 1$ if and only if $\mathcal{A}$ succeeds in guessing the challenge bit (i.e. $b' = b$ occurs), we have

$$\mathsf{Adv}^{\mathsf{circ}}_{\mathsf{SKE}, \mathcal{B}_{\mathsf{c}}, 1}(\lambda) = \Big| \Pr[\beta' = 1 | \beta = 1] - \Pr[\beta' = 1 | \beta = 0] \Big| = \Big| \Pr[\mathsf{SUC}_1] - \Pr[\mathsf{SUC}_2] \Big|.$$
$$\square \text{ (\textbf{Lemma} 2)}$$

Lemma 3. *There exists a PPT $(0.6\ell_{\mathsf{sk}})$-noisy-leakage-respecting adversary $\mathcal{B}_{\mathsf{w}}$ such that $\mathsf{Adv}^{\mathsf{wlr}}_{\mathsf{PKE}, \mathcal{B}_{\mathsf{w}}, 0.6\ell_{\mathsf{sk}}}(\lambda) = 2 \cdot |\Pr[\mathsf{SUC}_2] - 1/2|$.*

Proof Sketch of Lemma 3. The reduction algorithm $\mathcal{B}_{\mathsf{w}}$ for the proof of this lemma proceeds very similarly to $\mathcal{B}$ used in the proof of Theorem 5, with the following differences:

- $\mathcal{B}_{\mathsf{w}}$ embeds its instance pk' into the position (i^*, v^*) output by $\mathcal{A}_0$ (rather than $(i^*, 1 \oplus \mathsf{k}[i^*])$), which means that $(\mathsf{pk}', \mathsf{sk}')$ now corresponds to $(\mathsf{pk}_{i^*,v^*}, \mathsf{sk}_{i^*,v^*})$; $\mathcal{B}_{\mathsf{w}}$ generates the key pair of the opposite position, namely $(\mathsf{pk}_{i^*,1\oplus v^*}, \mathsf{sk}_{i^*,1\oplus v^*})$ by itself.
- $\mathcal{B}_{\mathsf{w}}$ defines the set P by $P := \{j \in [\ell_{\mathsf{sk}}] | \mathsf{sk}_{i^*,1\oplus v^*}[j] = v^*\}$, and uses it to define the leakage function $f_P(\cdot)$ exactly $\mathcal{B}$ in the proof of Theorem 5 does. Note that since we have the correspondence $\mathsf{sk}' = \mathsf{sk}_{i^*,v^*}$, the leakage $f_P(\mathsf{sk}')$ is $(\mathsf{sk}_{i^*,v^*}[j])_{j \in P}$.
- For every $j \in [\ell_{\mathsf{sk}}]$, $\mathcal{B}_{\mathsf{w}}$ generates $\mathsf{e}_{i^*,j}$ by

$$\mathsf{e}_{i^*,j} \leftarrow \begin{cases} \texttt{flip} & \text{if } j \in P \wedge \mathsf{sk}'[j] = 1 \oplus v^* \\ \mathsf{E}(\mathsf{k}, 0) & \text{otherwise} \end{cases}.$$

Then, by the definition of P and the correspondence $\mathsf{sk}' = \mathsf{sk}_{i^*,v^*}$, we have

$$j \in P \wedge \mathsf{sk}'[j] = 1 \oplus v^* \iff (\mathsf{sk}_{i^*,1\oplus v^*}[j], \mathsf{sk}_{i^*,v^*}[j]) = (v^*, 1 \oplus v^*)$$
$$\iff (\mathsf{sk}_{i^*,0}[j], \mathsf{sk}_{i^*,1}[j]) = (1,0).$$

Thus, $\mathsf{e}_{i^*,j}$ is generated exactly as in Game 2.

Then, it is straightforward to see that $\mathcal{B}_w$ is $(0.6\ell_{sk})$-noisy-leakage-respecting and simulates Game 2 perfectly for $\mathcal{A}$, and its advantage in attacking the weak noisy-leakage-resilience of PKE is exactly $2 \cdot |\Pr[\mathsf{SUC}_2] - 1/2|$.   □ (**Lemma** 3)

Combining Lemmas 2 and 3 with Eq. 2, we can conclude that there exist PPT adversaries $\mathcal{B}_c$ and $\mathcal{B}_w$ satisfying Eq. 1.   □ (**Theorem** 6)

5   Implications of Our TE Scheme

In this section, we explain the implications of our TE scheme in Sect. 4.

Completeness of Circular Security for KDM Security in the Single-Key Setting. Note that our construction of TE is a fully black-box construction from the building blocks. Moreover, by appropriately setting parameters, we can construct a PKE scheme with simple key generation whose secret key length is ℓ_{sk} and that satisfies weak $(0.6\ell_{sk})$-noisy-leakage-resilience, based on any IND-CPA secure PKE scheme via Lemma 1. Hence, the following theorem follows from the combination of Theorems 4, 5, and 6, and Lemma 1.

Theorem 7. *If there exist an IND-CPA secure PKE scheme and a $CIRC^{(1)}$ secure bit-SKE scheme, then for any polynomial* $\mathsf{size} = \mathsf{size}(\lambda)$, *there exists a* $\mathcal{B}_{\mathsf{size}}$-$KDM^{(1)}$-*CPA secure PKE scheme. Furthermore, there exists a fully black-box construction of a $\mathcal{P}$-$KDM^{(1)}$-CPA secure PKE scheme from an IND-CPA secure PKE scheme and a $CIRC^{(1)}$ secure bit-SKE scheme.*

Combining Theorem 7 with Theorem 3, we obtain the following completeness theorem for KDM security in the single-key setting. This improves the results of [3] and [22] in terms of assumptions.

Theorem 8. *If there exists an IND-CPA secure PKE scheme and a $CIRC^{(1)}$ secure bit-SKE scheme, then for any polynomial* $\mathsf{size} = \mathsf{size}(\lambda)$, *there exists a* $\mathcal{B}_{\mathsf{size}}$-$KDM^{(1)}$-*CCA secure PKE scheme.*

In Sect. 7, we will show that a similar completeness theorem for KDM security in the multi-key setting can be established. For the result, we will rely on the results on IND-CCA secure PKE and a reusable DV-NIZK argument system[9] for NP languages stated below.

Additional Results on IND-CCA PKE and DV-NIZK. As stated in Theorem 7, a $\mathcal{P}$-$KDM^{(1)}$-CPA secure PKE scheme can be constructed from an IND-CPA secure PKE and a $CIRC^{(1)}$ secure bit-SKE scheme in a fully black-box manner. Hence, combined with Theorem 2, we obtain the following result on IND-CCA secure PKE, which improves the results of [23] and [19] in terms of assumptions.

---

[9] The formal definitions for IND-CCA security and a reusable DV-NIZK argument system are given in the full version.

Theorem 9. *There exists a fully black-box construction of an IND-CCA secure PKE scheme from an IND-CPA secure PKE scheme and a $CIRC^{(1)}$ secure bit-SKE scheme.*

Finally, combining Theorem 7 with the results in [22, 25] that a reusable DV-NIZK argument system for all NP languages can be constructed from the combination of IND-CPA secure PKE and $\mathcal{P}$-$KDM^{(1)}$-CPA secure SKE, we also obtain the following result that improves [22] and [25] in terms of assumptions.

Theorem 10. *If there exists an IND-CPA secure PKE scheme and a $CIRC^{(1)}$ secure bit-SKE scheme, then there exists a reusable DV-NIZK argument system for all NP languages.*

6   Conformed Targeted Encryption

In this section, we introduce an encryption primitive that we call *conformed targeted encryption (CTE)*. This is an extension of an ordinary TE, and has some similar flavor to *augmented TE* formalized by Barak et al. [5]. Our definitional choice of CTE is made so that (1) it can be achieved from the combination of an IND-CPA secure PKE scheme and a circular secure bit-SKE scheme, and (2) it is sufficient as a building block for constructing a KDM-CCA secure PKE scheme in the multi-key setting.

In Sect. 6.1, we give the definitions for CTE and explain its difference with augmented TE formalized by Barak et al.. In Sect. 6.2, we show how our TE scheme presented in Sect. 4 can be extended to be a CTE scheme satisfying all the requirements.

6.1   Definitions

Syntax and Correctness. A *conformed targeted encryption* (CTE) scheme TE consists of the six algorithms $(\mathsf{CKG}, \mathsf{CEnc}, \mathsf{CDec}, \widehat{\mathsf{CDec}}, \mathsf{CSEnc}, \mathsf{CSDec})$:

- CKG, CEnc, and CDec are defined similarly to the key generation, encryption, and decryption algorithms of a TE scheme, respectively, except that in addition to a public/secret key pair $(\mathsf{pk}, \mathsf{sk})$, CKG also outputs a trapdoor td. This process is written as $(\mathsf{pk}, \mathsf{sk}, \mathsf{td}) \leftarrow \mathsf{CKG}(1^\lambda)$.
- $\widehat{\mathsf{CDec}}$ is the trapdoor-decryption algorithm that takes td, an index $i \in [\ell_{\mathsf{sk}}]$, a bit $v \in \{0, 1\}$, and a ciphertext ct (supposedly generated by CEnc) as input, and outputs a message m.
- CSEnc and CSDec are the additional *secret-key* encryption and decryption algorithms, respectively, where they use a secret key sk generated by CKG. We denote $\widetilde{\mathsf{ct}}$ to indicate that it is a ciphertext generated by CSEnc.

As the correctness for a CTE scheme, we require that for all $\lambda \in \mathbb{N}$ and $(\mathsf{pk}, \mathsf{sk}, \mathsf{td}) \leftarrow \mathsf{CKG}(1^\lambda)$, the following conditions are satisfied:

1. $\mathsf{CDec}(\mathsf{pk}, \mathsf{sk}, i, \mathsf{CEnc}(\mathsf{pk}, i, \mathsf{sk}[i], \mathsf{m})) = \mathsf{m}$ holds for all $i \in [\ell_{\mathsf{sk}}]$ and m.

2. $\widehat{\mathsf{CDec}}(\mathsf{td}, i, v, \mathsf{CEnc}(\mathsf{pk}, i, v, \mathsf{m})) = \mathsf{m}$ holds for all $(i, v) \in [\ell_{\mathsf{sk}}] \times \{0, 1\}$ and m.
3. $\mathsf{CDec}(\mathsf{pk}, \mathsf{sk}, i, \mathsf{ct}) = \widehat{\mathsf{CDec}}(\mathsf{td}, i, \mathsf{sk}[i], \mathsf{ct})$ holds for all $i \in [\ell_{\mathsf{sk}}]$ and ct (not necessarily in the support of CEnc).
4. $\mathsf{CSDec}(\mathsf{sk}, \mathsf{CSEnc}(\mathsf{sk}, \mathsf{m})) = \mathsf{m}$ holds for all m.

Note that the first condition of correctness ensures that $(\mathsf{CKG}, \mathsf{CEnc}, \mathsf{CDec})$ constitutes a TE scheme when td in the output of CKG is discarded. We also remark that the third condition of correctness is required to hold for all values of ct not necessarily in the support of CEnc. Looking ahead, this property plays an important role in our construction of KDM-CCA secure PKE in Sect. 7.

Security Definitions for CTE. For a CTE scheme, we require two security notions: *security against the receiver* and *special weak circular security (in the multi-key setting).*[10] The former is defined in exactly the same way as that for TE, except that we just discard and ignore the trapdoor td generated from CKG. Thus, we omit its formal description.

The latter security notion, special weak circular security, requires that the additional secret-key encryption/decryption algorithms $(\mathsf{CSEnc}, \mathsf{CSDec})$ satisfy a weak form of circular security in the multi-key setting. Specifically, in the n-key setting, we require that messages encrypted by CSEnc be hidden even in the presence of public keys $\{\mathsf{pk}^s\}_{s \in [n]}$, trapdoors $\{\mathsf{td}^s\}_{s \in [n]}$, and *encryptions of a "key cycle"* $\{\mathsf{CSEnc}(\mathsf{sk}^s, \mathsf{sk}^{(s \bmod n)+1})\}_{s \in [n]}$. We call it *weak* since except for giving $\{(\mathsf{pk}^s, \mathsf{td}^s)\}_{s \in [n]}$ to an adversary, our definition is the same as the definition of weak circular security formalized by Cash, Green, and Hohenberger [13].

Formally, let $n = n(\lambda)$ be a polynomial. For a CTE scheme $(\mathsf{CKG}, \mathsf{CEnc}, \mathsf{CDec}, \widehat{\mathsf{CDec}}, \mathsf{CSEnc}, \mathsf{CSDec})$, n, and an adversary $\mathcal{A}$, consider the experiment $\mathsf{Expt}^{\mathsf{sp-wcirc}}_{\mathsf{CTE}, \mathcal{A}, n}(\lambda)$ described in Fig. 6. Note that in the experiment, $\mathcal{O}_{\mathsf{CSEnc}}$ is an ordinary (challenge) encryption oracle. Thus, except for the encryptions of a key cycle $\{\mathsf{CSEnc}(\mathsf{sk}^s, \mathsf{sk}^{(s \bmod n)+1})\}_{s \in [n]}$, $\mathcal{A}$ is *not* allowed to directly obtain encryptions of key-dependent messages.

Definition 6 (Special Weak Circular Security). *Let $n = n(\lambda)$ be a polynomial. We say that a CTE scheme* CTE *satisfies special weak circular security in the n-key setting (special weak $CIRC^{(n)}$ security) if for all PPT adversaries $\mathcal{A}$, we have* $\mathsf{Adv}^{\mathsf{sp-wcirc}}_{\mathsf{CTE}, \mathcal{A}, n}(\lambda) := 2 \cdot |\Pr[\mathsf{Expt}^{\mathsf{sp-wcirc}}_{\mathsf{CTE}, \mathcal{A}, n}(\lambda) = 1] - 1/2| = \mathsf{negl}(\lambda).$

Relation to Augmented TE. As mentioned earlier, Barak et al. [5] introduced the notion of *augmented TE*, and used it to construct a $\mathcal{B}_{\mathsf{size}}$-KDM$^{(n)}$-CPA-secure PKE scheme for any polynomials $n = n(\lambda)$ and $\mathsf{size} = \mathsf{size}(\lambda)$. An augmented TE scheme is a TE scheme with the additional *public-key* encryption/decryption algorithms, for which Barak et al. assumed circular security in the n-key setting.

---

[10] We can also consider security against outsiders for CTE. However, we do not formalize it since we need not use it in our construction of KDM-CCA secure PKE.

$\mathsf{Expt}_{\mathsf{CTE},\mathcal{A},n}^{\mathsf{sp-wcirc}}(\lambda):$
$\quad \forall s \in [n] : (\mathsf{pk}^s, \mathsf{sk}^s, \mathsf{td}^s) \leftarrow \mathsf{CKG}(1^\lambda)$
$\quad (\widetilde{\mathsf{ct}}^s)_{s \in [n]} \leftarrow \mathsf{EncCycle}((\mathsf{sk}^s)_{s \in [n]})$
$\quad b \xleftarrow{\mathsf{r}} \{0, 1\}$
$\quad b' \leftarrow \mathcal{A}^{\mathcal{O}_{\mathsf{CSEnc}}(\cdot, \cdot, \cdot)}((\mathsf{pk}^s, \mathsf{td}^s, \widetilde{\mathsf{ct}}^s)_{s \in [n]})$
$\quad \text{Return } (b' \stackrel{?}{=} b).$

$\mathsf{EncCycle}((\mathsf{sk}^s)_{s \in [n]}):$
$\quad \forall s \in [n] : \widetilde{\mathsf{ct}}^s \leftarrow \mathsf{CSEnc}(\mathsf{sk}^s, \mathsf{sk}^{(s \bmod n)+1})$
$\quad \text{Return } (\widetilde{\mathsf{ct}}^s)_{s \in [n]}.$

$\mathcal{O}_{\mathsf{CSEnc}}(\alpha, \mathsf{m}_0, \mathsf{m}_1): \quad // \ \alpha \in [n], |\mathsf{m}_0| = |\mathsf{m}_1|$
$\quad \widetilde{\mathsf{ct}} \leftarrow \mathsf{CSEnc}(\mathsf{sk}^\alpha, \mathsf{m}_b)$
$\quad \text{Return } \widetilde{\mathsf{ct}}.$

Fig. 6. The experiment for defining special weak circular security for a CTE scheme.

(Their definition requires that encryptions of a key cycle of length n are indistinguishable from encryptions of some fixed messages.)

We observe that their security proof goes through even if (1) the additional encryption/decryption algorithms are of secret-key, and (2) we only require *weak* circular security in the n-key setting [13], which requires that IND-CPA security holds in the presence of encryptions of a key cycle of length n.

Our formalization for CTE is based on these observations, but CTE has an additional syntactical extension involving a trapdoor generated in the key generation algorithm, together with the additional correctness requirements. This plays an important role in the security proof for our $\mathcal{B}_{\mathsf{size}}\text{-KDM}^{(n)}\text{-CCA}$ secure PKE scheme presented in Sect. 7. We also remark that we do not require CTE to satisfy security against outsiders, while it is necessary for augmented TE used in the construction of KDM-CPA secure PKE in [5]. Our construction of KDM-CCA secure PKE does not require security against outsiders for the underlying CTE scheme because of the other building blocks. (See Sect. 7.)

6.2 Construction

Let $n = n(\lambda)$ be a polynomial for which we would like our CTE scheme CTE to satisfy special weak $\mathrm{CIRC}^{(n)}$ security. Let $\mathsf{PKE} = (\mathsf{KG}, \mathsf{Enc}, \mathsf{Dec})$ and $\mathsf{SKE} = (\mathsf{K}, \mathsf{E}, \mathsf{D})$ be PKE and SKE schemes as in Sect. 4, respectively, where we now require SKE to be $\mathrm{CIRC}^{(n)}$ secure.

Our construction of a CTE scheme $\mathsf{CTE} = (\mathsf{CKG}, \mathsf{CEnc}, \mathsf{CDec}, \widehat{\mathsf{CDec}}, \mathsf{CSEnc}, \mathsf{CSDec})$ based on PKE and SKE, is a simple extension of our TE scheme $\mathsf{TE} = (\mathsf{TKG}, \mathsf{TEnc}, \mathsf{TDec})$ presented in Sect. 4. Specifically, each algorithm of CTE operates as follows:

- CKG computes a public/secret key pair $(\mathsf{PK}, \mathsf{SK})$ in exactly the same way as TKG, and additionally outputs $\mathsf{td} := (\mathsf{pk}_{i,v}, \mathsf{sk}_{i,v})_{i \in [\ell_k], v \in \{0,1\}}$ as a trapdoor.
- CEnc and CDec are exactly TEnc and TDec, respectively.
- $\widehat{\mathsf{CDec}}(\mathsf{td}, i, v, \mathsf{ct}) := \mathsf{Dec}(\mathsf{pk}_{i,v}, \mathsf{sk}_{i,v}, \mathsf{ct})$.
- CSEnc and CSDec use E and D to encrypt/decrypt a message/ciphertext in a bit-wise fashion. More specifically, $\mathsf{CSEnc}(\mathsf{SK} = \mathsf{k}, \mathsf{m} \in \{0,1\}^\mu)$ outputs $\widetilde{\mathsf{ct}} = (\widetilde{\mathsf{ct}}_t)_{t \in [\mu]}$, where $\widetilde{\mathsf{ct}}_t \leftarrow \mathsf{E}(\mathsf{k}, \mathsf{m}[t])$ for each $t \in [\mu]$; $\mathsf{CDec}(\mathsf{SK} = \mathsf{k}, \widetilde{\mathsf{ct}} = (\widetilde{\mathsf{ct}}_t)_{t \in [\mu]})$ computes $\mathsf{m}[t] \leftarrow \mathsf{D}(\mathsf{k}, \widetilde{\mathsf{ct}}_t)$ for each $t \in [\mu]$, and outputs m.

Correctness. The first condition of correctness is exactly the same as the correctness for TE. The third condition of correctness holds because sk' computed in CDec(PK, SK = k, i, ·) is $\mathsf{sk}_{i,\mathsf{k}[i]}$ as we saw for the correctness of TE. The second and fourth conditions of correctness are trivially satisfied because of the correctness of PKE and SKE, respectively.

Security. The following theorems guarantee that CTE satisfies the two kinds of security notions for CTE. We omit the proof of Theorem 11 since it is exactly the same as that of Theorem 5.

Theorem 11. *If* PKE *is weakly* $(0.6\ell_{\mathsf{sk}})$-*noisy-leakage-resilient, then* CTE *satisfies security against the receiver.*

Theorem 12. *Let* $n = n(\lambda)$ *be a polynomial. If* SKE *is* $CIRC^{(n)}$ *secure, then* CTE *satisfies special weak* $CIRC^{(n)}$ *security.*

Proof Sketch of Theorem 12. This is straightforward to see by noting that CSEnc directly uses E to encrypt a given message in a bit-wise fashion, and the trapdoor td consists only of key pairs of the underlying PKE scheme PKE and thus is independent of a secret key SK = k.

More specifically, for $s \in [n]$, let $\mathsf{SK}^s = \mathsf{k}^s$ denote the s-th secret key. Then, consider a modified security experiment, which proceeds similarly to the experiment for the special weak $CIRC^{(n)}$ security of CTE, except that for every $s \in [n]$, all invocations of $\mathsf{E}(\mathsf{k}^s, ·)$ (which include those during the execution of $\mathsf{EncCycle}((\mathsf{SK}^s = \mathsf{k}^s)_{s\in[n]})$, those during the execution of $(\mathsf{PK}^s, \mathsf{SK}^s = \mathsf{k}^s, \mathsf{td}^s) \leftarrow \mathsf{CKG}(1^\lambda)$, and those for encryption queries from an adversary) are replaced with $\mathsf{E}(\mathsf{k}^s, 0)$. Note that this modified experiment is independent of the challenge bit b, and thus any adversary has zero advantage. Furthermore, by the $CIRC^{(n)}$ security of SKE, for any PPT adversary, its advantage in the original special weak $CIRC^{(n)}$ security experiment is negligibly close to that in the modified experiment. □ (**Theorem** 12)

7   KDM-CCA Security in the Multi-key Setting

In this section, we show the completeness of circular security in the multi-key setting. Specifically, we show the following theorem:

Theorem 13. *Let* $n = n(\lambda)$ *be a polynomial. Assume that there exist an IND-CPA secure* PKE *scheme and a* $CIRC^{(n)}$ *secure bit-SKE scheme. Then, for any polynomial* size = $\mathsf{size}(\lambda)$, *there exists a* $\mathcal{B}_{\mathsf{size}}$-$KDM^{(n)}$-*CCA secure* PKE *scheme.*

Note that this result improves the result by Kitagawa and Matsuda [22] (recalled as Theorem 3) in terms of the strength of assumptions and the number of keys.

As explained earlier, we will show the above theorem by constructing a $\mathcal{B}_{\mathsf{size}}$-$KDM^{(n)}$-CCA secure PKE scheme from the building blocks that are all implied by an IND-CPA secure PKE scheme and a $CIRC^{(n)}$ secure bit-SKE scheme. Our construction can be seen as combining the construction ideas from the bounded-KDM$^{(n)}$-CPA secure PKE scheme from an augmented TE scheme by Barak et al. [5] and the bounded-KDM$^{(1)}$-CCA secure PKE scheme from an IND-CPA secure PKE scheme and a projection-KDM$^{(1)}$-CPA secure SKE scheme by Kitagawa and Matsuda [22]. The latter construction in fact uses an IND-CCA secure PKE scheme, a garbling scheme, and a reusable DV-NIZK argument system as additional building blocks, which are implied by the assumption used in [22]. Construction-wise, roughly speaking, our construction is obtained by replacing the underlying IND-CPA secure scheme of the Kitagawa-Matsuda construction with a CTE scheme.

Construction. To construct a $\mathcal{B}_{\text{size}}$-KDM$^{(n)}$-CCA secure PKE scheme, we use the following building blocks all of which are implied by the combination of an IND-CPA secure PKE scheme and a CIRC$^{(n)}$ secure SKE scheme:

- Let CTE = (CKG, CEnc, CDec, $\widehat{\text{CDec}}$, CSEnc, CSDec) be a CTE scheme whose secret key length is ℓ_{sk}. Let $\ell_{\tilde{\text{e}}}$ denote the length of a ciphertext when encrypting a message of length ℓ_{sk} by using CSEnc. We denote the randomness space of CEnc by $\mathcal{R}$.
- Let PKE$_{\text{cca}}$ = (KG$_{\text{cca}}$, Enc$_{\text{cca}}$, Dec$_{\text{cca}}$) be an IND-CCA secure PKE scheme.
- Let GC = (Garble, Eval, Sim) be a garbling scheme for circuits.[11]
- Let DVNIZK = (DVKG, P, V) be a reusable DV-NIZK argument system for the following NP language L:[12]

$$L = \left\{ \left(\text{pk}, (\text{ct}_{i,v})_{i \in [\ell_{\text{sk}}], v \in \{0,1\}} \right) \middle| \begin{array}{c} \exists (\text{lab}_i, r_{i,0}, r_{i,1})_{i \in [\ell_{\text{sk}}]} \text{ s.t.} \\ \forall (i, v) \in [\ell_{\text{sk}}] \times \{0,1\}: \\ \text{ct}_{i,v} = \text{CEnc}(\text{pk}, i, v, \text{lab}_i; r_{i,v}) \end{array} \right\}.$$

Let $\mu = \mu(\lambda)$ be a polynomial that denotes the length of messages to be encrypted by our constructed PKE scheme. Let $n = n(\lambda)$ and $\text{size} = \text{size}(\lambda) \geq \max\{n \cdot \ell_{\text{sk}}, \mu\}$ be polynomials for which we wish to achieve $\mathcal{B}_{\text{size}}$-KDM$^{(n)}$-CCA security. Finally, let $\text{pad} = O(n \cdot (|\text{CSDec}| + \ell_{\tilde{\text{e}}}) + \text{size}) \geq \text{size}$ be the size parameter for the underlying garbling scheme (which is the size of a circuit that will be specified in the security proof), where $|\text{CSDec}|$ denotes the size of the circuit computing CSDec.

Using these ingredients, we construct our proposed PKE scheme PKE$_{\text{kdm}}$ = (KG$_{\text{kdm}}$, Enc$_{\text{kdm}}$, Dec$_{\text{kdm}}$) whose message space is $\{0,1\}^\mu$ as described in Fig. 7.

Correctness. The correctness of PKE$_{\text{kdm}}$ follows from that of the building blocks. Specifically, let (PK, SK) = ((pk, pk$_{\text{cca}}$, pk$_{\text{dv}}$, $\widetilde{\text{ct}}$), sk) be a key pair output by KG$_{\text{kdm}}$, let m $\in \{0,1\}^\mu$ be any message, and let CT $\leftarrow$ Enc$_{\text{kdm}}$(PK, m) be an honestly generated ciphertext. Due to the correctness of CTE, PKE$_{\text{cca}}$, and DVNIZK,

---

[11] For the formal security definition of a garbling scheme, see the full version.

[12] Intuitively, a statement $(\text{pk}, (\text{ct}_{i,v})_{i \in [\ell_{\text{sk}}], v \in \{0,1\}})$ of the language L constitutes a $(\ell_{\text{sk}} \times 2)$-matrix of ciphertexts such that the pair $(\text{ct}_{i,0}, \text{ct}_{i,1})$ in the i-th row encrypt the same plaintext lab_i for each $i \in [\ell_{\text{sk}}]$.

$\mathsf{KG_{kdm}}(1^\lambda):$	$\mathsf{Enc_{kdm}}(\mathsf{PK}, \mathsf{m}):$
$\quad (\mathsf{pk}, \mathsf{sk}, \mathsf{td}) \leftarrow \mathsf{CKG}(1^\lambda)$	$\quad (\mathsf{pk}, \mathsf{pk_{cca}}, \mathsf{pk_{dv}}, \widetilde{\mathsf{ct}}) \leftarrow \mathsf{PK}$
$\quad (\mathsf{pk_{cca}}, \mathsf{sk_{cca}}) \leftarrow \mathsf{KG_{cca}}(1^\lambda)$	$\quad (\widetilde{\mathsf{Q}}, (\mathsf{lab}_i)_i) \leftarrow \mathsf{Sim}(1^\lambda, \mathsf{pad}, \mathsf{m})$
$\quad (\mathsf{pk_{dv}}, \mathsf{sk_{dv}}) \leftarrow \mathsf{DVKG}(1^\lambda)$	$\quad \forall (i, v) \in [\ell_{\mathsf{sk}}] \times \{0, 1\}:$
$\quad \widetilde{\mathsf{ct}} \leftarrow \mathsf{CSEnc}(\mathsf{sk}, (\mathsf{sk_{cca}}, \mathsf{sk_{dv}}))$	$\quad\quad r_{i,v} \xleftarrow{r} \mathcal{R}$
$\quad \mathsf{PK} \leftarrow (\mathsf{pk}, \mathsf{pk_{cca}}, \mathsf{pk_{dv}}, \widetilde{\mathsf{ct}}); \quad \mathsf{SK} \leftarrow \mathsf{sk}$	$\quad\quad \mathsf{ct}_{i,v} \leftarrow \mathsf{CEnc}(\mathsf{pk}, i, v, \mathsf{lab}_i; r_{i,v})$
$\quad$ Return $(\mathsf{PK}, \mathsf{SK}).$	$\quad x \leftarrow (\mathsf{pk}, (\mathsf{ct}_{i,v})_{i,v})$
$\mathsf{Dec_{kdm}}(\mathsf{PK}, \mathsf{SK} = \mathsf{sk}, \mathsf{CT}): \quad (\star)$	$\quad w \leftarrow (\mathsf{lab}_i, r_{i,0}, r_{i,1})_i$
$\quad (\mathsf{pk}, \mathsf{pk_{cca}}, \mathsf{pk_{dv}}, \widetilde{\mathsf{ct}}) \leftarrow \mathsf{PK}$	$\quad \pi \leftarrow \mathsf{P}(\mathsf{pk_{dv}}, x, w)$
$\quad (\mathsf{sk_{cca}}, \mathsf{sk_{dv}}) \leftarrow \mathsf{CSDec}(\mathsf{sk}, \widetilde{\mathsf{ct}})$	$\quad \mathsf{CT} \leftarrow \mathsf{Enc_{cca}}(\mathsf{pk_{cca}}, (\widetilde{\mathsf{Q}}, (\mathsf{ct}_{i,v})_{i,v}, \pi))$
$\quad (\widetilde{\mathsf{Q}}, (\mathsf{ct}_{i,v})_{i,v}, \pi) \leftarrow \mathsf{Dec_{cca}}(\mathsf{pk_{cca}}, \mathsf{sk_{cca}}, \mathsf{CT})$	$\quad$ Return $\mathsf{CT}.$
$\quad x \leftarrow (\mathsf{pk}, (\mathsf{ct}_{i,v})_{i,v})$	
$\quad$ If $\mathsf{V}(\mathsf{sk_{dv}}, x, \pi) = \mathsf{reject}$ then return $\bot$.	
$\quad \forall i \in [\ell_{\mathsf{sk}}]: \mathsf{lab}_i \leftarrow \mathsf{CDec}(\mathsf{pk}, \mathsf{sk}, i, \mathsf{ct}_{i,\mathsf{sk}[i]})$	
$\quad$ Return $\mathsf{m} \leftarrow \mathsf{Eval}(\widetilde{\mathsf{Q}}, (\mathsf{lab}_i)_i).$	

Fig. 7. The construction of a $\mathcal{B}_{\mathsf{size}}$-KDM$^{(n)}$-CCA secure PKE scheme $\mathsf{PKE_{kdm}}$ from a CTE scheme CTE, an IND-CCA secure PKE scheme $\mathsf{PKE_{cca}}$, a garbling scheme for circuits GC, and a reusable DV-NIZK argument system DVNIZK. The notations like $(X_{i,v})_{i,v}$ and $(X_i)_i$ are abbreviations for $(X_{i,v})_{i \in [\ell_{\mathsf{sk}}], v \in \{0,1\}}$ and $(X_i)_{i \in [\ell_{\mathsf{sk}}]}$, respectively. $^{(\star)}$ If CSDec, CDec, or Dec$_{\mathsf{cca}}$ returns $\bot$, then Dec$_{\mathsf{kdm}}$ returns $\bot$ and terminate.

each decryption/verification done in the execution of $\mathsf{Dec_{kdm}}(\mathsf{PK}, \mathsf{SK}, \mathsf{CT})$ never fails, and just before the final step of $\mathsf{Dec_{kdm}}$, the decryptor can recover a garbled circuit $\widetilde{\mathsf{Q}}$ and the labels $(\mathsf{lab}_i)_i$, which is generated as $(\widetilde{\mathsf{Q}}, (\mathsf{lab}_i)_i) \leftarrow \mathsf{Sim}(1^\lambda, \mathsf{pad}, \mathsf{m})$. Then, by the correctness of GC, we have $\mathsf{Eval}(\widetilde{\mathsf{Q}}, (\mathsf{lab}_i)_i) = \mathsf{m}$.

Security. The following theorem guarantees the $\mathcal{B}_{\mathsf{size}}$-KDM$^{(n)}$-CCA security of $\mathsf{PKE_{kdm}}$. Combined with Theorems 9, 10, 11, and 12, it implies Theorem 13.

Theorem 14. *Let $n = n(\lambda)$, $\mu = \mu(\lambda)$, and* $\mathsf{size} = \mathsf{size}(\lambda) \geq \max\{n \cdot \ell_{\mathsf{sk}}, \mu\}$ *be any polynomials. Also, let* $\mathsf{pad} = O(n \cdot (|\mathsf{CSDec}| + \ell_{\widetilde{\mathsf{e}}}) + \mathsf{size}) \geq \mathsf{size}$ *(which is the size of a circuit that will be specified in the proof), where $|\mathsf{CSDec}|$ denotes the size of the circuit computing CSDec. Assume that CTE satisfies security against the receiver and special weak $CIRC^{(n)}$ security, $\mathsf{PKE_{cca}}$ is IND-CCA secure, GC is a secure garbling scheme, and DVNIZK is a reusable DV-NIZK argument system (satisfying soundness and zero-knowledge) for the NP language L. Then, $\mathsf{PKE_{kdm}}$ is $\mathcal{B}_{\mathsf{size}}$-KDM$^{(n)}$-CCA secure.*

Overview of the Proof. Due to the space limitation, the formal proof is given in the full version. Here, we give an overview of the proof.

The proof uses a sequence of games argument. The first game is the original $\mathcal{B}_{\mathsf{size}}$-KDM$^{(n)}$-CCA experiment regarding $\mathsf{PKE_{kdm}}$. Let $\mathcal{A}$ be a PPT adversary, and for $s \in [n]$, let $(\mathsf{PK}^s = (\mathsf{pk}^s, \mathsf{pk_{cca}^s}, \mathsf{pk_{dv}^s}, \widetilde{\mathsf{ct}}^s), \mathsf{SK}^s = \mathsf{sk}^s)$ denote the s-th public/secret key pair.

We first invoke the zero-knowledge of DVNIZK to change the security game so that the simulator $\mathcal{S} = (\mathcal{S}_1, \mathcal{S}_2)$ is used to generate each $(\mathsf{pk}_{\mathsf{dv}}^s, \mathsf{sk}_{\mathsf{dv}}^s)$ at key generation, and generate π in the response to KDM-encryption queries.

Next, we deal with the KDM-encryption queries (α, f_0, f_1), and make the behavior of the KDM-encryption oracle (essentially) independent of the secret keys $\{\mathsf{sk}^s\}_{s \in [n]}$. If there existed only a single key pair $(\mathsf{PK}, \mathsf{SK} = \mathsf{sk})$, then we could change the generation of the CTE-ciphertexts $(\mathsf{ct}_{i,v})_{i,v}$ in the KDM-encryption oracle so that we garble the KDM function f_b by $(\widetilde{\mathsf{Q}}, (\mathsf{lab}_{i,v})_{i,v}) \leftarrow$ Garble$(1^\lambda, f_b)$ and then encrypt $\mathsf{lab}_{i,v}$ by $\mathsf{ct}_{i,v} \leftarrow \mathsf{CEnc}(\mathsf{pk}^s, i, v, \mathsf{lab}_{i,v})$ for every $(i, v) \in [\ell_{\mathsf{sk}}] \times \{0, 1\}$. Since $\mathsf{Eval}(\widetilde{\mathsf{Q}}, (\mathsf{lab}_{i,\mathsf{sk}[i]})_{i \in [\ell_{\mathsf{sk}}]}) = f_b(\mathsf{sk})$, this can go unnoticed by $\mathcal{A}$ due to the security of GC and the security against the receiver of CTE, and the behavior of the resulting KDM-encryption oracle becomes independent of the secret key sk. However, we cannot take this rather simple approach in the multi-key setting, since the KDM-function f_b here is a function that takes all keys $\{\mathsf{sk}^s\}_{s \in [n]}$ as input, while we need to garble a circuit that takes a single key sk^α as input. Here, we rely on the clever technique of Barak et al. [5] to transform the KDM function f_b to a circuit Q so that $\mathsf{Q}(\mathsf{sk}^\alpha) = f_b((\mathsf{sk}^s)_{s \in [n]})$ holds, by using encryptions of the key cycle $\{\widetilde{e}^s = \mathsf{CSEnc}(\mathsf{sk}^s, \mathsf{sk}^{(s \bmod n)+1})\}_{s \in [n]}$. Specifically, Q has α, f_b, and $\{\widetilde{e}^s\}_{s \in [n]}$ hardwired, and it on input sk^α decrypts the encryptions of the key cycle one-by-one to recover all keys $\{\mathsf{sk}^s\}_{s \in [n]}$ and then outputs $f_b((\mathsf{sk}^s)_{s \in [n]})$. Then, we can garble Q instead of garbling f_b directly, and the argument goes similarly to the above. This change necessitates that the subsequent games generate the encryptions of the key cycle.

Then, we deal with the decryption queries (α, CT), and make the behavior of the decryption oracle independent of the secret keys $\{\mathsf{sk}^s\}_{s \in [n]}$. To achieve this, notice that the only essential part that we need to use the secret key sk^α in the decryption procedure is the step of executing $\mathsf{lab}_i \leftarrow \mathsf{CDec}(\mathsf{pk}^\alpha, \mathsf{sk}^\alpha, \mathsf{ct}_{i,\mathsf{sk}[i]})$ for every $i \in [\ell_{\mathsf{sk}}]$. To eliminate the dependency on sk^α in this step, in the next game we replace the above step with $\mathsf{lab}_i \leftarrow \widehat{\mathsf{CDec}}(\mathsf{td}^\alpha, i, \mathsf{sk}^\alpha[i], \mathsf{ct}_{i,\mathsf{sk}^\alpha[i]})$ for every $i \in [\ell_{\mathsf{sk}}]$. This makes no change in the behavior of the decryption oracle due to the third condition of the correctness of CTE. Next, we further change this step to always decrypt the "0-side" ciphertext $\mathsf{ct}_{i,0}$ as $\mathsf{lab}_i \leftarrow \widehat{\mathsf{CDec}}(\mathsf{td}^\alpha, i, 0, \mathsf{ct}_{i,0})$ for every $i \in [\ell_{\mathsf{sk}}]$. Now the behavior of the decryption oracle becomes independent of the secret keys $\{\mathsf{sk}^s\}_{s \in [n]}$. The behavior of the decryption oracle could differ between the change only if $\widehat{\mathsf{CDec}}(\mathsf{td}^\alpha, i^*, 0, \mathsf{ct}_{i^*,0}) \neq \widehat{\mathsf{CDec}}(\mathsf{td}^\alpha, i^*, 1, \mathsf{ct}_{i^*,1})$ holds for some $i^* \in [\ell_{\mathsf{sk}}]$ and yet the proof π recovered from CT is valid. Let us call such a query a bad decryption query. If $\mathcal{A}$ does not make a bad decryption query, this change of the behavior of the decryption oracle cannot be noticed by $\mathcal{A}$. Similarly to [22], we bound the probability of a bad query occurring to be negligible using a deferred analysis technique and postpone to bound it in a later (in fact the final) game, together with the second correctness condition of CTE. See the formal proof for this argument.

Now, since the behavior of the KDM-encryption and decryption oracles become independent of the secret keys $\{\mathsf{sk}^s\}_{s \in [n]}$, the remaining steps in which we use the secret keys are to generate $\{\widetilde{\mathsf{ct}}^s\}_{s \in [n]}$ in public keys, and to generate the encryptions of the key cycle $\{\widetilde{\mathsf{e}}^s\}_{s \in [n]}$. Then, we can rely on the special weak $\mathrm{CIRC}^{(n)}$ security of CTE to ensure that $\widetilde{\mathsf{ct}}^s$ is indistinguishable from an encryption of a garbage that contains no information on $(\mathsf{sk}^s_{\mathsf{cca}}, \mathsf{sk}^s_{\mathsf{dv}})$ in the presence of the trapdoors $\{\mathsf{td}^s\}_{s \in [n]}$ and the encryptions of the key cycle $\{\widetilde{\mathsf{e}}^s\}_{s \in [n]}$. Finally, we invoke the IND-CCA security of $\mathsf{PKE}_{\mathsf{cca}}$ to conclude that $\mathcal{A}$'s advantage in the final game is negligible.

For all the details, see the formal proof in the full version.

Acknowledgement. A part of this work was supported by JST CREST Grant Number JPMJCR19F6 and JSPS KAKENHI Grant Number 19H01109.

References

1. Acar, T., Belenkiy, M., Bellare, M., Cash, D.: Cryptographic agility and its relation to circular encryption. In: Gilbert, H. (ed.) EUROCRYPT 2010. LNCS, vol. 6110, pp. 403–422. Springer, Heidelberg (2010). https://doi.org/10.1007/978-3-642-13190-5_21

2. Adão, P., Bana, G., Herzog, J., Scedrov, A.: Soundness of formal encryption in the presence of key-cycles. In: di Vimercati, S.C., Syverson, P., Gollmann, D. (eds.) ESORICS 2005. LNCS, vol. 3679, pp. 374–396. Springer, Heidelberg (2005). https://doi.org/10.1007/11555827_22

3. Applebaum, B.: Key-dependent message security: generic amplification and completeness. In: Paterson, K.G. (ed.) EUROCRYPT 2011. LNCS, vol. 6632, pp. 527–546. Springer, Heidelberg (2011). https://doi.org/10.1007/978-3-642-20465-4_29

4. Backes, M., Pfitzmann, B., Scedrov, A.: Key-dependent message security under active attacks - BRSIM, UC-soundness of symbolic encryption with key cycles. In: 20th IEEE Computer Security Foundations Symposium, CSF, Venice, Italy, 6–8 July 2007, pp. 112–124 (2007)

5. Barak, B., Haitner, I., Hofheinz, D., Ishai, Y.: Bounded key-dependent message security. In: Gilbert, H. (ed.) EUROCRYPT 2010. LNCS, vol. 6110, pp. 423–444. Springer, Heidelberg (2010). https://doi.org/10.1007/978-3-642-13190-5_22

6. Bellare, M., Boldyreva, A., Staddon, J.: Randomness re-use in multi-recipient encryption schemeas. In: Desmedt, Y.G. (ed.) PKC 2003. LNCS, vol. 2567, pp. 85–99. Springer, Heidelberg (2003). https://doi.org/10.1007/3-540-36288-6_7

7. Black, J., Rogaway, P., Shrimpton, T.: Encryption-scheme security in the presence of key-dependent messages. In: Nyberg, K., Heys, H. (eds.) SAC 2002. LNCS, vol. 2595, pp. 62–75. Springer, Heidelberg (2003). https://doi.org/10.1007/3-540-36492-7_6

8. Boneh, D., Halevi, S., Hamburg, M., Ostrovsky, R.: Circular-secure encryption from decision Diffie-Hellman. In: Wagner, D. (ed.) CRYPTO 2008. LNCS, vol. 5157, pp. 108–125. Springer, Heidelberg (2008). https://doi.org/10.1007/978-3-540-85174-5_7

9. Boyle, E., Kohl, L., Scholl, P.: Homomorphic secret sharing from lattices without FHE. In: Ishai, Y., Rijmen, V. (eds.) EUROCRYPT 2019. LNCS, vol. 11477, pp. 3–33. Springer, Cham (2019). https://doi.org/10.1007/978-3-030-17656-3_1

10. Camenisch, J., Lysyanskaya, A.: Dynamic accumulators and application to efficient revocation of anonymous credentials. In: Yung, M. (ed.) CRYPTO 2002. LNCS, vol. 2442, pp. 61–76. Springer, Heidelberg (2002). https://doi.org/10.1007/3-540-45708-9_5

11. Canetti, R., et al.: Fiat-Shamir: from practice to theory. In: 51st ACM STOC, pp. 1082–1090 (2019)

12. Canetti, R., Chen, Y., Reyzin, L., Rothblum, R.D.: Fiat-Shamir and correlation intractability from strong KDM-secure encryption. In: Nielsen, J.B., Rijmen, V. (eds.) EUROCRYPT 2018. LNCS, vol. 10820, pp. 91–122. Springer, Cham (2018). https://doi.org/10.1007/978-3-319-78381-9_4

13. Cash, D., Green, M., Hohenberger, S.: New definitions and separations for circular security. In: Fischlin, M., Buchmann, J., Manulis, M. (eds.) PKC 2012. LNCS, vol. 7293, pp. 540–557. Springer, Heidelberg (2012). https://doi.org/10.1007/978-3-642-30057-8_32

14. Dodis, Y., Reyzin, L., Smith, A.: Fuzzy extractors: how to generate strong keys from biometrics and other noisy data. In: Cachin, C., Camenisch, J.L. (eds.) EUROCRYPT 2004. LNCS, vol. 3027, pp. 523–540. Springer, Heidelberg (2004). https://doi.org/10.1007/978-3-540-24676-3_31

15. Gentry, C.: Fully homomorphic encryption using ideal lattices. In: 41st ACM STOC, pp. 169–178 (2009)

16. Goldreich, O., Izsak, R.: Monotone circuits: one-way functions versus pseudorandom generators. Theory Comput. 8(1), 231–238 (2012)

17. Goyal, R., Koppula, V., Waters, B.: Separating semantic and circular security for symmetric-key bit encryption from the learning with errors assumption. In: Coron, J.-S., Nielsen, J.B. (eds.) EUROCRYPT 2017. LNCS, vol. 10211, pp. 528–557. Springer, Cham (2017). https://doi.org/10.1007/978-3-319-56614-6_18

18. Guo, S., Malkin, T., Oliveira, I.C., Rosen, A.: The power of negations in cryptography. In: Dodis, Y., Nielsen, J.B. (eds.) TCC 2015. LNCS, vol. 9014, pp. 36–65. Springer, Heidelberg (2015). https://doi.org/10.1007/978-3-662-46494-6_3

19. Hajiabadi, M., Kapron, B.M.: Reproducible circularly-secure bit encryption: applications and realizations. In: Gennaro, R., Robshaw, M. (eds.) CRYPTO 2015. LNCS, vol. 9215, pp. 224–243. Springer, Heidelberg (2015). https://doi.org/10.1007/978-3-662-47989-6_11

20. Hajiabadi, M., Kapron, B.M.: Toward fine-grained blackbox separations between semantic and circular-security notions. In: Coron, J.-S., Nielsen, J.B. (eds.) EUROCRYPT 2017. LNCS, vol. 10211, pp. 561–591. Springer, Cham (2017). https://doi.org/10.1007/978-3-319-56614-6_19

21. Håstad, J., Impagliazzo, R., Levin, L.A., Luby, M.: A pseudorandom generator from any one-way function. SIAM J. Comput. 28(4), 1364–1396 (1999)

22. Kitagawa, F., Matsuda, T.: CPA-to-CCA transformation for KDM security. In: Hofheinz, D., Rosen, A. (eds.) TCC 2019. LNCS, vol. 11892, pp. 118–148. Springer, Cham (2019). https://doi.org/10.1007/978-3-030-36033-7_5

23. Kitagawa, F., Matsuda, T., Tanaka, K.: CCA security and trapdoor functions via key-dependent-message security. In: Boldyreva, A., Micciancio, D. (eds.) CRYPTO 2019. LNCS, vol. 11694, pp. 33–64. Springer, Cham (2019). https://doi.org/10.1007/978-3-030-26954-8_2

24. Koppula, V., Ramchen, K., Waters, B.: Separations in circular security for arbitrary length key cycles. In: Dodis, Y., Nielsen, J.B. (eds.) TCC 2015. LNCS, vol. 9015, pp. 378–400. Springer, Heidelberg (2015). https://doi.org/10.1007/978-3-662-46497-7_15

25. Lombardi, A., Quach, W., Rothblum, R.D., Wichs, D., Wu, D.J.: New constructions of reusable designated-verifier NIZKs. In: Boldyreva, A., Micciancio, D. (eds.) CRYPTO 2019. LNCS, vol. 11694, pp. 670–700. Springer, Cham (2019). https://doi.org/10.1007/978-3-030-26954-8_22

26. Naor, M., Segev, G.: Public-key cryptosystems resilient to key leakage. In: Halevi, S. (ed.) CRYPTO 2009. LNCS, vol. 5677, pp. 18–35. Springer, Heidelberg (2009). https://doi.org/10.1007/978-3-642-03356-8_2

27. Reingold, O., Trevisan, L., Vadhan, S.: Notions of reducibility between cryptographic primitives. In: Naor, M. (ed.) TCC 2004. LNCS, vol. 2951, pp. 1–20. Springer, Heidelberg (2004). https://doi.org/10.1007/978-3-540-24638-1_1

28. Rothblum, R.D.: On the circular security of bit-encryption. In: Sahai, A. (ed.) TCC 2013. LNCS, vol. 7785, pp. 579–598. Springer, Heidelberg (2013). https://doi.org/10.1007/978-3-642-36594-2_32

29. Yao, A.C.-C.: How to generate and exchange secrets (extended abstract). In: 27th FOCS, pp. 162–167 (1986)

Post-quantum Cryptography

Scalable Ciphertext Compression Techniques for Post-quantum KEMs and Their Applications

Shuichi Katsumata[1]([✉]), Kris Kwiatkowski[2]([✉]), Federico Pintore[3]([✉]),
and Thomas Prest[2]([✉])

[1] National Institute of Advanced Industrial Science and Technology (AIST),
Tokyo, Japan
shuichi.katsumata@aist.go.jp
[2] PQShield, Oxford, UK
{kris.kwiatkowski,thomas.prest}@pqshield.com
[3] Mathematical Institute, University of Oxford, Oxford, UK
federico.pintore@maths.ox.ac.uk

Abstract. A *multi-recipient* key encapsulation mechanism, or mKEM, provides a scalable solution to securely communicating to a large group, and offers savings in both bandwidth and computational cost compared to the trivial solution of communicating with each member individually. All prior works on mKEM are only limited to classical assumptions and, although some generic constructions are known, they all require specific properties that are not shared by most post-quantum schemes. In this work, we first provide a simple and efficient generic construction of mKEM that can be instantiated from versatile assumptions, including post-quantum ones. We then study these mKEM instantiations at a practical level using 8 post-quantum KEMs (which are lattice and isogeny-based NIST candidates), and CSIDH, and show that compared to the trivial solution, our mKEM offers savings of at least one order of magnitude in the bandwidth, and make encryption time shorter by a factor ranging from 1.92 to 35. Additionally, we show that by combining mKEM with the TreeKEM protocol used by MLS – an IETF draft for secure group messaging – we obtain significant bandwidth savings.

1 Introduction

Secure communication within a system of several users is becoming indispensable in our everyday lives. One leading example is the recent trend in secure group messaging (Zoom, Signal, WhatsApp, and so on) to handle large groups – up to 50000 users according to the IETF draft of the Message Layer Security (MLS) architecture [38, Section 3.1]. The scenario is that users in a system, each holding their public and secret key, frequently exchange messages with a group of users. More than often, the solution adopted is the trivial approach of individually encrypting the same message M using the public keys associated with

ⓒ International Association for Cryptologic Research 2020
S. Moriai and H. Wang (Eds.): ASIACRYPT 2020, LNCS 12491, pp. 289–320, 2020.
https://doi.org/10.1007/978-3-030-64837-4_10

the respective recipients in the group.[1] However, this trivial approach makes the required *bandwidth* and *computational costs* grow by a factor N (where N is the number of recipients), compared to sending a message to a single recipient. Therefore, as the number of recipients increases, this trivial solution has poor scalability.

An additional motivation for lowering the bandwidth and computational costs is the current phase of gradual transition towards *post-quantum* cryptography—a type of cryptography that is known to be resilient against quantum adversaries. Most, if not all, post-quantum secure schemes are known to incur bandwidth and/or computational overheads compared to classical schemes. For example, all key encapsulation mechanisms (KEMs) still considered for standardization by NIST require an order of magnitude more bandwidth than ECDH [9] at a comparable classical security level. Therefore, lowering the cost of communication with multiple recipients even when the number of recipients N is only moderately large, say $N \geq 10$, will already be of value.

Multi-recipient Key Encapsulation Mechanism (mKEM), coined by Smart [40][2], is a primitive designed with the above motivations in mind. On a high level, an mKEM is like a standard KEM that securely sends *the same* session key K to a group of recipients. Subsequently, the sender transmits *a single* ciphertext to all the recipients by encrypting the message M using K as a secret key for a secret-key encryption scheme. The latter procedure corresponds to the standard DEM. The main requirement that makes mKEM appealing is that the bandwidth and computational resources required to send the session key K are less than those required when individually encrypting K using the recipients' public keys. To be precise, we can trivially construct an mKEM from any public-key encryption (PKE) scheme by encrypting the same session key K with respect to all the recipients' public keys. However, this trivial construction will be as inefficient as the aforementioned trivial solution (modulo the efficient DEM component), and therefore, the main goal for mKEM is to offer a more efficient alternative.

Due to its practically appealing and theoretically interesting nature, the study of mKEM has attracted much attention, e.g., [8,24,26,33,35,42]. Also, similar variants of mKEM, such as *multi-message* multi-recipient *public-key encryption* [11–13,33], have been considered prior to mKEM with similar motivations in mind, and have illustrated the importance of investigating the multi-recipient settings. As a consequence, by now many exciting results regarding mKEMs have appeared. However, we like to point out *three* unsatisfactory issues remaining with burdening the current state of affairs. First, to the best of our knowledge, all the literature on mKEMs is based on classical assumptions (e.g., Diffie-Hellman type assumptions) which are believed to not endure quantum adversaries. We are aware of one recent work [17] that claims the construction of an IND-CCA secure mKEM from the learning parity with noise (LPN) assumption, which is believed

---

[1] To be more precise, it is common to rely on the KEM/DEM framework [19,22] to lower the reliance on the more inefficient public key cryptography.

[2] We note that very similar variants of mKEM have been considered prior to this work [11–13,33]. More details follow.

to be quantumly secure. However, while going over their results, we noticed that their scheme is insecure since there is a trivial break in their claimed IND-CCA security. In particular, the ciphertexts are easily malleable. Second, earlier works such as [8,24,35] provide a somewhat generic construction of mKEM from a (single-recipient) PKE, but require the underlying PKE to satisfy rather specific properties that seems somewhat tailored to classical Diffie-Hellman type assumptions. For instance, [8] requires a notion of *weak reproducibility*, which informally states that there is an efficient procedure to re-randomize a ciphertext under a certain public key to a ciphertext under another public key. Unfortunately, such properties are not known to exist for post-quantum assumptions, such as lattice-based assumptions. Therefore, we still do not have a truly general framework for constructing mKEMs from standard building blocks. Here, "standard" building blocks mean blocks that are potentially instantiable from many hardness assumptions.

Summarizing thus far, the first question we are interested in this work is:

(Theoretical Question) Are there any simple and efficient generic constructions of mKEM *that can be based on versatile assumptions, including post-quantum assumptions?*

The third issue, which is orthogonal to the above concerns, is that all previous works on mKEM do not come with any implementations. Notably, most literature only points out the efficiency gain in a rather theoretical manner and does not provide comparisons with the trivial solution (i.e., running KEM in parallel). Since these gains depend on the concrete mKEM implementation and also on the choice of KEM used in the trivial solution, the benefit of using an mKEM is unclear without proper comparison. Considering the practical oriented nature of mKEM, we believe understanding the concrete gain of using an mKEM instead of using the trivial solution would help in illustrating the practical relevance of this primitive and in providing insight on when to use an mKEM.

Therefore, the second question we are interested in this work is:

(Practical Question) What is the concrete gain of using an mKEM *compared to the trivial solution? What are the concrete applications of* mKEMs?

1.1   Our Contributions and Techniques

Theoretical Contribution. We provide a new simple and efficient generic construction of an IND-CCA secure multi-recipient KEM (mKEM) from any IND-CPA secure multi-recipient PKE (mPKE).[3] The construction is proven secure in the classical *and* quantum random oracle model ((Q)ROM). Here, mPKE is a variant of mKEM where a user can encrypt any same message M (rather than a random session key K) to multiple recipients. We then show that IND-CPA secure mPKEs

---

[3] As standard in practice, we consider indistinguishability under chosen ciphertext attacks (IND-CCA) to be the default security requirement on our resulting scheme.

can be constructed very easily from most assumptions known to imply standard PKEs (including classical Diffie-Hellman type assumptions). The construction of an IND-CPA secure mPKE is in most cases a simple modification of a standard IND-CPA secure PKE to the multi-recipient setting. Concretely, we show how to construct mPKEs based on lattices and isogenies. Compared to previous works [8,24,35] which provide some types of generic constructions of mKEM, ours require an mPKE whereas they only require a single-recipient PKE. However, we only require very natural properties from the underlying mPKE, such as IND-CPA. Considering that our mPKE can be instantiated with diverse assumptions (including but not limited to post-quantum assumptions) in a very natural way from standard PKEs, we believe our generic construction to be more versatile and handy than previous ones. We point out that our mKEM achieves both implicit and explicit rejection.

Moreover, we introduce a new notion of *recipient anonymity* which we believe to be of independent interest. The notion captures the fact that the ciphertext does not leak the set of intended group members or recipients. We provide a mild additional property for the underlying IND-CPA secure mPKE, under which our above generic construction naturally implies a recipient-anonymous IND-CCA secure mKEM. Our lattice and isogeny-based instantiations satisfy the extra property without any modification. An overview of our generic construction is provided in the following section.

Practical Contribution. An immediate consequence of our theoretical contribution is that it opens the door to a large number of post-quantum instantiations of mKEM. A natural next step is to study these mKEM instantiations at a practical level and compare them to the trivial solution of running standard KEMs in parallel. Doing this work is precisely one of our practical contributions. As it turns out, at least 9 post-quantum schemes are compatible with our construction of mKEM: 7 lattice-based NIST candidates, the only isogeny-based NIST candidate SIKE, and the CSIDH scheme. We performed a systematic study of the bandwidth efficiency and found that for all of these schemes, our mKEM variants are more compact than the trivial solution with the original schemes by *at least one order of magnitude* (for a clearly defined metric). In addition, for a subset of these 9 schemes (CSIDH, FrodoKEM, Kyber, SIKE), we implemented their mKEM counterparts and compared their performance (cycle count). We found our mKEM variants to be (asymptotically) faster than the trivial solution with original schemes by factors ranging from 1.92 to more than 35.

Additionally, we show that we can use the mKEM primitive for the TreeKEM protocol obtaining significant bandwidth savings. To give some context, the importance of TreeKEM could be best understood by looking at its parent protocol, MLS [10,38], a IETF draft for secure (group) messaging. MLS has gained considerable industrial traction and has attracted a fair amount of academic scrutiny. TreeKEM constitutes the cryptographic backbone of MLS, as well as its main bottleneck in bandwidth and computational efficiency. Indeed, given N users, it requires each of them to compute and send $O(\log N)$ ciphertexts at regular intervals. We highlight a simple but powerful interplay between TreeKEM and mKEM, and show that by applying our technique we can reduce communication cost by a factor between 1.8 and 4.2 compared to using standard KEMs.

Our Techniques: Generic Construction of IND-CCA **Secure** mKEM. On a high level, our generic construction can be seen as a generalization of the Fujisaki-Okamoto (FO) transform [23]. The FO transform (roughly) converts any IND-CPA secure PKE into an IND-CCA secure KEM. There are several variants of the FO transform and most of the variants are secure in the ROM [18, 22, 25, 37] and/or QROM [15, 25, 29–32, 39, 41, 43]. The high-level construction is as follows: to encrypt, we sample a random message $M \leftarrow \mathcal{M}$ and derive randomness for the underlying encryption algorithm of the PKE by hashing M with a hash function G modeled as a (Q)RO. That is, $ct \leftarrow PKE.Enc(pk, M; G(M))$. The session key is then set as $K := H(M)$, where H is another hash function modeled as a (Q)RO. To decrypt, we first decrypt $M' \leftarrow PKE.Dec(sk, ct)$ and then only accept $K = H(M')$ if M' re-encrypts back to ct, that is, we check $ct = PKE.Enc(pk, M'; G(M'))$. Although the actual proof is rather complicated, intuitively, it achieves IND-CCA security since the adversary must have queried G to have constructed a valid ciphertext ct. Therefore, in the ROM, to answer a decapsulation-oracle query, the simulator runs through all the messages that have been queried to G to check if any of them re-encrypts to ct. Since the simulator no longer requires sk to simulate the decapsulation oracle, we can invoke the IND-CPA security of the underlying PKE.

Our idea is to generalize the FO transform to the mPKE/mKEM setting. At first glance, this may seem to not work. Indeed, an mPKE typically comes with a *multi*-encryption algorithm with the following syntax: $mEnc(pp, (pk_i)_{i \in [N]}, M; r) \rightarrow ct$, where ct is targeted to the set of N recipients with public keys $(pk_i)_{i \in [N]}$. There is also an extraction algorithm mExt which takes as input an index $i \in [N]$ and ct, and outputs the ciphertext component ct_i targeted to the i-th recipient, say R_i, holding pk_i. Recipient R_i can then run the decryption algorithm on ct_i using its secret key sk_i. The reason why the FO transform cannot be directly applied to mPKE becomes clear. Assume $r = G(M)$ and that recipient R_i decrypted to M. Then, to check validity of ct_i, R_i must re-encrypt the *entire* ciphertext ct by running $mEnc(pp, (pk_i)_{i \in [N]}, M; r)$. Therefore, the decapsulation time will depend on N, which is highly undesirable.

To get around this issue, in this work we consider a slight variant of mPKE with a *decomposable* flavor. Informally, a decomposable multi-encryption algorithm mEnc takes randomness of the form $r = (r_0, r_1, \cdots, r_N)$ as input, and creates a public-key-*independent* ciphertext $ct_0 \leftarrow mEnc^i(r_0)$ and public-key-*dependent* ciphertexts $\widehat{ct}_i \leftarrow mEnc^d(pk_i, M; r_0, r_i)$. The resulting ciphertext for recipient R_i is then $ct_i = (ct_0, \widehat{ct}_i)$. We view this as a natural formalization of mPKE as it is satisfied by all the mPKE constructions that we are aware of. Moreover, this feature is desirable in practice as it allows to parallelize part of the encryption algorithm. Now, to perform the FO transform, we derive $r_0 = G(M)$ and $r_i = G(pk_i, M)$. It is evident that R_i can re-encrypt and check the validity of its ciphertext. Notably, the decapsulation time is now independent of N. With this new formalization, the proof in the (classical) ROM follows in a straightforward manner (with minor modification) from the standard FO transform [25].

However, the security proof of our mKEM in the *quantum* ROM (QROM) requires more work. Prior proof strategies in the QROM for standard IND-CCA secure KEMs based on the FO transform – which fix the description of the QROM at the outset of the game [15, 25, 29–31, 39, 41] – seem to be an ill fit for mPKE. This is because in the multi-recipient setting, the decapsulation oracle is required to output a different (implicit) rejection value for each of the users when the ciphertext is invalid, and to output the same session key K when the ciphertext is valid. Due to this discrepancy between invalid and valid ciphertexts (i.e., the former requires to output different random values, whereas the latter requires to output the same random value), previous proof techniques that always output random values fail. Note that in the single-user setting, regardless of the ciphertext being valid or invalid, the decapsulation oracle could output random values without being detected by the adversary, and hence, this obstacle was absent. To overcome this, we use the recently introduced *compressed oracles* technique [43]. This allows the simulator to perform *lazy sampling* and to check the validity of the ciphertext submitted to the decapsulation oracle without interfering with the adversary's state. Although the high-level structure of the proof is similar to the classical case, much subtle care is required in the QROM case as the simulator must not disturb the adversary's state. We note that Zhandry [43] showed security of one variant of the FO transform which converts a *perfectly* correct IND-CPA secure PKE to an IND-CCA secure PKE.

2   Preliminaries

2.1   Hard Problems for Lattices

For any natural number d and q, let R_q denote the ring $\mathbb{Z}[X]/(q, X^d + 1)$. The learning with errors (LWE) problem is defined below.

Definition 1 (Learning with Errors (LWE)). *Let d, q, n_1, n_2, n_3 be natural numbers, and D_s and D_e be distributions over R_q. We say that the advantage of algorithm $\mathcal{A}$ in solving the (decisional) $\mathsf{LWE}_{n_1,n_2,n_3}$ problem over the ring R_q is*

$$\mathsf{Adv}^{\mathsf{LWE}}_{n_1,n_2,n_3}(\mathcal{A}) := \big| \Pr[\boldsymbol{A} \leftarrow R_q^{n_1 \times n_2}, \boldsymbol{S} \leftarrow D_s^{n_2 \times n_3}, \boldsymbol{E} \leftarrow D_e^{n_1 \times n_3} : 1 \leftarrow \mathcal{A}(\boldsymbol{A}, \boldsymbol{AS} + \boldsymbol{E})]$$
$$- \Pr[\boldsymbol{A} \leftarrow R_q^{n_1 \times n_2}, \boldsymbol{B} \leftarrow R_q^{n_1 \times n_3} : 1 \leftarrow \mathcal{A}(\boldsymbol{A}, \boldsymbol{B})] \big|.$$

We say the $\mathsf{LWE}_{n_1,n_2,n_3}$ problem is hard if, for any (possibly quantum) efficient adversary $\mathcal{A}$, its advantage is negligible.

We also consider a variant of the LWE problem, called learning with rounding (LWR) problem [7], where the least significant bits are removed. The benefit of this variant is that we no longer require to sample the noise, as it is removed. Below the function $\lfloor \cdot \rceil_p : \mathbb{Z}_q \to \mathbb{Z}_p$, where $q > p \geq 2$, is defined as $\lfloor x \rceil_p = \lfloor (p/q) \cdot x \rceil \mod p$. The definition of the LWR problem follows.

Definition 2 (Learning with Rounding (LWR)). *Let* d, p, q, n_1, n_2, n_3 *be natural numbers such that* $q > p$, *and* D_s *a distributions over* R_q. *We say that the advantage of algorithm* $\mathcal{A}$ *in solving the (decisional)* $\mathsf{LWR}_{n_1,n_2,n_3}$ *problem over the rings* R_p *and* R_q *is*

$$\mathsf{Adv}^{\mathsf{LWR}}_{n_1,n_2,n_3}(\mathcal{A}) := |\ \Pr[\mathbf{A} \leftarrow R_q^{n_1 \times n_2}, \mathbf{S} \leftarrow D_s^{n_2 \times n_3} : 1 \leftarrow \mathcal{A}(\mathbf{A}, \lfloor \mathbf{A}\mathbf{S} \rceil_p)]$$
$$- \Pr[\mathbf{A} \leftarrow R_q^{n_1 \times n_2}, \mathbf{B} \leftarrow R_p^{n_1 \times n_3} : 1 \leftarrow \mathcal{A}(\mathbf{A}, \mathbf{B})]|\ .$$

We say the $\mathsf{LWR}_{n_1,n_2,n_3}$ *problem is hard if, for any (possibly quantum) efficient adversary* $\mathcal{A}$, *its advantage is negligible.*

2.2 Hard Problems for Isogenies

In the following sections we propose two different isogeny-based schemes: one stemming from the SIDH key exchange [21] and the other from the CSIDH key exchange [16]. Both key exchanges share common mathematical tools, but several technical differences make them, and their descendants, substantially different. As a consequence, schemes in the SIDH family rely on hardness assumptions different from those used for schemes in the CSIDH family. Our schemes make no exception, as they use distinct security assumptions.

SIDH-Based Assumption. Let p be an odd prime of the form $2^{e_2}3^{e_3} - 1$, with $e_2, e_3 \in \mathbb{N}$ and $2^{e_2} \approx 3^{e_3}$. For a supersingular elliptic curve E over $\mathbb{F}_{p^2}$ we will denote by $B_2 = \{P_2, Q_2\}$ and $B_3 = \{P_3, Q_3\}$ bases for $E[2^{e_2}]$ and $E[3^{e_3}]$, respectively. Under the hypothesis that $|E(\mathbb{F}_{p^2})| = (2^{e_2}3^{e_3})^2$, both torsion subgroups $E[2^{e_2}]$ and $E[3^{e_3}]$ are contained in $E(\mathbb{F}_{p^2})$. Given the curve E and $s \in \mathbb{Z}_{2^{e_2}}$, by $\mathsf{pk}_2(s)$ we denote the tuple $(E/\langle R_2 = P_2 + [s]Q_2\rangle, \phi_{\langle R_2\rangle}(P_3), \phi_{\langle R_2\rangle}(Q_3))$, where $\phi_{\langle R_2\rangle}$ is the isogeny from E having kernel $\langle R_2\rangle$. Analogously, for $r \in \mathbb{Z}_{3^{e_3}}$ we define $\mathsf{pk}_3(r)$ as $(E/\langle R_3 = P_3 + [r]Q_3\rangle, \phi_{\langle R_3\rangle}(P_2), \phi_{\langle R_3\rangle}(Q_2))$.

The security of our scheme relies on a decisional variant, named SSDDH [21], of the SSCDH assumption. The latter is used by one of NIST second-round candidate KEMs, called SIKE [28], which is deduced from the key exchange SIDH.

Definition 3 (Supersingular Decisional Diffie-Hellman (SSDDH)). *Let* E *be a supersingular elliptic curve over* $\mathbb{F}_{p^2}$ *such that* $|E(\mathbb{F}_{p^2})| = (2^{e_2}3^{e_3})^2$. *We say that the advantage of algorithm* $\mathcal{A}$ *in solving the* $\mathsf{SSDDH}_{p,E,B_2,B_3}$ *problem is*

$$\mathsf{Adv}^{\mathsf{SSDDH}}_{p,E,B_2,B_3}(\mathcal{A}) := |\ \Pr[s \leftarrow \mathbb{Z}_{2^{e_2}}, r \leftarrow \mathbb{Z}_{3^{e_3}} :$$
$$1 \leftarrow \mathcal{A}(\mathsf{pk}_2(s), \mathsf{pk}_3(r), E/\langle P_2 + [s]Q_2, P_3 + [r]Q_3\rangle)]$$
$$- \Pr[(s, s') \leftarrow (\mathbb{Z}_{2^{e_2}})^2, (r, r') \leftarrow (\mathbb{Z}_{3^{e_3}})^2 :$$
$$1 \leftarrow \mathcal{A}(\mathsf{pk}_2(s), \mathsf{pk}_3(r), E/\langle P_2 + [s']Q_2, P_3 + [r']Q_3\rangle)]|\ .$$

We say the $\mathsf{SSCDH}_{p,E,B_2,B_3}$ *problem is hard if, for any (possibly quantum) efficient adversary* $\mathcal{A}$, *its advantage is negligible.*

CSIDH-Based Assumption. The CSIDH key exchange works with supersingular elliptic curves and isogenies as well, but they are defined over a prime field $\mathbb{F}_p$. Despite offering weaker security guarantees than SIDH, CSIDH enjoys a simpler design based on the action of a group G on a set of curves. The simplicity of its design makes it easy to use CSIDH for constructing cryptographic primitives. Details on the CSIDH assumption we use are provided in the full version.

3   Multi-recipient PKE and KEM

3.1   Decomposable Multi-recipient Public Key Encryption

Definition 4 (Decomposable Multi-Recipient Public Key Encryption).
A (single-message) decomposable multi-recipient public key encryption (mPKE) over a message space $\mathcal{M}$ and ciphertext spaces $\mathcal{C}$ and $\mathcal{C}_{\mathsf{single}}$ consists of the following five algorithms $\mathsf{mPKE} = (\mathsf{mSetup}, \mathsf{mGen}, \mathsf{mEnc}, \mathsf{mExt}, \mathsf{mDec})$:

- $\mathsf{mSetup}(1^\kappa) \to \mathsf{pp}$: *The setup algorithm on input the security parameter 1^κ outputs a public parameter* pp.
- $\mathsf{mGen}(\mathsf{pp}) \to (\mathsf{pk}, \mathsf{sk})$: *The key generation algorithm on input a public parameter* pp *outputs a pair of public key and secret key* $(\mathsf{pk}, \mathsf{sk})$.
- $\mathsf{mEnc}(\mathsf{pp}, (\mathsf{pk}_i)_{i \in [N]}, \mathsf{M}; \mathsf{r}_0, \mathsf{r}_1, \cdots, \mathsf{r}_N) \to \boldsymbol{ct} = (\mathsf{ct}_0, (\widehat{\mathsf{ct}}_i)_{i \in [N]})$: *The (decomposable) encryption algorithm running with randomness* $(\mathsf{r}_0, \mathsf{r}_1, \cdots, \mathsf{r}_N)$, *splits into a pair of algorithms* $(\mathsf{mEnc}^\mathsf{i}, \mathsf{mEnc}^\mathsf{d})$:
    - $\mathsf{mEnc}^\mathsf{i}(\mathsf{pp}; \mathsf{r}_0) \to \mathsf{ct}_0$: *On input a public parameter* pp *and randomness* r_0, *it outputs a (public key Independent) ciphertext* ct_0.
    - $\mathsf{mEnc}^\mathsf{d}(\mathsf{pp}, \mathsf{pk}_i, \mathsf{M}; \mathsf{r}_0, \mathsf{r}_i) \to \widehat{\mathsf{ct}}_i$: *On input a public parameter* pp, *a public key* pk_i, *a message* $\mathsf{M} \in \mathcal{M}$, *and randomness* $(\mathsf{r}_0, \mathsf{r}_i)$, *it outputs a (public key Dependent) ciphertext* $\widehat{\mathsf{ct}}_i$.
- $\mathsf{mExt}(i, \boldsymbol{ct}) \to \mathsf{ct}_i = (\mathsf{ct}_0, \widehat{\mathsf{ct}}_i)$ *or* $\bot$: *The deterministic extraction algorithm on input an index $i \in \mathbb{N}$ and a (multi-recipient) ciphertext $\boldsymbol{ct} \in \mathcal{C}$, outputs either a (single-recipient) ciphertext* $\mathsf{ct}_i = (\mathsf{ct}_0, \widehat{\mathsf{ct}}_i) \in \mathcal{C}_{\mathsf{single}}$ *or a special symbol* $\bot_{\mathsf{Ext}}$ *indicating extraction failure.*
- $\mathsf{mDec}(\mathsf{sk}, \mathsf{ct}_i) \to \mathsf{M}$ *or* $\bot$: *The deterministic decryption algorithm on input a secret key sk and a ciphertext $\mathsf{ct}_i \in \mathcal{C}_{\mathsf{single}}$, outputs either $\mathsf{M} \in \mathcal{M}$ or a special symbol* $\bot \notin \mathcal{M}$.

Although we can consider *non-decomposable* multi-recipient PKEs, we only focus on decomposable schemes as they are compatible with the Fujisaki-Okamoto (FO) transform [23]. Informally, the FO transform relies on the recipient being able to recover the encryption randomness from the ciphertext and to check validity of the ciphertext by re-encrypting with the recovered randomness. Therefore, in the multi-recipient setting, if we do not impose decomposable encryption, then the recipient may require all the public keys that were used in constructing $\boldsymbol{ct}$ to be able to re-encrypt. However, this is clearly undesirable since the decryption time may now depend on the number of public keys used to encrypt, and furthermore, the size of the ciphertext will grow by appending all the public keys used. Therefore, in this paper, when we say mPKE, we always assume it is decomposable. We require the following properties from a mPKE.

Definition 5 (Correctness). *A* mPKE *is* δ-*correct if*

$$\delta \geq \mathbb{E} \left[\max_{M \in \mathcal{M}} \Pr \left[\begin{array}{c} \mathsf{ct}_0 \leftarrow \mathsf{mEnc}^i(\mathsf{pp}), \widehat{\mathsf{ct}} \leftarrow \mathsf{mEnc}^d(\mathsf{pp}, \mathsf{pk}, M) : \\ M \neq \mathsf{mDec}(\mathsf{sk}, (\mathsf{ct}_0, \widehat{\mathsf{ct}})) \end{array} \right] \right], \quad (1)$$

where the expectation is taken over $\mathsf{pp} \leftarrow \mathsf{mSetup}(1^\kappa)$ *and* $(\mathsf{pk}, \mathsf{sk}) \leftarrow \mathsf{mGen}(\mathsf{pp})$.

We also define the notion of *well-spreadness* [23] which states informally that the ciphertext has high min-entropy.

Definition 6 (γ-Spreadness). *Let* mPKE *be a decomposable multi-recipient* PKE *with message space* $\mathcal{M}$ *and ciphertext spaces* $\mathcal{C}$ *and* $\mathcal{C}_{\mathsf{single}}$. *For all* $\mathsf{pp} \in \mathsf{Setup}(1^\kappa)$, *and* $(\mathsf{pk}, \mathsf{sk}) \in \mathsf{Gen}(\mathsf{pp})$, *define*

$$\gamma(\mathsf{pp}, \mathsf{pk}) := -\log_2 \left(\max_{\mathsf{ct} \in \mathcal{C}_{\mathsf{single}}, M \in \mathcal{M}} \Pr_{r_0, r} \left[\mathsf{ct} = (\mathsf{mEnc}^i(\mathsf{pp}; r_0), \mathsf{mEnc}^d(\mathsf{pp}, \mathsf{pk}, M; r_0, r)) \right] \right).$$

We call mPKE γ-*spread if* $\mathbb{E}[\gamma(\mathsf{pp}, \mathsf{pk})] \geq \gamma$, *where the expectation is taken over* $\mathsf{pp} \leftarrow \mathsf{mSetup}(1^\kappa)$ *and* $(\mathsf{pk}, \mathsf{sk}) \leftarrow \mathsf{mGen}(\mathsf{pp})$.

Finally, we define the notion of indistinguishability of chosen plaintext attacks (IND-CPA) for mPKE.

Definition 7 (IND-CPA). Let mPKE be a decomposable multi-recipient PKE with message space $\mathcal{M}$ and ciphertext space $\mathcal{C}$. We define IND-CPA by a game illustrated in Fig. 1 and say the (possibly quantum) adversary $\mathcal{A} = (\mathcal{A}_1, \mathcal{A}_2)$ *wins* if the game outputs 1. We define the advantage of $\mathcal{A}$ against IND-CPA security of mPKE parameterized by $N \in \mathbb{N}$ as $\mathsf{Adv}^{\mathsf{IND\text{-}CPA}}_{\mathsf{mPKE}, N}(\mathcal{A}) = |\Pr[\mathcal{A} \ wins] - 1/2|$.

Remark 1 (Insider corruption). We point out that insider corruptions for mPKE are not considered [8,40]. This is because if an adversary obtains a secret key corresponding to any of the public keys used to encrypt, then it can trivially recover the encrypted message.

Remark 2 (Inefficient m-PKE from any standard (single-recipient) PKE). Our definition of mPKE captures the trivial solution of sending different ciphertexts obtained with a standard single-recipient PKE to multiple recipients. That is, independently encrypting the same message to all recipients using their respective public keys. In the above syntax of mPKE, this amounts to setting mEnc^i as a null function and setting r_0 as an empty string. Also, mExt will simply pick the relevant ciphertext component for the particular recipient. Therefore, in the context of ciphertext compression, the goal is to obtain a mPKE with better efficiency/ciphertext-size compared to this trivial method.

Remark 3 (Number of recipients). In general, the number of recipients $N = \mathrm{poly}(\kappa)$ can be chosen arbitrary by the sender (or adversary). Some schemes may require an upper bound on N since the concrete provably-secure parameters may have a dependance on N, e.g., the reduction loss degrades by a factor of $1/N$. Our proposal does not require such an upper bound since N only shows up in a statistical manner, and so we can handle large N, say $N = 2^{15}$, without having any large impact on the concrete parameter choice.

3.2 Multi-recipient Key Encapsulation Mechanism

Definition 8 (Multi-recipient Key Encapsulation Mechanism). *A (single-message) multi-recipient key encapsulation mechanism (mKEM) over a key space $\mathcal{K}$ and ciphertext space $\mathcal{C}$ consists of the following five algorithms* mKEM = (mSetup, mGen, mEncaps, mExt, mDecaps)*:*

GAME IND-CPA
1: pp $\leftarrow$ mSetup(1^κ)
2: **for** $i \in [N]$ **do**
3:    ($\mathsf{pk}_i, \mathsf{sk}_i$) $\leftarrow$ mGen(pp)
4: ($\mathsf{M}_0^*, \mathsf{M}_1^*, \mathsf{state}$) $\leftarrow \mathcal{A}_1(\mathsf{pp}, (\mathsf{pk}_i)_{i \in [N]})$
5: $b \leftarrow \{0,1\}$
6: $\mathbf{ct}^* \leftarrow$ mEnc(pp, $(\mathsf{pk}_i)_{i \in [N]}, \mathsf{M}_b^*$)
7: $b' \leftarrow \mathcal{A}_2(\mathsf{pp}, (\mathsf{pk}_i)_{i \in [N]}, \mathbf{ct}^*, \mathsf{state})$
8: **return** $[b = b']$

GAME IND-CCA
1: pp $\leftarrow$ mSetup(1^κ)
2: **for** $i \in [N]$ **do**
3:    ($\mathsf{pk}_i, \mathsf{sk}_i$) $\leftarrow$ mGen(pp)
4: ($\mathsf{K}_0^*, \mathbf{ct}^*$) $\leftarrow$ mEncaps(pp, $(\mathsf{pk}_i)_{i \in [N]}$)
5: $\mathsf{K}_1^* \leftarrow \mathcal{K}$
6: $b \leftarrow \{0,1\}$
7: $b' \leftarrow \mathcal{A}^{\mathcal{D}}(\mathsf{pp}, (\mathsf{pk}_i)_{i \in [N]}, \mathbf{ct}^*, \mathsf{K}_b^*)$
8: **return** $[b = b']$

Decapsulation Oracle $\mathcal{D}(i, \mathsf{ct})$
1: $\mathsf{ct}_i^* := \mathsf{mExt}(i, \mathbf{ct}^*)$
2: **if** $\mathsf{ct} = \mathsf{ct}_i^*$ **then**
3:    **return** $\perp$
4: $\mathsf{K} := \mathsf{mDecaps}(\mathsf{sk}_i, \mathsf{ct})$
5: **return** K

Fig. 1. IND-CPA of mPKE and IND-CCA of mKEM.

- mSetup(1^κ) $\rightarrow$ pp: *The setup algorithm on input the security parameter 1^κ outputs a public parameter* pp.
- mGen(pp) $\rightarrow$ (pk, sk): *The key generation algorithm on input a public parameter* pp *outputs a pair of public key and secret key* (pk, sk).
- mEncaps(pp, $(\mathsf{pk}_i)_{i \in [N]}$) $\rightarrow$ (K, $\mathbf{ct}$): *The encapsulation algorithm on input a public parameter* pp*, and N public keys $(\mathsf{pk}_i)_{i \in [N]}$, outputs a key* K *and a ciphertext* $\mathbf{ct}$.
- mExt($i, \mathbf{ct}$) $\rightarrow \mathsf{ct}_i$: *The deterministic extraction algorithm on input an index $i \in \mathbb{N}$ and a ciphertext $\mathbf{ct}$, outputs either ct_i or a special symbol $\perp_{\mathsf{Ext}}$ indicating extraction failure.*

- mDecaps(sk, ct$_i$) → K *or* ⊥: *The deterministic decryption algorithm on input a secret key* sk *and a ciphertext* ct$_i$, *outputs either* K ∈ $\mathcal{K}$ *or a special symbol* ⊥ ∉ $\mathcal{K}$.

Definition 9 (Correctness). *A* mKEM *is* δ_N-*correct if*

$$\delta_N \geq \Pr\left[(K, \boldsymbol{ct}) \leftarrow \mathsf{mEnc}(\mathsf{pp}, (\mathsf{pk}_i)_{i\in[N]}), (\mathsf{ct}_i \leftarrow \mathsf{mExt}(i, \boldsymbol{ct}))_{i\in[N]}\right.$$
$$\left. : \exists i \in [N] \ s.t. \ K \neq \mathsf{mDec}(\mathsf{sk}, \mathsf{ct}_i)\right],$$

where the probability is taken over pp ← mSetup *and* (pk$_i$, sk$_i$) ← mGen(pp) *for all* $i \in [N]$.

We define the notion of indistinguishability of chosen ciphertext attacks (IND-CCA) for mKEM.

Definition 10 (IND-CCA). Let mKEM be a multi-recipient KEM. We define IND-CCA by a game illustrated in Fig. 1 and say the (possibly quantum) adversary $\mathcal{A}$ (making only classical decapsulation queries to $\mathcal{D}$) *wins* if the game outputs 1. We define the advantage of $\mathcal{A}$ against IND-CCA security of mKEM parameterized by $N \in \mathbb{N}$ as $\mathsf{Adv}^{\mathsf{IND\text{-}CCA}}_{\mathsf{mKEM},N}(\mathcal{A}) = |\Pr[\mathcal{A} \ wins] - 1/2|$.

3.3 Recipient Anonymity for mPKE and mKEM

In many practical scenarios, it is often convenient to have an additional guarantee of recipient anonymity, which stipulates that the ciphertext does not leak any information about the set of intended recipients. Informally, we say mPKE (mKEM) is IND-Anon-CPA (IND-Anon-CCA) if there exists a fake encryption (encapsulation) algorithm mEnc (mEncaps), which takes as input only the number of recipients and outputs a fake ciphertext indistinguishable from an honestly generated ciphertext. The definition is formally provided in the full version.

4 FO Transform: (IND-CPA mPKE) ⇒ (IND-CCA mKEM)

4.1 Generic Construction via FO Transform

We provide a generic transformation of an IND-CPA secure mPKE to an IND-CCA secure mKEM following the (generalized) Fujisaki-Okamoto transform. This is illustrated in Fig. 2. The scheme provides *implicit* rejection as opposed to *explicit* rejection, where in the latter type, the decapsulation algorithm outputs a special symbol ⊥ to explicitly indicate decapsulation failure. We discuss later how to tweak our scheme to get explicit rejection with no additional cost. In Fig. 2, G_1, G_2, H, H' are hash functions modeled as random oracles in the security proof. They can be simulated by a single random oracle by using appropriate domain separation. Finally, we include an ℓ-bit seed to perform implicit rejection by viewing H'(seed, ·) as a pseudorandom function in the (Q)ROM.

The following theorem classically and quantumly reduce the IND-CCA security of mKEM to the IND-CPA security of mPKE, where the classical reduction is tight. The proof for each theorem is provided in the subsequent sections.

mSetup(1^κ)
1: pp ← mSetup$^\mathrm{p}$(1^κ)
2: return pp

mGen(pp)
1: (pk, sk$^\mathrm{p}$) ← mGen$^\mathrm{p}$(pp)
2: seed ← $\{0,1\}^\ell$
3: sk := (sk$^\mathrm{p}$, seed)
4: return (pk, sk)

mExt(i, ct)
1: ct$_i$ ← mExt$^\mathrm{p}$(i, ct)
2: return ct$_i$

mEncaps(pp, (pk$_i$)$_{i \in [N]}$)
1: M ← $\mathcal{M}$
2: ct$_0$:= mEnc$^\mathrm{i}$(pp; G$_1$(M))
3: for $i \in [N]$ do
4:    $\widehat{\mathrm{ct}}_i$:= mEnc$^\mathrm{d}$(pp, pk$_i$, M;
         G$_1$(M), G$_2$(pk$_i$, M))
5: K := H(M)
6: return (K, ct := (ct$_0$, ($\widehat{\mathrm{ct}}_i$)$_{i \in [N]}$))

mDecaps(sk, ct)
1: sk := (sk$^\mathrm{p}$, seed)
2: M := mDec(sk$^\mathrm{p}$, ct)
3: if M = ⊥ then
4:    return K := H'(seed, ct)
5: ct$_0$:= mEnc$^\mathrm{i}$(pp; G$_1$(M))
6: $\widehat{\mathrm{ct}}$:= mEnc$^\mathrm{d}$(pp, pk, M; G$_1$(M), G$_2$(pk, M))
7: if ct $\neq$ (ct$_0$, $\widehat{\mathrm{ct}}$) then
8:    return K := H'(seed, ct)
9: else
10:    return K := H(M)

Fig. 2. An IND-CCA secure mKEM from a decomposable IND-CPA secure mPKE = (mSetup$^\mathrm{p}$, mGen$^\mathrm{p}$, mEnc = (mEnc$^\mathrm{i}$, mEnc$^\mathrm{d}$), mExt$^\mathrm{p}$, mDec). We include the superscript $^\mathrm{p}$ to make the code more readable.

Theorem 1 (Classical: IND-CPA mPKE ⇒ IND-CCA mKEM). *Assume mPKE with message space $\mathcal{M}$ is δ-correct and γ-spread. Then, for any classical PPT IND-CCA adversary $\mathcal{A}$ issuing at most $q_\mathcal{D}$ queries to the decapsulation oracle $\mathcal{D}$, a total of at most q_G queries to G$_1$ and G$_2$, and at most $q_\mathsf{H}, q'_\mathsf{H}$ queries to H and H', there exists a classical PPT adversary $\mathcal{B}_\mathsf{IND}$ such that*

$$\mathsf{Adv}^{\mathsf{IND\text{-}CCA}}_{\mathsf{mKEM},N}(\mathcal{A}) \leq 2 \cdot \mathsf{Adv}^{\mathsf{IND\text{-}CPA}}_{\mathsf{mPKE},N}(\mathcal{B}_\mathsf{IND}) + (2q_\mathsf{G} + q_\mathcal{D} + 2) \cdot \delta + q_\mathcal{D} \cdot 2^{-\gamma}$$
$$+ \frac{(q_\mathsf{G} + q_\mathsf{H})}{|\mathcal{M}|} + q'_\mathsf{H} \cdot N \cdot 2^{-\ell}.$$

where the running time of $\mathcal{B}_\mathsf{IND}$ is about that of $\mathcal{A}$, and ℓ is the number of bits of the seed composing a private key.

Theorem 2 (Quantum: IND-CPA mPKE ⇒ IND-CCA mKEM). Assume mPKE with message space $\mathcal{M}$ is δ-correct and γ-spread. Then, for any quantum PT IND-CCA adversary $\mathcal{A}$ issuing at most $q_\mathcal{D}$ classical queries to the decapsulation oracle $\mathcal{D}$, a total of at most q_G quantum queries to G$_1$ and G$_2$, and at most $q_\mathsf{H}, q'_\mathsf{H}$ quantum queries to H and H', there exists a quantum PT adversary $\mathcal{B}_\mathsf{IND}$ such that

$$\mathsf{Adv}^{\mathsf{IND\text{-}CCA}}_{\mathsf{mKEM},N}(\mathcal{A}) \leq \sqrt{2 \cdot (q_\mathsf{G} + 1) \cdot \mathsf{Adv}^{\mathsf{IND\text{-}CPA}}_{\mathsf{mPKE},N}(\mathcal{B}_\mathsf{IND})} + \frac{4(q_\mathsf{G} + 1)}{\sqrt{|\mathcal{M}|}}$$
$$+ 12 \cdot (q_\mathsf{G} + q_\mathcal{D} + 1)^2 \cdot \delta + q_\mathcal{D} \cdot (9\sqrt{2^{-\gamma}} + 2^{\mu-2}) + q'_\mathsf{H} \cdot N \cdot 2^{\frac{-\ell+1}{2}},$$

where the running time of $\mathcal{B}_{\mathsf{IND}}$ is about that of $\mathcal{A}$, ℓ is the number of bits of the seed composing a private key, and $\mu = \max_{(r_0, r) \in \mathcal{R}}\{|r_0|, |r|\}$ where $\mathcal{R}$ is the randomness space of mPKE.

Remark 4 (Implicit vs explicit rejection). In our construction in Fig. 2, we use *implicit* rejection. That is, mDecaps does not explicitly output $\bot$ to indicate that the input ciphertext was invalid. This may be suitable in practice when we do not want to let the adversary know that decapsulation failed. However, we note that our proof is agnostic to this choice, and in particular, the same proof can be shown in case we want *explicit rejection*, where mDecaps outputs $\bot$ in case either $\mathsf{M} = \bot$ or ct is not the same as the reencrypted ciphertext $(\mathsf{ct}_0, \widehat{\mathsf{ct}}_i)$. Concretely, we obtain an IND-CCA secure mKEM with explicit rejection by simply outputting $\bot$ rather than outputting $\mathsf{H}'(\mathsf{seed}, \mathsf{ct})$ in Fig. 2. We emphasize that this tweak cannot be made in general since the security proofs may hinge on the fact that the adversary does not learn decapsulation failures (see [15,39]).

4.2   Proof for Classical Case

Proof (Proof of Theorem 1). Let $\mathcal{A}$ be a classical PPT adversary against the IND-CCA security of mKEM. We upper bound its advantage by considering the following game sequence. We denote by E_i the event $\mathcal{A}$ wins in Game_i.

- Game_1: This is the real IND-CCA security game: $\mathsf{Adv}_{\mathsf{mKEM}, N}^{\mathsf{IND\text{-}CCA}}(\mathcal{A}) = |\Pr[\mathsf{E}_1] - 1/2|$.

- Game_2: In this game, we replace the computation of $\mathsf{H}'(\mathsf{seed}_i, \cdot)$ by a random function $\widehat{\mathsf{H}}_i'(\cdot)$ in case $\mathsf{M} = \bot$ or $\mathsf{ct} \neq (\mathsf{ct}_0, \widehat{\mathsf{ct}})$ occurs when answering the decapsulation oracle with input $i \in [N]$. Here, $\widehat{\mathsf{H}}_i'(\cdot)$ is a random function that cannot be accessed by the adversary. Since this modification remains unnoticed by the adversary unless $\mathsf{H}'(\mathsf{seed}, \cdot)$ is queried for any $\mathsf{seed} \in \{\mathsf{seed}_i\}_{i \in [N]}$, we have $|\Pr[\mathsf{E}_1] - \Pr[\mathsf{E}_2]| \leq \frac{q_{\mathsf{H}}' \cdot N}{2^\ell}$.

- Game_3: In this game, we enforce that no decryption failure occurs. Namely, we modify the random oracle so that the output is distributed randomly over the space of randomness that leads to no decryption failures. By the correctness of mPKE, we have $|\Pr[\mathsf{E}_2] - \Pr[\mathsf{E}_3]| \leq (q_{\mathsf{G}} + q_{\mathcal{D}} + 1) \cdot \delta$.

(The next Game_4, Game_5 and Game_6 aim to get rid of the secret keys sk_i to answer $\mathcal{A}$'s decapsulation oracle queries.)

- Game_4: In this game, we add an additional check when answering the decapsulation oracle query. This is illustrated in Fig. 3 where the red underline indicates the modification. Here, $\mathcal{L}_{\mathsf{G}}$ is a list that stores the random oracle queries made to G_1 and G_2. We have $\mathsf{M} \in \mathcal{L}_{\mathsf{G}}$ if either G_1 was queried on M or G_2 was queried on $(\mathsf{pk}, \mathsf{M})$ for any pk. The only difference occurs when $\mathcal{A}$ queries a ciphertext $\mathsf{ct} = (\mathsf{ct}_0, \widehat{\mathsf{ct}}_i)$ such that $\mathsf{M} := \mathsf{mDec}(\mathsf{sk}_i^{\mathsf{p}}, \mathsf{ct})$ has not been queried to the random oracles G_1 and G_2 but $\mathsf{ct}_0 = \mathsf{mEnc}^i(\mathsf{pp}; \mathsf{G}_1(\mathsf{M}))$

Game$_4$: Decap. Oracle $\mathcal{D}(i, \mathsf{ct} \neq \mathsf{ct}_i^*)$

1: $\mathsf{sk}_i := (\mathsf{sk}_i^\mathsf{p}, \mathsf{seed}_i)$
2: $\mathsf{M} := \mathsf{mDec}(\mathsf{sk}_i^\mathsf{p}, \mathsf{ct})$
3: **if** $\mathsf{M} \notin \mathcal{L}_\mathsf{G}$ **then**
4:     **return** $\mathsf{K} := \widehat{\mathsf{H}}_i'(\mathsf{ct})$

5: **if** $\mathsf{M} = \bot$ **then**
6:     **return** $\mathsf{K} := \widehat{\mathsf{H}}_i'(\mathsf{ct})$
7: $\mathsf{ct}_0 := \mathsf{mEnc}^\mathsf{i}(\mathsf{pp}; \mathsf{G}_1(\mathsf{M}))$
8: $\widehat{\mathsf{ct}}_i := \mathsf{mEnc}^\mathsf{d}(\mathsf{pp}, \mathsf{pk}_i, \mathsf{M}; \mathsf{G}_1(\mathsf{M}), \mathsf{G}_2(\mathsf{pk}_i, \mathsf{M}))$
9: **if** $\mathsf{ct} \neq (\mathsf{ct}_0, \widehat{\mathsf{ct}}_i)$ **then**
10:     **return** $\mathsf{K} := \widehat{\mathsf{H}}_i'(\mathsf{ct})$
11: **else**
12:     **return** $\mathsf{K} := \mathsf{H}(\mathsf{M})$

Game$_5$: Decap. Oracle $\mathcal{D}(i, \mathsf{ct} \neq \mathsf{ct}_i^*)$

1: **for** $\mathsf{M} \in \mathcal{L}_\mathsf{G}$ **do**
2:     $\mathsf{ct}_0 := \mathsf{mEnc}^\mathsf{i}(\mathsf{pp}; \mathsf{G}_1(\mathsf{M}))$
3:     $\widehat{\mathsf{ct}}_i := \mathsf{mEnc}^\mathsf{d}(\mathsf{pp}, \mathsf{pk}_i, \mathsf{M};$
        $\mathsf{G}_1(\mathsf{M}), \mathsf{G}_2(\mathsf{pk}_i, \mathsf{M}))$
4:     **if** $\mathsf{ct} = (\mathsf{ct}_0, \widehat{\mathsf{ct}}_i)$ **then**
5:         **return** $\mathsf{K} := \mathsf{H}(\mathsf{M})$
6: **return** $\mathsf{K} := \widehat{\mathsf{H}}_i(\mathsf{ct})$

Fig. 3. Decapsulation oracles of Game$_4$ and Game$_5$. We enforce ct is not $\mathsf{ct}_i^* :=$ $\mathsf{mExt}(i, \mathbf{ct}^*)$ at the input level for simplicity.

and $\widehat{\mathsf{ct}}_i = \mathsf{mEnc}^\mathsf{d}(\mathsf{pp}, \mathsf{pk}_i, \mathsf{M}; \mathsf{G}_1(\mathsf{M}), \mathsf{G}_2(\mathsf{pk}_i, \mathsf{M}))$. Since $\mathsf{G}_1(\mathsf{M})$ and $\mathsf{G}_2(\mathsf{pk}_i, \mathsf{M})$ are information theoretically hidden from $\mathcal{A}$, we can use γ-spreadness of mPKE to conclude $|\Pr[\mathsf{E}_3] - \Pr[\mathsf{E}_4]| \leq q_\mathcal{D} \cdot 2^{-\gamma}$.

– Game$_5$: In this game, we further modify the way a decapsulation-oracle query is answered. This is illustrated in Fig. 3, where notice that we no longer require the secret keys sk_i to answer the queries.

   If the decapsulation oracle in Game$_4$ outputs $\mathsf{K} := \mathsf{H}(\mathsf{M})$, then $\mathsf{M} \in \mathcal{L}_\mathsf{G}$ and $\mathsf{ct} = (\mathsf{ct}_0, \widehat{\mathsf{ct}}_i)$ holds. Therefore, the decapsulation oracle in Game$_5$ outputs K as well. On the other hand, assume the decapsulation oracle in Game$_5$ outputs $\mathsf{K} := \mathsf{H}(\mathsf{M})$ for some $\mathsf{M} \in \mathcal{L}_\mathsf{G}$ such that $\mathsf{ct} = (\mathsf{ct}_0, \widehat{\mathsf{ct}}_i)$ where $\mathsf{ct}_0 := \mathsf{mEnc}^\mathsf{i}(\mathsf{pp}; \mathsf{G}_1(\mathsf{M}))$ and $\widehat{\mathsf{ct}}_i := \mathsf{mEnc}^\mathsf{d}(\mathsf{pp}, \mathsf{pk}_i, \mathsf{M}; \mathsf{G}_1(\mathsf{M}), \mathsf{G}_2(\mathsf{pk}_i, \mathsf{M}))$. Then, since we have no correctness error (due to Game$_3$), ct must decrypt to M. Hence, this implies that the decapsulation oracle Game$_4$ outputs the same K as well. Combining the arguments together, we get $\Pr[\mathsf{E}_4] = \Pr[\mathsf{E}_5]$.

– Game$_6$: In this game, we undo the change we made in Game$_3$ and alter the output of the random oracles G_1 and G_2 to be over all the randomness space. Due to the same argument as before, we have $|\Pr[\mathsf{E}_5] - \Pr[\mathsf{E}_6]| \leq (q_\mathsf{G} + 1) \cdot \delta_N$.

(The following final Game$_7$ aims to get rid of M^* in the challenge ciphertext.)

– Game$_7$: In this game, we sample the random message $\mathsf{M}^* \leftarrow \mathcal{M}$ to be used to generate the challenge ciphertext at the beginning. We then define Query as the event that $\mathcal{A}$ queries the random oracles $\mathsf{H}(\cdot)$, $\mathsf{G}_1(\cdot)$, or $\mathsf{G}_2(\star, \cdot)$ on input M^*, where $\star$ denotes an arbitrary element. When Query occurs, we abort the game and force $\mathcal{A}$ to output a random bit. We show in the full version that $|\Pr[\mathsf{E}_6] - \Pr[\mathsf{E}_7]| \leq 2 \cdot \mathsf{Adv}_{\mathsf{mPKE}, N}^{\mathsf{IND\text{-}CPA}}(\mathcal{B}_{\mathsf{IND}}) + \frac{(q_\mathsf{G} + q_\mathsf{H})}{|\mathcal{M}|}$ for some classical PPT adversary $\mathcal{B}_{\mathsf{IND}}$ with similar runtime as $\mathcal{A}$.

   In Game$_7$, the view of the adversary is independent of the challenge bit b. Therefore, we have $\Pr[\mathsf{E}_7] = \frac{1}{2}$. This concludes the proof.

4.3 Proof for Quantum Case

The proof structure for the quantum case follows very closely the classical case. Minimal background on quantum computation is provided in the full version, and we refer for more details to other works, such as [6, 20, 27, 43].

The main difference between our proof and prior proofs for IND-CCA secure KEM in the QROM, e.g., [15, 25, 29–31, 39, 41], is that we use the *lazy sampling* with *compressed* quantum oracles introduced in [43]. This allows the simulator to check the validity of the ciphertext submitted to the decapsulation oracle without interfering with the adversary's state. Specifically, other than how we specify and interact with the random oracle, the proof structure is essentially the same as the classical case. We refer to the full version for the full proof.

4.4 Adding Recipient Anonymity

The construction provided in Sect. 4.1 immediately give rise to a *recipient anonymous* mKEM if we additionally assume the underlying IND-CPA secure mPKE is IND-Anon-CPA secure. In particular, we define the fake encapsulation algorithm $\overline{\mathsf{mEncaps}}$ (see Sect. 3.3) as: sample $\mathsf{K} \leftarrow \mathcal{K}$, run $\mathbf{ct} \leftarrow \overline{\mathsf{mEnc}}(\mathsf{pp}, N)$, and output $(\mathsf{K}, \mathbf{ct})$, where $\overline{\mathsf{mEnc}}$ is the fake encryption algorithm of the underlying mPKE (see Sect. 3.3). The only modification to the proofs of Theorems 1 and 2 is that we add an additional game at the end where we invoke the IND-Anon-CPA security game. Since, by the end of both proofs, the key K^* are distributed uniformly random, it remains to guarantee that $\mathbf{ct}^*$ is distributed independently of the public keys $(\mathsf{pk}_i)_{i \in [N]}$. We omit the full proof as it directly reduces from the IND-Anon-CPA security game.

5   Multi-recipient KEM from Post-quantum Assumptions

We provide two types of IND-CCA secure mKEM instantiations: one scheme based on lattices, and two schemes based on isogenies (in the SIDH and CSIDH setting). Specifically, we provide two types of IND-CPA secure mPKEs and use Theorems 1 and 2 to generically convert them into IND-CCA secure mKEMs in the ROM and QROM, respectively. As we see in Sect. 6, both types of instantiations are designed to fit with many of the NIST round 2 candidate (single-recipient) PKE/KEMs.

5.1   Multi-recipient KEM from Lattices

In this section, we show that the lattice-based (single-recipient) PKE based on the Lindner-Peikert framework [34] provides a natural mPKE with the required properties. Since we are able to reuse a large part of the ciphertext for lattice-based schemes, we get a notable efficiency gain compared to the trivial mPKE/mKEM which runs PKE/KEM independently for each recipient (as discussed in Remark 2).

The mPKE scheme based on the Lindner-Peikert framework [34] is provided in Fig. 4. Here, Encode (resp. Decode) is an efficiently computable bijective function that maps elements from the message space (resp. $R_q^{\bar{m} \times m}$) to $R_q^{\bar{m} \times m}$ (resp. message space). The details of Encode and Decode are scheme specific and not significant for this section. We show the mPKE scheme in Fig. 4 has all the properties required for applying the "multi-recipient" Fujisaki-Okamoto transform (Theorems 1 and 2). First, it is straightforward to see that we can easily set the parameters as to have δ-correctness and γ-spreadness for exponentially small δ and $2^{-\gamma}$. Moreover, practical schemes such as NIST candidates also allow for exponentially small δ and $2^{-\gamma}$. It remains to show that the Linder-Peikert framework provides not only a secure PKE but also a secure mPKE.

Algorithm 1 mSetup(1^κ)

Input: Security parameter 1^κ
Output: Public parameter pp
1: $\mathbf{A} \leftarrow R_q^{n \times n}$
2: **return** pp := $\mathbf{A}$

Algorithm 2 mGen(pp)

Input: Public parameter pp = $\mathbf{A}$
Output: Public key pk, a secret key sk
1: $\mathbf{S} \leftarrow D_s^{n \times m}$
2: $\mathbf{E} \leftarrow D_e^{n \times m}$
3: $\mathbf{B} \leftarrow \mathbf{AS} + \mathbf{E}$ ▷ $\mathbf{B} \in R_q^{n \times m}$
4: **return** pk := $\mathbf{B}$, sk := $\mathbf{S}$

Algorithm 3 mEnc(pp, $(\mathsf{pk}_i)_{i \in [N]}$, M)

Input: Public parameter pp = $\mathbf{A}$, set of public keys $(\mathsf{pk}_i = \mathbf{B}_i)_{i \in [N]}$, message M
Output: Ciphertext ct = $(\mathsf{ct}_0, (\widehat{\mathsf{ct}}_i)_{i \in [N]})$
1: $r_0 := (\mathbf{R}, \mathbf{E}') \leftarrow D_s^{\bar{m} \times n} \times D_e^{\bar{m} \times n}$
2: $\mathsf{ct}_0 := \mathsf{mEnc}^i(\mathsf{pp}; r_0)$
3: **for** $i \in [N]$ **do**
4:      $r_i := \mathbf{E}_i'' \leftarrow D_e^{\bar{m} \times m}$
5:      $\widehat{\mathsf{ct}}_i := \mathsf{mEnc}^d(\mathsf{pp}, \mathsf{pk}_i, M; r_0, r_i)$
6: **return** ct := $(\mathsf{ct}_0, \widehat{\mathsf{ct}}_1, \ldots, \widehat{\mathsf{ct}}_N)$

Algorithm 4 mEnc^d(pp, pk_i, M; r_0, r_i)

Input: Public parameter pp = $\mathbf{A}$, public key $\mathsf{pk}_i = \mathbf{B}_i$, message M, randomness $r_0 = (\mathbf{R}, \mathbf{E}')$ and $r_i = \mathbf{E}_i''$
Output: (Public key dependent) ciphertext $\widehat{\mathsf{ct}}_i$
1: $\mathbf{V}_i \leftarrow \mathbf{R}\mathbf{B}_i + \mathbf{E}_i'' + \mathsf{Encode}(M)$ ▷
     $\mathbf{V}_i \in R_q^{\bar{m} \times m}$
2: **return** $\widehat{\mathsf{ct}}_i := \mathbf{V}_i$

Algorithm 5 mEnc^i(pp; r_0)

Input: Public parameter pp = $\mathbf{A}$, randomness $r_0 = (\mathbf{R}, \mathbf{E}')$
Output: (Public key independent) ciphertext ct_0
1: $\mathbf{U} \leftarrow \mathbf{R}\mathbf{A} + \mathbf{E}'$ ▷ $\mathbf{U} \in R_q^{\bar{m} \times n}$
2: **return** $\mathsf{ct}_0 := \mathbf{U}$

Algorithm 6 mDec(sk, ct)

Input: Secret key sk = $\mathbf{S}$, ciphertext ct = $(\mathbf{U}, \mathbf{V})$
Output: Message M
1: $\mathbf{M} \leftarrow \mathbf{V} - \mathbf{US}$ ▷ $\mathbf{M} \in R_q^{\bar{m} \times m}$
2: **return** M := Decode($\mathbf{M}$)

Fig. 4. Lattice-based mPKE via the Lindner-Peikert framework [34]. mExt with input index i is defined by picking the relevant components $(\mathsf{ct}_0, \widehat{\mathsf{ct}}_i)$ from ct.

IND-(Anon-)CPA *Security.* It is straightforward to see that IND-CPA security follows naturally from the LWE assumption. The proof of the following lemma is given in the full version for completeness.

Lemma 1 *Assume* mPKE *as shown in Fig. 4. Then, for any (classical/quantum)* IND-CPA *adversary* $\mathcal{A}$, *there exist (classical/quantum) adversaries* $\mathcal{B}_1$ *and* $\mathcal{B}_2$ *such that*

$$\mathsf{Adv}^{\mathsf{IND\text{-}CPA}}_{\mathsf{mPKE},N}(\mathcal{A}) \leq \mathsf{Adv}^{\mathsf{LWE}}_{n,n,Nm}(\mathcal{B}_1) + \mathsf{Adv}^{\mathsf{LWE}}_{(n+Nm),n,\bar{m}}(\mathcal{B}_2).$$

Moreover, as a simple consequence of the proof of the above lemma, we have IND-Anon-CPA for free. In particular, the fake encryption algorithm $\overline{\mathsf{mEnc}}$ simply outputs a random element in $R_q^{\bar{m} \times n} \times (R_q^{\bar{m} \times m})^N$.

Remark 5 (Using LWR *instead of* LWE*).* The mPKE presented in Fig. 4 readily generalizes to the LWRsetting. The only difference is that instead of adding the noise terms (i.e., $\mathbf{E}, \mathbf{E}', \mathbf{E}''_i$), we round. For instance, the public key pk will be $\lfloor \mathbf{AS} \rceil_p \in R_p^{n \times m}$ rather than $\mathbf{AS} + \mathbf{E} \in R_q^{n \times m}$. It is easy to show that mPKE has γ-spreadness, is δ-correct and IND-CPA secure assuming the LWR assumption.

5.2   Multi-recipient KEMs from Isogenies

Retracing the steps that lead to the hashed version of ElGamal encryption from the Diffie-Hellman key exchange, public-key encryption schemes can be deduced from both SIDH [21] and CSIDH. Building on such encryption schemes, we present two isogeny-based IND-CPA secure mPKEs. Both of them satisfy the generic properties required in Theorems 1 and 2 for obtaining an IND-CCA secure mKEM. Since a unified presentation of the two schemes would be rather convoluted, for the sake of readability we differentiate their explanations. We note that both schemes require a family of universal hash functions $\mathcal{H} = \{\mathsf{H}_k : \mathcal{X} \subset \mathbb{F} \to \{0,1\}^w\}_{k \in K}$ indexed by a finite set K, where $\mathbb{F}$ denotes a finite field. The scheme based on SIDH is detailed below, while, due to space limitation, the CSIDH-based mPKE is provided in the full version.

Isogeny-Based mPKE via SIDH. The mPKE deduced from SIDH is provided in Fig. 5. We highlight that the public parameter pp output by mSetup on input a security parameter 1^κ consists of: a prime p of the form $2^{e_2} 3^{e_3} - 1$; a supersingular elliptic curve E defined over $\mathbb{F}_{p^2}$ and such that $|E(\mathbb{F}_{p^2})| = (2^{e_2} 3^{e_3})^2$; bases $B_2 = \{P_2, Q_2\}$ and $B_3 = \{P_3, Q_3\}$ for $E[2^{e_2}]$ and $E[3^{e_3}]$, respectively; a hash function H uniformly sampled from a family of universal hash functions $\mathcal{H} = \{\mathsf{H}_k : \mathcal{X} \subset \mathbb{F}_{p^2} \to \{0,1\}^w\}_{k \in K}$. Here $\mathcal{X}$ is the set of all supersingular j-invariants in $\mathbb{F}_{p^2}$, for which holds $|\mathcal{X}| = p/12 + \epsilon$, with $\epsilon \in \{0, 1, 2\}$ [21]. Furthermore, Encode (resp. Decode) is an efficiently computable bijective function from the message space (resp. $\{0,1\}^w$) to $\{0,1\}^w$ (resp. message space). The details of Encode and Decode are not significant for this section, since they are scheme specific.

The perfect correctness of the SIDH-based public-key encryption scheme from which our mPKE is deduced implies that the latter has δ-correctness, with $\delta = 0$.

Algorithm 7 $\mathsf{mSetup}(1^\kappa)$

Input: Security parameter 1^κ
Output: Public parameter pp
1: Select $e_2, e_3, E, B_2 = \{P_2, Q_2\}, B_3 = \{P_3, Q_3\}$
2: $\mathsf{H} \leftarrow \mathcal{H}$
3: **return** $\mathsf{pp} := (E, \{(e_j, B_j)\}_{j=2,3}, \mathsf{H})$

Algorithm 8 $\mathsf{mGen}(\mathsf{pp})$

Input: Public parameter $\mathsf{pp} = (E, \{(e_j, B_j)\}_{j=2,3}, \mathsf{H})$
Output: Public key pk, a secret key sk
1: $(P_2, Q_2) \leftarrow B_2, (P_3, Q_3) \leftarrow B_3$
2: $s \leftarrow \mathbb{Z}_{3^{e_3}}$
3: $R_3 \leftarrow P_3 + [s]Q_3$
4: $E_3 \leftarrow E/\langle R_3 \rangle$
5: $U_2 \leftarrow \phi_{\langle R_3 \rangle}(P_2), V_2 \leftarrow \phi_{\langle R_3 \rangle}(Q_2)$
6: **return** $\mathsf{pk} := (E_3, U_2, V_2), \mathsf{sk} := s$

Algorithm 9 $\mathsf{mEnc}(\mathsf{pp}, (\mathsf{pk}_i)_{i \in [N]}, \mathsf{M})$

Input: Public parameter $\mathsf{pp} = (E, \{(e_j, B_j)\}_{j=2,3}, \mathsf{H})$, set of public keys $(\mathsf{pk}_i = (E_3^{(i)}, U_2^{(i)}, V_2^{(i)}))_{i \in [N]}$, message M
Output: Ciphertext $\mathbf{ct} = (\mathsf{ct}_0, (\widehat{\mathsf{ct}}_i)_{i \in [N]})$
1: $r_0 := r \leftarrow \mathbb{Z}_{2^{e_2}}$
2: $\mathsf{ct}_0 := \mathsf{mEnc}^i(\mathsf{pp}; r_0)$
3: **for** $i \in [N]$ **do**
4:    $\widehat{\mathsf{ct}}_i := \mathsf{mEnc}^d(\mathsf{pp}, \mathsf{pk}_i, \mathsf{M}; r_0)$
5: **return** $\mathbf{ct} := (\mathsf{ct}_0, \widehat{\mathsf{ct}}_1, \dots, \widehat{\mathsf{ct}}_N)$

Algorithm 10 $\mathsf{mEnc}^d(\mathsf{pp}, \mathsf{pk}_i, \mathsf{M}; r_0)$

Input: Public parameter $\mathsf{pp} = (E, \{(e_j, B_j)\}_{j=2,3}, \mathsf{H})$, public key $\mathsf{pk}_i = (E_3^{(i)}, U_2^{(i)}, V_2^{(i)})$, message M, randomness $r_0 = r$
Output: (Public key dependent) ciphertext $\widehat{\mathsf{ct}}_i$
1: $T_i \leftarrow U_2^{(i)} + [r]V_2^{(i)}$
2: $J_i \leftarrow \mathsf{jInvariant}(E_3^{(i)}/\langle T_i \rangle)$
3: $F_i \leftarrow \mathsf{H}(J_i) \oplus \mathsf{Encode}(\mathsf{M})$
4: **return** $\widehat{\mathsf{ct}}_i := F_i$

Algorithm 11 $\mathsf{mEnc}^i(\mathsf{pp}; r_0)$

Input: Public parameter $\mathsf{pp} = (E, \{(e_j, B_j)\}_{j=2,3}, \mathsf{H})$, randomness $r_0 = r$
Output: (Public key independent) ciphertext ct_0
1: $(P_2, Q_2) \leftarrow B_2, (P_3, Q_3) \leftarrow B_3$
2: $R_2 \leftarrow P_2 + [r]Q_2$
3: $E_2 \leftarrow E/\langle R_2 \rangle$
4: $U_3 \leftarrow \phi_{\langle R_2 \rangle}(P_3), V_3 \leftarrow \phi_{\langle R_2 \rangle}(Q_3)$
5: **return** $\mathsf{ct}_0 := (E_2, U_3, V_3)$

Algorithm 12 $\mathsf{mDec}(\mathsf{sk}, \mathsf{ct})$

Input: Public parameter $\mathsf{pp} = (E, \{(e_j, B_j)\}_{j=2,3}, \mathsf{H})$, secret key $\mathsf{sk} = s$, ciphertext $\mathsf{ct} = (E_2, U_3, V_3, F)$
Output: Message M
1: $R' \leftarrow U_3 + [s]V_3$
2: $E' \leftarrow E_2/\langle R' \rangle$
3: $J' \leftarrow \mathsf{jInvariant}(E')$
4: $\mathbf{M} \leftarrow F \oplus \mathsf{H}(J')$
5: **return** $\mathsf{M} := \mathsf{Decode}(\mathbf{M})$

Fig. 5. SIDH-based mPKE via hashed ElGamal [21]. mExt with input index i is defined by picking the relevant components $(\mathsf{ct}_0, \widehat{\mathsf{ct}}_i)$ from $\mathbf{ct}$. Note that mEnc^d does not require any randomness r_i for $i \in [N]$.

In addition, for a given security parameter 1^κ, the prime $p = 2^{e_2} 3^{e_3} - 1$ in the public parameter $\mathsf{pp} \leftarrow \mathsf{mGen}(1^\kappa)$ is fixed [28]. The first component of each element in $\mathcal{C}_{\mathsf{single}}$ contains a curve 2^{e_2}-isogenous to E. We denote by W the set

$\{j(E/\langle P_2 + [r]Q_2\rangle)|r \in \mathbb{Z}_{2^{e_2}}\}$ of all such curves. Since $p/12 + \epsilon \gg |W|$, one expects that the number of pairs of distinct coefficients $r, \tilde{r} \in \mathbb{Z}_{2^{e_2}}$ such that $j(E/\langle P_2 + [r]Q_2\rangle) = j(E/\langle P_2 + [\tilde{r}]Q_2\rangle)$ is very small [1]. Hence, we can assume that $|W| = 2^{e_2}$ and deduce $\gamma(\mathsf{pp}, \mathsf{pk}) \geq e_2$. This value is independent of the public key pk and E, B_2, B_3 in pp, therefore the mPKE scheme has γ-spreadness with $\gamma = e_2$. We observe that $1/2^{e_2} \approx 1/\sqrt{p}$, which is negligible in the security parameter κ ($e_2 \geq \kappa$ for any set of SIDH parameters [28]).

IND-(Anon-)CPA *Security.* The IND-CPA security of the SIDH-based mPKE follows from the SSDDH assumption and the Leftover Hash Lemma. The proof of the following lemma is given in the full version for completeness.

Lemma 2 *Assume* mPKE *as shown in Fig. 5. Then, for any (classical/quantum)* IND-CPA *adversary* $\mathcal{A}$*, there exists a (classical/quantum) adversary* $\mathcal{B}$ *such that*

$$\mathsf{Adv}^{\mathsf{IND\text{-}CPA}}_{\mathsf{mPKE},N}(\mathcal{A}) \leq N \cdot \left(\mathsf{Adv}^{\mathsf{SSDDH}}_{p,E,B_2,B_3}(\mathcal{B}) + \frac{1}{2}\sqrt{2^w/p} \right). \tag{2}$$

We note that in concrete instantiations, $\log_2 p$ assumes one of the values $434, 503, 610$, while the corresponding w is $128, 192$ or 256, respectively [28]. Therefore the quantity $(1/2)\sqrt{2^w/p}$ is bounded by 2^{152} for each pair (p, w) and it can be safely discarded in the right term of Eq. (2). Moreover, as a simple consequence of the concrete proof of the above lemma, we have IND-Anon-CPA for free. In particular, the fake encryption algorithm $\overline{\mathsf{mEnc}}$ simply outputs a tuple composed by a ciphertext ct_0 and N uniformly random elements in $\{0,1\}^w$.

Isogeny-Based mPKE via CSIDH. Since the high level structure of our CSIDH-based mPKE is similar to our SIDH-based mPKE, we refer the full details to full version. We consider the action of a cyclic group G on a set of supersingular elliptic curves. However, it can be easily adapted to the case where the structure of G is unknown.

6 Instantiating mKEM with NIST Candidates and CSIDH

In this section, we concretely instantiate the generic mKEM framework laid out in previous sections. We take the PKEs underlying 8 existing lattice-based and isogeny-based NIST KEMs (as well as CSIDH). We first modify them into efficient mPKEs (following Sect. 5) and then into mKEMs via our generic transformation (Theorem 1 and 2). We note that we did not consider the corresponding mKEM for the CISDH mPKE, for reasons explained later. We compare these mKEMs to the trivial solution that uses (single-recipient) KEMs in parallel, and show that our mKEMs provide efficiency gains, both in communication and computation, of an order of magnitude.

Until the end of this document, we denote by $|\mathsf{x}|$ the bytesize of an object x, where x may be any cryptographic object (a public key, a ciphertext, etc.)

6.1 Comparison Methodology

Our goal is to provide an accurate assessment of the gains provided by various mKEM instantiations. A natural way to do that is to compare the performances of these mKEMs (with N recipients) with N instantiations of the original (single-recipient) KEMs. This comparison can be done via two metrics:

(C1) Communication cost. How much data does the encryptor broadcast when using mKEM with N recipients, and how does it compare to N instances of the original KEM (one per recipient)?
(C2) Computational cost. How many cycles does one instance of mKEM with N recipients cost, and how does it compare to N instances of KEM?

For (C1), we measure the ratio:

$$\frac{\text{Data broadcast when using } N \text{ instances of the original KEM}}{\text{Data broadcast when using mKEM with } N \text{ recipients}}. \tag{3}$$

With mKEM the encryptor broadcasts a single multi-ciphertext of size $|ct_0| + \sum_{i \in [N]} |\widehat{ct}_i| = |ct_0| + N|\widehat{ct}_i|$, whereas with N instances of KEM he broadcasts N ciphertexts $ct = (ct_0, \widehat{ct}_i)$ – except for NewHope, see Footnote 4 – for a total size $N|ct_0| + N|\widehat{ct}_i|$. Therefore, the ratio converges to a value independent of N when N tends to infinity. Specifically, the value (3) is:

$$\frac{N|ct_0| + N|\widehat{ct}_i|}{|ct_0| + N|\widehat{ct}_i|} \quad \xrightarrow[N \to \infty]{} \quad 1 + \frac{|ct_0|}{|\widehat{ct}_i|}. \tag{4}$$

Let $k_{\text{comm}} = 1 + \frac{|ct_0|}{|\widehat{ct}_i|}$. This value measures asymptotically "how much more compact" mKEM is compared to the original KEM, and serves as our metric for (C1). Similarly, the following value serves as our metric for (C2):

$$k_{\text{cycles}} = \lim_{N \to \infty} \frac{\text{Cycles spent to run } N \text{ instances of the original KEM}}{\text{Cycles spent to run mKEM with } N \text{ recipients}} \tag{5}$$

We note that k_{cycles} is far less absolute than k_{comm} as a metric, since the number of cycles depend on the implementation of a scheme, the architecture of the target platform, etc. However, it is a useful indicator of the efficiency gain that one can expect by using mKEM. All cycles measurements in this section are performed on a processor i7-8665U (Whiskey Lake) @ 1.90 GHz, with Turbo Boost disabled.

6.2 Instantiation with Lattice-Based NIST Candidates

In this section, we provide concrete instantiations of the high-level scheme described in Sect. 5.1. Our efforts are facilitated by the fact that 7 lattice-based NIST candidate KEMs are deduced from PKEs that follow the Lindner-Peikert framework:

- Kyber;
- FrodoKEM;
- LAC;
- NewHope;
- Round5;
- Saber;
- ThreeBears.

Full specifications of these 7 schemes are available at [36]. Out of these, FrodoKEM, Kyber, LACand NewHopefollow the most closely the Lindner-Peikert framework, since they are based on LWE, Module-LWE, Ring-LWEand Ring-LWE, respectively. Round5and Saberare based on variants of LWR. This implies a few changes on Fig. 4, since the addition of noise error is replaced in some instances by rounding. See Rem. 4 for a short discussion on this change. Finally, ThreeBearsis based on an extremely recent variant called Module Integer-LWE. In addition, each scheme has different parameters and uses different tweaks. A widespread trick is for $\widehat{\mathsf{ct}}_i$ to drop the least significant bits of $\mathbf{V}_i$, since the message M is encoded in the most significant bits. This reduces the size of a (multi-)ciphertext. Note that bit dropping is more beneficial to mKEMs than to KEMs as it reduces $|\widehat{\mathsf{ct}}_i|$, hence a larger bandwidth impact for mKEMs – see (4).

These 7 KEMs and the PKEs they are based on serve as the bases for our mKEM constructions. We tweaked them in order to fit the frameworks described in Fig. 4 (IND-CPA mPKE) and Fig. 2 (conversion into an IND-CCA mKEM). Note that our tweaks break compatibility with the specifications of the aforementioned schemes, for two reasons. First, we fix the public matrix $\mathbf{A}$ in order to fit Fig. 4 (see Remark 6 below). Second, the transform of Fig. 2 is completely different from the ones used in the 7 aforementioned KEMs, which themselves differ from each other. As a consequence, comparing our mKEMs to these KEMs is not an entirely apples-to-apples comparison, as the 7 KEMs we cited claim some additional properties such as contributivity or security in specific threat models (see Remark 6). For our mKEMs, we do not claim to achieve any security notion besides those proven in this document.

Remark 6 (Reusing the public matrix). A difference between Fig. 4 and the aforementioned NIST schemes is that the latter use PKEs for which the matrix $\mathbf{A}$ is made part of the public key pk. That is, each user has its $\mathbf{A}$ rather than sharing it. The main argument for this choice is to hinder *all-for-the-price-of-one attacks* [2, Section 3]. The associated threat model considers an attacker that has enough cryptanalytic capabilities to break *one* hard instance of a lattice problem, but not much more. This is an arguably specific security model, one that implicitly considers that the parameter set of the scheme may not be cryptographically secure. In order to enable our mKEM instantiations, we instead make $\mathbf{A}$ part of the public parameter pp, as per Fig. 4. This can be done with minimal changes to the PKEs used by the original KEMs, and has no impact on their concrete security analysis.

Communication Costs. Table 1 provides a comparison of NIST KEMs with their mKEM variants. Sending N ciphertexts costs $N \cdot |\mathsf{ct}|$ bytes for a NIST KEM, whereas using its mKEM counterpart costs $|\mathsf{ct}_0| + N \cdot |\widehat{\mathsf{ct}}_i|$. The gain in bandwidth $k_{\mathsf{comm}}$is of one order of magnitude (sometimes two). Schemes based on module lattices (Saber, Kyber, ThreeBears) and standard lattices (FrodoKEM) see the most dramatic gains (as high as a factor 169 times for FrodoKEM).

Table 1. Bandwidth impact of our solution on various schemes. Sizes are in bytes.

Scheme	$|ct_0|$	$|\widehat{ct}_i|$	$|ct|$	k_{comm}
FrodoKEM-640	9600	120	9720	81
FrodoKEM-976	15616	128	15744	123
FrodoKEM-1344	21504	128	21632	169
Kyber-512	640	96	736	7.67
Kyber-768	960	128	1088	8.5
Kyber-1024	1408	160	1568	9.8
LAC-128	512	200	712	3.56
LAC-192	1024	164	1188	7.24
LAC-256	1024	400	1424	3.56
NewHope-512-CCA-KEM	896	192	1120	5.83
NewHope-1048-CCA-KEM	1792	384	2208	5.75
Round5 R5ND_1KEMb	429	110	539	4.9
Round5 R5ND_3KEMb	756	74	830	11.22
Round5 R5ND_5KEMb	940	142	1082	7.62
LightSaber	640	96	736	7.67
Saber	960	128	1088	8.5
FireSaber	1280	192	1472	7.67
BabyBear	780	137	917	6.69
MamaBear	1170	137	1307	9.54
PapaBear	1560	137	1697	12.38

Unlike other lattice-based KEMs, the CCA variant of NewHopeadds a hash to the ciphertext. So in this particular case $|ct| = |ct_0| + |\widehat{ct}_i| + \{32, 64\}$.

Computational Costs. Due to time constraints, we only implemented mKEM on two lattice-based schemes: FrodoKEM and Kyber. Nevertheless, we believe these examples already showcase the efficiency gain provided by our techniques. Starting from reference implementations available on Github[4,5], we tweaked them to obtain mKEMs. As shown by Table 2, our mKEM variants perform (multi-)encapsulation between one and two orders of magnitude faster than their original KEM counterparts. We provide additional experiments in the full version and show that the target platform can play an important role in the performance gain.

[4] https://github.com/Microsoft/PQCrypto-LWEKE.
[5] https://github.com/pq-crystals/kyber/.

Table 2. Encapsulation times of FrodoKEM and Kyber vs their mKEM variants. Times are in cycles and are normalized by the number of recipients (here, 1000).

Scheme	Trivial KEM	Our mKEM	k_{cycles}
FrodoKEM-640	4948835	251405	19.68
FrodoKEM-976	10413149	387733	26.86
FrodoKEM-1344	18583122	519973	35.74
Kyber-512	181297	42647	4.25
Kyber-768	279210	52471	5.32
Kyber-1024	414774	61808	6.71

6.3 Instantiation with Isogeny-Based Schemes

In this section, we focus on isogeny-based instantiations of mKEM and mPKE. Concerning SIKE, we obtain an mKEM from the mPKE of Fig. 5, and we compare it with the trivial solution consisting in N instances of SIKE. For CSIDH, we compare our mPKE in the full version with N instances of the CSIDH-based hashed ElGamal. Since CSIDH is a key-exchange, we simply construct a trivial IND-CPA secure PKE from it (rather than constructing an IND-CCA secure KEM) and compare it with our mPKE from Sect. 5.2.

To obtain proof-of-concept implementation of mPKE for CSIDH and mKEM for SIKE, we have modified implementation available in the NOBS library[6].

Communication Cost. Our construction provides the most significant gain when used with SIKE/p434. In this case our mKEM variant can be over 20 times more efficient (Table 3).

Table 3. Bandwidth impact of our mKEM on isogeny schemes. Sizes are in bytes.

Scheme	$|ct_0|$	$|\widehat{ct}_i|$	$|ct|$	k_{comm}
SIKE/p434	330	16	346	21.63
SIKE/p503	378	24	402	16.75
SIKE/p751	564	32	596	18.63
SIKE/p434_compressed	196	16	209	13.25
SIKE/p503_compressed	224	24	248	10.33
SIKE/p751_compressed	331	32	363	11.34
cSIDH PKE/p512	64	16	80	5

---

[6] https://github.com/henrydcase/nobs.

Computational Costs. In SIKE and CSIDH-based hashed ElGamal, the computational cost is dominated by isogeny computations. In both schemes, encapsulation/encryption requires the computation of two smooth-degree isogenies. Assuming SIKE key compression is not used, we can assume that both computations have a similar cost C. When running SIKE/CSIDH-based hashed ElGamal for N recipients, the total computation cost is roughly $2 \cdot N \cdot C$. By applying our mKEM/mPKE this cost reduces to $(N + 1) \cdot C$. So, the expectation is that our approach will be roughly two times faster. The results from the benchmarking in Table 4 confirms the expected speed-up. It is worth noticing that the gain from using mKEM is expected to be bigger when using SIKE with key compression. That is because computing $|\mathsf{ct}_0|$ is a slower operation than computing $|\widehat{\mathsf{ct}}_i|$.

Table 4. Encapsulation times of SIKE vs its mKEM variant and encryption times of CSIDH-based hashed ElGamal vs its mPKE variant. Times are in cycles and are normalized by the number of recipients (here, 100).

Scheme	Trivial KEM	Our mKEM	k_{cycles}
SIKE/p434	1657655212	759202275	2.18
SIKE/p503	2301014376	1037469650	2.22
SIKE/p751	6900791605	3150069659	2.19
cSIDH/p512	37455411429	19438021692	1.92

7   Application to Secure Group Messaging

In this section, we show how our mKEM can be used to optimize the *TreeKEM* protocol [3,5,14] used within secure group messagings. The resulting protocol has a lower communication cost than the standard version of TreeKEM [5,14].

7.1   Syntax and Notations for Group Messaging

We first introduce group messaging-related notions. We observe that group messaging is an extensive topic; we keep our presentation minimal and introduce notions that are strictly required for our argument. More in-depth discussions on group messaging can be found in e.g. [3,5,10,14].

   Continuous group key agreement (CGKA), which generalizes the notion of continuous key agreement (CKA, see [4]), forms the backbone of secure *group* messaging (SGM) protocols. Informally, one can think of CGKA as a group key exchange where the group members dynamically change and the (group) session keys need to be re-established in each epoch to maintain strong security. Once a session key is established for a given epoch, a user can then use the key to securely communicate with the group members. Therefore, a SGM protocol can be described as a continuum of running CGKA and exchanging secured messages.

Definition 11 (Continuous Group Key Agreement. *[5]*). *A continuous group key agreement* CGKA = (Init, Create, Add, Remove, Update, Process) *consists of the following algorithms:*

- **Initialization.** Init *takes an ID* ID *and outputs an initial state* state.
- **Group creation.** Create *takes a state* state, *a list of IDs* $(ID_i)_{i \in [N]}$ *and outputs a new state* state′ *and a control message* W.
- **Add.** Add *takes a state* state, *an ID* ID *and outputs a new state* state′ *and control messages* W, T.
- **Remove.** Remove *takes a state* state, *an ID* ID *and outputs a new state* state′ *and a control message* T.
- **Update.** Update *takes a state* state *and outputs a new state* state′ *and a control message* T.
- **Process.** Process*takes a state* state *and outputs a new state* state′ *and an update secret* I.

Above, Updateallows a user to update the session key on behalf of the whole group (it is run on every epoch to maintain strong security), and Processallows each group member to process the updated session key. Four properties are required from a CGKA: correctness, privacy, forward privacy (FS), and post-compromise security (PCS). At a high level, FS states that if any group member is compromised at some point, then all previous session keys remain hidden from the attacker; and PCS states that after every compromised group member performs an update, the session key becomes secret again. As the precise definitions are not relevant to our work, we refer to [5, Section 3.2] for more details.

In the following, we focus on TreeKEM; a specific instantiation of CGKA that forms the building block of the SGM protocol MLS [10]. It was first described in [14] and various improvements have been proposed in [3,5]. TreeKEM is at the heart of the MLS protocol [10], and is arguably one of MLS' main efficiency bottlenecks due to the large number of public key material sent. To be more concrete, our efforts are directed at optimizing the Update algorithm of TreeKEM; this algorithm constitutes an efficiency bottleneck (in computation and communication) of TreeKEM as it is performed on a regular basis (in contrast to Create, Add and Remove, which are performed upon punctual events). In effect, improving the efficiency of Update will improve the efficiency of TreeKEM (and hence the MLS protocol) on a similar scale. Details on TreeKEM follows.

Dendrologic Notations. In a (binary or m-ary) tree T, a *leaf* is a node with no child, an *internal node* is a node that is not a leaf, and the *root* root is the unique node that has no parent. By synecdoche, we may abusively refer to a node by its label; for example in Fig. 6, "1" denotes the bottom left node.

Let u be a node in a tree T. Its siblings, siblings(u), is the set of nodes $v \neq u$ in T with the same parent as u. Its *path*, path(u), is the set of nodes between u and root, including u but excluding root. Its *co-path*, copath(u), is the set of siblings of nodes in its path: copath(u) = $\bigcup_{v \in \text{path}(u)}$ siblings(v). For example, in

Fig. 6, the only sibling of "1" is "2", its path is the set of red nodes (⬤), and its co-path is the set of green nodes (⬤).

TreeKEM. In TreeKEM, a (binary or m-ary) tree T is constructed with the N group members as its leaves. As an example, Fig. 6 illustrates the tree T associated to a group of 16 users (numbered from 1 to 16). Let PRG be a pseudorandom generator. Then, to each node i is associated a secret seed seed_i and a keypair $(\mathsf{pk}_i, \mathsf{sk}_i) = \mathsf{mGen}(\mathsf{pp}; \mathsf{PRG}(\mathsf{seed}_i)_\mathsf{L})$, where $\mathsf{PRG}(\cdot)_\mathsf{L}$ (resp. $\mathsf{PRG}(\cdot)_\mathsf{R}$) denotes the left (resp. right) half output of the PRG. In particular, mGen is run on randomness $\mathsf{PRG}(\mathsf{seed}_i)_\mathsf{L}$. The root does not need a keypair, but its seed will in effect be the group secret I (i.e., session key). The *TreeKEM invariant* states that a group member u knows seed_i if and only if $i \in \mathsf{path}(u)$. When a user u performs an update (via Update), he does the following:

(U1) Generate a new secret seed seed_u for u.
(U2) For each $i \in \mathsf{path}(u)$, update its keypair: $(\mathsf{pk}_i, \mathsf{sk}_i) = \mathsf{mGen}(\mathsf{pp}; \mathsf{PRG}(\mathsf{seed}_i)_\mathsf{L})$, and compute a new secret seed for its parent: $\mathsf{seed}_{\mathsf{parent}(i)} = \mathsf{PRG}(\mathsf{seed}_i)_\mathsf{R}$.
(U3) For each $i \in \mathsf{path}(u)$, compute the ciphertext

$$\mathbf{ct}_i \leftarrow \mathsf{mEncaps}(\mathsf{pp}, (\mathsf{pk}_j)_{j \in \mathsf{siblings}(i)}; \mathsf{seed}_{\mathsf{parent}(i)}). \tag{6}$$

Note that $\mathsf{mEncaps}$ is derandomized here. For our construction in Fig. 2, this is equivalent to setting the random message $\mathsf{M}_i = \mathsf{PRG}(\mathsf{seed}_{\mathsf{parent}(i)})$.
(U4) Send the update package $(\mathsf{pk}_i, \mathbf{ct}_i)_{i \in \mathsf{path}(u)}$ to the server, which dispatches it to the other group members (this is known as *server-side fan-out*).

Upon receiving the update package, a user v processes it (via $\mathsf{Process}$) as follows:

(P1) Update each pk_i he received.
(P2) Compute the closest common ancestor w of u and v, then recover seed_w by decapsulating the adequate $\mathbf{ct}_i$.
(P3) Recover the secret seeds of all remaining common ancestors of u and v by computing $\mathsf{seed}_{\mathsf{parent}(i)} = \mathsf{PRG}(\mathsf{seed}_i)_\mathsf{R}$. The update secret is $I = \mathsf{seed}_{\mathsf{root}}$

This description is more generic than previous ones [3,5,10,14] in the following sense. All existing instantiations of TreeKEM take T to be a binary tree, in which case there is no need for a mKEM as a single-recipient KEM suffices. Note that while our description uses mKEM as a building block, it is easily adapted to work with an mPKE. Figure 6 illustrates the "classical" instantiation of TreeKEM. Each update contains at most $\lceil \log_2(N) \rceil$ public keys and as many ciphertexts, so its bytesize is at most:

$$\lceil \log_2(N) \rceil \cdot \left(|\mathsf{pk}| + |\mathbf{ct}_0| + |\widehat{\mathbf{ct}}_i| \right) \tag{7}$$

m-ary TreeKEM. We now show how to obtain significant efficiency gains by instantiating TreeKEM with an m-ary tree combined with mKEM. As mentioned

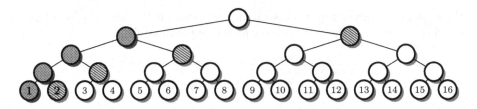

Fig. 6. TreeKEM (Color figure online)

in [14], TreeKEM can be instantiated with an m-ary tree instead of binary; see Fig. 7 for an example where "1" issues a package update. At first, it is not obvious that this is more efficient than the instantiation of Fig. 6, since in our example the update package now contains 2 public keys (one for each node (⊛) in the path) and 6 ciphertexts (one for each node (⊘) in the co-path).

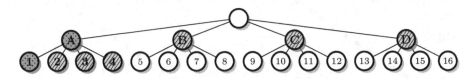

Fig. 7. 4-ary TreeKEM (Color figure online)

We make the following observation: when a user u issues an update, the update package may encapsulate several times the same information. Precisely, for each $i \in \mathsf{path}(u)$, the update package encapsulates $\mathsf{seed}_{\mathsf{parent}(i)}$ under the key pk_j for each $j \in \mathsf{siblings}(i)$. In the example of Fig. 7, this means that an update package issued by 1 encapsulates seed_A under $\mathsf{pk}_2, \mathsf{pk}_3, \mathsf{pk}_4$, and $\mathsf{seed}_{\mathsf{root}}$ under $\mathsf{pk}_B, \mathsf{pk}_C, \mathsf{pk}_D$. The bandwidth gain happens exactly here: since the same value seed_A is encapsulated under $\mathsf{pk}_2, \mathsf{pk}_3, \mathsf{pk}_4$, one can use mKEM to perform this (multi-)encapsulation. And similarly at each level of the tree. Hence the total size of an update package is at most: $\lceil \log_m(N) \rceil \cdot \left(|\mathsf{pk}| + |\mathsf{ct}_0| + (m-1) \cdot |\widehat{\mathsf{ct}}_i| \right)$. One can see that this generalizes (7) to any integer $m > 2$. It is clear that whenever $|\mathsf{pk}| + |\mathsf{ct}_0| \gg |\widehat{\mathsf{ct}}_i|$, it is advantageous efficiency-wise to take $m > 2$. This is illustrated in the next section.

7.2 Concrete Instantiations of m-ary TreeKEM

We now illustrate the substantial communication gains that can be obtained in practice with the method described above. A good rule of thumb is to take $m - 1 \approx \frac{|\mathsf{pk}| + |\mathsf{ct}_0|}{|\widehat{\mathsf{ct}}_i|}$. According to (7), the bytesize of an update package for binary TreeKEM will then be approximately $\lceil \log_2(N) \rceil \cdot m \cdot |\widehat{\mathsf{ct}}_i|$. On the other hand, the bytesize for our proposal is about $\lceil \log_m(N) \rceil \cdot 2(m-1) \cdot |\widehat{\mathsf{ct}}_i|$. Compared to the standard TreeKEM, our proposal improves communication cost by a factor equal to the ratio of the two values, which is approximately:

$$\frac{\lceil \log_2(N) \rceil \cdot m \cdot |\widehat{\mathsf{ct}}_i|}{\lceil \log_m(N) \rceil \cdot 2(m-1) \cdot |\widehat{\mathsf{ct}}_i|} \xrightarrow[N \to \infty]{} \frac{m}{2(m-1)} \cdot \log_2(m)$$
$$= \quad O(\log m).$$

Our solution provides a gain $O(\log m)$ compared to TreeKEM. A concrete comparison is provided by Fig. 8, which compares the bytesize of an update package for binary TreeKEM - using FrodoKEM, Kyber, SIKEor cSIDHas a (single-recipient) KEM/PKE - and m-ary TreeKEM - using the mKEM/mPKE obtained from FrodoKEM, Kyber, SIKEor cSIDH, respectively. For the schemes considered, our proposal improves the communication cost for large groups by a factor between 1.8 and 4.2.

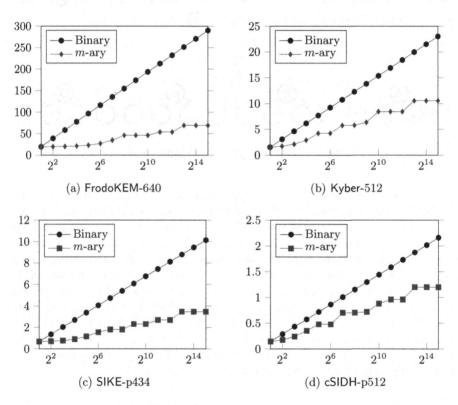

(a) FrodoKEM-640

(b) Kyber-512

(c) SIKE-p434

(d) cSIDH-p512

Fig. 8. Comparing the classic "binary" TreeKEM with m-ary TreeKEM, when instantiated with four schemes: FrodoKEM, Kyber, SIKEand cSIDH. In each case, the x-axis represent the number N of group members (from 2 to 2^{15}) and the y-axis represent the maximal size of an update package in kilobytes. The arity m depends on the scheme and the group size N, and is omitted for readability.

Acknowledgement. Shuichi Katsumata was supported by JST CREST Grant Number JPMJCR19F6 and JSPS KAKENHI Grant Number JP19H01109. Kris Kwiatkowski and Thomas Prest were supported by the Innovate UK Research Grant 104423 (PQ Cybersecurity). The authors would like to thank Takashi Yamakawa for helpful discussions on QROM.

References

1. Adj, G., Cervantes-Vázquez, D., Chi-Domínguez, J.J., Menezes, A., Rodríguez-Henríquez, F.: On the cost of computing isogenies between supersingular elliptic curves. In: Cid, C., Jacobson Jr., M. (eds.) SAC 2018. LNCS, vol. 11349, pp. 322–343. Springer, Cham (2019). https://doi.org/10.1007/978-3-030-10970-7_15

2. Alkim, E., Ducas, L., Pöppelmann, T., Schwabe, P.: Post-quantum key exchange - a new hope. In: USENIX Security, pp. 327–343 (2016)

3. Alwen, J., et al.: Keep the dirt: tainted TreeKEM, an efficient and provably secure continuous group key agreement protocol. Cryptology ePrint Archive, Report 2019/1489 (2019)

4. Alwen, J., Coretti, S., Dodis, Y.: The double ratchet: security notions, proofs, and modularization for the signal protocol. In: Ishai, Y., Rijmen, V. (eds.) EUROCRYPT 2019. LNCS, vol. 11476, pp. 129–158. Springer, Cham (2019). https://doi.org/10.1007/978-3-030-17653-2_5

5. Alwen, J., Coretti, S., Dodis, Y., Tselekounis, Y.: Security analysis and improvements for the IETF MLS standard for group messaging. Cryptology ePrint Archive, Report 2019/1189 (2019)

6. Ambainis, A., Hamburg, M., Unruh, D.: Quantum security proofs using semiclassical oracles. In: Boldyreva, A., Micciancio, D. (eds.) CRYPTO 2019. LNCS, vol. 11693, pp. 269–295. Springer, Cham (2019). https://doi.org/10.1007/978-3-030-26951-7_10

7. Banerjee, A., Peikert, C., Rosen, A.: Pseudorandom functions and lattices. In: Pointcheval, D., Johansson, T. (eds.) EUROCRYPT 2012. LNCS, vol. 7237, pp. 719–737. Springer, Heidelberg (2012). https://doi.org/10.1007/978-3-642-29011-4_42

8. Barbosa, M., Farshim, P.: Randomness reuse: extensions and improvements. In: Galbraith, S.D. (ed.) Cryptography and Coding 2007. LNCS, vol. 4887, pp. 257–276. Springer, Heidelberg (2007). https://doi.org/10.1007/978-3-540-77272-9_16

9. Barker, E., et al.: Recommendation for pair-wise key establishment schemes using discrete logarithm cryptography. Technical Report; National Institute of Standards and Technology (NIST), Gaithersburg, MD, USA, p. 15158 (2006) (2012). https://doi.org/10.6028/NIST.SP.800-56Ar3

10. Barnes, R., Beurdouche, B., Millican, J., Omara, E., Cohn-Gordon, K., Robert, R.: The Messaging Layer Security (MLS) Protocol. Internet-Draft draft-IETF-MLS-protocol-09, Internet Engineering Task Force. In: Work in Progress (2020)

11. Baudron, O., Pointcheval, D., Stern, J.: Extended notions of security for multicast public key cryptosystems. In: Montanari, U., Rolim, J.D.P., Welzl, E. (eds.) ICALP 2000. LNCS, vol. 1853, pp. 499–511. Springer, Heidelberg (2000). https://doi.org/10.1007/3-540-45022-X_42

12. Bellare, M., Boldyreva, A., Micali, S.: Public-key encryption in a multi-user setting: security proofs and improvements. In: Preneel, B. (ed.) EUROCRYPT 2000. LNCS, vol. 1807, pp. 259–274. Springer, Heidelberg (2000). https://doi.org/10.1007/3-540-45539-6_18

13. Bellare, M., Boldyreva, A., Staddon, J.: Randomness re-use in multi-recipient encryption schemeas. In: Desmedt, Y.G. (ed.) PKC 2003. LNCS, vol. 2567, pp. 85–99. Springer, Heidelberg (2003). https://doi.org/10.1007/3-540-36288-6_7

14. Bhargavan, K., Barnes, R., Rescorla, E.: TreeKEM: asynchronous decentralized key management for large dynamic groups a protocol proposal for messaging layer security (MLS). Research report, Inria Paris (2018)

15. Bindel, N., Hamburg, M., Hövelmanns, K., Hülsing, A., Persichetti, E.: Tighter proofs of CCA security in the quantum random oracle model. In: Hofheinz, D., Rosen, A. (eds.) TCC 2019. LNCS, vol. 11892, pp. 61–90. Springer, Cham (2019). https://doi.org/10.1007/978-3-030-36033-7_3

16. Castryck, W., Lange, T., Martindale, C., Panny, L., Renes, J.: CSIDH: an efficient post-quantum commutative group action. In: Peyrin, T., Galbraith, S. (eds.) ASIACRYPT 2018. LNCS, vol. 11274, pp. 395–427. Springer, Cham (2018). https://doi.org/10.1007/978-3-030-03332-3_15

17. Cheng, H., Li, X., Qian, H., Yan, D.: CCA secure multi-recipient KEM from LPN. In: Naccache, D., et al. (eds.) ICICS 2018. LNCS, vol. 11149, pp. 513–529. Springer, Cham (2018). https://doi.org/10.1007/978-3-030-01950-1_30

18. Jean-Sébastien, C., Handschuh, H., Joye, M., Paillier, P., Pointcheval, D., Tymen, C.: GEM: a generic chosen-ciphertext secure encryption method. In: Preneel, B. (ed.) CT-RSA 2002. LNCS, vol. 2271, pp. 263–276. Springer, Heidelberg (2002). https://doi.org/10.1007/3-540-45760-7_18

19. Cramer, R., Shoup, V.: Design and analysis of practical public-key encryption schemes secure against adaptive chosen ciphertext attack. SIAM J. Comput. **33**(1), 167–226 (2003)

20. Czajkowski, J., Majenz, C., Schaffner, C., Zur, S.: Quantum lazy sampling and game-playing proofs for quantum indifferentiability. Cryptology ePrint Archive, Report 2019/428 (2019)

21. De Feo, L., Jao, D., Plût, J.: Towards quantum-resistant cryptosystems from supersingular elliptic curve isogenies. J. Math. Cryptol. **8**, 209–247 (2014)

22. Dent, A.W.: A designer's guide to KEMs. In: Paterson, K.G. (ed.) Cryptography and Coding 2003. LNCS, vol. 2898, pp. 133–151. Springer, Heidelberg (2003). https://doi.org/10.1007/978-3-540-40974-8_12

23. Fujisaki, E., Okamoto, T.: Secure integration of asymmetric and symmetric encryption schemes. In: Wiener, M. (ed.) CRYPTO 1999. LNCS, vol. 1666, pp. 537–554. Springer, Heidelberg (1999). https://doi.org/10.1007/3-540-48405-1_34

24. Hiwatari, H., Tanaka, K., Asano, T., Sakumoto, K.: Multi-recipient public-key encryption from simulators in security proofs. In: Boyd, C., González Nieto, J. (eds.) ACISP 2009. LNCS, vol. 5594, pp. 293–308. Springer, Heidelberg (2009). https://doi.org/10.1007/978-3-642-02620-1_21

25. Hofheinz, D., Hövelmanns, K., Kiltz, E.: A modular analysis of the Fujisaki-Okamoto transformation. In: Kalai, Y., Reyzin, L. (eds.) TCC 2017. LNCS, vol. 10677, pp. 341–371. Springer, Cham (2017). https://doi.org/10.1007/978-3-319-70500-2_12

26. Hofheinz, D., Kiltz, E.: Secure hybrid encryption from weakened key encapsulation. In: Menezes, A. (ed.) CRYPTO 2007. LNCS, vol. 4622, pp. 553–571. Springer, Heidelberg (2007). https://doi.org/10.1007/978-3-540-74143-5_31

27. Hövelmanns, K., Kiltz, E., Schäge, S., Unruh, D.: Generic authenticated key exchange in the quantum random oracle model. In: Kiayias, A., Kohlweiss, M., Wallden, P., Zikas, V. (eds.) PKC 2020. LNCS, vol. 12111, pp. 389–422. Springer, Cham (2020). https://doi.org/10.1007/978-3-030-45388-6_14

28. Jao, D., et al.: SIKE. Technical report, National Institute of Standards and Technology (2019). https://csrc.nist.gov/projects/post-quantum-cryptography/round-2-submissions

29. Jiang, H., Zhang, Z., Chen, L., Wang, H., Ma, Z.: IND-CCA-secure key encapsulation mechanism in the quantum random oracle model, revisited. In: Shacham, H., Boldyreva, A. (eds.) CRYPTO 2018. LNCS, vol. 10993, pp. 96–125. Springer, Cham (2018). https://doi.org/10.1007/978-3-319-96878-0_4

30. Jiang, H., Zhang, Z., Ma, Z.: Key encapsulation mechanism with explicit rejection in the quantum random oracle model. In: Lin, D., Sako, K. (eds.) PKC 2019. LNCS, vol. 11443, pp. 618–645. Springer, Cham (2019). https://doi.org/10.1007/978-3-030-17259-6_21

31. Jiang, H., Zhang, Z., Ma, Z.: Tighter security proofs for generic key encapsulation mechanism in the quantum random oracle model. In: Ding, J., Steinwandt, R. (eds.) PQCrypto 2019. LNCS, vol. 11505, pp. 227–248. Springer, Cham (2019). https://doi.org/10.1007/978-3-030-25510-7_13

32. Kuchta, V., Sakzad, A., Stehlé, D., Steinfeld, R., Sun, S.-F.: Measure-rewind-measure: tighter quantum random oracle model proofs for one-way to hiding and CCA security. In: Canteaut, A., Ishai, Y. (eds.) EUROCRYPT 2020. LNCS, vol. 12107, pp. 703–728. Springer, Cham (2020). https://doi.org/10.1007/978-3-030-45727-3_24

33. Kurosawa, K.: Multi-recipient public-key encryption with shortened ciphertext. In: Naccache, D., Paillier, P. (eds.) PKC 2002. LNCS, vol. 2274, pp. 48–63. Springer, Heidelberg (2002). https://doi.org/10.1007/3-540-45664-3_4

34. Lindner, R., Peikert, C.: Better key sizes (and attacks) for LWE-based encryption. In: Kiayias, A. (ed.) CT-RSA 2011. LNCS, vol. 6558, pp. 319–339. Springer, Heidelberg (2011). https://doi.org/10.1007/978-3-642-19074-2_21

35. Matsuda, T., Hanaoka, G.: Key encapsulation mechanisms from extractable hash proof systems, revisited. In: Kurosawa, K., Hanaoka, G. (eds.) PKC 2013. LNCS, vol. 7778, pp. 332–351. Springer, Heidelberg (2013). https://doi.org/10.1007/978-3-642-36362-7_21

36. NIST. Post-quantum cryptography - round 2 submissions. https://csrc.nist.gov/projects/post-quantum-cryptography/round-2-submissions

37. Okamoto, T., Pointcheval, D.: REACT: rapid enhanced-security asymmetric cryptosystem transform. In: Naccache, D. (ed.) CT-RSA 2001. LNCS, vol. 2020, pp. 159–174. Springer, Heidelberg (2000). https://doi.org/10.1007/3-540-45353-9_13

38. Omara, E., Beurdouche, B., Rescorla, E., Inguva, S., Kwon, A., Duric, A.: The Messaging Layer Security (MLS) Architecture. Internet-Draft draft-IETF-MLS-architecture-04, Internet Engineering Task Force. In: Work in Progress (2020)

39. Saito, T., Xagawa, K., Yamakawa, T.: Tightly-secure key-encapsulation mechanism in the quantum random oracle model. In: Nielsen, J.B., Rijmen, V. (eds.) EUROCRYPT 2018. LNCS, vol. 10822, pp. 520–551. Springer, Cham (2018). https://doi.org/10.1007/978-3-319-78372-7_17

40. Smart, N.P.: Efficient key encapsulation to multiple parties. In: Blundo, C., Cimato, S. (eds.) SCN 2004. LNCS, vol. 3352, pp. 208–219. Springer, Heidelberg (2005). https://doi.org/10.1007/978-3-540-30598-9_15

41. Targhi, E.E., Unruh, D.: Post-quantum security of the Fujisaki-Okamoto and OAEP transforms. In: Hirt, M., Smith, A. (eds.) TCC 2016. LNCS, vol. 9986, pp. 192–216. Springer, Heidelberg (2016). https://doi.org/10.1007/978-3-662-53644-5_8

42. Yang, Z.: On constructing practical multi-recipient key-encapsulation with short ciphertext and public key. SCN **8**(18), 4191–4202 (2015)

43. Zhandry, M.: How to record quantum queries, and applications to quantum indifferentiability. In: Boldyreva, A., Micciancio, D. (eds.) CRYPTO 2019. LNCS, vol. 11693, pp. 239–268. Springer, Cham (2019). https://doi.org/10.1007/978-3-030-26951-7_9

Post-Quantum Verification
of Fujisaki-Okamoto

Dominique Unruh[(✉)]

University of Tartu, Tartu, Estonia
unruh@ut.ee

Abstract. We present a computer-verified formalization of the post-quantum security proof of the Fujisaki-Okamoto transform (as analyzed by Hövelmanns, Kiltz, Schäge, and Unruh, PKC 2020). The formalization is done in quantum relational Hoare logic and checked in the qrhl-tool (Unruh, POPL 2019).

1 Introduction

In this paper, we present the first formal verification of the post-quantum security of the Fujisaki-Okamoto transform.

Cryptographic security proofs tend to be complex, and, due to their complexity, error prone. Small mistakes in a proof can be difficult to notice and may invalidate the whole proof. For example, the proof of the OAEP construction [7] went through a number of fixes [13, 14, 27] until it was finally formally proven in [4] after years of industrial use. The PRF/PRP switching lemma was a standard textbook example for many years before it was shown that the standard proof is flawed [8]. And more recently, an attack on the ISO standardized blockcipher mode OCB2 [19] was found [18], even though OCB2 was believed to be proven secure by [24].

While a rigorous and well-structured proof style (e.g., using sequences of games as advocated in [8, 28]) can reduce the potential for hidden errors and imprecisions, it is still very hard to write a proof that is 100% correct. (Especially when proof techniques such as random oracles [9] or rewinding [30, 36] are used.) And especially if a mistake in a proof happens in a step that seems very intuitive, it is quite likely that the mistake will also not be spotted by a reader.

This problem is exacerbated in the case of post-quantum security (i.e., security against quantum adversaries): Post-quantum security proofs need to reason about quantum algorithms (the adversary). Our intuition is shaped by the experience with the classical world, and it is easy to have a wrong intuition about quantum phenomena. This makes it particularly easy for seemingly reasonable but incorrect proof steps to stay undetected in a post-quantum security proof.

In a nutshell, to ensure high confidence in a post-quantum security proof, it is not sufficient to merely have it checked by a human. Instead, we advocate formal (or computer-aided) verification: the security proof is verified by software that checks every proof step. In this paper, we present the first such formal veri-

© International Association for Cryptologic Research 2020
S. Moriai and H. Wang (Eds.): ASIACRYPT 2020, LNCS 12491, pp. 321–352, 2020.
https://doi.org/10.1007/978-3-030-64837-4_11

fication, namely of a variant of the Fujisaki-Okamoto transform [12] as analyzed by Hövelmanns, Kiltz, Schäge, and Unruh [17].

Post-Quantum Security. Quantum computers have long been known to be a potential threat to cryptographic protocols, in particular public key encryption. Shor's algorithm [26] allows us to efficiently solve the integer factorization and discrete logarithm problems, thus breaking RSA and ElGamal and variants thereof. This breaks all commonly used public key encryption and signature schemes. Of course, as of today, there are no quantum computers that even come close to being able to execute Shor's algorithm on reasonable problem sizes. Yet, there is constant progress towards larger and more powerful quantum computers (see, e.g., the recent breakthrough by Google [2]). In light of this, it is likely that quantum computers will be able to break today's public key encryption and signature schemes in the foreseeable future. Since the development, standardization, and industrial deployment of a cryptosystem can take many years, we need to develop and analyze future post-quantum secure protocols already today. One important step in this direction is the NIST post-quantum competition [23] that will select a few post-quantum public-key encryption and signature schemes for industrial standardization.

Quantum Random Oracles. One important proof technique in cryptography are random oracles [6]. In a proof in the random oracle model, we idealize hash functions by assuming that every hash function is simply a uniformly random function. (All algorithms including the adversary get oracle access to that function.) Based on this assumption, security proofs become considerably simpler. In some cases, we only know security proofs in the random oracle model. Of course, this comes at a cost: This assumption is an idealization; concluding that a protocol that is secure in the random oracle model is also secure using a real-world hash function is merely a heuristic argument. (And this heuristic is known to be false in certain contrived cases, e.g., [11].)

As first explicitly pointed out by [9], in the quantum setting, the random oracle becomes more involved: To get a realistic modeling, the adversary needs to be given superposition access to the random oracle, i.e., the adversary can evaluate the random oracle/hash function in a quantum superposition of many possible inputs. Due to this, quantum random oracle proofs are much harder than in the classical setting.

Of importance for this paper is the O2H theorem [1]. The O2H theorem tells us – very roughly – that the probability of noticing whether a specific output $H(x)$ of the random oracle has been changed ("reprogrammed") can be bounded in terms of the probability of guessing that input x. This technique is used in a number of QROM proofs, in particular those for the FO transform described next.

Fujisaki-Okamoto. A common approach for constructing public key encryption schemes is the Fujisaki-Okamoto (FO) transform [12] or a variant thereof. The FO transform takes a public-key encryption scheme with some weak passive security notion (such as IND-CPA or one-way security) and transforms it into an actively secure public-key encryption or KEM[1] scheme (IND-CCA security). On a very high level, instead of executing the encryption algorithm with

---

[1] A KEM, key encapsulation scheme, is similar to an encryption scheme but specialized for use in hybrid encryption schemes.

true randomness, the FO transform hashes the plaintext and uses the resulting hash value as the randomness for the encryption algorithm. This removes some of the flexibility the attacker has when constructing fake ciphertexts and makes chosen-ciphertext attacks impossible. The advantage of the FO transform is that it gets us IND-CCA security at no or almost no increase in ciphertext size or computational cost. The disadvantage is that the FO transform is only proven in the random oracle model, which means that there is a heuristic element to its security proof. Due to its high efficiency, the FO transform or some variations thereof is used in basically all public key encryption candidates in the NIST competition. Because of this, it is very important to understand the post-quantum security of the FO transform. However, due to the intricacies of the quantum random oracle model, proving the security of the FO transform is not as easy as in the classical setting. The first positive result was made by Ebrahimi Targhi and Unruh [29] who proved the security of an FO variant that includes one more hash value in the ciphertext. That result was adapted by [15] to several other FO variants, but still using an additional hash. ([15] also gives an excellent overview over the different FO variants.) The first result to prove post-quantum security of FO without an additional hash was given by Saito, Xagawa, and Yamakawa [25]. To achieve this, they introduced a new intermediate security notion called "disjoint simulatability". However, [25] relies on the assumption that the underlying passively-secure encryption scheme has perfect correctness, i.e., the probability of incorrectly decrypting honestly generated ciphertexts is zero. Unfortunately, this is not the case with typical lattice-based encryption schemes (they have a negligible failure probability), making the results of [25] inapplicable to many relevant encryption schemes such as, to the best of our knowledge, all lattice-based NIST candidates. This situation was resolved by Hövelmanns, Kiltz, Schäge, and Unruh [17] who show the security of an FO variant (without additional hash) that is secure even in the presence of decryption failures. (This result is the one we formalize in this work. We will refer to [17], specifically to the part concerned with the FO transformation, as HKSU in the following.)

Formal Verification of Cryptography. As mentioned above, a state-of-the-art approach for writing cryptographic security proofs are sequences of games. This approach is also well suited for formal verification. A number of frameworks/tools use this approach for verifying classical cryptography, e.g., EasyCrypt [3]. EasyCrypt requires the user to explicitly specify the games that constitute the security proof (as is done in a pen-and-paper proof), and to additionally provide justification for the fact that two consecutive games are indeed related as claimed. This justification will often be considerably more detailed than in a pen-and-paper proof where the fact that two slightly different games are equivalent will often be declared to be obvious.

Their approach for proving the relationship of consecutive games is to give a proof in relational Hoare logic. Relational Hoare logic is a logic that allows us to express the relationship between two programs by specifying a relational precondition and a relational postcondition. A relational Hoare judgment of the form $\{A\}c \sim \mathfrak{d}\{B\}$ intuitively means that if the variables of the programs c and $\mathfrak{d}$ are

related as described by the precondition A before execution, and we execute c and
ɔ, then afterwards their variables will be related as described by B. A very simple example would be $\{x_1 \leq x_2\}x \leftarrow x + 1 \sim x \leftarrow x + 1\{x_1 \leq x_2\}$. This means
that if the variable x in the left program is smaller-equal than in the right one,
and both programs increase x, then x in the left program will still be smaller-equal
than in the right one. As this example shows, relational Hoare logic can express
more complex relationships than simple equivalence of two games. This makes the
approach very powerful. To reason about cryptography, one needs a variant of relational Hoare logic that supports probabilistic programs. Such a probabilistic relational Hoare logic (pRHL) was developed for this purpose by Barthe, Grégoire, and
Zanella Béguelin [5]. EasyCrypt uses pRHL for proving the relationship between
cryptographic games.

Formal Verification of Quantum Cryptography. When considering the verification of post-quantum cryptography, one might wonder whether the tools developed for classical cryptography may not already be sufficient. Unfortunately, this
is not the case. The soundness of the existing tools is proven relative to classical
semantics of the protocols and of the adversary. In fact, at least for EasyCrypt,
Unruh [32] gave an explicit example of a protocol which can be shown secure in
EasyCrypt but which is known not to be secure against quantum adversaries. For
the purpose of verifying quantum cryptography, Unruh [32] introduced a generalization of pRHL, quantum relational Hoare logic (qRHL) that allows to prove
relational statements about quantum programs. (We will describe qRHL in more
detail in Sect. 2.) Unruh [32] also developed a tool `qrhl-tool` for reasoning in
qRHL for the purpose of verifying quantum cryptography. However, except for a
toy example, the post-quantum security of a very simple encryption scheme, to
the best of our knowledge, no post-quantum security proof has been formally verified before this work. `qrhl-tool` uses a hybrid approach: Reasoning about qRHL
judgments is hardcoded in the tool, but verification conditions (i.e., auxiliary subgoals, e.g., implications between invariants) are outsourced to the theorem prover
Isabelle/HOL [22].

Our Contribution. In this work, we formally verified the security proof of the
FO transformation from HKSU [17].[2] The FO-variant analyzed by HKSU is a
state-of-the-art construction for building efficient public-key encryption schemes,
and can be applied to many of the NIST submissions to get IND-CCA secure
encryption schemes (e.g., Frodo [20] or Kyber [10]).

---

[2] To be precise, we formalize the security proof from the February 2019 version [16]
of [17]. The proof has been improved upon in later revisions of the paper. In particular, the requirement of injective encryption (see Footnote 5) has been removed.
We formalized the earlier version of the proof since the formalization was already
under way when the proof was updated. Their new proof does not use substantially
different techniques, and we believe that formalizing their new proof in qRHL would
not pose any challenges different from the ones encountered in this work. However,
since their new proof is an almost complete rewrite (i.e., a different proof), it is
not possible to simply update our formalization. Instead, a new development from
scratch would be needed.

Our formalization follows the overall structure of HKSU (i.e., it uses roughly the same games) but introduces many additional intermediate games. (Altogether, our proof defines 136 programs, which covers games, oracles, and explicitly constructed adversaries in reductions.) The formalization has 3455 lines of proof in qRHL and 1727 lines of proof in Isabelle/HOL for auxiliary lemmas. (Not counting comments and blank lines or files autogenerated by search & replace from others.) We mostly follow the structure of HKSU (but in many places we need to do some adjustments to achieve the level of rigor required for formal verification). In the process, we identified a few best practices for doing proofs in `qrhl-tool` that we list in Sect. 2.4.

We furthermore extended the `qrhl-tool` with a tactic o2h that implements an application of the Semiclassical O2H Theorem [1]. This is needed in HKSU, but the O2H Theorem is often in post-quantum crypto proofs, so we expect this addition to be very useful for future verifications, too. (Details are given in the full version [35].)

Organization. In Sect. 2, we review qRHL and the `qrhl-tool`. In Sect. 3, we review the result and part of the proof from HKSU. In Sect. 4, we go through the parts of the formalization that make up the specification of the main result. In Sect. 5, we discuss the formal proof. We conclude in Sect. 6. The source code of the formalization is provided in [33]. A full version with additional details is available at [35].

2 Quantum Relational Hoare Logic

In this section, we give an overview of quantum relational Hoare logic (qRHL). We will not give formal definitions or a set of reasoning rules. For these, refer to [32]. Instead, our aim is to give an intuitive understanding of the logic that allows to understand (most of) the reasoning steps in our formalization.

2.1 Quantum While Language

qRHL allows us to reason about the relationship between quantum programs (that encode cryptographic games). The programs are written in a simple while language that has the following syntax (where c and $\mathfrak{d}$ stand for programs):

$c, \mathfrak{d} := \mathbf{skip}, \quad c; \mathfrak{d}$	(no operation / sequential composition)
$x \leftarrow e, \quad x \overset{\$}{\leftarrow} e$	(classical assignment/sampling)
$\mathbf{if}\ e\ \mathbf{then}\ c\ \mathbf{else}\ \mathfrak{d}, \quad \mathbf{while}\ e\ \mathbf{do}\ c$	(conditional/loop)
$q_1 \ldots q_n \overset{q}{\leftarrow} e$	(initialization of quantum registers)
$\mathbf{apply}\ e\ \mathbf{to}\ q_1 \ldots q_n$	(quantum application)
$x \leftarrow \mathbf{measure}\ q_1 \ldots q_n\ \mathbf{with}\ e$	(measurement)
$\{\mathbf{local}\ V; c\}$	(local variable declaration)

The language distinguishes two kinds of variables, quantum and classical. In the above syntax, classical variables are denoted by $\mathbf{x}$ and quantum variables by $\mathbf{q}$. The command $\mathbf{x} \leftarrow e$ evaluates the expression e (which can be any well-typed mathematical expression involving only classical variables) and assigns the value to $\mathbf{x}$. In contrast $\mathbf{x} \xleftarrow{\$} e$ evaluates e which is supposed to evaluate to a distribution $\mathcal{D}$, and then samples the new value of $\mathbf{x}$ according to $\mathcal{D}$. If- and while-statements branch depending on a classical expression e.

To initialize quantum variables, we use $\mathbf{q}_1 \ldots \mathbf{q}_n \xleftarrow{\mathsf{q}} e$. Here e is evaluated to return a quantum state (i.e., a classical expression returning the description of a quantum state). Then $\mathbf{q}_1 \ldots \mathbf{q}_n$ are jointly initialized with that state. E.g., we can write $\mathbf{q} \xleftarrow{\mathsf{q}} |\mathbf{x}\rangle$ (where $\mathbf{x}$ is a classical bit variable) to initialize a quantum bit $\mathbf{q}$.

Given an expression e that computes a unitary U, we use **apply** e **to** $\mathbf{q}_1 \ldots \mathbf{q}_n$ to apply U jointly to $\mathbf{q}_1 \ldots \mathbf{q}_n$. E.g., **apply** CNOT **to** $\mathbf{q}_1 \mathbf{q}_2$.

$\mathbf{x} \leftarrow$ **measure** $\mathbf{q}_1 \ldots \mathbf{q}_n$ **with** e evaluates e to get a description of a measurement, measures $\mathbf{q}_1 \ldots \mathbf{q}_n$ jointly with that measurement and assigns the result to $\mathbf{x}$. Typically, e might be something like `computational_basis`, denoting a computational basis measurement.

Finally, $\{$**local** $V; \mathbf{c}\}$ declares the variables V as local inside $\mathbf{c}$. (This is an extension of the language from [34].)

2.2 QRHL Judgements

Recall from the introduction that in relational Hoare logics, judgments are of the form $\{\mathsf{A}\}\mathbf{c} \sim \mathbf{d}\{\mathsf{B}\}$ where $\mathbf{c}, \mathbf{d}$ are programs, and A, B are relational predicates (the pre- and postcondition). In particular, $\{\mathsf{A}\}\mathbf{c} \sim \mathbf{d}\{\mathsf{B}\}$ means that if the variables of $\mathbf{c}, \mathbf{d}$ (jointly) satisfy A before execution, then they (jointly) satisfy B after execution.

Predicates. The same idea is used in qRHL but the concept of predicates becomes more complex because we want to express something about the state of quantum variables. In fact, predicates in qRHL are subspaces of the Hilbert space of all possible states of the quantum variables of the two programs. We will illustrate this by an example:

Say $\mathbf{q}$ is a quantum variable in the first program $\mathbf{c}$. We refer to $\mathbf{q}$ as $\mathbf{q}_1$ to distinguish it from a variable with the same name in program $\mathbf{d}$. Say we want to express the fact that $\mathbf{q}_1$ is in state $|+\rangle$. That means that the whole system (i.e., all quantum variables together), are in a state of the form $|+\rangle_{\mathbf{q}_1} \otimes |\Psi\rangle_{\mathbf{vars}}$ where **vars** are all other variables (of $\mathbf{c}$ and $\mathbf{d}$), except $\mathbf{q}_1$. The set of all states of this form forms a subspace of the Hilbert space of all possible states of the quantum variables. Thus $\mathsf{A} := \{|+\rangle_{\mathbf{q}_1} \otimes |\Psi\rangle_{\mathbf{vars}} : |\Psi\rangle \in \mathcal{H}_{\mathbf{vars}}\}$ (with $\mathcal{H}_{\mathbf{vars}}$ denoting the corresponding Hilbert space) is a subspace and thus a valid predicate for use in a qRHL judgment. For example, we could then write $\{\mathsf{A}\}$**apply** X **to** $\mathbf{q} \sim$ **skip**$\{\mathsf{A}\}$ to express the fact that, if $\mathbf{q}$ is in state $|+\rangle$ in the left program, and we apply X (a quantum bit flip) to $\mathbf{q}$, then afterwards q is still in state $|+\rangle$. Of course, writing A explicitly as a set is very cumbersome. (And, in the setting of formal verification, one would then have no syntactic guarantees that the resulting set is indeed a valid predicate.) Instead, we have the shorthand span$\{|+\rangle\}$ »q_1 to denote the above predicate A. (More generally, S»$q_1 \dots q_n$ means that $q_1 \dots q_n$ are jointly in a state in S.)

We can build more complex predicates by combining existing ones. E.g., if A, A' are predicates, then A ∩ B is a predicate that intuitively denotes the fact that both A and B hold. We will also often have to compare predicates. A ⊆ B means that A is a subspace of B for all values of the classical variables. Intuitively, this means A implies B.

Predicates with Classical Variables. In most cases, however, we do not only have quantum variables, but also classical variables. Especially in a post-quantum cryptography setting, the majority of variables in a predicate tends to be classical. Support for classical variables in qRHL predicates is straightforward: A predicate A can be an expression containing classical variables. Those are then substituted with the current values of those variables, and the result is a subspace that describes the state of the quantum variables as explained above. For example, we can write the predicate span$\{|x_2\rangle\}$ »q_1. This would mean that q_1 (a qubit in the left program) is in state $|x_2\rangle$.

This already allows us to build complex predicates, but it is rather inconvenient if we want to express something about the classical variables only, e.g., if we want to express that $x_1 = x_2$ always holds. To express such classical facts, we use an additional shorthand: $\mathfrak{Cla}[b]$ is defined to be $\mathcal{H}$ (the full Hilbert space) if $b = \texttt{true}$, and defined to be 0 (the subspace containing only 0) if $b = \texttt{false}$. Why is this useful? Consider the predicate $\mathfrak{Cla}[x_1 = x_2]$. If $x_1 = x_2$, this evaluates to $\mathfrak{Cla}[\texttt{true} = \mathcal{H}]$. Since $\mathcal{H}$ contains all possible states, the state of the quantum variables will necessarily be contained in $\mathfrak{Cla}[\texttt{true}]$, hence the predicate is satisfied. If $x_1 \neq x_2$, $\mathfrak{Cla}[x_1 = x_2]$ evaluates to $\mathfrak{Cla}[\texttt{false} = 0]$, and the state of the quantum variables will not be contained in $\mathfrak{Cla}[\texttt{false}]$, hence the predicate will not be satisfied. Thus, $\mathfrak{Cla}[x_1 = x_2]$ is satisfied iff $x_1 = x_2$; the state of the quantum variables does not matter. In general $\mathfrak{Cla}[e]$ allows us to translate any classical predicate e into a quantum predicate. (And this predicate can then be combined with quantum predicates, e.g., $\mathfrak{Cla}[x_1 = x_2] \cap$ span$\{|+\rangle\}$ »q_1.)

Quantum Equality. One very important special case of predicates are equalities. We will often need to express that the variables of the left and right programs have the same values. We have already seen how to do this for classical variables. For quantum variables, the situation is more complex. We cannot write $\mathfrak{Cla}[q_1 = q_2]$, this is not even a meaningful expression (inside $\mathfrak{Cla}[\dots]$, only classical variables are allowed). Instead, we need to define a *subspace* that in some way expresses the fact that two quantum variables are equal. The solution proposed in [32] is: Let $q_1 \equiv_{\mathsf{quant}} q_2$ denote the subspace of all states that are invariant under exchanging q_1 and q_2 (i.e., invariant under applying a swap operation). Then $q_1 \equiv_{\mathsf{quant}} q_2$ is a quantum predicate. And – this is less easy to see but shown in [32] – $q_1 \equiv_{\mathsf{quant}} q_2$ does indeed capture the idea that q_1 and q_2 have the same value in a meaningful way. We can now write, for example, $\mathfrak{Cla}[x_1 = x_2] \cap (q_1 \equiv_{\mathsf{quant}} q_2)$ to denote the fact that the variables x (classical) and q (quantum) have the same value in both programs. In particular, if $\mathbf{c}$ only contains those two variables, we have $\{\mathfrak{Cla}[\mathbf{x}_1 = \mathbf{x}_2] \cap (\mathbf{q}_1 \equiv_{\text{quant}} \mathbf{q}_2)\}\mathbf{c} \sim \mathbf{c}\{\mathfrak{Cla}[\mathbf{x}_1 = \mathbf{x}_2] \cap (\mathbf{q}_1 \equiv_{\text{quant}} \mathbf{q}_2)\}$. What if there are more quantum variables? The advantage of the quantum equality is that we hardly ever need to recall the actual definition in terms of swap invariance. All we need to remember is that $\mathbf{q}_1 \equiv_{\text{quant}} \mathbf{q}_2$ is a quantum predicate/subspace that intuitively encodes equality of $\mathbf{q}_1$ and $\mathbf{q}_2$.

The most common form of predicate that we will see is $A_= :=$ $\mathfrak{Cla}[\mathbf{x}_1^{(1)} = \mathbf{x}_2^{(1)} \wedge \cdots \wedge \mathbf{x}_1^{(1)} = \mathbf{x}_2^{(1)}] \cap (\mathbf{q}_1^{(1)} \ldots \mathbf{q}_1^{(m)} \equiv_{\text{quant}} \mathbf{q}_2^{(1)} \ldots \mathbf{q}_2^{(m)})$. In fact, if both sides have the same program $\mathbf{c}$ (and $\mathbf{c}$ contains no variables besides the ones mentioned in $A_=$), then $\{A_=\}\mathbf{c} \sim \mathbf{c}\{A_=\}$ holds. Intuitively, this means: if the inputs of two programs are equal, the outputs are equal.

2.3   Reasoning in qRHL

To derive qRHL judgments, one will hardly ever go directly through the definition of qRHL itself. Instead one derives complex qRHL judgments from elementary ones. For example, to derive the elementary $\{\mathfrak{Cla}[\mathbf{x}_1 = 0]\}\mathbf{x} \leftarrow \mathbf{x} + 1 \sim$ $\mathbf{skip}\{\mathfrak{Cla}[\mathbf{x}_1 = 1]\}$, we use the ASSIGN1 rule [32] that states $\{B\{e_1/\mathbf{x}_1\}\}\mathbf{x} \leftarrow e \sim$ $\mathbf{skip}\{B\}$. (Here e_1 is the expression e where all variables $\mathbf{y}$ are replaced by $\mathbf{y}_1$. And $B\{e_1/\mathbf{x}_1\}$ means every occurrence of $\mathbf{x}_1$ in B is replaced by e_1.) With $B :=$ $\mathfrak{Cla}[\mathbf{x}_1 = 1]$, we get from ASSIGN1: $\{\mathfrak{Cla}[\mathbf{x}_1 + 1 = 1]\}\mathbf{x} \leftarrow e \sim \mathbf{skip}\{\mathfrak{Cla}[\mathbf{x}_1 = 1]\}$. Since $\mathbf{x}_1 + 1 = 1$ is logically equivalent to $\mathbf{x}_1 = 1$ (assuming the type of $\mathbf{x}$ is, e.g., integers or reals), this statement is equivalent to $\{\mathfrak{Cla}[\mathbf{x}_1 = 0]\}\mathbf{x} \leftarrow \mathbf{x} + 1 \sim$ $\mathbf{skip}\{\mathfrak{Cla}[\mathbf{x}_1 = 1]\}$. (This is an example of reasoning in the "ambient logic": Besides application of qRHL rules, we need to use "normal" mathematics to derive facts about predicates. This is external to qRHL itself.)

One can then combine several judgments into one, using, e.g., the SEQ rule: "If $\{A\}\mathbf{c} \sim \mathfrak{d}\{B\}$ and $\{B\}\mathbf{c}' \sim \mathfrak{d}'\{C\}$ holds, then $\{A\}\mathbf{c}; \mathbf{c}' \sim \mathfrak{d}; \mathfrak{d}'\{C\}$ holds." For example, once we have derived $\{\mathfrak{Cla}[\mathbf{true}]\}\mathbf{x} \leftarrow 1 \sim \mathbf{skip}\{\mathfrak{Cla}[\mathbf{x}_1 = 1]\}$ and $\{\mathfrak{Cla}[\mathbf{x}_1 = 1]\}\mathbf{skip} \sim \mathbf{y} \leftarrow 1\{\mathfrak{Cla}[\mathbf{x}_1 = \mathbf{y}_2]\}$, we conclude using SEQ that $\{\mathfrak{Cla}[\mathbf{true}]\}\mathbf{x} \leftarrow 1 \sim \mathbf{y} \leftarrow 1\{\mathfrak{Cla}[\mathbf{x}_1 = \mathbf{y}_2]\}$. (We use here implicitly that $\mathbf{x} \leftarrow 1; \mathbf{skip}$ is the same as $\mathbf{x} \leftarrow 1$ and analogously for $\mathbf{skip}; \mathbf{y} \leftarrow 1$.)

We will not give the full list of rules here, see [32] and the manual of [31] for a comprehensive list.

One common approach to prove more complex qRHL judgments is backward reasoning: One starts by stating the judgment one wants to prove, say $G_1 :=$ $\{\mathfrak{Cla}[\mathbf{true}]\}\mathbf{x} \leftarrow 1 \sim \mathbf{y} \leftarrow 1\{\mathfrak{Cla}[\mathbf{x}_1 = \mathbf{y}_2]\}$. Then one applies one qRHL rule to the very last statement on the left or right, say $\mathbf{y} \leftarrow 1$. By application of the SEQ and ASSIGN2 rule, we see that $G_2 := \{\mathfrak{Cla}[\mathbf{true}]\}\mathbf{x} \leftarrow 1 \sim \mathbf{skip}\{\mathfrak{Cla}[\mathbf{x}_1 = 1]\}$ implies G_1. So we have reduced our current goal to showing G_2. (Using a reasoning step that can be fully automated.) By application of SEQ and ASSIGN1, we see that $G_3 := \{\mathfrak{Cla}[\mathbf{true}]\}\mathbf{skip} \sim \mathbf{skip}\{\mathfrak{Cla}[1 = 1]\}$ implies G_2. So our new proof goal is G_3. And finally, G_3 is implied by $G_4 := (\mathfrak{Cla}[\mathbf{true}] \subseteq \mathfrak{Cla}[1 = 1])$. So our final goal is G_4 which is a trivial statement in ambient logic because $1 = 1$ is $\mathbf{true}$. Hence the proof concludes and G_1 holds. The advantage of this approach is that it is fully mechanical in many cases, e.g., for sequences of assignments and applications of unitaries. The proof tool qrhl-tool (see the next section) follows exactly this approach.

So far, we have gotten a glimpse how to derive qRHL judgments. In a cryptographic proof, however, we are interested not in qRHL judgments but in statements about probabilities. Fortunately, we can derive those directly from a qRHL judgment using the QRHLELIMEQ rule. It states (somewhat simplified): Assuming $\mathbf{X}$ and $\mathbf{Q}$ are all the variables occurring in $\mathfrak{c}, \mathfrak{d}$, then $\{\mathfrak{Cla}[\mathbf{X}_1 = \mathbf{X}_2] \cap (\mathbf{Q}_1 \equiv_{\mathsf{quant}} \mathbf{Q}_2)\}\mathfrak{c} \sim \mathfrak{d}\{\mathfrak{Cla}[e_1 \implies f_2]\}$ implies $\Pr[e : \mathfrak{c}] \leq \Pr[f : \mathfrak{d}]$ (and similarly for $=$ instead of $\leq$). (Here $\Pr[e : \mathfrak{c}]$ denotes the probability that the Boolean expression e is true after executing $\mathfrak{c}$, and analogously $\Pr[f : \mathfrak{d}]$.) Thus to derive an inequality or equality of probabilities of program outcomes, we convert it into a qRHL proof goal with QRHLELIMEQ, and then use the reasoning rules of qRHL to derive that qRHL judgment. This is, on a high level, how crypto proofs in qRHL are done (modulo many concrete details).

2.4 The qrhl-tool

While reasoning using qRHL in pen-and-paper proofs is possible in principle, qRHL was specifically designed for formal verification on the computer. To that end, an interactive theorem prover for qRHL was developed, qrhl-tool [31, 32]. To execute our formalization, version 0.5 is required. See README.txt there for instructions on how to check/edit our formalization, and manual.pdf for detailed information. In the following, we recap the most important facts about the tool.

In addition to that review, we also list some "best practices" for developing proofs in the tool, based on our experience while formalizing HKSU.

Architecture of the Tool. qrhl-tool has a hybrid architecture: It embeds the theorem prover Isabelle/HOL, and all reasoning in the ambient logic is done by Isabelle/HOL. The tool handles qRHL judgments directly. As a consequence, proofs are written in two files: .thy files contain native Isabelle/HOL code and can reason only about ambient logic (no support for qRHL itself). Those .thy files are also used to specify the logical background of the formalization (e.g., declaring constants such as the encryption function in our development). .qrhl files are executed natively by qrhl-tool and contain specifications of programs, as well as proofs in qRHL. They can also contain proofs in ambient logic (arbitrary Isabelle/HOL tactics can be invoked) but this is only suitable for simple proofs in ambient logic. Complex ambient logic facts are best proven as an auxiliary lemma in the .thy files. It is possible to split a proof into many files by including one .qrhl file from another using the include command.

The tool can be run in two modes, batch and interactive mode. In batch mode, a given .qrhl file is checked on the command-line and the run aborts with an error if the proof is incorrect. In interactive mode, an Emacs/ProofGeneral-based user interface allows us to edit and execute the proofs.

BEST PRACTICE: *Create one file* **variables.qrhl** *that declares all program variables and loads the* **.thy** *files. Furthermore, create a separate file* **p.qrhl** *for every* *declared program p , and a separate file* `lemma_l.qrhl` *for every lemma l. This allows us to execute proofs without too much runtime overhead and at the same time allows us to find quickly which entity is declared where.* ◇

Declarations. All program variables that occur in any analyzed program need to be declared globally (even if the variable is used only as a local variable). This is done using `classical/quantum/ambient var x : type` where `type` is any type understood by Isabelle/HOL. (`ambient var` declares an unspecified constant value that can be used in programs and in ambient logic subgoals.) Programs are declared by `program name := { code }` where `code` is a quantum program as described in Sect. 2.1. For describing games this approach is sufficient, but when specifying adversaries or oracles or helper functions, we would like to define procedures that take arguments and have return values. Unfortunately, such procedure calls are not supported by the language underlying qRHL yet. What has to be done instead is to pass values to/from procedures via global variables. A program X can be invoked by another program using `call X`,[3] and we need to write the program X so that it communicates with the invoking program via global variables that are set aside for this purpose. While this approach is not very convenient, we found that with disciplined variable use, no bigger problems arise.

One highly important feature in more advanced cryptographic definitions and proofs are oracles. Roughly speaking, an oracle is a program O that is given as an argument to another program A, so that the other program can execute it whenever needed. (For example, an adversary A may get access to a decryption oracle `Dec` that decrypts messages passed to it.) Programs that take oracles are supported by `qrhl-tool`. One can declare a program via, e.g., `program prog(O1,O2) := {code}` where `code` can contain, e.g., a `call O1` statement. Then `prog` is a program that needs to be instantiated with oracles when invoked, e.g.: `call prog(Enc,Dec)`.

Finally, to model adversaries we need to declare programs of unspecified code. (This then means that anything that is proven holds for any adversary.) The command `adversary A` declares an adversary A that can be invoked via `call A`. Additional arguments to the `adversary` command allow to specify global variables that the adversary may access, and whether A expects oracles.

BEST PRACTICE: *When declaring a program that is intended as a subroutine (e.g., an oracle or an adversary), make explicit which global variables are used as inputs/outputs to simulate procedure calls. (E.g., an adversary might be annotated with a comment "Input: c (ciphertext). Output: b (guessed bit). Internal state:* `stateA`*.")*

All variables (especially quantum variables) that are used that are not needed between consecutive invocations should be made local at the beginning of the program using the `local` *program statement.*

---

[3] Semantically, `call X` is not a separate language feature. It just means that the source code of X is included verbatim at this point.

When invoking a program taking an oracle (e.g., `call A(queryH)` where queryH expects inputs/outputs in variables `Hin, Hout`), the input/output variables should be made local at that call. (E.g., `{ local Hin, Hout; call A(queryH);}`.) Otherwise, `qrhl-tool` will not be able to determine that `Hin, Hout` are not changed globally, even if the code of A internally already contains a `local` statement.

`print programname` can be used in interactive mode to check the list of variables used by a program.

Following these rules may make many proofs somewhat longer (due to additional boilerplate for removing `local` commands) but it removes a lot of potential for conflicts in variable use. (Especially with quantum variables: due to the idiosyncrasies of the quantum equality, any quantum variable used non-locally by a subprogram will have to be carried around explicitly in all quantum equalities.)

◇

Note that qRHL did not initially support local variables. The addition of local variables to `qrhl-tool` and the corresponding theory [34] were prompted by our experiences in the present formalization. Without local variables, it becomes very difficult to maintain a larger formalization involving quantum equalities.

Proving Lemmas. Finally, to state a lemma one can either state a lemma in ambient logic (extended with syntax `Pr[...]` for talking about the results of program executions), or qrhl subgoals. The command `lemma name: formula` states the former, the command `qrhl name: {precondition} call X; ~ call Y; {postcondition}` the latter. The syntax `Pr[e : prog(rho)]` denotes the probability that the Boolean expression `e` is true after running `prog` with initial quantum state `rho`. Most of the time we will thus state lemmas of the form `Pr[b=1 : prog1(rho)] = Pr[b=1 : prog2(rho)]` where `rho` is an ambient variable (meaning, the initial state is arbitrary). This can be converted into a qRHL subgoal using the tactic `byqrhl` (implementing the rule QRHLELIMEQ).

Once one has stated a qRHL proof goal, the proof proceeds via backwards reasoning as described in Sect. 2.3. For example, to remove the last assign statement from a goal (and rewrite the postcondition accordingly) as done in Sect. 2.3, one writes `wp left/right` (or `wp n m` for the last n/m statements on the left/right). Once all statements are gone (`skip` on both sides), the tactic `skip` replaces {A}`skip` ~ `skip`{B} by the ambient logic goal A ⊆ B. Another important tactic is `conseq pre/post: C` which replaces the current pre-/postcondition by C (and adds a ambient logic subgoal to prove that this replacement is justified). This allows to clean up subgoals and increases readability. The tactic `simp` simplifies the current goal using the Isabelle/HOL simplifier.

BEST PRACTICE: *To make proofs more maintainable, before each tactic invocation add a comment which line of code it addresses. E.g., `wp left` will always affect the last command of the left program. If that command is, e.g., x `<- 1+y`, add the comment #x. This ensures that if a change in a program definition breaks an existing proof, it is easier to find out where the proof script went out of sync.*

Additionally, at regular intervals add the tactic `conseq post: X` commands where X is the current postcondition (possibly, but not necessarily simplified). This serves both as a documentation of the current state of the proof, and it *makes maintenance easier because the proof will fail at the first point where the postcondition is not what was expected anymore (as opposed to failing at a later point).* ◇

Isabelle/HOL Micro Primer. For an introduction to Isabelle/HOL we recommend [21]. Here, we only give some minimal information to help reading the code fragments in the paper (Figs. 7, 8 and 9). This micro primer does not does not allow us to understand the definitions given in this paper in depth. In particular, to understand them in depth one needs to know the predefined constants in Isabelle/HOL and in the qrhl-tool. But with the syntax given here, it should at least be possible to make educated guesses about the meanings of the definitions.

All constants in Isabelle/HOL are typed. A function f taking arguments of types $t_1, \ldots, t_n$ and returning t has type $t_1 \Rightarrow \cdots \Rightarrow t_n \Rightarrow t$. To invoke f with arguments $a_1, \ldots, a_n$, we write f a_1 a_2 ... a_n. (Not $f(a_1, \ldots, a_n)$.) To declare (axiomatically) the existence of a new constant c of type *type*, we write

₁ **axiomatization** c :: *type* **where** *facts*

Here the optional **facts** are logical propositions that we assume about c. For example, we can declare the existence of a commutative binary operation op on natural numbers via

₁ **axiomatization** op :: "nat⇒nat⇒nat" **where** comm: "op x y = op y x"

Instead of axiomatizing constants, we can also define them in terms of existing constants. This cannot introduce logical inconsistencies. The syntax for this is

₁ **definition** c :: *type* **where** "c *arguments* = *definition*"

Instead of = we can also write ↔ when defining a proposition (i.e., if the return type is **bool**). For example, if we wanted to define the operation op above as twice the sum of its arguments, we could write:

₁ **definition** op :: "nat⇒nat⇒nat" **where** "op x y = 2 * (x + y)"

The parts before **where** are optional and will be inferred if necessary.

This summary of the operation of qrhl-tool does not, of course, replace a reading of the manual. However, it should give a first impression as well as help in reading Sects. 4–5.

3   Fujisaki-Okamato á la HKSU

In this section, we describe the FO variant analyzed by HKSU [17] and their proof. We stress that the proof we analyzed (and describe here) is the one from the earlier version [16] of HKSU, it has been rewritten since we started our formalization.

$\mathsf{DS_{real}}$
01 $(pk, sk) \leftarrow \mathsf{Keygen}()$
02 $m \xleftarrow{\$} \mathcal{M}$
03 $c \leftarrow \mathsf{Enc}(pk, m)$
04 $b \leftarrow A(pk, c)$

$\mathsf{DS_{fake}}$
05 $(pk, sk) \leftarrow \mathsf{Keygen}()$
06 $c \leftarrow \overline{\mathsf{Enc}}(pk)$
07 $b \leftarrow A(pk, c)$

Fig. 1. Games from definition of disjoint simulatability. In the random oracle model, A is additionally given oracle access to all random oracles.

The goal of the FO transform is to transform an encryption scheme that is passively secure into a chosen-ciphertext secure key encapsulation mechanism (KEM). The variant analyzed by HKSU can be described modularly by consecutively applying three transformations (called Punc, T, and $\mathsf{U}_m^{\not\perp}$) to the passively secure encryption scheme.

3.1 Transformation Punc

We start with a base public-key encryption scheme $(\mathsf{Keygen}_0, \mathsf{Enc}_0, \mathsf{Dec}_0)$ with message space $\mathcal{M}_0$. We assume the base scheme to be IND-CPA secure. (We assume further that decryption is deterministic, but we do not assume that decryption succeeds with probability 1, or that decrypting a valid ciphertext returns the original plaintext with probability 1.)

The first step is to construct a scheme with disjoint simulatability (DS). DS security [25] means that there exists a fake encryption algorithm $\overline{\mathsf{Enc}}$ that (without being given a plaintext) returns ciphertexts that are indistinguishable from valid encryptions of random messages, but that are guaranteed to be distinct from any valid ciphertext with high probability.

More precisely:

Definition 1 (Disjoint simulatability). *We call* $(\mathsf{Keygen}, \mathsf{Enc}, \mathsf{Dec})$ *with message space* $\mathcal{M}$ *and randomness space* $\mathcal{R}$ *DS secure iff for any quantum-polynomial-time* A, $|\Pr[b = 1 : \mathsf{DS_{real}}] - \Pr[b = 1 : \mathsf{DS_{fake}}]|$ *is negligible, for the games defined in Fig. 1.*

We say $(\mathsf{Keygen}, \mathsf{Enc}, \mathsf{Dec})$ *is* ε-disjoint iff for all possible public keys pk, $\Pr[(\exists m \in \mathcal{M}, r \in \mathcal{R}. \ c = \mathsf{Enc}(pk, m; r)) : c \leftarrow \overline{\mathsf{Enc}}(pk)] \leq \varepsilon$.

The transformation Punc is very straightforward: The encryption scheme is not really modified (i.e., the resulting $\mathsf{Keygen}, \mathsf{Enc}, \mathsf{Dec}$ are the same in the base scheme). But the message space is reduced by one element. I.e., we simply declare one plaintext $\hat{m}$ as invalid, hence encryptions of that plaintext will be disjoint from valid ciphertexts, and thus we can produce fake encryptions $\overline{\mathsf{Enc}}$ by encrypting $\hat{m}$. We summarize Punc in Fig. 2. The proof that the resulting scheme is both DS and IND-CPA secure is very straightforward, and we omit it here. (But we have formalized it, of course.)

$$\mathsf{Enc} := \mathsf{Enc}_0, \ \mathsf{Dec} := \mathsf{Dec}_0, \ \mathsf{Keygen} := \mathsf{Keygen}_0,$$

$$\mathcal{M} \subsetneq \mathcal{M}_0, \ \hat{m} \in \mathcal{M}_0 \setminus \mathcal{M}, \qquad \overline{\mathsf{Enc}}(pk) := \mathsf{Enc}_0(pk, \hat{m}).$$

Fig. 2. Transformation Punc. Input scheme: $(\mathsf{Enc}_0, \mathsf{Dec}_0, \mathsf{Keygen}_0)$ with message space $\mathcal{M}_0$. Output scheme: $(\mathsf{Enc}, \mathsf{Dec}, \mathsf{Keygen})$ with message space $\mathcal{M}_0$ and fake encryption algorithm $\overline{\mathsf{Enc}}$.

$$\mathsf{Keygen}' := \mathsf{Keygen}, \ \mathcal{M}' := \mathcal{M}, \ \overline{\mathsf{Enc}'} := \overline{\mathsf{Enc}}, \qquad \mathsf{Enc}'(pk, m) := \mathsf{Enc}(pk, m; G(m)).$$

$$\mathsf{Dec}'(sk, c) := \textbf{if } m = \bot \textbf{ or } \mathsf{Enc}'(pk, m) \neq c \textbf{ then return } \bot \textbf{ else return } m$$

$$(\textbf{where } m := \mathsf{Dec}(sk, c)).$$

Fig. 3. Transformation T. Input scheme: $(\mathsf{Enc}, \mathsf{Dec}, \mathsf{Keygen})$ with message space $\mathcal{M}$ and fake encryption algorithm $\overline{\mathsf{Enc}}$. Output scheme: $(\mathsf{Enc}', \mathsf{Dec}', \mathsf{Keygen}')$ with message space $\mathcal{M}'$ and fake encryption algorithm $\overline{\mathsf{Enc}'}$. $G : \mathcal{M} \to \mathcal{R}$ is a hash function (modeled as a random oracle).

3.2   Transformation T

Transformation Punc gave us a DS secure encryption scheme Enc. However, as the starting point for the transformation $\mathsf{U}_m^{\not\perp}$ below, we need a deterministic encryption scheme (that is still DS secure).

Transformation T achieves this by a simple technique: Instead of running Enc normally (i.e., $\mathsf{Enc}(pk, m; r)$ with r uniformly from the randomness space $\mathcal{R}$), the modified encryption algorithm Enc' computes the randomness r from the message m as $r := G(m)$. Here G is a hash function (modeled as a random oracle).

Transformation T also strengthens the decryption algorithm: The decryption algorithm resulting from T rejects any invalid ciphertexts (i.e., any ciphertext that is not in the range of Enc'). This is achieved by adding an extra check to the decryption algorithm Dec': After decrypting a ciphertext c to m, m is reencrypted and compared with the ciphertext c. Since Enc' is deterministic, this will always succeed for honestly generated ciphertexts, but it will always fail for invalid ones.

We summarize transformation T in Fig. 3.

Security of Transformation T. HKSU shows the following:

Theorem 1 (DS security of Enc', informal). *If* Enc *is ε-disjoint, so is* Enc'. *If* Enc *is DS secure and IND-CPA secure, then* Enc' *is DS secure.*

(In HKSU, the result is given with concrete security bounds.)

The core idea of the proof is to show that the adversary cannot distinguish between uniform randomness (as used in Enc) and randomness $r := G(m^*)$ where m^* is the challenge message (as used in Enc'). This is shown by bounding the probability for guessing m^* and then using the Semiclassical O2H theorem [1] to bound the distinguishing probability.

Keygen$_{FO}$() :	Encaps(pk):	Decaps(sk, c) with $sk = (sk', k)$:
01 $(pk, sk') \leftarrow$ Keygen$'()$	05 $m \xleftarrow{\$} \mathcal{M}'$	09 $m := $ Dec$'(sk', c)$
02 $k \xleftarrow{\$} \mathcal{K}_{PRF}$	06 $c \leftarrow$ Enc$'(pk, m)$	10 **if** $m = \bot$
03 $sk := (sk', k)$	07 $K := H(m)$	11 **then return** $K :=$ PRF(k, c)
04 **return** (pk, sk)	08 **return** (K, c)	12 **else return** $K := H(m)$

Fig. 4. Transformation $\mathsf{U}_m^{\not\perp}$. Input scheme: (Enc$'$, Dec$'$, Keygen$'$) with message space $\mathcal{M}'$ and fake encryption algorithm $\overline{\mathsf{Enc}'}$. Output scheme: (Keygen$_{FO}$, Encaps, Decaps) with key space $\mathcal{K}$. (The key space is the space of encapsulated keys, not of public/secret key pairs.) PRF is a pseudorandom function with key space $\mathcal{K}_{PRF}$. $H : \mathcal{M}' \to \mathcal{K}$ is a hash function (modeled as a random oracle).

We omit the proof from this exposition (we will focus on the more complex proof of transformation $\mathsf{U}_m^{\not\perp}$ below). The full proof can be found in [16].

3.3 Transformation $\mathsf{U}_m^{\not\perp}$

Finally, the transformation $\mathsf{U}_m^{\not\perp}$ takes the deterministic DS secure encryption scheme and transforms it into a KEM. In a KEM, we have an encapsulation algorithm Encaps that, instead of accepting a plaintext as input, uses a random (symmetric) key K as plaintext (intended for use in a symmetric encryption scheme) and returns both that key and the ciphertext. (We stress that K must not be confused with the public/secret keys of the KEM.) And the decapsulation algorithm Decaps takes the ciphertext and returns the key, like a decryption does.

The encapsulation algorithm constructed by transformation $\mathsf{U}_m^{\not\perp}$ picks a uniform $m \xleftarrow{\$} \mathcal{M}'$ and encrypts it (resulting in a ciphertext c). However, instead of using m directly as the symmetric key, the key is set to be $K := H(m)$. (Here H is a hash function modeled as a random oracle.)

Decapsulating c is straightforward: By decrypting c we get m back, and then we can compute the key $K := H(m)$. However, there is a subtlety in case of decryption failures: If $m = \bot$, then Decaps does not return $\bot$, but instead returns a key K that is indistinguishable from one that would result from a successful decryption. (This is called "implicit rejection", as opposed to "explicit rejection" that would return $\bot$.) This key K is generated from the ciphertext as $K := $ PRF(k, c) where PRF is a pseudorandom function.[4] And the PRF-key k is part of the secret key of the KEM. We describe the transformation $\mathsf{U}_m^{\not\perp}$ in Fig. 4.

Security of Transformation $\mathsf{U}_m^{\not\perp}$. HKSU does not show the security of transformation $\mathsf{U}_m^{\not\perp}$ (in the sense of showing that Encaps is secure if Enc$'$ satisfies certain properties), but instead directly analyzes the result of applying both T

---

[4] Note that HKSU [16] instead uses a *secret* random function H_r. (Not a public random function like the random oracle.) But it is understood that this secret random function is to be implemented by a PRF. Here, we directly use the PRF since we want to avoid keeping the proof step that replaces the PRF by a random function implicit.

Game IND-CCA$_0$	Game IND-CCA$_1$	Oracle DECAPS($c \neq c^*$)
01 $(pk, sk) \leftarrow$ Keygen$_{FO}()$	04 $(pk, sk) \leftarrow$ Keygen$_{FO}()$	08 $K \leftarrow$ Decaps(sk, c)
02 $(K^*, c^*) \leftarrow$ Encaps(pk)	05 $(K^*, c^*) \leftarrow$ Encaps(pk)	09 **return** K
03 $b \leftarrow A^{\text{DECAPS}}(pk, c^*, K^*)$	06 $K^* \overset{\$}{\leftarrow} \mathcal{K}$	
	07 $b \leftarrow A^{\text{DECAPS}}(pk, c^*, K^*)$	

Fig. 5. Games in the definition of IND-CCA security. In the random oracle model, A is additionally given oracle access to all random oracles.

and $\mathsf{U}_m^{\not\perp}$. That is, they show that Encaps is secure if Enc satisfies certain properties. HKSU does not completely modularize the proof (i.e., it does not separately analyze T and $\mathsf{U}_m^{\not\perp}$) but shows the following:

Theorem 2. *Assume* Enc *has injective encryption[5] and is IND-CPA secure and DS secure and ε-disjoint, and has ε'-correctness.[6] (For negligible $\varepsilon, \varepsilon'$) Then* Encaps *(as constructed by transformations* T *and* $\mathsf{U}_m^{\not\perp}$ *from* Enc*) is IND-CCA secure.*

The result stated in HKSU includes concrete security bounds. We also recall the definition of IND-CCA security for KEMs used in the preceding theorem:

Definition 2. *A KEM* (Keygen$_{FO}$, Encaps, Decaps) *with key space $\mathcal{K}$ is IND-CCA secure iff for any quantum-polynomial-time adversary A, $|\Pr[b = 1 : \text{IND-CCA}_0] - \Pr[b = 1 : \text{IND-CCA}_1]|$ is negligible, using the games from Fig. 5.*

Intuitively, this means that A cannot distinguish between the true key K^* contained in the ciphertext c^* and a uniformly random key K^*.

Note that in this definition, we slightly deviate from HKSU: In HKSU, only one game is given. This game picks randomly whether to play IND-CCA$_0$ or IND-CCA$_1$ from our definition. The security definition then requires that the adversary guesses which game is played with probability negligibly close to $\frac{1}{2}$. (We call this a "bit-guessing-style definition") In contrast, our definition requires the adversary to distinguish with its output bit between two games. (We call this a "distinguishing-style definition".) It is well-known that bit-guessing-style and distinguishing-style definitions are equivalent. But in the context of formal verification, it seems (according to our experiences) easier to work with distinguishing-style definitions.

Security Proof of Transformation $\mathsf{U}_m^{\not\perp}$. We give a compressed overview of the proof of Theorem 2 from HKSU. For details, see [16].

---

[5] This means that for any $m_0 \neq m_1$ in the message space, $\text{Enc}(pk, m_0) \neq \text{Enc}(pk, m_1)$ with probability 1. Note that this does not imply the possibility of correct decryption: While information theoretically, the plaintext is determined by the ciphertext, it may be computationally infeasible to determine the correct plaintext with probability 1, even given the secret key.

[6] This means that for random $(pk, sk) \leftarrow$ Keygen() and worst-case m, Dec(sk, Enc(pk, m)) $= m$ with probability at least $1 - \varepsilon$. See [16] for a precise definition.

Fix an adversary A. By definition of IND-CCA security (Definition 2), we need to bound $|\Pr[b = 1 : \mathsf{IND\text{-}CCA_0}] - \Pr[b = 1 : \mathsf{IND\text{-}CCA_1}]|$ for the games from Fig. 5.

We use essentially the same games in this proof as HKSU, with one difference: Since we decided to define IND-CCA security via a distinguishing-style definition, we need to adapt the games accordingly. All arguments from HKSU carry over trivially to our changed presentation.

The first step is to rewrite $\mathsf{IND\text{-}CCA_0}$ by unfolding the definitions of $\mathsf{Keygen_{FO}}$, Encaps, Decaps. (I.e., we make all constructions introduced by T and $\mathsf{U}_m^{\not\perp}$ explicit.) In addition, we replace the PRF by a uniformly random function H_r (that is not accessible to the adversary). The resulting game is:

Game 0	$\textsc{Decaps}(c \neq c^*)$
01 $G \xleftarrow{\$} (\mathcal{M} \to \mathcal{R}),\ H_r \xleftarrow{\$} (\mathcal{C} \to \mathcal{K})$	08 $m := \mathsf{Dec}(sk, c)$
02 $H \xleftarrow{\$} (\mathcal{M} \to \mathcal{K})$	09 **if** $m = \perp$ **or** $\mathsf{Enc}(pk, m; G(m)) \neq c$
03 $(pk, sk) \leftarrow \mathsf{Keygen}()$	10 **then return** $K := H_r(c)$
04 $m^* \xleftarrow{\$} \mathcal{M}$	11 **else return** $K := H(m)$
05 $c^* \leftarrow \mathsf{Enc}(pk, m^*; G(m^*))$	
06 $K^* := H(m^*)$	
07 $b \leftarrow A^{\textsc{Decaps},H,G}(pk, c^*, K^*)$	

Here $(A \to B)$ is the set of functions from A to B. And $\mathcal{C}$ is the ciphertext space.

From the fact that PRF is a pseudorandom function, we get that $|\Pr[b = 1 : \mathsf{IND\text{-}CCA_0}] - \Pr[b = 1 : \text{Game } 0]|$ is negligible.

Next, we chose the random oracle H differently: Instead of chosing H uniformly, we define it as the composition of a uniformly random function H_q and the encryption function $\mathsf{Enc}(pk, -; G(-))$. (The $-$ stands for the function argument.) Since Enc has injective encryption, $\mathsf{Enc}(pk, -; G(-))$ is injective, and thus H is still uniformly distributed. We get the following game (changed lines are marked with boldface line numbers):

Game 1	$\textsc{Decaps}(c \neq c^*)$
01 $G \xleftarrow{\$} (\mathcal{M} \to \mathcal{R}),\ H_r \xleftarrow{\$} (\mathcal{C} \to \mathcal{K})$	09 $m := \mathsf{Dec}(sk, c)$
02 $H_q \leftarrow (\mathcal{C} \to \mathcal{K})$	10 **if** $m = \perp$ **or** $\mathsf{Enc}(pk, m; G(m)) \neq c$
03 $H := H_q(\mathsf{Enc}(pk, -; G(-)))$	11 **then return** $K := H_r(c)$
04 $(pk, sk) \leftarrow \mathsf{Keygen}()$	**12 else return** $K := H_q(c)$
05 $m^* \xleftarrow{\$} \mathcal{M}$	
06 $c^* \leftarrow \mathsf{Enc}(pk, m^*; G(m^*))$	
07 $K^* := H_q(c^*)$	
08 $b \leftarrow A^{\textsc{Decaps},H,G}(pk, c^*, K^*)$	

Note that we additionally replaced two invocations $H(m^*)$, $H(m)$ by $H_q(c^*)$, $H_q(c)$. By construction, the new invocations return the same values. We have $\Pr[b = 1 : \text{Game } 0] = \Pr[b = 1 : \text{Game } 1]$.

In the next game hop, we change the decapsulation oracle. Instead of returning $H_r(c)$ or $H_q(c)$, depending on the result of the decryption, we now always return $H_q(c)$. The resulting game is:

Game 2   DECAPS($c \neq c^*$)
Unchanged from Game 1.   **01 return $K := H_q(c)$**

Since H_r and H_q are both random functions, at the first glance it might seem that this change does not matter at all, the return value is still random. However, H_q is indirectly accessible to the adversary via H! A more careful case analysis reveals that the adversary can distinguish the two games if it finds a message m with "bad randomness". That is, a message m such that $\mathsf{Dec}(sk, \mathsf{Enc}(pk, m; r)) \neq m$ where $r := G(m)$. If such bad randomness did not exist (i.e., when using a perfectly correct base scheme), this case would never happen. However, we do not assume perfect correctness. The solution from HKSU is to first replace the uniformly chosen $G \xleftarrow{\$} (\mathcal{M} \to \mathcal{R})$ by a G that outputs only good randomness (short: a "good G"). I.e., for each m, $G(m) := r$ is chosen uniformly from the set of all r with $\mathsf{Dec}(sk, \mathsf{Enc}(pk, m; r)) = m$. Once we have such a good G, bad randomness does not occur any more, and we can show that switching between H_r and H_q cannot be noticed (zero distinguishing probability). And then we replace G back by $G \xleftarrow{\$} (\mathcal{M} \to \mathcal{R})$.

To show that replacing the uniform G by a good G, HKSU reduces distinguishing the two situations to distinguishing a sparse binary function F from a constant-zero function F_0 (given as an oracle). And for that distinguishing problem (called GDPB), they give a lemma that shows the impossibility of distinguishing the F and F_0. Altogether, we get that $|\Pr[b = 1 : \text{Game 1}] - \Pr[b = 1 : \text{Game 2}]|$ is negligible.

Our formalization deviates somewhat from that proof: Instead of using the lemma about GDPB (which we would have to implement in the tool, first), we use the O2H Theorem [1] to show this indistinguishability. (We had to implement the O2H Theorem anyway because it is used in the analysis of transformation T.)

Note that this makes our bound somewhat worse. In HKSU, the proof step involving GDPB leads to a summand of $O(q^2\delta)$ in the final bound, while we achieve $O(q\sqrt{\delta})$ instead (last but one summand of (1)). Here q is the number of queries and δ the correctness error of the underlying scheme.

In the next game, we change how the challenge ciphertext c^* is generated. Instead of encrypting m^*, we simply produce a fake ciphertext $c^* \leftarrow \overline{\mathsf{Enc}}(pk)$. The resulting game is:

Game 3   DECAPS($c \neq c^*$)
01 $G \xleftarrow{\$} (\mathcal{M} \to \mathcal{R})$, $H_r \xleftarrow{\$} (\mathcal{C} \to \mathcal{K})$ 09 **return $K := H_q(c)$**
02 $H_q \leftarrow (\mathcal{C} \to \mathcal{K})$
03 $H := H_q(\mathsf{Enc}(pk, -; G(-)))$
04 $(pk, sk) \leftarrow \mathsf{Keygen}()$
05 $m^* \xleftarrow{\$} \mathcal{M}$
06 $c^* \leftarrow \overline{\mathsf{Enc}}(pk)$
07 $K^* := H_q(c^*)$
08 $b \leftarrow A^{\text{DECAPS}, H, G}(pk, c^*, K^*)$

By DS security of Enc, this fake encryption cannot be distinguished from a real encryption. (Note that the secret key is not used any more in Game 2.) Hence $|\Pr[b = 1 : \text{Game 2}] - \Pr[b = 1 : \text{Game 3}]|$ is negligible.

Finally, we change how K^* is chosen. Instead of picking $K^* := H_q(c^*)$, we chose K^* uniformly:

Game 4

01 $G \xleftarrow{\$} (\mathcal{M} \to \mathcal{R})$, $H_r \xleftarrow{\$} (\mathcal{C} \to \mathcal{K})$

02 $H_q \leftarrow (\mathcal{C} \to \mathcal{K})$

03 $H := H_q(\text{Enc}(pk, -; G(-)))$

04 $(pk, sk) \leftarrow \text{Keygen}()$

05 $m^* \xleftarrow{\$} \mathcal{M}$

06 $c^* \leftarrow \overline{\text{Enc}}(pk)$

07 $K^* \xleftarrow{\$} \mathcal{K}$

08 $b \leftarrow A^{\text{DECAPS},H,G}(pk, c^*, K^*)$

$\text{DECAPS}(c \neq c^*)$

09 **return** $K := H_q(c)$

Since H_q is a random function, this change can only be noticed if $H_q(c^*)$ is queried somewhere else. The adversary has access to H_q via H, but through H it can only query H_q on values that are in the range of Enc. But since c^* was constructed as a fake encryption $\overline{\text{Enc}}(pk)$, the ε-disjointness of $\overline{\text{Enc}}$ guarantees that c^* is, with overwhelming probability, not in the range of Enc. In that case, $H_q(c^*)$ is independent from anything the adversary might query. Thus $|\Pr[b = 1 : \text{Game 3}] - \Pr[b = 1 : \text{Game 4}]|$ is negligible.

So far, we have shown that the games IND-CCA$_0$ and Game 4 are indistinguishable. To show indistinguishability of IND-CCA$_0$ and IND-CCA$_1$, we write down a similar sequence of games Game 0' to Game 4' where K^* is chosen uniformly (as in IND-CCA$_1$). We then have indistinguishability of IND-CCA$_1$ and Game 4'. Game 4 and Game 4' are identical, thus IND-CCA$_0$ and IND-CCA$_1$ are indistinguishable, finishing the proof of IND-CCA security of Encaps.

```
1  lemma security_encFO:
2    abs(Pr[b=1: indcca_encFO_0(rho)] - Pr[b=1: indcca_encFO_1(rho)])
3    <=
4    abs (Pr[b=1:PRF_real (rho)] - Pr[b=1:PRF_ideal (rho)])
5    + abs (Pr[b=1:PRF_real'(rho)] - Pr[b=1:PRF_ideal'(rho)])
6    + abs (Pr[b=1:indcpa_enc0_0'''(rho)] - Pr[b=1:indcpa_enc0_1'''(rho)])
7    + 2 * sqrt(1+q) * sqrt(abs(Pr[b=1:indcpa_enc0_0''(rho)]
8                              - Pr[b=1:indcpa_enc0_1''(rho)])
9                      + 4 * q / card (msg_space()))
10   + abs (Pr[b=1:indcpa_enc0_0'(rho)] - Pr[b=1:indcpa_enc0_1'(rho)])
11   + 2 * sqrt(1+q) * sqrt(abs(Pr[b=1:indcpa_enc0_0(rho)]
12                             - Pr[b=1:indcpa_enc0_1(rho)])
13                     + 4 * q / card (msg_space()))
14   + 8 * sqrt(4 * (q+qD+2) * (q+qD+1)
15                   * correctness params0 keygen0 enc0 dec0 msg_space0)
16   + 2 * correctness params0 keygen0 enc0 dec0 msg_space0.
```

Fig. 6. The main theorem. File: `lemma_security_encFO.qrhl`

4   Formalizing HKSU – the Specification

A proof (formal or pen-and-paper) will consist of two separate parts: A specification of the result that is proven, and the proof itself. This separation is
important because if we trust that the proof is correct, we only need to read the
specification. In a pen-and-paper proof, this specification will usually consist of
the theorem together with all information required for interpreting the theorem,
i.e., all definitions that the theorem refers to, and all assumptions (if they are
not stated within the theorem itself). In the case of formal verification, we tend
to trust the proof (because it has been verified by the computer) but we have to
check the specification – does it indeed encode what we intended to prove?

In this section we go through the specification part of our HKSU formalization (available at [33]). It consists roughly of five parts: The main theorem. The
specification of the encryption algorithm and other functions in Isabelle/HOL.
The specification of the security definitions (security games). The specification
of the adversary. And the specification of the reduction-adversaries (we explain
below why this is a relevant part of the specification).

The Main Theorem. The source code for the main theorem is shown in
Fig. 6. Line 2 is the IND-CCA advantage $\mathsf{Adv}_{\mathsf{CCA}}$ of the adversary attacking the
KEM Encaps resulting from the transformations Punc, T, $\mathsf{U}_m^{\not\perp}$. (See Sect. 3.3.)
$\mathsf{Adv}_{\mathsf{CCA}}$ is defined as the difference between the probability of adversary-output
$b = 1$ in games `indcca_encF0_0` and `indcca_encF0_1`. We will see those games
below. In 4 we have the advantage $\mathsf{Adv}_{\mathsf{PRF}}$ of a reduction-adversary[7] against the
pseudorandom function PRF, expressed as the probability-difference between
games `PRF_real` and `PRF_ideal`. In 5, we have basically the same but with
respect to a different reduction-adversary. We have two reduction-adversaries for
PRF since we used the pseudorandomness twice in the proof. Since the adversary is hardcoded in the games,[8] we express this in terms of further games
`PRF_real'` and `PRF_ideal'`. In 6 we have the IND-CPA advantage $\mathsf{Adv}_{\mathsf{CPA}}'''$
of a reduction-adversary against the base scheme Enc$_0$, expressed in terms of
games `indcpa_enc0_0'''` and `indcpa_enc0_1'''`. Similarly, we have advan-
tages $\mathsf{Adv}_{\mathsf{CPA}}''$ in lines 7–8, $\mathsf{Adv}_{\mathsf{CPA}}'$ in 6, and $\mathsf{Adv}_{\mathsf{CPA}}$ in lines 7–8, against further
reduction-adversaries. The term $\delta :=$ `correctness params0 ...` in lines 11
and 12 refers to the correctness of Enc$_0$, i.e., we assume Enc$_0$ to be δ-correct.
(Cf. Footnote 6 for the meaning and Fig. 7 for the formalization of `correctness`.)
Finally, `card (msg_space())` is the cardinality of the message space $\mathcal{M}$ of Enc.
q_G, q_H, q_D are the number of queries made to the three oracles, and $q := q_G + 2q_H$.

---

[7] By reduction-adversary, we mean an adversary that we have explicitly constructed.

[8] Due to a lack of a proper module system in `qrhl-tool`, we have a lot of code duplication. A module system for games and adversaries such as in EasyCrypt would be
a valuable addition to `qrhl-tool` and would have simplified our proofs considerably.

```
 1 definition "force_into M x = (if x∈M then x else SOME m. m∈M)"
 2
 3 definition correctness_pkskm where "correctness_pkskm enc dec p pk sk m
 4   = Prob (enc p pk m) {c. dec p sk c ≠ Some m}"
 5
 6 definition correctness_pksk where "correctness_pksk enc dec msg_space p pk sk
 7   = (SUP m∈msg_space p. correctness_pkskm enc dec p pk sk m)"
 8
 9 definition correctness where "correctness P keygen enc dec msg_space =
10   expectation' P (λp. expectation' (keygen p)
11     (λ(pk,sk). correctness_pksk enc dec msg_space p pk sk))"
12
13 definition "injective_enc_pk p enc msg_space pk ⟷
14   (∀m1∈msg_space p. ∀m2∈msg_space p.
15     disjnt (supp (enc p pk m1)) (supp (enc p pk m2)))"
16
17 definition "injective_enc P keygen enc msg_space ⟷
18   (∀p∈supp P. ∀(pk,sk)∈supp (keygen p). injective_enc_pk p enc msg_space pk)"
19
20 axiomatization qD qG qH :: nat
21   where "qD ≥ 1" and "qG ≥ 1" and "qH ≥ 1"
22
23 definition "q = qG + 2 * qH"
```

Fig. 7. Some definitions from `General_Definitions.thy`. See Page 11 for a micro primer on Isabelle/HOL syntax.

With the notation we introduced in this explanation, we can write the main theorem more readably:

$$\mathsf{Adv}_{\mathsf{CCA}} \leq \mathsf{Adv}_{\mathsf{PRF}} + \mathsf{Adv}'_{\mathsf{PRF}} + \mathsf{Adv}'''_{\mathsf{CPA}} + 2\sqrt{1+q}\sqrt{\mathsf{Adv}''_{\mathsf{CPA}} + 4q/|\mathcal{M}|}$$
$$+ \mathsf{Adv}'_{\mathsf{CPA}} + 2\sqrt{1+q}\sqrt{\mathsf{Adv}_{\mathsf{CPA}} + 4q/|\mathcal{M}|}$$
$$+ 8\sqrt{4(q+qD+2)(q+qD+1)\delta} + 2\delta. \qquad (1)$$

Encryption Algorithm and Other Definitions. In order to make sense of the main theorem, we first need to check the definitions of the KEM and the building blocks used in its construction. The simplest is the pseudorandom function PRF, defined in Fig. 8, lines 1–2. The `axiomatization` command declares two constants PRF (the PRF) and keygenPRF (the key generation algorithm for the PRF, given as a distribution over keys). It furthermore axiomatizes the fact the key generation is a total distribution (axiom `keygenPRF_total`). (We do not need to axiomatize the security of PRF; its security is used implicitly by having $\mathsf{Adv}_{\mathsf{PRF}}$ occur in the main theorem.)

Similarly, we axiomatize the encryption scheme Enc_0 in lines 4–16. All encryption schemes in our work consist of a public parameter distribution (we only use this here for chosing the random oracles), a key generation, an encryption, a decryption algorithm, and a message space (which we allow to depend on the public parameters). The base scheme does not have public parameters, so we define params0 as the point distribution that always returns the dummy value () (4). The key generation keygen0 (lines 6–9) takes the public parameter and returns a distribution of public/secret key pairs. We assume that key generation is a total distribution (axiom `weight_keygen0`). Additionally we assume a function pk_of_sk that returns the corresponding pk for every sk in the support of

```
 1  axiomatization PRF :: "prfkey⇒ciph⇒key" and keygenPRF :: "prfkey distr"
 2  where keygenPRF_total: "weight keygenPRF = 1"
 3
 4  definition "params0 = point_distr ()"
 5
 6  axiomatization keygen0 :: "unit ⇒ (pk * sk) distr"
 7            and pk_of_sk :: "sk ⇒ pk"
 8  where pk_of_sk: "(pk,sk) ∈ supp (keygen ()) ⟹ pk_of_sk sk = pk"
 9    and weight_keygen0: "weight (keygen0 ()) = 1"
10
11  axiomatization enc0r :: "unit ⇒ pk ⇒ msg ⇒ rand ⇒ ciph"
12  definition "enc0 _ pk m = map_distr (enc0r () pk m) (uniform UNIV)"
13  axiomatization dec0 :: "unit ⇒ sk ⇒ ciph ⇒ msg option"
14
15  axiomatization msg_space0 :: "unit ⇒ msg set"
16  where nonempty_msg_space0: "msg_space0 () ≠ {}"
17
18  axiomatization where
19    enc0_injective: "injective_enc params0 keygen0 enc0 msg_space0"
```

Fig. 8. Building blocks: Base scheme and pseudorandom function. File: `Base_Scheme.thy` (last line: `F0_Specification.thy`). See Page 11 for a micro primer on Isabelle/HOL syntax.

keygen.[9] We define the encryption by first defining `enc0r`, a function that takes the public parameters, public key, message, and explicit randomness to compute a ciphertext (11). From this we define `enc0` as the distribution resulting from applying `enc0r` to the uniform distribution on the randomness (12). Decryption (`dec0`, 13) may fail, hence the return type is `msg option`, which means it can be `None` or `Some m` with a message m. Finally, `msg_space0` is a non-empty set (lines 15–16). We have an additional axiom `enc0_injective` (lines 18–19) which encodes the assumption that our base scheme is injective. (Cf. Footnote 5 for the meaning and Fig. 7 for the formalization of `injective_enc`.)

The transformations Punc, T, and $U_m^{\not\perp}$ are given in Fig. 9. As with our base scheme, we always define a deterministic encryption/encapsulation that takes explicit randomness first. The final KEM consists of the functions `keygenF0`, `encapsF0`, `decapsF0`, etc. We omit a discussion of the details of the function definitions, they follow our exposition in Sect. 3.

Security Definitions/Games. Next we have to understand the games that define the various advantages in the main theorem. We start with the IND-CCA security of Encaps. Adv_{CCA} was defined as the difference in probabilities that an adversary A (`Adv_INDCCA_encF0` in our case) outputs $b = 1$ in games `indcca_encF0_0/1`. The formalization of these games is given in Fig. 10. It is a direct encoding of the games in Fig. 5, with several small differences: Since we do not support procedures with parameters and return values, we use the global variables `in_pk` and `in_cstar` and `Kstar` for the inputs pk and c^* and K^*. And the global variable b is used for the return value (guessing bit). Below, when defining the adversary, we will then make sure the adversary gets access

---

[9] This assumption is not explicit in HKSU but clearly necessary for defining the decryption in transformation T: since the decryption re-encrypts, it needs to know the public key.

```
 1 definition "params = params0"
 2 definition "keygen = keygen0"
 3 definition "encr = enc0r"
 4 definition "dec P sk c = (case dec0 P sk c of Some m ⇒ if m ∈
   msg_space P then Some m else None | None ⇒> None)"
 5 definition "fakeenc _ pk = enc0 () pk puncture"
 6 definition "enc _ pk m = map_distr (encr () pk m) (uniform UNIV)"
 7
 8 definition paramsT where "paramsT = uniform UNIV"
 9 definition "keygenT G = keygen ()"
10 definition "encrT G pk m = encr () pk m (G m)"
11 definition "encT G pk m = point_distr (encrT G pk m)"
12 definition "decT G sk c = (case dec () sk c of None ⇒ None
13    | Some m ⇒ if encrT G (pk_of_sk sk) m = c then Some m else None)"
14 definition "fakeencT G = fakeenc ()"
15 definition "msg_spaceT G = msg_space ()"
16
17 definition paramsFO where "paramsFO = uniform UNIV"
18 definition keyspaceFO where "keyspaceFO _ = UNIV"
19 definition "keygenFO = (λ(G,H). map_distr (λ((pk,sk),prfk). (pk,(sk,prfk)))
20             (product_distr (keygenT G) keygenPRF))"
21 definition "encapsrFO = (λ(G,H) pk r. (H(r), encrT G pk r))"
22 definition "encapsFO GH pk = map_distr (encapsrFO GH pk)
23             (uniform (msg_spaceT (fst GH)))"
24 definition "decapsFO = (λ(G,H) (sk,prfk) c. case decT G sk c of
25    None ⇒ Some (PRF prfk c) | Some m ⇒ Some(H(m)))"
```

Fig. 9. Functions resulting from transformations Punc, T, $U_m^{\neq}$. Files: Punc_Specification.thy (l.1–6), T_Specification.thy (l.8–15), FO_Specification.thy (l.7–25). See Page 11 for a micro primer on Isabelle/HOL syntax.

to those global variables.[10] Access to the oracle decapsQuery is by passing it to the adversary as one of the oracles. Communication with decapsQuery is through variables c (input) and K' (output). It checks explicitly whether $c \neq c^*$ and returns None otherwise. (In Fig. 5, it was not made explicit how we enforce $c \neq c^*$.) Additionally, we model the access to the random oracles G, H by giving A access to queryG, queryH. queryG operates on global variables Gin, Gout and applies the unitary transformation Uoracle G on them. (Uoracle is a built-in function that transforms a function G into a unitary $|x,y\rangle \mapsto |x,y \oplus G(x)\rangle$.) Analogously queryH.

Similarly we define the games used in the rhs (right hand side) of the main theorem. The games PRF_real and PRF_ideal defining PRF-security for adversary Adv_PRF are given in Fig. 11. Again, we define oracles to either evaluate a pseudo-random function PRF or a random function RF and pass them to the adversary. The adversary Adv_PRF is explicitly defined in terms of Adv_INDCCA_encFO as part of our reduction, but its implementation details do not matter for us (except for some necessary sanity checks, see below). The primed variants Adv_real' and Adv_ideal' are identical except that they use a different reduction-adversary.

---

[10] We do not use pk and cstar directly for passing pk and c^* since that would mean giving A access to those variables. Then A could change the value of pk and c^* but the oracle decapsQuery relies on having the original values of pk and c^*.

```
 1 program indcca_encFO_0 := {        21 program queryG := {
 2   (G,H) <$ paramsFO;                22   on Gin,Gout apply (Uoracle G);
 3   (pk,skfo) <$ keygenFO (G,H);      23 }.
 4   (Kstar,cstar) <$ encapsFO (G,H) pk; 24
 5   in_pk <- pk;                      25 program queryH := {
 6   in_cstar <- cstar;               26   on Hin,Hout apply (Uoracle H);
 7   call Adv_INDCCA_encFO             27 }.
 8     (queryG,queryH,decapsQuery);    28
 9 }.                                  29 program decapsQuery := {
10                                     30   if (c=cstar) then
11 program indcca_encFO_1 := {        31     K' <- None;
12   (G,H) <$ paramsFO;               32   else
13   (pk,skfo) <$ keygenFO (G,H);     33     K' <- decapsFO (G,H) skfo c;
14   (Kstar,cstar) <$ encapsFO (G,H) pk; 34 }.
15   Kstar <$ uniform (keyspaceFO (G,H));
16   in_pk <- pk;
17   in_cstar <- cstar;
18   call Adv_INDCCA_encFO
19     (queryG,queryH,decapsQuery);
20 }.
```

Fig. 10. IND-CCA security definition for Encaps. Files: `indcca_encfo_0.qrhl`, `indcca_encfo_1.qrhl`, `decapsQuery.qrhl`, `queryG.qrhl`, `queryH.qrhl`.

```
 1 program PRF_real := {              10 program queryPRF := {
 2   prfk <$ keygenPRF;               11   K <- PRF prfk c;
 3   call Adv_PRF(queryPRF);          12 }.
 4 }.                                 13
 5                                    14 program queryRF := {
 6 program PRF_ideal := {             15   K <- RF c;
 7   RF <$ uniform UNIV;              16 }.
 8   call Adv_PRF(queryRF);
 9 }.
```

Fig. 11. Pseudorandomness game for `Adv_PRF`. Files `PRF_real.qrhl`, `PRF_ideal.qrhl`, `queryPRF.qrhl`, `queryRF.qrhl`.

```
 1 program indcpa_enc0_0 := {         14 program indcpa_enc0_1 := {
 2   (pk,sk) <$ keygen0 ();           15   (pk,sk) <$ keygen0 ();
 3   in_pk <- pk;                     16   in_pk <- pk;
 4   call Adv_INDCPA_enc0_1;          17   call Adv_INDCPA_enc0_1;
 5   m0star <- force_into             18   m0star <- force_into
 6     (msg_space0()) m0star;         19     (msg_space0()) m0star;
 7   m1star <- force_into             20   m1star <- force_into
 8     (msg_space0()) m1star;         21     (msg_space0()) m1star;
 9   cstar <$ enc0 () pk m0star;      22   cstar <$ enc0 () pk m1star;
10   in_pk <- pk;                     23   in_pk <- pk;
11   in_cstar <- cstar;              24   in_cstar <- cstar;
12   call Adv_INDCPA_enc0_2;          25   call Adv_INDCPA_enc0_2;
13 }.                                 26 }.
```

Fig. 12. IND-CPA security definition of Enc_0 for `Adv_INDCPA_enc0_1/2`. Files `indcpa_enc0_1.qrhl`, `indcpa_enc0_0.qrhl`.

Similarly, we define IND-CPA security of Enc_0 against `Adv_INDCPA_enc0_1/2` in Fig. 12. The primed variants are identical except that they use a different adversary.

The Adversary. In the games `indcca_encFO_1/2`, we use the adversary $A :=$ `Adv_INDCCA_encFO`. Since we want the main theorem to hold for arbitrary adversaries, we need to declare the adversary as an unspecified program. This is done

```
1  adversary Adv_INDCCA_encFO
2      vars classA, quantA, b, in_pk, in_cstar, Kstar
3      inner Hin, Hout, Gin, Gout, c, K'  calls ?,?,?.
```

Fig. 13. Adversary declaration. File: `Adv_INDCCA_encFO.qrhl`.

in Fig. 13. It declares that the adversary has access to the variables `classA`, `quantA`, `b`, `in_pk`, `in_cstar`, `Kstar`, i.e., we say the adversary has those free variables. Here `classA`, `quantA` are the global state of the adversary (quantum and classical part), and the others are the variables used for inputs/outputs of the adversary. Furthermore, the adversary needs to be able to access the variables `Hin`, `Hout`, `Gin`, `Gout`, `c`, `K'` that are used as inputs/outputs for its oracles `decapsQuery`, `queryG`, `queryH` (see above). Those variables are not declared as free variables (i.e., the adversary will have to hide them under a `local` command) but may be used internally, in particular before or after invoking the oracle. Finally, `calls ?,?,?` means that the adversary takes three oracles.

However, we are not interested in arbitrary adversaries, but in ones that always terminate and that make $\leq q_G, q_H, q_D$ queries to its various oracles. For this, we add various axioms to the file `axioms.qrhl`, stating the termination and the number of queries performed when instantiated with various oracles. The file with all axioms is discussed in the full version [35]. Unfortunately, this file contains a lot of repetitions because `qrhl-tool` does not allow us to allquantify over the oracles, so we need to state the axioms for any oracle we want to instantiate the adversary with.[11]

Reduction-Adversaries. Finally, to fully check whether the main theorem states what we want it to state (namely, that the KEM Encaps is secure assuming that the underlying encryption scheme Enc_0 and the PRF are secure), we also need to inspect the reduction-adversaries. This is because the main theorem basically says: If `Adv_INDCCA_encFO` breaks Encaps, then one of the adversaries in the games on the rhs breaks Enc_0 or PRF. (I.e., one of `Adv_PRF`, `Adv_PRF'`, `Adv_INDCPA_enc0/1`, etc.) But this is vacuously true – it is easy to construct an adversary that breaks Enc_0 or PRF. Namely, that adversary could run in exponential-time and perform a brute-force attack. Or that adversary could directly access the global variables containing, e.g., the secret key. So, while the exact details of what the reduction-adversaries do are not important, we need to check: Are the reduction-adversaries quantum-polynomial-time if `Adv_INDCCA_encFO` is? (Or even some more refined runtime relationship if we want tight concrete security bounds.) And do the reduction-adversaries access only variables that are not used by the security games themselves? The latter can be checked using the `print` command in interactive mode that prints all variables of a program (e.g., `print Adv_PRF`). This shows that the adversaries in the PRF games only access `cstar`, `classA`, `b`, `c`, `K'`, `quantA`, and in particular not `prfk` or `RF`. And the adversaries in the IND-CPA games access only

---

[11] Another place where a more advanced module system would help, cf. Footnote 8.

Find, mstar, S, in_cstar, in_pk, classA, b, is_puncture, G, quantA, but not the forbidden sk, pk, cstar.[12] To check the runtime of the adversaries, there is currently no better way than to manually inspect the code of all adversaries explicitly to see whether they do anything that increases the runtime too much. To the best of our knowledge, this is the state-of-the-art also in classical crypto verification. We believe that coming up with formal verification support for runtime analysis in qrhl-tool and similar tools is a very important next step. If this would be solved, the reduction-adversaries could be removed from the list of things we need to check as part of the specification.

By checking all the above points, we can have confidence that the formal proof indeed proves the right thing. (There are quite a lot of points to check, but we stress that in a pen-and-paper proof, the situation is similar – one needs to check whether all security definitions are correct, etc.)

5   Formalizing HKSU – The Proof

Since the formal proof is much too long to go through in detail, we only show a few select elements here to given an impression. HKSU shows security of three transformations Punc, T, $U_m^{\not\perp}$. The proof follows the overall structure of HKSU, lemma_ds_security.qrhl and lemma_indcpa_security.qrhl establishing DS and IND-CPA security of Punc, lemma_ds_encT_security.qrhl establishing DS security of T, and lemma_encFO_indcca.qrhl establishing IND-CCA security of the combination of T and $U_m^{\not\perp}$. Finally lemma_security_encFO.qrhl combines all those results into one overall result, the "main theorem" discussed in Sect. 4.

lemma_encFO_indcca.qrhl establishes IND-CCA security using the same sequence of games as described in Sect. 3.3, encoded as programs game0FO, ..., game4FO, game3FO', ..., game0FO' in the eponymous files.

Game 1 to Game 2. We zoom in some more onto the proof of the relationship between Game 1 and Game 2 (lemma_game1FO_game2FO.qrhl). We follow the basic intuition from Sect. 3.3, and split the proof of that step into the following subgames (all in eponymous .qrhl files):

(1) game1FO: Game 1 from Sect. 3.3.
(2) game1FO_goodbad: In this game, we prepare for replacing uniform G by a good G. For this purpose, instead of picking G uniformly, we pick a good Ggood (i.e., picking Ggood(m) uniformly from the good randomnesses for every m) and a bad Gbad, and a set S of messages. We define $G(m)$ to be Ggood(m) if $m \notin$ S and Gbad(m) otherwise. By choosing the distribution of S properly, we have that the resulting G is still uniform.
    We additionally remove all direct access to G, and make sure that queryG is used everywhere instead. This is necessary for bringing the game into the shape needed in the following step. This means all classical queries to

---

[12] Again, a more refined module system would allow us to automatically derive that certain variable-disjointness conditions hold, cf. Footnote 8.

G (e.g., in the creation of the challenge ciphertext) need to be replaced by quantum queries with subsequent measurements (we define a wrapper oracle ClassicalQueryG(queryG) for this), and we cannot simply define the function H in terms of G (see Game 1, line 03 in Sect. 3.3). Instead, we need to construct an oracle queryH_Hq that implements superposition queries of H in terms of superposition queries of G (via queryG). This makes this proof step considerably more complex than many of the other game steps.

That $\Pr[b = 1]$ does not change is shown in lemma_game1FO_goodbad.qrhl.

(3) game1FO_goodbad_o2h_right: We rewrite the previous game to have the right shape for the O2H theorem. The O2H theorem allows us to replace one oracle by another one that differs only in a few (hard to find) places. In order to apply the O2H theorem [1] (or the o2h tactic in qrhl-tool), the game needs to have a very specific form: count $\leftarrow 0; \overset{\$}{\leftarrow} (S, G, G', z')\mathcal{D};$ {localV; call $A_{O2H}(\text{Count}(\text{query}))$} for an oracle Count that counts queries in variable count and query that implements superposition queries to G'. The distribution $\mathcal{D}$ and the program A_{O2H} can be chosen freely. In our case we choose $\mathcal{D} := \text{goodbad\_o2h\_distr}$ such that G' is G from the previous game, and G is Ggood, and we choose $A_{O2H} = \text{Adv\_O2H\_Game1FO}$ to simulate the rest of the game. We show that the probability of $\Pr[b = 1]$ does not change (lemma_game1FO_goodbad_o2h_right.qrhl).

(4) game1FO_goodbad_o2h_left: We replace queries to G' by queries to G (recall that G was, in the previous game, made to return only good randomness). The Semiclassical O2H theorem [1] (implemented via our tactic o2h) allows us to do this replacement. In the resulting game $\Pr[b = 1]$ will differ by an amount that can be bounded in terms of the probability of finding an element in S. Bounding this probability involves a side-chain of games that we omit here. Altogether, lemma_game1FO_o2h_concrete.qrhl gives a concrete bound on the difference of $\Pr[b = 1]$.

(5) game1FO_goodbad_o2h_left': We remove the query-counting wrapper oracle Count that was introduced for the o2h tactic. We do this in a separate game step because it would be in the way in the next step. The probability $\Pr[b = 1]$ does not change (lemma_game1FO_goodbad_o2h_left'.qrhl).

(6) game1FO_goodbad_o2h_left_class: We unwrap the adversary Adv_O2H_Game1FO again which we introduced in (5). We also undo the various replacements done in (2) (which ensured that G was never used directly) to make the game simpler for the following steps. The probability $\Pr[b = 1]$ does not change (lemma_game1FO_goodbad_o2h_left_class.qrhl).

(7) game1FO_goodbad_badpk: In (2), we ignored one problem: Even if there is just one m without any good randomness, then it is not well-defined to pick G uniformly from the set of good G's because that set is empty.[13] For that reason, in (2), we actually defined $G(m)$ to be good *if good randomness exists*. But this definition breaks the next step below which relies on the fact that all randomness is good. Our solution is to introduce a predicate

---

[13] This problem also exists in HKSU but was not noticed there.

bad_pk pk sk that tells us whether there is an m (for that key pair) without good randomness. We then change the definition of the game to make a case distinction on bad_pk pk sk. If true, the new game behaves in a way that makes the next proof step trivially true. If false, the new game behaves as before. The probability for bad_pk pk sk is bounded by the correctness error of Enc_0, so we can bound the difference of $\Pr[b = 1]$ in lemma_game1FO_goodbad_badpk.qrhl.

(8) game2FO_goodbad_range: In the previous games, the choice whether *Decaps* returns $H_r(c)$ or $H_q(c)$ depended on whether we have a reencryption failure or not. (See *Decaps* in Game 1 in Sect. 3.3.) Instead, we use $H_r(c)$ or $H_q(c)$ depending on whether c is in the range of Enc'. We can show that, assuming good randomness, these two conditions are equivalent. Since G contains only good randomness, $\Pr[b = 1]$ does not change (lemma_game1FO_game2FO_o2h.qrhl).

(9) game2FO_goodbad_o2h_left': In the previous game, Decaps returns $H_r(c)$ if c is not in the range of Enc'. We replace this by always returning $H_q(c)$ as in Game 2 (Sect. 3.3). By analysis of the game, we can see that H_q is used in other places of the game only on the range of Enc' = encT, hence $H_q(c)$ and $H_r(c)$ are both fresh randomness if c is not in the range. Hence the replacement does not change $\Pr[b = 1]$ (lemma_game2FO_goodbad_range.qrhl).

(10) The rest of the proof steps are analogous to those done in (2)–(6), in reverse order until we reach game2FO.

Verification of ClassicalQueryG. To finish our illustration, we give the details of one of the subproofs of step (2), namely the proof that accessing G directly is the same querying G via ClassicalQueryG(queryG). The source of ClassicalQueryG is given in Fig. 14, lines 1–6. It initializes Gin with $|gin\rangle$, Gout with $|gout\rangle$, calls the query oracle (which will query G in superposition), and measures Gout into gout. Lines 8–11 claim that after doing so (in the right program) we will have gout2 = G2(gin2). And furthermore, that this preserves quantum equality of quantA, aux between the left and right side. Lines 13–14 inlines the definitions of the programs that we use, and lines 15–16 removes the local variable declarations. (The subgoal now has the same pre-/postcondition as before, but the right program is the code of ClassicalQueryG without the local statement.) Then wp right (17) consumes the statement gout <- measure Gout with computational_basis, and the postcondition becomes (after simplification) what is written in lines 18–19. Basically, this proof step tells us that having $|gin2, G2\,gin2\rangle$ in Gin2, Gout2 is sufficient for having gout2 = G2(gin2) after measurement. Next (lines 21–24) we consume "on Gin,Gout apply (Uoracle G)" from queryG (see Fig. 10, evaluation of G in superposition) and show that now it is sufficient to have $|gin2, 0\rangle$ in Gin2, Gout2. In lines 25–29, we remove the initialization Gout <q ket 0, now the necessary condition is to have $|gin\rangle$ in Gin2. And in lines 30–32, we remove Gin <q ket gin, removing the last requirement. Now left and right program are both skip and the pre-/postcondition are identical. The skip tactic (33) solves such a qRHL subgoal.

```
1  program ClassicalQueryG (query) := {
2    local Gin, Gout;
3    Gin <q ket gin;
4    Gout <q ket 0;
5    call query;
6    gout <- measure Gout with computational_basis; }.
7
8  qrhl ClassicalQueryG_queryG:
9    {top ⊓ ⟦quantA1,aux1⟧ ≡q ⟦quantA2,aux2⟧}
10     skip; ˜ call ClassicalQueryG (queryG);
11   {Cla⟦gout2 = G2(gin2)⟧ ⊓ ⟦quantA1,aux1⟧ ≡q ⟦quantA2,aux2⟧}.
12
13   inline ClassicalQueryG.
14   inline queryG.
15   local remove right.
16     simp!.
17   wp right.
18   conseq post: ⟦quantA1,aux1⟧ ≡q ⟦quantA2,aux2⟧
19                  ⊓ Span {ket (gin2, G2 gin2)}»⟦Gin2, Gout2⟧.
20     simp! aux5a aux5b.
21   wp right.
22   conseq post: ⟦quantA1,aux1⟧ ≡q ⟦quantA2,aux2⟧
23                  ⊓ Span {ket (gin2, 0)}»⟦Gin2, Gout2⟧.
24     simp! applyOpSpace_Span.
25   wp right.
26   conseq post: ⟦quantA1,aux1⟧ ≡q ⟦quantA2,aux2⟧
27                  ⊓ Span {ket gin2}»⟦Gin2⟧.
28   rule aux6.
29     simp!.
30   wp right.
31   conseq post: ⟦quantA1,aux1⟧ ≡q ⟦quantA2,aux2⟧.
32     simp! leq_space_div.
33   skip.
34   simp!.
35 qed.
```

Fig. 14. Verification of `ClassicalQueryG`. Files: `ClassicalQueryG.qrhl` (l.1–6), `lemma_ClassicalQueryG_queryG.qrhl` (l.8–35).

6 Conclusion

In this work, we have shown how to formally verify the HKSU security proof of a Fujisaki-Okamoto variant.

The experience shows that formal proofs of post-quantum secure schemes seem definitely possible using the approach in the `qrhl-tool`. Besides challenges due to the early development stage of the tool, probably the most troublesome part is reasoning about quantum computations. E.g., in one technical lemma[14] we show that a superposition query to the function $H := H_q(\mathsf{Enc}(pk, -; G(-)))$ as defined in Game 1, line 03 in Sect. 3.3 can be implemented by the simply quantum circuit that performs a superposition query to G, a superposition query to $H_q(\mathsf{Enc}(pk, -; -))$ and another superposition query to G for uncomputation.[15] The simplification of the resulting verification condition is a 200 lines Isabelle proof that takes almost ten minutes to execute (on the authors laptop).[16] Given

---

[14] File `lemma_queryH_invariant.qrhl`.

[15] This quantum circuit is formalized as a program in file `queryH_Hq.qrhl`.

[16] File `FO_Proofs_Very_Slow.thy`.

the simplicity of the fact that is proven, we feels this proof should be fully automatic and finish almost instantaneously.

What other post-quantum security proofs are possible using the same methodology? We feel that proofs of other post-quantum secure cryptographic schemes both in the standard model and the random oracle model should be feasible as well, as long as they do not use any advanced random oracle reasoning techniques beyond the O2H Theorem. How hard or easy it is to handle other proof techniques for the random oracle, or proof techniques that involve rewinding (which is notoriously challenging in the quantum setting) is not clear at this point. Similarly, it is not clear at this point how easily security proofs that involve reasoning about quantum information theory (such as quantum key distribution proofs, for example) can be formalized.

Possible directions for future research include:

- Formalizations of security proofs of the actual NIST candidates. While HKSU is quite close to some of the NIST candidates, to have highest assurance, we should analyze the schemes exactly as standardized and not merely schemes that are very similar to them. While unlikely, even a small difference such as the order in which the different inputs to a hash functions are concatenated might make a scheme insecure.
- Improved methods for reasoning about the quantum parts of the schemes, in particular methods for evaluating quantum computations such as the one mentioned in the beginning of this section. (Sequences of applications of unitaries in the program translate to multiplications of operators in the pre-/postconditions.)
- Support for other post-quantum security proof techniques beside the O2H Theorem. (E.g., rewinding, other random-oracle proof techniques.) Ideally, those proof techniques should be derived in the tool directly from first principles.
- Formal verification of "fully quantum" protocols such as quantum key distribution, quantum money, etc.

Acknowledgments. We thanks Kathrin Hövelmanns for valuable discussions. This work was supported by the US Air Force AOARD grant "Verification of Quantum Cryptography" (FA2386-17-1-4022), by the ERC consolidator grant CerQuS, by the Estonian Research Council grant PRG946, and by the Estonian Centre of Exellence in IT (EXCITE) funded by ERDF.

References

1. Ambainis, A., Hamburg, M., Unruh, D.: Quantum security proofs using semi-classical oracles. In: Boldyreva, A., Micciancio, D. (eds.) CRYPTO 2019. LNCS, vol. 11693, pp. 269–295. Springer, Cham (2019). https://doi.org/10.1007/978-3-030-26951-7_10

2. Arute, F., et al.: Quantum supremacy using a programmable superconducting processor. Nature **574**(7779), 505–510 (2019)
3. Barthe, G., Grégoire, B., Heraud, S., Béguelin, S.Z.: Computer-aided security proofs for the working cryptographer. In: Rogaway, P. (ed.) CRYPTO 2011. LNCS, vol. 6841, pp. 71–90. Springer, Heidelberg (2011). https://doi.org/10.1007/978-3-642-22792-9_5
4. Barthe, G., Grégoire, B., Lakhnech, Y., Zanella Béguelin, S.: Beyond provable security verifiable IND-CCA security of OAEP. In: Kiayias, A. (ed.) CT-RSA 2011. LNCS, vol. 6558, pp. 180–196. Springer, Heidelberg (2011). https://doi.org/10.1007/978-3-642-19074-2_13
5. Barthe, G., Grégoire, B., Zanella Béguelin, S.: Formal certification of code-based cryptographic proofs. In: POPL, pp. 90–101. ACM (2009)
6. Bellare, M., Rogaway, P.: Random oracles are practical: A paradigm for designing efficient protocols. In: CCS '93, pp. 62–73. ACM (1993)
7. Bellare, M., Rogaway, P.: Optimal asymmetric encryption. In: De Santis A. (eds.) Advances in Cryptology – EUROCRYPT'94, Lecture Notes in Computer Science, vol. 950. Springer, Berlin, vol. 950, pp. 92–111. (1994) https://doi.org/10.1007/BFb0053428
8. Bellare, M., Rogaway, P.: The security of triple encryption and a framework for code-based game-playing proofs. In: Vaudenay, S. (ed.) EUROCRYPT 2006. LNCS, vol. 4004, pp. 409–426. Springer, Heidelberg (2006). https://doi.org/10.1007/11761679_25
9. Boneh, D., Dagdelen, Ö., Fischlin, M., Lehmann, A., Schaffner, C., Zhandry, M.: Random oracles in a quantum world. In: Lee, D.H., Wang, X. (eds.) ASIACRYPT 2011. LNCS, vol. 7073, pp. 41–69. Springer, Heidelberg (2011). https://doi.org/10.1007/978-3-642-25385-0_3
10. Bos, J., et al.: CRYSTALS - kyber: a CCA-secure module-lattice-based KEM. IACR ePrint 2017/634 (2017)
11. Canetti, R., Goldreich, O., Halevi, S.: The random oracle methodology, revisited. In: STOC 1998, pp. 209–218. ACM (1998)
12. Fujisaki, E., Okamoto, T.: How to enhance the security of public-key encryption at minimum cost. IEICE Trans. Fund. Electron. Commun. Comput. Sci. **E83–A**(1), 24–32 (2000)
13. Fujisaki, E., Okamoto, T., Pointcheval, D., Stern, J.: RSA-OAEP is secure under the RSA assumption. In: Kilian, J. (ed.) CRYPTO 2001. LNCS, vol. 2139, pp. 260–274. Springer, Heidelberg (2001). https://doi.org/10.1007/3-540-44647-8_16
14. Fujisaki, E., Okamoto, T., Pointcheval, D., Stern, J.: RSA-OAEP is secure under the RSA assumption. J. Crypto **17**(2), 81–104 (2004)
15. Hofheinz, D., Hövelmanns, K., Kiltz, E.: A modular analysis of the Fujisaki-Okamoto transformation. In: Kalai, Y., Reyzin, L. (eds.) TCC 2017. LNCS, vol. 10677, pp. 341–371. Springer, Cham (2017). https://doi.org/10.1007/978-3-319-70500-2_12
16. Hövelmanns, K., Kiltz, E., Schäge, S., Unruh, D.: Generic authenticated key exchange in the quantum random oracle model. IACR ePrint 2018/928, rev. February 14, 2019 (2019), preliminary version of [17]
17. Hövelmanns, K., Kiltz, E., Schäge, S., Unruh, D.: Generic authenticated key exchange in the quantum random oracle model. In: Kiayias, A., Kohlweiss, M., Wallden, P., Zikas, V. (eds.) PKC 2020. LNCS, vol. 12111, pp. 389–422. Springer, Cham (2020). https://doi.org/10.1007/978-3-030-45388-6_14

18. Inoue, A., Iwata, T., Minematsu, K., Poettering, B.: Cryptanalysis of OCB2: attacks on authenticity and confidentiality. In: Boldyreva, A., Micciancio, D. (eds.) CRYPTO 2019. LNCS, vol. 11692, pp. 3–31. Springer, Cham (2019). https://doi.org/10.1007/978-3-030-26948-7_1

19. ISO: Information technology - security techniques - authenticated encryption. International Standard ISO/IEC 19772 (2009)

20. Naehrig, M., et al.: Frodokem. Technical Report, National Institute of Standards and Technology (2017)

21. Nipkow, T.: Programming and proving in isabelle/hol. https://isabelle.in.tum.de/website-Isabelle2019/dist/Isabelle2019/doc/prog-prove.pdf (2019), version for Isabelle 2019

22. Nipkow, T., Wenzel, M., Paulson, L.C. (eds.): Isabelle/HOL. LNCS, vol. 2283. Springer, Heidelberg (2002). https://doi.org/10.1007/3-540-45949-9

23. NIST: Post-quantum crypto standardization - call for proposals. http://csrc.nist.gov/groups/ST/post-quantum-crypto/call-for-proposals-2016.html (2016)

24. Rogaway, P.: Efficient instantiations of tweakable blockciphers and refinements to modes OCB and PMAC. In: Lee, P.J. (ed.) ASIACRYPT 2004. LNCS, vol. 3329, pp. 16–31. Springer, Heidelberg (2004). https://doi.org/10.1007/978-3-540-30539-2_2

25. Saito, T., Xagawa, K., Yamakawa, T.: Tightly-secure key-encapsulation mechanism in the quantum random oracle model. In: Nielsen, J.B., Rijmen, V. (eds.) EUROCRYPT 2018. LNCS, vol. 10822, pp. 520–551. Springer, Cham (2018). https://doi.org/10.1007/978-3-319-78372-7_17

26. Shor, P.W.: Algorithms for quantum computation: discrete logarithms and factoring. In: FOCS 1994, pp. 124–134. IEEE (1994)

27. Shoup, V.: OAEP reconsidered. J. Crypto **15**(4), 223–249 (2002)

28. Shoup, V.: Sequences of games: a tool for taming complexity in security proofs. Cryptology ePrint 2004/332 (2004)

29. Targhi, E.E., Unruh, D.: Post-quantum security of the Fujisaki-Okamoto and OAEP transforms. In: Hirt, M., Smith, A. (eds.) TCC 2016. LNCS, vol. 9986, pp. 192–216. Springer, Heidelberg (2016). https://doi.org/10.1007/978-3-662-53644-5_8

30. Unruh, D.: Quantum proofs of knowledge. In: Pointcheval, D., Johansson, T. (eds.) EUROCRYPT 2012. LNCS, vol. 7237, pp. 135–152. Springer, Heidelberg (2012). https://doi.org/10.1007/978-3-642-29011-4_10

31. Unruh, D.: dominique-unruh/qrhl-tool: Proof assistant for qRHL. GitHub, https://github.com/dominique-unruh/qrhl-tool (2017–2020), binaries of the correct version are at https://github.com/dominique-unruh/qrhl-tool/releases/tag/v0.5

32. Unruh, D.: Quantum relational Hoare logic. Proc. ACM Program. Lang. **3**, 1–31 (2019)

33. Unruh, D.: GitHub, https://github.com/dominique-unruh/hksu-verification/tree/asiacrypt2020 (2020), source code of the proofs described here

34. Unruh, D.: Local variables and quantum relational hoare logic. arXiv:2007.14155 [cs.LO] (2020)

35. Unruh, D.: Post-quantum verification of Fujisaki-Okamoto. IACR ePrint 2020/962 (2020), full version of this paper

36. Watrous, J.: Zero-knowledge against quantum attacks. SIAM J. Comput. **39**(1), 25–58 (2009)

A New Decryption Failure Attack
Against HQC

Qian Guo[1,2(✉)] and Thomas Johansson[1(✉)]

[1] Department of Electrical and Information Technology, Lund University,
P.O. Box 118, 221 00 Lund, Sweden
{qian.guo,thomas.johansson}@eit.lth.se
[2] Department of Informatics, University of Bergen,
P.O. Box 7803, 5020 Bergen, Norway

Abstract. HQC is an IND-CCA2 KEM running for standardization in NIST's post-quantum cryptography project and has advanced to the second round. It is a code-based scheme in the class of public key encryptions, with given sets of parameters spanning NIST security strength 1, 3 and 5, corresponding to 128, 192 and 256 bits of classic security.

In this paper we present an attack recovering the secret key of an HQC instance named hqc-256-1. The attack requires a single precomputation performed once and then never again. The online attack on an HQC instance then submits about 2^{64} special ciphertexts for decryption (obtained from the precomputation) and a phase of analysis studies the subset of ciphertexts that are not correctly decrypted. In this phase, the secret key of the HQC instance is determined.

The overall complexity is estimated to be 2^{246} if the attacker balances the costs of precomputation and post-processing, thereby claiming a successful attack on hqc-256-1 in the NIST setting. If we allow the precomputation cost to be 2^{254}, which is below exhaustive key search on a 256 bit secret key, the computational complexity of the later parts can be no more than 2^{64}. This is a setting relevant to practical security since the large precomputation needs to be done only once. Also, we note that the complexity of the precomputation can be lower if the online attack is allowed to submit more than 2^{64} ciphertexts for decryption.

Keywords: Code-based cryptography · IND-CCA · NIST post-quantum standardization · Decryption errors · HQC · Reaction attack

1 Introduction

Integer factorization and the discrete logarithm problem have been cornerstone problems for asymmetric cryptography, but this is changing due to quantum computers, as their ability to efficiently solve such mathematical problems through Shor's algorithm [42] compromises the security of currently used asymmetric primitives. These developments have created the emergence of the area of

© International Association for Cryptologic Research 2020
S. Moriai and H. Wang (Eds.): ASIACRYPT 2020, LNCS 12491, pp. 353–382, 2020.
https://doi.org/10.1007/978-3-030-64837-4_12

post-quantum cryptography and it motivated NIST to organize a post-quantum cryptography standardization project, with the ultimate goal of standardizing new quantum-resistant public-key crypto primitives. Submissions rely on problems from various fields within post-quantum cryptography, such as lattice-based, code-based and multivariate cryptography.

We specifically consider code-based cryptosystems. By this term, we mean cryptosystems where the algorithmic primitive uses an error correcting code. The primitive typically add an error to a codeword of the code and the primitive relies on the difficulty of decoding the received word back to the codeword. The first of those systems was a public key encryption scheme proposed by McEliece in 1978 [35]. The private key is a random binary irreducible Goppa code and the public key is a generator matrix of a randomly permuted and scrambled version of the original generator matrix for that code. The ciphertext is a codeword with some errors added, and only the knowledge of the private key (the Goppa code) can efficiently remove those errors. More formally, it is based on the difficulty of the syndrome decoding problem[1], which was proved to be NP-hard in [12]. After 40 years, some parameters have been adjusted, but no serious attack is known, even when using a quantum computer.

The birth of post-quantum cryptography made code-based cryptography a very interesting and the second most research-intense area after lattice-based crypto. Let us mention some recent code-based public key cryptosystems. The landmark paper presenting QC-MDPC [37] showed how the size of the public key could be made small, compared to the original McEliece scheme.

The different code-based proposals in the NIST process like NIST PQC candidates BIKE [5], LEDAcrypt [9], HQC [2], and others, showed that fully IND-CCA2 secure schemes could be built, using Fujisaki-Okamoto transform [22] or some similar conversion. They could also provide provable security in the sense that a proof of security related to a difficult decoding problem was given. The above mentioned schemes rely on decoding problems in the Hamming metric, whereas the schemes ROLLO [6] and RQC [3] rely on problems using the rank metric.

There are 17 remaining second-round candidates for public-key encryption and key-establishment algorithms in the NIST PQC project, among them six code-based schemes. The HQC submission [2] considered in this paper is such an IND-CCA2 KEM proposal running for standardization in NIST's post-quantum cryptography project and has advanced to the second round[2]. It is a code-based scheme in the class of public key encryptions, with given sets of parameters spanning NIST security strength 1, 3 and 5, corresponding to 128, 192 and 256 bits of classic security.

As for many of the code-based schemes (as well as for lattice-based schemes), there is no absolute guarantee that the decryption algorithm will succeed to decrypt to the transmitted message. Rather, there is a small probability of error

---

[1] A stronger hardness assumption in the average case is required.

[2] NIST announced the round-3 candidates in July 2020 and HQC is one of the eight alternate candidates.

for the decryption process, which for HQC is $<2^{-128}$ or even smaller. This work studies an attack that uses the possibility of having decryption errors as a part of the cryptanalysis process to finally determine the secret key.

1.1   Related Works

On code-based schemes without CCA2 conversion we have a few attacks in literature that require more than the CPA assumption. Using a *partially known plaintext attack* [16], one can reduce the code dimension in the decoding and thus achieve a lower complexity. In a *resend attack*, Alice resends the same message twice, or possible two related messages. The message can then be efficiently found [14]. A *reaction attack* [29] is a weaker version of a chosen ciphertext attack. The attacker sends a ciphertext or modifies an intercepted one and observes the reaction of the recipient (correct decryption or failure, but not the result of decryption). Again, one can in certain cases efficiently find the message corresponding to an intercepted ciphertext. Note that all these attacks are message recovery attacks.

In [26], an attack in the form of a reaction attack was given on the QC-MDPC scheme. The interesting fact for this attack was that it could be applied on the CCA version of the QC-MDPC scheme and still be successful; and it was a *key-recovery attack*. The journal version [27] expanded some details of the attack, e.g. the secret key recovery.

Following this work, many attacks on similar schemes were reported, for example on QC-LDPC [20], and attacks on LRPC [7,41]. All these attacks require that the decryption failure rate is fairly large, and subsequently the new schemes were designed with a much lower failure probability.

A similar development can be found for lattice-based schemes. For the lattice-based scheme NTRU (NTRUEncrypt) some problems due to decryption failures were identified already in [32,33]. More recently, several CCA type attacks using decryption failures on lattice-based schemes without CCA transforms has been reported, Fluhrer [21], Bernstein [13], on New-hope in CT-RSA 2019 [10], and mis-use attacks found in [8].

Attacking CCA secure lattice-based schemes through decryption failures in the spirit of [26] has been less successful. However, recently, CCA attacks based on failures were modeled and some initial attack attempts on an NTRU version were presented [17,25]. The most recent work in this direction is the attack on the LAC proposal [34] given in [28].

The proposed attack in this paper shares some similarities with these attacks in the sense that it uses a first precomputation phase to generate a set of encrypted messages for which the corresponding error vectors are causing the decryption failure probability to be much larger that the average case. The online attack then makes a statistical analysis of the information obtained from the ciphertexts that failed to decrypt and extracts enough information to recover the secret key.

There are also major differences, one being that HQC is a code-based scheme. Another major difference is that the LAC attack can only target weak secret keys (e.g. one out of 2^{64} key pairs), whereas this attack on HQC targets any public key.

A relevant research direction is to investigate failure amplification tricks, including [38] in the code-based regime and [18] in the lattice-based regime. These techniques seem not directly to apply to attacking HQC.

1.2 Contributions

In this paper we present a CCA attack recovering the secret key of an HQC instance named hqc-256-1. The attack requires a single precomputation performed once and then never again. The online attack then submits about 2^{64} special ciphertexts for decryption (obtained from the precomputation) and a statistical analysis step processes information from the subset of ciphertexts that are not correctly decrypted. In this phase, the secret key of the HQC instance is determined. The overall complexity is estimated to be 2^{246} when the online decryption calls are limited to 2^{64}. With the given attack, this parameter choice hqc-256-1 can be attacked faster than exhaustive key search for a single key. One could also allow a large precomputation to reduce the post-processing cost since the single precomputation is performed only once. One example is to perform a precomputation of about 2^{254}, which is still below exhaustive key search on a 256 bit secret key. The computational complexity of the online and the post-processing steps is no more than the cost of submitting 2^{64} ciphertexts for decryption. Also, the complexity of the precomputation can be lower if the online attack is allowed to submit more than 2^{64} ciphertexts for decryption.

Last, we should note that once the precomputation is completed, the attack can be mounted on any HQC public keys when this cryptosystem is deployed. In this case, the precomputation complexity of the attack can be amortized. Therefore, several other parameter choices of HQC can be successfully targeted as well, in the sense that *all* the attacked keys can be recovered with complexity below the claimed security level. The amortized complexity is similar to Hellman's "cost per solution" [30], and the vulnerability comes from that the attacked HQC parameter sets cannot provide sufficient security compared with that of time-memory trade-off attacks on their block cipher counterpart such as AES. This attack model is not considered in the attacking framework in the NIST PQC standardization project. However, it could have high practical relevance since a scheme will be widely deployed if it becomes a standard. Time-memory trade-off attacks are relevant in practice and this attack model should be discussed also in the PKC area.

1.3 Organizations

The remaining of the paper is organized as follows. We briefly describe the HQC scheme in Sect. 2. Then we give a high-level description of the attack, explaining the basic underlying ideas in Sect. 3. In Sect. 4 we then give a more formal and detailed description of the attack and provide a theoretical basis for estimating the required complexity. Section 5 specifically considers the security of several other HQC parameter sets. Section 6 discusses some aspects of the HQC scheme that are to the advantage of the attacker and related countermeasures. Section 7 concludes the paper.

2 Description of HQC

We briefly describe the HQC proposal [2] as submitted to the second round of the NIST post-quantum cryptography standardization process. HQC stands for Hamming Quasi-Cyclic and the underlying scheme was published in [36]. For more details we refer to the original design document [2] as we give only a brief description of the scheme. In particular, no description of the underlying difficult problems or the proofs of security are given in this section.

2.1 Notation

The scheme processes binary vectors of some length n, so such a vector $\mathbf{y} = (y_0, y_1, \ldots y_{n-1}) \in \mathbb{F}_2^n$, where $y_i \in \mathbb{F}_2$, for $i = 0, 1, \ldots, n - 1$. By $\omega(\mathbf{y})$ we mean the Hamming weight of the vector $\mathbf{y}$, i.e., the number of nonzero coordinates. Since the field is $\mathbb{F}_2$, one can replace the operation of $-$ by $+$. Given a set $\mathcal{S}$, we use $\#\mathcal{S}$ to denote its cardinality.

Let $\mathcal{R} = \mathbb{F}_2[X]/(X^n - 1)$. An element $y(x) \in \mathcal{R}$ is a polynomial of degree at most $n - 1$ expressed through the coefficients $y(x) = y_0 + y_1 x + \cdots + y_{n-1} x^{n-1}$. We will interchange between the expression of a vector $\mathbf{y}$ as a row vector and the corresponding polynomial $y(x)$. We may also write $\mathbf{y} \xleftarrow{\$} \mathcal{R}$, meaning that we randomly select a binary vector $\mathbf{y}$ also considered as a polynomial.

For two vectors $\mathbf{u}, \mathbf{v} \in \mathbb{F}_2^n$ we define their product $\mathbf{u} \cdot \mathbf{v}$ as the coefficients of the polynomial $u(x)v(x) \in \mathcal{R}$. This product can also be expressed using circulant matrices. For a vector $\mathbf{y} \in \mathbb{F}_2^n$, the circulant matrix induced by $\mathbf{y}$ is denoted $\mathbf{rot}(\mathbf{y})$ and defined as

$$\mathbf{rot}(\mathbf{y}) = \begin{pmatrix} y_0 & y_{n-1} & \cdots & y_1 \\ y_1 & y_0 & \cdots & y_2 \\ \vdots & \vdots & \ddots & \vdots \\ y_{n-1} & y_{n-2} & \cdots & y_0 \end{pmatrix}.$$

The multiplication $\mathbf{uv}$ can now alternatively be written as

$$\mathbf{uv} = \mathbf{u} \cdot \mathbf{rot}(\mathbf{v})^T = \mathbf{v} \cdot \mathbf{rot}(\mathbf{u})^T,$$

where $(\cdot)^T$ denotes transpose.

We give some basic definitions and properties from coding theory and refer to [2] or any textbook on the subject. A linear code $\mathcal{C}$ of length n and dimension k (an $[n, k]$ code) is a subspace of $\mathbb{F}_2^n$ of dimension k. A matrix $\mathbf{G} \in \mathbb{F}_2^{k \times n}$ is a generator matrix of the code if

$$\mathcal{C} = \{\mathbf{mG}, \mathbf{m} \in \mathbb{F}_2^k\}.$$

A matrix $\mathbf{H} \in \mathbb{F}_2^{(n-k)\times n}$ is a parity check matrix of the code if

$$\mathcal{C} = \{\mathbf{v} \in \mathbb{F}_2^n, \text{such that } \mathbf{v}\mathbf{H}^{\mathbf{T}} = \mathbf{0}\}.$$

Fix a parity check matrix and let $\mathbf{v} \in \mathbb{F}_2^n$. Then the syndrome of $\mathbf{v}$ is the value $\mathbf{v}\mathbf{H}^{\mathbf{T}}$. If $\mathbf{v} \in \mathcal{C}$ then the syndrome is $\mathbf{0}$. The minimum distance d of the code is the minimum weight taken over all nonzero codewords in the code. Such a code is capable of correcting $\delta = \lfloor \frac{d-1}{2} \rfloor$ errors. This means that if a codeword is disturbed by adding a binary vector known to be of weight at most δ, then there is an algorithm that can find and remove this noise and return the codeword.

A repetition code, denoted $\mathbb{1}_n$, is an $[n,1]$ code that has a generator matrix of the form $\mathbf{G} = [1]$. It means transmitting a single bit and repeating it n times. Such a code can then correct up to $\delta_r = \lfloor \frac{n-1}{2} \rfloor$ errors. BCH codes are a very common class of codes as they achieve a good error correction capability. We do not need to define them, but rather just note that there is an efficient algorithm for correcting errors. By $BCH(n_1, k_1, \delta)$ we denote a BCH code that is capable of correcting up to δ errors.

Finally, a tensor product code $\mathcal{C}$, denoted $\mathcal{C}_1 \otimes \mathcal{C}_2$, is a code built from two codes $\mathcal{C}_1$ and $\mathcal{C}_2$. If $\mathcal{C}_1$ is an $[n_1, k_1, d_1]$ code and $\mathcal{C}_2$ is an $[n_2, k_2, d_2]$ code then the tensor product code $\mathcal{C}$ is an $[n_1 n_2, k_1 k_2, d_1 d_2]$ code. You can view the length $n_1 n_2$ codewords in $\mathcal{C}_1 \otimes \mathcal{C}_2$ as a $n_1 \times n_2$ array, where every row is a codeword in $\mathcal{C}_1$ and every column is a codeword in $\mathcal{C}_1$. We will only be concerned with the construction $\mathrm{BCH}(n_1, k, \delta) \otimes \mathbb{1}_{n_2}$. It means that every position in the BCH codeword is repeated n_2 times. The decoding procedure first decodes every repetition code by simply counting the number of zeros (or ones). Then the output is used as the value for each position in the BCH code, which is then decoded. In particular, if we want to find an error that will not decode correctly, we need to have at least $\delta_r = \lfloor \frac{n_2+1}{2} \rfloor$ errors in each of at least $\delta + 1$ different columns (repetition codes).

2.2 The HQC Scheme

The public key encryption (PKE) version of HQC is shown in Fig. 1. HQC makes use of the tensor product code of two different codes, one being a BCH code and the other being a simple repetition code. The code is denoted by $\mathcal{C}$ and has a corresponding generator matrix $\mathbf{G} \in \mathbb{F}_2^{k\times n}$. We return to the details of the tensor product code later.

The scheme follows the steps of many lattice-based schemes, but here errors are considered in the Hamming metric. The key generation randomly selects a public $\mathbf{h} \in \mathcal{R}$ and two private vectors $\mathbf{x}, \mathbf{y} \in \mathcal{R}$ with very low Hamming weight. It computes $\mathbf{s} = \mathbf{x} + \mathbf{h} \cdot \mathbf{y}$ as the second part of the public key, which presumably looks like a randomly chosen vector.

In the encryption one generates noise $\mathbf{e}, \mathbf{r}_1, \mathbf{r}_2 \in \mathcal{R}$ with very low Hamming weight and computes $\mathbf{u} = \mathbf{r}_1 + \mathbf{h} \cdot \mathbf{r}_2$ and $\mathbf{v} = \mathbf{m}\mathbf{G} + \mathbf{s} \cdot \mathbf{r}_2 + \mathbf{e}$, which is returned as the ciphertext.

In decryption, one has access to the secret key $\mathbf{y}$ and computes $\mathbf{v} - \mathbf{u} \cdot \mathbf{y}$. The decoder for the code then finally removes all the noise. An expansion of the expression shows

$$\mathbf{v} - \mathbf{u} \cdot \mathbf{y} = \mathbf{m}\mathbf{G} + (\mathbf{x} + \mathbf{h} \cdot \mathbf{y}) \cdot \mathbf{r}_2 + \mathbf{e} - (\mathbf{r}_1 + \mathbf{h} \cdot \mathbf{r}_2) \cdot \mathbf{y} = \mathbf{m}\mathbf{G} + \mathbf{e}',$$

where

$$\mathbf{e}' = \mathbf{x} \cdot \mathbf{r}_2 - \mathbf{y} \cdot \mathbf{r}_1 + \mathbf{e}. \tag{1}$$

Throughout the paper, we denote the i-th entry of $\mathbf{e}$ ($\mathbf{e}'$) by e_i (e_i'). If the Hamming weight of $\mathbf{e}'$ is not too large, the decoder will be able to decode and return the correct message $\mathbf{m}$. As all parts of the expression for $\mathbf{e}'$ are of very low weight, also $\mathbf{e}'$ will be of somewhat low weight.

- Setup(1^λ): generates the global parameters param $= (n, k, \delta, \omega, \omega_\mathbf{r}, \omega_\mathbf{e})$.

- KeyGen(param): sample $\mathbf{h} \xleftarrow{\$} \mathcal{R}$, the generator matrix $\mathbf{G} \in \mathbb{F}_2^{k \times n}$ of $\mathcal{C}$, sk $= (\mathbf{x}, \mathbf{y}) \xleftarrow{\$} \mathcal{R}^2$ such that $\omega(\mathbf{x}) = \omega(\mathbf{y}) = \omega$, sets pk $= (\mathbf{h}, \mathbf{s} = \mathbf{x} + \mathbf{h} \cdot \mathbf{y})$, and returns (pk, sk).

- Encrypt(pk, m): generates $\mathbf{e} \xleftarrow{\$} \mathcal{R}$, $\mathbf{r} = (\mathbf{r}_1, \mathbf{r}_2) \xleftarrow{\$} \mathcal{R}^2$ such that $\omega(\mathbf{e}) = \omega_\mathbf{e}$ and $\omega(\mathbf{r}_1) = \omega(\mathbf{r}_2) = \omega_\mathbf{r}$, sets $\mathbf{u} = \mathbf{r}_1 + \mathbf{h} \cdot \mathbf{r}_2$ and $\mathbf{v} = \mathbf{m}\mathbf{G} + \mathbf{s} \cdot \mathbf{r}_2 + \mathbf{e}$, returns $\mathbf{c} = (\mathbf{u}, \mathbf{v})$.

- Decrypt(sk, c): returns $\mathcal{C}$.Decode($\mathbf{v} - \mathbf{u} \cdot \mathbf{y}$).

Fig. 1. Description of the proposal HQC.PKE [2].

A transform [31] is then applied to HQC.PKE to achieve IND-CCA2 for the KEM/DEM version of HQC (see HQC.KEM in Fig. 2). The KEM version can be converted to an IND-CCA2 PKE using generic transforms.

In the description, $\mathcal{G}, \mathcal{H}$ and $\mathcal{K}$ are different hash functions, e.g. SHA512. Also, $\mathcal{E}$ denotes the IND-CPA secure HQC.PKE primitive including randomness input.

The noise term written as $\mathbf{e}' = \mathbf{x} \cdot \mathbf{r}_2 - \mathbf{y} \cdot \mathbf{r}_1 + \mathbf{e}$ is a sparse vector, but not extremely sparse. The decryption is guaranteed to succeed if $\omega(\mathbf{e}')$ is an error that is within the decoding capability of the employed error-correcting code. So the code must be very powerful and be able to correct many errors. In the HQC scheme, the error correcting code with generator matrix $\mathbf{G}$ is the tensor product code $\mathcal{C} = \text{BCH}(n_1, k, \delta) \otimes \mathbb{1}_{n_2}$. This is a powerful code employed to reduce the decryption failure probability. It guarantees to correct any error of weight up to $\delta \cdot (n_2 + 1)/2$, but will most likely also correct errors of somewhat higher weight.

2.3   Parameter Settings

The proposed parameters of different instances of HQC are shown in Table 1. The parameter n is a prime number slightly larger than $n_1 \times n_2$, ω is the weight of the secret and $\omega_\mathbf{r}, \omega_\mathbf{e}$ is the weight of the noise vectors.

- Setup(1^λ): generates the global parameters param $= (n, k, \delta, \omega, \omega_{\mathbf{r}}, \omega_{\mathbf{e}})$. here k will be the length of the symmetric key being exchanged, typically $k = 256$.

- KeyGen(param): exactly as in HQC.PKE.

- Encapsulate(pk): generate $\mathbf{m} \xleftarrow{\$} \mathbb{F}_2^k$, which will serve as the seed to derive the shared key. Derive the randomness $\theta \xleftarrow{\$} \mathcal{G}(\mathbf{m})$. Generate the ciphertext $\mathbf{c} \leftarrow (\mathbf{u}, \mathbf{v}) = \mathcal{E}.\text{Encrypt}(\text{pk}, \mathbf{m}, \theta)$, and derive the symmetric key $K \leftarrow \mathcal{K}(\mathbf{m}, \mathbf{c})$. Let $\mathbf{d} \leftarrow \mathcal{H}(\mathbf{m})$, and send $(\mathbf{c}, \mathbf{d})$.

- Decapsulate(sk,c, d): decrypt $\mathbf{m}' \leftarrow \mathcal{E}.\text{Decrypt}(\text{sk}, \mathbf{c})$, compute $\theta' \leftarrow \mathcal{G}(\mathbf{m}')$, and (re-)encrypt $\mathbf{m}'$ to get $\mathbf{c}' \leftarrow \mathcal{E}.\text{Encrypt}(\text{pk}, \mathbf{m}', \theta')$. If $\mathbf{c} \neq \mathbf{c}'$ or $\mathbf{d} \neq \mathcal{H}(\mathbf{m}')$ then abort. Otherwise, derive the shared key $K \leftarrow \mathcal{K}(\mathbf{m}, \mathbf{c})$.

Fig. 2. Description of the proposal HQC.KEM [2].

Table 1. Proposed parameters for HQC.

	n_1	n_2	n	k	δ	ω	$\omega_{\mathbf{r}} = \omega_{\mathbf{e}}$	Security	p_{fail}
hqc-128-1	796	31	24,677	256	60	67	77	128	$<2^{-128}$
hqc-192-1	766	57	43,669	256	57	101	117	192	$<2^{-128}$
hqc-192-2	766	61	46,747	256	57	101	117	192	$<2^{-192}$
hqc-256-1	766	83	63,587	256	57	133	153	256	$<2^{-128}$
hqc-256-2	796	85	67,699	256	60	133	153	256	$<2^{-192}$
hqc-256-3	796	89	70,853	256	60	133	153	256	$<2^{-256}$

3   Basic Ideas for the Attack

In this section we try to describe the underlying ideas behind the attack and the detailed analysis is done in the following sections. The first step is to find out how we can produce decryption failures and to do that we need to study the details of the decoding procedure. The scheme uses the tensor product code $\mathcal{C} = \text{BCH}(n_1, k, \delta) \otimes \mathbb{1}_{n_2}$ which means that the received vector can be split in n_1 parts each of length n_2. The decoding is done in two steps. First, each subvector of length n_2 corresponding to a repetition code is decoded to a single bit $\{0, 1\}$. This leaves a length n_1 vector which is decoded through a decoder for the BCH code to correct up to δ errors. This means that in order to have an overall decoding error, one has to get at least $\delta + 1$ of the repetition codes to make an individual decoding error. Such an individual error appears if the noise $\mathbf{e}'$ has more ones than zeros in the n_2 positions corresponding to that particular repetition code.

Let us now look at a typical error pattern $\mathbf{e}'$ to be decoded. Since the noise term can be written as $\mathbf{e}' = \mathbf{x} \cdot \mathbf{r}_2 - \mathbf{y} \cdot \mathbf{r}_1 + \mathbf{e}$, almost all nonzero contribution comes from the two product terms. If we for example use the parameters for hqc-256-1 then $\mathbf{x}$ has weight 133, $\mathbf{r}_2$ has weight 153, and the product between them will have weight close to $133 \cdot 153$, say about weight 20000. Adding another

Fig. 3. How decoding is split in two parts.

such error contribution from $\mathbf{y} \cdot \mathbf{r}_1$ of the similar weight results in a typical error vector of weight around 27000 and length 63587. The ones in $\mathbf{e}'$ are distributed roughly with the same probability for all positions thus also roughly with the same probability in each repetition code (Fig. 3).

So how can we increase the overall probability of a decoding error? The idea is that we use a lot of precomputation to test many different messages and look at what error vectors they create (through the hash functions that gives the error vectors in the CCA version). The problem is to figure out what kind of error vectors will increase the overall probability of a decoding error. One answer to this problem is to consider the set of vectors where we have a lot of ones close together in the vector. More specifically, we keep and store only messages for which the generated $\mathbf{r}_2$ vector contains an interval (chunk) of length l_1 containing many ones, say at least l_0 ones. An example of a parameter choice might be $l_1 = 55$ and $l_0 = 38$. Now, let us look at the contribution of $\mathbf{x} \cdot \mathbf{r}_2$ to the error $\mathbf{e}'$. So $\mathbf{x}$ has weight 133, meaning that the result of $\mathbf{x} \cdot \mathbf{r}_2$ is the sum of 133 different rotated versions of $\mathbf{r}_2$. The average distance between ones in $\mathbf{x}$ is almost 500. This means that length l_1 intervals of many ones in the 133 rotated versions of $\mathbf{r}_2$ almost never coincide in positions, but leave (almost) 133 intervals of many ones in the result of $\mathbf{x} \cdot \mathbf{r}_2$. In more detail, a single interval of many ones may either end up completely inside a single repetition code or it will contribute in two adjacent repetition codes. This depends on the exact starting position of the interval of many ones as well as the positions of the ones in the secret $\mathbf{x}$. This is all depicted in Fig. 4, where we can see the top interval of many ones (illustrated as a box) affecting two adjacent repetition codes whereas the second top interval in the figure affects only a single repetition code.

In any case, the result is that the ones in $\mathbf{e}'$ are no longer uniformly distributed, but some repetition codes will have many errors and others very few. Concentrating the errors to a subset of the repetition codes drastically changes the overall probability of a decoding error. Whereas an average error vector has probability much smaller than 2^{-128} of not being correctly decoded, errors of the above form with $l_1 = 55$ and $l_0 = 38$ show an overall decoding error probability of 2^{-14}!

We now assume that we have observed a number of decryption errors by feeding the decryption oracle these special messages and recording their corresponding error vectors generated in the encryption. The second task in the attack is to recover some part of the secret key $\mathbf{x}, \mathbf{y}$. We do that by the following observation. We consider a position i and look at whether it is likely that

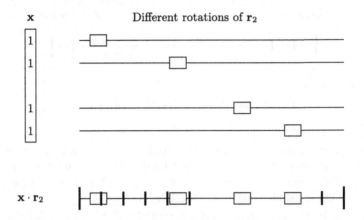

Fig. 4. The appearance of ones in $\mathbf{x} \cdot \mathbf{r}_2$ when $\mathbf{r}_2$ contains an interval of many ones.

$x_i = 1$. If this is the case and an interval of many ones starts at position j for a particular $\mathbf{r}_2$, then we will have a contribution of many ones starting at position $i + j$. Since we got a decryption error it is much more likely that the repetition codes corresponding to position $i + j$ and l_1 positions onwards, will decode in error, compared to the general case.

Now, since the overall error is $\mathbf{e}' = \mathbf{x} \cdot \mathbf{r}_2 - \mathbf{y} \cdot \mathbf{r}_1 + \mathbf{e}$ another observation is that if a repetition code is not decoding correctly, it is likely that the independent noise part $\mathbf{e}$ is "helping out to make a decoding error". If the contribution from the $\mathbf{x} \cdot \mathbf{r}_2$ term for $x_i = 1$ gives a chunk of many ones in a repetition code that is assumed not to decoding correctly, then the corresponding $\mathbf{e}$ values will be more likely to be zero if there is already a one contributed from the interval of many ones. Similarly, the corresponding $\mathbf{e}$ values will be more likely to be one if there is a zero contribution from the interval of many ones, or if the position is outside the interval.

These two observations put together gives us a strategy of examining the Hamming weight of the given $\mathbf{e}$ vector in the repetition codes corresponding to position $i + j$. Basically, if the Hamming weight of these parts taken over many different such $\mathbf{e}$ vectors is following the above observation, then we can come to the conclusion that $x_i = 1$, otherwise we set $x_i = 0$. We come back to the details of this procedure in the next section.

There is some dependence for positions that are closely located, so it is actually a good approach to only establish many positions for which we have $x_i = 0$. Then we can use an information set decoding algorithm to solve for $\mathbf{x}, \mathbf{y}$ using the knowledge from the public key. The complexity of this procedure has very limited complexity.

4   Attack Model and Detailed Steps

We follow the newly-proposed attack using decryption failures adopting the weak-ciphertext attack model from [17], although no assumption on weak keys is used. The attack consists of three main steps. Firstly, we prepare 'weak' ciphertexts with the noise tuple $(\mathbf{r_1}, \mathbf{r_2}, \mathbf{e})$ of a specific form. We then submit these ciphertexts to the decryption oracle and collect the decryption errors that occur. The last step is to perform a statistical analysis (e.g., hypothesis testing) to extract the key information. We will also include classical solving algorithms in code-based cryptography like Information Set Decoding (ISD) to improve the key-recovery efficiency.

4.1   Weak-Ciphertext Preparation

We select a set (denoted $\mathcal{A}$) of 'weak' ciphertexts and the corresponding noise tuples $(\mathbf{r_1}, \mathbf{r_2}, \mathbf{e})$ with $\mathbf{r_2}$ having a consecutive l_1 positions with at least l_0 ones in this chunk. Let A_i denote the event that this consecutive chunk exists and starts from the i-th position. We estimate the probability of this event as

$$\Pr[A_i] = \frac{\binom{w_r}{l_0} \cdot \binom{n-w_r}{l_1-l_0}}{\binom{n}{l_1}}.$$

The overall probability of finding such a chunk in a length n vector, denoted as p, can then be estimated as

$$p = \Pr[\cup_i A_i] \approx \sum_i \Pr[A_i] - \sum_{i,j} \Pr[A_i \cap A_j]. \qquad (2)$$

Thus, we expect that we need p^{-1} computations (hash calls to $\mathcal{G}$) to generate one 'weak' ciphertext with the chosen form. For hqc-256-1, as shown in the second column of Table 2, the precomputation costs differ for different choices of l_1 and l_0. This cost is bounded by 2^{191} if we set $l_1 = 53$ and $l_0 = 29$. Note that even though the precomputation is searching a larger space than allowed in the scheme, if we set $l_1 = 55$ and $l_0 \geq 36$, we include and discuss these parameter choices for the purpose of simulation of parts of the attack.

4.2   Collecting Errors

We send the selected ciphertexts in set $\mathcal{A}$ to the decryption oracle for decryption and store the tuple $(\mathbf{r_1}, \mathbf{r_2}, \mathbf{e})$ for ciphertexts leading to a decryption error. An important task is to estimate the decryption error rate for the chosen parameters.

The Convolution of Probability Distributions. Let $X_i = 1$ be the event that decoding output of the i-th repetition code is erroneous, for $i \in \{0, \dots, n_1 - 1\}$. We denote this event by p_i, i.e., $p_i = \Pr[X_i = 1]$, and thus, the probability $\Pr[X_i = 0]$ is $(1 - p_i)$. Let $\mathcal{D}$ denote the event that the tuple $(\mathbf{r_1}, \mathbf{r_2}, \mathbf{e})$ leads to

Table 2. The estimated decryption error rate (DER) for hqc-256-1. The starting position is 0.

l_1	l_0	$\log_2(p^{-1})$	The DER (in $\log_2(\cdot)$) in estimation
55	38	276	−14.72
55	37	266	−17.65
55	36	256	−20.84
53	29	191	−48.61
63	30	191	−48.03
66	30	188	−49.17
55	26	163	−63.91
45	16	86	−112.6

a decryption error. If we assume that all the X_i's are independent[3], then we can recursively estimate the probability of $\mathcal{D}$ as

$$\Pr[\sum_{i=0}^{n_1-1} X_i > \delta] = p_{n_1-1} \cdot \Pr[\sum_{i=0}^{n_1-2} X_i \geq \delta] + (1 - p_{n_1-1}) \cdot \Pr[\sum_{i=0}^{n_1-2} X_i > \delta]. \quad (3)$$

This method is referred to as the convolution of probability distributions.

The computed decryption error probabilities (DER) for different choices of l_1 and l_0 are shown in the third column of Table 2. We see that for the simulation purpose, the decryption error probability can be as low as 2^{-14} if $l_1 = 55$ and $l_0 = 38$; for a theoretical attack, the decryption error probability is estimated to be $2^{-48.61}$ if $l_1 = 53$ and $l_0 = 29$. The p_i's can be computed and also tested in simulation. The exact calculation of the p_i's for a given error pattern in $\mathcal{A}$ is considered later in the section. In practice, we run a large number of trials to empirically test the values of p_i and then use the convolution of probability distributions to compute the decryption error probabilities (DER). In a later part (see Table 5) we report on testing the accuracy of this estimation approach and obtained simulation results are close to the estimation. This estimation approach is actually a bit conservative from the attacker's viewpoint.

4.3 Statistical Analysis

After collecting all the tuples $(\mathbf{r_1}, \mathbf{r_2}, \mathbf{e})$ that lead to a decryption error, we attempt to recover partial secret key information on $\mathbf{x}$. In this part, we first present the empirical statistical dependence observed for a key recovery attack

---

[3] The independence assumption will lead to a conservative estimation from the attacker's viewpoint. The reason is this assumption can cause a DER estimation smaller than the true value, which fits the results [19,28] on LAC and has been verified by simulation in Table 5.

and develop theoretical estimations on this dependence. The developed theory nicely explains the observed distinguishing property and shows that the property is even stronger when the DER drops. We also discuss techniques and tricks employed in this statistical test step.

Observation. Assume for simplicity that all chunks of many ones in $\mathbf{r_2}$ start in position 0. Our approach to recover partial secret key information is to investigate and compute the frequency of $\{e_i = 1|\mathcal{D}\}$, where $0 \le i \le n_1 n_2 - 1$ and $\mathcal{D}$ means that the tuple $(\mathbf{r_1}, \mathbf{r_2}, \mathbf{e})$ leads to a decryption error.

The basic observation is that if $x_{i_0} = 1$, then with high probability (due to the sparsity of $\mathbf{x}$), only one nonzero entry is in the interval $[n_2 \cdot t, n_2 \cdot (t+1))$, for $t = \lfloor i_0/n_2 \rfloor$. Then $\#\{e_i = 1|\mathcal{D}\}$ for $i \in [i_0, i_0 + l_1]$ is smaller than for the values corresponding to the other positions in the interval $[n_2 \cdot t, n_2 \cdot (t+1))$. We can observe no difference (i.e., behave like the random) for an interval $\mathcal{I}$ corresponding to a repetition code without an i_0 such that $i_0 \in \mathcal{I}$ and $x_{i_0} = 1$. We refer to the prior as *CASE I* and the latter as *CASE II*.

The controlled window of length l_1 can be divided into two halves and contributes to two consecutive but different repetition decoding intervals. In this case we can still observe these (possibly weaker) frequency differences.

Visual Illustration from Experiments. This phenomenon is visually illustrated in Fig. 5, where the simulation results for targeting the hqc-256-1 parameters by setting $l_1 = 55$ and $l_0 = 38$ are provided. The DER is simulated to be $2^{-14.3}$. We select at random two CASE I repetition code intervals and two CASE II repetition code intervals, which are plotted in the top two sub-figures and the bottom two sub-figures in Fig. 5, respectively. In the first two plots we re-order the positions by putting the length l_1 controlled window at the beginning. We then derive four length $n_2 - l_1$ vectors with entry i being the summation of l_1 consecutive positions starting from i in the re-ordered repetition code intervals. One can in this way visually observe the differences of CASE I and CASE II in the repetition code intervals.

This figure shows that one can recover key information if a sufficient number of decryption failures are provided. The above presented distinguisher, however, is far from optimal. We will now present a better maximum likelihood distinguisher that will also give an estimate of the required number of decryption failures.

Theoretical Estimation on $\Pr[e_j = 1|\mathcal{D}]$. Let us examine $\Pr[e_j = 1|\mathcal{D}]$ for $0 \le j \le n_1 n_2 - 1$ through

$$\Pr[e_j = 1|\mathcal{D}] = \Pr[X_i = 1|\mathcal{D}]\Pr[e_j = 1|X_i = 1, \mathcal{D}] + \Pr[X_i = 0|\mathcal{D}]\Pr[e_j = 1|X_i = 0, \mathcal{D}],$$

where $X_i = 1$ represents the event that the i-th repetition decoding is erroneous, and vice versa, for $i = \lfloor j/n_2 \rfloor$. We denote the i-th repetition code interval as $\mathcal{I}_i$, where $\mathcal{I}_i = [i \cdot n_2, (i+1) \cdot n_2)$.

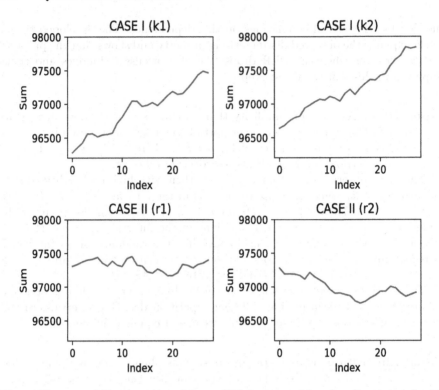

Fig. 5. The sum of l_1 consecutive $\#\{e_i = 1|\mathcal{D}\}$ in a repetition decoding interval with re-ordering. The top two sub-figures plot CASE I intervals and the last two figures plot the opposite case. $735,000$ decryption errors are collected with DER $2^{-14.3}$. The CASE I and CASE II intervals could be distinguished.

We assume that the events $(e_j = 1|X_i = 1)$ and $(\mathcal{D}|X_i = 1)$ are independent, as e_j roughly only depends on X_i and not any other X_j for $j \neq i$. Then we derive that

$$\Pr[e_j = 1|X_i = 1, \mathcal{D}] = \frac{\Pr[e_j = 1, \mathcal{D}|X_i = 1]}{\Pr[\mathcal{D}|X_i = 1]} \approx \Pr[e_j = 1|X_i = 1],$$

Also, $\Pr[e_j = 1|X_i = 0, \mathcal{D}] \approx \Pr[e_j = 1|X_i = 0]$. Then we can rewrite as

$$\begin{aligned}
\Pr[e_j = 1|\mathcal{D}] \approx & \Pr[X_i = 1|\mathcal{D}]\Pr[e_j = 1|X_i = 1] \\
& + \Pr[X_i = 0|\mathcal{D}]\Pr[e_j = 1|X_i = 0] \\
= & \Pr[X_i = 1|\mathcal{D}](\Pr[e_j = 1|X_i = 1] - \Pr[e_j = 1|X_i = 0]) \\
& + \Pr[e_j = 1|X_i = 0].
\end{aligned}$$

We note that

$$\Pr[X_i = 1|\mathcal{D}] = \frac{\Pr[X_i = 1, \mathcal{D}]}{\Pr[\mathcal{D}]} = \frac{p_i \cdot \Pr[\sum_{j \neq i} X_j \geq \delta]}{\Pr[\mathcal{D}]}.$$

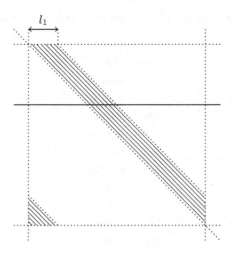

Fig. 6. The matrix representation of $\mathbf{r}_1$ in case that the controlled interval starts from Position 0.

We also know that

$$\Pr[e_j = 1, X_i = 1] = \Pr[e_j = 1, \sum_{k \in \mathcal{I}_i} e'_k > \delta_r]$$

$$= \Pr[e_j = 1, e'_j = 1] \cdot \Pr[\sum_{k \neq j, k \in \mathcal{I}_i} e'_k > \delta_r - 1]$$

$$+ \Pr[e_j = 1, e'_j = 0] \cdot \Pr[\sum_{k \neq j, k \in \mathcal{I}_i} e'_k > \delta_r]$$

and

$$\Pr[e_j = 1 | X_i = 1] = \frac{\Pr[e_j = 1, X_i = 1]}{\Pr[e_j = 1, X_i = 1] + \Pr[e_j = 0, X_i = 1]}. \tag{4}$$

We can analogously compute $\Pr[e_j = 1 | X_i = 0]$ as

$$\Pr[e_j = 1 | X_i = 0] = \frac{\Pr[e_j = 1] - \Pr[e_j = 1, X_i = 1]}{1 - \Pr[X_i = 1]}, \tag{5}$$

where $\Pr[e_j = 1] = \omega_{\mathbf{e}}/n$.

Thus, all the intermediate probability values can be obtained via recursively computing the convolution of probability distributions if p_i, $\Pr[e_j = 1, e'_j = 1]$, $\Pr[e_j = 1, e'_j = 0]$, and $\Pr[e'_k = 1]$ are known. We next show how to estimate p_i, $\Pr[e_j = 1, e'_j = 1]$, $\Pr[e_j = 1, e'_j = 0]$, and $\Pr[e'_k = 1]$.

Computation of Probabilities p_i: Firstly, the probability p_i can also be computed using the convolution of probability distributions of $\Pr[e_j = 1] : j \in \mathcal{I}_i$, but a simpler strategy is to test the values experimentally, since these probability

Table 3. The computed $\Pr[X_i = 1 | \mathcal{D}]$ from the simulation results on hqc-256-1 with $l_1 = 53$ and $l_0 = 29$.

l'	Index	$\Pr[X_i = 1 | \mathcal{D}]$
0	25	0.00506
	71	0.00504
	166	0.00504
	250	0.00502
	365	0.00500
	590	0.00506
53	68	0.3089
	127	0.3087
	186	0.3089
	356	0.3089
	482	0.3089
	695	0.3089

values are relatively significant. An important observation shown in Table 3 is that the computed $\Pr[X_i = 1 | \mathcal{D}]$ is a function of the length l' of the controlled window in the repetition code interval. Here $l' = 0$ corresponds to the random case and $l' = l_1$ corresponds to having a full length l_1 chunk. Intermediate values appear when a chunk of many ones is split in two different repetition code intervals. In this table, the computed $\Pr[X_i = 1 | \mathcal{D}]$ from the simulation results regarding the hqc-256-1 parameters, where $l_1 = 53$ and $l_0 = 29$ and the controlled interval starting form position 0. We choose at random 6 repetition code intervals with controlled length 0 and repetition code intervals with the full controlled length 53. The second column shows the index of the selected repetition code interval and the last column shows the computed probability $\Pr[X_i = 1 | \mathcal{D}]$. We see the computed probabilities are close in the same group and have a huge gap between the two groups with different l'.

Computation of Remaining Probabilities: Secondly, with assumptions of certain independence, if the contribution from the marked strip in Fig. 6 is correctly guessed, then one can apply similar arguments as Proposition 1.4.1 in [2] to derive closed formulas to estimate the probabilities $\Pr[e'_k = 1]$, $\Pr[e_j = 1, e'_j = 1]$, and $\Pr[e_j = 1, e'_j = 0]$.

Proposition 1 (Proposition 1.4.1 in [2]). *Let* $\mathbf{x} = (X_0, \ldots, X_{n-1})$ *(resp.* $\mathbf{r} = (R_0, \ldots, R_{n-1})$*) be a random vector where* X_i *(resp.* R_i*) are independent Bernoulli variables of parameters* p *(resp.* $p_{\mathbf{r}}$*),* $\Pr[X_i = 1] = p$ *and* $\Pr[R_i = 1] = p_{\mathbf{r}}$*. Assuming* $\mathbf{x}$ *and* $\mathbf{r}$ *are independent, and denoting* $\mathbf{z} = \mathbf{x} \cdot \mathbf{r} = (Z_0, \ldots, Z_{n-1})$ *as defined as the multiplication of* $\mathbf{x}$ *and* $\mathbf{r}$ *in* $\mathcal{R}$*, we have*

$$\hat{p} = \Pr[Z_k = 1] = \frac{1}{2} - \frac{1}{2}(1 - 2pp_{\mathbf{r}})^n. \tag{6}$$

Table 4. The simulated probabilities v.s. the estimated probabilities on hqc-256-1. The starting position is 0. The distinguishing property is stronger when the DER level drops.

l_1	l_0	In estimation			In simulation			The DER level
		p_{random}	p_{high}	p_{low}	p_{random}	p_{high}	p_{low}	(in $\log_2(\cdot)$)
55	38	0.002406	0.002412	0.002401	0.002404	0.002460	0.002347	-14
55	36	0.002406	0.002419	0.002393	0.002404	0.002468	0.002340	-20
53	29	0.002408	0.002446	0.002369	$-$	$-$	$-$	-48

Thus, the contribution of $\mathbf{y} \cdot \mathbf{r}_2$ can be modeled as a Bernoulli random variable with probability $\hat{p}$. For a position j, if we guess the sub-vector $\mathbf{x}_{part}$ of $\mathbf{x}$ corresponding to the controlled interval of length l_1 shown in the marked strip, its contribution denoted Υ_{part} to e'_j is then known. Let ω_{part} be the weight of $\mathbf{x}_{part}$, we then model the position in the remaining sub-vector of $\mathbf{x}$ as a Bernoulli random variable with probability $\frac{\omega - \omega_{part}}{n - l_1}$. We model the position in the unmarked part of $\mathbf{r}_1$ as a Bernoulli random variable with probability $\frac{\omega_r - l_0}{n - l1}$. The contribution of $\mathbf{x} \cdot \mathbf{r}_1 - \Upsilon_{part}$ is modeled as a Bernoulli random variable with probability $\tilde{p}$, where

$$\tilde{p} = \frac{1}{2} - \frac{1}{2}(1 - 2 \cdot \frac{\omega - \omega_{part}}{n - l_1} \cdot \frac{\omega_r - l_0}{n - l_1})^{n - l_1}.$$

We derive the following proposition.

Proposition 2. *We have that,*

$$\Pr[e'_k - \Upsilon_{part} = 0, e_k = 1] = \frac{\omega_e}{n} \cdot (\hat{p} \cdot (1 - \tilde{p}) + (1 - \hat{p}) \cdot \tilde{p}), \quad (7)$$

$$\Pr[e'_k - \Upsilon_{part} = 1, e_k = 1] = \frac{\omega_e}{n} \cdot (\hat{p} \cdot \tilde{p} + (1 - \hat{p}) \cdot (1 - \tilde{p})), \quad (8)$$

$$\Pr[e'_k - \Upsilon_{part} = 1, e_k = 0] = \left(1 - \frac{\omega_e}{n}\right) \cdot (\hat{p} \cdot (1 - \tilde{p}) + (1 - \hat{p}) \cdot \tilde{p}), \quad (9)$$

and

$$\Pr[e'_k - \Upsilon_{part} = 0, e_k = 0] = \left(1 - \frac{\omega_e}{n}\right) \cdot (\hat{p} \cdot \tilde{p} + (1 - \hat{p}) \cdot (1 - \tilde{p})). \quad (10)$$

Putting all the formulas together, we can compute the probability $\Pr[e_j = 1|\mathcal{D}]$ in the different cases. The distinguishing property can then be depicted as in Fig. 7. We plotted two repetition decoding intervals, a CASE II interval at the right with a probability of $\Pr[e_j = 1|\mathcal{D}]$ denoted by p_{random} and a CASE I interval at the left. For the latter, for the position outside a window of length l_1 corresponding to the controlled section, we know that the contribution of Υ_{part} is always 0, thus showing a higher probability of $\Pr[e_j = 1|\mathcal{D}]$ than p_{random} denoted by p_{high}; otherwise, the contribution Υ_{part} can be either 0 or 1, showing a higher or lower probability of $\Pr[e_j = 1|\mathcal{D}]$, respectively. We denote the lower probability of $\Pr[e_j = 1|\mathcal{D}]$ by p_{low}.

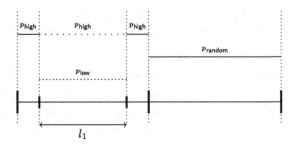

Fig. 7. Graphic illustration of the distinguishing property.

Example 1: We apply the theoretical analysis on hqc-256-1 with results as shown in Table 4. When the starting position is 0, $l_1 = 55$ and $l_0 = 38$, for a CASE II repetition decoding window, we estimate that $\Pr[e_j = 1|\mathcal{D}]$ is 0.002406 (p_{random}); for a CASE I repetition decoding window, we estimate that $\Pr[e_j = 1|\mathcal{D}]$ is 0.002401 (p_{low}) for the case $\Upsilon_{\text{part}} = 1$, and $\Pr[e_j = 1|\mathcal{D}]$ is 0.002412 (p_{high}) for the case $\Upsilon_{\text{part}} = 0$. The difference (or called bias) between p_{high} and p_{low} becomes larger for parameters with lower estimated decryption error rates (say $l_0 = 29$).

The remaining problem is to correctly guess the contribution Υ_{part} from the marked strip, which is a hypothesis testing problem revealing partial information on the secret key $\mathbf{x}$.

Maximum Likelihood Ratio Test. We describe the maximum likelihood ratio test to correctly guess the contribution Υ_{part}. We guess a small chunk of $\mathbf{x}$ and then obtain the corresponding Υ_{part}. We then group the positions according to its guessed contribution Υ_{part} and to decide if the resulted distribution is more close to the theoretically derived one, i.e., with a high $\Pr[e_j = 1|\mathcal{D}]$ for $\Upsilon_{\text{part}} = 0$ and withe a low $\Pr[e_j = 1|\mathcal{D}]$ for $\Upsilon_{\text{part}} = 1$, or more close to the random case (i.e. CASE II).

In the implementation, we test bit-by-bit, i.e., running through all the positions of $\mathbf{x}$ and for each position, using maximum likelihood test to decide if that position should be zero, under the assumption that the rest positions are all zero. This approach is definitely the simplest strategy, and is demonstrated to be efficient in simulation. There exist many other possible approaches for this statistical test step.

Double Distinguishing. In the previous discussion, we prepare the weak ciphertext set $\mathcal{A}$ whose $\mathbf{r_2}$ part has a consecutive l_1 positions with l_0 ones, to recover partial information of $\mathbf{x}$. Also, we can prepare another set (denoted $\mathcal{A}'$) of weak ciphertexts whose $\mathbf{r_1}$ part has a consecutive l_1 positions with l_0 ones, to recover partial information of $\mathbf{y}$. Due to the 2^{64} constraint on the number of the submitted ciphertexts, we let $\mathcal{A}'$ and $\mathcal{A}$ be both of size 2^{63}. One call to the encryption function will return both the $\mathbf{r_1}$ and $\mathbf{r_2}$ parts. Thus, if 2^γ encryptions are required to detect a ciphertext in $\mathcal{A}$ (or $\mathcal{A}'$) with the desired pattern, we only need $2^{\gamma+63}$ encryption calls in total to prepare the two sets.

4.4 Information Set Decoding

This step will be applied if no full key-recovery is achieved after the statistical analysis. The basic idea is that, with the partial information obtained from the statistical analysis step, recovering the secret key $\mathsf{sk} = (\mathbf{x}, \mathbf{y})$ from the public key $\mathsf{pk} = (\mathbf{h}, \mathbf{s} = \mathbf{x} + \mathbf{h} \cdot \mathbf{y})$ is a simple task.

To be more specific, if one knows from the previous step the l positions in $\mathbf{x}$ and also l positions in $\mathbf{y}$ that are zero with the highest probability, then a new decoding problem with code length $2l$ and dimension n can be derived. This problem can be much easier to solve as the chosen positions are rarely non-zero.

The plain ISD [40] algorithm works very well if the guessed positions are reliable. This process could possibly be accelerated by applying advanced information set decoding algorithms like Stern's algorithm [43] and BJMM [11]. In addition, the previous hypothesis testing step provides soft information of the secret key, so the ISD variant with bit reliability [39] and the soft-Stern algorithm [23, 24] could be employed to accelerate this post-processing step.

4.5 Simulation Results on hqc-256-1

We in this part present implementation results on hqc-256-1. In the later analysis we will stick with the empirical distributions from the largest simulation we conducted. This analysis is conservative from an attacker's viewpoint, since the distinguishing property is stronger when the DER drops.

The Tested Bias. We have tested the different probabilities of p_{high}, p_{low}, and p_{random}, computed in the previous parts. The comparison between the theoretical results and the simulated results is shown in Table 4. We could see that for a fixed l_1 (here $l_1 = 55$), when the value of l_0 drops (meaning that the precomputation cost drops and also the decryption error probability), the differences (also named bias) between two of the probabilities increase. Most importantly, the simulated bias is much larger than then estimated bias. For instance, we observed a gap of 0.000055 between p_{high} and p_{random}, while only of 0.000006 in the theoretical estimation, when setting $l_1 = 55$ and $l_0 = 38$.

This table (Table 4) verifies our theoretical analysis, i.e., explaining the reason of observing the different probabilities in CASE I and CASE II, though the real bias is much larger than the one computed. Due to the crypt-analytic nature of this work, we want to upper-bound the complexity of the newly proposed attack. In the later analysis, thus, we make a conservative choice by employing the empirical distributions obtained from the largest simulation we conducted. Note that these chosen probabilities ($p_{\mathsf{random}}, p_{\mathsf{high}}, p_{\mathsf{low}}$) correspond to the case that the decryption error probability is about 2^{-22}. Though the true bias when launching the attack for parameters (of $l_1 = 53$ and $l_0 = 29$) with decryption

Table 5. The simulated DER v.s. the estimated DER (with starting position 0).

l_1	l_0	The DER (in $\log_2(\cdot)$) in estimation	The DER (in $\log_2(\cdot)$) in simulation
55	38	-14.72	-14.3
55	37	-17.65	-17.2
55	36	-20.84	-20.3

error probability of about 2^{-48} is beyond our capability to simulate, it will be larger than the one in our simulation.

The Accuracy of the Convolution Method. We have tested the accuracy of the estimation using the convolution of probability distributions as shown in Table 5. The estimation is always slightly lower than the simulated decryption error rate, caused by the weak dependence between different positions. We see that the ratio between the simulated DER and the estimated DER becomes larger when the error rate is smaller, and it is already $2^{0.54}$ when the DER is about 2^{-20}. We expect to have the ratio to be 2 when considering the case that the DER is smaller than 2^{-48}.

Estimation from Different Starting Positions. We have observed that the estimated decryption error rates fluctuate slightly if the starting position differs. The mean over all starting positions is $2^{-48.98}$ for $l_1 = 53$ and $l_0 = 29$. Since the estimation is slightly conservative, we could expect to collect $2^{64-49+1} = 2^{16}$ decryption errors in practice.

A Full Test. We run simulation to demonstrate that 2^{16} decryption errors, i.e., 2^{15} decryption errors for each test when employing the double distinguishing procedure, are enough for a full-key recovery with complexity bounded by the 2^{64} online decryption oracle queries. As discussed before, if one launches the attack with decryption error probability of about 2^{-48}, the bias will be larger and lead to a reduced attack complexity.

In the simulation, we pick $l_1 = 40$ and $l_0 = 34$ leading to a simulated decryption error probability of $2^{-21.8}$. As it is slightly smaller than $2^{-20.3}$, the simulated decryption error probability when setting $l_1 = 55$ and $l_0 = 36$, it is reasonable to have the bias of the simulated probabilities $(p_{\mathsf{random}}, p_{\mathsf{high}}, p_{\mathsf{low}}) = (0.2404, 0.2467, 0.2333)$ also slightly larger. We then roughly compute the divergence, which is $2^{-13.17}$, between the probability distributions over an interval of length 83 in CASE I and CASE II. Since we only need to detect positions that are highly probable to be 0 and the noise vector is very sparse, the sample number 2^{15} is theoretically large enough.

We test the bits of the secret vector $\mathbf{x}$ and assume that it works for $\mathbf{y}$ as well since the double distinguishing procedure just repeats the same test. To be specific, we run $2^{36.8}$ encryptions using randomly generated ciphertexts with the r_2 part having the desired pattern. We then obtain the likelihood that one position of x is zero by the bit-by-bit test. It is interesting to see that in the 46875 most reliable positions that are decided to be zero, only 22 positions are actually one, and these positions all have a non-zero neighbor which falsifies the assumption of our test, i.e., only one bit is one and the rest are all zero. A test can be more efficient if it can handle in a smarter manner the close-by non-zero pairs in the secret.

Since only one position error occurs in the 16056 most reliable positions, we could have 14500 error-free positions effortlessly. Assuming that we have the same test result for the y vector, we then need to solve a new decoding problem with code-length 64750, dimension 35587, and the error weight 44. This new problem can be solved with complexity 2^{50} Gaussian Eliminations, by using the plain ISD algorithm. The overall complexity of the post-processing can be bounded by 2^{57} Gaussian Eliminations, which is negligible compared with the cost of the online decryption oracle calls.

We also test that the post-processing complexity increases to 2^{165} Gaussian Eliminations if the number of decryption errors is reduced by a factor of 6.

4.6   Summarizing the Complexity of Attacking hqc-256-1

We summarize the attack on hqc-256-1. Firstly, if the attacker chooses the attaching parameters $l_1 = 53$ and $l_0 = 29$, then he will obtain 2^{16} decryption errors after sending out 2^{64} decryption oracles calls, i.e., 2^{15} errors for each test when the double distinguishing procedure are applied. We then in simulation test that this amount of decryption errors are sufficient for a full key recovery.

Note that in the above analysis, we employ the bias tested empirically from simulations with decryption error rate of only 2^{-22}, which is stronger in the attacking scenario with decryption error rate of 2^{-48}. Unlike the precomputation phase and the online decryption phase, the statistical analysis phase and the post-processing phase using the ISD algorithms require computational costs that are sensitive to the bias. Though the current complexity number claimed is already below the cost of the online phase, the true cost should be even smaller since it drops drastically if the bias increases. This trend has been well verified in the simulation.

We conclude that 2^{16} decryption errors are enough to correct a number of entries in x and y so that the full key can be recovered in a later ISD step with complexity negligible to the 2^{64} online decryption requests. Thus, the complexity of this CCA attack on hqc-256-1 can be estimated as 2^{64} online decryption requests, after one large precomputation of 2^{254}.

If we remove the constraint that an attack can only submit 2^{64} ciphertexts for decryption, the precomputation cost can be lower. The precomputation cost for one ciphertext and its corresponding decryption error rate are shown in Table 2. Since the bias will be even stronger when the DER becomes smaller, 2^{16} decryption errors are more than sufficient in these parameter settings. If an attacker is allowed to submit 2^{80} decryption requests, then the precomputation

Table 6. The trade-off between the precomputation cost and the number of online decryption oracle queries for hqc-256-1. We assume that 2^{16} decryption failures are sufficient for a full-key recovery.

l_1	l_0	Online DOQs (in $\log_2(\cdot)$)	Precomputation cost (in $\log_2(\cdot)$)
53	29	64	254
55	26	80	242
45	16	128	213

cost can drop to 2^{242} when setting $l_1 = 55$ and $l_0 = 26$. The cost even drops to 2^{213} if 2^{128} ciphertexts are allowed to be decrypted online. We summarize the trade-off between the precomputation cost and the number of online decryption oracle queries (DOQs) in Table 6, when assuming that 2^{16} decryption failures are sufficient for a full-key recovery.

When the Overall Complexity Includes the Precomputation Cost. In the previous analysis, we ensure the complexity of the online querying and the post-processing to be bounded by the 2^{64} decryption oracle calls. This cost also bounds the whole attacking complexity since the large precomputation only needs to be done once and therefore should not be included in the attacking complexity of one particular attack. We now consider a different optimization goal to optimize the complexity including the precomputation cost. Thus, the attacker could employ a heavier post-processing to reduce the precomputation cost.

As stated in Sect. 4.5, we tested that one could reduce the required number of decryption errors by a factor of 6 and still kept the post-processing complexity far below 2^{220}. We then select $(l_1, l_0) = (61, 29)$ and estimate the DER to be $2^{-51.5}$ by the convolution method. We obtain enough decryption errors if allowing 2^{64} decryption oracle calls, and the corresponding precomputation cost is 2^{248} due to the double distinguishing procedure.

In Table 4, we see that the simulated bias is larger than the estimated bias. We can extrapolate the distribution when the DER is close to 2^{-50} if a simple model where p_{random} is almost unchanged and $p_{\mathsf{T}}^{\mathsf{sim}} \approx p_{\mathsf{T}}^{\mathsf{esti}} + \delta$ are adopted. Here $\mathsf{T} \in \{\mathsf{high}, \mathsf{low}\}$, $p_{\mathsf{T}}^{\mathsf{sim}}$ means the simulated p_{T} and $p_{\mathsf{T}}^{\mathsf{esti}}$ means the estimated p_{T}. By this simple model, we could select $(l_1, l_0) = (63, 29)$ and give a sharper estimation that the precomputation cost of 2^{246} could be enough for a full key-recovery.

Comparing with AES256 in the TMTO Model. We emphasize the practical relevance of ensuring the complexity in the real attacking phase to be bounded by the 2^{64} online decryption oracle queries. In this case, a large precomputation is done and the real-time complexity T and the memory constraint M can be set to be 2^{64}. Therefore, by splitting the cost into the precomputation and the online parts, a natural model to compare with is the famous Hellman's

Table 7. The estimated decryption failure probability.

	l_1	l_0	$\log_2(p^{-1})$	The DER (in $\log_2(\cdot)$) in estimation
hqc-128-1	20	16	110	-46.25
hqc-192-1	41	24	157	-47.56
hqc-192-2	50	28	187	-48.36

time-memory trade-off (TMTO) attack on block ciphers [30]. It is well-known that the trade-off relationship for Hellman's TMTO attack is

$$TM^2 = 2^{2\lambda},$$

where T is the time complexity, M is the memory complexity, and λ is the claimed security level. It can be easily checked that, for our attack on hqc-256-1, the value of TM^2 is much smaller than 2^{512}.

NIST classified the range of the security strengths from symmetric cryptographic primitives like AES (see [1]). We conclude, also from the perspective of time-memory trade-off attacks, that hqc-256-1 cannot provide sufficient security compared with block ciphers such as AES256. Similar discussions on several other HQC parameter sets will be presented in the next section.

5 On Other HQC Parameters

Comparing with AES in the TMTO Model. We adopt the assumption that 2^{16} decryption errors – for the case that the decryption error probability is close to 2^{-48} – are sufficient for recovering the key with complexity negligible to the 2^{64} online decryption oracle calls, as we discussed in the previous section. This assumption for hqc-192-1 was verified in simulation. Table 7 shows the estimated DER from the convolution of probability distributions for three HQC parameter sets, hqc-128-1, hqc-192-1, and hqc-192-2. For all the three parameter sets, it is possible to attack with complexity bounded by 2^{64} online decryption oracle calls. We can set the time and memory constraints to be 2^{64} and the new attacks are much better than Hellman's TMTO relationship for a block cipher.

Thus, we similarly claim that all the three parameter sets cannot provide sufficient security regarding the TMTO attacks.

When the Precomputation Can Be Amortized. The precomputation is excluded from the time complexity constraint T in the TMTO model. We could consider a different model of attacking more keys and amortizing the precomputation complexity. In other words, the precomputation is still done once and never again; the attacker then use the precomputed weak ciphertexts to attack all the public keys once the HQC cryptosystem is deployed. If HQC is used for a very long period, we could assume that the attacker can have 2^{64} public keys to target. His goal is to recover all the keys with complexity below $2^{64+\lambda}$, where λ is the claimed security level. If so, the amortized complexity is below 2^{λ} for recovering one key. Moreover, the memory cost for storing the precomputed noise seeds is also amortized.

The idea of attacking many keys for a lower RAM and precomputation cost than attacking each key separately was originally discussed by Hellman, also in his seminal work [30]. Note that this model is different from the usual multi-target model where only one key among the 2^{64} keys needs to be recovered, whose counterpart for block ciphers (e.g., AES) is discussed as time/memory/data trade-off attacks in [15] for recovering one out of many possible keys.

The previous section shows that hqc-256-1 can be solved with 2^{254} precomputation, which can be amortized to 2^{190} for recovering 2^{64} keys in the new model. Due to the double distinguishing procedure, we see from Table 7 that the precomputation costs for hqc-128-1, hqc-192-1 and hqc-192-2 are $2^{110+63=173}$, 2^{220}, and 2^{250}, respectively. If 2^{64} keys are attacked in this model, the amortized precomputation complexity can be estimated as 2^{109}, 2^{156}, and 2^{186}, respectively, each of which is below its claimed security level. If one makes an extreme assumption that there is an infinite number of HQC keys to attack, then the complexity per key is only 2^{64}, dominated by that of the online attacking phase.

Experiments. We tested our assumption for hqc-192-1 in simulation that 2^{16} decryption errors are sufficient in our attack scenario. For the ease of simulation, we also select parameters leading to a DER close to 2^{-20}. Firstly, we have detected a stronger bias for hqc-192-1, e.g., the absolution value of $(p_{high} - p_{random})$ is almost twice as large as the simulated value for hqc-256-1. We then collected 2^{15} decryption errors and performed a full test similar to the version described in Sect. 4.5. As expected, the experimental results are even better, and the post-processing complexity is estimated to be less than 2^{49} Gaussian Eliminations using the plain ISD.

We also tested the accuracy of the convolution method by running $2^{37.3}$ encryptions. The simulated DER is $2^{-19.29}$, larger than the estimated DER of $2^{-20.55}$ by a factor of about $2^{1.3}$. In this sense, our attack complexity estimation is conservative and the actual complexity could be slightly lower.

6   Discussion and Countermeasures

In [4], NIST commented on HQC that "HQC presents a strong argument that its decryption failure rate is low enough to obtain chosen ciphertext security. This is the strongest argument, at present, of CCA security among the second-round candidate code-based cryptosystems, where information set decoding is the limiting attack for both private key recovery and message recovery (BIKE, HQC, and LEDAcrypt)." The newly proposed attack partly proves and disproves these comments at least for certain parameter sets.

From one perspective, we do not falsify the designers' claim on the DER analysis (for instance, we do not break their claim that the averaged decryption error probability (DER) is below 2^{-128} for hqc-256-1)[4]. Our experiments to test the accuracy of the convolution method can be treated as a partial verification that the error-correcting implementation in HQC matches its theoretical estimation, i.e., the correlation among positions is much weaker (than that in LAC [19,28]).

On the other hand, our attack shows that the (CCA) security claim of HQC is problematic. In the NIST setting – with only 2^{64} online chosen ciphertext submission and only one public key is assumed – the proposed parameters of hqc-256-1 with DER below 2^{-128} is insufficient to ensure the claimed CCA security level. One should consider parameter settings with even lower DER. The problem becomes even more severe in the model where more keys are assumed and the precomputation cost can be amortized.

Secure Parameters. The current attack version does not affect the security claim of hqc-256-2 and hqc-256-3.

Protection. The attacks on hqc-128-1, hqc-192-1 and hqc-192-2 with amortized precomputation cost can be thwarted by employing the multi-target protection technique, i.e., using $\mathcal{G}(pk, m)$ rather than only $\mathcal{G}(m)$ where $\mathcal{G}$ is a hash function, in the random noise generation process. We suggest the designers to include this technique in a later version. For the highest security level, we suggest to use the other parameter settings, hqc-256-2 and hqc-256-3, that are invulnerable to the new attacks.

Not a Weak-Key Attack. Note that the current attack version includes no weak-key analysis, which has been proven a big threat [28] to the LAC [34] scheme. We leave this problem for further research.

More Discussions on the Attack Models. In this paper, we have discussed the attack with three different models, i.e., the NIST setting, the model that the precomputation cost can be amortized, and the TMTO model that the precomputation cost is excluded from the trade-off formula. The last two models are of practical relevance.

To be specific, the precomputation cost is done only once and is done *before* the adversary gets a target to attack. It can be used for all targets in the future. Later the adversary may get one or many targets to attack and the online complexity to find the key is only 2^{64}. Also, the targeted keys can be in different HQC systems. We see that the second model and the TMTO model are not the same as a multitarget attack model in general.

---

[4] Actually, by computing the convolution of distributions, we estimate the decryption error rates for the selected keys in simulation to be 2^{-163} for hqc-192-1 and 2^{-151} for hqc-256-1, which supports their official claim of DER smaller than 2^{-128}. Since the gap between the two estimation method (2^{-151} v.s. 2^{-128}) is large, it may be too conservative to only multiply a factor of 2 to adjust DER estimation value in Sect. 4.5.

The TMTO attacks are not considered in the current NIST PQC framework but could be considered relevant because if precomputation is for free, a TMTO attack is the best known attack on all versions of HQC (and other NIST candidates), by attacking the random seed to public key setup. In such a case the NIST security definition would relate to a generic TMTO attack instead of a simple exhaustive key search.

It is stated in the NIST submission requirements that "Any attack that breaks the relevant security definition must require computational resources comparable to or greater than those required for key search on a block cipher with a 128-bit key (e.g. AES128)", and NIST goes on "any attack must require computational resources comparable to or greater than the stated threshold, with respect to ALL metrics that NIST deems to be potentially relevant to practical security". Similar requirements are explicitly stated for other security levels. Thus, if NIST considers the TMTO attack model to be a relevant metric, then hqc-128-1, hqc-192-1, and hqc-192-2 are all affected.

7   Concluding Remarks

We have presented a new CCA attack on the HQC proposal that has advanced to the second round in the NIST post-quantum cryptography standardization project. For hqc-256-1, the secret key can be recovered with complexity 2^{248} estimated by using simulation data (or 2^{246} using an extrapolation model), if only 2^{64} online decryption oracle calls are submitted. This analysis questions the security claim of hqc-256-1 in the NIST setting. Moreover, we could bound the online and post-processing complexity to 2^{64} online decryption oracle calls, if a large precomputation of 2^{254} is included. The precomputation cost needs to be done only once and can be smaller if more decryption oracle calls are allowed. We also presented attacks on hqc-128-1, hqc-192-1, and hqc-192-2 with amortized precomputation complexity below the claimed security levels, respectively, if multiple keys are assumed. Compared with AES in the TMTO attack model, all the four parameter sets, hqc-128-1, hqc-192-1, hqc-192-2, and hqc-256-1 are insufficient for providing security w.r.t. the claimed security levels. There are safe parameter choices like hqc-256-2 and hqc-256-3.

We present this attack version to demonstrate the vulnerability of the broken HQC parameter settings; the attack, however, can be further optimized. Firstly, employing better ISD algorithms with bit reliability like the Soft-Stern [23,24] will allow reduced post-processing complexity. Secondly, performing larger implementation will lead to a more accurate complexity estimation with a smaller complexity number, as the bias will be stronger if the error rate becomes even lower. Thirdly, a more sophisticated distinguisher better dealing with the close-by ones would reduce the required number of errors, thereby reducing the attack complexity further. Last, one could design a more powerful weak-key version similar to the attack [28] on LAC, which only works for a small fraction of keys.

It is interesting to apply similar ideas to other proposals in the NIST PQC project, e.g., the rank-based proposal Rollo [6]. This attacking approach can be generally applied to code-based primitives using the tensor product codes built from BCH codes and the repetition codes. This error-correcting scheme is also employed in Lepton [44], a round-1 candidate in the NIST PQC project. The attack may need to be adjusted when considering other coding implementations, which would be interesting for future research.

Acknowledgments. The authors would like to thank the anonymous reviewers from Asiacrypt 2020 for their helpful comments. This work was supported in part by the Swedish Research Council (Grant No. 2019-04166), by the Swedish Foundation for Strategic Research (Grant No. RIT17-0005), and by the Norwegian Research Council (Grant No. 247742/070). The computations/simulations were performed on resources provided by UNINETT Sigma2 - the National Infrastructure for High Performance Computing and Data Storage in Norway, and by Swedish National Infrastructure for Computing.

References

1. Submission requirements and evaluation criteria for the post-quantum cryptography standardization process. https://csrc.nist.gov/CSRC/media/Projects/Post-Quantum-Cryptography/documents/call-for-proposals-final-dec-2016.pdf. Accessed 05 Feb 2020
2. Aguilar Melchor, C., et al.: HQC. Technical report. National Institute of Standards and Technology (2019). https://csrc.nist.gov/projects/post-quantum-cryptography/round-2-submissions
3. Aguilar Melchor, C., et al.: RQC. Technical report. National Institute of Standards and Technology (2019). https://csrc.nist.gov/projects/post-quantum-cryptography/round-2-submissions
4. Alagic, G., et al.: Status report on the first round of the NIST post-quantum cryptography standardization process (2019). https://doi.org/10.6028/NIST.IR.8240
5. Aragon, N., et al.: BIKE. Technical report. National Institute of Standards and Technology (2019). https://csrc.nist.gov/projects/post-quantum-cryptography/round-2-submissions
6. Aragon, N., et al.: ROLLO. Technical report. National Institute of Standards and Technology (2019). https://csrc.nist.gov/projects/post-quantum-cryptography/round-2-submissions
7. Aragon, N., Gaborit, P.: A key recovery attack against LRPC using decryption failures. In: Coding and Cryptography, International Workshop, WCC, vol. 2019 (2019)
8. Băetu, C., Durak, F.B., Huguenin-Dumittan, L., Talayhan, A., Vaudenay, S.: Misuse attacks on post-quantum cryptosystems. In: Ishai, Y., Rijmen, V. (eds.) EUROCRYPT 2019. Misuse attacks on post-quantum cryptosystems, vol. 11477, pp. 747–776. Springer, Cham (2019). https://doi.org/10.1007/978-3-030-17656-3_26
9. Baldi, M., Barenghi, A., Chiaraluce, F., Pelosi, G., Santini, P.: LEDAcrypt. Technical report. National Institute of Standards and Technology (2019). https://csrc.nist.gov/projects/post-quantum-cryptography/round-2-submissions
10. Bauer, A., Gilbert, H., Renault, G., Rossi, M.: Assessment of the key-reuse resilience of NewHope. In: Matsui, M. (ed.) CT-RSA 2019. LNCS, vol. 11405, pp. 272–292. Springer, Cham (2019). https://doi.org/10.1007/978-3-030-12612-4_14

11. Becker, A., Joux, A., May, A., Meurer, A.: Decoding random binary linear codes in $2^{n/20}$: how $1 + 1 = 0$ improves information set decoding. In: Pointcheval, D., Johansson, T. (eds.) EUROCRYPT 2012. LNCS, vol. 7237, pp. 520–536. Springer, Heidelberg (2012). https://doi.org/10.1007/978-3-642-29011-4_31

12. Berlekamp, E.R., McEliece, R.J., van Tilborg, H.C.A.: On the inherent intractability of certain coding problems (corresp.). IEEE Trans. Inf. Theory **24**(3), 384–386 (1978). https://doi.org/10.1109/TIT.1978.1055873

13. Bernstein, D.J., Bruinderink, L.G., Lange, T., Panny, L.: HILA5 pindakaas: on the CCA security of lattice-based encryption with error correction. Cryptology ePrint Archive, Report 2017/1214 (2017). https://eprint.iacr.org/2017/1214

14. Berson, T.A.: Failure of the McEliece public-key cryptosystem under message-resend and related-message attack. In: Kaliski, B.S. (ed.) CRYPTO 1997. LNCS, vol. 1294, pp. 213–220. Springer, Heidelberg (1997). https://doi.org/10.1007/BFb0052237

15. Biryukov, A., Mukhopadhyay, S., Sarkar, P.: Improved time-memory trade-offs with multiple data. In: Preneel, B., Tavares, S. (eds.) SAC 2005. LNCS, vol. 3897, pp. 110–127. Springer, Heidelberg (2006). https://doi.org/10.1007/11693383_8

16. Canteaut, A., Sendrier, N.: Cryptanalysis of the original McEliece cryptosystem. In: Ohta, K., Pei, D. (eds.) ASIACRYPT 1998. LNCS, vol. 1514, pp. 187–199. Springer, Heidelberg (2000). https://doi.org/10.1007/3-540-49649-1_16

17. D'Anvers, J.-P., Guo, Q., Johansson, T., Nilsson, A., Vercauteren, F., Verbauwhede, I.: Decryption failure attacks on IND-CCA secure lattice-based schemes. In: Lin, D., Sako, K. (eds.) PKC 2019. LNCS, vol. 11443, pp. 565–598. Springer, Cham (2019). https://doi.org/10.1007/978-3-030-17259-6_19

18. D'Anvers, J.-P., Rossi, M., Virdia, F.: *(One) Failure Is Not an Option*: bootstrapping the search for failures in lattice-based encryption schemes. In: Canteaut, A., Ishai, Y. (eds.) EUROCRYPT 2020. LNCS, vol. 12107, pp. 3–33. Springer, Cham (2020). https://doi.org/10.1007/978-3-030-45727-3_1

19. D'Anvers, J.-P., Vercauteren, F., Verbauwhede, I.: The impact of error dependencies on Ring/Mod-LWE/LWR based schemes. In: Ding, J., Steinwandt, R. (eds.) PQCrypto 2019. LNCS, vol. 11505, pp. 103–115. Springer, Cham (2019). https://doi.org/10.1007/978-3-030-25510-7_6

20. Fabšič, T., Hromada, V., Stankovski, P., Zajac, P., Guo, Q., Johansson, T.: A reaction attack on the QC-LDPC McEliece cryptosystem. In: Lange, T., Takagi, T. (eds.) PQCrypto 2017. LNCS, vol. 10346, pp. 51–68. Springer, Cham (2017). https://doi.org/10.1007/978-3-319-59879-6_4

21. Fluhrer, S.: Cryptanalysis of ring-LWE based key exchange with key share reuse. Cryptology ePrint Archive, Report 2016/085 (2016). http://eprint.iacr.org/2016/085

22. Fujisaki, E., Okamoto, T.: Secure integration of asymmetric and symmetric encryption schemes. In: Wiener, M. (ed.) CRYPTO 1999. LNCS, vol. 1666, pp. 537–554. Springer, Heidelberg (1999). https://doi.org/10.1007/3-540-48405-1_34

23. Guo, Q., Johansson, T., Mårtensson, E., Stankovski, P.: Information set decoding with soft information and some cryptographic applications. In: 2017 IEEE International Symposium on Information Theory, ISIT 2017, Aachen, Germany, 25–30 June 2017, pp. 1793–1797 (2017). https://doi.org/10.1109/ISIT.2017.8006838

24. Guo, Q., Johansson, T., Mårtensson, E., Wagner, P.S.: Some cryptanalytic and coding-theoretic applications of a soft stern algorithm. Adv. Math. Commun. **13**(4), 559–578 (2019). https://doi.org/10.3934/amc.2019035

25. Guo, Q., Johansson, T., Nilsson, A.: A generic attack on lattice-based schemes using decryption errors with application to ss-ntru-pke. IACR Cryptology ePrint Archive 2019, 43 (2019). https://eprint.iacr.org/2019/043
26. Guo, Q., Johansson, T., Stankovski, P.: A key recovery attack on MDPC with CCA security using decoding errors. In: Cheon, J.H., Takagi, T. (eds.) ASIACRYPT 2016. LNCS, vol. 10031, pp. 789–815. Springer, Heidelberg (2016). https://doi.org/10.1007/978-3-662-53887-6_29
27. Guo, Q., Johansson, T., Wagner, P.S.: A key recovery reaction attack on QC-MDPC. IEEE Trans. Inf. Theory **65**(3), 1845–1861 (2019). https://doi.org/10.1109/TIT.2018.2877458
28. Guo, Q., Johansson, T., Yang, J.: A novel CCA attack using decryption errors against LAC. In: Galbraith, S.D., Moriai, S. (eds.) ASIACRYPT 2019. LNCS, vol. 11921, pp. 82–111. Springer, Cham (2019). https://doi.org/10.1007/978-3-030-34578-5_4
29. Hall, C., Goldberg, I., Schneier, B.: Reaction attacks against several public-key cryptosystem. In: Varadharajan, V., Mu, Y. (eds.) ICICS 1999. LNCS, vol. 1726, pp. 2–12. Springer, Heidelberg (1999). https://doi.org/10.1007/978-3-540-47942-0_2
30. Hellman, M.E.: A cryptanalytic time-memory trade-off. IEEE Trans. Inf. Theory **26**(4), 401–406 (1980). https://doi.org/10.1109/TIT.1980.1056220
31. Hofheinz, D., Hövelmanns, K., Kiltz, E.: A modular analysis of the Fujisaki-Okamoto transformation. In: Kalai, Y., Reyzin, L. (eds.) TCC 2017. LNCS, vol. 10677, pp. 341–371. Springer, Cham (2017). https://doi.org/10.1007/978-3-319-70500-2_12
32. Howgrave-Graham, N., et al.: The impact of decryption failures on the security of NTRU encryption. In: Boneh, D. (ed.) CRYPTO 2003. LNCS, vol. 2729, pp. 226–246. Springer, Heidelberg (2003). https://doi.org/10.1007/978-3-540-45146-4_14
33. Howgrave-Graham, N., Silverman, J.H., Singer, A., Whyte, W.: NAEP: provable security in the presence of decryption failures. Cryptology ePrint Archive, Report 2003/172 (2003). http://eprint.iacr.org/2003/172
34. Lu, X., et al.: LAC. Technical report. National Institute of Standards and Technology (2019). https://csrc.nist.gov/projects/post-quantum-cryptography/round-2-submissions
35. McEliece, R.J.: A public-key cryptosystem based on algebraic coding theory. JPL DSN Prog. Rep. **44**, 114–116 (1978)
36. Melchor, C.A., Blazy, O., Deneuville, J., Gaborit, P., Zémor, G.: Efficient encryption from random quasi-cyclic codes. IEEE Trans. Inf. Theory **64**(5), 3927–3943 (2018). https://doi.org/10.1109/TIT.2018.2804444
37. Misoczki, R., Tillich, J., Sendrier, N., Barreto, P.S.L.M.: MDPC-McEliece: New McEliece variants from moderate density parity-check codes. In: Proceedings of the 2013 IEEE International Symposium on Information Theory, Istanbul, Turkey, 7–12 July 2013, pp. 2069–2073. IEEE (2013). https://doi.org/10.1109/ISIT.2013.6620590
38. Nilsson, A., Johansson, T., Wagner, P.S.: Error amplification in code-based cryptography. IACR Tran. Cryptogr. Hardw. Embed. Syst. **2019**, 238–258 (2019)
39. Pessl, P., Mangard, S.: Enhancing side-channel analysis of binary-field multiplication with bit reliability. In: Sako, K. (ed.) CT-RSA 2016. LNCS, vol. 9610, pp. 255–270. Springer, Cham (2016). https://doi.org/10.1007/978-3-319-29485-8_15
40. Prange, E.: The use of information sets in decoding cyclic codes. IRE Trans. Inf. Theory **8**(5), 5–9 (1962). https://doi.org/10.1109/TIT.1962.1057777

41. Samardjiska, S., Santini, P., Persichetti, E., Banegas, G.: A reaction attack against cryptosystems based on LRPC codes. In: Schwabe, P., Thériault, N. (eds.) LAT-INCRYPT 2019. LNCS, vol. 11774, pp. 197–216. Springer, Cham (2019). https://doi.org/10.1007/978-3-030-30530-7_10

42. Shor, P.W.: Algorithms for quantum computation: discrete logarithms and factoring. In: 35th Annual Symposium on Foundations of Computer Science, pp. 124–134, 20–22 November 1994. IEEE Computer Society Press, Santa Fe, NM, USA (1994)

43. Stern, J.: A method for finding codewords of small weight. In: Cohen, G., Wolfmann, J. (eds.) Coding Theory 1988. LNCS, vol. 388, pp. 106–113. Springer, Heidelberg (1989). https://doi.org/10.1007/BFb0019850

44. Yu, Y., Zhang, J.: Lepton. Technical report. National Institute of Standards and Technology (2017). https://csrc.nist.gov/projects/post-quantum-cryptography/round-1-submissions

Cryptanalysis

A Bit-Vector Differential Model for the Modular Addition by a Constant

Seyyed Arash Azimi[1]([✉]), Adrián Ranea[2], Mahmoud Salmasizadeh[3], Javad Mohajeri[3], Mohammad Reza Aref[1], and Vincent Rijmen[2,4]

[1] Department of Electrical Engineering, Sharif University of Technology, Tehran, Iran
arash_azimi@ee.sharif.edu, aref@sharif.edu
[2] imec-COSIC, KU Leuven, Leuven, Belgium
{adrian.ranea,vincent.rijmen}@esat.kuleuven.be
[3] Electronic Research Institute, Sharif University of Technology, Tehran, Iran
{salmasi,mohajer}@sharif.edu
[4] Department of Informatics, UiB, Bergen, Norway

Abstract. ARX algorithms are a class of symmetric-key algorithms constructed by Addition, Rotation, and XOR, which achieve the best software performances in low-end microcontrollers. To evaluate the resistance of an ARX cipher against differential cryptanalysis and its variants, the recent automated methods employ constraint satisfaction solvers, such as SMT solvers, to search for optimal characteristics. The main difficulty to formulate this search as a constraint satisfaction problem is obtaining the differential models of the non-linear operations, that is, the constraints describing the differential probability of each non-linear operation of the cipher. While an efficient bit-vector differential model was obtained for the modular addition with two variable inputs, no differential model for the modular addition by a constant has been proposed so far, preventing ARX ciphers including this operation from being evaluated with automated methods.

In this paper, we present the first bit-vector differential model for the n-bit modular addition by a constant input. Our model contains $O(\log_2(n))$ basic bit-vector constraints and describes the binary logarithm of the differential probability. We also represent an SMT-based automated method to look for differential characteristics of ARX, including constant additions, and we provide an open-source tool ArxPy to find ARX differential characteristics in a fully automated way. To provide some examples, we have searched for related-key differential characteristics of TEA, XTEA, HIGHT, and LEA, obtaining better results than previous works. Our differential model and our automated tool allow cipher designers to select the best constant inputs for modular additions and cryptanalysts to evaluate the resistance of ARX ciphers against differential attacks.

Keywords: Modular addition by a constant · Differential probability · ARX · SMT · Automated search · Bit-vector theory

S. A. Azimi and A. Ranea—These authors contributed equally to this work.

S. Moriai and H. Wang (Eds.): ASIACRYPT 2020, LNCS 12491, pp. 385–414, 2020.
https://doi.org/10.1007/978-3-030-64837-4_13

1 Introduction

Low-end devices such as RFID tags, sensor networks, and the Internet of Things (IoT) are becoming ubiquitous. In 2018, Gartner, Inc. forecasted that there will be more than 25 billion connected devices forming the IoT by 2021 [1]. Traditional cryptographic algorithms are not suitable for these resource-constrained devices, and several lightweight cryptographic algorithms have been recently proposed to meet this growing demand. In this regard, the National Institute of Standards and Technology (NIST) has started a process to evaluate and standardize lightweight cryptographic algorithms [2].

ARX primitives, composed exclusively of modular Additions, cyclic Rotations, and XORs, are a promising class of lightweight cryptographic algorithms with the most efficient software implementations on low-end microcontrollers [3]. There are many noteworthy ARX algorithms, such as the hash function BLAKE [4], the stream cipher Salsa20 [5], the MAC algorithm Chaskey [6] and notable block ciphers like HIGHT [7], LEA [8], SPECK [9] or SPARX [10]. Usually, ciphers that are exclusively composed of ARX operations and other common bit-vector operations (e.g., modular multiplication or logical shifts) are also considered in the class of ARX ciphers, such as IDEA [11], TEA [12], or XTEA [13].

The security of ARX ciphers is evaluated by analysing their robustness against various attacks. Some of the most successful attacks applied to ARX algorithms are differential cryptanalysis and their variants, such as boomerang or related-key differential attacks [8,14]. These attacks exploit differences in the inputs that propagate through the cipher with high probability. The standard approach to show an ARX cipher is secure against differential attacks is by finding the optimal characteristics (i.e., trails of differences with the highest probabilities) that cover most of the rounds of the cipher and checking that their probabilities are negligible [7,8]. When the best attack in the design stage is a differential attack, the number of rounds of the cipher is determined by the number of rounds that optimal characteristics can cover with non-negligible probability. Thus, searching for optimal characteristics is a crucial step in the design and security analysis of a cipher.

Two main techniques have been applied to search for optimal characteristics of ARX algorithms: branch-and-bound algorithms [15,16] based on Matsui's algorithm [17], and the recent automated methods based on constraint satisfaction problems, such as SMT (Satisfiability Modulo Theories) or MILP (Mixed Integer Linear Programming) problems [18,19]. Automated methods formulate the characteristic search problem as a constraint satisfaction problem and delegate the solving task to one of the powerful off-the-shelf constraint satisfaction solvers available nowadays [20,21]. The main difficulty to formulate the search problem lies in the *differential models* of the non-linear operations, that is, the constraints describing the differential probability of the non-linear operations of the cipher.

ARX ciphers can be efficiently described using the bit-vector theory of SMT, and several bit-vector differential models have been proposed so far [22–24]. For the modular addition with two n-bit operands, the foremost non-linear operation in ARX primitives, Lipmaa and Moriai found a bit-vector algorithm for computing the differential probability with complexity $O(\log_2 n)$ [22]. This algorithm can be straightforwardly translated to a bit-vector differential model, and it has been used in several SMT-based methods to search for characteristics of ARX ciphers [18,24,25].

However, no bit-vector differential model has been proposed for the modular addition with a constant input, preventing from searching for characteristics of ARX ciphers that contain constant additions. Lipmaa's algorithm is restricted to the modular addition with two operands, and it cannot be applied when one of the inputs is fixed to a constant as we will discuss later. Machado proposed an algorithm to compute the differential probability of the constant addition [26], but it cannot be translated to an efficient bit-vector differential model due to its recursive nature and the use of floating-point arithmetic.

Contributions. We propose an efficient bit-vector differential model for the modular addition by an n-bit constant. Our model contains $O(\log_2 n)$ basic bit-vector constraints and it is composed of a bit-vector formula that determines whether a differential over the constant addition has non-zero probability and a bit-vector function that computes the binary logarithm of the differential probability. Our bit-vector model exploits the properties of the carry chain of the modular addition and relies on efficient well-known bit-vector functions, such as the hamming weight or the bit-reversal, and new bit-vector functions that we have developed for the binary logarithm.

Furthermore, we describe an SMT-based automated method to search for characteristics of ARX ciphers including constant additions. Our method is composed of an iterated search of optimal characteristics of round-reduced versions of the cipher and an automated encoding technique which formulates the SMT problems from the Single Static Assignment (SSA) form of the cipher. We have implemented our method in an open-source tool ArxPy[1], which fully automated the search of ARX characteristics. ArxPy offers a simple interface to represent any ARX cipher, different types of characteristics to search, and a complete documentation. To provide some examples, we have applied our characteristic search method to several ARX ciphers containing constant additions. In particular, we have searched for different types of related-key characteristics of TEA, XTEA, HIGHT and LEA. With our automated approach, we have revisited results previously found with manual and ad-hoc techniques, and we have obtained better characteristics in terms of probability and number of rounds.

With our bit-vector model for the constant addition, the SMT-based automated method, and our open-source tool ArxPy, we provide cipher designers with the resources to design ARX ciphers including constant additions that are secure against differential attacks. Thus, cipher designers can choose the best constants for the modular additions and optimize the number of rounds to strike a balance between security and efficiency.

---

[1] https://github.com/ranea/ArxPy.

Outline. The notation and preliminaries are introduced in Sect. 2, and the bit-vector model for the modular addition by a constant is described in Sect. 3. Section 4 illustrates the formulation of the characteristic search as a sequence of SMT problems, SMT-based search method, and the encoding of bit-vector SMT problems for ARX characteristics. Section 5 presents the characteristics found for TEA, XTEA, HIGHT, and LEA using our automated approach and finally Sect. 6 concludes the paper and addresses future works.

2 Preliminaries

2.1 Notations

Let x be an integer such that its n-bit vector representation when $0 \leq x < 2^n$ is $x = (x[n-1], \ldots, x[0])$, where $x[0]$ and $x[n-1]$ denote respectively the least and the most significant bit. For ease of notation, we define $x[i] = 0$ when $i < 0$ and the symbol $*$ stands for an undetermined bit. The usual integer operations are denoted by $(+, -, \times, /)$ and the *basic* bit-vector operations are gathered in Table 1.

A mathematical expression only involving bit-vector variables and basic bit-vector operations is called a bit-vector expression. A bit-vector formula is a bit-vector expression returning True or False, such as Equals, whereas an n-bit vector function is a bit-vector expression returning an n-bit vector. In order to measure the complexity of the bit-vector differential model that we propose in this paper, we define the *bit-vector complexity* of a bit-vector expression as the number of basic bit-vector operations that the expression is composed of.

Table 1. Basic bit-vector operations for n-bit vectors.

$x[i, j]$	the bit-vector $(x[i], \ldots, x[j])$, $n > i \geq j \geq 0$
$\neg x$	bit-wise NOT of x
$x \parallel y$	concatenation of x and y
$x \wedge y$	bit-wise AND of x and y
$x \vee y$	bit-wise OR of x and y
$x \oplus y$	bit-wise XOR of x and y
$x \ll i$	(logical) left shift of x by i bits
$x \gg i$	right shift of x by i bits
$x \lll i$	left cyclic rotation of x by i bits
$x \ggg i$	right cyclic rotation of x by i bits
$x \boxplus y$	modular addition of x and y
$x \boxminus y$	modular subtraction of x and y
Equals(x, y)	bit-vector equality of x and y, returning True if x and y are the same, otherwise False

In the literature of the bit-vector theory, the set of basic bit-vector operations usually includes the operations gathered in Table 1 and few additional operations, such as modular multiplication or modular division [27]. However, modular multiplication and modular division are much more costly than the other operations in practice, and we have excluded them from our set of basic bit-vector operations, which resembles the unit-cost RAM model used in [22].

Apart from the basic bit-vector operations listed in Table 1, we will also employ the following well-known bit-vector functions: $\mathsf{Carry}, \mathsf{Rev}, \mathsf{RevCarry}, \mathsf{HW}$ and LZ. The carry function $c = \mathsf{Carry}(x, y)$ returns the n-bit carry chain of the n-bit modular addition $x \boxplus y$. It is defined iteratively as $c[0] = 0$ and $c[i + 1] = (x[i] \wedge y[i]) \oplus (x[i] \wedge c[i]) \oplus (y[i] \wedge c[i])$. Note that the carry has bit-vector complexity $O(1)$, since $\mathsf{Carry}(x, y) = x \oplus y \oplus (x \boxplus y)$.

The bit-reversal function $\mathsf{Rev}(x)$ reverses the order of bits of x, i.e., $\mathsf{Rev}(x) = (x[0], x[1], \ldots, x[n-1])$. We will use this function to define the reverse carry, $\mathsf{RevCarry}(x, y) = \mathsf{Rev}(\mathsf{Carry}(\mathsf{Rev}(x), \mathsf{Rev}(y)))$. The hamming weight $\mathsf{HW}(x)$ returns an n-bit vector denoting the number of non-zero bits of the n-bit input x. Lastly, the leading zeros function $\mathsf{LZ}(x)$ marks the leading zeros of an n-bit input x, that is, for $0 \le i < n$ we have $\mathsf{LZ}(x)[i] = 1 \iff x[n-1, i] = 0$. Note that the functions $\mathsf{Rev}, \mathsf{RevCarry}, \mathsf{HW}$ and LZ can be computed using a divide and conquer approach with bit-vector complexity $O(\log_2 n)$ [28].

2.2 Differential Cryptanalysis

A block cipher is a family of permutations parameterized by a κ-bit key k, mapping n-bit plaintexts p to n-bit ciphertexts c. Most block ciphers consist of a key scheduling algorithm KS, which derives round keys $k_1, \ldots, k_r$ from the master key k, and an encryption algorithm E_k, which processes the plaintext by iterating a round function f and injecting a round key at each round, i.e., $E_k = f_{k_r} \circ \cdots \circ f_{k_1}$.

Block ciphers are shown to be secure by analysing their resistance against all known attacks. One of the most powerful attacks, specially to ARX primitives, is differential cryptanalysis [29]. Basically, it exploits non-random propagation of differences in the input to recover the secret key.

Let F be an n-bit to n-bit function and (Δ_p, Δ_c) be the XOR of a pair of inputs (p, p') and their corresponding outputs (c, c'), i.e., $\Delta_p = p \oplus p'$ and $\Delta_c = c \oplus c'$. The pair (Δ_p, Δ_c) is called a differential and its probability is defined as

$$\Pr[\Delta_p \xrightarrow{F} \Delta_c] = \frac{\#\{p : F(p) \oplus F(p \oplus \Delta_p) = \Delta_c\}}{2^n}.$$

A differential is valid if it has non-zero probability. In this case, its weight is defined as

$$\mathsf{weight}_F(\Delta_p, \Delta_c) = -\log_2(\Pr[\Delta_p \xrightarrow{F} \Delta_c]).$$

The differential $0 \xrightarrow{F} 0$ has probability 1 for any function F, and a differential with non-zero input difference over a random n-bit permutation has probability 2^{-n}. Differential cryptanalysis [29] exploits a differential over the n-bit block cipher with probability $p > 2^{-n}$ to recover the secret key with roughly $O(p^{-1})$ encryption calls.

Related-key differential cryptanalysis [30] extends differential cryptanalysis by considering key differences. A related-key differential is given by a pair of differentials over the key schedule and the encryption function respectively,

$$(\Delta_k \xrightarrow{\text{KS}} (\Delta_{k_1}, \ldots, \Delta_{k_r})), \quad (\Delta_p \xrightarrow{E} \Delta_c),$$

where the ciphertext difference is computed using the related round-key pairs,

$$\Delta_c = (f_{k_r} \circ \cdots \circ f_{k_1})(p) \oplus (f_{k_r \oplus \Delta_{k_r}} \circ \cdots \circ f_{k_1 \oplus \Delta_{k_1}})(p \oplus \Delta_p).$$

The probability of a related-key differential is the product of the probability of key schedule differential p_{KS} and the probability of encryption differential p_E.

A related-key attack exploits a related-key differential with $p_{\text{KS}} > 2^{-\kappa}$ and $p_E > 2^{-n}$ to recover the secret key with complexity $O((p_{\text{KS}} \times p_E)^{-1})$. The attacker takes about p_{KS}^{-1} key pairs to find one key, on average, that satisfies the key schedule differential. Next and for each key pair, the attacker runs a differential attack over the encryption using $O(p_E^{-1})$ encryption calls.

Related-key differential cryptanalysis requires a very powerful attacker that can query the encryption function $E_{k \oplus \Delta_k}$ for many keys $k \oplus \Delta_k$. In fact, if an adversary can query $E_{k \oplus \Delta_k}$ for 2^m key differences Δ_k, any block cipher is vulnerable to a related-key attack with complexity $O(2^m + 2^{n-m})$ [31]. Thus, we distinguish between weak related-key differentials (i.e., $p_{\text{KS}} < 1$) and strong related-key differentials (i.e., $p_{\text{KS}} = 1$), which can be exploited in practice with a single related-key pair. Furthermore, we call equivalent keys as pairs of related keys $(k, k \oplus \Delta_k)$ such that $\forall p, E_k(p) = E_{k \oplus \Delta_k}(p \oplus \Delta_p) \oplus \Delta_c$, for some (Δ_p, Δ_c). Note that a related-key differential with $p_E = 1$ leads to $2^{\kappa} p_{\text{KS}}$ pairs of equivalent keys.

Searching for Differentials. The most difficult step to launch a differential attack is finding a differential with high probability. The main approach is to analyse how differences propagate through the round function and search for a characteristic, that is, a trail of differences

$$\Omega = (\Delta_p = \Delta_{x_0} \xrightarrow{f_{k_1}} \Delta_{x_1} \to \cdots \to \Delta_{x_{r-1}} \xrightarrow{f_{k_r}} \Delta_{x_r} = \Delta_c).$$

Similar to differentials, a characteristic Ω is valid if it has non-zero probability and its weight is defined as $-\log_2(\Pr[\Omega])$. Furthermore, we denote a related-key characteristic by a pair of characteristics $(\Omega_{\text{KS}}, \Omega_E)$, where Ω_{KS} is the key schedule characteristic containing the trail of differences from the master key to the round keys and Ω_E is the encryption characteristic containing the trail of differences through the encryption.

Obtaining the exact probability of a characteristic is computationally infeasible. Thus, two assumptions are commonly made. First, it is assumed that the differential probabilities over each round are independent, which allows to compute the weight of a characteristic by summing the round weights, i.e.,

$$\text{weight}(\Omega) = \sum_{i=0}^{r} \text{weight}(\Delta_{x_i} \to \Delta_{x_{i+1}}).$$

Second, it is assumed that the probability of a characteristic does not strongly depend on the choice of the secret key, also known as the hypothesis of stochastic equivalence [32], which allows to compute the weight of a characteristic by averaging over all keys.

On top of that, designers also assume that the probability of a differential (Δ_p, Δ_c) is close to the probability of the best characteristic $(\Delta_p \to \cdots \to \Delta_c)$, and they prove a cipher is secure against differential cryptanalysis by showing that characteristics with high probability cannot cover most rounds of the cipher. While these assumptions do not always hold, currently this is the best systematic approach to argue security against differential cryptanalysis, and this heuristic approach is widely used for ARX ciphers in practice [18,19,23,25,33,34].

SMT Solvers. A recent approach to search for characteristics of ARX ciphers is by formulating the search problem as an SMT problem in the bit-vector theory [18,23–25,35]. Satisfiability Modulo Theories (SMT) refers to the problem of determining whether a first order formula is satisfiable with respect to some logical theory. SMT problems are a generalization of SAT problems; while the latter problems are expressed in propositional logic, SMT formulas can be expressed in richer logics, such as the theory of bit-vectors or the theory of integers.

SMT has grown in recent years into a very active research field and several off-the-shelf SMT solvers are available nowadays [20]. Most SMT solvers can not only determine the satisfiability of a problem but also obtain an assignment of the variables that satisfies the problem. This feature allows SMT solvers to be applied in search problems.

An SMT problem in the bit-vector theory is given by a set of bit-vector variables and a set of bit-vector formulas or constraints. The constraints can be defined with the usual logical operations (e.g., Equals, NotEquals, Implies, etc.) and with the usual bit-vector operations (e.g., $\oplus, \boxplus, \lll$, etc.).

2.3 Differential Models

To represent a characteristic in a constraint satisfaction problem, it is necessary to find a *differential model* of the round function f. For an SMT problem in the bit-vector theory, a differential model of a function $y = f(x)$ is given by a bit-vector formula $\text{valid}_f(\Delta_x, \Delta_y)$ and a bit-vector function $\text{weight}_f(\Delta_x, \Delta_y)$. The formula $\text{valid}_f(\Delta_x, \Delta_y)$ is True if and only if the differential $(\Delta_x \to \Delta_y)$ over f is valid, and the function $\text{weight}_f(\Delta_x, \Delta_y)$ returns the weight of a valid differential $(\Delta_x \to \Delta_y)$.

Characteristics over ARX ciphers are usually defined by considering the difference after each ARX operation. The differential models of the XOR and the cyclic rotations are very simple since these operations propagate differences deterministically, that is,

$$\Delta_{x_1}, \Delta_{x_2} \xrightarrow{f(x_1,x_2)=x_1\oplus x_2} \Delta_{x_1}\oplus\Delta_{x_2}, \qquad \Delta_x \xrightarrow{f_a(x)=x\oplus a} \Delta_x,$$

$$\Delta_x \xrightarrow{f_a(x)=x\lll a} \Delta_x \lll a, \qquad \Delta_x \xrightarrow{f_a(x)=x\ggg a} \Delta_x \ggg a.$$

For the modular addition with two n-bit inputs, $y = f(x_1, x_2) = x_1 \boxplus x_2$, the algorithm by Lipmaa et al. [22] can be translated into the following differential model with bit-vector complexity $O(\log_2 n)$.

Theorem 1. *Let* $((\Delta_{x_1}, \Delta_{x_2}), \Delta_y)$ *be a differential over the modular addition* $y = x_1 \boxplus x_2$ *and denote* $\overleftarrow{x} = x \lll 1$ *and* $\mathsf{eq}(a, b, c) = (\neg a \oplus b) \wedge (\neg a \oplus c)$. *Then, the differential is valid if and only if the bit-vector formula*

$$\mathsf{valid}_{\boxplus}((\Delta_{x_1}, \Delta_{x_2}), \Delta_y) = \mathsf{Equals}(0, \mathsf{eq}(\overleftarrow{\Delta_{x_1}}, \overleftarrow{\Delta_{x_2}}, \overleftarrow{\Delta_y}) \wedge (\Delta_{x_1}\oplus\Delta_{x_2}\oplus\Delta_y\oplus\overleftarrow{\Delta_{x_2}}))$$

is True. *In this case, the differential weight is given by the bit-vector function*

$$\mathsf{weight}_{\boxplus}((\Delta_{x_1}, \Delta_{x_2}), \Delta_y) = \mathsf{HW}(\neg \mathsf{eq}(\Delta_{x_1}, \Delta_{x_2}, \Delta_y) \lll 1).$$

For the modular addition with a constant input $\boxplus_a(x) = x \boxplus a$, Machado obtained the following algorithm to compute the differential probability [26].

Theorem 2. *Let* (u, v) *be a differential over the n-bit constant addition* $\boxplus_a$. *Then, the differential probability is given by*

$$\Pr[u \xrightarrow{\boxplus_a} v] = \varphi_0 \times \cdots \times \varphi_{n-1},$$

where φ_i *depends on the* δ_{i-1} *and* S_i, *each one defined for* $0 \le i < n$ *by*

$$S_i = (u[i-1], v[i-1], u[i]\oplus v[i]),$$

$$\delta_i = \begin{cases} (a[i-1]+\delta_{i-1})/2, & S_i = 000 \\ 0, & S_i = 001 \\ a[i-1], & S_i \in \{010, 100, 110\} \\ \delta_{i-1}, & S_i \in \{011, 101\} \\ 1/2, & S_i = 111 \end{cases}$$

$$\varphi_i = \begin{cases} 1, & S_i = 000 \\ 0, & S_i = 001 \\ 1/2, & S_i \in \{010, 011, 100, 101\} \\ 1 - (a[i-1]+\delta_{i-1}-2a[i-1]\delta_{i-1}), & S_i = 110 \\ (a[i-1]+\delta_{i-1}-2a[i-1]\delta_{i-1}), & S_i = 111, \end{cases}$$

For $i = -1$, S_i *and* δ_i *are defined by* $S_{-1} = \bot$ *and* $\delta_{-1} = 0$.

Unfortunately, the algorithm illustrated in Theorem 2 is not suitable for constraint satisfaction problems due to its recursive nature and the use of floating-point arithmetic.

Some authors [36, Corollary 2] [37] have adapted the differential model of the 2-input addition (i.e., the modular addition with two independent inputs) for the constant addition by setting the difference of the second operand to zero, that is,

$$
\begin{aligned}
\mathsf{valid}_{\boxplus_a}(\Delta_x, \Delta_y) &\leftarrow \mathsf{valid}_{\boxplus}((\Delta_x, 0), \Delta_y)\,, \\
\mathsf{weight}_{\boxplus_a}(\Delta_x, \Delta_y) &\leftarrow \mathsf{weight}_{\boxplus}((\Delta_x, 0), \Delta_y)\,.
\end{aligned}
\tag{1}
$$

The approximation given by Eq. (1) models the differential $(\Delta_x \xrightarrow{\boxplus_a} \Delta_y)$ by averaging over all a. While this approach can be used to model the constant addition by a round key, since the characteristic probability is also computed by averaging over all keys, for a fixed constant this approach is rather inaccurate.

Surprisingly, the differential properties of the 2-input addition and the constant addition are very different. The 2-input addition was shown to be CCZ-equivalent to a quadratic function [38], that is, the differential properties of the 2-input addition are the same of some quadratic function. In particular, the set of inputs (x_1, x_2) satisfying a differential $((\Delta_{x_1}, \Delta_{x_2}) \to \Delta_y)$ over the 2-input addition forms a subspace of $\mathbb{F}_2^n$, which allows to describe its differential model using few basic operations.

On the other hand, the constant addition is not CCZ-equivalent to a quadratic function, since the set of inputs (x_1, x_2) satisfying a differential (Δ_x, Δ_y) over $\boxplus_a$ does not form a subspace for many a. In other words, the probability of a differential over the constant addition is not necessarily of the form $2^{-\alpha}$ for a positive integer α, and finding a differential model for the constant input addition is a much harder problem.

We checked experimentally how accurate was the approximation given by Eq. (1) for 8-bit constants a. For most values of a, validity formulas differ roughly in 2^{13} out of all 2^{16} differentials, and for those differentials where they did not differ, the difference between their weights was significantly high in average.

Consequently, no differential model of the constant addition suitable for constraint satisfaction problems has been proposed so far. In the next section we present the first differential model of the constant addition for SMT problems in the bit-vector theory.

3   Bit-Vector Differential Model of the Constant Addition

We present a bit-vector differential model of the constant addition, composed of a bit-vector formula to determine whether a given differential is valid and a bit-vector function that computes the weight of the valid differential. Our model takes benefit from Theorem 2 [26]; however, we avoid bit iterations, floating-point arithmetic, multiplications and look-up tables, in order to obtain efficient bit-vector constraints to be used in bit-vector SMT problems.

Before we illustrate our model, we remark an essential property of Theorem 2. When the state S_i is not 110 or 111, the probability of the step i, φ_i, depends exclusively on S_i; otherwise, φ_i depends on S_i and δ_{i-1}. When $S_i = 11*$, $S_{i-1} \in \{010, 100, 110, 000\}$ and for the first three cases, δ_{i-1} is equal to $a[i-2]$. However, considering the forth case, i.e., $S_{i-1} = 000$, δ_{i-1} depends on δ_{i-2} and this dependency will proceed until we obtain a state $S_{i-\ell_i} \neq 000$ for some positive integer ℓ_i. Thus, δ_{i-1} has the following expression when $S_i = 11*$,

$$\delta_{i-1} = \frac{a[i-\ell_i-1]}{2^{\ell_i-1}} + \sum_{j=2}^{\ell_i} \frac{a[i-j]}{2^{j-1}} . \qquad (2)$$

Therefore, when $S_i = 11*$, φ_i also depends on the previous states $S_{i-1} \cdots, S_{i-\ell_i}$, which motivates the following definition.

Definition 1. *Let $S_i = 11*$. The chain Γ_i is defined as the smallest set of previous states $\{S_{i-1}, S_{i-2}, \cdots, S_{i-\ell_i}\}$ that completely determine φ_i, and the positive integer ℓ_i is called the length of Γ_i.*

Given a chain $\Gamma_i = \{S_{i-1}, S_{i-2}, \cdots, S_{i-\ell_i}\}$, note that $S_{i-\ell_i} \neq 000$ and the remaining states in the chain (if any) are all equal to 000.

3.1   Validity

Let (u, v) be a differential over $\boxplus_a$, the modular addition by n-bit constant a. According to Theorem 2, the differential probability of (u, v) can be expressed as $\varphi_0 \times \cdots \times \varphi_{n-1}$. Thus, (u, v) is a valid differential, i.e., with non-zero probability, if and only if all φ_i are non-zero. If $\varphi_i = 0$, note that S_i must be $001, 110$ or 111. While $S_i = 001$ always implies $\varphi_i = 0$, the other two cases require an extra condition to result in $\varphi_i = 0$, as shown in the next lemma.

Lemma 1. *Let the state S_i be 11b, for $b \in \{0, 1\}$. Then, φ_i is equal to 0 if and only if $\neg b \oplus a[i-1] = a[i-2] = \cdots = a[i-\ell_i-1]$.*

Proof. Having $S_i = 11b$, $\varphi_i = 0$ if and only if $\neg b = \delta_{i-1} \oplus a[i-1]$. Let ℓ_i be the chain length of S_i. The case for $\ell_i = 1$ is trivial, since $\delta_{i-1} = a[i-2]$. To achieve $\delta_{i-1} = a[i-1] \oplus \neg b$ when $\ell_i > 1$, the non-negative rational number δ_{i-1} must be equal to 0 or 1. Since δ_{i-1} is a monotonically increasing function of $(a[i-2], \ldots, a[i-\ell_i-1])$ regarding Eq. (2), δ_{i-1} reaches its extrema in $(0, \ldots, 0)$ and $(1, \ldots, 1)$, that is,

$$\delta_{i-1} = c \iff a[i-2] = a[i-3] = \cdots = a[i-\ell_i-1] = c, \quad \forall c \in \{0, 1\},$$

Thus, $\delta_{i-1} = a[i-1] \oplus \neg b \iff \delta_{i-1} = a[i-2] = \cdots = a[i-\ell_i].$ $\qquad \square$

The next lemma provides a bit-vector expression to check Lemma 1 by exploiting the fact that the carry chain allows a bit to affect the bits to its left.

Lemma 2. *Consider the following n-bit values,*

$$s_{00*} = \neg(u \ll 1) \wedge \neg(v \ll 1), \quad s_{**1} = u \oplus v, \quad a' = (a \oplus (a \ll 1)) \ll 1,$$
$$c = \mathsf{Carry}\big(s_{00*} \wedge \neg a', \neg(s_{00*} \ll 1)\big), \quad g = (s_{**1} \oplus a') \wedge (c \vee \neg(s_{00*} \ll 1)).$$

Then, for all states $S_i = 11*$, we have $\varphi_i = 0$ if and only if $g[i] = 1$.

Proof. Let $S_i = 11\mathrm{b}$ with chain length ℓ_i. Note that $a'[i] = a[i-1] \oplus a[i-2]$ and that $s_{00*}[i] = 1$ (resp. $s_{**1}[i] = 1$) if and only if $S_i = 00*$ (resp. $S_i = **1$).

The first operand of $g[i]$, i.e., $(s_{**1} \oplus a')[i]$, is equal to one if and only if $\mathrm{b} = \neg(a[i-1] \oplus a[i-2])$. For $\ell_i = 1$ it is easy to see that $S_{i-1} \neq 00*$; therefore, the second operand of $g[i]$ is 1, and by Lemma 1 $g[i] = 1$ if and only if $\varphi_i = 0$.

When $\ell_i > 1$, $S_{i-1} = 000$ and the second major operand of $g[i]$ reduces to c. In particular, the two major operands of the Carry function of c are given by

$$(s_{00*} \wedge \neg a')[i, i - \ell_i] = (\neg(a[i-1] \oplus a[i-2]), \ldots, \neg(a[i-\ell_i] \oplus a[i-\ell_i-1]), 0),$$
$$\neg(s_{00*} \ll 1)[i, i - \ell_i] = (0, \ldots, 0, 1, *).$$

Thus, $c[i] = c[i-1] \wedge \neg a'[i-1]$ and $c[i - \ell_i + 1] = c[i - \ell_i] \wedge \neg s_{00*}[i - \ell_i - 1] = 0$; otherwise, for $0 \leq j \leq i - \ell_i - 1$ we will obtain $s_{00*}[j] = 0$ which does not conform to $S_0 = 00*$. By unrolling the recursive definition of $c[i]$, we see that $c[i] = \neg a'[i-1] \wedge \cdots \wedge \neg a'[i - \ell_i + 1]$. In other words, $c[i] = 1$ if and only if $a[i-2] = \cdots = a[i - \ell_i - 1]$. Together with the condition for $(s_{**1} \oplus a')[i] = 1$, we have that $g[i] = 1$ exactly when $\varphi_i = 0$, regarding Lemma 1. □

Lemma 2 provides a bit-vector variable g that detects the states $S_i = 11*$ leading to invalidity. The next theorem presents the final bit-vector formula for the validity by taking into account the states $S_i = 001$ as well.

Theorem 3. *Let (u, v) be a differential over the n-bit constant addition $\boxplus_a$. Consider the n-bit value g defined in Lemma 2 and the following n-bit values*

$$s_{001} = \neg(u \ll 1) \wedge \neg(v \ll 1) \wedge (u \oplus v), \quad s_{11*} = (u \ll 1) \wedge (v \ll 1).$$

*Then, the bit-vector formula $\mathsf{valid}_{\boxplus_a}(u, v) = \mathsf{Equals}(s_{001} \vee (s_{11*} \wedge g), 0)$ is **True** if and only if the differential (u, v) is valid.*

Proof. By the definition of s_{001} and s_{11*}, $s_{001}[i] = 1$ (respectively $s_{11*}[i] = 1$) if and only if $S_i = 001$ (respectively $S_i = 11*$). Moreover, $\varphi_i = 0$ exactly when $S_i = 001$, or when $S_i = 11*$ and $g[i] = 1$ (Lemma 2). Thus, $\varphi_i = 0$ if and only if $s_{001} \vee (s_{11*} \wedge g)[i] = 1$. □

Since the number of basic bit-vector operations of our bit-vector validity formula is independent of the bit-size of the inputs, the bit-vector complexity of $\mathsf{valid}_{\boxplus_a}$ is $O(1)$.

3.2   Weight of a Valid Differential

In this section, we propose a bit-vector function that computes the weight of a valid differential over the constant addition. Working with differential weights has the advantage that multiple differential weights can be combined by adding them up, while probabilities need to be multiplied, a very costly operation in a bit-vector SMT problem.

The weight of a valid differential over the constant addition is an irrational value in general, and it cannot be represented as a fixed-sized bit-vector. Thus, our bit-vector function computes a close approximation of the weight, and we provide almost tight bounds for the approximation error.

Through the rest of the section, let (u, v) be a valid differential over the n-bit constant addition $\boxplus_a$. According to Theorem 2, the weight can be obtained by

$$\mathsf{weight}_{\boxplus_a}(u, v) = -\log_2\left(\prod_{i=0}^{n-1} \varphi_i\right) = -\sum_{i=0}^{n-1} \log_2(\varphi_i). \tag{3}$$

Let $\mathcal{I}$ denote the set of indices corresponding to the states 11* with chain length bigger than one, i.e., $\mathcal{I} = \{1 \le i \le n-1 \mid S_i = \mathtt{11*}, \ell_i > 1\}$. For $i \notin \mathcal{I}$, the probability φ_i only depends on the current state S_i and φ_i is either 1 or $1/2$. Since $\varphi_i = 1/2$ when $S_i \in \{\mathtt{01*}, \mathtt{10*}\}$, it is easy to see that

$$-\sum_{i \notin \mathcal{I}} \log_2(\varphi_i) = \mathsf{HW}((u \oplus v) \ll 1). \tag{4}$$

Equation 4 describes the sum of $\log_2(\varphi_i)$ when $i \notin \mathcal{I}$ as a bit-vector expression with complexity $O(\log_2 n)$. To describe the logarithmic summation when $i \in \mathcal{I}$ as a bit-vector, we will first show how to split φ_i as the quotient of two integers.

Lemma 3. *Let $i \in \mathcal{I}$ and let p_i be the positive integer defined by*

$$p_i = \begin{cases} a[i-2, i-\ell_i] + a[i-\ell_i-1], & u[i] \oplus v[i] \oplus a[i-1] = 1 \\ 2^{\ell_i-1} - (a[i-2, i-\ell_i] + a[i-\ell_i-1]), & u[i] \oplus v[i] \oplus a[i-1] = 0 \end{cases}$$

where $\ell_i > 1$ is the chain length of the state $S_i = \mathtt{11*}$. Then, $\varphi_i = \dfrac{p_i}{2^{\ell_i-1}}$.

Proof. Considering the definition of φ_i when $S_i = \mathtt{11*}$,

$$\varphi_i = \begin{cases} \delta_{i-1}, & u[i] \oplus v[i] \oplus a[i-1] = 1 \\ 1 - \delta_{i-1}, & u[i] \oplus v[i] \oplus a[i-1] = 0 \end{cases}$$

and following the definition of δ_{i-1} given by Eq. (2),

$$2^{\ell_i-1}\delta_i = \sum_{j=0}^{\ell_i-2} 2^j a[i-\ell_i+j] + a[i-\ell_i-1] = a[i-2, i-\ell_i] + a[i-\ell_i-1],$$

we obtain that $\varphi_i = p_i/2^{\ell_i-1}$. Moreover, having $0 < \varphi_i \le 1$ and $\ell_i > 1$ results in $0 < p_i \le 2^{\ell_i-1}$. Thus, p_i is always a positive integer.   □

Due to Lemma 3, we can decompose the logarithmic summation over $\mathcal{I}$ as

$$\sum_{i\in\mathcal{I}} \log_2(\varphi_i) = \sum_{i\in\mathcal{I}} \log_2(p_i) - \sum_{i\in\mathcal{I}}(\ell_i - 1).$$

The next lemma shows how to describe the summation involving the chain lengths with basic bit-vector operations.

Lemma 4. *Consider the n-bit vector $s_{000} = \neg(u \ll 1) \wedge \neg(v \ll 1)$. Then,*

$$\sum_{i\in\mathcal{I}}(\ell_i - 1) = \mathsf{HW}\big(s_{000} \wedge \neg\mathsf{LZ}(\neg s_{000})\big).$$

Proof. Recall that there are exactly $(\ell_i - 1)$ states in each chain Γ_i such that

$$S_{i-1} = S_{i-2} = \cdots = S_{i-(\ell_i-1)} = 000.$$

Therefore, we have $\sum_{i\in\mathcal{I}}(\ell_i - 1) = \#\{S_j | S_j = 000 \text{ and } \exists i \in \mathcal{I} \text{ s.t. } S_j \in \Gamma_i\}$. When $S_j = 000$, the next state S_{j+1} will be a member of the set $\{000, 11*\}$. As a result, it is easy to see that for an arbitrary j, if S_j is equal to 000, then either S_j is included in some chain $\Gamma_i, i \in \mathcal{I}$, or S_j belongs to the set Γ' defined by

$$\Gamma' = \{S_{n-1} = 000, \cdots, S_{n-k} = 000\},$$

for some $k > 0$, where $S_{n-k-1} \neq 000$. Concerning Definition 1, one can observe that Γ' is not a chain. Therefore, $\sum_{i\in\mathcal{I}}(\ell_i - 1) = \#\{S_j | S_j = 000 \text{ and } S_j \notin \Gamma'\}$.

Since we are assuming that the differential is valid, there are no states $S_j = 001$, and $s_{000}[j] = 1$ if and only if $S_j = 000$. On the other hand, the function LZ can be used to detect the states from the set Γ'. In particular, $\mathsf{LZ}(\neg s_{000})[i]$ is equal to 1 if and only if $S_i \in \Gamma'$. Therefore, we obtain

$$\sum_{i\in\mathcal{I}}(\ell_i - 1) = \mathsf{HW}\big(s_{000} \wedge (\neg\mathsf{LZ}(\neg s_{000}))\big).$$

$\square$

Representing the sum of $\log_2(p_i)$ by a bit-vector expression is the most complex and challenging part of our differential model. Thus, we will proceed in several steps. First, we will show how to obtain a bit-vector w that contains all the p_i as some sub-vectors.

Lemma 5. *Consider the following n-bit values,*

$$s_{000} = \neg(u \ll 1) \wedge \neg(v \ll 1), \quad s'_{000} = s_{000} \wedge \neg\mathsf{LZ}(\neg s_{000}),$$

$$t = \neg s'_{000} \wedge (s'_{000} \gg 1), \quad t' = s'_{000} \wedge (\neg(s'_{000} \gg 1)),$$

$$s = ((a \ll 1) \wedge t) \boxplus (a \wedge (s'_{000} \gg 1)), \quad q = ((\neg((a \ll 1) \oplus u \oplus v)) \gg 1) \wedge t',$$

$$d = \mathsf{RevCarry}(s'_{000}, q) \vee q, \quad w = (q \boxminus (s \wedge d)) \vee (s \wedge \neg d).$$

Then, for all states $S_i = 11*$ with $i \in \mathcal{I}$, $w[i-1, i-\ell_i] = p_i$.

Proof. For each $i \in \mathcal{I}$ and $0 \le j < n$, note that $s'_{000}[j] = 1$ exactly when $S_j = 000$ and $S_j \in \Gamma_i$, and $t[j] = 1$ (resp. $t'[j] = 1$) if and only if $S_j = S_{i-\ell_i}$ (resp. $S_j = S_{i-1}$). Denoting $s = s_1 \boxplus s_2$, where $s_1 = (a \ll 1) \wedge t$ and $s_2 = a \wedge (s'_{000} \gg 1)$, when $i \in \mathcal{I}$ the sub-vectors

$$s_1[i-1, i-\ell_i - 1] = (0, 0, \qquad \ldots, 0, \qquad a[i-\ell_i - 1], 0),$$
$$s_2[i-1, i-\ell_i - 1] = (0, a[i-2], \ldots, a[i-\ell_i+1], a[i-\ell_i], \quad 0),$$

result in $s[i-1, i-\ell_i] = a[i-2, i-\ell_i] + a[i-\ell_i - 1]$. In particular, $s[i-1, i-\ell_i] \le 2^{\ell_i - 1}$ and the equality holds when $s[i-1, i-\ell_i] = 10\ldots0$.

It is easy to see that $q[i-1] = \neg(a[i-2] \oplus u[i-1] \oplus v[i-1])$ when $i \in \mathcal{I}$ and q is zero elsewhere. Then, the sub-vectors $d[i-1, i-\ell_i]$ are composed of repeated copies of $q[i-1]$ when $i \in \mathcal{I}$, as shown by the following sub-vectors

$$s'_{000}[i, i-\ell_i - 1] = (0, 1, \qquad 1, \qquad \ldots, 1, \qquad 0, \qquad *),$$
$$q[i, i-\ell_i - 1] = (0, q[i-1], 0, \qquad \ldots, 0, \qquad 0, \qquad *),$$
$$\mathrm{RevCarry}(s'_{000}, q)[i, i-\ell_i - 1] = (*, 0, \qquad q[i-1], \ldots, q[i-1], q[i-1], 0),$$
$$d[i, i-\ell_i - 1] = (*, q[i-1], q[i-1], \ldots, q[i-1], q[i-1], *).$$

The only exception for the above equations is when $i - \ell_i = -1$, where the two least significant bits of the above sub-vectors will be equal to zero.

Let $w = w_1 \wedge w_2$, where $w_1 = q \boxminus (s \wedge d)$ and $w_2 = s \wedge \neg d$. Regarding the acquired patterns for q and d, we prove the following inequalities for $i \in \mathcal{I}$

$$(s \wedge d)[i-1, i-\ell_i] \le q[i-1, i-\ell_i],$$
$$(s \wedge d)[i-\ell_i - 1, 0] \le q[i-\ell_i - 1, 0],$$

which imply the identity $w_1[i-1, i-\ell_i] = q[i-1, i-\ell_i] \boxminus (s \wedge d)[i-1, i-\ell_i]$.

The first inequality can be derived from the fact that $s[i-1, i-\ell_i] \le 10\ldots0$. For the second inequality, consider the index set $\mathcal{J} = \{j | \forall i \in I, S_j \notin \Gamma_i\}$. Then, the second inequality holds since for $j \in \mathcal{J}$ and $c \in \{0, 1\}$ we can see that

$$s'_{000}[j+1-c] = 0 \implies s_1[j-c] = s_2[j-c] = 0.$$

We are now ready to evaluate $w[i-1, i-\ell_i]$ when $i \in \mathcal{I}$. If $q[i-1] = 0$, then $d[i-1, i-\ell_i] = (0, \ldots, 0)$, $w_1[i-1, i-\ell_i]$ reduces to 0, and

$$w[i-1, i-\ell_i] = w_2[i-1, i-\ell_i] = a[i-2, i-\ell_i] + a[i-\ell_i - 1].$$

If $q[i-1] = 1$, then $d[i-1, i-\ell_i] = (1, \ldots, 1)$, $w_2[i-1, i-\ell_i]$ reduces to 0, and

$$w[i-1, i-\ell_i] = w_1[i-1, i-\ell_i] = (1, 0, \ldots, 0) \boxminus s[i-1, i-\ell_i]$$
$$= 2^{\ell_i - 1} - (a[i-2, i-\ell_i] + a[i-\ell_i - 1]).$$

Hence, for $q[i-1] = \neg(a[i-1] \oplus u[i] \oplus v[i])$ and regarding Lemma 3, we obtain that $w[i-1, i-\ell_i] = p_i$. $\qquad \square$

Recall that both LZ and RevCarry have bit-vector complexity $O(\log_2 n)$. Therefore, w can be described with $O(\log_2 n)$ basic bit-vector operations.

Since p_i is not always a power of two, $\log_2(p_i)$ cannot be represented by a fixed-sized bit-vector. Thus, we will use the following approximation for the binary logarithm of a positive integer x,

$$\mathsf{apxlog}_2(x) \triangleq m + \frac{\mathsf{Truncate}(x[m-1,0])}{2^4}, \tag{5}$$

where $m = \lfloor \log_2(x) \rfloor$ and $\mathsf{Truncate}(z)$ for an m-bit vector z is defined by

$$\mathsf{Truncate}(z) = \begin{cases} z[m-1, m-4], & m \geq 4 \\ z[m-1,0] \parallel \overbrace{(0,\ldots,0)}^{4-m}, & m < 4 \end{cases}$$

In other words, apxlog_2 includes the integer part of the logarithm and takes the four bits right after the most significant one as the "fraction" bits. While Truncate can be generalized to consider more fraction bits, we will show later that four fraction bits are enough to minimize the bounds of our approximation error.

To describe $\sum_{i \in \mathcal{I}} \mathsf{apxlog}_2(p_i)$ with basic bit-vector operations, we will introduce in the next proposition two new bit-vector functions ParallelLog and ParallelTrunc. Given a bit-vector x with sub-vectors delimited by a bit-vector y, $\mathsf{ParallelLog}(x,y)$ computes the sum of the integer part of the logarithm of the delimited sub-vectors, whereas $\mathsf{ParallelTrunc}(x,y)$ calculates the sum of the four most significant bits of the delimited sub-vectors.

Proposition 1. *Let x and y be n-bit vectors such that y has r sub-vectors*

$$y[i_t, j_t] = (1, 1, \ldots, 1, 0), \quad t = 1, \ldots, r$$

where $i_1 > j_1 > i_2 > j_2 > \cdots > i_r > j_r \geq 0$, and y is equal to zero elsewhere. We define the bit-vector functions ParallelLog and ParallelTrunc by

$$\mathsf{ParallelLog}(x,y) = \mathsf{HW}(\mathsf{RevCarry}(x \wedge y, y))$$
$$\mathsf{ParallelTrunc}(x,y) = (\mathsf{HW}(z_0) \ll 3) \boxplus (\mathsf{HW}(z_1) \ll 2) \boxplus (\mathsf{HW}(z_2) \ll 1) \boxplus \mathsf{HW}(z_3)$$

where $z_\lambda = x \wedge (y \gg 0) \wedge \cdots \wedge (y \gg \lambda) \wedge \neg(y \gg (\lambda + 1))$.

a) If $x[i_t, j_t] > 0$ for $t = 1, \ldots, r$, then

$$\sum_{t=1}^{r} \lfloor \log_2(x[i_t, j_t]) \rfloor = \mathsf{ParallelLog}(x, y).$$

b) If at least $\lfloor \log_2(n) \rfloor + 4$ bits are dedicated to $\mathsf{ParallelTrunc}(x, y)$, then

$$\sum_{t=1}^{r} \mathsf{Truncate}(x[i_t, j_t + 1]) = \mathsf{ParallelTrunc}(x, y).$$

Proof. Case a) Let $m = \lfloor \log_2(x[i_1, j_1]) \rfloor$ and $c = \mathsf{RevCarry}(x \wedge y, y)$. Note that $c[n-1, i_1] = 0$, since $y[n-1, i_1+1] = 0$. For $m \geq 1$, we obtain the sub-vectors

$$
\begin{array}{rccccccc}
& i_1, \ldots, & j_1+m+1, & j_1+m, & j_1+m-1, & \ldots, & j_1+1, & j_1, & j_1-1 \\
y[i_1, j_1-1] = (1, \ldots, & & 1, & 1, & 1, & \ldots, & 1, & 0, & *), \\
(x \wedge y)[i_1, j_1-1] = (0, \ldots, & & 0, & 1, & *, & \ldots, & *, & 0, & *), \\
c[i_1, j_1-1] = (0, \ldots, & & 0, & 0, & 1, & \ldots, & 1, & 1, & 0).
\end{array}
$$

In particular, $c[i_1, j_1]$ has m bits set to one. If $m = 0$, $x[i_1, j_1 + 1] = 0$ and $y[j_1] = 0$, which implies that there is no carry chain, i.e., $c[i_1, j_1] = 0$. Therefore, in both cases $\mathsf{HW}(c)[i_1, j_1]) = m = \lfloor \log_2(x[i_1, j_1]) \rfloor$.

Note that the reversed carry chain stops at j_1, and $c[j_1 - 1, i_2] = 0 \cdots 0$. Therefore, the same argument can be applied for $t = 2, \ldots, r$, obtaining

$$
\mathsf{HW}(c[i_t, j_t]) = \lfloor \log_2(x[i_t, j_t]) \rfloor, \quad c[j_t - 1, i_{t+1}] = 0.
$$

Finally, it is easy to see that $c[j_r - 1, 0] = 0$, concluding the proof for this case.

Case b) First note that for $\lambda = 0, \ldots, 3$ and $t = 1, \ldots, r$, the variable z_λ is

$$
z_\lambda[i] = \begin{cases} x[i], & \text{if } i = i_t - \lambda > j_t \\ 0, & \text{otherwise} \end{cases}
$$

Therefore, the hamming weight of z_λ computes the following summation:

$$
\mathsf{HW}(z_\lambda) = \sum_{\substack{t \\ i_t - \lambda > j_t}} x[i_t - \lambda].
$$

While we define HW as a bit vector function returning an n-bit output given an n-bit input, $\lfloor \log_2(n) \rfloor + 1$ bits are sufficient to represent the output of HW. Therefore, by representing each $\mathsf{HW}(z_\lambda) \ll (3-\lambda)$ in a $(\lfloor \log_2(n) \rfloor + 4)$-bit variable h_λ, the bit-vector expression $h_0 \boxplus h_1 \boxplus h_2 \boxplus h_3$ does not overflow, and we obtain

$$
\sum_{t=1}^{r} \mathsf{Truncate}(x[i_t, j_t + 1]) = \sum_{t=1}^{r} \sum_{\substack{\lambda=0 \\ i_t - \lambda > j_t}}^{3} x[i_t - \lambda] \times 2^{3-\lambda} = h_0 \boxplus h_1 \boxplus h_2 \boxplus h_3,
$$

which concludes the proof. □

Since both HW and Rev have $O(\log_2 n)$ bit-vector complexities, so do the functions $\mathsf{ParallelLog}$ and $\mathsf{ParallelTrunc}$. The next lemma applies $\mathsf{ParallelLog}$ and $\mathsf{ParallelTrunc}$ to provide a bit-vector expression of the sum of $\mathsf{apxlog}_2(p_i)$.

Lemma 6. *Let r and f be the bit-vectors given by*

$$
r = \mathsf{ParallelLog}((w \wedge s'_{000}) \ll 1, s'_{000} \ll 1),
$$
$$
f = \mathsf{ParallelTrunc}(w \ll 1, \mathsf{RevCarry}((w \wedge s'_{000}) \ll 1, s'_{000} \ll 1)).
$$

If at least $\lfloor \log_2(n) \rfloor + 5$ bits are dedicated to r and f, then

$$
2^4 \sum_{i \in \mathcal{I}} \mathsf{apxlog}_2(p_i) = (r \ll 4) \boxplus f.
$$

Proof. Regarding Lemma 5, $w[i-1, i-\ell_i]$ represents the ℓ_i-bit vector of p_i and $s'_{000}[i-1, i-\ell_i]$ conforms to the pattern $(1, \cdots, 1, 0)$ for any $i \in \mathcal{I}$. Therefore,

$$\sum_{i \in \mathcal{I}} \lfloor \log_2(p_i) \rfloor = \mathsf{HW}(\mathsf{RevCarry}((w \wedge s'_{000}) \ll 1, s'_{000} \ll 1)),$$

following Proposition 1. For the second case, let c be the n-bit vector given by $c = \mathsf{RevCarry}((w \wedge s'_{000}) \ll 1, s'_{000} \ll 1)$. Denoting by $j = i - l_i$ and $m = \lfloor \log_2(p_i) \rfloor$ for a given $i \in \mathcal{I}$, note that $p_i[m]$ is the most significant active bit of p_i and

$$
\begin{array}{rcccccccc}
 & & i{+}1, \ldots, j{+}m{+}2, & j{+}m{+}1, & j{+}m, & \ldots, & j{+}2, & j{+}1, & j \\
(w \ll 1)[i{+}1, j] = & (0, \ldots, & 0 & p_i[m], & p_i[m{-}1], & \ldots, & p_i[1], & p_i[0] & 0), \\
c[i{+}1, j] = & (0, \ldots, & 0 & 0, & 1, & \ldots, & 1, & 1 & 0).
\end{array}
$$

Thus $c[j+m, j]$ conforms to the pattern $(1, \cdots, 1, 0)$ and Proposition 1 leads to

$$\sum_{\substack{i \in \mathcal{I} \\ m = \lfloor \log_2(p_i) \rfloor}} \mathsf{Truncate}(p_i[m-1, 0]) = \mathsf{ParallelTrunc}(w \ll 1, c).$$

For any n-bit variables x and y, it is easy to see that $\mathsf{ParallelLog}(x, y) < n$. Thus, $\lfloor \log_2(n) \rfloor + 4$ bits are sufficient to represent $(r \ll 4)$, and f can also be represented with the same number of bits following Proposition 1. Therefore, by representing $(r \ll 4)$ and f in $(\lfloor \log_2(n) \rfloor + 5)$-bit variables, the bit-vector expression $(r \ll 4) \boxplus f$ does not overflow.   □

Recall that the differential weight of constant addition can be decomposed as

$$\mathsf{weight}_{\boxplus_a}(u, v) = -\sum_{i \notin \mathcal{I}} \log_2(\varphi_i) - \sum_{i \in \mathcal{I}} \log_2\left(\frac{1}{2^{\ell_i - 1}}\right) - \sum_{i \in \mathcal{I}} \log_2(p_i).$$

If the binary logarithm of p_i is replaced by our approximation of the binary logarithm $\mathsf{apxlog}_2(p_i)$, we obtain the following approximation of the weight,

$$\mathsf{apxweight}_{\boxplus_a}(u, v) \triangleq -\sum_{i \notin \mathcal{I}} \log_2(\varphi_i) - \sum_{i \in \mathcal{I}} \log_2\left(\frac{1}{2^{\ell_i - 1}}\right) - \sum_{i \in \mathcal{I}} \mathsf{apxlog}_2(p_i). \quad (6)$$

Our weight approximation can be computed with the bit-vector function $\mathsf{BvWeight}$ described in Algorithm 1, as shown in the lemma.

Algorithm 1. Bit-vector function $\mathsf{BvWeight}(u, v, a)$.

Require: (u, v, a)
Ensure: $\mathsf{BvWeight}(u, v, a)$
$\quad s_{000} \leftarrow \neg(u \ll 1) \wedge \neg(v \ll 1)$
$\quad s'_{000} \leftarrow s_{000} \wedge \neg\mathsf{LZ}(\neg s_{000})$
$\quad t \leftarrow \neg s'_{000} \wedge (s'_{000} \gg 1)$
$\quad t' \leftarrow s'_{000} \wedge (\neg(s'_{000} \gg 1))$
$\quad s \leftarrow ((a \ll 1) \wedge t) \boxplus (a \wedge (s'_{000} \gg 1))$
$\quad q \leftarrow ((\neg((a \ll 1) \oplus u \oplus v)) \gg 1) \wedge t'$
$\quad d \leftarrow \mathsf{RevCarry}(s'_{000}, q) \vee q$
$\quad w \leftarrow (q \boxminus (s \wedge d)) \vee (s \wedge \neg d)$
$\quad int \leftarrow \mathsf{HW}((u \oplus v) \ll 1) \boxplus \mathsf{HW}(s'_{000}) \boxminus \mathsf{ParallelLog}((w \wedge s'_{000}) \ll 1, s'_{000} \ll 1)$
$\quad frac \leftarrow \mathsf{ParallelTrunc}(w \ll 1, \mathsf{RevCarry}((w \wedge s'_{000}) \ll 1, s'_{000} \ll 1))$
$\quad$**return** $(int \ll 4) \boxminus frac$

Lemma 7. *If at least $\lfloor \log_2(n) \rfloor + 5$ bits are dedicated to $\mathsf{BvWeight}(u, v, a)$, then*

$$2^4 \mathsf{apxweight}_{\boxplus_a}(u, v) = \mathsf{BvWeight}(u, v, a).$$

Proof. Regarding Eq. 4 and Lemmas 4 and 6 we respectively obtain

$$-\sum_{i \notin \mathcal{I}} \log_2(\varphi_i) = \mathsf{HW}((u \oplus v) \ll 1), \quad -\sum_{i \in \mathcal{I}} \log_2\left(\frac{1}{2^{\ell_i - 1}}\right) = \mathsf{HW}(s'_{000}),$$

$$2^4 \sum_{i \in \mathcal{I}} \mathsf{apxlog}_2(p_i) = (\mathsf{ParallelLog}((w \wedge s'_{000}) \ll 1, s'_{000} \ll 1) \ll 4) \boxplus frac.$$

All in all, we get the following identities,

$$2^4 \mathsf{apxweight}_{\boxplus_a}(u, v) = 2^4((int \ll 4) \boxminus frac) = \mathsf{BvWeight}(u, v, a).$$

$\square$

Note that the four least significant bits of $\mathsf{BvWeight}(u, v, a)$ correspond to the fraction bits of the approximate weight. In other words, the output of $\mathsf{BvWeight}(u, v, a)$ represents the rational value

$$\sum_{i=0}^{\lfloor \log_2(n) \rfloor + 4} 2^{i-4} \mathsf{BvWeight}(u, v, a)[i].$$

The bit-vector complexity of $\mathsf{BvWeight}$ is dominated by the complexity of $\mathsf{LZ}, \mathsf{Rev}, \mathsf{HW}, \mathsf{ParallelLog}$ and $\mathsf{ParallelTrunc}$. Since these operations can be computed with $O(\log_2 n)$ basic bit-vector operations, so does $\mathsf{BvWeight}$.

Theorem 4 shows that $\mathsf{BvWeight}$ leads to a close approximation of the differential weight and provides explicit bounds for the approximation error.

Theorem 4. *Let (u, v) be a valid differential over the n-bit constant addition $\boxplus_a$, let* $\mathsf{weight}_{\boxplus_a}(u, v)$ *be the differential weight of (u, v), and let* BvWeight *be the bit-vector function defined by Algorithm 1. Then, the approximation error,*

$$E = \mathsf{weight}_{\boxplus_a}(u, v) - \mathsf{apxweight}_{\boxplus_a}(u, v) = \mathsf{weight}_{\boxplus_a}(u, v) - 2^{-4}\mathsf{BvWeight}(u, v, a)$$

is bounded by $-0.029 \cdot n \le E \le 0$.

The next subsection is devoted to the proof of Theorem 4, where we will also analyse the error caused by our approximated binary logarithm.

3.3   Error Analysis - Proof of Theorem 4

In this subsection, we will prove Theorem 4 by gradually analysing the error produced by our approximation of the binary logarithm. As we can see from Eqs. (3) and (6), the gap between $\mathsf{weight}_{\boxplus_a}(u, v)$ and $\mathsf{apxweight}_{\boxplus_a}(u, v)$ is

$$\mathsf{weight}_{\boxplus_a}(u, v) - \mathsf{apxweight}_{\boxplus_a}(u, v) = -\sum_{i \in \mathcal{I}} \big(\log_2(p_i) - \mathsf{apxlog}_2(p_i)\big).$$

Note that the integer part of apxlog_2 is equal to the integer part of $\log_2$ and the error is caused by the fraction part of the logarithm. While $\mathsf{apxlog}_2(x)$ considers four bits of the input x for the fraction part, we generalize the definition of $\mathsf{apxlog}_2(x)$ to include variable number of bits of x. Given a positive integer x and the corresponding $m = \lfloor \log_2(x) \rfloor$, we define apxlog_2^κ as

$$\mathsf{apxlog}_2^\kappa(x) = \begin{cases} m + x[m-1, 0]/2^m, & m \le \kappa \\ m + x[m-1, x-\kappa]/2^\kappa, & m > \kappa \end{cases}$$

The non-negative integer κ is called the precision of the fraction part, and for $\kappa = 4$ we have $\mathsf{apxlog}_2^4(x) = \mathsf{apxlog}_2(x)$, which is defined in Eq. (5).

The following lemma bounds the approximation error of apxlog_2 when $\kappa \ge \lfloor \log_2(x) \rfloor$, with a similar proof as [39] for the sake of completeness. The main idea is that after extracting integer part of the logarithm in base 2, one can estimate $\log_2(1 + \gamma)$ by γ when $0 \le \gamma < 1$.

Lemma 8. *Consider a positive integer x and the binary logarithm approximation $\log_2(x) \approx m + x[m-1, 0]/2^m$, where $m = \lfloor \log_2(x) \rfloor$. Then, the approximation error $e = \log_2(x) - (m + x[m-1, 0]/2^m)$ is bounded by $0 \le e \le B$, where $B = 1 - \big(1 + \ln(\ln(2))\big)/\ln(2) \approx 0.086$.*

Proof. Let $x = 2^m + b$, where b is a non-negative integer such that $0 \le b < 2^m$. Therefore, $x[m-1, 0] = x - 2^m = b$ and the error is given by

$$e = \log_2(x) - (m + \frac{x[m-1, 0]}{2^m}) = \log_2(2^m + b) - (m + \frac{b}{2^m}) = \log_2(1 + \frac{b}{2^m}) - \frac{b}{2^m}.$$

For $\gamma = b/2^m$, we obtain $0 \le \gamma < 1$ and $e = \log_2(1 + \gamma) - \gamma$. Note that e is a concave function of γ where $e \ge 0$ if and only if $0 \le \gamma \le 1$. By deriving $e = e(\gamma)$, one can see that $\max(e) = B = 1 - \big(1 + \ln(\ln(2))\big)/\ln(2) \approx 0.086$ is reached when $\gamma = 1/\ln(2) - 1 \approx 0.44$. $\square$

The bound B is an almost tight bound, e.g., when $x = 3$, the obtained error is $\log_2(3) - (1 + \frac{1}{2}) \cong 0.085$. Similar to apxlog_2^κ, we generalize $\mathsf{apxweight}_{\boxplus_a}$ as

$$\mathsf{apxweight}_{\boxplus_a}^\kappa(u, v) = -\left(\sum_{i \in \mathcal{I}} \mathsf{apxlog}_2^\kappa(p_i) + \sum_{i \in \mathcal{I}} \log_2\left(\frac{1}{2^{\ell_i - 1}}\right) + \sum_{i \notin \mathcal{I}} \log_2(\varphi_i) \right),$$

where $\mathsf{apxweight}_{\boxplus_a}^4(u, v) = \mathsf{apxweight}_{\boxplus_a}(u, v)$ is defined by Eq. (6).

Finally, we prove Theorem 4 by generalizing the definition of approximated weight error $E_\kappa = \mathsf{weight}_{\boxplus_a}(u, v) - \mathsf{apxweight}_{\boxplus_a}^\kappa(u, v)$ and showing that if we dedicate at least 4 bits to the fraction precision κ, the approximation error is always bounded by $-0.086 \cdot (n/3) \le E_\kappa \le 0$.

Proof (Theorem 4). First, we mention that $\log_2(\varphi_i)$ is an integer number when $S_i \ne \mathbf{11*}$ or for $S_i = \mathbf{11*}$ we see $\ell_i < 3$. For these cases, $\log_2(\varphi_i) = \lfloor \log_2(\varphi_i) \rfloor$ and the approximation error is equal to zero.

Next, for each $i \in \mathcal{I}$ when $\ell_i \ge 3$, let $p_i = 2^{m_i} + b_i$ such that m_i and b_i are two non-negative integers, $m_i \le \ell_i - 2$ and $0 \le b_i < 2^{m_i}$. If $\ell_i \le \kappa + 2$, we obtain $m_i \le \kappa$ and $\mathsf{apxlog}_2^\kappa(p_i) = m_i + b_i \cdot 2^{-m_i}$. Thus, the resulting error

$$e_i = \log_2(p_i) - \mathsf{apxlog}_2^\kappa(p_i) = \log_2(p_i) - (m_i + b_i \cdot 2^{-m_i})$$

is exactly the same as the error defined in Proposition 8, and $0 \le e_i \le B \approx 0.086$.

On the other hand, for $m_i > \kappa$, i.e., $\ell_i \ge \kappa + 3$, let $p_i = 2^{m_i} + t_i \cdot 2^{m_i - \kappa} + \zeta_i$, where t_i and ζ_i are two non-negative integers such that $0 \le t_i < 2^\kappa$ as well as $0 \le \zeta_i < 2^{m_i - \kappa}$. In this case, the approximated binary logarithm is $\mathsf{apxlog}_2^\kappa(p_i) = m_i + t_i \cdot 2^{-\kappa}$. We now define a new error e_i' as

$$e_i' = \log_2(p_i) - \mathsf{apxlog}_2^\kappa(p_i) = \log_2(1 + t_i \cdot 2^{-\kappa} + \zeta_i \cdot 2^{-m_i}) - t_i \cdot 2^{-\kappa}.$$

Due to the fact that $\zeta_i \ge 0$, we can see that

$$e_i' = \log_2(p_i) - (m_i + t_i \cdot 2^{-\kappa}) \ge \log_2(p_i) - (m_i + t_i \cdot 2^{-\kappa} + \zeta_i \cdot 2^{-m_i}) = e_i \ge 0.$$

Since $\zeta_i < 2^{m_i - \kappa}$ and by reforming the error, we obtain the upper bound of e_i'

$$e_i' \le \log_2(1 + t_i \cdot 2^{-\kappa} + 2^{-\kappa}) - t_i \cdot 2^{-\kappa} = (\log_2(1 + \gamma_i') - \gamma_i') + 2^{-\kappa},$$

where $\gamma_i' = (t_i + 1) \cdot 2^{-\kappa}$ and $2^{-\kappa} \le \gamma_i' < 1$. Regarding Proposition 8, the new error e_i' is bounded by $0 \le e_i' \le B + 2^{-\kappa}$. Finally, by defining the conditional index set $\mathcal{I}_\alpha^\beta = \{i \in \mathcal{I} \mid \alpha \le \ell_i \le \beta\}$ we obtain

$$E_\kappa = \mathsf{weight}_{\boxplus_a}(u, v) - \mathsf{apxweight}_{\boxplus_a}^\kappa(u, v)$$

$$= -\sum_{i \in \mathcal{I}} (\log_2(p_i) - \mathsf{apxlog}_2^\kappa(p_i)) = -\left(\sum_{i \in \mathcal{I}_3^{\kappa+2}} e_i + \sum_{i \in \mathcal{I}_{\kappa+3}^n} e_i' \right)$$

$$\ge -\left(B \sum_{i \in \mathcal{I}_3^{\kappa+2}} 1 + (B + 2^{-\kappa}) \sum_{i \in \mathcal{I}_{\kappa+3}^n} 1 \right) \ge -\left(\frac{B}{3} \sum_{i \in \mathcal{I}_3^{\kappa+2}} \ell_i + \left(\frac{B + 2^{-\kappa}}{\kappa + 3} \right) \sum_{i \in \mathcal{I}_{\kappa+3}^n} \ell_i \right).$$

For $\kappa \geq 4$, we can see that $\dfrac{B + 2^{-\kappa}}{\kappa + 3} \leq \dfrac{B}{3}$, resulting in

$$0 \geq E_\kappa \geq -\left(\frac{B}{3} \sum_{i \in \mathcal{I}_3^n} \ell_i\right) \geq -(\frac{B}{3}n) \approx -0.029n \,.$$

Since for $\kappa = 4$, we have $E_4 = E = \mathsf{weight}_{\boxplus_a}(u, v) - \mathsf{apxweight}_{\boxplus_a}(u, v)$, the above inequalities hold for the approximation error E as well.   □

While dedicating $\kappa = 4$ bits as the fraction precision is enough to obtain the same error bounds as $\kappa > 4$, considering $\kappa < 4$ creates a trade-off between the lower bound of the error and the complexity of Algorithm 1. As an example, choosing $\kappa = 3$ removes one HW call in Algorithm 1. However, by following the proof of Theorem 4 for $\kappa = 3$, the error will be lower bounded by $-0.035n$, which potentially is an acceptable trade-off.

The differential model of the constant addition as well as the approximation error will be used in the automated method that we will present in the next section to search for characteristics of ARX ciphers.

4   SMT-Based Search of Characteristics

In this section, we describe how to formulate the search of an optimal characteristic as a sequence of SMT problems, which can be solved by an off-the-shelf SMT solver such as Boolector [40] or STP [41]. This approach was originally used by Mouha and Preneel to search for single-key characteristics of Salsa20 [18].

To search for characteristics up to probability 2^{-n}, the probability space is decomposed into n intervals $I_w = \left(2^{-w-1}, 2^{-w}\right]$, where $w = 0, 1, \ldots, n - 1$, and for each interval, the decision problem of whether there exists a characteristic with probability $p \in I_w$ is encoded as an SMT problem. Note that a characteristic Ω has probability $p \in I_w$ if and only if its integer weight $\lfloor \mathsf{weight}(\Omega) \rfloor$ is equal to w. Sect. 4.1 describes the encoding process for an ARX cipher.

The SMT problems are provided to the SMT solver, which checks their satisfiability in increasing weight order. When the SMT solver finds the first satisfiable problem, an assignment of the variables that makes the problem satisfiable is obtained, and the search finishes. The assignment contains a characteristic with integer weight $\hat{w}$, and it is optimal in the sense that there are no characteristics with integer weight strictly smaller than $\hat{w}$. If the n SMT problems are found to be unsatisfiable, then it is proved there are no characteristics with probability higher than 2^{-n}.

To speed up the search, we perform the search iteratively on round-reduced versions of the cipher. First, we search for an optimal characteristic for a small number of rounds r; let $\hat{w}$ denote its integer weight. Then, we search for an optimal $(r+1)$-round characteristic, but skipping the SMT problems with weight strictly less than $\hat{w}$. Since these SMT problems were found to be unsatisfiable for r rounds, they will also be unsatisfiable for $r + 1$ rounds. This procedure is repeated until the total number of rounds is reached. Our strategy prioritises SMT problems with low weight and small number of rounds, which are faster to solve. In addition, our search also finds optimal characteristics of round-reduced versions, which can be used in other differential-based attacks, such as the rectangle or rebound attacks [42,43].

This automated method can be used to search for either single-key or related-key characteristics. Furthermore, additional SMT constraints can be added to the SMT problems in order to search for different types of characteristics. For related-key characteristics, this method search by default characteristics minimizing the total weight $\mathsf{weight}(\Omega) = \mathsf{weight}(\Omega_{KS}) + \mathsf{weight}(\Omega_E)$. Strong related-key characteristics can be searched by adding the constraint $\mathsf{weight}(\Omega_{KS}) = 0$ in the SMT problems. Similarly, equivalent keys can be found by adding the constraint $\mathsf{weight}(\Omega_E) = 0$.

In some cases, the integer weight computed by the SMT solver is not the exact integer weight of the characteristic, but a bound of the error ϵ is known. For example, for an ARX cipher with constant additions, the weight of the constant additions is computed in the SMT problems using Theorem 4, which introduces an error that can be bounded (Theorem 4). Nonetheless, this method can find the optimal characteristic in this case by finding all the characteristics with integer weights $\{\hat{w}, \hat{w} + 1, \ldots, \hat{w} + \lfloor \epsilon \rfloor\}$, where $\hat{w}$ is the integer weight of the first characteristic found by the SMT solver.

This method only ensures optimality if the differential probabilities over each round are independent and the characteristic probability does not strongly depend on the choice of the secret key. When these assumptions do not hold for a cipher, we empirically compute the weight of each characteristic found by sampling many input pairs satisfying the input difference and counting those satisfying the difference trail. In this case, this method provides a practical heuristic to find characteristics with high probability, and it is one of the best systematic approaches for some families of ciphers, such as ARX.

4.1   Encoding the SMT Problems

In this section, we explain how to formulate the decision problem of determining whether there exists a characteristic Ω with integer weight W of an ARX cipher as an SMT problem in the bit-vector theory.

First, the ARX cipher is represented in Static Single Assignment (SSA) form, that is, as an ordered list of instructions $y \leftarrow f(x)$ such that each variable is assigned exactly once and each instruction is a modular addition, a rotation or an XOR.

For each variable x in the SSA representation, a bit-vector variable Δ_x denoting the difference of x is defined in the SMT problem. Then, for every instruction $y \leftarrow f(x)$, the weight and the differential model of f are added to the SMT problem as a bit-vector variable w and bit-vector constraints $\mathsf{valid}_{f_i}(\Delta_x, \Delta_y)$ and $\mathsf{Equals}(w, \mathsf{weight}_{f_i}(\Delta_x, \Delta_y))$, following Table 2.

Finally, the following bit-vector constraints are added to the SMT problem,

$$\mathsf{NotEquals}(\Delta_p, 0)\,, \quad \mathsf{Equals}(W, w_1 \boxplus \cdots \boxplus w_r)\,,$$

Table 2. Bit-vector differential models of ARX operations.

$y = f_a(x)$	Validity	Weight
$y = x_1 \oplus x_2$	$\mathsf{Equals}(\Delta_y, \Delta_{x_1} \oplus \Delta_{x_2})$	0
$y = x \oplus a$	$\mathsf{Equals}(\Delta_y, \Delta_x)$	0
$y = x \lll a$	$\mathsf{Equals}(\Delta_y, \Delta_x \lll a)$	0
$y = x \ggg a$	$\mathsf{Equals}(\Delta_y, \Delta_x \ggg a)$	0
$y = x_1 \boxplus x_2$	Theorem 1	Theorem 1
$y = x \boxplus a$	Theorem 3	Theorem 4

where Δ_p denotes the input difference and $(w_1, \ldots, w_r)$ denote the weight of each operation. The first constraint excludes the trivial characteristic with zero input difference, while the second constraint fixes the weight of the characteristic to the target weight. Note that the bit-size of the weights might need to be increased to prevent an overflow in the modular addition of the last constraint.

4.2   Implementation

We have developed an open-source[2] tool to find characteristics of ARX ciphers implementing the method described in the previous sections. ArxPy provides high-level functions that automate the search of optimal characteristics, a simple interface to represent ARX ciphers, and a complete documentation in HTML format, among other features.

ArxPy workflow is represented in Fig. 1. The user first defines the ARX cipher using the interface provided by ArxPy and chooses the parameters of the search

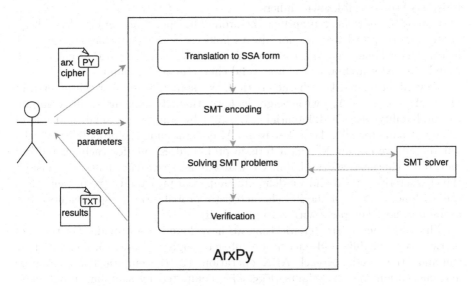

Fig. 1. Workflow of ArxPy

---

[2] https://github.com/ranea/ArxPy.

(e.g., the type of the characteristic to search, the SMT solver to use, etc.). Then, `ArxPy` automatically translates the python implementation of the ARX cipher into SSA form, encodes the SMT problems associated to the type of search selected by the user, and solves the SMT problems by querying the SMT solver. For each satisfiable SMT problem found, `ArxPy` reconstructs the characteristic from the assignment of the variables that satisfies the problem and empirically verifies the weight of the characteristic. Finally, `ArxPy` returns the results of the search to the user.

Internally, `ArxPy` is implemented in Python 3 and uses the libraries `SymPy` [44] to obtain the SSA representation through symbolic execution and `PySMT` [45] for the communication with the SMT solvers. Thus, all the SMT solvers supported by `PySMT` can be directly used for `ArxPy`.

5   Experiments

We have applied our method for finding characteristics to some ARX ciphers that include constant additions. In particular, we have searched for related-key characteristics of TEA, XTEA, HIGHT and LEA.

Due to the difficulty of searching for characteristics of ciphers with constant additions this far, cipher designers have avoided constant additions in the encryption functions so that they can search for single-key characteristics, the most threatening ones. Only a few ciphers include constant additions in the encryption function, and their ad-hoc structures makes them more suitable to be analysed with other types of differences, such as additive differences in the case of TEA [15]. As a result, we have focused on searching related-key characteristics of some well-known ciphers.

However, the usual assumptions (i.e., round independence and the hypothesis of stochastic equivalence) do not always hold for related-key characteristics, as in this case. Thus, we empirically verify each characteristic and stopped each round-reduced search after the first valid characteristic is found.

To verify a related-key characteristic Ω, we split Ω in smaller characteristics $\Omega_i = (\Delta_{x_i} \to \cdots \to \Delta_{y_i})$ with weight w_i lower than 20, and empirically compute the probability of each differential $(\Delta_{x_i}, \Delta_{y_i})$ by sampling a small multiple of 2^{w_i} input pairs for 2^{10} related-key pairs. After combining the probability of each differential, we obtain 2^{10} characteristic probabilities, one for each related-key pair. If the characteristic probability is non-zero for several key pairs, we consider the characteristic valid and we define its empirical probability (resp. weight) as the arithmetic mean of the 2^{10} characteristic probabilities (resp. weights), but excluding those key pairs with zero probability.

Thus, for each characteristic that we have found, we provide: (1) the theoretical key schedule and encryption integer weights (w_{KS}, w_E), computed by summing the weight of each ARX operation; (2) the empirical key schedule and encryption integer weights $(\overline{w_{\mathsf{KS}}}, \overline{w_E})$, computed by sampling input pairs as explained before; and (3) the percentage of key pairs that lead to non-zero probability in the weight verification. In the extended version, we provide the round weights and round differences for the characteristics covering the most rounds.

For the experiments, we have used ArxPy equipped with the SMT solver Boolector [40], winner of the SMT competition SMT-COMP 2019 in the bit-vector track [46]. We run the search for one week on a single core of an Intel Xeon 6244 at 3.60 GHz. Table 3 lists the characteristics we have found and compares them with the previous longest-known characteristics. Note that better characteristics could be found if the round-reduced searches are not stopped after the first valid characteristic or if more time is employed.

Table 3. Best related-key characteristics of XTEA, HIGHT and LEA.

Cipher	Ch. Type	Rounds	$(w_{KS}, \overline{w_{KS}})$	$(w_E, \overline{w_E})$	% valid keys	Reference
XTEA	Strong related-key	16	0	32	–	[47]
		16	(0,0)	(37, 32)	46%	This paper
		18	(0,0)	(57, 49)	48%	This paper
	Weak related-key	18	17	19	–	[47,48]
		18	(4, 3)	(16, 14)	100%	This paper
		27	(6, 5)	(40, 39)	7%	This paper
HIGHT	Strong related-key	10	0	12	–	[49]
		10	(0, 0)	(12, 9)	34%	This paper
		15	(0, 0)	(45, 42)	8%	This paper
	Weak related-key	12	2	19	–	[50]
		12	(2, 3)	(19, 17)	40%	This paper
		14	(13, 9)	(14, 11)	17%	This paper
LEA	Weak related-key	11	–	–	–	[8]
		6	(1, 1)	(24, 22)	100%	This paper
		7	(2, 4)	(36, 34)	100%	This paper

TEA. Designed by Wheeler and Needham, TEA [12] is a block cipher with 64-bit block size and 128-bit key size. It iterates 64 times an ARX round function including constant additions and logical shifts. Since the logical shifts propagate XOR differences deterministically, the encoding method presented in Sect. 4.1 can be easily extended to include these operations.

The best related-key characteristics were obtained by Kelsey, Schneier, and Wagner in [51]. They found a 2-round iterative strong related-key characteristic Ω with weight $(w_k, w_e) = (0, 1)$, which they extended to a 60-round characteristic with weight $(0, 30)$. They also discovered in [30] that each TEA key has 3 other equivalent keys.

Using ArxPy, we revisited the results by Kelsey et al., but in a fully automated way. We found three related-key characteristic with weight zero over the full cipher, confirming that each key is equivalent to exactly three other keys.

Excluding these three characteristics, we also obtained a 60-round strong related-key characteristic with weight (0, 30), and all the 60-round SMT problems with smaller weights were found to be unsatisfiable. Since a 60-round related-key characteristic is sufficient to mount the related-key differential cryptanalysis on full-round TEA [51], there is no need to search for characteristics containing more rounds of TEA and we stop at 60 rounds.

XTEA. To fix the weakness of TEA against related-key attacks, the same designers propose XTEA [13]. This block cipher has a 64-bit block size and a 128-bit key size. The ARX round function includes logical shifts, but the key schedule is composed exclusively of constant additions.

The longest related-key characteristics found so far are the 16-round strong related-key differential with weight 32, manually found by Lu in [47], and the 18-round weak related-key characteristic with weights $(w_{KS}, w_E) = (19, 19)$, manually found by Lee et al. [48] but later improved to (17, 19) by Lu [47].

The results of our automated search are listed in Table 3. In the strong related-key search we found an 18-round characteristic with weight 57; all the SMT problems for 19 rounds were found to be unsatisfiable. In the weak related-key search, we found characteristics up to 27 rounds, where the 27-round characteristic has total weight $6 + 40 = 46$. No equivalent keys were found for XTEA.

HIGHT. Adopted as an international standard by ISO/IEC [52], HIGHT [7] is a lightweight cipher with block size of 64 bits and a key size of 128 bits. The encryption function performs an initial and final key-whitening transformations, and iterates 32 times a round function including XORs, 2-input additions and rotations; the constant additions are performed in the key schedule.

The longest related-key characteristics found for HIGHT are a 10-round strong characteristic with weight 12 found by Lu [49], and a 12-round weak characteristic with weights $(w_{KS}, w_E) = (2, 19)$ found by Koo et al. [50].

In our automated search, we found related-key characteristic up to 15 rounds, listed in Table 3. The longest strong related-key characteristic we found covered 15 rounds with weights (0, 45), whereas the longest weak related-key characteristic covered 14 rounds with total weight $13 + 14 = 27$.

LEA. Among the family of ARX ciphers LEA [8], we have analysed LEA-128, the version with 128-bit block size, 24 rounds and 128-bit key size. The encryption round function of LEA performs 2-input additions, rotations and XORs, whereas the key schedule contains constant additions and rotations.

The designers of LEA found related-key characteristics up to 11 rounds, but only specifying that the 11-round characteristics are valid for a small part of the key space and without providing the weights of such characteristics [8]. Excluding these characteristics, there are no others examples of related-key characteristics of LEA. In our automated search, we found weak related-key characteristic up to 7 rounds valid for the full key space, listed in Table 3. Strong characteristics with weight smaller than 128 were found up to 4 rounds, and all the strong related-key SMT problems for 5 rounds were found unsatisfiable. No equivalent keys were found for LEA.

6   Conclusion

In this paper we proposed the first bit-vector differential model of the n-bit modular addition with a constant. We described a bit-vector formula, with bit-vector complexity $O(1)$, that determines whether a differential is valid and a bit-vector function, with complexity $O(\log_2 n)$, that provides a close approximation of the differential weight. In this regard, we carefully studied our approximation error and obtained almost tight bounds.

Moreover, we described an SMT-based automated method to search for characteristics of ARX ciphers including constant additions. Our method formulates the search problem as a sequence of SMT problems in the bit-vector theory, which are encoded from the SSA representation of the cipher and the bit-vector differential models of each operation. We have implemented our method in `ArxPy`, an open-source tool to find characteristic of ARX ciphers in a fully automated way. To show some examples, we have applied our automated method to search for equivalent keys and related-key characteristics of TEA, XTEA, HIGHT, and LEA. For TEA, we revisited previous results obtained in a manual approach, whereas for XTEA, HIGHT and LEA we improved the previous best-known related-key characteristics in both the strong-key and weak-key settings.

Our differential model relies on a bit-vector friendly approximation on the binary logarithm. Thus, future works could explore other approximations improving the bit-vector complexity or the approximation error, which could also be applied to other SMT problems involving the binary logarithm. While we have focused on the modular addition by a constant, there are other simple operations for which no differential model have been proposed so far, such as the modular multiplication. Obtaining differential models for more operations will allow designing ciphers with more flexibility, leading to new designs that potentially are more efficient.

Acknowledgements. Adrián Ranea is supported by a PhD Fellowship from the Research Foundation – Flanders (FWO). The authors would like to thank the anonymous reviewers for their comments and suggestions.

References

1. Omale, G.: Gartner identifies top 10 strategic IoT technologies and trends (2018). https://www.gartner.com/en/newsroom/press-releases/2018-11-07-gartner-identifies-top-10-strategic-iot-technologies-and-trends
2. National Institute of Standards and Technology. Lightweight cryptography project. https://csrc.nist.gov/Projects/Lightweight-Cryptography
3. Dinu, D., Corre, L.Y., Khovratovich, D., Perrin, L., Großschädl, J., Biryukov, A.: Triathlon of lightweight block ciphers for the internet of things. J. Cryptographic Eng. **9**(3), 283–302 (2019)
4. Aumasson, J.-P., Henzen, L., Meier, W., Phan, R.C.-W.: Sha-3 proposal blake. Submission to NIST (round 3), 92 (2008)

5. Bernstein, D.J.: The Salsa20 family of stream ciphers. In: Robshaw, M., Billet, O. (eds.) New Stream Cipher Designs. LNCS, vol. 4986, pp. 84–97. Springer, Heidelberg (2008). https://doi.org/10.1007/978-3-540-68351-3_8

6. Mouha, N., Mennink, B., Van Herrewege, A., Watanabe, D., Preneel, B., Verbauwhede, I.: Chaskey: an efficient MAC algorithm for 32-bit microcontrollers. In: Joux, A., Youssef, A. (eds.) SAC 2014. LNCS, vol. 8781, pp. 306–323. Springer, Cham (2014). https://doi.org/10.1007/978-3-319-13051-4_19

7. Hong, D., et al.: HIGHT: a new block cipher suitable for low-resource device. In: Goubin, L., Matsui, M. (eds.) CHES 2006. LNCS, vol. 4249, pp. 46–59. Springer, Heidelberg (2006). https://doi.org/10.1007/11894063_4

8. Hong, D., Lee, J.-K., Kim, D.-C., Kwon, D., Ryu, K.H., Lee, D.-G.: LEA: a 128-bit block cipher for fast encryption on common processors. In: Kim, Y., Lee, H., Perrig, A. (eds.) WISA 2013. LNCS, vol. 8267, pp. 3–27. Springer, Cham (2014). https://doi.org/10.1007/978-3-319-05149-9_1

9. Beaulieu, R., Shors, D., Smith, J., Treatman-Clark, S., Weeks, B., Wingers, L.: The SIMON and SPECK families of lightweight block ciphers. IACR Cryptology ePrint Archive 2013, 404 (2013)

10. Dinu, D., Perrin, L., Udovenko, A., Velichkov, V., Großschädl, J., Biryukov, A.: Design strategies for ARX with provable bounds: SPARX and LAX. In: Cheon, J.H., Takagi, T. (eds.) ASIACRYPT 2016. LNCS, vol. 10031, pp. 484–513. Springer, Heidelberg (2016). https://doi.org/10.1007/978-3-662-53887-6_18

11. Lai, X., Massey, J.L.: A proposal for a new block encryption standard. In: Damgård, I.B. (ed.) EUROCRYPT 1990. LNCS, vol. 473, pp. 389–404. Springer, Heidelberg (1991). https://doi.org/10.1007/3-540-46877-3_35

12. Wheeler, D.J., Needham, R.M.: TEA, a tiny encryption algorithm. In: Preneel, B. (ed.) FSE 1994. LNCS, vol. 1008, pp. 363–366. Springer, Heidelberg (1995). https://doi.org/10.1007/3-540-60590-8_29

13. Needham, R., Wheeler, D.: Tea extensions. Technical report, Computer Laboratory, University of Cambridge (1997)

14. Koo, B., Roh, D., Kim, H., Jung, Y., Lee, D.-G., Kwon, D.: CHAM: a family of lightweight block ciphers for resource-constrained devices. In: Kim, H., Kim, D.-C. (eds.) ICISC 2017. LNCS, vol. 10779, pp. 3–25. Springer, Cham (2018). https://doi.org/10.1007/978-3-319-78556-1_1

15. Biryukov, A., Velichkov, V.: Automatic search for differential trails in ARX ciphers. In: Benaloh, J. (ed.) CT-RSA 2014. LNCS, vol. 8366, pp. 227–250. Springer, Cham (2014). https://doi.org/10.1007/978-3-319-04852-9_12

16. Biryukov, A., Velichkov, V., Le Corre, Y.: Automatic search for the best trails in ARX: application to block cipher SPECK. In: Peyrin, T. (ed.) FSE 2016. LNCS, vol. 9783, pp. 289–310. Springer, Heidelberg (2016). https://doi.org/10.1007/978-3-662-52993-5_15

17. Matsui, M.: On correlation between the order of S-boxes and the strength of DES. In: De Santis, A. (ed.) EUROCRYPT 1994. LNCS, vol. 950, pp. 366–375. Springer, Heidelberg (1995). https://doi.org/10.1007/BFb0053451

18. Mouha, N., Preneel., B.: Towards finding optimal differential characteristics for ARX: Application to Salsa20. IACR Cryptology ePrint Archive, 2013:328 (2013). http://eprint.iacr.org/2013/328

19. Fu, K., Wang, M., Guo, Y., Sun, S., Hu, L.: MILP-based automatic search algorithms for differential and linear trails for speck. In: Peyrin, T. (ed.) FSE 2016. LNCS, vol. 9783, pp. 268–288. Springer, Heidelberg (2016). https://doi.org/10.1007/978-3-662-52993-5_14

20. Barrett, C., Tinelli, C.: Satisfiability modulo theories. Handbook of Model Checking, pp. 305–343. Springer, Cham (2018). https://doi.org/10.1007/978-3-319-10575-8_11
21. Lodi, A.: Mixed integer programming computation. In: Jünger, M., et al. (eds.) 50 Years of Integer Programming 1958-2008, pp. 619–645. Springer, Heidelberg (2010). https://doi.org/10.1007/978-3-540-68279-0_16
22. Lipmaa, H., Moriai, S.: Efficient algorithms for computing differential properties of addition. In: Matsui, M. (ed.) FSE 2001. LNCS, vol. 2355, pp. 336–350. Springer, Heidelberg (2002). https://doi.org/10.1007/3-540-45473-X_28
23. Kölbl, S., Leander, G., Tiessen, T.: Observations on the SIMON block cipher family. In: Gennaro, R., Robshaw, M. (eds.) CRYPTO 2015. LNCS, vol. 9215, pp. 161–185. Springer, Heidelberg (2015). https://doi.org/10.1007/978-3-662-47989-6_8
24. Liu, Y., De Witte, G., Ranea, A., Ashur, T.: Rotational-XOR cryptanalysis of reduced-round SPECK. IACR Trans. Symmetric Cryptol. **2017**(3), 24–36 (2017). https://doi.org/10.13154/tosc.v2017.i3.24-36
25. Song, L., Huang, Z., Yang, Q.: Automatic differential analysis of ARX block ciphers with application to SPECK and LEA. In: Liu, J.K., Steinfeld, R. (eds.) ACISP 2016. LNCS, vol. 9723, pp. 379–394. Springer, Cham (2016). https://doi.org/10.1007/978-3-319-40367-0_24
26. Machado, A.W.: Differential probability of modular addition with a constant operand. IACR Cryptology ePrint Archive, 2001:52 (2001). http://eprint.iacr.org/2001/052
27. Kovásznai, G., Fröhlich, A., Biere, A.: Complexity of fixed-size bit-vector logics. Theory Comput. Syst. **59**(2), 323–376 (2016)
28. Warren Jr., H.S.: Hacker's Delight. Addison-Wesley, Boston (2003)
29. Biham, E., Shamir, A.: Differential cryptanalysis of des-like cryptosystems. J. Cryptol. **4**(1), 3–72 (1991). https://doi.org/10.1007/BF00630563
30. Kelsey, J., Schneier, B., Wagner, D.: Key-schedule cryptanalysis of IDEA, G-DES, GOST, SAFER, and triple-DES. In: Koblitz, N. (ed.) CRYPTO 1996. LNCS, vol. 1109, pp. 237–251. Springer, Heidelberg (1996). https://doi.org/10.1007/3-540-68697-5_19
31. Winternitz, R.S., Hellman, M.E.: Chosen-key attacks on a block cipher. Cryptologia **11**(1), 16–20 (1987)
32. Lai, X., Massey, J.L., Murphy, S.: Markov ciphers and differential cryptanalysis. In: Davies, D.W. (ed.) EUROCRYPT 1991. LNCS, vol. 547, pp. 17–38. Springer, Heidelberg (1991). https://doi.org/10.1007/3-540-46416-6_2
33. Sun, S., Hu, L., Wang, P., Qiao, K., Ma, X., Song, L.: Automatic security evaluation and (related-key) differential characteristic search: application to SIMON, PRESENT, LBlock, DES(L) and other bit-oriented block ciphers. In: Sarkar, P., Iwata, T. (eds.) ASIACRYPT 2014. LNCS, vol. 8873, pp. 158–178. Springer, Heidelberg (2014). https://doi.org/10.1007/978-3-662-45611-8_9
34. Sun, S., et al.: Analysis of AES, skinny, and others with constraint programming. IACR Trans. Symmetric Cryptol. **2017**(1), 281–306 (2017). https://doi.org/10.13154/tosc.v2017.i1.281-306
35. Aumasson, J.-P., Jovanovic, P., Neves, S.: Analysis of NORX: investigating differential and rotational properties. In: Aranha, D.F., Menezes, A. (eds.) LATIN-CRYPT 2014. LNCS, vol. 8895, pp. 306–324. Springer, Cham (2015). https://doi.org/10.1007/978-3-319-16295-9_17

36. Lipmaa, H.: On differential properties of pseudo-Hdamard transform and related mappings (extended abstract). In: Menezes, A., Sarkar, P. (eds.) INDOCRYPT 2002. LNCS, vol. 2551, pp. 48–61. Springer, Heidelberg (2002). https://doi.org/10.1007/3-540-36231-2_5

37. Bagherzadeh, E., Ahmadian, Z.: Milp-based automatic differential searches for LEA and HIGHT. IACR Cryptology ePrint Archive, 2018:948 (2018). https://eprint.iacr.org/2018/948

38. Schulte-Geers, E.: On CCZ-equivalence of addition mod 2^n. Des. Codes Cryptogr. **66**(1–3), 111–127 (2013). https://doi.org/10.1007/s10623-012-9668-4

39. Mitchell, J.N.: Computer multiplication and division using binary logarithms. IRE Trans. Electr. Comput. (4), 512–517 (1962)

40. Niemetz, A., Preiner, M., Biere, A.: Boolector 2.0 system description. J. Satisfiab. Boolean Model. Comput **9**, 53–58 (2015)

41. Ganesh, V., Dill, D.L.: A decision procedure for bit-vectors and arrays. In: Damm, W., Hermanns, H. (eds.) CAV 2007. LNCS, vol. 4590, pp. 519–531. Springer, Heidelberg (2007). https://doi.org/10.1007/978-3-540-73368-3_52

42. Wagner, D.: The boomerang attack. In: Knudsen, L. (ed.) FSE 1999. LNCS, vol. 1636, pp. 156–170. Springer, Heidelberg (1999). https://doi.org/10.1007/3-540-48519-8_12

43. Biham, E., Dunkelman, O., Keller, N.: The rectangle attack — rectangling the serpent. In: Pfitzmann, B. (ed.) EUROCRYPT 2001. LNCS, vol. 2045, pp. 340–357. Springer, Heidelberg (2001). https://doi.org/10.1007/3-540-44987-6_21

44. Meurer, A., et al.: Sympy: symbolic computing in python. Peer J. Comput. Sci. **3**:e103 (2017). ISSN 2376–5992. https://doi.org/10.7717/peerj-cs.103

45. Gario, M., Micheli, A.: Pysmt: a solver-agnostic library for fast prototyping of smt-based algorithms. In: SMT Workshop 2015 (2015)

46. Hadarean, L., Hyvarinen, A., Niemetz, A., Reger, G.: 14th International Satisfiability Modulo Theories Competition (smt-comp 2019): Rules and Procedures (2019)

47. Jiqiang, L.: Related-key rectangle attack on 36 rounds of the XTEA block cipher. Int. J. Inf. Sec. **8**(1), 1–11 (2009)

48. Lee, E., Hong, D., Chang, D., Hong, S., Lim, J.: A weak key class of XTEA for a related-key rectangle attack. In: Nguyen, P.Q. (ed.) VIETCRYPT 2006. LNCS, vol. 4341, pp. 286–297. Springer, Heidelberg (2006). https://doi.org/10.1007/11958239_19

49. Lu, J.: Cryptanalysis of reduced versions of the HIGHT block cipher from CHES 2006. In: Nam, K.-H., Rhee, G. (eds.) ICISC 2007. LNCS, vol. 4817, pp. 11–26. Springer, Heidelberg (2007). https://doi.org/10.1007/978-3-540-76788-6_2

50. Koo, B., Hong, D., Kwon, D.: Related-key attack on the full HIGHT. In: Rhee, K.-H., Nyang, D.H. (eds.) ICISC 2010. LNCS, vol. 6829, pp. 49–67. Springer, Heidelberg (2011). https://doi.org/10.1007/978-3-642-24209-0_4

51. Kelsey, J., Schneier, B., Wagner, D.: Related-key cryptanalysis of 3-WAY, Biham-DES,CAST, DES-X, NewDES, RC2, and TEA. In: Han, Y., Okamoto, T., Qing, S. (eds.) ICICS 1997. LNCS, vol. 1334, pp. 233–246. Springer, Heidelberg (1997). https://doi.org/10.1007/BFb0028479

52. ISO/IEC 18033-3:2010. Information technology - Security techniques - Encryption algorithms - Part 3: Block ciphers. Standard, International Organization for Standardization, March 2010

Mind the Propagation of States

New Automatic Search Tool for Impossible Differentials and Impossible Polytopic Transitions

Xichao Hu[1,2], Yongqiang Li[1,2(✉)], Lin Jiao[3], Shizhu Tian[1,2],
and Mingsheng Wang[1,2]

[1] State Key Laboratory of Information Security, Institute of Information
Engineering, Chinese Academy of Sciences, Beijing, China
{huxichao,tianshizhu,wangmingsheng}@iie.ac.cn,
yongq.lee@gmail.com
[2] School of Cyber Security, University of Chinese Academy of Sciences,
Beijing, China
[3] State Key Laboratory of Cryptology, Beijing, China
jiaolin_jl@126.com

Abstract. Impossible differentials cryptanalysis and impossible polytopic cryptanalysis are the most effective approaches to estimate the security of block ciphers. However, the previous automatic search methods of their distinguishers, impossible differentials and impossible polytopic transitions, neither consider the impact of key schedule in the single-key setting and the differential property of large S-boxes, nor apply to the block ciphers with variable rotations.

Thus, unlike previous methods which focus on the propagation of the difference or s-difference, we redefine the impossible differentials and impossible $(s+1)$-polytopic transitions according to the propagation of state, which allow us to break through those limitations of the previous methods. Theoretically, we prove that traditional impossible differentials and impossible $(s+1)$-polytopic transitions are equivalent to part of our redefinitions, which have advantages from broader view. Technically, we renew the automatic search model and design an SAT-based tool to evaluate our redefined impossible differentials and impossible $(s+1)$-polytopic transitions efficiently.

As a result, for GIFT64, we get the 6-round impossible differentials which cannot be detected by all previous tools. For PRINTcipher, we propose the first modeling method for the key-dependent permutation and key-dependent S-box. For MISTY1, we derive 902 4-round impossible differentials by exploiting the differential property of S-boxes. For RC5, we present the first modeling method for the variable rotation and get 2.5-round impossible differentials for each version of it. More remarkable, our tool can be used to evaluate the security of given cipher against the impossible differentials, and we prove that there exists no 5-round 1 input active word and 1 output active word impossible differentials for AES-128 even consider the relations of 3-round keys. Besides, we also get the impossible $(s+1)$-polytopic transitions for PRINTcipher, GIFT64, PRESENT, and RC5, all of which can cover more rounds than their corresponding impossible differentials as far as we know.

© International Association for Cryptologic Research 2020
S. Moriai and H. Wang (Eds.): ASIACRYPT 2020, LNCS 12491, pp. 415–445, 2020.
https://doi.org/10.1007/978-3-030-64837-4_14

Keywords: Impossible differentials · Impossible polytopic transitions · $(s+1)$-ploygon · SAT

1   Introduction

Impossible differential cryptanalysis was proposed by Biham et al. and Knudsen respectively, where Biham et al. used it to analyze the security of Skipjack [4], and Knudsen utilized it to analyze the security of DEAL [14]. Up to now, impossible differential cryptanalysis has been applied to lots of block ciphers, such as AES [18], SIMON [8], XTEA [9], and so on. There is no doubt that it is one of the most effective cryptanalytic approaches to evaluate the security of block ciphers.

In the impossible differential cryptanalysis, attackers derive the right keys by discarding the wrong keys that lead to the impossible differentials inherent to the given cipher. Thus how to find an impossible differential as longer as possible is the most essential and critical problem in regard to this kind of attacks.

Impossible $(s+1)$-polytopic cryptanalysis was proposed by Tiessen [29], which is a generalization of impossible differential cryptanalysis. Unlike the impossible differentials are constructed by considering the interdependencies of the differences of two plaintexts and the accordingly two ciphertexts, the distinguishers of impossible $(s+1)$-polytopic cryptanalysis, named impossible $(s+1)$-polytopic transitions, are constructed by considering the interdependencies between the s-differences of $(s+1)$ plaintexts and $(s+1)$ ciphertexts [1].

In the last 20 years, using automatic tools to search the distinguishers becomes a new trend. The first automatic tool for the impossible differentials is presented by Kim et al. [13], named $\mathcal{U}$-method. Then, Luo et al. [17] extended it as UID-method. After that, Wu and Wang [31] introduced another method using the idea of solving equations, called $\mathcal{WW}$-method. However, those tools to search impossible differentials cannot describe the details of S-boxes, which waste plenty of differential property of the propagation.

This problem is settled with the application of the Mixed Integer Linear Programming (MILP) method to symmetric cryptography. The MILP problem is a mathematical optimization problem that finds the minimum or maximum value of some objective function under the conditions of linear equations and inequalities of integer variables. Mouha et al. [22] first introduced it to symmetric cryptography to find the lower bound on the number of active S-boxes for both differential and linear cryptanalysis. Later, Sun et al. [28] proposed the modelling method to depict the valid differential propagation of small S-boxes (typically 4 bits), and Fu et al. [12] presented the modelling method to depict all the valid differential/linear characteristics propagations of modular addition. Thus, the differential propagation of any round for the small S-boxes based block ciphers and ARX block ciphers can be modeled by a set of linear inequalities accurately.

---

[1] **Convention.** In our paper, the impossible $(s+1)$-polytopic transition is uniformly defined for $(s \geq 2)$, excluding the case of the impossible differential, since it has been studied in-depth separately.

On that basis, Cui et al. [10] proposed a MILP-based tool to search the impossible differentials for lightweight block ciphers, and an algorithm to verify the impossible differentials. Soon after, Sasaki and Todo [27] presented a MILP-based tool to search the impossible differential for SPN block ciphers. In particular, they proposed the best search method at present for large S-boxes based block ciphers, named the *arbitrary S-box* mode, which only treats the large S-boxes as permutations in order to make their tool valid to detect the contradiction in linear components.

However, the previous automatic search tools for impossible differentials have the following limitations in general.

- Previous tools cannot take into account the key schedule in the single-key setting.
- Previous tools cannot consider the differential property of large S-boxes.
- Previous tools cannot be applied to the block ciphers with variable rotation.

As to impossible polytopic transitions, there was only a search method proposed for DES and AES in the original paper [29]. However, due to the limitation that the searching spaces increase rapidly with the number of rounds, this method can only be confined to a small number of rounds. Besides, this tool cannot take into account the key schedule in the single-key setting and be applied to the block ciphers with variable rotations either.

Our Contributions. In this paper, we define a series of new notations, s-polygon to describe a tuple with s states, s-polygonal trail to depict the propagation of s-polygon, possible s-polygons and impossible s-polygons to depict the relations between two s-polygons.

Then, unlike the traditional impossible differentials and impossible $(s + 1)$-polytopic transitions that are constituted according to the propagation of difference and s-difference, we redefine the impossible differentials and impossible $(s + 1)$-polytopic transitions based on the propagation of the s-polygon[2]. Thus, the key schedule in the single-key setting can be considered in the construction of redefined impossible differentials and impossible $(s+1)$-polytopic transitions. We define the i-impossible differential (resp. i-impossible $(s + 1)$-polytopic transition) to represent the redefined impossible differential (resp. impossible $(s+1)$-polytopic transition) which is constituted in the round key independent setting and d-impossible differential (resp. d-impossible $(s + 1)$-polytopic transition) to

---

[2] This idea can be traced back to [21]. In [21], Mironov et al. used the idea of the transition of states to search two states that satisfy a fixed differential path, which is the critical step to find a collision of the hash function. Recently, two papers [16,26] that also used the idea of the transition of states appeared in the ePrint. As we understand, [16] applied the transition of two states to the non-linear layer. [26] utilized the idea to determine whether a given differential path of ARX based block ciphers is compatible or not. In our paper, we exploit the idea of the transition of multi-states to search the impossible differential and the impossible $(s+1)$-polytopic transition for block ciphers.

represent the redefined impossible differential (resp. impossible $(s+1)$-polytopic transition) which is constituted by considering the key schedule.

Next, we study the relation between our redefined impossible differential (resp. impossible $(s+1)$-polytopic transition) and traditional impossible differential (resp. impossible $(s+1)$-polytopic transition). We show that the i-impossible differential (resp. i-impossible $(s+1)$-polytopic transition) is equivalent to traditional impossible differential (resp. impossible $(s+1)$-polytopic transition) which is constructed by taking into account the inside property of S-boxes for the block ciphers with SPN or Feistel structures and the block cipher MISTY1.

Finally, we model the propagations of states by the statements in the CVC format of STP[3] (a solver of the SAT problem) for each operation, and design an SAT-based unified automatic tool for searching the redefined impossible differential and impossible $(s + 1)$-polytopic transition. Since traditional impossible differential is equivalent to the i-impossible differential and traditional impossible $(s+1)$-polytopic transition is equivalent to the i-impossible $(s+1)$-polytopic transition, our tool can be used to search the traditional impossible differential and traditional impossible $(s + 1)$-polytopic transition. Furthermore, our tool has the following advantages.

Able to Search the Distinguishers by Considering the Impact of Key Schedule in the Single-Key Setting. Our automatic search tool focuses on the propagations of states, which are impacted by the value of key. By adding the constraints of key variables according to the key schedule, it can be used to search the impossible differentials and impossible $(s+1)$-polytopic transitions in the single-key setting confirming the key schedule. As far as we know, this is the first automatic search tool that considers the impact of key schedule in the single-key setting for impossible differentials and impossible $(s + 1)$-polytopic transitions.

Able to Search the Distinguishers for the Block Ciphers with Variable Rotation. In this paper, by exploiting the conditional term of the CVC format, we propose a novel method to model the propagations of states for variable rotation. This method allows us to search the impossible differentials and impossible $(s + 1)$-polytopic transitions for block ciphers with variable rotation automatically. As far as we know, this is the first automatic search method for such type of block ciphers.

Able to Search Impossible Differentials for Block Ciphers with Large S-boxes by Considering the Differential Property of Large S-boxes. We make use of the conditional terms to model the propagations of states for large S-boxes. This way allows us to search the impossible differentials for the block ciphers with large S-boxes by considering the differential property of large S-boxes. As far as we know, this is the first automatic tool to search the impossible differentials for such ciphers taking account in the differential property of large S-boxes.

---

[3] http://stp.github.io/.

New Proving Tool for Resisting Impossible Differentials in Aspect of Cipher Design. Our tool not only can be used to evaluate the security of block ciphers against traditional impossible differentials for block ciphers with large S-box in the case of considering the differential property of large S-boxes, but also can be used to evaluate the security of block ciphers (includes block ciphers with key-dependent permutation) against the impossible differentials in the case of considering the key schedule in the single-key setting. It is very favorable in aspect of block ciphers design and assessment.

We apply our tool to various block ciphers, these results can be divided into three aspects[4].

Deriving New Impossible Differentials

- For GIFT64 [2], we get the 6-round impossible differentials, which cannot be detected by Sun et al.'s method or Sasaki et al.'s method. This result shows that, our tool can detect more contradictions than the previous methods.
- For PRINTcipher48/96 [15], we can not only give the first modeling method for the key-dependent permutation, but also give the first direct modeling method for the key-dependent S-box, which is consisted of the key-dependent permutation and the fixed S-box. Take either of the two modeling methods, by considering all the details of the key schedule, we found 730 4-round impossible differentials for PRINTcipher48 and 234 5-round impossible differentials for PRINTcipher96.
- For MISTY1 [20], we found 902 4-round i-impossible differentials by exploiting the differential property of S-boxes, while only 28 4-round i-impossible differentials were got by implementing the *arbitrary S-box* mode of Sasaki et al.'s method.
- For RC5-32/64/128 [24], we propose the first modeling method for variable rotation, which allows us to get the 2.5-round impossible differentials for them in the key independent setting.

Evaluating the Resistance Against the Impossible Differentials. Besides applying our tool directly, we also propose three phases technique and inside value technique to speed up our proving process.

---

[4] **Illustrantion.** Note that, when to search the r-round distinguishers by considering the key schedule in our model, different beginning round lead to different final models, since the round constants are different from each round. To a common format, we place the distinguishers of our model in the 1st round by default (except GIFT64, since the round key is not XORed with plaintext in the first round, we place the distinguishers in the 2nd). That is, when we say a distinguisher is an r-round distinguisher, it is an r-round distinguisher placed from 1st round to the r-th round. Similarly, when we say there exists no r-round impossible differentials in the search space, it means that for all the input differences and output differences where the input differences placed at the 1st round and the output differences placed at the r-th round, the differences cannot be connected. Actually, in other cases that the distinguishers do not begin with the 1st round, the distinguisher can be searched similarly.

- For GIFT64, PRESENT [6], Midori64 [1], PRINTcipher48, and PRINTcipher96, we prove that, in the search space where the input difference only actives one S-box in the first substitution and the output difference only actives one S-box in the last substitution, there exists no 7-round, 7-round, 6-round, 5-round, and 6-round impossible differentials for GIFT64, PRESENT, Midori64, PRINTcipher48, and PRINTcipher96 even taking account in the details of the key schedule.
- For AES [11], by adopting the new proposed three phases technique, we prove that even considering the relations of middle three-round keys, there still exists no 5-round 1 input active word and 1 output active word impossible differentials.
- For 5-round MISTY1 [20] with the FL layers placed at the even rounds, by adopting the three phases technique and inside value technique, we prove that there exists no 1 input active bit and 1 output active bit impossible differentials.

Resulting in New Impossible $(s+1)$-Polytopic Transition $(s \geq 2)$. Besides applying our tool directly, we further propose the step by step strategy to speed up the search.

- For PRINTcipher, by considering all the details of the key schedule, we obtain the 6-round d-impossible 3-polytopic transition and 7-round d-impossible 4-polytopic transition for PRINTcipher48, and 7-round d-impossible 3-polytopic transition and 8-round d-impossible 4-polytopic transition for PRINTcipher96. Moreover, we investigate the impact of the restraints of the **xor** keys (i.e. the keys which are xored with the state) and **control** keys (i.e. the keys which are used to control the key-dependent permutation). The result shows that, both the restraints of the xor keys and control keys will lead to more contradictions.
- For GIFT64, we get a 7-round d-impossible 3-polytopic transition.
- For RC5-32, we get 108 3-round i-impossible 3-polytopic transitions. Similarly, we get a 3-round i-impossible 3-polytopic transition for RC5-64.
- For PRESENT, we get a 7-round i-impossible 4-polytopic transition.

Outline. We introduce the notations and related work in Sect. 2. Our redefined impossible differentials and impossible $(s+1)$-polytopic transitions and the relations between our redefinitions and traditional definitions are shown in Sect. 3. The SAT modeling methods and our search algorithm are detailed in Sect. 4. We apply our method to impossible differentials from the cryptanalysis aspect and design aspect in Sect. 5 and Sect. 6, respectively. In Sect. 7, we apply our method to impossible polytopic transitions. In Sect. 8, we conclude this paper.

2 Preliminaries

2.1 Notations

The following notations are used in this paper.

- $\boldsymbol{x}^{m,s}$: the tuple $(x_0, \ldots, x_{s-1})$, where $x_i \in \mathbb{F}_2^m$ $(0 \le i \le s-1)$.
- $\boldsymbol{x}_i^{m,s}$: the tuple $(x_{i,0}, \ldots, x_{i,s-1})$, where $x_{i,j} \in \mathbb{F}_2^m$ $(0 \le j \le s-1)$.
- $\boldsymbol{x}^{m,s} \| \boldsymbol{y}^{m,s}$: the tuple $(x_0 \| y_0, \ldots, x_{s-1} \| y_{s-1})$, where $x_i, y_i \in \mathbb{F}_2^m$ $(0 \le i \le s-1)$.
- $\boldsymbol{x}^{m,s+1} \triangleright \boldsymbol{\alpha}^{m,s}$: the tuple $\boldsymbol{x}^{m,s+1}$ satisfy $x_0 \oplus x_{j+1} = \alpha_j$ $(0 \le j \le s-1)$.
- $0^p 1^q$: the concatenation of p successive 0s and q successive 1s.
- $a^p b^q$: the concatenation of p-bit constant a and q-bit constant b.
- $W(a)$: the hamming weight of a, i.e., the 1's number in the bit representation of a.
- e_I^n: an n bits value, whose i-th bit is 1 for $i \in I$, and 0 otherwise.
- $BC(n, m, l)$: the set of all iterated block ciphers whose block size is n-bit, master key size is m-bit, and round key size is l-bit.
- $E_k^r(x)$: the output of encryption $E \in BC(n, m, l)$ on the state $x \in \mathbb{F}_2^n$ after r-round under $k \in (\mathbb{F}_2^l)^r$.
- $E_k^r(\boldsymbol{x}^{n,s})$: the tuple $(E_k^r(x_0), \ldots, E_k^r(x_{s-1}))$.
- IKS_r^l: the set $\{(k_1, \ldots, k_r) | k_i \in \mathbb{F}_2^l, 1 \le i \le r\}$.
- $DKS_r^{m,l}$: the set $\{(k_1, \ldots, k_r) | k \in \mathbb{F}_2^m, k_i \in \mathbb{F}_2^l, k_i = G_i(k), 1 \le i \le r\}$, where G_i denotes the key schedule to generate the round key k_i from the master key k for a block cipher $E \in BC(n, m, l)$.

2.2 A Brief Introduction of Impossible Differentials and Impossible $(s + 1)$-Polytopic Transitions

Impossible differential is the distinguisher of impossible differential cryptanalysis, and impossible $(s+1)$-polytopic transition is the distinguisher of the impossible polytopic cryptanalysis. Here, we only recall the definitions of impossible $(s + 1)$-polytopic transition, since impossible differential is the special case of $s = 1$. First, let us recall the definition of s-polytope and s-difference.

Definition 1 (s-polytope [29]). An s-polytope in $\mathbb{F}_2^n$ is an s-tuple of values in $\mathbb{F}_2^n$.

Definition 2 (s-difference [29]). An s-difference over $\mathbb{F}_2^n$ is an s-tuple of values in $\mathbb{F}_2^n$. For an $(s+1)$-polytope $(m_0, m_1, \ldots, m_s)$, the corresponding s-difference is defined as $(m_0 \oplus m_1, m_0 \oplus m_2, \ldots, m_0 \oplus m_s)$.

Next, we recall the propagation rule of s-difference and the valid $(s + 1)$-polytopic trail.

Definition 3 (The Propagation Rule of The s-difference [29]). Let $f : \mathbb{F}_2^n \to \mathbb{F}_2^q$ be a function. For the input s-difference $\boldsymbol{\alpha}^{n,s}$ and the output s-difference $\boldsymbol{\beta}^{q,s}$, if there exists x such that, $f(x \oplus \alpha_i) \oplus f(x) = \beta_i (0 \le i \le s-1)$, we call that $\boldsymbol{\alpha}^{n,s}$ can propagate to $\boldsymbol{\beta}^{q,s}$, denoted as $\boldsymbol{\alpha}^{n,s} \xrightarrow{f} \boldsymbol{\beta}^{q,s}$. Otherwise, we call that $\boldsymbol{\alpha}^{n,s}$ cannot propagate to $\boldsymbol{\beta}^{q,s}$, denoted as $\boldsymbol{\alpha}^{n,s} \not\xrightarrow{f} \boldsymbol{\beta}^{q,s}$.

Definition 4 (Valid $(s + 1)$-polytopic Trail [29]). Let $f : \mathbb{F}_2^n \to \mathbb{F}_2^n$ be a function that is the iterated composition of round functions $f_i : \mathbb{F}_2^n \to \mathbb{F}_2^n$:

$$f := f_r \circ \cdots \circ f_2 \circ f_1.$$

Let $\boldsymbol{\alpha}_0^{n,s}$ be the input s-difference and $\boldsymbol{\alpha}_r^{n,s}$ be the output s-difference. Then, a valid $(s+1)$-polytopic trail for $(\boldsymbol{\alpha}_0^{n,s}, \boldsymbol{\alpha}_r^{n,s})$ on f is an $(r+1)$-tuple $(\boldsymbol{\alpha}_0^{n,s}, \boldsymbol{\alpha}_1^{n,s}, \ldots, \boldsymbol{\alpha}_r^{n,s})$, where $\boldsymbol{\alpha}_i^{n,s} \overset{f_{i+1}}{\to} \boldsymbol{\alpha}_{i+1}^{n,s} (0 \leq i \leq r - 1)$.

By exploiting the definition of the valid $(s+1)$-polytopic trail, the definitions of possible $(s+1)$-polytopic transition and impossible $(s+1)$-polytopic transition can be re-expressed as follows.

Definition 5 (Possible $(s + 1)$-polytopic Transition [29]). A pair of input and output s-differences $(\boldsymbol{\Delta}_i^{n,s}, \boldsymbol{\Delta}_0^{n,s})$ is called an r-round possible $(s + 1)$-polytopic transition if and only if there exists an r-round valid $(s + 1)$-polytopic trail for $(\boldsymbol{\Delta}_i^{n,s}, \boldsymbol{\Delta}_0^{n,s})$.

Definition 6 (Impossible $(s+1)$-polytopic Transition [29]). A pair of input and output s-differences $(\boldsymbol{\Delta}_i^{n,s}, \boldsymbol{\Delta}_0^{n,s})$ is called an r-round impossible $(s + 1)$-polytopic transition if and only if there exists no r-round valid $s + 1$-polytopic trail for $(\boldsymbol{\Delta}_i^{n,s}, \boldsymbol{\Delta}_0^{n,s})$.

2.3   SAT Problem and STP

The Boolean Satisfiability Problem (SAT) is a classic scientific computation problem aiming to determine whether a given boolean formula has a solution. STP is the openly available solver for the SAT problem, which supports the CVC format as the file-based input formats.

When to solve an SAT problem, we first model it by the statements in CVC format and save those statements as a file. Then, we invoke the STP for this file. If the target SAT problem has no solution, STP will return "Valid.". Otherwise, it will return a solution of the SAT problem and "Invalid.".

In particular, it is worth to mention that the CVC format supports the conditional term, i.e., the statement "IF a THEN b ELSE c ENDIF", where a is a boolean term, and b and c are bitvector terms. By exploiting the conditional term, we give our modeling methods for S-boxes and variable rotation in Sects. 4.1.

3   New Definitions of Impossible Differentials and Impossible $(s + 1)$-Polytopic Transitions

In this section, we define the notations of s-polygon, possible s-polygons, and impossible s-polygons. Based on this, we redefine the impossible differentials and impossible $(s+1)$-polytopic transitions. Then, we study the relations between our redefinitions and traditional definitions of impossible differentials and impossible $(s + 1)$-polytopic transitions.

3.1 New Definitions of Impossible Differentials and Impossible $(s+1)$-Polytopic Transitions

Let us think over the definitions of traditional impossible differentials and impossible $(s+1)$-polytopic transitions. For $E \in BC(n, m, l)$, suppose $(\boldsymbol{\Delta}_i{}^{n,s}, \boldsymbol{\Delta}_o{}^{n,s})$ is an r-round traditional impossible $(s+1)$-polytopic transition of it. Then, for $\forall k \in (F_2^l)^r$, $\forall \boldsymbol{x}_i{}^{n,s+1} \triangleright \boldsymbol{\Delta}_i{}^{n,s}$ and $\forall \boldsymbol{y}_i{}^{n,s+1} \triangleright \boldsymbol{\Delta}_o{}^{n,s}$, it holds $E_k^r(\boldsymbol{x}_i{}^{n,s+1}) \neq \boldsymbol{y}_i{}^{n,s+1}$. In particular, if (Δ_i, Δ_0) is an r-round impossible differential. Then, for $\forall k \in (F_2^l)^r$, $\forall x \in \mathbb{F}_2^n$ and $\forall y \in \mathbb{F}_2^n$, it holds $(E_k^r(x), E_k^r(x \oplus \Delta_i)) \neq (y, y \oplus \Delta_o)$. Thus, it is important to research the relations between two (resp. $s+1$) input states and two (resp. $s+1$) output states for forming the impossible differentials (resp. impossible $(s+1)$-polytopic transitions). To investigate such relations, we define the s-polygon firstly.

Definition 7 (s-polygon). For $\forall E \in BC(n, m, l)$, its s-polygon is a tuple with s elements, where each element belongs to $\mathbb{F}_2^n$.

For an iterated block cipher, the s-polygon propagates through round by round, which constitutes the s-polygonal trail.

Definition 8 (s-polygonal Trail). Let $E \in BC(n, m, l)$ and $r \in \mathbb{Z}$. For any s-polygon $\boldsymbol{x}^{n,s}$ and $\forall k = (k_1, \ldots, k_r) \in (\mathbb{F}_2^l)^r$, we have the following chain of propagation:

$$\boldsymbol{x}^{n,s} \to E_{(k_1)}^1(\boldsymbol{x}^{n,s}) \to E_{(k_1,k_2)}^2(\boldsymbol{x}^{n,s}) \to \cdots \to E_k^r(\boldsymbol{x}^{n,s}).$$

We call $(\boldsymbol{x}^{n,s}, E_{(k_1)}^1(\boldsymbol{x}^{n,s}), \ldots, E_k^r(\boldsymbol{x}^{n,s}))$ an r-round s-polygonal trail. Moreover, if $k \in IKS_r^l$, the trail is called an r-round i-s-polygonal trail; if $k \in DKS_r^{m,l}$, the trail is called an r-round d-s-polygonal trail.

Based on the definitions of s-polygon and s-polygonal trail, according to the compatibility of a pair of input and output s-polygons, the possible s-polygon and impossible s-polygon are defined as follows.

Definition 9 (Possible s-polygons). Let $E \in BC(n, m, l)$, a pair of input and output s-polygons $(\boldsymbol{x}^{n,s}, \boldsymbol{y}^{n,s})$ is called r-round possible s-polygons of E, if there exists $k = (k_1, \ldots, k_r) \in (\mathbb{F}_2^l)^r$ and s-polygonal trail $(\boldsymbol{x}^{n,s}, E_{(k_1)}^1(\boldsymbol{x}^{n,s}), \ldots, E_k^r(\boldsymbol{x}^{n,s}))$ s.t. $y_i = E_k^r(x_i)(0 \leq i \leq s-1)$. Moreover, if $k \in IKS_r^l$, $(\boldsymbol{x}^{n,s}, \boldsymbol{y}^{n,s})$ is called r-round i-possible s-polygons; if $k \in DKS_r^{m,l}$, $(\boldsymbol{x}^{n,s}, \boldsymbol{y}^{n,s})$ is called r-round d-possible s-polygons.

Definition 10 (Impossible s-polygons). Let $E \in BC(n, m, l)$, a pair of input and output s-polygons $(\boldsymbol{x}^{n,s}, \boldsymbol{y}^{n,s})$ is called r-round i-impossible s-polygons (resp. r-round d-impossible s-polygons) of E, if $(\boldsymbol{x}^{n,s}, \boldsymbol{y}^{n,s})$ is not the r-round i-possible s-polygons (resp. r-round d-possible s-polygons).

Now, based on the definition of impossible s-polygons, we propose two definitions of impossible $(s+1)$-polytopic transitions: i-impossible $(s+1)$-polytopic transition and d-impossible $(s+1)$-polytopic transition.

Definition 11 (The i-impossible (resp.d-impossible) $(s + 1)$-polytopic Transition). Let $E \in BC(n, m, l)$, a pair of input and output tuples $(\alpha^{n,s}, \beta^{n,s})$ is called an r-**round** i-**impossible (resp.d-impossible) $(s + 1)$-polytopic transition**, if for $\forall x^{n,s+1} \rhd \alpha^{n,s}$ and $\forall y^{n,s+1} \rhd \beta^{n,s}$, $(x^{n,s+1}, y^{n,s+1})$ are r-round i-impossible (resp.d-impossible) $(s + 1)$-polygons.

Here, we give the definitions of i-impossible differential and d-impossible differential independently for clarity, while actually impossible differential is a particular case of impossible $(s + 1)$-polytopic transition.

Definition 12 (The i-impossible (resp. d-impossible) Differential). Let $E \in BC(n, m, l)$, $\alpha \in \mathbb{F}_2^n$, and $\beta \in \mathbb{F}_2^n$, (α, β) is called an r-**round** i-**impossible (resp. d-impossible) differential**, if for $\forall (x_0, x_1) \in \{(\alpha_0, \alpha_1) \in \mathbb{F}_2^n \times \mathbb{F}_2^n | \alpha_0 \oplus \alpha_1 = \alpha\}$ and $\forall (y_0, y_1) \in \{(\beta_0, \beta_1) \in \mathbb{F}_2^n \times \mathbb{F}_2^n | \beta_0 \oplus \beta_1 = \beta\}$, (x_0, x_1) and (y_0, y_1) are r-round i-impossible (resp. d-impossible) 2-polygons.

According to the definitions of d-possible $(s + 1)$-polygons and i-possible $(s + 1)$-polygons, the relation between i-impossible $(s + 1)$-polytopic transition and d-impossible $(s + 1)$-polytopic transition is obviously as follows.

Theorem 1. Let $E \in BC(n, m, l)$. Then an i-impossible $(s+1)$-polytopic transition of E must be a d-impossible $(s+1)$-polytopic transition of E. In particular, an i-impossible differential of E must be a d-impossible differential of E.

3.2 The Equivalence of i-impossible $(s + 1)$-Polytopic Transitions and Traditional Impossible $(s + 1)$-Polytopic Transitions

SPN structure and Feistel structure are widely used in the design of block ciphers. In this subsection, we show that the i-impossible $(s+1)$-polytopic transitions are equivalent to traditional impossible $(s + 1)$-polytopic transitions for the block ciphers with SPN structure or Feistel structure. Moreover, with the same approach, the equivalence also holds for the block cipher MISTY1. Note that, since impossible differentials are the particular case of impossible $(s + 1)$-polytopic transitions, we are not going to state the equivalency for impossible differentials solely here.

First, for narrative purposes, we define a class of round function, which is widely used in block ciphers.

Definition 13 (Common Round Function). A function F_r is called common round function(CRF), if it can be represented as $F_r = (P_r' \circ S_r \circ P_r \circ K_r) \circ \cdots \circ (P_1' \circ S_1 \circ P_1 \circ K_1) \circ (P_0' \circ S_0 \circ P_0)$, where $S_i (0 \leq i \leq r)$ denotes the substitution layer which is composed of a set of S-boxes in parallel, $P_i (0 \leq i \leq r)$ and $P_i' (0 \leq i \leq r)$ denote the linear permutation layers, and $K_i (1 \leq i \leq r)$ denotes the key mixing layer, where the key is fully Xored with the state. In particular, in the case of $r = 0$, denote $F_0 = (P_0' \circ S_0 \circ P_0)$.

The above definition of CRF includes a lot of round functions, which are broadly used in block ciphers. For example, the round function of AES [11] is of the "SP" structure, in which the substitution layer precedes the linear layer. It is the CRF in the case of $r = 0$ and P_0 is the identical permutation. The round function of Prince [7] in the last half rounds is of the "PS" structure, in which the linear layer precedes the substitution layer. It is the CRF in the case of $r = 0$ and P_0' is the identical permutation. The round function of RoadRunneR [3] is of the "SPKSPKSPKS" structure. It is the CRF in the case of $r = 3$ and P_3 is the identical permutation.

Since the common round function is widely used in block ciphers, we study the relationship between the valid $(s + 1)$-polytopic transitions and i-possible $(s + 1)$-polygons of it.

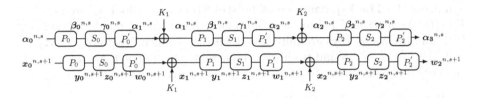

Fig. 1. The Valid $(s + 1)$-polytopic Trail and $(s + 1)$-polygonal Trail for CRF

Theorem 2 (The Equivalence of CRF). Let F_r be a CRF. Then, $(\boldsymbol{\alpha_0}^{n,s}, \boldsymbol{\alpha_{r+1}}^{n,s})$ is a valid polytopic transition of F_r if and only if there exist i-possible $(s+1)$-polygons $(\boldsymbol{x_0}^{n,s+1}, \boldsymbol{w_r}^{n,s+1})$ of F_r, where $\boldsymbol{x_0}^{n,s+1} \triangleright \boldsymbol{\alpha_0}^{n,s}$ and $\boldsymbol{w_r}^{n,s+1} \triangleright \boldsymbol{\alpha_{r+1}}^{n,s}$.

Proof. We only prove this theorem in the case of $r = 2$. The other cases can be proved analogously.

Suppose $(\boldsymbol{\alpha_0}^{n,s}, \boldsymbol{\alpha_3}^{n,s})$ is a valid polytopic transition of F_2. Then there exists a valid $(s+1)$-polytopic trail $(\boldsymbol{\alpha_0}^{n,s}, \boldsymbol{\alpha_1}^{n,s}, \boldsymbol{\alpha_2}^{n,s}, \boldsymbol{\alpha_3}^{n,s})$, as shown in the upper half of Fig. 1. For $0 \leq i \leq 2$, since $(\boldsymbol{\beta_i}^{n,s}, \boldsymbol{\gamma_i}^{n,s})$ is a possible $(s + 1)$-polytopic transition of S_i, there exists a_i such that $S_i(a_i) \oplus S_i(a_i \oplus \beta_{i,j}) = \gamma_{i,j} (0 \leq j \leq s - 1)$. Let $\boldsymbol{y_i}^{n,s+1} = (y_{i,0}, \ldots, y_{i,s})$ and $\boldsymbol{z_i}^{n,s+1} = (z_{i,0}, \ldots, z_{i,s})$, where $y_{i,0} = a_i$, $y_{i,j+1} = a_i \oplus \beta_{i,j}$, $z_{i,0} = S_i(a_i)$ and $z_{i,j+1} = S(a_i) \oplus \gamma_{i,j}$, then we have $S(y_{i,j}) = z_{i,j} (0 \leq j \leq s)$. Denote $\boldsymbol{x_i}^{n,s+1} = (x_{i,0}, \ldots, x_{i,s})$ and $\boldsymbol{w_i}^{n,s+1} = (w_{i,0}, \ldots, w_{i,s})$, where $x_{i,j} = P_i^{-1}(y_{i,j})$ and $w_{i,j} = P_i'(z_{i,j}) (0 \leq j \leq s)$. Since $\alpha_{i,j} = P_i^{-1}(\beta_{i,j})$, we have $x_{i,0} \oplus x_{i,j+1} = \alpha_{i,j} (0 \leq j \leq s - 1)$. Similar, we have $w_{i,0} \oplus w_{i,j+1} = \alpha_{i+1,j} (0 \leq j \leq s - 1)$. Thus, for $1 \leq i \leq 2$, we have $w_{i-1,0} \oplus w_{i-1,j+1} = \alpha_{i,j} = x_{i,0} \oplus x_{i,j+1} (0 \leq j \leq s - 1)$. Let $K_i = w_{i-1,0} \oplus x_{i,0}$, then we have $x_{i,j} = w^{i-1,j} \oplus K_i (0 \leq j \leq s)$. Therefore, we have constructed i-possible $(s+1)$-polygons of F_2, which is $(\boldsymbol{x_0}^{n,s+1}, \boldsymbol{w_2}^{n,s+1})$ with $\boldsymbol{w_2}^{n,s+1} \triangleright \boldsymbol{\alpha_3}^{n,s}$ and $\boldsymbol{x_0}^{n,s+1} \triangleright \boldsymbol{\alpha_0}^{n,s}$, as shown in the lower half of Fig. 1.

Since all the procedures above are invertible, it is easy to show that if there exist $\boldsymbol{x_0}^{n,s+1} \triangleright \boldsymbol{\alpha_0}^{n,s}$ and $\boldsymbol{w_2}^{n,s+1} \triangleright \boldsymbol{\alpha_3}^{n,s}$, such that $(\boldsymbol{x_0}^{n,s+1}, \boldsymbol{w_2}^{n,s+1})$ is the i-possible $(s+1)$-polygons of F_2, then $(\boldsymbol{\alpha_0}^{n,s}, \boldsymbol{\alpha_3}^{n,s})$ is the valid polytopic transition of F_2. □

With the same technique, we also can show the equivalence between traditional impossible $(s + 1)$-polytopic transition and the i-impossible $(s + 1)$-polytopic transition for the block ciphers with SPN structure and Feistel structure as follows. The specific process of proofs are shown in the Full Version of our paper in the ePrint because of space cause.

Theorem 3 (The Equivalence of SPN Structure Block Ciphers). Let $E \in BC(n, m, l)$ be an SPN structure block cipher whose round function is a CRF, and the round keys are fully Xored with the state. Then, $(\alpha_0^{n,s}, \alpha_r^{n,s})$ is an r-round traditional impossible $(s + 1)$-polytopic transition if and only if it is an r-round i-impossible $(s + 1)$-polytopic transition.

Theorem 4 (The Equivalence of Feistel Structure Block Ciphers). Let $E \in BC(2n, m, l)$ be a Feistel structure block cipher whose round function is a CRF and the round keys are fully Xored with the branch. Then, $(\alpha_0^{n,s}||\beta_0^{n,s}, \alpha_r^{n,s}||\beta_r^{n,s})$ is an r-round traditional impossible $(s + 1)$-polytopic transition if and only if it is an r-round i-impossible $(s + 1)$-polytopic transition.

The block cipher MISTY1 [20] is designed by adopting the theory of provable security [23]. We can also show that traditional impossible $(s + 1)$-polytopic transition is equivalent to the i-impossible $(s + 1)$-polytopic transition for the block cipher MISTY1 as the following theorem. The specific process of proof is also shown in the Full Version of our paper.

Theorem 5 (The Equivalence of The Block Cipher MISTY1). Let E denote the block cipher MISTY1. Then, $(\alpha_0^{32,s}||\beta_0^{32,s}, \alpha_r^{32,s}||\beta_r^{32,s})$ is an r-round traditional impossible $(s + 1)$-polytopic transition if and only if it is an r-round i-impossible $(s + 1)$-polytopic transition.

The Avantages of i-Impossible Differentials and i-Impossible $(s + 1)$-Polytopic Transitions. Since i-impossible differentials (resp. i-impossible $(s+1)$-polytopic transitions) are equivalent to traditional impossible differentials (resp. traditional impossible $(s+1)$-polytopic transitions), our method gives new view of traditional impossible differentials and impossible $(s + 1)$-polytopic transitions, which allows us to get the distinguishers for the block cipher with large S-boxes or variable rotation in the key independent setting using full knowledge of their differential or s-differential property. In particular, by exploiting this new view, we can evaluate the security of block ciphers against traditional impossible differentials for block ciphers with large S-box in the case of considering the differential property of large S-boxes.

4   Automatic Search Method

In this section, we propose an unified automatic search algorithm for our redefined impossible differentials and impossible $(s+1)$-polytopic transitions. Firstly, we give the statements in CVC format to model the propagation of the state under each operation.

4.1   Model the Propagation of the State by Statements in CVC Format

Here, we model the propagation of the state under the operations (Generalized-) Copy, (Generalized-) Xor, (Generalized-) Modular Addition, Linear Transformations, S-box and Variable Rotation by statements in CVC format.

Model 1 ((Generalized-)Copy). Let F be a (Generalized-)Copy function, where the input x takes value from $\mathbb{F}_2^q$, and the output is calculated as $(y_0, y_1, \ldots, y_{t-1}) = (x, x, \ldots, x)$. Then, the following statements can describe the propagation of the state under the (Generalized-)Copy operation.

$$
\begin{cases}
\text{ASSERT}(y_0 = x); \\
\text{ASSERT}(y_1 = x); \\
\quad \vdots \\
\text{ASSERT}(y_{t-1} = x);
\end{cases}
$$

Model 2 ((Generalized-)Xor). Let F be a (Generalized-)Xor function, where the input $(x_0, x_1, \ldots, x_{t-1})$ take values from $(\mathbb{F}_2^q)^t$, and the output is calculated as $y = \oplus_{i=0}^{i=t-1} x_i$. Then, the following statement can describe the propagation of the state under the (Generalized-)Xor operation.[5]

$$\text{ASSERT}(y = \text{BVXOR}(\cdots (\text{BVXOR}(\text{BVXOR}(x_0, x_1), x_2), \ldots, x_{t-1}));$$

Model 3 ((Generalized-)Modular Addition). Let F be a (Generalized-) Modular Addition function, where the input $(x_0, x_1, \ldots, x_{t-1})$ take values from $(\mathbb{F}_2^q)^t$, and the output is calculated as $y = \boxplus_{i=0}^{i=t-1} x_i$.[6] Then, the following statement can describe the propagation of the state under the (Generalized-)Modular Addition operation.

$$\text{ASSERT}(y = \text{BVPLUS}(q, x_0, \ldots, x_{t-1}));$$

The linear transformations of block ciphers have various representations, such as the permutation layer of PRESENT [6], and the MDS matrix in AES [11]. Since all the representations of linear transformations can be converted to the binary matrix multiplication, we only show the modeling method for the binary matrix multiplication here.

Model 4 (Binary Matrix Multiplication). Let $M = (m_{i,j})_{0 \le i \le s-1, 0 \le j \le t-1}$ be a binary matrix, where the input $x = (x_0, x_1, \ldots, x_{t-1})$ take values from $\mathbb{F}_2^t$, and the output of multiplication $y = (y_0, y_1, \ldots, y_{s-1})$ is calculated as

$$
y_i = \begin{cases}
x_k, & \text{if } m_{i,k} = 1 \text{ and } |\{j | m_{i,j} \ne 0\}| = 1, \\
\oplus_{\{j | m_{i,j} \ne 0\}} x_j, & \text{otherwise.}
\end{cases}
$$

Then, the statements to describe the propagation of the state under binary matrix multiplication operation can be combined by the modeling methods for Copy and (Generalized-) Xor.

---

[5] BVXOR: Bitwise XOR function which is supported by the CVC format of STP.
[6] BVPLUS: Bitvector Add function which is supported by the CVC format of STP.

S-box is often used to provide confusion for block ciphers. By exploiting the conditional term, we can describe the propagation of the state under it specifically.

Algorithm 1. *Function for Modeling S-box*

1: **Input**: S, x, y
2: **Output**: *The statement to describe the propagation of the state under S-box*
3: $statement_1 = S[0]$
4: **for** $j = 1$ to $2^t - 1$ **do**
5:     $statement_1 = $ "IF $x = j$ THEN $S[j]$ ELSE $statement_1$"
6: **endfor**
7: $statement = $ "ASSERT($y = statement_1$);"
8: **return** $statement$

Model 5 (S-box). Let S be an S-box which substitutes t-bit to s-bit, where the input x takes values from $\mathbb{F}_2^t$, and the output $y \in \mathbb{F}_2^s$ is calculated as $y = S(x)$. Then the statement generated by Algorithm 1 can describe the propagation of the state under S-box operation.

Variable rotation is a novel operation used in some typical block ciphers, such as RC5 [24] and RC6 [25]. Due to the output of variable rotation operation is closely related to the input values, it is hard to model the propagation of difference and s-difference under it. In our new model, we exploit the conditional term to describe the propagation of the state under the variable rotation.

Algorithm 2. *Function for Modeling Variable Rotation*

1: **Input**: q, x, y, z
2: **Output**: The statement to describe the propagation of the state under variable rotation
3: $statement_1 = x$
4: **for** $j = 1$ to $q - 1$ **do**
5:     $statement_1 = $ "IF $(y \bmod q) = j$ THEN $x \lll_j$ ELSE $statement_1$"
6: **endfor**
7: $statement = $ "ASSERT($z = statement_1$);"
8: **return** $statement$

Model 6 (Variable Rotation). Let F be a variable rotation function, the input (x, y) take values from $\mathbb{F}_2^q \times \mathbb{F}_2^q$, and the output is calculated as $z = x \lll_y \in \mathbb{F}_2^q$. Then, the statement generated by the Algorithm 2 can describe the propagation of the state under variable rotation operation.

4.2 The Automatic Search Method for Redefined Impossible Differentials and Impossible $(s + 1)$-Polytopic Transitions

In this subsection, we show our automatic search algorithm for the i-impossible (resp. d-impossible) $(s + 1)$-polytopic transitions. Since an i-impossible (resp. d-impossible) differential is an i-impossible (resp. d-impossible) 2-polytopic transition, the automatic search algorithm for i-impossible (resp. d-impossible) differentials can be derived from the algorithm for i-impossible (resp. d-impossible) $(s + 1)$-polytopic transitions with $s = 1$. First, we propose our method for determining whether a pair of input and output s-differences is an i-impossible (resp. d-impossible) $(s + 1)$-polytopic transition. Then, we discuss the selection of parameter s and the search space of our method.

The i-Impossible (resp. d-Impossible) $(s + 1)$-Polytopic Transition Determining Method.
Our method for determining whether a pair of input and output s-differences $(\alpha^{n,s}, \beta^{n,s})$ is an i-impossible (resp. d-impossible) $(s+1)$-polytopic transition can be divided into two phases: statements generated phase and STP invoked phase. In the statements generated phase, we generate a system of statements as a file to describe the $(s + 1)$-polygons $x^{n,s+1}$ propagate to $y^{n,s+1}$ with $x^{n,s+1} \rhd \alpha^{n,s}$ and $y^{n,s+1} \rhd \beta^{n,s}$. In the STP invoked phase, we invoke the STP for the file to determine whether $(\alpha^{n,s}, \beta^{n,s})$ is an i-impossible (resp. d-impossible) $(s+1)$-polytopic transition.

Specification of the statements generated phase.
The algorithm shown in Algorithm 3 generates the statements for judging whether a pair of input and output s-differences $(\alpha^{n,s}, \beta^{n,s})$ is an r-round impossible $(s + 1)$-polytopic transition.

Algorithm 3. Generating statements in CVC format

1: **Input:** the number of rounds r, the input s-difference $\alpha^{n,s}$, the output s-difference $\beta^{n,s}$ and keyflag$\in$ {True, False}
2: **Output:** System of statements in CVC format
3: Declare the input and output $(s + 1)$-polygons of $x^{n,s+1}$ and $y^{n,s+1}$.
4: Declare the intermediate variables and key variables.
5: **for** $i = 0$ to s **do**
6:    Model the r-round propagation of (x_i, y_i).
7: **endfor**
8: Generate the constraint of $x^{n,s+1}$ such that $x^{n,s+1} \rhd \alpha^{n,s}$.
9: Generate the constraint of $y^{n,s+1}$ such that $y^{n,s+1} \rhd \beta^{n,s}$.
10: **if** keyflag **then**
11:    Generate the constraint of key variables according to key shedule.
12: **endif**
13: Add the statements "QUERY(FALSE);" and "COUNTEREXAMPLE;".

We present certain illustrations for Algorithm 3 as follows.

- Line 3–4. Declare the variables which are used in the system of statements, including the variables which are used to represent the input $(s + 1)$-polygon and output $(s+1)$-polygon, the intermediate variables and key variables used to describe the propagation from the input $(s + 1)$-polygon to the output $(s + 1)$-polygon.
- Line 5–7. According to the propagation rules for each operation which are given in Sect. 4.1, model the propagation from the input $(s + 1)$-polygon $x^{n,s+1}$ to the output $(s + 1)$-polygon $y^{n,s+1}$ with the aid of the intermediate variables and key variables.
- Line 8–9. Generate the statements in CVC format such that the input $(s+1)$-polygon $x^{n,s+1}$ satisfies the input s-difference $\alpha^{n,s}$ and the output $(s + 1)$-polygon $y^{n,s+1}$ satisfies the output s-difference $\beta^{n,s}$.
- L ine 10–12. If "keyflag=True", then the algorithm generates the statements to constraint the key variables according to the key schedule. In this case, the algorithm generates the statements to judge whether a pair of input and output s-differences $(\alpha^{n,s}, \beta^{n,s})$ is an r-round d-impossible $(s + 1)$-polytopic transition; Otherwise, it generates the statements to judge whether a pair of input and output s-differences $(\alpha^{n,s}, \beta^{n,s})$ is an r-round i-impossible $(s+1)$-polytopic transition.
- Line 13. The statements "QUERY(FALSE);" and "COUNTEREXAMPLE;" are added to the system of statements. This is a common method in STP to determine whether an SAT problem has a solution. By adding those two statements, if the SAT problem has solutions, the STP will return one of the solutions and the statement "Invalid."; Otherwise, it returns "Valid.".

Specification of the Invoke STP Phase.
We invoke the STP for the file which is consisted of the system of statements. If the statements generated in the case of *keyflag=True*, then the s-differences $(\alpha^{n,s}, \beta^{n,s})$ is an r-round d-impossible $(s + 1)$-polytopic transition when the STP returns "Valid.", and $(\alpha^{n,s}, \beta^{n,s})$ is not an r-round d-impossible $(s + 1)$-polytopic transition when the STP returns an r-round d-$(s+1)$-polygonal trail and "Invalid.". Similarly, if the statements generated in the case of *keyflag=False*, then the s-differences $(\alpha^{n,s}, \beta^{n,s})$ is an r-round i-impossible $(s + 1)$-polytopic transition when the STP returns "Valid.", and $(\alpha^{n,s}, \beta^{n,s})$ is not an r-round i-impossible $(s + 1)$-polytopic transition when the STP returns an r-round i-$(s + 1)$-polygonal trail and "Invalid.".

Work as a Proof Tool. Once the search space fixed, we can run our tool for all the input and output s-differences in such space. If none of the input and output s-differences is an r-round i-impossible (resp. d-impossible) $(s + 1)$-polytopic transition, we can declare that there exists no r-round i-impossible (resp. d-impossible) $(s + 1)$-polytopic transition in this space.

The Select of Parameter s and Search Space.
In our automatic search method for impossible $(s + 1)$-polytopic transition, the total time cost mainly depends on the size of the search space and the time

cost for determining whether an element in the search space is an impossible $(s + 1)$-polytopic transition.

The time cost for determining whether an element in the search space is an impossible $(s + 1)$-polytopic transition is closely related to operations contained in the block cipher and the value of parameter s we selected. In our experiment, we choose s at most 4, since the search time will cost quite a lot if s increases beyond this range.

For the search space, traditional automatic tools focus on search the μ input active bits (resp. nibbles) and ν output active bits (resp. nibbles) impossible differentials. Since the impossible $(s+1)$-polytopic transition is the generation of impossible differential, we define the $(\mu_0, \ldots, \mu_{s-1})$ active bits and $(\mu_0, \ldots, \mu_{s-1})$ active nibbles to generate the search space.

Definition 14 ($(\mu_0, \ldots, \mu_{s-1})$ Active Bits). For a block cipher $E \in BC(n, m, l)$, we call the s-difference $\boldsymbol{\alpha}^{n,s}$ satisfied the $(\mu_0, \ldots, \mu_{s-1})$ active bits, if there are μ_i bits of the binary representation of $\alpha_i (0 \leq i \leq s-1)$ are non-zero.

Definition 15 ($(\mu_0, \ldots, \mu_{s-1})$ Active Nibbles). For a block cipher $E \in BC(n, m, l)$ whose S-box size is q, for any s-difference $\boldsymbol{\alpha}^{n,s}$, the binary representation of α_i $(0 \leq i \leq s - 1)$ can be divided into $\frac{n}{q}$ pieces, where $\alpha_{i,j} = \{\alpha_{i,q \cdot j}, \ldots, \alpha_{i,q \cdot j+q-1}\}$ $(0 \leq j \leq \frac{n}{q} - 1)$. We call the s-difference $\boldsymbol{\alpha}^{n,s}$ satisfied the $(\mu_0, \ldots, \mu_{s-1})$ active nibbles, if there are μ_i pieces of $\alpha_i (0 \leq i \leq s-1)$ have non-zero items.

Our method focuses on searching the $(\mu_0, \ldots, \mu_{s-1})$ input active bits and $(\nu_0, \ldots, \nu_{s-1})$ output active bits or $(\mu_0, \ldots, \mu_{s-1})$ input active nibbles and $(\nu_0, \ldots, \nu_{s-1})$ output active nibbles, or the subset of those two spaces according to the experimental result. Due to the limitation of the size of the executable search space, we mainly search some small values of active bits and active nibbles. Assume the value μ'_i $(0 \leq i \leq g)$ appears φ_i times in the tuple $(\mu_0, \ldots, \mu_{s-1})$ and value ν'_i $(0 \leq i \leq h)$ appears ϕ_i times in the tuple $(\nu_0, \ldots, \nu_{s-1})$. Then, for a block cipher $E \in BC(n, m, l)$, the number of pairs of input and output s-differences with $(\mu_0, \ldots, \mu_{s-1})$ input active bits and $(\nu_0, \ldots, \nu_{s-1})$ output active bits is

$$\binom{\binom{n}{\mu'_0}}{\varphi_0} \times \cdots \times \binom{\binom{n}{\mu'_g}}{\varphi_g} \times \binom{\binom{n}{\nu'_0}}{\phi_0} \times \cdots \times \binom{\binom{n}{\nu'_h}}{\phi_h} \sim O(n^{\mu'_0 \varphi_0 + \cdots + \mu'_g \varphi_g + \nu'_0 \phi_0 + \cdots + \nu'_h \phi_h}).$$

For a block cipher $E \in BC(n, m, l)$ whose S-box size is q, let $p = \frac{n}{q}$, the number of pairs of input and output s-differences with $(\mu_0, \ldots, \mu_{s-1})$ input active nibbles and $(\nu_0, \ldots, \nu_{s-1})$ output active nibbles is

$$\binom{\binom{p}{\mu'_0} \cdot (2^q - 1)}{\varphi_0} \times \cdots \times \binom{\binom{p}{\mu'_g} \cdot (2^q - 1)}{\varphi_g} \times \binom{\binom{p}{\nu'_0} \cdot (2^q - 1)}{\phi_0} \times \cdots \times \binom{\binom{p}{\nu'_h} \cdot (2^q - 1)}{\phi_h},$$

which is $O(p^{\mu'_0 \varphi_0 + \cdots + \mu'_g \varphi_g + \nu'_0 \phi_0 + \cdots + \nu'_h \phi_h} \cdot 2^{q \cdot (\mu'_0 + \cdots + \mu'_g + \nu'_0 + \cdots + \nu'_h)})$.

According to the above analysis, the size of the search space is still large even we only search for small values of active bits and active nibbles for impossible $(s+1)$-polytopic transitions with small value of parameter s. For example, if we search the $(1,1)$ input active bits and $(1,1)$ output active bits for the impossible 3-polytopic transition of a block cipher whose block size is 64, the number of pairs of input and output s-differences is $\binom{\binom{64}{1}}{2} \times \binom{\binom{64}{1}}{2} = 4064256 \approx 2^{22}$. Thus, we propose the following step by step strategy, which is quite helpful to search the impossible $(s+1)$-polytopic transitions when the search space is too large.

Step by Step Strategy. The core of this strategy is to search the impossible $(s+1)$-polytopic$(s \geq 2)$ transition based on the result of the impossible s-polytopic transition. To be specific, for a block cipher $E \in BC(n, m, l)$, if we know that $(\alpha^{n,s-1}, \beta^{n,s-1})$ is an impossible s-polytopic transition, then we search the impossible $(s+1)$-polytopic$(s \geq 2)$ transition in the set

$$\{(\alpha_0, \ldots, \alpha_{s-2}, \alpha) \times (\beta_0, \ldots, \beta_{s-2}, \beta) | \text{the active bits (nibbles) of } \alpha \text{ and } \beta \text{ is } u$$
and v respectively$\}$,

where u and v are the predetermined values.

5 Applications to Impossible Differentials from the Aspect of Cryptanalysis

In this section, we apply our method to various block ciphers, including the block cipher GIFT64 [2], the key-dependent permutation (or the key-dependent S-box) based block cipher PRINTcipher [15], the large S-boxes based block cipher MISTY1 [20], and the variable rotation based block cipher RC5 [24]. Only concise descriptions of those block ciphers are specified here. For more details, please refer to their coresponding references. All the experiments in this paper are conducted on this platform: Intel(R) Xeon(R) CPU E5-2650 v2 @2.60 GHz, 64.00G RAM, 64-bit Windows 7 system. The source codes are available in https://github.com/HugeChaos/Impossible-differentials-and-impossible-polyto pic-transitions.

5.1 GIFT64

GIFT64 was designed by Banik el at. [2], it is a 64-bit block cipher with 128-bit master key. Interestingly, its round key is 32-bit while it adopts the SPN structure.

Previous Best Result. In [2], they searched the impossible differentials by limiting the input difference activates only one of the first four S-boxes and the output difference activates only one S-box. The maximum number of rounds of impossible differentials they got in this search space is 6.

Advantage of Our Tool. Compared with the previous tools, our tools can search the impossible differentials taking into account the key schedule.

Configurations for the Tool. Firstly, in the search space where the input and output difference activates only one S-box, the maximum number of rounds of the impossible differentials we got is also 6. Then, we try to find the 6-round impossible differentials in which the contradiction cannot be detected by the previous method. To achieve this purpose, we randomly pick the input differences activate at most the right 16 bits and the output differences activate at most the i-th ($i \in \{0, 4, 8, 12, 17, 21, 25, 29, 34, 38, 42, 46, 51, 55, 59, 63\}$) bit. In this way, it allows at most the 0th, 4th, 8th and 12th S-box to be active in the 2nd round by propagating the input difference in the forward direction, and at most the 0th, 1st, 2nd and 3rd S-box to be active in the 5th round by propagating the output difference in the backward direction. After 65536 random tests, we find 3 6-round impossible differentials that the previous tools cannot detect.

Example of 6-Round d-Impossible Differentials. One of the 6-round d-impossible differentials is

$$0x0000000000000600 \xrightarrow{6-round} 0x0000004020000110.$$

Automatic Verification for Above Example of Impossible Differential of GIFT64. Since this impossible differential cannot be detected by the propagation of difference, verifying this impossible differential by manual is difficult, we modify the verification algorithm in [10] and apply it to verify this impossible differential. The details of our verification are shown in the Full Version of our paper.

5.2   PRINTcipher

PRINTcipher [15] is proposed by Lars et al. at CHES 2010, consisting of two versions: PRINTcipher48 and PRINTcipher96. PRINTcipher48 is a block cipher with 48-bit block and 80-bit key. PRINTcipher96 is a block cipher with 96-bit block and 160-bit key.

Advantage of Our Tool. Previous tools cannot apply to PRINTcipher directly due to that they cannot handle the operation of key-dependent permutation. By making use of the conditional term, we propose the first modeling method to describe the propagation of state for key-dependent permutation: *ASSERT(y2@y1@y0 = (IF k1@k0 = 0bin11 THEN x0@x1@x2 ELSE (IF k1@k0 = 0bin10 THEN x2@x0@x1 ELSE (IF k1@k0 = 0bin01 THEN x1@x2@x0 ELSE x2@x1@x0 ENDIF) ENDIF) ENDIF));*
where $x2||x1||x0$ is the input variable, $y2||y1||y0$ is the output variable, and $k1||k0$ is the control key. This modeling method allows us to search the impossible differentials for PRINTcipher by considering the impact of all the details of key schedule. Besides, the PRINTcipher also can be regarded as the key-dependent S-box based block cipher, where the key-dependent S-box is consisted of the key-dependent permutation and the fixed S-box. We also propose the first modeling method to describe the propagation of state for key-dependent S-box directly, which is shown in the Full Version of our paper.

434   X. Hu et al.

Configurations for the Tool. By considering all the details of key schedule, we search the impossible differentials for PRINTcipher48 and PRINTcipher96 in the space where the input difference activates only one S-box in the first substitution layer and the output difference activates only one S-box in the last substitution layer . Finally, we found 730 4-round d-impossible differentials for PRINTcipher48 and 234 5-round d-impossible differentials for PRINTcipher96 in total.

Example of d-Impossible Differentials of PRINTcipher. One of the 730 4-round d-impossible differentials of PRINTcipher48 is

$$0x000000000001 \xrightarrow{4-round} 0x000000000008.$$

One of the 234 5-round d-impossible differentials of PRINTcipher96 is

$$0x000000000000000200000000 \xrightarrow{5-round} 0x000000000000000000001000.$$

Manual Verification for the Above Example of Impossible Differential of PRINTcipher. As the impossible differentials are detected by considering the key schedule, the verification is completely different from the previous impossible differentials. First, we have the following observation for the composition of key-dependent permutation and S-box.

Observation 1. *Let $SP_k = S \circ P_k$, where S denotes the S-box of PRINTcipher and P_k denotes the key-dependent permutation. Then, $1 \xrightarrow{SP_0} \{1,3,5,7\}$, $1 \xrightarrow{SP_1} \{1,3,5,7\}$, $1 \xrightarrow{SP_2} \{2,3,6,7\}$, and $1 \xrightarrow{SP_3} \{4,5,6,7\}$. On the contrary, we have $\{1,3,5,7\} \xrightarrow{SP_0} 1$, $\{1,3,5,7\} \xrightarrow{SP_1} 1$, $\{2,3,6,7\} \xrightarrow{SP_2} 1$, and $\{4,5,6,7\} \xrightarrow{SP_3} 1$.*

Then, we verify the 4-round example of impossible differential of PRINTcipher48 in case that 0th or 5th S-box in the 3rd round is active. More details of the proof are given in the Full Version of our paper. The 5-round example of PRINTcipher96 can be verified similarly.

5.3   MISTY1

The block cipher MISTY1 was designed by Matsui [20]. It is a 64-bit block cipher which adopts the theory of provable security [23] against differential attack [5] and linear attack [19].

The Result by Sasaki et al.'s Method. Sasaki et al.'s method is the most advanced previous method to search the impossible differentials for block ciphers with large S-boxes. We employ this method to search the 1 input active bit and 1 output active bit impossible differentials by limiting the input difference activates only the right branch and the output difference activates only the left branch. After $32 \times 32 = 1024$ tests, the maximum number of rounds we got is 4 and a total of 28 4-round impossible differentials are found.

Advantage of Our Tool. Compared with previous tools, our tool is the first tool that can search the impossible differentials for large S-boxes based block ciphers taking into account the differential property of the S-boxes in the independent key setting.

Configurations for the Tool. We run our tool to search the i-impossible differentials in the search space as that by Sasaki et al.'s method. Finally, we found 902 4-round i-impossible differentials, and all the 4-round impossible differentials derived by Sasaki et al.'s method are detected by our tool.

List of 4-Round i-Impossible Differentials. All the 4-round impossible differentials we found are shown in the Table 1, where $\mathbb{Z}_{32} = \{0, 1, \ldots, 31\}$ and $A = \{33, 35, 36, 46, 49, 50, 51, 52, 53, 57, 58, 62\}$.

Table 1. 4-round impossible differentials of MISTY-1

ID	ΔP	ΔC	Number
001	$e_i^{64}(i \in \mathbb{Z}_{32}/\{3, 12, 19, 28\})$	e_{32}^{64}	28
002	$e_i^{64}(i \in \mathbb{Z}_{32}/\{14, 30\})$	e_{34}^{64}	30
003	$e_i^{64}(i \in \mathbb{Z}_{32}/\{7, 23\})$	e_{37}^{64}	30
004	$e_i^{64}(i \in \{0, 9, 11, 12, 13, 14, 15, 16, 25, 27, 28, 29, 30, 31\})$	e_{38}^{64}	14
005	$e_i^{64}(i \in \{1, 4, 5, 6, 7, 10, 17, 20, 21, 22, 23, 26\}$	e_{43}^{64}	12
006	$e_i^{64}(i \in \{4, 5, 6, 7, 10, 20, 21, 22, 23, 26\})$	e_{44}^{64}	10
007	$e_i^{64}(i \in \{0, 3, 4, 5, 6, 7, 8, 10, 16, 19, 20, 21, 22, 23, 24, 26\}$	e_{45}^{64}	16
008	$e_i^{64}(i \in \mathbb{Z}_{32}/\{12, 28\})$	e_{48}^{64}	30
009	$e_i^{64}(i \in \mathbb{Z}_{32}/\{6, 22\})$	e_{54}^{64}	30
010	$e_i^{64}(i \in \mathbb{Z}_{32})$	$e_j^{64}(j \in A)$	384
011	$e_i^{64}(i \in \mathbb{Z}_{32}/\{12+j, 28+j\})$	$e_{55+j}^{64}(j \in \{0, 1\})$	60
012	$e_i^{64}(i \in \mathbb{Z}_{32}/\{11, 27\})$	$e_j^{64}(j \in \{47, 63\})$	60
013	$e_i^{64}(i \in \mathbb{Z}_{32}/\{11, 12, 13, 27, 28, 29\})$	$e_j^{64}(j \in \{59, 60, 61\})$	78
014	$e_i^{64}(i \in \mathbb{Z}_{32}/\{12+j, 28+j\})$	$e_{39+j}^{64}(j \in \{0, 1, 2, 3\})$	120

Manual Verification for the 4-Round i-Impossible Differentials (e_i^{64}, e_{52}^{64}) $(i \in \mathbb{Z}_{32})$ **of MISTY1.** First, we study the property of the FL and FO function of MISTY1.

Observation 2. *Let F denote the FL function of MISTY1, if the input difference is one of e_i^{32}, e_{i+16}^{32}, and $e_{i,i+16}^{32}$ ($0 \le i \le 15$), all possible output difference of F is $\{e_i^{32}, e_{i+16}^{32}, e_{i,i+16}^{32}\}$. Moreover, all possible output difference of F^2 is also $\{e_i^{32}, e_{i+16}^{32}, e_{i,i+16}^{32}\}$, where F^2 denotes the composition of two FL function.*

Proposition 1. *Let F denote the FO function of MISTY1 and $\gamma_i (0 \le i \le 1)$ be the 16-bit variables, for $\forall (\gamma_1 || \gamma_0) \in \{\beta | e_{20}^{32} \xrightarrow{F} \beta\}$, the weight of γ_1 must be greater than 1.*

Then, we verify the 4-round i-impossible differentials $(e_i^{64}, e_{52}^{64})(i \in \mathbb{Z}_{32})$ of MISTY1, which is finished in the Full Version of our paper.

5.4 RC5

RC5 is designed by Rivest in 1994 [24]. The block size of it can be 32, 64, or 128 bits. For each block size n, the version is denoted as RC5-n($n = 32, 64, 128$).

Advantage of Our Tool. The operation variable rotation highly depends on the value of state, which cannot be handled by the previous automatic search tools for impossible differentials. In our model, by exploiting the modeling method we proposed in Sect. 4.1, we give the first automatic method for searching the impossible differentials of RC5.

Configurations of Our Tool. The key schedule of RC5 is very complex. Thus, we focus on searching i-impossible differentials. By observing the structure of RC5-n, the difference $e_{(i,i+\frac{n}{2})}^n$ propagates to the difference $e_{(i+\frac{n}{2})}^n$ after 0.5-round in the encryption direction. Thus, we search the i-impossible differentials for RC5-n($n = 32, 64, 128$) by limiting the input difference and output difference in the set $(e_{(i,i+\frac{n}{2})}^n, e_{(j)}^n)(0 \leq i \leq \frac{n}{2} - 1, 0 \leq j \leq n - 1)$.

List of 2.5-round i-Impossible Differentials. As a result, our tool found 12 i-impossible differentials for RC5-32, 27 i-impossible differentials for RC5-64, and 58 i-impossible differentials for RC5-128. This is the first result of impossible differentials for RC5. All the results are shown in Table 2.

Table 2. 2.5-Round i-impossible Differentials of RC5

Block Size	ΔP	ΔC	Number
32	$e_{(i,i+16)}^{32}(4 \leq i \leq 15)$	$e_{(15)}^{32}$	12
64	$e_{(i,i+32)}^{64}(5 \leq i \leq 31)$	$e_{(31)}^{64}$	27
128	$e_{(i,i+64)}^{128}(6 \leq i \leq 63)$	$e_{(63)}^{128}$	58

Manual Verification for the i-Impossible Differential $(e_{(\frac{n}{2}-1,n-1)}^n, e_{(\frac{n}{2})-1}^n)$ of RC5-n. First, we study the relation of a pair of input values and a pair of output values for the operation variable rotation, and have that the parity of $W(z \oplus w)$ is the same as $W(x \oplus u)$, where $z = x \lll y, w = u \lll v$, $x, y, z, u, v, w \in \mathbb{F}_2^m$. Then, we verify the 2.5-round i-impossible differential $(e_{(15,31)}^{32}, e_{(15)}^{32})$ of RC5-32, $(e_{(31,63)}^{64}, e_{(31)}^{64})$ of RC5-64, and $(e_{(63,127)}^{128}, e_{(63)}^{128})$ of RC5-128 together. The details of our manual process are shown in the Full Version of our paper.

6 Applications to Impossible Differentials from the Aspect of Design

In this section, we apply our tool to evaluate the security of lightweight block ciphers against the d-impossible differentials directly. For block ciphers with large S-boxes, we propose the three phases technique and inside value technique, which improve the security evaluation efficiency against the impossible differentials.

Three Phases Technique. For a block cipher, proving that all the input differences in Λ and output differences in Θ are the r-round possible differentials may be time-consuming. To overcome this dilemma, we pick two sets Φ and Ψ satisfied: for $\forall \alpha \in \Lambda$, there exists $\alpha_0 \in \Phi$ such that α can propagate to α_0 after r_1 rounds in the forward direction, and for $\forall \beta \in \Theta$, there exists $\beta_0 \in \Psi$ such that β can propagate to β_0 after r_2 rounds in the backward direction. In this way, we just need to prove all the difference of the Φ and Ψ are the $(r - r_1 - r_2)$-round possible differentials.

Inside Value Technique. For a block cipher, proving (α, β) is an r-round i-possible (resp. d-possible) differential directly may be time-consuming. To solve this problem, we prove that $(0, \alpha)$ and $(0, \beta)$ is an i-possible (resp. d-possible) 2-polygon instead. Our experimental results show that this technique speeds up our proof process.

6.1 Direct Application to GIFT64, PRESENT, Midori64, PRINTcipher48, and PRINTcipher96

By exploiting our tool, we prove that, in the search space where the input difference activates only one S-box in the first substitution and the output difference activates only one S-box in the last substitution, there exists no 7-round, 7-round, 6-round, 5-round, and 6-round impossible differential for GIFT64, PRESENT, Midori64, PRINTcipher48, and PRINTcipher96 even considering the details of the key schedule.

6.2 Three Phases Technique: Apply to AES-128

AES-128 is the most famous standard block cipher designed by Vincent Rijmen and Joan Daemen [11]. It is a 128-bit block cipher with 128-bit key. AES-128 adopts the SPN structure. Its 128-bit internal state s can be represented as a 4×4 matrix of bytes $s_{i,j} \in \mathbb{F}_2^8$ ($0 \leq i, j \leq 3$), each values in the finite fields $\mathbb{F}_2^8$. For more details of AES, please refer to [11].

Previous Result. Wang el at. [30] have proved that there exists no 5-round 1 input active word and 1 output active word impossible differentials for AES-128 without the last MC operation even considering all the details of the S-box in the key independent setting. But, the influence of the key schedule for the impossible differentials about AES-128 is still unknown.

Our Method. Determine whether a pair of input and output differences is the 5-round impossible differential by considering all the details of the relations of the round keys is very time-consuming. To resolve this issue, we adopt the three phases technique to finish our proof. First, according to the following two observations and further the propositions by studying the differential property of the S-box of AES, we propagate the input difference one round in the forward direction and the output difference two rounds in the backward direction. Then, we run our algorithm to show that those differences after the propagation can be connected through two rounds of AES even considering the relation of 3-round keys.

Observation 3. *Let S denote the S-box of AES, define $DDT_{in}(\beta) = \{\alpha | \exists x \in \mathbb{F}_2^8, s.t. S(x) \oplus S(x \oplus \alpha) = \beta\}$, then we have $DDT_{in}(0x01) \cup DDT_{in}(0x02) \cup DDT_{in}(0xec) = \mathbb{F}_2^8$.*

Observation 4. *Let S denote the S-box of AES, define $DDT_{out}(\alpha) = \{\beta | \exists x \in \mathbb{F}_2^8, s.t. \beta = S(x) \oplus S(x \oplus \alpha)\}$, then we have $DDT_{out}(0x01) \cup DDT_{out}(0x02) \cup DDT_{out}(0xf7) = \mathbb{F}_2^8$. Moreover, we have*

$$\{0x0d, 0x1a, 0xff\} = \{0x0d \times 0x01, 0x0d \times 0x02, 0x0d \times 0xf7\} \in DDT_{out}(0x01),$$
$$\{0x0b, 0x16, 0xfb\} = \{0x0b \times 0x01, 0x0b \times 0x02, 0x0b \times 0xf7\} \in DDT_{out}(0x03),$$
$$\{0x09, 0x12, 0x0e\} = \{0x09 \times 0x01, 0x09 \times 0x02, 0x09 \times 0xf7\} \in DDT_{out}(0x06),$$
$$\{0x0e, 0x1c, 0xfd\} = \{0x0e \times 0x01, 0x0e \times 0x02, 0x0e \times 0xf7\} \in DDT_{out}(0x09).$$

Proposition 2. *Let $F_1 = MC \circ SR \circ SB \circ ARK$, any difference $D_\alpha^{i,j}$ $(0 \le i \le 3, 0 \le j \le 3, \alpha \in \mathbb{F}_2^8/\{0\})$ can propagate to at least one of the differences of $MC \circ SR(D_{0x01}^{i,j})$, $MC \circ SR(D_{0x02}^{i,j})$, and $MC \circ SR(D_{0xec}^{i,j})$ through F_1.*

Proposition 3. *Let $F_2 = ARK \circ SR \circ SB \circ ARK \circ MC \circ SR \circ SB$ and*

$$P = \begin{pmatrix} 0x09 & 0x03 & 0x01 & 0x06 \\ 0x06 & 0x09 & 0x03 & 0x01 \\ 0x01 & 0x06 & 0x09 & 0x03 \\ 0x03 & 0x01 & 0x06 & 0x09 \end{pmatrix}.$$

Let $k = (j + i) \bmod 4$. Then, for any difference $D_\alpha^{i,j}$ $(0 \le i \le 3, 0 \le j \le 3, \alpha \in \mathbb{F}_2^8/\{0\})$, the difference $G_{i,j} := D_{P_{0,i}}^{0,k} + D_{P_{1,i}}^{1,(k+1)mod4} + D_{P_{2,i}}^{2,(k+2)mod4} + D_{P_{3,i}}^{3,(k+3)mod4}$ can propagate to it through F_2.

Proof. Let Q be the inverse matrix of the MDS used in AES[7]. According to Observation 4, for $\forall z \in \{0x01, 0x02, 0x7f\}$, we have $G_{i,j} \xrightarrow{SR \circ SB} D_{Q_{0,i} \times z}^{0,k} +$

---
[7]

$$Q = \begin{pmatrix} 0x0e & 0x0b & 0x0d & 0x09 \\ 0x09 & 0x0e & 0x0b & 0x0d \\ 0x0d & 0x09 & 0x0e & 0x0b \\ 0x0b & 0x0d & 0x09 & 0x0e \end{pmatrix}.$$

$D_{Q_{1,i} \times z}^{1,k} + D_{Q_{2,i} \times z}^{2,k} + D_{Q_{3,i} \times z}^{3,k}$, since the S-box is applied to each byte of the state in parallel in the SB operation. Then based on the definition of Q, we have $MC(D_{Q_{0,i} \times z}^{0,k} + D_{Q_{1,i} \times z}^{1,k} + D_{Q_{2,i} \times z}^{2,k} + D_{Q_{3,i} \times z}^{3,k}) = D_z^{i,k}$. According to Observation 4, for any difference $D_\alpha^{i,j}$ ($0 \le i \le 3, 0 \le j \le 3, \alpha \in \mathbb{F}_2^8/\{0\}$), at least one of $D_{0x01}^{i,k}$, $D_{0x02}^{i,k}$, and $D_{0x7f}^{i,k}$ can propagate to it through $SR \circ SB$. Thus, for any difference $D_\alpha^{i,j}$ ($0 \le i \le 3, 0 \le j \le 3, \alpha \in \mathbb{F}_2^8/\{0\}$), the difference $G_{i,j}$ can propagate to it through F_2. □

Our Experiment. Let $F_3 = ARK \circ (MC \circ SR \circ SB \circ ARK)^2$. For $0 \le i, j, s, t \le 3$, by considering the relations of K_1, K_2, and K_3 according to the key schedule, we run our tool to determine whether all the differences of $MC \circ SR(D_{0x01}^{i,j})$, $MC \circ SR(D_{0x02}^{i,j})$, and $MC \circ SR(D_{0xec}^{i,j})$ can propagate to $G_{s,t}$ through F_3. After a total of $16 \times 16 \times 3 = 768$ tests, our result shows that all the differences of $MC \circ SR(D_{0x01}^{i,j})$, $MC \circ SR(D_{0x02}^{i,j})$, and $MC \circ SR(D_{0xec}^{i,j})$ can propagate to $G_{s,t}$ through F_3 in our setting, which leads to the following theorem.

Theorem 6. For 5-round AES-128 without the last MC operation, there exists no 1 input active word and 1 output active word impossible differentials by considering the relations of K_1, K_2, and K_3.

6.3 Combination of Three Phases Technique and Inside Value Technique: Application to MISTY1

Previous Result. Since MISTY1 adopts the 7-bit and 9-bit S-boxes, no automatic search tool could be used to evaluate its security taking account into the differential property of S-boxes so far.

Our Approach. We combine the three phases technique and inside value technique to accelerate our tool in this part. Denote $\beta_0||\alpha_0$ be the 1 input active bit difference and $\beta_5||\alpha_5$ be the 1 output active bit difference, and $FO_{(KI,KO)}$ be the FO function, where KI and KO are the secret keys in the FO function. Let

$$\beta_1||\alpha_1 = \begin{cases} e_{i+32}^{64}, \text{ if } (\beta_0||\alpha_0) = e_i^{64}(0 \le i \le 31), \\ (FO_{0,0}(0) \oplus FO_{0,0}(e_{i-32}^{32}))||e_{i-32}^{32}, \text{ if } \beta_0||\alpha_0 = e_i^{64}(32 \le i \le 63). \end{cases}$$

$$\beta_4||\alpha_4 = \begin{cases} e_i^{32}||(FO_{0,0}(0) \oplus FO_{0,0}(e_i^{32}))e_{i+32}^{64}, \text{ if } (\beta_5||\alpha_5) = e_i^{64}(0 \le i \le 31), \\ e_{i-32}^{64}, \text{ if } \beta_5||\alpha_5 = e_i^{64}(32 \le i \le 63). \end{cases}$$

That is, we propagate the difference $\beta_0||\alpha_0$ through one round to $\beta_1||\alpha_1$ in the forward direction and the difference $\beta_5||\alpha_5$ through one round to $\beta_4||\alpha_4$ in the backward direction. Then, we prove that $(0, \beta_1||\alpha_1)$ and $(0, \beta_4||\alpha_4)$ is the i-possible 2-polygons.

Our Experiment. We run our tool to determine whether the input 2-polygons $(0, \beta_1||\alpha_1)$ and the output 2-polygons $(0, \beta_4||\alpha_4)$ are the i-possible 2-polygons for 3 rounds MISTY1. After a total of $64 \times 64 = 4096$ tests, our result shows that all the input 2-polygons $(0, \beta_1||\alpha_1)$ and the output 2-polygons $(0, \beta_4||\alpha_4)$ are the i-possible 2-polygons for 3-round MISTY1, which leads to the following theorem.

Theorem 7. For 5-round MISTY1 in which the FL layers were placed at the even rounds, there exists no 1 input active bit and 1 output active bit impossible differentials in the key independent setting.

7   Applications to Impossible $(s + 1)$-Polytopic $(s \geq 2)$ Transitions

In this section, we run our tool to search the impossible $(s+1)$-polytopic$(s \geq 2)$ transitions for PRINTcipher, GIFT64, PRESENT, and RC5. All the contradictions of the distinguishers in this section can be detected by our verification algorithm, the details are shown in the Full Version of our paper in the supplementary materials. First, for S-boxes based block ciphers, we define some search spaces for the input and output s-differences.

Search Space$_1$: In this space, the input 2-difference (b_1, b_2) is the $(1, 1)$ active bit which only activates the two right S-boxes in the first round, and the output 2-difference (e_1, e_2) is the $(1, 1)$ active bit.

Search Space$_2$: In this space, the input 2-difference (b_1, b_2) is the $(1, 1)$ input active bit which only activates the first right S-box in the first round and the 2-difference (e_1, e_2) is the $(1, 1)$ output active bit which activates the same S-box in the last round.

Search Space$_i$ $(i = 3, 4)$: In this space, the input 3-difference is of pattern $(b_1, b_2, b_1 \oplus b_2)$ and the output 3-difference is of pattern $(e_1, e_2, e_1 \oplus e_2)$, where (b_1, b_2) and (e_1, e_2) are in Search space$_{i-2}$.

7.1   The d-Impossible Polytopic Transitions of PRINTcipher

In this part, we show our method to search the impossible 3-polytopic transitions and impossible 4-polytopic transitions for PRINTcipher48 and PRINTcipher96 by considering all the details of the key schedule. Besides, we also study the influence of the Xor key and control key for the d-impossible 3-polytopic transitions of PRINTcipher48.

For the d-impossible 3-polytopic transitions of PRINTcipher48, we search such distinguishers in the Search space$_1$. After a total of $\binom{6}{1} \times \binom{48}{1} = 16920$ tests, the maximum number of rounds of d-impossible 3-polytopic transitions in this search space is 6, and a total of 1471 6-round d-impossible 3-polytopic transitions are found. One of them is

$$(0x000000000001, 0x000000010000) \xrightarrow{6-round} (0x000000000002, 0x000000000200).$$

Impact of the constraints of the Xor keys. In our search above, we restrict the Xor keys and control keys according to the key schedule. To investigate the impact of the constraints of the Xor keys, we further release the constraints of the Xor keys and keep the constraints of the control keys. Then, we run our tool to search the 6-round impossible 3-polytopic transitions in Search space$_1$. Finally, we get 1448 6-round impossible 3-polytopic transitions. This result shows that, the constraint of the Xor keys leads to more contradictions for constructing the impossible 3-polytopic transitions.

Impact of the Constraints of the Control Keys. Similarly, we keep the constraints of the Xor keys and release the constraints of the control keys over again. Then, we run our tool to search the 6-round impossible 3-polytopic transitions in Search space$_1$. Finally, we found that there exists no 6-round impossible 3-polytopic transitions in such search space. This result shows that the constraints of the control keys have a very significant impact on constructing the impossible 3-polytopic transitions.

Those two results show that, both the Xor keys and control keys may have influences on the results of impossible $(s + 1)$-polytopic transitions. Thus, in the search of impossible $(s + 1)$-polytopic transitions, we should consider the details of key schedule as much as possible if the time cost permits.

For the d-impossible 4-polytopic transitions of PRINTcipher48, we search such distinguishers in Search space$_3$. Finally, we found one 7-round d-impossible 4-polytopic transition of PRINTcipher48 as follows and stop our tool due to the limitation of search time.

$$(0x000000000001, 0x000000010000, 0x000000010001) \xrightarrow{7-round} \nrightarrow$$
$$(0x000000000001, 0x000000000200, 0x000000000201).$$

For the d-impossible 3-polytopic transitions of PRINTcipher96, we search such distinguishers in Search space$_1$. Finally, we find one 7-round d-impossible 3-polytopic transition of PRINTcipher96 as follows and stop our tool due to the limitation of search time.

$$(0x000000000000000000000001, 0x000000000000000100000000) \xrightarrow{7-round} \nrightarrow$$
$$(0x000000000000000000000001, 0x000000000000000008000000)$$

For the d-impossible 4-polytopic transitions of PRINTcipher96, we search such distinguishers in Search space$_3$. Finally, we find one 8-round d-impossible 4-polytopic transition of PRINTcipher96 as follows (as the left 48-bit of each value are 0, we only show the right 48 bits here) and stop our tool due to the limitation of search time.

$$(0x000000000001, 0x000100000000, 0x000100000001) \xrightarrow{8-round} \nrightarrow$$
$$(0x000000000001, 0x000000000200, 0x000000000201).$$

7.2 The 7-Round d-Impossible 3-Polytopic Transition of GIFT64

For GIFT64, we search the d-impossible 3-polytopic transitions in Search space$_2$ Finally, we find one 7-round d-impossible 3-polytopic transition as follows and stop our tool due to the limitation of search time.

$$(0x0000000000000001, 0x0000000000000002) \xrightarrow{7-round} \nrightarrow$$
$$(0x0000000000000001, 0x0000000000000008).$$

7.3   The 7-Round i-Impossible 4-Polytopic Transition of PRESENT

For the i-impossible 4-polytopic transitions of PRESENT, we search such distinguishers in Search space$_4$. Finally, we find one 7-round d-impossible 4-polytopic transition of PRESENT as follows and stop our tool due to the limitation of search time.

$$(0x0000000000000001, 0x0000000000000002, 0x0000000000000003) \overset{7-round}{\nrightarrow}$$
$$(0x0000000000000001, 0x0000000000010000, 0x0000000000010001).$$

7.4   The 3-Round i-Impossible 3-Polytopic Transition of RC5-32 and RC5-64

In this subsection, we show our method for searching the i-impossible 3-polytopic transition of RC5-32 and RC5-64 by adopting the step by step strategy.

For RC5-32, since $(0x80008000, 0x00008000)$ is the 2.5-round impossible differential, we search the i-impossible 3-polytopic transitions by limiting the input 2-difference (b_1, b_2) in the set $\{(0x80008000, e_{i,i+16}^{32})|0 \le i \le 15\}$ and the output 2-difference (e_1, e_2) in the set $\{(0x00008000, e_i^{32})|0 \le i \le 31\}$. Finally, we find 108 3-round i-impossible 3-polytopic transitions and result in that there exists no 3.5-round i-impossible 3-polytopic transitions in such search space. One of the transitions is

$$(0x80008000, 0x00100010) \overset{3-round}{\nrightarrow} (0x80000000, 0x00200000).$$

By adopting the same method for RC5-32, we find one 3-round i-impossible 3-polytopic transition as follows.

$$(0x8000000080000000, 0x0000002000000020) \overset{3-round}{\nrightarrow}$$
$$(0x8000000000000000, 0x0000004000000000).$$

8   Conclusion

In this paper, we redefine the impossible differentials and impossible $(s+1)$-polytopic transitions based on the notation of s-polygon, and design a unity SAT-based automatic tool to search them. We apply our tool to various block ciphers. These results show that our tool can not only be used to search the distinguishers by considering the key schedule in the single-key setting, but also make the most of the inside property of large S-boxes or variable rotation for several typical classes of block ciphers.

Moreover, we derive an interesting result that, with the increase of the parameter s, the number of rounds in which the impossible $(s+1)$-polytopic transition exists also increases. Although due to the limitations of computing power, we can only search the impossible $(s+1)$-polytopic transition with a small value of s. But, the result indicates a challenge clearly that the impossible $(s+1)$-polytopic transition may bring threats for block ciphers with the development of the solver of the SAT and the computing power, and it is better to resist this kind of cryptanalysis in a theoretical way of cipher design.

Acknowledgements. We are very grateful to the anonymous reviewers for their helpful comments. This work is supported by the National Natural Science Foundation of China (No. 61772517, 61902030, 61772516), Beijing Municipal Science & Technology Commission (No. Z191100007119004), and Youth Innovation Promotion Association CAS.

References

1. Banik, S., et al.: Midori: a block cipher for low energy. In: Iwata, T., Cheon, J.H. (eds.) ASIACRYPT 2015. LNCS, vol. 9453, pp. 411–436. Springer, Heidelberg (2015). https://doi.org/10.1007/978-3-662-48800-3_17

2. Banik, S., Pandey, S.K., Peyrin, T., Sasaki, Yu., Sim, S.M., Todo, Y.: GIFT: a small present. In: Fischer, W., Homma, N. (eds.) CHES 2017. LNCS, vol. 10529, pp. 321–345. Springer, Cham (2017). https://doi.org/10.1007/978-3-319-66787-4_16

3. Baysal, A., Şahin, S.: RoadRunneR: a small and fast bitslice block cipher for low cost 8-bit processors. In: Güneysu, T., Leander, G., Moradi, A. (eds.) LightSec 2015. LNCS, vol. 9542, pp. 58–76. Springer, Cham (2016). https://doi.org/10.1007/978-3-319-29078-2_4

4. Biham, E., Biryukov, A., Shamir, A.: Cryptanalysis of skipjack reduced to 31 rounds using impossible differentials. In: Stern, J. (ed.) EUROCRYPT 1999. LNCS, vol. 1592, pp. 12–23. Springer, Heidelberg (1999). https://doi.org/10.1007/3-540-48910-X_2

5. Biham, E., Shamir, A.: Differential cryptanalysis of des-like cryptosystems. J. Cryptol. 4(1), 3–72 (1991)

6. Bogdanov, A., et al.: PRESENT: an ultra-lightweight block cipher. In: Paillier, P., Verbauwhede, I. (eds.) CHES 2007. LNCS, vol. 4727, pp. 450–466. Springer, Heidelberg (2007). https://doi.org/10.1007/978-3-540-74735-2_31

7. Borghoff, J., et al.: PRINCE – a low-latency block cipher for pervasive computing applications. In: Wang, X., Sako, K. (eds.) ASIACRYPT 2012. LNCS, vol. 7658, pp. 208–225. Springer, Heidelberg (2012). https://doi.org/10.1007/978-3-642-34961-4_14

8. Boura, C., Naya-Plasencia, M., Suder, V.: Scrutinizing and improving impossible differential attacks: applications to CLEFIA, Camellia, LBlock and SIMON. In: Sarkar, P., Iwata, T. (eds.) ASIACRYPT 2014. LNCS, vol. 8873, pp. 179–199. Springer, Heidelberg (2014). https://doi.org/10.1007/978-3-662-45611-8_10

9. Chen, J., Wang, M., Preneel, B.: impossible differential cryptanalysis of the lightweight block ciphers TEA, XTEA and HIGHT. In: Mitrokotsa, A., Vaudenay, S. (eds.) AFRICACRYPT 2012. LNCS, vol. 7374, pp. 117–137. Springer, Heidelberg (2012). https://doi.org/10.1007/978-3-642-31410-0_8

10. Cui, T., Jia, K., Kai, F., Chen, S., Wang, M.: New automatic search tool for impossible differentials and zero-correlation linear approximations. IACR Cryptology ePrint Archive 2016, p. 689 (2016)

11. Daemen, J., Rijmen, V.: The Design of Rijndael: AES - The Advanced Encryption Standard. Information Security and Cryptography. Springer, Heidelberg (2002). https://doi.org/10.1007/978-3-662-04722-4

12. Fu, K., Wang, M., Guo, Y., Sun, S., Hu, L.: MILP-based automatic search algorithms for differential and linear trails for speck. In: Peyrin, T. (ed.) FSE 2016. LNCS, vol. 9783, pp. 268–288. Springer, Heidelberg (2016). https://doi.org/10.1007/978-3-662-52993-5_14

13. Kim, J., Hong, S., Sung, J., Lee, S., Lim, J., Sung, S.: Impossible differential cryptanalysis for block cipher structures. In: Johansson, T., Maitra, S. (eds.) INDOCRYPT 2003. LNCS, vol. 2904, pp. 82–96. Springer, Heidelberg (2003). https://doi.org/10.1007/978-3-540-24582-7_6
14. Knudsen, L.: Deal - a 128-bit block cipher. In: NIST AES Proposal (1998)
15. Knudsen, L., Leander, G., Poschmann, A., Robshaw, M.J.B.: PRINTCIPHER: a block cipher for IC-printing. In: Mangard, S., Standaert, F.-X. (eds.) CHES 2010. LNCS, vol. 6225, pp. 16–32. Springer, Heidelberg (2010). https://doi.org/10.1007/978-3-642-15031-9_2
16. Liu, F., Isobe, T., Meier, W.: Automatic verification of differential characteristics: application to reduced gimli. In: Micciancio, D., Ristenpart, T. (eds.) CRYPTO 2020. LNCS, vol. 12172, pp. 219–248. Springer, Cham (2020). https://doi.org/10.1007/978-3-030-56877-1_8
17. Luo, Y., Lai, X., Zhongming, W., Gong, G.: A unified method for finding impossible differentials of block cipher structures. Inf. Sci. **263**, 211–220 (2014)
18. Mala, H., Dakhilalian, M., Rijmen, V., Modarres-Hashemi, M.: Improved impossible differential cryptanalysis of 7-round AES-128. In: Gong, G., Gupta, K.C. (eds.) INDOCRYPT 2010. LNCS, vol. 6498, pp. 282–291. Springer, Heidelberg (2010). https://doi.org/10.1007/978-3-642-17401-8_20
19. Matsui, M.: Linear cryptanalysis method for DES cipher. In: Helleseth, T. (ed.) EUROCRYPT 1993. LNCS, vol. 765, pp. 386–397. Springer, Heidelberg (1994). https://doi.org/10.1007/3-540-48285-7_33
20. Matsui, M.: New block encryption algorithm MISTY. In: Biham, E. (ed.) FSE 1997. LNCS, vol. 1267, pp. 54–68. Springer, Heidelberg (1997). https://doi.org/10.1007/BFb0052334
21. Mironov, I., Zhang, L.: Applications of SAT solvers to cryptanalysis of hash functions. In: Biere, A., Gomes, C.P. (eds.) SAT 2006. LNCS, vol. 4121, pp. 102–115. Springer, Heidelberg (2006). https://doi.org/10.1007/11814948_13
22. Mouha, N., Wang, Q., Gu, D., Preneel, B.: Differential and linear cryptanalysis using mixed-integer linear programming. In: Wu, C.-K., Yung, M., Lin, D. (eds.) Inscrypt 2011. LNCS, vol. 7537, pp. 57–76. Springer, Heidelberg (2012). https://doi.org/10.1007/978-3-642-34704-7_5
23. Nyberg, K., Knudsen, L.R.: Provable security against a differential attack. J. Cryptol. **8**(1), 27–37 (1995). https://doi.org/10.1007/BF00204800
24. Rivest, R.L.: The RC5 encryption algorithm. In: Preneel, B. (ed.) FSE 1994. LNCS, vol. 1008, pp. 86–96. Springer, Heidelberg (1995). https://doi.org/10.1007/3-540-60590-8_7
25. Rivest, R.L., Robshaw, M.J.B., Yin, Y.L.: RC6 as the AES. In: The Third Advanced Encryption Standard Candidate Conference, 13–14 April 2000, New York, pp. 337–342. National Institute of Standards and Technology (2000)
26. Sadeghi, S., Rijmen, V., Bagheri, N.: Proposing an milp-based method for the experimental verification of difference trails. IACR Cryptol. ePrint Arch. **2020**, 632 (2020)
27. Sasaki, Yu., Todo, Y.: New impossible differential search tool from design and cryptanalysis aspects. In: Coron, J.-S., Nielsen, J.B. (eds.) EUROCRYPT 2017. LNCS, vol. 10212, pp. 185–215. Springer, Cham (2017). https://doi.org/10.1007/978-3-319-56617-7_7

28. Sun, S., Hu, L., Wang, P., Qiao, K., Ma, X., Song, L.: Automatic security evaluation and (related-key) differential characteristic search: application to SIMON, PRESENT, LBlock, DES(L) and other bit-oriented block ciphers. In: Sarkar, P., Iwata, T. (eds.) ASIACRYPT 2014. LNCS, vol. 8873, pp. 158–178. Springer, Heidelberg (2014). https://doi.org/10.1007/978-3-662-45611-8_9
29. Tiessen, T.: Polytopic cryptanalysis. In: Fischlin, M., Coron, J.-S. (eds.) EUROCRYPT 2016. LNCS, vol. 9665, pp. 214–239. Springer, Heidelberg (2016). https://doi.org/10.1007/978-3-662-49890-3_9
30. Wang, Q., Jin, C.: Upper bound of the length of truncated impossible differentials for AES. Des. Codes Crypt. **86**(7), 1541–1552 (2017). https://doi.org/10.1007/s10623-017-0411-z
31. Wu, S., Wang, M.: Automatic search of truncated impossible differentials for word-oriented block ciphers. In: Galbraith, S., Nandi, M. (eds.) INDOCRYPT 2012. LNCS, vol. 7668, pp. 283–302. Springer, Heidelberg (2012). https://doi.org/10.1007/978-3-642-34931-7_17

An Algebraic Formulation of the Division Property: Revisiting Degree Evaluations, Cube Attacks, and Key-Independent Sums

Kai Hu[1,4], Siwei Sun[2,5], Meiqin Wang[1,4(✉)], and Qingju Wang[3]

[1] School of Cyber Science and Technology, Shandong University,
Qingdao, Shandong, China
hukai@mail.sdu.edu.cn, mqwang@sdu.edu.cn
[2] State Key Laboratory of Information Security, Institute of Information
Engineering, Chinese Academy of Sciences, Beijing, China
siweisun.isaac@gmail.com
[3] SnT, University of Luxembourg, Esch-sur-Alzette, Luxembourg
qingju.wang@uni.lu
[4] Key Laboratory of Cryptologic Technology and Information Security, Ministry
of Education, Shandong University, Qingdao, Shandong, China
[5] School of Cyber Security, University of Chinese Academy of Sciences,
Beijing, China

Abstract. Since it was proposed in 2015 as a generalization of integral properties, the division property has evolved into a powerful tool for probing the structures of Boolean functions whose algebraic normal forms are not available. We capture the most essential elements for the detection of division properties from a pure algebraic perspective, proposing a technique named as *monomial prediction*, which can be employed to determine the presence or absence of a monomial in any product of the coordinate functions of a vectorial Boolean function f by counting the number of the so-called *monomial trails* across a sequence of simpler functions whose composition is f. Under the framework of the monomial prediction, we formally prove that most algorithms for detecting division properties in literature raise no false alarms but may miss. We also establish the equivalence between the monomial prediction and the three-subset bit-based division property without unknown subset presented at EUROCRYPT 2020, and show that these two techniques are perfectly accurate.

The monomial prediction technique can be regarded as a purification of the definitions of the division properties without resorting to external multisets. This algebraic formulation gives more insights into division properties and inspires new search strategies. With the monomial prediction, we obtain the *exact* algebraic degrees of TRIVIUM up to 834 rounds for the first time. In the context of cube attacks, we are able to explore a larger search space in limited time and recover the exact algebraic normal forms of complex superpolies with the help of a divide-and-conquer

Due to page limits, all appendixes and some tables of this paper are provided in our full version [11].

© International Association for Cryptologic Research 2020
S. Moriai and H. Wang (Eds.): ASIACRYPT 2020, LNCS 12491, pp. 446–476, 2020.
https://doi.org/10.1007/978-3-030-64837-4_15

strategy. As a result, we identify more cubes with smaller dimensions, leading to improvements of some near-optimal attacks against 840-, 841- and 842-round TRIVIUM.

Keywords: Division property · Monomial prediction · Detection algorithm · Algebraic degree · Cube attack · TRIVIUM

1   Introduction

The division property [25] was first proposed by Todo at EUROCRYPT 2015 to uncover and exploit the spectrum of properties hidden between the two extremes—the ALL and BLANCE properties in the traditional integral cryptanalysis [6,16] targeting word-oriented primitives. Compared with the traditional integral cryptanalysis, the division property presents a more refined way for cryptanalysts to identify balanced output bits, where the algebraic degree information of the local components of the target is fully utilized. Its powerfulness and potential were undoubtedly demonstrated by the break of the full MISTY1 [24]. Subsequently, by considering the division property at the bit level, Todo and Morii [27] introduced the bit-based division property to find balanced bits of the round-reduced SIMON. Moreover, to capture also constant output bits and some cancellation characteristics ignored by the conventional bit-based division property, the so-called three-subset bit-based division property was proposed in the same work [27].

This seemingly natural and obvious migration from words to bits (1-bit word) not only makes division properties applicable to bit-oriented designs, but also reveals the intimate relationship between division properties and the algebraic normal forms (ANF) of the target [26], well-beyond merely the algebraic degree. This relationship hints at how the division property can be employed to probe the ANF of a complex Boolean function whose explicit formula is typically not available. As expected, the division property was shown to be useful in (partially) determining the algebraic structures of the superpolies arising in cube attacks [9,26,29,30]. Essentially, every cryptanalysis attempt based on the division property employs some procedures which we call *detection algorithms*.

Detection Algorithms. Given a Boolean function f, a detection algorithm for a certain property $\mathcal{P}$ is a procedure used to determine whether $\mathcal{P}$ holds for f. The property $\mathcal{P}$ can be as simple as "f is a constant" or as complicated as "the sum of f over all possible values of certain variables is zero regardless of the values of some other variables". Given a Boolean function f and a detection algorithm for $\mathcal{P}$, four possibilities are in order:

- *Hit*: $\mathcal{P}$ holds and the output of the algorithm is positive;
- *Miss*: $\mathcal{P}$ holds but the output of the algorithm is negative;
- *False alarm*: $\mathcal{P}$ does not hold but the output of the algorithm is positive;
- *Correct reject*: $\mathcal{P}$ does not hold and the output of the algorithm is negative.

At this point, we remind the readers that a lot of research that has been done on division property so far is about the construction of detection algorithms, loosely speaking, for the balance (or more generally the key-independent constant) property, or more essentially, the absence of certain monomials. A no-false-alarm algorithm can be employed by an attacker (e.g., to find balanced output bits), while a no-miss algorithm can be employed by a designer in security proofs. Our ultimate goal is to devise a perfect and efficient detection algorithm that never misses and never raises false alarms.

Our Contributions. Capturing the algebraic essentials of many attempts to make the detection of division properties more accurate, we propose a new technique called *monomial prediction*. This is a perfect detection algorithm for detecting the presence and absence of any monomial x^u in the product y^v of any output bits of a vectorial Boolean function $y = f(x)$ by counting the number of the so-called *monomial trails* connecting x^u and y^v across a sequence of simpler vectorial Boolean functions whose composition is f. We then establish an equivalence between the monomial prediction approach and the recently proposed three-subset bit-based division property without unknown subset at EUROCRYPT 2020 [9]. We also show that all the predecessors of [9] (except the *lazy propagation* method [27]) can be categorized as no-false-alarm detection algorithms.

The monomial prediction technique can be regarded as a new language for describing the division properties. The original language for the division properties is somehow indirect and vague since a property (the division property) of an object (a vectorial Boolean function) is defined via its effects on external objects (multisets) rather than via its own intrinsic natures. The monomial prediction delivers a definition of division properties fully getting rid of the external multisets. This new treatment not only gives us a unified view on the two-subset bit-based division property, three-subset bit-based division property, and three-subset division property without unknown subset, but also naturally leads to new search strategies. We revisit several well-known applications of the division property with the monomial prediction approach, and identify some improvements over the state-of-the-art.

By showing the presence of monomials with a certain degree and the absence of monomials with larger degrees, we obtain the *exact* algebraic degree of the output bits of TRIVIUM up to 834 rounds for the first time. Our results show that the algebraic degree of 834-round TRIVIUM is only 78, which is much lower than the previous estimations by Liu at CRYPTO 2017 [18], where the upper bound of 793-round TRIVIUM has already reached 79. Along the way, we observe and report on an interesting and somewhat counter-intuitive phenomenon: The algebraic degree of TRIVIUM can drop as the number of rounds grows. For example, the degree of 807-round TRIVIUM has been proven to achieve 71, but the degree of the next round drops to 70.

For a Boolean function f, we can check the presence and absence of all monomials that are divisible by the cube term to recover the superpoly in the cube attack. With the help of a divide-and-conquer strategy, our algorithm achieves high efficiency and scales well, making it possible to test many cubes in a limited time. As a result, we are able to identify some cubes with smaller dimensions for TRIVIUM than the previous best works, for instance, in [8,9] all the cubes chosen for 840-, 841- and 842-round TRIVIUM are of dimension 78, which take 2^{78} encryptions of TRIVIUM to recover one bit information of the key, and take 2^{79} TRIVIUM encryption to recover the remaining key bits by exhaustive search. Thus the total complexity of the key-recovery attack is estimated as $2^{78} + 2^{79} \approx 2^{79.6}$. Using our technique, for 840-round TRIVIUM, we can recover superpolies with three different cubes that have dimension of only 75, which reduces the complexity for recovering the key to $2^{77.8}$ encryption. For 841-round TRIVIUM, we recover two superpolies with two different cubes of dimension 76, which reduces the complexity for recovering the full key to $2^{78.6}$ encryption. For 842-round TRIVIUM, with two different cubes of dimension 76 together with their superpolies, we can recover the full key with time complexity $2^{78.6}$. We summarize our cube attacks on TRIVIUM in Table 1.

Table 1. The complexity of cube attacks on 840-, 841- and 842-round TRIVIUM measured by the encryption of TRIVIUM. #Cube means the number of cubes used in the offline phase of the cube attack.

#Round	Offline phase			Online phase	Total time	Reference
	#Cube	Dimension	#Key			
840	1	78	1	2^{79}	$2^{79.6}$	[9]
	3	75, 75, 75	3	2^{77}	$2^{77.8}$	Sect. 5.2
841	1	78	1	2^{79}	$2^{79.6}$	[9]
	2	76, 76	2	2^{78}	$2^{78.6}$	Sect. 5.2
842	1	78	1	2^{79}	$2^{79.6}$	[8]
	2	76, 76	2	2^{78}	$2^{78.6}$	Sect. 5.2

Remark. Before going any further, we would like to briefly discuss the relationship between the monomial prediction and division properties. When used as detection algorithms for the key-independent sum property, both monomial prediction and the three-subset bit-based division property without unknown subsets are perfect. Originally, the division properties are defined over the multisets that the target cipher acts on, while the monomial prediction technique is fully formulated via the algebraic structure of the cipher itself. Our philosophy is that the effect of a cipher on multisets should be regarded as the manifestations of the cipher's intrinsic property, which should not be mixed with the definition of this property. A unified view naturally emerges with the monomial prediction technique for all previous division properties, since all of them are the manifestations of the properties of the ANFs of the target cipher. Finally, we would like to mention that Hebborn et al. [10] show that the three-subset bit-based division property without unknown subsets allows to decide whether or not a specific monomial appears in the ANF with the help of the *parity set* proposed in [2]. So we say that the monomial prediction and the division properties achieve the same goal through different routes.

Organization. In Sect. 2, we introduce necessary notations and preliminaries. The principle of the monomial prediction approach is established in Sect. 3. This leads to the applications to the degree evaluation in Sect. 4 and to cube attacks in Sect. 5. In Sect. 6, we establish the equivalence between the three-subset bit-based division property without unknown subsets and the monomial prediction technique, and theoretically prove that they are perfect in detecting the key-independent sum property. Also, we theoretically show that other algorithms for division properties raise no false alarms. Section 7 concludes and discusses potential future work.

2   Preliminaries

We use bold italic lowercase letters to represent bit vectors, and $\mathbf{0}$ represents a bit vector with all elements being 0. For an n-bit vector $\boldsymbol{u} \in \mathbb{F}_2^n$, its i-th coordinate is denoted by u_i, and thus $\boldsymbol{u} = (u_0, \cdots, u_{n-1})$. The complementary vector of $\boldsymbol{u}$ is denoted by $\bar{\boldsymbol{u}}$ where $u_i \oplus \bar{u}_i = 1$ for $0 \leq i < n$. The Hamming weight of $\boldsymbol{u}$ is $wt(\boldsymbol{u}) = \sum_{i=0}^{n-1} u_i$. For any n-bit vectors $\boldsymbol{u}$ and $\boldsymbol{u}'$, we define $\boldsymbol{u} \succeq \boldsymbol{u}'$ if $u_i \geq u_i'$ for all i, otherwise, $\boldsymbol{u} \not\succeq \boldsymbol{u}'$. Similarly, we define $\boldsymbol{u} \preceq \boldsymbol{u}'$ if $u_i \leq u_i'$ for all i, $\boldsymbol{u} \prec \boldsymbol{u}'$ if $u_i < u_i'$ for all i and $\boldsymbol{u} \succ \boldsymbol{u}'$ if $u_i > u_i'$ for all i.

Let $f : \mathbb{F}_2^n \to \mathbb{F}_2$ be a Boolean function in $\mathbb{F}_2[x_0, x_1, \ldots, x_{n-1}]/(x_0^2 - x_0, x_1^2 - x_1, \ldots, x_{n-1}^2 - x_{n-1})$ whose *algebraic normal form* (ANF) is

$$f(\boldsymbol{x}) = f(x_0, x_1, \ldots, x_{n-1}) = \bigoplus_{\boldsymbol{u} \in \mathbb{F}_2^n} a_{\boldsymbol{u}} \prod_{i=0}^{n-1} x_i^{u_i},$$

where $a_{\boldsymbol{u}} \in \mathbb{F}_2$, and

$$\boldsymbol{x}^{\boldsymbol{u}} = \pi_{\boldsymbol{u}}(\boldsymbol{x}) = \prod_{i=0}^{n-1} x_i^{u_i} \text{ with } x_i^{u_i} = \begin{cases} x_i, & \text{if } u_i = 1, \\ 1, & \text{if } u_i = 0, \end{cases}$$

is called a monomial. If the coefficient of $\boldsymbol{x}^{\boldsymbol{u}}$ in f is 1, we say $\boldsymbol{x}^{\boldsymbol{u}}$ is *contained* by f, denoted by $\boldsymbol{x}^{\boldsymbol{u}} \to f$. Otherwise, $\boldsymbol{x}^{\boldsymbol{u}}$ is not contained by f, we denote it by $\boldsymbol{x}^{\boldsymbol{u}} \nrightarrow f$. In the remaining paper, we will use $\boldsymbol{x}^{\boldsymbol{u}}$ and $\pi_{\boldsymbol{u}}(\boldsymbol{x})$ interchangeably to avoid using the awkward notation $x^{(i)^{\boldsymbol{u}^{(j)}}}$ when both $\boldsymbol{x}$ and $\boldsymbol{u}$ have superscripts.

Example 1. Let $f(x_0, x_1) = x_0 x_1 \oplus x_0 \oplus 1$, then we have $x_0 x_1 \to f$, $x_0 \to f$, $1 \to f$, and $x_1 \nrightarrow f$.

Let $\boldsymbol{y} = (y_0, \cdots, y_{m-1}) = \boldsymbol{f}(\boldsymbol{x}) = (f_0(\boldsymbol{x}), \cdots, f_{m-1}(\boldsymbol{x}))$ be a vectorial Boolean function from $\mathbb{F}_2^n$ to $\mathbb{F}_2^m$. For $\boldsymbol{v} = (v_0, v_1, \ldots, v_{m-1}) \in \mathbb{F}_2^m$, a monomial $\boldsymbol{y}^{\boldsymbol{v}}$ of $\boldsymbol{y}$ can be symbolically expressed as a polynomial of the variable $\boldsymbol{x}$:

$$\boldsymbol{y}^{\boldsymbol{v}} = \prod_{i=0}^{m-1} (f_i(\boldsymbol{x}))^{v_i} = \bigoplus_{\boldsymbol{u} \in \mathbb{F}_2^n} a_{\boldsymbol{u}} \boldsymbol{x}^{\boldsymbol{u}}, a_{\boldsymbol{u}} \in \mathbb{F}_2.$$

In the following, we show how to determine whether $\boldsymbol{x}^u \rightarrow \boldsymbol{y}^v$ for a given monomial $\boldsymbol{x}^u$.

3 Monomial Prediction

Let $\boldsymbol{f} : \mathbb{F}_2^n \rightarrow \mathbb{F}_2^m$ be a vectorial Boolean function sending $\boldsymbol{x} = (x_0, \cdots, x_{n-1})$ to $\boldsymbol{y} = (y_0, \cdots, y_{m-1})$ with $y_i = f_i(\boldsymbol{x})$. By the *monomial prediction* we mean the problem of determining the presence or absence of a particular monomial $\boldsymbol{x}^u$ in $\boldsymbol{y}^v$, that is, whether $\boldsymbol{x}^u \rightarrow \boldsymbol{y}^v$. This is a trivial problem if the ANF of $\boldsymbol{f}$ is available. However, in the context of the symmetric-key cryptography, in most cases, the ANF of the targeted $\boldsymbol{f}$ is too complicated to be computed (or even to be stored) in practice. Typically, the only fact we know is that $\boldsymbol{f}$ is built by composition from a sequence of vectorial Boolean functions whose ANFs are known, i.e.,

$$\boldsymbol{y} = \boldsymbol{f}(\boldsymbol{x}) = \boldsymbol{f}^{(r-1)} \circ \boldsymbol{f}^{(r-2)} \circ \cdots \circ \boldsymbol{f}^{(0)}(\boldsymbol{x}).$$

Now, how do we determine whether $\boldsymbol{x}^u \rightarrow \boldsymbol{y}^v$?

Let $\boldsymbol{x}^{(i)}$ and $\boldsymbol{x}^{(i+1)}$ be the input and output variables of $\boldsymbol{f}^{(i)} : \mathbb{F}_2^{n_i} \rightarrow \mathbb{F}_2^{n_{i+1}}$, respectively. Then $\boldsymbol{x}^{(i+1)} = \boldsymbol{f}^{(i)}(\boldsymbol{x}^{(i)})$ for $0 \leq i < r$, and thus $\boldsymbol{x}^{(i)}$ can be represented as a vectorial Boolean function of $\boldsymbol{x}^{(j)}$ with $j < i$:

$$\boldsymbol{x}^{(i)} = \boldsymbol{f}^{(i-1)} \circ \cdots \circ \boldsymbol{f}^{(j+1)} \circ \boldsymbol{f}^{(j)}(\boldsymbol{x}^{(j)}), \text{ for } 1 \leq i \leq r.$$

Since the ANF of $\boldsymbol{x}^{(i+1)} = \boldsymbol{f}^{(i)}(\boldsymbol{x}^{(i)})$ is available, one can determine whether $\pi_{\boldsymbol{u}^{(i)}}(\boldsymbol{x}^{(i)}) \rightarrow \pi_{\boldsymbol{u}^{(i+1)}}(\boldsymbol{x}^{(i+1)})$ for any $\boldsymbol{u}^{(i)}$ and $\boldsymbol{u}^{(i+1)}$, which gives rise to the concept of the *monomial trail*.

Definition 1 (Monomial Trail). *Let* $\boldsymbol{x}^{(i+1)} = \boldsymbol{f}^{(i)}(\boldsymbol{x}^{(i)})$ *for* $0 \leq i < r$. *We call a sequence of monomials* $(\pi_{\boldsymbol{u}^{(0)}}(\boldsymbol{x}^{(0)}), \pi_{\boldsymbol{u}^{(1)}}(\boldsymbol{x}^{(1)}), \ldots, \pi_{\boldsymbol{u}^{(r)}}(\boldsymbol{x}^{(r)}))$ *an r-round monomial trail connecting* $\pi_{\boldsymbol{u}^{(0)}}(\boldsymbol{x}^{(0)})$ *and* $\pi_{\boldsymbol{u}^{(r)}}(\boldsymbol{x}^{(r)})$ *with respect to the composite function* $\boldsymbol{f} = \boldsymbol{f}^{(r-1)} \circ \boldsymbol{f}^{(r-2)} \circ \cdots \circ \boldsymbol{f}^{(0)}$ *if*

$$\pi_{\boldsymbol{u}^{(0)}}(\boldsymbol{x}^{(0)}) \rightarrow \cdots \rightarrow \pi_{\boldsymbol{u}^{(i)}}(\boldsymbol{x}^{(i)}) \rightarrow \cdots \rightarrow \pi_{\boldsymbol{u}^{(r)}}(\boldsymbol{x}^{(r)}).$$

If there is at least one monomial trail connecting $\pi_{\boldsymbol{u}^{(0)}}(\boldsymbol{x}^{(0)})$ *and* $\pi_{\boldsymbol{u}^{(r)}}(\boldsymbol{x}^{(r)})$, *we write* $\pi_{\boldsymbol{u}^{(0)}}(\boldsymbol{x}^{(0)}) \rightsquigarrow \pi_{\boldsymbol{u}^{(r)}}(\boldsymbol{x}^{(r)})$. *Otherwise,* $\pi_{\boldsymbol{u}^{(0)}}(\boldsymbol{x}^{(0)}) \not\rightsquigarrow \pi_{\boldsymbol{u}^{(r)}}(\boldsymbol{x}^{(r)})$.

Note that a monomial trail is always specified with respect to a given composition sequence $\boldsymbol{f}^{(r-1)} \circ \boldsymbol{f}^{(r-2)} \circ \cdots \circ \boldsymbol{f}^{(0)}$. When this sequence is obvious from the context, we will omit it to keep the presentation concise. Also, we always assume in default that

$$\boldsymbol{x}^{(r)} = \boldsymbol{f}^{(r-1)}(\boldsymbol{x}^{(r-1)}) = \boldsymbol{f}^{(r-1)} \circ \boldsymbol{f}^{(r-2)}(\boldsymbol{x}^{(r-2)}) = \cdots = \boldsymbol{f}^{(r-1)} \circ \cdots \circ \boldsymbol{f}^{(0)}(\boldsymbol{x}^{(0)}).$$

Example 2. Let $z = (z_0, z_1) = f^{(1)}(y_0, y_1) = (y_0 y_1, y_0 \oplus y_1)$, $y = (y_0, y_1) = f^{(0)}(x_0, x_1, x_2) = (x_0 \oplus x_1 \oplus x_2, x_0 x_1 \oplus x_0 \oplus x_2)$ and $f = f^{(1)} \circ f^{(0)}$.

Consider the monomial $(x_0, x_1, x_2)^{(1,0,0)} = x_0$. Since the ANF of $f^{(0)}$ is available, we can compute all monomials of y, i.e.,

$$(y_0, y_1)^{(0,0)} = 1, (y_0, y_1)^{(1,0)} = y_0 = \underline{x_0} \oplus x_1 \oplus x_2, (y_0, y_1)^{(0,1)} = y_1 = x_0 x_1 \oplus \underline{x_0} \oplus x_2,$$

$$(y_0, y_1)^{(1,1)} = y_0 y_1 = x_0 x_1 x_2 \oplus x_0 x_1 \oplus x_1 x_2 \oplus \underline{x_0} \oplus x_2.$$

Then

$$x_0 \to y_0, \ x_0 \to y_1, \ x_0 \to y_0 y_1$$

are all the three monomial trails of $f^{(0)}$ connecting x_0 and monomials of y.

Similarly, we can compute all the monomials of z as follows,

$$(z_0, z_1)^{(0,0)} = 1, (z_0, z_1)^{(1,0)} = z_0 = \underline{y_0 y_1}, (z_0, z_1)^{(0,1)} = z_1 = \underline{y_0} \oplus y_1,$$

$$(z_0, z_1)^{(1,1)} = z_0 z_1 = 0.$$

There are three monomial trails of f connecting x_0 and monomials of z:

$$x_0 \to y_0 \to z_1, \quad x_0 \to y_1 \to z_1, \quad x_0 \to y_0 y_1 \to z_0.$$

Lemma 1. $\pi_{u^{(0)}}(x^{(0)}) \rightsquigarrow \pi_{u^{(r)}}(x^{(r)})$ *if* $\pi_{u^{(0)}}(x^{(0)}) \to \pi_{u^{(r)}}(x^{(r)})$, *and thus* $\pi_{u^{(0)}}(x^{(0)}) \not\rightsquigarrow \pi_{u^{(r)}}(x^{(r)})$ *implies* $\pi_{u^{(0)}}(x^{(0)}) \not\to \pi_{u^{(r)}}(x^{(r)})$.

Proof. We prove it by induction on r. Assuming this lemma holds for $r < s$, we are going to show that it also holds for $r = s$. First, we expand $\pi_{u^{(s)}}(x^{(s)})$ on $x^{(s-1)}$ as

$$\pi_{u^{(s)}}(x^{(s)}) = \bigoplus_{\pi_{u^{(s-1)}}(x^{(s-1)}) \to \pi_{u^{(s)}}(x^{(s)})} \pi_{u^{(s-1)}}(x^{(s-1)}).$$

Since $\pi_{u^{(0)}}(x^{(0)}) \to \pi_{u^{(s)}}(x^{(s)})$, there is at least one $\pi_{u^{(s-1)}}(x^{(s-1)})$ contained by $\pi_{u^{(s)}}(x^{(s)})$ satisfying $\pi_{u^{(0)}}(x^{(0)}) \to \pi_{u^{(s-1)}}(x^{(s-1)})$. According to our assumption, $\pi_{u^{(0)}}(x^{(0)}) \rightsquigarrow \pi_{u^{(s-1)}}(x^{(s-1)})$, then $\pi_{u^{(0)}}(x^{(0)}) \rightsquigarrow \pi_{u^{(s)}}(x^{(s)})$. $\square$

According to Lemma 1, $\pi_{u^{(0)}}(x^{(0)}) \to \pi_{u^{(r)}}(x^{(r)})$ is sufficient for $\pi_{u^{(0)}}(x^{(0)}) \rightsquigarrow \pi_{u^{(r)}}(x^{(r)})$. However, the conversion is not true in general. Considering Example 2, although $x_0 \rightsquigarrow z_1$, we have $x_0 \not\to z_1$ since

$$z_1 = y_0 \oplus y_1 = \underline{x_0} \oplus x_1 \oplus x_2 \oplus x_0 x_1 \oplus \underline{x_0} \oplus x_2 = x_0 x_1 \oplus x_1.$$

The reason is that two x_0's (underlined in the above equation) cancel each other. In the following, we will demonstrate that whether $\pi_{u^{(0)}}(x^{(0)}) \to \pi_{u^{(r)}}(x^{(r)})$ is determined by the number of monomial trails connecting them rather than the existence of the monomial trail, which raises the definition below.

Definition 2 (Monomial Hull). *For f with a specific composition sequence, the monomial hull of $\pi_{u^{(0)}}(x^{(0)})$ and $\pi_{u^{(r)}}(x^{(r)})$, denoted by $\pi_{u^{(0)}}(x^{(0)}) \bowtie \pi_{u^{(r)}}(x^{(r)})$, is the set of all monomial trails connecting them. The number of trails in the monomial hull is called the **size** of the hull and is denoted by $|\pi_{u^{(0)}}(x^{(0)}) \bowtie \pi_{u^{(r)}}(x^{(r)})|$.*

Example 3. Consider Example 2, the monomial hull of x_0 and z_1 is the set

$$x_0 \bowtie z_1 = \{x_0 \to y_0 \to z_1, x_0 \to y_1 \to z_1\}.$$

Thus the size of $x_0 \bowtie z_1$ is 2. Furthermore, since $x_0 \not\to z_0 z_1$, $x_0 \bowtie z_0 z_1 = \emptyset$ and $|x_0 \bowtie z_0 z_1| = 0$.

For $i \geq 1$, if $\pi_{\boldsymbol{u}^{(0)}}(\boldsymbol{x}^{(0)}) \rightsquigarrow \pi_{\boldsymbol{u}^{(i)}}(\boldsymbol{x}^{(i)})$, $|\pi_{\boldsymbol{u}^{(0)}}(\boldsymbol{x}^{(0)}) \bowtie \pi_{\boldsymbol{u}^{(i)}}(\boldsymbol{x}^{(i)})|$ can be calculated recursively as follows,

Lemma 2. *For $i \geq 1$, if $\pi_{\boldsymbol{u}^{(0)}}(\boldsymbol{x}^{(0)}) \rightsquigarrow \pi_{\boldsymbol{u}^{(i)}}(\boldsymbol{x}^{(i)})$,*

$$|\pi_{\boldsymbol{u}^{(0)}}(\boldsymbol{x}^{(0)}) \bowtie \pi_{\boldsymbol{u}^{(i)}}(\boldsymbol{x}^{(i)})| = \begin{cases} 1, & i = 1, \\ \displaystyle\sum_{\substack{\pi_{\boldsymbol{u}^{(i-1)}}(\boldsymbol{x}^{(i-1)}) \\ \to \pi_{\boldsymbol{u}^{(i)}}(\boldsymbol{x}^{(i)})}} |\pi_{\boldsymbol{u}^{(0)}}(\boldsymbol{x}^{(0)}) \bowtie \pi_{\boldsymbol{u}^{(i-1)}}(\boldsymbol{x}^{(i-1)})|, & i \geq 2. \end{cases}$$

The time has come to address the monomial prediction problem we mentioned at the beginning of this section.

Proposition 1. $\pi_{\boldsymbol{u}^{(0)}}(\boldsymbol{x}^{(0)}) \to \pi_{\boldsymbol{u}^{(r)}}(\boldsymbol{x}^{(r)})$ *if and only if* $|\pi_{\boldsymbol{u}^{(0)}}(\boldsymbol{x}^{(0)}) \bowtie \pi_{\boldsymbol{u}^{(r)}}(\boldsymbol{x}^{(r)})|$ *is odd.*

Proof. We prove it by induction on r. Assuming this proposition holds for $r < s$, we are going to show that it also holds for $r = s$. First, we expand $\pi_{\boldsymbol{u}^{(s)}}(\boldsymbol{x}^{(s)})$ on $\boldsymbol{x}^{(s-1)}$ as

$$\pi_{\boldsymbol{u}^{(s)}}(\boldsymbol{x}^{(s)}) = \bigoplus_{\pi_{\boldsymbol{u}^{(s-1)}}(\boldsymbol{x}^{(s-1)}) \to \pi_{\boldsymbol{u}^{(s)}}(\boldsymbol{x}^{(s)})} \pi_{\boldsymbol{u}^{(s-1)}}(\boldsymbol{x}^{(s-1)}).$$

Consequently, we have

$$|\pi_{\boldsymbol{u}^{(0)}}(\boldsymbol{x}^{(0)}) \bowtie \pi_{\boldsymbol{u}^{(s)}}(\boldsymbol{x}^{(s)})| = \sum_{\substack{\pi_{\boldsymbol{u}^{(s-1)}}(\boldsymbol{x}^{(s-1)}) \\ \to \pi_{\boldsymbol{u}^{(s)}}(\boldsymbol{x}^{(s)})}} |\pi_{\boldsymbol{u}^{(0)}}(\boldsymbol{x}^{(0)}) \bowtie \pi_{\boldsymbol{u}^{(s-1)}}(\boldsymbol{x}^{(s-1)})|.$$

Moreover, $\pi_{\boldsymbol{u}^{(0)}}(\boldsymbol{x}^{(0)}) \to \pi_{\boldsymbol{u}^{(s)}}(\boldsymbol{x}^{(s)})$ if and only if there are odd number of $\pi_{\boldsymbol{u}^{(s-1)}}(\boldsymbol{x}^{(s-1)})$ contained by $\pi_{\boldsymbol{u}^{(s)}}(\boldsymbol{x}^{(s)})$ such that $\pi_{\boldsymbol{u}^{(0)}}(\boldsymbol{x}^{(0)}) \to \pi_{\boldsymbol{u}^{(s-1)}}(\boldsymbol{x}^{(s-1)})$, or equivalently, according to the induction hypothesis we made at the beginning, there are odd number of $\pi_{\boldsymbol{u}^{(s-1)}}(\boldsymbol{x}^{(s-1)})$ contained by $\pi_{\boldsymbol{u}^{(s)}}(\boldsymbol{x}^{(s)})$ such that $|\pi_{\boldsymbol{u}^{(0)}}(\boldsymbol{x}^{(0)}) \bowtie \pi_{\boldsymbol{u}^{(s-1)}}(\boldsymbol{x}^{(s-1)})|$ is odd. Finally, Proposition 1 is true for $r = s$ since $|\pi_{\boldsymbol{u}^{(0)}}(\boldsymbol{x}^{(0)}) \bowtie \pi_{\boldsymbol{u}^{(s)}}(\boldsymbol{x}^{(s)})|$ is odd if and only if

$$\sum_{\pi_{\boldsymbol{u}^{(s-1)}}(\boldsymbol{x}^{(s-1)}) \to \pi_{\boldsymbol{u}^{(s)}}(\boldsymbol{x}^{(s)})} |\pi_{\boldsymbol{u}^{(0)}}(\boldsymbol{x}^{(0)}) \bowtie \pi_{\boldsymbol{u}^{(s-1)}}(\boldsymbol{x}^{(s-1)})| \text{ is odd.}$$

$\square$

3.1   Derived Function

When applying the monomial prediction technique to cryptanalysis, we may consider functions that are derived from a vectorial Boolean function f by fixing some variables of f to known constants. In this case, the derived function has fewer variables than the original function f. Also, the remaining variables are not treated equally. Some of them are public (IV bits, plaintext bits, tweak bits, etc.), while some of them are secret (key bits). To highlight the semantic difference of the variables and distinguish between the variables fixed to 0 and those fixed to 1, we introduce the notion of *variable masks*. Together with the original function f, these masks completely determine the derived function, and tells us which variables of the derived function are public and which are secret.

Remark. The only purpose of introducing the concept of the derived function is to have a unified approach to specify the functions to which our techniques are applied. It has no theoretical significance and the readers who do not care about the details of the attacks on concrete targets can safely skip this part to avoid being overloaded by unnecessary notations. Actually, skipping this part is encouraged and the readers can look back when necessary.

Variable Masks and Derived Function. Let Γ^0, Γ^1, Γ^p, and $\Gamma^s \in \mathbb{F}_2^n$ be constant vectors such that $\{0 \le i < n : \Gamma_i^0 = 1\}$, $\{0 \le i < n : \Gamma_i^1 = 1\}$, $\{0 \le i < n : \Gamma_i^p = 1\}$, and $\{0 \le i < n : \Gamma_i^s = 1\}$ form a partition of $\{0, \cdots, n-1\}$, which are called variable masks. For a vectorial Boolean function $f(x)$ from $\mathbb{F}_2^n$ to $\mathbb{F}_2^m$, we can derive a new function f_d from f with the variable masks by setting certain variables of f to constants according to the following rule for $i \in \{0, 1, \cdots, n-1\}$:

$$\begin{cases} x_i \leftarrow 0, & \text{if } \Gamma_i^0 = 1, \\ x_i \leftarrow 1, & \text{if } \Gamma_i^1 = 1. \end{cases}$$

The remaining x_i's are still treated as variables but with different access permissions: x_i's with $\Gamma_i^p = 1$ are public variables and can be manipulated by the attackers, while x_i's with $\Gamma_i^s = 1$ are secret variables. Although in practice secret variables typically represent secret key bits and are actually fixed to unknown constants, in our framework we still regard them as symbolic objects rather than constants. The concept of the derived function should be best understood by a concrete example.

Example 4. For $y = f(x_0, x_1, x_2, x_3, k_0, k_1, k_2, k_3)$ where x_0, x_1, x_2, x_3 are four public input bits and k_0, k_1, k_2, k_3 are four secret input bits. If we fix x_0 to 0 and x_1 to 1, the resulting function mapping $(0, 1, x_2, x_3, k_0, k_1, k_2, k_3)$ to

$$f(0, 1, x_2, x_3, k_0, k_1, k_2, k_3)$$

is a derived function from f with the following variable masks

$$\Gamma^0 = (1, 0, 0, 0, 0, 0, 0, 0), \quad \Gamma^1 = (0, 1, 0, 0, 0, 0, 0, 0),$$
$$\Gamma^p = (0, 0, 1, 1, 0, 0, 0, 0), \quad \Gamma^s = (0, 0, 0, 0, 1, 1, 1, 1).$$

In the following sections, we typically first give a function f which can be directly obtained from the description of the targeted cipher, and then we specify the associated variable masks. Finally, the techniques presented in this work are applied to the corresponding derived function.

In the case of $\boldsymbol{f}_d$, we should note $\boldsymbol{x}^v \equiv 1$ for any $\boldsymbol{v} \preceq \boldsymbol{\Gamma}^1$, then $\boldsymbol{x}^{u \oplus v} = \boldsymbol{x}^u \cdot \boldsymbol{x}^v = \boldsymbol{x}^u$ for any $\boldsymbol{v} \preceq \boldsymbol{\Gamma}^1$ and the Proposition 1 can be converted to the following proposition.

Proposition 2. *Let $\boldsymbol{f}_d$ be the derived function of f with $\boldsymbol{\Gamma}^0, \boldsymbol{\Gamma}^1, \boldsymbol{\Gamma}^p, \boldsymbol{\Gamma}^s$. For $\boldsymbol{x}^{(r)} = \boldsymbol{f}_d(\boldsymbol{x}^{(0)})$ and $\boldsymbol{u}^{(0)} \preceq \boldsymbol{\Gamma}^p \oplus \boldsymbol{\Gamma}^s$, $\pi_{\boldsymbol{u}^{(0)}}(\boldsymbol{x}^{(0)}) \to \pi_{\boldsymbol{u}^{(r)}}(\boldsymbol{x}^{(r)})$ if and only if*

$$\sum_{v \preceq \boldsymbol{\Gamma}^1} |\pi_{\boldsymbol{u}^{(0)} \oplus v}(\boldsymbol{x}^{(0)}) \bowtie \pi_{\boldsymbol{u}^{(r)}}(\boldsymbol{x}^{(r)})| \bmod 2 = 1.$$

4   Application I: Degree Evaluation

Since the algebraic degree of a symmetric-key primitive significantly affects its security against cryptanalytic techniques such as algebraic attacks [20], higher-order differential attacks [15,17], interpolation attacks [14], and integral attacks [6,16], methods and tools for degree evaluation have been an important topic in the community all along. To put our approach into perspective, we highlight several important works in this line of research. At EUROCRYPT 2002, Canteaut and Videau developed a method for upper bounding the algebraic degree of composite functions [5], which was improved by Boura et al. [3] at FSE 2011. In [1], the authors identified a simple closed formula bounding the number of rounds necessary to achieve full degree for the block ciphers with secret components. At CRYPTO 2017, Liu presented a general framework known as *numeric mapping*, which is exclusively used for estimating the algebraic degrees of the cryptosystems based on the nonlinear feedback shift register (NFSR) [18].

Another approach for the degree evaluation is based on the division property. The accuracy of this approach is determined by the accuracy of the "propagation rules" of the underlying detection algorithms for division properties. When the detection algorithm is *perfect* (The meaning of perfect will be more concrete in Sect. 6), its estimation is exact. In the following, we show that the monomial prediction technique achieves this exactness.

4.1   Compute Exact Algebraic Degree of a Boolean Function

The algebraic degree of a Boolean function f is defined as follows,

$$\deg(f) = \max_{\pi_{\boldsymbol{u}^{(0)}}(\boldsymbol{x}^{(0)}) \to f} wt(\boldsymbol{u}^{(0)}). \tag{1}$$

To determine the algebraic degree of f, we only need to prove the existence of a monomial $\pi_{\boldsymbol{u}^{(0)}}(\boldsymbol{x}^{(0)})$ such that $\pi_{\boldsymbol{u}'}(\boldsymbol{x}^{(0)}) \nrightarrow f$ for any $\boldsymbol{u}'$ with $wt(\boldsymbol{u}') > d$, which can be done in two steps:

1. Find a monomial $\pi_{u^{(0)}}(x^{(0)}) \rightsquigarrow f$ with $wt(u) = d$ and prove $\pi_{u'}(x^{(0)}) \nrightarrow f$ for any $wt(u') > d$.
2. Compute $|\pi_{u^{(0)}}(x^{(0)}) \bowtie f|$ to confirm the presence of $\pi_{u^{(0)}}(x^{(0)})$, if the value is odd, then $\deg(f) = d$, else, we need to repeat the process until we find a desired monomial of f.

The Mixed Integer Linear Programming (MILP) approach has been extensively used to probe the structure of Boolean functions in previous works such as [9,22,26,28–31]. In this work, we also employ the MILP-based approach to search for the monomials of f. In this MILP model, the objective function of the model is to maximize $wt(u^{(0)})$ according to Eq. (1). One solution of the MILP model is a sequence of $(u^{(0)}, u^{(1)}, \ldots, u^{(r)})^1$, such that

$$\pi_{u^{(0)}}(x^{(0)}) \rightarrow \pi_{u^{(1)}}(x^{(1)}) \rightarrow \cdots \rightarrow \pi_{u^{(r)}}(x^{(r)}).$$

To confirm the presence of $\pi_{u^{(0)}}(x^{(0)})$ as in the above Step 2, we use the PoolSearchMode of Gurobi to compute $|\pi_{u^{(0)}}(x^{(0)}) \bowtie f|$.

PoolSearchMode of Gurobi. To judge whether the size of a monomial hull is an odd number, we frequently need to find all solutions of a MILP model. Following Hao et al.'s work at EUROCRYPT 2020 [9], we also employ the PoolSearchMode of Gurobi[2] to perform solution enumerations. The PoolSearchMode is a mode implemented by Gurobi to systematically search for multiple solutions. Let $\mathcal{M}$ be a MILP model, we use

$$\mathcal{M}.\texttt{PoolSearchMode} \leftarrow 1$$

to signal that the PoolSearchMode is turned on. All the source codes are available at https://github.com/hukaisdu/MonomialPrediction.

4.2 Application to TRIVIUM

Specification of TRIVIUM. TRIVIUM [4] is an NFSR-based stream cipher with a 288-bit internal state $x = (x_0, x_1, \ldots, x_{287})$ divided into three registers (denoted as Reg 0, Reg 1 and Reg 2 in Fig. 1). The 80-bit secret key K is loaded to the first register (Reg 0), and the 80-bit initialization vector IV is loaded to the second register. The other bits of the three registers are set to 0 except the last three bits of the third register. Namely, we have

$$(x_0, x_1, \ldots, x_{92}) \leftarrow (K[0], K[1], \ldots, K[79], 0, \ldots, 0),$$
$$(x_{93}, x_{94}, \ldots, x_{176}) \leftarrow (IV[0], IV[2], \ldots, IV[79], 0, \ldots, 0),$$
$$(x_{177}, x_{178}, \ldots, x_{287}) \leftarrow (0, 0, \ldots, 0, 1, 1, 1).$$

---

[1] In this section, we focus on the Boolean function, so $u^{(r)}$ is always a unit vector.
[2] https://www.gurobi.com.

Let $h : \mathbb{F}_2^5 \to \mathbb{F}_2$ be a Boolean function such that $h(\alpha_0, \alpha_1, \alpha_2, \alpha_3, \alpha_4) = \alpha_0 \oplus \alpha_1\alpha_2 \oplus \alpha_3 \oplus \alpha_4$. The pseudo code of the update function is given by

$$t_1 \leftarrow h(x_{65}, x_{90}, x_{91}, x_{92}, x_{170}) = x_{65} \oplus x_{90}x_{91} \oplus x_{92} \oplus x_{170},$$
$$t_2 \leftarrow h(x_{161}, x_{174}, x_{175}, x_{176}, x_{263}) = x_{161} \oplus_{174} x_{175} \oplus x_{176} \oplus x_{263},$$
$$t_3 \leftarrow h(x_{242}, x_{285}, x_{286}, x_{287}, x_{68}) = x_{242} \oplus x_{285}x_{286} \oplus x_{287} \oplus x_{68}.$$

The state of the next clock is computed as

$$(x_0, x_1, \ldots, x_{92}) \leftarrow (t_3, x_0, \ldots, x_{91}),$$
$$(x_{93}, x_{94}, \ldots, x_{176}) \leftarrow (t_1, x_{93}, \ldots, x_{175}),$$
$$(x_{177}, x_{178}, \ldots, x_{287}) \leftarrow (t_2, x_{177}, \ldots, x_{286}).$$

During the initialization, the state is updated 1152 times without producing any output. After the initialization, one bit key is produced per application of the update function by the key stream generation function $g : \mathbb{F}_2^{288} \to \mathbb{F}_2$ as

$$z \leftarrow g(x_0, x_1, \ldots, x_{287}) = x_{65} \oplus x_{92} \oplus x_{161} \oplus x_{176} \oplus x_{242} \oplus x_{287}.$$

MILP Model for a Monomial Trail of TRIVIUM. Let $\boldsymbol{x}^{(0)}$ denote the initial state of TRIVIUM and $\boldsymbol{x}^{(i+1)}$ denote the state after the i-th update function $\boldsymbol{f}^{(i)}$. The output bit after r-round TRIVIUM[3] z_r is a Boolean function of $\boldsymbol{x}^{(0)}$ which is denoted by $z_r = f(\boldsymbol{x}^{(0)})$. Naturally, f is the composition of the update functions and the key stream generation function as

$$z_r = f(\boldsymbol{x}^{(0)}) = g \circ \boldsymbol{f}^{(r-1)} \circ \boldsymbol{f}^{(r-2)} \circ \cdots \circ \boldsymbol{f}^{(0)}(\boldsymbol{x}^{(0)})$$
$$= g(\boldsymbol{x}^{(r)}) = x_{65}^{(r)} \oplus x_{92}^{(r)} \oplus x_{161}^{(r)} \oplus x_{176}^{(r)} \oplus x_{242}^{(r)} \oplus x_{287}^{(r)}. \tag{2}$$

To construct the MILP model for the monomial trail of TRIVIUM, we should study the ANFs of $\boldsymbol{f}^{(i)}$ and g and model the monomial trail locally for them.

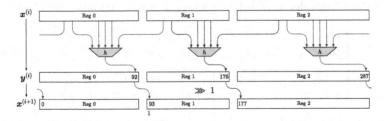

Fig. 1. The illustration of $\boldsymbol{f}^{(i)}$. In the first phase, if $j \notin \{92, 176, 287\}$, $y_j^{(i)} = x_j^{(i)}$. In the second phase, $x_{(j+1) \bmod 288}^{(i+1)} = y_j^{(i)}$.

---

[3] When saying (reduced) r-round of TRIVIUM, we mean the update function $\boldsymbol{f}$ is called r times and then the key stream generation function g is finally performed.

According to Fig. 1, $\boldsymbol{f}^{(i)}$ can be represented by parallel bit-permutations and three H functions such as

$$x^{(i+1)}_{j+1 \bmod 288} = x^{(i)}_j, \text{ if } j \notin \{65,90,91,92,170,161,174,175,176,263,242,285,286,287,68\}, \quad (3)$$

$$(x^{(i+1)}_{66}, x^{(i+1)}_{91}, x^{(i+1)}_{92}, x^{(i+1)}_{93}, x^{(i+1)}_{171}) = H(x^{(i)}_{65}, x^{(i)}_{90}, x^{(i)}_{91}, x^{(i)}_{92}, x^{(i)}_{170}) \quad (4)$$

$$(x^{(i+1)}_{162}, x^{(i+1)}_{175}, x^{(i+1)}_{176}, x^{(i+1)}_{177}, x^{(i+1)}_{264}) = H(x^{(i)}_{161}, x^{(i)}_{174}, x^{(i)}_{175}, x^{(i)}_{176}, x^{(i)}_{263}) \quad (5)$$

$$(x^{(i+1)}_{243}, x^{(i+1)}_{286}, x^{(i+1)}_{287}, x^{(i+1)}_{0}, x^{(i+1)}_{69}) = H(x^{(i)}_{242}, x^{(i)}_{285}, x^{(i)}_{286}, x^{(i)}_{287}, x^{(i)}_{68}) \quad (6)$$

where $H : \mathbb{F}_2^5 \to \mathbb{F}_2^5$ defined as follows,

$$(\beta_0, \beta_1, \beta_2, \beta_3, \beta_4) = H(\alpha_0, \alpha_1, \alpha_2, \alpha_3, \alpha_4) = (\alpha_0, \alpha_1, \alpha_2, \alpha_0 \oplus \alpha_1 \alpha_2 \oplus \alpha_3 \oplus \alpha_4, \alpha_4).$$

H can be decomposed into a sequence of smaller functions such as COPY, AND and XOR, which is shown in Fig. 2.

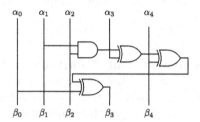

Fig. 2. The decomposition of H function by COPY, AND and XOR.

MILP Model for the Monomial Trail of $\boldsymbol{f}^{(i)}$. The operations in Eq. (3) are simple bit-permutations which can be handled by directly changing the positions of the variables, thus no inequalities are required for this condition. To model H function, we generate inequalities to model the monomial trials of COPY, AND and XOR. For COPY, consider $x \xrightarrow{\text{COPY}} (x, x)$ where x is a bit variable, we have

$$\begin{cases} x^0(=1) \to x^0 \cdot x^0(=1), & x^0(=1) \nrightarrow x^0 \cdot x^1(=x) \\ x^0(=1) \nrightarrow x^1 \cdot x^0(=x), & x^0(=1) \nrightarrow x^1 \cdot x^1(=x) \\ x^1(=x) \nrightarrow x^0 \cdot x^0(=1), & x^1(=x) \to x^0 \cdot x^1(=x) \\ x^1(=x) \to x^1 \cdot x^0(=x), & x^1(=x) \to x^1 \cdot x^1(=x) \end{cases}.$$

Then there are four valid monomial trails of COPY, i.e., (0, 0, 0), (1, 0, 1), (1, 1, 0) and (1, 1, 1). Similarly, AND has two monomial trials (0, 0, 0) and (1, 1, 1), while XOR has three monomial trials (0, 0, 0), (1, 0, 1) and (0, 1, 1).

To generate inequalities for monomial trails of each function, we follow Sun et al.'s approach in [23] to derive linear inequalities by Sage[4] and then use the

---

[4] https://www.sagemath.org.

greedy algorithm to simplify them. At last, a set of 15 inequalities $\mathcal{L}$ with 5 auxiliary variables (given in Appendix A of [11]) is sufficient to describe the H function. Thus we need 45 linear inequalities and 15 auxiliary variables to model $\boldsymbol{f}^{(i)}$. In Appendix B (Ref. [11]), we provide an alternative method to describe the monomial trails of H with less inequalities, where H is treated as a whole. Note that Proposition 1 implies that the decomposition with different granularity levels of the target Boolean function will not affect the parity of the number of the monomial trails of the Boolean function.

MILP Model for the Monomial trail of g. Since g is a simple Boolean function that contains 6 monomials (Eq. (2)), a set of simple constraints as

$$\begin{cases} u_{65}^{(r)} + u_{92}^{(r)} + u_{161}^{(r)} + u_{176}^{(r)} + u_{242}^{(r)} + u_{287}^{(r)} = 1, \\ u_j^{(r)} = 0, \text{ if } j \notin \{65, 92, 161, 176, 242, 287\}. \end{cases} \tag{7}$$

will complete our modeling.

In Algorithm 1, we demonstrate how to generate the MILP model for TRIV-IUM, where $\mathcal{L}$ represents the inequalities for the model of H. Note in some cases we may want to manipulate the first (e.g., line 16 of Algorithm 2) and last terms (e.g., line 11 of Algorithm 3) of the monomial trail. Then the MILP model in Algorithm 1 excludes the model of g, instead the variables representing the

---

Algorithm 1: $(\mathcal{M}, \boldsymbol{u}^{(0)}, \boldsymbol{u}^{(r)}) = \mathsf{GenerateTriviumModel}(r)$

Input: r, the targeted number of rounds of TRIVIUM

Output: The MILP model $\mathcal{M}$ for r-round TRIVIUM and the MILP variables representing the initial state $\boldsymbol{u}^{(0)}$

1 Declare an empty MILP model $\mathcal{M}$;

2 $\mathcal{M}.var \leftarrow u_0^{(0)}, u_1^{(0)}, \ldots, u_{287}^{(0)}$;

3 $\mathcal{M}.var \leftarrow u_0, u_1, \ldots, u_{287}$;

4 $\boldsymbol{u} \leftarrow \boldsymbol{u}^{(0)}$;

5 **for** $i = 0; i < r; i \leftarrow i + 1$ **do**

6 $\quad \mathcal{M}.var \leftarrow v_{65}, v_{90}, v_{91}, v_{92}, v_{170}, w_0, w_1, w_2, w_4, t$;

7 $\quad \mathcal{M}.con \leftarrow \mathcal{L}(u_{65}, u_{90}, u_{91}, u_{92}, u_{170}, v_{65}, v_{90}, v_{91}, v_{92}, v_{170}, w_0, w_1, w_2, w_4, t)$;

8 $\quad u_i \leftarrow v_i, i \in \{65, 90, 91, 92, 170\}$;

9 $\quad \mathcal{M}.var \leftarrow v_{161}, v_{174}, v_{175}, v_{176}, v_{263}, w_0, w_1, w_2, w_4, t$;

10 $\quad \mathcal{M}.con \leftarrow$
$\quad\quad \mathcal{L}(u_{161}, u_{174}, u_{175}, u_{176}, u_{263}, v_{161}, v_{174}, v_{175}, v_{176}, v_{263}, w_0, w_1, w_2, w_4, t)$;

11 $\quad u_i \leftarrow v_i, i \in \{161, 174, 175, 176, 263\}$;

12 $\quad \mathcal{M}.var \leftarrow v_{242}, v_{285}, v_{286}, v_{287}, v_{68}, w_0, w_1, w_2, w_4, t$;

13 $\quad \mathcal{M}.con \leftarrow$
$\quad\quad \mathcal{L}(u_{242}, u_{285}, u_{286}, u_{287}, u_{68}, v_{242}, v_{285}, v_{286}, v_{287}, v_{68}, w_0, w_1, w_2, w_4, t)$;

14 $\quad u_i \leftarrow v_i, i \in \{242, 285, 286, 287, 68\}$;

15 $\quad u_{i+1 \bmod 288} \leftarrow u_i$;

16 $\boldsymbol{u}^{(r)} \leftarrow \boldsymbol{u}$;

17 **return** $\mathcal{M}, \boldsymbol{u}^{(0)}, \boldsymbol{u}^{(r)}$;

---

first monomial $\pi_{u^{(0)}}(x^{(0)})$ and the last monomial $\pi_{u^{(r)}}(x^{(r)})$ are also returned in order for later usage.

Degree of TRIVIUM. The output bit $z_r = f(x^{(0)})$ after r-round TRIVIUM is a Boolean function of the initial state $x^{(0)}$. If we regard the IV bits as public variables and the key bits as secret variables, the initial setup of the state implies the following derived function with four variable masks $\Gamma^0, \Gamma^1, \Gamma^p, \Gamma^s$:

$$\Gamma_i^0 = \begin{cases} 1, & \text{if } 80 \leq i \leq 92 \text{ or } 173 \leq i \leq 284, \\ 0, & \text{otherwise.} \end{cases} \qquad \Gamma_i^1 = \begin{cases} 1, & \text{if } 285 \leq i \leq 287, \\ 0, & \text{otherwise.} \end{cases}$$

$$\Gamma_i^p = \begin{cases} 1, & \text{if } 93 \leq i \leq 172, \\ 0, & \text{otherwise.} \end{cases} \qquad \Gamma_i^s = \begin{cases} 1, & \text{if } 0 \leq i \leq 79, \\ 0, & \text{otherwise.} \end{cases}$$

In accordance, the derived function and its variable masks can be used to modify the algebraic degree expression given in Eq. (1), therefore the algebraic degree of z_r can be computed as

$$\deg(z_r) = \max_{\substack{u^{(0)} \preceq \Gamma^p \oplus \Gamma^s \\ \pi_{u^{(0)}}(x^{(0)}) \to z_r}} \left\{ \sum_{\Gamma_i^p = 1} u_i^{(0)} \right\} = \max_{\substack{u^{(0)} \preceq \Gamma^p \oplus \Gamma^s \\ \pi_{u^{(0)}}(x^{(0)}) \to z_r}} \left\{ \sum_{93 \leq i \leq 172} u_i^{(0)} \right\}.$$

By calling Algorithm 1, Algorithm 2 finds the monomial with the potential maximum degree satisfying $\pi_{u^{(0)}}(x^{(0)}) \rightsquigarrow z_r$. Thereafter, $|\pi_{u^{(0)}}(x^{(0)}) \bowtie z_r|$ is computed under the `PoolSearchMode` to determine if $\pi_{u^{(0)}}(x^{(0)}) \to z_r$ holds. Once $\pi_{u^{(0)}}(x^{(0)}) \to z_r$ is confirmed, we derive the exact algebraic degree of r-round TRIVIUM.

Our Results. With the help of the monomial prediction we are able to evaluate the exact algebraic degree of TRIVIUM up to 834 rounds and the results are listed in Table 5 in Appendix E (Ref. [11]). Interestingly, for the first time, we notice a counter-intuitive phenomenon that the algebraic degree of TRIVIUM is not monotonously increasing with rounds. For example, the degrees of 806-, 807- and 808-round TRIVIUM are 69, 71, 70, respectively. It implies that some monomials with the maximum degree are canceled in the subsequent round. Such degree drops are highlighted in Table 5.

A comparison of monomial prediction and the numeric mapping technique for upper bounding the degree of NFSR ciphers [18] is illustrated in Fig. 3. As the number of iterated rounds gets larger, the gap between the upper bound and the exact degree becomes more significant. For the degree of the 793-round TRIVIUM, the numeric mapping technique gives an upper bound of 79, while the monomial prediction method tells us that the exact degree is only 67.

Algorithm 2: $\deg = \mathsf{SearchDegree}(r)$

Input: r, the targeted number of rounds of TRIVIUM
Output: The degree of r-round TRIVIUM

/* Search For $\pi_{\boldsymbol{u}^{(0)}}(\boldsymbol{x}^{(0)}) \rightsquigarrow f$ */

1   $(\mathcal{M}_0, \boldsymbol{u}^{(0)}, \boldsymbol{u}^{(r)}) \leftarrow \mathsf{GenerateTriviumModel}(r)$

2   **for** $i = 0; i < 288; i \leftarrow i + 1$ **do**
3   **if** Γ_i^0 *is 1* **then**
4       $u_i^{(0)} \leftarrow 0$

5   **for** $i = 0; i < 288; i \leftarrow i + 1$ **do**
6   **if** $i \notin \{65, 92, 161, 176, 242, 287\}$ **then**
7       $\mathcal{M}_0.con \leftarrow u_i^{(r)} = 0;$

8   $\mathcal{M}_0.con \leftarrow u_{65}^{(r)} + u_{92}^{(r)} + u_{161}^{(r)} + u_{176}^{(r)} + u_{242}^{(r)} + u_{287}^{(r)} = 1;$

9   $\mathcal{M}_0.obj \leftarrow \max(u_{93}^{(0)} + u_{94}^{(0)} + \cdots + u_{172}^{(0)});$

10 **while** *true* **do**
11    $\mathcal{M}_0.optimize();$
12   **if** $\mathcal{M}_0.status$ *is* `OPTIMAL` **then**
      /* Compute $|\pi_{\boldsymbol{u}^{(0)}}(\boldsymbol{x}^{(0)}) \bowtie f|$ */
13      $(\mathcal{M}_1, \boldsymbol{u}'^{(0)}, \boldsymbol{u}'^{(r)}) \leftarrow \mathsf{GenerateTriviumModel}(r)$
14      $\mathcal{M}_1.\texttt{SolutionPoolMode} \leftarrow 1;$
15   **for** $i = 0; i < 288; i \leftarrow i + 1$ **do**
16        $u_i'^{(0)} \leftarrow u_i^{(0)}.val;$
17   **for** $i = 0; i < 288; i \leftarrow i + 1$ **do**
18   **if** $i \notin \{65, 92, 161, 176, 242, 287\}$ **then**
19          $\mathcal{M}_1.con \leftarrow u_i'^{(r)} = 0;$
20      $\mathcal{M}_1.con \leftarrow u_{65}'^{(r)} + u_{92}'^{(r)} + u_{161}'^{(r)} + u_{176}'^{(r)} + u_{242}'^{(r)} + u_{287}'^{(r)} = 1;$
21      $\mathcal{M}_1.optimize();$
22   **if** $\mathcal{M}_1.status$ *is* `OPTIMAL` **then**
23   **if** $\mathcal{M}_1.solnum$ *is odd* **then**
24   **return** $\mathcal{M}_0.objval;$
25   **else**
         /* Note the values of the last 3 bits are all 1 */
26          $\mathcal{M}_0.con \leftarrow remove(u_0'^{(0)}, u_1'^{(0)}, \ldots, u_{284}'^{(0)})$
27          $\mathcal{M}_0.update();$

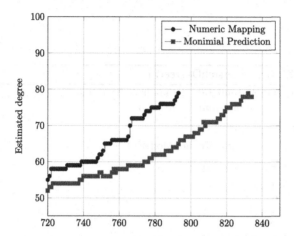

Fig. 3. The exact degree derived by monomial prediction and the upper bound derived by numeric mapping [18].

We also perform the degree evaluations with the two-subset bit-based division property [27] to estimate the upper bound of the degree of r-round TRIVIUM. The results show that the division property is quite precise. From 1- to 834-round TRIVIUM, there are only 14 cases where the division property fails to hit the exact degrees, which are listed in Table 2.

Table 2. The gaps among the exact degree, the upper bound obtained by the two-subset bit-based division property and the numeric mapping for several special cases of TRIVIUM up to 834-round. For the other cases, the result obtained by the two-subset bit-based division property equals to the exact degree.

#Round	508	509	514	515	719	770	773	783	789	806	810	816	831	833
Exact degree	13	13	15	15	51	59	59	62	63	69	71	72	78	78
Division property	14	14	16	16	52	60	60	63	64	70	72	73	79	79
Numeric mapping	16	16	16	17	55	72	72	76	76	>80	>80	>80	>80	>80

5   Application II: Cube Attacks

The cube attack was proposed by Dinur and Shamir [7] at EUROCRYPT 2009. Let $f(\boldsymbol{x})$ be a Boolean function from $\mathbb{F}_2^n$ to $\mathbb{F}_2$, and $\boldsymbol{u} \in \mathbb{F}_2^n$ be a constant vector. Then $f(\boldsymbol{x})$ can be represented uniquely as

$$f(\boldsymbol{x}) = \boldsymbol{x}^{\boldsymbol{u}} p(\boldsymbol{x}) + q(\boldsymbol{x}),$$

where each term of $q(\boldsymbol{x})$ is not divisible by $\boldsymbol{x}^{\boldsymbol{u}}$. Note that in our notations, the set $I_{\boldsymbol{u}} = \{0 \le i \le n-1 : u_i = 1\} \subseteq \{0, \cdots, n-1\}$ and the monomial $\boldsymbol{x}^{\boldsymbol{u}}$ correspond to the *cube indices* and *cube term* that are commonly used in the literature of cube attacks[5]. If we compute the sum of f over the cube $\mathbb{C}_u = \{x \in \mathbb{F}_2^n : x \preceq u\}$, we have

$$\bigoplus_{x \in \mathbb{C}_u} f(x) = \bigoplus_{x \in \mathbb{C}_u} (x^u p(x) + q(x)) = p(x),$$

where $p(x)$ is called the *superpoly* of the cube $\mathbb{C}_u$, and $p(x)$ only involves variables x_j with $j \in I_{\bar{u}} = \{0 \leq i \leq n - 1 : u_i = 0\}$.

The superpoly recovery plays a critical role in the cube attack. The attacker recovers the superpoly in the offline phase, and then in the online phase, he/she queries the encryption oracle with the cube, and finally gets the value of the superpoly. If the superpoly is a balanced Boolean function, a bit information of the secret key can be obtained. The remaining key bits can be recovered by the exhaustive search.

At the early stage in the applications of cube attacks, the superpoly recovery is achieved experimentally by summing the outputs over certain "good" cubes, and therefore the sizes of cubes are largely confined in a practical range. Moreover, superpolies derived from small cubes have to be extremely simple (typically linear or quadratic functions [7,19]) in order to be recovered in a probabilistic way.

In [26], the division property was first introduced to enhance cube attacks, which allows us to identify the key bits that do not present in the superpoly. This approach is deterministic and can be used to analyze cubes whose sizes are beyond practical reach. By setting the key bits that are not involved in the superpoly to arbitrary constants and varying the remaining l key bits, one can obtain the truth table of the superpoly for a subsequent key-recovery attack with complexity $2^{|I|+l}$. At CRYPTO 2018, Wang et al. proposed the flag technique and term enumeration technique to recover directly all the monomials of the superpoly based on the two-subset bit-based division property, which further lowers the complexity of the superpoly recovery and thus attacks of more rounds on several targets are mounted [29].

However, in [26,29], it was assumed that every identified secret key variable or the monomial must be involved in the superpoly. If such an assumption does not hold, the superpoly can be much simpler than estimated, or even falls into the extreme case: $p(x) \equiv 0$. In fact it has been reported in [8,9,30,32] that some of previous key-recovery attacks are actually distinguishers. To get rid of this assumption, Wang et al. for the first time proposed a systematic method based on the three-subset bit-based division property to recover the exact superpoly [30]. In [9], the method was refined as the three-subset bit-based division property without unknown subsets and was modeled under the `PoolSearchMode` of Gurobi. As a result, they recovered the exact superpolies for 840-, 841- and 842-round Trivium.

5.1   Apply Monomial Prediction to Superpoly Recovery

It is natural to apply the monomial prediction to the recovery of the superpoly. For $f : \mathbb{F}_2^n \to \mathbb{F}_2$, we define a constant vector $u \in \mathbb{F}_2^n$ and let the corresponding

---

[5] When there is no ambiguity, we denote the cube indices as I and its size as $|I|$.

cube term be $\boldsymbol{x}^u$. To recover the superpoly which is a polynomial of x_i's with $\bar{u}_i = 1$, we find all the possible monomials like $\boldsymbol{x}^{u \oplus w} = \boldsymbol{x}^u \cdot \boldsymbol{x}^w$ where $\boldsymbol{w} \preceq \bar{u}$ satisfying $\boldsymbol{x}^{u \oplus w} \rightarrow f$. Then the superpoly of $\boldsymbol{x}^u$ is

$$p(\boldsymbol{x}) = \bigoplus_{\substack{\boldsymbol{w} \preceq \bar{u} \\ \boldsymbol{x}^{u \oplus w} \rightarrow f}} \boldsymbol{x}^w = \left(\bigoplus_{\substack{\boldsymbol{w} \preceq \bar{u} \\ \boldsymbol{x}^{u \oplus w} \rightarrow f}} \boldsymbol{x}^{u \oplus w} \right) / \boldsymbol{x}^u.$$

To find all $\boldsymbol{x}^{u \oplus w} \rightarrow f$ for $\boldsymbol{w} \preceq \bar{u}$, we could take the `PoolSearchMode` of Gurobi solver to find all solutions satisfying $\boldsymbol{x}^{u \oplus w} \rightsquigarrow f$. Next, we store all the $\boldsymbol{x}^{u \oplus w}$ into a hash table which are indexed by $(\boldsymbol{u}, \boldsymbol{w})$, the size of each possible $\boldsymbol{x}^{u \oplus w} \bowtie f$ for $\boldsymbol{w} \preceq \bar{u}$ can be counted naturally.

Speedup and Memory Reduction: A Divide-and-Conquer Strategy. In this paper, we only study the composite function f, where

$$f = \boldsymbol{f}^{(r-1)} \circ \boldsymbol{f}^{(r-2)} \circ \cdots \circ \boldsymbol{f}^{(0)}.$$

According to Lemma 2, if $\pi_{\boldsymbol{u}^{(0)}}(\boldsymbol{x}^{(0)}) \rightsquigarrow f$, then for $0 < i < r$,

$$|\pi_{\boldsymbol{u}^{(0)}}(\boldsymbol{x}^{(0)}) \bowtie f| \equiv \sum_{\pi_{\boldsymbol{u}^{(r-i)}}(\boldsymbol{x}^{(r-i)}) \rightarrow f} |\pi_{\boldsymbol{u}^{(0)}}(\boldsymbol{x}^{(0)}) \bowtie \pi_{\boldsymbol{u}^{(r-i)}}(\boldsymbol{x}^{(r-i)})| \pmod 2. \quad (8)$$

Generally speaking, computing $|\pi_{\boldsymbol{u}^{(0)}}(\boldsymbol{x}^{(0)}) \bowtie \pi_{\boldsymbol{u}^{(r-i)}}(\boldsymbol{x}^{(r-i)})|$ one by one is much easier than computing $|\pi_{\boldsymbol{u}^{(0)}}(\boldsymbol{x}^{(0)}) \bowtie f|$ when i is significantly smaller than r. In this paper, we always expand f firstly and then obtain the speedups and memory reductions by the divide-and-conquer strategy.

5.2 Application to TRIVIUM

Let $z_r = f(\boldsymbol{x}^{(0)})$ be the output of the r-round TRIVIUM with $\boldsymbol{x}^{(0)} \in \mathbb{F}_2^{288}$. When the cube attack is applied to TRIVIUM, only the cube variables indexed by the cube indices I and the secret key bits are regarded as symbolic variables in our analysis, and all other input variables are fixed to constants. Therefore, we are actually analyzing the derived function of f with the variable masks $\boldsymbol{\Gamma}^0$, $\boldsymbol{\Gamma}^1$, $\boldsymbol{\Gamma}^p$, and $\boldsymbol{\Gamma}^s$ given as follows:

$$
\Gamma_i^0 = \begin{cases} 1, & \text{if } x_i \equiv 0, \\ 0, & \text{otherwise.} \end{cases} \qquad
\Gamma_i^1 = \begin{cases} 1, & \text{if } x_i \equiv 1, \\ 0, & \text{otherwise.} \end{cases}
$$
$$
\Gamma_i^p = \begin{cases} 1, & \text{if } i \in I, \\ 0, & \text{otherwise.} \end{cases} \qquad
\Gamma_i^s = \begin{cases} 1, & \text{if } 0 \le i \le 79, \\ 0, & \text{otherwise.} \end{cases} \quad (9)
$$

To recover the superpoly corresponding to the cube indices $I = \{0 \le i \le 287 : \Gamma_i^p = 1\}$, we need to find all $\pi_{\boldsymbol{\Gamma}^p \oplus w}(\boldsymbol{x}^{(0)}) \rightarrow f$ for all $\boldsymbol{w} \preceq \boldsymbol{\Gamma}^s$.

In practice, we take the divide-and-conquer strategy based on Eq. (8) to keep the consumption of computational resources under control. Let the internal state of the i-th round TRIVIUM be $\boldsymbol{x}^{(i)}$. We first express z_r as a polynomial of $\boldsymbol{x}^{(r-r_0)}$ for some r_0. According to Proposition 3, when r_0 is not very large, the expression of z_r in $\boldsymbol{x}^{(r-r_0)}$ can be got by the monomial prediction technique [6].

---

[6] According to our experiments, a reasonable range of r_0 is from 200 to 300.

Proposition 3. *Let* $z_r = f(\boldsymbol{x}^{(0)})$, *and*

$$\mathbb{U}_{r-r_0} = \{\boldsymbol{u}^{(r-r_0)} : |\pi_{\boldsymbol{u}^{(r-r_0)}}(\boldsymbol{x}^{(r-r_0)}) \bowtie f| \bmod 2 = 1 \}, \quad then$$

$$f = \bigoplus_{\boldsymbol{u}^{(r-r_0)} \in \mathbb{U}_{r-r_0}} \pi_{\boldsymbol{u}^{(r-r_0)}}(\boldsymbol{x}^{(r-r_0)}).$$

Based on Proposition 3, an algorithm to express r-round TRIVIUM in $\boldsymbol{x}^{(r-r_0)}$ is presented in Algorithm 4 in Appendix D (Ref. [11]).

Remark. We can also get the expression by symbolic computation. We choose the monomial prediction technique because most variables and constraints needed to complete this step are already presented in our model, which significantly reduces the burden of extra coding efforts.

Algorithm 3 shows how we recover the superpoly of a certain cube based on the divide-and-conquer strategy. The divide-and-conquer strategy leads to remarkable speedups and memory reductions in practice, which makes it possible

---

Algorithm 3: $\mathbb{U}_k = \mathsf{ComputeSuperpoly}(r, \boldsymbol{\Gamma}^0, \boldsymbol{\Gamma}^1, \boldsymbol{\Gamma}^p, \boldsymbol{\Gamma}^s)$

Input: The targeted number of rounds r and the four variables masks for f_d
Output: A set $\mathbb{U}_k$ for the monomials in superpoly like $\pi_{\boldsymbol{\Gamma}^p \oplus \boldsymbol{w}}(\boldsymbol{x}^{(0)})$ for $\boldsymbol{w} \preceq \boldsymbol{\Gamma}^s$

1 Allocate a hash table T;
2 $\mathbb{U}_{r-r_0} \leftarrow \mathsf{ExpandTrivium}(r, r_0);$ // Practically, we set $r_0 = 200$
3 **for** *each* $\boldsymbol{u'}^{(r-r_0)} \in \mathbb{U}_{r-r_0}$ **do**
4 $\quad$ $(\mathcal{M}, \boldsymbol{u}^{(0)}, \boldsymbol{u}^{(r-r_0)}) \leftarrow \mathsf{GenerateModel}(r - r_0);$
5 $\quad$ $\mathcal{M}.\mathsf{PoolSearchMode} \leftarrow 1;$
6 $\quad$ **for** $i = 0; i < 288; i \leftarrow i + 1$ **do**
7 $\quad\quad$ **if** Γ_i^0 *is 1* **then**
8 $\quad\quad\quad$ $u_i^{(0)} \leftarrow 0;$
9 $\quad\quad$ **if** Γ_i^p *is 1* **then**
10 $\quad\quad\quad$ $u_i^{(0)} \leftarrow 1;$
11 $\quad$ $\boldsymbol{u}^{(r-r_0)} \leftarrow \boldsymbol{u'}^{(r-r_0)};$
12 $\quad$ $\mathcal{M}.optimize();$
13 $\quad$ **if** $\mathcal{M}.status$ *is* `OPTIMAL` **then**
   $\quad\quad$ /* Store all the solutions in hash table and count $\qquad\qquad$ */
14 $\quad\quad$ **for** $i = 0; i < \mathcal{M}.solnum; i \leftarrow i + 1$ **do**
15 $\quad\quad\quad$ $\mathcal{M}.SolutionNumber \leftarrow i;$
16 $\quad\quad\quad$ $T[(u_0^{(0)}, u_1^{(0)}, \ldots, u_{79}^{(0)})] \leftarrow T[(u_0^{(0)}, u_1^{(0)}, \ldots, u_{79}^{(0)})] + 1;$

17 **for** $i = 0; i < H.linenumber; i \leftarrow i + 1$ **do**
18 $\quad$ **if** $T[i] \bmod 2$ *is 1* **then**
19 $\quad\quad$ $\mathbb{U}_k \leftarrow \mathbb{U}_k \cup \{i\};$

20 **return** $\mathbb{U}_k$

---

to test more cubes with limited resources. As a result, we identify some cubes with smaller dimensions for TRIVIUM, and thus improve upon several currently known best attacks on TRIVIUM. We list our experimental results with different smaller-dimension cubes in Table 3 (Ref. [11]). To verify our program, we re-conduct the experiments in [9] using the same cube indices for 840- and 841-round TRIVIUM and obtain the same superpolies.

Cube Attack on 840-Round TRIVIUM. We find the superpolies p_{I_1}, p_{I_2} and p_{I_3} for three different cube indices I_1, I_2 and $I_3{}^7$, whose dimensions are 75, 76, and 76, respectively.

Taking the cube of dimension 75 as $I_1 = \{0, 1, \ldots, 69, 71, 73, 75, 77, 79\}$ with

$$IV[70] = IV[72] = IV[74] = IV[76] = IV[78] = 0,$$

we recover a balanced superpoly for 840-round TRIVIUM that has 41 terms and of the algebraic degree 4. The independent monomial of the superpoly is labeled by the red text.

$p_{I_1} = k_{79} \oplus k_{77} \oplus k_{78}k_{77} \oplus k_{76}k_{75} \oplus k_{76}k_{63} \oplus k_{75}k_{74}k_{63} \oplus k_{73}k_{63} \oplus k_{72}k_{63} \oplus k_{71}k_{63} \oplus$
$\quad k_{72}k_{71}k_{63} \oplus k_{71}k_{70}k_{63} \oplus k_{70}k_{69}k_{63} \oplus k_{63}k_{61} \oplus k_{63}k_{60} \oplus k_{61}k_{60} \oplus k_{63}k_{59} \oplus$
$\quad k_{63}k_{59}k_{58} \oplus k_{61}k_{59}k_{58} \oplus k_{63}k_{57} \oplus k_{63}k_{57}k_{56} \oplus k_{52} \oplus k_{50} \oplus k_{63}k_{50} \oplus k_{63}k_{49} \oplus$
$\quad k_{63}k_{46} \oplus k_{63}k_{45} \oplus k_{63}k_{44} \oplus k_{63}k_{33} \oplus k_{61}k_{33} \oplus k_{63}k_{32} \oplus k_{63}k_{31} \oplus k_{63}k_{26} \oplus$
$\quad k_{71}k_{63}k_{12} \oplus k_{70}k_{69}k_{63}k_{12} \oplus k_{63}k_{59}k_{12} \oplus k_{63}k_{58}k_{12} \oplus k_{63}k_{57}k_{12} \oplus k_{63}k_{58}k_{57}k_{12} \oplus$
$\quad k_{63}k_{50}k_{12} \oplus k_{63}k_{44}k_{12} \oplus k_{63}k_{26}k_{12}.$

Taking the cube of dimension 76 as $I_2 = \{0, 1, \ldots, 71, 73, 75, 77, 79\}$ with

$$IV[72] = IV[74] = IV[76] = IV[78] = 0,$$

we recover a balanced superpoly for 840-round TRIVIUM that has 4 terms and algebraic degree of 2, and give it as follows

$$p_{I_2} = 1 \oplus k_{64} \oplus k_{63}k_{62} \oplus k_{37}.$$

Taking the cube of dimension 76 as $I_3 = \{0, 1, \ldots, 69, 71, 72, 73, 75, 77, 79\}$ with

$$IV[70] = IV[74] = IV[76] = IV[78] = 0,$$

we recover a balanced superpoly for 840-round TRIVIUM that has 6 terms and algebraic degree of 3 as below,

$$p_{I_3} = 1 \oplus k_{63} \oplus k_{59} \oplus k_{59}k_{50} \oplus k_{59}k_{49}k_{48} \oplus k_{59}k_{23}.$$

Let $\mathbb{C}_I = \{x \in \mathbb{F}_2^{288} : x \preceq \Gamma^p\}$, where Γ^p is set as Eq. (9). since $I_2 = I_1 \cup \{70\}$,

$$p_{I_2} = \bigoplus_{x \in \mathbb{C}_{I_2}} f(x) = \bigoplus_{x \in \mathbb{C}_{I_1}, IV[70]=1} f(x) \oplus \bigoplus_{x \in \mathbb{C}_{I_1}, IV[70]=0} f(x),$$

---

[7] For convenience, every element in the cube indices $I_i, 0 \le i \le 11$ in this subsection is the index of IV, i.e. from 0 to 79.

and

$$p_{I_1} = \bigoplus_{x \in \mathbb{C}_{I_1}} f(x) = \bigoplus_{x \in \mathbb{C}_{I_1}, IV[70]=0} f(x),$$

then we can deduce that $p_{I_4} = p_{I_1} \oplus p_{I_2}$ is the superpoly for the cube indices $I_4 = \{0, 1, \ldots, 69, 71, 73, 75, 77, 79\}$ with

$$IV[72] = IV[74] = IV[76] = IV[78] = 0, IV[70] = 1.$$

Similarly, we can deduce that $p_{I_5} = p_{I_1} \oplus p_{I_3}$ is the superpoly for the cube indices $I_5 = \{0, 1, \ldots, 69, 71, 73, 75, 77, 79\}$ with

$$IV[70] = IV[74] = IV[76] = IV[78] = 0, IV[72] = 1.$$

p_{I_1}, p_{I_4} and p_{I_5} are balanced Boolean functions because there are monomials that are independent of other monomials, respectively. Therefore, we can recover 3 bits of key information by using $3 \times 2^{75} \approx 2^{76.6}$ time complexity. The dominant part of the whole key recovery attack is the exhaustive search after the recovery of the 3-bit key information, which is 2^{77} time complexity. So in total, the time complexity for this 840-round TRIVIUM is $2^{76.6} + 2^{77} \approx 2^{77.8}$.

Cube Attack on 841-Round TRIVIUM. We find the superpolies p_{I_6} and p_{I_7} for the set of cube indices I_6 and I_7, whose dimensions are 76 and 77, respectively. Taking the cube of dimension 76 as $I_6 = \{0, 1, \ldots, 69, 71, 73, 74, 75, 77, 79\}$ with

$$IV[70] = IV[72] = IV[76] = IV[78] = 0,$$

we recover a balanced superpoly p_6 for 841-round TRIVIUM that has 3632 terms and algebraic degree of 9. Since the number of terms in p_{I_6} (and other superpolies, e.g., p_{I_7}, p_{I_9} and $p_{I_{10}}$ are too many, we provide them at https://github.com/hukaisdu/MonomialPrediction/blob/master/superpoly.pdf.

Taking the cube of dimension 77 as $I_7 = \{0, 1, \ldots, 71, 73, 74, 75, 77, 79\}$ with

$$IV[72] = IV[76] = IV[78] = 0,$$

we recover a balanced superpoly p_{I_7} for 841-round TRIVIUM that has 1400 terms and algebraic degree of 8.

Similar with p_{I_4}, $p_{I_8} = p_{I_6} \oplus p_{I_7}$ is the superpoly for the cube indices $I_8 = \{0, 1, \ldots, 69, 71, 73, 7475, 77, 79\}$ with

$$IV[72] = IV[76] = IV[78] = 0, IV[70] = 1.$$

Hence, we can recover 2 bits of the key information with time complexity $2^{77} = 2 \times 2^{76}$. The dominant part of the whole key recovery attack is the exhaustive search after 2-bit key recovery, which is 2^{78} time complexity. Therefore, totally the time complexity of the attack on the 841-round TRIVIUM is $2^{78} + 2^{77} \approx 2^{78.6}$.

Cube Attack on 842-Round TRIVIUM. We find the superpolies p_{I_9} and $p_{I_{10}}$ for the set of cube indices I_9 and I_{10}, whose dimensions are 76 and 77, respectively.

Taking the cube of dimension 76 as $I_9 = \{0, 1, \ldots, 71, 73, 75, 77, 79\}$ with

$$IV[72] = IV[74] = IV[76] = IV[78] = 0,$$

we recover a balanced superpoly for 842-round TRIVIUM that has 5147 terms and algebraic degree of 8.

Taking the cube of dimension 77 as $I_{10} = \{0, 1, \ldots, 73, 75, 77, 79\}$ with

$$IV[74] = IV[76] = IV[78] = 0,$$

we recover a balanced superpoly p_{10} for 842-round TRIVIUM that has 4174 terms and algebraic degree of 8.

Similar with p_{I_4}, $p_{I_{11}} = p_{I_9} \oplus p_{I_{10}}$ is the superpoly of the cube indices $I_{11} = \{0, 1, \ldots, 71, 73, 75, 77, 79\}$ with $IV[74] = IV[76] = IV[78] = 0, IV[72] = 1$. Therefore, we can recover 2 bits of key information by using $2^{77} = 2 \times 2^{76}$ time complexities. The dominant part of the whole key recovery attack is the exhaustive search after 2-bit key recovery, which is 2^{78} time complexity. Totally, the time complexity is $2^{78} + 2^{77} \approx 2^{78.6}$.

6   Division Property from an Algebraic Viewpoint

Since 2015, various division properties together with their "propagation rules" are proposed in the literature, including the word-based division property [21,25], the two-subset bit-based division property [27] (a.k.a. the conventional bit-based division property), the three-subset bit-based division property [27], and the recent three-subset bit-based division property without unknown subset [9,30]. Based on these properties with their associated propagation rules, detection algorithms or tools can be built. In a narrow sense, these detection algorithms are used to detect whether the sum of an output bit of a symmetric-key primitive over a carefully constructed input data set is *key-independent*, that is, the sum is a constant (0 or 1) for any key.

We now look at the detection algorithms for the *key-independent* property from an algebraic viewpoint. Before we go any further, we would like to mention that the first attempt to formulate the division property in an algebraic way was made by Boura and Canteaut at CRYPTO 2016 [2]. However, they only focused themselves on local components rather than on the global (keyed) Boolean functions. Furthermore, Biryukov, Khovratovich, and Perrin proposed the multiset-algebraic cryptanalysis which can also be seen as an algebraic treatment of the division property [1]. But they focused more on the algebraic degree only. Now, let us proceed to show the following conclusions:

- A *perfect* detection algorithm for the *key-independent* property can be constructed based on the monomial prediction (i.e., this algorithm never raises false alarms and never misses).
- The word-based division property [25], two-subset bit-based division property [27] and three-subset bit-based division property [27] together with their propagation rules lead to *no-false-alarm* detection algorithms for the *key-independent* property (however, these algorithms can miss).

- The three-subset bit-based division property without unknown subset with its propagation rules [9] forms a *perfect* detection algorithm for the *key-independent* property, and an equivalence between it and the monomial prediction technique can be established.

6.1   A Perfect Detection Algorithm Based on Monomial Prediction

For a composite function $f : \mathbb{F}_2^n \to \mathbb{F}_2^m, x^{(r)} = f(x^{(0)})$, we define a constant vector $u \in \mathbb{F}_2^n$ then we derive a structure of the input values $\mathbb{X} = \{x \in \mathbb{F}_2^n : x \preceq u\}$. We want to detect whether

$$\lambda = \bigoplus_{x \in \mathbb{X}} \pi_{u^{(r)}}(f(x))$$

is independent of the variables x_i's with $\bar{u}_i = 1$ denoted by $\bar{u}$-(in)dependent. From the viewpoint of presence and absence of monomials, we have

$$\lambda = \begin{cases} \bar{u}\text{-dependent,} & \text{if } \pi_{u \oplus w}(x^{(0)}) \to \pi_{u^{(r)}}(x^{(r)}) \text{ for some } 0 \prec w \preceq \bar{u} \\ \bar{u}\text{-independent,} & \text{if } \pi_{u \oplus w}(x^{(0)}) \nrightarrow \pi_{u^{(r)}}(x^{(r)}) \text{ for all } 0 \prec w \preceq \bar{u} \end{cases}$$

Hence, for f, the monomial prediction can detect whether λ is independent of x_i with $\bar{u}_i = 1$ precisely in theory by computing $|\pi_{u \oplus w}(x^{(0)}) \bowtie \pi_{u^{(r)}}(x^{(r)})|$ for every possible $0 \prec w \preceq \bar{u}$.

Application to Derived Function. When applying the monomial prediction to a practical cipher, some part of the public variables will be fixed as a constant value. Let $\Gamma^0, \Gamma^1, \Gamma^p$ and Γ^s be four constant vectors indicating the 0-constant public variables, 1-constant public variables, the non-constant public variables and the secret variables, respectively. Then we study the derived function f_d of f with $\Gamma^0, \Gamma^1, \Gamma^p, \Gamma^s$. In the integral attack, the chosen plaintext set is

$$\mathbb{X}_0 = \{x \oplus \Gamma^1 \in \mathbb{F}_2^n : x \preceq \Gamma^p\}. \tag{10}$$

And we are interested in whether

$$\Lambda = \bigoplus_{x \in \mathbb{X}_0} \pi_{u^{(r)}}(f_d(x)).$$

is independent of the secret variables x_i with $\Gamma_i^s = 1$, denoted by key-(in)dependent. Similarly,

$$\Lambda = \begin{cases} \text{key-dependent,} & \text{if } \pi_{\Gamma^p \oplus w}(x^{(0)}) \to \pi_{u^{(r)}}(x^{(r)}) \text{ for some } 0 \prec w \preceq \Gamma^s \\ \text{key-independent,} & \text{if } \pi_{\Gamma^p \oplus w}(x^{(0)}) \nrightarrow \pi_{u^{(r)}}(x^{(r)}) \text{ for all } 0 \prec w \preceq \Gamma^s \end{cases}$$

Hence, by computing $|\pi_{\Gamma^p \oplus w}(x^{(0)}) \bowtie \pi_{u^{(r)}}(x^{(r)})|$ for every possible $0 \prec w \preceq \Gamma^s$, we can predict whether Λ is or not key-independent.

6.2   No-False-Alarm Detection Algorithms

Although the monomial prediction can predict the key-independent property precisely, computing the size of a monomial hull is commonly difficult, especially for a block cipher because the size of the monomial hull is usually huge. Furthermore, for attackers, integral property of any bits (it is not necessary to find all) is useful in distinguishing attacks. Therefore, some trade-off between the efficiency and precision is necessary and reasonable.

Following this idea of trade-off, we show a simple observation. Recall Lemma 1, if $\pi_{\boldsymbol{u}}(\boldsymbol{x}^{(0)}) \not\rightarrow \pi_{\boldsymbol{u}^{(r)}}(\boldsymbol{x}^{(r)})$, we have $\pi_{\boldsymbol{u}}(\boldsymbol{x}^{(0)}) \twoheadrightarrow \pi_{\boldsymbol{u}^{(r)}}(\boldsymbol{x}^{(r)})$. Then if we are able to make the claim that $\varLambda$ is key-independent according to $\pi_{\boldsymbol{\varGamma}^p \oplus \boldsymbol{w}}(\boldsymbol{x}^{(0)}) \not\rightarrow \pi_{\boldsymbol{u}^{(r)}}(\boldsymbol{x}^{(r)})$ for any $\boldsymbol{w} \preceq \boldsymbol{\varGamma}^s$, the detection algorithm we employ will never raise false alarms.

Definition 3 (No-False-Alarm Approximations). *For two detection algorithms $\mathcal{A}_1$ and $\mathcal{A}_2$, if $\mathcal{A}_1$ claims a certain property $\mathcal{P}$ holds, $\mathcal{A}_2$ must also claim $\mathcal{P}$ holds, then we say $\mathcal{A}_1$ is a no-false-alarm approximation of $\mathcal{A}_2$.*

Next we prove that the two-subset bit-based division property is a no-false-alarm approximation of the monomial prediction.

Definition 4 (Two-Subset Bit-Based Division Property [27]). *Let $\mathbb{X}$ be a multiset whose elements are n-bit vectors and $\mathbb{K}$ be a set whose elements are n-bit vectors. When the multiset $\mathbb{X}$ has the division property $\mathcal{D}_{\mathbb{K}}^{1^n}$, it fulfills the following conditions:*

$$\bigoplus_{\boldsymbol{x} \in \mathbb{X}} \pi_{\boldsymbol{u}}(\boldsymbol{x}) = \begin{cases} unknown, & \text{if there exist } \boldsymbol{k} \in \mathbb{K} \text{ s.t. } \boldsymbol{u} \succeq \boldsymbol{k}, \\ 0, & \text{otherwise.} \end{cases}$$

Let $\boldsymbol{f}_d$ be the derived function of $\boldsymbol{f}$ with $\boldsymbol{\varGamma}^0, \boldsymbol{\varGamma}^1, \boldsymbol{\varGamma}^p, \boldsymbol{\varGamma}^s$. Suppose the initially chosen set (multiset) of the plaintext is $\mathbb{X}_0$ as defined in Eq. (10) and the multiset of the ciphertext is $\mathbb{X}_r = \{\boldsymbol{y} : \boldsymbol{y} = \boldsymbol{f}_d(\boldsymbol{x}), \boldsymbol{x} \in \mathbb{X}_0\}$. Then we first compute the division property of $\mathbb{X}_0$ as $\mathcal{D}_{\mathbb{K}_0}^{1^n}$, where

$$\mathbb{K}_0 = \{\boldsymbol{k} \in \mathbb{F}_2^n : \boldsymbol{k} \succeq \boldsymbol{\varGamma}^p\}. \tag{11}$$

To compute the division property of $\mathbb{X}_r$, i.e., $\mathcal{D}_{\mathbb{K}_r}^{1^n}$, we will trace all the propagation from the vectors in $\mathbb{K}_0$. The propagation rules for the two-subset bit-based division property are listed in [13,27,31].

Proposition 4. *The two-subset bit-based division property is a no-false-alarm approximation of the monomial prediction in detecting the balance property, therefore the two-subset bit-based division property claims $\bigoplus_{\boldsymbol{x}^{(r)} \in \mathbb{X}_r} \pi_{\boldsymbol{k}^{(r)}}(\boldsymbol{x}^{(r)}) \equiv 0$ without false alarms.*

Proof. Firstly, for any $\boldsymbol{k}^{(0)} \in \mathbb{K}_0$, $\pi_{\boldsymbol{k}^{(0)}}(\boldsymbol{x}^{(0)}) = \pi_{\boldsymbol{\varGamma}^p \oplus \boldsymbol{w}}(\boldsymbol{x}^{(0)})$ where $\boldsymbol{w} = \boldsymbol{\varGamma}^p \oplus \boldsymbol{k}^{(0)} \preceq \boldsymbol{\varGamma}^1 \oplus \boldsymbol{\varGamma}^s$. Next, we consider the propagation from these vectors in $\mathbb{K}_0$. Note all kinds of components of a cipher can be seen as an S-box: $\boldsymbol{y} = \boldsymbol{S}(\boldsymbol{x})$, and the propagation of the S-box for the two-subset bit-based division property has been concluded as a rule: Let $\mathcal{D}_{\mathbb{K}_{in}}^{1^n}$ and $\mathcal{D}_{\mathbb{K}_{out}}^{1^n}$ be the input and output two-subset bit-based division property of $\boldsymbol{S}$, respectively. If $\boldsymbol{u} \in \mathbb{K}_{in}$ can propagates to $\boldsymbol{v} \in \mathbb{K}_{out}$, there must be $\boldsymbol{u}' \succeq \boldsymbol{u}$ satisfying $\pi_{\boldsymbol{u}'}(\boldsymbol{x}) \to \boldsymbol{y}^{\boldsymbol{v}}$. Since the monomial trail requires $\boldsymbol{x}^{\boldsymbol{u}} \to \boldsymbol{y}^{\boldsymbol{v}}$, then from the same $\boldsymbol{u}$, the two-subset bit-based division property can propagate to a larger range of vectors $\boldsymbol{v}$.

Hence, if $\boldsymbol{k}^{(r)} \notin \mathbb{K}_r$, we have $\pi_{\boldsymbol{k}}(\boldsymbol{x}^{(0)}) \not\rightsquigarrow \pi_{\boldsymbol{k}^{(r)}}(\boldsymbol{x}^{(r)})$ for all $\boldsymbol{k} \in \mathbb{K}_0$. Therefore, $\pi_{\boldsymbol{k}^{(r)}}(\boldsymbol{x}^{(r)})$ does not contain any terms like $\pi_{\boldsymbol{\Gamma}^p \oplus \boldsymbol{w}}(\boldsymbol{x}^{(0)}) = \pi_{\boldsymbol{w}}(\boldsymbol{x}^{(0)})\pi_{\boldsymbol{\Gamma}^p}(\boldsymbol{x}^{(0)})$ for $\boldsymbol{w} \preceq \boldsymbol{\Gamma}^1 \oplus \boldsymbol{\Gamma}^s$, naturally,

$$\bigoplus_{\boldsymbol{x}^{(r)} \in \mathbb{X}_r} \pi_{\boldsymbol{k}^{(r)}}(\boldsymbol{x}^{(r)}) = \bigoplus_{\boldsymbol{x}^{(0)} \in \mathbb{X}_0} \pi_{\boldsymbol{k}^{(r)}}(\boldsymbol{f}_d(\boldsymbol{x}^{(0)})) \equiv 0.$$

□

According to the proof, it can be checked even if $\boldsymbol{k}^{(r)} \in \mathbb{K}_r$, we cannot determine whether $\pi_{\boldsymbol{k}^{(0)}}(\boldsymbol{x}^{(0)}) \rightsquigarrow \pi_{\boldsymbol{k}^{(r)}}(\boldsymbol{x}^{(r)})$ (let alone $\pi_{\boldsymbol{k}^{(0)}}(\boldsymbol{x}^{(0)}) \to \pi_{\boldsymbol{k}^{(r)}}(\boldsymbol{x}^{(r)})$), while the two-subset division property claims that the parity is an unknown value, i.e., the two-subset bit-based division property may miss some balance properties.

Similarly, we can prove that the three-subset bit-based division property and the word-based division property are also no-false-alarm approximation of the monomial prediction. The proofs are provided in Appendix C (Ref. [11]).

6.3   The Three-Subset Bit-Based Division Property Without Unknown Subset is Perfect

In [30], Wang et al. found that we can only focus on a part of the propagation of the three-subset bit-based division property when processing a public-update cipher. Later in [9], Hao et al. formulated this method to the three-subset bit-based division property without unknown subset. In this subsection, we show it is perfect in detecting the key-independent property.

Definition 5 (Three-Subset Bit-Based Division Property w/o Unknown Subset [9,30]). *Let $\mathbb{X}$ and $\mathbb{L}$ be two multisets whose elements are n-bit vectors. When the multiset $\mathbb{X}$ has the three-subset bit-based division property without unknown subset $\mathcal{T}_{\mathbb{L}}^{1^n}$, it fulfills the following conditions:*

$$\bigoplus_{\boldsymbol{x} \in \mathbb{X}} \pi_{\boldsymbol{\ell}}(\boldsymbol{x}) = \begin{cases} 1, & \text{if there are } \textit{odd-number } \boldsymbol{\ell} \text{ in } \mathbb{L}, \\ 0, & \text{if there are } \textit{even-number } \boldsymbol{\ell} \text{ in } \mathbb{L}. \end{cases}$$

Let $\boldsymbol{f}_d$ be the derived function of $\boldsymbol{f}$ with $\boldsymbol{\Gamma}^0, \boldsymbol{\Gamma}^1, \boldsymbol{\Gamma}^p, \boldsymbol{\Gamma}^{s}$[8]. Suppose the initial chosen set (multiset) of the plaintext is $\mathbb{X}_0$ in Eq. (10), and the multiset of the

---

[8] In [9], the definition of the three-subset division property without unknown subset made no distinction between the public and secret variables, equivalently, $\boldsymbol{\Gamma}^s = \boldsymbol{0}$ and $\boldsymbol{\Gamma}^p$ indicates all variables.

ciphertext is $\mathbb{X}_r = \{\boldsymbol{y} : \boldsymbol{y} = \boldsymbol{f}_d(\boldsymbol{x}), \boldsymbol{x} \in \mathbb{X}_0\}$. Then we first compute the division property of $\mathbb{X}_0$ as $\mathcal{T}_{\mathbb{L}_0}^{1^n}$ [30], where

$$\mathbb{L}_0 = \{\boldsymbol{\ell} \in \mathbb{F}_2^n : \boldsymbol{\Gamma}^p \preceq \boldsymbol{\ell} \preceq \boldsymbol{\Gamma}^p \oplus \boldsymbol{\Gamma}^1\}. \tag{12}$$

To compute the division property of $\mathbb{X}_r$, i.e., $\mathcal{T}_{\mathbb{L}_r}^{1^n}$, we will trace all the propagation from the vectors in $\mathbb{L}_0$. The propagation rules for three-subset bit-based division property without unknown subset are listed in [9,30].

Proposition 5.   *The three-subset bit-based division property without unknown subset predicts $\bigoplus_{\boldsymbol{x}^{(r)} \in \mathbb{X}_r} \pi_{\boldsymbol{\ell}^{(r)}}(\boldsymbol{x}^{(r)})$ for any $\boldsymbol{\ell}^{(r)}$ perfectly.*

Proof. Firstly, for any $\boldsymbol{\ell}^{(0)} \in \mathbb{L}_0$, $\pi_{\boldsymbol{\ell}^{(0)}}(\boldsymbol{x}^{(0)}) = \pi_{\boldsymbol{\Gamma}^p \oplus \boldsymbol{w}}(\boldsymbol{x}^{(0)})$ where $\boldsymbol{w} = \boldsymbol{\Gamma}^p \oplus \boldsymbol{\ell}^{(0)} \preceq \boldsymbol{\Gamma}^1$. Then $\pi_{\boldsymbol{\Gamma}^p \oplus \boldsymbol{w}}(\boldsymbol{x}^{(0)}) = \pi_{\boldsymbol{\Gamma}^p}(\boldsymbol{x}^{(0)})$. Next, we consider the propagation from these vectors in $\mathbb{L}_0$. Since all kinds of components of a cipher can be seen as an S-box: $\boldsymbol{y} = \boldsymbol{S}(\boldsymbol{x})$ and the propagation of the S-box for the three-subset bit-based division property without unknown subset has been concluded as a rule that guarantees $\boldsymbol{x}^u \to \boldsymbol{y}^v$ [30], we can trace the propagation and compute out $\mathbb{L}_r$. Therefore, for every vector $\boldsymbol{\ell}^{(r)} \in \mathbb{L}_r$, there is a monomial trail connecting $\pi_{\boldsymbol{\ell}^{(0)}}(\boldsymbol{x}^{(0)})$ and $\pi_{\boldsymbol{\ell}^{(r)}}(\boldsymbol{x}^{(r)})$ since $\boldsymbol{x}^u \to \boldsymbol{y}^v$ is also required by Definition 1. Let $\boldsymbol{\ell}^{(r)}$ appears N times in $\mathbb{L}_r$, then

$$N = \sum_{\boldsymbol{\ell} \in \mathbb{L}_0} |\pi_{\boldsymbol{\ell}}(\boldsymbol{x}^{(0)}) \bowtie \pi_{\boldsymbol{\ell}^{(r)}}(\boldsymbol{x}^{(r)})| = \sum_{\boldsymbol{w} \preceq \boldsymbol{\Gamma}^1} |\pi_{\boldsymbol{\Gamma}^p \oplus \boldsymbol{w}}(\boldsymbol{x}^{(0)}) \bowtie \pi_{\boldsymbol{\ell}^{(r)}}(\boldsymbol{x}^{(r)})|.$$

According to Proposition 2, $\pi_{\boldsymbol{\Gamma}^p}(\boldsymbol{x}^{(0)}) \to \pi_{\boldsymbol{\ell}^{(r)}}(\boldsymbol{x}^{(r)})$, if and only if $N \bmod 2 = 1$.   □

6.4   An Alternative Detection Algorithm for Division Property

The algebraic insights into the division property bring us much more flexibility in designing new detection algorithms for balance properties. Although the three-subset bit-based division property is more accurate than the two-subset bit-based division property [30], the latter is more MILP-friendly and needs simpler programming, therefore the two-subset version is more efficient. According to the existing literature, the three-subset bit-based division property can find several more balanced bits, but hardly surpass the two-subset version by rounds. Hence, the two-subset bit-based division property is still the dominant method in searching for the integral property.

From an algebraic viewpoint, we show how to design a new detection algorithm of division property which surpasses the capability but achieves the similar efficiency with the two-subset bit-based division property. For the derived function $\boldsymbol{f}_d$ with $\boldsymbol{\Gamma}^0, \boldsymbol{\Gamma}^1, \boldsymbol{\Gamma}^p, \boldsymbol{\Gamma}^s$, if we want to determine whether $\bigoplus_{\boldsymbol{x} \in \mathbb{X}_0} \pi_{\boldsymbol{u}^{(r)}}(\boldsymbol{f}_d(\boldsymbol{x}))$ is key-independent or not, we only need to check whether $\pi_{\boldsymbol{u}^{(r)}}(\boldsymbol{x}^{(r)})$ contains any term in

$$\mathbb{S}_0 = \{\pi_{\boldsymbol{\Gamma}^p \oplus \boldsymbol{w}}(\boldsymbol{x}^{(0)}) : \boldsymbol{0} \prec \boldsymbol{w} \preceq \boldsymbol{\Gamma}^s\}.$$

Table 3. Some experimental results of our new detection algorithm compared with the previous ones. All results are re-produced on the same platform.

Cipher	#Data	#Round	#Constant	Time	Method
SIMON32	2^{31}	15	–[†]	–	[31]
			3	27 s	[12]
			3	120 s	[30]
			3	3 s	Ours
SIMON32 (102)[‡]	2^{31}	20	1	3 s	[31]
			3	25 s	[12]
			3	3 s	Ours
SIMON48 (102)	2^{47}	28	3	8 s	[31]
			3	9 s	[12]
			3	8 s	Ours
SIMON64 (102)	2^{63}	36	1	23 s	[31]
			3	1.1 h	[12]
			3	30 s	Ours

[†] The two-subset bit-based division property cannot find the 15-round integral distinguisher for SIMON32.
[‡] SIMON32 (102) means the rotation constants are (1,0,2) rather than (8,1,2), see [31].

Consider $\mathbb{S}_r = \{\pi_{\boldsymbol{u}^{(r)}}(\boldsymbol{x}^{(r)}) : \pi_{\boldsymbol{u}^{(0)}}(\boldsymbol{x}^{(0)}) \rightsquigarrow \pi_{\boldsymbol{u}^{(r)}}(\boldsymbol{x}^{(r)})\}$, if $\pi_{\boldsymbol{u}^{(r)}}(\boldsymbol{x}^{(r)}) \notin \mathbb{S}_r$, then we know $\boldsymbol{f}_d$ does not contain any monomials in $\mathbb{S}_0$ since there is no monomial trail. Therefore $\bigoplus_{\boldsymbol{x} \in \mathbb{X}_0} \pi_{\boldsymbol{u}^{(r)}}(\boldsymbol{f}_d(\boldsymbol{x}))$ is a key-independent value.

To detect it, firstly, we construct the model of $\pi_{\boldsymbol{u}^{(0)}}(\boldsymbol{x}^{(0)}) \rightsquigarrow \pi_{\boldsymbol{u}^{(r)}}(\boldsymbol{x}^{(r)})$ by decomposing the target cipher like we do for TRIVIUM. Secondly, we impose another constraint on all the round key bits k_i on the MILP model $\mathcal{M}$ as

$$\mathcal{M} \leftarrow \sum_i k_i \geq 1.$$

Finally, we check the validity of this model. If the model is infeasible, then $\pi_{\boldsymbol{u}^{(r)}}(\boldsymbol{x}^{(r)})$ contains no monomial in $\mathbb{S}_0$ and $\bigoplus_{\boldsymbol{x} \in \mathbb{X}_0} \pi_{\boldsymbol{u}^{(r)}}(\boldsymbol{f}_d(\boldsymbol{x}))$ is key-independent. Since we do not need to compute the size of the monomial hull, the model is easy to solve. Some experiments are conducted to show the capability of this alternative detection algorithm, we list the results in Table 3.

7 Conclusion and Discussion

In this work, a pure algebraic treatment of the division property is presented, and we propose the monomial prediction technique which determines the presence or absence of a monomial by counting the number of monomial trails in the corresponding monomial hull. Based on this technique, we manage to obtain the exact algebraic degrees of TRIVIUM up to 834 rounds and improved key-recovery attacks on 840-, 841- and 842-round TRIVIUM.

Moreover, we categorize existing detection algorithms for division properties into perfect, no-false-alarm, and no-missing classes. In particular, we prove that the three-subset bit-based division property without unknown subset and monomial prediction are perfect. At this point, a natural question arises. Can we design an efficient no-missing detection algorithm for the division property that does not raise too many false alarms, which would be very useful for designers to theoretically determine the security bounds against attacks based on division properties.

Acknowledgements. We thank the anonymous reviewers for their valuable comments. This work is supported by the National Key Research and Development Program of China (No. 2018YFA0704702, 2018YFA0704704), the Major Scientific and Technological Innovation Project of Shandong Province, China (No. 2019JZZY010133), the Chinese Major Program of National Cryptography Development Foundation (MMJJ20180102), and the National Natural Science Foundation of China (61772519). The work of Qingju Wang is funded by the University of Luxembourg Internal Research Project (IRP) FDISC.

References

1. Biryukov, A., Khovratovich, D., Perrin, L.: Multiset-algebraic cryptanalysis of reduced Kuznyechik, Khazad, and secret SPNs. IACR Trans. Symmetric Cryptol. **2016**(2), 226–247 (2016)
2. Boura, C., Canteaut, A.: Another view of the division property. In: Robshaw, M., Katz, J. (eds.) CRYPTO 2016. LNCS, vol. 9814, pp. 654–682. Springer, Heidelberg (2016). https://doi.org/10.1007/978-3-662-53018-4_24
3. Boura, C., Canteaut, A., De Cannière, C.: Higher-order differential properties of KECCAK and *Luffa*. In: Joux, A. (ed.) FSE 2011. LNCS, vol. 6733, pp. 252–269. Springer, Heidelberg (2011). https://doi.org/10.1007/978-3-642-21702-9_15
4. De Cannière, Christophe, Preneel, Bart: Trivium. In: Robshaw, Matthew, Billet, Olivier (eds.) New Stream Cipher Designs. LNCS, vol. 4986, pp. 244–266. Springer, Heidelberg (2008). https://doi.org/10.1007/978-3-540-68351-3_18
5. Canteaut, A., Videau, M.: Degree of composition of highly nonlinear functions and applications to higher order differential cryptanalysis. In: Knudsen, L.R. (ed.) EUROCRYPT 2002. LNCS, vol. 2332, pp. 518–533. Springer, Heidelberg (2002). https://doi.org/10.1007/3-540-46035-7_34
6. Daemen, J., Knudsen, L., Rijmen, V.: The block cipher square. In: Biham, E. (ed.) FSE 1997. LNCS, vol. 1267, pp. 149–165. Springer, Heidelberg (1997). https://doi.org/10.1007/BFb0052343
7. Dinur, I., Shamir, A.: Cube attacks on tweakable black box polynomials. In: Joux, A. (ed.) EUROCRYPT 2009. LNCS, vol. 5479, pp. 278–299. Springer, Heidelberg (2009). https://doi.org/10.1007/978-3-642-01001-9_16
8. Hao, Y., Leander, G., Meier, W., Todo, Y., Wang, Q.: Modeling for three-subset division property without unknown subset. IACR Cryptology ePrint Archive, 2020:441 (2020)

9. Hao, Y., Leander, G., Meier, W., Todo, Y., Wang, Q.: Modeling for three-subset division property without unknown subset. In: Canteaut, A., Ishai, Y. (eds.) EUROCRYPT 2020. LNCS, vol. 12105, pp. 466–495. Springer, Cham (2020). https://doi.org/10.1007/978-3-030-45721-1_17

10. Hebborn, P., Lambin, B., Leander, G., Todo, Y.: Lower bounds on the degree of block ciphers. In: Moriai, S., Wang, H. (eds.) ASIACRYPT 2020 (to appear)

11. Hu, K., Sun, S., Wang, M., Wang, Q.: An algebraic formulation of the division property: revisiting degree evaluations, cube attacks, and key-independent sums (2020). https://eprint.iacr.org/2020/1048

12. Hu, K., Wang, M.: Automatic search for a variant of division property using three subsets. In: Matsui, M. (ed.) CT-RSA 2019. LNCS, vol. 11405, pp. 412–432. Springer, Cham (2019). https://doi.org/10.1007/978-3-030-12612-4_21

13. Kai, H., Wang, Q., Wang, M.: Finding bit-based division property for ciphers with complex linear layers. IACR Trans. Symmetric Cryptol. **2020**(1), 236–263 (2020)

14. Jakobsen, T., Knudsen, L.R.: The interpolation attack on block ciphers. In: Biham, E. (ed.) FSE 1997. LNCS, vol. 1267, pp. 28–40. Springer, Heidelberg (1997). https://doi.org/10.1007/BFb0052332

15. Knudsen, L.R.: Truncated and higher order differentials. In: Preneel, B. (ed.) FSE 1994. LNCS, vol. 1008, pp. 196–211. Springer, Heidelberg (1995). https://doi.org/10.1007/3-540-60590-8_16

16. Knudsen, L., Wagner, D.: Integral cryptanalysis. In: Daemen, J., Rijmen, V. (eds.) FSE 2002. LNCS, vol. 2365, pp. 112–127. Springer, Heidelberg (2002). https://doi.org/10.1007/3-540-45661-9_9

17. Lai, X.: Higher order derivatives and differential cryptanalysis. In: Blahut, R.E., Costello, D.J., Maurer, U., Mittelholzer, T. (eds.) Communications and Cryptography, pp. 227–233. Springer, Boston (1994). https://doi.org/10.1007/978-1-4615-2694-0_23

18. Liu, M.: Degree evaluation of NFSR-based cryptosystems. In: Katz, J., Shacham, H. (eds.) CRYPTO 2017. LNCS, vol. 10403, pp. 227–249. Springer, Cham (2017). https://doi.org/10.1007/978-3-319-63697-9_8

19. Mroczkowski, P., Szmidt, J.: The cube attack on stream cipher Trivium and quadraticity tests. Fundam. Inform. **114**(3–4), 309–318 (2012)

20. Murphy, S., Robshaw, M.J.B.: Essential algebraic structure within the AES. In: Yung, M. (ed.) CRYPTO 2002. LNCS, vol. 2442, pp. 1–16. Springer, Heidelberg (2002). https://doi.org/10.1007/3-540-45708-9_1

21. Sun, B., Hai, X., Zhang, W., Cheng, L., Yang, Z.: New observation on division property. Sci. China Inf. Sci. **60**(9), 1–3 (2016). https://doi.org/10.1007/s11432-015-0376-x

22. Sun, L., Wang, W., Wang, M.: Automatic search of bit-based division property for ARX ciphers and word-based division property. In: Takagi, T., Peyrin, T. (eds.) ASIACRYPT 2017. LNCS, vol. 10624, pp. 128–157. Springer, Cham (2017). https://doi.org/10.1007/978-3-319-70694-8_5

23. Sun, S., Hu, L., Wang, P., Qiao, K., Ma, X., Song, L.: Automatic security evaluation and (related-key) differential characteristic search: application to SIMON, PRESENT, LBlock, DES(L) and other bit-oriented block ciphers. In: Sarkar, P., Iwata, T. (eds.) ASIACRYPT 2014. LNCS, vol. 8873, pp. 158–178. Springer, Heidelberg (2014). https://doi.org/10.1007/978-3-662-45611-8_9

24. Todo, Y.: Integral cryptanalysis on full MISTY1. In: Gennaro, R., Robshaw, M. (eds.) CRYPTO 2015. LNCS, vol. 9215, pp. 413–432. Springer, Heidelberg (2015). https://doi.org/10.1007/978-3-662-47989-6_20

25. Todo, Y.: Structural evaluation by generalized integral property. In: Oswald, E., Fischlin, M. (eds.) EUROCRYPT 2015. LNCS, vol. 9056, pp. 287–314. Springer, Heidelberg (2015). https://doi.org/10.1007/978-3-662-46800-5_12
26. Todo, Y., Isobe, T., Hao, Y., Meier, W.: Cube attacks on non-blackbox polynomials based on division property. In: Katz, J., Shacham, H. (eds.) CRYPTO 2017. LNCS, vol. 10403, pp. 250–279. Springer, Cham (2017). https://doi.org/10.1007/978-3-319-63697-9_9
27. Todo, Y., Morii, M.: Bit-based division property and application to SIMON family. In: Peyrin, T. (ed.) FSE 2016. LNCS, vol. 9783, pp. 357–377. Springer, Heidelberg (2016). https://doi.org/10.1007/978-3-662-52993-5_18
28. Wang, Q., Grassi, L., Rechberger, C.: Zero-sum partitions of PHOTON permutations. In: Smart, N.P. (ed.) CT-RSA 2018. LNCS, vol. 10808, pp. 279–299. Springer, Cham (2018). https://doi.org/10.1007/978-3-319-76953-0_15
29. Wang, Q., Hao, Y., Todo, Y., Li, C., Isobe, T., Meier, W.: Improved division property based cube attacks exploiting algebraic properties of superpoly. In: Shacham, H., Boldyreva, A. (eds.) CRYPTO 2018. LNCS, vol. 10991, pp. 275–305. Springer, Cham (2018). https://doi.org/10.1007/978-3-319-96884-1_10
30. Wang, S., Hu, B., Guan, J., Zhang, K., Shi, T.: MILP-aided method of searching division property using three subsets and applications. In: Galbraith, S.D., Moriai, S. (eds.) ASIACRYPT 2019. LNCS, vol. 11923, pp. 398–427. Springer, Cham (2019). https://doi.org/10.1007/978-3-030-34618-8_14
31. Xiang, Z., Zhang, W., Bao, Z., Lin, D.: Applying MILP method to searching integral distinguishers based on division property for 6 lightweight block ciphers. In: Cheon, J.H., Takagi, T. (eds.) ASIACRYPT 2016. LNCS, vol. 10031, pp. 648–678. Springer, Heidelberg (2016). https://doi.org/10.1007/978-3-662-53887-6_24
32. Ye, C., Tian, T.: Revisit division property based cube attacks: Key-recovery or distinguishing attacks? IACR Trans. Symmetric Cryptol. 2019(3), 81–102 (2019)

An Algebraic Attack on Ciphers with Low-Degree Round Functions: Application to Full MiMC

Maria Eichlseder[1]($\boxtimes$), Lorenzo Grassi[1,2]($\boxtimes$), Reinhard Lüftenegger[1]($\boxtimes$),
Morten Øygarden[3]($\boxtimes$), Christian Rechberger[1]($\boxtimes$), Markus Schofnegger[1]($\boxtimes$),
and Qingju Wang[4]($\boxtimes$)

[1] IAIK, Graz University of Technology, Graz, Austria
{maria.eichlseder,reinhard.luftenegger,christian.rechberger,
markus.schofnegger}@iaik.tugraz.at, lgrassi@science.ru.nl
[2] Digital Security Group, Radboud University, Nijmegen, The Netherlands
[3] Simula UiB, Bergen, Norway
morten.oygarden@simula.no
[4] SnT, University of Luxembourg, Luxembourg City, Luxembourg
qingju.wang@uni.lu

Abstract. Algebraically simple PRFs, ciphers, or cryptographic hash functions are becoming increasingly popular, for example due to their attractive properties for MPC and new proof systems (SNARKs, STARKs, among many others).

In this paper, we focus on the algebraically simple construction MiMC, which became an attractive cryptanalytic target due to its simplicity, but also due to its use as a baseline in a competition for more recent algorithms exploring this design space.

For the first time, we are able to describe key-recovery attacks on all full-round versions of MiMC over $\mathbb{F}_{2^n}$, requiring half the code book. In the chosen-ciphertext scenario, recovering the key from this data for the n-bit full version of MiMC takes the equivalent of less than $2^{n-\log_2(n)+1}$ calls to MiMC and negligible amounts of memory.

The attack procedure is a generalization of higher-order differential cryptanalysis, and it is based on two main ingredients. First, we present a higher-order distinguisher which exploits the fact that the algebraic degree of MiMC grows significantly slower than originally believed. Secondly, we describe an approach to turn this distinguisher into a key-recovery attack without guessing the full subkey. Finally, we show that approximately $\lceil \log_3(2 \cdot R) \rceil$ more rounds (where $R = \lceil n \cdot \log_3(2) \rceil$ is the current number of rounds of MiMC-n/n) can be necessary and sufficient to restore the security against the key-recovery attack presented here.

The attack has been practically verified on toy versions of MiMC. Note that our attack does not affect the security of MiMC over prime fields.

Keywords: Algebraic attack · MiMC · Higher-order differential

© International Association for Cryptologic Research 2020
S. Moriai and H. Wang (Eds.): ASIACRYPT 2020, LNCS 12491, pp. 477–506, 2020.
https://doi.org/10.1007/978-3-030-64837-4_16

1   Introduction

The design of symmetric cryptographic constructions exhibiting a clear and ideally low-degree algebraic structure is motivated by many recent use cases, for
example the increasing popularity of new proof systems such as STARKs [8],
SNARKs (e.g., Pinocchio [44]), Bulletproofs [19], and other concepts like secure
multi-party computation (MPC). To provide good performance in these new
applications, ciphers and hash functions are designed in order to minimize specific characteristics (e.g., the total number of multiplications, the depth, or other
parameters related to the nonlinear operations). In contrast to traditional cipher
design, the size of the field over which these constructions are defined has only
a small impact on the final cost. In order to achieve this new performance goal,
some crucial differences arise between these new designs and traditional ones. For
example, we can consider the substitution (S-box) layer, that is, the operation
providing nonlinearity in the permutation: In these new schemes, the S-boxes
composing this layer are relatively large compared to the ones used in classical
schemes (e.g., they operate over 64 or 128 bits instead of 4 or 8 bits) and/or
they can usually be described by a simple low-degree nonlinear function (e.g.,
$x \mapsto x^d$ for some d). Examples of these schemes include LowMC [4], MiMC
[3], JARVIS/FRIDAY [6], GMiMC [2], HadesMiMC [31], *Vision/Rescue* [5], and
STARKAD/POSEIDON [30].

   The structure of these schemes has a significant impact on the attacks that
can be mounted. While statistical attacks (including linear [42] and differential
[11] ones) are among the most powerful techniques against traditional schemes,
algebraic attacks turned out to be especially effective against these new primitives. In other words, these constructions are naturally more vulnerable to algebraic attacks than those which do not exhibit a clear and simple algebraic structure. For example, this has been shown in [1], in which algebraic strategies covering the full-round versions of the attacked primitives are described. Although
the approaches can be quite different, most of them exploit the low degree of the
construction.

   In this paper, we focus on MiMC [3]. The MiMC design constructs a cryptographic permutation by iterated cubing, interleaved with additions of random
constants to break any symmetries. A secret key is added after every such round
to obtain a block cipher. The design of MiMC is very flexible and can work with
binary strings as well as integers modulo some prime number. Security analysis by the designers rules out various statistical attacks, and the final number
of rounds is derived from an analysis of attack vectors that exploit the simple
algebraic structure. We remark that the designers chose the number of rounds
with a minimal security margin for efficiency. For a more detailed specification
and a summary of previous analysis, we refer to Sect. 2.3.

   Since its publication in 2016, MiMC has become the preferred choice for many
use cases that benefit from a low multiplication count or algebraic simplicity

Table 1. Various attacks on MiMC. In this representation, n denotes the block size (and key size). The unit for the attack complexity is usually the cost of a single encryption (number of multiplications over $\mathbb{F}_{2^n}$ necessary for a single encyption). The SK and KR attacks can be implemented using chosen plaintexts CP and/or chosen ciphertexts CC. The memory complexity is negligible for all approaches listed.

Type	n	Rounds	Time	Data	Source
KR*	129	38	$2^{65.5}$	$2^{60.2}$ CP	[41]
SK	129	80	2^{128} XOR	2^{128} CP/CC	Sect. 4.1
SK	n	$\lceil \log_3(2^{n-1} - 1) \rceil - 1$	2^{n-1} XOR	2^{n-1} CP/CC	Sect. 4.1
KK	129	160 ($\approx 2 \times$ full)	–	2^{128}	Sect. 4.3
KK	n	$2 \cdot \lceil \log_3(2^{n-1} - 1) \rceil - 2$	–	2^{n-1}	Sect. 4.3
KR	129	82 (full)	$2^{122.64}$	2^{128} CC	Sect. 5
KR	255	161 (full)	$2^{246.67}$	2^{254} CC	Sect. 5
KR	n	$\lceil n \cdot \log_3(2) \rceil$ (full)	$\leq 2^{n - \log_2(n) + 1}$	2^{n-1} CC	Sect. 5

KR $\equiv$ Key-Recovery, KR* $\equiv$ attack on a variant of MiMC proposed in a low-memory scenario, SK $\equiv$ Secret-Key Distinguisher, KK $\equiv$ Known-Key Distinguisher

[32,45]. It also serves as a baseline for various follow-up designs evaluated in the context of the public "STARK-Friendly Hash Challenge" competition[1].

1.1 Our Contribution

As the main results in this paper, we present

(1) a new upper bound for the algebraic degree growth in key-alternating ciphers with low-degree round functions,
(2) a secret-key higher-order distinguisher on almost full MiMC over $\mathbb{F}_{2^n}$,
(3) a known-key zero-sum distinguisher on almost double the rounds of MiMC,
(4) the first key-recovery attack on *full-round* MiMC over $\mathbb{F}_{2^n}$.

We also show that the technique we use for MiMC is sufficiently generic to apply to any permutation fulfilling specific properties, which we will define in detail. Our attacks and distinguishers on MiMC, as well as other attacks in the literature, are listed in Table 1.

Secret-Key Higher-Order Distinguishers. After recalling some preliminary facts about higher-order differentials, in Sect. 3 we analyze the growth of the algebraic degree for key-alternating ciphers whose round function can be described as a low-degree polynomial over $\mathbb{F}_{2^n}$.

For an SPN cipher over a field $\mathbb{F}$ where each round has algebraic degree δ, the algebraic degree of the cipher is expected to grow essentially exponentially in δ. Several analyses made in the literature [17,18,20] confirm this growth for most

---
[1] https://starkware.co/hash-challenge/.

ciphers, except when the algebraic degree of the function is close to its maximum. As a result, the number of rounds necessary for security against higher-order differential attacks generally grows logarithmically in the size of $\mathbb{F}$. Different behaviour has been observed for certain non-SPN designs, such as some designs with partial nonlinear layers where the algebraic degree grows exponentially in some (not necessarily integer) value smaller than δ [26].

In Sect. 3, we show that if the round function can be described as an invertible low-degree polynomial function in $\mathbb{F}_{2^n}$, then the algebraic degree grows linearly with the number of rounds, and not exponentially as generally expected. More precisely, let d denote the exponent of the power function $x \mapsto x^d$ used to define the S-boxes. Then, we show that in the case of key-alternating ciphers over $\mathbb{F}_{2^n}$, the algebraic degree $\delta(r)$ as a function in the number of rounds r is

$$\delta(r) \in \mathcal{O}(\log_2(d^r)) = \mathcal{O}(r).$$

As an immediate consequence, our observation implies that roughly $n \cdot \log_d(2)$ rounds are necessary to provide security against higher-order differential attacks, much more than the expected $\approx \log_\delta(n-1)$ rounds.

Distinguishers on MiMC over $\mathbb{F}_{2^n}$. Our new bounds on the number of rounds necessary to provide security against higher-order differential cryptanalysis have a major impact on key-alternating ciphers with large S-boxes. A concrete example for this class of ciphers is MiMC [3], a key-alternating cipher defined over $\mathbb{F}_{2^n}$ (for odd $n \in \mathbb{N}$), where the round function is simply defined as the cube map $x \mapsto x^3$. Since any cubic function over $\mathbb{F}_{2^n}$ has algebraic degree 2, one may expect that approximately $\log_2(n)$ rounds are necessary to prevent higher-order differential attacks. Our new bound implies that a much larger number of rounds is required to provide security, namely approximately $n \cdot \log_3(2)$.

As a concrete example, in Sect. 4 we show that MiMC-n/n has a security margin of only 1 or 2 rounds against (secret-key) higher-order distinguishers (depending on n), which is much smaller than expected by the designers. Moreover, we can set up a known-key distinguisher for approximately double the number of rounds of MiMC, by showing that the same number of rounds is necessary to reach the maximum degree in the decryption direction. Our findings have been practically verified on toy versions.

We remark that the designers presented other non-random properties (including GCD and interpolation attacks) that can cover a similar number of rounds. The number of rounds proposed by the designers were chosen in order to provide security against key-recovery attacks based on these properties. As we are going to show, the number of rounds is not sufficient against our new attack based on a higher-order differential property.

Results using the Division Property. For completeness, in Sect. 4.5 we search for higher-order distinguishers for MiMC-n/n with the division property [46] proposed by Todo at Eurocrypt 2015, a powerful tool for finding the best integral distinguishers for block ciphers. By modeling the most recently proposed variant of the bit-based division property, which is called *three-subset bit-based division property without unknown subset* in [34], we are able to reproduce exactly the same higher-order distinguishers for cases with small n-bit S-boxes, where $n \in \{5, 7, 9\}$. However, as far as we know, it is an open problem to model the three-subset bit-based division property for a larger S-box of size bigger than 9 in practical time. Therefore, we conclude that the division property is unlikely to help us for the ciphers we focus on.

Key-Recovery Attack on MiMC-n/n and on Generic Ciphers. A trivial way to extend an r-round distinguisher to an $(r + 1)$-round key-recovery attack is based on guessing the last round key, partially decrypting/encrypting, and finally exploiting the distinguisher to filter wrong key guesses. Unfortunately, this strategy does not work for MiMC, since guessing the full last round key required to invert the large S-box is equivalent to exhaustive key search. Another key-recovery approach that has been combined with integral distinguishers is based on interpolating the Boolean polynomials that define the final rounds. However, this strategy requires evaluating the distinguisher several times to collect enough equations, which is not feasible for our distinguisher due to its large data complexity.

In Sect. 5, we show how to solve this problem. Instead of guessing the last round key, we set up an equation over $\mathbb{F}_{2^n}$ with the master key as a variable. To obtain this equation, we symbolically express the zero sum at the input to the last round as a polynomial function of the key, whose coefficients depend on the queried ciphertexts. We show how the resulting polynomial equation can be solved efficiently to recover the key. As a result, in the chosen-ciphertext case only, recovering the key from this data for the *full* n-bit version of MiMC takes the equivalent of less than $2^{n-\log_2(n)+1}$ calls to MiMC, 2^{n-1} chosen ciphertexts, and negligible amounts of memory. Moreover, we show that approximately $\lceil \log_3(2 \cdot R) \rceil$ more rounds (where $R = \lceil n \cdot \log_3(2) \rceil$ is the current number of rounds of MiMC-n/n) can be necessary and sufficient to restore the security against the key-recovery attack presented here. This would, for example, imply that we need to add 5 more rounds for the most used version MiMC-129/129 (which currently has 82 rounds).

A Generic Strategy. Our strategy is an instance of a broader class of algebraic key-recovery approaches based on solving equations in the key variables. As such, it shares some ideas with other algebraic approaches like optimized interpolation attacks. However, while most algebraic key-recovery approaches of the last years construct and solve systems of many Boolean linear equations, we use a single univariate equation of higher degree that can be solved with polynomial factoring algorithms such as Berlekamp's algorithm. In Sect. 6, we outline a more detailed and generic procedure for such an attack. It is interesting to note that a comparatively old technique which basically disappeared for the cryptanalysis of AES-like ciphers turns out to be very competitive for schemes with large S-boxes.

2   Preliminaries

In this section, we recall the most important results about polynomial representations of Boolean functions and summarize the currently best known results regarding the growth of the algebraic degree in the context of SP networks. We also provide the specification of MiMC and give an overview of previous cryptanalytic results.

We emphasize that in general it is only possible to give a *lower* bound regarding the number of rounds which we can attack using higher-order differential techniques, in the following denoted as "necessary number of rounds to provide security". While upper-bounding the algebraic degree is more important from an adversary's point of view, lower bounds on the degree are much more relevant when arguing about security against algebraic attacks (such as e.g. [24,38,40,49]) from a designer's viewpoint. However, at the current state of the art and to the best of our knowledge, it seems hard to find such a lower bound for a given cipher without investigating concrete instances experimentally – which, of course, limits the scope of any analysis.

2.1 Polynomial Representations over Binary Extension Fields

We denote addition (and subtraction) in binary extension fields by the symbol $\oplus$. For $n \in \mathbb{N}$, every function $F : \mathbb{F}_{2^n} \to \mathbb{F}_{2^n}$ can be uniquely represented by an n-tuple $(F_1, F_2, \ldots, F_n)$ of polynomials over $\mathbb{F}_2$ in n variables with a maximum degree of 1 in each variable. In this representation, F_i is of the form

$$F_i(X_1, \ldots, X_n) = \bigoplus_{u=(u_1,\ldots,u_n)\in\{0,1\}^n} \varphi_i(u) \cdot X_1^{u_1} \cdots \cdot X_n^{u_n}, \tag{1}$$

where the coefficients $\varphi_i(u)$ can be computed by the *Moebius transform*.

As is common, we denote functions $F : \mathbb{F}_2^n \to \mathbb{F}_2$ as *Boolean functions* and functions of the form $F : \mathbb{F}_2^n \to \mathbb{F}_2^m$, for $n, m \in \mathbb{N}$, as *vectorial Boolean functions*.

Definition 1. *The algebraic normal form (ANF) of a Boolean function $F : \mathbb{F}_2^n \to \mathbb{F}_2$, as given in Eq. (1), is the unique representation as a polynomial over $\mathbb{F}_2$ in n variables and with a maximum univariate degree of 1. The algebraic degree $\delta(F)$ of F – or δ for simplicity – is the degree of the above representation of F as a multivariate polynomial over $\mathbb{F}_2$. If $G : \mathbb{F}_2^n \to \mathbb{F}_2^n$ is a vectorial Boolean function and $(G_1, \ldots, G_n)$ is its representation as an n-tuple of multivariate polynomials over $\mathbb{F}_2$, then its algebraic degree $\delta(G)$ is defined as $\delta(G) := \max_{1\le i\le n} \delta(G_i)$.*

The link between the algebraic degree and the univariate degree of a vectorial Boolean function is well-known, and is for example established in [22]: the algebraic degree of $F : \mathbb{F}_{2^n} \to \mathbb{F}_{2^n}$ can be computed from its univariate polynomial representation, and is equal to the maximum hamming weight of the 2-ary expansion of its exponents.

Lemma 1. *Let $F : \mathbb{F}_{2^n} \to \mathbb{F}_{2^n}$ be a function and let $F(X) = \sum_{i=0}^{2^n-1} \varphi_i \cdot X^i$ denote the corresponding univariate polynomial description over $\mathbb{F}_{2^n}$. The algebraic degree $\delta(F)$ of F as a vectorial Boolean function is the maximum hamming weight[2] of its exponents, i.e., it is $\delta(F) = \max_{0\le i\le 2^n-1} \{\mathrm{hw}(i) \mid \varphi_i \ne 0\}$.*

---

[2] Given $x = \sum_{i=0}^{\chi} x_i \cdot 2^i$ for $x_i \in \{0, 1\}$, the hamming weight of x is $\mathrm{hw}(x) = \sum_{i=0}^{\chi} x_i$.

2.2   Higher-Order Differential Cryptanalysis

Higher-order differential attacks [38,40] form a prominent class of attacks exploiting the low algebraic degree of a nonlinear transformation such as a classical block cipher. If this degree is sufficiently low, an attack using multiple input texts and their corresponding output texts can be mounted. In more detail, if the algebraic degree of a Boolean function f is δ, then, when applying f to all elements of an affine vector space $\mathcal{V} \oplus c$ of dimension greater than δ and taking the sum of these values, the result is 0, i.e., $\bigoplus_{v \in \mathcal{V} \oplus c} f(v) = 0$.

Security Against Higher-Order Differential Attacks – State of the Art.
To prevent higher-order differential attacks against iterated block ciphers, one would usually want the maximum algebraic degree to be reached (well) within the suggested number of rounds. To achieve this goal, and to assess the security margins, it is crucial to estimate how the algebraic degree grows with the number of rounds.

The algebraic degree of composing two functions, $F, G : \mathbb{F}_2^n \to \mathbb{F}_2^n$, can be generically bounded by

$$\deg(F \circ G) \le \deg(F) \cdot \deg(G), \tag{2}$$

and hence an upper bound is found by iterative use of this on the round function. The resulting bound does, however, fail to reflect the real growth of the algebraic degree for many cryptosystems, and the problem of estimating the growth has been widely studied in the literature. After the initial work of Canteaut and Videau [20], a tighter upper bound was presented by Boura, Canteaut, and De Cannière [18] at FSE'11. There, the authors show how to deduce a new bound for the algebraic degree of iterated permutations for a special category of SP networks over $(\mathbb{F}_{2^n})^t$, which includes functions that have a number $t \ge 1$ of balanced S-boxes as their nonlinear layer. Specifically, the authors show that the algebraic degree of the considered SP network grows almost exponentially, except when it is close to its maximum.

Proposition 1 ([18]). *Let F be a function from $\mathbb{F}_2^N$ to $\mathbb{F}_2^N$ corresponding to the concatenation of t smaller S-boxes $S_1, \ldots, S_t$ defined over $\mathbb{F}_2^n$. Then, for any function G from $\mathbb{F}_2^N$ to $\mathbb{F}_2^N$, we have*

$$\deg(G \circ F(\cdot)) \le \min\left\{ \deg(F) \cdot \deg(G), N - \frac{N - \deg(G)}{\gamma} \right\}, \text{ where} \tag{3}$$

$$\gamma = \max_{i=1,\ldots,n-1} \frac{n-i}{n-\delta_i} \le n-1, \tag{4}$$

and where δ_i is the maximum degree of the product of any i coordinates of any of the smaller S-boxes.

Thus, the number of rounds necessary to prevent higher-order differential attacks is in general bigger than the one obtained using the trivial bound in Eq. (2).

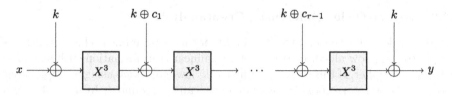

Fig. 1. The MiMC encryption function with r rounds.

2.3   Specification and Previous Analysis of MiMC

MiMC [3] is a key-alternating n-bit block cipher, where in each round the same n-bit key is added to the state. The nonlinear component of the construction is the evaluation of the cube function $f(x) = x^3$ over $\mathbb{F}_{2^n}$. Additionally, a different round constant is added in each round to break symmetries, where the first round constant is 0. The total number of rounds is then

$$r = \lceil n \cdot \log_3(2) \rceil,$$

and we refer to Fig. 1 for a graphical representation of the encryption function.

MiMC is defined to work over prime fields and binary fields. In this paper, we focus on the binary field versions of MiMC[3], for which the block size n has to be odd in order for the S-box to be a permutation.

MiMC:Related Attacks in the Literature. The designers recommend MiMC with $\lceil n \cdot \log_3(2) \rceil$ rounds [3]. They derive this number of rounds by considering a variety of different key-recovery attacks on MiMC. According to their analysis, the most powerful attacks are interpolation [36] and GCD attacks. About higher-order differential attacks, the authors claim that *"the large number of rounds ensures that the algebraic degree of MiMC in its native field will be maximum or almost maximum. This naturally thwarts higher-order differential attacks [...]"*.

The first attack on MiMC-n/n [41], presented at SAC 2019, targets a reduced-round version of MiMC proposed by the designers for a scenario in which the attacker has only limited memory, but it does not affect the security claims of full-round MiMC. The Feistel version of MiMC was attacked shortly after, by using generic properties of the used Feistel construction instead of exploiting properties of the primitive itself [16]. Finally, a specific attack on MiMC using Gröbner bases was considered in [1]. The authors state that by introducing a new intermediate variable in each round, the resulting multivariate system of equations is already a Gröbner basis and thus the first step of a Gröbner basis attack is for free. However, recovering univariate polynomials from this representation and then applying techniques like the GCD attack will result in a prohibitively large computational complexity, since the recovered polynomials will be of degree $\approx 3^r$ after r rounds. Hence, the authors conclude that MiMC cannot be attacked directly by using known Gröbner basis techniques.

---

[3] Since the only subspaces of $\mathbb{F}_p$, where p is a prime number, are $\{0\}$ and $\mathbb{F}_p$ itself, our attack does not affect the security of MiMC over prime fields.

3   Higher-Order Differentials of Key-Alternating Ciphers

Our bound on the growth of the algebraic degree does not depend on the cubing of the round function in MiMC, so we introduce the following generalization of the result on MiMC from Sect. 2.3.

3.1   Setting

Let $E_k^r : \mathbb{F}_{2^n} \to \mathbb{F}_{2^n}$ be a key-alternating cipher defined by

$$E_k^r(x) := k_r \oplus R(\cdots R(k_1 \oplus R(k_0 \oplus x))\cdots) \tag{5}$$

over $r \geq 1$ rounds, where $k_0, k_1, \ldots, k_r \in \mathbb{F}_{2^n}$ are derived from a master key $k \in \mathbb{F}_{2^n}$ using a key schedule. Each round function $R : \mathbb{F}_{2^n} \to \mathbb{F}_{2^n}$ is defined as some invertible univariate polynomial function

$$R(x) := \rho_0 \oplus \bigoplus_{i=1}^{d} \rho_i \cdot x^i \tag{6}$$

of univariate degree $d \geq 3$, where $\rho_i \in \mathbb{F}_{2^n}$ and $\rho_d \neq 0$. We will, without loss of generality, assume $d \leq d_{\text{inv}}$, where d_{inv} denotes the degree of the compositional inverse of R (otherwise, an attacker would target the decryption function instead). Furthemore, we assume that the round function has *low* univariate degree, i.e., low compared to the size of $\mathbb{F}_{2^n}$. In other words, we work with $d \ll 2^n - 1$.

3.2   Growth of the Degree

In this section, we show that the algebraic degree δ of a key-alternating cipher E_k^r grows much slower than commonly presented in the literature. More precisely, in some cases it can grow linearly in the number of rounds and not exponentially.

Proposition 2. *Let E_k^r be a an r-round key-alternating block cipher with a round function R of degree d, as defined in Eq. (5). If $r \leq \mathcal{R}_{lin} - 1$, where*

$$\mathcal{R}_{lin} = \lceil \log_d(2^{n-1} - 1) \rceil \approx (n-1) \cdot \log_d(2), \tag{7}$$

then the algebraic degree δ of E_k^r is at most $n - 2$. Then, a (secret-key) higher-order distinguisher using at most 2^{n-1} data can be applied to E_k^r.[4]

Proof. Due to the relation between the word-level degree and the algebraic degree, E_k^r reaches its maximum algebraic degree of $n - 1$ if at least one monomial with the exponent $2^n - 2^j - 1$ (for $0 \leq j < n$) appears in the polynomial representation. Indeed, note that all these monomials have an algebraic degree of $n - 1$. Since the smallest exponent of this form is $2^n - 2^{n-1} - 1 = 2^{n-1} - 1$,

---

[4] We denote our bound by $\mathcal{R}_{\text{lin}}$ to indicate the almost linear growth of the algebraic degree for this specific class of constructions.

and since the degree of E_k^r after r rounds is at most d^r, we require $d^r \geq 2^{n-1} - 1$ to make $x^{2^{n-1}-1}$ appear, or equivalently,

$$r \geq \lceil \log_d(2^{n-1} - 1) \rceil.$$

Hence, the degree is not maximal for $r < \lceil \log_d(2^{n-1} - 1) \rceil$ and a higher-order distinguisher using at most 2^{n-1} data can be applied.   □

The Difficulty of Lower-Bounding the Growth of the Degree. We point out that it is always possible to set up a (secret-key) higher-order distinguisher if the number of rounds is smaller than $\mathcal{R}_{\text{lin}}$. However, a number of rounds greater than or equal to $\mathcal{R}_{\text{lin}}$ does not necessarily provide security.

One of the main problems in order to derive a sufficient condition for the number of rounds that provides security is the difficulty of analyzing the non-vanishing coefficients in the polynomial representation of E_k^r. Note, in general it is not easy to give a condition guaranteeing that a particular monomial appears, since many factors (including the secret key, the constant addition, and the details of the S-box) influence the result.

Without going into the details, we consider the influence of the S-box in some concrete examples. Working with $R(x) = x^d$ for a certain $3 \leq d \leq 2^n - 2$ (where $d \neq 2^{d'}$ for $d' \in \mathbb{N}$), we focus for simplicity only on two extreme cases $d = 2^{d'} \pm 1$. By exploiting Lucas's Theorem[5]:

- If $d = 2^{d'} + 1$ for some $d' \in \mathbb{N}$, then the output of a single round is sparse:

$$(x \oplus y)^{2^{d'}+1} = x^{2^{d'}+1} \oplus x^{2^{d'}} \cdot y \oplus y^{2^{d'}} \cdot x \oplus y^{2^{d'}+1}$$

(note that it contains only 4 terms instead of $d + 1 = 2^{d'} + 2$).
- If $d = 2^{d'} - 1$ for some $d' \in \mathbb{N}$, then the output of a single round is full, since

$$(x \oplus y)^{2^{d'}-1} = \bigoplus_{i=0}^{2^{d'}-1} x^i \cdot y^{2^{d'}-1-i}.$$

Even if a single round is not sparse, the output of several combined rounds is not guaranteed to be full (even if it is in general dense). As a concrete example, while the output of $(x \oplus k_0)^3 \oplus k_1$ is full, the same is not true for

$$\begin{aligned}
((x \oplus k_0)^3 \oplus k_1)^3 \oplus k_2 &= x^9 \oplus x^8 \cdot k_0 \oplus x^6 \cdot k_1 \oplus x^4 \cdot k_0^2 \cdot k_1 \oplus x^3 \cdot k_1^2 \\
&\oplus x^2 \cdot (k_0 \cdot k_1^2 \oplus k_0^2 \cdot k_1^2 \oplus k_0^4 \cdot k_1) \oplus x \cdot k_0^8 \oplus c(k_0, k_1, k_2),
\end{aligned} \tag{8}$$

where both x^5 and x^7 are missing, and where $c(k_0, k_1, k_2)$ is a function that depends only on the keys. This simple example emphasizes the difficulty of analyzing the sparsity of the polynomial that defines E_k.

---

[5] By Lucas's Theorem, $\binom{n}{m} \equiv \prod_{i=0}^{k} \binom{n_i}{m_i}$ (mod 2), it follows that where $n = \sum_{i=0}^{k} n_i \cdot 2^i$ and $m = \sum_{i=0}^{k} m_i \cdot 2^i$ is the 2-ary expansion of n and m, respectively.

3.3   Comparison with Other Bounds

We now compare the new number of rounds necessary to provide security against secret-key higher-order distinguishers with other possible bounds. An alternative strategy is to apply generic bounds focusing on the algebraic degree of the round function, as recalled in Proposition 1. Recall that $\mathcal{R}_{\text{lin}}$ is the number of rounds from Proposition 2, and we will denote the number of round based on generic bounds by $\mathcal{R}_{\text{gen}}$. The comparison will make use of $\delta_{\text{lin}}(r)$, the upper bound on the algebraic degree after r rounds following Proposition 2. The upper bound from Eq. (3) will be denoted by $\delta_{\text{gen}}(r)$. Note that $\delta_{\text{gen}}(r)$ can, for example, take advantage of a slower growth in the algebraic degree, as in Eq. (8) by considering two rounds instead of one. Despite this, the overall trend of $\delta_{\text{gen}}(r)$ will still be exponential. On the other hand, if the round function can be described by a polynomial of low univariate degree d over $\mathbb{F}_{2^n}$, we expect a linear behaviour in $\delta_{\text{lin}}(r)$:

$$\delta_{\text{lin}}(r) \leq \lfloor \log_2(d^r + 1) \rfloor \approx r \cdot \log_2(d).$$

As a result, the round numbers $\mathcal{R}_{\text{lin}}$ and $\mathcal{R}_{\text{gen}}$ *necessary* to provide security grow respectively linearly and logarithmically in the size n of the field, namely

$$\mathcal{R}_{\text{lin}} \in \mathcal{O}(n) \qquad \text{and} \qquad \mathcal{R}_{\text{gen}} \in \mathcal{O}(\log_\delta(n)).$$

A concrete comparison of $\delta_{\text{lin}}(r)$ and $\delta_{\text{gen}}(r)$ for MiMC-129/129 is given in Fig. 2. In this setting we have $\delta_{\text{lin}}(r) = \lfloor \log_2(3^r + 1) \rfloor$, and $\delta_{\text{gen}}(r)$ has been derived using the observation that two rounds of MiMC have algebraic degree two (see [28, App. A] for more details). In particular, we find $\mathcal{R}_{\text{gen}} = 13$ and $\mathcal{R}_{\text{lin}} = 81$.

Remark. We emphasize that every (invertible) S-box/round function in $\mathbb{F}_2^n$ can be rewritten as a polynomial over $\mathbb{F}_{2^n}$. The crucial point here is that given a "random" S-box/round function over $\mathbb{F}_2^n$, the corresponding polynomial over $\mathbb{F}_{2^n}$ has in general a high univariate degree (e.g., $d \approx 2^n - \varepsilon$ for some small ε). In such a case, even if our argument still holds, the final result becomes meaningless, since $\log_d(2^n - 1) \approx \log_{2^n - \varepsilon}(2^n - 1) \approx 1$ is basically constant (i.e., it does not grow linearly with n). Hence, our results turn out to be relevant only for S-boxes/round functions for which the corresponding polynomial over $\mathbb{F}_{2^n}$ has "small" degree (namely, small compared to the field size, i.e., $d \ll 2^n$).

4   Distinguishers for Reduced-Round and Full MiMC

Exploiting the previous result, we now discuss the possibility to set up higher-order differential distinguishers and attacks on MiMC [3]. We show that

(1) MiMC has a security margin of only 1 or 2 round(s) against (secret-key) higher-order distinguishers, depending on n, and that
(2) a zero-sum known-key distinguisher can be set up for approximately double the number of rounds of MiMC.

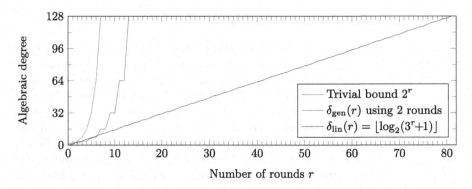

Fig. 2. Different upper bounds of the growth of the algebraic degree for MiMC-129/129. The trivial bound is 2^r. A tighter bound, $\delta_{\text{gen}}(r)$, exploits the observation that 2 rounds only have degree 2 (see Eq. (8)). Our new bound, $\delta_{\text{lin}}(r)$, is linear in the number of rounds.

4.1   Secret-Key Higher-Order Distinguisher for MiMC

The results just presented allow to set up a nontrivial (secret-key) higher-order distinguisher on $\lceil \log_3(2^{n-1} - 1) \rceil - 1$ rounds of MiMC, where $\lceil \log_3(2^{n-1} - 1) \rceil - 1 < \lceil n \cdot \log_3(2) \rceil$ for all n. Consequently, the security margin is reduced to

$$1 \le \lceil n \cdot \log_3(2) \rceil - \left(\lceil \log_3(2^{n-1} - 1) \rceil - 1 \right) \le 2$$

rounds. To give some concrete examples, MiMC has 1 round of security margin for $n \in \{33, 63, 255\}$, and 2 rounds of security margin for $n \in \{31, 65, 127, 129\}$.

4.2   Practical Results

In this section we compare the results from Proposition 2 with practical results from scaled-down versions of MiMC. The tests[6] have been performed in the following way: Instead of computing the ANF of a keyed permutation (which is expensive even for small field sizes), we evaluate the higher-order differential zero-sum property (as given in Sect. 2.2) for a specific input vector space. Namely, for random keys, random constants, and an input subspace of dimension $n - 1$, we look for the minimum number of rounds r for which the corresponding sum of the ciphertexts is different from zero. Such a number corresponds to the number of rounds necessary to prevent higher-order distinguishers. In order to avoid the influence of weak keys or round constants, we repeated the tests multiple times (with new random keys and round constants). The practical number of rounds we give in each row is *the smallest number of rounds among all tested keys and round constants necessary* to prevent higher-order distinguishers. This means that a potentially higher number of rounds can be attacked by choosing the keys and round constants in a particular way.

---

[6] The source code for the attacks and the tests is available on https://github.com/IAIK/mimc-analysis.

Table 2. Theoretical and practical round numbers *necessary* to prevent higher-order distinguishers for MiMC over $\mathbb{F}_{2^n}$.

Param.	Theoretical		Practical
n	$\mathcal{R}_{\text{lin}}$	$\mathcal{R}_{\text{gen}}$	$\mathcal{R}$
7	4	5	5
9	6	5	6
11	7	7	7
13	8	7	9
15	9	7	10
17	11	7	11
33	21	9	21
65	41	11	-
129	81	13	-

The results, denoted $\mathcal{R}$, are given in Table 2. We also present $\mathcal{R}_{\text{lin}}$ (from Proposition 2) and $\mathcal{R}_{\text{gen}}$ (see [28, App. A]) for comparison. We emphasize that the theoretical values predicted by $\mathcal{R}_{\text{lin}}$ match the practical results in about half of the cases, and are off by at most one.

4.3 Known-Key Zero-Sum Distinguisher for MiMC

A known-key distinguisher is a scenario introduced in [39] where the attacker knows the key, and it is important in all settings in which no secret material is present. To succeed, the attacker has to discover some property of the attacked cipher that holds with a probability higher than for an ideal cipher, or is believed to be hard to exhibit generically. The goal of a known-key zero-sum distinguisher is to find a set of plaintexts and ciphertexts whose sums are equal to zero. To do this, the idea is to exploit the inside-out approach. By choosing a subspace of texts $\mathcal{V}$, one simply defines the plaintexts as the r_{dec}-round decryption of $\mathcal{V}$ and the ciphertexts as the r_{enc}-round encryption of $\mathcal{V}$. Such a distinguisher can then cover $r_{\text{enc}} + r_{\text{dec}}$ rounds. Examples of this approach are given in the literature for KECCAK [7,10,18], Luffa [7,18], or PHOTON [50].

In the case of MiMC, the idea is to choose $\mathcal{V}$ as a subspace of $\mathbb{F}_{2^n}$ of dimension $n - 1$. The maximum number of encryption rounds r_{enc} for which it is possible to guarantee a zero sum has been given in the previous paragraph. Based on Sect. 4.2, we can set up a known-key distinguisher on (more than) full MiMC-n/n. For our distinguisher on MiMC, we first recall the following result from [17].

Proposition 3 (Corollary 3 of [17]). *Let F be a permutation of $\mathbb{F}_2^n$. Then, $\deg(F^{-1}) = n - 1$ if and only if $\deg(F) = n - 1$.*

Corollary 1. *Let r_{enc} be the number of rounds necessary for MiMC over $\mathbb{F}_{2^n}$ to reach its maximum algebraic degree in the encryption direction. The same* *number of rounds is necessary for reaching the maximum algebraic degree in the decryption direction, i.e., $r_{dec} = r_{enc} = \lceil \log_3(2^{n-1} - 1) \rceil$.*

It follows that, given a subspace $\mathcal{V} \subseteq \mathbb{F}_{2^n}$ of dimension $n - 1$, the sums of the corresponding texts after $r_{\text{dec}} - 1$ decryption rounds and $r_{\text{enc}} - 1$ encryption rounds are always equal to zero, i.e.,

$$\underbrace{\bigoplus_{w \in \mathcal{V} \oplus v} R^{-(r_{\text{dec}}-1)}(w) = 0}_{\text{Zero sum}} \xleftarrow{R^{-(r_{\text{dec}}-1)}} \mathcal{V} \oplus v \xrightarrow{R^{r_{\text{enc}}-1}} 0 = \underbrace{\bigoplus_{w \in \mathcal{V} \oplus v} R^{r_{\text{enc}}-1}(w)}_{\text{Zero sum}}$$

for each $v \in \mathbb{F}_{2^n}$. Hence, a known-key zero-sum distinguisher can be set up for

$$2 \cdot (\lceil \log_3(2^{n-1} - 1) \rceil - 1) \approx 2(n-1) \cdot \log_3(2) - 2 =$$
$$= \underbrace{n \cdot \log_3(2)}_{= \text{full MiMC}} + [(n-2) \cdot \log_3(2) - 2]$$

rounds of MiMC-n/n, which is much more than *full* MiMC-n/n.

4.4   Impact of the Known-Key Distinguisher on Full MiMC

Sponge Function. In [3], the authors propose a hash function by instantiating a sponge construction with MiMC$^\pi$, a fixed-key version of MiMC. The sponge hash function is indifferentiable from a random oracle up to $2^{c/2}$ calls to the internal permutation P (where c is the capacity) if P is modeled as a randomly chosen permutation [9]. Thus, even if it is not strictly necessary, it is desirable that MiMC is resistant against known-key distinguishers.

For completeness, we mention that even if there is a way to distinguish a permutation from a random one, it seems difficult to exploit a zero-sum distinguisher of the internal permutation of a sponge construction in order to attack the hash function. To give a concrete example, consider the case of KECCAK: As a consequence of the zero-sum distinguisher found on 18-round KECCAK-f[1600], the number of rounds has been increased from 18 to 24 in the second round of the SHA-3 competition in order to avoid "non-ideal" properties (see [10, 18] for more details). However, the best known attack on the KECCAK hash function can only be set up when using 6-/7-round KECCAK-f [33].

In any case, we remark that such distinguishers based on zero sums cannot be set up for an arbitrary number of rounds, and they do indeed exploit the internal properties of a primitive using the inside-out approach found in this paper and in other literature. Hence, they cannot be considered meaningless.

Other Approaches. Even though the original MiMC paper only specifies a sponge-based hash function using MiMC, there are various applications and/or specific considerations that would make a block-cipher-based approach more advantageous (like, for example, being forced to use a block size which is too small for a sponge-based approach). Another way to turn a block cipher into a hash function is to use a compression function like the Davies–Meyer one together with something like the Merkle–Damgård construction. Similar to the case of sponge constructions, the security of such an algorithm is proven in the ideal cipher model [12]. This choice is, however, not supported by the MiMC designers, who use our results to support their advice against using a block-cipher-based approach (even though such implementations can still be found[7]). It follows that, since the attacker has control of the key in such scenarios, it is desirable for MiMC to be resistant against known- and chosen-key distinguishers, even if it does not seem to be strictly necessary.

4.5   Results Using the Division Property

Finally, in [28, App. C] we present our practical results obtained using "Mixed Integer Linear Programming (MILP)", which models the propagation of the (conventional) bit-based division property.

The (conventional) bit-based division property [48] was proposed to investigate integral characteristics of block ciphers at a bit level. With this approach, the integral property of each bit is studied independently. Naturally, this strategy allows to capture more information of the propagation than the word-level version, and thus integral characteristics for more rounds can be found with this new technique. For example, the integral distinguishers of SIMON32 have been improved from 10 rounds [46] (the current best result at word level) to 14 rounds [52] (obtained by the experimental method cited before).

Instead of separating the parity into the two cases "0" and "unknown" as for the (conventional) bit-based division property, three-subset bit-based division property [48] was introduced to enhance the accuracy of the conventional one, where the parity is separated into three sets, i.e., "0", "1", and "unknown". It shows that the three-subset bit-based division property can indeed be more accurate than the two-subset bit-based division property for some ciphers [35,53]. However, it becomes harder to efficiently model the three-subset division property propagation even for ciphers with simple structures. Recently, [34] pointed out that the three-subset division property has a couple of known problems when applied to cube attacks, and proposed a modified three-subset bit-based division without the "unknown" set to overcome these problems. By modeling this modified version of the three-subset bit-based division property for our cases with small n-bit S-boxes, where $n \in \{5, 7, 9\}$, we confirm the practical results given in Table 2.

However, as far as we know, it is still an open problem to model the (modified) three-subset bit-based division property for a larger S-box of size bigger than 9. The S-boxes we focus on in this paper can be described as a (low-degree) polynomial function in $\mathbb{F}_{2^n}$, where n is much larger than 9. Therefore, *the division property, which is commonly believed as the most efficient tool to find the best integral distinguishers, might not help us as much for the ciphers we focus on.*

---

[7] https://github.com/HarryR/ethsnarks/blob/master/src/gadgets/mimc.hpp.

5   Key-Recovery Attack on MiMC

Since the security margin of MiMC with respect to a (secret-key) higher-order distinguisher is of only 1 or 2 round(s) depending on n, it is potentially possible to extend a distinguisher to a key-recovery attack. Given a subspace $\mathcal{V}$ of plaintexts whose sum is equal to zero after r rounds, we can consider $r+1$ rounds, partially guess the last subkey and decrypt, and filter wrong key guesses that do not satisfy the zero sum:

$$\mathcal{V} \oplus v \xrightarrow{R^r(\cdot)} \underbrace{\bigoplus_{w \in \mathcal{V} \oplus v} R^r(w) = 0}_{\text{Higher-order distinguisher}} \xleftarrow[\text{Key guessing}]{R^{-1}(\cdot)} \underbrace{\{R^{r+1}(w) \mid w \in \mathcal{V} \oplus v\}}_{\text{Ciphertexts}}.$$

However, since the subkeys of MiMC are equal to the master key plus constants, and due to the single full-state S-box, even a (partial) decryption of a single round requires guessing the full key. As a result, a key-recovery attack on full MiMC based on this strategy seems infeasible.

In this section, we present an alternative strategy that allows to break full-round MiMC. Since a trivial key-guessing approach is inefficient, our idea is to construct a polynomial of low degree, which we can then try to solve.

5.1   Strategy of the Attack

From Proposition 2 and Proposition 3, a zero sum can be set up for at least $\lceil (n-1)\log_3(2) \rceil - 1 = \lceil n \log_3(2) \rceil - \varepsilon$ rounds in the encryption and decryption direction with a vector space $\mathcal{V} \oplus v$ of dimension $n-1$, where $\varepsilon \in \{1, 2\}$. Recalling that $\lceil n \cdot \log_3(2) \rceil$ is the number of rounds of full MiMC, we define $r_{\mathrm{ZS}}, r_{\mathrm{KR}}$ as

$$r_{\mathrm{ZS}} = \lceil (n-1)\log_3(2) \rceil - 1 \quad \text{and} \quad r_{\mathrm{KR}} = 1 + (\lceil n \log_3(2) \rceil - \lceil (n-1)\log_3(2) \rceil),$$

where r_{ZS} is the number of rounds that we can cover with a zero sum, $r_{\mathrm{KR}} = \lceil n \cdot \log_3(2) \rceil - r_{\mathrm{ZS}} \in \{1, 2\}$.

Let $f^r(x, K)$ be the function corresponding to r rounds of $\mathrm{MiMC}_k(\cdot)$ (and $f^{-r}(x, K)$ be r rounds of decryption, $\mathrm{MiMC}_k^{-1}(\cdot)$), where x is the input text and K is a symbolic variable that represents the secret key k. We intend to use these functions to create a polynomial from which we can deduce k. More precisely, for a fixed vector space $\mathcal{V} \oplus v$, we consider the equations

$$\underbrace{\bigoplus_{x \in \mathrm{MiMC}_k^{-1}(\mathcal{V} \oplus v)} f^{r_{\mathrm{KR}}}(x, K) = 0}_{= F(K)} \quad \text{and} \quad \underbrace{\bigoplus_{x \in \mathrm{MiMC}_k(\mathcal{V} \oplus v)} f^{-r_{\mathrm{KR}}}(x, K) = 0}_{= G(K)}. \quad (9)$$

After having received all x values from an oracle, the attacker can construct one of the polynomials $F(K) = 0$ or $G(K) = 0$. The secret key k can now be determined by finding the roots of either of these polynomials.

In the case of MiMC, the degree of a single encryption round is 3, while the degree of a single decryption round is $(2^{n+1} - 1)/3$ (which is significantly larger than 3 for large n). Due to the slow degree growth in the encryption direction of MiMC, we will focus on finding the roots of $F(K)$ given in Eq. (9).

Finding the Roots of Univariate Polynomials. Let $F(X) \in \mathbb{F}_{2^n}[X]/\langle X^{2^n} + X \rangle$ be a univariate polynomial of degree D. Furthermore, let $M(D)$ denote a number such that multiplying two polynomials of degree $\leq D$ over $\mathbb{F}_{2^n}$ requires $\mathcal{O}(M(D))$ operations in $\mathbb{F}_{2^n}$. For instance, a straightforward method would yield $M(D) = D^2$, whereas $M(D) = D \cdot \log(D) \cdot \log\log(D)$ holds for methods based on fast Fourier transforms [21]. The *Berlekamp algorithm* for determining the roots of F is then expected to require $\mathcal{C} \in \mathcal{O}(M(D)\log(D)\log(2^n D))$ operations in $\mathbb{F}_{2^n}$ (see [29, Chapter 14.5]).

5.2 Details of the Attack

Assume $\mathcal{V} \oplus v$ is a coset of a subspace $\mathcal{V}$ of dimension $n - 1$. We define

$$\mathcal{W} = \text{MiMC}_k^{-1}(\mathcal{V} \oplus v) \equiv \{\text{MiMC}_k^{-1}(x) \in \mathbb{F}_{2^n} \mid x \in \mathcal{V} \oplus v\}$$

under a fixed secret key k. Here, we present the details of the attack for the cases $r_{\text{KR}} = 1$ and $r_{\text{KR}} = 2$, and we analyze the computational cost. We introduce the following notation:

$$\forall d \in \mathbb{N}: \qquad \mathscr{P}_d := \bigoplus_{x \in \mathcal{W}} x^d, \tag{10}$$

and whenever possible we will make use of the fact that squaring is a linear operation over $\mathbb{F}_{2^n}$. More specifically, computing $\mathscr{P}_{2d}$ only requires a single squaring operation once $\mathscr{P}_d$ is calculated:

$$\mathscr{P}_{2d} := \bigoplus_{x \in \mathcal{W}} x^{2d} = \left(\bigoplus_{x \in \mathcal{W}} x^d\right)^2 = \mathscr{P}_d^2. \tag{11}$$

This allows to reduce the total number of XOR operations.

Case: $r_{\text{KR}} = 1$. Since a single round of MiMC is described by $(x \oplus k)^3 = k^3 \oplus k^2 \cdot x \oplus k \cdot x^2 \oplus x^3$, the function $F(K)$ is given by

$$F(K) = K^2 \cdot \mathscr{P}_1 \oplus K \cdot \mathscr{P}_2 \oplus \mathscr{P}_3.$$

A complete pseudo code of the attack can be found in Algorithm 1, which makes it easy to see that the cost of the attack is well approximated by

- $|\mathcal{V}| = 2^{n-1}$ multiplications,
- $|\mathcal{V}| = 2^{n-1} + 1$ squarings,
- $2 \cdot |\mathcal{V}| + 1 = 2^n + 1$ n-bit XOR operations,
- cost of finding the roots of a univariate polynomial of degree 2.

Algorithm 1: Attack on MiMC – Case: $r_{\mathrm{KR}} = 1$.

Input: Vector subspace $\mathcal{V}$ of ciphertexts of dimension $\dim(\mathcal{V}) = n - 1$.
Output: Secret key k.

1   $\mathscr{P}_1, \mathscr{P}_2, \mathscr{P}_3 \leftarrow 0$.
2   **for** $x \in \mathcal{V} \oplus v$ **do**
3      $p \leftarrow \mathrm{MiMC}_k^{-1}(x)$ from the decryption oracle.
4      $\mathscr{P}_1 \leftarrow \mathscr{P}_1 \oplus p$.
5      $q \leftarrow p^2$.
6      $\mathscr{P}_3 \leftarrow \mathscr{P}_3 \oplus q \cdot p$.
7   $\mathscr{P}_2 \leftarrow (\mathscr{P}_1)^2$.
8   $F(K) = \mathscr{P}_1 \cdot K^2 \oplus \mathscr{P}_2 \cdot K \oplus \mathscr{P}_3$.
9   Find a solution k of $F(K) = 0$ – see Section 5.1 (filter multiple solutions by brute force).
10 **return** k.

Case: $r_{\mathrm{KR}} = 2$. The attack for the case $r_{\mathrm{KR}} = 2$ is similar. From Eq. (8) (using $k_0 = k$, $k_1 = k \oplus c_1$ and $k_2 = 0$), the function $F(K)$ is described by

$$F(K) = K^8 \cdot \mathscr{P}_1 \oplus K^5 \cdot \mathscr{P}_2 \oplus K^4 \cdot (\mathscr{P}_2 \cdot c_1 \oplus \mathscr{P}_1) \oplus K^3 \cdot (\mathscr{P}_4 \oplus \mathscr{P}_2)$$
$$\oplus K^2 \cdot (\mathscr{P}_4 \cdot c_1 \oplus \mathscr{P}_3 \oplus \mathscr{P}_1 \cdot c_1^2) \oplus K \cdot (\mathscr{P}_8 \oplus \mathscr{P}_6 \oplus \mathscr{P}_2 \cdot c_1^2) \oplus (\mathscr{P}_9 \oplus \mathscr{P}_6 \cdot c_1 \oplus \mathscr{P}_3 \cdot c_1^2),$$

where c_1 is the round constant of the first round. As also noted in Sect. 3.2, while $\mathscr{P}_9$ is the largest $\mathscr{P}_d$ in this expression, both $\mathscr{P}_5$ and $\mathscr{P}_7$ are missing, and hence do not need to be computed. A complete pseudo code of the attack can be found in Algorithm 2. Again, it is easy to see that the cost of the attack is well approximated by

- $2 \cdot |\mathcal{V}| + 6 = 2^n + 6$ multiplications,
- $2 \cdot |\mathcal{V}| + 4 = 2^n + 4$ squarings,
- $3 \cdot |\mathcal{V}| + 8 = 3 \cdot 2^{n-1} + 8$ n-bit XOR operations,
- cost of finding the roots of a univariate polynomial of degree 8.

5.3 Complexity Estimation

As we have just seen, our attack requires half of the code book (namely, 2^{n-1} chosen ciphertexts). Here we show that our attacks are better than exhaustive search (from the computational point of view). In order to do this, we measure the time complexities in equivalent encryption operations.

A single encryption round in MiMC requires one addition, one squaring operation, and one multiplication in the extension field. Since the cost of a single n-bit XOR operation is much smaller than the cost of a multiplication over $\mathbb{F}_{2^n}$, and since the number of XOR operations is similar to the number of multiplications, in the following we do not consider XOR operations. After this simplification, we find that the time complexity of $r_{\mathrm{KR}} = 1$ is dominated by 2^{n-1} squaring and multiplication operations or, equivalently, 2^{n-1} encryption rounds. A similar line of reasoning reveals that $r_{\mathrm{KR}} = 2$ is comparable to 2^n encryption rounds.

Algorithm 2: Attack on MiMC – Case: $r_{\text{KR}} = 2$.

Input: Vector subspace $\mathcal{V}$ of ciphertexts of dimension $\dim(\mathcal{V}) = n - 1$.
Output: Secret key k.

1   $\mathscr{P}_1, \mathscr{P}_2, \mathscr{P}_3, \ldots, \mathscr{P}_9 \leftarrow 0$.
2   **for** $x \in \mathcal{V} \oplus v$ **do**
3      $p \leftarrow \text{MiMC}_k^{-1}(x)$ from the decryption oracle.
4      $\mathscr{P}_1 \leftarrow \mathscr{P}_1 \oplus p$.
5      $q_2 \leftarrow p^2$.
6      $q_3 \leftarrow q_2 \cdot p$.
7      $\mathscr{P}_3 \leftarrow \mathscr{P}_3 \oplus q_3$.
8      $q_6 \leftarrow q_3^2$.
9      $\mathscr{P}_9 \leftarrow \mathscr{P}_9 \oplus q_6 \cdot q_3$.
10   $\mathscr{P}_2 \leftarrow (\mathscr{P}_1)^2$.
11   $\mathscr{P}_4 \leftarrow (\mathscr{P}_2)^2$.
12   $\mathscr{P}_6 \leftarrow (\mathscr{P}_3)^2$.
13   $\mathscr{P}_8 \leftarrow (\mathscr{P}_4)^2$.
14   $F(K) = K^8 \cdot \mathscr{P}_1 \oplus K^5 \cdot \mathscr{P}_2 \oplus K^4 \cdot (\mathscr{P}_2 \cdot c_1 \oplus \mathscr{P}_1) \oplus K^3 \cdot (\mathscr{P}_4 \oplus \mathscr{P}_2) \oplus K^2 \cdot (\mathscr{P}_4 \cdot c_1 \oplus \mathscr{P}_3 \oplus \mathscr{P}_1 \cdot c_1^2) \oplus K \cdot (\mathscr{P}_8 \oplus \mathscr{P}_6 \oplus \mathscr{P}_2 \cdot c_1^2) \oplus (\mathscr{P}_9 \oplus \mathscr{P}_6 \cdot c_1 \oplus \mathscr{P}_3 \cdot c_1^2)$.
15   Find a solution k of $F(K) = 0$ (filter multiple solutions by brute force).
16   **return** k.

Since the cost of solving a single low-degree equation is negligible, and one unit of encryption contains $\lceil n \cdot \log_3(2) \rceil$ rounds, it follows that the cost of our attacks is about

$$\frac{r_{\text{KR}} \cdot 2^{n-1}}{\lceil n \cdot \log_3(2) \rceil}$$

encryptions for $r_{\text{KR}} \in \{1, 2\}$. That is, the computational cost of the key-recovery part of our attacks is upper-bounded by $2^{n - \log_2(n) + 1}$, and hence the total cost is smaller than that of a brute-force attack (namely, 2^n encryptions) for each $n \geq 3$.

5.4   Practical Verification

We implemented Algorithm 1 and Algorithm 2 in the computer algebra system Magma, and verified both algorithms for all odd integers $n \in [5, 35]$. We note that Algorithm 1 ($r_{\text{KR}} = 1$) yields the correct answer for all the tested $5 \leq n \leq 35$, even if $\lceil n \log_3(2) \rceil \neq \lceil (n-1) \log_3(2) \rceil$. Namely, in practice it is possible to cover one more round with a zero sum than what we theoretically expect. In other words, $\lceil (n-1) \log_3(2) \rceil$ rounds of the decryption function of MiMC fail to obtain the maximum algebraic degree for these parameters, which is reached after $\lceil (n-1) \log_3(2) \rceil + 1$ rounds (see [28, App. B] for more details on the degree growth of MiMC^{-1}). Since we are not able to prove this behavior for larger values of n, we leave it as an open question whether Algorithm 1 can be applied to MiMC for odd integers $n > 35$.

Considerations on Data and Computational Costs of This Attack. A possible drawback of our attack is the cost. Since we are not able to provide an estimation of the growth of the degree in the decryption direction, we can only exploit the fact that a certain number of rounds are necessary in order to achieve maximum degree. It follows that the attacker is forced to use half of the code book in order to set up the attack, which also has an impact on the computational cost.

Even if our attack is not practical, we believe it provides valuable theoretical insight. It is also in line with several other attacks found in the literature, which are set up under a similar assumption on the data and/or computational cost. To give some concrete examples, consider the case of zero-correlation attacks [14], which exploit linear approximations that hold with probability $\frac{1}{2}$. The crucial limitation for basic zero-correlation linear cryptanalysis is that it requires half of the code book. Only follow-up works have been able to reduce this data requirement, including the more powerful distinguisher called multiple zero-correlation (MPZC) linear distinguisher proposed in [15], which exploits the fact that there are numerous zero-correlation linear approximations in susceptible ciphers. While needing (close to) the full code book is an inherent property of zero-correlation attacks, the reason for the high data complexity in our case is purely due to the specification of MiMC and the attacked number of rounds, and not due to an inherent property of our attack.

Splice-and-cut meet-in-the-middle attacks and biclique attacks are other examples of attacks that often come with time complexities relatively close to exhaustive search. Indeed, an extension of the biclique approach first described in [13] has a brute-force phase for a number of rounds as part of the attack. It can in principle work for any number of rounds and is hence best described as a particular optimization of brute-force key guessing. However, later variants then showed examples where the gain over brute force was in the order of millions [37]. Still, we note that the complexity of biclique attacks scales differently than our attack, whose runtime cost depends strongly on the details of the target cipher MiMC.

Finally, we point out that any attack that is better than brute force is relevant, even if it requires unrealistic amounts of data or storage. Indeed, the main goal of cryptanalysis is finding a "certificated weakness", that is, an evidence that the cipher does not perform as advertised. In other words, in academic cryptography, a weakness or a break in a scheme is usually defined quite conservatively: It may require impractical amounts of time, memory, or data.

The Number of Rounds Needed for Security. It may be of interest to estimate the number of rounds needed for MiMC to be resistant against this attack. To this end, we bound the operations needed to compute all monomials of odd degree, up to a maximum degree D.

Lemma 2. *Let $1 \leq D \leq 2^n - 1$ and $x \in \mathbb{F}_{2^n}$. The overall number of operations needed to compute all odd powers x^i for $i \in [3, D]$ is given by 1 squaring and $\lfloor \frac{D-1}{2} \rfloor$ multiplications.*

Proof. From x, calculate and store $q := x^2$. The odd powers of x can now be successively computed as $x^{i+2} = x^i \cdot q$ for all odd integers i in the interval $[1, D-2]$. This yields a total of 1 squaring and $\lfloor \frac{D-1}{2} \rfloor$ multiplications.   □

Assume for simplicity that $\lceil n \cdot \log_3(2) \rceil - 1$ rounds can be covered by a zero sum, and that the cost of solving the final polynomial equation is negligible. As before, we expect the time complexity to be dominated by the number of operations needed to construct the polynomial $F(K)$. Since the degree of this polynomial is upper-bounded by $3^{r_{KR}}$, by Lemma 2 at most $[(3^{r_{RK}} - 1)/2] \cdot 2^{n-1}$ multiplications are required to compute all monomials with odd exponents in $F(K)$ (where all monomials with even exponents are computed via Eq. (11)).

Since one encryption of MiMC costs $\lceil n \cdot \log_3(2) \rceil$ multiplications, the number of extra rounds ρ for MiMC must satisfy

$$(3^{\rho+1} - 1) \cdot 2^{n-2} \geq 2^n \cdot (\lceil n \cdot \log_3(2) \rceil + \rho)$$

in order to provide security against the attack just presented. This would, for example, require at least $\rho = 5$ extra rounds for $n = 129$ (more generally, if R is the number of rounds of MiMC-n/n, then $\rho \approx \lceil \log_3(2 \cdot R) \rceil$ more rounds are sufficient to restore the security[8]). We remark that *this rough estimation is not intended to replace the number of rounds proposed by the designers.*

6   An Algebraic Attack on Ciphers with Low-Degree Round Functions

Here we generalize the key-recovery attack on MiMC described in Sect. 5 and discuss a generic attack strategy for any block cipher working over $(\mathbb{F}_{2^n})^t$, where $n, t \in \mathbb{N}$, $t \geq 2$ and $n \geq 3$.

6.1   Setting

We consider an r-round block cipher $E_k^r : (\mathbb{F}_{2^n})^t \to (\mathbb{F}_{2^n})^t$ with

$$E_k^r(x) = (R_r \circ R_{r-1} \circ \cdots \circ R_1)(x \oplus k),$$

and where $R, R_i : (\mathbb{F}_{2^n})^t \to (\mathbb{F}_{2^n})^t$ are defined by $R_i(x) = R(x) \oplus k^{(i)}$. Here, R denominates the (nonlinear) round function. Since E_k^r consists of t components, we can write

$$E_k^r(x) = (E_{k,1}^r(x), \ldots, E_{k,t}^r(x)),$$

where $E_{k,i}^r : (\mathbb{F}_{2^n})^t \to \mathbb{F}_{2^n}$. We denote the compositional inverse of E_k^r by E_k^{-r}. We assume that

---

[8] In more details, $\rho \geq \log_3(4 \cdot (R + \rho) + 1) - 1$. The previous estimation is obtained by assuming $\rho \leq R/2$.

(1) the i-th round key $k^{(i)} \in (\mathbb{F}_{2^n})^t$ is derived from the master key $k = (k_1, \ldots, k_t) \in (\mathbb{F}_{2^n})^t$ by some *low-degree* (e.g., linear) key schedule,

(2) the round function R can be described by a polynomial

$$R(x = (x_1, \ldots, x_t)) = \bigoplus_{\substack{j=(j_1, \ldots, j_t) \in \{0,1,\ldots,2^n-1\}^t \\ j_1 + \cdots + j_t \leq d}} \alpha_j \cdot x_1^{j_1} \cdot \cdots \cdot x_t^{j_t}$$

of *low-degree* d with coefficients $\alpha_j \in (\mathbb{F}_{2^n})^t$.

Our attack requires the symbolic evaluation of the encryption function $E_k^{r'}$ for a small number of rounds r' to be relatively easy, which motivates the requirements of a low-degree round function R and a low-degree key schedule. This ensures that the polynomial representation of $E_k^{r'}$ can be computed efficiently. In both cases, *low-degree* means *low compared to the size of the field* $\mathbb{F}_{2^n}$, i.e., $d \ll 2^n - 1$. A cipher in the literature that satisfies above assumptions and does indeed use low-degree round functions is, e.g., HadesMiMC [31].

6.2   Strategy of the Attack

The idea of our generic attack is to recover the secret master key k of a cipher E_k^r by exploiting a given higher-order distinguisher over the subset $\mathcal{X} \subseteq (\mathbb{F}_{2^n})^t$ covering $1 \leq r_{\mathrm{ZS}} < r$ rounds in the encryption or the decryption direction. For the sake of simplicity, we follow the approach of the attack on MiMC in Sect. 5 and assume that the higher-order distinguisher covers r_{ZS} rounds in the decryption direction.

In our attack, we symbolically evaluate $E_k^{r_{\mathrm{KR}}}(y)$ with respect to the remaining $r_{\mathrm{KR}} := r - r_{\mathrm{ZS}}$ rounds in the encryption direction and obtain polynomials ($1 \leq i \leq t$)

$$E_{(K_1, \ldots, K_t), i}^{r_{\mathrm{KR}}}(Y) \in \mathbb{F}_{2^n}[K_1, \ldots, K_t, Y_1, \ldots, Y_t]$$

over $\mathbb{F}_{2^n}$ with the master key words K_j and plaintext variables $(Y_1, \ldots, Y_t) =: Y$ as indeterminates – in short, one polynomial for each of the t components of $E_k^{r_{\mathrm{KR}}}(y)$. In general, we work with $r_{KR} \ll r_{ZS}$, since the symbolic evaluation of $E_k^{r_{\mathrm{KR}}}(y)$ is expensive.

Having a zero sum after r_{ZS} rounds in the decryption direction with respect to the subset $\mathcal{X} \subseteq (\mathbb{F}_{2^n})^t$ means that

$$\bigoplus_{x \in \mathcal{X}} E_k^{-r_{\mathrm{ZS}}}(x) = 0.$$

The main observation behind our attack is the following: We exploit the relation[9]

$$0 = \bigoplus_{x \in \mathcal{X}} E_k^{-r_{\mathrm{ZS}}}(x) = \bigoplus_{x \in \mathcal{X}} \left(E_k^{r_{\mathrm{KR}}} \circ E_k^{-r} \right)(x) = \bigoplus_{y \in E_k^{-r}(\mathcal{X})} E_k^{r_{\mathrm{KR}}}(y) \qquad (12)$$

----

[9] Note that in this representation, $E_k^r = E_k^{r_{\mathrm{ZS}}} \circ E_k^{r_{\mathrm{KR}}}$ and $E_k^{-r_{\mathrm{ZS}}} = E_k^{r_{\mathrm{KR}}} \circ E_k^{-r}$.

Algorithm 3: Attack on a generic cipher E_k^r over $(\mathbb{F}_{2^n})^t$.

Input: Number of rounds r of the cipher E_k^r, number of rounds r_{ZS} in the decryption direction and a subset $\mathcal{X} \subseteq (\mathbb{F}_{2^n})^t$ satisfying the zero sum $\bigoplus_{x \in \mathcal{X}} E_k^{-r_{ZS}}(x) = 0$.

Output: Secret key $k = (k_1, \ldots, k_t)$.

1 $r_{KR} \leftarrow r - r_{ZS}$.
2 **for each** $1 \leq i \leq t$ **do**
3   Compute the symbolic evaluation
    $f_i = f_i(Y_1, \ldots, Y_t, K_1, \ldots, K_t) = E_{(K_1, \ldots, K_t), i}^{r_{KR}}(Y_1, \ldots, Y_t)$ of word i in the encryption direction for r_{KR} rounds.
4   **for each** monomial $Y_1^{i_1} \ldots Y_t^{i_t} \cdot K_1^{j_1} \ldots K_t^{j_t}$ in f_i with $i_1 + \cdots + i_t \geq 1$ **do**
5     $\mathscr{P}_{i_1, \ldots, i_t} \leftarrow 0$.
6   **for each** $x \in \mathcal{X}$ **do**
7      $y = (y_1, \ldots, y_t) \leftarrow E_k^{-r}(x)$, via the decryption oracle.
8      $\mathscr{P}_{i_1, \ldots, i_t} \leftarrow \mathscr{P}_{i_1, \ldots, i_t} \bigoplus y_1^{i_1} \cdot \ldots \cdot y_t^{i_t}$.
9   Replace $Y_1^{i_1} \ldots Y_t^{i_t} \cdot K_1^{j_1} \ldots K_t^{j_t}$ with $\mathscr{P}_{i_1, \ldots, i_t} \cdot K_1^{j_1} \cdot \ldots \cdot K_t^{j_t}$.
10   $F_i(K_1, \ldots, K_t) \leftarrow f_i(K_1, \ldots, K_t)$.
11 Find a solution $k = (k_1, \ldots, k_t)$ of $F_1(k_1, \ldots, k_t) = \cdots = F_t(k_1, \ldots, k_t) = 0$.
12 **return** $k = (k_1, \ldots, k_t)$.

---

to set up the following equations $(1 \leq i \leq t)$ over $\mathbb{F}_{2^n}$ in the variables $k_1, \ldots, k_t$:

$$F_i(k_1, \ldots, k_t) := \bigoplus_{y \in E_k^{-r}(\mathcal{X})} E_{(k_1, \ldots, k_t), i}^{r_{KR}}(y) = 0. \tag{13}$$

Again, $E_{(k_1, \ldots, k_t), i}^{r_{KR}}(y)$ denotes the symbolic evaluation of the i-th word after r_{KR} rounds in the encryption direction with the master key words as variables $k_1, \ldots, k_t$ and evaluated at $y \in \mathbb{F}_{2^n}$. Once we have set up the equation system arising from Eq. (13), we apply Gröbner basis techniques to solve this system over $\mathbb{F}_{2^n}$ for the key variables $k_1, \ldots, k_t$.

In Algorithm 3 we summarize the approach of our generic attack and present a pseudo code of the attack procedure. For completeness, a rough complexity estimation of the attack is derived in [28, App. E].

6.3   Comparison with Related Work

Interpolation Attacks. Originally introduced as a standalone attack, interpolation attacks [36] are algebraic attacks that express the (potentially round-reduced) cipher as a polynomial equation with unknown, key-dependent coefficients, and recover these coefficients from known inputs and outputs. More recently, this approach has been combined as a key-recovery approach together with integral distinguishers.

Attack on CAST. In an attack [43] on the CAST cipher the authors use a higher-order differential distinguisher to set up an equation system and finally solve this systems for the key variables. In contrast to our attack, the authors of [43] work with linear equation systems over $\mathbb{F}_2$. While this is sufficient for CAST, working at bit level is in general more expensive than working on word level when analyzing ciphers that are natively defined at word level.

Optimized Interpolation Attacks. One type of optimized interpolation attacks was described in [23], where the authors find attacks on reduced-round versions of LowMC which are more efficient than previous attacks based on key guessing [25]. A similar attack was also used to break the full-round version of the FRIT permutation in an Even–Mansour setting [26]. The overall strategy of this interpolation attack is to find a distinguisher (for example a constant sum in the encryption direction in the case of LowMC) with which one attacks the construction by finding the unknown monomials of the sums of the symbolic representations in the inverse direction. By determining these (key-dependent) monomials, the full key can eventually be found. Since the approach in [23] shares some similarities with our proposal, we describe the differences between these two strategies in detail.

The main difference regarding the two strategies concerns the way in which the system of equations $F_i(K) = 0$ is constructed and consequently solved:

- In [23], the idea is to construct the function using a "standard" interpolation technique. Specifically, the attacker does not care about the specification of the monomials of F, which are simply considered as unknowns. Hence, the idea is to recover (interpolate) the unknown coefficients of $F_K(C)$, and then use various ad-hoc techniques (which are not part of the framework described in this section) in order to recover the actual secret key.
- In our case, we heavily exploit the simple algebraic structure of the round function in order to construct the system of equations $F_i(K) = 0$. In other words, the system of equations is constructed by using a symbolic evaluation and not by interpolation techniques.

We emphasize that the possibility to set up one of the two attacks does not imply the possibility to set up the other one. For example, it seems hard to use the attack presented in [23] against full-round MiMC, while we show that our strategy can break it. Indeed, since we already need 2^{n-1} data for the distinguishing property (i.e., half of the code book), we do not see how to apply the approach from [23] to MiMC without further increasing the data complexity due to data needed for the interpolation step.

Attack on Pyjamask. Only recently, a similar attack on Pyjamask, competing in the ongoing NIST call for lightweight authenticated encryption, has been presented [27]. The authors propose an attack on the full block cipher Pyjamask-96 by combining higher-order differentials with an in-depth ad-hoc analysis of the system of equations obtained for 2.5 rounds of Pyjamask-96. As is the case for CAST, the attack is set up at bit level.

Cube Attacks. Although our attack and cube attacks [24] exploit low degrees in the polynomial description of a cipher, they are quite different from a conceptual point of view and can be regarded as two different cryptanalytic methods. To justify this conclusion, we briefly present the idea behind cube attacks and contrast them with our attack ideas.

Given a cipher with input variables $x_0, \ldots, x_{n-1}$ as the public variables (IV bits, plaintext bits, tweak bits, etc.), and $x_n, \ldots, x_{n+m-1}$ as the secret variables (key bits), the output of the cipher can be regarded as a polynomial $f = f(x)$ in $x = (x_0, \ldots, x_{n+m-1})$. For every set $I \subset \{0, \ldots, n-1\}$, f can be uniquely decomposed into

$$f = t_I \cdot f_{S(I)} + q,$$

where $t_I := \prod_{i \in I} x_i$ denotes the product of all variables indexed by elements in I, the polynomial $f_{S(I)}$ does not contain any variables from t_I, and where q misses at least one variable from t_I. The polynomial $f_{S(I)}$ is also called the *superpoly* with respect to I. For any subset $I \subseteq \{0, \ldots, n-1\}$ of size $|I|$, the authors of [24] call the set C_I of $2^{|I|}$ vectors, where all the $|I|$ variables indexed by I range over all possible combinations of elements in $\mathbb{F}_2$ and the remaining $n + m - |I|$ variables remain undetermined, a $|I|$-*dimensional Boolean cube*. Then the sum of f over all values in the cube C_I yields the equation of polynomials

$$\bigoplus_{v \in C_I} f(v) = f_{S(I)}.$$

Cube attacks consist of two steps. First, attackers recover the superpoly in the offline phase. In this phase, the attacker might need to try sufficiently many cubes and assignments for the remaining public variables such that the superpoly $f_{S(I)}$ is a balanced function of the secret variables. Moreover, determining the actual coefficients of $f_{S(I)}$ requires the additional assumption that the attacker is allowed to tweak both public and secret variables. Then, with this usable superpoly, during the online phase, the attacker leaves the secret variables undetermined and queries the encryption oracle with every value $c \in C_I$ and gets $f(c) \in \mathbb{F}$. Eventually, the attacker computes

$$f_I := \bigoplus_{c \in C_I} f(c).$$

The secret key information can be recovered by solving the corresponding equation system $f_I = f_{S(I)}$.

Compared with our attack, cube attacks involve an initial step of finding balanced superpolies that contain independent secret variables. Apart from that, cube attacks do *not* exploit the algebraic structure of a cipher, since they rely on the assumption of tweakable black box polynomials. In this sense, our attack is different, since it makes heavy use of the algebraic structure of a cipher when symbolically evaluating a certain number of rounds. Furthermore, cube attacks use the assumption that both key and plaintext variables are tweakable, while we rely on the assumption that some rounds of the cipher can be efficiently evaluated symbolically (which is why we work with low-degree round functions).

7   Concluding Remarks and Future Work

Reducing the Cost of the Attack. As shown in [28, App. E], two steps – namely, (1st) the construction of the system of equations $F_i(k_1, \ldots, k_t) = 0$ for $1 \le i \le t$ and (2nd) solving such a system – mainly constitute the cost of the attack. In general, it could make sense to balance the costs of the two steps in order to either minimize the total cost of the attack or maximize the number of rounds that can be broken.

In more detail, consider the case in which the cost of the attack is well approximated by the cost of *constructing* the system of equations $F_i(K) = 0$. Since this cost grows with the size of the subspace $\mathcal{V}$, one strategy could be to consider a smaller subset $\mathcal{X}$.[10] Obviously, this implies in general the possibility to cover fewer rounds r_{ZS} using a higher-order distinguisher, which means that more rounds r_{KR} must be covered in general. However, the overall cost of the attack may benefit from this strategy. On the other hand, the case in which the attack cost is well approximated by the cost of *solving* the system of equations $F_i(K) = 0$ requires the opposite strategy.

Moreover, we point out that the attacks can be improved by exploiting the details of the cipher. To give a concrete example, consider the case of MiMC given in Algorithm 1: The attack and its computational complexity benefit from the fact that $F(K)$ does not depend on $\mathscr{P}_5$ or $\mathscr{P}_7$. As another example, consider the case of an SPN cipher where the round function is defined as

$$R(x = (x_1, \ldots, x_t)) = M \times (S(x_1), S(x_2), \ldots, S(x_t)),$$

where $M \in (\mathbb{F}_{2^n})^{t \times t}$ and $S : \mathbb{F}_{2^n} \to \mathbb{F}_{2^n}$ (here, '$\times$' denotes matrix-vector multiplication). The cost of the attack can potentially be reduced by taking into account the fact that all monomials in the polynomial representation R depend only on a single variable x_i.

Further Generalization: Ciphers over $\mathbb{F}_p$. Finally, the attack strategy can be generalized to include ciphers over $(\mathbb{F}_p)^t$ for a prime p. This is of particular importance since many of the new applications named in the introduction (e.g., STARKs and MPC) natively work over $\mathbb{F}_p$, which means that many of the recently proposed primitives are natively constructed over $\mathbb{F}_p$. We remark that the strategy of the attack does not depend on the details of the field $\mathbb{F}$. Hence, the only thing that seems to preclude this possibility seems to be a lack of knowledge regarding efficient distinguishers over $(\mathbb{F}_p)^t$. Indeed, while it is well-known how to find a higher-order distinguisher over Boolean fields (e.g., by exploiting division property tools present in the literature [47,51,53]), the same is not yet true for prime fields.

---

[10] We note that we cannot adopt this strategy for MiMC since we are not able to predict the growth of the degree of MiMC^{-1}. With such an estimation, the strategy proposed here can potentially reduce the cost of the attack.

Acknowledgements. The authors thank the anonymous reviewers for their valuable comments and suggestions. Qingju Wang is funded by the University of Luxembourg Internal Research Project (IRP) FDISC. This project has received funding from the European Union's Horizon 2020 research and innovation programme (H2020 ICT 825225: Safe-DEED) and the European Research Council (ERC 681402: SOPHIA).

References

1. Albrecht, M.R., Cid, C., Grassi, L., Khovratovich, D., Lüftenegger, R., Rechberger, C., Schofnegger, M.: Algebraic cryptanalysis of STARK-friendly designs: application to MARVELlous and MiMC. In: Galbraith, S.D., Moriai, S. (eds.) ASIACRYPT 2019. LNCS, vol. 11923, pp. 371–397. Springer, Cham (2019). https://doi.org/10.1007/978-3-030-34618-8_13

2. Albrecht, M.R., Grassi, L., Perrin, L., Ramacher, S., Rechberger, C., Rotaru, D., Roy, A., Schofnegger, M.: Feistel structures for MPC, and more. In: Sako, K., Schneider, S., Ryan, P.Y.A. (eds.) ESORICS 2019. LNCS, vol. 11736, pp. 151–171. Springer, Cham (2019). https://doi.org/10.1007/978-3-030-29962-0_8

3. Albrecht, M., Grassi, L., Rechberger, C., Roy, A., Tiessen, T.: MiMC: efficient encryption and cryptographic hashing with minimal multiplicative complexity. In: Cheon, J.H., Takagi, T. (eds.) ASIACRYPT 2016. LNCS, vol. 10031, pp. 191–219. Springer, Heidelberg (2016). https://doi.org/10.1007/978-3-662-53887-6_7

4. Albrecht, M.R., Rechberger, C., Schneider, T., Tiessen, T., Zohner, M.: Ciphers for MPC and FHE. In: Oswald, E., Fischlin, M. (eds.) EUROCRYPT 2015. LNCS, vol. 9056, pp. 430–454. Springer, Heidelberg (2015). https://doi.org/10.1007/978-3-662-46800-5_17

5. Aly, A., Ashur, T., Ben-Sasson, E., Dhooghe, S., Szepieniec, A.: Design of Symmetric-Key Primitives for Advanced Cryptographic Protocols. IACR Cryptology ePrint Archive, Report 2019/426 (2019)

6. Ashur, T., Dhooghe, S.: MARVELlous: a STARK-Friendly Family of Cryptographic Primitives. IACR Cryptology ePrint Archive, Report 2018/1098 (2018)

7. Aumasson, J.P., Meier, W.: Zero-sum distinguishers for reduced Keccak-f and for the core functions of Luffa and Hamsi (2009), presented at the Rump Session of CHES 2009, https://131002.net/data/papers/AM09.pdf

8. Ben-Sasson, E., Bentov, I., Horesh, Y., Riabzev, M.: Scalable, transparent, and post-quantum secure computational integrity. IACR Cryptology ePrint Archive **2018**, 46 (2018)

9. Bertoni, G., Daemen, J., Peeters, M., Van Assche, G.: On the indifferentiability of the sponge construction. In: Smart, N. (ed.) EUROCRYPT 2008. LNCS, vol. 4965, pp. 181–197. Springer, Heidelberg (2008). https://doi.org/10.1007/978-3-540-78967-3_11

10. Bertoni, G., Daemen, J., Peeters, M., Van Assche, G.: Note on zero-sum distinguishers of Keccak-f. http://keccak.noekeon.org/NoteZeroSum.pdf

11. Biham, E., Shamir, A.: Differential cryptanalysis of DES-like cryptosystems. In: Menezes, A.J., Vanstone, S.A. (eds.) CRYPTO 1990. LNCS, vol. 537, pp. 2–21. Springer, Heidelberg (1991). https://doi.org/10.1007/3-540-38424-3_1

12. Black, J., Rogaway, P., Shrimpton, T.: Black-box analysis of the block-cipher-based hash-function constructions from PGV. In: Yung, M. (ed.) CRYPTO 2002. LNCS, vol. 2442, pp. 320–335. Springer, Heidelberg (2002). https://doi.org/10.1007/3-540-45708-9_21

13. Bogdanov, A., Khovratovich, D., Rechberger, C.: Biclique cryptanalysis of the full AES. In: Lee, D.H., Wang, X. (eds.) ASIACRYPT 2011. LNCS, vol. 7073, pp. 344–371. Springer, Heidelberg (2011). https://doi.org/10.1007/978-3-642-25385-0_19

14. Bogdanov, A., Rijmen, V.: Linear hulls with correlation zero and linear cryptanalysis of block ciphers. Des. Codes Cryptogr. **70**(3), 369–383 (2014). https://doi.org/10.1007/s10623-012-9697-z

15. Bogdanov, A., Wang, M.: Zero correlation linear cryptanalysis with reduced data complexity. In: Canteaut, A. (ed.) FSE 2012. LNCS, vol. 7549, pp. 29–48. Springer, Heidelberg (2012). https://doi.org/10.1007/978-3-642-34047-5_3

16. Bonnetain, X.: Collisions on feistel-MiMC and univariate GMiMC. IACR Cryptology ePrint Archive **2019**, 951 (2019)

17. Boura, C., Canteaut, A.: On the influence of the algebraic degree of F^{-1} on the algebraic degree of G ∘ F. IEEE Trans. Inf. Theor. **59**(1), 691–702 (2013)

18. Boura, C., Canteaut, A., De Cannière, C.: Higher-order differential properties of KECCAK and *Luffa*. In: Joux, A. (ed.) FSE 2011. LNCS, vol. 6733, pp. 252–269. Springer, Heidelberg (2011). https://doi.org/10.1007/978-3-642-21702-9_15

19. Bünz, B., Bootle, J., Boneh, D., Poelstra, A., Wuille, P., Maxwell, G.: Bulletproofs: short proofs for confidential transactions and more. In: IEEE Symposium on Security and Privacy, pp. 315–334. IEEE Computer Society (2018)

20. Canteaut, A., Videau, M.: Degree of composition of highly nonlinear functions and applications to higher order differential cryptanalysis. In: Knudsen, L.R. (ed.) EUROCRYPT 2002. LNCS, vol. 2332, pp. 518–533. Springer, Heidelberg (2002). https://doi.org/10.1007/3-540-46035-7_34

21. Cantor, D.G., Kaltofen, E.: On fast multiplication of polynomials over arbitrary algebras. Acta Inf. **28**(7), 693–701 (1991)

22. Carlet, C., Charpin, P., Zinoviev, V.A.: Codes, bent functions and permutations suitable for DES-like cryptosystems. DCC **15**(2), 125–156 (1998)

23. Dinur, I., Liu, Y., Meier, W., Wang, Q.: Optimized interpolation attacks on LowMC. In: Iwata, T., Cheon, J.H. (eds.) ASIACRYPT 2015. LNCS, vol. 9453, pp. 535–560. Springer, Heidelberg (2015). https://doi.org/10.1007/978-3-662-48800-3_22

24. Dinur, I., Shamir, A.: Cube attacks on tweakable black box polynomials. In: Joux, A. (ed.) EUROCRYPT 2009. LNCS, vol. 5479, pp. 278–299. Springer, Heidelberg (2009). https://doi.org/10.1007/978-3-642-01001-9_16

25. Dobraunig, C., Eichlseder, M., Mendel, F.: Higher-order cryptanalysis of LowMC. In: Kwon, S., Yun, A. (eds.) ICISC 2015. LNCS, vol. 9558, pp. 87–101. Springer, Cham (2016). https://doi.org/10.1007/978-3-319-30840-1_6

26. Dobraunig, C., Eichlseder, M., Mendel, F., Schofnegger, M.: Algebraic cryptanalysis of variants of FRIT. In: Paterson, K.G., Stebila, D. (eds.) SAC 2019. LNCS, vol. 11959, pp. 149–170. Springer, Cham (2020). https://doi.org/10.1007/978-3-030-38471-5_7

27. Dobraunig, C., Rotella, Y., Schoone, J.: Algebraic and higher-order differential cryptanalysis of Pyjamask-96. IACR Trans. Symmetric Cryptology **2020**(1), 289–312 (2020)

28. Eichlseder, M., Grassi, L., Lüftenegger, R., Øygarden, M., Rechberger, C., Schofnegger, M., Wang, Q.: An algebraic attack on ciphers with low-degree round functions: application to full MiMC. IACR Cryptol. ePrint Arch. **2020**, 182 (2020)

29. von zur Gathen, J., Gerhard, J.: Modern Computer Algebra, (3ed) Cambridge University Press, New York (2013)

30. Grassi, L., Kales, D., Khovratovich, D., Roy, A., Rechberger, C., Schofnegger, M.: Starkad and Poseidon: New Hash Functions for Zero Knowledge Proof Systems. Cryptology ePrint Archive, Report 2019/458 (2019)

31. Grassi, L., Lüftenegger, R., Rechberger, C., Rotaru, D., Schofnegger, M.: On a generalization of substitution-permutation networks: the HADES design strategy. In: Canteaut, A., Ishai, Y. (eds.) EUROCRYPT 2020. LNCS, vol. 12106, pp. 674–704. Springer, Cham (2020). https://doi.org/10.1007/978-3-030-45724-2_23

32. Grassi, L., Rechberger, C., Rotaru, D., Scholl, P., Smart, N.P.: Mpc-friendly symmetric key primitives. In: ACM Conference on Computer and Communications Security, pp. 430–443. ACM (2016)

33. Guo, J., Liao, G., Liu, G., Liu, M., Qiao, K., Song, L.: Practical collision attacks against round-reduced SHA-3. J. Cryptology **33**(1), 228–270 (2020)

34. Hao, Y., Leander, G., Meier, W., Todo, Y., Wang, Q.: Modeling for three-subset division property without unknown subset. In: Canteaut, A., Ishai, Y. (eds.) EUROCRYPT 2020. LNCS, vol. 12105, pp. 466–495. Springer, Cham (2020). https://doi.org/10.1007/978-3-030-45721-1_17

35. Hu, K., Wang, M.: Automatic search for a variant of division property using three subsets. In: Matsui, M. (ed.) CT-RSA 2019. LNCS, vol. 11405, pp. 412–432. Springer, Cham (2019). https://doi.org/10.1007/978-3-030-12612-4_21

36. Jakobsen, T., Knudsen, L.R.: The interpolation attack on block ciphers. FSE. LNCS **1267**, 28–40 (1997)

37. Khovratovich, D., Leurent, G., Rechberger, C.: Narrow-bicliques: cryptanalysis of full Idea. In: Pointcheval, D., Johansson, T. (eds.) EUROCRYPT 2012. LNCS, vol. 7237, pp. 392–410. Springer, Heidelberg (2012). https://doi.org/10.1007/978-3-642-29011-4_24

38. Knudsen, L.R.: Truncated and higher order differentials. In: Preneel, B. (ed.) FSE 1994. LNCS, vol. 1008, pp. 196–211. Springer, Heidelberg (1995). https://doi.org/10.1007/3-540-60590-8_16

39. Knudsen, L.R., Rijmen, V.: Known-key distinguishers for some block ciphers. In: Kurosawa, K. (ed.) ASIACRYPT 2007. LNCS, vol. 4833, pp. 315–324. Springer, Heidelberg (2007). https://doi.org/10.1007/978-3-540-76900-2_19

40. Lai, X.: Higher Order Derivatives and Differential Cryptanalysis. In: Blahut, R.E., Costello, D.J., Maurer, U., Mittelholzer, T. (eds.) Communications and Cryptography. The Springer International Series in Engineering and Computer Science (Communications and Information Theory), vol. 276, pp. 227–233, Springer, Boston (1994) https://doi.org/10.1007/978-1-4615-2694-0_23

41. Li, C., Preneel, B.: Improved interpolation attacks on cryptographic primitives of low algebraic degree. In: Paterson, K.G., Stebila, D. (eds.) SAC 2019. LNCS, vol. 11959, pp. 171–193. Springer, Cham (2020). https://doi.org/10.1007/978-3-030-38471-5_8

42. Matsui, M.: Linear cryptanalysis method for DES cipher. In: Helleseth, T. (ed.) EUROCRYPT 1993. LNCS, vol. 765, pp. 386–397. Springer, Heidelberg (1994). https://doi.org/10.1007/3-540-48285-7_33

43. Moriai, S., Shimoyama, T., Kaneko, T.: Higher order differential attack of a CAST cipher. In: Vaudenay, S. (ed.) FSE 1998. LNCS, vol. 1372, pp. 17–31. Springer, Heidelberg (1998). https://doi.org/10.1007/3-540-69710-1_2

44. Parno, B., Howell, J., Gentry, C., Raykova, M.: Pinocchio: Nearly practical verifiable computation. In: IEEE Symposium on Security and Privacy, pp. 238–252. IEEE Computer Society (2013)

45. Rotaru, D., Smart, N.P., Stam, M.: Modes of operation suitable for computing on encrypted data. IACR Trans. Symmetric Cryptol. **2017**(3), 294–324 (2017)

46. Todo, Y.: Structural evaluation by generalized integral property. In: Oswald, E., Fischlin, M. (eds.) EUROCRYPT 2015. LNCS, vol. 9056, pp. 287–314. Springer, Heidelberg (2015). https://doi.org/10.1007/978-3-662-46800-5_12

47. Todo, Y., Isobe, T., Hao, Y., Meier, W.: Cube attacks on non-blackbox polynomials based on division property. In: Katz, J., Shacham, H. (eds.) CRYPTO 2017. LNCS, vol. 10403, pp. 250–279. Springer, Cham (2017). https://doi.org/10.1007/978-3-319-63697-9_9

48. Todo, Y., Morii, M.: Bit-based division property and application to SIMON family. In: Peyrin, T. (ed.) FSE 2016. LNCS, vol. 9783, pp. 357–377. Springer, Heidelberg (2016). https://doi.org/10.1007/978-3-662-52993-5_18

49. Vielhaber, M.: Breaking ONE.FIVIUM by AIDA an algebraic IV differential attack. IACR Cryptology ePrint Archive 2007, 413 (2007)

50. Wang, Q., Grassi, L., Rechberger, C.: Zero-sum partitions of PHOTON permutations. In: Smart, N.P. (ed.) CT-RSA 2018. LNCS, vol. 10808, pp. 279–299. Springer, Cham (2018). https://doi.org/10.1007/978-3-319-76953-0_15

51. Wang, Q., Hao, Y., Todo, Y., Li, C., Isobe, T., Meier, W.: Improved division property based cube attacks exploiting algebraic properties of superpoly. In: Shacham, H., Boldyreva, A. (eds.) CRYPTO 2018. LNCS, vol. 10991, pp. 275–305. Springer, Cham (2018). https://doi.org/10.1007/978-3-319-96884-1_10

52. Wang, Q., Liu, Z., Varıcı, K., Sasaki, Yu., Rijmen, V., Todo, Y.: Cryptanalysis of reduced-round SIMON32 and SIMON48. In: Meier, W., Mukhopadhyay, D. (eds.) INDOCRYPT 2014. LNCS, vol. 8885, pp. 143–160. Springer, Cham (2014). https://doi.org/10.1007/978-3-319-13039-2_9

53. Wang, S., Hu, B., Guan, J., Zhang, K., Shi, T.: MILP-aided method of searching division property using three subsets and applications. In: Galbraith, S.D., Moriai, S. (eds.) ASIACRYPT 2019. LNCS, vol. 11923, pp. 398–427. Springer, Cham (2019). https://doi.org/10.1007/978-3-030-34618-8_14

Improvements of Algebraic Attacks for Solving the Rank Decoding and MinRank Problems

Magali Bardet[4,5], Maxime Bros[1(✉)], Daniel Cabarcas[6], Philippe Gaborit[1], Ray Perlner[2], Daniel Smith-Tone[2,3], Jean-Pierre Tillich[4], and Javier Verbel[6]

[1] Univ. Limoges, CNRS, XLIM, UMR 7252, 87000 Limoges, France
maxime.bros@unilim.fr
[2] National Institute of Standards and Technology, Gaithersburg, USA
[3] University of Louisville, Louisville, USA
[4] Inria, 2 rue Simone Iff, 75012 Paris, France
[5] LITIS, University of Rouen Normandie, Mont-Saint-Aignan, France
[6] Universidad Nacional de Colombia Sede Medellín, Medellín, Colombia

Abstract. In this paper, we show how to significantly improve algebraic techniques for solving the MinRank problem, which is ubiquitous in multivariate and rank metric code based cryptography. In the case of the structured MinRank instances arising in the latter, we build upon a recent breakthrough [11] showing that algebraic attacks outperform the combinatorial ones that were considered state of the art up until now. Through a slight modification of this approach, we completely avoid Gröbner bases computations for certain parameters and are left only with solving linear systems. This does not only substantially improve the complexity, but also gives a convincing argument as to why algebraic techniques work in this case. When used against the second round NIST-PQC candidates ROLLO-I-128/192/256, our new attack has bit complexity respectively 71, 87, and 151, to be compared to 117, 144, and 197 as obtained in [11]. The linear systems arise from the nullity of the maximal minors of a certain matrix associated to the algebraic modeling. We also use a similar approach to improve the algebraic Min-Rank solvers for the usual MinRank problem. When applied against the second round NIST-PQC candidates GeMSS and Rainbow, our attack has a complexity that is very close to or even slightly better than those of the best known attacks so far. Note that these latter attacks did not rely on MinRank techniques since the MinRank approach used to give complexities that were far away from classical security levels.

Keywords: Post-quantum cryptography · NIST-PQC candidates · Rank metric code-based cryptography · Algebraic attack

1 Introduction

Rank Metric Code-Based Cryptography. In the last decade, rank metric code-based cryptography has proved to be a powerful alternative to traditional

© International Association for Cryptologic Research 2020
S. Moriai and H. Wang (Eds.): ASIACRYPT 2020, LNCS 12491, pp. 507–536, 2020.
https://doi.org/10.1007/978-3-030-64837-4_17

code-based cryptography based on the Hamming metric. This thread of research started with the GPT cryptosystem [22] based on Gabidulin codes [21], which are rank metric analogues of Reed-Solomon codes. However, the strong algebraic structure of those codes was successfully exploited for attacking the original GPT cryptosystem and its variants with the Overbeck attack [34] (see [32] for the latest developments). This is similar to the Hamming metric situation where essentially all McEliece cryptosystems based on Reed-Solomon codes or variants of them have been broken. However, recently a rank metric analogue of the NTRU cryptosystem [28] has been designed and studied, starting with the pioneering paper [23]. NTRU relies on a lattice with vectors of rather small Euclidean norm. It is precisely those vectors that allow an efficient decoding/deciphering process. The decryption of the cryptosystem proposed in [23] relies on LRPC codes with rather short vectors in the dual code, but this time for the rank metric. This cryptosystem can also be viewed as the rank metric analogue of the MDPC cryptosystem [31] relying on short dual code vectors for the Hamming metric.

This new way of building rank metric code-based cryptosystems has led to a sequence of proposals [5,6,23,25], culminating in submissions to the NIST post-quantum competition [2,3], whose security relies solely on decoding codes in rank metric with a ring structure similar to those used in lattice-based cryptography. Interestingly enough, one can also build signature schemes using the rank metric; even though early attempts which relied on masking the structure of a code [9,26] have been broken [16], a promising recent approach [8] only considers random matrices without structural masking.

Decoding $\mathbb{F}_{q^m}$-Linear Codes in Rank Metric. In other words, in rank metric code-based cryptography we are now only left with assessing the difficulty of the decoding problem in rank metric. The trend there is to consider linear codes of length n over an extension $\mathbb{F}_{q^m}$ of degree m of $\mathbb{F}_q$, i.e., $\mathbb{F}_{q^m}$-linear subspaces of $\mathbb{F}_{q^m}^n$. Let $(\beta_1, \ldots, \beta_m)$ be any basis of $\mathbb{F}_{q^m}$ as a $\mathbb{F}_q$-vector space. Then words of those codes can be interpreted as matrices with entries in the ground field $\mathbb{F}_q$ by viewing a vector $\boldsymbol{x} = (x_1, \ldots, x_n) \in \mathbb{F}_{q^m}^n$ as a matrix $Mat(\boldsymbol{x}) = (X_{ij})_{i,j}$ in $\mathbb{F}_q^{m \times n}$, where $(X_{ij})_{1 \leq i \leq m}$ is the column vector formed by the coordinates of x_j in $(\beta_1, \ldots, \beta_m)$, i.e., $x_j = \beta_1 X_{1j} + \cdots + \beta_m X_{mj}$. Then the "rank" metric d on $\mathbb{F}_{q^m}^n$ is the rank metric on the associated matrix space, namely

$$d(\boldsymbol{x}, \boldsymbol{y}) := |\boldsymbol{y} - \boldsymbol{x}|_{\text{RANK}}, \quad \text{where we define } |\boldsymbol{x}|_{\text{RANK}} := \text{Rank}\,(\text{Mat}(\boldsymbol{x})).$$

Hereafter, we will use the following terminology.

Problem 1 ((m, n, k, r)-decoding problem).
    Input: an $\mathbb{F}_{q^m}$-basis $(\boldsymbol{c}_1, \ldots, \boldsymbol{c}_k)$ of a subspace $\mathcal{C}$ of $\mathbb{F}_{q^m}^n$, an integer $r \in \mathbb{N}$, and a vector $\boldsymbol{y} \in \mathbb{F}_{q^m}^n$ such that $|\boldsymbol{y} - \boldsymbol{c}|_{\text{RANK}} \leq r$ for some $\boldsymbol{c} \in \mathcal{C}$.
    Output: $\boldsymbol{c} \in \mathcal{C}$ and $\boldsymbol{e} \in \mathbb{F}_{q^m}^n$ such that $\boldsymbol{y} = \boldsymbol{c} + \boldsymbol{e}$ and $|\boldsymbol{e}|_{\text{RANK}} \leq r$.

This problem is known as the Rank Decoding problem, written RD. It is equivalent to the Rank Syndrome Decoding problem, for which one uses the parity check matrix of the code. There are two approaches to solve RD instances: the combinatorial ones such as [10, 24] and the algebraic ones. For some time it was thought that the combinatorial approach was the most threatening attack on such schemes especially when q is small, until [11] showed that even for $q = 2$ the algebraic attacks outperform the combinatorial ones. If the conjecture made in [11] holds, the complexity of solving by algebraic attacks the decoding problem is of order $2^{O(r \log n)}$ with a constant depending on the code rate $R = k/n$.

Even if the decoding problem is not known to be NP-complete for these $\mathbb{F}_{q^m}$-linear codes, there is a randomized reduction to an NP-complete problem [27] (namely to decoding in the Hamming metric). The region of parameters which is of interest for the NIST submissions corresponds to $m = \Theta(n)$, $k = \Theta(n)$ and $r = \Theta(\sqrt{n})$.

The MinRank Problem. The MinRank problem was first mentioned in [13] where its NP-completeness was also proven. We will consider here the homogeneous version of this problem which corresponds to

Problem 2 (MinRank problem).
   Input: an integer $r \in \mathbb{N}$ and K matrices $\boldsymbol{M}_1, \ldots, \boldsymbol{M}_K \in \mathbb{F}_q^{m \times n}$.
   Output: field elements $x_1, x_2, \ldots, x_K \in \mathbb{F}_q$ that are not all zero such that

$$\text{Rank}\left(\sum_{i=1}^{K} x_i \boldsymbol{M}_i\right) \leq r.$$

It plays a central role in public key cryptography. Many multivariate schemes are either directly based on the hardness of this problem [15] or strongly related to it as in [35–37] and the NIST post-quantum competition candidates Gui [17], GeMSS [14] or Rainbow [18]. It first appeared in this context as part of Kipnis-Shamir's attack [29] against the HFE cryptosystem [35]. It is also central in rank metric code-based cryptography, because the RD problem reduces to MinRank as explained in [19] and actually the best algorithms for solving this problem are really MinRank solvers taking advantage of the $\mathbb{F}_{q^m}$ underlying structure as in [11]. However the parameter region generally differs. When the RD problem arising from rank metric schemes is treated as a MinRank problem we generally have $K = \Theta(n^2)$ and r is rather small $r = \Theta(\sqrt{n})$ whereas for the multivariate cryptosystems $K = \Theta(n)$ but r is much bigger.

The current best known algorithms for solving the MinRank problem have exponential complexity. Many of them are obtained by an algebraic approach too consisting in modeling the MinRank problem by an algebraic system and solving it with Gröbner basis techniques. The main modelings are the Kipnis-Shamir modeling [29] and the minors modeling [20]. The complexity of solving MinRank using these modelings has been investigated in [19, 20, 38]. In particular [38] shows that the bilinear Kipnis-Shamir modeling behaves much better than generic bilinear systems with respect to Gröbner basis techniques.

Our Contribution. Here we follow on from the approach in [11] and propose a slightly different modeling to solve the RD problem. Roughly speaking the algebraic approach in [11] is to set up a bilinear system satisfied by the error we are looking for. This system is formed by two kinds of variables, the "coefficient" variables and the "support" variables. It is implicitly the modeling considered in [33]. The breakthrough obtained in [11] was to realize that

- the coefficient variables have to satisfy "maximal minor" equations: the maximal minors of a certain $r \times (n - k - 1)$ matrix (i.e. the $r \times r$ minors) with entries being linear forms in the coefficient variables have to be equal to 0.
- these maximal minors are themselves linear combinations of maximal minors c_T of an $r \times n$ matrix C whose entries are the coefficient variables.

This gives a linear system in the c_T's provided there are enough linear equations. Moreover the original bilinear system has many solutions and there is some freedom in choosing the coefficient variables and the support variables. With the choice made in [11] the information we obtain about the c_T's is not enough to recover the coefficient variables directly. In this case the last step of the algebraic attack still has to compute a Gröbner basis for the algebraic system consisting of the original system plus the information we have on the c_T's.

Our new approach starts by noticing that there is a better way to use the freedom on the coefficient variables and the support variables: we can actually specify so many coefficient variables that all those that remain unknown are essentially equal to some maximal minor c_T of C. With this we avoid the Gröbner basis computation: we obtain from the knowledge of the c_T's the coefficient variables and plugging in theses values in the original bilinear system we are left with solving a linear system in the support variables. This new approach gives a substantial speed-up in the computations for solving the system. It results in the best practical efficiency and complexity bounds that are currently known for the decoding problem; in particular, it significantly improves upon [11]. We present attacks for ROLLO-I-128, ROLLO-I-192, and ROLLO-I-256 with bit complexity respectively in 70, 86, and 158, to be compared to 117, 144, and 197 obtained in [11]. The difference with [11] is significant since as there is no real quantum speed-up for solving linear systems, the best quantum attacks for ROLLO-I-192 remained the quantum attack based on combinatorial attacks, when our new attacks show that ROLLO parameters are broken and need to be changed.

Our analysis is divided into two categories: the "overdetermined" and the "underdetermined" case. An (m, n, k, r)-decoding instance is overdetermined if

$$m \binom{n - k - 1}{r} \geq \binom{n}{r} - 1. \tag{1}$$

This really corresponds to the case where we have enough linear equations by our approach to find all the c_T's (and hence all the coefficient variables). In that case we obtain a complexity in

$$\mathcal{O}\left(m \binom{n - p - k - 1}{r} \binom{n - p}{r}^{\omega - 1}\right) \tag{2}$$

operations in the field $\mathbb{F}_q$, where ω is the constant of linear algebra and $p = \max\{i : i \in \{1..n\}, m\binom{n-i-k-1}{r} \geq \binom{n-i}{r} - 1\}$ represents, in case the overdetermined condition (1) is comfortably fulfilled, the use of punctured codes. This complexity clearly supersedes the previous results of [11] in terms of complexity and also by the fact that it does not require generic Gröbner Basis algorithms. In a rough way for $r = \mathcal{O}\left(\sqrt{n}\right)$ (the type of parameters used for ROLLO and RQC), the recent improvements on algebraic attacks can be seen as this: before [11] the complexity for solving RD involved a term in $\mathcal{O}(n^2)$ in the upper part of a binomial coefficient, the modeling in [11] replaced it by a term in $\mathcal{O}\left(n^{\frac{3}{2}}\right)$ whereas our new modeling involves a term in $\mathcal{O}(n)$ at a similar position. This leads to a gain in the exponential coefficient of order 30% compared to [11] and of order 50% compared to approaches before [11]. Notice that for ROLLO and RQC only parameters with announced complexities 128 and 192 bits satisfied condition (1) but not parameters with announced complexities 256 bits.

When condition (1) is not fulfilled, the instance can either be underdetermined or be brought back to the overdetermined area by an hybrid approach using exhaustive search with exponential complexity to guess few variables in the system. In the underdetermined case, our approach is different from [11]. Here we propose an approach using reduction to the MinRank problem and a new way to solve it. Roughly speaking we start with a quadratic modeling of MinRank that we call "support minors modeling" which is bilinear in the aforementioned coefficient and support variables and linear in the so called "linear variables". The last ones are precisely the x_i's that appear in the MinRank problem. Recall that the coefficient variables are the entries of a $r \times n$ matrix C. The crucial observation is now that for all positive integer b all maximal minors of any $(r + b) \times n$ matrix obtained by adding to C any b rows of $\sum_i x_i M_i$ are equal to 0. These minors are themselves linear combinations of terms of the form mc_T where c_T is a maximal minor of C and m a monomial of degree b in the x_i's. We can predict the number of independent linear equations in the mc_T's we obtain this way and when the number of such equations is bigger than the number of mc_T's we can recover their values and solve the MinRank problem by linearization. This new approach is not only effective in the underdetermined case of the RD problem it can also be quite effective for some multivariate proposals made to the NIST competition. In the case of the RD problem, it improves the attacks on [7] made in [11] for the parameter sets with the largest values of r (corresponding to parameters claiming 256 bits of security). The multivariate schemes that are affected by this new attack are for instance GeMSS and Rainbow. On GeMSS it shows MinRank attacks together with this new way of solving MinRank come close to the best known attacks against this scheme. On Rainbow it outperforms slightly the best known attacks for certain high security parameter sets.

At last, not only do these two new ways of solving algebraically the RD or MinRank problem outperform previous algebraic approaches in certain parameter regimes, they are also much better understood: we do not rely on heuristics based on the first degree fall as in [11,38] to analyze its complexity, but it really amounts to solve a linear system and understand the number of independent linear equations that we obtain which is something for which we have been able to give accurate formulas predicting the behavior we obtain experimentally.

2 Notation

In what follows, we use the following notation and definitions:

- Matrices and vectors are written in boldface font M.
- The transpose of a matrix M is denoted by M^T.
- For a given ring $\mathcal{R}$, the set of matrices with n rows, m columns and coefficients in $\mathcal{R}$ is denoted by $\mathcal{R}^{n \times m}$.
- $\{1..n\}$ stands for the set of integers from 1 to n.
- For a subset $I \subset \{1..n\}$, $\#I$ stands for the number of elements in I.
- For two subsets $I \subset \{1..n\}$ and $J \subset \{1..m\}$, we write $M_{I,J}$ for the submatrix of M formed by its rows (resp. columns) with index in I (resp. J).
- For an $m \times n$ matrix M we use the shorthand notation $M_{*,J} = M_{\{1..m\},J}$ and $M_{i,j}$ for the entry in row i and column j.
- $|M|$ is the determinant of a matrix M, $|M|_{I,J}$ is the determinant of the submatrix $M_{I,J}$ and $|M|_{*,J}$ is the determinant of $M_{*,J}$.
- $\alpha \in \mathbb{F}_{q^m}$ is a primitive element, that is to say that $(1, \alpha, \dots, \alpha^{m-1})$ is a basis of $\mathbb{F}_{q^m}$ seen as an $\mathbb{F}_q$-vector space.
- For $v = (v_1, \dots, v_n) \in \mathbb{F}_{q^m}^n$, the *support* of v is the $\mathbb{F}_q$-vector subspace of $\mathbb{F}_{q^m}$ spanned by the vectors $v_1, \dots, v_n$. Thus this support is the column space of the matrix $Mat(v)$ associated to v (for any choice of basis), and its dimension is precisely $\mathrm{Rank}(Mat(v))$.
- An $[n, k]$ $\mathbb{F}_{q^m}$-linear code is an $\mathbb{F}_{q^m}$-linear subspace of $\mathbb{F}_{q^m}^n$ of dimension k.

3 Algebraic Modeling of the MinRank and the Decoding Problem

3.1 Modeling of MinRank

The modeling for MinRank we consider here is related to the modeling used for decoding in the rank metric in [11]. The starting point is that, in order to solve *Problem 2*, we look for a nonzero solution $(S, C, x) \in \mathbb{F}_q^{m \times r} \times \mathbb{F}_q^{r \times n} \times \mathbb{F}_q^K$ of

$$SC = \sum_{i=1}^{K} x_i M_i. \tag{3}$$

S is an unknown matrix whose columns give a basis for the column space of the matrix $\sum_{i=1}^{K} x_i M_i$ of rank $\leq r$ we are looking for. The j-th column of C represents the coordinates of the j-th column of the aforementioned matrix in this basis. We call the entries of S the *support variables*, and the entries of C the *coefficient variables*. Note that in the above equation, the variables x_i only occur linearly. As such, we will dub them the *linear variables*.

Let r_j be the j-th row of $\sum_{i=1}^{K} x_i M_i$. (3) implies that each row r_j is in the rowspace of C (or in coding theoretic terms r_j should belong to the code $\mathcal{C} := \{uC, u \in \mathbb{F}_q^r\}$). The following $(r+1) \times n$ matrix C'_j is therefore of rank $\leq r$:

$$C'_j = \begin{pmatrix} r_j \\ C \end{pmatrix}.$$

Therefore, all the maximal minors of this matrix are equal to 0. These maximal minors can be expressed via cofactor expansion with respect to their first row. In this way, they can be seen as bilinear forms in the x_i's and the $r \times r$ minors of C. These minors play a fundamental role in the whole paper and we use the following notation for them.

Notation 1. *Let $T \subset \{1..n\}$ with $\#T = r$. Let c_T be the maximal minor of C corresponding to the columns of C that belong to T, i.e.*

$$c_T := |C|_{*,T} \,.$$

These considerations lead to the following algebraic modeling.

Modelling 1 (Support Minors modeling). *We consider the system of bilinear equations, given by canceling the maximal minors of the m matrices C'_j:*

$$\left\{ f = 0 \,\middle|\, f \in \mathbf{MaxMinors}\begin{pmatrix} r_j \\ C \end{pmatrix}, \; j \in \{1..m\} \right\}. \tag{4}$$

This system contains:

- $m\binom{n}{r+1}$ *bilinear equations with coefficients in $\mathbb{F}_q$,*
- $K + \binom{n}{r}$ *unknowns: $\boldsymbol{x} = (x_1, \cdots, x_K)$ and the c_T's, $T \subset \{1..n\}$ with $\#T = r$.*

We search for the solutions x_i, c_T's in $\mathbb{F}_q$.

Remark 1.

1. One of the point of having the c_T as unknowns instead of the coefficients C_{ij} of C is that, if we solve (4) in the x_i and the C_{ij} variables, then there are many solutions to (4) since when $(\boldsymbol{x}, C)$ is a solution for it, then $(\boldsymbol{x}, AC)$ is also a solution for any invertible matrix A in $\mathbb{F}_q^{r \times r}$. With the c_T variables we only expect a space of dimension 1 for the c_T corresponding to the transformation $c_T \mapsto |A|\, c_T$ that maps a given solution of (4) to a new one.
2. Another benefit brought by replacing the C_{ij} variables by the c_T's is that it decreases significantly the number of possible monomials for writing the algebraic system (4) (about $r!$ times less). This allows for solving this system by linearization when the number of equations of the previous modeling exceeds the number of different $x_i c_T$ monomials minus 1, namely when

$$m\binom{n}{r+1} \geq K\binom{n}{r} - 1. \tag{5}$$

This turns out to be "almost" the case for several multivariate cryptosystem proposals based on the MinRank problem where K is generally of the same order as m and n.

3.2 The Approach Followed in [11] to Solve the Decoding Problem

In what follows, we consider the (m, n, k, r)-decoding problem for a code $\mathcal{C}$ of length n, dimension k over $\mathbb{F}_{q^m}$ with a $\boldsymbol{y} \in \mathbb{F}_{q^m}^n$ at distance r from $\mathcal{C}$ and look for $\boldsymbol{c} \in \mathcal{C}$ and $\boldsymbol{e}$ such that $\boldsymbol{y} = \boldsymbol{c} + \boldsymbol{e}$ and $|\boldsymbol{e}| = r$. We assume that there is a unique solution to this problem (which is relevant for our cryptographic schemes). The starting point is the Ourivksi-Johansson approach, consisting in considering the linear code $\widetilde{\mathcal{C}} = \mathcal{C} + \langle \boldsymbol{y} \rangle$. From now on, let $\widetilde{G} = (\boldsymbol{I}_{k+1} \ \boldsymbol{R})$ (respectively $\widetilde{H} = (-\boldsymbol{R}^\mathsf{T} \ \boldsymbol{I}_{n-k-1})$) be the generator matrix in systematic form (respectively a parity-check matrix) of the extended code $\widetilde{\mathcal{C}}$. By construction, $\boldsymbol{e}$ belongs to $\widetilde{\mathcal{C}}$ as well as all its multiples $\lambda \boldsymbol{e}$, $\lambda \in \mathbb{F}_{q^m}$. Looking for non-zero codewords in $\widetilde{\mathcal{C}}$ of rank weight r has at least $q^m - 1$ different solutions, namely all the $\lambda \boldsymbol{e}$ for $\lambda \in \mathbb{F}_{q^m}^\times$.

It is readily seen that finding such codewords can be done by solving the (homogeneous) MinRank problem with $\boldsymbol{M}_{ij} := Mat(\alpha^{i-1}\boldsymbol{c}_j)$ (we adopt a bivariate indexing of the $\boldsymbol{M}_i$'s which is more convenient here) for $(ij) \in \{1..m\} \times \{1..k+1\}$ and where $\boldsymbol{c}_1, \cdots, \boldsymbol{c}_{k+1}$ is an $\mathbb{F}_{q^m}$-basis of $\widetilde{\mathcal{C}}$. This is because the $\alpha^{i-1}\boldsymbol{c}_j$'s form an $\mathbb{F}_q$-basis of $\widetilde{\mathcal{C}}$. However, the problem with this approach is that $K = (k+1)m = \Theta\left(n^2\right)$ for the parameters relevant to cryptography. This is much more than for the multivariate cryptosystems based on MinRank and (5) is far from being satisfied here. However, as observed in [11], it turns out in this particular case, it is possible because of the $\mathbb{F}_{q^m}$ linear structure of the code, to give an algebraic modeling that only involves the entries of $\boldsymbol{C}$. It is obtained by introducing a parity-check matrix for $\widetilde{\mathcal{C}}$, that is a matrix $\boldsymbol{H}$ whose kernel is $\widetilde{\mathcal{C}}$:

$$\widetilde{\mathcal{C}} = \{\boldsymbol{c} \in \mathbb{F}_{q^m}^n : \boldsymbol{c}\boldsymbol{H}^\mathsf{T} = 0\}.$$

In our $\mathbb{F}_{q^m}$ linear setting the solution $\boldsymbol{e}$ we are looking for can be written as

$$\boldsymbol{e} = \left(1 \ \alpha \ldots \alpha^{m-1}\right) \boldsymbol{S}\boldsymbol{C}, \tag{6}$$

where $\boldsymbol{S} \in \mathbb{F}_q^{m \times r}$ and $\boldsymbol{C} \in \mathbb{F}_q^{r \times n}$ play the same role as in the previous subsection: $\boldsymbol{S}$ represents a basis of the support of $\boldsymbol{e}$ in $\left(\mathbb{F}_q^m\right)^r$ and $\boldsymbol{C}$ the coordinates of $\boldsymbol{e}$ in this basis. By writing that $\boldsymbol{e}$ should belong to $\widetilde{\mathcal{C}}$ we obtain that

$$\left(1 \ \alpha \ldots \alpha^{m-1}\right) \boldsymbol{S}\boldsymbol{C}\boldsymbol{H}^\mathsf{T} = \boldsymbol{0}_{n-k-1}. \tag{7}$$

This gives an algebraic system using only the coefficient variables as shown by

Proposition 1 ([11], **Theorem 2**). *The maximal minors of the $r \times (n-k-1)$ matrix $\boldsymbol{C}\boldsymbol{H}^\mathsf{T}$ are all equal to 0.*

Proof. Consider the following vector in $\mathbb{F}_q^r$: $\boldsymbol{e}' := \left(1 \ \alpha \ldots \alpha^{m-1}\right) \boldsymbol{S}$ whose entries generate (over $\mathbb{F}_q$) the subspace generated by the entries of $\boldsymbol{e}$ (i.e. its support). Substituting $\left(1 \ \alpha \ldots \alpha^{m-1}\right) \boldsymbol{S}$ for $\boldsymbol{e}'$ in (7) yields $\boldsymbol{e}'\boldsymbol{C}\boldsymbol{H}^\mathsf{T} = \boldsymbol{0}_{n-k-1}$. This shows that the $r \times n$ matrix $\boldsymbol{C}\boldsymbol{H}^\mathsf{T}$ is of rank $\leq r - 1$. $\qquad \square$

These minors $CH^\intercal$ are polynomials in the entries of C with coefficients in $\mathbb{F}_{q^m}$. Since these entries belong to $\mathbb{F}_q$, the nullity of each minor gives m algebraic equations corresponding to polynomials with coefficients in $\mathbb{F}_q$. This involves the following operation.

Notation 2. *Let $\mathcal{S} := \{\sum_j a_{ij} m_{ij} = 0, 1 \leq i \leq N\}$ be a set of polynomial equations where the m_{ij}'s are the monomials in the unknowns that are assumed to belong to $\mathbb{F}_q$, whereas the a_{ij}'s are known coefficients that belong to $\mathbb{F}_{q^m}$. We define the a_{ijk}'s as $a_{ij} = \sum_{k=0}^{m-1} a_{ijk} \alpha^k$, where the a_{ijk}'s belong to $\mathbb{F}_q$. From this we can define the system "unfolding" over $\mathbb{F}_q$ as*

$$\mathbf{UnFold}(\mathcal{S}) := \left\{ \sum_j a_{ijk} m_{ij} = 0, 1 \leq i \leq N, 0 \leq k \leq m-1 \right\}.$$

The important point is that the solutions of $\mathcal{S}$ over $\mathbb{F}_q$ are exactly the solutions of $\mathbf{UnFold}(\mathcal{S})$ over $\mathbb{F}_q$, so that in that sense the two systems are equivalent.

By using the Cauchy-Binet formula, it is proved [11, Prop. 1] that the maximal minors of $CH^\intercal$, which are polynomials of degree $\leq r$ in the coefficient variables C_{ij}, can actually be expressed as *linear* combinations of the c_T's. In other words we obtain $m\binom{n-k-1}{r}$ linear equations over $\mathbb{F}_q$ by "unfolding" the $\binom{n-k-1}{r}$ maximal minors of $CH^\intercal$. We denote such a system by

$$\mathbf{UnFold}\left(\{f = 0 | f \in \mathbf{MaxMinors}(CH^\intercal)\}\right). \tag{8}$$

It is straightforward to check that some variables in C and S can be specialized. The choice which is made in [11] is to specialize S with its r first rows equal to the identity ($S_{\{1..r\},*} = I_r$), its first column to $\mathbf{1}^\intercal = (1, 0, \dots, 0)^\intercal$ and C has its first column equal to $\mathbf{1}^\intercal$. It is proved in [11, Section 3.3] that if the first coordinate of e is nonzero and the top $r \times r$ block of S is invertible, then the previous specialized system has a unique solution. Moreover, this will always be the case up to a permutation of the coordinates of the codewords or a change of $\mathbb{F}_{q^m}$-basis.

It is proved in [11, Prop. 2] that a degree-r Gröbner basis of the unfolded polynomials **MaxMinors** is obtained by solving the corresponding linear system in the c_T's. However, this strategy of specialization does not reveal the entries of C (it only reveals the values of the c_T's). To finish the calculation it still remains to compute a Gröbner basis of the whole algebraic system as done in [11, Step 5, §6.1]). There is a simple way to avoid this computation by specializing the variables of C in a different way. This is the new approach we explain now.

3.3 The New Approach : Specializing the Identity in C

As in the previous approach we note that if (S, C) is a solution of (7) then (SA^{-1}, AC) is also a solution of it for any invertible matrix A in $\mathbb{F}_q^{r \times r}$. Now, when the first r columns of a solution C form a invertible matrix, we will still have a solution with the specialization

$$C = \left(I_r \ C' \right).$$

We can also specialize the first column of S to $\mathbf{1}^{\intercal} = \left(1\,0\ldots 0\right)^{\intercal}$. If the first r columns of C are not independent, it suffices as in [11, Algo. 1] to make several different attempts of choosing r columns. The point of this specialization is that

- the corresponding c_T's are equal to the entries C_{ij} of C up to an unessential factor $(-1)^{r+i}$ whenever $T = \{1..r\}\backslash\{i\} \cup \{j\}$ for any $i \in \{1..r\}$ and $j \in \{r+1..n\}$. This follows on the spot by writing the cofactor expansion of the minor $c_T = |C|_{*,\{1..r\}\backslash\{i\}\cup\{j\}}$. Solving the linear system in the c_T's corresponding to (8) yields now directly the coefficient variables C_{ij}. This avoids the subsequent Gröbner basis computation, since once we have C we obtain S directly by solving (7) which has become a linear system.
- it is readily shown that any solution of (8) is actually a projection on the C_{ij} variables of a solution (S, C) of the whole system (see Proposition 3). This justifies the whole approach.

In other words we are interested here in the following modeling

Modelling 2. *We consider the system of linear equations, given by unfolding all maximal minors of $\left(I_r\ C'\right)H^{\intercal}$:*

$$\mathbf{UnFold}\left(\left\{f = 0\middle| f \in \mathbf{MaxMinors}\left(\left(I_r\ C'\right)H^{\intercal}\right)\right\}\right). \qquad (9)$$

This system contains:

- $m\binom{n-k-1}{r}$ *linear equations with coefficients in $\mathbb{F}_q$,*
- $\binom{n}{r} - 1$ *unknowns: the c_T's, $T \subset \{1..n\}$ with $\#T = r$, $T \neq \{1..r\}$.*

We search for the solutions c_T's in $\mathbb{F}_q$.

Note that from the specialization, $c_{\{1..r\}} = 1$ is not an unknown. For the reader's convenience, let us recall the specific form of these equations which is obtained by unfolding the following polynomials (see [11, Prop. 2] and its proof).

Proposition 2. $\mathbf{MaxMinors}(CH^{\intercal})$ *contains $\binom{n-k-1}{r}$ polynomials of degree r over $\mathbb{F}_{q^m}$, indexed by the subsets $J \subset \{1..n-k-1\}$ of size r, that are the*

$$P_J = \sum_{\substack{T_1 \subset \{1..k+1\}, T_2 \subset J, \\ \#T_1 + \#T_2 = r \\ T = T_1 \cup (T_2+k+1)}} (-1)^{\sigma_J(T_2)} \left|R\right|_{T_1, J\backslash T_2} c_T, \qquad (10)$$

where the sum is over all subsets $T_1 \subset \{1..k+1\}$ and T_2 subset of J, with $\#T_1 + \#T_2 = r$, and $\sigma_J(T_2)$ is an integer depending on T_2 and J. We denote by $T_2 + k + 1$ the set $\{i + k + 1 : i \in T_2\}$.

Let us show now that the solutions of this linear system are projections of the solutions of the original system. For this purpose, let us bring in

- The original system (7) over $\mathbb{F}_{q^m}$ obtained with the aforementioned specialization

$$\mathcal{F}_C = \left\{\left(1\ \alpha\ \cdots\ \alpha^{m-1}\right)\left(\mathbf{1}^{\intercal}\ S'\right)\left(I_r\ C'\right)H^{\intercal} = \mathbf{0}_{n-k-1}\right\}, \qquad (11)$$

where $\mathbf{1}^{\intercal} = \left(1\,0\ldots 0\right)^{\intercal}$, $S = \left(\mathbf{1}^{\intercal}\ S'\right)$ and $C = \left(I_r\ C'\right)$.

- The system in the coefficient variables we are interested in
$$\mathcal{F}_M = \Big\{ f = 0 \Big| f \in \mathbf{MaxMinors}\left(\left(\boldsymbol{I}_r \; \boldsymbol{C}' \right) \boldsymbol{H}^{\mathsf{T}} \right) \Big\}.$$

- Let $V_{\mathbb{F}_q}(\mathcal{F}_C)$ be the set of solutions of (11) with all variables in $\mathbb{F}_q$, that is
$$V_{\mathbb{F}_q}(\mathcal{F}_C) = \Big\{ (\boldsymbol{S}^*, \boldsymbol{C}^*) \in \mathbb{F}_q^{m(r-1)+r(n-r)} \; : \; (1 \, \alpha \, \cdots \, \alpha^{m-1})(\mathbf{1}^{\mathsf{T}} \, \boldsymbol{S}^*)(\boldsymbol{I}_r \, \boldsymbol{C}^*)$$
$$\boldsymbol{H}^{\mathsf{T}} = \boldsymbol{0} \Big\}.$$

- Let $V_{\mathbb{F}_q}(\mathcal{F}_M)$ be the set of solutions of $\mathcal{F}_M$ with all variables in $\mathbb{F}_q$, i.e.
$$V_{\mathbb{F}_q}(\mathcal{F}_M) = \Big\{ \boldsymbol{C}^* \in \mathbb{F}_q^{r(n-r)} : \mathrm{Rank}_{\mathbb{F}_{q^m}}\left(\left(\boldsymbol{I}_r \; \boldsymbol{C}^* \right) \boldsymbol{H}^{\mathsf{T}} \right) < r \Big\}.$$

With these notations at hand, we now show that solving the decoding problem is left to solve the **MaxMinors** system depending only on the $\boldsymbol{C}$ variables.

Proposition 3. *If $\boldsymbol{e}$ can be uniquely decoded and has rank r, then*

$$V_{\mathbb{F}_q}(\mathcal{F}_M) = \Big\{ \boldsymbol{C}^* \in \mathbb{F}_q^{r(n-r)} : \exists \boldsymbol{S}^* \in \mathbb{F}_q^{m(r-1)} \text{ s.t. } (\boldsymbol{S}^*, \boldsymbol{C}^*) \in V_{\mathbb{F}_q}(\mathcal{F}_C) \Big\}, \quad (12)$$

that is $V_{\mathbb{F}_q}(\mathcal{F}_M)$ is the projection of $V_{\mathbb{F}_q}(\mathcal{F}_C)$ on the last $r(n-r)$ coordinates.

Proof. Let $(\boldsymbol{S}^*, \boldsymbol{C}^*) \in V_{\mathbb{F}_q}(\mathcal{F}_C)$, then $\left(1 \, S_2^* \ldots S_r^* \right) = \left(1 \, \alpha \, \cdots \, \alpha^{m-1} \right) \left(\mathbf{1}^{\mathsf{T}} \, \boldsymbol{S}^* \right)$ belongs to the left kernel of the matrix $\left(\boldsymbol{I}_r \, \boldsymbol{C}^* \right) \boldsymbol{H}^{\mathsf{T}}$. Hence this matrix has rank less than r, and $\boldsymbol{C}^* \in V_{\mathbb{F}_q}(\mathcal{F}_M)$. Reciprocally, if $\boldsymbol{C}^* \in V_{\mathbb{F}_q}(\mathcal{F}_M)$, then the matrix $\left(\boldsymbol{I}_r \, \boldsymbol{C}^* \right) \boldsymbol{H}^{\mathsf{T}}$ has rank less than r, hence its left kernel over $\mathbb{F}_{q^m}$ contains a non zero element $(S_1^*, \ldots, S_r^*) = (1, \alpha, \ldots, \alpha^{m-1}) \boldsymbol{S}^*$ with the coefficients of $\boldsymbol{S}^*$ in $\mathbb{F}_q$. But S_1^* cannot be zero, as it would mean that $(0, S_2^*, \ldots, S_r^*) \left(\boldsymbol{I}_r \, \boldsymbol{C}^* \right)$ is an error of weight less than r solution of the decoding problem, and we assumed there is only one error of weight exactly r solution of the decoding problem. Then, $(S_1^{*-1}(S_2^*, \ldots, S_r^*), \boldsymbol{C}^*) \in V_{\mathbb{F}_q}(\mathcal{F}_C)$. $\qquad \square$

4   Solving RD: Overdetermined Case

In this section, we show that, when the number of equations is sufficiently large, we can solve the system given in Modeling 2 with only linear algebra computations, by linearization on the c_T's.

4.1   The Overdetermined Case

The linear system given in Modeling 2 is described by the following matrix **MaxMin** with rows indexed by $(J, i) : J \subset \{1..n-k-1\}, \#J = r, 0 \leq i \leq m-1$ and columns indexed by $T \subset \{1..n\}$ of size r, with the entry in row (J, i) and column T being the coefficient in α^i of the element $\pm |\boldsymbol{R}|_{T_1, J \setminus T_2} \in \mathbb{F}_{q^m}$. More precisely, we have

$$\mathbf{MaxMin}[(J, i), T] = \begin{cases} 0 & \text{if } T_2 \not\subset J \\ [\alpha^i](-1)^{\sigma_J(T_2)}(|\boldsymbol{R}|_{T_1, J \setminus T_2}) & \text{if } T_2 \subset J, \end{cases} \quad (13)$$

$$\text{with} \quad T_1 = T \cap \{1..k+1\},$$
$$\text{and} \quad T_2 = (T \cap \{k+2..n\}) - (k+1).$$

The matrix **MaxMin** can have rank $\binom{n}{r} - 1$ at most; indeed if it had a maximal rank of $\binom{n}{r}$, this would imply that all c_T's are equal to 0, which is in contradiction with the assumption $c_{\{1..r\}} = 1$.

Proposition 4. *If* **MaxMin** *has rank* $\binom{n}{r} - 1$, *then the right kernel of* **MaxMin** *contains only one element* $(c \; 1) \in \mathbb{F}_q^{\binom{n}{r}}$ *with value 1 on its component corresponding to* $c_{\{1..r\}}$. *The components of this vector contain the values of the* c_T's, $T \neq \{1..r\}$. *This gives the values of all the variables* $C_{i,j} = (-1)^{r+i} c_{\{1..r\}\setminus\{i\}\cup\{j\}}$.

Proof. If **MaxMin** has rank $\binom{n}{r} - 1$, then as there is a solution to the system, a row echelon form of the matrix has the shape

$$\begin{pmatrix} I_{\binom{n}{r}-1} & -c^{\mathsf{T}} \\ 0 & 0 \end{pmatrix}$$

with c a vector in $\mathbb{F}_q$ of size $\binom{n}{r} - 1$: we cannot get a jump in the stair of the echelon form as it would imply that $\mathcal{F}_M$ has no solution. Then $(c \; 1)$ is in the right kernel of **MaxMin**. $\qquad\square$

It is then easy to recover the variables S from (11) by linear algebra. The following algorithm recovers the error if there is one solution to the system (11). It is shown in [11, Algorithm 1] how to deal with the other cases, and this can be easily adapted to the specialization considered in this paper.

Input: Code $\mathcal{C}$, vector y at distance r from $\mathcal{C}$, such that $m\binom{n-k-1}{r} \geq \binom{n}{r} - 1$
and **MaxMin** has rank $\binom{n}{r} - 1$
Output: The error e of weight r such that $y - e \in \mathcal{C}$
Construct **MaxMin**, the $m\binom{n-k-1}{r} \times \binom{n}{r}$ matrix over $\mathbb{F}_q$ associated to the system $\mathcal{F}_M$;
Let $(c \; 1)$ be the only such vector in the right kernel of **MaxMin** ;
Compute the values $C^* = (C_{i,j}^*)_{i,j}$ from c;
Compute the values $(S_1^*, \ldots, S_r^*) \in \mathbb{F}_{q^m}^r$ by solving the linear system

$$(S_1, \ldots, S_r) C^* H^{\mathsf{T}} = 0$$

and taking the unique value with $S_1^* = 1$;
return $(1, S_2^*, \ldots, S_r^*) C^*$;

    Algorithm 1: (m, n, k, r)-decoding in the overdetermined case.

Proposition 5. *When* $m\binom{n-k-1}{r} \geq \binom{n}{r} - 1$ *and* **MaxMin** *has rank* $\binom{n}{r} - 1$, *then Algorithm 1 recovers the error in complexity*

$$\mathcal{O}\left(m \binom{n-k-1}{r} \binom{n}{r}^{\omega-1} \right) \qquad (14)$$

operations in the field $\mathbb{F}_q$, *where* ω *is the constant of linear algebra.*

Proof. To recover the error, the most consuming part is the computation of the left kernel of the matrix **MaxMin** in $\mathbb{F}_q^{m\binom{n-k-1}{r}\times\binom{n}{r}}$, in the case where $m\binom{n-k-1}{r} \geq \binom{n}{r} - 1$.
This complexity is bounded by Eq. (14). $\square$

We ran a lot of experiments with random codes $\mathcal{C}$ such that $m\binom{n-k-1}{r} \geq \binom{n}{r} - 1$, and the matrix **MaxMin** was always of rank $\binom{n}{r} - 1$. That is why we propose the following heuristic about the rank of **MaxMin**.

Heuristic 1 (Overdetermined case). *When* $m\binom{n-k-1}{r} \geq \binom{n}{r} - 1$, *with overwhelming probability, the rank of the matrix* **MaxMin** *is* $\binom{n}{r} - 1$.

Figure 1 gives the experimental results for $q = 2$, $r = 3, 4, 5$ and different values of n. We choose to keep m prime and close to $n/1.18$ to have a data set containing the parameters of the ROLLO-I cryptosystem. We choose for k the minimum between $\frac{n}{2}$ and the largest value leading to an overdetermined case. We have $k = \frac{n}{2}$ as soon as $n \geq 22$ for $r = 3$, $n \geq 36$ for $r = 4$, $n \geq 58$ for $r = 5$. The figure shows that the estimated complexity is a good upper bound for the computation's complexity. It also shows that this upper bound is not tight. Note that the experimental values are the complexity of the whole attack, including building the matrix that requires to compute the minors of $\boldsymbol{R}$. Hence for small values of n, it may happen that this part of the attack takes more time than solving the linear system. This explains why, for $r = 3$ and $n < 28$, the experimental curve is above the theoretical one.

Figure 2 shows the theoretical complexity for the same parameter regime as Fig. 1 which fit the overdetermined case. The graph starts from the first value of n where $(n/1.18, n, 2k, r)$ is in the overdetermined case. We can see that theoretically, the cryptosystem ROLLO-I-128 with parameters $(79, 94, 47, 5)$ needs 2^{73} bit operations to decode an error, instead of the announced 2^{128} bits of security. In the same way, ROLLO-I-192 with parameters $(89, 106, 53, 6)$ would have 86 bits of security instead of 192. The parameters $(113, 134, 67, 7)$ for ROLLO-I-256 are not in the overdetermined case.

There are two classical improvements that can be used to lower the complexity of solving an algebraic system. The first one consists in selecting a subset of all equations, when some of them are redundant, see Sect. 4.2. The second one is the hybrid attack that will be explained in Sect. 4.3.

4.2   Improvement in the "Super"-Overdetermined Case by Puncturing

We consider the case when the system is "super"-overdetermined, i.e. when the number of rows in **MaxMin** is really larger than the number of columns. In that case, it is not necessary to consider all equations, we just need the minimum number of them to be able to find the solution.

To select the good equations (i.e. the ones that are likely to be linearly independent), we can take the system **MaxMinors** obtained by considering code

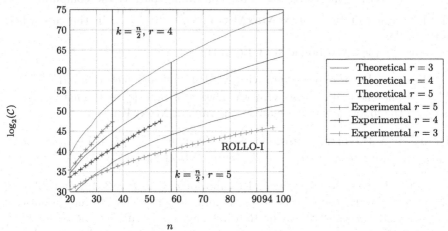

Fig. 1. Theoretical vs Experimental value of the complexity of the computation. The computations are done using `magma v2.22-2` on a machine with an Intel® Xeon® 2.00 GHz processor (*Any mention of commercial products is for information only and does not imply endorsement by NIST*). We measure the experimental complexity in terms of clock cycles of the CPU, given by the `magma` function `ClockCycles()`. The theoretical value is the binary logarithm of $m\binom{n-k-1}{r}\binom{n}{r}^{2.81-1}$. m is the largest prime less than $n/1.18$, k is the minimum of $n/2$ (right part of the graph) and the largest value for which the system is overdetermined (left part).

$\widetilde{C}$ punctured on the p last coordinates, instead of the entire code. Puncturing code $\widetilde{C}$ is equivalent to shortening the dual code, i.e. considering the system

$$\mathbf{MaxMinors}\left(\boldsymbol{C}_{*,\{1..n-p\}}(\boldsymbol{H}^{\mathsf{T}})_{\{1..n-p\},\{1..n-k-1-p\}}\right). \tag{15}$$

as we take $\boldsymbol{H}$ to be systematic on the last coordinates. This system is formed by a sub-sequence of polynomials in **MaxMinors** that do not contain the variables $c_{i,j}$ with $n - p + 1 \leq j \leq n$. This system contains $m\binom{n-p-k-1}{r}$ equations in $\binom{n-p}{r}$ variables c_T with $T \subset \{1..n - p - k - 1\}$. If we take the maximal value of p such that $m\binom{n-p-k-1}{r} \geq \binom{n-p}{r} - 1$, we can still apply Algorithm 1 but the complexity is reduced to

$$\mathcal{O}\left(m\binom{n-p-k-1}{r}\binom{n-p}{r}^{\omega-1}\right) \tag{16}$$

operations in the field $\mathbb{F}_q$.

4.3   Reducing to the Overdetermined Case: Hybrid Attack

Another classical improvement consists in using an hybrid approach mixing exhaustive search and linear resolution, like in [12]. This consists in specializing some variables of the system to reduce an underdetermined case to an

Theoretical complexity for $r = 5, 6, 7$ in the *overdetermined* cases when $n = 2k$.

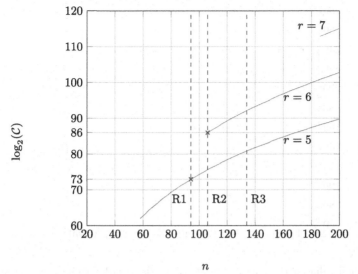

Fig. 2. Theoretical value of the complexity of the computation in the overdetermined cases, which is the binary logarithm of $m\binom{n-k-1}{r}\binom{n}{r}^{2.81-1}$. m is the largest prime less than $n/1.18$, $n = 2k$. The axis "R1, R2, R3" correspond to the values of n for the cryptosystems ROLLO-I-128; ROLLO-I-192 and ROLLO-I-256.

overdetermined one. For instance, if we specialize a columns of the matrix C, we are left with solving q^{ar} linear systems **MaxMin** of size $m\binom{n-k-1}{r} \times \binom{n-a}{r}$, and the global cost is

$$\mathcal{O}\left(q^{ar}m\binom{n-k-1}{r}\binom{n-a}{r}^{\omega-1}\right) \qquad (17)$$

operations in the field $\mathbb{F}_q$. In order to minimize the previous complexity (17), one chooses a to be the smallest integer such that the condition $m\binom{n-k-1}{r} \geq \binom{n-a}{r}-1$ is fulfilled. Figure 3 page 16 gives the best theoretical complexities obtained for $r = 5 \dots 9$ with the best values of a and p, for $n = 2k$. Table 1 page 24 gives the complexities of our attack (column "**This paper**") for all the parameters in the ROLLO and RQC submissions to the NIST competition; for the sake of clarity, we give the previous complexity from [11].

5   Solving RD and MinRank: Underdetermined Case

This section analyzes the support minors modeling approach (Modeling 1).

Theoretical complexity for $r = 5 \ldots 9$ when $n = 2k$.

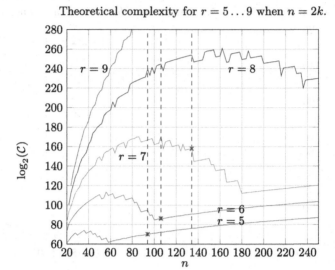

Fig. 3. Theoretical value of the complexity of RD in the overdetermined case (using punctured codes or specialization). $\mathcal{C}$ is the smallest value between (17) and (16). m is the largest prime less than $n/1.18$, $n = 2k$. The dashed axes correspond to the values of n for the cryptosystems ROLLO-I-128; ROLLO-I-192 and ROLLO-I-256.

5.1 Solving (3) by Direct Linearization

The number of monomials that can appear in Modeling 1 is $K\binom{n}{r}$ whereas the number of equations is $m\binom{n}{r+1}$. When the solution space of (3) is of dimension 1, we expect to solve it by direct linearization whenever:

$$m\binom{n}{r+1} \geq K\binom{n}{r} - 1. \tag{18}$$

We did a lot of experiments as explained in Sect. 5.6, and they suggest that it is the case.

Remark 2. Note that, in what follows, the Eq. (18) will sometimes be referred as the "$b = 1$ case".

5.2 Solving Support Minors Modeling at a Higher Degree, $q > b$

In the case where Eq. (18) does not hold we may produce a generalized version of Support Minors Modeling, multiplying the Support Minors Modeling equations by homogeneous degree $b - 1$ monomials in the linear variables, resulting in a system of equations that are homogeneous degree 1 in the variables c_T and homogeneous degree b in the variables x_i. The strategy will again be to linearize over monomials. Unlike in the simpler $b = 1$ case, for $b \geq 2$ we cannot assume that all $m\binom{n}{r+1}\binom{K+b-2}{b-1}$ equations we produce in this way are linearly independent up to the point where we can solve the system by linearization. In fact, we can construct explicit linear relations between the equations starting at $b = 2$.

In this section, we will focus on the simpler $q > b$ case. We will deal with the common $q = 2$ case in Sect. 5.3. There is however an unavoidable complication which occurs whenever we consider $b \geq q$, $q \neq 2$.

We can construct linear relations between the equations from determinantal identities involving maximal minors of matrices whose first rows are some of the r_j's concatenated with C. For instance we may write the trivial identity for any subset J of columns of size $r + 2$:

$$\begin{vmatrix} r_j \\ r_k \\ C \end{vmatrix}_{*,J} + \begin{vmatrix} r_k \\ r_j \\ C \end{vmatrix}_{*,J} = 0.$$

Notice that this gives trivially a relation between certain equations corresponding to $b = 2$ since a cofactor expansion along the first row of $\begin{vmatrix} r_j \\ r_k \\ C \end{vmatrix}_{*,J}$ shows that this maximal minor is indeed a linear combination of terms which is the multiplication of a linear variable x_i with a maximal minor of the matrix $\begin{pmatrix} r_k \\ C \end{pmatrix}$ (in other words an equation corresponding to $b = 2$). A similar result holds for $\begin{vmatrix} r_k \\ r_j \\ C \end{vmatrix}_{*,J}$ where a cofactor expansion along the first row yields terms formed by a linear variable x_i multiplied by a maximal minor of the matrix $\begin{pmatrix} r_j \\ C \end{pmatrix}$. This result can be generalized by considering symmetric tensors $(S_{j_1,\cdots,j_r})_{\substack{1 \leq j_1 \leq m \\ 1 \leq j_r \leq m}}$ of dimension m of rank $b \geq 2$ over $\mathbb{F}_q$. Recall that these are tensors that satisfy

$$S_{j_1,\cdots,j_b} = S_{j_{\sigma(1)},\cdots,j_{\sigma(b)}}$$

for any permutation σ acting on $\{1..b\}$. This is a vector space that is clearly isomorphic to the space of homogeneous polynomials of degree b in $y_1, \cdots, y_m$ over $\mathbb{F}_q$. The dimension of this space is therefore $\binom{m+b-1}{b}$. We namely have

Proposition 6. *For any symmetric tensor* $(S_{j_1,\cdots,j_b})_{\substack{1 \leq j_1 \leq m \\ 1 \leq j_b \leq m}}$ *of dimension* m *of rank* $b \geq 2$ *over* $\mathbb{F}_q$ *and any subset* J *of* $\{1..n\}$ *of size* $r + b$, *we have:*

$$\sum_{j_1=1}^{m} \cdots \sum_{j_b=1}^{m} S_{j_1,\cdots,j_b} \begin{vmatrix} r_{j_1} \\ \cdots \\ r_{j_b} \\ C \end{vmatrix}_{*,J} = 0.$$

Proof. Notice first that the maximal minor $\begin{vmatrix} r_{j_1} \\ \cdots \\ r_{j_b} \\ C \end{vmatrix}_{*,J}$ is equal to 0 whenever at least two of the j_i's are equal. The left-hand sum reduces therefore to a sum of terms of the form $\sum_{\sigma \in S_b} S_{\sigma(j_1),\cdots,\sigma(j_b)} \begin{vmatrix} r_{\sigma(j_1)} \\ \cdots \\ r_{\sigma(j_b)} \\ C \end{vmatrix}_{*,J}$ where all the j_i's are different. Notice now that from the fact that S is a symmetric tensor we have

$$\sum_{\sigma \in S_b} S_{\sigma(j_1),\cdots,\sigma(j_b)} \begin{vmatrix} r_{\sigma(j_1)} \\ \cdots \\ r_{\sigma(j_b)} \\ C \end{vmatrix}_{*,J} = S_{j_1,\cdots,j_b} \sum_{\sigma \in S_b} \begin{vmatrix} r_{\sigma(j_1)} \\ \cdots \\ r_{\sigma(j_b)} \\ C \end{vmatrix}_{*,J}$$
$$= 0$$

because the determinant is an alternating form and there as many odd and even permutations in the symmetric group of order b when $b \geq 2$.   □

This proposition can be used to understand the dimension D of the space of linear equations we obtain after linearizing the equations we obtain for a certain b. For instance for $b = 2$ we obtain $m\binom{n}{r+1}K$ linear equations (they are obtained by linearizing the equations resulting from multiplying all the equations of the support minors modeling by one of the K linear variables). However as shown by Proposition 6 all of these equations are not independent and we have $\binom{n}{r+2}\binom{m+1}{2}$ linear relations coming from all relations of the kind

$$\sum_{j=1}^{m}\sum_{k=1}^{m} S_{j,k} \begin{vmatrix} r_j \\ r_k \\ C \end{vmatrix}_{*,J} = 0. \tag{19}$$

In our experiments, these relations turnt out to be independent yielding that the dimension D of this space should not be greater than $m\binom{n}{r+1}K - \binom{n}{r+2}\binom{m+1}{2}$. Experimentally, we observed that we indeed had

$$D_{\exp} = m\binom{n}{r+1}K - \binom{n}{r+2}\binom{m+1}{2}.$$

For larger values of b things get more complicated but again Proposition 6 plays a key role here. Consider for example the case $b = 3$. We have in this case $m\binom{n}{r+1}\binom{K+1}{2}$ equations obtained by multiplying all the equations of the support minors modeling by monomials of degree 2 in the linear variables. Again these equations are not all independent, there are $\binom{m+1}{2}\binom{n}{r+2}K$ equations obtained by mutiplying all the linear relations between the $b = 2$ equations derived from (19) by a linear variable, they are of the form

$$x_i \sum_{j=1}^{m}\sum_{k=1}^{m} S_{j,k} \begin{vmatrix} r_j \\ r_k \\ C \end{vmatrix}_{*,J} = 0. \tag{20}$$

But all these linear relations are themselves not independent as can be checked by using Proposition 6 with $b = 3$, we namely have for any symmetric tensor $S_{i,j,k}$ of rank 3:

$$\sum_{i=1}^{m}\sum_{j=1}^{m}\sum_{k=1}^{m} S_{i,j,k} \begin{vmatrix} r_i \\ r_j \\ r_k \\ C \end{vmatrix}_{*,J} = 0. \tag{21}$$

This induces linear relations among the equations (20), as can be verified by a cofactor expansion along the first row of the left-hand term of (21) which yields an equation of the form

$$\sum_{i=1}^{m} x_i \sum_{j=1}^{m}\sum_{k=1}^{m} S_{j,k}^{i} \begin{vmatrix} r_j \\ r_k \\ C \end{vmatrix}_{*,J} = 0$$

where the $\boldsymbol{S}^i = (S^i_{j,k})_{\substack{1 \le j \le m \\ 1 \le k \le m}}$ are symmetric tensors of order 2. We would then expect that the dimension of the set of linear equations obtained from (20) is only $\binom{m+1}{2}\binom{n}{r+2}K - \binom{n}{r+3}\binom{m+2}{3}$ yielding an overall dimension D of order

$$D = m\binom{n}{r+1}\binom{K+1}{2} - \binom{m+1}{2}\binom{n}{r+2}K + \binom{n}{r+3}\binom{m+2}{3},$$

which is precisely what we observe experimentally. This argument extends also to higher values of b, so that, if linear relations of the form considered above are the only relevant linear relations, then the number of linearly independent equations available for linearization at a given value of b is:

Heuristic 2

$$D_{\text{exp}} = \sum_{i=1}^{b}(-1)^{i+1}\binom{n}{r+i}\binom{m+i-1}{i}\binom{K+b-i-1}{b-i}. \tag{22}$$

Experimentally, we found this to be the case with overwhelming probability (see Sect. 5.6) with the only general exceptions being:

1. When D_{exp} exceeds the number of monomials for a smaller value of b, typically 1, the number of equations is observed to be equal to the number of monomials for all higher values of b as well, even if D_{exp} does not exceed the total number of monomials at these higher values of b.
2. When the MinRank Problem has a nontrivial solution and cannot be solved at $b = 1$, we find the maximum number of linearly independent equations is not the total number of monomials but is less by 1. This is expected, since when the underlying MinRank problem has a nontrivial solution, then the Support Minors Modeling equations have a 1 dimensional solution space.
3. When $b \ge r + 2$, the equations are not any more linearly independent, and we give an explanation in Sect. 5.4.

In summary, in the general case $q > b$, the number of monomials is $\binom{n}{r}\binom{K+b-1}{b}$ and we expect to be able to linearize at degree b whenever $b < r + 2$ and

$$\binom{n}{r}\binom{K+b-1}{b} - 1 \le \sum_{i=1}^{b}(-1)^{i+1}\binom{n}{r+i}\binom{m+i-1}{i}\binom{K+b-i-1}{b-i} \tag{23}$$

Note that, for $b = 1$, we recover the result (18). As this system is very sparse, with $K(r+1)$ monomials per equation, one can solve it using Wiedemann algorithm [39]; thus the complexity to solve MinRank problem when $b < q$, $b < r + 2$ is

$$\mathcal{O}\left(K(r+1)\left(\binom{n}{r}\binom{K+b-1}{b}\right)^2\right) \tag{24}$$

where b is the smallest positive integer so that the condition (23) is fulfilled.

5.3   The $q = 2$ Case

The same considerations apply in the $q = 2$ case, but due to the field equations, $x_i^2 = x_i$, for systems with $b \geq 2$, a number of monomials will collapse to a lower degree. This results in a system which is no longer homogeneous. Thus, in this case it is most profitable to combine the equations obtained at a given value of b with those produced using all smaller values of b. Similar considerations to the general case imply that as long as $b < r + 2$ we will have

$$D_{\exp} = \sum_{j=1}^{b} \sum_{i=1}^{j} (-1)^{i+1} \binom{n}{r+i} \binom{m+i-1}{i} \binom{K}{j-i}. \qquad (25)$$

equations with which to linearize the $\sum_{j=1}^{b} \binom{n}{r}\binom{K}{j}$ monomials that occur at a given value of b. We therefore expect to be able to solve by linearization when $b < r + 2$ and b is large enough that

$$\sum_{j=1}^{b} \binom{n}{r}\binom{K}{j} - 1 \leq \sum_{j=1}^{b} \sum_{i=1}^{j} (-1)^{i+1} \binom{n}{r+i} \binom{m+i-1}{i} \binom{K}{j-i}. \qquad (26)$$

Similarly to the general case for any q described in the previous section, the complexity to solve MinRank problem when $q = 2$ and $b < r + 2$ is

$$\mathcal{O}\left(K(r+1) \left(\sum_{j=1}^{b} \binom{n}{r}\binom{K}{j} \right)^2 \right) \qquad (27)$$

where b is the smallest positive integer so that the condition (26) is fulfilled.

5.4   Toward the $b \geq r + 2$ Case

We can also construct additional nontrivial linear relations starting at $b = r + 2$. The simplest example of this sort of linear relations occurs when $m > r + 1$. Note that each of the Support Minors modeling equations at $b = 1$ is bilinear in the x_i variables and a subset consisting of $r + 1$ of the variables c_T. Note also, that there are a total of m equations derived from the same subset (one for each row of $\sum_{i=0}^{K} x_i M_i$.) Therefore, if we consider the Jacobian of the $b = 1$ equations with respect to the variables c_T, the m equations involving only $r + 1$ of the variables c_T will form a submatrix with m rows and only $r + 1$ nonzero columns. Using a Cramer-like formula, we can therefore construct left kernel vectors for these equations; its coefficients would be degree $r + 1$ polynomials in the x_i variables. Multiplying the equations by this kernel vector will produce zero, because the $b = 1$ equations are homogeneous, and multiplying equations from a bilinear system by a kernel vector of the Jacobian of that system cancels all the highest degree terms. This suggests that Eq. (22) needs to be modified when we consider values of b that are $r + 2$ or greater. These additional linear relations do not appear to be relevant in the most interesting range of b for attacks on any of the cryptosystems considered, however.

5.5   Improvements for Generic Minrank

The two classical improvements Sect. 4.2 in the "super"-overdetermined cases the hybrid attack and Sect. 4.3 can also apply for Generic Minrank.

We can consider applying the Support Minors Modeling techniques to sub-matrices $\sum_{i=1}^{K} \boldsymbol{M}'_i x_i$ of $\sum_{i=1}^{K} \boldsymbol{M}_i x_i$. Note that if $\sum_{i=1}^{K} \boldsymbol{M}_i x_i$ has rank $\leq r$, so does $\sum_{i=1}^{K} \boldsymbol{M}'_i x_i$, so assuming we have a unique solution x_i to both systems of equations, it will be the same. Generically, we will keep a unique solution in the smaller system as long as the decoding problem has a unique solution, i.e. as long as the Gilbert-Varshamov bound $K \leq (m - r)(n - r)$ is satisfied.

We generally find that the most beneficial settings use matrices with all m rows, but only $n' \leq n$ of the columns. This corresponds to a puncturing of the corresponding matrix code over $\mathbb{F}_q$. It is always beneficial for the attacker to reduce n' to the minimum value allowing linearization at a given degree b, however, it can sometimes lead to an even lower complexity to reduce n' further and solve at a higher degree b.

On the other side, we can run exhaustive search on a variables x_i in $\mathbb{F}_q$ and solve q^a systems with a smaller value of b, so that the resulting complexity is smaller than solving directly the system with a higher value of b. This optimization is considered in the attack against ROLLO-I-256 (see Table 1); more details about this example are given in Sect. 6.1.

5.6   Experimental Results for Generic Minrank

We verified experimentally that the value of $D_{\exp}$ correctly predicts the number of linearly independent polynomials. We constructed random systems (with and without a solution) for $q = 2, 13$, with $m = 7, 8$, $r = 2, 3$, $n = r + 3, r + 4, r + 5$, $K = 3, \ldots, 20$. Most of the time, the number of linearly independent polynomials was as expected. For $q = 13$, we had a few number of non-generic systems (usually less than 1% over 1000 random samples), and only in square cases where the matrices have a predicted rank equal to the number of columns. For $q = 2$ we had a higher probability of linear dependencies, due to the fact that over small fields, random matrices have a non-trivial probability to be non invertible. Anyway, as soon as the field is big enough or the number $D_{\exp}$ is large compared to the number of columns, all our experiments succeeded over 1000 samples.

5.7   Using Support Minors Modeling Together with MaxMin for RD

Recall that from MaxMin, we obtain $m\binom{n-k-1}{r}$ homogeneous linear equations in the c_T's. These can be used to produce additional equations over the same monomials as used for Support Minors Modeling with $K = m(k + 1)$. However here, unlike in the overdetermined case, it is not interesting to specialize the matrix $\boldsymbol{C}$. Indeed, in that case it is sufficient to assume that the first component of $\boldsymbol{e}$ is nonzero, then we can specialize to $(*, 0, \ldots, 0)^{\mathsf{T}}$ the first column of $\boldsymbol{SC}$. Now, Eq. (3) gives $m-1$ linear equations involving only the x_i's, that allows us to eliminate $m - 1$ variables x_i's from the system and reduces the number of linear variables to $K = mk + 1$. We still expect a space of dimension 1 for the $x^\alpha c_T$'s, and this will be usefull for the last step of the attack described in Sect. 5.8.

When $q > b$, we multiply the equations from MaxMin by degree b monomials in the x_i's. When $q = 2$, this can be done by multiplying the MaxMin equations by monomials of degree b or less. All these considerations lead to a similar heuristic as Heuristic 1, i.e. linearization is possible for $q > b$, $0 < b < r + 2$ when:

$$\binom{n}{r}\binom{mk+b}{b} - 1 \leq$$

$$m\binom{n-k-1}{r}\binom{mk+b}{b} + \sum_{i=1}^{b}(-1)^{i+1}\binom{n}{r+i}\binom{m+i-1}{i}\binom{mk+b-i}{b-i},$$

and for $q = 2$, $0 < b < r + 2$ whenever:

$$A_b - 1 \leq B_c + C_b \tag{28}$$

where

$$A_b := \sum_{j=1}^{b}\binom{n}{r}\binom{mk+1}{j}$$

$$B_b := \sum_{j=1}^{b}\left(m\binom{n-k-1}{r}\binom{mk+1}{j}\right)$$

$$C_b := \sum_{j=1}^{b}\sum_{i=1}^{j}\left((-1)^{i+1}\binom{n}{r+i}\binom{m+i-1}{i}\binom{mk+1}{j-i}\right).$$

For the latter, it leads to a complexity of

$$\mathcal{O}\left((B_b + C_b)A_b^{\omega-1}\right) \tag{29}$$

where b is the smallest positive integer so that the condition (28) is fulfilled. This complexity formula correspond to solving a linear system with A_b unknowns and $B_b + C_b$ equations, recall that ω is the constant of linear algebra.

For a large range of parameters, this system is particularly sparse, so one could take advantage of that to use Wiedemann algorithm [39]. More precisely, for values of m, n, r and k of ROLLO or RQC parameters (see Table 3 and Table 4) for which the condition (28) is fulfilled, we typically find that $b \approx r$.

In this case, B_b equations consist of $\binom{k+r+1}{r}$ monomials, C_b equations consist of $(mk + 1)(r + 1)$ monomials, and the total space of monomials is of size A_b. The Wiedemann's algorithm complexity can be written in term of the average number of monomials per equation, in our case it is

$$D_b := \frac{B_b\binom{k+r+1}{r} + C_b(mk+1)(r+1)}{B_b + C_b}.$$

Thus the linearized system at degree b is sufficiently sparse that Wiedemann outperforms Strassen for $b \geq 2$. Therefore the complexity of support minors modeling bootstrapping MaxMin for RD is

$$\mathcal{O}\left(D_b A_b^2\right) \tag{30}$$

where b is still the smallest positive integer so that the condition (28) is fulfilled. A similar formula applies for the case $q > b$.

5.8   Last Step of the Attack

To end the attack on MinRank using Support Minors modeling or the attack on RD using MaxMinors modeling in conjunction with Support Minors modeling, one needs to find the value of each unknown. When direct linearization at degree b works, we get $\boldsymbol{v} = (v_{\alpha,T}^*)_{\alpha,T}$ one nonzero vector containing one possible value for all $x^\alpha c_T$, where the x^α's are monomials of degree $b - 1$ in the x_i's, and all the other solutions are multiples of $\boldsymbol{v}$ (as the solution space has dimension 1).

In order to extract the values of all the x_i's and thus finish the attack, one needs to find one i_0 and one T_0 such that $x_{i_0} \neq 0$ and $c_{T_0} \neq 0$. This is easily done by looking for a nonzero entry v^* of $\boldsymbol{v}$ corresponding to a monomial $x_{i_0}^{b-1} c_{T_0}$. At this point, we know that there is a solution of the system with $x_{i_0} = 1$ and $c_{T_0} = v^*$. Then by computing the quotients of the entries in $\boldsymbol{v}$ corresponding to the monomials $x_i x_{i_0}^{b-2} c_{T_0}$ and $x_{i_0}^{b-1} c_{T_0}$ we get the values of

$$x_i = \frac{x_i}{x_{i_0}} = \frac{x_i x_{i_0}^{b-2} c_{T_0}}{x_{i_0}^{b-1} c_{T_0}}, \quad 1 \leq i \leq K. \tag{31}$$

Doing so, one gets the values of all the x_i's. This finishes the attack. This works without any assumption on MinRank, and with the assumption that the first coordinate of $\boldsymbol{e}$ is nonzero for RD. If it is not the case, one uses another coordinate of $\boldsymbol{e}$.

6   Complexity of the Attacks for Different Cryptosystems and Comparison with Generic Gröbner Basis Approaches

6.1   Attacks Against the Rank Decoding Problem

Table 1 presents the best complexity of our attacks (see Sects. 4 and 5) against RD and gives the binary logarithm of the complexities (column **"This paper"**) for all the parameters in the ROLLO and RQC submissions to the NIST competition and Loidreau cryptosystem [30]; for the sake of clarity, we give the previous best known complexity from [11] (last column). The third column gives the original rate for being overdeterminate. The column 'a' indicates the number of specialized columns in the hybrid approach (Sect. 4.3), when the system is not overdetermined. Column 'p' indicates the number of punctured columns in the "super"-overdetermined cases (Sect. 4.2). Column 'b' indicates that we use Support Minors Modeling in conjunction with MaxMin (Sect. 5.7).

Let us give more details on how we compute the best complexity, in Table 1, for ROLLO-I-256 whose parameters are $(m, n, k, r) = (113, 134, 67, 7)$. The attack from Sect. 4 only works with the hybrid approach, thus requiring $a = 8$ and resulting in a complexity of 158 bits (using (17) and $\omega = 2.81$). On the other hand, the attack from Sect. 5.7 needs $b = 2$ which results in a complexity of 154 (this time using Wiedemann's algorithm). However, if we specialize $a = 3$ columns in C, we get $b = 1$ and the resulting complexity using Wiedemann's algorithm is 151.

Table 1. Complexity of the attack against RD for different cryptosystems. A "*" in column "**This paper**" means that the best complexity uses Widemann's algorithm, otherwise Strassen's algorithm is used.

	(m, n, k, r)	$\frac{m\binom{n-k-1}{r}}{\binom{n}{r}-1}$	a	p	b	This paper	[11]
Loidreau ([30])	$(128, 120, 80, 4)$	1.28	0	43	0	**65**	98
ROLLO-I-128	$(79, 94, 47, 5)$	1.97	0	9	0	**71**	117
ROLLO-I-192	$(89, 106, 53, 6)$	1.06	0	0	0	**87**	144
ROLLO-I-256	$(113, 134, 67, 7)$	0.67	3	0	1	**151***	197
ROLLO-II-128	$(83, 298, 149, 5)$	2.42	0	40	0	**93**	134
ROLLO-II-192	$(107, 302, 151, 6)$	1.53	0	18	0	**111**	164
ROLLO-II-256	$(127, 314, 157, 7)$	0.89	0	6	1	**159***	217
ROLLO-III-128	$(101, 94, 47, 5)$	2.52	0	12	0	**70**	119
ROLLO-III-192	$(107, 118, 59, 6)$	1.31	0	4	0	**88**	148
ROLLO-III-256	$(131, 134, 67, 7)$	0.78	0	0	1	**131***	200
RQC-I	$(97, 134, 67, 5)$	2.60	0	18	0	**77**	123
RQC-II	$(107, 202, 101, 6)$	1.46	0	10	0	**101**	156
RQC-III	$(137, 262, 131, 7)$	0.93	3	0	0	**144**	214

6.2 Attacks Against the MinRank Problem

Table 2 shows the complexity of our attack against generic MinRank problems for GeMSS and Rainbow, two cryptosystems at the second round of the NIST competition. Our new attack is compared to the previous MinRank attacks, which use minors modeling in the case of GeMSS [14], and a linear algebra search [18] in the case of Rainbow. Concerning Rainbow, the acronyms RBS and DA stand from Rainbow Band Separation and Direct Algebraic respectively; the column "Best/Type" shows the complexity of the previous best attack against Rainbow, which was not based on MinRank before our new attack (except for Ia). All new complexities are computed by finding the number of columns n' and the degree b that minimize the complexity, as described in Sect. 5.

Table 2. Complexity comparison between the new and the previous attacks against GeMSS and Rainbow parameters [18].

GeMSS(D, n, Δ, v)	n/m	K	r	n'	b	Complexity		
						New	Previous	Type
GeMSS128($513, 174, 12, 12$)	174	162	34	61	2	**154**	522	MinRank
GeMSS192($513, 256, 22, 20$)	265	243	52	94	2	**223**	537	MinRank
GeMSS256($513, 354, 30, 33$)	354	324	73	126	3	**299**	1254	MinRank
RedGeMSS128($17, 177, 15, 15$)	177	162	35	62	2	**156**	538	MinRank
RedGeMSS192($17, 266, 23, 25$)	266	243	53	95	2	**224**	870	MinRank
RedGeMSS256($17, 358, 34, 35$)	358	324	74	127	3	**301**	1273	MinRank
BlueGeMSS128($129, 175, 13, 14$)	175	162	35	63	2	**158**	537	MinRank
BlueGeMSS192($129, 265, 22, 23$)	265	243	53	95	2	**224**	870	MinRank
BlueGeMSS256($129, 358, 34, 32$)	358	324	74	127	3	**301**	1273	MinRank

Rainbow($GF(q), v_1, o_1, o_2$)	n	K	r	n'	b	New	Previous	Best / Type
Ia($GF(16), 32, 32, 32$)	96	33	64	82	3	155	161	145 / RBS
IIIc($GF(256), 68, 36, 36$)	140	37	104	125	5	**208**	585	215 / DA
Vc($GF(256), 92, 48, 48$)	188	49	140	169	5	**272**	778	275 / DA

6.3 Our Approach vs. Using Generic Gröbner Basis Algorithms

Since our approach is an algebraic attack, it relies on solving a polynomial system, thus it looks like a Gröbner basis computation. In fact, we do compute a Gröbner basis of the system, as we compute the unique solution of the system, which represents its Gröbner basis.

Nevertheless, our algorithm is not a generic Gröbner basis algorithm as it only works for the special type of system studied in this paper: the RD and MinRank systems. As it is specifically designed for this purpose and for the reasons detailed below, it is more efficient than a generic algorithm.

There are three main reasons why our approach is more efficient than a generic Gröbner basis algorithm:

- We compute formally (that is to say at no extra cost except the size of the equations) new equations of degree r (the **MaxMinors** ones) that are already in the ideal, but not in the vector space

$$\mathcal{F}_r := \langle uf : u \text{ monomial of degree } r - 2, \ f \text{ in the set of initial polynomials} \rangle.$$

In fact, a careful analysis of a Gröbner basis computation with a standard strategy shows that those equations are in $\mathcal{F}_{r+1}$, and that the first degree fall for those systems is $r + 1$. Here, we apply linear algebra directly on a small number of polynomials of degree r (see the next two items for more details), whereas a generic Gröbner basis algorithm would compute many polynomials of degree $r + 1$ and then reduce them in order to get those polynomials of degree r.

- A classical Gröbner basis algorithm using linear algebra and a standard strategy typically constructs Macaulay matrices, where the rows correspond to polynomials in the ideal and the columns to monomials of a certain degree. Here, we introduce variables c_T that represent maximal minors of C, and thus represent not one monomial of degree r, but $r!$ monomials of degree r. As we compute the Gröbner basis by using only polynomials that can be expressed in terms of those variables (see the last item below), this reduces the number of columns of our matrices by a factor around $r!$ compared to generic Macaulay-like matrices.

- The solution can be found by applying linear algebra only to some specific equations, namely the MaxMinors ones in the overdetermined case, and in the underdetermined case, equations that have degree 1 in the c_T variables, and degree $b-1$ in the x_i variables (see Sect. 5.2). This enables us to deal with polynomials involving only the c_T variables and the x_i variables, whereas a generic Gröbner basis algorithm would consider all monomials up to degree $r + b$ in the x_l and the $c_{i,j}$ variables. This drastically reduces the number of rows and columns in our matrices.

For all of those reasons, in the overdetermined case, only an elimination on our selected MaxMinors equations (with a "compacted" matrix with respect to the columns) is sufficient to get the solution; so we essentially avoid going up to the degree $r + 1$ to produce those equations, we select a small number of rows, and gain a factor $r!$ on the number of columns.

In the underdetermined case, we find linear equations by linearization on some well-chosen subspaces of the vector space $\mathcal{F}_{r+b}$. We have theoretical reasons to believe that our choice of subspace should lead to the computation of the solution (as usual, this is a "genericity" hypothesis), and it is confirmed by all our experiments.

7   Examples of New Parameters for ROLLO-I and RQC

In light of the attacks presented in this article, it is possible to give a few examples of new parameters for the rank-based cryptosystems, submitted to the NIST competition, ROLLO and RQC. With these new parameters, ROLLO and RQC would be resistant to our attacks, while still remaining attractive, for example with a loss of only about 50% in terms of key size for ROLLO-I.

For cryptographic purpose, parameters have to belong to an area which does not correspond to the overdetermined case and such that the hybrid approach would make the attack worse than in the underdetermined case.

Alongside the algebraic attacks in this paper, the best combinatorial attack against RD is in [4]; its complexity for (m, n, k, r) decoding is

$$\mathcal{O}\left((nm)^2 q^{r\left\lceil \frac{m(k+1)}{n}\right\rceil - m}\right).$$

In the following tables, we consider $\omega = 2.81$. We also use the same notation as in ROLLO and RQC submissions' specifications [1,7]. In particular, n is the block-length and not the length of the code which can be either $2n$ or $3n$. Moreover, for ROLLO (Table 3):

- **over/hybrid** is the cost of the hybrid attack; the value of a is the smallest to reach the overdetermined case, $a = 0$ means that parameters are already in the overdetermined case,
- **under** is the case of underdetermined attack.
- **comb** is the cost of the best combinatorial attack mentioned above,
- **DFR** is the binary logarithm of the Decoding Failure Rate,

and for RQC (Table 4):

- **hyb2n(a):** hybrid attack for length $2n$, the value of a is the smallest to reach the overdetermined case, $a = 0$ means that parameters are already in the overdetermined case,
- **hyb3n(a):** non-homogeneous hybrid attack for length $3n$, a is the same as above. This attack corresponds to an adaptation of our attack to a non-homogeneous error of the RQC scheme, more details are given in [1],
- **und2n:** underdetermined attack for length $2n$,
- **comb3n:** combinatorial attack for length $3n$.

Table 3. New parameters and attacks complexities for ROLLO-I.

Instance	q	n	m	r	d	pk size (B)	DFR	over/hybrid	a	p	under	b	comb
new2ROLLO-I-128	2	83	73	7	8	757	-27	233	18	0	180	3	213
new2ROLLO-I-192	2	97	89	8	8	1057	-33	258*	17	0	197*	3	283*
new2ROLLO-I-256	2	113	103	9	9	1454	-33	408*	30	0	283*	6	376*

Table 4. New parameters and attacks complexities for RQC.

Instance	q	n	m	k	w	w_r	δ	pk (B)	hyb2n(a)	hyb3n(a)	und2n	b	comb3n
newRQC-I	2	113	127	3	7	7	6	1793	160(6)	211(0)	158	1	205
newRQC-II	2	149	151	5	8	8	8	2812	331(24)	262(0)	224	3	289
newRQC-III	2	179	181	3	9	9	7	4049	553(44)	321(5)	324	6	401

8 Conclusion

In this paper, we improve on the results by [11] on the Rank Decoding problem by providing a better analysis which permits to avoid the use of generic Gröbner bases algorithms and permits to completely break rank-based cryptosystems parameters proposed to the NIST Standardization Process, when the analysis in [11] only attacked them slightly.

We generalize this approach to the case of the MinRank problem for which we obtain the best known complexity with algebraic attacks.

Overall, the results proposed in this paper give a new and deeper understanding of the connections and the complexity of two problems of great interest in post-quantum cryptography: the Rank Decoding and the MinRank problems.

Acknowledgements. We would like to warmly thank the reviewers, who did a wonderful job by carefully reading our article and giving us useful feedback.

This work has been supported by the French ANR project CBCRYPT (ANR-17-CE39-0007) and the MOUSTIC project with the support from the European Regional Development Fund and the Regional Council of Normandie.

Javier Verbel was supported for this work by Colciencias scholarship 757 for PhD studies and the University of Louisville facilities.

We would like to thank John B Baena, and Karan Khathuria for useful discussions. We thank the Facultad de Ciencias of the Universidad Nacional de Colombia sede Medellín for granting us access to the Enlace server, where we ran some of the experiments.

References

1. Aguilar Melchor, C., et al.: Rank quasi cyclic (RQC). Second round submission to the NIST post-quantum cryptography call, April 2020
2. Aguilar Melchor, C., et al.: First round submission to the NIST post-quantum cryptography call, November 2017
3. Aguilar Melchor, C., et al.: Rank quasi cyclic (RQC). First round submission to the NIST post-quantum cryptography call, November 2017
4. Aragon, N., Gaborit, P., Hauteville, A., Tillich, J.P.: A new algorithm for solving the rank syndrome decoding problem. In: Proceedings of the IEEE ISIT (2018)
5. Aragon, N., et al.: LAKE - Low rAnk parity check codes Key Exchange. First round submission to the NIST post-quantum cryptography call, November 2017
6. Aragon, N., et al.: LOCKER - LOw rank parity ChecK codes EncRyption. First round submission to the NIST post-quantum cryptography call, November 2017
7. Aragon, N., et al.: ROLLO (merger of Rank-Ouroboros, LAKE and LOCKER). Second round submission to the NIST post-quantum cryptography call, April 2020
8. Aragon, N., Blazy, O., Gaborit, P., Hauteville, A., Zémor, G.: Durandal: a rank metric based signature scheme. In: Ishai, Y., Rijmen, V. (eds.) EUROCRYPT 2019. LNCS, vol. 11478, pp. 728–758. Springer, Cham (2019). https://doi.org/10.1007/978-3-030-17659-4_25
9. Aragon, N., Gaborit, P., Hauteville, A., Ruatta, O., Zémor, G.: RankSign - a signature proposal for the NIST's call. First round submission to the NIST post-quantum cryptography call, November 2017
10. Aragon, N., Gaborit, P., Hauteville, A., Tillich, J.P.: A new algorithm for solving the rank syndrome decoding problem. In: 2018 IEEE International Symposium on Information Theory (ISIT), pp. 2421–2425. IEEE (2018)
11. Bardet, M., et al.: An algebraic attack on rank metric code-based cryptosystems. In: Canteaut, A., Ishai, Y. (eds.) EUROCRYPT 2020. LNCS, vol. 12107, pp. 64–93. Springer, Cham (2020). https://doi.org/10.1007/978-3-030-45727-3_3
12. Bettale, L., Faugere, J.C., Perret, L.: Hybrid approach for solving multivariate systems over finite fields. J. Math. Cryptol. **3**(3), 177–197 (2009)

13. Buss, J.F., Frandsen, G.S., Shallit, J.O.: The computational complexity of some problems of linear algebra. J. Comput. Syst. Sci. **58**(3), 572–596 (1999)
14. Casanova, A., Faugère, J., Macario-Rat, G., Patarin, J., Perret, L., Ryckeghem, J.: GeMSS: A Great Multivariate Short Signature. Second round submission to the NIST post-quantum cryptography call, April 2019
15. Courtois, N.T.: Efficient zero-knowledge authentication based on a linear algebra problem MinRank. In: Boyd, C. (ed.) ASIACRYPT 2001. LNCS, vol. 2248, pp. 402–421. Springer, Heidelberg (2001). https://doi.org/10.1007/3-540-45682-1_24
16. Debris-Alazard, T., Tillich, J.-P.: Two attacks on rank metric code-based schemes: RankSign and an IBE scheme. In: Peyrin, T., Galbraith, S. (eds.) ASIACRYPT 2018. LNCS, vol. 11272, pp. 62–92. Springer, Cham (2018). https://doi.org/10. 1007/978-3-030-03326-2_3
17. Ding, J., Chen, M.S., Petzoldt, A., Schmidt, D., Yang, B.Y.: Gui. First round submission to the NIST post-quantum cryptography call, November 2017
18. Ding, J., Chen, M.S., Petzoldt, A., Schmidt, D., Yang, B.Y.: Rainbow. Second round submission to the NIST post-quantum cryptography call, April 2019
19. Faugère, J.-C., Levy-dit-Vehel, F., Perret, L.: Cryptanalysis of MinRank. In: Wagner, D. (ed.) CRYPTO 2008. LNCS, vol. 5157, pp. 280–296. Springer, Heidelberg (2008). https://doi.org/10.1007/978-3-540-85174-5_16
20. Faugère, J., Safey El Din, M., Spaenlehauer, P.: Computing loci of rank defects of linear matrices using Gröbner bases and applications to cryptology. In: International Symposium on Symbolic and Algebraic Computation, ISSAC 2010, Munich, Germany, 25–28 July 2010, pp. 257–264 (2010)
21. Gabidulin, E.M.: Theory of codes with maximum rank distance. Problemy Peredachi Informatsii **21**(1), 3–16 (1985)
22. Gabidulin, E.M., Paramonov, A.V., Tretjakov, O.V.: Ideals over a non-commutative ring and their application in cryptology. In: Davies, D.W. (ed.) EUROCRYPT 1991. LNCS, vol. 547, pp. 482–489. Springer, Heidelberg (1991). https://doi.org/10.1007/3-540-46416-6_41
23. Gaborit, P., Murat, G., Ruatta, O., Zémor, G.: Low rank parity check codes and their application to cryptography. In: Proceedings of the Workshop on Coding and Cryptography WCC 2013, Bergen, Norway (2013)
24. Gaborit, P., Ruatta, O., Schrek, J.: On the complexity of the rank syndrome decoding problem. IEEE Trans. Inf. Theory **62**(2), 1006–1019 (2016)
25. Gaborit, P., Ruatta, O., Schrek, J., Zémor, G.: New results for rank-based cryptography. In: Pointcheval, D., Vergnaud, D. (eds.) AFRICACRYPT 2014. LNCS, vol. 8469, pp. 1–12. Springer, Cham (2014). https://doi.org/10.1007/978-3-319-06734-6_1
26. Gaborit, P., Ruatta, O., Schrek, J., Zémor, G.: RankSign: an efficient signature algorithm based on the rank metric. In: Mosca, M. (ed.) PQCrypto 2014. LNCS, vol. 8772, pp. 88–107. Springer, Cham (2014). https://doi.org/10.1007/978-3-319-11659-4_6
27. Gaborit, P., Zémor, G.: On the hardness of the decoding and the minimum distance problems for rank codes. IEEE Trans. Inf. Theory **62**(12), 7245–7252 (2016)
28. Hoffstein, J., Pipher, J., Silverman, J.H.: NTRU: a ring-based public key cryptosystem. In: Buhler, J.P. (ed.) ANTS 1998. LNCS, vol. 1423, pp. 267–288. Springer, Heidelberg (1998). https://doi.org/10.1007/BFb0054868
29. Kipnis, A., Shamir, A.: Cryptanalysis of the HFE public key cryptosystem by relinearization. In: Wiener, M. (ed.) CRYPTO 1999. LNCS, vol. 1666, pp. 19–30. Springer, Heidelberg (1999). https://doi.org/10.1007/3-540-48405-1_2

30. Loidreau, P.: A new rank metric codes based encryption scheme. In: Lange, T., Takagi, T. (eds.) PQCrypto 2017. LNCS, vol. 10346, pp. 3–17. Springer, Cham (2017). https://doi.org/10.1007/978-3-319-59879-6_1

31. Misoczki, R., Tillich, J.P., Sendrier, N., Barreto, P.S.L.M.: MDPC-McEliece: New McEliece variants from moderate density parity-check codes (2012)

32. Otmani, A., Kalachi, H.T., Ndjeya, S.: Improved cryptanalysis of rank metric schemes based on Gabidulin codes. Des. Codes Cryptogr. **86**(9), 1983–1996 (2017). https://doi.org/10.1007/s10623-017-0434-5

33. Ourivski, A.V., Johansson, T.: New technique for decoding codes in the rank metric and its cryptography applications. Probl. Inf. Transm. **38**(3), 237–246 (2002)

34. Overbeck, R.: A new structural attack for GPT and variants. In: Dawson, E., Vaudenay, S. (eds.) Mycrypt 2005. LNCS, vol. 3715, pp. 50–63. Springer, Heidelberg (2005). https://doi.org/10.1007/11554868_5

35. Patarin, J.: Hidden fields equations (HFE) and isomorphisms of polynomials (IP): two new families of asymmetric algorithms. In: Maurer, U. (ed.) EUROCRYPT 1996. LNCS, vol. 1070, pp. 33–48. Springer, Heidelberg (1996). https://doi.org/10.1007/3-540-68339-9_4

36. Petzoldt, A., Chen, M.-S., Yang, B.-Y., Tao, C., Ding, J.: Design principles for HFEv- based multivariate signature schemes. In: Iwata, T., Cheon, J.H. (eds.) ASIACRYPT 2015. LNCS, vol. 9452, pp. 311–334. Springer, Heidelberg (2015). https://doi.org/10.1007/978-3-662-48797-6_14

37. Porras, J., Baena, J., Ding, J.: ZHFE, a new multivariate public key encryption scheme. In: Mosca, M. (ed.) PQCrypto 2014. LNCS, vol. 8772, pp. 229–245. Springer, Cham (2014). https://doi.org/10.1007/978-3-319-11659-4_14

38. Verbel, J., Baena, J., Cabarcas, D., Perlner, R., Smith-Tone, D.: On the Complexity of "Superdetermined" Minrank Instances. In: Ding, J., Steinwandt, R. (eds.) PQCrypto 2019. LNCS, vol. 11505, pp. 167–186. Springer, Cham (2019). https://doi.org/10.1007/978-3-030-25510-7_10

39. Wiedemann, D.: Solving sparse linear equations over finite fields. IEEE Trans. Inf. Theory **32**(1), 54–62 (1986)

Lower Bounds on the Degree
of Block Ciphers

Phil Hebborn[1], Baptiste Lambin[1(✉)], Gregor Leander[1], and Yosuke Todo[1,2(✉)]

[1] Horst Görtz Institute for IT Security, Ruhr University Bochum, Bochum, Germany
{phil.hebborn,gregor.leander}@rub.de, baptiste.lambin@protonmail.com
[2] NTT Secure Platform Laboratories, Tokyo, Japan
yosuke.todo.xt@hco.ntt.co.jp

Abstract. Only the method to estimate the upper bound of the algebraic degree on block ciphers is known so far, but it is not useful for the designer to guarantee the security. In this paper we provide meaningful lower bounds on the algebraic degree of modern block ciphers.

Keywords: Block cipher · Algebraic degree · Minimum degree · Lower bounds · Division property · Parity set

1 Introduction

Along with stream ciphers and, more recently, permutation based cryptography, block ciphers are among the most efficient cryptographic primitives. As such block ciphers are one of the cornerstones of our cryptographic landscape today and indeed are used to ensure the security for a large fraction of our daily communication. In a nutshell, a block cipher should be an, efficient to implement, family of permutations that cannot be distinguished from a randomly selected family of permutations without guessing the entire secret key. The community has, in general, a rather good understanding of the security of block ciphers and arguments of their security have become significantly more precise and, using tool-based approaches for many aspects, significantly less error-prone. However, for some of the most basic properties a block cipher should fulfill, good arguments are still missing. One of those properties is the algebraic degree of a permutation, resp. the degree of a family of permutations. For a randomly drawn permutation, the degree is $n - 1$ almost certainly. Thus, in order to be indistinguishable from a random permutation, a block cipher should also have degree $n - 1$. This observation, and generalisations of it, leads indeed to a class of attacks called integral attacks, introduced already in [10,14]. Very similar concepts are known as high-order differential attacks [15] and cube-attacks [11].

It is highly desirable to be able to argue that a given block-cipher has degree $n - 1$, or in general high degree. However, so far, we only have upper bounds on the degree of our ciphers. Those bounds, see e.g., [15] and in particular [6,8] are very efficient to compute in most cases and far from trivial.

S. Moriai and H. Wang (Eds.): ASIACRYPT 2020, LNCS 12491, pp. 537–566, 2020.
https://doi.org/10.1007/978-3-030-64837-4_18

Unfortunately, upper bounds on the degree are not very helpful for a designer of a cipher, as this is not what is needed to argue about the security of a given design. What we actually need, and what has not been achieved so far, is to give meaningful *lower bounds* on the degree.

Algebraic Degree of Keyed (Vectorial) Functions. Before we describe our results, we will define precisely the degree and discuss how lower and upper bounds have to be understood in order to avoid confusion, see e.g., [9] for more background on Boolean functions. Consider a general set-up of a (parameterized, vectorial) Boolean function

$$F_k : \mathbb{F}_2^n \to \mathbb{F}_2^m$$

with $k \in \mathbb{F}_2^\ell$. Any such function can be uniquely described by its algebraic normal form as

$$F_k(x) = \sum_{u \in \mathbb{F}_2^n} p_u(k) x^u$$

where x^u is short for $\prod_i x_i^{u_i}$ and $p_u(k)$ are functions

$$p_u : \mathbb{F}_2^\ell \to \mathbb{F}_2^m$$

mapping keys to values in $\mathbb{F}_2^m$. If there is no parameter, i.e., no key, then all p_u degenerate naturally to constants and if, on top, it is not a vectorial Boolean function, i.e., if $m = 1$, these constants are just bits, i.e., $p_u \in \mathbb{F}_2$. The definition of (algebraic) degree is the same in all cases and is given as

$$\deg(F) := \max_u \{\mathrm{wt}(u) \mid p_u \neq 0\}.$$

Here $\mathrm{wt}(u)$ denotes the Hamming weight of u, i.e., the number of 1 and this weight corresponds to the number of variables multiplied in x^u.

For clarity, consider the case of a keyed vectorial function. The degree of F is d or higher if there exist a u of Hamming weight d such that p_u is not zero, i.e., not the constant zero function.

A *lower bound* d on the degree of F implies that there exists at least one key and at least one output bit which is of degree at least d. An *upper bound* d on the degree of F implies that for all keys all output bits are of degree at most d.

For cryptographic purposes, the degree as defined above is not always satisfactory. An attacker can always pick the weakest spot, e.g., an output bit of lowest degree. A vectorial function of high degree might still have very low degree in one specific output bit or, more general, in a specific linear combination of output bits. This motivates the notion of minimum degree. For this, one considers all non-zero linear combination of output bits $\langle \beta, F \rangle$ and the minimum degree of all those Boolean functions

$$\mathrm{minDeg}(F) = \min_{\beta \neq 0} \deg(\langle \beta, F \rangle).$$

A *lower bound* d on the minimum degree of a function implies that for all component functions $\langle \beta, F \rangle$ there exist a key such that the degree of the component function is at least d. An *upper bound* d on the minimum degree of a function implies that there exist at least one component function that has degree at most d for all keys.

Table 1. Summary of the number of rounds to get full degree/full minimum degree/appearance of all max-degree monomials. We also label "tight" when they fit with the upper bounds.

	Full degree	Full minimum degree	All max-degree monomials
GIFT-64	8 (tight)	10	11
SKINNY64	10 (tight)	11 (tight)	13
PRESENT	8 (tight)	10	11

	Note
AES	Algebraic degree is at least 116 in 4 rounds

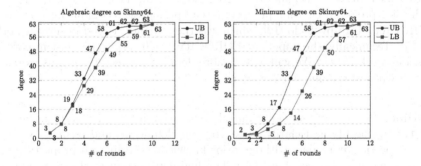

Fig. 1. Algebraic degree and minimum degree on SKINNY64, where UB and LB denote upper bound and lower bound, respectively.

Our Results. In this paper we present – for the first time – non-trivial lower bounds on the degree and minimum degree of various block ciphers with the sole assumption of independent round-keys. More precisely, we assume that after each round a new round key is added to the full state.

We hereby focus in particular on the block ciphers that are used most frequently as building blocks in the ongoing NIST lightweight project[1], namely GIFT-64, SKINNY64, and AES. Furthermore, we investigate PRESENT. Our results are summarized in Table 1. To give a concrete example of our results, consider the block cipher SKINNY64 [4]. We are able to show that 10 and 11 rounds are sufficient to get full, i.e., 63, degree and minimum degree, respectively. Together with the known upper bounds, we get a rather good view on the actual degree development of SKINNY64 with increasing number of rounds (see Fig. 1).

---

[1] https://csrc.nist.gov/Projects/lightweight-cryptography.

Besides the degree and the minimum degree, we also elaborate on the appearance of all n possible monomials of maximal degree, i.e., degree $n - 1$. While this is not captured by a natural notion of degree, it does capture large classes of integral attacks. With respect to this criterion, we also show that 13 rounds are enough for SKINNY64.

Technical Contribution. Our results are based on the concept of division property and require a non-negligible, but in all cases we consider, practical computational effort. They can be derived within a few hours on a single PC. All code required for our results will be made publicly available.

The main technical challenge in our work (and many previous works based on division property) is to keep the model solvable and the number of division trails in a reasonable range. For our purpose, we solve this by optimizing the division property of the key, a freedom that was (i) previously not considered and (ii) allows to speed-up our computations significantly.

Previous Works. This paper has strong ties with all the previous works related to division property. Division property is a cryptanalysis technique introduced at EUROCRYPT'15 by Todo [19], which was then further refined in several works [20,21]. Technically, the papers at EUROCRYPT'20 [12] is the most important previous work for us. We will give a more detailed review of previous works in Sect. 2 when also fixing our notation.

Outline. We present our notation related to the division property in Sect. 2. We try to simplify and clarify some previous definitions and results. We hope that in particular readers without prior knowledge on division property might find it accessible. In Sect. 3 we provide a high-level overview of our results and how they were achieved. As mentioned above, the main technical contribution is the optimization for a suitable division-property for the key, which is explained in Sect. 4. Our applications and the detailed results for the ciphers studied are given in Sect. 5. Being the first paper to derive meaningful lower bounds on ciphers by relying only on independent round-keys, our work leaves many open questions and room for improvements. We elaborate on this in Sect. 6 concluding our work.

Finally we note that all our implementations are available at

https://github.com/LowerBoundsAlgDegree/LowerBoundsAlgDegree.

2   Notation and Preliminaries

Let us start by briefly fixing some basic notation. We denote by $\mathbb{F}_2$ the finite field with two elements, basically a bit, and by $\mathbb{F}_2^n$ the n-dimensional vector space over $\mathbb{F}_2$, i.e., the set of n-bit vectors with the XOR operation as the addition. For $x, y \in \mathbb{F}_2^n$ we denote by $\langle x, y \rangle = \sum_i x_i y_i$ the canonical inner product.

For a function $F : \mathbb{F}_2^n \to \mathbb{F}_2^m$ given as $F(x) = (F^{(1)}(x), \ldots, F^{(m)}(x))$ with $F^{(i)} : \mathbb{F}_2^n \to \mathbb{F}_2$, the $F^{(i)}$ are referred to as the *coordinate functions* of F and any linear combination $\langle \beta, F(x) \rangle$ of those as a *component function* of F. We use $+$ to denote all kind of additions (of sets, vectors, polynomials, monomials) as it should be clear from context.

In this section we start by recalling the development of division property since its first introduction by Todo [18]. The technique has been proven very helpful in many applications and led to a large variety of results. The notion of trails [22] has been an important technical improvement that itself already has undergone several iterations. We try to simplify notations and at the same time make some previous definitions and results more rigid and precise. The aim is to be self contained and accessible to readers without prior knowledge on division property. Before doing so, we briefly recapture the previous developments.

2.1   Previous Works on Division Properties

This paper has strong ties with all the previous works related to division property and as such, we would like to precisely describe where our work fits and what are the precise relations and differences with the division property. Division property is a cryptanalysis technique introduced at EUROCRYPT'15 by Todo as a technique to study the parity of x^u [19]. This initial variant is by now referred to as the *conventional division property* (CDP). This was further refined to the *bit-based division property* (BDP) by Todo and Morii at FSE'16 [21]. The core idea of the division property is to evaluate whether the ANF of a block cipher contains some specific monomials. More precisely, given a monomial m in the plaintext variables, the BDP can essentially allows us to derive one of two possible results: either the ANF of a block cipher does *not* contain any *multiple* of the monomial m, or we simply do not know anything (i.e., we cannot prove the existence or non-existence of the monomial or its multiples). Another way to see the BDP is that, for a given set $\mathbb{X}$, it splits the space $\mathbb{F}_2^n$ into two distinct parts, depending on the value of the sum $s_u = \sum_{x \in \mathbb{X}} x^u, u \in \mathbb{F}_2^n$:

- A set $\mathbb{K} \subset \mathbb{F}_2^n$ such that for any $u \in \mathbb{K}$, we do not know the value of s_u.
- For the remaining $u \in \mathbb{F}_2^n \setminus \mathbb{K}$, we know that $s_u = 0$.

While this was already powerful enough to find new integral distinguishers (e.g. [18,20]), the *imperfect* nature of the division property means that some known integral distinguisher could not be explained using the division property. This was noticed by Todo and Morii in their FSE'16 paper, as a 15-round distinguisher over the block cipher SIMON [3] could not be explained with BDP. They thus extended the concept to *three-subset division property* (3SDP) to cover this distinguisher. Now, for a given monomial, the 3SDP can give us one of the following:

- The ANF does not contains any multiple of the monomial.
- The ANF contains exactly this monomial.
- We cannot prove neither existence nor non-existence of the monomials.

The term three-subset comes from the fact that we now split $\mathbb{F}_2^n$ into three parts: one where we know that $s_u = 0$, one where we know that $s_u = 1$ (aka, the $\mathbb{L}$ set), and the results is unknown for the remaining u's (aka, the $\mathbb{K}$ set). Again, there is still a loss of information and there are some cases where we do not get any information.

The main reason for this loss of information comes from the fact that previous techniques give results that are independent from the key used, hence the inability to precisely compute (parts of) the ANF. This fact was noticed and exploited at EUROCRYPT'20 by Hao et al. [12], where they introduced the *three-subset division property without unknown subset* (3SDPwoU). Their idea was to remove the "unknown subset", splitting $\mathbb{F}_2^n$ into two parts, either $s_u = 0$ or $s_u = 1$, however the implication for this is that we can no longer ignore the key. While they applied this technique to stream ciphers, they mentioned that this technique might be used for block ciphers, but left as an open problem.

It is worth noting that this idea of splitting $\mathbb{F}_2^n$ into two parts where either $s_u = 0$ or $s_u = 1$ has also been studied as another view of the division property by Boura and Canteaut at CRYPTO'16 [7] using the term parity set. However, they did not focus on actual algorithmic aspects. For our results, the focus on algorithmic aspects and in particular the notation of division trails is essential.

To summarize, originating with the division property, many variants such as BDP, 3SDP, and the parity set (which is essentially the same as the 3SDPwoU) have been proposed. After many algorithmic improvements for BDP and 3SDP, nowadays, it enables us to evaluate the most extreme variant, parity set, which allows to decide whether or not a specific monomial appears in the ANF.

2.2 Division Properties and the ANF

Any function $F : \mathbb{F}_2^n \to \mathbb{F}_2^n$ can be uniquely expressed with its algebraic normal form.

$$F(x) = \sum_u \lambda_u x^u$$

where $\lambda_u \in \mathbb{F}_2^n$. It is well known that the coefficients can be computed via the identity

$$\lambda_u = \sum_{x \preceq u} F(x) \tag{1}$$

where $x \preceq u$ if and only if $x_i \leq u_i$ for all i where elements of $\mathbb{F}_2$ are seen as integers.

We start by recalling the division property, more accurately the definition of parity set, as given in [7].

Definition 1 (Parity Set). *Let* $\mathbb{X} \subseteq \mathbb{F}_2^n$ *be a set. We define the* parity set *of* $\mathbb{X}$ *as*

$$\mathcal{U}(\mathbb{X}) := \left\{ u \in \mathbb{F}_2^n \text{ such that } \sum_{x \in \mathbb{X}} x^u = 1 \right\}$$

The power of the division property as introduced in [19] is that (i) it is often easier to trace the impact of a function on its parity set than on the set itself and (ii) the evolution of certain parity sets is related to the algebraic normal form of the functions involved.

Defining the addition of two subsets $\mathbb{X}, \mathbb{Y} \subseteq F_2^n$ by

$$\mathbb{X} + \mathbb{Y} := (\mathbb{X} \cup \mathbb{Y}) \setminus (\mathbb{X} \cap \mathbb{Y})$$

the set of all subsets of $\mathbb{F}_2^n$ becomes a binary vector space of dimension 2^n. Note that this addition is isomorphic to adding the binary indicator vectors of the sets. Also note that if an element is contained both in $\mathbb{X}$ and $\mathbb{Y}$ is not contained in the sum.

From this perspective $\mathcal{U}$ is a linear mapping and the division property can be seen as a change of basis. In particular for $\mathbb{X}_i \subset F_2^n$ it holds that

$$\mathcal{U}\left(\sum \mathbb{X}_i\right) = \sum \mathcal{U}(\mathbb{X}_i)$$

It was shown in [7] that there is a one to one correspondence between sets and its parity set, that is the mapping

$$\mathcal{U} : \mathbb{X} \mapsto \mathcal{U}(\mathbb{X})$$

is a bijection and actually its own inverse, i.e.,

$$\mathcal{U}(\mathcal{U}(\mathbb{X})) = \mathbb{X}.$$

Those properties follow from the linearity of $\mathcal{U}$ and the following lemma. The proof is added for completeness and to get familiar with the notation.

Lemma 1. *Let $\mathcal{U}$ be the mapping defined above and ℓ be an element in $\mathbb{F}_2^n$. Then*

1. $\mathcal{U}(\{\ell\}) = \{u \in \mathbb{F}_2^n \mid u \preceq \ell\}$
2. $\mathcal{U}(\{x \in \mathbb{F}_2^n \mid x \preceq \ell\}) = \{\ell\}$

Proof. For the first property, we note that $x^u = 1$ if and only if $u \preceq x$. Thus we get

$$\mathcal{U}(\{\ell\}) = \left\{ u \in \mathbb{F}_2^n \text{ such that } \sum_{x \in \{\ell\}} x^u = 1 \right\}$$
$$= \{u \in \mathbb{F}_2^n \text{ such that } \ell^u = 1\}$$
$$= \{u \in \mathbb{F}_2^n \mid u \preceq \ell\}$$

For the second property, we see that $\sum_{x \in \mathbb{F}_2^n \mid x \preceq \ell} x^u = 1$ if and only if $u = \ell$. Let A_u be the number of elements $x \preceq \ell$ such that $x^u = 1$ we get

$$A_u = |\{x \preceq \ell \mid x^u = 1\}| = |\{x \preceq \ell \mid u \preceq x\}| = |\{x \in \mathbb{F}_2^n \mid u \preceq x \preceq \ell\}|$$

and it holds that A_u is odd if and only if $\ell = u$, which completes the proof. □

We next introduce the propagation of the division property and the notion of the division trail. More formally, as our focus is the parity set, its propagation is identical to the propagation of the so-called $\mathbb{L}$ set in 3SDP introduced in [21]. Moreover, the division trail is identical to the three-subset division trail introduced in [12].

The division property provides the propagation rule for some basic operations, such as XOR or AND, and the propagation has been defined in this context as a bottom-up approach. The propagation rule allows us to evaluate any ciphers without deep knowledge for underlying theory for the division property, and it is one of advantages as a cryptanalytic tool. On the other hand, for a mathematical definition of the propagation, a top-down approach, starting with a general function and deriving the propagation rules as concrete instances, is helpful.

Definition 2 (Propagation). *Given $F : \mathbb{F}_2^n \to \mathbb{F}_2^m$ and $a \in \mathbb{F}_2^n, b \in \mathbb{F}_2^m$ we say that the division property a propagates to the division property b, denoted by*

$$a \xrightarrow{F} b$$

if and only if

$$b \in \mathcal{U}(F(\mathcal{U}(\{a\})))$$

Here the image of a set $\mathbb{X}$ under F is defined as

$$F(\mathbb{X}) := \sum_{a \in \mathbb{X}} \{F(a)\},$$

that is again using the addition of sets as defined above.

The propagation is defined without specifying each concrete operation in Definition 2. For any application, Definition 2 will never be applied directly. Nevertheless, only using this definition reveals one important property of the propagation very simply. Given $U_1 = \mathcal{U}(\mathbb{X})$, for any function F, $U_2 = \mathcal{U}(F(\mathbb{X}))$ is evaluated as

$$U_2 = \mathcal{U}(F(\mathbb{X})) = \sum_{x \in \mathbb{X}} \mathcal{U}(F(\{x\})) = \sum_{a \in \mathcal{U}(\mathbb{X})} \mathcal{U}(F(\mathcal{U}(\{a\}))) = \sum_{\substack{a \in U_1 \\ a \xrightarrow{F} b}} \{b\}. \quad (2)$$

This shows that our definition fits to the intuitive meaning of propagation: In order to determine U_2 after applying the function F, it is enough to consider what happens with individual elements of U_1 to start with. Here again, we like to emphasize that the sum in Eq. 2 is modulo two, that is, if an element appears an even number of times on the right side, it actually does not appear in U_2. Of course, to evaluate the propagation in real, we need to mention the concrete propagation $a \xrightarrow{F} b$, and we also give the following proposition, which allows to easily deduce the possible propagation given the ANF of a function.

Proposition 1. *Let $F : \mathbb{F}_2^n \to \mathbb{F}_2^m$ be defined as*

$$F(x_1, \ldots, x_n) = (y_1, \ldots, y_m) = y$$

where y_i are multivariate polynomials over $\mathbb{F}_2$ in the variables x_i. For $a \in \mathbb{F}_2^n$ and $b \in \mathbb{F}_2^m$, it holds that $a \xrightarrow{F} b$ if and only if y^b contains the monomial x^a.

Proof. By Definition 2, we have $a \xrightarrow{F} b$ if and only if $b \in \mathcal{U}(F(\mathcal{U}(\{a\})))$. Using Lemma 1, we can see that

$$\mathbb{Y} := F(\mathcal{U}(\{a\})) = \{F(x) \mid x \preceq a, x \in \mathbb{F}_2^n\}.$$

Hence $b \in \mathcal{U}(\mathbb{Y})$ exactly means $\sum_{x \preceq a} F^b(x) = 1$. Note that F^b is a Boolean function over the variables $x_1, \ldots, x_n$ whose ANF is exactly y^b, that is

$$F^b(x) = \sum_{u \in \mathbb{F}_2^n} \lambda_u x^u = y^b.$$

Using the well known relation between a function and the coefficients of its ANF, having $\sum_{x \preceq a} F^b(x) = 1$ directly gives that $\lambda_a = 1$, i.e., the monomial x^a appears in the ANF of F^b, said ANF being exactly y^b. $\qquad\square$

We remark that all propagation rules already introduced in [21] are generated by assigning concrete function to F. We refer the reader to [21] for more details about these propagation rules

Following previous work, we now generalize the definition above to the setting where F is actually given as the composition of many functions

$$F = F_R \circ \cdots \circ F_2 \circ F_1.$$

Definition 3 (Division Trail). *Given $F : \mathbb{F}_2^n \to \mathbb{F}_2^n$ as*

$$F = F_R \circ \cdots \circ F_2 \circ F_1$$

and $a_0 \ldots a_R \in \mathbb{F}_2^n$ we call $(a_0, \ldots, a_R)$ a division trail for the compositions of F into the F_i if and only if

$$\forall i \in \{1, \ldots, R\}, a_{i-1} \xrightarrow{F_i} a_i.$$

We denote such a trail by

$$a_0 \xrightarrow{F_1} a_1 \xrightarrow{F_2} \cdots \xrightarrow{F_R} a_R.$$

Using the same considerations as in Eq. 2, we can now state the main reason of why considering trails is useful.

Theorem 1. *Given $F : \mathbb{F}_2^n \to \mathbb{F}_2^n$ as*

$$F = F_R \circ \cdots \circ F_2 \circ F_1$$

and $\mathbb{X} \subseteq \mathbb{F}_2^n$. Then

$$\mathcal{U}(F(\mathbb{X})) = \sum_{\substack{a_0, \ldots, a_R \\ a_0 \in \mathcal{U}(\mathbb{X}), a_0 \xrightarrow{F_1} a_1 \xrightarrow{F_2} \cdots \xrightarrow{F_R} a_R}} \{a_R\}$$

The important link between the division property and the ANF is the following observations and is actually a special case of Proposition 1.

Corollary 1. *Let* $F : \mathbb{F}_2^n \to \mathbb{F}_2^n$ *be a function with algebraic normal form*

$$F(x) = \sum_{u \in \mathbb{F}_2^n} \lambda_u x^u$$

where $\lambda_u = (\lambda_u^{(1)}, \ldots, \lambda_u^{(n)}) \in \mathbb{F}_2^n$. *Furthermore, let* $\mathbb{X}$ *be the set such that* $\mathcal{U}(\mathbb{X}) = \{\ell\}$. *Then*

$$\lambda_\ell^{(i)} = 1 \iff e_i \in \mathcal{U}(F(\mathbb{X}))$$

Proof. If $\mathcal{U}(\mathbb{X}) = \{\ell\}$, by Lemma 1 we have

$$\mathbb{X} = \{x \in \mathbb{F}_2^n \mid x \preceq \ell\}.$$

Now by Eq. (1) we get

$$\lambda_\ell^{(i)} = \sum_{x \preceq \ell} F^{(i)}(x) = \sum_{x \in \mathbb{X}} F^{(i)}(x)$$

$$= \sum_{x \in F(\mathbb{X})} x^{e_i} = \begin{cases} 1 & \text{if } e_i \in \mathcal{U}(F(\mathbb{X})) \\ 0 & \text{otherwise} \end{cases}$$

which concludes the proof. $\qquad\square$

Theorem 1 and Corollary 1 finally result in the following corollary.

Corollary 2. *Let* $F : \mathbb{F}_2^n \to \mathbb{F}_2^n$ *be a function with algebraic normal form*

$$F(x) = \sum_{u \in \mathbb{F}_2^n} \lambda_u x^u$$

where $\lambda_u = (\lambda_u^{(1)}, \ldots, \lambda_u^{(n)}) \in \mathbb{F}_2^n$ *and* $F = F_R \circ \cdots \circ F_2 \circ F_1$. *Then* $\lambda_\ell^{(i)} = 1$ *if and only if the number of trails*

$$\ell \xrightarrow{F_1} a_1 \xrightarrow{F_2} \cdots \xrightarrow{F_R} e_i$$

is odd.

Proof. Follows immediately from the statements above. $\qquad\square$

This is what is actually solved using SAT solvers and/or mixed integer linear programming techniques. Before going into the details of the algorithmic approach, we explain why the case of a keyed function does not significantly change the perspective in our application in the next section.

3   High-Level Approach

Conceptually, there is no difference between key variables and input variables when it comes to division properties as used here and outlined in the previous section. It is only about splitting the set of variables into two (or potentially more) sets and changing the notation accordingly. Consider a function

$$E : \mathbb{F}_2^n \times \mathbb{F}_2^m \to \mathbb{F}_2^n$$
$$(x, k) \mapsto E(x, k)$$

When thinking of E as a block cipher, we usually rephrase this as a family of functions indexed by k, i.e., we consider

$$E_k : \mathbb{F}_2^n \to \mathbb{F}_2^n$$
$$\text{where } E_k(x) = E(x, k).$$

The algebraic normal form (ANF) of E and E_k are not identical, but related. Starting with the ANF of E expressed as

$$E(x, k) = \sum_{u \in \mathbb{F}_2^n, v \in \mathbb{F}_2^m} \lambda_{u,v} x^u k^v, \tag{3}$$

we get the ANF of E_k by rearranging terms as

$$E_k(x) = \sum_{u \in \mathbb{F}_2^n} \left(\sum_{v \in \mathbb{F}_2^m} \lambda_{u,v} k^v \right) x^u = \sum_{u \in \mathbb{F}_2^n} p_u(k) x^u,$$

where

$$p_u(k) = \sum_{v \in \mathbb{F}_2^m} \lambda_{u,v} k^v$$

are the key-dependent coefficients of the ANF of function E_k.

Note that the degree of E and E_k, which we already defined in Sect. 1 are usually different as

$$\deg(E) = \max_{u \in \mathbb{F}_2^n, v \in \mathbb{F}_2^m} \{\mathrm{wt}(u) + \mathrm{wt}(v) \mid \lambda_{u,v} \neq 0\}$$

while

$$\deg(E_k) = \max_{u \in \mathbb{F}_2^n} \{\mathrm{wt}(u) \mid p_u(k) \neq 0\}.$$

Here, clearly, we are interested in the later.

In order to lower bound the degree of E_k by some value d, we have to find a vector u of hamming weight d, such that $p_u(k)$ is non-zero. For a given u, there are two basic approaches to do so.

Fixed Key. Conceptually, the easiest way to lower bound the degree of E_k is to simply choose a random key k and, using Corollary 2 for computing one ANF coefficient of large degree. If this is feasible for a random key and the corresponding coefficient is actually 1, the degree must be larger or equal than d. If, however, the corresponding coefficient is zero, nothing can be concluded and one might have to repeat either for a different key or a different coefficient, or both. The advantage of this approach is its conceptual simplicity and that it can take an arbitrary key-scheduling into account. The significant drawback is that this approach becomes quickly impossible in practice. We elaborate on our initial findings using this approach in Sect. 6.

Variable Key. Luckily, we can use another approach. Namely, in order to show that the degree of E_k is at least d, it is sufficient to identify a single $u \in \mathbb{F}_2^n$ of Hamming weight d and an arbitrary $v \in \mathbb{F}_2^m$ such that $\lambda_{u,v} \neq 0$ (see Eq. 3) as this implies $p_u(k) \neq 0$. While this approach might seem more difficult at first glance, computationally it is significantly easier, especially when independent round-keys are assumed.

By definition, the keyed function E_k has degree at least d if for one $u \in \mathbb{F}_2^n$ of weight d and any $v \in \mathbb{F}_2^m$ the coefficient vector

$$\lambda_{u,v} = (\lambda_{u,v}^{(1)}, \ldots, \lambda_{u,v}^{(n)}) \in \mathbb{F}_2^n.$$

is non zero. So actually it is enough if, for one such u of weight d, an arbitrary v and any $1 \leq i \leq n$ it holds that $\lambda_{u,v}^{(i)} = 1$.

3.1 Minimum Degree

However, from an attacker perspective it is sufficient if there exists a single output bit of low degree. Thus, a stronger bound on the degree would potentially show that for all i there exist a u of weight d and an arbitrary v such that $\lambda_{u,v}^{(i)} = 1$. This would ensure that for each output bit there exists a key such that the degree of this output bit is at least d.

Again, this is not enough, as the attacker could equally look at any linear combination of output bits of her choice. The above result does not imply any bound on the degree of such linear combinations. Indeed, we would like to show that for each linear combination, there exists a key such that the degree of this linear combination is at least d. This is exactly captured in the definition of minimum degree.

Definition 4. *The* minimum degree *of a function $F : \mathbb{F}_2^n \to \mathbb{F}_2^n$ is defined as*

$$minDeg(F) = \min_{\beta \in \mathbb{F}_2^n, \beta \neq 0} \deg\langle \beta, F \rangle$$

Now, while for the degree it was sufficient to identify a single suitable coefficient $\lambda_{u,v}^{(i)}$ equal to one, things are more intricate here. There are, in principle,

$2^n - 1$ component functions $\langle \beta, F \rangle$ to be studied. Indeed, considering a single (u, v) pair and the corresponding $\lambda_{u,v}$ coefficient is not sufficient, as choosing any β such that $\langle \beta, \lambda_{u,v} \rangle = 0$ results in a component function that does not contain the monomial $k^v x^u$ in its ANF. It is this canceling of high degree monomials that has to be excluded for lower bounding the minimum degree.

In order to achieve this it is sufficient (and actually necessary) to find a set

$$S = \{(u_1, v_1), \ldots, (u_t, v_t)\}$$

of pairs (u, v) of size $t \geq n$ and compute the value of $\lambda_{u,v}^{(i)}$ for all i and all $(u, v) \in S$. This will lead to a binary matrix

$$M_S(E_k) = \begin{pmatrix} \lambda_{u_1,v_1}^{(1)} & \lambda_{u_2,v_2}^{(1)} & \cdots & \lambda_{u_t,v_t}^{(1)} \\ \lambda_{u_1,v_1}^{(2)} & \lambda_{u_2,v_2}^{(2)} & \cdots & \lambda_{u_t,v_t}^{(2)} \\ & & \vdots & \\ \lambda_{u_1,v_1}^{(n)} & \lambda_{u_2,v_2}^{(n)} & \cdots & \lambda_{u_t,v_t}^{(n)} \end{pmatrix}.$$

What has to be excluded, in order to bound the minimum degree is that columns of this matrix can be combined to the all zero vector, as in this case all monomials $k^{v_i} x^{u_i}$ cancel in the corresponding linear combination. Clearly, this is possible if and only if the columns are linear dependent. This observation is summarized in the following proposition.

Proposition 2. *A keyed function E_k has minimum degree at least d if and only if there exist a set S such that the matrix $M_S(E_k)$ has rank n and*

$$d \leq \min_{(u,v) \in S} \text{wt}(u)$$

3.2 Appearance of All High-Degree Monomials

Returning to the attacker perspective, it is clear that bounds on the minimum degree are more meaningful than bounds on the algebraic degree. However, it is also clear that even those are not enough to exclude the existence of integral attacks. In particular, even so the minimum degree of a function is $n - 1$, it could be the case that a certain monomial x^u of degree $n - 1$ never occurs in the ANF of the linear combination $\langle \beta, E_k(x) \rangle$ of output bits. That is, a minimum degree of $n - 1$ does not exclude that $\langle \beta, \lambda_{u,v} \rangle = 0$ for a fixed u and all v.

In order to ensure that this does not happen we have to show that for each fixed u of weight $n - 1$ there exist vectors v_i such that $M_{S_u}(E_k)$ has full rank for

$$S_u = \{(u, v_1), \ldots, (u, v_t)\}.$$

Here, we are (i) more restricted in the choice of the pairs in S as we always have to use the same fixed u and (ii) have to repeat the process n times, once for each u of weight $n - 1$.

Interestingly, the appearance of all high-degree monomials excludes a large class of integral distinguishers. Namely, for a cipher where all high-degree monomials appear (for at least one key), there will not be integral distinguisher by fixing bits that work for all keys. This is a consequence of the following observation that separates the pre-whitening key from the remaining round keys.

Proposition 3. *Let $E_k : \mathbb{F}_2^n \to \mathbb{F}_2^n$ be a cipher with ANF*

$$E_k(x) = \sum_{u \in \mathbb{F}_2^n} p_u(k) x^u$$

and consider a version of E_k with an additional pre-whitening key k_0, i.e.

$$E_{k,k_0}(x) := E_k(x + k_0)$$

with ANF

$$E_{k,k_0}(x) = \sum_{v \in \mathbb{F}_2^n} q_v(k, k_0) x^v$$

If, for all u of weight $n-1$ the coefficient $p_u(k)$, is non-constant, it follows that $q_v(k, k_0)$ is non-constant for all v of weight less than n.

Proof. We first express $q_v(k, k_0)$ in terms of p_u. We get

$$E_{k,k_0}(x) = E_k(x + k_0) = \sum_{u \in \mathbb{F}_2^n} p_u(k)(x + k_0)^u$$

$$= \sum_{u \in \mathbb{F}_2^n} p_u(k) \left(\sum_{v \preceq u} x^v k_0^{u \oplus v} \right) = \sum_{v \in \mathbb{F}_2^n} \left(\sum_{u \succeq v} p_u(k) k_0^{u \oplus v} \right) x^v$$

This shows that

$$q_v(k, k_0) = \sum_{u \succeq v} p_u(k) k_0^{u \oplus v}$$

Now, for any v of weight at most $n-1$, there exists at least one $u' \succeq v$ of weight $n-1$ in the sum above. By the assumption on E_k it holds that $p_{u'}(k)$ is not constant. Therefore, q_v is not constant as a function in k and k_0, which concludes the proof.   □

3.3   The Key Pattern

Computing the values of $\lambda_{u,v}^{(i)}$ is certainly not practical for arbitrary choice of (u, v) and i. There is not a lot of freedom in the choice of u, especially not if we aim at showing the appearance of all high degree monomials. However, there is a huge freedom in the choice of v, that is in the key monomial k^v that we consider.

It is exactly the careful selection of suitable v that has a major impact on the actual running time and finally allows us to obtain meaningful results in practical time. It is also here where assuming independent round-keys is needed. Consider that case of a key-alternating block cipher depicted below[2]

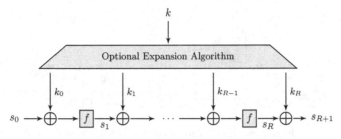

When considering independent round-keys, the key monomial k^v actually consists of

$$k^v = k_0^{v^{(0)}} k_1^{v^{(1)}} \dots k_R^{v^{(R)}}.$$

Here, we can select for each round-key k_i a suitable vector $v^{(i)}$ freely.

Returning to Corollary 2 and the division property, recall that $\lambda_{u,v}^{(i)} = 1$ if and only if the number of division trails $(u,v) \to e_i$ is odd. The vector v and therefore its parts $v = (v^{(0)}, \dots, v^{(R)})$ correspond to (parts of) the input division property. We will refer to v and its parts as the *key-pattern*. The number of trails, and therefore the computational effort, is highly dependent on this choice. This is the main technical challenge we solve, which is described in the following Sect. 4.

4   How to Search Input/Key/Output Patterns

As we already discussed above, we need to find u (called an *input pattern*) and $(v_0, \dots, v_R)$ (called a *key pattern*), in which the number of trails from $(u, v_0, \dots, v_R)$ to some unit vector e_i (called a *output pattern*) is odd and, equally important, efficiently computable. To do so, we will mainly rely on the use of automatic tools such as MILP and SAT. We refer the reader to [12] for the modeling in MILP and to [16] for the modeling in SAT (note that this paper shows how to modelize BDP in SAT, but it can easily be adapted in our context).

Once we get such an input/key/output pattern, it is very easy to verify the lower bound of the degree using standard techniques. We simply enumerate all trails and check the parity of the number of trails[3].

Therefore, the main problem that we need to solve is how to select suitable input/key/output patterns. In general, we search key patterns whose Hamming weight is as high as possible. The number of trails is highly related to the number of appearances of the same monomial when they are expanded without canceling in each round. Intuitively, we can expect such a high-degree monomial is unlikely to appear many times. Unfortunately, even if the key pattern is chosen with high weight, the number of trails tends to be even or extremely large when these patterns are chosen without care.

---

[2] Thanks to TikZ for Cryptographers [13].

[3] We also provide a simple code to verify our results about lower bounds.

Parasite Sub-Trails. To understand the difficulty and our strategy to find proper input/key/output patterns, we introduce an example using SKINNY64.

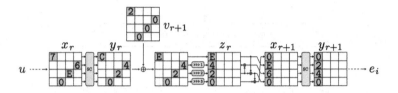

Fig. 2. Extraction from the trail of SKINNY64

Assume that we want to guarantee that the lower bound of algebraic degree of R-round SKINNY64 is 63. Given an input/key/output pattern, let us assume that there is a trail that contains the trail shown in Fig. 2 somewhere in the middle as a sub-trail. This sub-trail only focuses on the so-called super S-box involving the 4th anti-diagonal S-boxes in the $(r + 1)$th round and the 1st-column S-boxes in the $(r + 2)$th round. A remarkable, and unfortunately very common, fact is that this sub-trail never yields an odd-number of trails because we always have the following two different sub-trails.

$$T1 : \ 0x76E0 \xrightarrow{SC} 0xC420 \xrightarrow{ART(+0x2000)} 0xE420 \xrightarrow{MC} 0x0E60 \xrightarrow{SC} 0x0240$$

$$T2 : \ 0x76E0 \xrightarrow{SC} 0x1420 \xrightarrow{ART(+0x2000)} 0x3420 \xrightarrow{MC} 0x0360 \xrightarrow{SC} 0x0240$$

The trail shown in Fig. 2 is $T1$, and we always have another trail $T2$. Like this, when the number of sub-trails is even under the fixed input, key, and output pattern of the sub-trail, we call it an *inconsistent sub-trail*. Moreover, inconsistent sub-trails are independent of other parts of the trail and might occur in several parts of trails simultaneously. Assuming that there are 10 inconsistent sub-trails, the number of the total trails is at least 2^{10}. In other words, *inconsistent sub-trails increase the number of total trails exponentially*.

Heuristic Approach. It is therefore important to avoid trails containing inconsistent sub-trails. Instead of getting input/key/output pattern, the goal of the first step in our method is to find a trail, where all sub-trails relating to each super S-box are consistent, i.e., there is no inconsistent sub-trail as long as each super S-box is evaluated independently. Note that this goal is not sufficient for our original goal, and the number of total trails might still be even. Therefore, once we get such a trail, we extract the input/key/output pattern from the found trail, and check the total number of trails with this pattern.

We have several approaches to find such a trail. As we are actually going to search for these patterns and enumerate the number of trails using MILP or SAT solvers, the most straightforward approach is to generate a model to represent the propagation by each super S-box accurately. However, modeling a 16-bit keyed S-box has never been done before. Considering the difficulty to model even an 8-bit S-box, it is unlikely to be a successful path to follow.

Another approach is to use the well-known modeling technique, where the S-box and MixColumns are independently modeled, and exclude inconsistent sub-trail in each super S-box only after detecting them in a trail[4]. This approach is promising, but the higher the number of rounds gets, the less efficient it is as the number of super S-boxes we need to check the consistency increases. Indeed, as far as we tried, this approach is not feasible to find proper patterns for 11-round SKINNY64.

The method that we actually used is a heuristic approach that builds the trail round by round. Let x_r, y_r, and z_r be an intermediate values for the input of the $(r + 1)$th S-box layer, output of the $(r + 1)$th S-box layer, and input of the $(r + 1)$th MixColumns in each trail, respectively. Our main method consists of the following steps.

1. Given $e_i(= y_{R-1})$, determine (x_{R-2}, v_{R-1}), where the Hamming weight of x_{R-2} and v_{R-1} is as high as possible and the number of trails from x_{R-2} to e_i is odd and small (1 if possible).
2. Compute $(x_{R-3}, v_{R-2}, y_{R-2})$, where the Hamming weight of x_{R-3} and v_{R-2} is as high as possible and the number of trails from x_{R-3} to y_{R-2} is odd (1 if possible). Then, check if the number of trails from x_{R-3} to e_i is odd (1 if possible) under (v_{R-2}, v_{R-1}).
3. Repeat the procedure above to R_{mid} rounds. This results in a key pattern $(v_{R_{mid}+1}, \dots, v_{R-1})$, where the number of trails from $x_{R_{mid}}$ to e_i is odd and small (again, 1 in the best case).
4. Compute $(v_1, \dots, v_{R_{mid}})$ such that the number of trails from $u(= x_0)$ to $y_{R_{mid}}$ is odd.
5. Compute the number of trails satisfying $(u, v_1, \dots, v_{R-1}) \rightarrow e_i$.

Our method can be regarded as the iteration of the local optimization. As we already discussed in the beginning of this section, we can expect that the number of trails from pattern with high weight is small. The first three steps, called *trail extension* in our paper, are local optimization in this context from the last round. Note that these steps are neither a deterministic nor an exhaustive methods. In other words, the trail extension is randomly chosen from a set of optimal or semi-optimal choices. Sometimes, there is an unsuccessful trail extension, e.g., it requires too much time to extend the trail after a few rounds or we run into trails that cannot reach the input pattern u. The heuristic and randomized algorithm allows, in case we faces such unsuccessful trail extensions, to simply restart the process from the beginning.

As far as we observe some ciphers, unsuccessful trail extensions happens with higher probability as the trail approaches the first round. Therefore, after some R_{mid} rounds, we change our strategy, and switch to the more standard way of searching for $(u, v_1, \dots, v_{R_{mid}})$, e.g., $R_{mid} = 5$ or 6 is used in SKINNY64.

---

[4] When we use Gurobi MILP solver, we can easily implement this behavior by using callback functions.

More formally, we search trails from u to $y_{R_{mid}}$ while excluding inconsistent sub-trails. Note that this is possible now because this trail has to cover less rounds. Once we find such a trail, we extract the key-patterns $(u, v_1, \ldots, v_{R_{mid}})$ from the trail and check if the number of trails from $(u, v_1, \ldots, v_{R_{mid}})$ to $y_{R_{mid}}$ is odd. If so, we finally extract the entire input/key/output pattern and verify the number of trails satisfying $(u, v_1, \ldots, v_{R-1}) \rightarrow e_i$.

Our algorithm is not generic, and it only searches "the most likely spaces" at random. Therefore, it quickly finds the proper pattern only a few minutes sometimes, but sometimes, no pattern is found even if we spend one hour and more.

We like to stress again that, once we find input/key/output patterns whose number of trails is odd, verifying the final number of trails is easy and standard, and for this we refer the reader to the code available at https://github.com/LowerBoundsAlgDegree/LowerBoundsAlgDegree.

How to Compute Minimum-Degree. The minimum degree is more important for cryptographers than the algebraic degree. To guarantee the lower bound of the minimum degree, we need to create patterns whose resulting matrix $M_S(E_k)$ has full rank.

Our method allows us to get the input/key/output pattern, i.e., compute $\lambda_{u,v}^{(i)}$ for the specific tuple (u, v, i). However, to construct this matrix, we need to know all bits of $\lambda_{u,v}$. And, the use of the input/key pattern for different output patterns is out of the original use of our method. Therefore, it might allow significantly many trails that we cannot enumerate them with practical time.

To solve this issue, we first restrict ourselves to use a non-zero key pattern v_{R-1} for the last-but one round during the trail extension. This is motivated by the observation that, usually, a single round function is not enough to mix the full state. Therefore it is obvious that the ANF of some output bits is independent of some key-bits $k_r^{v_{R-1}}$.

Equivalently, many output bits of $\lambda_{u,v}$ are trivially 0, i.e., the number of trails is always 0. Thus, the matrix $M_S(E_k)$ is a block diagonal matrix

$$M_S(E_k) = \begin{pmatrix} M_{S_1}(E_k) & 0 & \cdots & 0 \\ 0 & M_{S_2}(E_k) & \cdots & 0 \\ \vdots & \vdots & \ddots & \vdots \\ 0 & 0 & \cdots & M_{S_m}(E_k) \end{pmatrix}.$$

As such, $M_S(E_k)$ has the full rank when $M_{S_i}(E_k)$ has the full rank for all i. This technique allows us to generate input/key/output patterns for the full-rank matrix efficiently.

Even if we use non-zero v_{R-1}, we still need to get full-rank block matrices. Luckily, there is an important (algorithmic) improvement that we like to briefly mention here. In many cases, it is not needed to compute the entire set of entries of a matrix $M_S(F)$ to conclude it has full rank. As an example, consider the matrix

$$M_S(F) = \begin{pmatrix} 1 & 0 & * \\ 0 & 1 & 0 \\ 0 & 0 & 1 \end{pmatrix}$$

where $*$ is an undetermined value. Then $M_S(F)$ has full rank, no matter what the value of $*$ actually is. Even so this observation is rather simple, it is often an important ingredient to save computational resources.

How to Compute All High-Degree Monomials. Guaranteeing the appearance of all high-degree monomials is more important for cryptographers than minimum degree. Conceptually, it is not so difficult. We simply use a specific u in the 4th step instead of any u whose Hamming weight is $n - 1$ and guarantee the lower bound of the minimum degree. Then, we repeat this procedure for all us with Hamming weight $n - 1$.

How to Compute Lower Bounds for Intermediate Rounds. While the most interesting result for cryptographers is to show the full algebraic degree and full minimum degree, it is also interesting to focus on the degree or minimum degree in the intermediate rounds and determine how the lower bounds increase.

In our paper, these lower bounds are computed by using the input/key/output pattern, which is originally generated to guarantee the full degree and minimum degree. For example, when we prove the lower bound of r rounds, we first enumerate all trails on this pattern, and extract x_{R-r} whose number of trails $(x_{R-r}, v_{R-r+1}, \ldots, v_{R-1}) \to e_i$ is odd. Let $X_{R-r}^{(i)}$ be the set of all extracted values, and a lower bounds of the algebraic degree for r rounds is given by

$$\max_i \max_{u \in X_{R-r}^{(i)}} wt(u).$$

A more involved technique is needed for the minimum degree. We first construct the matrix $M_S(E_k)$ for R rounds, where for non-diagonal elements, we set 0 if there is no trail, and we set $*$ if there is trail. If this matrix has the full rank, we always have the full-rank matrix even when we focus on intermediate rounds. In this case, a lower bounds of the minimum degree for r rounds is given by

$$\min_i \max_{u \in X_{R-r}^{(i)}} wt(u).$$

How to Compute Upper Bounds. While some work has been done previously to find upper bounds on the algebraic degree [6,8], we want to point out that we can easily compute such upper bounds using our MILP models, and our results in Sect. 5 show that the resulting upper bounds are quite precise, especially for the algebraic degree. Indeed, to prove an upper bound for R rounds and for the i-th coordinate function, we simply generate a model for R rounds, fix the output value of the trail to the unit vector e_i and then simply ask the solver to maximize $wt(u)$. This maximum value thus leads to an upper bound

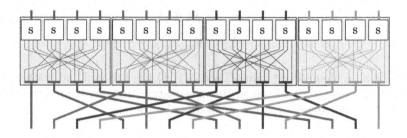

Fig. 3. Round function of GIFT-64 using SSB-friendly description

on the degree, since it is the maximum weight that u can have so that there is at least one trail. Then, once we collected an upper bound ub_i for each coordinate function, we easily get an upper bound on the algebraic degree of the vectorial function as $\max_i ub_i$. To get an upper bound on the minimum degree, recall that the minimum degree is defined as the minimal algebraic degree of any linear combination of all coordinate functions. Thus, in particular, this minimum degree is at most equal to the minimal upper bound we have on each coordinate function, i.e., using the upper bounds on each coordinate function as before, we simply need to compute $\min_i ub_i$.

5   Applications

Clearly, we want to point out that the result about the lower bounds do not depend on how we model our ciphers. That is, the parity of the number of trails must be the same as long as we create the correct model. However the number of trails itself highly depends on the way we model, e.g., the number is 0 for one model but it is 1,000,000 for another model. As enumerating many trails is a time consuming and difficult problem, we have to optimize the model.

For example, we could use only the COPY, XOR and AND operations to describe the propagation through the S-box. However this would lead to more trails than necessary, while directly modeling the propagation using the convex hull method as in [22] significantly reduces the induced number of trails.

We already mentioned earlier that we consider independent round-keys added to the full state. In particular for GIFT and SKINNY, the cipher we study are strictly speaking actually not GIFT and SKINNY. However, we stress that this is a rather natural assumption that is widely used for both design and cryptanalysis of block ciphers.

5.1   GIFT

GIFT is a lightweight block cipher published at CHES'17 by Banik et al. [2]. Two variants of this block cipher exists depending on the block length (either 64-bit or 128-bit) and use a 128-bit key in both case. Its round function and the Super S-boxes are depicted in Fig. 3. Note that in the original design, the round key is added only to a part of the state.

Table 2. Propagation table for the S-box of GIFT

	0	1	2	4	8	3	5	6	9	A	C	7	B	D	E	F
0	x	x														
1		x	x	x						x						
2		x		x												
4		x	x	x		x										
8		x	x													
3		x	x						x	x						
5		x					x	x		x	x	x	x	x	x	x
6						x		x								
9			x			x	x	x	x			x				
A			x	x	x			x	x			x				
C						x	x									
7								x				x	x	x	x	x
B								x				x	x	x		
D				x	x	x						x	x		x	x
E			x				x	x	x	x		x				
F																x

Modeling. The round function of GIFT-64 is very simple and only consist of an S-box layer and a bit permutation layer. We give the propagation table of this S-box in Table 2, namely, an x in row u and column v means that $u \xrightarrow{S} v$ where S is the GIFT-64 S-box. For example, the column 0x1 corresponds to the monomials appearing in the ANF of the first output bit of the S-box. We can obtain linear inequalities to modelize this table according to the technique given in [22].

The bit permutation is simply modelized by reordering the variables accordingly.

Algebraic Degree. We applied our algorithm for GIFT-64 and obtained that the algebraic degree of all coordinate functions is maximal (i.e., 63) after 9 rounds. However, we can go even further and prove that 32 of the coordinate functions are of degree 63 after only 8 rounds. As such, the algebraic degree of GIFT-64 as a vectorial function is maximal after only 8 rounds. In Fig. 4 on the left side, we give the lower and upper bounds for the algebraic degree of GIFT-64, and we will give the detailed lower and upper bounds for each coordinate function in the full version of the paper.

Note that we thus have two data-sets: one for 8 rounds and another one for 9 rounds. To get the curve for the lower bounds on algebraic degree, we simply "merged" the data-sets and extracted the best lower bound for each coordinate function and for each number of rounds. Thus this curve shows the best results we were able to get.

While the execution time can widely vary depending on a lot of factors, in practice our algorithm proved to be quite efficient when applied to GIFT-64. Indeed, to prove that each output bit is of maximal degree after 9 rounds as well as computing the lower bounds for a smaller number of rounds, we needed less than one hour on a standard laptop, and about 30 min to find all coordinate functions with algebraic degree 63 after 8 rounds (and again, also computing all lower bounds for less rounds).

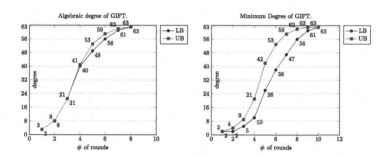

Fig. 4. Algebraic degree and minimum degree for GIFT-64

Minimum Degree. In about one hour of computation on a standard laptop, we were able to show that the minimum degree is maximal after 10 rounds. In Fig. 4 on the right side we show the lower and upper bounds on the minimum degree for each number of rounds from 1 to 10.

All Maximal Degree Monomials. As described in Sect. 3.2 we were able to show that *all* 63-degree monomials appear after 11 rounds for any linear combination of the output bits. This computation was a bit more expensive than the previous one, yet our results were obtained within about 64 h.

5.2 SKINNY64

SKINNY is a lightweight block cipher published at CRYPTO'16 by Beierle et al. [4]. SKINNY supports two different block lengths (either 64 bits or 128 bits). The round function adopts the so-called AES-like structure, where significantly lightweight S-box and MixColumns are used.

Please refer to Fig. 2 for the figure of the round function of our variant of SKINNY64.

Modeling. We introduce how to create the model to enumerate trails. For the S-box, the method is the same as for GIFT, i.e. using the technique from [22]. Therefore, here, we focus on MixColumns.

Table 3. Algebraic degree and minimum degree on SKINNY64

		1R	2R	3R	4R	5R	6R	7R	8R	9R	10R	11R
degree	UB	3	8	19	33	47	58	61	62	62	63	63
	LB	3	8	18	29	39	49	55	59	61	63	–
minDeg	UB	2	3	8	17	33	47	58	61	62	62	63
	LB	2	2	5	8	14	26	39	50	57	61	63

Naively, propagation through linear layers would be done with a combination of COPY and XOR propagations as in [12]. However, this leads to more trails that we need to count, which thus increase the overall time needed for our algorithm. Therefore, we use that MixColumns of SKINNY can be seen as the parallel application of several small linear S-boxes, denoted by L-box hereinafter. Formally, MixColumns is the multiplication over $\mathbb{F}_{2^4}$, but equivalently, we can see this operation over $\mathbb{F}_2$, where it is the multiplication with the following block matrix over $\mathbb{F}_2$

$$\begin{pmatrix} I_4 & 0 & I_4 & I_4 \\ I_4 & 0 & 0 & 0 \\ 0 & I_4 & I_4 & 0 \\ I_4 & 0 & I_4 & 0 \end{pmatrix},$$

where I_4 is the identity matrix over $\mathbb{F}_2$ of dimension 4. By carefully examining the structure of this matrix, we can actually notice that it can be written as the parallel application of 4 L-boxes, which is defined as

$$L(x_1, x_2, x_3, x_4) = (x_1 \oplus x_3 \oplus x_4, x_1, x_2 \oplus x_3, x_1 \oplus x_3),$$

Hence, instead of using the COPY and XOR operations, we consider that it is actually the parallel application of this L-box. Thus, the modelization for MixColumns is done in the same way as for S-boxes using the technique from [22].

Algebraic Degree. Before we discuss the algebraic degree of SKINNY, we introduce a *column rotation equivalence*. We now focus on SKINNY, where all round keys are independent and XORed with the full state. Then, the impact on the round constant is removed, and each column has the same algebraic normal form with different input. Overall, we remove the last ShiftRows and MixColumns, and the output bit is the output of the last S-box layer. Then, in the context of the division property, once we find a trail $(u, v_0, \ldots, v_R) \rightarrow e_i$, we always have a trail $(u^{\lll 32 \cdot i}, v_0^{\lll 32 \cdot i}, \ldots, v_R^{\lll 32 \cdot i}) \rightarrow e_{i+32 \cdot i})$, where $u^{\lll 32 \cdot i}$ is a value after rotating u by i columns. The column rotation equivalence enables us to see that it is enough to check the first column only.

We evaluated the upper bound of the algebraic degree for each coordinate function in the first column. The UB of degree in Table 3 shows the maximum upper bound among upper bounds for 16 coordinate functions, as well as the best lower bounds we managed to compute. The detailed results for the UB and LB of each coordinate function will be given in the full version of the paper.

In 10 rounds, the lower bound is the same as the upper bound. In other words, the full degree in 10 rounds is tight, and we can guarantee the upper bound of the algebraic degree is never less than 63 in 10-round SKINNY under our assumption.

Minimum Degree. The upper bound of the algebraic degree for bits in the 2nd row is 62 in 10 rounds. Therefore, 10 rounds are clearly not enough when we consider the full minimum degree. As we already discussed in Sect. 3.1, we need to construct 64 input/key patterns whose matrix $M_S(E_k)$ has the full rank.

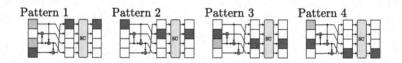

Fig. 5. Deterministic trail extension for the last MixColumns and S-box

To guarantee the lower bounds of the minimum degree, the method shown in Sect. 4 is used. In SKINNY64, when v_{R-2} is non-zero, the resulting matrix becomes a block diagonal matrix, where each block is 16×16 matrix. Moreover, thanks to the column rotation equivalence, we always have input/key patterns such that each block matrix is identical. Therefore, only getting one full-rank 16×16 block matrix is enough to guarantee the lower bound of minimum degree.

Unfortunately, the use of the technique described in Sect. 4 is not sufficient to find patterns efficiently. We use another trick called a *deterministic trail extension*, where we restrict the trail extension for the last MixColumns and S-box such that it finds key patterns whose matrix is the full rank efficiently. Figure 5 summarizes our restriction, where the cell labeled deep red color must have non-zero value in the trail. We assume that taking the input of each pattern is necessary for the trail to exist. Then, taking Pattern 1 (resp. Pattern 3) implies that $\lambda_{u,v}^{(i)}$ can be 1 only when i indicates bits in the 1st nibble (resp. 3rd nibble). Taking Pattern 2 allows non-zero $\lambda_{u,v}^{(i)}$ for i which indicates bits in the 1st, 2nd, and 4th nibbles. Taking Pattern 4 allows non-zero $\lambda_{u,v}^{(i)}$ for i which indicates bits in the 1st, 3rd, and 4th nibbles. In summary, we can expect the following matrix

$$
M_{S_1}(E_k) = \begin{pmatrix} A & * & 0 & * \\ 0 & B & 0 & 0 \\ 0 & 0 & C & * \\ 0 & * & 0 & D \end{pmatrix},
$$

where 0 is 4×4 zero matrix, and $*$ is an arbitrary 4×4 matrix. We can notice that this matrix is full rank if A, B, C, and D are full rank.

By using these techniques, we find 16 input/key patterns to provide the lower bound of the minimum degree on SKINNY64 (see minDeg in Table 3). In 11 rounds, the lower bound is the same as the upper bound, thus having full minimum degree in 11 rounds is tight. In other words, we can guarantee the upper bound of the minimum degree is never less than 63 in 11-round SKINNY under our assumption.

All Maximum-Degree Monomials. To guarantee the appearance of all maximum-degree monomials, much more computational power must be spent. The column rotation equivalence allows us to reduce the search space, but it is still 64 times the cost of the minimum degree. After spending almost one week of computations, we can get input/key patterns to prove the appearance of all maximum-degree monomials in 13-round SKINNY64. All input/key patterns are listed in https://github.com/LowerBoundsAlgDegree/LowerBoundsAlgDegree.

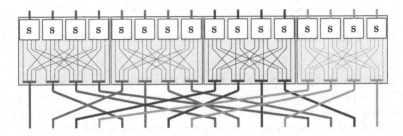

Fig. 6. Round function of PRESENT using SSB-friendly description

5.3   PRESENT

PRESENT is another lightweight block cipher published at CHES'07 [5], with a 64-bit block size and two variants depending on the key-length : either 80 bits or 128 bits. Its round function is very similar to the round function of GIFT and is also built using a 4-bit S-box and a bit permutation, see Fig. 6.

Modeling. As for GIFT-64, the S-box is modelized using the technique from [22] and the bit permutation can easily be modelized by reordering variables.

Algebraic Degree. Using our algorithm, we were able to show that all output bits have an algebraic degree of 63 after 9 rounds in about nine hours, including the lower bounds for a smaller number of rounds. Even better, for 8 rounds, we were able to show that 54 out of all 64 coordinate functions are actually already of degree 63. We give the resulting lower and upper bounds for the algebraic degree of PRESENT on the left side of Fig. 7. As for GIFT-64, these curves were obtained by taking the best bounds over all coordinate functions, and the detailed bounds for each coordinate function will be given in the full version of the paper.

Minimum Degree. Note that while directly using the PRESENT specification would still allow us to get some results for the minimum degree, we found out a way to largely improve the speed of the search for this case. Similarly to SKINNY64, we used a deterministic trail extension for the last S-box layer. We will give the full details about this observation and how we managed it in the full version.

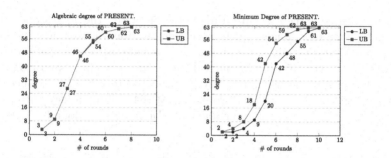

Fig. 7. Algebraic degree and minimum degree for PRESENT

In short, we change the S-box in the last S-box layer to a linearly equivalent one S' (thus preserving the correctness of our results for the minimum degree) and add additional constraints to help finding "good" key patterns during the search. While these constraints could slightly restrict the search space, in practice it proved to be a very efficient trick to speed up the search and was enough to prove the full minimum degree over 10 rounds. The same trick is used for the all monomial property since it is essentially the same as for the minimum degree, only repeated several time for each possible input monomial. In the end, within about nine hours, we were able to show that the minimum degree is also maximal after 10 rounds using this trick. In Fig. 7 on the right side, we give the lower and upper bounds for the minimum degree over 1 to 10 rounds.

All Maximal Degree Monomials. Showing that all 63-degree monomials appear after 11 rounds for any linear combinations of output bits required quite a bit more computational power, however we were still able to show this result in about 17 days of computation.

5.4 AES

Despite many proposals of lightweight block ciphers, AES stays the most widely-used block cipher. The application to AES of our method is thus of great interest.

However, our method uses automatic tools such as MILP or SAT and such tools are not always powerful for block ciphers using 8-bit S-boxes like AES. As therefore expected, our method also has non-negligible limitation, and it is difficult to prove the full, i.e., 127, lower bound of algebraic degree. Yet, our method can still derive new and non-trivial result regarding the AES.

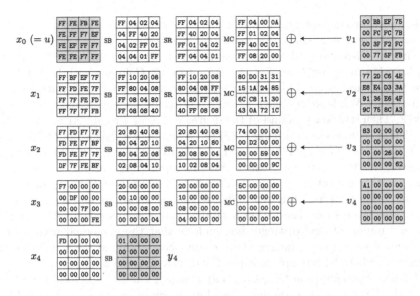

Fig. 8. Trail on 5-round AES

Modeling. We first construct linear inequalities to model the propagation table for the AES S-box, where we used the modeling technique shown in [1]. While a few dozens of linear inequalities are enough to model 4-bit S-boxes, 3,660 inequalities are required to model the AES S-box. Moreover, the model for Mix-Columns is also troublesome because the technique using L-boxes like SKINNY is not possible. The only choice is a naive method, i.e., we would rely on the COPY + XOR rules for the division property [21]. Unfortunately, this method requires 184, which is equal to the weight of the matrix over $\mathbb{F}_2$, temporary variables, and such temporary variables increase the number of trails. In particular, when the weight of the output pattern in MixColumns is large, the number of sub-trails exponentially increases even when we focus on one MixColumns.

Algebraic Degree. Due to the expensive modeling situation, proving full algebraic degree is unlikely to be possible. Nevertheless, this model still allows us to get non-trivial results. We exploit that the number of sub-trails can be restrained to a reasonable size when the weight of the output pattern in MixColumns is small. Namely, we extend the trail such that only such trails are possible.

Figure 8 shows one trail for 5-round AES. When the input/key/output pattern, shown in red, is fixed, the number of trails is odd. Moreover, we confirmed that the number of trails for reduced-number of rounds is odd, e.g., in 3-round AES, the number of trails $(x_2, v_3, v_4) \rightarrow y_4$ is odd.

This result provides us some interesting and non-trivial results.

On 3-round AES, the input of this trail is 16 values with Hamming weight 7. In other words, the lower bound of the degree is $16 \times 7 = 112$. Considering well-known 3-round integral distinguisher exploits that the monomial with all bits in each byte is missing, this lower bound is tight.

From the 4-round trail, we can use the input, which includes 0xFF. Unfortunately, using many 0xFF implies the output of MixColumns with higher Hamming weight, and as we already discussed, the resulting number of trails increases dramatically. While we can have 12 0xFF potentially, we only extend the trail to 4 0xFF. Then, the lower bound of the degree is 116 in 4-round AES.

The first column in x_1 has 0xFFFFFFFF. When we use the naive COPY+XOR rules, there are many trails from 0xFFFFFFFF to 0xFFFFFFFF via MixColumns. However, this trail must be possible and this input (resp. output) cannot propagate to other output (resp. input). Therefore, we bypass only this propagation without using COPY+XOR rule. This technique allows us to construct x_0 in Fig. 8. One interesting observation is all diagonal elements take 0xFF, and well-known 4-round integral distinguisher exploits that the monomial with all bits in diagonal elements is missing. Our result shows 5-round AES includes the monomial, where 84 bits are multiplied with the diagonal monomial.

While we can give non-trivial and large enough lower bound for 3-round and 4-round AES, the results are not satisfying. Many open questions are still left, e.g., how to prove the full degree, full minimum degree, the appearance of all high-degree monomials.

6   Conclusion

Cryptographers have so far failed to provide meaningful lower bounds on the degree of block cipher, and in this paper, we (partially) solve this long-lasting problem and give, for the first time, such lower bounds on a selection of block ciphers. Interestingly, we can now observe that the upper bounds are relatively tight in many cases. This was hoped for previously, but not clear at all before our work.

Obviously, there are some limitations and restrictions of our current work that, in our opinion, are good topics for future works. The main restriction is the applicability to other ciphers. For now, all ciphers studied so far needed some adjustment in the procedure to increase the efficiency and derive the results. It would be great if a unified and improved method could avoid those hand made adjustments. This restriction is inherently related to our heuristic search approach for the key-pattern. A better search, potentially based on new insights into how to choose the key-pattern in an optimal way, is an important topic for future research. Moreover, if we focus on the appearance of all maximal degree monomials, we still have a gap between the best integral distinguishers and our results. Thus, either our bounds or the attacks might be improved in the future. Finally, for now, computing good bounds for fixed key variants of the ciphers is not possibly with our ideas so far. This is in particular important for cryptographic permutations where we fail for now to argue about lower bounds for the degree. Only in the case of PRESENT, we were able to compute a non-trivial lower bound on the algebraic degree in the fixed key setting for a few bits for 10 rounds. Here, we counted the number of trails using a #SAT solver[5] [17]. Especially for other ciphers with a more complicated linear layer like SKINNY, we were not able to show a lower bound on any output bit.

Acknowledgment. This work was partially funded by the DFG, German Research Foundation) under Germany's Excellence Strategy - EXC 2092 CASA – 390781972 and the by the German Federal Ministry of Education and Research (BMBF, project iBlockchain – 16KIS0901K).

References

1. Abdelkhalek, A., Sasaki, Y., Todo, Y., Tolba, M., Youssef, A.M.: MILP modeling for (large) s-boxes to optimize probability of differential characteristics. IACR Trans. Symmetric Cryptol. **2017**(4), 99–129 (2017). https://doi.org/10.13154/tosc.v2017.i4.99-129
2. Banik, S., Pandey, S.K., Peyrin, T., Sasaki, Y., Sim, S.M., Todo, Y.: GIFT: a small present. In: Fischer, W., Homma, N. (eds.) CHES 2017. LNCS, vol. 10529, pp. 321–345. Springer, Cham (2017). https://doi.org/10.1007/978-3-319-66787-4_16
3. Beaulieu, R., Shors, D., Smith, J., Treatman-Clark, S., Weeks, B., Wingers, L.: The SIMON and SPECK families of lightweight block ciphers. IACR Cryptol. ePrint Arch. **2013**, 404 (2013). http://eprint.iacr.org/2013/404
4. Beierle, C., et al.: The SKINNY family of block ciphers and its low-latency variant MANTIS. In: Robshaw, M., Katz, J. (eds.) CRYPTO 2016. LNCS, vol. 9815, pp. 123–153. Springer, Heidelberg (2016). https://doi.org/10.1007/978-3-662-53008-5_5
5. Bogdanov, A., et al.: PRESENT: an ultra-lightweight block cipher. In: Paillier, P., Verbauwhede, I. (eds.) CHES 2007. LNCS, vol. 4727, pp. 450–466. Springer, Heidelberg (2007). https://doi.org/10.1007/978-3-540-74735-2_31
6. Boura, C., Canteaut, A.: On the influence of the algebraic degree of f^{-1} on the algebraic degree of G ∘ F. IEEE Trans. Inf. Theory **59**(1), 691–702 (2013). https://doi.org/10.1109/TIT.2012.2214203
7. Boura, C., Canteaut, A.: Another view of the division property. In: Robshaw, M., Katz, J. (eds.) CRYPTO 2016. LNCS, vol. 9814, pp. 654–682. Springer, Heidelberg (2016). https://doi.org/10.1007/978-3-662-53018-4_24
8. Boura, C., Canteaut, A., De Cannière, C.: Higher-order differential properties of KECCAK and *Luffa*. In: Joux, A. (ed.) FSE 2011. LNCS, vol. 6733, pp. 252–269. Springer, Heidelberg (2011). https://doi.org/10.1007/978-3-642-21702-9_15
9. Carlet, C., Crama, Y., Hammer, P.L.: Vectorial boolean functions for cryptography. In: Crama, Y., Hammer, P.L. (eds.) Boolean Models and Methods in Mathematics, Computer Science, and Engineering, pp. 398–470. Cambridge University Press (2010). https://doi.org/10.1017/cbo9780511780448.012
10. Daemen, J., Knudsen, L., Rijmen, V.: The block cipher square. In: Biham, E. (ed.) FSE 1997. LNCS, vol. 1267, pp. 149–165. Springer, Heidelberg (1997). https://doi.org/10.1007/BFb0052343
11. Dinur, I., Shamir, A.: Cube attacks on tweakable black box polynomials. In: Joux, A. (ed.) EUROCRYPT 2009. LNCS, vol. 5479, pp. 278–299. Springer, Heidelberg (2009). https://doi.org/10.1007/978-3-642-01001-9_16

---

[5] A #SAT solver is optimized to count the number of solutions for a given Boolean formula.

12. Hao, Y., Leander, G., Meier, W., Todo, Y., Wang, Q.: Modeling for three-subset division property without unknown subset. In: Canteaut, A., Ishai, Y. (eds.) EUROCRYPT 2020. LNCS, vol. 12105, pp. 466–495. Springer, Cham (2020). https://doi.org/10.1007/978-3-030-45721-1_17

13. Jean, J.: TikZ for Cryptographers. https://www.iacr.org/authors/tikz/ (2016)

14. Knudsen, L., Wagner, D.: Integral cryptanalysis. In: Daemen, J., Rijmen, V. (eds.) FSE 2002. LNCS, vol. 2365, pp. 112–127. Springer, Heidelberg (2002). https://doi.org/10.1007/3-540-45661-9_9

15. Lai, X.: Higher order derivatives and differential cryptanalysis. In: Blahut, R.E., Costello, D.J., Maurer, U., Mittelholzer, T. (eds.) Communications and Cryptography. The Springer International Series in Engineering and Computer Science, vol. 276, pp. 227–233. Springer, Boston (1994). https://doi.org/10.1007/978-1-4615-2694-0_23

16. Sun, L., Wang, W., Wang, M.: Automatic search of bit-based division property for ARX ciphers and word-based division property. In: Takagi, T., Peyrin, T. (eds.) ASIACRYPT 2017. LNCS, vol. 10624, pp. 128–157. Springer, Cham (2017). https://doi.org/10.1007/978-3-319-70694-8_5

17. Thurley, M.: sharpSAT – counting models with advanced component caching and implicit BCP. In: Biere, A., Gomes, C.P. (eds.) SAT 2006. LNCS, vol. 4121, pp. 424–429. Springer, Heidelberg (2006). https://doi.org/10.1007/11814948_38

18. Todo, Y.: Integral cryptanalysis on full MISTY1. In: Gennaro, R., Robshaw, M. (eds.) CRYPTO 2015. LNCS, vol. 9215, pp. 413–432. Springer, Heidelberg (2015). https://doi.org/10.1007/978-3-662-47989-6_20

19. Todo, Y.: Structural evaluation by generalized integral property. In: Oswald, E., Fischlin, M. (eds.) EUROCRYPT 2015. LNCS, vol. 9056, pp. 287–314. Springer, Heidelberg (2015). https://doi.org/10.1007/978-3-662-46800-5_12

20. Todo, Y.: Integral cryptanalysis on full MISTY1. J. Cryptol. 30(3), 920–959 (2016). https://doi.org/10.1007/s00145-016-9240-x

21. Todo, Y., Morii, M.: Bit-based division property and application to SIMON family. In: Peyrin, T. (ed.) FSE 2016. LNCS, vol. 9783, pp. 357–377. Springer, Heidelberg (2016). https://doi.org/10.1007/978-3-662-52993-5_18

22. Xiang, Z., Zhang, W., Bao, Z., Lin, D.: Applying MILP method to searching integral distinguishers based on division property for 6 lightweight block ciphers. In: Cheon, J.H., Takagi, T. (eds.) ASIACRYPT 2016. LNCS, vol. 10031, pp. 648–678. Springer, Heidelberg (2016). https://doi.org/10.1007/978-3-662-53887-6_24

Towards Closing the Security Gap
of Tweak-aNd-Tweak (TNT)

Chun Guo[1], Jian Guo[2], Eik List[3(✉)], and Ling Song[4,5]

[1] School of Cyber Science and Technology, Shandong University, Qingdao, China
chun.guo@sdu.edu.cn
[2] Division of Mathematical Sciences, School of Physical and Mathematical Sciences,
Nanyang Technological University, Singapore, Singapore
guojian@ntu.edu.sg
[3] Bauhaus-Universität Weimar, Weimar, Germany
eik.list@uni-weimar.de
[4] Jinan University, Guangzhou, China
songling.qs@gmail.com
[5] Institute of Information Engineering, Chinese Academy of Sciences,
Beijing, China

Abstract. Tweakable block ciphers (TBCs) have been established as a valuable replacement for many applications of classical block ciphers. While several dedicated TBCs have been proposed in the previous years, generic constructions that build a TBC from a classical block cipher are still highly useful, for example, to reuse an existing implementation. However, most generic constructions need an additional call to either the block cipher or a universal hash function to process the tweak, which limited their efficiency.

To address this deficit, Bao et al. proposed Tweak-aNd-Tweak (TNT) at EUROCRYPT'20. Their construction chains three calls to independent keyed permutations and adds the unmodified tweak to the state in between the calls. They further suggested an efficient instantiation TNT-AES that was based on round-reduced AES for each of the permutations. Their work could prove $2n/3$-bit security for their construction, where n is the block size in bits. Though, in the absence of an upper bound, their analysis had to consider all possible attack vectors with up to 2^n time, data, and memory. Still, closing the gap between both bounds remained a highly interesting research question.

In this work, we show that a variant of Mennink's distinguisher on CLRW2 with $O(\sqrt{n}2^{3n/4})$ data and $O(2^{3n/2})$ time from TCC'18 also applies to TNT. We reduce its time complexity to $O(\sqrt{n}2^{3n/4})$, show the existence of a second similar distinguisher, and demonstrate how to transform the distinguisher to a key-recovery attack on TNT-AES[5, *, *] from an impossible differential. From a constructive point of view, we adapt the rigorous STPRP analysis of CLRW2 by Jha and Nandi to show $O(2^{3n/4})$ TPRP security for TNT. Thus, we move towards closing the gap between the previous proof and attacks for TNT as well as its proposed instance.

© International Association for Cryptologic Research 2020
S. Moriai and H. Wang (Eds.): ASIACRYPT 2020, LNCS 12491, pp. 567–597, 2020.
https://doi.org/10.1007/978-3-030-64837-4_19

Keywords: Cryptanalysis · Block cipher · Tweakable block cipher · AES · Impossible differential

1   Introduction

Tweakable Block Ciphers (TBCs) differ from classical block ciphers in the sense that they take a public input called tweak that can increase the security or the performance of higher-level schemes effectively, e.g., in encryption modes [KR11,PS16], MACs [IMPS17,Nai15], or in authenticated-encryption schemes [IMPS17,JNP16]. Initially, TBCs have been built from classical block ciphers and universal hash functions, starting with Liskov et al.'s constructions [LRW02] LRW1 and LRW2. Various works enlarged the portfolio of generic TBC constructions, e.g. the cascade CLRW2 [LST12], Mennink's constructions $\widetilde{F}[1]$ and $\widetilde{F}[2]$ [Men15], XHX [JLM+17], XHX2 [LL18], or the constructions by Wang et al. [WGZ+16]. These proposals processed the tweak either with a universal hash function or an additional call to the classical block cipher.

As An Alternative Approach, several works proposed dedicated TBCs in the previous decade. In particular, the TWEAKEY framework [JNP14b] found wide adoption, e.g. in Deoxys-BC, Joltik-BC [JNP14b], or Skinny [BJK+16]. Though, since TWEAKEY treats key and tweak equally, any update needs a call to (significant parts of) the TWEAKEY schedule. However, tweak updates occur usually considerably more frequently than key updates. For example, modes like CTRT or ΘCB3 employ a different tweak in each primitive call. Thus, performant tweak-update functions can boost efficiency. KIASU-BC [JNP14a] or CRAFT [BLMR19] avoid tweak schedules, but need further analysis. Moreover, some applications cannot easily be equipped with novel dedicated TBCs but would profit rather from efficient transformations that turn an existing block-cipher implementation into a TBC. For this purpose, generic constructions such as CLRW2 are still relevant. Yet, it would be desirable if its internal hash function could be eliminated to avoid its implementation and the storage of its keys.

Tweak-aNd-Tweak (TNT) is a recent proposal by Bao et al. [BGGS20] for generating a TBC from three block ciphers $E_{K_1}, E_{K_2}, E_{K_3} : \mathcal{K} \times \mathbb{F}_2^n \to \mathbb{F}_2^n$, where $\mathbb{F}_2$ is the Galois Field of characteristic 2 and $\mathcal{K}$ a non-empty set of keys. The encryption of TNT is defined as

$$\mathsf{TNT}[E_{K_1}, E_{K_2}, E_{K_3}](T, M) \stackrel{\text{def}}{=} E_{K_3}(E_{K_2}(E_{K_1}(M) \oplus T) \oplus T).$$

where the tweak space is $\mathcal{T} = 2^n$. The intermediate values are illustrated in Fig. 1. We will use ΔM, ΔT, etc. to refer to the differences between two values M and M', T and T', and so on. This extends naturally to the other variables. Given ideal secret permutations $\pi_1, \pi_2, \pi_3 \in \mathsf{Perm}(\mathbb{F}_2^n)$, where $\mathsf{Perm}(\mathcal{X})$ is the set of all permutations over a set $\mathcal{X}$, Bao et al. [BGGS20] showed that TNT is a secure tweakable permutation for at least $O(2^{2n/3})$ queries.

TNT-AES instantiates the individual keyed permutations in TNT with round-reduced variants of AES. More precisely, TNT-AES$[r_1, r_2, r_3]$ denotes the version

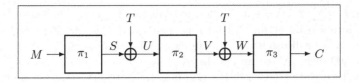

Fig. 1. The encryption of a message M under a tweak T with $\mathsf{TNT}[\pi_1, \pi_2, \pi_3]$.

where π_i uses r_i rounds of the AES, for $1 \leq i \leq 3$, and the tweak matches the state size of the AES, i.e. $\mathcal{T} = \mathcal{B} = (\mathbb{F}_2^8)^{4 \times 4}$, and $n = 128$. The concrete proposal was TNT-AES[6, 6, 6] [BGGS20]. While the earlier proposal contained no explicit claim, it suggested that TNT should be treated as a secure tweakable block cipher for up to $O(2^{2n/3})$ queries and TNT-AES should provide n-bit security, even in the related-key chosen-tweak setting: "Following the proven security bound of TNT, TNT-AES offers $2n/3$-bit security, i.e., there exists no key-recovery attack, given that the data (the combination of tweak and plaintext with no restriction on individual input) and time complexities are bounded by $2^{2 \cdot 128/3} \simeq 2^{85}$. Due to the fact that there is no attack against TNT matching the $2^{2n/3}$ bound, all our security analysis against TNT-AES are following the $2^n = 2^{128}$ bound for both data and time" [BGGS20, Sect. 5.2]. The best attack in [BGGS20] was a related-tweak boomerang distinguisher on TNT-AES[∗, 5, ∗] with 21 active S-boxes. The asterisks indicate that the analysis holds for arbitrary values for r_1 and r_3.

Contribution. This work aims at narrowing the security gap from both sides. We show in Sect. 2 that a variant of Mennink's distinguisher on CLRW2 [Men18] also applies to TNT, which yields a theoretical TPRP (i.e., chosen-tweak, chosen-plaintext) distinguisher in $O(\sqrt{n}2^{3n/4})$ time, data, and memory complexity. As improvements, we reduce the complexity of Mennink's information-theoretic distinguisher from $O(2^{3n/2})$ to $O(2^{3n/4})$ computations. More precisely, we show two similar TPRP distinguishers that we call parallel-road and cross-road distinguishers. We use one of them to mount a partial key-recovery attack on the instance TNT-AES[5, ∗, ∗] with an impossible differential in Sect. 3. Since it needs more message pairs, its complexity exceeds $O(2^{3n/4})$ but is still considerably below 2^n computations and data. We emphasize that we do not break the proposed version TNT-AES[6, 6, 6] of [BGGS20].

From a constructive point of view, we show that the rigorous STPRP (i.e., chosen plain- and ciphertext queries) analysis by Jha and Nandi on CLRW2, that showed security for up to $O(2^{3n/4})$ queries, can be adapted to a TPRP proof of TNT with similar complexity. Thus, we move a considerable step towards closing the gap between proofs and attacks for TNT and its proposed instance.

Notation. We use uppercase characters for variables and functions, lowercase characters for indices, calligraphic characters for sets and distributions, and sans-serif characters for random variables. For $n \in \mathbb{N}$, let $[n] =^{\text{def}} \{1, 2, \dots, n\}$ and $[0..n] =^{\text{def}} \{0, 1, \dots, n\}$. For a bit string $X \in \mathbb{F}_2^n$, let $X = (X_{n-1}X_{n-2} \dots X_0)$ be its individual bits. We assume that the most significant bit is the leftmost, and the least significant bit is the rightmost bit, s.t. the integer representation

x of X is $x = \sum_i 2^i \cdot X_i$. For $x < 2^n$, we will use $X = \langle x \rangle_n$ as conversion of an integer x into a n-bit string X that represents x. For non-negative integers $\leq n$ and $X \in \mathbb{F}_2^n$, we will use $\mathsf{lsb}_x(X)$ as function that returns the least significant x bits of X and $\mathsf{msb}_x(X)$ to return the most significant x bits of X. $(n)_k$ denotes the falling factorial $n!/(n-k)!$. For non-negative integers $x + y = n$ and $Z \in \mathbb{F}_2^n$, we will use $(X, Y) \xleftarrow{x,y} Z$ to denote that $X \| Y = Z$ where $|X| = x$ and $|Y| = y$. Similar to Perm, we define $\widetilde{\mathsf{Perm}}(\mathcal{T}, \mathcal{X})$ as the set of all tweakable permutations $\widetilde{\pi} : \mathcal{T} \times \mathcal{X} \to \mathcal{X}$ over $\mathcal{X}$ with tweak space $\mathcal{T}$.

Practical Implications. While an STPRP proof is desirable, the implications of higher TPRP security already provide a valuable gain for TBC-based schemes that do not need the primitive's inverse. Considering authenticated encryption schemes, examples of such schemes include SCT [PS16], ZAE [IMPS17], ZOTR [BGIM19], or the TBC-based variants of OTR ($\mathbb{OTR}$) [Min14] and COFB (iCOFB) [CIMN17, CIMN20]. Considering MACs, there exist various such constructions, e.g. ZMAC [IMPS17] and its derivates [LN17, Nai18]. The security of those schemes is limited by the minimum of $O(2^{\min(n, (n+t)/2)})$ queries and the TPRP security of the underlying primitive. Since the latter is the bottleneck, its improvement yields directly higher security guarantees for the schemes.

AES. We assume that the reader is familiar with the AES. We use R to refer to the round function, X^i for the state after i rounds, starting with X^0 as the plaintext, and K^0 for the initial round key. We use X_{SB}^i, X_{SR}^i, and X_{MC}^i to refer to the state directly after the SubBytes, ShiftRows, and MixColumns operation in the i-th round, respectively. Moreover, $X^i[j]$ refers to the j-th byte of X^i. For $\mathcal{I} \subseteq \{0, 1, 2, 3\}$, we adopt the subspaces for diagonals $\mathcal{D}_\mathcal{I}$, columns $\mathcal{C}_\mathcal{I}$, inverse (or anti-)diagonals $\mathcal{ID}_\mathcal{I}$, and mixed spaces $\mathcal{M}_\mathcal{I}$ from Grassi et al. [GRR16].

2 Distinguishers on TNT

Here, we briefly describe two distinguishers on TNT with $O(\sqrt{n} \cdot 2^{3n/4})$ queries, which implies an upper bound on the (query) security of TNT of at most $O(q^4/(\sqrt{n} \cdot 2^{3n}))$. Our distinguishers are illustrated in Fig. 2. We do not claim that our observations are novel. Instead, both are applications of [LNS18] and [Men18]. The latter, however, is an information-theoretic distinguisher that uses $O(\sqrt{n} \cdot 2^{3n/4})$ queries, but the description by Mennink demands $O(2^{3n/2})$ offline operations to identify the required pairs.

We note that Sibleyras' work [Sib20] proposes generic key-recovery attacks for LRW2 and cascades that also hold for CLRW2. Those attacks slightly reduce the time complexity of Mennink's attack, but require more queries, roughly $2^{2(n+k)/3}$, and are hence in $O(2^n)$ for plausible values of the key size $k \geq n/2$.

2.1 General Setup

Let $M^0, M^1 \in \mathbb{F}_2^n$ be two distinct messages and $\mathcal{T}^0$ and $\mathcal{T}^1$ be two sets of $q = 2^{3n/4+x}$ pairwise distinct random tweaks T_j for $0 \leq j < q$ in each set, where

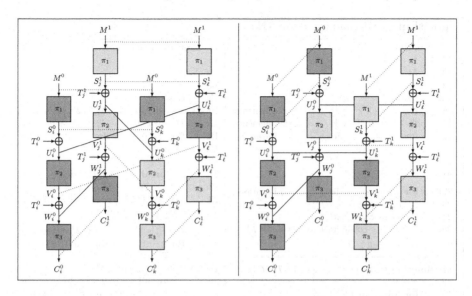

Fig. 2. Cross- (left) and parallel-road (right) distinguishers on TNT. Solid horizontal lines are probabilistic equalities that hold with probability around 2^{-n} each. Dotted lines hold either by choice or by design once the solid-line equalities are fulfilled.

$\mathcal{T}^i$ associates all tweaks with a fixed message M^i for $\mathcal{T}^i$ for $i = 0, 1$. We describe two ways to combine two pairs to quartets each that differ in the way where the messages are used. Figure 2 may illustrate why we call them parallel- and cross-road distinguishers. For both distinguishers, we want two pairs, (M_i, T_i) and (M_j, T_j) as well as (M_k, T_k) and (M_ℓ, T_ℓ), with the same tweak difference $\Delta T_{i,j} = T_i \oplus T_j = \Delta T_{k,\ell} = T_k \oplus T_\ell$, and for which $C_i = C_j$ and $C_k = C_\ell$.

2.2 Cross-Road Distinguisher

Here, we denote the queries and intermediate variables

- related to $(M^0, T_i^0) \in \mathcal{T}^0$ also as $(S_i^0, U_i^0, V_i^0, W_i^0, C_i^0)$,
- those related to $(M^1, T_j^1) \in \mathcal{T}^1$ also as $(S_j^1, U_j^1, V_j^1, W_j^1, C_j^1)$,
- those related to $(M^0, T_k^0) \in \mathcal{T}^0$ also as $(S_k^0, U_k^0, V_k^0, W_k^0, C_k^0)$, and
- those related to $(M^1, T_\ell^1) \in \mathcal{T}^1$ also as $(S_\ell^1, U_\ell^1, V_\ell^1, W_\ell^1, C_\ell^1)$.

Clearly, we want $i \neq k$ and $j \neq \ell$ as well as $(i, j) \neq (k, \ell)$.

Procedure. We define two construction functions:

$$\tau_0(i) \stackrel{\text{def}}{=} 0^{n/4-x} \parallel \langle i \rangle_{3n/4+x}, \quad \text{and} \quad \tau_1(j) \stackrel{\text{def}}{=} \langle j \rangle_{3n/4+x} \parallel 0^{n/4-x}.$$

The resulting tweak structures are illustrated in Fig. 3. The distinguisher procedure is given on the left-hand side of Algorithm 1. Let $\theta \geq 0$ be a threshold. The threshold depends on the desired error (and success) probability and will be discussed in Sect. 3.3. The distinguisher can be described as:

Algorithm 1. Distinguishers on TNT.

```
11: function CROSSROAD                          11: function PARALLELROAD
12:     K ← 𝔽₂ᵏ                                  12:     K ← 𝔽₂ᵏ
13:     M⁰ ← 𝔽₂ⁿ                                 13:     M⁰ ← 𝔽₂ⁿ
14:     M¹ ← 𝔽₂ⁿ                                 14:     M¹ ← 𝔽₂ⁿ
15:     coll ← 0                                 15:     coll ← 0
16:     𝓛 ← [] × [0..2ⁿ − 1]   ▷ 2ⁿ elements     16:     𝓛 ← [] × [0..2ⁿ − 1]   ▷ 2ⁿ elements
17:     𝒟 ← 0 × [0..2ⁿ − 1]   ▷ 2ⁿ elements      17:     𝒟 ← 0 × [0..2ⁿ − 1]   ▷ 2ⁿ elements
18:     for i ← 0..q − 1 do   ▷ q iterations     18:     for i ← 0..q − 1 do   ▷ q iterations
19:         Tᵢ⁰ ← τ₀(i)                          19:         Tᵢ⁰ ← τ₀(i)
20:         Cᵢ⁰ ← ℰₖ(Tᵢ⁰, M⁰)                    20:         Cᵢ⁰ ← ℰₖ(Tᵢ⁰, M⁰)
21:         𝓛[Cᵢ⁰] ⟵∪ {Tᵢ⁰}                      21:         for all Tⱼ⁰ in 𝓛[Cᵢ⁰] do
22:     for j ← 0..q − 1 do   ▷ q iterations     22:             ΔTᵢ,ⱼ⁰ ← Tᵢ⁰ ⊕ Tⱼ⁰
23:         Tⱼ¹ ← τ₁(j)                          23:             𝒟[ΔTᵢ,ⱼ⁰] ← 𝒟[ΔTᵢ,ⱼ⁰] + 1
24:         Cⱼ¹ ← ℰₖ(Tⱼ¹, M¹)                    24:         𝓛[Cᵢ⁰] ⟵∪ {Tᵢ⁰}
25:         coll ← coll+findNumColls(𝓛,𝒟,Tⱼ¹,Cⱼ¹) 25:     𝓛 ← [] × [0..2ⁿ − 1]   ▷ 2ⁿ elements
26:     return coll ≥ θ                          26:     for k ← 0..q − 1 do   ▷ q iterations
                                                 27:         Tₖ¹ ← τ₁(k)
31: function FINDNUMCOLLS(𝓛, 𝒟, Tⱼ¹, Cⱼ¹)        28:         Cₖ¹ ← ℰₖ(Tₖ¹, M¹)
32:     c ← 0                                    29:         for all Tₗ¹ in 𝓛[Cₖ¹] do
33:     for all Tᵢ⁰ in 𝓛[Cⱼ¹] do                 30:             ▷ 2ⁿ/² calls over all executions
34:         ▷ 2ⁿ/² calls over all executions     31:             ΔTₖ,ₗ¹ ← Tₖ¹ ⊕ Tₗ¹
35:         ΔTᵢ,ⱼ ← Tᵢ⁰ ⊕ Tⱼ¹                    32:             coll ← coll + 𝒟[ΔTₖ,ₗ¹]
36:         c ← c + 𝒟[ΔTᵢ,ⱼ]                     33:         𝓛[Cₖ¹] ⟵∪ {Tₖ¹}
37:         𝒟[ΔTᵢ,ⱼ] ← 𝒟[ΔTᵢ,ⱼ] + 1             34:     return coll ≥ θ
38:     return c
```

1. Initialize two lists $\mathcal{L}$ and $\mathcal{D}$ and initialize a counter coll $= 0$.
2. For $i \in [0..q - 1]$:
    - Use $\tau_0(i)$ as tweak-construction function to generate queries (M^0, T_i^0). Encrypt them to obtain $C_i^0 \leftarrow \mathcal{E}_K(T_i^0, M^0)$. Insert T_i^0 to $\mathcal{L}[C_i^0]$.
3. For $j \in [0..q - 1]$:
    - Use $\tau_1(j)$ as tweak-construction function to generate queries (M^1, T_j^1). Encrypt them to obtain $C_j^1 \leftarrow \mathcal{E}_K(T_j^1, M^1)$.
    3.1. For each $T_i^0 \in \mathcal{L}[C_j^1]$:
        - Derive $\Delta T_{i,j} = T_i^0 \oplus T_j^1$. Derive the number of pairs (T_k^0, T_ℓ^1) with the same tweak difference from $\mathcal{D}[\Delta T_{i,j}]$, add this number c to the total number of colliding quartets, coll, and increment $\mathcal{D}[\Delta T_{i,j}]$.
4. If coll $> \theta$, return "real" and "random" otherwise.

Since the i-th and k-th query share the same message M^0, it follows that $S_i^0 = S_k^0$; a similar argument holds from $M_j^1 = M_\ell^1$ to $S_j^1 = S_\ell^1$. With probability 2^{-n}, it holds that $S_i^0 \oplus S_\ell^1 = T_i^0 \oplus T_\ell^1$. In this case, it follows that $U_i^0 = U_\ell^1$. By combination, there exist approximately $(2^{3n/4+x})^2 \cdot 1/(2^n - 1) \simeq 2^{n/2+2x}$ ordered collision pairs $U_i^0 = U_\ell^1$ between (M^0, T_i^0) and (M^1, T_ℓ^1). There exist $(2^{3n/4+x} - 1)^2 \cdot 1/(2^n - 1) \simeq 2^{n/2+2x}$ ordered collision pairs $U_k^0 = U_j^1$ between (M^0, T_k^0) and (M^1, T_j^1). Note that this is a conditional probability; since $S_k^0 = S_i^0$ and $S_j^1 = S_\ell^1$, it follows from $T_k^0 \oplus T_j^1 = S_k^0 \oplus S_j^1$ that $T_k^0 \oplus T_j^1 = T_i^0 \oplus T_\ell^1$. Those

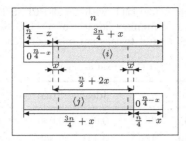

Fig. 3. Construction of the tweak sets.

will be mapped to $V_i^0 = V_\ell^1$ and $V_k^0 = V_j^1$. Thus, by combination, there are $\binom{2^{n/2+2x}}{2} \simeq 2^{n+4x-1}$ pairs of pairs (quartets) with $T_i^0 \oplus T_\ell^1$ and $T_k^0 \oplus T_j^1$. With probability 2^{-n}, a quartet has $V_i^0 \oplus V_\ell^1 = T_k^0 \oplus T_j^1$, which implies $W_i^0 = W_j^0$. Since $V_i^0 = V_\ell^1$ and $V_k^0 = V_j^1$, this implies that $W_k^0 = W_\ell^0$ also holds. We obtain

$$\binom{2^{n/2+2x}}{2} \cdot 2^{-n} \simeq 2^{4x-1} \text{ quartets.}$$

Similarly, we expect $(2^{3n/4+x})^2 \cdot 2^{-n} \simeq 2^{n/2+2x}$ pairs $C_i^0 = C_j^1$ formed by accident, which can be combined to

$$\binom{2^{n/2+2x}}{2} \cdot 2^{-n} \simeq 2^{4x-1} \text{ quartets.}$$

For a random tweakable permutation, only the latter events occur, whereas we have two sources in the real world. Thus, we can expect twice as many quartets in the real construction compared to the ideal world.

Experimental Verification. To improve the understanding, we followed Mennink's approach and also implemented the distinguisher for small permutations. We used TNT with three independent instances of Small-PRESENT-n [Lea10], the small-scale variants of PRESENT [BKL+07], with the original key schedule of PRESENT as proposed there, where the original round keys K^i are truncated to their rightmost (least significant) n bits for $n \in \{16, 20, 24\}$. We employed the full 31 rounds as for the original PRESENT cipher. For the real construction, we sampled uniformly and independently 1 000 random keys, one per experiment, and two random messages. The tweaks were constructed as in Fig. 3. For the ideal world, we sampled the ciphertexts uniformly and independently at random and verified that no message-pair for the same tweak amid any experiment collides. The results of our implementation are summarized in Table 1a. The source code of all experiments can be found freely available to the public.[1]

---

[1] https://gitlab.com/elist/tnt.

Table 1. Average #quartets for TNT with Small-PRESENT-n as permutations π_i ("real") and pseudorandom sampling ("ideal") over $1\,000$ experiments with random keys, two random messages, and 2^t tweaks per message in each experiment.

(a) Cross-road distinguisher.

n	t	Ideal	Real	n	t	Ideal	Real	n	t	Ideal	Real
16	11	0.026	0.061	20	14	0.032	0.055	24	17	0.034	0.066
16	12	0.485	1.009	20	15	0.494	0.960	24	18	0.482	1.009
16	13	7.967	15.970	20	16	8.087	16.162	24	19	7.979	16.174
16	14	127.458	255.133	20	17	128.057	255.739	24	20	127.941	255.661

(b) Parallel-road distinguisher.

n	t	Ideal	Real	n	t	Ideal	Real	n	t	Ideal	Real
16	11	0.015	0.050	20	14	0.024	0.057	24	17	0.016	0.063
16	12	0.232	0.787	20	15	0.274	0.749	24	18	0.233	0.726
16	13	4.076	12.127	20	16	3.892	11.952	24	19	4.016	12.170
16	14	64.274	192.275	20	17	64.405	191.398	24	20	63.686	191.599

2.3   Parallel-Road Distinguisher

Our second distinguisher is described in the right-hand side of Algorithm 1 and is illustrated on the right-hand side of Fig. 2. The core difference is the choice of sets for collisions. While the first distinguisher used collisions from different messages, the second one uses collisions from ciphertexts from the same set. Here, we denote the queries and intermediate variables

- related to $(M^0, T_i^0) \in \mathcal{T}^0$ also as $(S_i^0, U_i^0, \dots)$,
- those related to $(M^0, T_j^0) \in \mathcal{T}^0$ also as $(S_j^0, U_j^0, \dots)$,
- those related to $(M^1, T_k^1) \in \mathcal{T}^1$ also as $(S_k^1, U_k^1, \dots)$, and
- those related to $(M^1, T_\ell^1) \in \mathcal{T}^1$ also as $(S_\ell^1, U_\ell^1, \dots)$.

By combination, we obtain about $(2^{3n/4+x})^2 \cdot 2^{-n} \simeq 2^{n/2+2x}$ collisions $U_i^0 = U_k^1$ between (M^0, T_i^0) and (M^1, T_k^1), and the approximately same number of collisions $U_j^1 = U_\ell^1$ between (M^1, T_j^1) and (M^1, T_ℓ^1). Those will be mapped to $V_i^0 = V_k^1$ and $V_j^0 = V_\ell^1$. We can form $\binom{2^{n/2+2x}}{2} \simeq 2^{n+4x-1}$ pairs of pairs (quartets). With probability 2^{-n}, a quartet has $V_i^0 \oplus V_j^0 = T_i^0 \oplus T_j^0$, which implies $W_i^0 = W_j^0$. Since $V_i^0 = V_k^1$ and $V_j^1 = V_\ell^1$, it follows that $W_k^1 = W_\ell^1$ holds. Thus, we obtain 2^{4x-1} quartets. Moreover, we expect $\binom{2^{3n/4+x}}{2} \cdot 2^{-n} \simeq 2^{n/2+2x-1}$ pairs $C_i^0 = C_j^0$ that are formed randomly and can be combined with $2^{n/2+2x-1}$ pairs $C_k^1 = C_\ell^1$. We obtain

$$(2^{n/2+2x-1})^2 \cdot 2^{-n} \simeq 2^{4x-2} \text{ quartets} \tag{1}$$

Algorithm 2. More efficient variant of the parallel-road distinguisher on TNT.

11: **function** PARALLELROAD	28: $\mathcal{L} \leftarrow [] \times [0..q-1]$ ▷ q elements
12: $K \twoheadleftarrow \mathbb{F}_2^k$	29: **for** $k \leftarrow 0..q-1$ **do** ▷ q iterations
13: $M^0 \twoheadleftarrow \mathbb{F}_2^n$	30: $T_k^1 \leftarrow \tau_1(k)$
14: $M^1 \twoheadleftarrow \mathbb{F}_2^n$	31: $C_k^1 \leftarrow \mathcal{E}_K(T_k^1, M^1)$
15: coll $\leftarrow 0$	32: $(b_k^1, c_k^1) \xleftarrow{n/4, 3n/4} C_k^1$
16: $\mathcal{L} \leftarrow [] \times [0..q-1]$ ▷ q elements	33: **for all** (T_ℓ^1, b_ℓ^1) in $\mathcal{L}[c_k^1]$ **do**
17: $\mathcal{D} \leftarrow [] \times [0..q-1]$ ▷ q elements	34: **if** $b_k^1 = b_\ell^1$ **then** ▷ $C_k^1 = C_\ell^1$
18: **for** $i \leftarrow 0..q-1$ **do** ▷ q iterations	35: $\Delta T_{k,\ell}^1 \leftarrow T_k^1 \oplus T_\ell^1$
19: $T_i^0 \leftarrow \tau_0(i)$	36: $(s_{k,\ell}^1, t_{k,\ell}^1) \xleftarrow{n/4, 3n/4} \Delta T_{k,\ell}^1$
20: $C_i^0 \leftarrow \mathcal{E}_K(T_i^0, M^0)$	37: **for all** $s_{i,j}^0$ in $\mathcal{D}[t_{k,\ell}^1]$ **do**
21: $(b_i^0, c_i^0) \xleftarrow{n/4, 3n/4} C_i^0$	▷ $\Delta T_{i,j}^0 = \Delta T_{k,\ell}^1$
22: **for all** (T_j^0, b_j^0) in $\mathcal{L}[c_i^0]$ **do**	38: **if** $s_{i,j}^0 = s_{k,\ell}^1$ **then**
23: **if** $b_i^0 = b_j^0$ **then** ▷ $C_i^0 = C_j^0$	39: coll $\leftarrow$ coll $+ 1$
24: $\Delta T_{i,j}^0 \leftarrow T_i^0 \oplus T_j^0$	40: $\mathcal{L}[c_k^1] \xleftarrow{\cup} \{(T_k^1, b_k^1)\}$
25: $(s_{i,j}^0, t_{i,j}^0) \xleftarrow{n/4, 3n/4} \Delta T_{i,j}^0$	41: **return** coll $\geq \theta$
26: $\mathcal{D}[t_{i,j}^0] \xleftarrow{\cup} \{s_{i,j}^0\}$	
27: $\mathcal{L}[c_i^0] \xleftarrow{\cup} \{(T_i^0, b_i^0)\}$	

formed at random. In sum, this yields

$$2^{4x-1} + 2^{4x-2} = 3 \cdot 2^{4x-2} \text{ quartets}$$

in the real construction, which implies that we can expect roughly three times as many quartets in the real construction compared to a random tweakable permutation wherin only the latter events occur.

Experimental Verification. We implemented the distinguisher with Small-PRESENT and state and tweak sizes of $n \in \{16, 20, 24\}$ bits. The results are summarized in Table 1b.

2.4 Efficiency

Mennink's [Men18] distinguisher evaluated the number of quartets for each tweak difference $\Delta \in \mathbb{F}_2^n$. From the choice of pairs given τ_0 and τ_1, there existed $2^{n/2+2x}$ possible pairs (C_i^0, C_j^1) for each tweak difference. Thus, the naive way needed $2^n \cdot 2^{n/2+2x} \simeq O(2^{3n/2+2x})$ operations to exhaust all 2^n possible tweak differences. To reduce the computational complexity below $O(2^n)$, we give an improved description of the parallel-road distinguisher.

    The lists $\mathcal{L}$ and $\mathcal{D}$ needed to reserve 2^n cells each, which was the bottleneck. To reduce the complexity, we shrink $\mathcal{L}$ to a list of $2^{3n/4}$ sub-lists, where $\mathcal{L}[x]$ holds a sub-list of tweaks T_i^0 s.t. $\mathsf{lsb}_{3n/4}(C_i^0) = \langle x \rangle_{3n/4}$. This means that we truncate the $n/4$ most significant bits (MSB) of C_i^0. Additionally, we store also the $n/4$ truncated bits as part of the entry: $(T_i^0, \mathsf{msb}_{n/4}(C_i^0))$. Similarly, we no longer store a list of 2^n counters in $\mathcal{D}$. Instead, each entry will be a sub-list of full tweak differences. Thus, $\mathcal{D}[x]$ contains $2^{3n/4}$ slots, where $\Delta T_{i,j}$ is stored in the sub-list at location $\mathsf{lsb}_{3n/4}(\Delta T_{i,j}) = \langle x \rangle_{3n/4}$. Clearly, the length of the sub-list at $\mathcal{D}[x]$ equals the previous counter value that was stored in $\mathcal{D}[x]$ before.

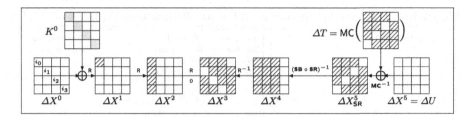

Fig. 4. Key recovery and impossible differential trail through $1 + 4$ rounds of AES. Hatched bytes are active; filled bytes are targeted key bytes; indices in bytes denote that a set index is encoded into them.

On average, Line 22 of Algorithm 2 is called

$$\binom{2^{3n/4+x}}{2} \cdot 2^{-3n/4} \simeq 2^{3n/4+2x-1}$$

times. The second test in the if-statement on $n/4$ bits is fulfilled in about $2^{n/2+2x-1}$ calls. Thus, the first loop from Line 18 in Algorithm 2 has roughly $2^{3n/4+2x}$ operations on average. A similar argument holds for the second test in Line 33 of Algorithm 2. Thus, the second outer loop over q tweaks from Line 29 of Algorithm 2 also contains roughly $2^{3n/4+2x}$ operations on average. More detailed, the first $3n/4$-bit filter reduces again the number of pairs

$$\binom{2^{3n/4+x}}{2} \cdot 2^{-3n/4} \simeq 2^{3n/4+2x-1}$$

times. The second test in the if-statement on $n/4$ bits is fulfilled in $2^{n/2+2x-1}$ times on average. The $3n/4$-bit tweak-difference filter lets the check in Line 34 in Algorithm 2 be successful $2^{n/4+4x-2}$ times for $(2^{3n/4+2x-1})^2$ pairs. Thus, it will be called at most $2^{3n/4+x} + 2^{n/2+2x} + 2^{n/4+4x-2}$ and the overall computational complexity is in $O(2^{3n/4+2x})$.

3   An Impossible-Differential Attack on TNT-AES[5, *, *]

We combine the well-known impossible differential on four-round AES for key-recovery attacks on versions of TNT-AES. We describe the key-recovery phase in the first round and both key recovery and impossible differential in π_1.

3.1   Core Idea

The core idea is based on the following assumption. The $O(\sqrt{n} \cdot 2^{3n/4})$-distinguisher works iff we can find pairs that collide in U. Let us consider the parallel-road distinguisher. It needs pairs (M^0, M^1) whose difference $\pi_1(M^0) \oplus \pi_1(M^1) = S^0 \oplus S^1$ equals the difference of their corresponding tweaks: $S^0 \oplus S^1 = T_i^0 \oplus T^1$, which implies that $U^0 = U^1$. The adversary can choose differences ΔT of its choice as well as plaintexts with certain input differences. If it can manage to exclude that ΔT occurs for the message inputs of its choice, then, the distinguisher cannot happen. This implies that $U^0 \neq U^1$ for all choices of M^0 and M^1. As a result, the values $V_i^0, V_j^0, V_k^1, V_\ell^1$ are pairwise unique for each quartet and the number of colliding pairs will then match that of a random tweakable permutation.

For this purpose, the adversary considers tweaks such that their differences ΔT are output differences of an impossible differential. Then, each correct quartet from the distinguisher is possible only if the message was not encrypted through the first (few) round(s) to an input difference of the impossible differential, which allows discarding all keys that would have encrypted it in this way. We need a sufficient number of pairs such that for all key candidates, we will expect a correct quartet (for TNT-AES), except for the correct key.

We use the impossible differential from Fig. 4, where ΔX_{MC}^5 (the difference after five rounds) is identical to ΔT. Let $\mathcal{I} = \{0, 1, 2\}$ and let $\mathcal{M}_\mathcal{I}$ denote the mixed space after applying MixColumns to a vector space that is active in the first three inverse diagonals (cf. [GRR16]). Our choice leaves a space of $2^{96} - 1$ differences for $\Delta T \in \mathcal{M}_\mathcal{I}$ and call $\mathcal{T}$ the space of desired tweak differences.

3.2 Messages

We need message pairs with the impossible difference after π_1. Since the difference has 32 zero bits, a zero difference in the rightmost inverse diagonal has a probability of 2^{-32}. We try to recover $K^0[0, 5, 10, 15]$. For a message pair (M^i, M^j) that produces the impossible difference after π_1, we can discard all key candidates that would lead to a difference of $\Delta X^1 =^{\text{def}} \mathsf{R}(M^i) \oplus \mathsf{R}(M^j)$ that is active in only a single byte after the first round. On average, there exist $4 \cdot 2^8 = 2^{10}$ possible output differences ΔX^1. Since $M^i \oplus M^j$ is fixed, approximately one input-output mapping exists for the AES S-box on average. Hence, 2^{10} keys produce an impossible ΔX^1 on average and can be discarded. Assuming that the discarded keys are uniformly randomly and independently distributed, the probability that a key candidate can be discarded from a given pair (M^i, M^j) is 2^{-22}. Under standard assumptions, we need N_{pairs} pairs to reduce the number of key candidates to 2^{32-a}, where a is the advantage in bits:

$$(1 - 2^{-22})^{N_{\text{pairs}}} \leq 2^{-a}. \tag{2}$$

Equation (2) yields approximately $2^{23.47}$, $2^{24.47}$, $2^{25.47}$, and $2^{26.47}$ necessary message pairs that fulfill the impossible difference after π_1 to obtain an advantage of $a = 4$, 8, 16, and 32 bits, respectively. If we fix the position of the inactive diagonal, we need $2^{26.47} \cdot 2^{32} \simeq 2^{58.47}$ message pairs, or $2 \cdot 2^{29.24} \simeq 2^{30.24}$ pairwise distinct messages. The number of message pairs with less than four active input bytes is negligible. We define $2^s \simeq \lceil 2^{29.24} \rceil$. We employ a space of a single plaintext diagonal, where we can focus on the first diagonal $\mathcal{D}_{\{0\}}$. The remaining diagonals are fixed to constants. We want a certain tweak difference that is zero in the final inverse diagonal. We add computational effort by choosing many

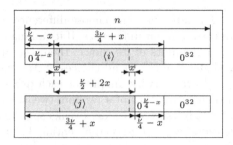

Fig. 5. Encoding the indices i and j into the tweaks to build the tweak sets $\mathcal{T}^i$ and $\mathcal{T}^j$ corresponding to the messages M^i and M^j.

messages that we partially compensate for by fixing those 32 bits to constants in all tweaks and define $\nu =^{\mathrm{def}} n - 32 = 96$ for the AES.

Expected Number of Pairs. To each message M^i, we associate a tweak set $\mathcal{T}^i$, where we use the same tweaks for each message. Among the pairs in a single set $(M, \mathcal{T}^i)$ and $(M, \mathcal{T}^j)$, the probability for $C^i = C^j$ is approximately 2^{-n}.

Using 2^t tweaks in a set, we obtain $\binom{2^t}{2} \cdot 2^{-n} \simeq 2^{2t-n-1}$ pairs. Given two messages that do **not** have the desired tweak difference after π_1, we can combine the pairs, where each pair collides in its ciphertexts, to $(2^{2t-n-1})^2$ quartets, which have the correct tweak difference after π_1 with probability $2^{3n/4} = 2^{-96}$. Thus, the number of quartets become

$$(2^{2t-n-1})^2 \cdot 2^{-3n/4} \simeq 2^{4t-11n/4-2} \simeq 2^{4t-354}. \tag{3}$$

For messages that produce the desired difference after π_1, i.e., have 32 zero bits in the rightmost inverse diagonal, we can form $2^t \cdot 2^t \cdot 2^{-3n/4} \simeq 2^{2t-3n/4}$ pairs after π_1 since only the 96-bit tweak difference must match that of the message difference at that point. From those pairs, we can build quartets that collide with probability 2^{-n} after π_2. Thus, the number of quartets becomes

$$\binom{2^{2t-3n/4}}{2} \cdot 2^{-n} \simeq 2^{4t-5n/2-1} \simeq 2^{4t-321}. \tag{4}$$

Note that the number of quartets in Eq. (3) differs significantly from the 2^{4x-2} of Eq. (1) since we restrict the valid tweak differences. Here, we need more message pairs so that enough of them possess the desired 32-bit condition of the zero-difference anti-diagonal after π_1. Thus, the here-proposed attack is **less** efficient but allows us to recover a part of the secret key.

3.3   Success Probability, Advantage, and Data Complexity

Samajder and Sarkar [SS17] gave rigorous upper bounds on the data complexities for differential and linear cryptanalysis that improved previous results. For the parallel-road distinguisher, $2 \cdot 2^t$ message-tweak tuples in total produce

$2^{4t-5n/2-1} + 2^{4t-11n/4-2}$ quartets for the real world, and $2^{4t-11n/4-2}$ quartets in the ideal world on average. Thus, we can define for the probability of quartets

$$p_{cor} \simeq 2^{-321} + 2^{-354} \quad \text{and} \quad p_{wrong} \simeq 2^{-354}.$$

Let θ be a threshold and H_0 be the hypothesis that a given message pair M^i, M^j has the 32-bit zero difference after π_1 in the rightmost anti-diagonal. We say that H_0 holds if $N^{i,j}_{quartets} > \theta$. Otherwise, we reject H_0.

Let $\alpha =^{\text{def}} \Pr[N^{i,j}_{quartets} < \theta | M^i \oplus M^j \in \mathcal{T}]$ be the Type-I error, i.e., a pair with correct difference has too few quartets. This event is not essential, but yields more surviving wrong key candidates. Let $\beta =^{\text{def}} \Pr[N^{i,j}_{quartets} \geq \theta | M^i \oplus M^j \notin \mathcal{T}]$ be the Type-II error, i.e., a pair with wrong difference after π_1 has more quartets than the threshold and is incorrectly classified as correct. The latter event is crucial since the pair might suggest the correct key as wrong and the attack will fail. Therefore, the success probability is given by

$$1 - \sum_{i<j} \Pr\left[N^{i,j}_{quartets} \geq \theta\right] \cdot 2^{-22} \leq 1 - \left(2^{58.47} \cdot \Pr\left[N^{i,j}_{quartets} \geq \theta\right] \cdot 2^{-22}\right).$$

Thus, β should be far below $2^{-36.5}$. From [SS17, Proposition 5.1], it follows that the number of quartets (for each message pair) should fulfill

$$N_{quartets} \geq \frac{3\left(\sqrt{p_{cor} \ln\left(\frac{1}{\alpha}\right)} + \sqrt{p_{wrong} \ln\left(\frac{2}{\beta}\right)}\right)^2}{\left(p_{cor} - p_{wrong}\right)^2}. \tag{5}$$

Since the distinguisher produces $N_{quartets} = 2^{4t-2}$ quartets, we can derive $t = (\log_2(N_{quartets}) + 2)/4$. Results of t for plausible values of α and β are listed in Table 2. For Hypothesis 3, Samajder and Sarkar [SS17] suggest a threshold of

$$\theta = \sqrt{3N_{quartets} \cdot p_{wrong} \cdot \ln\left(\frac{2}{\beta}\right)},$$

which is given in Table 2 for the sake of simplicity. Equation (5) targets single-differential key-recovery attacks.

Remark 1. We point out that Samajder and Sarkar also studied an upper bound for the data complexity of distinguishers in [SS17, Proposition 8.1]:

$$N_{quartets} \geq \frac{v^2 \ln\left(\frac{1}{P_e}\right)}{2\left(D\left(\mathcal{P} \| \mathcal{Q}\right) + D\left(\mathcal{Q} \| \mathcal{P}\right)\right)^2}. \tag{6}$$

Though, [SS17, Sect. 10] showed that Eq. (5) yields a better upper bound for single-differential cryptanalysis. Details can be found in their work.

Table 2. Logarithmic data complexity per set t and logarithmic threshold values θ for varying error probabilities.

	$-\log_2(\beta)/\log_2(\theta)$					
$-\log_2(\alpha)$	38	39	41	45	53	69
1	80.882/–	80.882/–	80.882/–	80.882/–	80.882/–	80.882/–
2	81.382/−0.201	81.382/−0.201	81.382/−0.201	81.382/−0.201	81.382/−0.200	81.382/−0.200
4	81.882/3.204	81.882/3.204	81.882/3.204	81.882/3.204	81.882/3.204	81.882/3.204
8	82.382/5.730	82.382/5.730	82.382/5.730	82.382/5.730	82.382/5.730	82.382/5.730
16	82.882/8.012	82.882/8.012	82.882/8.012	82.882/8.012	82.882/8.012	82.882/8.012
32	83.382/10.183	83.382/10.183	83.382/10.183	83.382/10.183	83.382/10.183	83.382/10.183

Data Complexity. Choosing a sufficiently high threshold for the number of quartets allows identifying message pairs with the desired difference after π_1. Only those pairs are needed for subkey filtering. $t = 83.39$ gives approximately $2^{12.56}$ quartets on average, which implies $2 \cdot 2^{29.24} \cdot 2^{83.39} \simeq 2^{113.63}$ messages.

We employ Mennink's way of constructing tweaks. In each set, the tweaks iterate over $2^{83.39}$ values in the leftmost three anti-diagonals in the state X_{SR}^5 before the MixColumns operation of Round 5 is applied to each tweak. We define that $\mu_0(i) : \mathbb{Z}_{2^{84}} \to (\mathbb{F}_{2^8})^{4\times 4}$ encodes the integer i into the 12 bytes 0, 1, 2, 4, 5, 7, 8, 10, 11, 13, 14, 15, from most to least significant bits and define $\mu_1(j) : \mathbb{Z}_{2^{84}} \to (\mathbb{F}_{2^8})^{4\times 4}$ encodes $(j \ll 12)$ (left shift by 12 bits) into the 12 bytes 0, 1, 2, 4, 5, 7, 8, 10, 11, 13, 14 , 15, from most to least significant bits. This is illustrated in Figs. 4 and 5. In total, we need $2 \cdot 2^s \cdot 2^t \simeq 2^{113.63}$ message-tweak pairs.

3.4   Procedure

The attack proceeds as follows:

1. Zeroize 2^{2s} counters $N_{\text{quartets}}^{i,j}$, and prepare lists $\mathcal{L}^0$, $\mathcal{D}^0$, $\mathcal{L}^1$, and $\mathcal{D}^1$. Initialize a list $\mathcal{K}$ of 2^{32} true flags that represent the values of $K^0[0, 5, 10, 15]$.
2. Construct the messages M^i and tweak sets $\mathcal{T}^i$ as described above and ask for the encryption of all tweak-message tuples. Each message-tweak set can be considered separately.
3. For 2^s messages $M^i, 0 \le i < 2^s$:
   3.1 Call the first loop of the parallel-road distinguisher. For tweak set $\mathcal{T}^i$, store the results into $\mathcal{L}^{0,i}[c_k^{0,i}]$, for all $0 \le k < 2^t$. The 2^{2t-n-1} pairs are stored in $\mathcal{D}^{0,i}$.
4. For 2^s messages $M^j, 2^s \le j < 2^{s+1}$:
   4.1 Call the second loop of the parallel-road distinguisher and store their results into $\mathcal{L}^{1,j}[c_k^{1,j}]$ for each tweak set $\mathcal{T}^j$ and $0 \le k < 2^t$. On average, 2^{2t-n-1} ciphertext pairs per tweak set need lookups in $\mathcal{D}^{1,j}$.
   4.2 For each message M^i:
      i. Look up $\mathcal{D}^{0,i}$ for matches of the tweak difference. Increase the counter $N_{\text{quartets}}^{i,j}$ if there are matches.

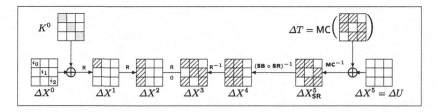

Fig. 6. Key recovery and impossible differential trail through $1 + 4$ rounds of SMALL-AES 36. Hatched bytes are active; filled bytes are targeted key bytes; indices in bytes denote that a set index is encoded into them.

5. For all counters $N_{\text{quartets}}^{i,j}$ that are above the threshold θ, derive the $4 \cdot 2^8 \simeq 2^{10}$ round-key candidates $K^0[0, 5, 10, 15]$ that would encrypt $M^i \oplus M^j$ to a single-byte difference after the first round.
6. For all round-key candidates set the corresponding entry in $\mathcal{K}$ to false.
7. Output the entries of $\mathcal{K}$ that are still marked as true.

3.5 Computational and Memory Complexity

The total computational complexity is given by

1. $2 \cdot 2^{29.24} \cdot 2^{83.39} \simeq 2^{113.63}$ encryptions.
2. About $2^{29.24} \cdot 2^{83.39} \simeq 2^{112.63}$ memory insertions and lookups to obtain all pairs of equal ciphertexts in the sets $\mathcal{T}^{0,i}$ that are used to fill $\mathcal{D}^{0,i}$.
3. About $2^{29.24} \cdot 2^{83.39} \simeq 2^{112.63}$ memory insertions and lookups to obtain all pairs of equal ciphertexts in the sets $\mathcal{T}^{1,j}$.
4. About $2^s \cdot 2^{2t-1-n} \simeq 2^{29.24} \cdot 2^{2 \cdot 83.39 - 1 - 128} \simeq 2^{67}$ lookups into the sets $\mathcal{D}^{0,i}$.
5. We expect to have an advantage of at least $a \simeq 32$ bits. Thus, there will be at most 2^{96} remaining key candidates on average.

Thus, we have $2^{113.63} + 2^{96} \simeq 2^{113.63}$ encryptions and $2^{112.63} + 2^{112.63} + 2^{80.1} \simeq 2^{113.63}$ memory accesses. The memory complexity is upper bounded by storing $2^{112.63}$ ciphertext-tweak tuples in the lists $\mathcal{L}^{0,i}$ and $\mathcal{L}^{1,j}$ each and the same amount of tweak differences in $\mathcal{D}^{0,i}$ and $\mathcal{D}^{1,j}$, which is upper bounded by the memory for $2^{113.63}$ states and 2^{32} key candidates.

3.6 Experiments

For verification purposes, we considered a reduced version of the AES. A natural starting point is the 64-bit version, SMALL-AES [CMR05], where each cell is an element in $\mathbb{F}_{2^4}$. Since the complexity of $O(2^{3n/4}) = O(2^{48})$ operations and memory, multiplied by 100 keys is still hardly feasible, we reduced the cipher further to a 3×3-matrix structure of cells with 36-bit state, which we will denote as SMALL-AES36. We borrow almost all components from SMALL-AES, except for the MixColumns operation. In SMALL-AES36, MixColumns employs the circulant MDS matrix $\text{circ}(1, 1, 2)$, with elements in the field $\mathbb{F}_{2^4}/p(\mathbf{x})$ with

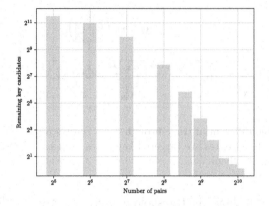

	Key recovery		
#Pairs	μ	σ	a
32	2897.14	128.49	0.50
64	2025.67	131.33	1.02
128	992.78	90.57	2.04
256	234.67	38.19	4.13
384	57.34	13.82	6.16
512	14.44	5.25	8.15
640	4.71	2.30	9.76
768	1.85	0.97	11.11
896	1.34	0.66	11.58
1024	1.09	0.28	11.88

Fig. 7. Mean (μ) and standard deviation (σ) for the number of key candidates, as well as the advantage in bits (a), for 100 experiments of SMALL-AES36 each with varying numbers of message pairs with the desired difference ΔT after π_1 and random keys.

$p(\mathbf{x}) = (\mathbf{x}^4 + \mathbf{x} + 1)$. We verified that the matrix is MDS in the given field with a python script.

The key-recovery phase targets the first diagonal of the first round key K^0. We iterate over all 2^{12} messages of the first diagonal and consider all message pairs (M^i, M^j) for distinct i, j that yield more than θ collisions for filtering. Each set $\mathcal{T}^{i,0}$ employs 2^t tweaks. Again, we use a variant of Mennink's tweak encoding: The t-bit tweaks $\langle i \rangle_{24} = (i_0, i_1, i_2, i_3, i_4, i_5)$ are encoded as $\mathsf{MC}(i_0, i_1, 0, i_2, 0, i_3, 0, i_4, i_5)$ in the cells 0-8, as shown in Fig. 6.

Expected Number of Messages. We experimented with varying numbers of message pairs that fulfilled the desired tweak differences ΔT. The results are illustrated in Fig. 7. We experimented with $1\,000$ random keys and 2^{12} messages that iterated over all values of the first diagonal and used a random value of the other cells. On average, we observed approximately $2^{11.1}$ message pairs with the desired difference after π_1, which yielded a probability of $2^{-11.9} \simeq 2^{12}$ that matches our expectation since we have 12 bit conditions in ΔX_{SR}^5.

Expected Number of Quartets. The distribution of quartets among message pairs with and without the desired difference is shown in Table 3.

Recall Eqs. (3) and (4). In our reduced AES version, we have a 24-bit tweak space, which must replace the $3n/4$ terms in those equations. In the following, we use $2^t = 2^{24+x}$. First, assume that $t \leq 24$ for a message pair that does **not** fulfill the correct difference after π_1. Then, we can combine $\binom{2^t}{2}$ tweaks pairs for one message and obtain 2^{-n} pairs that collide in their ciphertexts. We can combine those pairs for both messages to quartets, and have a probability of 2^{-24} that the tweak differences match for both pairs. If $t > 24$, we have $\binom{2^{24+x}}{2} \cdot 2^{-n}$ pairs per message whose ciphertexts collide. Building quartets, their tweak differences will match with probability $2^{-x} \cdot 2^{-24}$. Hence, we obtain

$$\begin{cases} (2^{2t-n-1})^2 \cdot 2^{-24} \simeq 2^{4t-96-2} \simeq 2^{4t-98} & \text{if } t \leq 24 \\ (2^{2t-n-1})^2 \cdot 2^{-x-24} \simeq 2^{4t-96-2-x} \simeq 2^{4t-98-x} & \text{otherwise.} \end{cases} \quad (7)$$

For a message pair that produces the desired difference after π_1, we have $2^{t-x} \cdot 2^{t-x}$ tweaks in their tweak sets that lead to a collision with probability 2^{-24} after π_1, and thus to $2^{2t-2x-24}$ pairs. Note that we can combine only the tweak sets that share the same 12-bit value in the anti-diagonal $\mathsf{MC}^{-1}(\Delta T)[2, 4, 6]$. If $t = 24 + x$ for non-negative x, there are 2^x times such pairs on average: $2^{2t-2x-24}$ for every value in the anti-diagonal, assuming 2^x is integer. Thus, we have

$$\begin{cases} \binom{2^{2t-24}}{2} \cdot 2^{-n} \simeq 2^{4t-48-36-1} \simeq 2^{4t-85} & \text{if } t \leq 24 \\ \binom{2^x \cdot 2^{2t-2x-24}}{2} \cdot 2^{-n} \simeq 2^{4t-2x-48-36-1} \simeq 2^{4t-2x-85} & \text{otherwise.} \end{cases} \quad (8)$$

quartets. For the messages with the desired difference after π_1, we observe approximately 2^3, 2^7, 2^{11}, 2^{13}, 2^{15}, and 2^{17} quartets with the standard deviation matching about the square root, for 2^t message-tweak tuples per message, and $t \in \{22, \ldots, 27\}$. This matches our expectations in Eq. (8) including the break at $t = 24$. For $t \leq 24$, one can observe an increasing factor of 2^4 quartets for each increment of t, which becomes 2^2 for $t > 24$.

For message pairs without the desired difference after π_1, the numbers of quartets are far below those of pairs with the desired difference, with means of 2^{-10}, 2^{-6}, 2^{-2}, 2^1, and 2^4, and 2^7. Again, the factor from t to $t+1$ changes from 2^4 if $t \leq 24$, to a factor of 2^3 times more quartets from t to $t+1$ when $t > 24$, as expected.

The standard deviations are about the square root of the expectations, which matches Bernoulli distributions. The major insight is that the gap in the number of quartets is huge enough – in the order of 2^{13}, 2^{12}, and 2^{11} for $t = 24, 25, 26$ – to reasonably choose a threshold and not have a single non-desired message pair that could mistakenly filter out the correct partial key.

4   Provable Security Preliminaries

4.1   Provable Security Notations

Given a sequence $\mathcal{X} = (X_1, \ldots, X_q)$, we use $\mathcal{X}^q$ to indicate that it consists of q elements; $\widehat{\mathcal{X}}^q = \{X_1, \ldots, X_q\}$ denotes their set and $\mu(\mathcal{X}^q, X)$ the multiplicity of an element X in $\mathcal{X}^q$. For an index set $\mathcal{I} \subseteq [q]$ and $\mathcal{X}^q$, $\mathcal{X}^{\mathcal{I}} =^{\text{def}} (X_i)_{i \in \mathcal{I}}$. For a pair of sequences $\mathcal{X}^q$ and $\mathcal{Y}^q$, $(\mathcal{X}^q, \mathcal{Y}^q)$ denotes the two-ary q-tuple $((X_1, Y_1), \ldots, (X_q, Y_q))$. An n-ary q-tuple is defined naturally. A two-ary tuple $(\mathcal{X}^q, \mathcal{Y}^q)$ is said to be permutation-compatible, denoted as $\mathcal{X}^q \leftrightsquigarrow \mathcal{Y}^q$, iff $X_i = X_j \Leftrightarrow Y_i = Y_j$. A three-ary tuple $(\mathcal{T}^q, \mathcal{X}^q, \mathcal{Y}^q)$ is said to be tweakable-permutation-compatible, denoted as $(\mathcal{T}^q, \mathcal{X}^q) \leftrightsquigarrow (\mathcal{T}^q, \mathcal{Y}^q)$, iff $(T_i, X_i) = (T_j, X_j) \Leftrightarrow (T_i, Y_i) = (T_j, Y_j)$. For any function $F : \mathcal{X} \to \mathcal{Y}$ and $\mathcal{X}^q$, $F(\mathcal{X}^q)$ denotes $(F(X_i), \ldots, F(X_q))$. For a set $\mathcal{X}$, $X \leftarrow \mathcal{X}$ means that X is sampled uniformly at random and independently from other variables from $\mathcal{X}$. Moreover, let $\exists^*$ mean "there exist distinct".

Table 3. Probabilities (μ) and standard deviations (σ) for #quartets of messages with the desired difference after π_1, from m experiments with random keys each and 2^t distinct tweaks per message.

		With desired difference?			
		With		Without	
t	m	$\log_2(\mu)$	$\log_2(\sigma)$	$\log_2(\mu)$	$\log_2(\sigma)$
22	10 000	2.994	1.511	-10.480	-5.241
23	1 000	6.997	3.550	-6.158	-2.991
24	100	11.005	5.502	-1.837	-0.907
25	100	12.998	6.479	1.233	0.664
26	100	15.001	7.437	3.986	2.097
27	100	17.002	8.395	6.987	3.497

A distinguisher **A** is an algorithm that tries to distinguish between two worlds $\mathcal{O}_{real}$ and $\mathcal{O}_{ideal}$ via black-box interaction with one of them chosen randomly and invisible from **A**. At the end of its interaction, **A** has to output a decision bit. $\mathbf{Adv}_{\mathcal{O}_{ideal};\mathcal{O}_{real}}(\mathbf{A})$ denotes the advantage of **A** to distinguish between both. We consider information-theoretic distinguishers that are bounded only in terms of the number of queries and message material that they can ask to the available oracles. $\mathbf{Adv}_{\mathcal{O}_{ideal};\mathcal{O}_{real}}(q) \overset{\text{def}}{=} \max_{\mathbf{A}} \left\{ \mathbf{Adv}_{\mathcal{O}_{ideal};\mathcal{O}_{real}}(\mathbf{A}) \right\}$ denotes the maximum of advantages over all possible adversaries **A** that are allowed to ask at most q queries to its oracles. Later, we exclude trivial distinguishers, i.e., distinguishers who ask duplicate queries or queries to which the answer is already known.

4.2 Expectation Method

Let **A** be a computationally unbounded deterministic distinguisher that tries to distinguish between a real world $\mathcal{O}_{real}$ and an ideal world $\mathcal{O}_{ideal}$. The queries and responses of the interaction of **A** with its oracles are collected in a transcript τ. It may also contain additional information which would make the adversary only stronger. By Θ_{real} and Θ_{ideal}, we denote random variables for the transcript when **A** interacts with the real world or the ideal world, respectively. Since **A** is deterministic, the probability of **A**'s decision depends only on the oracle and the transcript. A transcript τ is called attainable if its probability in the ideal world is non-zero.

The expectation method is a generalization of the popular H-coefficient method by Patarin [Pat08], which is a simple corollary of the following result.

Lemma 1 (Expectation Method [HT16]). Let Ω be a set of all transcripts that can be partitioned into two disjoint non-empty sets of good transcripts, GOODT and bad transcripts, BADT. For some $\epsilon_{bad} > 0$ and a non-negative function $\epsilon_{\text{ratio}} : \Omega \to [0, \infty)$, suppose $\Pr[\Theta_{\text{ideal}} \in \text{BADT}] \leq \epsilon_{\text{bad}}$ and for any $\tau \in \text{GOODT}$, it holds that $\Pr[\Theta_{\text{real}} = \tau]/\Pr[\Theta_{\text{ideal}} = \tau] \geq 1 - \epsilon_{\text{ratio}}$. Then, for any distinguisher $\mathbf{A}$ that tries to distinguish between $\mathcal{O}_{\text{real}}$ and $\mathcal{O}_{\text{ideal}}$, it holds:

$$\mathbf{Adv}_{\mathcal{O}_{\text{ideal}};\mathcal{O}_{\text{real}}}(\mathbf{A}) \leq \epsilon_{\text{bad}} + \mathbb{E}\left[\epsilon_{\text{ratio}}(\Theta_{\text{ideal}})\right].$$

4.3 Mirror Theory

Patarin [Pat10] defined the Mirror Theory as an approach to estimate the number of solutions of a linear system of equalities and linear inequalities in cyclic groups. He followed a recursive sophisticated proof [Pat08, Pat10] that was brought to the attention of a wider audience by Mennink and Neves [MN17]. Jha and Nandi [JN20] revisited it for a tight proof of CLRW2 [LRW02]. We follow their description that itself referred to Mennink and Neves' interpretation of the Mirror theory. For $q \geq 1$, let $\mathcal{L}$ be a system of linear equations of the form

$$\{ e_1 : U_1 \oplus V_1 = \lambda_1, \quad \ldots, \quad e_q : U_q \oplus V_q = \lambda_q \},$$

where U_i and V_i are the unknowns, λ_i the knowns, and $U_i, V_i, \lambda_i \in \mathbb{F}_2^n$. We denote their sets as $\mathcal{U}^q$ and $\mathcal{V}^q$, respectively. Moreover, $\mathcal{L}$ contains a set of inequalities that uniquely determine $\widehat{\mathcal{U}}^q$ and $\widehat{\mathcal{V}}^q$, respectively. We assume that $\widehat{\mathcal{U}}^q$ and $\widehat{\mathcal{V}}^q$ are indexed in arbitrary order by index sets $[q_u]$ and $[q_v]$, where $q_u = |\widehat{\mathcal{U}}^q|$ and $q_v = |\widehat{\mathcal{V}}^q|$. Then, we can define two surjective index maps

$$\varphi_u : \begin{cases} [q] \to [q_u] \\ i \to j \text{ iff } U_i = \widehat{U}_j. \end{cases} \qquad \varphi_v : \begin{cases} [q] \to [q_v] \\ i \to j \text{ iff } V_i = \widehat{V}_j. \end{cases}$$

Thus, $\mathcal{L}$ is uniquely determined by $(\varphi_u, \varphi_v, \lambda^q)$ and vice versa. Let $\mathcal{G}(\mathcal{L}) \overset{\text{def}}{=} ([q_u], [q_v], \mathcal{E})$ be a labeled bipartite graph corresponding to $\mathcal{L}$, where

$$\mathcal{E} \overset{\text{def}}{=} \{(\varphi_u(i), \varphi_v(i), \lambda_i) : i \in [q]\}$$

is the set of edges and λ_i the edge labels. Thus, each equation in $\mathcal{L}$ corresponds to a unique labeled edge if there exist no duplicate equations in $\mathcal{L}$. We need three definitions to use the fundamental theorem of the Mirror Theory.

Definition 1 (Cycle-freeness). We call $\mathcal{L}$ cycle-free iff $\mathcal{G}(\mathcal{L})$ is acyclic.

Definition 2 (Maximal Block Size). Two equations e_i and e_j for distinct i, j are in the same component iff the corresponding edges (vertices) in $\mathcal{G}(\mathcal{L})$ are in the same graph component. The size of any component $\mathcal{C} \in \mathcal{L}$, denoted $\xi(\mathcal{C})$, is given by the number of vertices in the corresponding component of $\mathcal{G}(\mathcal{L})$. The maximal component size of $\mathcal{G}(\mathcal{L})$ is denoted by $\xi_{\max}(\mathcal{L})$ or short by $\xi_{\max}$.

Definition 3 (Non-degeneracy). $\mathcal{L}$ is called non-degenerate iff there exists no path of length ≥ 2 in $\mathcal{G}(\mathcal{L})$ such that the labels along its edges sum to zero.

Theorem 1 (Fundamental Theorem of the Mirror Theory [Pat10]). Let $\mathcal{L}$ be a system of equations over the unknowns $(\mathcal{U}^q, \mathcal{V}^q)$ that is (i) cycle-free, (ii) non-degenerate, and (iii) possesses a maximal component size of $\xi_{\max}$ with $\xi_{\max}^2 \cdot \max\{q_u, q_v\} \leq 2^n$. Then, the number of solutions $(U_1, \dots, U_{q_u}, V_1, \dots, V_{q_v})$ of $\mathcal{L}$, denoted as h_q, such that $U_i \neq U_j$ and $V_i \neq V_j$ for all $i \neq j$, satisfies

$$h_q \geq \frac{(2^n)_{q_u} \cdot (2^n)_{q_v}}{(2^n)^q}. \tag{9}$$

h_q is multiplied by a factor of $(1 - \epsilon)$ for some $\epsilon > 0$ at the end. For $\xi \geq 2$ and $\epsilon > 0$, we denote as the (ξ, ϵ)-restricted Mirror-Theory theorem the variant with $\xi_{\max} = \xi$ and $h_q \geq (1 - \epsilon) \cdot h_q^*$, where h_q^* is the right-hand side of Eq. (9).

4.4 Transcript Graph

For TNT, a transcript τ will consist of the queries and responses (T_i, M_i, C_i) as well as intermediate values. We will later use a transcript of TNT as the tuple of tuples $(\mathcal{T}^q, \mathcal{M}^q, \mathcal{C}^q, \mathcal{X}^q, \mathcal{Y}^q, \mathcal{V}^q)$ that will collect the values T_i, M_i, etc., for $1 \leq i \leq q$, respectively. The roles of the individual variables are shown in Fig. 9.

Given a transcript τ, a transcript graph is a graph-isomorphic unique bipartite representation of the mappings in τ. For our purpose, the relevant transcript graph will reflect the mappings of $\mathcal{X}^q$ and $\mathcal{U}^q$. The transcript τ is therefore isomorphic to a graph on $(\mathcal{X}^q, \mathcal{U}^q)$.

Definition 4. A transcript graph $\mathcal{G} = (\mathcal{X}^q, \mathcal{U}^q, \mathcal{E}^q)$ that is associated with $(\mathcal{X}^q, \mathcal{U}^q)$ is denoted as $\mathcal{G}(\mathcal{X}^q, \mathcal{U}^q)$ and defined as $\mathcal{X} =^{\mathrm{def}} \{(X_i, 0) : i \in [q]\}$, $\mathcal{U} =^{\mathrm{def}} \{(U_i, 1) : i \in [q]\}$, and $\mathcal{E} =^{\mathrm{def}} \{((X_i, 0), (U_i, 1)) : i \in [q]\}$. A label λ_i is associated with the edge $((X_i, 0), (U_i, 1)) \in \mathcal{E}$.

The resulting graph may contain parallel edges. The 0 and 1 in $(X_i, 0)$ and $(U_i, 1)$ will be dropped for simplicity. If for distinct $i, j \in [q]$, it holds that $X_i = X_j$ (or $U_i = U_j$), we denote that as shared vertex $X_{i,j}$ (or $U_{i,j}$). Since there is a bijection of each edge $(X_i, U_i) \in \mathcal{E}$ to i, we can also represent the edge by i.

4.5 Extended Mirror Theory

Jha and Nandi [JN20] applied the mirror theory to the tweakable-permutation setting. We briefly recall their main result and the necessary notations.

In an edge-labeled bipartite graph $\mathcal{G} = (\mathcal{Y}, \mathcal{V}, \mathcal{E})$, an edge (Y, V, λ) is isolated iff both Y and V have degree one. A component $\mathcal{S} \subseteq \mathcal{G}$ is called a star iff $\xi(\mathcal{S}) \geq 3$ (recall that $\xi(\mathcal{S})$ is the number of vertices in $\mathcal{S}$) and there is a unique vertex $V \in \mathcal{S}$ with degree $\xi(\mathcal{S}) - 1$. V is called the center of $\mathcal{S}$. $\mathcal{S}$ is called a $\mathcal{Y}$-star (or $\mathcal{V}$-star) if its center $Y \in \mathcal{Y}$ (or $V \in \mathcal{V}$). Consider an equation system $\mathcal{L}$

$$\{e_1 : Y_1 \oplus V_1 = \lambda_1, \quad e_2 : Y_2 \oplus V_2 = \lambda_2, \quad \dots, \quad e_q : Y_q \oplus V_q = \lambda_q\},$$

such that each component in $\mathcal{G}(\mathcal{L})$ is either an isolated edge or a star. Let c_1, c_2, and c_3 denote the number of isolated, $\mathcal{Y}$-star, and $\mathcal{V}$-star components, respectively. Moreover, $q_1 = c_1$, q_2, and q_3 denote the number of their equations. The equations in $\mathcal{L}$ can be arranged in arbitrary order. The isolated edges are indexed first, followed by the star components. Jha and Nandi show the following:

Theorem 2 (Theorem 5.1 in [JN20]). Let $\mathcal{L}$ be as above with $q < 2^{n-2}$ and $\xi_{\max} q \leq 2^{n-1}$. Then, the number of tuples $(\mathcal{Y}^{q_\mathcal{Y}}, \mathcal{V}^{q_\mathcal{V}})$ that satisfy $\mathcal{L}$ with $Y_i \neq Y_j$ and $V_i \neq V_j$ for all $i \neq j$ satisfies

$$h_q \geq \left(1 - \frac{13q^4}{2^{3n}} - \frac{2q^2}{2^{2n}} - \left(\sum_{i=1}^{c_2+c_3} \eta_{c_i+1}^2\right) \frac{4q^2}{2^{2n}}\right) \cdot \frac{(2^n)_{q_1+c_2+q_3} \cdot (2^n)_{q_1+q_2+c_3}}{\prod_{\lambda' \in \lambda^2} (2^n)_{\mu(\lambda^q, \lambda')}},$$

where $\eta_j = \xi_j - 1$ and ξ_j denotes the number of vertices of the j-th component for $j \in [c_1 + c_2 + c_3]$.

4.6 Universal Hashing

Let $\mathcal{X}$ and $\mathcal{Y}$ be non-empty sets or spaces in the following, and let $\mathcal{H} = \{H | H : \mathcal{X} \to \mathcal{Y}\}$ be a family of hash functions.

Definition 5 (Almost-Universal Hash Function [CW79]). We say that $\mathcal{H}$ is ϵ-almost-universal (ϵ-AU) if, for all distinct $X, X' \in \mathcal{X}$, it holds that $\Pr[H(X) = H(X')] \leq \epsilon$, where the probability is taken over $H \leftarrow \mathcal{H}$.

Definition 6 (Almost-XOR-Universal Hash Function [Kra94, Rog95]). Let $\mathcal{Y} \subseteq \mathbb{F}_2^*$. We say that $\mathcal{H}$ is ϵ-almost-XOR-universal (ϵ-AXU) if, for all distinct $X, X' \in \mathcal{X}$ and arbitrary $\Delta \in \mathcal{Y}$, it holds that $\Pr[H(X) \oplus H(X') = \Delta] \leq \epsilon$, where the probability is taken over $H \leftarrow \mathcal{H}$.

Let $\mathcal{H} : \{H | H : \mathcal{T} \to \mathbb{F}_2^n\}$ be a family ϵ-almost-universal hash functions and $H \leftarrow \mathcal{H}$ be an instance. Let $\mathcal{X}^q \stackrel{\text{def}}{=} H(\mathcal{T}^q)$ be the sequence of outputs X_i from $H(T_i)$, for $i \in [q]$ queries. In the following, [JN20] defined, in an abstract way, variables ν_i for the number of occurrences of the hash value i, and defined coll for the number of colliding pairs in $\mathcal{X}^q$.

Lemma 2 (Lemma 4.3 in [JN20]). Since $\mathbb{E}[\text{coll}] \leq \binom{q}{2}\epsilon$, it holds that

$$\mathbb{E}\left[\sum_{i=1}^{r} \nu_i^2\right] = 2 \cdot \mathbb{E}[\text{coll}] + \sum_{i=1}^{r} \nu_i \leq 4 \cdot \mathbb{E}[\text{coll}] \leq 2q^2\epsilon.$$

Thus, Lemma 2 says that the number of collisions is limited by $2q^2\epsilon$ on expectation. Furthermore, the corollary below upper bounds the number of occurrences of any single hash value. The proof in [JN20] stems from Markov's inequality.

Corollary 1 (Corollary 4.1 in [JN20]). Let $\nu_{\max} = \max\{\nu_i : i \in [r]\}$. Then, for some $a \geq 1$, it holds that $\Pr[\nu_{\max} \geq a] \leq \frac{2q^2\epsilon}{a^2}$.

588   C. Guo et al.

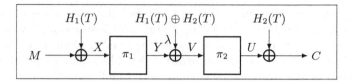

Fig. 8. CLRW2.

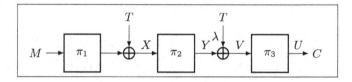

Fig. 9. TNT with relabeled variables.

The following lemma from [JN20] bounds the probability that four distinct inputs to two ϵ-AU hash functions yield three alternating collisions.

Lemma 3 (Alternating-collisions Lemma in [JN20]). Let $H_1, H_2 \twoheadleftarrow \mathcal{H}$ be independently sampled ϵ-AU hash functions with domain $\mathcal{X}$. Let $X_1, \ldots, X_q \in \mathcal{X}^q$ be pairwise distinct inputs. Then, it holds, over $H_1, H_2 \twoheadleftarrow \mathcal{H}$, that

$$\Pr\left[\exists^* i, j, k, \ell \in [q] : H_1(X_i) = H_1(X_j) \wedge H_2(X_j) = H_2(X_k) \wedge H_1(X_k) = H_1(X_\ell)\right]$$

is at most $q^2 \epsilon^{1.5}$.

5 TPRP Proof of TNT

We followed the footsteps of the STPRP proof of CLRW2 by [JN20] closely to show Theorem 3. We provide an extract that highlights where both constructions and proofs differ. Thus, we do not claim novelty of the proof approach but show that it applies also to TNT in encryption direction only with minor adaptions.

Theorem 3 (TPRP Security of TNT). Let $q \leq 2^{n-2}$, and $E_{K_1}, E_{K_2}, E_{K_3} : \mathcal{K} \times \mathbb{F}_2^n \to \mathbb{F}_2^n$ be block ciphers with $K_1, K_2, K_3 \twoheadleftarrow \mathcal{K}$. Then,

$$\mathbf{Adv}_{\mathsf{TNT}[E_{K_1}, E_{K_2}, E_{K_3}]}^{\mathsf{TPRP}}(q) \leq \frac{91q^4}{2^{3n}} + \frac{2q^2}{2^{2n}} + \frac{4q^2}{2^{1.5n}} + 3 \cdot \mathbf{Adv}_E^{\mathsf{PRP}}(q).$$

First, we can replace the secret-key block ciphers $E_{K_1}, E_{K_2}, E_{K_3}$ with $K_1, K_2, K_3 \twoheadleftarrow \mathcal{K}$ by random permutations $\pi_1, \pi_2, \pi_3 \twoheadleftarrow \mathsf{Perm}(\mathbb{F}_2^n)$. For TNT, the advantage between both settings is upper bounded by

$$\mathbf{Adv}_{\mathsf{TNT}[E_{K_1}, E_{K_2}, E_{K_3}]}^{\mathsf{TPRP}} \leq 3 \cdot \mathbf{Adv}_E^{\mathsf{PRP}}(q) + \mathbf{Adv}_{\mathsf{TNT}[\pi_1, \pi_2, \pi_3]}^{\mathsf{TPRP}}(q).$$

We consider the information-theoretic setting with a computationally unbounded distinguisher **A**. W.l.o.g., we assume that **A** is deterministic and non-trivial.

5.1 Oracle Descriptions

The Real Oracle. $\mathcal{O}_{\text{real}}$ runs $\mathsf{TNT}[\pi_1, \pi_2, \pi_3]$. The transcript random variable Θ_{real} yields the transcript as the tuple $(\mathcal{T}^q, \mathcal{M}^q, \mathcal{C}^q, \mathcal{X}^q, \mathcal{Y}^q, \mathcal{V}^q)$ where for all queries $i \in [q]$, the values T_i, M_i, C_i, X_i, Y_i, V_i, U_i, λ_i refer to the variables as given in Fig. 9, which can be compared to those in CLRW2 in Fig. 8. The sets $\mathcal{U}^q = \mathcal{C}^q$ and $\lambda^q = \mathcal{T}^q$ can be derived directly from the transcript.

The Ideal Oracle. $\mathcal{O}_{\text{ideal}}$ implements $\widetilde{\Pi} \twoheadleftarrow \widetilde{\mathsf{Perm}}(\mathbb{F}_2^n, \mathbb{F}_2^n)$. Moreover, we treat the first permutation and tweak addition in TNT as equivalent to the first hash function in CLRW2. Thus, the ideal oracle samples $\pi_1 \twoheadleftarrow \mathsf{Perm}(\mathbb{F}_2^n)$ and gives all values X_i to **A** after **A** finished its interactions but before it outputs its decision bit. The transcript looks as before, where T_i, M_i, C_i are the inputs and outputs from $C_i = \widetilde{\Pi}(T_i, M_i)$ or $M_i = \widetilde{\Pi}^{-1}(T_i, C_i)$, $\lambda_i = T_i$, $X_i \leftarrow \pi_1(M_i) \oplus T_i$, $U_i \leftarrow C_i$. The values of the sets $\mathcal{X}^q$, $\mathcal{U}^q$, and $\mathcal{T}^q$ are defined honestly.

Jha and Nandi [JN20] characterized so-called bad hash keys. Given the partial transcript $(\mathcal{T}^q, \mathcal{M}^q, \mathcal{C}^q, \mathcal{X}^q)$ – plus for CLRW2 also the hash functions H_1 and H_2 – they defined a number of conditions when (H_1, H_2) where considered good or bad, respectively, and defined the sets $\mathcal{H}_{\text{good}}$ and $\mathcal{H}_{\text{bad}}$ for this purpose. While TNT omits hash functions, the predicates were not conditions on the hash keys but instead on equalities of internal variables that can also occur in TNT. Therefore, we consider their cases analogously. A hash key was defined to be bad iff one of the following predicates was true:

1. badH_1: $\exists^* i, j \in [q]$ such that $X_i = X_j \wedge U_i = U_j$.
2. badH_2: $\exists^* i, j \in [q]$ such that $X_i = X_j \wedge T_i = T_j$.
3. badH_3: $\exists^* i, j \in [q]$ such that $U_i = U_j \wedge T_i = T_j$.
4. badH_4: $\exists^* i, j, k, \ell \in [q]$ such that $X_i = X_j \wedge U_j = U_k \wedge X_k = X_\ell$.
5. badH_5: $\exists^* i, j, k, \ell \in [q]$ such that $U_i = U_j \wedge X_j = X_k \wedge U_k = U_\ell$.
6. badH_6: $\exists k \geq 2^n/2q$, $\exists^* i_1, i_2, \ldots, i_k \in [q]$ such that $X_{i_1} = \cdots = X_{i_k}$.
7. badH_7: $\exists k \geq 2^n/2q$, $\exists^* i_1, i_2, \ldots, i_k \in [q]$ such that $U_{i_1} = \cdots = U_{i_k}$.

In the absence of hash keys, we cannot label those as H being bad or good. Thus, we call them bad and good hash equivalent instead.

Bad Hash Equivalent: If one of the events badH_1 through badH_7 occurs, the ideal oracle samples the values $\mathcal{Y}^q$ and $\mathcal{V}^q$ as $Y_i = V_i = 0$ for all $i \in [q]$.

Good Hash Equivalent: In the other case, it will be useful to study the transcript graph $\mathcal{G}(\mathcal{X}^q, \mathcal{U}^q)$ of the associations $(\mathcal{X}^q, \mathcal{U}^q)$ that arises from the transcript when no badH event occurs. Figure 10 shows all possible types of components in $\mathcal{G}(\mathcal{X}^q, \mathcal{U}^q)$. There, (star) components of the Types (2) and (3) contain exactly one vertex with a degree of ≥ 2. Components of Types (4) and (5) can contain one vertex with a degree of ≥ 2 in $\mathcal{U}$ and one such vertex in $\mathcal{X}$.

Lemma 4 (Lemma 6.1 in [JN20]). The transcript graph $\mathcal{G}(\mathcal{X}^q, \mathcal{U}^q)$ ($\mathcal{G}$ for short, hereafter) by a good hash equivalent has the following properties:

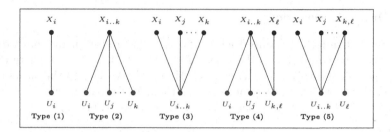

Fig. 10. Components types of a transcript graph corresponding to a good hash equivalent. Type (1) is the only component with a single edge. Types (2) and (3) are $\mathcal{X}$- and $\mathcal{U}$-star components, respectively. Types (4) and (5) are the only components that are neither isolated nor stars since they can have vertices of degree ≥ 2 in both $\mathcal{X}$ and $\mathcal{U}$.

1. $\mathcal{G}$ is simple, acyclic, and possesses no isolated vertices.
2. $\mathcal{G}$ has no two adjacent edges i and j such that $T_i \oplus T_j = 0$.
3. $\mathcal{G}$ has no component of size $\geq 2^n/2q$ edges.
4. $\mathcal{G}$ has no component with more than one vertex of degree ≥ 2 in neither $\mathcal{X}$ or $\mathcal{U}$ (though, it can have one vertex with degree ≥ 2 in $\mathcal{X}$ and one in $\mathcal{U}$).

The proof is given in [JN20].

For the sake of completeness, we describe the sampling process of $\mathcal{Y}^q$ and $\mathcal{V}^q$ in the case of a good hash equivalent. This is the same process as for CLRW2 in [JN20]. Therefore, this part is only a revisit and attributed to [JN20]:

The indices $i \in [q]$ are collected in index sets $\mathcal{I}_1, \ldots, \mathcal{I}_5$, corresponding to the edges in all Type-1, $\ldots$, Type-5 components, respectively. The five sets are disjoint and $[q] = \bigcup_{i=1}^5 \mathcal{I}_i$. Let $\mathcal{I} = \bigcup_{i=1}^3 \mathcal{I}_i$ and consider the system of equations

$$\mathcal{L} \stackrel{\text{def}}{=} \{Y_i \oplus V_i = T_i : i \in \mathcal{I}\},$$

where $Y_i = Y_j$ (respectively $V_i = V_j$) holds iff $X_i = X_j$ (respectively $U_i = U_j$) for all $i, j \in [q]$. The solution set of $\mathcal{L}$ is precisely the set

$$\mathcal{S} \stackrel{\text{def}}{=} \{(\mathcal{Y}^\mathcal{I}, \mathcal{V}^\mathcal{I}) : \mathcal{Y}^\mathcal{I} \rightsquigarrow \mathcal{X}^\mathcal{I} \wedge \mathcal{V}^\mathcal{I} \rightsquigarrow \mathcal{U}^\mathcal{I} \wedge \mathcal{Y}^\mathcal{I} \oplus \mathcal{V}^\mathcal{I} = \mathcal{T}^\mathcal{I}\}.$$

Given these definitions, the ideal-world oracle $\mathcal{O}_{\text{ideal}}$ samples $(\mathcal{Y}^q, \mathcal{V}^q)$ as follows:

- $(\mathcal{Y}^\mathcal{I}, \mathcal{V}^\mathcal{I}) \twoheadleftarrow \mathcal{S}$. This means, $\mathcal{O}_{\text{ideal}}$ samples uniformly one valid assignment from the set of all valid assignments.
- Let $\mathcal{G} \backslash \mathcal{I}$ denote the subgraph of $\mathcal{G}$ after the removal of edges and vertices corresponding to $i \in \mathcal{I}$. For each component $\mathcal{C} \subset \mathcal{G} \backslash \mathcal{I}$:
  - If $(X_i, U_i) \in \mathcal{C}$ corresponds to the edge in $\mathcal{C}$ where both X_i and U_i have a degree ≥ 2. Then, $Y_i \twoheadleftarrow \mathbb{F}_2^n$ and $V_i = Y_i \oplus T_i$.
  - For each edge $(X_{i'}, U_{i'}) \neq (X_i, U_i) \in \mathcal{C}$, either $X_{i'} = X_i$ or $U_{i'} = U_i$. Take the case that $X_{i'} = X_i$. Then, $Y_{i'} = Y_i$ and $V_{i'} = Y_{i'} \oplus T_{i'}$. In the other case $U_{i'} = U_i$. Then, $V_{i'} = V_i$ and $Y_{i'} = V_{i'} \oplus T_{i'}$.

Then, the transcript in the ideal world is completely defined, maintaining both the consistency of equations of the form $Y_i \oplus V_i = T_i$ as in the real world and the permutation consistency within each component for **good** hash equivalents. Still, there can be collisions among the values of $\mathcal{Y}$ or among the values of $\mathcal{V}$ from different components.

5.2 Definition of Bad Transcripts

The analysis of **bad** transcripts and of **bad** hash equivalents, in particular, is the core aspect wherein the analyses of CLRW2 and TNT differ. However, there can be collisions among the values of $\mathcal{Y}$ or among the values of $\mathcal{V}$ from different components that have to be treated in **bad** transcripts. Their treatment can be done similarly as in [JN20]. They are essential for the proof of TNT and listed in this subsection only for the sake of completeness, but we refer to [JN20] for their proof.

The set of transcripts Ω is the set of all tuples $\tau = (\mathcal{T}^q, \mathcal{M}^q, \mathcal{C}^q, \mathcal{X}^q, \mathcal{Y}^q, \mathcal{V}^q)$ defined as before. Recall that $\mathcal{U}^q = \mathcal{C}^q$ holds for TNT. Following [JN20], a bad transcript definition needs the following preprocessing steps:

1. Eliminate all tuples $(\mathcal{X}^q, \mathcal{U}^q, \mathcal{T}^q)$ such that both $\mathcal{Y}^q$ and $\mathcal{V}^q$ are trivially restricted by linear dependencies.
2. Eliminate all tuples $(\mathcal{X}^q, \mathcal{U}^q, \mathcal{V}^q, \mathcal{Y}^q)$ such that $\mathcal{X}^q \not\rightsquigarrow \mathcal{Y}^q$ or $\mathcal{U}^q \not\rightsquigarrow \mathcal{V}^q$.

A transcript τ is called a **bad** hash-equivalent transcript if one of the conditions badH_1 through badH_7 holds. We define a compound event $\mathsf{badH} =^{\mathrm{def}} \bigcup_{i=1}^{7} \mathsf{badH}_i$ that ensures that the first requirement is fulfilled.

For the second requirement, all conditions that might lead to $\mathcal{X}^q \not\rightsquigarrow \mathcal{Y}^q$ or $\mathcal{U}^q \not\rightsquigarrow \mathcal{V}^q$ have to be addressed. The transcript is trivially inconsistent if one of them is fulfilled and we consider that badH does not hold in the following. If the transcript is still **bad**, it is called sampling-induced **bad** iff one of the following conditions from [JN20] holds, for some $\alpha \in \{1, \ldots, 5\}$ and $\beta \in \{\alpha, \ldots, 5\}$:

- $\mathsf{ycoll}_{\alpha,\beta}$: $\exists i \in \mathcal{I}_\alpha, j \in \mathcal{I}_\beta$ such that $X_i \neq X_j \wedge Y_i = Y_j$ and
- $\mathsf{vcoll}_{\alpha,\beta}$: $\exists i \in \mathcal{I}_\alpha, j \in \mathcal{I}_\beta$ such that $U_i \neq U_j \wedge V_i = V_j$,

where $\mathcal{I}_i$ is defined as before. It holds that

$$\mathsf{badsamp} \overset{\mathrm{def}}{=} \bigcup_{\alpha \in [5], \beta \in \{\alpha, \ldots, 5\}} \left(\mathsf{ycoll}_{\alpha,\beta} \cup \mathsf{vcoll}_{\alpha,\beta} \right).$$

By varying α and β over all 30 values, one obtains 30 conditions that could yield that $\mathcal{X}^q \not\rightsquigarrow \mathcal{Y}^q$ or $\mathcal{U}^q \not\rightsquigarrow \mathcal{V}^q$. Some of these conditions cannot be satisfied due to the sampling mechanism. Those are

$$\mathsf{ycoll}_{1,1}, \mathsf{ycoll}_{1,2}, \mathsf{ycoll}_{1,3}, \mathsf{ycoll}_{2,2}, \mathsf{ycoll}_{2,3}, \mathsf{ycoll}_{3,3},$$
$$\mathsf{vcoll}_{1,1}, \mathsf{vcoll}_{1,2}, \mathsf{vcoll}_{1,3}, \mathsf{vcoll}_{2,2}, \mathsf{vcoll}_{2,3}, \mathsf{vcoll}_{3,3}.$$

A transcript is called bad if it is a bad hash-equivalent or bad sampling-induced transcript. All other transcripts are called good and all good transcripts are attainable. It holds that

$$\Pr\left[\Theta_{\text{ideal}} \in \text{BADT}\right] \leq \Pr_{\Theta_{\text{ideal}}}\left[\text{badH}\right] + \Pr_{\Theta_{\text{ideal}}}\left[\text{badsamp}\right].$$

5.3   Analysis of Bad Transcripts

The analysis of bad transcript is the core point where the analysis of CLRW2 and TNT differ. This is mainly because TNT lacks hash functions, but adds the unmodified tweak to the state between the permutation calls. As a result, hash collisions as in CLRW2 cannot occur for distinct tweaks.

Lemma 5. For TNT, it holds in the ideal world that

$$\Pr\left[\text{badH}\right] \leq \frac{4q^2}{2^{1.5n}} + \frac{32q^4}{2^{3n}}.$$

Proof. We study the probabilities of the individual events badH in the following. Prior, we note that $F(T_i, M_i) =^{\text{def}} \pi_1(M_i) \oplus T_i$ is ϵ-AU for $\epsilon \leq 1/(2^n - 1) \leq 2^{1-n}$, and at most $1/(2^n - (q - 1))$ if $q - 1$ values M_i had been queried before. Since $q \leq 2^{n-2}$, it holds that $\epsilon \leq 4/(3 \cdot 2^n)$.

- **badH$_1$.** This event holds if for some distinct i, j both $X_i = X_j$ and $U_i = U_j$. If $T_i = T_j$, it must hold that $M_i \neq M_j$, which implies that $X_i \neq X_j$ and the event cannot hold. If $T_i \neq T_j$, $X_i = X_j$ implies $Y_i = Y_j$ and $U_i = U_j$ implies $V_i = V_j$. Thus, it would have to hold that $T_i = T_j$, which is a contradiction. Hence, the probability is zero.
- **badH$_2$.** This event holds if for some distinct i, j both $X_i = X_j$ and $T_i = T_j$. Since $T = T$, it must follow that $M_i = M_j$. Though, since **A** does not ask duplicate queries, this implies that $X_i \neq X_j$. So, the probability is zero.
- **badH$_3$.** This event holds if for some distinct i, j both $U_i = U_j$ and $T_i = T_j$. Again, the latter condition implies that $M_i \neq M_j$. $U_i = U_j$ implies that $V_i = V_j$, which implies that $Y_i = Y_j$, $X_i = X_j$, and $\pi_1(M_i) = \pi_1(M_j)$, which is a contradiction and therefore has zero probability.
- **badH$_4$.** This event holds if for some distinct i, j, k, ℓ, $X_i = X_j$, $U_j = U_k$, and $X_k = X_\ell$. The values of X are results from an ϵ-universal hash function. The values U are sampled uniformly at random in the ideal world from a set of at least $2^n - q$ values for the current tweak. Thus, its sampling process can be interpreted to be ϵ-AU with $\epsilon \leq 1/(2^n - q)$. We can apply Lemma 3 to obtain

$$\Pr\left[\text{badH}_4\right] \leq q^2 \epsilon^{1.5} \leq \frac{4^{1.5} q^2}{(3 \cdot 2^n)^{1.5}} \leq \frac{2q^2}{2^{1.5n}}.$$

- **badH$_5$.** This event holds if for some distinct i, j, k, ℓ, $U_i = U_j$, $X_j = X_k$, and $U_k = U_\ell$. From a similar argumentation as for badH$_4$, it holds that

$$\Pr\left[\text{badH}_5\right] \leq \frac{2q^2}{2^{1.5n}}.$$

– **badH$_6$.** This event holds if there exist distinct $i_1, \ldots, i_k \in [q]$ for $k \geq 2^n/2q$ such that $X_{i_1} = \cdots = X_{i_k}$. Since $(T_i, M_i) \neq (T_j, M_j)$ for none of the indices, we can use Corollary 1 with $a = 2^n/2q$ to upper bound it by

$$\Pr\left[\mathsf{badH_6}\right] \leq \frac{8q^4\epsilon}{2^{2n}} \leq \frac{16q^4}{2^{3n}}.$$

– **badH$_7$.** This event holds if there exist distinct $i_1, \ldots, i_k \in [q]$ for $k \geq 2^n/2q$ such that $U_{i_1} = \cdots = U_{i_k}$. From a similar argumentation as for badH$_6$, we get

$$\Pr\left[\mathsf{badH_7}\right] \leq \frac{16q^4}{2^{3n}}.$$

Lemma 5 follows then from the sum of probabilities of all badH events.   □

Lemma 6. For TNT, it holds in the ideal world that

$$\Pr\left[\mathsf{badsamp}\right] \leq \frac{14q^4}{2^{3n}}.$$

The proof is exactly as in [JN20] and is deferred to the full version of this work.

5.4   Analysis of Good Transcripts

Lemma 7. For an arbitrary good transcript τ, it holds that

$$\frac{\Pr\left[\Theta_{\mathrm{real}} = \tau\right]}{\Pr\left[\Theta_{\mathrm{ideal}} = \tau\right]} \geq 1 - \frac{45q^4}{2^{3n}} - \frac{2q^2}{2^{2n}}.$$

Again, the proof can follow a similar argumentation as the analysis of good transcripts in [JN20] and is therefore deferred to the full version of this work.

6   Summary and Discussion

This work tried to conduct a step towards closing the security gap of TNT. We showed in Sect. 2 that a variant of Mennink's distinguisher from [Men18] also applies to TNT, which yields a theoretical distinguisher in $O(\sqrt{n} \cdot 2^{3n/4})$ time, data, and memory complexity. For this purpose, we reduce the complexity of Mennink's information-theoretic distinguisher from $O(2^{3n/2})$ to $O(2^{3n/4})$ computations and show that at least two similar distinguishers exist. Thereupon, we use the distinguisher to mount a partial key-recovery attack on the instance TNT-AES$[5, *, *]$ from an impossible differential. This attack is described in Sect. 3. Since it needs multiple pairs, its complexity is higher than $O(2^{3n/4})$. We emphasize that our analysis does not break the proposed version of TNT-AES$[6, 6, 6]$ from [BGGS20].

From a constructive point of view, we followed the rigorous analysis by Jha and Nandi on CLRW2. We show in Sect. 5 that their STPRP security proof of CLRW2 for up to $O(2^{3n/4})$ queries can be adapted to an TPRP proof of TNT with similar complexity. We could build on the approach by Jha and Nandi on CLRW2 since we restricted the adversary's queries to the forward direction only. Thus, the first permutation and tweak addition masks the inputs, similar to the first hash function in CLRW2. Since an equivalent is missing at the ciphertext side, one cannot directly derive STPRP security. However, a four-round variant of TNT would possess such hash-function-like masking at the ciphertext-side. This implies that a four-round variant that adds a fourth independent permutation π_4 and encrypts M under T as

$$\mathsf{TNT4}[\pi_1, \pi_2, \pi_3, \pi_4](T, M) \stackrel{\text{def}}{=} \pi_4(\pi_3(\pi_2(\pi_1(M) \oplus T) \oplus T) \oplus T),$$

would directly inherit the $O(2^{3n/4})$ STPRP security from CLRW2. Still, it remains a highly interesting work to conduct an STPRP analysis of the three-round construction TNT. In particular, the Mirror-theory approach seems not easily adaptable since the sampling process in the ideal world is unclear.

From our studies, we see strong indications that TNT is STPRP-secure for approximately $O(2^{3n/4})$ queries if the primitives are secure – although, we were not able to show it at this point of time. However, we found the problem of sampling the variables from both sides consistently in the middle non-trivial. An alternative strategy could be a more precise, but also considerably more sophisticated, study of the original χ^2-based proof of TNT from [BGGS20].

Acknowledgments. We are highly thankful to Zhenzhen Bao and Mridul Nandi for the fruitful discussions as well as the reviewers from Asiacrypt 2020 for their inspiring comments, all of which lead to significant improvements in this work. This research has been partially supported by Nanyang Technological University in Singapore under Grant 04INS000397C230, Singapore's Ministry of Education under Grants RG18/19 and MOE2019-T2-1-060, the National Natural Science Foundation of China (No. 61961146004, 61802399, 61802400, 61732021 and 61772519) and the Youth Innovation Promotion Association CAS.

References

[BGGS20] Bao, Z., Guo, C., Guo, J., Song, L.: TNT: how to tweak a block cipher. In: Canteaut, A., Ishai, Y. (eds.) EUROCRYPT 2020. LNCS, vol. 12106, pp. 641–673. Springer, Cham (2020). https://doi.org/10.1007/978-3-030-45724-2_22

[BGIM19] Bao, Z., Guo, J., Iwata, T., Minematsu, K.: ZOCB and ZOTR: tweakable blockcipher modes for authenticated encryption with full absorption. IACR Trans. Symmetric Cryptol. **2019**(2), 1–54 (2019)

[BJK+16] Beierle, C., et al.: The SKINNY family of block ciphers and its low-latency variant MANTIS. In: Robshaw, M., Katz, J. (eds.) CRYPTO 2016. LNCS, vol. 9815, pp. 123–153. Springer, Heidelberg (2016). https://doi.org/10.1007/978-3-662-53008-5_5

[BKL+07] Bogdanov, A., et al.: PRESENT: an ultra-lightweight block cipher. In: Pail-
          lier, P., Verbauwhede, I. (eds.) CHES 2007. LNCS, vol. 4727, pp. 450–466.
          Springer, Heidelberg (2007). https://doi.org/10.1007/978-3-540-74735-2_31
[BLMR19] Beierle, C., Leander, G., Moradi, A., Rasoolzadeh, S.: CRAFT: lightweight
          tweakable block cipher with efficient protection against DFA attacks. IACR
          Trans. Symmetric Cryptol. **2019**(1), 5–45 (2019)
[CIMN17] Chakraborti, A., Iwata, T., Minematsu, K., Nandi, M.: Blockcipher-based
          authenticated encryption: how small can we go? In: Fischer, W., Homma, N.
          (eds.) CHES 2017. LNCS, vol. 10529, pp. 277–298. Springer, Cham (2017).
          https://doi.org/10.1007/978-3-319-66787-4_14
[CIMN20] Chakraborti, A., Iwata, T., Minematsu, K., Nandi, M.: Blockcipher-based
          authenticated encryption: how small can we go? J. Cryptol. **33**(3), 703–741
          (2019). https://doi.org/10.1007/s00145-019-09325-z
[CMR05]   Cid, C., Murphy, S., Robshaw, M.J.B.: Small scale variants of the AES. In:
          Gilbert, H., Handschuh, H. (eds.) FSE 2005. LNCS, vol. 3557, pp. 145–162.
          Springer, Heidelberg (2005). https://doi.org/10.1007/11502760_10
[CW79]   Carter, L., Wegman, M.N.: Universal classes of hash functions. J. Comput.
          Syst. Sci. **18**(2), 143–154 (1979)
[GRR16]   Grassi, L., Rechberger, C., Rønjom, S.: Subspace trail cryptanalysis and its
          applications to AES. IACR Trans. Symmetric Cryptol. **2016**(2), 192–225
          (2016)
[HT16]   Hoang, V.T., Tessaro, S.: Key-alternating ciphers and key-length extension:
          exact bounds and multi-user security. In: Robshaw, M., Katz, J. (eds.)
          CRYPTO 2016. LNCS, vol. 9814, pp. 3–32. Springer, Heidelberg (2016).
          https://doi.org/10.1007/978-3-662-53018-4_1
[IMPS17] Iwata, T., Minematsu, K., Peyrin, T., Seurin, Y.: ZMAC: a fast tweakable
          block cipher mode for highly secure message authentication. In: Katz, J.,
          Shacham, H. (eds.) CRYPTO 2017. LNCS, vol. 10403, pp. 34–65. Springer,
          Cham (2017). https://doi.org/10.1007/978-3-319-63697-9_2
[JLM+17] Jha, A., List, E., Minematsu, K., Mishra, S., Nandi, M.: XHX – a framework
          for optimally secure tweakable block ciphers from classical block ciphers
          and universal hashing. In: Lange, T., Dunkelman, O. (eds.) LATINCRYPT
          2017. LNCS, vol. 11368, pp. 207–227. Springer, Cham (2019). https://doi.
          org/10.1007/978-3-030-25283-0_12
[JN20]   Jha, A., Nandi, M.: Tight security of cascaded LRW2. J. Cryptol. **33**, 1272–
          1317 (2020). https://doi.org/10.1007/s00145-020-09347-y
[JNP14a] Jean, J., Nikolić, I., Peyrin, T.: KIASU v1.1 (2014). First-round submission
          to the CAESAR competition
[JNP14b] Jean, J., Nikolić, I., Peyrin, T.: Tweaks and keys for block ciphers: the
          TWEAKEY framework. In: Sarkar, P., Iwata, T. (eds.) ASIACRYPT 2014.
          LNCS, vol. 8874, pp. 274–288. Springer, Heidelberg (2014). https://doi.
          org/10.1007/978-3-662-45608-8_15
[JNP16]   Jean, J., Nikolić, I., Peyrin, T.: Deoxys v1.41, 12 October 2016. Third-
          round submission to the CAESAR competition. http://competitions.cr.yp.
          to/caesar-submissions.html
[KR11]   Krovetz, T., Rogaway, P.: The software performance of authenticated-
          encryption modes. In: Joux, A. (ed.) FSE 2011. LNCS, vol. 6733, pp.
          306–327. Springer, Heidelberg (2011). https://doi.org/10.1007/978-3-642-
          21702-9_18

[Kra94] Krawczyk, H.: LFSR-based hashing and authentication. In: Desmedt, Y.G. (ed.) CRYPTO 1994. LNCS, vol. 839, pp. 129–139. Springer, Heidelberg (1994). https://doi.org/10.1007/3-540-48658-5_15

[Lea10] Leander, G.: Small scale variants of the block cipher PRESENT. IACR Cryptology ePrint Archive 2010/143 (2010)

[LL18] Lee, B.H., Lee, J.: Tweakable block ciphers secure beyond the birthday bound in the ideal cipher model. In: Peyrin, T., Galbraith, S. (eds.) ASIACRYPT 2018. LNCS, vol. 11272, pp. 305–335. Springer, Cham (2018). https://doi.org/10.1007/978-3-030-03326-2_11

[LN17] List, E., Nandi, M.: ZMAC+ - an efficient variable-output-length variant of ZMAC. IACR Trans. Symmetric Cryptol. **2017**(4), 306–325 (2017)

[LNS18] Leurent, G., Nandi, M., Sibleyras, F.: Generic attacks against beyond-birthday-bound MACs. In: Shacham, H., Boldyreva, A. (eds.) CRYPTO 2018. LNCS, vol. 10991, pp. 306–336. Springer, Cham (2018). https://doi.org/10.1007/978-3-319-96884-1_11

[LRW02] Liskov, M., Rivest, R.L., Wagner, D.: Tweakable block ciphers. In: Yung, M. (ed.) CRYPTO 2002. LNCS, vol. 2442, pp. 31–46. Springer, Heidelberg (2002). https://doi.org/10.1007/3-540-45708-9_3

[LST12] Landecker, W., Shrimpton, T., Terashima, R.S.: Tweakable blockciphers with beyond birthday-bound security. In: Safavi-Naini, R., Canetti, R. (eds.) CRYPTO 2012. LNCS, vol. 7417, pp. 14–30. Springer, Heidelberg (2012). https://doi.org/10.1007/978-3-642-32009-5_2

[Men15] Mennink, B.: Optimally secure tweakable blockciphers. In: Leander, G. (ed.) FSE 2015. LNCS, vol. 9054, pp. 428–448. Springer, Heidelberg (2015). https://doi.org/10.1007/978-3-662-48116-5_21

[Men18] Mennink, B.: Towards tight security of cascaded LRW2. In: Beimel, A., Dziembowski, S. (eds.) TCC 2018. LNCS, vol. 11240, pp. 192–222. Springer, Cham (2018). https://doi.org/10.1007/978-3-030-03810-6_8

[Min14] Minematsu, K.: Parallelizable rate-1 authenticated encryption from pseudorandom functions. In: Nguyen, P.Q., Oswald, E. (eds.) EUROCRYPT 2014. LNCS, vol. 8441, pp. 275–292. Springer, Heidelberg (2014). https://doi.org/10.1007/978-3-642-55220-5_16

[MN17] Mennink, B., Neves, S.: Encrypted Davies-Meyer and its dual: towards optimal security using mirror theory. In: Katz, J., Shacham, H. (eds.) CRYPTO 2017. LNCS, vol. 10403, pp. 556–583. Springer, Cham (2017). https://doi.org/10.1007/978-3-319-63697-9_19

[Nai15] Naito, Y.: Full PRF-secure message authentication code based on tweakable block cipher. In: Au, M.-H., Miyaji, A. (eds.) ProvSec 2015. LNCS, vol. 9451, pp. 167–182. Springer, Cham (2015). https://doi.org/10.1007/978-3-319-26059-4_9

[Nai18] Naito, Y.: On the efficiency of ZMAC-type modes. In: Camenisch, J., Papadimitratos, P. (eds.) CANS 2018. LNCS, vol. 11124, pp. 190–210. Springer, Cham (2018). https://doi.org/10.1007/978-3-030-00434-7_10

[Pat08] Patarin, J.: The "coefficients H" technique. In: Avanzi, R.M., Keliher, L., Sica, F. (eds.) SAC 2008. LNCS, vol. 5381, pp. 328–345. Springer, Heidelberg (2009). https://doi.org/10.1007/978-3-642-04159-4_21

[Pat10] Patarin, J.: Introduction to mirror theory: analysis of systems of linear equalities and linear non equalities for cryptography. IACR Cryptology ePrint Archive 2010/287 (2010)

[PS16] Peyrin, T., Seurin, Y.: Counter-in-tweak: authenticated encryption modes for tweakable block ciphers. In: Robshaw, M., Katz, J. (eds.) CRYPTO 2016. LNCS, vol. 9814, pp. 33–63. Springer, Heidelberg (2016). https://doi.org/10.1007/978-3-662-53018-4_2

[Rog95] Rogaway, P.: Bucket hashing and its application to fast message authentication. In: Coppersmith, D. (ed.) CRYPTO 1995. LNCS, vol. 963, pp. 29–42. Springer, Heidelberg (1995). https://doi.org/10.1007/3-540-44750-4_3

[Sib20] Sibleyras, F.: Generic attack on iterated tweakable FX constructions. In: Jarecki, S. (ed.) CT-RSA 2020. LNCS, vol. 12006, pp. 1–14. Springer, Cham (2020). https://doi.org/10.1007/978-3-030-40186-3_1

[SS17] Samajder, S., Sarkar, P.: Rigorous upper bounds on data complexities of block cipher cryptanalysis. J. Math. Cryptol. **11**(3), 147–175 (2017)

[WGZ+16] Wang, L., Guo, J., Zhang, G., Zhao, J., Gu, D.: How to build fully secure tweakable blockciphers from classical blockciphers. In: Cheon, J.H., Takagi, T. (eds.) ASIACRYPT 2016. LNCS, vol. 10031, pp. 455–483. Springer, Heidelberg (2016). https://doi.org/10.1007/978-3-662-53887-6_17

Symmetric Key Cryptography

Minimizing the Two-Round Tweakable Even-Mansour Cipher

Avijit Dutta[✉]

Institute for Advancing Intelligence, TCG-CREST, Kolkata, India
avirocks.dutta13@gmail.com

Abstract. In CRYPTO 2015, Cogliati et al. have proposed one-round tweakable Even-Mansour (1-TEM) cipher constructed out of a single n-bit public permutation π and a uniform and almost XOR-universal hash function H as $(k, t, x) \mapsto \mathsf{H}_k(t) \oplus \pi(\mathsf{H}_k(t) \oplus x)$, where t is the tweak, and x is the n-bit message. Authors have shown that its two-round extension, which we refer to as 2-TEM, obtained by cascading 2-independent instances of the construction gives $2n/3$-bit security and r-round cascading gives $rn/r+2$-bit security. In ASIACRYPT 2015, Cogliati and Seurin have shown that four-round tweakable Even-Mansour cipher, which we refer to as 4-TEM, constructed out of four independent n-bit permutations $\pi_1, \pi_2, \pi_3, \pi_4$ and two independent n-bit keys k_1, k_2, defined as

$$k_1 \oplus t \oplus \pi_4(k_2 \oplus t \oplus \pi_3(k_1 \oplus t \oplus \pi_2(k_2 \oplus t \oplus \pi_1(k_1 \oplus t \oplus x)))),$$

is secure upto $2^{2n/3}$ adversarial queries. In this paper, we have shown that if we replace two independent permutations of 2-TEM (Cogliati et al., CRYPTO 2015) with a single n-bit public permutation, then the resultant construction still guarantees security upto $2^{2n/3}$ adversarial queries. Using the results derived therein, we also show that replacing the permutation (π_4, π_3) with (π_1, π_2) in the above equation preserves security upto $2^{2n/3}$ adversarial queries.

Keywords: Tweakable block cipher · Key alternating cipher · Tweakable Even-Mansour cipher · H-Coefficient

1 Introduction

BLOCK CIPHER AND TWEAKABLE BLOCK CIPHER. A block cipher is a fundamental cryptographic primitive and a workhorse in symmetric key cryptography. A block cipher $\mathsf{E} : \mathcal{K} \times \mathcal{M} \to \mathcal{M}$ with key space $\mathcal{K}$ and message space $\mathcal{M}$ is a family of permutations over $\mathcal{M}$ indexed by key $k \in \mathcal{K}$. A tweakable block cipher (TBC) is similar to a block cipher except that it takes an additional public input parameter t, called *tweak*. The signature of a tweakable block cipher is $\widetilde{\mathsf{E}} : \mathcal{K} \times \mathcal{T} \times \mathcal{M} \to \mathcal{M}$ with key space $\mathcal{K}$, tweak space $\mathcal{T}$ and message space $\mathcal{M}$ such that for each $k \in \mathcal{K}$ and each tweak $t \in \mathcal{T}$, $m \mapsto \widetilde{\mathsf{E}}(k, t, m)$ is a permutation over $\mathcal{M}$. A block cipher is different from a tweakable block cipher in

© International Association for Cryptologic Research 2020
S. Moriai and H. Wang (Eds.): ASIACRYPT 2020, LNCS 12491, pp. 601–629, 2020.
https://doi.org/10.1007/978-3-030-64837-4_20

the sense that for each key k, the former is a permutation over $\mathcal{M}$ whereas the latter is a family of permutations over $\mathcal{M}$ indexed by $t \in \mathcal{T}$. The purpose of introducing tweak was to bring the inherent variability in the cipher in about the same way a nonce or an IV brings variability in a block cipher based encryption mode. After a rigorous formalization of tweakable block ciphers by Liskov, Rivest and Wagner [25], it has recently become one of the fundamental symmetric key primitives and has been found to be used in multiple applications like message authentication codes [8, 26, 32], length preserving tweakable enciphering mode [13, 18, 19, 40], online ciphers [1, 20, 37] and various authenticated encryption modes [25, 26, 34]. Offering higher security guarantee is one of the reasons that various cryptographic modes of operations are now build on top of a tweakable block cipher than conventional block ciphers [8, 26, 34].

Before the formalization of TBC by Liskov et al. [25], there were few tweakable block ciphers which were designed from scratch. For example, block ciphers like Hasty Pudding cipher [38], Mercy cipher [11], Threefish (which is used in Skein hash function [15]) natively supports tweaks. Along with the formalization of the primitive, Liskov et al. [25] also proposed two generic constructions of a TBC out of a conventional block cipher in a black-box fashion and proved their birthday bound security, i.e., when the adversary is allowed to make roughly $2^{n/2}$ queries to the encryption or decryption oracle, where n is the block size of the block cipher. Since then, designing TBC in a black-box mode (i.e., build from a standard block cipher) has become one of the main avenues of symmetric key research [4, 29, 36]. Recently, a number of beyond birthday bound secure constructions build on top of block ciphers have also been emerged [23, 24, 27, 30]. Security of all these constructions have been proven in the standard model (i.e., assuming that the underlying block cipher is a pseudorandom permutation), except for constructions proposed in [24, 27] that were analyzed in the ideal cipher model.

However, in the black box mode of TBC design, where changing the tweak enforces to change the key of the underlying block cipher [30], are tend to be avoided for efficiency reasons, as re-keying a block cipher is often a costly operation. Hence, most of the existing proposals of designing a TBC out of a block cipher have the property that changing the tweak should not alter the key of the block cipher. In this regard, LRW1 and LRW2, proposed by Liskov et al. [25], are two such examples of birthday bound secure TBC which are build on top of a conventional block cipher and do not have the re-keying issue. Later on, Landecker et al. [23] proposed a beyond birthday bound secure TBC designed on top of a block cipher by just simply cascading two independent instances of LRW2 construction. Authors of [23] have shown that cascaded LRW2 (CLRW2) is secure against any adaptive adversary that makes roughly at most $2^{2n/3}$ encryption and decryption queries[1]. This line of research was later extended by Lampe and Seurin [22], who showed $rn/r + 2$-bit security by cascading r-independent

---

[1] Later, a flaw in the security proof was found in the original paper of Landecker et al. [23], which was fixed by Procter [35]. However, a different way of fixing the proof was proposed by Landecker et al. in the revised version of [23].

LRW2 instances and they conjectured a tight $rn/r + 1$-bit security. Later on, Mennink [28] showed $3n/4$-bit tight security bound on CLRW2. However, Mennink's analysis is based on 4-wise independent almost-xor universal (axu) hash function and each tweak value should occur for at most $2^{n/4}$ times. These non-trivial bottlenecks are lifted in a recent work of Jha and Nandi [21].

TBC DESIGN FROM LOWER LEVEL PRIMITIVES. There have been several proposals of designing beyond the birthday bound TBC on top of a block cipher [23,24,27]. But unfortunately none of the them seem to be truly practical [9]. Thus, in an another line of work, researchers study how to build TBC from some lower level primitives like public permutations instead from a conventional block cipher. This was undertaken by Goldenberg et al. [16], who showed how to incorporate tweak in a feistel based cipher. This was later extended to generalized feistel ciphers by Iwata and Mitsuda [31]. In parallel to feistel based ciphers, a similar study was undertaken for iterated Even-Mansour (IEM) cipher [3,6], a super class of popular SPN based networks. An r-round iterated Even-Mansour cipher based on a tuple of r independent permutations $(\pi_1, \ldots, \pi_r)$ and a tuple of $r + 1$ independent keys $(k_0, \ldots, k_r)$ is defined as follows: for $x \in \{0,1\}^n$,

$$\mathsf{IEM}_{\mathbf{k}}^{\pi}(x) = k_r \oplus \pi_r(k_{r-1} \oplus \pi_{r-1}(\ldots \pi_2(k_1 \oplus \pi_1(k_0 \oplus x))\ldots)).$$

Similar to the feistel based designs, it is a natural quest to investigate how to incorporate tweaks in IEM cipher. In other words, how to mix the tweak and the key in an IEM cipher. We generally refer to this cipher as *Tweakable Even-Mansour* (TEM) cipher.

To address the question of incorporating tweaks in an IEM cipher, Cogliati and Seurin [10] and independently Farshim and Proecter [14] analyzed the simple case with n-bit key and n-bit tweak and showed that one can simply xor the tweak and the key in each round of IEM cipher to get a secure tweakable block cipher. However, they showed that such an approach gives no security for one and two rounds. Moreover, they had proved birthday bound security for three rounds and in fact, due to a result by Bellare and Kohno [2], it can be seen that xoring an n-bit tweak with an n-bit key in each round of IEM construction does not give security beyond the birthday bound. Therefore, to achieve beyond the birthday bound security, we should go for a complex mixing functions of tweak and key. Even if the function is linear, it should prevent the TBC construction from being of the form $\mathsf{E}(k \oplus t, m)$ for some block cipher E with n-bit key and n-bit tweak.

BEYOND BIRTHDAY BOUND TEM. Designing beyond the birthday bound secure TEM was first undertaken by Cogliati et al. [7]. They used almost-xor universal hash functions as mixing functions of key and tweak as shown in Fig. 1. In particular, the mixing function is of the form $\mathsf{H}_{k_i}(t)$, where k_i the key and t is the tweak.

Cogliati et al. have shown that one round TEM with non-linear mixing function gives $n/2$-bit security and 2-round gives $2n/3$-bit security. In general, they also gave a non-tight asymptotic security bound on r-round TEM with $rn/r+2$-

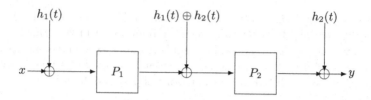

Fig. 1. 2-round tweakable Even-Mansour cipher with non-linear tweak and key mixing [7]. h_1, h_2 are two independent almost-xor universal hash functions.

bit security. Out of a particular relevance in this paper, we refer to Cogliati et al.'s 2-round TEM with non-linear mixing function as 2-TEM.

However, implementing an axu hash function might be costly [9]. For example multiplication based hashing [39] is a classic example of an axu hash function and implementing field multiplication is practically not efficient. Thus, a linear mixing function of key and tweak is always preferable over a non-linear one. Therefore, one would ask for whether it is possible to design a beyond birthday bound secure TEM with linear mixing function. In this regard, Cogliati and Seurin (CS) [9] have showed that with $2n$-bit keys and an n-bit tweak, one can realize a beyond the birthday bound secure TEM by simply xoring the key and the tweak in an alternating fashion in a 4-round IEM cipher (in the way as LED-128 [17] is designed) as depicted in Fig. 2. Again, out of a particular relevance in this paper, we refer to this construction as 4-TEM.

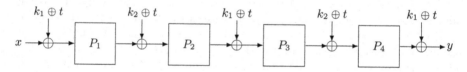

Fig. 2. 4-round tweakable Even-Mansour cipher with linear tweak and key mixing function [9]. k_1, k_2 are two independently sampled n-bit keys, t is an n-bit tweak and P_1, P_2, P_3, P_4 are independent n-bit public random permutations.

CS [9] have shown that 4-TEM gives $2n/3$-bit security. However, realizing a beyond birthday bound secure TEM with n-bit tweak and n-bit key is open till date.

We would like to mention here that all the existing beyond birthday bound secure TEM constructions use independent permutations. Iterated Even-Mansour (resp. Tweakable Even-Mansour) cipher stands as a theoretical model for formally arguing the security of SPN based block ciphers (resp. tweakable block ciphers). However, almost every constructions following SPN paradigm fix a permutation P and keeps iterating it for multiple times to generate the output. Thus, the theoretical abstractions for SPN based tweakable block ciphers where independent round permutations are used, deviates from practical instantiations.

Hence, it is natural to study the security of the TEM ciphers using a single permutation. In this regard, Chen et al. [5] studied the beyond birthday bound security of single permutation based two-round iterated Even-Mansour cipher. Hence, it is natural to investigate whether we can design a single permutation based TEM cipher that achieves beyond the birthday bound security.

OUR CONTRIBUTION. Inspired from the work of Chen et al. [5], we study the security of single permutation based 2-TEM cipher. In particular, we study the security of 2-TEM, as depicted in Fig. 1, where $P_1 = P_2 = \pi$, π is an n-bit public random permutation. We show that single permutation based 2-TEM construction is secure against all adversaries that make roughly $2^{2n/3}$ queries. As a second part of the contribution, we have also reduced the number of permutations from four to two in 4-TEM and show that the resulting construction is secure against any adversaries that make roughly $2^{2n/3}$ queries. In particular, we study the beyond birthday bound security of 4-TEM as depicted in Fig. 2, where $P_1 = P_4 = \pi_1$ and $P_2 = P_3 = \pi_2$, π_1 and π_2 are two independent n-bit public random permutations (Fig. 3).

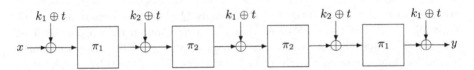

Fig. 3. 4-round tweakable Even-Mansour cipher with linear tweak and key mixing function. k_1, k_2 are two independently sampled n-bit keys, t is an n-bit tweak and π_1 and π_2 are independent n-bit public random permutations.

However, we would like to mention here that for both of our contributions, we have not reduced the number of independent keys used in the construction, i.e., for 2-TEM, we require two independent hash keys and for 4-TEM we require two independent n-bit keys. A natural open problem is to investigate that whether one can reduce the number of keys of the construction as well without degrading the security.

2   Preliminaries

BASIC NOTATIONS. For a set $\mathcal{X}$, $x \leftarrow_\$ \mathcal{X}$ denotes that x is sampled uniformly at random from $\mathcal{X}$ and is independent to all other random variables defined so far. For any natural number q, $[q]$ denotes the set $\{1, \ldots, q\}$. We denote an empty set as ϕ. We say two sets $\mathcal{X}$ and $\mathcal{Y}$ are disjoint if $\mathcal{X} \cap \mathcal{Y} = \phi$. We denote their union as $\mathcal{X} \sqcup \mathcal{Y}$ (which we refer to as *disjoint union*). Let $\mathfrak{X} = (\mathcal{X}_1, \ldots, \mathcal{X}_s)$ be a finite collection of finite sets. We say $\mathfrak{X}$ is a *disjoint collection* if for each $j \neq j' \in [s]$, $\mathcal{X}_j$ and $\mathcal{X}_{j'}$ are disjoint. The size of $\mathfrak{X}$, denoted as $|\mathfrak{X}| = |\mathcal{X}_1| + \ldots + |\mathcal{X}_s|$. For a disjoint collection $\mathfrak{X} = (\mathcal{X}_1, \ldots, \mathcal{X}_s, \mathcal{X}_{s+1})$, we write $\mathfrak{X} \setminus \mathcal{X}_s$ to denote the collection $(\mathcal{X}_1, \ldots, \mathcal{X}_s)$. For two disjoint collections $\mathfrak{X} = (\mathcal{X}_1, \ldots, \mathcal{X}_s)$ and

$\mathfrak{Y} = (\mathcal{Y}_1, \ldots, \mathcal{Y}_{s'})$, we say $\mathfrak{X}$ is *inter disjoint* with $\mathfrak{Y}$ if for all $j \in [s], j' \in [s']$, $\mathcal{X}_j$ is disjoint with $\mathcal{Y}_{j'}$. If $\mathfrak{X}$ is inter disjoint with $\mathfrak{Y}$, then we denote their union as $\mathfrak{X} \sqcup \mathfrak{Y}$. Moreover, $|\mathfrak{X} \sqcup \mathfrak{Y}| = |\mathfrak{X}| + |\mathfrak{Y}|$. For a set $\mathcal{S}$ and for a finite disjoint collection of finite sets $\mathfrak{X} = (\mathcal{X}_1, \ldots, \mathcal{X}_s)$, we write $\mathcal{S} \setminus \mathfrak{X}$ to denote $\mathcal{S} \setminus (\mathcal{X}_1 \sqcup \ldots \sqcup \mathcal{X}_s)$. For a tuple $\widetilde{x} = (x_1, x_2, \ldots, x_q)$, where each $x_i \in \mathcal{S}$ for some finite set $\mathcal{S}$, $\delta_{\widetilde{x}}(x)$ denotes the number of times $x \in \mathcal{S}$ appears in the tuple $\widetilde{x}$.

For any natural number n, $\{0, 1\}^n$ denotes the set of all binary strings of length n. We denote $|\{0, 1\}^n|$ as $N = 2^n$ throughout the paper. For integers $1 \leq b \leq a$, $(a)_b$ denotes $a(a-1) \ldots (a-b+1)$, where $(a)_0 = 1$ by convention. We denote the set of all n-bit permutations π as $\mathcal{P}_n$. Let $\mathcal{Z}_1 = (z_1^1, \ldots, z_q^1)$ and $\mathcal{Z}_2 = (z_1^2, \ldots, z_q^2)$ be two finite tuples of length q such that for each $i \in [q]$, $z_i^1, z_i^2 \in \{0, 1\}^n$. We say an n bit permutation $\pi \in \mathcal{P}_n$ maps $\mathcal{Z}_1$ to $\mathcal{Z}_2$, denoted as $\mathcal{Z}_1 \overset{\pi}{\mapsto} \mathcal{Z}_2$, if for all $i \in [q]$, $\pi(z_i^1) = z_i^2$. We say $\mathcal{Z}_1$ is *permutation compatible* to $\mathcal{Z}_2$ if there exists at least one $\pi \in \mathcal{P}_n$ such that $\mathcal{Z}_1 \overset{\pi}{\mapsto} \mathcal{Z}_2$.

For a given tuple of ordered pairs $\mathcal{Q} = ((x_1, y_1), \ldots, (x_q, y_q))$, where each x_i are pairwise distinct n-bit strings and each y_i are pairwise distinct n bit strings, we define the following two sets: $\mathsf{Dom}(\mathcal{Q}) = \{x_i \in \{0, 1\}^n : (x_i, y_i) \in \mathcal{Q}\}$ and $\mathsf{Ran}(\mathcal{Q}) = \{y_i \in \{0, 1\}^n : (x_i, y_i) \in \mathcal{Q}\}$. Clearly, $|\mathsf{Dom}(\mathcal{Q})| = |\mathsf{Ran}(\mathcal{Q})| = q$. We say that an n-bit permutation $\pi \in \mathcal{P}_n$ extends $\mathcal{Q}$, which we denote as $\pi \mapsto \mathcal{Q}$, if for all $i \in [q], \pi(x_i) = y_i$. We say that $\mathcal{Q}$ is *extendable* if there exists at least one $\pi \in \mathcal{P}_n$ such that $\pi \mapsto \mathcal{Q}$. One can naturally generalize this *extendable* notion for more than one tuple of ordered pairs. Let $\widetilde{\mathcal{Q}} = (\mathcal{Q}_1, \ldots, \mathcal{Q}_s)$ such that for each $j \in [s]$, $\mathcal{Q}_j$ is defined as $\mathcal{Q}_j = ((x_1^j, y_1^j), \ldots, (x_{q_j}^j, y_{q_j}^j))$, where each x_i^j are pairwise distinct n-bit strings and each y_i^j are pairwise distinct n-bit strings. Now, for each $j \in [s]$, we define the following two sets: $\mathsf{Dom}(\mathcal{Q}_j) = \{x_i^j : (x_i^j, y_i^j) \in \mathcal{Q}_j\}$ and $\mathsf{Ran}(\mathcal{Q}_j) = \{y_i^j : (x_i^j, y_i^j) \in \mathcal{Q}_j\}$. Clearly, for each $j \in [s]$, $|\mathsf{Dom}(\mathcal{Q}_j)| = |\mathsf{Ran}(\mathcal{Q}_j)| = q_j$. We say that an n-bit permutation $\pi \in \mathcal{P}_n$ extends $\widetilde{\mathcal{Q}}$, which we denote as $\pi \mapsto \widetilde{\mathcal{Q}}$, if for all $j \in [s], \pi \mapsto \mathcal{Q}_j$. For the sake of notational simplicity, we will be using the following: if for all $j \neq j' \in [s]$, $\mathsf{Dom}(\mathcal{Q}_j)$ is disjoint with $\mathsf{Dom}(\mathcal{Q}_{j'})$ and $\mathsf{Ran}(\mathcal{Q}_j)$ is disjoint with $\mathsf{Ran}(\mathcal{Q}_{j'})$, then $\mathfrak{X} = (\mathsf{Dom}(\mathcal{Q}_1), \ldots, \mathsf{Dom}(\mathcal{Q}_s))$ and $\mathfrak{Y} = (\mathsf{Ran}(\mathcal{Q}_1), \ldots, \mathsf{Ran}(\mathcal{Q}_s))$ becomes two disjoint collection of finite sets and in that case, as an alternative notation of $\pi \mapsto \widetilde{\mathcal{Q}}$, we write $\mathfrak{X} \overset{\pi}{\mapsto} \mathfrak{Y}$. If $\mathcal{S} = \{s_1, \ldots, s_q\} \subseteq \{0, 1\}^n$ and $\mathcal{D} = \{d_1, \ldots, d_q\} \subseteq \{0, 1\}^n$ are two finite sets of equal cardinality, then we write $(\mathcal{S}, \mathcal{D})$ to denote the sequence of ordered pairs: $((s_1, d_1), \ldots, (s_q, d_q))$.

2.1 A Simple Result on Probability

Having set up the basic notations, in this section, we state two simple yet useful probability results that we will be frequently using while proving the security of the construction.

Proposition 1. *Let* $\widetilde{Q} = (\mathcal{Q}_1, \ldots, \mathcal{Q}_{s+1})$ *be an* $s+1$ *tuple of ordered pairs such that for* $j \in [s+1]$, $\mathcal{Q}_j$ *is defined as* $\mathcal{Q}_j = ((x_1^j, y_1^j), \ldots, (x_{q_j}^j, y_{q_j}^j))$. *Moreover, for each* $j, j' \in [s+1]$, $\mathsf{Dom}(\mathcal{Q}_j) \cap \mathsf{Dom}(\mathcal{Q}_{j'}) = \phi$ *and* $\mathsf{Ran}(\mathcal{Q}_j) \cap \mathsf{Ran}(\mathcal{Q}_{j'}) = \phi$.

Therefore, $\mathfrak{X} = (\mathsf{Dom}(\mathcal{Q}_1), \ldots, \mathsf{Dom}(\mathcal{Q}_{s+1}))$ *and* $\mathfrak{Y} = (\mathsf{Ran}(\mathcal{Q}_1), \ldots, \mathsf{Ran}(\mathcal{Q}_{s+1}))$ *be two disjoint collection of finite sets such that for each* $j \in [s+1]$, $|\mathsf{Dom}(\mathcal{Q}_j)| = |\mathsf{Ran}(\mathcal{Q}_j)| = q_j$. *Then, we have*

$$\Pr[\pi \leftarrow_\$ \mathcal{P}_n : \mathfrak{X} \backslash \mathsf{Dom}(\mathcal{Q}_{s+1}) \overset{\pi}{\mapsto} \mathfrak{Y} \backslash \mathsf{Ran}(\mathcal{Q}_{s+1}) \mid \pi \mapsto \mathcal{Q}_{s+1}] = \frac{1}{(N - q_{s+1})_{q_1 + \ldots + q_s}}.$$

By setting $s = 1$ in the above proposition gives the following simple corollary:

Corollary 1. *For two sets* $\mathcal{Q}_1$ *and* $\mathcal{Q}_2$, *where* $\mathcal{Q}_1 = ((x_1^1, y_1^1), \ldots, (x_{q_1}^1, y_{q_1}^1))$ *of cardinality* q_1 *and* $\mathcal{Q}_2 = ((x_1^2, y_1^2), \ldots, (x_{q_2}^2, y_{q_2}^2))$ *of cardinality* q_2, *such that* $\mathsf{Dom}(\mathcal{Q}_1) \cap \mathsf{Dom}(\mathcal{Q}_2) = \phi$ *and* $\mathsf{Ran}(\mathcal{Q}_1) \cap \mathsf{Ran}(\mathcal{Q}_2) = \phi$. *Then, we have*

$$\Pr[\pi \leftarrow_\$ \mathcal{P}_n : \pi \mapsto \mathcal{Q}_1 \mid \pi \mapsto \mathcal{Q}_2] = \frac{1}{(N - q_2)_{q_1}}.$$

2.2   Security Definition

In this section, we recall the security definition of tweakable block ciphers, almost xor universal hash function and tweakable Even Mansour cipher.

TWEAKABLE BLOCK CIPHERS. A *tweakable block cipher* (TBC) with key space $\mathcal{K}$, tweak space $\mathcal{T}$ and domain $\mathcal{X}$ is a mapping $\widetilde{\mathsf{E}} : \mathcal{K} \times \mathcal{T} \times \mathcal{X} \rightarrow \mathcal{X}$ such that for all key $k \in \mathcal{K}$ and all tweak $t \in \mathcal{T}$, $x \mapsto \widetilde{\mathsf{E}}(k, t, x)$ is a permutation of $\mathcal{X}$. We denote $\mathsf{TBC}(\mathcal{K}, \mathcal{T}, \mathcal{X})$ the set of all tweakable block ciphers with tweak space $\mathcal{T}$ and message space $\mathcal{X}$. A *tweakable permutation* with tweak space $\mathcal{T}$ and domain $\mathcal{X}$ is a mapping $\widetilde{\pi} : \mathcal{T} \times \mathcal{X} \rightarrow \mathcal{X}$ such that for all tweak $t \in \mathcal{T}$, $x \mapsto \widetilde{\pi}(t, x)$ is a permutation of $\mathcal{X}$. We write $\mathsf{TP}(\mathcal{T}, n)$ denotes the set of all tweakable permutations with tweak space $\mathcal{T}$ and n-bit messages.

AXU, UNIVERSAL AND ALMOST REGULAR HASH FUNCTION. Let $\mathcal{K}_h$ and $\mathcal{X}$ be two non-empty finite sets and H be a keyed function $\mathsf{H} : \mathcal{K}_h \times \mathcal{X} \rightarrow \{0,1\}^n$. Then, (i) H is said to be an ϵ-almost xor universal hash function if for any distinct $x, x' \in \mathcal{X}$ and for any $\Delta \in \{0,1\}^n$,

$$\Pr[k_h \leftarrow_\$ \mathcal{K}_h : \mathsf{H}_{k_h}(x) \oplus \mathsf{H}_{k_h}(x') = \Delta] \leq \epsilon.$$

H is said to be an ϵ-almost regular hash function if for any $x \in \mathcal{X}$ and for any $\Delta \in \{0,1\}^n$,

$$\Pr[k_h \leftarrow_\$ \mathcal{K}_h : \mathsf{H}_{k_h}(x) = \Delta] \leq \epsilon.$$

TWEAKABLE EVEN-MANSOUR. We first fix some integer $n, r \geq 1$. Let $\mathcal{K}$ and $\mathcal{T}$ be two non-empty finite sets and let $\Psi = (\Psi_0, \ldots, \Psi_r)$ be $r + 1$-tuple of functions from $\mathcal{K} \times \mathcal{T}$ to $\{0,1\}^n$. Then, an r-round tweakable Even-Mansour cipher $\mathsf{TEM}[n, r, \Psi]$, constructed from a r-tuple of n-bit independent permutations $\pi = (\pi_1, \ldots, \pi_r)$, specifies a tweakble block cipher, with key space $\mathcal{K}$, tweak space $\mathcal{T}$ and message space $\{0,1\}^n$, denoted as TEM^π that maps a key $\mathbf{k}$, tweak $\mathbf{t}$ and a plaintext $x \in \{0,1\}^n$ to the ciphertext defined as:

$$\mathsf{TEM}^\pi(\mathbf{k}, \mathbf{t}, x) = \Psi_r(\mathbf{k}, \mathbf{t}) \oplus \pi_r(\ldots \pi_2(\Psi_1(\mathbf{k}, \mathbf{t}) \oplus \pi_1(\Psi_0(\mathbf{k}, \mathbf{t}) \oplus x)) \ldots). \quad (1)$$

Note that, 2-TEM is a special class of Eq. (1) where $r = 2$, $\mathbf{k} = (k_1, k_2)$ and $\Psi_0(\mathbf{k}, t) = H_{k_1}(t), \Psi_1(\mathbf{k}, t) = H_{k_1}(t) \oplus H_{k_2}(t)$ and $\Psi_2(\mathbf{k}, t) = H_{k_2}(t)$, where $H = \{H_{k_h}\}_{k_h \in \mathcal{K}_h}$ is a family of almost-xor universal and almost-regular hash functions that maps elements from $\mathcal{T}$ to $\{0, 1\}^n$. Similarly, 4-TEM is a special class of Eq. (1) where $r = 4$, $\mathbf{k} = (k_1, k_2)$ and $\Psi_0(\mathbf{k}, t) = k_1 \oplus t, \Psi_2(\mathbf{k}, t) = k_2 \oplus t, \Psi_3(\mathbf{k}, t) = k_1 \oplus t, \Psi_4(\mathbf{k}, t) = k_2 \oplus t$ and $\Psi_5(\mathbf{k}, t) = k_1 \oplus t$.

SECURITY DEFINITION OF TEM. We study the indistinguishability of r-round tweakable Even-Mansour construction $\mathsf{TEM}[n, r, H]$ in the random permutation model where we consider an adaptive distinghisher A that interacts with a tuple of $r + 1$ oracles $(\widetilde{\mathcal{O}}, \boldsymbol{\pi})$, where $\widetilde{\mathcal{O}}$ is a tweakable permutations with tweak space $\mathcal{T}$ and message space $\{0, 1\}^n$ and $\boldsymbol{\pi} = (\pi_1, \ldots, \pi_r)$ are n-bit public random permutations. The goal of the distinguisher is to distinguish between the following two worlds: in the real world it interacts with the oracle $(\mathsf{TEM}_{\mathbf{k}}^{\boldsymbol{\pi}}, \boldsymbol{\pi})$, where the key $\mathbf{k}$ is sampled uniformly at random from some finite key space $\mathcal{K}$. In the ideal world, it interacts with $(\widetilde{\pi}_0, \boldsymbol{\pi})$, where $\widetilde{\pi}_0$ is uniformly sampled from $\mathsf{TP}(\mathcal{T}, n)$ and $\boldsymbol{\pi}$ is a tuple of n-bit public random permutations independent of $\widetilde{\pi}_0$. We refer $\mathsf{TEM}_{\mathbf{k}}^{\boldsymbol{\pi}}/\widetilde{\pi}_0$ as the construction oracle and $\boldsymbol{\pi}$ as the primitive oracles. We assume that A is not only adaptive, but is also bi-directional (i.e., it can make forward and inverse queries to its oracle). Moreover, A is also allowed to query the primitive oracles in an interleave fashion with the construction oracle queries. We define the strong tweakable pseudo-random permutation (stprp) advantage of $\mathsf{TEM}[n, r, \Psi]$ as

$$\mathbf{Adv}_{\mathsf{TEM}}^{\mathrm{tsprp}}(A) \overset{\Delta}{=} |\ \Pr[A^{(\mathsf{TEM}_{\mathbf{k}}^{\boldsymbol{\pi}}, \boldsymbol{\pi})} \Rightarrow 1] - \Pr[A^{(\widetilde{\pi}_0, \boldsymbol{\pi})} \Rightarrow 1]\ |, \qquad (2)$$

where $A^{\mathcal{O}} \Rightarrow 1$ denotes the event that A outputs 1 after interacting with the oracle $\mathcal{O}$. The first probability in Eq. (2) is defined over the randomness of $\mathbf{k}$ and $\boldsymbol{\pi}$, whereas the second probability is defined over the randomness of $\widetilde{\pi}_0$ and $\boldsymbol{\pi}$. In the rest of the paper we assume that A is computationally unbounded and hence a deterministic distinguisher. We call such a distinguisher as *information theoretic* distinguisher. We also assume that A does not repeat queries and never makes pointless queries[2]. As we study the security analysis of single permutation variant of 2-TEM and two independent permutations variant of 4-TEM, from now onwards, we concentrate on only these two constructions.

2.3   H-Coefficient Technique

H-Coefficient technique [6,33] is an important tool to upper bound the statistical distance between the answers of two interactive systems and is typically used to prove the information theoretic pseudo randomness of constructions. We discuss this result in the light of tweakable Even-Mansour cipher. Let us consider an information theoretic deterministic distinguisher A with access to the following tuple of oracles: in the real world it interacts with $(\mathsf{TEM}_{\mathbf{k}}^{\boldsymbol{\pi}}, \boldsymbol{\pi})$ and in the ideal world it interacts with $(\widetilde{\pi}_0, \boldsymbol{\pi})$. After this interaction is over, A outputs a decision

---

[2] Queries whose answer can be deduced from previous query-responses.

bit. The collection of all queries and responses that is made to and from the oracle during the interaction of A with $\mathcal{O}$, is summarized in a transcript (τ_c, τ_p), where τ_c is the transcript that summarizes the interaction with construction oracle and τ_p summarizes the interaction with primitive oracles. More formally, $\tau_c = \{(t_1, x_1, y_1), \ldots, (t_q, x_q, y_q)\}$ is the set of all construction queries and responses and $\tau_p = \{(u_1, v_1), \ldots, (u_p, v_p)\}$ is the set of all primitive queries and responses, where A makes q construction queries and p primitive queries. Since A is bi-directional, A can make either forward construction query (t, x) and receives response y or can make inverse construction query (t, y) and receives response x. Similarly, for primitive query A can either make forward query u to its primitive π and receives response y or can make inverse query v to π^{-1} and receives response u. Since, we assume that A never makes pointless queries, none of the transcripts contain any duplicate elements. We also assume that A repeats tweaks in the construction query. Hence, we assume that there are μ distinct tweaks $(t_1, t_2, \ldots, t_\mu)$ in the set of construction queries and q_i denotes the number of construction queries with i-th tweak such that

$$\sum_{i=1}^{\mu} q_i = q.$$

We modify the experiment by releasing internal information to A after it has finished the interaction but has not output yet the decision bit. In the real world, we reveal the key $\mathbf{k}$ which is used in the construction and in the ideal world, we sample a dummy key $\mathbf{k}$ uniformly at random from the keyspace and reveal it to the distinguisher. In all the following, the complete transcript is $(\tau_c, \tau_p, \mathbf{k})$. Note that, the modified experiment only makes the distinguisher more powerful and hence the distinguishing advantage of A in this experiment is no way less than its distinguishing advantage in the former one.

Let D_{re} (resp. D_{id}) denotes the random variable representing the real world and the ideal world transcript respectively. The probability of realizing a transcript $(\tau_c, \tau_p, \mathbf{k})$ in the ideal (resp. real) world is called *ideal (resp. real) interpolation probability*. A transcript $(\tau_c, \tau_p, \mathbf{k})$ is said to be *attainable* with respect to A if its ideal interpolation probability is non zero. We denote the set of all such attainable transcripts by Θ. Following these notations, we state the main theorem of H-Coefficient Technique as follows.

Theorem 1 (H-Coefficient Technique). *Let* $\Theta = \Theta_g \sqcup \Theta_b$ *be some partition of the set of attainable transcripts. Suppose there exists* $\epsilon_{ratio} \geq 0$ *such that for any* $\tau = (\tau_c, \tau_p, \mathbf{k}) \in \Theta_g$,

$$\frac{\mathsf{p}_{re}(\tau)}{\mathsf{p}_{id}(\tau)} \triangleq \frac{\Pr[D_{re} = \tau]}{\Pr[D_{id} = \tau]} \geq 1 - \epsilon_{ratio},$$

and there exists $\epsilon_{bad} \geq 0$ *such that* $\Pr[D_{id} \in \Theta_b] \leq \epsilon_{bad}$. *Then,*

$$\mathbf{Adv}_{\mathsf{TEM}}^{\mathsf{tsprp}}(A) \leq \epsilon_{ratio} + \epsilon_{bad}. \tag{3}$$

Having explained the H-Coefficient technique in the view of our construction, we now state the following result from [7,9].

Lemma 1. *Let* $\tau = (\tau_c, \tau_p, \mathbf{k}) \in \Theta$ *be an attainable transcript. Let* $\mathsf{p}(\tau) \triangleq \Pr[\pi \leftarrow_\$ \mathcal{P}_n : \mathrm{TEM}_{\mathbf{k}}^{\pi} \mapsto \tau_c \mid \pi \mapsto \tau_p]$. *Then, we have*

$$\frac{\mathsf{p}_{\mathsf{re}}(\tau)}{\mathsf{p}_{\mathsf{id}}(\tau)} = \mathsf{p}(\tau) \cdot \prod_{i=1}^{\mu} (N)_{q_i}$$

Therefore, to apply Theorem 1, for a properly defined good transcript τ, we need to compare $\mathsf{p}(\tau)$ and $\prod_{i=1}^{\mu} (N)_{q_i}$.

2.4   Sum Capture Lemma

In this section, we state an important probabilistic result, dubbed as *sum capture lemma*. In the following, we state two variants of the sum-capture lemma. The first variant will be used in the security proof of single permutation variant of 2-TEM and the other variant will be used in the security proof of two independent permutations variant of 4-TEM.

SUM-CAPTURE LEMMA-VARIANT I. We use the sum capture lemma by Chen et al. [5]. Informally, the result states that for a random subset $\mathcal{S}$ of $\{0,1\}^n$ of size q_0 and for any two arbitrary subsets $\mathcal{A}$ and $\mathcal{B}$ of $\{0,1\}^n$, the size of the set

$$\mu(\mathcal{S}, \mathcal{A}, \mathcal{B}) \triangleq |\{(s, a, b) \in \mathcal{S} \times \mathcal{A} \times \mathcal{B} : s = a \oplus b\}|,$$

is at most $q_0|\mathcal{A}||\mathcal{B}|/N$, except with negligible probability.

Lemma 2 (Sum-Capture Lemma). *Let* $n, q_0 \in \mathbb{N}$ *such that* $9n \leq q_0 \leq N/2$. *Let* $\mathcal{S}$ *be a random subset of* $\{0,1\}^n$ *of size* q_0. *Then, for any two subsets* $\mathcal{A}$ *and* $\mathcal{B}$ *of* $\{0,1\}^n$, *we have*

$$\Pr[\exists \mathcal{A}, \mathcal{B} : \mu(\mathcal{S}, \mathcal{A}, \mathcal{B}) \geq \frac{q_0|\mathcal{A}||\mathcal{B}|}{N} + \frac{2q_0^2\sqrt{|\mathcal{A}||\mathcal{B}|}}{N} + 3\sqrt{nq_0|\mathcal{A}||\mathcal{B}|}] \leq \frac{2}{N}, \quad (4)$$

where the randomness is defined over the set $\mathcal{S}$.

SUM-CAPTURE LEMMA-VARIANT II. We use the sum capture lemma by Cogliati et al. [9], which is dubbed as *Extended Sum-Capture Lemma* [9]. Informally, the result states that for a fixed automorphism Φ and a probabilistic adversary A, the size of the set

$$\mu(\mathcal{Q}, \mathcal{U}, \mathcal{V}) \triangleq |\{((t, x, y), u, v) \in \mathcal{Q} \times \mathcal{U} \times \mathcal{V} : x \oplus u = \Phi(y \oplus v)\}|,$$

is at most $q|\mathcal{U}||\mathcal{V}|/N$, except with negligible probability, where the set $\mathcal{Q} = \{(t_1, x_1, y_1), \ldots, (t_q, x_q, y_q)\}$ denotes the interaction of A with an uniform random tweakable permutation $\tilde{\pi}$.

Lemma 3 (Extended Sum-Capture Lemma). *Let Φ be a fixed automorphism and $\mathcal{T}$ be a fixed non-empty finite set. Let $\widetilde{\pi}$ be a uniform tweakable random permutation in $\mathsf{TP}(\mathcal{T}, n)$ and A be some probabilistic adversary that makes two sided adaptive queries to $\widetilde{\pi}$. Let $\mathcal{Q} = \{(t_1, x_1, y_1), \ldots, (t_q, x_q, y_q)\}$ be the transcript of the interaction of A with $\widetilde{\pi}$ and for any two subsets $\mathcal{U} \subseteq \{0,1\}^n, \mathcal{V} \subseteq \{0,1\}^n$, let us define*

$$\mu(\mathcal{Q}, \mathcal{U}, \mathcal{V}) \triangleq |\{((t, x, y), u, v) \in \mathcal{Q} \times \mathcal{U} \times \mathcal{V} : x \oplus u = \Phi(y \oplus v)\}|.$$

Then, for $9n \leq q \leq N/2$, we have

$$\Pr[\exists \mathcal{U}, \mathcal{V} : \mu(\mathcal{Q}, \mathcal{U}, \mathcal{V}) \geq \frac{q|\mathcal{U}||\mathcal{V}|}{N} + \frac{2q^2\sqrt{|\mathcal{U}||\mathcal{V}|}}{N} + 3\sqrt{nq|\mathcal{U}||\mathcal{V}|}] \leq \frac{2}{N}, \quad (5)$$

where the randomness is defined over the set $\mathcal{Q}$ and the random coin of A.

When we apply Lemma 3 in our security analysis, we consider the automorphism Φ to be an identity function.

3   BBB Security of Single Permutation Variant of 2-TEM

3.1   Security Statement

In this section, we state the security result of single permutation based 2-TEM cipher. Let H be a family of ϵ-almost-xor universal and ϵ-almost-regular hash functions that maps elements from tweak space $\mathcal{T}$ to $\{0,1\}^n$. Then, single permutation based 2-TEM is defined as

$$\text{2-TEM}_{h_1, h_2}^{\pi}(t, x) = \pi(\pi(x \oplus h_1(t)) \oplus h_1(t) \oplus h_2(t)) \oplus h_2(t) = y,$$

where $\pi \in \mathcal{P}_n$ is an n-bit public random permutation, $(h_1, h_2) \leftarrow\!\!\$\, \mathsf{H}^2$ are two independently sampled hash functions, $t \in \mathcal{T}$ is the tweak and $x \in \{0,1\}^n$ is the plaintext. For convenience, we refer the single permutation based 2-TEM construction as 2-TEM$^+$. The main result of this section is to prove the following:

Theorem 2. *Let A be any adaptive deterministic distinguisher that makes q many construction queries with μ distinct tweaks and p many primitive queries in both the forward and the backward directions. Let H be an ϵ-almost-xor universal and ϵ-almost regular hash function that maps elements from tweak space $\mathcal{T}$ to $\{0,1\}^n$. Then,*

$$\mathbf{Adv}_{\text{2-TEM}^+}^{\text{tsprp}}(\mathsf{A}) \leq \left(\frac{3qp^2}{N^2} + \frac{2pq^2}{N^2} + \frac{5q^3}{3N^2} + \frac{6p\sqrt{q}}{N} + \frac{11q^{3/2}}{N} + \frac{14q}{N^{2/3}} + \frac{38q^2}{N^{4/3}} + \frac{6q}{N}\right.$$

$$\left. + \frac{4q(p + 6\sqrt{q} + 3q)^2}{N^2} + \frac{24\sqrt{nq}}{N^{1/3}} + \frac{48\sqrt{q}}{N^{1/3}}\right).$$

In particular, if the almost-xor universal and the almost-regular advantage of H is roughly 2^{-n}, then one can see that 2-TEM$^+$ is secure roughly upto $2^{2n/3}$ adversarial queries.

In the rest of the section we prove Theorem 2. Our security proof relies on H-Coefficient technique. As a result, the first step of our proof would be to identify bad transcripts and upper bound their probability in the ideal world. Followed by this, we will show that for a good transcript τ, its real interpolation probability is very close to its ideal interpolation probability.

3.2   Definition and Probability of Bad Transcripts

In this section, we define and bound the probability of bad transcripts in the ideal world. For a transcript $\tau = (\tau_c, \tau_p, k_1, k_2)$, we define $U = \mathsf{Dom}(\tau_p)$, the domain of primitive queries and $V = \mathsf{Ran}(\tau_p)$, the range of primitive queries. Moreover, for a pair of keys (k_1, k_2) and for any $t \in \mathcal{T}$, we write $h_1(t)$ to denote $\mathsf{H}_{k_1}(t)$ and $h_2(t)$ to denote $\mathsf{H}_{k_2}(t)$. For a transcript $\tau = (\tau_c, \tau_p, k_1, k_2)$, we associate the following parameters:

$$\alpha_1 \stackrel{\Delta}{=} |\{(t, x, y) \in \tau_c : x \oplus h_1(t) \in U\}|$$
$$\alpha_2 \stackrel{\Delta}{=} |\{(t, x, y) \in \tau_c : y \oplus h_2(t) \in V\}|$$
$$\beta_1 \stackrel{\Delta}{=} |\{(t, x, y) \neq (t', x', y') \in \tau_c : x \oplus h_1(t) = x' \oplus h_1(t')\}|$$
$$\beta_2 \stackrel{\Delta}{=} |\{(t, x, y) \neq (t', x', y') \in \tau_c : y \oplus h_2(t) = y' \oplus h_2(t')\}|$$

Definition 1 (Bad Transcript). *An attainable transcript $\tau' = (\tau_c, \tau_p, k_1, k_2)$ is called a **bad** transcript if any one of the following condition holds:*

- B.1: $\exists\ i \in [q], j, j' \in [p]$ such that $x_i \oplus h_1(t_i) = u_j, y_i \oplus h_2(t_i) = v_{j'}$.
- B.2: $\exists\ i \in [q], j, j' \in [p]$ such that $x_i \oplus h_1(t_i) = u_j, v_j \oplus h_1(t_i) \oplus h_2(t_i) = u_{j'}$.
- B.3: $\exists\ i \in [q], j, j' \in [p]$ such that $y_i \oplus h_2(t_i) = v_j, u_j \oplus h_1(t_i) \oplus h_2(t_i) = v_{j'}$.
- B.4: $\exists\ i, i' \in [q], j \in [p]$ such that $x_i \oplus h_1(t_i) = u_j, v_j \oplus h_1(t_i) \oplus h_2(t_i) = x_{i'} \oplus h_1(t_{i'})$.
- B.5: $\exists\ i, i' \in [q], j \in [p]$ such that $y_i \oplus h_2(t_i) = v_j, u_j \oplus h_1(t_i) \oplus h_2(t_i) = y_{i'} \oplus h_2(t_{i'})$.
- B.6: $\exists\ i, i' \in [q], j \in [p]$ such that $x_i \oplus h_1(t_i) = u_j, y_i \oplus h_2(t_i) = y_{i'} \oplus h_2(t_{i'})$.
- B.7: $\exists\ i, i' \in [q], j \in [p]$ such that $y_i \oplus h_2(t_i) = v_j, x_i \oplus h_1(t_i) = x_{i'} \oplus h_1(t_{i'})$.
- B.8: $\exists\ i, i' \in [q]$ such that $x_i \oplus h_1(t_i) = x_{i'} \oplus h_1(t_{i'}), h_1(t_i) \oplus h_2(t_i) = h_1(t_{i'}) \oplus h_2(t_{i'})$.
- B.9: $\exists\ i, i' \in [q]$ such that $y_i \oplus h_2(t_i) = y_{i'} \oplus h_2(t_{i'}), h_1(t_i) \oplus h_2(t_i) = h_1(t_{i'}) \oplus h_2(t_{i'})$.
- B.10: $\exists\ i, i', i'' \in [q]$ such that $x_i \oplus h_1(t_i) = x_{i'} \oplus h_1(t_{i'}), y_i \oplus h_2(t_i) = y_{i''} \oplus h_2(t_{i''})$.
- B.11: $\exists\ i, i' \in [q], j, j' \in [p]$ such that $x_i \oplus h_1(t_i) = u_j, x_{i'} \oplus h_1(t_{i'}) = u_{j'}, v_j \oplus h_1(t_i) \oplus h_2(t_i) = v_{j'} \oplus h_1(t_{i'}) \oplus h_2(t_{i'})$.

- B.12: $\exists\ i, i' \in [q], j, j' \in [p]$ such that $y_i \oplus h_2(t_i) = v_j, y_{i'} \oplus h_2(t_{i'}) = v_{j'}, u_j \oplus h_1(t_i) \oplus h_2(t_i) = u_{j'} \oplus h_1(t_{i'}) \oplus h_2(t_{i'})$.
- B.13: $\mathcal{D} \triangleq |\{(t_i, x_i, y_i), (t_j, x_j, y_j), (t_k, x_k, y_k) \in \tau_c : y_i \oplus h_2(t_i) \oplus h_2(t_j) = x_k \oplus h_1(t_k) \oplus h_1(t_j)\}| \geq 3q^3/N + 3q\sqrt{nq}$.
- B.14: $\alpha_1 \geq \sqrt{q}$
- B.15: $\alpha_2 \geq \sqrt{q}$.
- B.16: $\beta_1 \geq \sqrt{q} \lor \beta_2 \geq \sqrt{q}$.

Recall that, we denote Θ_b (resp. Θ_g) the set of bad (resp. good) transcripts. We bound the probability of bad transcripts in the ideal world as follows.

Lemma 4 (Bad Lemma). Let $\tau = (\tau_c, \tau_p, k_1, k_2)$ be any attainable transcript. Let D_{id} and Θ_b be defined as above. Then

$$\Pr[\mathsf{D}_{id} \in \Theta_b] \leq \epsilon_{bad} = \frac{3qp^2}{N^2} + \frac{2pq^2}{N^2} + \frac{3q^2}{2N^2} + \frac{q^3}{6N^2} + \frac{2p\sqrt{q}}{N} + \frac{q}{N} + \frac{q^{3/2}}{N}.$$

Proof. Let $\tau = (\tau_c, \tau_p, k_1, k_2)$ be any attainable transcript. Recall that, in the ideal world k_1 and k_2 are drawn uniformly at random from the keyspace. Using the union bound, we have

$$\Pr[\mathsf{D}_{id} \in \Theta_b] \leq \underbrace{\left(\sum_{\substack{i=1, \\ i \neq 4,5,13}}^{16} \Pr[\text{B}.i] \right)}_{\text{A}} + \underbrace{(\Pr[\text{B}.4] + \Pr[\text{B}.5] + \Pr[\text{B}.13])}_{\text{B}}. \qquad (6)$$

We bound part (A) in exactly the similar way as done in [7] and hence we omit it. However, for the sake of completeness, we give its detail proof in [12]. Ahead of the calculation, we have

$$\text{A} \leq \frac{3qp^2}{N^2} + \frac{3q^2}{2N^2} + \frac{q^3}{6N^2} + \frac{2p\sqrt{q}}{N} + \frac{q+2}{N} + \frac{q^{3/2}}{N}. \qquad (7)$$

To bound, part (B) in the following, we begin with bounding event B.4 and B.5 as follows:

BOUNDING B.4 AND B.5. We consider the event B.4. For a fixed $(t_i, x_i, y_i) \neq (t_{i'}, x_{i'}, y_{i'}) \in \tau_c$ and for a fixed $(u_j, v_j) \in \tau_p$, one has by the regularity of H and h_1 and h_2 are drawn independent to each other,

$$\Pr[h_1(t_i) = x_i \oplus u_j, h_2(t_i) = v_j \oplus h_1(t_i) \oplus x_{i'} \oplus h_1(t_{i'})] \leq \frac{1}{N^2}.$$

By summing over all possible choices of $(t_i, x_i, y_i), (t_{i'}, x_{i'}, y_{i'}) \in \tau_c, (u_j, v_j) \in \tau_p$, we have

$$\Pr[\text{B}.4] \leq \frac{pq^2}{2N^2}. \qquad (8)$$

Similarly, for B.5 one obtains,

$$\Pr[\text{B}.5] \leq \frac{pq^2}{2N^2}. \qquad (9)$$

BOUNDING B.13. For bounding B.13, we introduce the following sets: $\mathcal{H}_1 = \{x \oplus h_1(t) : (t, x, y) \in \tau_c\}$ and $\mathcal{H}_2 = \{y \oplus h_2(t) : (t, x, y) \in \tau_c\}$ and $\mathcal{H}_3 = \{h_1(t) \oplus h_2(t) : (t, x, y) \in \tau_c\}$. Then,

$$|\mathcal{D}| = |\{(h_3, h_1, h_2)) \in \mathcal{H}_3 \times \mathcal{H}_1 \times \mathcal{H}_2 : h_3 = h_1 \oplus h_2\}|.$$

Therefore, to bound the probability of the event B.13, it is enough to bound the probability of the following event:

$$\mathsf{E} \triangleq |\{(h_3, h_2, h_1) \in \mathcal{H}_3 \times \mathcal{H}_1 \times \mathcal{H}_2 : h_3 = h_1 \oplus h_2\}| \geq \frac{3q^3}{N} + 3q\sqrt{nq}.$$

From Lemma 2, the probability of event E is bounded above by $2/N$. Hence,

$$\Pr[\text{B.13}] \leq \frac{2}{N}. \tag{10}$$

From Eq. (6)–Eq. (10), the result follows.   □

3.3   Analysis of Good Transcripts

In this section, we state that for a good transcript $\tau = (\tau_c, \tau_p, k_1, k_2)$ such that τ_c has μ distinct tweaks, realizing τ is almost as likely in the real world as in the ideal world. More formally,

Lemma 5. (Good Lemma). *Let $\tau = (\tau_c, \tau_p, k_1, k_2) \in \Theta_g$ be a good transcript such that τ_c has μ distinct tweaks. Let D_{re} and D_{id} be defined as above. Then,*

$$\frac{\Pr[\mathsf{D}_{re} = \tau]}{\Pr[\mathsf{D}_{id} = \tau]} \geq 1 - \left(\frac{4p\sqrt{q}}{N} + \frac{10q^{3/2}}{N} + \frac{14q}{N^{2/3}} + \frac{4q(p + 6\sqrt{q} + 3q)^2}{N^2} + \frac{38q^2}{N^{4/3}} + \frac{5q}{N} \right.$$
$$\left. + \frac{24\sqrt{nq}}{N^{1/3}} + \frac{48\sqrt{q}}{N^{1/3}} \right).$$

Proof of this lemma is the most difficult part of the paper. Hence, we devote the following separate section for proving it. Therefore, by applying H-Coefficient technique (i.e., Theorem 1) with Lemma 4 and Lemma 5, the result follows.   □

4   Proof of Good Lemma

In this section, we prove that for a good transcript $\tau = (\tau_c, \tau_p, k_1, k_2)$, realizing it in the real world is as likely as realizing it in the ideal world. Note that, we have shown in Lemma 1 that to compute the ratio of real to ideal interpolation probability for a good transcript τ, one needs to compare

$$\mathsf{p}(\tau) \triangleq \Pr[\pi \leftarrow_{\$} \mathcal{P}_n : 2\text{-TEM}_{k_1, k_2}^{+\pi} \mapsto \tau_c \mid \pi \mapsto \tau_p]$$

with $(N)_{q_1} \cdot (N)_{q_2} \dots (N)_{q_\mu}$, where recall that μ is the distinct number of tweaks $(t_1, \dots, t_\mu)$ and q_i is the number of times tweak t_i appears in the construction queries $\tau_c \in \tau$. Therefore, it is enough to establish a lower bound of $\mathsf{p}(\tau)$.

4.1   Establishing Lower Bound on $p(\tau)$

First of all, recall that U is the set of all domain points of primitive queries and V is the set of all range points of it. For a good transcript $(\tau_c, \tau_p, k_1, k_2)$, we define the following two sets: $\Im = \{x_i \oplus h_1(t_i) : (t_i, x_i, y_i) \in \tau_c\}$ and $\mathfrak{D} = \{y_i \oplus h_2(t_i) : (t_i, x_i, y_i) \in \tau_c\}$. Since, τ is a good transcript, we can partition the set of construction queries $\tau_c \in \tau$ into a finite number of disjoint groups as follows:

(a) $\mathcal{Q}_U \triangleq \{(t, x, y) \in \tau_c : x \oplus h_1(t) \in U\}$, (b) $\mathcal{Q}_V \triangleq \{(t, x, y) \in \tau_c : y \oplus h_2(t) \in V\}$

(c) $\mathcal{Q}_X \triangleq \{(t, x, y) \in \tau_c : \delta_\Im(x \oplus h_1(t)) > 1, x \oplus h_1(t) \notin U\}$

(d) $\mathcal{Q}_Y \triangleq \{(t, x, y) \in \tau_c : \delta_\mathfrak{D}(y \oplus h_2(t)) > 1, y \oplus h_2(t) \notin V\}$

(e) $\mathcal{Q}_0 \triangleq \{(t, x, y) \in \tau_c : \delta_\Im(x \oplus h_1(t)) = \delta_\mathfrak{D}(y \oplus h_2(t)) = 1, x \oplus h_1(t) \notin U, y \oplus h_2(t) \notin V\}$

Having defined the sets, we now claim that the sets are disjoint and they exhaust the entire set of attainable good transcripts.

Proposition 2. *Let* $\tau = (\tau_c, \tau_p, k_1, k_2) \in \Theta_g$ *be a good transcript. Then the sets* $(\mathcal{Q}_U, \mathcal{Q}_V, \mathcal{Q}_X, \mathcal{Q}_Y, \mathcal{Q}_0)$ *are pairwise disjoint.*

Proof. First of all, according to the definition of the sets, $\mathcal{Q}_U \cap \mathcal{Q}_X = \phi, \mathcal{Q}_U \cap \mathcal{Q}_0 = \phi, \mathcal{Q}_V \cap \mathcal{Q}_Y = \phi, \mathcal{Q}_V \cap \mathcal{Q}_0 = \phi$. Moreover, $\mathcal{Q}_X \cap \mathcal{Q}_0 = \phi, \mathcal{Q}_Y \cap \mathcal{Q}_0 = \phi$. Now, $\mathcal{Q}_U \cap \mathcal{Q}_V = \phi$, otherwise bad condition B.1 would be satisfied. Similarly, $\mathcal{Q}_U \cap \mathcal{Q}_Y = \phi$ (resp. $\mathcal{Q}_V \cap \mathcal{Q}_X = \phi$), otherwise bad condition B.6 (resp. B.7) would be satisfied. Moreover, $\mathcal{Q}_X \cap \mathcal{Q}_Y = \phi$ otherwise bad condition B.10 would be satisfied. Moreover, it is easy to see that a good transcript τ belongs to exactly one of these five sets. □

Note that, since τ is a good transcript, we have,

$$\alpha_1 \triangleq |\mathcal{Q}_U| \leq \sqrt{q}, \quad \alpha_2 \triangleq |\mathcal{Q}_V| \leq \sqrt{q}.$$

Let E_U denotes the event 2-TEM$_{k_1,k_2}^{+\pi} \mapsto \mathcal{Q}_U$. Similarly, E_V denotes the event 2-TEM$_{k_1,k_2}^{+\pi} \mapsto \mathcal{Q}_U$, E_X denotes the event 2-TEM$_{k_1,k_2}^{+\pi} \mapsto \mathcal{Q}_X$, E_Y denotes the event 2-TEM$_{k_1,k_2}^{+\pi} \mapsto \mathcal{Q}_Y$ and finally, E_0 denotes the event 2-TEM$_{k_1,k_2}^{+\pi} \mapsto \mathcal{Q}_0$. Now, it is easy to see that

$$p(\tau) = \Pr[\mathsf{E}_U \wedge \mathsf{E}_V \wedge \mathsf{E}_X \wedge \mathsf{E}_Y \wedge \mathsf{E}_0 \mid \pi \mapsto \tau_p]$$
$$= \underbrace{\Pr[\mathsf{E}_U \wedge \mathsf{E}_V \mid \pi \mapsto \tau_p]}_{p_1(\tau)} \cdot \underbrace{\Pr[\mathsf{E}_X \wedge \mathsf{E}_Y \wedge \mathsf{E}_0 \mid \mathsf{E}_U \wedge \mathsf{E}_V \wedge \pi \mapsto \tau_p]}_{p_2(\tau)} \quad (11)$$

Thus, it is enough to establish a good lower bound on $p_1(\tau)$ and $p_2(\tau)$ for a good transcript τ.

4.2   Lower Bound of $p_1(\tau)$

To lower bound $p_1(\tau)$, we define the following sets:

$$S_1 \triangleq \{x \oplus h_1(t) : (t,x,y) \in \mathcal{Q}_U\}, \quad S_2 \triangleq \{x \oplus h_1(t) : (t,x,y) \in \mathcal{Q}_V\}$$
$$\mathcal{D}_1 \triangleq \{y \oplus h_2(t) : (t,x,y) \in \mathcal{Q}_U\}, \quad \mathcal{D}_2 \triangleq \{y \oplus h_2(t) : (t,x,y) \in \mathcal{Q}_V\}$$

Note that, $|S_1| = \alpha_1$ and $|\mathcal{D}_2| = \alpha_2$. Moreover, $S_1 \subseteq U, \mathcal{D}_2 \subseteq V$. Without loss of generality, let us assume that $x_i \oplus h_1(t_i) = u_i$ for $(t_i, x_i, y_i) \in \mathcal{Q}_U$ and similarly, $y_i \oplus h_2(t_i) = v_i$ for $(t_i, x_i, y_i) \in \mathcal{Q}_V$. Now, we define two additional sets:

$$\mathcal{X}_1 \triangleq \{v_1 \oplus h_1(t_1) \oplus h_2(t_1), \ldots, v_{\alpha_1} \oplus h_1(t_{\alpha_1}) \oplus h_2(t_{\alpha_1})\}$$
$$\mathcal{X}_2 \triangleq \{u_1 \oplus h_1(t_1) \oplus h_2(t_1), \ldots, u_{\alpha_2} \oplus h_1(t_{\alpha_2}) \oplus h_2(t_{\alpha_2})\}$$

In the following we state that every element of $\mathcal{D}_1$ is distinct and does not collide with any primitive query output. Similarly, every element of S_2 is distinct and does not collide with any primitive query input.

Proposition 3. *Every element of $\mathcal{D}_1$ is distinct and does not collide with any primitive query output. Similarly, every element of S_2 is distinct and does not collide with any primitive query input.*

Proof of this proposition can be found in [12]. The above result says that $|\mathcal{D}_1| = \alpha_1$ and $|S_2| = \alpha_2$. Now, we have the following proposition which states that every element of $\mathcal{X}_1$ and $\mathcal{X}_2$ are distinct and $\mathcal{X}_1$ is pairwise disjoint with S_1 and S_2. Similarly, every element of $\mathcal{X}_2$ is distinct and pairwise disjoint with $\mathcal{D}_1$ and $\mathcal{D}_2$. Proof of the result can be found in [12].

Proposition 4. *Every element of $\mathcal{X}_1$ is distinct and $\mathcal{X}_1 \cap S_1 = \phi, \mathcal{X}_1 \cap S_2 = \phi$. Moreover, every element of $\mathcal{X}_2$ is distinct and $\mathcal{X}_2 \cap \mathcal{D}_1 = \phi, \mathcal{X}_2 \cap \mathcal{D}_2 = \phi$.*

Now, from Proposition 3 and Proposition 4, we have $|S_1| = |\mathcal{X}_1| = |\mathcal{D}_1| = \alpha_1$ and $|S_2| = |\mathcal{X}_2| = |\mathcal{D}_2| = \alpha_2$. Also recall that $|U| = |V| = p$. Now, we consider the following two sequences:

$$\mathcal{X}_1 \mathcal{D}_1 \triangleq ((v_i \oplus h_1(t_i) \oplus h_2(t_i), y_i \oplus h_2(t_i))_i : v_i \oplus h_1(t_i) \oplus h_2(t_i) \in \mathcal{X}_1, y_i \oplus h_2(t_i) \in \mathcal{D}_1).$$

$$S_2 \mathcal{X}_2 \triangleq ((x_i \oplus h_1(t_i), u_i \oplus h_1(t_i) \oplus h_2(t_i))_i : x_i \oplus h_1(t_i) \in S_2, u_i \oplus h_1(t_i) \oplus h_2(t_i) \in \mathcal{X}_2).$$

From Proposition 3 and Proposition 4, it follows that the domain of $\mathcal{X}_1 \mathcal{D}_1$ is disjoint with the domain of $S_2 \mathcal{X}_2$. Moreover, they are individually disjoint with U. Similarly, the range of $\mathcal{X}_1 \mathcal{D}_1$ is disjoint with the range of $S_2 \mathcal{X}_2$. Moreover, they are individually disjoint with V. Therefore, we have $\mathfrak{X} = (U, \mathcal{X}_1, S_2)$ and $\mathfrak{Y} = (V, \mathcal{D}_1, \mathcal{X}_2)$ are disjoint collections. Thus, from Proposition 2 one has,

$$p_1(\tau) \triangleq \Pr[\pi \leftarrow_\$ \mathcal{P}_n : \mathfrak{X} \setminus U \xrightarrow{\pi} \mathfrak{Y} \setminus V \mid \pi \mapsto \tau_p] = \frac{1}{(N-p)_{\alpha_1 + \alpha_2}}. \tag{12}$$

4.3 Lower Bound on $p_2(\tau)$

In the last section, we have seen that π has been fixed on $\alpha_1 + \alpha_2$ input-output (apart from p input-output primitive pairs). Moreover, the collection of input and output sets of π that have been explored in the last section is $\mathfrak{X} = (U, \mathcal{X}_1, \mathcal{S}_2)$ and $\mathfrak{Y} = (V, \mathcal{D}_1, \mathcal{X}_2)$. Now, to bound $p_2(\tau)$ for τ, we first define few sets:

$$\mathcal{S}_1' \triangleq \{x \oplus h_1(t) : (t, x, y) \in \mathcal{Q}_X\}, \quad \mathcal{S}_2' \triangleq \{x \oplus h_1(t) : (t, x, y) \in \mathcal{Q}_Y\}.$$

$$\mathcal{D}_1' \triangleq \{y \oplus h_2(t) : (t, x, y) \in \mathcal{Q}_X\}, \quad \mathcal{D}_2' \triangleq \{y \oplus h_2(t) : (t, x, y) \in \mathcal{Q}_Y\}.$$

Let $\alpha_1' = |\mathcal{S}_1'|, \alpha_2' = |\mathcal{D}_1'|$. Moreover, $\alpha_1'' = |\mathcal{S}_2'|, \alpha_2'' = |\mathcal{D}_2'|$. Let us enumerate the set $\mathcal{S}_1'$ and $\mathcal{D}_2'$ as follows: $\mathcal{S}_1' = \{s_{1,1}', \ldots, s_{1,\alpha_1'}'\}$ and $\mathcal{D}_2' = \{d_{2,1}'', \ldots, d_{2,\alpha_2''}''\}$. Our goal is to construct the set $P(\mathcal{S}_1'), P^{-1}(\mathcal{D}_1'), P(\mathcal{S}_2')$ and $P^{-1}(\mathcal{D}_2')$, where

$$P(\mathcal{S}_1') \triangleq \{\pi(x \oplus h_1(t)) : x \oplus h_1(t) \in \mathcal{S}_1'\}.$$

$$P^{-1}(\mathcal{D}_1') \triangleq \{\pi^{-1}(y \oplus h_2(t)) : y \oplus h_2(t) \in \mathcal{D}_1'\}.$$

Similarly, the set $P(\mathcal{S}_2')$ and $P^{-1}(\mathcal{D}_2')$ are defined. It is to be noted that initially these sets are undefined as the permutation is not sampled yet. Recall that, β_1 refers to the number of input-colliding pair of construction queries and β_2 refers to the number of output-colliding pair of construction queries. Therefore, we can write,

$$\beta_1 = \sum_{\substack{x \in \{0,1\}^n: \\ \delta_{\mathfrak{I}}(x) > 1}} \delta_{\mathfrak{I}}(x), \quad \beta_2 = \sum_{\substack{x \in \{0,1\}^n: \\ \delta_{\mathfrak{O}}(x) > 1}} \delta_{\mathfrak{O}}(x),$$

where recall that $\mathfrak{I} = \{x \oplus h_1(t) : (t, x, y) \in \tau_c\}$ and $\mathfrak{O} = \{y \oplus h_2(t) : (t, x, y) \in \tau_c\}$. Moreover, we have the following bound on α_1'.

$$\alpha_1' \leq \sum_{\substack{x \in \{0,1\}^n: \\ \delta_{\mathfrak{I}}(x) > 1}} 1 \leq \sum_{\substack{x \in \{0,1\}^n: \\ \delta_{\mathfrak{I}}(x) > 1}} \frac{\delta_{\mathfrak{I}}(x)}{2} = \frac{\beta_1}{2} \leq \frac{\sqrt{q}}{2}.$$

Similarly, one can derive $\alpha_2'' \leq \beta_2/2 \leq \sqrt{q}/2$. Now, we consider the elements of $\mathcal{D}_1'$. We claim that each element of $\mathcal{D}_1'$ is distinct. This is because if two of them collides then that would satisfy condition B.10. This gives us the following upper bound on α_2', which is derived as follows:

$$\alpha_2' \leq \sum_{i=1}^{\alpha_1'} \delta_{\mathfrak{I}}(s_{1,i}') \leq \sum_{\substack{x \in \{0,1\}^n: \\ \delta_{\mathfrak{I}}(x) > 1}} \delta_{\mathfrak{I}}(x) = \beta_1 \leq \sqrt{q}.$$

By a similar reasoning, one can derive $\alpha_1'' \leq \beta_2 \leq \sqrt{q}$. Moreover, since, each element of $\mathcal{D}_1'$ is distinct, $\alpha_1' = |\mathcal{Q}_X|$. Similarly, as each element of $\mathcal{S}_2'$ is distinct, $\alpha_2'' = |\mathcal{Q}_Y|$. Now, to lower bound $p_2(\tau)$, we need to define two more additional sets as follows:

$$\mathcal{U} \triangleq \{x \oplus h_1(t) : (t, x, y) \in \mathcal{Q}_0\}, \quad \mathcal{V} \triangleq \{y \oplus h_2(t) : (t, x, y) \in \mathcal{Q}_0\}.$$

Since, $(\mathcal{Q}_U, \mathcal{Q}_V, \mathcal{Q}_X, \mathcal{Q}_Y, \mathcal{Q}_0)$ forms a partition of a good construction query transcript τ_c, it is obvious that

$$q' \stackrel{\Delta}{=} |\mathcal{Q}_0| = q - (|\mathcal{Q}_U| + |\mathcal{Q}_V| + |\mathcal{Q}_X| + |\mathcal{Q}_Y|) = q - (\alpha_1 + \alpha_2 + \alpha_1'' + \alpha_2).$$

Thus, we have $q' = |\mathcal{U}| = |\mathcal{V}|$. Let us enumerate the set $\mathcal{U}$ and $\mathcal{V}$ as follows: $\mathcal{U} = \{\widetilde{u}_{1,i,j} : 1 \leq i \leq \mu, 1 \leq j \leq q_i'\}$ and $\mathcal{V} = \{\widetilde{v}_{2,i,j} : 1 \leq i \leq \mu, 1 \leq j \leq q_i'\}$, where recall that μ is the distinct number of tweaks $(t_1, \ldots, t_\mu)$ and q_i' is the number of construction queries $(t, x, y) \in \mathcal{Q}_0$ with tweak value t_i. Besides constructing $P(\mathcal{S}_1'), P(\mathcal{S}_2'), P^{-1}(\mathcal{D}_1')$ and $P^{-1}(\mathcal{D}_2')$, we also construct two additional sets:

$$P(\mathcal{U}) \stackrel{\Delta}{=} \{\pi(x \oplus h_1(t)) : (t, x, y) \in \mathcal{Q}_0\}.$$
$$P^{-1}(\mathcal{V}) \stackrel{\Delta}{=} \{\pi^{-1}(y \oplus h_2(t)) : (t, x, y) \in \mathcal{Q}_0\}.$$

Let $\mathfrak{X}^+ = (\mathcal{S}_1', \mathcal{S}_2', , \mathcal{U})$ and $\mathfrak{Y}^+ = (\mathcal{D}_1', \mathcal{D}_2', \mathcal{V})$. Now, we state the following proposition that says that $\mathfrak{X}^+$ is a disjoint collection and it is inter disjoint with $\mathfrak{X}$. Moreover, $\mathfrak{Y}^+$ is a disjoint collection and it is inter disjoint with $\mathfrak{Y}$. Due to the lack of space, we give its proof in [12].

Proposition 5. $\mathfrak{X}^+$ *is a disjoint collection and it is inter disjoint with* $\mathfrak{X}$. *Moreover,* $\mathfrak{Y}^+$ *is a disjoint collection and it is inter disjoint with* $\mathfrak{Y}$.

From Proposition 5, $\mathfrak{X}^+$ is inter disjoint with $\mathfrak{X}$ and $\mathfrak{Y}^+$ is inter disjoint with $\mathfrak{Y}$. Thus, we have $\mathfrak{X}^{++} = \mathfrak{X}^+ \sqcup \mathfrak{X}$ and $\mathfrak{Y}^{++} = \mathfrak{Y}^+ \sqcup \mathfrak{Y}$. It is easy to see that,

$$\Delta_1 \stackrel{\Delta}{=} |\mathfrak{X}^{++}| = p + q' + \alpha_1 + \alpha_2 + \alpha_1' + \alpha_1''$$
$$\Delta_2 \stackrel{\Delta}{=} |\mathfrak{Y}^{++}| = p + q' + \alpha_1 + \alpha_2 + \alpha_2' + \alpha_2''.$$

<u>OUR GOAL:</u> Now, our goal is to construct the set $P(\mathcal{S}_1'), P(\mathcal{S}_2'), P(\mathcal{U})$ and $P^{-1}(\mathcal{D}_1'), P^{-1}(\mathcal{D}_2')$ and $P^{-1}(\mathcal{V})$ in such a way so that

1. $(\mathcal{S}_1', P(\mathcal{S}_1'))$ becomes extendable
2. $(\mathcal{S}_2', P(\mathcal{S}_2'))$ becomes extendable
3. $(\mathcal{U}, P(\mathcal{U}))$ becomes extendable

Similarly,

1. $(P^{-1}(\mathcal{D}_1'), \mathcal{D}_1')$ becomes extendable
2. $(P^{-1}(\mathcal{D}_2'), \mathcal{D}_2')$ becomes extendable
3. $(P^{-1}(\mathcal{V}), \mathcal{V})$ becomes extendable

Note that $\mathfrak{X}^+ +$ and $\mathfrak{Y}^+ +$ are the set of elements of the domain and range of the partially completed permutation π respectively until the construction of the sets $P(\mathcal{S}_1'), P(\mathcal{S}_2'), P(\mathcal{U})$ and $P^{-1}(\mathcal{D}_1'), P^{-1}(\mathcal{D}_2')$ and $P^{-1}(\mathcal{V})$. Moreover, the elements of $P(\mathcal{S}_1')$ uniquely determines the elements of $P^{-1}(\mathcal{D}_1')$, elements of $P^{-1}(\mathcal{D}_2')$ uniquely determines the elements of $P(\mathcal{S}_2')$ and elements of $P(\mathcal{U})$ uniquely determines the elements of $P^{-1}(\mathcal{V})$. Hence, we sample the elements of $P(\mathcal{S}_1')$ in such a way so that it preserves the permutation compatibility between

$\mathcal{S}'_1$ and $P(\mathcal{S}'_1)$ and between $P^{-1}(\mathcal{D}'_1)$ and $\mathcal{D}'_1$. Similarly, we sample the elements of $P^{-1}(\mathcal{D}'_2)$ in such a way so that it preserves the permutation compatibility between $\mathcal{D}'_2$ and $P^{-1}(\mathcal{D}'_2)$ and between $\mathcal{S}'_2$ and $P(\mathcal{S}'_2)$. Finally, we sample the elements of $P(\mathcal{U})$ in such a way so that it preserves the permutation compatibility between $\mathcal{U}$ and $P(\mathcal{U})$ and between $\mathcal{V}$ and $P^{-1}(\mathcal{V})$. To this end, we define the following sets: for each $u, v \in \{0,1\}^n$,

$$\mathcal{X}_u = \{(t,x,y) \in \tau_c : x \oplus h_1(t) = u\}$$
$$\mathcal{Y}_v = \{(t,x,y) \in \tau_c : y \oplus h_2(t) = v\}$$

STEP-I: CONSTRUCT SET $P(\mathcal{S}'_1)$ AND $P^{-1}(\mathcal{D}'_1)$. Let $\mathcal{N}_1$ be the number of tuple of distinct values $(v'_{1,1}, \ldots, v'_{1,\alpha'_1})$ in $\{0,1\}^n \setminus \mathfrak{Y}^{++}$ such that it satisfies the following two conditions:

- for each $i \in [\alpha'_1]$ and for each $(t,x,y) \in \mathcal{X}_{s'_{1,i}}$, $v'_{1,i} \oplus h_1(t) \oplus h_2(t) \notin \mathfrak{X}^{++}$
- for each $i \in [\alpha'_1]$, for each $(t,x,y) \in \mathcal{X}_{s'_{1,i}}$, for each $j < i$ and for each $(t',x',y') \in \mathcal{X}_{s'_{1,j}}$, $v'_{1,i} \oplus h_1(t) \oplus h_2(t) \neq v'_{1,j} \oplus h_1(t') \oplus h_2(t')$

Let $\mathcal{Z}_1$ be the set of all tuple of distinct values $(v'_{1,1}, \ldots, v'_{1,\alpha'_1})$ in $\{0,1\}^n \setminus \mathfrak{Y}^{++}$ that satisfies the above two conditions. Note that, $|\{0,1\}^n \setminus \mathfrak{Y}^{++}| = (N - (p + q' + \alpha_1 + \alpha_2 + \alpha'_2 + \alpha''_2))$. Moreover, the first condition excludes at most $(p + q' + \alpha_1 + \alpha_2 + \alpha'_1 + \alpha''_1)|\mathcal{X}_{s'_{1,i}}|$ values for $v'_{1,i}$ and the last condition excludes at most $|\mathcal{X}_{s'_{1,i}}| \cdot (|\mathcal{X}_{s'_{1,1}}| + \ldots + |\mathcal{X}_{s'_{1,i-1}}|) \leq \alpha'_2 \cdot |\mathcal{X}_{s'_{1,i}}|$ values for $v'_{1,i}$. Thus, one has

$$|\mathcal{Z}_1| = \mathcal{N}_1 \geq \prod_{i=0}^{\alpha'_1 - 1} \left(N - \Delta_2 - i - (\Delta_1 + \alpha'_2)|\mathcal{X}_{s'_{1,i+1}}| \right). \tag{13}$$

We set $P(\mathcal{S}'_1) = \{v'_{1,1}, \ldots, v'_{1,\alpha'_1}\}$ and $P^{-1}(\mathcal{D}'_1) = \{v'_{1,i} \oplus h_1(t) \oplus h_2(t) : i \in [\alpha'_1], (t,x,y) \in \mathcal{X}_{s'_{1,i}}\}$. Note that such assignment makes $(\mathcal{S}'_1, P(\mathcal{S}'_1))$ extendable and $(P^{-1}(\mathcal{D}'_1), \mathcal{D}'_1)$ extendable. It is easy to see that $P(\mathcal{S}'_1)$ is disjoint with each set of $\mathfrak{Y}^{++}$ and $P^{-1}(\mathcal{D}'_1)$ is disjoint with each set of $\mathfrak{X}^{++}$. Thus, we have, $\mathfrak{X}^{3+} = \mathfrak{X}^{++} \sqcup P^{-1}(\mathcal{D}'_1)$ and $\mathfrak{Y}^{3+} = \mathfrak{Y}^{++} \sqcup P(\mathcal{S}'_1)$. Moreover, $\Delta_3 \stackrel{\Delta}{=} |\mathfrak{X}^{3+}| = \Delta_1 + \alpha'_2$ and $\Delta_4 \stackrel{\Delta}{=} |\mathfrak{Y}^{3+}| = \Delta_2 + \alpha'_1$.

STEP-II: CONSTRUCT SET $P(\mathcal{S}'_2)$ AND $P^{-1}(\mathcal{D}'_2)$. To begin the construction of the sets, we would like to note here that $\mathfrak{X}3+$ and $\mathfrak{Y}^{3+}$ are the set of elements of domain and range of the partially completed permutation π until the construction of the sets $P(\mathcal{S}'_2), P(\mathcal{U})$ and $P^{-1}(\mathcal{D}'_2)$ and $P^{-1}(\mathcal{V})$. Let $\mathcal{N}_2$ be the number of tuple of distinct values $(u''_{2,1}, \ldots, u''_{2,\alpha''_2})$ in $\{0,1\}^n \setminus \mathfrak{X}^{3+}$ such that it satisfies the following two conditions:

- for each $i \in [\alpha''_2]$ and each $(t,x,y) \in \mathcal{Y}_{d''_{2,i}}$, $u''_{2,i} \oplus h_1(t) \oplus h_2(t) \notin \mathfrak{Y}^{3+}$
- for each $i \in [\alpha''_2]$, for each $(t,x,y) \in \mathcal{Y}_{d''_{2,i}}$, for each $j < i$ and for each $(t',x',y') \in \mathcal{Y}_{d''_{1,j}}$, $u''_{1,i} \oplus h_1(t) \oplus h_2(t) \neq u''_{1,j} \oplus h_1(t') \oplus h_2(t')$

Let $\mathcal{Z}_2$ be the set of all tuple of distinct values $(u''_{2,1}, \ldots, u''_{2,\alpha'_2})$ in $\{0,1\}^n \setminus \mathfrak{X}^{3+}$ that satisfies the above two conditions. Note that, $|\{0,1\}^n \setminus \mathfrak{X}^{3+}| = (N - (\Delta_1 + \alpha'_2))$. Moreover, the first condition excludes at most $(\Delta_2 + \alpha'_1)|\mathcal{Y}_{d''_{2,i}}|$ values for $u''_{2,i}$ and the last condition excludes at most $|\mathcal{Y}_{d''_{2,i}}| \cdot (|\mathcal{Y}_{d''_{2,1}}| + \ldots + |\mathcal{Y}_{d''_{2,i-1}}|) \leq \alpha''_1 \cdot |\mathcal{Y}_{d''_{2,i}}|$ values for $u''_{2,i}$. Thus, one has

$$|\mathcal{Z}_2| = \mathcal{N}_2 \geq \prod_{i=0}^{\alpha''_2 - 1} \left(N - \Delta_3 - i - (\Delta_4 + \alpha''_1)|\mathcal{Y}_{d''_{2,i+1}}| \right). \tag{14}$$

We set $P^{-1}(\mathcal{D}'_2) = \{u''_{2,1}, \ldots, u''_{2,\alpha''_2}\}$ and $P(\mathcal{S}'_2) = \{u''_{2,i} \oplus h_1(t) \oplus h_2(t) : i \in [\alpha''_2], (t,x,y) \in \mathcal{Y}_{d''_{2,i}}\}$. Note that such assignment makes $(\mathcal{S}'_2, P(\mathcal{S}'_2))$ extendable and $(\mathcal{D}'_2, P^{-1}(\mathcal{D}'_2))$ extendable.

It is easy to see that $P(\mathcal{S}'_2)$ is disjoint with each set of $\mathfrak{Y}^{3+}$ and $P^{-1}(\mathcal{D}'_2)$ is disjoint with each set of $\mathfrak{X}^{3+}$. Thus, we have, $\mathfrak{X}^{4+} = \mathfrak{X}^{3+} \sqcup P^{-1}(\mathcal{D}'_2)$ and $\mathfrak{Y}^{4+} = \mathfrak{Y}^{3+} \sqcup P(\mathcal{S}'_2)$. Moreover, $\Delta \overset{\Delta}{=} |\mathfrak{X}^{4+}| = \Delta_3 + \alpha''_2 = \Delta_4 + \alpha''_1 = |\mathfrak{Y}^{4+}|$. Let $\mathfrak{X}_0 = \mathfrak{X}^{+4} \setminus \mathcal{U}$ and $\mathfrak{Y}_0 = \mathfrak{Y}^{+4} \setminus \mathcal{U}$. For a fixed choice of elements from $\mathcal{Z}_1$ and $\mathcal{Z}_2$, we have,

$$\widehat{p} = \Pr[\pi \leftarrow_\$ \mathcal{P}_n : \mathfrak{X}_0 \setminus \mathfrak{X} \overset{\pi}{\mapsto} \mathfrak{Y}_0 \setminus \mathfrak{Y} \mid \mathfrak{X} \overset{\pi}{\mapsto} \mathfrak{Y}] = \frac{1}{(N - (p + \alpha_1 + \alpha_2))_{\Delta'}}, \tag{15}$$

where $\Delta' = \Delta - (p + q' + \alpha_1 + \alpha_2)$. Now, we come to the last step in the construction of sets, i.e., we construct set $P(\mathcal{U})$ and $P^{-1}(\mathcal{V})$.

STEP-III: CONSTRUCT SET $P(\mathcal{U})$ AND $P^{-1}(\mathcal{V})$. Recall that $q' = q - (\alpha_1 + \alpha_2 + \alpha''_1 + \alpha''_2)$. Let us consider the following parameter:

$$M = \frac{q'}{N^{1/3}}$$

such that $q' - 3M = q'/2$, which holds true for $n \geq 9$. Let $p' = (p + \alpha_1 + \alpha_2 + \alpha'_1 + \alpha'_2 + \alpha''_1 + \alpha''_2)$ and $q'' = q' - 2\alpha$ for some α such that $0 \leq \alpha \leq M$. We know that $(q_1 + \ldots + q_\mu) = q$. Now, for each $i \in [\mu]$, we define q''_i and q'_i such that $q''_i \leq q'_i \leq q_i$ and

$$\sum_{i=1}^{\mu} q'_i = q', \quad \sum_{i=1}^{\mu} q''_i = q'', \quad q''_i = q'_i - \theta_i, \quad \text{for some } \theta_i, 1 \leq i \leq \mu$$

Let $\mathcal{Z}_0$ be the tuple of distinct values that makes $(\mathcal{U}, P(\mathcal{U}))$ extendable and $(P^{-1}(\mathcal{V}), \mathcal{V})$ extendable. Let $\mathcal{N}_0$ be the number of such tuples. Then, we have the following result:

Lemma 6. *Let* $\mathcal{N}_0, p', q', q''_i, \alpha, M$ *be defined as above. Moreover,* μ *is the distinct number of tweaks appearing in the construction query transcript. Then,*

$$\mathcal{N}_0 \geq \sum_{0 \leq \alpha \leq M} \frac{(q')_{2\alpha}}{\alpha!} \cdot (1 - \epsilon_0) \cdot \prod_{i=1}^{\mu} \left(N - 2p' - 2q' - 2\alpha - 2\sum_{k=1}^{i-1} q''_k \right)_{q''_i},$$

where $\epsilon_0 = 4q/N^{2/3} + 24q^2/N^{4/3} + 24\sqrt{nq}/N^{1/3} + 48\sqrt{q}/N^{1/3}$. Moreover, $P(\mathcal{U})$ is disjoint with each set of $\mathcal{Y}^{4+}$, $P^{-1}(\mathcal{V})$ is disjoint with each set of $\mathcal{X}^{4+}$. Even more, the number of input-ouput pairs on which a random permutation π becomes fixed to map $\mathcal{U}$ to $P(\mathcal{U})$ and $P^{-1}(\mathcal{V})$ to $\mathcal{V}$ is $3\alpha + 2q''$

Note that, the number of way of choosing the tuple looks different than that of $\mathcal{N}_1$ and $\mathcal{N}_2$ (which looks alike). This is because, we are allowing collisions between $P(\mathcal{U})$ and $\mathcal{V}$ or $P^{-1}(\mathcal{V})$ and $\mathcal{U}$. In other words, if $P(\mathcal{U}) \cap \mathcal{V} = \phi$ or $P^{-1}(\mathcal{V}) \cap \mathcal{U} = \phi$, then we end up with birthday bound term. Due to this enforcement of collision, the counting of the set $\mathcal{Z}_0$ becomes involved. A proof of the result can be found in [12].

From Lemma 6 and Eq. (15) and for a fixed choice of elements from $\mathcal{Z}_0, \mathcal{Z}_1$ and $\mathcal{Z}_2$, we have,

$$\hat{p}_2 = \Pr[\pi \xleftarrow{\$} \mathcal{P}_n : \mathcal{X}_0 \setminus \mathcal{X} \xrightarrow{\pi} \mathcal{Y}_0 \setminus \mathcal{Y} \bigwedge \pi \mapsto (\mathcal{U}, P(\mathcal{U})) \bigwedge \pi \mapsto (P^{-1}(\mathcal{V}), \mathcal{V}) \mid \mathcal{X} \xrightarrow{\pi} \mathcal{Y}]$$

$$= \frac{1}{(N - p - \alpha_1 - \alpha_2)_{\Delta' + 3\alpha + 2q''}} \tag{16}$$

From Eq. (13), Eq. (14), Eq. (16) and Lemma 6, we have,

$$p_2(\tau) = \mathcal{N}_0 \cdot \mathcal{N}_1 \cdot \mathcal{N}_2 \cdot \frac{1}{(N - p - \alpha_1 - \alpha_2)_{\Delta' + 3\alpha + 2q''}}, \tag{17}$$

where $\Delta' = \Delta - (p + q' + \alpha_1 + \alpha_2)$.

4.4   Final Step of the Proof

In this section we finalize the proof by combining the results derived in Sect. 4.2 and Sect. 4.3. We once again recall here the following parameters:

$$\Delta_1 = p + q' + \alpha_1 + \alpha_2 + \alpha_1' + \alpha_1''$$
$$\Delta_2 = p + q' + \alpha_1 + \alpha_2 + \alpha_2' + \alpha_2''$$
$$\Delta_3 = p + q' + \alpha_1 + \alpha_2 + \alpha_1' + \alpha_1'' + \alpha_2's$$
$$\Delta_4 = p + q' + \alpha_1 + \alpha_2 + \alpha_2' + \alpha_2'' + \alpha_1'$$
$$\Delta = p + q' + \alpha_1 + \alpha_2 + \alpha_1' + \alpha_1'' + \alpha_2' + \alpha_2''$$

Moreover, we would like to recall that $\alpha_1' \leq \sqrt{q}, \alpha_2' \leq \sqrt{q}, \alpha_1'' \leq \sqrt{q}$ and $\alpha_2'' \leq \sqrt{q}$. Now, from Eq. (11), Eq. (12) and Eq. (17), we have

$$p(\tau) \cdot \prod_{i=1}^{\mu} (N)_{q_i} = \mathcal{N}_0 \cdot \mathcal{N}_1 \cdot \mathcal{N}_2 \cdot \frac{\prod_{i=1}^{\mu} (N)_{q_i}}{(N-p)_{\Delta + 3\alpha + 2q'' - p - q'}}$$

$$= \underbrace{\frac{\mathcal{N}_1}{(N-p)_{\alpha_1'}}}_{\mathsf{N}_1} \cdot \underbrace{\frac{\mathcal{N}_2}{(N-p-\alpha_1')_{\alpha_2''}}}_{\mathsf{N}_2} \cdot \underbrace{\frac{\mathcal{N}_0 \cdot \prod_{i=1}^{\mu} (N)_{q_i}}{(N-p-\alpha_1'-\alpha_2'')_{\alpha_1+\alpha_2+\alpha_1''+\alpha_2'+3\alpha+2q''}}}_{\mathsf{N}_0}$$

Ahead of the calculation, we have

$$\mathbb{N}_1 \geq \left(1 - \left(\frac{2p\sqrt{q}}{N} + \frac{3q^{3/2}}{N} + \frac{3q}{N}\right)\right) \tag{18}$$

$$\mathbb{N}_2 \geq \left(1 - \left(\frac{2p\sqrt{q}}{N} + \frac{3q^{3/2}}{N} + \frac{2q}{N}\right)\right) \tag{19}$$

$$\mathbb{N}_0 \geq \left(1 - \frac{4q^{3/2}}{N} - \frac{10q}{N^{2/3}} - \frac{4q(p + 6\sqrt{q} + 3q)^2}{N^2} - \frac{14q^2}{N^{4/3}} - \epsilon_0\right). \tag{20}$$

where $\epsilon_0 = 4q/N^{2/3} + 24q^2/N^{4/3} + 24\sqrt{nq}/N^{1/3} + 48\sqrt{q}/N^{1/3}$. Derivation of these bounds can be found in [12]. Finally, from Eq. (18), Eq. (19) and Eq. (20), we have

$$\frac{\mathsf{p}(\tau)}{1/\prod\limits_{i=1}^{\mu}(N)_{q_i}} \geq \left(1 - \underbrace{\left(\frac{4p\sqrt{q}}{N} + \frac{10q^{3/2}}{N} + \frac{10q}{N^{2/3}} + \frac{4q(p + 6\sqrt{q} + 3q)^2}{N^2} + \frac{14q^2}{N^{4/3}} + \frac{5q}{N}\right) - \epsilon_0}_{\epsilon_1}\right)$$

Therefore, for a good transcript τ and from Lemma 1 and Lemma 6, we have

$$\frac{\mathsf{p}_{\mathrm{re}}(\tau)}{\mathsf{p}_{\mathrm{id}}(\tau)} \geq 1 - \left(\frac{4p\sqrt{q}}{N} + \frac{10q^{3/2}}{N} + \frac{14q}{N^{2/3}} + \frac{4q(p + 6\sqrt{q} + 3q)^2}{N^2} + \frac{38q^2}{N^{4/3}} + \frac{5q}{N}\right.$$
$$\left. + \frac{24\sqrt{nq}}{N^{1/3}} + \frac{48\sqrt{q}}{N^{1/3}}\right).$$

This proves Lemma 5.   □

5   BBB Security of Two Permutations Variant of 4-TEM

5.1   Security Statement

In this section, we state the security result of two permutation based 4-TEM construction. Let $k_1, k_2 \leftarrow_\$ \{0,1\}^n$ be two independently chosen random n-bit keys. Then, the two permutations variant of 4-TEM is defined as

$$\text{4-TEM}_{k_1,k_2}^{\pi_1,\pi_2}(t,x) = k_1 \oplus t \oplus \pi_1(k_2 \oplus t \oplus \pi_2(k_1 \oplus t \oplus \pi_2(k_2 \oplus t \oplus \pi_1(k_1 \oplus t \oplus x)))),$$

where $\pi_1, \pi_2 \in \mathcal{P}_n$ be two independently sampled n-bit public random permutations, $k_1 \leftarrow_\$ \{0,1\}^n$, $k_2 \leftarrow_\$ \{0,1\}^n$ be two independently sampled n-bit key, $t \in \{0,1\}^n$ is the tweak and $x \in \{0,1\}^n$ is the plaintext. For convenience, we refer the two permutations based 4-TEM construction as 4-TEM$^+$. The main result of this section is to prove the following:

Theorem 3. *Let* A *be any adaptive deterministic distinguisher that makes* q *many construction queries with* μ *distinct tweaks and* p *many primitive queries in both the forward and the backward directions. Then,*

$$\mathbf{Adv}_{\text{4-TEM+}}^{\mathrm{tsprp}}(\mathsf{A}) \leq \left(\frac{3qp^2}{N^2} + \frac{31pq^2}{N^2} + \frac{21p\sqrt{q}}{N} + \frac{31q^{3/2} + 2p^{3/2})}{N} + \frac{3p\sqrt{nq} + 2}{N} + \frac{14q}{N^{2/3}}\right.$$
$$\left. + \frac{4q(p + 6\sqrt{q} + 3q)^2}{N^2} + \frac{38q^2}{N^{4/3}} + \frac{5q}{N} + \frac{24\sqrt{nq}}{N^{1/3}} + \frac{48\sqrt{q}}{N^{1/3}} + \frac{4q\sqrt{p}}{N} + \frac{4q^3}{N^2}\right).$$

5.2 Definition and Probability of Bad Transcripts

For a transcript $\tau = (\tau_c, \tau_{p_1}, \tau_{p_1}, k_1, k_2)$, we define $U^{(b)} = \mathsf{Dom}(\tau_{p_b}) = \{u^{(b)} \in \{0,1\}^n : (u^{(b)}, v^{(b)}) \in \tau_{p_b}\}$, the domain of primitive queries and $V^{(b)} = \mathsf{Ran}(\tau_{p_b}) = \{v^{(b)} \in \{0,1\}^n : (u^{(b)}, v^{(b)}) \in \tau_{p_b}\}$, the range of primitive queries for $b \in \{1,2\}$. For a transcript $\tau = (\tau_c, \tau_{p_1}, \tau_{p_1}, k_1, k_2)$, we associate the following parameters:

$$\nu_1 \stackrel{\Delta}{=} |\{((t,x,y),(u^{(1)},v^{(1)})) \in \tau_c \times \tau_{p_1} : k_1 = x \oplus t \oplus u^{(1)}\}|$$
$$\nu_2 \stackrel{\Delta}{=} |\{((t,x,y),(u^{(2)},v^{(2)})) \in \tau_c \times \tau_{p_2} : k_1 = u^{(2)} \oplus v^{(2)} \oplus t\}|$$
$$\nu_3 \stackrel{\Delta}{=} |\{((t,x,y),(u^{(2)},v^{(2)})) \in \tau_c \times \tau_{p_2} : k_1 \oplus k_2 = x \oplus v^{(2)}\}|$$
$$\nu_3 \stackrel{\Delta}{=} |\{((t,x,y),(u^{(2)},v^{(2)})) \in \tau_c \times \tau_{p_2} : k_1 \oplus k_2 = y \oplus u^{(2)}\}|$$
$$\nu_4 \stackrel{\Delta}{=} |\{((t,x,y),(u^{(1)},v^{(1)})) \in \tau_c \times \tau_{p_1} : k_1 = y \oplus t \oplus u^{(1)}\}|$$
$$\nu_5 \stackrel{\Delta}{=} |\{((t,x,y),(t',x',y'),(u^{(2)},v^{(2)})) \in (\tau_c)^2 \times \tau_{p_2} : k_1 \oplus k_2 = x \oplus t \oplus v^{(2)} \oplus t'\}|$$

Moreover, we also have

$$\nu_5' \stackrel{\Delta}{=} |\{((t,x,y),(t',x',y'),(u^{(2)},v^{(2)})) \in (\tau_c)^2 \times \tau_{p_2} : k_1 \oplus k_2 = y \oplus t \oplus u^{(2)} \oplus t'\}|$$
$$\nu_{2,3} \stackrel{\Delta}{=} |\{((t,x,y),(u^{(2)},v^{(2)}),(u'^{(2)},v'^{(2)})) \in \tau_c \times (\tau_{p_2})^2 : k_1 = u^{(2)} \oplus v'^{(2)} \oplus t\}|$$
$$\nu_6 \stackrel{\Delta}{=} |\{((t,x,y),(t',x',y'),(u^{(1)},v^{(1)}),(u^{(2)},v^{(2)})) \in (\tau_c)^2 \times \tau_{p_1} \times \tau_{p_2} :$$
$$x \oplus k_1 \oplus t = u^{(1)}, v^{(1)} \oplus v^{(2)} \oplus t \oplus t' = k_1 \oplus k_2\}|$$
$$\nu_7 \stackrel{\Delta}{=} |\{((u^{(2)},v^{(2)}),(u'^{(2)},v'^{(2)})) \in (\tau_{p_2})^2 : (u^{(2)},v^{(2)}) \neq (u'^{(2)},v'^{(2)})$$
$$u^{(2)} \oplus v^{(2)} = u'^{(2)} \oplus v'^{(2)}\}|$$

Definition 2 (Bad Transcript). *An attainable transcript $\tau' = (\tau_c, \tau_{p_1}, \tau_{p_2}, k_1, k_2)$ is called a **bad** transcript if any one of the following condition holds:*

- B.1: $\exists\, i \in [q], j, j' \in [p]$ such that $k_1 \oplus t_i = x_i \oplus u_j^{(1)} = y_i \oplus v_{j'}^{(1)}$.
- B.2: $\exists\, i \in [q], j, j' \in [p]$ such that $x_i \oplus k_1 \oplus t_i = u_j^{(1)}, v_j^{(1)} \oplus k_2 \oplus t_i = u_{j'}^{(2)}$.
- B.3: $\exists\, i \in [q], j, j' \in [p]$ such that $y_i \oplus k_1 \oplus t_i = v_j^{(1)}, u_j^{(1)} \oplus k_2 \oplus t_i = v_{j'}^{(2)}$.
- B.4: $\nu_1 \geq \sqrt{q}$.
- B.5: $\nu_2 \geq \sqrt{q}$.
- B.6: $\nu_3 \geq \sqrt{q}$.
- B.7: $\nu_3' \geq \sqrt{q}$.
- B.8: $\nu_4 \geq \sqrt{q}$.
- B.9: $\nu_5 \geq p\sqrt{q}$.
- B.10: $\nu_5' \geq p\sqrt{q}$.
- B.11: $\nu_{2,3} \geq p\sqrt{q}$.
- B.12: $\nu_6 \geq p\sqrt{q}$.
- B.13: $\nu_7 \geq \sqrt{p}$.

Recall that, we denote Θ_b (resp. Θ_g) the set of bad (resp. good) transcripts. Then we have the following result:

Lemma 7 (Bad Lemma). *Let* $\tau = (\tau_c, \tau_{p_1}, \tau_{p_2}, k_1, k_2)$ *be any attainable transcript. Let* D_{id} *and* Θ_b *be defined as above. Then*

$$\Pr[\mathsf{D}_{id} \in \Theta_b] \leq \epsilon_{bad} = \frac{3qp^2}{N^2} + \frac{3pq^2}{N^2} + \frac{5p\sqrt{q}}{N} + \frac{2(q^{3/2} + p^{3/2})}{N} + \frac{3p\sqrt{nq} + 2}{N}.$$

Proof of this lemma can be found in [12].

5.3   Analysis of Good Transcripts

In this section, we state that for a good transcript $\tau = (\tau_c, \tau_{p_1}, \tau_{p_2}, k_1, k_2)$ such that τ_c has μ distinct tweaks, realizing τ is almost as likely in the real world as in the ideal world. More formally,

Lemma 8 (Good Lemma). *Let* $\tau = (\tau_c, \tau_{p_1}, \tau_{p_2}, k_1, k_2) \in \Theta_g$ *be a good transcript such that* τ_c *has* μ *distinct tweaks. Let* D_{re} *and* D_{id} *be defined as above. Then,*

$$\frac{\Pr[\mathsf{D}_{re} = \tau]}{\Pr[\mathsf{D}_{id} = \tau]} \geq 1 - \left(\frac{16p\sqrt{q}}{N} + \frac{29q^{3/2}}{N} + \frac{14q}{N^{2/3}} + \frac{4q(p + 6\sqrt{q} + 3q)^2}{N^2} + \frac{38q^2}{N^{4/3}} + \frac{5q}{N} \right.$$
$$\left. + \frac{24\sqrt{nq}}{N^{1/3}} + \frac{48\sqrt{q}}{N^{1/3}} + \frac{28pq^2}{N^2} + \frac{4q\sqrt{p}}{N} + \frac{4q^3}{N^2} \right).$$

By the grace of Lemma 1, we need to compute the following: for a good transcript $\tau = (\tau_c, \tau_{p_1}, \tau_{p_2}, k_1, k_2)$,

$$\mathsf{p}(\tau) \stackrel{\Delta}{=} \Pr[(\pi_1, \pi_2) \leftarrow_\$ (\mathcal{P}_n)^2 : 4\text{-TEM}^{+\pi_1, \pi_2}_{k_1, k_2} \mapsto \tau_c \mid \pi_1 \mapsto \tau_{p_1}, \pi_2 \mapsto \tau_{p_2}]. \quad (21)$$

The proof proceeds in two steps: in the first step we will lower bound that a randomly sampled permutation π_1 satisfy some *good* condition (definition is given below). Then, assuming π_1 is good, we will lower bound over the choice of π_2, $4\text{-TEM}^{+\pi_1, \pi_2}_{k_1, k_2} \mapsto \tau_c$. For the second step, we will directly appeal to the result developed for 2-TEM^+ in previous sections.

Definition 3. *A permutation* $\pi_1 \in \mathcal{P}_n$ *such that* $\pi_1 \mapsto \tau_{p_1}$ *is said to be bad if it satisfies at least one of the following conditions:*

- C.1: $\exists\, i \in [q], j, j' \in [p]$ *such that* $\pi_1(x_i \oplus k_1 \oplus t_i) \oplus k_2 \oplus t_i = u_j^{(2)}, \pi_1^{-1}(y_i \oplus k_1 \oplus t_i) \oplus k_2 \oplus t_i = v_{j'}^{(2)}$.
- C.2: $\exists\, i \in [q], j, j' \in [p]$ *such that* $\pi_1(x_i \oplus k_1 \oplus t_i) \oplus k_2 \oplus t_i = u_j^{(2)}, v_j^{(2)} \oplus k_1 \oplus t_i = u_{j'}^{(2)}$.
- C.3: $\exists\, i \in [q], j, j' \in [p]$ *such that* $\pi_1^{-1}(y_i \oplus k_1 \oplus t_i) \oplus k_2 \oplus t_i = v_j^{(2)}, u_j^{(2)} \oplus k_1 \oplus t_i = v_{j'}^{(2)}$.
- C.4: $\exists\, i, i' \in [q], j \in [p]$ *such that* $\pi_1(x_i \oplus k_1 \oplus t_i) \oplus k_2 \oplus t_i = u_j^{(2)}, v_j^{(2)} \oplus k_1 \oplus t_i = \pi_1(x_{i'} \oplus k_1 \oplus t_{i'}) \oplus k_2 \oplus t_{i'}$.
- C.5: $\exists\, i, i' \in [q], j \in [p]$ *such that* $\pi_1(y_i \oplus k_1 \oplus t_i) \oplus k_2 \oplus t_i = v_j^{(2)}, u_j^{(2)} \oplus k_1 \oplus t_i = \pi_1^{-1}(y_{i'} \oplus k_1 \oplus t_{i'}) \oplus k_2 \oplus t_{i'}$.

– C.6: $\exists\, i, i' \in [q], j \in [p]$ such that $\pi_1(x_i \oplus k_1 \oplus t_i) \oplus k_2 \oplus t_i = u_j^{(2)}, \pi_1^{-1}(y_i \oplus k_1 \oplus t_i) \oplus t_i = \pi_1^{-1}(y_{i'} \oplus k_1 \oplus t_{i'}) \oplus t_{i'}.$

– C.7: $\exists\, i, i' \in [q], j \in [p]$ such that $\pi_1^{-1}(y_i \oplus k_1 \oplus t_i) \oplus k_2 \oplus t_i = v_j^{(2)}, \pi_1(x_i \oplus k_1 \oplus t_i) \oplus t_i = \pi_1(x_{i'} \oplus k_1 \oplus t_{i'}) \oplus t_{i'}.$

– C.8: $\exists\, i, i' \in [q]$ such that $\pi_1(x_i \oplus k_1 \oplus t_i) \oplus t_i = \pi_1(x_{i'} \oplus k_1 \oplus t_{i'}) \oplus t_{i'}, t_i = t_{i'}.$

– C.9: $\exists\, i, i' \in [q]$ such that $\pi_1^{-1}(y_i \oplus k_1 \oplus t_i) \oplus t_i = \pi_1^{-1}(y_{i'} \oplus k_1 \oplus t_{i'}) \oplus t_{i'}, t_i = t_{i'}.$

– C.10: $\exists\, i, i', i'' \in [q]$ such that $\pi_1(x_i \oplus k_1 \oplus t_i) \oplus t_i = \pi_1(x_{i'} \oplus k_1 \oplus t_{i'}) \oplus t_{i'}, \pi_1^{-1}(y_i \oplus k_1 \oplus t_i) \oplus t_i = \pi_1^{-1}(y_{i''} \oplus k_1 \oplus t_{i''}) \oplus t_{i''}.$

– C.11: $\exists\, i, i' \in [q], j, j' \in [p]$ such that $\pi_1(x_i \oplus k_1 \oplus t_i) \oplus k_2 \oplus t_i = u_j^{(2)}, pi_1(x_{i'} \oplus k_1 \oplus t_{i'}) \oplus k_2 \oplus t_{i'} = u_{j'}^{(2)}, v_j^{(2)} \oplus t_i = v_{j'}^{(2)} \oplus t_{i'}.$

– C.12: $\exists\, i, i' \in [q], j, j' \in [p]$ such that $\pi_1^{-1}(y_i \oplus k_1 \oplus t_i) \oplus k_2 \oplus t_i = v_j^{(2)}, \pi_1^{-1}(y_{i'} \oplus k_1 \oplus t_{i'}) \oplus k_2 \oplus t_{i'} = v_{j'}^{(2)}, u_j^{(2)} \oplus t_i = u_{j'}^{(2)} \oplus t_{i'}.$

– C.13: $\mathcal{D} \triangleq |\{(t_i, x_i, y_i), (t_j, x_j, y_j), (t_k, x_k, y_k) \in \tau_c : \pi_1^{-1}(y_i \oplus k_1 \oplus t_i) \oplus k_2 \oplus t_i \oplus k_1 \oplus t_j = \pi_1(x_k \oplus k_1 \oplus t_k) \oplus k_2 \oplus t_k \oplus k_1 \oplus t_j\}| \geq 3q^3/N + 3q\sqrt{nq}.$

– C.14: $\alpha_1 \triangleq |\{((t, x, y), (u^{(2)}, v^{(2)})) \in \tau_c \times \tau_{p_2} : \pi_1(x \oplus k_1 \oplus t) \oplus k_2 \oplus t = u^{(2)}\}| \geq \sqrt{q}.$

– C.15: $\alpha_2 \triangleq |\{((t, x, y), (u^{(2)}, v^{(2)})) \in \tau_c \times \tau_{p_2} : \pi_1^{-1}(y \oplus k_1 \oplus t) \oplus k_2 \oplus t = v^{(2)}\}| \geq \sqrt{q}.$

– C.16: $\beta_1 \triangleq |\{((t, x, y), (t', x', y')) \in (\tau_c)^2 : (t, x, y) \neq (t', x', y'), \pi_1(x \oplus k_1 \oplus t) \oplus t = \pi_1(x' \oplus k_1 \oplus t') \oplus t'\}| \geq \sqrt{q}.$

– C.17: $\beta_2 \triangleq |\{((t, x, y), (t', x', y')) \in (\tau_c)^2 : (t, x, y) \neq (t', x', y'), \pi_1^{-1}(y \oplus k_1 \oplus t) \oplus t = \pi_1^{-1}(y' \oplus k_1 \oplus t') \oplus t'\}| \geq \sqrt{q}.$

Let $\mathcal{P}_b$ be the set of all permutations π_1 such that $\pi_1 \mapsto \tau_{p_1}$ and satisfies at least one of the above events. Let $\mathcal{P}_g = \mathcal{P}_n \setminus \mathcal{P}_b$. Then, we have the following lemma.

Lemma 9. *Let $\mathcal{P}_b$ be the set of bad permutations π_1 such that $\pi_1 \mapsto \tau_{p_1}$. Then,*

$$\Pr[\pi_1 \leftarrow_\$ \mathcal{P}_n : \pi_1 \in \mathcal{P}_b] \leq \frac{28pq^2}{N^2} + \frac{12p\sqrt{q}}{N} + \frac{19q^{3/2}}{N} + \frac{4q\sqrt{p}}{N} + \frac{4q^3}{N^2}.$$

We include the proof of the lemma in [12]. Having stated the result, we now move to the second step of the proof.

SECOND STEP OF THE PROOF. We fix a permutation $\pi_1 \in \mathcal{P}_n$ that satisfies $\pi_1 \mapsto \tau_{p_1}$. Then, we define a new query transcript and denote the following:

$$\widetilde{\tau}_c \triangleq \{(t, \pi_1(x \oplus t \oplus k_1), \pi_1^{-1}(y \oplus t \oplus k_1) : (t, x, y) \in \tau_c\}.$$
$$\widetilde{\mathsf{p}}(\tau, \pi_1) \triangleq \Pr[\pi_2 \leftarrow_\$ \mathcal{P}_n : 4\text{-TEM}_{k_1, k_2}^{+\pi_2} \mapsto \widetilde{\tau}_c \mid \pi_2 \mapsto \tau_{p_2}].$$

Once π_1 is fixed, $4\text{-TEM}_{k_1, k_2}^{+\pi_1, \pi_2} \mapsto \tau_c$ is equivalent to $4\text{-TEM}_{k_1, k_2}^{+\pi_2} \mapsto \widetilde{\tau}_c$. Therefore, following Lemma 5 of [9], we have for a good transcript τ,

$$\frac{\Pr[D_{re} = \tau]}{\Pr[D_{id} = \tau]} \geq \sum_{\pi_1 \in \mathcal{P}_g} \frac{\widetilde{\mathsf{p}}(\tau, \pi_1)}{(N - p)! \prod_{i=1}^{\mu} 1/(N)_{q_i}}, \tag{22}$$

where recall that q_i is the number of construction queries in τ_c with tweak value t_i. Moreover, note that the query transcripts $\tau' = (\tau_c, \tau_{p_2})$ satisfies exactly the conditions defining a good transcript as per Definition 1. Moreover, for a good permutation π_1, the ratio $\widetilde{p}(\tau, \pi_1)/ \prod_{i=1}^{\mu} 1/(N)_{q_i}$ is exactly the ratio of the probabilities to get τ' in the real and in the ideal world. Hence, we can apply Lemma 5 to yield

$$\frac{\widetilde{p}(\tau, \pi_1)}{\prod_{i=1}^{\mu} 1/(N)_{q_i}} \geq 1 - \left(\frac{4p\sqrt{q}}{N} + \frac{10q^{3/2}}{N} + \frac{14q}{N^{2/3}} + \frac{4q(p + 6\sqrt{q} + 3q)^2}{N^2} + \frac{38q^2}{N^{4/3}} + \frac{5q}{N} \right.$$

$$\left. + \frac{24\sqrt{nq}}{N^{1/3}} + \frac{48\sqrt{q}}{N^{1/3}} \right). \tag{23}$$

FINALIZING THE PROOF. Let

$$\epsilon = \frac{4p\sqrt{q}}{N} + \frac{10q^{3/2}}{N} + \frac{14q}{N^{2/3}} + \frac{4q(p + 6\sqrt{q} + 3q)^2}{N^2} + \frac{38q^2}{N^{4/3}} + \frac{5q}{N} + \frac{24\sqrt{nq}}{N^{1/3}} + \frac{48\sqrt{q}}{N^{1/3}}.$$

$$\epsilon_0 = \frac{28pq^2}{N^2} + \frac{12p\sqrt{q}}{N} + \frac{19q^{3/2}}{N} + \frac{4q\sqrt{p}}{N} + \frac{4q^3}{N^2}.$$

From Eq. (22) and Eq. (23), we have

$$\frac{\Pr[\mathsf{D}_{\mathrm{re}} = \tau]}{\Pr[\mathsf{D}_{\mathrm{id}} = \tau]} \geq \left(1 - \epsilon\right) \sum_{\pi_1 \in \mathcal{P}_g} \frac{1}{(N - p)!} = \left(1 - \epsilon\right) \cdot \Pr[\pi_1 \in \mathcal{P}_g]$$

$$= \left(1 - \epsilon\right) \cdot \left(1 - \Pr[\pi_1 \in \mathcal{P}_b]\right) \overset{(1)}{\geq} \left(1 - \epsilon\right) \cdot \left(1 - \epsilon_0\right)$$

$$\geq \left(1 - \epsilon - \epsilon_0\right),$$

where (1) follows from Lemma 9. By substituting the value of ϵ_0 and ϵ, the result follows. $\qquad\square$

6   Conclusion

This work shows that single permutation based 2-TEM and two-independent permutations based 4-TEM are beyond birthday bound secure TEM. As already mentioned that it would be interesting to investigate the security of 2-TEM$^+$ and 4-TEM$^+$ with reduced number of keys. We also conjecture that single permutation based 4-TEM (i.e., make all permutations of 4-TEM identical) is also beyond the birthday bound secure, but we currently we do not know how to prove its security.

Acknowledgement. This work has been done in Indian Institute of Technology, Kharagpur.

References

1. Andreeva, E., Bogdanov, A., Luykx, A., Mennink, B., Tischhauser, E., Yasuda, K.: Parallelizable and authenticated online ciphers. In: Sako, K., Sarkar, P. (eds.) ASIACRYPT 2013. LNCS, vol. 8269, pp. 424–443. Springer, Heidelberg (2013). https://doi.org/10.1007/978-3-642-42033-7_22
2. Bellare, M., Kohno, T.: A theoretical treatment of related-key attacks: RKA-PRPs, RKA-PRFs, and applications. In: Biham, E. (ed.) EUROCRYPT 2003. LNCS, vol. 2656, pp. 491–506. Springer, Heidelberg (2003). https://doi.org/10.1007/3-540-39200-9_31
3. Bogdanov, A., Knudsen, L.R., Leander, G., Standaert, F.-X., Steinberger, J., Tischhauser, E.: Key-alternating ciphers in a provable setting: encryption using a small number of public permutations. In: Pointcheval, D., Johansson, T. (eds.) EUROCRYPT 2012. LNCS, vol. 7237, pp. 45–62. Springer, Heidelberg (2012). https://doi.org/10.1007/978-3-642-29011-4_5
4. Chakraborty, D., Sarkar, P.: A general construction of tweakable block ciphers and different modes of operations. In: Lipmaa, H., Yung, M., Lin, D. (eds.) Inscrypt 2006. LNCS, vol. 4318, pp. 88–102. Springer, Heidelberg (2006). https://doi.org/10.1007/11937807_8
5. Chen, S., Lampe, R., Lee, J., Seurin, Y., Steinberger, J.: Minimizing the two-round Even-Mansour cipher. In: Garay, J.A., Gennaro, R. (eds.) CRYPTO 2014. LNCS, vol. 8616, pp. 39–56. Springer, Heidelberg (2014). https://doi.org/10.1007/978-3-662-44371-2_3
6. Chen, S., Steinberger, J.: Tight security bounds for key-alternating ciphers. In: Nguyen, P.Q., Oswald, E. (eds.) EUROCRYPT 2014. LNCS, vol. 8441, pp. 327–350. Springer, Heidelberg (2014). https://doi.org/10.1007/978-3-642-55220-5_19
7. Cogliati, B., Lampe, R., Seurin, Y.: Tweaking Even-Mansour ciphers. In: Gennaro, R., Robshaw, M. (eds.) CRYPTO 2015. LNCS, vol. 9215, pp. 189–208. Springer, Heidelberg (2015). https://doi.org/10.1007/978-3-662-47989-6_9
8. Cogliati, B., Lee, J., Seurin, Y.: New constructions of macs from (tweakable) block ciphers. IACR Trans. Symmetric Cryptol. **2017**(2), 27–58 (2017)
9. Cogliati, B., Seurin, Y.: Beyond-birthday-bound security for tweakable Even-Mansour ciphers with linear tweak and key mixing. In: Iwata, T., Cheon, J.H. (eds.) ASIACRYPT 2015. LNCS, vol. 9453, pp. 134–158. Springer, Heidelberg (2015). https://doi.org/10.1007/978-3-662-48800-3_6
10. Cogliati, B., Seurin, Y.: On the provable security of the iterated Even-Mansour cipher against related-key and chosen-key attacks. In: Oswald, E., Fischlin, M. (eds.) EUROCRYPT 2015. LNCS, vol. 9056, pp. 584–613. Springer, Heidelberg (2015). https://doi.org/10.1007/978-3-662-46800-5_23
11. Crowley, P.: Mercy: a fast large block cipher for disk sector encryption. In: Goos, G., Hartmanis, J., van Leeuwen, J., Schneier, B. (eds.) FSE 2000. LNCS, vol. 1978, pp. 49–63. Springer, Heidelberg (2001). https://doi.org/10.1007/3-540-44706-7_4
12. Dutta, A.: Minimizing the two-round tweakable Even-Mansour cipher. Cryptol. ePrint Archive, Report 2020/1076 (2020). https://eprint.iacr.org/2020/1076
13. Dutta, A., Nandi, M.: Tweakable HCTR: a BBB secure tweakable enciphering scheme. In: Chakraborty, D., Iwata, T. (eds.) INDOCRYPT 2018. LNCS, vol. 11356, pp. 47–69. Springer, Cham (2018). https://doi.org/10.1007/978-3-030-05378-9_3
14. Farshim, P., Procter, G.: The related-key security of iterated Even–Mansour ciphers. In: Leander, G. (ed.) FSE 2015. LNCS, vol. 9054, pp. 342–363. Springer, Heidelberg (2015). https://doi.org/10.1007/978-3-662-48116-5_17

15. Ferguson, N., et al.: The skein hash function family. SHA3 Submission to NIST (Round 3) (2010)
16. Goldenberg, D., Hohenberger, S., Liskov, M., Schwartz, E.C., Seyalioglu, H.: On tweaking Luby-Rackoff blockciphers. In: Kurosawa, K. (ed.) ASIACRYPT 2007. LNCS, vol. 4833, pp. 342–356. Springer, Heidelberg (2007). https://doi.org/10.1007/978-3-540-76900-2_21
17. Guo, J., Peyrin, T., Poschmann, A., Robshaw, M.J.B.: The LED block cipher. IACR Cryptol. ePrint Archive, 2012:600 (2012)
18. Halevi, S., Rogaway, P.: A tweakable enciphering mode. In: Boneh, D. (ed.) CRYPTO 2003. LNCS, vol. 2729, pp. 482–499. Springer, Heidelberg (2003). https://doi.org/10.1007/978-3-540-45146-4_28
19. Halevi, S., Rogaway, P.: A parallelizable enciphering mode. In: Okamoto, T. (ed.) CT-RSA 2004. LNCS, vol. 2964, pp. 292–304. Springer, Heidelberg (2004). https://doi.org/10.1007/978-3-540-24660-2_23
20. Jha, A., Nandi, M.: On rate-1 and beyond-the-birthday bound secure online ciphers using tweakable block ciphers. Cryptogr. Commun. **10**(5), 731–753 (2018). https://doi.org/10.1007/s12095-017-0275-0
21. Jha, A., Nandi, M.: Tight security of cascaded LRW2. IACR Cryptol. ePrint Arch. 2019:1495 (2019)
22. Lampe, R., Seurin, Y.: Tweakable blockciphers with asymptotically optimal security. In: Moriai, S. (ed.) FSE 2013. LNCS, vol. 8424, pp. 133–151. Springer, Heidelberg (2014). https://doi.org/10.1007/978-3-662-43933-3_8
23. Landecker, W., Shrimpton, T., Terashima, R.S.: Tweakable blockciphers with beyond birthday-bound security. In: Safavi-Naini, R., Canetti, R. (eds.) CRYPTO 2012. LNCS, vol. 7417, pp. 14–30. Springer, Heidelberg (2012). https://doi.org/10.1007/978-3-642-32009-5_2
24. Lee, B.H., Lee, J.: Tweakable block ciphers secure beyond the birthday bound in the ideal cipher model. In: Peyrin, T., Galbraith, S. (eds.) ASIACRYPT 2018. LNCS, vol. 11272, pp. 305–335. Springer, Cham (2018). https://doi.org/10.1007/978-3-030-03326-2_11
25. Liskov, M., Rivest, R.L., Wagner, D.: Tweakable block ciphers. In: Yung, M. (ed.) CRYPTO 2002. LNCS, vol. 2442, pp. 31–46. Springer, Heidelberg (2002). https://doi.org/10.1007/3-540-45708-9_3
26. List, E., Nandi, M.: Revisiting Full-PRF-secure PMAC and using it for beyond-birthday authenticated encryption. In: Handschuh, H. (ed.) CT-RSA 2017. LNCS, vol. 10159, pp. 258–274. Springer, Cham (2017). https://doi.org/10.1007/978-3-319-52153-4_15
27. Mennink, B.: Optimally secure tweakable blockciphers. In: Leander, G. (ed.) FSE 2015. LNCS, vol. 9054, pp. 428–448. Springer, Heidelberg (2015). https://doi.org/10.1007/978-3-662-48116-5_21
28. Mennink, B.: Towards tight security of cascaded LRW2. In: Beimel, A., Dziembowski, S. (eds.) TCC 2018. LNCS, vol. 11240, pp. 192–222. Springer, Cham (2018). https://doi.org/10.1007/978-3-030-03810-6_8
29. Minematsu, K.: Improved security analysis of XEX and LRW modes. In: Biham, E., Youssef, A.M. (eds.) SAC 2006. LNCS, vol. 4356, pp. 96–113. Springer, Heidelberg (2007). https://doi.org/10.1007/978-3-540-74462-7_8
30. Minematsu, K.: Beyond-birthday-bound security based on tweakable block cipher. In: Dunkelman, O. (ed.) FSE 2009. LNCS, vol. 5665, pp. 308–326. Springer, Heidelberg (2009). https://doi.org/10.1007/978-3-642-03317-9_19

31. Mitsuda, A., Iwata, T.: Tweakable pseudorandom permutation from generalized feistel structure. In: Baek, J., Bao, F., Chen, K., Lai, X. (eds.) ProvSec 2008. LNCS, vol. 5324, pp. 22–37. Springer, Heidelberg (2008). https://doi.org/10.1007/978-3-540-88733-1_2

32. Naito, Y.: Full PRF-secure message authentication code based on tweakable block cipher. In: Au, M.-H., Miyaji, A. (eds.) ProvSec 2015. LNCS, vol. 9451, pp. 167–182. Springer, Cham (2015). https://doi.org/10.1007/978-3-319-26059-4_9

33. Patarin, J.: The "Coefficients H" technique. In: Avanzi, R.M., Keliher, L., Sica, F. (eds.) SAC 2008. LNCS, vol. 5381, pp. 328–345. Springer, Heidelberg (2009). https://doi.org/10.1007/978-3-642-04159-4_21

34. Peyrin, T., Seurin, Y.: Counter-in-tweak: authenticated encryption modes for tweakable block ciphers. In: Robshaw, M., Katz, J. (eds.) CRYPTO 2016. LNCS, vol. 9814, pp. 33–63. Springer, Heidelberg (2016). https://doi.org/10.1007/978-3-662-53018-4_2

35. Procter, G.: A note on the CLRW2 tweakable block cipher construction. IACR Cryptol. ePrint Arch. 2014:111 (2014)

36. Rogaway, P.: Efficient instantiations of tweakable blockciphers and refinements to modes OCB and PMAC. In: Lee, P.J. (ed.) ASIACRYPT 2004. LNCS, vol. 3329, pp. 16–31. Springer, Heidelberg (2004). https://doi.org/10.1007/978-3-540-30539-2_2

37. Rogaway, P., Zhang, H.: Online ciphers from tweakable blockciphers. In: Kiayias, A. (ed.) CT-RSA 2011. LNCS, vol. 6558, pp. 237–249. Springer, Heidelberg (2011). https://doi.org/10.1007/978-3-642-19074-2_16

38. Schroeppel, R.: The hasty pudding cipher

39. Sarkar, P.: A new multi-linear universal hash family. Des. Codes Cryptogr. **69**(3), 351–367 (2013). https://doi.org/10.1007/s10623-012-9672-8

40. Wang, P., Feng, D., Wu, W.: HCTR: a variable-input-length enciphering mode. In: Feng, D., Lin, D., Yung, M. (eds.) CISC 2005. LNCS, vol. 3822, pp. 175–188. Springer, Heidelberg (2005). https://doi.org/10.1007/11599548_15

Beyond Birthday Bound Secure Fresh Rekeying: Application to Authenticated Encryption

Bart Mennink[✉]

Digital Security Group, Radboud University, Nijmegen, The Netherlands
b.mennink@cs.ru.nl

Abstract. Fresh rekeying is a well-established method to protect a primitive or mode against side-channel attacks: an easy to protect but cryptographically not so involved function generates a subkey from the master key, and this subkey is then used for the block encryption of a single or a few messages. It is an efficient way to achieve side-channel protection, but current solutions only achieve birthday bound security in the block size of the cipher and thus halve its security (except if more involved primitives are employed). We present generalized solutions to parallel block cipher rekeying that, for the first time, achieve security beyond the birthday bound in the block size n. The first solution involves, next to the subkey generation, one multiplication and the core block cipher call and achieves $2^{2n/3}$ security. The second solution makes two block cipher calls, and achieves optimal 2^n security. Our third solution uses a slightly larger subkey generation function but requires no adaptations to the core encryption and also achieves optimal security. The construction seamlessly generalizes to permutation based fresh rekeying. Central to our schemes is the observation that fresh rekeying and generic tweakable block cipher design are two very related topics, and we can take lessons from the advanced results in the latter to improve our understanding and development of the former. We subsequently use these rekeying schemes in a constructive manner to deliver three authenticated encryption modes that achieve beyond birthday bound security and are easy to protect against side-channel attacks.

Keywords: Fresh rekeying · Block cipher · Generalization · Beyond birthday bound · Optimal

1 Introduction

The security of cryptographic constructions is typically analyzed in a black-box model. The analysis is based on the assumption that the adversary adheres to the conditions and limitations set by the security model, and that it only obtains information about the cryptographic function by model-wise permitted evaluations of that function. The emerging threat of side-channel attacks questions the

© International Association for Cryptologic Research 2020
S. Moriai and H. Wang (Eds.): ASIACRYPT 2020, LNCS 12491, pp. 630–661, 2020.
https://doi.org/10.1007/978-3-030-64837-4_21

credibility of this approach. Side-channel attackers obtain *additional* information about a cryptographic function, typically via passive attacks such as timing attacks [52], differential power analysis [54], or electromagnetic radiation [56]. With black-box security of cryptographic schemes improving, side-channel security is often the weak spot. In particular, a cryptographic function could achieve very strong black-box security, but its security may be nullified if its implementation is in an unprotected environment.

Securing a cryptographic function against side-channel attacks is a serious challenge. One way of doing so is at the implementation level, namely through hiding [62] or masking [24,31,44,85]. However, these approaches are often design-specific and could be prohibitively expensive. An alternative approach is to change the mode at the protocol level, i.e., to develop the protocol in such a way that secret-key material is used scarcely and its usage is easier to protect.

One of the most basic and practically appealing expositions of this idea is fresh parallel rekeying. In this approach one does not use a block cipher in its naive fashion, but rather uses a subkey generation function on top of that. This subkey generation function has access to the master key (hence needs strong side-channel protection) but does not need to be a cryptographically strong primitive. The block cipher evaluation itself must of course be cryptographically strong, but only uses every subkey once or a few number of times, and does not need strong side-channel protection. In practical cases, the subkey generation needs to be protected against the stronger differential power analysis (DPA) whereas the core encryption only needs to be protected against simple power analysis (SPA) and related techniques [9,93]. This concept is called a "leveled implementation" [79]. The first appearance of the idea of rekeying was by Abdalla and Bellare [1], and it was independently introduced and proposed as side-channel countermeasure by Borst [21, Section 6.6.1]. The approach was recently reconsidered and popularized by Medwed et al. [64]: they suggest multiplication as subkey generation (but, see Sect. 7). In this way, the cryptographic strength and the side-channel resistance of the scheme are virtually disconnected into a light but strongly protected multiplication and a strong but lightly protected core encryption. Medwed et al. [63] generalized it to a multi-party variant, but later, Dobraunig et al. [28] demonstrated that Medwed et al.'s solutions allowed for birthday bound key recoveries in the block size of the cipher. Dobraunig et al. [30] later resolved this by introducing two fresh rekeying solutions: one based on the subkey generation function and two block cipher calls that is still birthday bound secure (though optimally key recovery secure), and one based on a subkey generation function and a tweakable block cipher call that is optimally secure (in the ideal model). Patented ideas on the topic appeared in [35,53]. We refer to Sect. 3 for a detailed survey of the schemes and their relation.

One might argue that the idea to separate cryptographic building blocks into a part that must be DPA-protected and a part that must be SPA-protected has been overtaken by time. Most notably, single trace attacks have improved over the last decades, in particular with the soft-analytical side-channel attacks enhanced with belief propagation [37,50,92]. These attacks, however, focus on unprotected implementations of which the behavior was known prior to the attack (e.g., how the implementation responds to known inputs with known key). In practical applications, such as smart cards, this is usually not the case. More fundamentally, in [37, Section 6] it is already confirmed that for noisy implementations, multiple traces simply give more information to an attacker than a single trace, and likewise [50, Section 1] conclude that DPA attacks are more powerful in the context of noisy implementation. From this viewpoint, it is fair to conclude that in practical settings, multiple traces simply give more information to an attacker than a single trace. The separation of schemes into a DPA-protected part and an SPA-protected part is thus a very valuable approach towards efficient cryptography.

None of the solutions so far is particularly desirable: rekeying a plain block cipher halves its security (this applies to the schemes of Medwed et al. [63,64] and the first one of Dobraunig et al. [30]), and beyond birthday bound security is only achieved using heavier machinery, namely a tweakable block cipher (this applies to the second one of Dobraunig et al. [30]). Of course, dedicated tweakable block cipher designs such as SKINNY or MANTIS [11] or QARMA [4] exist, but this solution is unsatisfying for securing implementations of the plain AES or lightweight block ciphers like PRESENT [19], CLEFIA [90], Midori [5], GIFT [6], and others [10,20,39,89].

Strikingly, it turns out that the idea of fresh rekeying is very related to generic tweakable block cipher design [60]: not only in its appearance as underlying primitive in Dobraunig et al.'s second construction, but more importantly from a bigger picture (see also [38]). Contrary to the field of rekeying, generic tweakable block cipher design has faced extensive research, in particular in the design and understanding of beyond birthday bound secure solutions. This direction was initiated by Landecker et al. [58], and optimally secure solutions (in the ideal model) were given by Mennink [65], Wang et al. [94], and Jha et al. [49]. A detailed survey of the state of the art and the relations among these schemes is given in Sect. 4.

1.1   Beyond Birthday Bound Security Block Cipher Rekeying

We tackle the problem of developing beyond birthday bound secure yet efficient parallel rekeying solutions of block ciphers. First, one may suggest that an instantiation of Dobraunig et al.'s tweakable block cipher based construction with a beyond birthday bound secure tweakable block cipher immediately reaches our goal, but this is not true: the analysis of Dobraunig et al. is performed in the ideal tweakable cipher model and thus only holds under the assumption that the tweakable block cipher is perfectly random. No generic construction can be perfectly secure, and as we will demonstrate in Sect. 5.2, composition may already collapse at the birthday bound. Instead, a *direct analysis* is necessary. In addition, Dobraunig et al. built a rekeying scheme *on top of* a tweakable block cipher, but it appears that one can use (variants of) tweakable block ciphers *as* rekeying schemes. Although the difference is subtle, this gives an efficiency gain as we will see later on (in Sect. 8).

Therefore, in Sect. 5, we investigate how to use beyond birthday bound secure tweakable block ciphers more efficiently in the context of rekeying. This is a delicate task: not all state of the art solutions are suitable. The first scheme is based on the simplest beyond birthday bound secure tweakable block cipher from Mennink [65], along with some cosmetic simplifications that appear unnecessary in the composition. The scheme, called $R1$, consists of one subkey generation function, one multiplication, and one block cipher call. It is depicted in Fig. 1, and achieves security up to complexity $2^{2n/3}$, where n is the block size of the cipher. The second solution is an instantiation of Dobraunig et al.'s scheme with an optimally secure tweakable block cipher from Wang et al. [94], along with some necessary changes to avoid that security collapses at $2^{n/2}$. The adjusted scheme, called $R2$, is depicted in Fig. 2 and achieves optimal 2^n security.

Albeit the two solutions achieve beyond birthday bound security and are reasonably efficient, they may be unsatisfying in certain settings. This is in part as they use a block cipher whose key size and block size are the same, but also as they consist of a sequential evaluation of three operations (subkey generation, then multiplication/block cipher, then block cipher). For our third generalized solution, we depart from state of the art on rekeying, and note that the tweakable block cipher XHX from Jha et al. [49] in itself is already well-suited for rekeying. Our third scheme $R3$ is a simplification and adaptation of XHX in such a way that it is easy to understand and analyze and at the same time general enough to be broadly applicable in a side-channel setting. The resulting scheme is introduced in Sect. 6 and depicted in Fig. 3. It uses a larger key than $R1$ and $R2$, but performs subkey generation more efficiently and flexibly, and consists of only two functions (subkey generation, then block cipher). In addition, key size reduction is possible. The scheme achieves optimal 2^n security. The scheme easily generalizes to a permutation based variant, concretely a rekeying scheme for Even-Mansour [33], in birthday bound security in the state size of the permutation, where we remark that the state of a permutation is typically much larger than the block size of a block cipher (see Sect. 6).

We elaborate on instantiations of the schemes in Sect. 7, where we also discuss possible key size reduction of $R3$, and we describe and discuss the costs of the schemes relative to the state of the art in Sect. 8. This comparison, summarized in Table 1, indicates that our schemes $R1$, $R2$, and $R3$, compare favorably. For example: $R2$ is equally expensive as the block cipher based solution of Dobraunig et al., yet optimally secure. The scheme $R1$, in turn, achieves a lower level of provable security than $R2$, but it is also cheaper and intuitively more appealing. Scheme $R3$, finally, has higher subkey generation cost and a priori larger key, but it achieves optimal security and is more generic.

1.2   Application: Rekeying-Based Authenticated Encryption

Tweakable block ciphers have played an important role in the design and analysis of authenticated encryption schemes. Either implicitly or explicitly, 18 out of 57 submissions to the CAESAR competition for the development of a portfolio of authenticated encryption schemes [22] were based on a tweakable block cipher.

The reason for this is a technical one: in analyzing the authenticated encryption mode, one can discard many technicalities and argue security of the mode assuming that the tweakable block cipher is secure. Then, these technicalities are dealt with at the tweakable block cipher level, which is by design a smaller and easier to handle object.

In Sect. 9, we benefit from the solid state of the art on authenticated encryption, and use our observation that generic tweakable block cipher design and fresh parallel rekeying are very related. We take the ΘCB authenticated encryption mode of Krovetz and Rogaway [55] as application, and instantiate it with our rekeying schemes $R1$, $R2$, and $R3$. The three resulting modes are parallelizable, have a security bound dominated by that of the underlying tweakable rekeying scheme (hence, $2^{2n/3}$, 2^n, and 2^n, respectively), and are *by design easy to protect against side-channel attacks* (as $R1$, $R2$, and $R3$ are). We compare the solutions among each other, with OCB3, with DTE [16,17], and other alternatives in Sect. 9.3.

It is important to note that the gains we achieve here are independent of the fact that we used ΘCB: they are purely caused by the use of our rekeying schemes. Further applications can be found in tweakable block cipher based MAC or AE schemes such as ZMAC [47] or ZOCB/ZOTR [7], and the achieved efficiency and security gains are comparable to that of the application outlined in Sect. 9.

1.3 Outline

Section 2 includes the preliminaries of this work. An in-depth survey of rekeying schemes is given in Sect. 3 and of tweakable block ciphers in Sect. 4. The first two schemes, $R1$ and $R2$, are given in Sect. 5. The third scheme, $R3$, is given in Sect. 6. We elaborate on instantiations of the schemes in Sect. 7, and perform a cost analysis of the schemes in Sect. 8. In Sect. 9, we apply our findings to authenticated encryption and instantiate ΘCB with our rekeying solutions. The work is concluded in Sect. 10.

2 Preliminaries

For natural $n \in \mathbb{N}$, $\{0,1\}^n$ denotes the set of all n-bit strings. $\{0,1\}^*$ denotes the set of arbitrarily sized strings. For a finite set $\mathcal{X}$, $x \xleftarrow{\$} \mathcal{X}$ denotes the random sampling of an element x from $\mathcal{X}$. For natural $m, n \in \mathbb{N}$ such that $m \leq n$, we denote by $(n)_m = n(n-1)\cdots(n-m+1)$ the falling factorial.

2.1 (Tweakable) Block Ciphers

For $\kappa, \rho, n \in \mathbb{N}$, a block cipher $E : \{0,1\}^\kappa \times \{0,1\}^n \to \{0,1\}^n$ is a mapping such that for every key $k \in \{0,1\}^\kappa$, the function $E_k(\cdot) = E(k, \cdot)$ is a permutation on n-bit strings. Its inverse is denoted $E_k^{-1}(\cdot)$. A tweakable block cipher $\widetilde{E} : \{0,1\}^\kappa \times \{0,1\}^\rho \times \{0,1\}^n \to \{0,1\}^n$ is a mapping such that for every key $k \in \{0,1\}^\kappa$ and every tweak $r \in \{0,1\}^{\rho}$, the function $\widetilde{E}_k(r, \cdot) = \widetilde{E}(k, r, \cdot)$ is a permutation on n-bit strings. Its inverse is denoted $\widetilde{E}_k^{-1}(r, \cdot)$.

Note that a block cipher is a family of 2^{κ} n-bit permutations, and a tweakable block cipher is a family of $2^{\kappa+\rho}$ n-bit permutations (gluing together key and tweak). For arbitrary $\mu, n \in \mathbb{N}$, we denote by $\text{tperm}(\mu, n)$ the set of all families of 2^{μ} n-bit permutations.

2.2 Universal Hashing

For $\kappa, \rho, n \in \mathbb{N}$, let $h : \{0,1\}^{\kappa} \times \{0,1\}^{\rho} \rightarrow \{0,1\}^n$ be a family of keyed hash functions. Let $\alpha \geq 0$. We say that h is α-uniform if for any $x \in \{0,1\}^{\rho}$ and $y \in \{0,1\}^n$:

$$\mathbf{Pr}_k \left(h(k, x) = y \right) \leq \alpha,$$

where the probability is taken over $k \xleftarrow{\$} \{0,1\}^{\kappa}$. For $m \leq n$, we say that h is α-m-partial-XOR-uniform if for any distinct $x, x' \in \{0,1\}^{\rho}$ and $y \in \{0,1\}^m$:

$$\mathbf{Pr}_k \left(h(k, x) \oplus h(k, x') = 0^{n-m} \| y \right) \leq \alpha,$$

where the probability is taken over $k \xleftarrow{\$} \{0,1\}^{\kappa}$. Partial-XOR-uniformity is a generalization of the well-known XOR-uniformity condition on hash function families. It was introduced in [73]. We simply refer to α-XOR-uniformity in case $m = n$.

2.3 Rekeying Schemes and Security Model

A rekeying scheme $R : \{0,1\}^{\kappa'} \times \{0,1\}^{\rho} \times \{0,1\}^n \rightarrow \{0,1\}^n$ is a mathematical function that gets as input a key $k \in \{0,1\}^{\kappa'}$, a tweak $r \in \{0,1\}^{\rho}$, and bijectively encrypts an input m to a ciphertext c. The tweak r is typically restricted to be a counter, nonce, or random value. For secret k, R should behave as a family of n-bit permutations indexed by r: for different choices of r the outcomes are uniformly random, whereas identical r's will give distinct outputs naturally. This means that a rekeying scheme has the same functionality as a tweakable block cipher, and we can inherit the security model.

The security of a rekeying scheme R considers a distinguisher D that has bi-directional query access to either R_k for $k \xleftarrow{\$} \{0,1\}^{\kappa'}$ or to $\tilde{\pi} \xleftarrow{\$} \text{tperm}(\rho, n)$, and tries to distinguish both worlds. The capabilities of the distinguisher are typically bounded by the number of queries it can make to its oracle, q, and the time it can use for offline computations, p. (We do not take storage into account.) In our work, we consider R to be based on a block cipher $E : \{0,1\}^{\kappa} \times \{0,1\}^n \rightarrow \{0,1\}^n$, and logically, the distinguisher may want to evaluate E offline as much as possible. Assuming that one evaluation of E takes one unit of time, it can make at most p evaluations of E offline. In our setting, we will consider security of R in the ideal cipher model, which means that the distinguisher has query access to $E \xleftarrow{\$} \text{tperm}(\kappa, n)$ and can make p queries to it. Besides these queries, we allow D to have unlimited time, we consider it computationally unbounded. We end up with the following definition.

Definition 1. *Let $\kappa', \kappa, \rho, n \in \mathbb{N}$. Consider $R : \{0,1\}^{\kappa'} \times \{0,1\}^{\rho} \times \{0,1\}^n \to \{0,1\}^n$ based on a block cipher $E \in \mathrm{tperm}(\kappa, n)$. Let D be any computationally unbounded distinguisher. The "strong tweakable pseudorandom permutation security" security of R is defined as*

$$\mathbf{Adv}_R^{\mathrm{stprp}}(D) = \left| \mathbf{Pr}_{k,E}\left(D^{R_k^{\pm}, E^{\pm}} = 1 \right) - \mathbf{Pr}_{\tilde{\pi},E}\left(D^{\tilde{\pi}^{\pm}, E^{\pm}} = 1 \right) \right|, \quad (1)$$

where the probabilities are taken over $k \xleftarrow{\$} \{0,1\}^{\kappa'}$, $E \xleftarrow{\$} \mathrm{tperm}(\kappa, n)$, and $\tilde{\pi} \xleftarrow{\$} \mathrm{tperm}(\rho, n)$. The superscript "$\pm$" indicates that the distinguisher has bidirectional access to the oracle.

Above model poses no restriction on the choice of r by the distinguisher: it can freely choose it. In practical rekeying schemes, however, r is typically restricted to be a counter, nonce, or random value, as explicitly outlined in the schemes below. This does not change the security model, yet it does influence the security analysis and the scope of the schemes.

3   State of the Art on Rekeying Schemes

Throughout this section, let $E : \{0,1\}^{\kappa} \times \{0,1\}^n \to \{0,1\}^n$ be a block cipher. If the block cipher is used many times under the same key, a poorly protected block cipher may leak this key. Abdalla and Bellare [1] formalized the idea of rekeying, where a particular function is used to generate subkeys for E. They introduced two variants, a parallel and a serial one; we will only be concerned with the parallel one. Using a PRF $F : \{0,1\}^{\kappa'} \times \{0,1\}^{\rho} \to \{0,1\}^{\kappa}$, they considered

$$\begin{aligned} \mathrm{AB} : \{0,1\}^{\kappa'} \times \{0,1\}^{\rho} \times \{0,1\}^n &\to \{0,1\}^n, \\ (k, r, m) &\mapsto E(F(k,r), m), \end{aligned} \quad (2)$$

where r is in principle a counter (the scheme could also be implemented with random r, but this may induce extra collisions for F). The approach was introduced independently, and suggested for side-channel protection, by Borst [21, Section 6.6.1]. Abdalla and Bellare proved that if F is a secure PRF and E is a secure cipher, AB is a perfectly secure rekeying mechanism (as a pseudorandom function).

Medwed et al. [64] initiated the investigation of the minimal conditions needed on the block cipher and the subkey generation to obtain side-channel security. They introduced a function

$$\begin{aligned} \mathrm{MSGR} : \{0,1\}^{\kappa'} \times \{0,1\}^{\rho} \times \{0,1\}^n &\to \{0,1\}^n, \\ (k, r, m) &\mapsto E(h(k,r), m), \end{aligned} \quad (3)$$

for some function $h : \{0,1\}^{\kappa'} \times \{0,1\}^{\rho} \rightarrow \{0,1\}^{\kappa}$, and where r is necessarily a random value for each evaluation. The idea of the scheme is that E is cryptographic machinery that does not need to be equipped with strong side-channel protection (just against SPA) and h is a function that does not need to have strong cryptographic properties but it processes the master key and hence needs to resist strong side-channel attacks (SPA and DPA). For a block cipher with 256-bit key, Medwed et al. suggested to take $\kappa' = \kappa = 256$, and to define h as multiplication in $\mathrm{GF}_{2^8}[\mathbf{x}]/f(\mathbf{x})$ for $f(\mathbf{x}) = \mathbf{x}^d + 1$ for $d \in \{4, 8, 16\}$. In other words, $h(k,r) = r \cdot k$ in above-mentioned ring. The scheme does not come with a theoretical security analysis, but the authors do provide extensive side-channel analysis. The scheme was later generalized to the multi-party setting by Medwed et al. [63].

In their introduction, Medwed et al. [64] did not draw the equivalence with the scheme of Abdalla and Bellare. Most importantly, h does not behave as a PRF. Dobraunig et al. [28] subsequently described a birthday bound key recovery attack on both schemes of Medwed et al. [63,64].[1] The attack is based on the idea that if a session key is recovered, the master key can be derived by invertibility of h. In other words, the attack relies on two weaknesses of MSGR:

(i) a subkey can be recovered in total complexity around $2^{n/2}$;
(ii) once a subkey is recovered, the master key can be recovered by invertibility of h.

Later, Dobraunig et al. [30] presented two solutions to remedy the situation. The first one does so by enhancing the subkey generation function, and works for $\kappa = n$:

$$\begin{aligned}\mathrm{DKM}^{+}1 : \{0,1\}^{\kappa'} \times \{0,1\}^{\rho} \times \{0,1\}^{n} &\rightarrow \{0,1\}^{n}\,, \\ (k,r,m) &\mapsto E(E(h(k,r),r) \oplus r \oplus h(k,r), m)\,.\end{aligned} \qquad (4)$$

Also in this scheme, h needs to be secured against SPA and DPA, whereas the block cipher only needs to be SPA secure. The value r can be random or a counter. $\mathrm{DKM}^{+}1$ differs from MSGR by having a one-way subkey generation function, and reducing the security to that of AB. To wit, the subkey generation function in $\mathrm{DKM}^{+}1$ is the function h followed by the Miyaguchi-Preneel compression function [82]. Nonetheless, the resulting subkey generation only behaves like a PRF up to the birthday bound: the authors prove that if h is bijective for either the left or the right of its inputs fixed and if E is an ideal cipher, the resulting scheme is secure up to complexity $2^{n/2}$. For h, they suggest multiplication in $\mathrm{GF}_2[\mathbf{x}]/f(\mathbf{x})$ for any irreducible polynomial $f(\mathbf{x})$ of degree n.

The second scheme of Dobraunig et al. [30] achieves security beyond the birthday bound, but it is based on a *tweakable* block cipher $\widetilde{E} : \{0,1\}^{\kappa} \times \{0,1\}^{\rho} \times \{0,1\}^{n} \rightarrow \{0,1\}^{n}$:

---

[1] They pointed out that the attack strategy also works on stateless schemes, such as Kocher's [53]. The attack is detailed in [30].

$$\text{DKM}^+2 : \{0,1\}^{\kappa'} \times \{0,1\}^\rho \times \{0,1\}^n \to \{0,1\}^n \, ,$$
$$(k,r,m) \mapsto \widetilde{E}(h(k,r),r,m) \, . \tag{5}$$

One can see this construction as an abstraction of DKM^+1 by "uniting" the two block cipher calls into a single tweakable block cipher call. The value r can, again, be random or a counter. This construction is perfectly secure under the assumption that h is bijective for either the left or the right of its inputs fixed and that $\widetilde{E}$ is an ideal tweakable block cipher.

For future discussion, it is of importance to understand how the schemes of Dobraunig et al. [30] improve over the one of Medwed et al. [64]. The first scheme, DKM^+1, improves over MSGR by resolving weakness (ii) above, namely by assuring that the subkey generation is non-invertible. It may still be possible to recover a session key in complexity $2^{n/2}$; this is no problem, but de facto contributes to the fact that the scheme only achieves $2^{n/2}$ security. The second scheme, DKM^+2, resolves both weaknesses (i) and (ii) and is the first scheme in the line to achieve beyond birthday bound security, but at a considerable cost: it assumes that $\widetilde{E}$ is an ideal tweakable block cipher. This particularly means that it is only meaningful for instantiation with a dedicated tweakable block cipher design (assumed to be perfectly secure). Any instantiation with a generic tweakable block cipher design (such as the ones in next section) violates the "ideal tweakable block cipher" assumption, and does not necessarily induce a secure scheme; to the contrary, as we will demonstrate in Sect. 5.2.

4   State of the Art on Tweak-Rekeyable Tweakable Block Ciphers

Throughout this section, let $E : \{0,1\}^\kappa \times \{0,1\}^n \to \{0,1\}^n$ be a block cipher. A tweakable block cipher extends a conventional one by the extra input of a "tweak" $r \in \{0,1\}^\rho$: the tweakable block cipher behaves as an independent block cipher for every tweak. The initial formalization of a tweakable block cipher is by Liskov et al. [60]. As part of their formalization, Liskov et al. suggested that changing the tweak should be cheaper than changing the key. Their formalization included two designs, most notably a construction currently known as LRW2:

$$\text{LRW2} : \{0,1\}^{\kappa+\kappa'} \times \{0,1\}^\rho \times \{0,1\}^n \to \{0,1\}^n \, ,$$
$$(k_1 \| k_2, r, m) \mapsto E(k_1, m \oplus h(k_2, r)) \oplus h(k_2, r) \, , \tag{6}$$

where $h : \{0,1\}^{\kappa'} \times \{0,1\}^\rho \to \{0,1\}^n$ is a universal hash function family. Various generalizations of the scheme have appeared [23,70,87]. A cascade of multiple LRW2's was proven to be secure beyond the birthday bound [57,58,68,84].

Cascading, however, makes the scheme more expensive, and alternatives to achieving beyond birthday bound secure tweakable block ciphers have been considered. Minematsu [71] introduced the following scheme based on block cipher E and a PRF $F : \{0,1\}^{\kappa'} \times \{0,1\}^{\rho} \to \{0,1\}^{\kappa}$:

$$\text{Min} : \{0,1\}^{\kappa'} \times \{0,1\}^{\rho} \times \{0,1\}^{n} \to \{0,1\}^{n}, \tag{7}$$
$$(k, r, m) \mapsto E(F(k, r), m),$$

where, depending on the application, the user can choose the tweak input r. Minematsu proved security up to $\max\{2^{n/2}, 2^{n-\rho}\}$ and the bound is known to be tight [67]. Note that Min is equivalent to AB but the security bounds are different: this is because Minematsu poses no restriction on repeated usage of r.

Mennink [65] introduced two constructions that achieve beyond birthday bound security with minimal key material. Both constructions assume $\kappa = \rho = n$ (but we will keep using κ, ρ, n as this more clearly describes the roles of the different sets). The first construction makes one call to E and one multiplication:

$$\text{Men1} : \{0,1\}^{\kappa} \times \{0,1\}^{\rho} \times \{0,1\}^{n} \to \{0,1\}^{n}, \tag{8}$$
$$(k, r, m) \mapsto E(k \oplus r, m \oplus r \cdot k) \oplus r \cdot k,$$

where multiplication is in $\text{GF}_2[\mathbf{x}]/f(\mathbf{x})$ for any irreducible polynomial $f(\mathbf{x})$ of degree n. The scheme is proven secure up to total complexity $2^{2n/3}$ in the ideal cipher model. Mennink's second construction,

$$\text{Men2} : \{0,1\}^{\kappa} \times \{0,1\}^{\rho} \times \{0,1\}^{n} \to \{0,1\}^{n}, \tag{9}$$
$$(k, r, m) \mapsto E(k \oplus r, m \oplus E(2 \cdot k, r)) \oplus E(2 \cdot k, r),$$

makes two block cipher calls (instead of one block cipher call and one multiplication) and is proven to achieve optimal 2^{n} security in the ideal cipher model [65,66].[2] One can simply take $E(k,r)$ for mask, provided that one restricts the tweak to $r \neq 0$.

Clearly, Men1 and Men2 are not so interesting from a leakage resilience point of view: the key input to the (possibly unprotected) block cipher is $k \oplus r$ from which k can be recovered with knowledge of r. Nevertheless, the work of Mennink [65] set the stage for a line of research on tweak-rekeyable schemes, where the key input to the internal primitive may change depending on the tweak. Wang et al. [94] generalized the construction Men2 to 32 variants $\text{WGZ}^{+}i$ for $i \in \{1, \ldots, 32\}$ that are based on two block cipher calls and achieve optimal 2^{n} security. The approach is systematic and gives an exhaustive list of all "interesting" solutions. We will highlight one of them, $\text{WGZ}^{+}12$, which we consider to be the simplest and most elegant scheme, as well as the most suitable one for our purposes (the reason being that for $\text{WGZ}^{+}12$ the masking $E(0,k)$ needs to be computed only once). Also this construction assumes $\kappa = \rho = n$:

$$\text{WGZ}^{+}12 : \{0,1\}^{\kappa} \times \{0,1\}^{\rho} \times \{0,1\}^{n} \to \{0,1\}^{n}, \tag{10}$$
$$(k, r, m) \mapsto E(k \oplus r, m \oplus E(0, k)) \oplus E(0, k).$$

---

[2] The conference version [65] contained a bug, pointed out by Wang et al. [94]; we took the adjusted function from the full version [66].

Naito [74] introduced XKX, a generalization of Min specifically targeting authenticated encryption. In addition to the PRF $F : \{0,1\}^{\kappa'} \times \{0,1\}^{\rho} \to \{0,1\}^{\kappa}$, it uses a hash function family $h : \{0,1\}^{\kappa''} \times \{0,1\}^{\rho'} \to \{0,1\}^n$ and is defined as

$$
\begin{aligned}
\text{XKX} : \{0,1\}^{\kappa'+\kappa''} \times \{0,1\}^{\rho+\rho'} &\times \{0,1\}^n \to \{0,1\}^n\,, \\
(k_1\|k_2, N\|r, m) &\mapsto E(F(k_1, N), m \oplus h(k_2, r)) \oplus h(k_2, r)\,.
\end{aligned}
\tag{11}
$$

Here, N is a nonce and r a counter, such that $N\|r$ is unique for every query. The PRF F is then instantiated using the sum of permutations [14,15,18,27,46, 61,77,78].

Jha et al. presented the generalized construction XHX [49]. It uses a universal hash function family $h : \{0,1\}^{\kappa'} \times \{0,1\}^{\rho} \to \{0,1\}^{\kappa} \times \{0,1\}^n \times \{0,1\}^n$, and is defined as

$$
\begin{aligned}
\text{XHX} : \{0,1\}^{\kappa'} \times \{0,1\}^{\rho} &\times \{0,1\}^n \to \{0,1\}^n\,, \\
(k, r, m) &\mapsto E(u, m \oplus v) \oplus w, \text{ where } (u, v, w) \leftarrow h(k, r)\,.
\end{aligned}
\tag{12}
$$

They subsequently consider h to be constructed of three universal hash function families h_1, h_2, h_3, all receiving subkeys k_1, k_2, k_3 derived from k using the block cipher E. The construction generalizes Men2 as well as the 32 WGZ^+i constructions. Jha et al. [49] derive minimal conditions on the functions and on the subkey generation for XHX to be secure, and prove that security up to $2^{(\kappa+n)/2}$ is achieved. Note that the XHX scheme is quite general (and in fact it is not described in full generality here), but this generality goes at the cost of simplicity, and in fact, if E-based subkey generation for h is omitted the scheme simplifies drastically. Also, security turns out not to be sacrificed if one uses identical masking before and after the block cipher, i.e., if one sets $v = w$.

It is important to note that, although Minematsu's Min and Naito's XKX can still be proven secure in the standard cipher model, the analyses of Mennink's Men1 and Men2, Wang et al.'s WGZ^+i, and Jha et al.'s XHX are performed in the ideal cipher model. This difference comes from the fact that the adversary can change tweaks, subsequently influence the key input to the block cipher, and the model of related-key secure block ciphers has to be deployed in order to get standard model security. The construction can subsequently never be properly proven to be beyond birthday bound secure. Mennink [67] performed an extensive theoretical analysis of this phenomenon and demonstrated that provably optimal security is impossible in the standard model, under the assumption that no non-tweak-rekeyable scheme based on approximately σ block cipher calls achieves security beyond $2^{\sigma n/(\sigma+1)}$. This assumption, in turn, is still open, and the security of cascaded LRW2 is known to reside on the edge of this bound [68]. Cogliati [25] recently considered multi-user beyond birthday bound security of tweakable block ciphers, and presented refinements of [68] in the case of block ciphers whose key space is larger than the block size.

5 Improved DKM$^+$2 Instantiations

The rekeying scheme DKM$^+$1 [30] (see (4)) is seen as a specific instantiation of AB, namely by putting PRF F:

$$F : \{0,1\}^{\kappa'} \times \{0,1\}^{\rho} \to \{0,1\}^{\kappa}, \tag{13}$$
$$(k,r) \mapsto E(h(k,r),r) \oplus r \oplus h(k,r).$$

Instead, in hindsight it is more reasonable to think of it as an instantiation of DKM$^+$2 for an inconveniently designed tweakable block cipher design:

$$\widetilde{E} : \{0,1\}^{\kappa} \times \{0,1\}^{\rho} \times \{0,1\}^{n} \to \{0,1\}^{n},$$
$$(k,r,m) \mapsto E(E(k,r) \oplus r \oplus k, m).$$

As a tweakable block cipher, this function can be broken in complexity $2^{n/2}$. In the remainder of this section, we start from DKM$^+$2 and consider two of the most suitable ways of instantiating the tweakable block cipher.

5.1 First Scheme

The simplest choice, following Sect. 4, is to instantiate DKM$^+$2 with the Men1 tweakable block cipher [65] (see (8)). We call this scheme $R1$. It is based on a block cipher $E : \{0,1\}^{\kappa} \times \{0,1\}^{n} \to \{0,1\}^{n}$ and internally uses a hash function family $h : \{0,1\}^{\kappa'} \times \{0,1\}^{\rho} \to \{0,1\}^{\kappa}$, where $\kappa = \rho = n$ (and typically, but not necessarily, $\kappa' = \kappa$):

$$R1 : \{0,1\}^{\kappa'} \times \{0,1\}^{\rho} \times \{0,1\}^{n} \to \{0,1\}^{n}, \tag{14}$$
$$(k,r,m) \mapsto E(h(k,r), m \oplus r \cdot h(k,r)) \oplus r \cdot h(k,r),$$

where multiplication is in $\mathrm{GF}_2[\mathbf{x}]/f(\mathbf{x})$ for any irreducible polynomial $f(\mathbf{x})$ of degree n. The scheme is depicted in Fig. 1. We remark that this is not *exactly* a composition of DKM$^+$2 with Men1: such a composition would have $h(k,r) \oplus r$ as key input to E. As we have included subkey generation $h(k,r)$ to the scheme, the addition of r is not needed.

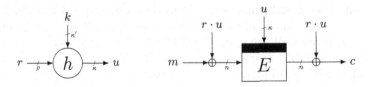

Fig. 1. Generalized rekeying construction $R1$ of (14) with $\kappa = \rho = n$: subkey generation (left) and core encryption (right).

Intuitively, as DKM$^+$2 is optimally 2^n secure and Men1 is $2^{2n/3}$ secure, one expects $R1$ to be $2^{2n/3}$ secure. Unfortunately, one cannot simply claim security of $R1$ in such a hybrid argument. The reason is that DKM^+2 is proven secure under the assumption that $\widetilde{E}$ is an ideal tweakable block cipher, and Men1 does not meet this criterion. Fortunately, however, a dedicated proof would be similar to that of Men1, the overlay of DKM^+2 coming at limited effort.

Formally, in the security model of Definition 1, we will prove that $R1$ achieves security up to complexity $2^{2n/3}$. The proof is given in the full version [69]. It is inspired by that of Mennink [65], but it is not quite the same due to the usage of the subkey generation function. In fact, the security of $R1$ *cannot* be concluded from the security results on DKM^+2 and Men1. The proof of $R1$ is, as that of [65], based on the Szemerédi-Trotter theorem [91], which claims that if one takes q lines and p points in a two-dimensional finite field $\mathbb{F}^2$, the number of point-line incidences is at most $\min\{q^{1/2}p + q, qp^{1/2} + p\}$.

Theorem 1. *Let* $\kappa', \kappa, \rho, n \in \mathbb{N}$ *with* $\kappa = \rho = n$. *Let* $h : \{0,1\}^{\kappa'} \times \{0,1\}^\rho \to \{0,1\}^\kappa$ *be a family of keyed hash functions that is injective for fixed* $k \in \{0,1\}^{\kappa'}$ *and* α-*uniform. Let* D *be a distinguisher making at most* q *construction queries and* p *primitive queries. Then,*

$$\mathbf{Adv}_{R1}^{\mathrm{stprp}}(D) \leq 2\min\{q^{1/2}p + q, qp^{1/2} + p\}\alpha. \tag{15}$$

Note that for $q = p$, the bound simplifies to $2(q^{3/2} + q)\alpha$. There exist hash function families h that meet the conditions for $\alpha = 2^{-\kappa}$ (see Sect. 7). Recalling that $\kappa = n$, this implies $2^{2n/3}$ security.

The condition that h needs to be injective for fixed $k \in \{0,1\}^{\kappa'}$ can be traded for the requirement that for any distinct $r, r' \in \{0,1\}^\rho$ and $y \in \{0,1\}^\kappa$,

$$\mathbf{Pr}_k\left(h(k,r) = h(k,r') = y\right) \leq \alpha^2. \tag{16}$$

This relaxation will add $\binom{q}{2}\alpha^2$ to the security bound. The proof is trivial: it simply considers the event $h(k,r) = h(k,r') = y$ as a bad event for any two construction queries.

5.2   Second Scheme

The first scheme $R1$ is efficient, but achieves security up to $2^{2n/3}$ only. We consider an alternative instantiation of DKM^+2 with a tweakable block cipher based on two block cipher calls. We will *not* take Men2 [65] (see (9)), but rather one of the solutions of Wang et al., WGZ^+12 [94] (see (10)) to be precise, which we found more suitable. The resulting scheme $R2$ is based on the same primitives as $R1$ and is defined as follows:

$$\begin{aligned} R2 : \{0,1\}^{\kappa'} \times \{0,1\}^\rho \times \{0,1\}^n &\to \{0,1\}^n, \\ (k,r,m) &\mapsto E(h(k,r), m \oplus E(r, h(k,r))) \oplus E(r, h(k,r)). \end{aligned} \tag{17}$$

The scheme is depicted in Fig. 2.

It is important to note that the scheme is not *exactly* a composition of DKM^+2 with WGZ^+12. First of all, as for $R1$, the subkey input $h(k,r) \oplus r$

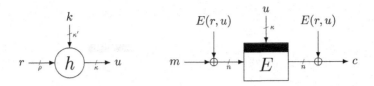

Fig. 2. Generalized rekeying construction $R2$ of (17) with $\kappa = \rho = n$: subkey generation (left) and core encryption (right).

is simplified to $h(k, r)$. More importantly, a literal composition would have $E(0, h(k, r))$ as masking rather than $E(r, h(k, r))$. This would make it easier to attack: an adversary can make q construction queries with $m = 0$ for varying r, and p primitive evaluations $E(0, l) = y$ for varying l, and the proof aborts at the point that the adversary has a correct guess $h(k, r) = l$, which happens with probability $qp/2^n$. This also perfectly marks the weak spot of the ideal tweakable cipher model used to prove DKM$^+$2: composition does not work as nicely as hoped for. It is also for the same reason that not any of the 32 WGZ^+i schemes could do the job, as became clear after experimentation.

In the full version [69], we will give a formal analysis in the security model of Definition 1 that $R2$ achieves security with complexity 2^n. The proof is inspired by that of Wang et al. [94], but it is more complex due to the changes in the construction and the usage of the subkey generation function. In fact, the security of $R2$ *cannot* be concluded from the security results on DKM$^+$2 and WGZ$^+$12.

Theorem 2. *Let $\kappa', \kappa, \rho, n \in \mathbb{N}$ with $\kappa = \rho = n$. Let $h : \{0,1\}^{\kappa'} \times \{0,1\}^{\rho} \to \{0,1\}^{\kappa}$ be a family of keyed hash functions that is α-uniform and α-XOR-uniform. Let D be a distinguisher making at most q construction queries and p primitive queries. Then,*

$$\mathbf{Adv}_{R2}^{\mathrm{stprp}}(D) \leq \frac{q(3q - 3 + 2p)\alpha}{2^n} + (q + p)\alpha + \frac{p}{2^n}. \quad (18)$$

For $q = p$ and for simplicity of reasoning taking h to meet the conditions for $\alpha = 2^{-\kappa} = 2^{-n}$ (see Sect. 7), the bound simplifies to $\frac{5q^2}{2^{2n}} + \frac{3q}{2^n}$. This implies security up to complexity 2^n.

6   Simpler Optimally Secure Block Cipher Rekeying

The links between fresh rekeying and generic tweakable block cipher design are apparent, but in-depth analyses of the problems in both directions have been performed mostly disjointly, and the equivalence has never been properly drawn and exploited. This is, in part, caused by the fact that the design incentives are different. For example, whereas Minematsu's tweakable block cipher Min [71] (see (7)) is identical to Abdalla and Bellare's AB [1] (see (2)) and almost identical to Medwed et al.'s rekeying scheme MSGR [64] (see (3)), schemes like Men1 and

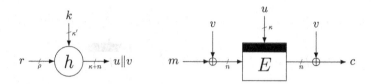

Fig. 3. Generalized rekeying construction $R3$ of (19): subkey generation (left) and core encryption (right).

Men2 do not achieve leakage resilience in the sense that MSGR, DKM$^+$1, or DKM$^+$2 do, at least not with the same minimal leakage resilience assumptions.

Yet, there is resemblance in the directions, and we can take advantage of this in our quest to optimally secure block cipher rekeying. Our third generalized solution discards the earlier rekeying schemes in its entirety and takes inspiration of the state of the art on tweakable block ciphers. The resulting scheme is reminiscent of XHX [49] (see (12)) but we make significant simplifications to balance between generality, simplicity, and the possibility to achieve leakage resilience under reasonable conditions. Our rekeying construction for block cipher $E : \{0,1\}^\kappa \times \{0,1\}^n \to \{0,1\}^n$ internally uses a hash function family $h : \{0,1\}^{\kappa'} \times \{0,1\}^\rho \to \{0,1\}^\kappa \times \{0,1\}^n$, and is defined as

$$R3 : \{0,1\}^{\kappa'} \times \{0,1\}^\rho \times \{0,1\}^n \to \{0,1\}^n \,,$$
$$(k, r, m) \mapsto E(u, m \oplus v) \oplus v, \text{ where } u\|v \leftarrow h(k,r) \,. \tag{19}$$

The scheme is depicted in Fig. 3. Note that we pose no restrictions on κ', κ, ρ, n. We remark that XHX is a particularly useful choice in the context of lightweight applications. For instance, due to its beyond birthday bound security (in the block size) it has been the base of the tweakable block cipher in REMUS [45], a first-round submission to the NIST lightweight cryptography competition [75].

In the security model of Definition 1, we will prove that $R3$ achieves security up to complexity $2^{(\kappa+n)/2}$. The proof is given in the full version [69]; it is a simplification of that of Jha et al. [49].

Theorem 3. *Let $\kappa', \kappa, \rho, n \in \mathbb{N}$. Let $h : \{0,1\}^{\kappa'} \times \{0,1\}^\rho \to \{0,1\}^\kappa \times \{0,1\}^n$ be a family of keyed hash functions that is α-uniform and α-n-partial-XOR-uniform. Let D be a distinguisher making at most q construction queries and p primitive queries. Then,*

$$\mathbf{Adv}_{R3}^{\mathrm{stprp}}(D) \le q(q - 1 + 2p)\alpha \,. \tag{20}$$

As we will discuss in Sect. 7, there exists a hash function family h that meets the requested conditions for $\alpha = 2^{-(\kappa+n)}$. Equating $q = p$ for simplicity, above bound simplifies to $3q^2/2^{\kappa+n}$. This roughly gives security up to complexity $2^{(\kappa+n)/2}$.

We remark that using a universal hash function family with ($\kappa = n$)-bit output and setting

$$(k, r, m) \mapsto E(h(k,r), m \oplus h(k,r)) \oplus h(k,r)$$

does not allow to achieve security beyond the birthday bound. An adversary can make q evaluations with $m = 0$ and varying r. It can additionally make p primitive evaluations $E(l, l)$ for varying l. Any construction query collides with any primitive query if $h(k, r) = l$, which happens with probability $qp/2^n$.

Recall that in $R3$ we pose no restriction on κ. One could consider $\kappa = 0$: in this case, $E \in \mathrm{tperm}(0, n)$ is simply a permutation, and one can consider $R3$ to be a rekeying scheme for Even-Mansour [33]. Following Theorem 3, it achieves security up to around $2^{n/2}$, where n is the state size of the permutation. Practical permutations are typically much larger than block ciphers. For example, the AES [26] has a block size of $n = 128$ bits, but the Keccak/SHA-3 [34] permutation has a state size of $n = 1600$ bits.

7 Instantiations

Medwed et al. and Dobraunig et al. initially suggested multiplication for h. Later, it was demonstrated [12,13,40,80] that its use should be done with care as the algebraic structure enables certain types of attacks. A formal treatment was delivered by Dziembowski et al. [32]. In their introduction of a side-channel secure authenticated encryption scheme ISAP, Dobraunig et al. [29] suggested the sponge for subkey generation.

Nonetheless, for the sake of comparison in Sect. 8, we will adopt the approach of using finite field multiplication for h in our schemes. For $R1$ and $R2$, the same approach as that of Dobraunig et al. works. In detail, finite field multiplication in $\mathrm{GF}_2[\mathbf{x}]/f(\mathbf{x})$ for any irreducible polynomial $f(\mathbf{x})$ of degree n is known to be 2^{-n}-uniform and 2^{-n}-XOR-uniform (assuming $r \neq 0^\rho$). For $R3$, multiplication also works but one would need a hash function family with $(\kappa + n)$-bit range, meaning multiplication in $\mathrm{GF}_2[\mathbf{x}]/f(\mathbf{x})$ for irreducible polynomial $f(\mathbf{x})$ of degree $\kappa + n$. It is possible to improve the efficiency to smaller multiplications by instantiating h using two independent keys. Let $\kappa, n \in \mathbb{N}$ be the parameters of the underlying block cipher E, set $\rho \leq \min\{\kappa, n\}$ and $\kappa' = \kappa + n$, and consider the folklore construction

$$
\begin{aligned}
h_{\mathrm{mult}} : \{0,1\}^{\kappa'} \times \{0,1\}^\rho &\to \{0,1\}^\kappa \times \{0,1\}^n, \\
(k_1 \| k_2, r) &\mapsto (r \cdot k_1, r \cdot k_2),
\end{aligned}
\tag{21}
$$

where multiplication is in $\mathrm{GF}_2[\mathbf{x}]/f(\mathbf{x})$ for any irreducible polynomial $f(\mathbf{x})$ of degree n, and r is always injectively padded to obtain a string of size κ resp. n bits. Assuming $r \neq 0^\rho$, it is straightforward to prove that h_{mult} is $2^{-(\kappa+n)}$-uniform and $2^{-(\kappa+n)}$-n-partial-XOR-uniform.

Proposition 1. h_{mult} of (21) is $2^{-(\kappa+n)}$-uniform and $2^{-(\kappa+n)}$-n-partial-XOR-uniform.

Proof. Starting with $2^{-(\kappa+n)}$-uniformity, consider any $r \in \{0,1\}^\rho \backslash \{0^\rho\}$ and $(u,v) \in \{0,1\}^\kappa \times \{0,1\}^n$. Then,

$$\mathbf{Pr}_{k_1,k_2}\left(h_{\mathrm{mult}}(k_1\|k_2,r) = (u,v)\right) = \mathbf{Pr}_{k_1}\left(r \cdot k_1 = u\right) \cdot \mathbf{Pr}_{k_2}\left(r \cdot k_2 = v\right) = 1/2^{\kappa+n},$$

where the randomness is taken over $k_1 \xleftarrow{\$} \{0,1\}^\kappa$ and $k_2 \xleftarrow{\$} \{0,1\}^n$.

For $2^{-(\kappa+n)}$-n-partial-XOR-uniformity, consider any distinct $r,r' \in \{0,1\}^\rho$ and $v \in \{0,1\}^n$. Then,

$$
\begin{aligned}
&\mathbf{Pr}_{k_1,k_2}\left(h_{\mathrm{mult}}(k_1\|k_2,r) \oplus h_{\mathrm{mult}}(k_1\|k_2,r') = (0^\kappa,v)\right) \\
&= \mathbf{Pr}_{k_1}\left((r \oplus r') \cdot k_1 = 0^\kappa\right) \cdot \mathbf{Pr}_{k_2}\left((r \oplus r') \cdot k_2 = v\right) \\
&= 1/2^{\kappa+n},
\end{aligned}
$$

where the randomness is taken over $k_1 \xleftarrow{\$} \{0,1\}^\kappa$ and $k_2 \xleftarrow{\$} \{0,1\}^n$.   □

Alternative solutions, particularly for larger and possibly variable length values of ρ, are described in [49].

The universal hash function family h_{mult} is thus optimally secure, and yields a construction $R3$ that is secure as long as, roughly, $q^2 + 2qp \leq 2^{\kappa+n}$ (see Theorem 3). It has the disadvantage that two keys are needed. It is possible to reduce this key material. An obvious choice for this is to use the block cipher E. A direct simplification of the technique used in XHX suggests the following key generation that takes a single κ-bit key k:

$$h(k,r) = (r \cdot E(k,0),\, r \cdot E(k,1)),\tag{22}$$

assuming for a moment that $\kappa = n$.[3] This works fine as long as none of the construction queries or primitive queries made by the distinguisher matches the evaluations of $E(k,0)$ or $E(k,1)$. Incorporating this in the proof is simple but technically involved; we refer to [49] for details.

From the perspective of leakage resilience, there is not much gain in this approach: computing the subkeys every evaluation of $R3$ would imply that E needs to be DPA protected (it evaluates the master key multiple times for each query). Alternatively, the subkeys can be precomputed and stored, but in this case the advantage over simply generating and storing random subkeys (k_1,k_2) is marginal.

8   Cost Comparison

We perform a comparison of the symmetric-cryptographic solutions around, i.e., those of Abdalla and Bellare [1], Medwed et al. [64], Dobraunig et al. [30], and ours. The comparison is given in Table 1. The cost is split into a subkey generation cost and a core generation cost: the subkey generation must be secure

---

[3] If $\kappa < n$, one needs to truncate the first block. If $\kappa > n$ one may need extra calls $E(k,2), E(k,3), \ldots$ to generate subkey material.

against differential power analysis (DPA) whereas the core part needs to be secure against simple power analysis (SPA). All security bounds are derived in the ideal model for the core (that is, the ideal cipher model or ideal tweakable cipher model).

Here, for simplicity of comparison, we keep $\kappa = \rho = n$ and take the instantiation of h using finite field multiplications of Sect. 7. In particular, any evaluation of h in $R1$ and $R2$ is considered to cost one multiplication and any evaluation of h in $R3$ to cost two multiplications. The main characteristics of the comparison hold for arbitrary choice of h: de facto, that of $R3$ is simply considered to be twice as expensive as that of the others.

Table 1. Cost comparison. Here, F a random function, $\widetilde{E}$ is a tweakable block cipher, E a block cipher, and $\otimes$ finite field multiplication of n-bit elements. We estimate the cost of subkey generation h with finite field multiplications as outlined in Sect. 7. (We stress that instantiation can also be done using different hash function families, as long as the conditions of Theorems 1–3 are met.) Cost is split into "subkey" to generate a session key from the master key and "core" that corresponds to the core encryption performed using the session key. For the number of finite field multiplications, key size, and security bound, we assume that $\kappa = \rho = n$ for simplicity.

scheme	subkey		core			keysize	security
	F	$\otimes/h$	$\widetilde{E}$	E	$\otimes$		
AB (2)	1	0	0	1	0	n	2^n
MSGR (3)	0	1	0	1	0	n	$2^{n/2\star}$
DKM$^+$1 (4)	0	1	0	2	0	n	$2^{n/2}$
DKM$^+$2 (5)	0	1	1	0	0	n	2^n
R1 (14)	0	1	0	1	1	n	$2^{2n/3}$
R2 (17)	0	1	0	2	0	n	2^n
R3 (19)	0	2	0	1	0	$2n$	2^n

*the scheme permits master key recovery attacks in complexity $2^{n/2}$.

Clearly, DPA protection is most expensive, so in the subkey generation a minimal primitive is desirable. This, in particular, led Dobraunig et al. [30] to instantiating the PRF F in AB as (13). Yet, DKM$^+$1 only achieved birthday bound security. The transition to DKM$^+$2 was to replace the two block cipher calls by a tweakable block cipher: the resulting construction is optimally secure, yet, the security loss is implicit in the ideal tweakable block cipher. If the scheme is instantiated with a dedicated tweakable block cipher such as SKINNY or MANTIS [11] or QARMA [4], this is reasonable. On the other hand, instantiations using generic block cipher constructions cost at least two expensive operations (either two block cipher calls or a block cipher call and a multiplication, see Sect. 4) to become beyond birthday bound secure [65]. Stated differently, if DKM$^+$2's security is wished for using a conventional block cipher rather than a tweakable block cipher as underlying primitive, *at least two block cipher calls or at least a block cipher call and a multiplication are needed*.

Needless to say, it is preferable to have as few block cipher calls as possible. Instantiating DKM^+2 with Men1 gives $2n/3$-security using a single key, as given by our construction $R1$. We had to perform a dedicated analysis, as the analysis of the original DKM^+2 is in the ideal tweakable cipher model. Our construction $R2$ achieves optimal 2^n security at cost identical to DKM^+1.

Our construction $R3$ generalizes. Assuming $\kappa = n$ and using two independent n-bit keys (as suggested in Sect. 7), it achieves optimal 2^n security as well. Using a $2n$-bit key may be arguably worse from a practitioner's perspective, and in some settings $R1$ is preferable over $R3$. From a theoretical perspective, the use of an extra key in $R3$ is justifiable compared to the analysis of DKM^+2. To wit, both analyses are in the ideal model for the core primitive. This means that the formal security analysis of DKM^+2 is based on the random generation of $\widetilde{E} \xleftarrow{\$} \mathrm{tperm}(\kappa + \rho, n)$ and of $k \xleftarrow{\$} \{0,1\}^{\kappa}$,[4] i.e., the random elements are taken uniformly randomly from a pool of

$$(2^n!)^{2^{\kappa+\rho}} \cdot 2^{\kappa}$$

elements. In the analysis of $R3$, the security is based on the random generation of $E \xleftarrow{\$} \mathrm{tperm}(\kappa, n)$ and of $k_1 \| k_2 \xleftarrow{\$} \{0,1\}^{\kappa+n}$ (see Sect. 7), i.e., the random elements are taken uniformly randomly from a pool of

$$(2^n!)^{2^{\kappa}} \cdot 2^{\kappa+n}$$

elements. It is clear to see that this is a much smaller pool of randomness. As a general rule, the larger the pool of randomness, the stronger the security assumption, and the easier a security analysis is performed.

In addition, as discussed in Sect. 6, $R3$ also generalizes to permutation based rekeying, namely by setting $\kappa = 0$ and instantiating it with an n-bit permutation $P \xleftarrow{\$} \mathrm{tperm}(0, n)$. The resulting scheme generates a subkey at cost 1 evaluation of $\otimes/h$, and encrypts data at cost 1 evaluation of P. It has keysize n and achieves $2^{n/2}$ security.

9   Authenticated Encryption from Fresh Rekeying

Tweakable block ciphers have historically been used a lot in the context of authenticated encryption [3,41,55,72,81,87,88]. They serve as an intermediate construction in a generic security proof: one can argue security of the authenticated encryption scheme *via* the tweakable block cipher *to* the underlying block cipher. Leading in this respect is the ΘCB (formally named $\Theta CB3$) authenticated encryption mode that was proven secure relative to the security of its underlying tweakable block cipher [55]. It forms the base of OCB1-OCB3 if instantiated

---

[4] We take $\kappa' = \kappa$ here for the sake of a fair comparison of the two schemes.

with (a variant of) XEX [55,87,88], of OPP if instantiated with MEM [36], and Deoxys-I if instantiated with a dedicated tweakable block cipher [48].[5]

In this section, we will combine this approach with our insights that tweakable block ciphers and block cipher rekeying are related. In more detail, we will instantiate ΘCB with the rekeying schemes $R1$, $R2$, and $R3$, and compare the resulting solutions with state of the art side-channel secure authenticated encryption schemes. We remark that ΘCB purely serves as example here. The security and efficiency gains that are achieved in this section are attributed to the use of our rekeying schemes. Comparable results can be achieved when these rekeying schemes are used to instantiate other tweakable block cipher based MAC or AE schemes such as ZMAC [47] or ZOCB/ZOTR [7].

The model of authenticated encryption is discussed in Sect. 9.1 and we describe ΘCB in Sect. 9.2. We instantiate ΘCB with our rekeying schemes in Sect. 9.3, and discuss the security and efficiency of the resulting schemes from a side-channel protection point of view.

9.1   Authenticated Encryption

We will be concerned with authenticated encryption schemes defined by parameters $\kappa', \kappa, \rho, n, \tau \in \mathbb{N}$ such that $\tau \leq n$, and that internally use a block cipher $E \in \text{tperm}(\kappa, n)$.

An authenticated encryption scheme AE consists of an encryption function $\mathcal{E}$ and a decryption function $\mathcal{D}$. The encryption function $\mathcal{E}$ gets as input a key $k \in \{0,1\}^{\kappa'}$, initial value $iv \in \{0,1\}^n$, associated data $a \in \{0,1\}^*$, and message $m \in \{0,1\}^*$, and outputs a ciphertext $c \in \{0,1\}^{|m|}$ and a tag $t \in \{0,1\}^\tau$. Decryption $\mathcal{D}$ gets as input a key $k \in \{0,1\}^{\kappa'}$, initial value $iv \in \{0,1\}^n$, associated data $a \in \{0,1\}^*$, ciphertext $c \in \{0,1\}^*$, and tag $t \in \{0,1\}^\tau$, and it outputs a message $m \in \{0,1\}^{|c|}$ (if the authentication is correct) or a dedicated failure symbol $\bot$:

$$\mathcal{E}(k, iv, a, m) = (c, t),$$
$$\mathcal{D}(k, iv, a, c, t) = m \text{ or } \bot,$$

in such a way that for any (k, iv, a, m), we have $\mathcal{D}(k, iv, a, \mathcal{E}(k, iv, a, m)) = m$.

The security of an authenticated encryption scheme $AE = (\mathcal{E}, \mathcal{D})$ consists of confidentiality and authenticity (these could be merged into a single definition, but it is convenient to treat them separately). In confidentiality, a distinguisher D has query access to either $\mathcal{E}_k$ for $k \xleftarrow{\$} \{0,1\}^{\kappa'}$ or to a random function $\$$ that for each input (iv, a, m) returns a random $(c, t) \xleftarrow{\$} \{0,1\}^{|m|+\tau}$. As in Sect. 2.3, we consider security in the ideal cipher model, which means that the distinguisher also has bi-directional query access to $E \xleftarrow{\$} \text{tperm}(\kappa, n)$. It can make q queries

---

[5] This instantiation must be done with care, as a small oversight may make the scheme insecure. Recently, Inoue and Minematsu [43] (see also Inoue et al. [42]) pointed out an oversight in OCB2. Their attack (informally) relies on the observation that OCB2 consists of an instantiation of not only XEX but also a simpler variant XE, but without proper separation of both. The attack of Inoue and Minematsu does not apply to the schemes introduced in this section.

to its construction oracle, in total of size at most σ n-bit blocks, and it can make p queries to the ideal cipher. The q construction queries must be made for non-repeated iv (i.e., the iv is a nonce). Besides these queries, we allow D to have unlimited time, we consider it computationally unbounded.

For authenticity, the distinguisher D has query access to $\mathcal{E}_k$, and in addition to either $\mathcal{D}_k$ or a function $\perp$ that always returns the $\perp$-sign. As before, it has bi-directional access to the underlying ideal cipher $E \xleftarrow{\$} \text{tperm}(\kappa, n)$. Its goal is to generate a forgery: a query (iv, a, c, t) to $\mathcal{D}_k$ that returns a valid message m, in such a way that (iv, a, m) has not been queried to $\mathcal{E}_k$ before. The query and computational complexities of D are as before, with the difference that it is allowed to repeat an iv for decryption queries. It can make q_v forgery attempts.

We obtain the following definitions for confidentiality and authenticity.

Definition 2. *Let $\kappa', \kappa, n, \tau \in \mathbb{N}$. Consider $AE = (\mathcal{E}, \mathcal{D})$ based on a block cipher $E \in \text{tperm}(\kappa, n)$. Let D be any computationally unbounded distinguisher. The "confidentiality" of AE is defined as*

$$\mathbf{Adv}_{AE}^{\text{conf}}(D) = \left| \mathbf{Pr}_{k,E}\left(D^{\mathcal{E}_k, E^{\pm}} = 1 \right) - \mathbf{Pr}_{\$,E}\left(D^{\$, E^{\pm}} = 1 \right) \right|, \qquad (23)$$

and the "authenticity" of AE is defined as

$$\mathbf{Adv}_{AE}^{\text{auth}}(D) = \left| \mathbf{Pr}_{k,E}\left(D^{\mathcal{E}_k, \mathcal{D}_k, E^{\pm}} = 1 \right) - \mathbf{Pr}_E\left(D^{\mathcal{E}_k, \perp, E^{\pm}} = 1 \right) \right|, \qquad (24)$$

where the probabilities are taken over $k \xleftarrow{\$} \{0,1\}^{\kappa'}$, $E \xleftarrow{\$} \text{tperm}(\kappa, n)$, and the function $\$$ that returns a random $(c, t) \in \{0,1\}^{|m|+\tau}$ for each input (iv, a, m). The distinguisher is not allowed to make two encryption queries for the same iv, and it is not allowed to query $\mathcal{D}_k / \perp$ on the outcome of an earlier query to $\mathcal{E}_k$. The superscript "$\pm$" indicates that the distinguisher has bi-directional access to the oracle.

9.2 ΘCB

The ΘCB authenticated encryption scheme was first described by Krovetz and Rogaway [55]. It is internally based on a tweakable block cipher $\widetilde{E} : \{0,1\}^{\kappa'} \times \{0,1\}^{\rho'} \times \{0,1\}^n \to \{0,1\}^n$ with $\rho' = n + \rho$. The encryption function of ΘCB for integral data is depicted in Fig. 4. We refer to [55] for a formal description of the function and its corresponding decryption function.   Krovetz and Rogaway proved optimal security of ΘCB under the assumption that the underlying tweakable block cipher is secure [55]. It is important to note that their result is in the *standard model*, but we will directly phrase it in the *ideal cipher model* (Definitions 1 and 2 are both in the ideal cipher model), where we look ahead and observe that our application is internally based on an ideal cipher $E \xleftarrow{\$} \text{tperm}(\kappa, n)$. For now, this does not bias the discussion; we will elaborate on this in Sect. 9.3.1.

Theorem 4. *Let $\kappa', \kappa, \rho, n, \tau \in \mathbb{N}$, and write $\rho' = n + \rho$. Consider ΘCB based on a tweakable block cipher $\widetilde{E} \in \text{tperm}(\kappa', \rho', n)$, that is in turn based on a block*

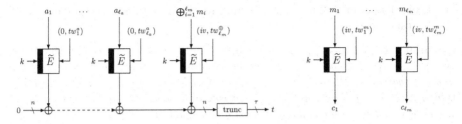

Fig. 4. The ΘCB encryption function $\mathcal{E}_k$ [87] for integral data. The associated data a and message m are padded into n-bit blocks. The tweak to each tweakable block cipher call consists of an n-bit string (either 0 or the initial value iv) and a ρ-bit string $tw_i^{a/\oplus/m}$ that unambiguously determines the position of the tweakable block cipher within the ΘCB construction.

cipher $E \in \mathrm{tperm}(\kappa, n)$. Let D be a distinguisher making at most q construction queries (in total of length at most σ blocks), q_v forgery attempts, and at most p offline evaluations of E. Then,

$$\mathbf{Adv}_{\Theta\mathrm{CB}}^{\mathrm{conf}}(D) \leq 0 \qquad + \mathbf{Adv}_{\widetilde{E}}^{\mathrm{stprp}}(D'), \qquad (25)$$

$$\mathbf{Adv}_{\Theta\mathrm{CB}}^{\mathrm{auth}}(D) \leq \frac{2^{n-\tau} q_v}{2^n - 1} + \mathbf{Adv}_{\widetilde{E}}^{\mathrm{stprp}}(D'), \qquad (26)$$

for some distinguisher D' making at most σ construction queries and p primitive queries.

As mentioned before, OCB1-OCB3 are designed by instantiating ΘCB with variants of XEX [87]. Here, we focus on OCB3 [55], which can be seen as being instantiated using the following *simplified* version of XEX:

$$\begin{aligned} \mathrm{XEX} : \{0,1\}^{\kappa} \times (\{0,1\}^n \times \{0,1\}^n) \times \{0,1\}^n &\to \{0,1\}^n, \\ (k, r\|a, m) &\mapsto E(k, m \oplus 2^a E(k, r)) \oplus 2^a E(k, r). \end{aligned} \qquad (27)$$

Here, exponentiation and multiplication are over an appropriate finite field, and the value $a \in \{0,1\}^{\rho}$ is first interpreted as a non-negative integer. In fact, the domain of a must be limited in some way to avoid colliding masks $2^a = 2^{a'}$, but this fine-tuning is irrelevant for the current discussion (refer to Rogaway [87] or Granger et al. [36]). In particular, in OCB3 the value a is updated according to the Gray code as this allows for optimization in the mask update. This tweakable block cipher is tightly birthday bound secure (in both the standard cipher model and the ideal cipher model), and from Theorem 4 it can be deduced that OCB3 is tightly birthday bound secure.

9.3 Instantiation of ΘCB with $R1$-$R3$

The security of ΘCB instantiated with $R1$, $R2$, or $R3$ follows readily from Theorem 4 on ΘCB and the security result on the respective rekeying scheme in Theorem 1, 2, or 3. The corresponding results are stated in Corollaries 1, 2, and 3, respectively.

Corollary 1. *Let $\kappa', \kappa, \rho, n, \tau \in \mathbb{N}$, and write $\rho' = n + \rho$. Let $h : \{0,1\}^{\kappa'} \times \{0,1\}^{\rho'} \to \{0,1\}^{\kappa}$ be a family of keyed hash functions that is α-uniform and α-n-partial-XOR-uniform. Consider ΘCB based on rekeying scheme $R1 \in \text{tperm}(\kappa', \rho', n)$ of (14), that is in turn based on a block cipher $E \in \text{tperm}(\kappa, n)$. Let D be a distinguisher making at most q construction queries (in total of length at most σ blocks), q_v forgery attempts, and at most p offline evaluations of E. Then,*

$$\mathbf{Adv}^{\text{conf}}_{\Theta CB\text{-}R1}(D) \leq 0 \qquad + 2\min\{\sigma^{1/2}p + \sigma, \sigma p^{1/2} + p\}\alpha, \qquad (28)$$

$$\mathbf{Adv}^{\text{auth}}_{\Theta CB\text{-}R1}(D) \leq \frac{2^{n-\tau}q_v}{2^n - 1} + 2\min\{\sigma^{1/2}p + \sigma, \sigma p^{1/2} + p\}\alpha. \qquad (29)$$

Corollary 2. *Let $\kappa', \kappa, \rho, n, \tau \in \mathbb{N}$, and write $\rho' = n + \rho$. Let $h : \{0,1\}^{\kappa'} \times \{0,1\}^{\rho'} \to \{0,1\}^{\kappa}$ be a family of keyed hash functions that is α-uniform and α-XOR-uniform. Consider ΘCB based on rekeying scheme $R2 \in \text{tperm}(\kappa', \rho', n)$ of (17), that is in turn based on a block cipher $E \in \text{tperm}(\kappa, n)$. Let D be a distinguisher making at most q construction queries (in total of length at most σ blocks), q_v forgery attempts, and at most p offline evaluations of E. Then,*

$$\mathbf{Adv}^{\text{conf}}_{\Theta CB\text{-}R2}(D) \leq 0 \qquad + \frac{\sigma(3\sigma - 3 + 2p)\alpha}{2^n} + (\sigma + p)\alpha + \frac{p}{2^n}, \qquad (30)$$

$$\mathbf{Adv}^{\text{auth}}_{\Theta CB\text{-}R2}(D) \leq \frac{2^{n-\tau}q_v}{2^n - 1} + \frac{\sigma(3\sigma - 3 + 2p)\alpha}{2^n} + (\sigma + p)\alpha + \frac{p}{2^n}. \qquad (31)$$

Corollary 3. *Let $\kappa', \kappa, \rho, n, \tau \in \mathbb{N}$, and write $\rho' = n + \rho$. Let $h : \{0,1\}^{\kappa'} \times \{0,1\}^{\rho'} \to \{0,1\}^{\kappa} \times \{0,1\}^{n}$ be a family of keyed hash functions that is α-uniform and α-n-partial-XOR-uniform. Consider ΘCB based on rekeying scheme $R3 \in \text{tperm}(\kappa', \rho', n)$ of (19), that is in turn based on a block cipher $E \in \text{tperm}(\kappa, n)$. Let D be a distinguisher making at most q construction queries (in total of length at most σ blocks), q_v forgery attempts, and at most p offline evaluations of E. Then,*

$$\mathbf{Adv}^{\text{conf}}_{\Theta CB\text{-}R3}(D) \leq 0 \qquad + \sigma(\sigma - 1 + 2p)\alpha, \qquad (32)$$

$$\mathbf{Adv}^{\text{auth}}_{\Theta CB\text{-}R3}(D) \leq \frac{2^{n-\tau}q_v}{2^n - 1} + \sigma(\sigma - 1 + 2p)\alpha. \qquad (33)$$

Efficiency-wise, the cost of authenticating and encrypting ℓ_a associated data blocks and ℓ_m message blocks (each of size n bits) using either of ΘCB-$R1$, ΘCB-$R2$, or ΘCB-$R3$ can be obtained by multiplying the cost of the corresponding underlying rekeying scheme from Table 1 by $\ell_a + \ell_m + 1$ (the number of times that the rekeying scheme is evaluated in one evaluation of the construction). As ΘCB itself is optimally secure (see Theorem 4), the security of the rekeying scheme will dominate that of the resulting construction: ΘCB-$R1$ achieves $2^{2n/3}$ security, and ΘCB-$R2$ and ΘCB-$R3$ achieve 2^n security. Even though $R3$ (and thus ΘCB-$R3$) has a larger key than $R1$ and $R2$, it achieves optimal security based on only one evaluation of the underlying ideal cipher, and it can arguably considered to be the best alternative of the three. Therefore, in the remainder, we focus on ΘCB-$R3$. The scheme is depicted in Fig. 5. We compare ΘCB-$R3$ with OCB3 and with alternative leakage resilient authenticated encryption schemes in Sects. 9.3.1 and 9.3.2, respectively.

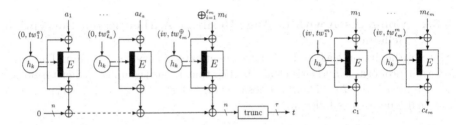

Fig. 5. The ΘCB-$R3$ encryption function $\mathcal{E}_k$ for integral data. The associated data a and message m are padded into n-bit blocks. The universal hash function h_k transforms a $(n+\rho)$-bit tweak into $(\kappa+n)$-bit subkey. The tweaks themselves are identical to those in ΘCB (see Fig. 4).

9.3.1 Comparison with OCB3

We acknowledge that the resulting construction ΘCB-$R3$ is more expensive than OCB3. Indeed, for the authenticated encryption of an input consisting of ℓ_a associated data blocks and ℓ_m message blocks (each of size n bits), OCB3 makes $\ell_a + \ell_m + 2$ block cipher calls, whereas ΘCB-$R3$ makes $\ell_a + \ell_m + 1$ block cipher calls and around $2(\ell_a + \ell_m + 1)$ universal hash function calls (taking the scaling of Sect. 8 on the number of universal hash function calls in $R3$ for granted).

On the other hand, Corollary 3 shows that our construction ΘCB-$R3$ achieves 2^n security whereas OCB3 achieves tight birthday bound security, only. The comparison must be taken with a grain of salt, though: OCB3 can be proven in the standard cipher model, but for ΘCB-$R3$ we have to resort to the ideal cipher model. That said, no standard model attack on ΘCB-$R3$ is known, and the difference seems to arise mostly due to the standard-versus-ideal phenomenon investigated by Mennink [67] in the context of tweakable block ciphers (cf. the last paragraph of Sect. 4).

More importantly, ΘCB-$R3$ is easier to protect against side-channel attacks than OCB3. For OCB3, all block cipher calls are performed for the same key, and the implementation of E needs to be DPA protected. In addition, a typical instantiation of OCB3 makes use of multiplications in the masking that are hard to protect due to their algebraic structure (recall the first paragraph of Sect. 7). In ΘCB-$R3$, only the "lighter" function h_k needs DPA protection. It is possible to incorporate a cheaper rekeying function in OCB3, for instance MSGR [64] (see (3)) [2], but the resulting authenticated encryption mode would only be birthday bound secure and security analysis must likewise be performed in the ideal cipher model.

We conclude by remarking that the efficiency of OCB3 in part comes from the fact that the computation of $E(k, iv)$ needs to be computed only once per evaluation of the construction. A similar efficiency improvement may be achieved in ΘCB-$R3$ by smart selection of h_k. In that case, the total cost of the evaluations of h_k in one evaluation of ΘCB-$R3$ may reduce to around $\ell_a + \ell_m + 2$.

9.3.2 Comparison with Leakage Resilient Authenticated Encryption Schemes

State of the art on leakage resilient authenticated encryption is slim. The most relevant proposal is by Berti et al. [16,17], that improves upon earlier proposals of Pereira et al. [79]. Their proposal DTE (Digest, Tag, and Encrypt), in a nutshell, operates as follows:

- Evaluate a hash function on the initial value iv and the message m;
- Transform the output through a side-channel-protected evaluation of E_k. The resulting value is the tag t;
- Transform the tag through another evaluation of the side-channel-protected evaluation of E_k. The resulting value is the subkey k_0;
- Evaluate a two-layer encryption part: the top layer evolves the subkey as $k_i = E_{k_{i-1}}(\text{const}_1)$ and the second layer derives a key stream block as $s_i = E_{k_{i-1}}(\text{const}_2)$, where const_1 and const_2 are two distinct constants.

Thus, for the authenticated encryption of a message of length ℓ_m n-bit blocks, DTE makes one cryptographic hash function evaluation on $\ell_m + 1$ blocks, two side-channel-protected E-calls, and $2\ell_m$ E-calls. Associated data of ℓ_a blocks can be covered by feeding these blocks to the cryptographic hash function as well. Assuming, for simplicity of counting, that hashing ℓ blocks is approximately as expensive as ℓ E-calls (this is the case for generic Merkle-Damgård hash functions based on the Davies-Meyer compression function), we obtain that DTE takes $\ell_a + \ell_m + 1$ unprotected E-calls, $2\ell_m$ SPA-protected E-calls, and 2 DPA-protected E-calls.

Comparing DTE with ΘCB-$R3$ is like comparing apples with oranges: the security models and incentives are different. In particular, DTE is proven to be misuse resistant and to achieve security against decryption leakages, a much stronger security requirement. Effectively, this leads to an efficiency gain in ΘCB-$R3$, in the number of primitive evaluations as well as in the fact that it is parallelizable. Furthermore, both security proofs require E to be an ideal cipher, but DTE is only birthday bound secure while ΘCB-$R3$ is optimally secure. Also, in ΘCB-$R3$, E needs only SPA-protection as long as h_k is DPA-protected;

DTE requires two evaluations of E to have strong side-channel protection (the remaining $\ell_a + 3\ell_m + 1$ can have lighter protection).

Dobraunig et al. [29] took a different avenue. Their proposal ISAP is sponge based: it uses the sponge with a very small rate to compress key material. ISAP relies on the philosophy that once the sponge has a state with sufficient entropy, it can perform authentication and encryption with a larger rate without any security sacrifice. ISAP is inherently sequential; in addition, it is infeasible to compare ΘCB-$R3$ with ISAP as its design rationale is different (block cipher versus permutation).

An alternative approach to design an authenticated encryption scheme is by generic composition of a MAC function and an authenticated encryption scheme. Barwell et al. [8] studied generic composition (MtE, M&E, EtM) under leakage and concluded that only the latter is leakage resilient. They present a generic solution, called SIVAT, a three-layer misuse resistant and leakage secure authenticated encryption scheme. The resulting construction can be instantiated with a PRF, an encryption scheme, plus a MAC function. Overall, Barwell et al. [8] target a different (stronger) security goal, and in part due to the generic nature of the approach, the resulting construction becomes more expensive.

10   Concluding Remarks

Depending on the subkey generation function, one may have to require the tweak to be unpredictable. In our formal security analyses, there is no issue, the adversary can freely choose it (provided that the tweakable block cipher is strong enough). The analysis does not limit the number of times a user may use a certain tweak, but one typically needs to limit it, in order to ensure that no subkey to the underlying block cipher is used too often. Indeed, in this case, for the functions to be side-channel secure it suffices for the block cipher to be secure against SPA (rather than DPA). It is possible to improve the bounds of Theorems 1–3 if the number of appearances per tweak is restricted. In the field of generic tweakable block cipher design and analysis, such a condition appeared before in [59, 68].

We remark that the rekeying solutions serve as an alternative to other strong side-channel countermeasures, at least for specific scenarios. Still, the primitives of the rekeying functions still require certain level of protection. It would be an interesting direction to investigate in what degree the cost of countermeasures gets reduced in practice.

It is fascinating to see that, as this work shows, two seemingly disjoint directions have such a strong relation that the knowledge from one direction (generic tweakable block cipher design) can be used to improve the state of the art of the other field (fresh rekeying). Other conclusions from the former field may likewise result in fruitful solutions to side-channel security, and it is worth exploring this direction. Conversely, there may be possibilities of using the extensive state of the art on, for example, leakage resilient pseudorandom number generators to classical cryptography.

Acknowledgments. The author would like to thank Christoph Dobraunig for his feedback and for the extensive discussions on this article. The author would like to thank the anonymous reviewers of ASIACRYPT 2020 for their valuable feedback.

References

1. Abdalla, M., Bellare, M.: Increasing the lifetime of a key: a comparative analysis of the security of re-keying techniques. In: Okamoto, T. (ed.) ASIACRYPT 2000. LNCS, vol. 1976, pp. 546–559. Springer, Heidelberg (2000). https://doi.org/10.1007/3-540-44448-3_42

2. Agrawal, M., et al.: RCB: leakage-resilient authenticated encryption via re-keying. J. Supercomputing **74**(9), 4173–4198 (2018)

3. Andreeva, E., Bogdanov, A., Luykx, A., Mennink, B., Tischhauser, E., Yasuda, K.: Parallelizable and authenticated online ciphers. In: Sako, K., Sarkar, P. (eds.) ASIACRYPT 2013. LNCS, vol. 8269, pp. 424–443. Springer, Heidelberg (2013). https://doi.org/10.1007/978-3-642-42033-7_22

4. Avanzi, R.: The QARMA block cipher family. IACR Trans. Symmetric Cryptol. **2017**(1), 4–44 (2017)

5. Banik, S., et al.: Midori: a block cipher for low energy. In: Iwata, T., Cheon, J.H. (eds.) ASIACRYPT 2015. LNCS, vol. 9453, pp. 411–436. Springer, Heidelberg (2015). https://doi.org/10.1007/978-3-662-48800-3_17

6. Banik, S., Pandey, S.K., Peyrin, T., Sasaki, Yu., Sim, S.M., Todo, Y.: GIFT: a small present. In: Fischer, W., Homma, N. (eds.) CHES 2017. LNCS, vol. 10529, pp. 321–345. Springer, Cham (2017). https://doi.org/10.1007/978-3-319-66787-4_16

7. Bao, Z., Guo, J., Iwata, T., Minematsu, K.: ZOCB and ZOTR: tweakable blockcipher modes for authenticated encryption with full absorption. IACR Trans. Symmetric Cryptol. **2019**(2), 1–54 (2019)

8. Barwell, G., Martin, D.P., Oswald, E., Stam, M.: Authenticated encryption in the face of protocol and side channel leakage. In: Takagi, T., Peyrin, T. (eds.) ASIACRYPT 2017. LNCS, vol. 10624, pp. 693–723. Springer, Cham (2017). https://doi.org/10.1007/978-3-319-70694-8_24

9. Battistello, A., Coron, J.-S., Prouff, E., Zeitoun, R.: Horizontal side-channel attacks and countermeasures on the ISW masking scheme. In: Gierlichs, B., Poschmann, A.Y. (eds.) CHES 2016. LNCS, vol. 9813, pp. 23–39. Springer, Heidelberg (2016). https://doi.org/10.1007/978-3-662-53140-2_2

10. Beaulieu, R., Shors, D., Smith, J., Treatman-Clark, S., Weeks, B., Wingers, L.: The SIMON and SPECK Families of Lightweight Block Ciphers. Cryptology ePrint Archive, Report 2013/404 (2013)

11. Beierle, C., et al.: The SKINNY family of block ciphers and its low-latency variant MANTIS. In: Robshaw and Katz [86], pp. 123–153 (2016)

12. Belaïd, S., Coron, J.-S., Fouque, P.-A., Gérard, B., Kammerer, J.-G., Prouff, E.: Improved side-channel analysis of finite-field multiplication. In: Güneysu, T., Handschuh, H. (eds.) CHES 2015. LNCS, vol. 9293, pp. 395–415. Springer, Heidelberg (2015). https://doi.org/10.1007/978-3-662-48324-4_20

13. Belaïd, S., Fouque, P.-A., Gérard, B.: Side-channel analysis of multiplications in GF($2^1$28). In: Sarkar, P., Iwata, T. (eds.) ASIACRYPT 2014. LNCS, vol. 8874, pp. 306–325. Springer, Heidelberg (2014). https://doi.org/10.1007/978-3-662-45608-8_17

14. Bellare, M., Impagliazzo, R.: A tool for obtaining tighter security analyses of pseudorandom function based constructions, with applications to PRP to PRF conversion. Cryptology ePrint Archive, Report 1999/024 (1999)

15. Bellare, M., Krovetz, T., Rogaway, P.: Luby-Rackoff backwards: increasing security by making block ciphers non-invertible. In: Nyberg, K. (ed.) EUROCRYPT 1998. LNCS, vol. 1403, pp. 266–280. Springer, Heidelberg (1998). https://doi.org/10. 1007/BFb0054132

16. Berti, F., Koeune, F., Pereira, O., Peters, T., Standaert, F.: Leakage-resilient and misuse-resistant authenticated encryption. Cryptology ePrint Archive, Report 2016/996 (2016)

17. Berti, F., Pereira, O., Peters, T., Standaert, F.: On leakage-resilient authenticated encryption with decryption leakages. IACR Trans. Symmetric Cryptol. **2017**(3), 271–293 (2017)

18. Bhattacharya, S., Nandi, M.: Revisiting variable output length XOR pseudorandom function. IACR Trans. Symmetric Cryptol. **2018**(1), 314–335 (2018)

19. Bogdanov, A., et al.: PRESENT: an ultra-lightweight block cipher. In: Paillier, P., Verbauwhede, I. (eds.) CHES 2007. LNCS, vol. 4727, pp. 450–466. Springer, Heidelberg (2007). https://doi.org/10.1007/978-3-540-74735-2_31

20. Borghoff, J., et al.: PRINCE – a low-latency block cipher for pervasive computing applications. In: Wang, X., Sako, K. (eds.) ASIACRYPT 2012. LNCS, vol. 7658, pp. 208–225. Springer, Heidelberg (2012). https://doi.org/10.1007/978-3-642-34961-4_14

21. Borst, J.: block ciphers: design, analysis, and side-channel analysis. Ph.D. thesis, Departement Elektrotechniek – ESAT/COSIC, Katholieke Universiteit Leuven, Leuven, Belgium, September 2001

22. CAESAR: Competition for Authenticated Encryption: Security, Applicability, and Robustness, May 2015. http://competitions.cr.yp.to/caesar.html

23. Chakraborty, D., Sarkar, P.: A general construction of tweakable block ciphers and different modes of operations. In: Lipmaa, H., Yung, M., Lin, D. (eds.) Inscrypt 2006. LNCS, vol. 4318, pp. 88–102. Springer, Heidelberg (2006). https://doi.org/10.1007/11937807_8

24. Chari, S., Jutla, C.S., Rao, J.R., Rohatgi, P.: Towards sound approaches to counteract power-analysis attacks. In: Wiener [95], pp. 398–412 (1999)

25. Cogliati, B.: Tweaking a block cipher: multi-user beyond-birthday-bound security in the standard model. Des. Codes Crypt. **86**(12), 2747–2763 (2018)

26. Daemen, J., Rijmen, V.: The Design of Rijndael: AES - The Advanced Encryption Standard. Springer, Heidelberg (2002). https://doi.org/10.1007/978-3-662-04722-4

27. Dai, W., Hoang, V.T., Tessaro, S.: Information-theoretic indistinguishability via the Chi-Squared method. In: Katz and Shacham [51], pp. 497–523 (2017)

28. Dobraunig, C., Eichlseder, M., Mangard, S., Mendel, F.: On the security of fresh rekeying to counteract side-channel and fault attacks. In: Joye, M., Moradi, A. (eds.) CARDIS 2014. LNCS, vol. 8968, pp. 233–244. Springer, Cham (2015). https://doi.org/10.1007/978-3-319-16763-3_14

29. Dobraunig, C., Eichlseder, M., Mangard, S., Mendel, F., Unterluggauer, T.: ISAP - towards side-channel secure authenticated encryption. IACR Trans. Symmetric Cryptol. **2017**(1), 80–105 (2017)

30. Dobraunig, C., Koeune, F., Mangard, S., Mendel, F., Standaert, F.-X.: Towards fresh and hybrid re-keying schemes with beyond birthday security. In: Homma, N., Medwed, M. (eds.) CARDIS 2015. LNCS, vol. 9514, pp. 225–241. Springer, Cham (2016). https://doi.org/10.1007/978-3-319-31271-2_14

31. Duc, A., Faust, S., Standaert, F.: Making masking security proofs concrete - or how to evaluate the security of any leaking device. In: Oswald and Fischlin [76], pp. 401–429 (2015)
32. Dziembowski, S., Faust, S., Herold, G., Journault, A., Masny, D., Standaert, F.: Towards sound fresh re-keying with hard (physical) learning problems. In: Robshaw and Katz [86], pp. 272–301 (2016)
33. Even, S., Mansour, Y.: A construction of a cipher from a single pseudorandom permutation. In: Imai, H., Rivest, R.L., Matsumoto, T. (eds.) ASIACRYPT 1991. LNCS, vol. 739, pp. 210–224. Springer, Heidelberg (1993). https://doi.org/10.1007/3-540-57332-1_17
34. FIPS 202: SHA-3 Standard: Permutation-Based Hash and Extendable-Output Functions (2015)
35. Gammel, B., Fischer, W., Mangard, S.: Generating a session key for authentication and secure data transfer. US Patent US 9,509,508 B2, November 2016
36. Granger, R., Jovanovic, P., Mennink, B., Neves, S.: Improved masking for tweakable blockciphers with applications to authenticated encryption. In: Fischlin, M., Coron, J.-S. (eds.) EUROCRYPT 2016. LNCS, vol. 9665, pp. 263–293. Springer, Heidelberg (2016). https://doi.org/10.1007/978-3-662-49890-3_11
37. Green, J., Roy, A., Oswald, E.: A systematic study of the impact of graphical models on inference-based attacks on AES. In: Bilgin, B., Fischer, J.-B. (eds.) CARDIS 2018. LNCS, vol. 11389, pp. 18–34. Springer, Cham (2019). https://doi.org/10.1007/978-3-030-15462-2_2
38. Guajardo, J., Mennink, B.: On side-channel resistant block cipher usage. In: Burmester, M., Tsudik, G., Magliveras, S., Ilić, I. (eds.) ISC 2010. LNCS, vol. 6531, pp. 254–268. Springer, Heidelberg (2011). https://doi.org/10.1007/978-3-642-18178-8_22
39. Guo, J., Peyrin, T., Poschmann, A., Robshaw, M.J.B.: The LED block cipher. In: Preneel and Takagi [83], pp. 326–341 (2011)
40. Guo, Q., Johansson, T.: A New Birthday-Type Algorithm for Attacking the Fresh Re-Keying Countermeasure. Cryptology ePrint Archive, Report 2016/225 (2016)
41. Hoang, V.T., Krovetz, T., Rogaway, P.: Robust authenticated-encryption AEZ and the problem that it solves. In: Oswald and Fischlin [76], pp. 15–44 (2015)
42. Inoue, A., Iwata, T., Minematsu, K., Poettering, B.: Cryptanalysis of OCB2: attacks on authenticity and confidentiality. In: Boldyreva, A., Micciancio, D. (eds.) CRYPTO 2019. LNCS, vol. 11692, pp. 3–31. Springer, Cham (2019). https://doi.org/10.1007/978-3-030-26948-7_1
43. Inoue, A., Minematsu, K.: Cryptanalysis of OCB2. Cryptology ePrint Archive, Report 2018/1040 (2018)
44. Ishai, Y., Sahai, A., Wagner, D.: Private circuits: securing hardware against probing attacks. In: Boneh, D. (ed.) CRYPTO 2003. LNCS, vol. 2729, pp. 463–481. Springer, Heidelberg (2003). https://doi.org/10.1007/978-3-540-45146-4_27
45. Iwata, T., Khairallah, M., Minematsu, K., Peyrin, T.: Remus v1.0. Submission to NIST Lightweight Cryptography (2019)
46. Iwata, T., Mennink, B., Vizár, D.: CENC is Optimally Secure. Cryptology ePrint Archive, Report 2016/1087 (2016)
47. Iwata, T., Minematsu, K., Peyrin, T., Seurin, Y.: ZMAC: a fast tweakable block cipher mode for highly secure message authentication. In: Katz and Shacham [51], pp. 34–65 (2017)
48. Jean, J., Nikolić, I., Peyrin, T., Seurin, Y.: Deoxys v1.41 (2016). Submission to CAESAR competition

49. Jha, A., List, E., Minematsu, K., Mishra, S., Nandi, M.: XHX – a framework for optimally secure tweakable block ciphers from classical block ciphers and universal hashing. In: Lange, T., Dunkelman, O. (eds.) LATINCRYPT 2017. LNCS, vol. 11368, pp. 207–227. Springer, Cham (2019). https://doi.org/10.1007/978-3-030-25283-0_12

50. Kannwischer, M.J., Pessl, P., Primas, R.: Single-trace attacks on Keccak. IACR Trans. Cryptogr. Hardw. Embed. Syst. 2020 (2020, to appear)

51. Katz, J., Shacham, H. (eds.): CRYPTO 2017–37th Annual International Cryptology Conference, Santa Barbara, CA, USA, 20–24 August 2017, Proceedings, Part III, LNCS, vol. 10403. Springer (2017)

52. Kocher, P.C.: Timing attacks on implementations of Diffie-Hellman, RSA, DSS, and other systems. In: Koblitz, N. (ed.) CRYPTO 1996. LNCS, vol. 1109, pp. 104–113. Springer, Heidelberg (1996). https://doi.org/10.1007/3-540-68697-5_9

53. Kocher, P.C.: Leak-resistant cryptographic indexed key update. US Patent 6,539,092, March 2003

54. Kocher, P.C., Jaffe, J., Jun, B.: Differential power analysis. In: Wiener [95], pp. 388–397 (1999)

55. Krovetz, T., Rogaway, P.: The software performance of authenticated-encryption modes. In: Joux, A. (ed.) FSE 2011. LNCS, vol. 6733, pp. 306–327. Springer, Heidelberg (2011). https://doi.org/10.1007/978-3-642-21702-9_18

56. Kuhn, M.G., Anderson, R.J.: Soft tempest: hidden data transmission using electromagnetic emanations. In: Aucsmith, D. (ed.) IH 1998. LNCS, vol. 1525, pp. 124–142. Springer, Heidelberg (1998). https://doi.org/10.1007/3-540-49380-8_10

57. Lampe, R., Seurin, Y.: Tweakable blockciphers with asymptotically optimal security. In: Moriai, S. (ed.) FSE 2013. LNCS, vol. 8424, pp. 133–151. Springer, Heidelberg (2014). https://doi.org/10.1007/978-3-662-43933-3_8

58. Landecker, W., Shrimpton, T., Terashima, R.S.: Tweakable blockciphers with beyond birthday-bound security. In: Safavi-Naini, R., Canetti, R. (eds.) CRYPTO 2012. LNCS, vol. 7417, pp. 14–30. Springer, Heidelberg (2012). https://doi.org/10.1007/978-3-642-32009-5_2

59. Lee, J., Luykx, A., Mennink, B., Minematsu, K.: Connecting tweakable and multi-key blockcipher security. Des. Codes Crypt. 86(3), 623–640 (2018)

60. Liskov, M., Rivest, R.L., Wagner, D.: Tweakable block ciphers. In: Yung, M. (ed.) CRYPTO 2002. LNCS, vol. 2442, pp. 31–46. Springer, Heidelberg (2002). https://doi.org/10.1007/3-540-45708-9_3

61. Lucks, S.: The sum of PRPs is a secure PRF. In: Preneel, B. (ed.) EUROCRYPT 2000. LNCS, vol. 1807, pp. 470–484. Springer, Heidelberg (2000). https://doi.org/10.1007/3-540-45539-6_34

62. Mangard, S., Oswald, E., Popp, T.: Power Analysis Attacks - Revealing the Secrets of Smart Cards. Springer, Boston (2007). https://doi.org/10.1007/978-0-387-38162-6

63. Medwed, M., Petit, C., Regazzoni, F., Renauld, M., Standaert, F.-X.: Fresh rekeying II: securing multiple parties against side-channel and fault attacks. In: Prouff, E. (ed.) CARDIS 2011. LNCS, vol. 7079, pp. 115–132. Springer, Heidelberg (2011). https://doi.org/10.1007/978-3-642-27257-8_8

64. Medwed, M., Standaert, F.-X., Großschädl, J., Regazzoni, F.: Fresh re-keying: security against side-channel and fault attacks for low-cost devices. In: Bernstein, D.J., Lange, T. (eds.) AFRICACRYPT 2010. LNCS, vol. 6055, pp. 279–296. Springer, Heidelberg (2010). https://doi.org/10.1007/978-3-642-12678-9_17

65. Mennink, B.: Optimally secure tweakable blockciphers. In: Leander, G. (ed.) FSE 2015. LNCS, vol. 9054, pp. 428–448. Springer, Heidelberg (2015). https://doi.org/10.1007/978-3-662-48116-5_21

66. Mennink, B.: Optimally Secure Tweakable Blockciphers. Cryptology ePrint Archive, Report 2015/363 (2015). Full version of [65]

67. Mennink, B.: Insuperability of the standard versus ideal model gap for tweakable blockcipher security. In: Katz, J., Shacham, H. (eds.) CRYPTO 2017. LNCS, vol. 10402, pp. 708–732. Springer, Cham (2017). https://doi.org/10.1007/978-3-319-63715-0_24

68. Mennink, B.: Towards tight security of cascaded LRW2. In: Beimel, A., Dziembowski, S. (eds.) TCC 2018. LNCS, vol. 11240, pp. 192–222. Springer, Cham (2018). https://doi.org/10.1007/978-3-030-03810-6_8

69. Mennink, B.: Beyond Birthday Bound Secure Fresh Rekeying: Application to Authenticated Encryption. Cryptology ePrint Archive, Report 2020/1082 (2020). Full version of this paper

70. Minematsu, K.: Improved security analysis of XEX and LRW modes. In: Biham, E., Youssef, A.M. (eds.) SAC 2006. LNCS, vol. 4356, pp. 96–113. Springer, Heidelberg (2007). https://doi.org/10.1007/978-3-540-74462-7_8

71. Minematsu, K.: Beyond-birthday-bound security based on tweakable block cipher. In: Dunkelman, O. (ed.) FSE 2009. LNCS, vol. 5665, pp. 308–326. Springer, Heidelberg (2009). https://doi.org/10.1007/978-3-642-03317-9_19

72. Minematsu, K.: Parallelizable rate-1 authenticated encryption from pseudorandom functions. In: Nguyen, P.Q., Oswald, E. (eds.) EUROCRYPT 2014. LNCS, vol. 8441, pp. 275–292. Springer, Heidelberg (2014). https://doi.org/10.1007/978-3-642-55220-5_16

73. Minematsu, K., Iwata, T.: Tweak-length extension for tweakable blockciphers. In: Groth, J. (ed.) IMACC 2015. LNCS, vol. 9496, pp. 77–93. Springer, Cham (2015). https://doi.org/10.1007/978-3-319-27239-9_5

74. Naito, Y.: Tweakable blockciphers for efficient authenticated encryptions with beyond the birthday-bound security. IACR Trans. Symmetric Cryptol. **2017**(2), 1–26 (2017)

75. NIST: Lightweight Cryptography, February 2019

76. Oswald, E., Fischlin, M. (eds.): EUROCRYPT 2015, Part I, LNCS, vol. 9056. Springer (2015)

77. Patarin, J.: A proof of security in $O(2^n)$ for the Xor of two random permutations. In: Safavi-Naini, R. (ed.) ICITS 2008. LNCS, vol. 5155, pp. 232–248. Springer, Heidelberg (2008). https://doi.org/10.1007/978-3-540-85093-9_22

78. Patarin, J.: Introduction to Mirror Theory: Analysis of Systems of Linear Equalities and Linear Non Equalities for Cryptography. Cryptology ePrint Archive, Report 2010/287 (2010)

79. Pereira, O., Standaert, F., Vivek, S.: Leakage-resilient authentication and encryption from symmetric cryptographic primitives. In: Ray, I., Li, N., Kruegel, C. (eds.) CCS 2015, pp. 96–108. ACM (2015)

80. Pessl, P., Mangard, S.: Enhancing side-channel analysis of binary-field multiplication with bit reliability. In: Sako, K. (ed.) CT-RSA 2016. LNCS, vol. 9610, pp. 255–270. Springer, Cham (2016). https://doi.org/10.1007/978-3-319-29485-8_15

81. Peyrin, T., Seurin, Y.: Counter-in-Tweak: authenticated encryption modes for tweakable block ciphers. In: Robshaw, M., Katz, J. (eds.) CRYPTO 2016. LNCS, vol. 9814, pp. 33–63. Springer, Heidelberg (2016). https://doi.org/10.1007/978-3-662-53018-4_2

82. Preneel, B., Govaerts, R., Vandewalle, J.: Hash functions based on block ciphers: a synthetic approach. In: Stinson, D.R. (ed.) CRYPTO 1993. LNCS, vol. 773, pp. 368–378. Springer, Heidelberg (1994). https://doi.org/10.1007/3-540-48329-2_31

83. Preneel, B., Takagi, T. (eds.): CHES 2011, LNCS, vol. 6917. Springer (2011)

84. Procter, G.: A Note on the CLRW2 Tweakable Block Cipher Construction. Cryptology ePrint Archive, Report 2014/111 (2014)

85. Prouff, E., Rivain, M.: Masking against side-channel attacks: a formal security proof. In: Johansson, T., Nguyen, P.Q. (eds.) EUROCRYPT 2013. LNCS, vol. 7881, pp. 142–159. Springer, Heidelberg (2013). https://doi.org/10.1007/978-3-642-38348-9_9

86. Robshaw, M., Katz, J. (eds.): CRYPTO 2016, Part II, LNCS, vol. 9815. Springer (2016)

87. Rogaway, P.: Efficient instantiations of tweakable blockciphers and refinements to modes OCB and PMAC. In: Lee, P.J. (ed.) ASIACRYPT 2004. LNCS, vol. 3329, pp. 16–31. Springer, Heidelberg (2004). https://doi.org/10.1007/978-3-540-30539-2_2

88. Rogaway, P., Bellare, M., Black, J., Krovetz, T.: OCB: a block-cipher mode of operation for efficient authenticated encryption. In: Reiter, M.K., Samarati, P. (eds.) CCS 2001, pp. 196–205. ACM (2001)

89. Shibutani, K., Isobe, T., Hiwatari, H., Mitsuda, A., Akishita, T., Shirai, T.: Piccolo: an ultra-lightweight blockcipher. In: Preneel and Takagi [83], pp. 342–357 (2011)

90. Shirai, T., Shibutani, K., Akishita, T., Moriai, S., Iwata, T.: The 128-bit blockcipher CLEFIA (extended abstract). In: Biryukov, A. (ed.) FSE 2007. LNCS, vol. 4593, pp. 181–195. Springer, Heidelberg (2007). https://doi.org/10.1007/978-3-540-74619-5_12

91. Szemerédi, E., Trotter Jr., W.T.: Extremal problems in discrete geometry. Combinatorica 3(3–4), 381–392 (1983)

92. Veyrat-Charvillon, N., Gérard, B., Standaert, F.-X.: Soft analytical side-channel attacks. In: Sarkar, P., Iwata, T. (eds.) ASIACRYPT 2014. LNCS, vol. 8873, pp. 282–296. Springer, Heidelberg (2014). https://doi.org/10.1007/978-3-662-45611-8_15

93. Walter, C.D.: Sliding windows succumbs to big Mac attack. In: Koç, Ç.K., Naccache, D., Paar, C. (eds.) CHES 2001. LNCS, vol. 2162, pp. 286–299. Springer, Heidelberg (2001). https://doi.org/10.1007/3-540-44709-1_24

94. Wang, L., Guo, J., Zhang, G., Zhao, J., Gu, D.: How to build fully secure tweakable blockciphers from classical blockciphers. In: Cheon, J.H., Takagi, T. (eds.) ASIACRYPT 2016. LNCS, vol. 10031, pp. 455–483. Springer, Heidelberg (2016). https://doi.org/10.1007/978-3-662-53887-6_17

95. Wiener, M.J. (ed.): CRYPTO '99, LNCS, vol. 1666. Springer (1999)

Tight Security Analysis of 3-Round Key-Alternating Cipher with a Single Permutation

Yusai Wu[1], Liqing Yu[1], Zhenfu Cao[1,2,3(✉)], and Xiaolei Dong[1]

[1] Shanghai Key Laboratory of Trustworthy Computing,
East China Normal University, Shanghai, China
yusaiwu@126.com, lqyups@126.com, {zfcao,dong-xl}@sei.ecnu.edu.cn
[2] Cyberspace Security Research Center, Peng Cheng Laboratory, Shenzhen, China
[3] Shanghai Institute of Intelligent Science and Technology, Tongji University,
Shanghai, China

Abstract. The tight security bound of the KAC (Key-Alternating Cipher) construction whose round permutations are independent from each other has been well studied. Then a natural question is how the security bound will change when we use fewer permutations in a KAC construction. In CRYPTO 2014, Chen et al. proved that 2-round KAC with a single permutation (2KACSP) has the same security level as the classic one (i.e., 2-round KAC). But we still know little about the security bound of incompletely-independent KAC constructions with more than 2 rounds. In this paper, we will show that a similar result also holds for 3-round case. More concretely, we prove that 3-round KAC with a single permutation (3KACSP) is secure up to $\Theta(2^{\frac{3n}{4}})$ queries, which also caps the security of 3-round KAC. To avoid the cumbersome graphical illustration used in Chen et al.'s work, a new representation is introduced to characterize the underlying combinatorial problem. Benefited from it, we can handle the knotty dependence in a modular way, and also show a plausible way to study the security of rKACSP. Technically, we abstract a type of problems capturing the intrinsic randomness of rKACSP construction, and then propose a high-level framework to handle such problems. Furthermore, our proof techniques show some evidence that for any r, rKACSP has the same security level as the classic r-round KAC in random permutation model.

1 Introduction

In provable-security setting, the construction of a practical cipher is often abstracted into a reasonable model with certain assumptions (e.g., the underlying primitives are random functions/permutations and independent from each other). Under those assumptions, we try to prove that the abstract construction is immune to all (known or unknown) attacks executed by an adversary with specific abilities. Then the provable-security results provide some heuristic support

© International Association for Cryptologic Research 2020
S. Moriai and H. Wang (Eds.): ASIACRYPT 2020, LNCS 12491, pp. 662–693, 2020.
https://doi.org/10.1007/978-3-030-64837-4_22

for the underlying design-criteria of the cipher, since the practical underlying primitives do not satisfy the assumptions in general.

As aforementioned, the provable-security results are closely related to the abstract assumptions. If the assumptions are closer to the actual implementations, then the corresponding results will be more persuasive. For example, most of the existing work reduces the security of SPN block ciphers to the classic KAC construction (see Eq. (2)), in which the underlying round permutations as well as the round keys are random and independent from each other. Unfortunately, most KAC-based practical ciphers use the same round function and generate the round keys from a shorter master-key (i.e., the underlying round permutations and round keys are not independent from each other at all). Thus, there is still a big gap between the existing provable-security results and the practical ciphers.

Opposite to the KAC construction with independent round permutations and round keys (i.e., the classic KAC construction), we refer to the one whose round permutations or round keys are not independent from each other as *incompletely-independent KAC* or *KAC with dependence*. It is well known that r-round KAC is $\Theta(2^{\frac{r}{r+1}n})$-secure in the random permutation model [CS14, HT16]. To characterize the actual SPN block ciphers, we should abstract a natural KAC construction (with dependence) satisfying two requirements: all the round permutations are the same and the round keys are generated from a shorter master-key by a certain deterministic algorithm. Hence, the ultimate question is whether there exists such a r-round incompletely-independent KAC construction which can still achieve $\Theta(2^{\frac{r}{r+1}n})$-security. In other words, we want to know whether the required randomness of KAC construction can be minimized without a significant loss of security.

Up to now, people know little about the incompletely-independent KAC constructions (even with very small number of rounds), since it becomes much more complicated when either the underlying round permutations or round keys are no longer independent. To our knowledge, the best work about the KAC with dependence was given by Chen et al. [CLL+18]. They proved that several types of 2-round KAC with dependence have almost the same security level as 2-round KAC construction. However, it is still open about the security of incompletely-independent KAC with more than 2 rounds in provable-security setting.

In this paper, we initiate the study on the incompletely-independent KAC with more than 2 rounds. Here, we mainly focus on a special class of KAC, in which all the round permutations are the same and the round keys are still independent from each other, and refer to it as *KACSP construction*. Given a permutation $P : \{0,1\}^n \rightarrow \{0,1\}^n$, as well as $r+1$ round keys $k_0, \ldots, k_r$, the r-round KACSP construction $r\text{KACSP}[P; k_0, \ldots, k_r]$ maps a message $x \in \{0,1\}^n$ to

$$k_r \oplus P\Big(k_{r-1} \oplus P\big(\cdots P(x \oplus k_0)\cdots\big)\Big). \tag{1}$$

Before turning into the results, we review the related existing work on classic KAC and KAC with dependence, respectively.

Results on Classic KAC. KAC construction is the generalization of the Even-Mansour construction [EM97] over multiple rounds. As one of the most popular ways to construct a practical cipher, the KAC construction captures the high-level structure of many SPN block ciphers, such as AES [DR02], PRESENT [BKL+07], LED [GPPR11] and so on. Given r permutations $P_1, \ldots, P_r \colon \{0,1\}^n \to \{0,1\}^n$, as well as $r+1$ round keys $k_0, \ldots, k_r$, the r-round KAC construction $r\mathrm{KAC}[P_1, \ldots, P_r; k_0, \ldots, k_r]$ maps a message $x \in \{0,1\}^n$ to

$$k_r \oplus P_r\Big(k_{r-1} \oplus P_{r-1}\big(\cdots P_1(x \oplus k_0) \cdots\big)\Big). \tag{2}$$

In the random permutation model, it was proved by Even and Mansour [EM97] that an adversary needs roughly $2^{\frac{n}{2}}$ queries to distinguish the 1-round KAC construction from a true random permutation. Their bound was matched by a distinguishing attack [Dae91] which needs about $2^{\frac{n}{2}}$ queries in total. Many years later, Bogdanov et al. [BKL+12] proved that r-round KAC is secure up to $2^{\frac{2n}{3}}$ queries and the result is tight for $r = 2$. Besides, they also conjectured that the security for r-round KAC should be $2^{\frac{rn}{r+1}}$ because of a simple generic attack. After that, Steinberger [Ste12] improved the bound to $2^{\frac{3n}{4}}$ queries for $r \geq 3$ by modifying the way to upper bound the statistical distance between two product distributions. In the same year, Lampe et al. [LPS12] used coupling techniques to show that $2^{\frac{rn}{r+1}}$ queries and $2^{\frac{rn}{r+2}}$ queries are needed for any nonadaptive and any adaptive adversary, respectively. The first asymptotically tight bound was proved by Chen et al. [CS14] through an elegant path-counting lemma. Recently, Hoang and Tessaro [HT16] refined the H-coefficient technique (named as the expectation method) and gave the first exact bound of KAC construction. At this point, the security bound of the classic KAC construction is solved perfectly.

Results on KAC with dependence. The development in the field of incompletely-independent KAC is much slower, since it usually becomes very involved when the underlying components are no longer independent from each other. Dunkelman et al. [DKS12] initiated the study of minimizing 1-round KAC construction, and showed that several strictly simpler variants provide the same level of security. After that, the best work was given by Chen et al. [CLL+14] in CRYPTO 2014. They proved that several types of incompletely-independent 2-round KAC have almost the same security level as the classic one. The result even holds when only a single permutation and a n-bit master-key are used, where n is the length of a plaintext/ciphertext. In their work, a generalized *sum-capture theorem*[1] is used to upper bound the probability of bad transcripts. And the

---

[1] Informally, the type of sum-capture theorems state that when choosing a random subset A of $\mathbb{Z}_2^n$ of size q, the value

$$\mu(A) = \max_{\substack{U, V \subseteq \mathbb{Z}_2^n \\ |U|=|V|=q}} |\{(a, u, v) \in A \times U \times V : a = u \oplus v\}|$$

is close to the expected value q^3/N. In the extended version of [CLL+18], the set A can be produced by a set of query-answer pairs, and an automorphism transformation is also allowed.

probability calculation related to good transcripts is reduced to a combinatorial problem. Using the similar techniques, Cogliati and Seurin [CS18] obtained the security bound of the single-permutation encrypted Davies-Meyer construction. Nevertheless, their work is still limited in the scope of 2-round constructions.

Recently, Dai et al. [DSST17] proved that the 5-round KAC with a non-idealized key-schedule is indifferentiable from an ideal cipher. The model employed in their work is however orthogonal to ours and hence the result is not directly comparable.

OUR CONTRIBUTIONS. In this paper, we initiate the study on the incompletely-independent KAC with more than 2 rounds and give a tight security bound of 3KACSP construction. Our contributions are conceptually novel and mainly two-fold:

1. We prove the tight security bound $\Theta(2^{\frac{3n}{4}})$ queries of 3KACSP, which is an open problem (proposed in [CLL+18]) for incompletely-independent KAC with more than 2 rounds. That is, we can use only one instead of three distinct permutations to construct 3-round KAC without a significant loss of security. Notably, our proof framework is general and theoretically workable for any rKACSP. Following the ideas of analyzing 3KACSP, we strongly believe that rKACSP is also $\Theta(2^{\frac{r}{r+1}n})$-secure in random permutation model, provided that the input/output size n is sufficiently large.
2. We develop a lot of general techniques to handle the dependence. Firstly, a new representation (see Sect. 3.3) is introduced to circumvent the cumbersome graphical illustration used in [CLL+18]. Benefited from it, we can handle the underlying combinatorial problem in a natural and intuitive way. Secondly, we abstract a type of combinatorial problems (i.e., Problem 1) capturing the intrinsic randomness of rKACSP, and also propose a high-level framework (see Sect. 5.1) to solve such problems. To instantiate the framework, we introduce some useful notions such as Core, *target-path*, *shared-edge*, and so on (see Sect. 3.3). Combining with the methods for constructing multiple shared-edges, we solve successfully the key problem in 3KACSP (see Sect. 5.2). At last, we also develop some new tricks (see Section 6 in the full version of this paper [WYCD20]) which are crucial in analyzing rKACSP ($r \geq 3$). Such tricks are not needed in 2KACSP, since it is relatively simple and does not have much dependence to handle.

It is rather surprising that the randomness of a single random permutation can provide such high level of security. From our proof, we can know an important reason is that, the information obtained by adversary is actually not so much. For instance, assume that n is big enough and an adversary can make $\Theta(2^{\frac{3n}{4}})$ queries to the random permutation, then the ratio of known points (i.e., roughly $2^{-\frac{n}{4}}$) is still very small. Furthermore, our work means a lot more than simply from 2 to 3, and we now show something new compared to Chen et al.'s work.

1. It is the first time to convert the analysis of rKACSP into a type of combinatorial problems, thus we can study the higher-round constructions in a

modular way. To solve such problems, we propose a general counting framework, and also successfully instantiate it for a 3-round case which is much more involved than the 2-round cases.

2. An important discovery is that we can adapt the tricks used in 2KACSP to solve the corresponding subproblems in 3KACSP, by designing proper assigning-strategy and $RoCs$(Range of Candidates, see Notation 5). We believe that the similar properties also hold in the analysis of general rKACSP.

3. A very big challenge in rKACSP$(r \geq 3)$ is to combine all the subproblems together into a desired bound. We do not need to consider that problem in the case of 2KACSP, since there is only one 2-round case in it. As a result, we develop some useful techniques to handle the dependence between the subproblems. Particularly, the key-points as shown at the beginning of Section 6 in the full version [WYCD20] are also essential in rKACSP$(r \geq 4)$.

Combining all above findings together, we point out that a plausible way to analyze rKACSP is by induction, and what's left is only to solve a single r-round case of Problem 1. That is, we actually reduce an extremely complex (maybe intractable) problem into a single combinatorial problem, which can be solved by our framework theoretically. From the view of induction, Chen et al. [CLL+18] proved the basis step, while we have done largely the non-trivial work of the inductive step. Besides the conceptually important results, the new notions and ideas used in our proof are rather general and not limited in the rKACSP setting. We hope that they can be applied to analyze more different cryptographic constructions with dependence.

OUTLINE OF THIS PAPER. We start in Sect. 2 by setting the basic notations, giving the necessary background on the H-coefficient technique, and showing some helpful lemmas. In Sect. 3, we state the main result of this paper and introduce the new representation used throughout the paper. After that, the main result is proved in Sect. 4 where we also illustrate the underlying combinatorial problem and give two technical lemmas. The core part is Sect. 5, where we propose the general framework and also show the high-level technical route to handle the key subproblem in 3KACSP. At last, we conclude and give some extra discussion in Sect. 6.

2   Preliminaries

2.1   Basic Notations

In this paper, we use capital letters such as $A, B, \ldots$ to denote sets. If A is a finite set, then $|A|$ denotes the cardinality of A, and $\overline{A}$ denotes the complement of A in the universal set (which will be clear from the context). For a finite set S, we let $x \leftarrow_{\$} S$ denote the uniform sampling from S and assigning the value to x. Let A and B be two sets such that $|A| = |B|$, then we denote $Bjt(A \rightarrow B)$ as the set of all bijections from A to B. If g and h are two well-defined bijections, then let $g \circ h(x) = h(g(x))$. Fix an integer $n \geq 1$, let $N = 2^n$, $I_n = \{0,1\}^n$, and $\mathcal{P}_n$ be the set of all permutations on $\{0,1\}^n$, respectively. If two integers s, t satisfy $1 \leq s \leq t$, then we will write $(t)_s = t(t-1)\cdots(t-s+1)$ and $(t)_0 = 1$ by convention.

Given $\mathcal{Q} = \{(x_1,y_1),\ldots,(x_q,y_q)\}$, where the x_i's (resp. y_i's) are pairwise distinct n-bit strings, as well as a permutation $P \in \mathcal{P}_n$, we say that the permutation P extends the set $\mathcal{Q}$, denoting $P \vdash \mathcal{Q}$, if $P(x_i) = y_i$ for $i = 1,\ldots,q$. Let $X = \{x \in I_n : (x,y) \in \mathcal{Q}\}$ and $Y = \{y \in I_n : (x,y) \in \mathcal{Q}\}$. We call X and Y respectively the domain and range of the set $\mathcal{Q}$.

Definition 1 ($\mathcal{Q}'$ is strongly-disjoint with $\mathcal{Q}$). *Let* $\mathcal{Q} = \{(x_1,y_1),\ldots,$ $(x_m,y_m)\}$ *and* $\mathcal{Q}' = \{(x_1',y_1'),\ldots,(x_n',y_n')\}$. *We denote* X,Y,X',Y' *as the domains and ranges of* $\mathcal{Q}$ *and* $\mathcal{Q}'$, *respectively. Then we say that* $\mathbf{\mathcal{Q}'}$ *is strongly-disjoint with* $\mathbf{\mathcal{Q}}$ *if* $X \cap X' = \emptyset$ *and* $Y \cap Y' = \emptyset$, *and denote it as* $\mathbf{\mathcal{Q}' \perp \mathcal{Q}}$.

2.2 Indistinguishability Framework

We will focus on the provable-security analysis of block ciphers in random permutation model, which allows the adversary to get access to the underlying primitives of the block ciphers. Consider the rKACSP construction (see Eq. (1)), a distinguisher $\mathcal{D}$ can interact with a set of 2 *permutation oracles* on n bits that we denote as (P_O, P_I). There are two worlds in terms of the instantiations of the 2 permutation oracles. If P is a random permutation and the round keys $\mathbf{K} = (k_0,\ldots,k_r)$ are randomly chosen from $I_{(r+1)n}$, we refer to $(r\text{KACSP}[P;\mathbf{K}], P)$ as *the "real" world*. If E is a random permutation independent from P, we refer to (E,P) as *the "ideal" world*. We usually refer to the first permutation P_O (instantiated by $r\text{KACSP}[P;\mathbf{K}]$ or E) as *the outer permutation*, and to permutation P_I (instantiated by P) as *the inner permutation*. Given a certain number of the queries to the 2 permutation oracles, the distinguisher $\mathcal{D}$ should distinguish whether the "real" world or the "ideal" world it is interacting with. The distinguisher $\mathcal{D}$ is adaptive such that it can query both sides of each permutation oracle, and also can choose the next query based on the query results it received. There is no computational limit on the distinguisher, thus we can assume *wlog* that the distinguisher is deterministic (with a priori query which maximizes its advantage) and never makes redundant queries (which means that it never repeats a query, nor makes a query $P_i(x)$ for $i \in \{I,O\}$, if it receives x as an answer of a previous query $P_i^{-1}(y)$, or vice-versa).

The *distinguishing advantage* of the adversary $\mathcal{D}$ is defined as

$$Adv(\mathcal{D}) = \left| \Pr[\mathcal{D}^{r\text{KACSP}[P;\mathbf{K}],P} = 1] - \Pr[\mathcal{D}^{E,P} = 1] \right|, \qquad (3)$$

where the first probability is taken over the random choice of P and $\mathbf{K}$, and the second probability is taken over the random choice of P and E. $\mathcal{D}^{(\cdot)}$ denotes that $\mathcal{D}$ can make both forward and backward queries to each permutation oracle according to the random permutation model described before.

For non-negative integers q_e and q_p, we define the insecurity of rKACSP against any adaptive distinguisher (even with unbounded computational source) who can make at most q_e queries to the outer permutation oracle (i.e., P_O) and q_p queries to the inner permutation oracle (i.e., P_I) as

$$Adv_{rKACSP}^{cca}(q_e, q_p) = \max_{\mathcal{D}} Adv(\mathcal{D}), \tag{4}$$

where the maximum is taken over all distinguishers $\mathcal{D}$ making exactly q_e queries to the outer permutation oracle and q_p queries to the inner permutation oracle.

2.3   The H-Coefficient Method

H-coefficient method [Pat08, CS14] is a powerful framework to upper bound the advantage of $\mathcal{D}$ and has been used to prove a number of results. We record all interactions between the adaptive distinguisher $\mathcal{D}$ and the oracles as an ordered list of queries which is also called a *transcript*. Each query in a transcript has the form of (i, b, z, z'), where $i \in \{I, O\}$ represents which permutation oracle being queried, b is a bit indicating whether this is a forward or backward query, z is the value queried and z' is the corresponding answer. For a fixed distinguisher $\mathcal{D}$, a transcript is called *attainable* if exists a tuple of permutations $(P_O, P_I) \in \mathcal{P}_n^2$ such that the interactions among $\mathcal{D}$ and (P_O, P_I) yield the transcript. Recall that the distinguisher $\mathcal{D}$ is deterministic and makes no redundant queries, thus we can convert a transcript into 2 following *lists of directionless queries* without loss of information

$$\mathcal{Q}_E = \{(x_1, y_1), \ldots, (x_{q_e}, y_{q_e})\},$$
$$\mathcal{Q}_P = \{(u_1, v_1), \ldots, (u_{q_p}, v_{q_p})\}.$$

We can reconstruct the transcript exactly through the 2 lists, since $\mathcal{D}$ is deterministic and each of its next action is determined by the previous oracle answers (which can be known from those lists) it has received. As a side note, the 2 lists contain the description of the deterministic distinguisher/algorithm $\mathcal{D}$ implicitly. Therefore, the above two representations of an attainable transcript are equivalent with regard to a fixed deterministic distinguisher $\mathcal{D}$. Based on Eq. (3), our goal is to know the values of the two probabilities. It can be verified that the first probability (i.e., the one related to the "real" world) is only determined by the number of coins which can produce the above 2 directionless lists, and the probability is irrelevant to the order of each query in the original transcript. Thus, it seems that the adaptivity of $\mathcal{D}$ is "dropped" (More details can be found in [CS14]). Through this conceptual transition, upper bounding the advantage of $\mathcal{D}$ is often reduced to certain probability problems. That is why the H-coefficient method works well in lots of provable-security problems, especially for an information-theoretic and adaptive adversary.

As what [CS14],[CLL+18] did, we will also be generous with the distinguisher $\mathcal{D}$ by giving it the actual key $\boldsymbol{K} = (k_0, \ldots, k_r)$ when it is interacting with the "real" world or a dummy key $\boldsymbol{K} \leftarrow_\$ I_{(r+1)n}$ when it is interacting with the "ideal" world at the end of its interaction. This treatment is reasonable since it will only increase the advantage of $\mathcal{D}$. Hence, a transcript τ we consider actually is a tuple $(\mathcal{Q}_E, \mathcal{Q}_P, \boldsymbol{K})$. We refer to $\hat{\tau} = (\mathcal{Q}_E, \mathcal{Q}_P)$ as the *permutation transcript* of τ and say that a transcript τ is *attainable* if its corresponding permutation transcript $\hat{\tau}$ is attainable. Let $\mathcal{T}$ denote the set of attainable transcripts. We denote T_{re}, resp. T_{id}, as the probability distribution of the transcript τ induced by the "real" world, resp. the "ideal" world. It should be pointed out that the two probability distributions depend on the distinguisher $\mathcal{D}$, since its description is embedded in the conversion between the aforementioned two representations. And we also use the same notation to denote the random variable distributed according to each distribution.

The H-coefficient method has lots of variants. In this paper, we will employ the standard "good versus bad" paradigm. More concretely, the set of attainable transcripts $\mathcal{T}$ is partitioned into a set of *"good"* transcripts $\mathcal{T}_1$ such that the probability to obtain some $\tau \in \mathcal{T}_1$ are close in the "real" world and in the "ideal" world, and a set of *"bad"* transcripts $\mathcal{T}_2$ such that the probability to obtain any $\tau \in \mathcal{T}_2$ is small in the "ideal" world. Finally, a well-known H-coefficient-type lemma is given as follows.

Lemma 1 (Lemma 1 of [CLL+18]). *Fix a distinguisher $\mathcal{D}$. Let $\mathcal{T} = \mathcal{T}_1 \sqcup \mathcal{T}_2$ be a partition of the set of attainable transcripts. Assume that there exists ε_1 such that for any $\tau \in \mathcal{T}_1$, one has*

$$\frac{\Pr[T_{re} = \tau]}{\Pr[T_{id} = \tau]} \geq 1 - \varepsilon_1,$$

and that there exists ε_2 such that $\Pr[T_{id} \in \mathcal{T}_2] \leq \varepsilon_2$. Then $Adv(\mathcal{D}) \leq \varepsilon_1 + \varepsilon_2$.

2.4   A Useful Lemma

Lemma 2 (3KACSP version, Lemma 2 of [CLL+18]). *Let $\tau = (\mathcal{Q}_E, \mathcal{Q}_P, \boldsymbol{K} = (k_0, k_1, k_2, k_3)) \in \mathcal{T}$ be an attainable transcript. Let $p(\tau) = \Pr[P \leftarrow_\$ \mathcal{P}_n : 3KACSP[P; \boldsymbol{K}] \vdash \mathcal{Q}_E \mid P \vdash \mathcal{Q}_P]$. Then*

$$\frac{\Pr[T_{re} = \tau]}{\Pr[T_{id} = \tau]} = (N)_{q_e} \cdot p(\tau).$$

Following Lemma 2, it is reduced to lower-bounding $p(\tau)$ if we want to determine the value of ε_1 in Lemma 1. In brief, $p(\tau)$ is the probability that $3KACSP[P; \boldsymbol{K}]$ extends $\mathcal{Q}_E$ when P is a random permutation extending $\mathcal{Q}_P$.

3   The Main Result and New Representation

3.1   3-Round KAC with a Single Permutation

Let n be a positive integer, and let $P : I_n \rightarrow I_n$ be a permutation on I_n. On input $x \in I_n$ and round keys $\boldsymbol{K} = (k_0, k_1, k_2, k_3) \in I_{4n}$, the block cipher 3KACSP returns $y = P\Big(P\big(P(x \oplus k_0) \oplus k_1\big) \oplus k_2\Big) \oplus k_3$. See Fig. 1 for an illustration of the construction of 3KACSP.

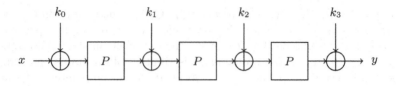

Fig. 1. Illustration of 3KACSP

3.2   Statement of the Result and Discussion

Since 3KACSP is a special case of 3-round KAC construction, its security is also capped by a distinguishing attack with $O(2^{\frac{3n}{4}})$ queries. We will show that the bound is tight by establishing the following theorem, which gives an asymptotical security bound of 3KACSP. Following the main theorem, we also give some comments. The proof of Theorem 1 can be found in Sect. 4, where we also illustrate the underlying combinatorial problem and give two technical lemmas.

Theorem 1 (Security Bound of 3KACSP). *Consider the 3KACSP construction, in which the underlying round permutation P is uniformly random sampled from $\mathcal{P}_n$ and the round keys $\boldsymbol{K} = (k_0, k_1, k_2, k_3)$ are uniformly random sampled from I_{4n}. Assume that $n \geq 32$ is sufficiently large, $\frac{28(q_e)^2}{N} \leq q_p \leq \frac{q_e}{5}$ and $2q_p + 5q_e \leq \frac{N}{2}$, then for any $6 \leq t \leq \frac{N^{1/2}}{8}$, the following upper bound holds:*

$$Adv_{3KACSP}^{cca}(q_e, q_p) \leq 98t \cdot \left(\frac{q_e}{N^{3/4}}\right) + 10t^2 \cdot \left(\frac{q_e}{N}\right) + \zeta(q_e),$$

where $\zeta(q_e) = \begin{cases} \frac{32}{t^2}, & \text{if } q_e \leq \frac{t}{6}N^{1/2} \\ \frac{9N}{q_e^2}, & \text{if } q_e \geq \frac{7t}{6}N^{1/2} \end{cases}$.

<u>Obtaining a concrete upper bound.</u> Due to the special form of error term $\zeta(q_e)$, a single constant t cannot optimize the bound for all q_e's simultaneously. The above result gives an upper bound for a range of q_e's once t is chosen, thus different constants t will give different upper bounds for a fixed q_e. That is, for each q_e, we can make the error term $\zeta(q_e)$ be arbitrarily small by choosing a proper t, as long as the n is big enough. In general, we prefer to choose a small t to obtain the bound, since the first two terms in it are proportional to t. As an explanatory example, we next will show how to choose the constant t, assume that the threshold value of $\zeta(q_e)$ is set to 0.01.

Firstly, we should determine the range of q_e's which are suitable for the minimum $t = 6$. It is easy to verify that, for the range of big $q_e \geq 30N^{1/2}$, it must has $\zeta(q_e) \leq 0.01$, since $\zeta(q_e) = \frac{9N}{q_e^2}$ for $q_e \geq 7N^{1/2}$ (when setting $t = 6$). But for a small q_e it needs a larger t, since we will use the function $\zeta(q_e) = \frac{32}{t^2}$ to obtain a desired $\zeta(q_e)$. For simplicity, we can set $t = 60$ for each $q_e \leq 10N^{1/2}$, because it has $\zeta(q_e) = \frac{32}{60^2} < 0.01$. Now what's left is to choose a proper t for covering the remain range of $10N^{1/2} < q_e < 30N^{1/2}$. Using again the function

$\zeta(q_e) = \frac{32}{t^2}$, we can crudely set $t = 180$, which implies that $\zeta(q_e) = \frac{32}{180^2} < 0.001$ for all $q_e \leq 30N^{1/2}$. As a side note, a slightly better choice is to choose $t = 6c$ for $q_e = cN^{1/2}$, where $10 < c < 30$.

From the above process, we obtain a concrete upper bound as follows.

$$Adv^{cca}_{3KACSP}(q_e, q_p) \leq \begin{cases} 588\left(\frac{q_e}{N^{3/4}}\right) + 360\left(\frac{q_e}{N}\right) + 0.01, & \text{for } q_e \geq 30N^{1/2} & (\text{Set } t = 6) \\ 17640\left(\frac{q_e}{N^{3/4}}\right) + 324000\left(\frac{q_e}{N}\right) + 0.001, & \text{for } 10N^{1/2} < q_e < 30N^{1/2} & (\text{Set } t = 180) \\ 5880\left(\frac{q_e}{N^{3/4}}\right) + 36000\left(\frac{q_e}{N}\right) + 0.01, & \text{for } q_e \leq 10N^{1/2} & (\text{Set } t = 60) \end{cases}$$

It is easy to see that $t = 6$ is available for almost all of the q_e's (i.e., except the fraction of $\frac{30}{N^{1/2}}$). That is, the bound $Adv \leq 588\left(\frac{q_e}{N^{3/4}}\right) + 360\left(\frac{q_e}{N}\right) + \frac{9N}{q_e^2}$ is suitable for almost q_e's. We also stress here that Theorem 1 is an asymptotical result (for sufficiently large n) and we are not focusing on optimizing parameters. The point is that it actually shows that $\Omega(N^{3/4})$ queries are needed to obtain a significant advantage against 3KACSP. Combining with the well-known matching attack, we conclude that the 3KACSP construction is $\Theta(2^{\frac{3n}{4}})$-secure.

DISCUSSION ABOUT THE RESULT. It should be pointed out that the deviation term $\zeta(q_e)$ and the assumption on q_p in Theorem 1 are artifacts of our proof, and have no effect on the final result.

1. The $\zeta(q_e)$ is simply caused by the inaccuracy of Chebyshev's Inequality (i.e., Lemma 5), rather than our proof methods nor the intrinsic flaws of 3KACSP. It is well-known that Chebyshev's Inequality is rather coarse and there must exist a more accurate tail-inequality (e.g., Chenoff Bound). The $\zeta(q_e)$ and t will disappear, as long as a bit more accurate tail-inequality is applied during the computation of Eq. (95) in full version [WYCD20]. That is, just by replacing with a better tail-inequality, our proof techniques actually can obtain a concrete bound such like $Adv \leq 98\left(\frac{q_e}{N^{3/4}}\right) + 10\left(\frac{q_e}{N}\right)$, i.e., $t = 1$ and $\zeta(q_e) = 0$ in Theorem 1. But to our knowledge, there is no explicit expression of the moment generating function for a hypergeometric distribution, hence we now have no idea how to obtain a Chernoff-Type bound.

2. The assumption on q_e and q_p is determined by the assigning-strategy and all the RoCs (there are dozens in total) designed in the formal proof. It means that a better choice corresponds to a weaker assumption. Theoretically, there exist choices which can eliminate the assumption without changing our proof framework. However, optimizing such a choice is rather unrealistic, since it is extremely hard to find even one feasible solution (as provided in our formal proof).

In a word, our results and proof techniques are strong enough to show that 3KACSP is $\Theta(N^{3/4})$-secure in random permutation model.

3.3 New Representation

In this subsection, we will propose a new representation which will be used throughout the paper. The representation improves our understanding of the underlying combinatorial problem, and is very helpful to handle the dependence caused by the single permutation. From our proof, it can be found that this new representation is natural to capture the intrinsic combinatorial problem, and the complicated graphical illustration used in [CLL+18] can also be avoided. More specifically, the new representation consists of several definitions.

Definition 2 (Directed-Edge). *Let A denote a set and $a, b \in A$. If a permutation Ψ on A maps a to b, then we denote it as $a \xrightarrow{\Psi} b$ and say that there is a $\boldsymbol{\Psi}$-directed-edge (or simply directed-edge if Ψ is clear from the context) from a to b. We also use $a \xrightarrow{\Psi} b$ to denote the ordered query-answer pair (a, b) of the permutation oracle Ψ. That is, if we make queries $\Psi(a)$ (resp. $\Psi^{-1}(b)$), then b (resp. a) will be the answer.*

*For a directed-edge $a \xrightarrow{\Psi} b$, we refer to a as the **previous-point** of b under Ψ, and to b as the **next-point** of a under Ψ, respectively. Naturally, the notation $a \xrightarrow{\Psi}$ means that the next-point of a under Ψ is undefined, and the notation $\xrightarrow{\Psi} b$ means that the previous-point of b under Ψ is undefined.*

Definition 2 aims to view the binary relation under a permutation as a set of directed-edges. Consider a permutation $P \in \mathcal{P}_n$, the list of directionless queries $\mathcal{Q}_P = \{(u_1, v_1), \ldots, (u_q, v_q)\}$ can be written as the set of P-directed-edges $\{u_1 \xrightarrow{P} v_1, \ldots, u_q \xrightarrow{P} v_q\}$. From now on, we will not distinguish the two representations.

Definition 3 (Directed-Path and Core). *Let $\varphi[\cdot] : \mathcal{P}_n \to \mathcal{P}_n$ be a block-cipher construction invoking one permutation $P \in \mathcal{P}_n$. Fix an attainable transcript $\tau = (\mathcal{Q}_E, \mathcal{Q}_P, \boldsymbol{K})$, where $\mathcal{Q}_E$ and $\mathcal{Q}_P$ are the lists of directionless queries of the outer and inner permutation oracle, respectively.*

For a specific $P \in \mathcal{P}_n$ and a string $a \in I_n$, the steps related to P in the calculation of $\varphi[P](a)$ can be denoted as a chain of P-directed-edges and has the form of $\langle f(a) \xrightarrow{P} a_1, \ldots, a_m \xrightarrow{P} g^{-1}(\varphi[P](a)) \rangle$, where $f(\cdot)$ and $g(\cdot)$ are invertible operations before the first invocation of P and after the last invocation of P in the construction $\varphi[\cdot]$, respectively.[2] We refer to such a chain as a $\left((a, \varphi[P](a)), \varphi[P] \right)$-directed-path, where a and $\varphi[P](a)$ are called as the source and destination of the directed-path, respectively. We may simply say a directed-path for convenience, if all things are clear from the context.

Let $\mathcal{Q}_E = \{(x_1, y_1), \ldots, (x_q, y_q)\}$, where x_i's (resp. y_i's) are pairwise distinct n-bit strings. We say a permutation $P \in \mathcal{P}_n$ is $\varphi[\cdot]$-correct with respect to $\mathcal{Q}_E$, if $\varphi[P] \vdash \mathcal{Q}_E$. That is, the $\varphi[P]$-directed-path starting from x_i must end at y_i (i.e., $y_i = \varphi[P](x_i)$) for a correct permutation P, where $i = 1, \cdots, q$. We refer to the set of P-directed-edges used in above q directed-paths as a $\varphi[P]$-Core with respect to $\mathcal{Q}_E$, and denote it as $\mathsf{Core}(\varphi[P] \vdash \mathcal{Q}_E)$. In addition, we use the notation $\mathsf{Core}(\varphi[\cdot] \vdash \mathcal{Q}_E)$ to denote a certain $\varphi[P]$-Core in general. And we may simply say a Core for convenience, if $\varphi[\cdot]$ and $\mathcal{Q}_E$ are clear from the context.

---

[2] In this paper, $f(\cdot)$ and $g(\cdot)$ are often the identity functions.

Definition 3 aims to highlight the steps related to P when calculating the value of $\varphi[P](a)$. In fact, the form of a directed-path is only determined by the construction $\varphi[\cdot]$.[3] That is, each $((*, *), \varphi[P])$-directed-path consists of m P-directed-edges, where m is the invoking number of P in the construction $\varphi[\cdot]$. Thus, we often use the notation $\varphi[\cdot]$-*directed-path* to denote a directed-path of the form in general. In addition, the calculation steps independent of P (e.g., the operations $f(\cdot)$ and $g(\cdot)$ in Definition 3) are always omitted, since we only care about the assignments of P. Of course, those omitted steps can still be inferred from the directed-path since they are deterministic. For instance, the calculation of $P(P(x) \boxplus 1) = y$ can be denoted as the directed-path $\langle x \xrightarrow{P} P(x), P(x) \boxplus 1 \xrightarrow{P} y \rangle$, in which the step from $P(x)$ to $P(x) \boxplus 1$ is omitted but can still be known from it. Next, we will give an explanatory example for the above definitions.

Example 1. Let P denote a permutation on $\mathcal{Z}_5 = \{0, 1, 2, 3, 4\}$, as well as $\mathcal{Q}_E = \{(0, 4), (1, 0)\}$, $\mathcal{Q}_P = \varnothing$ and $\varphi[P](x) = P(P(x) \boxplus 1)$, where $\boxplus$ represents the modulo-5 addition.

Case 1: If $P = \{0 \xrightarrow{P} 1, 1 \xrightarrow{P} 2, 2 \xrightarrow{P} 3, 3 \xrightarrow{P} 4, 4 \xrightarrow{P} 0\}$, then all directed-paths constructed by $\varphi[P]$ are $\langle 0 \xrightarrow{P} 1, 2 \xrightarrow{P} 3 \rangle$, $\langle 1 \xrightarrow{P} 2, 3 \xrightarrow{P} 4 \rangle$, $\langle 2 \xrightarrow{P} 3, 4 \xrightarrow{P} 0 \rangle$, $\langle 3 \xrightarrow{P} 4, 0 \xrightarrow{P} 1 \rangle$, and $\langle 4 \xrightarrow{P} 0, 1 \xrightarrow{P} 2 \rangle$. That is, the permutation $\varphi[P]$ maps 0 to 3, 1 to 4, 2 to 0, 3 to 1 and 4 to 2, respectively. Obviously, the P is not $\varphi[\cdot]$-correct with respect to $\mathcal{Q}_E$, since the $\varphi[P]$-directed-path $\langle 0 \xrightarrow{P} 1, 2 \xrightarrow{P} 3 \rangle$ leads 0 to 3 which is inconsistent with the source-destination pair $(0, 4) \in \mathcal{Q}_E$.

Case 2: If $P = \{0 \xrightarrow{P} 2, 1 \xrightarrow{P} 1, 2 \xrightarrow{P} 0, 3 \xrightarrow{P} 4, 4 \xrightarrow{P} 3\}$, then we have $\varphi[P] \vdash \mathcal{Q}_E$ because the directed-paths $\langle 0 \xrightarrow{P} 2, 3 \xrightarrow{P} 4 \rangle$ and $\langle 1 \xrightarrow{P} 1, 2 \xrightarrow{P} 0 \rangle$ lead 0 to 4 and 1 to 0, respectively. Also, we can know that $\mathsf{Core}(P) = \{0 \xrightarrow{P} 2, 1 \xrightarrow{P} 1, 2 \xrightarrow{P} 0, 3 \xrightarrow{P} 4\}$, and thus $|\mathsf{Core}(P)| = 4$.

Case 3: If $P = \{0 \xrightarrow{P} 3, 1 \xrightarrow{P} 0, 2 \xrightarrow{P} 1, 3 \xrightarrow{P} 2, 4 \xrightarrow{P} 4\}$, then it is easily to verify that $\varphi[P] \vdash \mathcal{Q}_E$, as well as $\mathsf{Core}(P) = \{0 \xrightarrow{P} 3, 1 \xrightarrow{P} 0, 4 \xrightarrow{P} 4\}$ and $|\mathsf{Core}(P)| = 3$.

Case 4: Similarly, if $P = \{0 \xrightarrow{P} 0, 1 \xrightarrow{P} 4, 2 \xrightarrow{P} 1, 3 \xrightarrow{P} 2, 4 \xrightarrow{P} 3\}$, then $\varphi[P] \vdash \mathcal{Q}_E$. Furthermore, it has $\mathsf{Core}(P) = \{0 \xrightarrow{P} 0, 1 \xrightarrow{P} 4\}$ and $|\mathsf{Core}(P)| = 2$.

Statement. For convenience, we will simply use the terms *edge* and *path* instead of *directed-edge* and *directed-path*, respectively. In addition, if x_α^β denotes the source of a path (where α and β are some symbols), then the notation y_α^β always denotes the corresponding destination of the path and vice-versa, and the correspondence can be easily inferred from the context.

We have known that a path can be used to denote a complete calculation given the construction, source and P. In fact, we often confront an incomplete path whose source and destination are fixed, provided that the permutation

---

[3] Recall that the adversary can obtain the keys after the querying phrase in our proof setting.

P is partially defined.[4] Namely, there are some edges *missing* in such a path. Particularly, we most interest in a special form of incomplete path which is called *target-path*.

Definition 4 (Target-Path). *Assume that P is partially defined, then a $((a, b), \varphi[P])$-target-path is a $\varphi[\cdot]$-path in which all the inner-nodes are undefined while the source a and the destination b are fixed. Thus, a target-path always has the form of* [5]

$$\langle a \xrightarrow{P} , \xrightarrow{P} , \cdots , \xrightarrow{P} , \xrightarrow{P} b\rangle.$$

In essence, the proof of main result is reduced to the task of completing a group of target-paths (i.e., Problem 1). That is why we refer to such type of paths as target-paths. In general, it is convenient to consider a group of (target-)paths having the same form. Then, the notion of *shared-edge* can also be introduced naturally.

Definition 5 (Group of Paths and Shared-Edge). *Fix a permutation P, which can be partially defined.*

We call the paths $((x_1, y_1), \varphi[P])$-path, $\ldots$, $((x_q, y_q), \varphi[P])$-path as a group of $\varphi[\cdot]$-paths, and denote it as $(\mathcal{Q}_E, \varphi[P])$-paths, where $\mathcal{Q}_E = \{(x_1, y_1), \ldots, (x_q, y_q)\}$ is the set of source-destination pairs. Also, we may simply use the notation $\mathcal{Q}_E$-paths if $\varphi[P]$ is clear from the context.

Similarly, we call the target-paths $((a_1, b_1), \varphi[P])$-target-path, $\ldots$, $((a_q, b_q), \varphi[P])$-target-path as a group of $\varphi[\cdot]$-target-paths, and denote it as $(\mathcal{Q}, \varphi[P])$-target-paths, where $\mathcal{Q} = \{(a_1, b_1), \ldots, (a_q, b_q)\}$ is the set of source-destination pairs.

*If an edge is used in at least 2 different paths, then we refer to it as a **shared-edge**.*

From now on, we can use Definition 5 to denote a group of (target-)paths conveniently. And it should be pointed out that the *shared-edge* is a key primitive in our proof, though the concept is rather simple and natural. Moreover, the notion of *partial-P* will be useful, since P is often partially defined.

Definition 6 (Partial-P and Partially-Sample). *Let P be a permutation on I_n, and let A be a subset of I_n. Then we refer to the set of edges $\{x_i \xrightarrow{P} P(x_i) : x_i \in A\}$ as the **partial-P** from A to $P(A)$.*

*Let S and T be two sets of elements whose next-points and previous-points are undefined under P, respectively. If $|S| = |T|$, then we can sample randomly a bijection $f \leftarrow_\$ Bjt(S \to T)$ and define $x \xrightarrow{P} f(x)$ for each $x \in S$. We refer to the above process as **sample partial-P randomly** from S to T, or **P is partially-sampled randomly** from S to T.*

---

[4] Informally, we say a permutation P is *partially defined*, if the correspondence of some points are undefined.

[5] For simplicity, we assume here that the operations $f(\cdot)$ and $g(\cdot)$ in construction $\varphi[\cdot]$ are both identity functions.

It should be pointed out that a partial-P is a subset of P, and also a set of P-edges. Now let's reconsider the sampling $P \leftarrow_\$ \mathcal{P}_n$ conditioned on $P \vdash \mathcal{Q}_P$, where $\mathcal{Q}_P = \{u_1 \xrightarrow{P} v_1, \ldots, u_q \xrightarrow{P} v_q\}$. If we denote $S = I_n \setminus \{u_1, \ldots, u_q\}$ and $T = I_n \setminus \{v_1, \ldots, v_q\}$, then the above sampling is equivalent to sample partial-P randomly from S to T. Furthermore, it is natural to view $\mathcal{Q}_P$ as the priori information of P. That is, we can fix the q edges of $\mathcal{Q}_P$ in advance, and then sample partial-P randomly from S to T.

4   Proof of Theorem 1

In this section, we will use the standard H-Coefficient method (i.e., Lemma 1) to prove our main result. That is, all attainable transcripts $\mathcal{T}$ should be partitioned into two disjoint parts: a set of "good" transcripts denoted as $\mathcal{T}_1$ and a set of "bad" transcripts denoted as $\mathcal{T}_2$. Determining the partition is often a subtle task, since it is intrinsically a trade-off between ε_1 and ε_2. If we add more conditions on good transcripts to make they have better property (i.e., with smaller ε_1), then the set of bad transcripts becomes larger accordingly (i.e., ε_2 becomes larger), or vice-versa.

Intuitively, the chance to obtain any $\tau \in \mathcal{T}_1$ in "real" world should be very close to the chance in "ideal" world, and it should be very rare to obtain any $\tau \in \mathcal{T}_2$ in the "ideal" world. For an attainable transcript $\tau = \big(\mathcal{Q}_E, \mathcal{Q}_P, \boldsymbol{K} = (k_0, k_1, k_2, k_3)\big)$, we know that (from Lemma 2) the quotient of $\Pr[T_{re} = \tau]$ and $\Pr[T_{id} = \tau]$ is determined by the value of

$$p(\tau) = \Pr\big[P \leftarrow_\$ \mathcal{P}_n : 3\text{KACSP}[P; \boldsymbol{K}] \vdash \mathcal{Q}_E \mid P \vdash \mathcal{Q}_P\big]. \tag{5}$$

That is, a transcript τ is whether "good" or not, can also be determined by the value of $p(\tau)$.

Therefore, we firstly illustrate the meaning of $p(\tau)$ through our new representation, and then give the definition of "bad" transcripts. In fact, it is also a good example to show that the knotty dependence can be sorted out if we use a proper representation. At the end of this section, we will prove Theorem 1 directly by combining two technical lemmas together.

4.1   Transcripts and $p(\tau)$

In this subsection, we firstly expound the meaning of $p(\tau)$ for a fixed transcript τ, and then give the concrete definition of "bad" transcripts. To reduce the complexity of notations, we now rewrite the $p(\tau)$ into another equivalent form.

A CONCEPTUAL TRANSFORMATION.   For an attainable transcript $\tau = (\mathcal{Q}_E, \mathcal{Q}_P, \boldsymbol{K})$, we modify the inner permutation P and its permutation transcript $\hat{\tau} = (\mathcal{Q}_E, \mathcal{Q}_P)$ as follows:

$$P' = P \oplus k_1,$$
$$\mathcal{Q}'_E = \{(x \oplus k_0, y \oplus k_1 \oplus k_3) : (x, y) \in \mathcal{Q}_E\},$$
$$\mathcal{Q}'_P = \{(u, v \oplus k_1) : (u, v) \in \mathcal{Q}_P\}.$$

Let

$$X = \{x' \in I_n : (x',y') \in \mathcal{Q}'_E\}, \quad Y = \{y' \in I_n : (x',y') \in \mathcal{Q}'_E\},$$
$$U = \{u' \in I_n : (u',v') \in \mathcal{Q}'_P\}, \quad V = \{v' \in I_n : (u',v') \in \mathcal{Q}'_P\}$$

denote the domains and the ranges of $\mathcal{Q}'_E$ and $\mathcal{Q}'_P$, respectively. Thus, $|\mathcal{Q}_E| = |\mathcal{Q}'_E| = |X| = |Y| = q_e$, and $|\mathcal{Q}_P| = |\mathcal{Q}'_P| = |U| = |V| = q_p$.

Accordingly, we also transform the 3KACSP construction into the 3KACSP' construction (as shown in Fig. 2), i.e., $P' \circ P' \circ (\oplus k_1 \oplus k_2) \circ P'$. The above modification is reasonable, since we show the actual key used in 3KACSP after the distinguisher $\mathcal{D}$ finishing the query phase (i.e., after obtaining $\mathcal{Q}_E$ and $\mathcal{Q}_P$). Thus, it is simply a conceptual transformation and only the notations should be changed. That is, we can consider that the distinguisher $\mathcal{D}$ is querying the outer permutation and inner permutation oracles instantiated by 3KACSP' and P', respectively. Then the resulting transcript is $\tau' = (\mathcal{Q}'_E, \mathcal{Q}'_P, \mathbf{K})$. From now on, we will not distinguish the transcripts τ and τ', since they can transform from each other easily. Thus, we have

$$p(\tau) = p(\tau') = \Pr[P' \leftarrow_\$ \mathcal{P}_n : \text{3KACSP}'[P';\mathbf{K}] \vdash \mathcal{Q}'_E | P' \vdash \mathcal{Q}'_P]. \qquad (6)$$

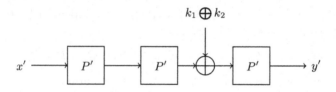

Fig. 2. 3KACSP': a conceptual transformation of 3KACSP

Notation 1 (Abbreviation). *Let A be a set of n-bit strings, and a be an element of A. From now on, we will abbreviate the expression $\mathsf{a} \oplus k_1 \oplus k_2$ as $\mathsf{a}_\oplus$ for convenience. Similarly, we also denote that $A_\oplus = \{\mathsf{a}_\oplus : \mathsf{a} \in A\}$.*

ILLUSTRATION OF $p(\tau')$. Next, we will show the underlying combinatorial problem of $p(\tau')$ intuitively. Fix arbitrarily a transcript $\tau' = (\mathcal{Q}'_E, \mathcal{Q}'_P, \mathbf{K})$, the event 3KACSP'$[P';\mathbf{K}] \vdash \mathcal{Q}'_E$ means that for each pair $(x',y') \in \mathcal{Q}'_E$, the 3KACSP'-path starting from x' ends exactly at y'. A complete 3KACSP'-path consists of 3 P'-edges, and has the form of

$$\langle x' \xrightarrow{P'} *_1, *_1 \xrightarrow{P'} *_2, (*_2)_\oplus \xrightarrow{P'} y' \rangle, \qquad (7)$$

where $*_1$ and $*_2$ are the 2 *inner-nodes* should be assigned.

Before turning into the value of $p(\tau')$, we consider a simpler case that $\mathcal{Q}'_P = \varnothing$ as first. Since no edge of the $\mathcal{Q}'_E$-paths has been fixed in advance, our task is simply to complete all the $(\mathcal{Q}'_E, \text{3KACSP}')$-target-paths, by sampling P' uniformly random from $\mathcal{P}_n$. In fact, we will see that it is exactly the Problem 1 instantiated by $\varphi[P'] = P' \circ P'_{\oplus} \circ P'$, $\mathcal{Q}_1 = \mathcal{Q}'_E$, $\mathcal{Q}_2 = \varnothing$, and can be solved directly by a general framework[6].

Unfortunately, it becomes much more complex when $\mathcal{Q}'_P \neq \varnothing$, since some 3KACSP'-target-paths will be "damaged". More specifically, a path will turn into "some other construction"-target-path, when some edges in it are fixed by $\mathcal{Q}'_P$. We now give some intuition about those paths. Assume that q_e and q_p are $O(N^{3/4})$ and $\boldsymbol{K}$ is uniformly random sampled from I_{4n}, then there are at most 4 types of paths. On average, there are $O(1)$ paths containing 3 fixed edges. Similarly, we know that there exist $O(N^{1/4})$ (resp. $O(N^{1/2})$) paths whose 2 edges (resp. 1 edge) are fixed in advance. And there are $O(N^{3/4})$ paths containing no fixed edge (i.e., they are 3KACSP'-target-paths). It can be found that the circumstances are more involved than before, since the constructions of missing-edges are no longer uniform. In other words, there may exist several different constructions of target-paths to be completed. Thus, we should analyze each of the constructions and complete them in turns.

In fact, we judge a transcript τ' is whether "good" or not, according to the $\mathcal{Q}'_E$-paths and the edges fixed by $\mathcal{Q}'_P$. Firstly, a transcript will be classified into the set of "bad" transcripts, if there exists some $\mathcal{Q}'_E$-path containing 3 fixed edges. Otherwise, we should further study the circumstances of paths and fixed edges determined by the transcript. More specifically, for such a transcript, we can classify the q_e paths between $\mathcal{Q}'_E$ into three groups (see Fig. 3 as an illustration) according to the number of fixed edges.

▶ **Group-2.** The paths containing 2 fixed edges belong to Group-2. More specifically, there are 3 subcases of such paths according to the position of fixed edges. Recall that U and V denote the domain and range of $\mathcal{Q}'_P$, respectively.

- *Group-2.1:* The paths whose first two edges are fixed. That is, Group-2.1 consists of the paths starting from the subset $X_{II} \subset X$, where

$$X_{II} \subset U \;\bigwedge\; \mathcal{Q}'_P(X_{II}) \subset U \;\bigwedge\; \left(\mathcal{Q}'_P(\mathcal{Q}'_P(X_{II}))\right)_{\oplus} \cap U = \varnothing$$

$$\Longleftrightarrow \forall x \in X_{II}, \exists\, w_1, w_2, \; s.t. \; (x, w_1), (w_1, w_2) \in \mathcal{Q}'_P \;\wedge\; (w_2)_{\oplus} \notin U.$$

- *Group-2.2:* The paths whose last two edges are fixed. That is, Group-2.2 consists of the paths ending at the subset $Y_B \subset Y$, where

$$Y_B \subset V \;\bigwedge\; \left(\mathcal{Q}'^{-1}_P(Y_B)\right)_{\oplus} \subset V \;\bigwedge\; \mathcal{Q}'^{-1}_P\left(\left(\mathcal{Q}'^{-1}_P(Y_B)\right)_{\oplus}\right) \cap V = \varnothing$$

$$\Longleftrightarrow \forall y \in Y_B, \exists\, w_1, w_2, \; s.t. \; (w_1, w_2), ((w_2)_{\oplus}, y) \in \mathcal{Q}'_P \;\wedge\; w_1 \notin V.$$

- *Group-2.3:* The paths whose first and third edges are fixed. That is, Group-2.3 consists of the paths starting from the subset $D_X \subset X$ to the corresponding $D_Y = \mathcal{Q}'_E(D_X) \subset Y$, where

$$D_X \subset U \;\bigwedge\; D_Y \subset V \;\bigwedge\; (\mathcal{Q}'_P(D_X)) \cap U = \varnothing \;\bigwedge\; ((\mathcal{Q}'_P)^{-1}(D_Y))_{\oplus} \cap V = \varnothing$$

$$\Longleftrightarrow \forall x \in D_X, \exists\, w_1, w_2, \; s.t. \; (x, w_1), (w_2, \mathcal{Q}'_E(x)) \in \mathcal{Q}'_P \;\wedge\; w_1 \notin U \;\wedge\; (w_2)_{\oplus} \notin V.$$

---

[6] The framework and the technical route can be found in Sect. 5.1 and 5.2, respectively.

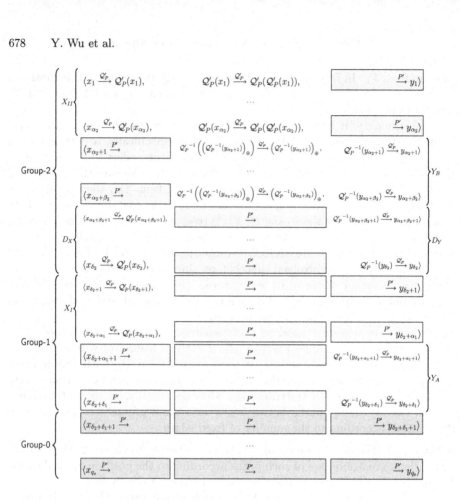

Fig. 3. Illustration of the missing-edges in $\mathcal{Q}'_E$-paths

Notation 2 (Group-2). *We denote* $|X_{II}| = \alpha_2$, $|Y_B| = \beta_2$, $|D_X| = |D_Y| = \gamma_2$, *and* $\delta_2 = \alpha_2 + \beta_2 + \gamma_2$. *Thus, Group-2 contains* δ_2 *paths in total, where* α_2 *paths belong to Group-2.1,* β_2 *paths belong to Group-2.2 and the other* γ_2 *paths belong to Group-2.3. For convenience, we assume wlog that* $X_{II} = \{x_1, \ldots, x_{\alpha_2}\}$, $Y_B = \{y_{\alpha_2+1}, \ldots, y_{\alpha_2+\beta_2}\}$, $D_X = \{x_{\alpha_2+\beta_2+1}, \ldots, x_{\delta_2}\}$ *and* $D_Y = \{y_{\alpha_2+\beta_2+1}, \ldots, y_{\delta_2}\}$.

▶ **Group-1.** The paths containing 1 fixed edge belong to Group-1. More specifically, there are 2 subcases of such paths according to the position of fixed edge. Recall that U and V denote the domain and range of $\mathcal{Q}'_P$, respectively.

  - *Group-1.1:* The paths whose first edge is fixed. That is, Group-1.1 consists of the paths starting from the subset $X_I \subset X$, where

$$X_I \subset U \bigwedge \mathcal{Q}'_P(X_I) \cap U = \emptyset$$
$$\Longleftrightarrow \forall x \in X_I, \exists\, w_1, \ s.t.\ (x, w_1) \in \mathcal{Q}'_P \ \wedge \ w_1 \notin U.$$

- *Group-1.2:* The paths whose third edge is fixed. That is, Group-1.2 consists of the paths ending at the subset $Y_A \subset Y$, where

$$Y_A \subset V \bigwedge \left(Q'^{-1}_P (Y_A) \right)_\oplus \cap V = \varnothing$$
$$\iff \forall y \in Y_A, \exists\, w_1, \text{ s.t. } (w_1, y) \in Q'_P \wedge (w_1)_\oplus \notin V.$$

Notation 3 (Group-1). *We denote $|X_I| = \alpha_1$, $|Y_A| = \beta_1$ and $\delta_1 = \alpha_1 + \beta_1$. Namely, Group-1 contains δ_1 paths in total, where α_1 paths belong to Group-1.1 and the other β_1 paths belong to Group-1.2. For convenience, we assume wlog that $X_I = \{x_{\delta_2+1}, \ldots, x_{\delta_2+\alpha_1}\}$ and $Y_A = \{y_{\delta_2+\alpha_1+1}, \ldots, y_{\delta_2+\delta_1}\}$.*

▶ **Group-0.** Each path belongs to Group-0 contains no fixed edge.

Notation 4 (Group-0). *We denote $\delta_0 = q_e - \delta_2 - \delta_1$. Thus, Group-0 contains δ_0 paths in total. Let X_0 and Y_0 denote the sets of sources and destinations of Group-0, respectively. For convenience, we assume wlog that $X_0 = \{x_i : \delta_2 + \delta_1 + 1 \le i \le q_e\}$ and $Y_0 = \{y_i : \delta_2 + \delta_1 + 1 \le i \le q_e\}$.*

For a fixed transcript τ', its circumstances of Q'_E-paths and fixed edges can be illustrated as Fig. 3, where the missing-edges are the ones marked with a colored square. At this point, it is clear that $p(\tau')$ (see Eq. (6)) represents the probability that, all missing-edges are filled by sampling P' uniformly random from the set of permutations extending Q'_P. Furthermore, the above problem becomes more straightforward if we use the notion of target-path (see Definition 4).

Definition 7 (Structure of Missing-Edges).
Let E_2 denote the event that the δ_2 paths of Group-2 are completed (i.e., the δ_2 missing-edges in Group-2 are filled).

Let E_{11} denote the event that the $\left(Q'_{E_{11}}, \varphi_{11}[\cdot] \right)$-target-paths are completed (i.e., the $2\alpha_1$ missing-edges in Group-1.1 are filled), where $Q'_{E_{11}} = \left\{ (Q'_P(x_i), y_i) : x_i \in X_I \right\}$ and $\varphi_{11}[P'] = P'_\oplus \circ P'$.

Let E_{12} denote the event that the $\left(Q'_{E_{12}}, \varphi_{12}[\cdot] \right)$-target-paths are completed (i.e., the $2\beta_1$ missing-edges in Group-1.2 are filled), where $Q'_{E_{12}} = \left\{ (x_i, Q'^{-1}_P(y_i)) : y_i \in Y_A \right\}$ and $\varphi_{12}[P'] = P' \circ P'_\oplus$.

Let E_0 denote the event that the $\left(Q'_{E_0}, \varphi_0[\cdot] \right)$-target-paths are completed (i.e., the $3\delta_0$ missing-edges in Group-0 are filled), where $Q'_{E_0} = \{ (x_i, y_i) : x_i \in X_0 \}$ and $\varphi_0[P'] = P' \circ P'_\oplus \circ P'$.

Immediately, we can know that

$$p(\tau') = \Pr[P' \leftarrow_\$ \mathcal{P}_n : E_2 \wedge E_{11} \wedge E_{12} \wedge E_0 | P' \vdash Q'_P]. \tag{8}$$

Obviously, lower-bounding the value of $p(\tau')$ is reduced to several subproblems which can be applied directly with the counting framework (proposed in Sect. 5.1). For a "good" transcript, we can successfully obtain an appropriate lower bound for each subproblem.[7]

---

[7] In fact, as shown in proof sketch of Lemma 3, we will handle each subproblem with an additional restriction.

<u>Definition of Bad Transcripts</u>. Now, we will give the concrete definition of "bad"/"good" transcripts. From the formal proof, it will be seen that each attainable permutation transcript $\hat{\tau}$ can be extended to a "good" transcript by adding a "good" key $\boldsymbol{K}$. Thus, it is equivalent to study the properties of "bad"/"good" keys for a fixed permutation transcript $\hat{\tau}$.

Definition 8 (Bad Transcripts and Bad Keys). *Fix arbitrarily a permutation transcript* $\hat{\tau} = (\mathcal{Q}_E, \mathcal{Q}_P)$. *If the extended transcript* $\tau' = (\mathcal{Q}'_E, \mathcal{Q}'_P, \boldsymbol{K})$ *satisfies* $\boldsymbol{K} \in \text{BadK} = \bigcup_{1 \leq i \leq 9} \text{BadK}_i$, *then we say the* $\tau = (\mathcal{Q}_E, \mathcal{Q}_P, \boldsymbol{K})$ *is a "bad" transcript and the* $\boldsymbol{K}$ *is a "bad" key for* $\hat{\tau}$. *Otherwise, we say the* τ *is a "good" transcript and the* $\boldsymbol{K}$ *is a "good" key for* $\hat{\tau}$. *More specifically, the definitions of* BadK_i $(1 \leq i \leq 9)$ *are shown as follows.*

$\boldsymbol{K} \in \text{BadK}_1 \iff$ There exists a $\mathcal{Q}'_E$-path containing 3 fixed edges.

$\boldsymbol{K} \in \text{BadK}_2 \iff \alpha_2 > \dfrac{q_e}{N^{1/2}} \bigvee \beta_2 > \dfrac{q_e}{N^{1/2}} \bigvee \gamma_2 > \dfrac{q_e}{N^{1/2}}$
$\qquad\qquad\qquad \bigvee \alpha_1 > \dfrac{q_e}{N^{1/4}} \bigvee \beta_1 > \dfrac{q_e}{N^{1/4}}$

$\boldsymbol{K} \in \text{BadK}_3 \iff U, \left(\mathcal{Q}'_P\left(\mathcal{Q}'_P(X_{II})\right)\right)_\oplus, \mathcal{Q}'^{-1}_E(Y_B)$ and $\mathcal{Q}'_P(D_X)$ are not
$\qquad\qquad\qquad$ pairwise disjoint $\bigvee V, \mathcal{Q}'_E(X_{II}), \mathcal{Q}'^{-1}_P\left(\left(\mathcal{Q}'^{-1}_P(Y_B)\right)_\oplus\right)$ and
$\qquad\qquad\qquad \left(\mathcal{Q}'^{-1}_P(D_Y)\right)_\oplus$ are not pairwise disjoint

$\boldsymbol{K} \in \text{BadK}_4 \iff |\mathcal{Q}'_P(X_I) \setminus (T_{11})_\oplus| > \dfrac{\alpha_1}{N^{1/4}} \bigvee |\mathcal{Q}'_E(X_I) \setminus (S_{11})_\oplus| > \dfrac{\alpha_1}{N^{1/4}}$
$\qquad\qquad\qquad$ when $\alpha_2, \beta_2, \gamma_2 \leq \dfrac{q_e}{N^{1/2}}$ and $\alpha_1, \beta_1 \leq \dfrac{q_e}{N^{1/4}}$

$\boldsymbol{K} \in \text{BadK}_5 \iff |\mathcal{Q}'_P(X_I) \cap (\mathcal{Q}'_E(X_I))_\oplus| > \dfrac{\alpha_1}{N^{1/4}}$ when $\alpha_2, \beta_2, \gamma_2 \leq \dfrac{q_e}{N^{1/2}}$
$\qquad\qquad\qquad$ and $\alpha_1, \beta_1 \leq \dfrac{q_e}{N^{1/4}}$

$\boldsymbol{K} \in \text{BadK}_6 \iff |\mathcal{Q}'^{-1}_E(Y_A) \setminus T_{12}| > \dfrac{\beta_1}{N^{1/4}} \bigvee |\mathcal{Q}'^{-1}_P(Y_A) \setminus (S_{12})_\oplus| > \dfrac{\beta_1}{N^{1/4}}$
$\qquad\qquad\qquad$ when $\alpha_2, \beta_2, \gamma_2 \leq \dfrac{q_e}{N^{1/2}}$ and $\alpha_1, \beta_1 \leq \dfrac{q_e}{N^{1/4}}$

$\boldsymbol{K} \in \text{BadK}_7 \iff |\mathcal{Q}'^{-1}_E(Y_A) \cap (\mathcal{Q}'^{-1}_P(Y_A))_\oplus| > \dfrac{\beta_1}{N^{1/4}}$ when $\alpha_2, \beta_2, \gamma_2 \leq \dfrac{q_e}{N^{1/2}}$
$\qquad\qquad\qquad$ and $\alpha_1, \beta_1 \leq \dfrac{q_e}{N^{1/4}}$

$\boldsymbol{K} \in \text{BadK}_8 \iff |X_0 \setminus T_0| > \dfrac{\delta_0}{N^{1/4}} \bigvee |X_0 \setminus (T_0)_\oplus| > \dfrac{\delta_0}{N^{1/4}}$
$\qquad\qquad\qquad \bigvee |Y_0 \setminus S_0| > \dfrac{\delta_0}{N^{1/4}} \bigvee |Y_0 \setminus (S_0)_\oplus| > \dfrac{\delta_0}{N^{1/4}}$ when $\alpha_2, \beta_2, \gamma_2$
$\qquad\qquad\qquad \leq \dfrac{q_e}{N^{1/2}}$ and $\alpha_1, \beta_1 \leq \dfrac{q_e}{N^{1/4}}$

$\boldsymbol{K} \in \text{BadK}_9 \iff |X_0 \cap Y_0| > \dfrac{\delta_0}{N^{1/4}} \bigvee |(X_0)_\oplus \cap Y_0| > \dfrac{\delta_0}{N^{1/4}}$ when $\alpha_2, \beta_2, \gamma_2$
$\qquad\qquad\qquad \leq \dfrac{q_e}{N^{1/2}}$ and $\alpha_1, \beta_1 \leq \dfrac{q_e}{N^{1/4}}$,

where S_i (resp. T_i) are the sets of n-bit strings whose next-points (resp. previous-points) are undefined when considering the subproblem related to E_i, for $i \in \{11, 12, 0\}$.[8]

It should be pointed out that the conditions for "bad" keys are not designed only for the "real" world. In fact, all discussion in Sect. 4.1 depends only on the relation between permutation transcript $\widehat{\tau}$ and $\boldsymbol{K}$ (which is dummy in the "ideal" world), and is irrelevant to which world we consider.

4.2 Two Technical Lemmas

In this subsection, we give two technical lemmas to upper-bound the values of ε_1 and ε_2 in Lemma 1, respectively. More specifically, Lemma 3 considers arbitrarily an attainable permutation transcript $\widehat{\tau}$, and lower-bounds the value of $\Pr[T_{re} = (\widehat{\tau}, \boldsymbol{K})])/(\Pr[T_{id} = (\widehat{\tau}, \boldsymbol{K})]$ for any "good" key $\boldsymbol{K}$. This is the major task in our formal proof. And Lemma 4 upper-bounds the value of $\Pr[\boldsymbol{K}$ is bad for $\widehat{\tau}]$ in "ideal" world, where $\widehat{\tau}$ can be any attainable permutation transcript.

Lemma 3. *Consider the 3KACSP construction, and fix arbitrarily an attainable permutation transcript $\widehat{\tau} = (\mathcal{Q}_E, \mathcal{Q}_P)$, where $|\mathcal{Q}_E| = q_e$ and $|\mathcal{Q}_P| = q_p$. Assume that $n \geq 32$, $6 \leq t \leq \frac{N^{1/2}}{8}$, $\frac{28(q_e)^2}{N} \leq q_p \leq \frac{q_e}{5}$ and $2q_p + 5q_e \leq \frac{N}{2}$. Following the Definition 8, if $\boldsymbol{K}$ is a good key for $\widehat{\tau}$, then we have the bound*

$$\frac{\Pr[T_{re} = (\widehat{\tau}, \boldsymbol{K})]}{\Pr[T_{id} = (\widehat{\tau}, \boldsymbol{K})]} \geq 1 - 97t \cdot \left(\frac{q_e}{N^{3/4}}\right) - 10t^2 \cdot \left(\frac{q_e}{N}\right) - \zeta(q_e).$$

OUTLINE OF THE PROOF. From Lemma 2 and the Eq. (8), we know that

$$\frac{\Pr[T_{re} = (\widehat{\tau}, \boldsymbol{K})]}{\Pr[T_{id} = (\widehat{\tau}, \boldsymbol{K})]} = (N)_{q_e} \cdot \Pr[P' \leftarrow_\$ \mathcal{P}_n : E_2 \wedge E_{11} \wedge E_{12} \wedge E_0 | P' \vdash \mathcal{Q}'_P]$$

$$\geq (N)_{q_e} \cdot \Pr[P' \leftarrow_\$ \mathcal{P}_n : E_2 \wedge \widetilde{E_{11}} \wedge \widetilde{E_{12}} \wedge \widetilde{E_0} | P' \vdash \mathcal{Q}'_P]$$

$$= (N)_{q_e}$$

$$\times \Pr[P' \leftarrow_\$ \mathcal{P}_n : E_2 | P' \vdash \mathcal{Q}'_P] \tag{9}$$

$$\times \Pr[P' \leftarrow_\$ \mathcal{P}_n : \widetilde{E_{11}} | P' \vdash \mathcal{Q}'_P \wedge E_2] \tag{10}$$

$$\times \Pr[P' \leftarrow_\$ \mathcal{P}_n : \widetilde{E_{12}} | P' \vdash \mathcal{Q}'_P \wedge E_2 \wedge \widetilde{E_{11}}] \tag{11}$$

$$\times \Pr[P' \leftarrow_\$ \mathcal{P}_n : \widetilde{E_0} | P' \vdash \mathcal{Q}'_P \wedge E_2 \wedge \widetilde{E_{11}} \wedge \widetilde{E_{12}}], \tag{12}$$

where $\widetilde{E_{11}}$ denotes the event $E_{11} \wedge |\mathsf{Core}(\varphi_{11}[P'] \vdash \mathcal{Q}'_{E_{11}})| \geq (2 - \frac{1}{N^{1/4}})\alpha_1$, $\widetilde{E_{12}}$ denotes the event $E_{12} \wedge |\mathsf{Core}(\varphi_{12}[P'] \vdash \mathcal{Q}'_{E_{12}})| \geq (2 - \frac{1}{N^{1/4}})\beta_1$, and $\widetilde{E_0}$ denotes the event $E_0 \wedge |\mathsf{Core}(\varphi_0[P'] \vdash \mathcal{Q}'_{E_0})| \geq (3 - \frac{2t}{N^{1/2}})\delta_0$.

---

[8] For completeness, we give directly the concrete definition here. A more natural way is showing some intuition on "good" transcripts before such a rigorous definition. The interested readers can refer to the Definitions 9 and 13 in full version [WYCD20] for more interpretations about the properties of "bad"/"good" keys.

We will see that it is easy to calculate the value of (9) when K is a "good" key for $\hat{\tau}$. Hence what's left is to lower-bound the values of (10)–(12) for any "good" transcript, respectively. Intrinsically, the 3 probabilities belong to the same type of combinatorial problems (i.e., the Problem 1). That means we can view Eqs. (10)–(12) as a 2-round, 2-round and 3-round instantiation of Problem 1, respectively. Interestingly, we find that the techniques used in [CLL+18] can be tailored to obtain desired values of the 2-round cases. Nonetheless, our 2-round cases are more involved and there are some new non-trivial tasks should be solved. Furthermore, the 3-round case is a whole new challenge, and is much more difficult than the 2-round ones. To handle it, we introduce a general framework in Sect. 5, where we also give the high-level technical route.

However, knowing how to solve (9)–(12) individually is still far from enough. It is a very big challenge to combine all the lower bounds together to obtain an appropriate result, since those subproblems affect each other by sharing the same resource of permutation P. There are numerous technical specifics should be handled, and we defer the formal proof of Lemma 3 to Section 6 of the full version [WYCD20].

Lemma 4. *Consider the "ideal" world, and fix arbitrarily an attainable permutation transcript* $\hat{\tau} = (\mathcal{Q}_E, \mathcal{Q}_P)$, *where* $|\mathcal{Q}_E| = q_e$ *and* $|\mathcal{Q}_P| = q_p$. *Following the Definition 8, if* $q_p \leq \frac{q_e}{5}$, *then it has*

$$\Pr[\mathbf{K} \xleftarrow{\$} I_{4n} : \mathbf{K} \text{ is bad for } \hat{\tau}] \leq 6 \cdot \left(\frac{q_e}{N^{3/4}}\right).$$

The formal proof of Lemma 4 is deferred to Section 7 of the full version [WYCD20].

4.3 Concluding the Proof of Theorem 1

At this point,we are ready to complete the proof of Theorem 1. It can be inferred that $\varepsilon_1 = 97t \cdot \left(\frac{q_e}{N^{3/4}}\right) + 10t^2 \cdot \left(\frac{q_e}{N}\right) + \zeta(q_e)$ and $\varepsilon_2 = 6 \cdot \left(\frac{q_e}{N^{3/4}}\right)$ from Lemma 3 and Lemma 4, respectively. Following the H coefficient method and Lemma 1, we finally obtain

$$
\begin{aligned}
Adv^{cca}_{3KACSP}(q_e, q_p) &\leq \varepsilon_1 + \varepsilon_2 \\
&\leq 97t \cdot \left(\frac{q_e}{N^{3/4}}\right) + 10t^2 \cdot \left(\frac{q_e}{N}\right) + \zeta(q_e) + 6 \cdot \left(\frac{q_e}{N^{3/4}}\right) \\
&\leq 98t \cdot \left(\frac{q_e}{N^{3/4}}\right) + 10t^2 \cdot \left(\frac{q_e}{N}\right) + \zeta(q_e),
\end{aligned}
$$

where we use the fact that $t \geq 6$ for the last inequality.

5 A Type of Combinatorial Problem

It is known that the proof of Lemma 3 can be reduced to several subproblems having a similar form. In fact, the analysis of $rKACSP$ can also be reduced to the same type of problems. That is a key perspective to simplify the task of studying the security of rKACSP.

In this section, we will only study how to solve such type of problems individually, while the tricks of balancing all the subproblems are deferred to the formal proof. More specifically, a general framework which can theoretically solve such problems is proposed. For the reason of space, we here only instantiate it for the 3-round case and the full version [WYCD20] also gives the 2-round instance as a warm-up.

First of all, the general definition of aforementioned problems is given as follows.

Problem 1 (Completing A Group of Target-Paths). Consider a group of $(\mathcal{Q}_1, \varphi[\cdot])$-target-paths, where $\mathcal{Q}_1$ is the set of source-destination pairs. Let $\mathcal{Q}_2$ denote the set of fixed edges, and it has $\mathcal{Q}_1 \perp \mathcal{Q}_2$. Then, how to lower-bound the value of

$$p = \Pr[P \leftarrow_\$ \mathcal{P}_n : \varphi[P] \vdash \mathcal{Q}_1 | P \vdash \mathcal{Q}_2]. \tag{13}$$

It should be pointed out that each target-path in the group has the same construction, and hence the same number of missing-edges. This number of missing-edges is the principal character of Problem 1. In addition, we do not care about the specific values of the source-destination pairs in $\mathcal{Q}_1$, as long as they satisfy some "good" properties and $\mathcal{Q}_1 \perp \mathcal{Q}_2$. More importantly, our work shows some evidence that, the problems with the same number of missing-edges can be solved by similar techniques.

Compared to Chen et al.'s ad-hoc work, our techniques stand in a higher level and unearth something more intrinsic. In a very high level, our method is reduced to constructing a certain number of shared-edges by assigning inner-nodes.

Statement. For simplicity, we assume that all edges defined in this section are well-defined and compatible from each other.

5.1 Counting Framework

In this subsection, we will study how to handle the Problem 1 with at least 2 missing-edges, since the case of 1 missing-edge is trivial. More specifically, a counting framework will be proposed based on the notions of Core (see Definition 3) and shared-edge (see Definition 5). Before that, we will give some intuition about the framework.

INTUITION. Let U and V denote the domain and range of $\mathcal{Q}_2$, respectively. Then, the sets $S = I_n \backslash U$ and $T = I_n \backslash V$ denote the sets of the strings whose next-points and previous-point are undefined, respectively. In fact, we will only use the edges from S to T to complete all the target-paths. Namely, the Cores we construct must be strongly-disjoint with $\mathcal{Q}_2$. The reason why we can still construct enough Cores is that, the number of known edges (i.e., $|\mathcal{Q}_2|$) is relatively rather small. For example, $|\mathcal{Q}_P| = O(N^{3/4})$ is far more smaller than N (i.e., roughly 1 out of $N^{1/4}$) when n is big enough.

Let $\mathcal{P}_C = \{P \in \mathcal{P}_n : \varphi[P] \vdash \mathcal{Q}_1 \wedge P \vdash \mathcal{Q}_2\}$ denote the set of all correct permutations extending $\mathcal{Q}_2$, and $\mathcal{C} = \{\widetilde{C} : \widetilde{C} \perp \mathcal{Q}_2 \wedge \exists P \in \mathcal{P}_C \text{ s.t. } \widetilde{C} = \mathsf{Core}(\varphi[P] \vdash \mathcal{Q}_1)\}$ denote the set of all possible Cores strongly-disjoint with $\mathcal{Q}_2$. From the definition, we know that each correct permutation $P \in \mathcal{P}_C$ must determine a $\mathsf{Core}(\varphi[P] \vdash \mathcal{Q}_1)$. On the other side, for a specific $\widetilde{C} \in \mathcal{C}$, there exist exactly $(N - |\mathcal{Q}_2| - |\widetilde{C}|)!$ different correct permutations $P \in \mathcal{P}_C$ such that $\mathsf{Core}(\varphi[P] \vdash \mathcal{Q}_1) = \widetilde{C}$. That is because such P must contain the $|\mathcal{Q}_2|$ edges fixed in $\mathcal{Q}_2$ and the $|\widetilde{C}|$ edges fixed in $\widetilde{C}$, while the rest of edges can be defined freely. We can know that the above $(|\mathcal{Q}_2| + |\widetilde{C}|)$ edges are distinct and have no conflict, since it has $\widetilde{C} \perp \mathcal{Q}_2$. Additionally, it is easy to know that the size of the sample space is equal to $(N - |\mathcal{Q}_2|)!$, thus we have

$$(13) = \frac{|\mathcal{P}_C|}{(N - |\mathcal{Q}_2|)!}$$

$$\geq \frac{\sum_{\widetilde{C} \in \mathcal{C}} |\{P \in \mathcal{P}_C : \mathsf{Core}(\varphi[P] \vdash \mathcal{Q}_1) = \widetilde{C}\}|}{(N - |\mathcal{Q}_2|)!}$$

$$= \frac{\sum_{\widetilde{C} \in \mathcal{C}} (N - |\mathcal{Q}_2| - |\widetilde{C}|)!}{(N - |\mathcal{Q}_2|)!}$$

$$= \frac{\sum_m \sum_{\widetilde{C} \in \mathcal{C} : |\widetilde{C}| = m} (N - |\mathcal{Q}_2| - m)!}{(N - |\mathcal{Q}_2|)!}$$

$$= \sum_m \frac{\left|\{\widetilde{C} \in \mathcal{C} : |\widetilde{C}| = m\}\right|}{(N - |\mathcal{Q}_2|)_m}. \tag{14}$$

Intrinsically, we classify the correct permutations according to the cardinality of the corresponding Core. In fact, we only interest in the Cores strongly-disjoint with $\mathcal{Q}_2$, since they are easier to be counted. From Eq. (14), it is known that the value of p can be lower-bounded, if we can count the number of Cores with a specific cardinality and also know how to sum all the related terms up.

THE COUNTING FRAMEWORK. Based on the above intuition, a 4-step counting framework is proposed in Fig. 4. Roughly, the first 3 steps aim to lower-bound the number of Cores with a specific cardinality, and the last step will handle the calculation of a summation. As shown in Fig. 4, our first task is to instantiate the Problem 1 with specific parameters (i.e., Step 1). Then, we should propose an appropriate assigning strategy for constructing a specific number of shared-edges, and hence obtain the Cores with the specific cardinality (i.e., Step 2). Also, we should count the number of possible assignments which can be constructed from the above strategy (i.e., Step 3). Thus, we actually establish a lower bound for the number of Cores with a specific cardinality. At last, we should calculate a summation to obtain the final result (i.e., Step 4).

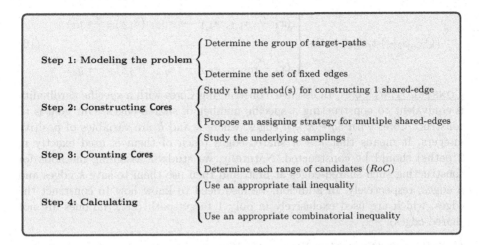

Fig. 4. Illustration of the counting framework

5.2 The Key Subproblem in 3KACSP

In this subsection, we will instantiate the counting framework for the 3-round case to show how it works. For brevity, we here only give the high-level technical route, and all the details will be completed in the formal proof. First of all, we abstract the 3-round subproblem in 3KACSP as follows.

Problem 2 (A Problem with 3 Missing-Edges). Let $\mathcal{Q}_E = \{(x_1, y_1), \ldots, (x_q, y_q)\}$ be the set of source-destination pairs of $\varphi_2[\cdot]$-target-paths, and $\mathcal{Q}_P = \{(u_1, v_1), \ldots, (u_p, v_p)\}$ be the set of known edges, where $\varphi_2[P] = P \circ P_\oplus \circ P$ and $\mathcal{Q}_P \perp \mathcal{Q}_E$. Then, how to lower-bound the value of

$$p_2 = \Pr[P \leftarrow_\$ \mathcal{P}_n : \varphi_2[P] \vdash \mathcal{Q}_E | P \vdash \mathcal{Q}_P]. \tag{15}$$

MODELING THE PROBLEM. Following the counting framework in Fig. 4, our first task is to make clear the group of target-paths (including the construction and source-destination pairs) and the set of fixed edges. Obviously, Problem 2 is exactly the Problem 1 instantiated by $\varphi[\cdot] = \varphi_2[\cdot]$, $\mathcal{Q}_1 = \mathcal{Q}_E$ and $\mathcal{Q}_2 = \mathcal{Q}_P$. We denote X and Y as the domain and range of $\mathcal{Q}_E$, respectively. And let $S = I_n \setminus \{u_1, \ldots, u_p\}$ and $T = I_n \setminus \{v_1, \ldots, v_p\}$ denote the sets of strings whose next-points and previous-points are undefined, respectively. Then, it has $|S| = |T| = N - p$.

As shown in (16), there are 2 *inner-nodes* (i.e., $*_{i,1}$ and $*_{i,2}$) to be assigned in each $(\mathcal{Q}_E, \varphi_2[\cdot])$-target-path. We refer to the 2 inner-nodes in such a target-path as 1st-*inner-node* and 2nd-*inner-node*, respectively. Since a well-defined assignment of all the inner-nodes (i.e., the tuple of $(*_{1,1}, *_{1,2}, \ldots, *_{q,1}, *_{q,2})$) is equivalent to a $\mathsf{Core}(\varphi_2[\cdot] \vdash \mathcal{Q}_E)$, we will not distinguish them from now on. Moreover, we will count the number of assignments of all the inner-nodes, to lower-bound the value of (15).

$$(\mathcal{Q}_E, \varphi_2[\cdot])\text{-target-paths} \begin{cases} \langle x_1 \xrightarrow{P} *_{1,1}, \ *_{1,1} \xrightarrow{P} *_{1,2}, \ (*_{1,2})_\oplus \xrightarrow{P} y_1 \rangle \\ \qquad\qquad\qquad \cdots \\ \langle x_q \xrightarrow{P} *_{q,1}, \ *_{q,1} \xrightarrow{P} *_{q,2}, \ (*_{q,2})_\oplus \xrightarrow{P} y_q \rangle \end{cases} \tag{16}$$

CONSTRUCTING Cores. In essence, constructing Cores with a specific cardinality is equivalent to constructing a specific number of shared-edges. Our goal is to construct Cores with $3q - k - h$ edges, where k and h are variables of positive integers. It means that $k + h$ shared-edges (each of them is used exactly in 2 paths) should be constructed. Naturally, we study 2 assigning methods for constructing such shared-edges at first, and then use them to save k edges and h edges, respectively. In addition, we also need to know how to construct the edges, which are used exclusively in only 1 target-path (i.e., the ones are not shared-edges).

Definition 9 (Exclusive-Element). *We say an inner-node is assigned by an* ***exclusive-element****, if it not creates any new shared-edge at this moment. In this paper, we always use a notation related to w (e.g., w_i) to denote an exclusive-element.*

Consider the $(\mathcal{Q}_E, \varphi_2[\cdot])$-target-paths in (16), we will only focus on the shared-edge involved exactly in 2 paths (i.e., each such shared-edge will save 1 edge). It is easy to verify that a shared-edge is established once a 1st-inner-node is assigned by an element from X or Y. Similarly, a shared-edge is also established once a 2nd-inner-node is assigned by an element from $X_\oplus$ or Y. Therefore, for constructing a shared-edge, we choose a target-path at first, and then assign a proper value to its 1st-inner-node or 2nd-inner-node. In either case, the chosen value determines the other path sharing an edge with the former one. To distinguish them, we refer to the later determined target-path as a negative-path (denoted as $path^-$), since it is determined passively by the assigning. Accordingly, we call the former path as a positive-path (denoted as $path^+$).

Next, we will further interpret the above process. Since both of the 2 inner-nodes can be used to establish shared-edges, we discuss the 2 cases separately. At first, we will show how to construct shared-edges by assigning 1st-inner-nodes.

▶ **1st-Inner-Node.** In fact, we will construct exactly 1 shared-edge for each $path^+$. That is, the 2nd-inner-node of a $path^+$ must be assigned by an exclusive-element. According to the position of the shared-edge(s) in $path^-$, there are 3 cases as follows.

– *Case 1:* Fix a target-path from x to y as the $path^+$ at first. If we assign $\ddot{x} \in X$ as its 1st-inner-node (i.e., the one with box), then the target-path from $\ddot{x}$ to $\ddot{y}$ becomes the corresponding $path^-$ whose first edge (i.e., the bold one) is the shared-edge. That is, the 1st-inner-node (i.e., the underline one) in $path^-$ must be the same exclusive-element (i.e., w) as the 2nd-inner-node in $path^+$. Additionally, if $\ddot{y}$ is not assigned to the 1st- nor 2nd- inner-node of any target-path, then we can assign an exclusive-element (i.e., $\widetilde{w}$) to the 2nd-inner-node of $path^-$. As a result, we obtain a Type^{1a} sharing-gadget (as shown in (17)) containing 2 paths, 1 shared-edge and 2 exclusive-elements. And we refer to the 2 paths as a $\text{Type}^{1a}\text{-}path^+$ and a $\text{Type}^{1a}\text{-}path^-$, respectively.

$$
\begin{array}{l}
\text{Type}^{1a} \\
\text{sharing-gadget}
\end{array}
\left\{
\begin{array}{ll}
\langle x \xrightarrow{P} \boxed{\ddot{x}}, \ \ddot{x} \xrightarrow{P} w, \ w_\oplus \xrightarrow{P} y \rangle & (path^+) \\
\langle \ddot{x} \xrightarrow{P} \underline{w}, \ w \xrightarrow{P} \widetilde{w}, \ \widetilde{w}_\oplus \xrightarrow{P} \ddot{y} \rangle & (path^-)
\end{array}
\right.
\tag{17}
$$

- *Case 2:* Fix a target-path from x to y as the $path^+$ at first. If we assign $\ddot{y} \in Y$ as its 1st-inner-node (i.e., the one with box), then the target-path from $\ddot{x}$ to $\ddot{y}$ becomes the corresponding $path^-$ whose third edge (i.e., the bold one) is the shared-edge. That is, the 2th-inner-node (i.e., the underline one) in $path^-$ must be assigned by $x_\oplus$. Additionally, if $\ddot{x}$ is not assigned to the 1st-inner-node of any target-path and $\ddot{x}_\oplus$ is not assigned to the 2nd-inner-node of any target-path, then we can assign an exclusive-element (i.e., $\widetilde{w}$) to the 1st-inner-node of $path^-$. As a result, we obtain a Type^{1b} sharing-gadget (as shown in (18)) containing 2 paths, 1 shared-edge and 2 exclusive-elements. And we refer to the 2 paths as a $\text{Type}^{1b}\text{-}path^+$ and a $\text{Type}^{1b}\text{-}path^-$, respectively.

$$
\begin{array}{l}
\text{Type}^{1b} \\
\text{sharing-gadget}
\end{array}
\left\{
\begin{array}{ll}
\langle x \xrightarrow{P} \boxed{\ddot{y}}, \ \ddot{y} \xrightarrow{P} w, \ w_\oplus \xrightarrow{P} y \rangle & (path^+) \\
\langle \ddot{x} \xrightarrow{P} \widetilde{w}, \ \widetilde{w} \xrightarrow{P} \underline{x_\oplus}, \ x \xrightarrow{P} \ddot{y} \rangle & (path^-)
\end{array}
\right.
\tag{18}
$$

- *Case 3:* Interestingly, a $path^-$ can share edges with 2 different $paths^+$ simultaneously. Fix the target-path from x_1 to y_1 as $path_1^+$, and fix the target-path from x_2 to y_2 as $path_2^+$. If we assign $\ddot{x}$ (resp. $\ddot{y}$) as the 1st-inner-node of $path_1^+$ (resp. $path_2^+$) (i.e., the ones with box), then the target-path from $\ddot{x}$ to $\ddot{y}$ becomes the $path^-$ of $path_1^+$ and $path_2^+$ simultaneously. That is, the 1st-inner-node in $path^-$ must be the same exclusive-element (i.e., w) as the 2nd-inner-node in $path_1^+$, and the 2nd-inner-node in $path^-$ must be assigned by $(x_2)_\oplus$. As a result, we obtain a Type^{1c} sharing-gadget (as shown in (19)) containing 3 paths, 2 shared-edge and 2 exclusive-elements. And we refer to the 3 paths as a $\text{Type}^{1c}\text{-}path_1^+$, a $\text{Type}^{1c}\text{-}path_2^+$ and a $\text{Type}^{1c}\text{-}path^-$, respectively.

$$
\begin{array}{l}
\text{Type}^{1c} \\
\text{sharing-gadget}
\end{array}
\left\{
\begin{array}{ll}
\langle x_1 \xrightarrow{P} \boxed{\ddot{x}}, \ \ddot{x} \xrightarrow{P} w, \ \ w_\oplus \xrightarrow{P} y_1 \rangle & (path_1^+) \\
\langle x_2 \xrightarrow{P} \boxed{\ddot{y}}, \ \ddot{y} \xrightarrow{P} \widetilde{w}, \ \ \widetilde{w}_\oplus \xrightarrow{P} y_2 \rangle & (path_2^+) \\
\langle \ddot{x} \xrightarrow{P} \underline{w}, \ w \xrightarrow{P} \underline{(x_2)_\oplus}, \ x_2 \xrightarrow{P} \ddot{y} \rangle & (path^-)
\end{array}
\right.
\tag{19}
$$

At this point, we have known how to construct a shared-edge for a $path^+$ by assigning its 1st-inner-node. Naturally, we can establish k such shared-edges if k $paths^+$ are considered. It is easy to verify that the following Method 1 actually establishes k shared-edges for the involved $paths^+$ and $paths^-$.[9]

---

[9] In brief, Step 1 establishes k shared-edges, while Step 2 produces no shared-edge.

Method 1 for constructing k shared-edges:

–**Step 1** Choose k proper target-paths as the $paths^+$, and then choose k proper elements from $X \cup Y$ as their 1st-inner-nodes, respectively. Namely, we choose a Type^{1a}/Type^{1b}/Type^{1c}-$path^-$ for each of the k $paths^+$.

–**Step 2** For the $paths^+$ and $paths^-$ determined in Step 1, we assign in turn each undefined inner-node with an exclusive-element.

We can see that Method 1 allows the $paths^-$ to be a mixture of Type^{1a}-, Type^{1b}- and Type^{1c}- $paths^-$. This is a *key point* to obtain an appropriate lower bound in our proof, since it enlarge the number of candidates for $paths^-$ (i.e., roughly double the one involved in 2-round case[10]). It should be pointed out that the number of $paths^-$ is determined by the 1st-inner-nodes of the k $paths^+$, and is not necessarily equal to k. In a sense, the k $paths^+$ with their 1st-inner-nodes determine almost "everything" about the involved $paths^+$ and $paths^-$.

▶ 2nd-**Inner-Node.** It is similar to construct a shared-edge by assigning the 2nd-inner-node of a $path^+$. We will also construct exactly 1 shared-edge for each $path^+$. That is, the 1st-inner-node of a $path^+$ must be assigned by an exclusive-element. According to the position of the shared-edge(s) in $path^-$, there are also 3 cases. For reason of the space, we omit the explanation here, and defer the details to the corresponding part of full version [WYCD20].

– *Case 1:*

$$
\begin{array}{ll}
\text{Type}^{2a} \\
\text{sharing-gadget}
\end{array}
\begin{cases}
\langle x \xrightarrow{P} w, \; w \xrightarrow{P} \boxed{\ddot{x}_\oplus}, \; \ddot{x} \xrightarrow{P} y \rangle & (path^+) \\
\langle \ddot{x} \xrightarrow{P} \underline{y}, \; y \xrightarrow{P} \widetilde{w}, \; \widetilde{w}_\oplus \xrightarrow{P} \ddot{y} \rangle & (path^-)
\end{cases}
\tag{20}
$$

– *Case 2:*

$$
\begin{array}{ll}
\text{Type}^{2b} \\
\text{sharing-gadget}
\end{array}
\begin{cases}
\langle x \xrightarrow{P} w, \; \boldsymbol{w} \xrightarrow{P} \boxed{\ddot{y}}, \; \ddot{y}_\oplus \xrightarrow{P} y \rangle & (path^+) \\
\langle \ddot{x} \xrightarrow{P} \widetilde{w}, \; \widetilde{w} \xrightarrow{P} \underline{w_\oplus}, \; \boldsymbol{w} \xrightarrow{P} \ddot{y} \rangle & (path^-)
\end{cases}
\tag{21}
$$

– *Case 3:*

$$
\begin{array}{ll}
\text{Type}^{2c} \\
\text{sharing-gadget}
\end{array}
\begin{cases}
\langle x_1 \xrightarrow{P} w, \; w \xrightarrow{P} \boxed{\ddot{x}_\oplus}, \; \ddot{x} \xrightarrow{P} y_1 \rangle & (path_1^+) \\
\langle x_2 \xrightarrow{P} \widetilde{w}, \; \widetilde{\boldsymbol{w}} \xrightarrow{P} \boxed{\ddot{y}}, \; (\ddot{y})_\oplus \xrightarrow{P} y_2 \rangle & (path_2^+) \\
\langle \ddot{x} \xrightarrow{P} \underline{y_1}, \; y_1 \xrightarrow{P} \underline{\widetilde{w}_\oplus}, \; \widetilde{w} \xrightarrow{P} \ddot{y} \rangle & (path^-)
\end{cases}
\tag{22}
$$

---

[10] More details can be found in the corresponding part of the full version [WYCD20], in which we also give the assigning strategy of 2-round case.

At this point, we have known how to construct a shared-edge for a $path^+$ by assigning its 2nd-inner-node. Naturally, we can establish h such shared-edges if h $paths^+$ are considered. It is easy to verify that the following Method 2 actually establishes h shared-edges for the involved $paths^+$ and $paths^-$.

Method 2 for constructing h shared-edges:

−Step 1 Choose h proper target-paths as the $paths^+$, and then choose h proper elements from $X_\oplus \cup Y$ as their 2nd-inner-nodes, respectively. Namely, we choose a $\text{Type}^{2a}/\text{Type}^{2b}/\text{Type}^{2c}$-$path^-$ for each of the h $paths^+$.

−Step 2 For the $paths^+$ and $paths^-$ determined in Step 1, we assign in turn each undefined inner-node with an exclusive-element.

Similarly, the number of $paths^-$ is determined by the 2nd-inner-nodes of the h $paths^+$, and is not necessarily equal to h. In a sense, the h $paths^+$ with their 2nd-inner-nodes determine almost "everything" about the involved $paths^+$ and $paths^-$.

Combing the Method 1 and Method 2, we propose the assigning strategy for constructing a Core with $3q - k - h$ edges. As shown in Fig. 5, Step 1 (resp. Step 2) establishes k (resp. h) shared-edges, and Step 3 produces no shared-edge. In brief, we fix k $paths^+$ and their 1st-inner-nodes firstly, then other h $paths^+$ and their 2nd-inner-nodes. At last, we assign all the undefined inner-nodes with proper exclusive-elements.

Assigning Strategy:

−Step 1 Choose k proper target-paths as the $paths^+$, and then choose k proper elements from $X \cup Y$ as their 1st-inner-nodes, respectively.

−Step 2 Apart from the paths involved in Step 1, we choose h proper target-paths as the $paths^+$, and then choose h proper elements from $X_\oplus \cup Y$ as their 2nd-inner-nodes, respectively.

−Step 3 Assign in turn each undefined inner-node with an exclusive-element.

Fig. 5. Assigning strategy for constructing a $\mathsf{Core}(\varphi_2[\cdot] \vdash \mathcal{Q}_E)$ with $3q - k - h$ edges

COUNTING Cores. Intrinsically, the assigning strategy consists of several samplings such as the $paths^+$, $paths^-$, and so on. To lower-bound the number of Cores constructed by Fig. 5, we should know how many elements can be chosen for each sampling. For convenience, we introduce the notation RoC to denote the *range of candidates* for a sampling.

Notation 5 (Range of Candidates). *Let A denote a finite set to be sampled, then we write $RoC(A)$ as a set of elements which can be chosen into A.*

That is, we should determine the size of each RoC to count the number of possible assignments. The analysis is rather cumbersome, and we defer it to the formal proof. Here, we can just assume that the lower bound of the number of Cores with $3q - k - h$ edges is given as follows.

$$\#\mathsf{Cores}_{3q-k-h} \geq LB(k, h), \tag{23}$$

where $\#\mathsf{Cores}_{3q-k-h}$ denotes the number of Cores with $3q - k - h$ edges, and $LB(k, h)$ is a function of k and h.

CALCULATING THE LOWER BOUND. At this point, we are ready to calculate a lower bound of (15). Since $|S| = |T| = N - p$, and from the Eq. (14) and (23), we finally obtain that

$$
\begin{aligned}
p_2 &\geq \sum_{k,h} \frac{LB(k, h)}{(N - p)_{3q-k-h}} \\
&\geq \sum_{\substack{0 \leq k \leq M \\ 0 \leq h \leq M}} \frac{LB(k, h)}{(N - p)_{3q-k-h}} \\
&= \underbrace{\sum_{\substack{0 \leq k \leq M \\ 0 \leq h \leq M}} MHyp_{N,a,b,c}(k, h)}_{\text{Use Lemma 5 to obtain a proper lower bound}} \cdot \underbrace{(\text{Major Terms})}_{\substack{\text{Use Lemma 6 to obtain} \\ \text{a proper lower bound} \\ \text{independent of } k \text{ and } h}} \cdot \underbrace{(\text{Minor Terms})}_{\substack{\text{Obtain directly a} \\ \text{proper lower bound} \\ \text{independent of } k \text{ and } h}},
\end{aligned}
$$

where $MHyp_{N,a,b,c}$ is a multivariate hypergeometric distribution random variable. It can be seen that a tail inequality (i.e., Lemma 5) and a combinatorial inequality (i.e., Lemma 6) will be used during the calculation.

Lemma 5 (Chebyshev's Inequality). *Let $X \sim Hyp_{N,a,b}$ be a hypergeometric distribution random variable, that is, $\Pr[X = k] = \frac{\binom{b}{k}\binom{N-b}{a-k}}{\binom{N}{a}} = \frac{(a)_k (b)_k (N-b)_{a-k}}{k!(N)_a}$. Then we have*

$$\Pr[X > \lambda] \leq \frac{ab(N - a)(N - b)}{(\lambda N - ab)^2 (N - 1)}. \tag{24}$$

Lemma 6. *Let N, a, b, c, d be positive integers such that $c + d = 2b$ and $2a + 2b \leq N$. Then*

$$\frac{(N)_a (N - 2b)_a}{(N - c)_a (N - d)_a} \times \frac{(N - \frac{b}{2})_a}{(N - b)_a} \geq 1 - \frac{8ab^3}{N^3}. \tag{25}$$

6   Conclusion and Discussion

The practical block-ciphers often iterate the same round function and use a key-schedule algorithm to produce round-keys, while there are a few theoretical results supporting such designing philosophy. Particularly, only a little provable-security work considers the dependence between components, since it always becomes very complicated.

In this paper, we study a family of KAC construction with dependence, and finally prove that 3KACSP construction has the same security level as the classic 3KAC construction. It means that the randomness of one random permutation and a random $4n$-bit string is enough to make the 3KAC construction achieve the ideal security. To our knowledge, it is the first time to obtain a tight bound about an incompletely-independent KAC construction with more than 2 rounds.

Besides the tight security analysis of 3KACSP, our most valuable contributions are the insights into the general rKACSP. Before our work, there is no proof method handling the knotty dependence in a high level. Compared to Chen et al.'s techniques, ours are more general and highly modular so that they can be easily generalized. More concretely, we abstract a type of combinatorial problems capturing the intrinsic randomness of rKACSP construction. To solve such problems, we also propose a general counting framework and successfully apply it to the cases with 2 and 3 missing-edges. Following the proof ideas in this work, we give some intuition on the analysis of rKACSP.

INTUITION ON rKACSP. Intuitively, when handling a "good" transcript, the paths between Q_E can be classified into r groups according to the number of fixed edges. Similar to 3KACSP, we denote the Group-i as the group of paths whose i edges are fixed by Q_P, where $0 \leq i \leq r - 1$. The subproblem of completing the paths in Group-i can be instantiated by Problem 1 with $r - i$ missing-edges. Inspired by the analysis of 3KACSP, the tricks used in $(r-i)$KACSP can be tailored to solve the corresponding subproblems related to Group-i, where $1 \leq i \leq r - 2$. By induction, what's left is only to solve a single r-round instance of Problem 1. Our counting framework, as well as the notions of shared-edges and assigning strategy can still work, but the circumstances of analysis would be very complicated.

To our conjecture, rKACSP construction is also $\Theta(2^{\frac{r}{r+1}n})$-secure in the random permutation model, which is a well-known result for classic rKAC construction.

Conjecture 1. Consider the rKACSP construction (see Eq. (1)), if P is a random permutation, as well as the round keys $\boldsymbol{K} = (k_0, \ldots, k_r)$ are random and independent from each other, then rKACSP is $\Theta\left(2^{\frac{r}{r+1}n}\right)$-secure in the random permutation model.

In fact, the bottleneck of pushing our work to higher-round case is simply the computational power. Following our ideas, the technical roadmap for analyzing rKACSP is rather clear, and one can solve it given sufficient energy. Honestly, we consider that the complexity of proof specifics will increase very fast (maybe exponentially) so that the proof may not be explicitly written out, but we strongly believe that Conjecture 1 is intrinsically correct. If the conjecture is true, then it is exactly a powerful support for the aforementioned broadly-used designing philosophy. Moreover, the proof complexity may just reveal the reason why there often exist gaps between the practical and theoretical results.

OPEN PROBLEMS. Currently, our results only apply when the round keys are random and independent from each other. Thus, it is unknown that whether we can reduce the randomness of round keys without a significant loss of security. Another challenging open problem is of course to generalize our results to larger number of rounds. In addition, the new representation and counting framework are rather generic, therefore we hope that they can be used in more scenarios.

Acknowledgements. This work has been submitted to several conferences successively, we would like to thank all the anonymous reviewers for their valuable comments which helped to improve the presentation of this paper.

This work was supported in part by the National Natural Science Foundation of China (Grant No. 61632012 and 61672239), in part by the Peng Cheng Laboratory Project of Guangdong Province (Grant No. PCL2018KP004), and in part by "the Fundamental Research Funds for the Central Universities".

References

[BKL+07] Bogdanov, A., et al.: PRESENT: an ultra-lightweight block cipher. In: Paillier, P., Verbauwhede, I. (eds.) CHES 2007. LNCS, vol. 4727, pp. 450–466. Springer, Heidelberg (2007). https://doi.org/10.1007/978-3-540-74735-2_31

[BKL+12] Bogdanov, A., Knudsen, L.R., Leander, G., Standaert, F.-X., Steinberger, J., Tischhauser, E.: Key-alternating ciphers in a provable setting: encryption using a small number of public permutations. In: Pointcheval, D., Johansson, T. (eds.) EUROCRYPT 2012. LNCS, vol. 7237, pp. 45–62. Springer, Heidelberg (2012). https://doi.org/10.1007/978-3-642-29011-4_5

[CLL+14] Chen, S., Lampe, R., Lee, J., Seurin, Y., Steinberger, J.: Minimizing the two-round Even-Mansour cipher. In: Garay, J.A., Gennaro, R. (eds.) CRYPTO 2014. LNCS, vol. 8616, pp. 39–56. Springer, Heidelberg (2014). https://doi.org/10.1007/978-3-662-44371-2_3

[CLL+18] Chen, S., Lampe, R., Lee, J., Seurin, Y., Steinberger, J.: Minimizing the two-round Even-Mansour cipher. J. Cryptolo. **31**(4), 1064–1119 (2018). https://doi.org/10.1007/s00145-018-9295-y

[CS14] Chen, S., Steinberger, J.: Tight security bounds for key-alternating ciphers. In: Nguyen, P.Q., Oswald, E. (eds.) EUROCRYPT 2014. LNCS, vol. 8441, pp. 327–350. Springer, Heidelberg (2014). https://doi.org/10.1007/978-3-642-55220-5_19

[CS18] Cogliati, B., Seurin, Y.: Analysis of the single-permutation encrypted Davies-Meyer construction. Des. Codes Crypt. **86**(12), 2703–2723 (2018). https://doi.org/10.1007/s10623-018-0470-9

[Dae91] Daemen, J.: Limitations of the Even-Mansour construction. In: Imai, H., Rivest, R.L., Matsumoto, T. (eds.) ASIACRYPT 1991. LNCS, vol. 739, pp. 495–498. Springer, Heidelberg (1993). https://doi.org/10.1007/3-540-57332-1_46

[DKS12] Dunkelman, O., Keller, N., Shamir, A.: Minimalism in cryptography: the Even-Mansour scheme revisited. In: Pointcheval, D., Johansson, T. (eds.) EUROCRYPT 2012. LNCS, vol. 7237, pp. 336–354. Springer, Heidelberg (2012). https://doi.org/10.1007/978-3-642-29011-4_21

[DR02] Daemen, J., Rijmen, V.: The Design of Rijndael: AES - The Advanced Encryption Standard. Information Security and Cryptography. Springer, Heidelberg (2002). https://doi.org/10.1007/978-3-662-04722-4

[DSST17] Dai, Y., Seurin, Y., Steinberger, J., Thiruvengadam, A.: Indifferentiability of iterated Even-Mansour ciphers with non-idealized key-schedules: five rounds are necessary and sufficient. In: Katz, J., Shacham, H. (eds.) CRYPTO 2017. LNCS, vol. 10403, pp. 524–555. Springer, Cham (2017). https://doi.org/10.1007/978-3-319-63697-9_18

[EM97] Even, S., Mansour, Y.: A construction of a cipher from a single pseudorandom permutation. J. Cryptol. **10**(3), 151–161 (1997). https://doi.org/10.1007/s001459900025

[GPPR11] Guo, J., Peyrin, T., Poschmann, A., Robshaw, M.: The LED block cipher. In: Preneel, B., Takagi, T. (eds.) CHES 2011. LNCS, vol. 6917, pp. 326–341. Springer, Heidelberg (2011). https://doi.org/10.1007/978-3-642-23951-9_22

[HT16] Hoang, V.T., Tessaro, S.: Key-alternating ciphers and key-length extension: exact bounds and multi-user security. In: Robshaw, M., Katz, J. (eds.) CRYPTO 2016. LNCS, vol. 9814, pp. 3–32. Springer, Heidelberg (2016). https://doi.org/10.1007/978-3-662-53018-4_1

[LPS12] Lampe, R., Patarin, J., Seurin, Y.: An asymptotically tight security analysis of the iterated Even-Mansour cipher. In: Wang, X., Sako, K. (eds.) ASIACRYPT 2012. LNCS, vol. 7658, pp. 278–295. Springer, Heidelberg (2012). https://doi.org/10.1007/978-3-642-34961-4_18

[Pat08] Patarin, J.: The "coefficients h" technique. In: Selected Areas in Cryptography, 15th International Workshop, SAC 2008, Sackville, New Brunswick, Canada, 14–15 August, Revised Selected Papers, pp. 328–345 (2008). https://doi.org/10.1007/978-3-642-04159-421

[Ste12] Steinberger, J.P.: Improved security bounds for key-alternating ciphers via Hellinger distance. IACR Cryptology ePrint Archive, 2012:481 (2012). http://eprint.iacr.org/2012/481

[WYCD20] Wu, Y., Yu, L., Cao, Z., Dong, X.: Tight security analysis of 3-round key-alternating cipher with a single permutation. Cryptology ePrint Archive, Report 2020/1073 (2020). https://eprint.iacr.org/2020/1073

Message Authentication Codes

Improved Security Analysis
for Nonce-Based Enhanced
Hash-then-Mask MACs

Wonseok Choi, Byeonghak Lee, Yeongmin Lee, and Jooyoung Lee[✉]

KAIST, Daejeon, Korea
{krwioh,lbh0307,dudals4780,hicalf}@kaist.ac.kr

Abstract. In this paper, we prove that the *nonce-based enhanced hash-then-mask MAC* (nEHtM) is secure up to $2^{\frac{3n}{4}}$ MAC queries and 2^n verification queries (ignoring logarithmic factors) as long as the number of faulty queries μ is below $2^{\frac{3n}{8}}$, significantly improving the previous bound by Dutta et al. Even when μ goes beyond $2^{\frac{3n}{8}}$, nEHtM enjoys graceful degradation of security.

The second result is to prove the security of PRF-based nEHtM; when nEHtM is based on an n-to-s bit random function for a fixed size s such that $1 \le s \le n$, it is proved to be secure up to any number of MAC queries and 2^s verification queries, if (1) $s = n$ and $\mu < 2^{\frac{n}{2}}$ or (2) $\frac{n}{2} < s < 2^{n-s}$ and $\mu < \max\{2^{\frac{s}{2}}, 2^{n-s}\}$, or (3) $s \le \frac{n}{2}$ and $\mu < 2^{\frac{n}{2}}$. This result leads to the security proof of truncated nEHtM that returns only s bits of the original tag since a truncated permutation can be seen as a pseudorandom function. In particular, when $s \le \frac{2n}{3}$, the truncated nEHtM is secure up to $2^{n-\frac{s}{2}}$ MAC queries and 2^s verification queries as long as $\mu < \min\{2^{\frac{n}{2}}, 2^{n-s}\}$. For example, when $s = \frac{n}{2}$ (resp. $s = \frac{n}{4}$), the truncated nEHtM is secure up to $2^{\frac{3n}{4}}$ (resp. $2^{\frac{7n}{8}}$) MAC queries. So truncation might provide better provable security than the original nEHtM with respect to the number of MAC queries.

Keywords: Message authentication codes · Beyond-birthday-bound security · Mirror theory · Graceful degradation · Truncation

1 Introduction

MACs. A message authentication code (MAC) is typically built from a block cipher, e.g., CBC-MAC [4], PMAC [6], OMAC [16], or from a cryptographic hash function, e.g., HMAC [2]. At a high level, many of these constructions follow the well-established *UHF-then-PRF* design paradigm: a message is first mapped

Jooyoung Lee was supported by a National Research Foundation of Korea (NRF) grant funded by the Korean government (Ministry of Science and ICT), No. NRF-2017R1E1A1A03070248.

© International Association for Cryptologic Research 2020
S. Moriai and H. Wang (Eds.): ASIACRYPT 2020, LNCS 12491, pp. 697–723, 2020.
https://doi.org/10.1007/978-3-030-64837-4_23

onto a short string through a universal hash function (UHF), and then encrypted through a fixed-input-length PRF to obtain a short tag. This method is simple, in particular, being deterministic and stateless, yet its security caps at the so-called birthday bound; any collision at the output of the UHF, which translates into a tag collision, is usually enough to break the security of the scheme. However, the birthday bound security might not be enough, in particular, when the MAC construction is instantiated with a lightweight block cipher such as PRESENT [7], LED [14] and GIFT [1] operating on small blocks. Better security bounds can be obtained by incorporating in the tag computation a nonce (a value that never repeats), e.g. in Wegman-Carter type MACs [5,9,29,31] or a random value [3, 11,17,18,24]. The focus of this paper is put on nonce-based MACs.

NONCE-MISUSE RESISTANT MACs. The Wegman-Carter MAC (based on a pseudorandom function) guarantees a strong security bound when nonces are never reused. However, only a single nonce repetition can completely break its security [20]. The problem is that it might be challenging to maintain the unique-ness of the nonce in certain environments, for example, when a nonce is chosen randomly from a small set, or when the state of the MAC is reset due to some fault in its implementation. For this reason, there has been a considerable amount of research on the construction of (nonce-based) MACs that provide security under nonce misuse [9,10,12,23,26].

In this line of research, Cogliati and Seurin [9] proposed EWCDM, and then Datta et al. [10] made a slight modification to it, dubbed DWCDM, in order to reduce the number of block cipher keys. Both constructions provide beyond-birthday-bound security in a nonce respecting settings, and secure up to the birthday bound even in a nonce misuse setting. Mennink and Neves [23] also proved the PRF-security of EWCDM up to $2^n/(67n)$ queries in a nonce respect-ing setting (without considering verification queries). However, their security degrades to the birthday bound as soon as only a single nonce is misused.

Recently, Dutta et al. [12] proposed a new construction of MACs, which is called *nonce-based Enhanced Hash-then-Mask* (nEHtM). They proved that nEHtM is secure up to $2^{\frac{2n}{3}}$ MAC queries and 2^n verification queries in a nonce respecting setting. Moreover, nEHtM enjoys graceful degradation of security in a nonce misuse setting. More precisely, with respect to the number of faulty nonces μ, their bound on the forging advantage includes $\mu q/2^n$ and $\mu v/2^n$ terms, where q and v denote the number of MAC queries and the number of verification queries, respectively. So the threshold number of MAC queries and verification queries linearly decreases as the number of faulty queries increases in a logarithmic scale.

OUR RESULTS. In this paper, we revisit the nEHtM construction; when nEHtM is based on a universal hash function H and a block cipher E, the tag for an $(n-1)$-bit nonce N and a message M is defined as

$$\mathsf{nEHtM}[H,E]_{K_h,K}(N,M) = E_K(0||N) \oplus E_K(1||(H_{K_h}(M) \oplus N))$$

using a hash key K_h and a block cipher key K (see Fig. 1).

We prove that nEHtM is secure up to $2^{\frac{3n}{4}}$ MAC queries and 2^n verification queries (ignoring logarithmic factors) as long as the number of faulty queries μ

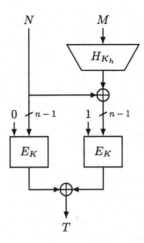

Fig. 1. nEHtM based on a universal hash function H and a block cipher E.

is below $2^{\frac{3n}{8}}$, significantly improving the previous bound by Dutta et al. Even when μ goes beyond $2^{\frac{3n}{8}}$, nEHtM enjoys graceful degradation of security. It is known that there is a forging attack on nEHtM using $2^{\frac{n}{2}}$ faulty queries [12], which means that μ cannot go beyond $2^{\frac{n}{2}}$. Figure 2 compares our new bound to the previous one given in [12].

The second result is to prove the security of PRF-based nEHtM. When the structure of nEHtM was first proposed in [24], it was based on independent pseudorandom functions using random IVs instead of nonces. Its security has been proved up to $2^{\frac{2n}{3}}$ MAC queries, and later Dutta et al. [11] tightly proved its $3n/4$-bit security with a matching attack. In this work, we study its security in a nonce respecting/misuse setting. More precisely, when nEHtM is based on a *single* n-to-s bit random function (with domain separation) for a fixed size s such that $1 \leq s \leq n$, it is proved to be secure up to any number of MAC queries and 2^s verification queries, if (1) $s = n$ and $\mu < 2^{\frac{n}{2}}$ or (2) $\frac{n}{2} < s < 2^{n-s}$ and $\mu < \max\{2^{\frac{s}{2}}, 2^{n-s}\}$, or (3) $s \leq \frac{n}{2}$ and $\mu < 2^{\frac{n}{2}}$. This result leads to the security proof of truncated nEHtM that returns only s bits of the original tag since a truncated permutation can be seen as a pseudorandom function. In particular, when $s \leq \frac{2n}{3}$, the truncated nEHtM is secure up to $2^{n-\frac{s}{2}}$ MAC queries and 2^s verification queries as long as $\mu < \min\{2^{\frac{s}{2}}, 2^{n-s}\}$. For example, when $s = \frac{n}{2}$ (resp. $s = \frac{n}{4}$), the truncated nEHtM is secure up to $2^{\frac{3n}{4}}$ (resp. $2^{\frac{7n}{8}}$) MAC queries. So truncation might provide better provable security than the original nEHtM with respect to the number of MAC queries.

PROOF TECHNIQUE. The main tool of our security proof is Mirror theory [27,28] that systematically estimates the number of solutions to a system of equations. However, we cannot directly apply Mirror theory to our problem in a black box manner; the original theory requires that $\xi_{max}^2 q \leq 2^n$, where ξ_{max} and q denote the maximum component size and the number of edges, respectively, when a system of equations is represented by a graph. Unfortunately, this restriction does not hold in our graph, possibly containing large components. Furthermore, our system includes non-equations corresponding to verification queries. For this reason, we need to refine and generalize Mirror theory. More precisely, we decompose our graph into four subgraphs - the union of the components containing at least one trail of length three, the union of "stars", the set of isolated edges, and the set of isolated vertices. For a subgraph whose components are small, we sharply estimate the number of solutions to the subgraph, while we probabilistically upper bound the number of larger components.

Recently, deterministic *double-block hash-then-sum* MACs have been proved to be tightly secure up $\frac{3n}{4}$ queries [21,22], while the security proof of nonce-based constructions turn out to be even more challenging since (faulty) nonces can be adaptively chosen by an adversary.

COMPARISON. Table 1 compares nEHtM with existing beyond-birthday-bound MACs based on a block cipher E and a δ-AXU-hash function H. "Nonce" indicates that whether it is nonce-based MAC or not. "# Keys" gives the total number of hash and block cipher keys. The number of queries and the maximum message length (in block) are denoted q and ℓ, respectively. Security is evaluated by assuming $\delta \approx \frac{\ell}{2^n}$ and $v = 0$. We always have the trivial bound $\mu < q$. We see that nEHtM is the first (nonce-based) MAC construction based on a block cipher that provides $\frac{3n}{4}$-bit provable security.

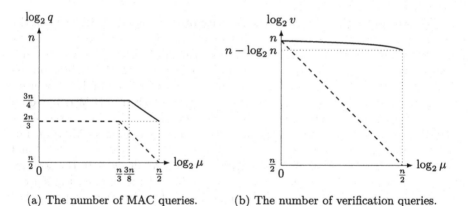

(a) The number of MAC queries.   (b) The number of verification queries.

Fig. 2. Comparison of the security bounds (in terms of the threshold number of MAC queries and verification queries) as functions of μ. The solid lines (resp. dashed lines) represent our bounds (resp. the previous bounds in [12]). In (b), we used parameter L satisfying $\mu^{2L} = L^L \cdot 2^{(L-1)n}$ for each μ (see Theorem 2).

Table 1. Comparison of nEHtM with existing beyond-birthday-bound MACs.

Scheme	Nonce	# Keys	Security		References
SUM-ECBC	✗	4	$\ell^{o(1)}q^{\frac{4}{3}}/2^n + \ell^4 q^{\frac{4}{3}}/2^{2n}$		[21,32]
PMAC-Plus	✗	3	$\ell^{\frac{2}{3}}q^{\frac{4}{3}}/2^n + \ell^2 q/2^n$		[21,33]
3kf9	✗	3	$\ell^{\frac{4}{3}}q^{\frac{4}{3}}/2^n + \ell^2 q^2/2^{2n} + \ell^6 q^4/2^{3n}$		[21,34]
LightMAC-Plus	✗	3	$q^{\frac{4}{3}}/2^n$		[21,25]
EWCDM	✓	3	$\ell q/2^n + q^{\frac{3}{2}}/2^n$ if $\mu = 0$ $\ell q^2/2^n$ if $\mu \geq 1$		[9]
DWCDM	✓	1	$\ell q/2^n + q/2^{\frac{2n}{3}}$ if $\mu = 0$ $\ell q^2/2^n$ if $\mu \geq 1$		[10]
nEHtM	✓	2	$\ell \mu q/2^n + \ell q^3/2^{2n}$		[12]
nEHtM	✓	2	$\ell \mu^2/2^n + \ell \mu q^{\frac{3}{2}}/2^{\frac{3}{2}} + \ell^{\frac{1}{2}}q^2/2^{\frac{3n}{2}}$		This work

2 Preliminaries

NOTATION. In all of the following, we fix a positive integer n such that $n \geq 3$. We denote 0^n (i.e., n-bit string of all zeros) by **0**. The set $\{0,1\}^n$ is sometimes regarded as a set of integers $\{0, 1, \ldots, 2^n - 1\}$ by converting an n-bit string $a_{n-1} \cdots a_1 a_0 \in \{0,1\}^n$ to an integer $a_{n-1}2^{n-1} + \cdots + a_1 2 + a_0$. We also identify $\{0,1\}^n$ with a finite field $\mathbf{GF}(2^n)$ with 2^n elements. For a positive integer q, we write $[q] = \{1, \ldots, q\}$.

Given a non-empty set $\mathcal{X}$, $x \leftarrow_\$ \mathcal{X}$ denotes that x is chosen uniformly at random from $\mathcal{X}$. The set of all functions from $\mathcal{X}$ to $\mathcal{Y}$ is denoted $\mathsf{Func}(\mathcal{X}, \mathcal{Y})$, and the set of all permutations of $\mathcal{X}$ is denoted $\mathsf{Perm}(\mathcal{X})$. The set of all permutations of $\{0,1\}^n$ is simply denoted $\mathsf{Perm}(n)$. The set of all sequences that consist of b pairwise distinct elements of $\mathcal{X}$ is denoted $\mathcal{X}^{*b}$. For integers $1 \leq b \leq a$, we will write $(a)_b = a(a-1)\cdots(a-b+1)$ and $(a)_0 = 1$ by convention. If $|\mathcal{X}| = a$, then $(a)_b$ becomes the size of $\mathcal{X}^{*b}$.

When two sets $\mathcal{X}$ and $\mathcal{Y}$ are disjoint, their (disjoint) union is denoted $\mathcal{X} \sqcup \mathcal{Y}$. For a set $\mathcal{X} \subset \{0,1\}^n$ and $\lambda \in \{0,1\}^n$, we will write $\mathcal{X} \oplus \lambda = \{x \oplus \lambda : x \in \mathcal{X}\}$. For a graph $\mathcal{G} = (\mathcal{V}, \mathcal{E})$, we will interchangeably write $|\mathcal{V}|$ and $|\mathcal{G}|$ for the number of vertices of $\mathcal{G}$.

ALMOST XOR UNIVERSAL HASH FUNCTIONS. Let $\delta > 0$, and let $H : \mathcal{K}_h \times \mathcal{M} \rightarrow \mathcal{X}$ be a keyed function for three non-empty sets $\mathcal{K}_h$, $\mathcal{M}$, and $\mathcal{X}$. H is said to be δ-almost XOR universal (AXU) if for any distinct $M, M' \in \mathcal{M}$ and $X \in \mathcal{X}$,

$$\Pr\left[K_h \leftarrow_\$ \mathcal{K}_h : H_{K_h}(M) \oplus H_{K_h}(M') = X\right] \leq \delta.$$

For a positive integer q, fix $M_1, \ldots, M_q \in \mathcal{M}$. For a random key $K_h \in \mathcal{K}_h$, let $X_i = H_{K_h}(M_i)$ for $i = 1, \ldots, q$. Then we can define an equivalence relation $\sim$ on $[q]$: for $\alpha, \beta \in [q]$, $\alpha \sim \beta$ if and only if $X_\alpha = X_\beta$. For some nonnegative integer r, let $\mathcal{P}_1, \ldots, \mathcal{P}_r$ denote the equivalence classes of $[q]$ with respect to $\sim$ such that

$p_i =^{\text{def}} |\mathcal{P}_i| \geq 2$ for $i = 1, \ldots, r$. Jha and Nandi [19] proved the following lemma, which is also useful in our security proof.

Lemma 1. *Let p_i, $i = 1 \ldots, r$, be the random variables as defined above. Then we have*

$$\mathsf{Ex}\left[\sum_{i=1}^{r} p_i^2\right] \leq 2q^2 \delta,$$

where the expectation is taken over the uniform distribution of $K_h \in \mathcal{K}_h$.

Proof. Let c denote the random variable that counts the number of "X-colliding" pairs. More precisely,

$$c \overset{\text{def}}{=} \left|\{(i,j) \in [q]^2 : i < j \text{ and } X_i = X_j\}\right|.$$

Then it is easy to show that

$$\sum_{i=1}^{r} p_i^2 = 2c + \sum_{i=1}^{r} p_i \leq 4c.$$

Furthermore, we have $\mathsf{Ex}[c] \leq \binom{q}{2}\delta$, which completes the proof.   □

PRFs AND PRPs. Let $F : \mathcal{K} \times \mathcal{X} \to \mathcal{Y}$ be a keyed function with key space $\mathcal{K}$, domain $\mathcal{X}$, and range $\mathcal{Y}$, where $\mathcal{X}$ is a subset of $\{0,1\}^*$. We will denote $F_K(X)$ for $F(K, X)$. A (q, t, l)-distinguisher against F is an algorithm $\mathcal{A}$ with oracle access to a function from $\mathcal{X}$ to $\mathcal{Y}$, making at most q oracle queries, each of length at most l in blocks, running in time at most t, and outputting a single bit. The advantage of $\mathcal{A}$ in breaking the PRF-security of F, i.e., in distinguishing F from a uniformly randomly chosen function $R \leftarrow_{\$} \mathsf{Func}(\mathcal{X}, \mathcal{Y})$, is defined as

$$\mathsf{Adv}_F^{\mathsf{prf}}(\mathcal{A}) = \left|\Pr\left[K \leftarrow_{\$} \mathcal{K} : \mathcal{A}^{F_K} = 1\right] - \Pr\left[R \leftarrow_{\$} \mathsf{Func}(\mathcal{X}, \mathcal{Y}) : \mathcal{A}^R = 1\right]\right|.$$

When $\mathcal{X} = \mathcal{Y}$ and $F(K, \cdot)$ is a permutation for each $K \in \mathcal{K}$, the PRP-security of F is defined as

$$\mathsf{Adv}_F^{\mathsf{prp}}(\mathcal{A}) = \left|\Pr\left[K \leftarrow_{\$} \mathcal{K} : \mathcal{A}^{F_K} = 1\right] - \Pr\left[R \leftarrow_{\$} \mathsf{Perm}(\mathcal{X}, \mathcal{Y}) : \mathcal{A}^R = 1\right]\right|.$$

For $\mathsf{atk} \in \{\mathsf{prf}, \mathsf{prp}\}$, we define $\mathsf{Adv}_F^{\mathsf{atk}}(q, t, l)$ as the maximum of $\mathsf{Adv}_F^{\mathsf{atk}}(\mathcal{A})$ over all (q, t, l)-distinguishers against F. We will consider PRP-security only for a block cipher whose input size is fixed (e.g., $\mathcal{X} = \{0,1\}^n$); in this case, we will simply drop the parameter l. On the other hand, when we consider information theoretic security, we will drop the parameter t.

NONCE-BASED MACs. Given four non-empty sets $\mathcal{K}$, $\mathcal{N}$, $\mathcal{M}$, and $\mathcal{T}$, a nonce-based keyed function with key space $\mathcal{K}$, nonce space $\mathcal{N}$, message space $\mathcal{M}$ and tag space $\mathcal{T}$ is simply a function $F : \mathcal{K} \times \mathcal{N} \times \mathcal{M} \to \mathcal{T}$. Stated otherwise, it is a keyed function whose domain is a cartesian product $\mathcal{N} \times \mathcal{M}$. We denote $F_K(N, M)$ for $F(K, N, M)$.

For $K \in \mathcal{K}$, let Auth_K be the MAC oracle which takes as input a pair $(N, M) \in \mathcal{N} \times \mathcal{M}$ and returns $F_K(N, M)$, and let Ver_K be the verification oracle which takes as input a triple $(N, M, T) \in \mathcal{N} \times \mathcal{M} \times \mathcal{T}$ and returns 1 ("accept") if $F_K(N, M) = T$, and 0 ("reject") otherwise. We assume that an adversary makes queries to the two oracles Auth_K and Ver_K for a secret key $K \in \mathcal{K}$. A MAC query (N, M) made by an adversary is called a *faulty query* if the adversary has already queried to the MAC oracle with the same nonce but with a different message.

A (μ, q, v, t)-adversary against the nonce-based MAC-security of F is an adversary $\mathcal{A}$ with oracle access to Auth_K and Ver_K, making at most q MAC queries to its first oracle with at most μ faulty queries and at most v verification queries to its second oracle, and running in time at most t. We say that $\mathcal{A}$ forges if any of its queries to Ver_K returns 1. The advantage of $\mathcal{A}$ against the nonce-based MAC-security of F is defined as

$$\mathsf{Adv}_F^{\mathsf{mac}}(\mathcal{A}) = \Pr\left[K \leftarrow_\$ \mathcal{K} : \mathcal{A}^{\mathsf{Auth}_K, \mathsf{Ver}_K} \text{ forges}\right].$$

where the probability is also taken over the random coins of $\mathcal{A}$, if any. The adversary is not allowed to ask a verification query (N, M, T) if a previous query (N, M) to Auth_K returned T. When $\mu = 0$, we say that $\mathcal{A}$ is nonce-respecting, otherwise $\mathcal{A}$ is said nonce-misusing. However, the adversary is allowed to repeat nonces in its verification queries.

We define $\mathsf{Adv}_F^{\mathsf{mac}}(\mu, q, v, t)$ as the maximum of $\mathsf{Adv}_F^{\mathsf{mac}}(\mathcal{A})$ over all (μ, q, v, t)-adversaries. When we consider information theoretic security, we will drop the parameter t.

NONCE-BASED ENHANCED HASH-THEN-MASK MACs. Let

$$H : \mathcal{K}_h \times \mathcal{M} \longrightarrow \{0, 1\}^{n-1}$$
$$(K_h, M) \longmapsto H_{K_h}(M)$$

be a keyed function. Given a block cipher

$$E : \mathcal{K} \times \{0, 1\}^n \longrightarrow \{0, 1\}^n$$
$$(K, X) \longmapsto E_K(X),$$

one can define the nEHtM MAC with key space $\mathcal{K}_h \times \mathcal{K}$, nonce space $\{0, 1\}^{n-1}$, message space $\mathcal{M}$ and tag space $\{0, 1\}^n$: for a key $(K_h, K) \in \mathcal{K}_h \times \mathcal{K}$, a nonce $N \in \{0, 1\}^{n-1}$, a message $M \in \mathcal{M}$, the tag is computed as follows:

$$\mathsf{nEHtM}[H, E]_{K_h, K}(N, M) = E_K(0\|N) \oplus E_K(1\|(H_{K_h}(M) \oplus N)).$$

More generally, the underlying block cipher can be replaced by a compression function $E : \mathcal{K} \times \{0, 1\}^n \longrightarrow \{0, 1\}^m$ for some $m < n$.

EXPECTATION METHOD. Consider the nEHtM construction based on H and E using keys (K_h, K). Suppose that a distinguisher $\mathcal{A}$ adaptively makes q MAC queries and v verification queries to either $(\mathsf{Auth}_{K_h, K}, \mathsf{Ver}_{K_h, K})$ for a random secret key $(K_h, K) \in \mathcal{K}_h \times \mathcal{K}$ (in the real world) or $(\mathsf{Rand}, \mathsf{Rej})$ (in the ideal world), where Rand returns an independent random value (instantiating a truly random function) and Rej always return 0 for every verification query. Furthermore, $\mathcal{A}$ records all the queries in

$$\tau_m \stackrel{\text{def}}{=} ((N_1, M_1, T_1), \ldots, (N_q, M_q, T_q)),$$
$$\tau_v \stackrel{\text{def}}{=} ((N_1', M_1', T_1', b_1'), \ldots, (N_v', M_v', T_v', b_v')),$$

where either $\mathsf{Auth}_{K_h,K}(N_i, M_i) = T_i$ or $\mathsf{Rand}(N_i, M_i) = T_i$ for $i = 1, \ldots, q$, and either $\mathsf{Ver}_{K_h,K}(N_i', M_i', T_i') = b_i'$ or $\mathsf{Rej}(N_i', M_i', T_i') = b_i'(= 0)$ for $i = 1, \ldots, v$, according to the world that $\mathcal{A}$ interacts with.

At the end of the interaction, we will provide the distinguisher $\mathcal{A}$ with the hash key K_h for free. In the ideal world, a dummy key K_h will be selected uniformly at random from $\mathcal{K}_h$, and given to $\mathcal{A}$. This will not degrade the adversarial distinguishing advantage since the distinguisher is free to ignore this additional information.

We will call

$$\tau = (K_h, \tau_m, \tau_v)$$

the *transcript* of the attack; it contains all the information that $\mathcal{A}$ has obtained at the end of the attack. When we consider an information theoretic distinguisher, we can assume that the distinguisher is deterministic without making any redundant query.

A transcript τ is called *attainable* if the probability to obtain this transcript in the ideal world is non-zero. Note that any key $K_h \in \mathcal{K}_h$ and any sequence of tags $(T_1, \ldots, T_q) \in (\{0,1\}^n)^q$ uniquely determine an attainable transcript containing them, and each attainable transcript appears in the ideal world with the same probability, namely $1/N^q$. We denote Γ the set of attainable transcripts. We also denote T_{re} (resp. T_{id}) the probability distribution of the transcript τ induced by the real world (resp. the ideal world). By extension, we use the same notation to denote a random variable distributed according to each distribution.

In this setting, it is obvious that $\mathcal{A}$'s distinguishing advantage upper bounds $\mathcal{A}$'s forging probability and when $v = 0$, we can derive PRF-security of the of nEHtM. In order to upper bound the distinguishing advantage, we will use Patarin's coefficient-H technique; we partition the set of attainable transcripts Γ into a set of "good" transcripts Γ_{good} such that the probabilities to obtain some transcript $\tau \in \Gamma_{\mathsf{good}}$ are close in the real world and the ideal world, and a set Γ_{bad} of "bad" transcripts such that the probability to obtain any $\tau \in \Gamma_{\mathsf{bad}}$ is small in the ideal world. The lower bound in the ratio of the probabilities to obtain a good transcript in both worlds will be given as a function of τ, and we will take its expectation. This refinement is called the *expectation method*, first introduced in [15], summarized in the following theorem.

Lemma 2. *Fix a forging adversary $\mathcal{A}$. Let $\Gamma = \Gamma_{\mathsf{good}} \sqcup \Gamma_{\mathsf{bad}}$ be a partition of the set of attainable transcripts, where there exists a non-negative function $\varepsilon_1(\tau)$ such that for any $\tau \in \Gamma_{\mathsf{good}}$,*

$$\frac{\Pr\left[\mathsf{T}_{\mathrm{re}} = \tau\right]}{\Pr\left[\mathsf{T}_{\mathrm{id}} = \tau\right]} \geq 1 - \varepsilon_1(\tau),$$

and there exists ε_2 such that $\Pr[\mathsf{T}_{\mathrm{id}} \in \Gamma_{\mathsf{bad}}] \leq \varepsilon_2$. Then one has

$$\mathsf{Adv}_{\mathsf{nEHtM}[H,E]}^{\mathrm{mac}}(\mathcal{A}) \leq \mathsf{Ex}[\varepsilon_1(\tau)] + \varepsilon_2,$$

where the expectation is taken over the distribution T_{id} in the ideal world.

Proof. Since the distinguisher's output is a (deterministic) function of the transcript, its distinguishing advantage is upper bounded by the statistical distance between T_{id} and T_{re}. So we have

$$\mathsf{Adv}_{\mathsf{nEHtM}[H,E]}^{\mathrm{mac}}(\mathcal{A}) \leq \|\mathsf{T}_{\mathrm{re}} - \mathsf{T}_{\mathrm{id}}\| \stackrel{\mathrm{def}}{=} \frac{1}{2} \sum_{\tau \in \Gamma} |\Pr[\mathsf{T}_{\mathrm{re}} = \tau] - \Pr[\mathsf{T}_{\mathrm{id}} = \tau]|.$$

Moreover we have:

$$\|\mathsf{T}_{\mathrm{re}} - \mathsf{T}_{\mathrm{id}}\| = \sum_{\substack{\tau \in \Gamma \\ \Pr[\mathsf{T}_{\mathrm{id}}=\tau]>\Pr[\mathsf{T}_{\mathrm{re}}=\tau]}} (\Pr[\mathsf{T}_{\mathrm{id}} = \tau] - \Pr[\mathsf{T}_{\mathrm{re}} = \tau])$$

$$= \sum_{\substack{\tau \in \Gamma \\ \Pr[\mathsf{T}_{\mathrm{id}}=\tau]>\Pr[\mathsf{T}_{\mathrm{re}}=\tau]}} \Pr[\mathsf{T}_{\mathrm{id}} = \tau] \left(1 - \frac{\Pr[\mathsf{T}_{\mathrm{re}} = \tau]}{\Pr[\mathsf{T}_{\mathrm{id}} = \tau]}\right)$$

$$\leq \sum_{\tau \in \Gamma_{\mathsf{good}}} \Pr[\mathsf{T}_{\mathrm{id}} = \tau]\varepsilon_1(\tau) + \sum_{\tau \in \Gamma_{\mathsf{bad}}} \Pr[\mathsf{T}_{\mathrm{id}} = \tau]$$

$$\leq \mathsf{Ex}[\varepsilon_1(\tau)] + \varepsilon_2.$$

$\square$

3   Extended Mirror Theory

The goal of this section is to lower bound the number of solutions to a certain type of system of equations and non-equations. For simplicity of notation, we will denote $N = 2^n$ *throughout this section.*

We will represent a system of equations and non-equations by a graph. Each vertex corresponds to an n-bit *distinct* unknowns. We will assume that the number of vertices is at most $N/4$, and by abuse of notation, identify the vertices with the values assigned to them. We distinguish two types of edges, namely, =-labeled edges and $\neq$-labeled edges that correspond to equations and non-equations, respectively. Each of the edge is additionally labeled by an element in $\{0,1\}^n$. So, if two vertices P and Q are adjacent by an edge with label $(\lambda, =)$ (resp. $(\lambda, \neq)$) for some $\lambda \in \{0,1\}^n$, then it would mean that $P \oplus Q = \lambda$ (resp. $P \oplus Q \neq \lambda$).

Consider a graph $\mathcal{G} = (\mathcal{V}, \mathcal{E}^= \sqcup \mathcal{E}^{\neq})$, where $\mathcal{E}^=$ and $\mathcal{E}^{\neq}$ denote the set of =-labeled edges and the set of $\neq$-labeled edges, respectively. Then $\mathcal{G}$ can be seen as a superposition of two subgraphs $\mathcal{G}^= =^{\text{def}} (\mathcal{V}, \mathcal{E}^=)$ and $\mathcal{G}^{\neq} =^{\text{def}} (\mathcal{V}, \mathcal{E}^{\neq})$. Let $P \overset{\lambda}{-} Q$ denote a $(\lambda, =)$-labeled edge in $\mathcal{G}^=$. For $\ell > 0$ and a trail[1]

$$\mathcal{L} : P_0 \overset{\lambda_1}{-} P_1 \overset{\lambda_2}{-} \cdots \overset{\lambda_\ell}{-} P_\ell$$

in $\mathcal{G}^=$, its label is defined as

$$\lambda(\mathcal{L}) \overset{\text{def}}{=} \lambda_1 \oplus \lambda_2 \oplus \cdots \oplus \lambda_\ell.$$

In this work, we will focus on a graph $\mathcal{G} = (\mathcal{V}, \mathcal{E}^= \sqcup \mathcal{E}^{\neq})$ with certain properties, as listed below.

1. $\mathcal{G}^=$ contains no cycle.
2. $\lambda(\mathcal{L}) \neq \mathbf{0}$ for any trail $\mathcal{L}$ in $\mathcal{G}^=$.
3. If P and Q are connected with a $(\lambda, \neq)$-labeled edge, then they are not connected by a λ-labeled trail in $\mathcal{G}^=$.

Any graph $\mathcal{G}$ satisfying the above properties will be called a *nice* graph. Given a nice graph $\mathcal{G} = (\mathcal{V}, \mathcal{E}^= \sqcup \mathcal{E}^{\neq})$, an assignment of *distinct* values to the vertices in $\mathcal{V}$ satisfying all the equations in $\mathcal{E}^=$ and all the non-equations in $\mathcal{E}^{\neq}$ is called a *solution* to $\mathcal{G}$. We remark that if we assign any value to a vertex P, then =-labeled edges determine the values of all the other vertices in the component containing P in $\mathcal{G}^=$, where the assignment is unique since $\mathcal{G}^=$ contains no cycle, and the values in the same component are all distinct since $\lambda(\mathcal{L}) \neq \mathbf{0}$ for any trail $\mathcal{L}$. Furthermore, any non-equation between two vertices in the same component will be redundant due to the third property above.

The number of possible assignments of distinct values to the vertices in $\mathcal{V}$ is $(N)_{|\mathcal{V}|}$. One might expect that when such an assignment is chosen uniformly at random, it would satisfy all the equations and non-equations in $\mathcal{G}$ with probability close to $1/N^q$, where q denotes the number of =-labeled edges (i.e., equations) in $\mathcal{G}^=$. Indeed, we can prove that the number of solutions to $\mathcal{G}$ is close to $\frac{(N)_{|\mathcal{V}|}}{N^q}$ up to a certain error (that can be negligible according to the parameters). We begin with a simple bound that holds for any type of graphs.

In the following lemma, we partition the set of vertices $\mathcal{V}$ into two disjoint sets, denoted $\mathcal{V}_{\text{kn}}$ and $\mathcal{V}_{\text{uk}}$, respectively, and fix an assignment of distinct values to the vertices in $\mathcal{V}_{\text{kn}}$. Subject to this assignment, the number of possible assignments of distinct values to the vertices in $\mathcal{V}_{\text{uk}}$ can be lower bounded (in a way that the entire assignment becomes a solution to $\mathcal{G}$).

Lemma 3. *For a positive integer q and a nonnegative integer v, let $\mathcal{G} = (\mathcal{V}, \mathcal{E}^= \sqcup \mathcal{E}^{\neq})$ be a nice graph such that $|\mathcal{E}^=| = q$ and $|\mathcal{E}^{\neq}| = v$. Suppose that*

1. *$\mathcal{V}$ is partitioned into two subsets, denoted $\mathcal{V}_{\text{kn}}$ and $\mathcal{V}_{\text{uk}}$;*
2. *there is no =-labeled edge that is incident to a vertex in $\mathcal{V}_{\text{kn}}$;*
3. *there is no $\neq$-labeled edge connecting two vertices in $\mathcal{V}_{\text{kn}}$.*

---

[1] A trail is a walk in which all edges are distinct.

Suppose that $\mathcal{G}_{uk}^{=} = (\mathcal{V}_{uk}, \mathcal{E}^{=})$ is decomposed into k components $\mathcal{C}_1, \dots, \mathcal{C}_k$ for some k. Given a fixed assignment of distinct values to the vertices in $\mathcal{V}_{kn}$, the number of solutions to $\mathcal{G}$, denoted $h(\mathcal{G})$, satisfies

$$\frac{h(\mathcal{G})N^q}{(N - |\mathcal{V}_{kn}|)_{|\mathcal{V}_{uk}|}} \geq 1 - \frac{|\mathcal{V}|^2}{N^2} \sum_{i=1}^{k} |\mathcal{C}_i|^2 - \frac{2v}{N}.$$

If every component of the graph contains exactly two vertices, then we can improve the bound as follows.

Lemma 4. *For a positive integer q and a nonnegative integer v, let $\mathcal{G} = (\mathcal{V}, \mathcal{E}^{=} \sqcup \mathcal{E}^{\neq})$ be a nice graph such that $|\mathcal{E}^{=}| = q$ and $|\mathcal{E}^{\neq}| = v$. Suppose that*

1. *$\mathcal{V}$ is partitioned into two subsets, denoted $\mathcal{V}_{kn}$ and $\mathcal{V}_{uk}$;*
2. *there is no =-labeled edge that is incident to a vertex in $\mathcal{V}_{kn}$;*
3. *there is no $\neq$-labeled edge connecting two vertices in $\mathcal{V}_{kn}$.*

Suppose that $\mathcal{G}_{uk}^{=} = (\mathcal{V}_{uk}, \mathcal{E}^{=})$ is decomposed into q components of size two. Given a fixed assignment of distinct values to the vertices in $\mathcal{V}_{kn}$, the number of solutions to $\mathcal{G}$, denoted $h(\mathcal{G})$, satisfies

$$\frac{h(\mathcal{G})N^q}{(N - |\mathcal{V}_{kn}|)_{|\mathcal{V}_{uk}|}} \geq 1 - \frac{4|\mathcal{V}_{kn}|^2 q}{N^2} - \frac{4|\mathcal{V}_{kn}|q^2}{N^2} - \frac{18q^2}{N^2} - \frac{32|\mathcal{V}_{kn}|q^3}{3N^3} - \frac{16q^4}{N^3} - \frac{2v}{N} - \frac{16qv}{N^2}.$$

The proof of Lemma 3 and 4 will be deferred to the full version due to the space limit. Finally, we consider a graph containing no =-labeled edges. So $\mathcal{G}^{=}$ consists only of isolated vertices.

Lemma 5. *For a nonnegative integer v, let $\mathcal{G} = (\mathcal{V}, \mathcal{E}^{\neq})$ be a nice graph such that $|\mathcal{E}^{\neq}| = v$. Suppose that*

1. *$\mathcal{V}$ is partitioned into two subsets, denoted $\mathcal{V}_{kn}$ and $\mathcal{V}_{uk}$;*
2. *there is no $\neq$-labeled edge connecting two vertices in $\mathcal{V}_{kn}$.*

Given a fixed assignment of distinct values to the vertices in $\mathcal{V}_{kn}$, the number of solutions to $\mathcal{G}$, denoted $h(\mathcal{G})$, satisfies

$$\frac{h(\mathcal{G})}{(N - |\mathcal{V}_{kn}|)_{|\mathcal{V}_{uk}|}} \geq 1 - \frac{2v}{N}.$$

Proof. The number of possible assignments of distinct values outside $\mathcal{V}_{kn}$ to the vertices in $\mathcal{V}_{uk}$ is $(N - |\mathcal{V}_{kn}|)_{|\mathcal{V}_{uk}|}$. Among these assignments, at most $(N - |\mathcal{V}_{kn}|)_{|\mathcal{V}_{uk}|-1}$ assignments violate any fixed $\neq$-labeled edge. Therefore, we have

$$h(\mathcal{G}) \geq (N - |\mathcal{V}_{kn}|)_{|\mathcal{V}_{uk}|} - v(N - |\mathcal{V}_{kn}|)_{|\mathcal{V}_{uk}|-1},$$

which means

$$\frac{h(\mathcal{G})}{(N - |\mathcal{V}_{kn}|)_{|\mathcal{V}_{uk}|}} \geq 1 - \frac{2v}{N}.$$

$\square$

Given an arbitrary nice graph $\mathcal{G}$, we will decompose $\mathcal{G}^=$ into four subgraphs, denoted $\mathcal{G}_3^=$, $\mathcal{G}_2^=$, $\mathcal{G}_1^=$ and $\mathcal{G}_0^=$, respectively, where

- $\mathcal{G}_3^= = (\mathcal{V}_3, \mathcal{E}_3^=)$ is the union of components containing at least one trail of length three;
- $\mathcal{G}_2^= = (\mathcal{V}_2, \mathcal{E}_2^=)$ is the union of components containing at least one trail of length two (i.e., stars), but not a trail of length three;
- $\mathcal{G}_1^= = (\mathcal{V}_1, \mathcal{E}_1^=)$ is the union of components of size two (i.e., trails of length one);
- $\mathcal{G}_0^= = (\mathcal{V}_0, \mathcal{E}_0^=)$ is the set of isolated vertices.

For $i = 0, 1, 2, 3$, let $\mathcal{E}_i^{\neq}$ denote the set of $\neq$-labeled edges connecting a vertex in $\mathcal{V}_i$ and one in $\bigsqcup_{j=i}^{3} \mathcal{V}_j$, and let

$$\mathcal{G}_i = \left(\bigsqcup_{j=i}^{3} \mathcal{V}_j, \bigsqcup_{j=i}^{3} \mathcal{E}_j^= \sqcup \bigsqcup_{j=i}^{3} \mathcal{E}_j^{\neq} \right).$$

In order to lower bound the number of solutions to $\mathcal{G}$, we will first lower bound the number of solutions to $\mathcal{G}_3$ and $\mathcal{G}_2$ using Lemma 3, and then $\mathcal{G}_1$ and $\mathcal{G}_0$ ($= \mathcal{G}$) using Lemma 4 and Lemma 5, respectively. In the following theorem, $\mathcal{G}_3$ and $\mathcal{G}_2$ can be any partition of the components containing trails of length two, but the current partition will be used later in our security proof.

Theorem 1. *For positive integers q and v, let $\mathcal{G} = (\mathcal{V}, \mathcal{E}^= \sqcup \mathcal{E}^{\neq})$ be a nice graph such that $|\mathcal{E}^=| = q$ and $|\mathcal{E}^{\neq}| = v$. With the notations defined as above, assume that $\mathcal{G}_2^=$ is decomposed into k components $\mathcal{C}_1, \ldots, \mathcal{C}_k$ for some k. Then the number of solutions to $\mathcal{G}$, denoted $h^*(\mathcal{G})$, satisfies*

$$\frac{h^*(\mathcal{G}) 2^{nq}}{(2^n)_{|\mathcal{V}|}} \geq 1 - \frac{|\mathcal{G}_3^=|^4}{2^{2n}} - \frac{(|\mathcal{G}_3^=| + |\mathcal{G}_2^=|)^2}{2^{2n}} \sum_{i=1}^{k} |\mathcal{C}_i|^2 - \frac{8(|\mathcal{G}_3^=| + |\mathcal{G}_2^=|)q^2}{2^{2n}}$$

$$- \frac{18q^2}{2^{2n}} - \frac{16q^4}{2^{3n}} - \frac{2v}{2^n} - \frac{16qv}{2^{2n}}$$

provided that $q \leq 2^{n-3}$.

The proof of Theorem 1 will be deferred to Appendix A.

4   Security of nEHtM Based on a Block Cipher

In this section, we consider nEHtM$[H, E]$ based on an $(n-1)$-bit δ-AXU hash function H and an n-bit block cipher E. A message M with an $(n-1)$-bit nonce N is encrypted as

$$E_K(0 \parallel N) \oplus E_K(1 \parallel (H_{K_h}(M) \oplus N))$$

by a hash key K_h and a block cipher key K (see Sect. 2).

Up to the PRP-security of E, the keyed permutation E_K can be replaced by a truly random permutation π. The goal of this section is to prove the security of nEHtM$[H, \pi]$ using Theorem 1. As a result, we have the following theorem.

Theorem 2. *Let $\delta > 0$, and let $H : \mathcal{K} \times \mathcal{M} \to \{0,1\}^n$ be a δ-almost universal hash function. For positive integers μ, q, v, and L such that $q + v \leq 2^{n-3}$, we have*

$$
\mathsf{Adv}^{\mathsf{mac}}_{\mathsf{nEHtM}[H,\pi]}(\mu, q, v) \leq \frac{10q^2\delta^{\frac{1}{2}}}{2^n} + \frac{16q^4}{2^{3n}} + 5\mu^2\delta + \frac{\mu^2}{2^n} + \frac{3\mu q^{\frac{3}{2}}\delta}{2^{\frac{n}{2}}} + \frac{6\mu^3\delta^{\frac{1}{2}}}{2^n}
$$

$$
+ \frac{24\mu q^2}{2^{2n}} + \frac{25\mu^4}{2^{2n}} + (2L+1)v\delta + \frac{2v}{2^n} + 2^n\left(\frac{e\mu^2}{L2^n}\right)^L + \varepsilon
$$

where

$$
\varepsilon = 6q\delta + \frac{q}{2^n} + 6q^2\delta^2 + \frac{q^2\delta}{2^n} + \frac{18q^2}{2^{2n}} + 4\mu\delta + \frac{24\mu^2\delta^{\frac{1}{2}}}{2^n}
$$

$$
+ \frac{4\mu^2q\delta}{2^n} + \frac{36\mu^3}{2^{2n}} + \frac{36\mu q^2\delta^{\frac{3}{2}}}{2^n} + \frac{54\mu^2q^2\delta}{2^{2n}} + \frac{16qv}{2^{2n}}.
$$

Note that ε contains all the negligible terms, not dominating the entire bound.

INTERPRETATION. Setting $\delta \leq \frac{\ell}{2^n}$ for a constant ℓ and $L = n$, we have

$$
\mathsf{Adv}^{\mathsf{mac}}_{\mathsf{nEHtM}[H,\pi]}(\mu, q, v) = \mathcal{O}\left(\frac{\ell^{\frac{1}{2}}q^2}{2^{\frac{3n}{2}}} + \frac{\ell\mu q^{\frac{3n}{2}}}{2^{\frac{3n}{2}}} + \frac{\ell\mu^2}{2^n} + \frac{\ell nv}{2^n}\right).
$$

4.1 Graph Representation of Transcripts

Suppose that an adversary $\mathcal{A}$ makes q MAC queries using at most μ faulty nonces, and makes v verification queries. Throughout the security proof, we will assume that

$$
q + v \leq 2^{n-3}.
$$

Let

$$
\tau_m = (N_i, M_i, T_i)_{1 \leq i \leq q},
$$

$$
\tau_v = (N'_j, M'_j, T'_j, b'_j)_{1 \leq j \leq v}
$$

denote the list of MAC queries and the list of verification queries, respectively. Note that $\mathcal{A}$ is given K_h for free at the end of the attack. Then, from the transcript

$$
\tau = (K_h, \tau_m, \tau_v),
$$

one can fix $X_i =^{\mathrm{def}} H_{K_h}(M_i) \oplus N_i$ for $i = 1, \ldots, q$, and $X'_j =^{\mathrm{def}} H_{K_h}(M'_j) \oplus N'_j$ for $j = 1, \ldots, v$.

The core of the security proof is to estimate the number of possible ways of fixing evaluations of π in a way that $\pi(0 \parallel N_i) \oplus \pi(1 \parallel X_i) = T_i$ for $i = 1, \ldots, q$, and $\pi(0 \parallel N'_j) \oplus \pi(1 \parallel X'_j) \neq T'_j$ for $j = 1, \ldots, v$. We will identify $\{\pi(0 \parallel N_i)\} \cup \{\pi(0 \parallel N'_j)\}$ with a set of unknowns

$$
\mathcal{P} = \{P_1, \ldots, P_{q_1}\}
$$

where $q_1 \leq q$, since there might be collisions between nonces. Similarly, we identify $\{\pi(1 \parallel X_i)\} \cup \{\pi(1 \parallel X'_j)\}$ with a set of unknowns

$$\mathcal{Q} = \{Q_1, \ldots, Q_{q_2}\}$$

for some $q_2 \leq q$.

For $i = 1, \ldots, q$, let $\pi(0 \parallel N_i) = P_j \in \mathcal{P}$ and let $\pi(1 \parallel X_i) = Q_k \in \mathcal{Q}$. Then P_j and Q_k are connected with a $(T_i, =)$-labeled edge. Similarly, for $i = 1, \ldots, v$, P_j and Q_k are connected with a $(T'_i, \neq)$-labeled edge if $\pi(0 \parallel N'_i) = P_j$ and $\pi(1 \parallel X'_i) = Q_k$. In this way, we obtain a graph on $\mathcal{V} \overset{\text{def}}{=} \mathcal{P} \sqcup \mathcal{Q}$, called the *transcript graph* of τ and denoted $\mathcal{G}_\tau$. By definition, $\mathcal{G}_\tau$ has no isolated vertices. Furthermore, $\mathcal{G}_\tau$ is a bipartite graph with independent sets $\mathcal{P}$ and $\mathcal{Q}$.

4.2 Bad Transcripts

For fixed positive numbers L_1 and L_2, a transcript $\tau = (K_h, \tau_m, \tau_v)$ is defined as *bad* if one of the following conditions holds.

- $\mathsf{bad}_1 \Leftrightarrow$ there exists $(i, j) \in [q]^{*2}$ such that $N_i = N_k$ for some $k(\neq i)$, $N_j = N_l$ for some $l(\neq j)$ and $X_i = X_j$.
- $\mathsf{bad}_2 \Leftrightarrow \mathsf{bad}_{2a} \vee \mathsf{bad}_{2b} \vee \mathsf{bad}_{2c} \vee \mathsf{bad}_{2d} \vee \mathsf{bad}_{2e}$, where
  - $\mathsf{bad}_{2a} \Leftrightarrow$ there exists $i \in [q]$ such that $T_i = \mathbf{0}$;
  - $\mathsf{bad}_{2b} \Leftrightarrow$ there exists $(i, j) \in [q]^{*2}$ such that $N_i = N_j$ and $T_i = T_j$;
  - $\mathsf{bad}_{2c} \Leftrightarrow$ there exists $(i, j) \in [q]^{*2}$ such that $X_i = X_j$ and $T_i = T_j$;
  - $\mathsf{bad}_{2d} \Leftrightarrow$ there exists $(i, j, k) \in [q]^{*3}$ such that $X_i = X_j$, $N_j = N_k$ and $T_i \oplus T_j \oplus T_k = \mathbf{0}$.
  - $\mathsf{bad}_{2e} \Leftrightarrow$ there exists $(i, j, k, l) \in [q]^{*4}$ such that $X_i = X_j$, $N_j = N_k$, $X_k = X_l$ and $T_i \oplus T_j \oplus T_k \oplus T_l = \mathbf{0}$.
- $\mathsf{bad}_3 \Leftrightarrow \mathsf{bad}_{3a} \vee \mathsf{bad}_{3b}$, where
  - $\mathsf{bad}_{3a} \Leftrightarrow$ there exist $i \in [q]$ and $j \in [v]$ such that $N_i = N'_j$, $X_i = X'_j$ and $T_i = T'_j$;
  - $\mathsf{bad}_{3b} \Leftrightarrow$ there exist $(i, j, k) \in [q]^{*3}$ and $l \in [v]$ such that $X_i = X_j$, $N_j = N_k$, $X_k = X'_l$, $N'_l = N_i$, and $T_i \oplus T_j \oplus T_k \oplus T'_l = \mathbf{0}$.
- $\mathsf{bad}_4 \Leftrightarrow |\{i \in [q] : X_i = X_j, N_j = N_k \text{ for some } j, k \text{ s.t. } j \neq i, k \neq j\}| \geq L_1$.
- $\mathsf{bad}_5 \Leftrightarrow |\{i \in [q] : X_i = X_j \text{ for some } j \text{ such that } j \neq i\}| \geq L_2$.

If a transcript τ is not bad, then it will be called a *good* transcript. For a good transcript τ, we observe that

1. $\mathcal{G}_\tau^=$, being a bipartite graph, contains no cycle without bad_1;
2. $\mathcal{G}_\tau^=$ contains no trail $\mathcal{L}$ such that $\lambda(\mathcal{L}) = \mathbf{0}$ without $\mathsf{bad}_1 \vee \mathsf{bad}_2$;
3. if two vertices are connected by a λ-labeled trail in $\mathcal{G}^=$, then they cannot be connected with a $(\lambda, \neq)$-labeled edge without $\mathsf{bad}_1 \vee \mathsf{bad}_3$.

Furthermore, we see that $\mathcal{G}_\tau^=$ contains no trail of length 5 without bad_1. With this observation, we conclude that for a good transcript τ,

1. the transcript graph $\mathcal{G}_\tau$ is nice (as defined in Sect. 3);
2. $|\mathcal{G}| \leq 2(q + v) \leq 2^{n-2}$.

These properties allow us to use Theorem 1 later. The following lemma upper bounds the probability of bad transcripts in the ideal world.

Lemma 6. *With the notations defined as above, it holds that*

$$\Pr[\mathsf{T}_{\mathsf{id}} \in \Gamma_{\mathsf{bad}}] \leq \frac{2\mu q \delta}{L_1} + \frac{q}{2^n} + \frac{q^2 \delta}{L_2} + \frac{q^2 \delta}{2^n} + 4\mu^2 \delta + \frac{\mu^2}{2^n} + \frac{3\mu q^{\frac{3n}{2}} \delta}{2^{\frac{n}{2}}}$$
$$+ \frac{4\mu^2 q \delta}{2^n} + (2L_3 + 1)v\delta + 2^n \left(\frac{e\mu^2}{L_3 2^n}\right)^{L_3}.$$

Proof. In order to analyze bad_{3b} later, we need to define a certain auxiliary event, which is parameterized by a positive number L_3; let

$$I_T \stackrel{\text{def}}{=} \{i \in [q] : N_i = N_j \text{ and } T_i \oplus T_j = T \text{ for some } j < i\}$$

for $T \in \{0,1\}^n$, and let
-aux $\Leftrightarrow$ there exists $T^* \in \{0,1\}^n$ such that $|I_{T^*}| > L_3$.

1. For fixed $T \in \{0,1\}^n$ and $i \in [q]$, suppose that $i \in I_T$. It means that the i-th query is faulty, and that $T_i \oplus T_j = T$ for any (previous) j-th query such that $N_i = N_j$, which happens with probability at most $\mu/2^n$. Therefore we have

$$\Pr[\text{aux}] \leq 2^n \binom{\mu}{L_3} \left(\frac{\mu}{2^n}\right)^{L_3} \leq 2^n \left(\frac{e\mu^2}{L_3 2^n}\right)^{L_3}.$$

2. The number of queries using any repeated nonce is at most 2μ. So the number of pairs $(i,j) \in [q]^{*2}$ such that $N_i = N_k$ for some $k(\neq i)$ and $N_j = N_{k'}$ for some $k'(\neq j)$ is at most $4\mu^2$. For each of such pairs, say (i,j), the probability that $X_i = X_j$ is at most δ. Therefore, we have

$$\Pr[\mathsf{bad}_1] \leq 4\mu^2 \delta.$$

3. The probability that $T_i = \mathbf{0}$ for some $i \in [q]$ is $\frac{q}{2^n}$; namely,

$$\Pr[\mathsf{bad}_{2a}] \leq \frac{q}{2^n}.$$

4. By symmetry, we can assume that $i < j$, which means that N_j is a faulty nonce. For each MAC query using a faulty nonce, there are at most μ other queries using the same nonce. So the number of pairs (i,j) such that $i < j$ and $N_i = N_j$ is at most μ^2. For each of such pairs (i,j), the probability that $T_i = T_j$ is $\frac{1}{2^n}$. Therefore, we have

$$\Pr[\mathsf{bad}_{2b}] \leq \frac{\mu^2}{2^n}.$$

Similarly, we can show that

$$\Pr[\mathsf{bad}_{2c}] \leq \frac{q^2 \delta}{2^n}.$$

5. Consider the case that $i > \max\{j, k\}$. On the i-th query, the number of pairs $(j, k) \in [q]^{*2}$ such that $N_j = N_k$ is at most $2\mu^2$. For each such pair (j, k), the probability that $T_i \oplus T_j \oplus T_k = \mathbf{0}$ and $X_i = X_j$ is $\frac{\delta}{2^n}$. By similar arguments for the other cases (i.e., $j > \max\{i, k\}$ and $k > \max\{i, j\}$), we see

$$\Pr\left[\mathsf{bad}_{2d}\right] \leq \frac{4\mu^2 q\delta}{2^n}.$$

6. Consider the case that $k > \max\{i, j, l\}$ and the k-th query makes bad_{2e}. For each $Z \in \mathcal{K}_h$, let

$$\mathcal{I}_Z \stackrel{\text{def}}{=} \left\{(i, j) \in [l-1]^{*2} : H_Z(M_i) \oplus H_Z(M_j) = N_i \oplus N_j\right\},$$

$$\mathcal{J}_Z \stackrel{\text{def}}{=} \left\{l \in [l-1] : H_Z(M_k) \oplus H_Z(M_l) = N_k \oplus N_l\right\}.$$

Since H is δ-almost XOR universal, we have $\sum_{Z \in \mathcal{K}_h} |\mathcal{I}_Z| \leq q^2 \delta |\mathcal{K}_h|$ and $\sum_{Z \in \mathcal{K}_h} |\mathcal{J}_Z| \leq q\delta |\mathcal{K}_h|$. Then the probability that the k-th query completes a trail of length 4 satisfying $T_i \oplus T_j \oplus T_k \oplus T_l = \mathbf{0}$ is upper bounded by

$$\sum_{Z \in \mathcal{K}_h} \Pr\left[K_h = Z\right] \cdot \min\left\{\frac{|\mathcal{I}_Z||\mathcal{J}_Z|}{2^n}, 1\right\} \leq \frac{1}{|\mathcal{K}_h|} \sum_{Z \in \mathcal{K}_h} \sqrt{\frac{|\mathcal{I}_Z||\mathcal{J}_Z|}{2^n}}$$

$$\leq \frac{1}{|\mathcal{K}_h|} \sqrt{\left(\sum_{Z \in \mathcal{K}_h} \frac{|\mathcal{I}_Z|}{2^n}\right)\left(\sum_{Z \in \mathcal{K}_h} |\mathcal{J}_Z|\right)} \leq \sqrt{\frac{q^3 \delta^2}{2^n}},$$

where the last inequality follows from the Cauchy-Schwarz inequality. Since the k-th query makes an inner edge of the trail, it should be a faulty query. Therefore this case happens with probability at most

$$\mu\sqrt{\frac{q^3 \delta^2}{2^n}}. \tag{1}$$

Next, consider the case that $l > \max\{i, j, k\}$ and the l-th query makes bad_{2e}. For each $Z \in \mathcal{K}_h$, let

$$\mathcal{R} \stackrel{\text{def}}{=} \left\{i \in [l-1] : N_i = N_j \text{ for some } j \in [l-1] \text{ such that } j \neq i\right\},$$

$$\mathcal{I}'_Z \stackrel{\text{def}}{=} \left\{(i, j) \in ([l-1] \times \mathcal{R}) : i \neq j \text{ and } H_Z(M_i) \oplus H_Z(M_j) = N_i \oplus N_j\right\},$$

$$\mathcal{J}'_Z \stackrel{\text{def}}{=} \left\{k \in \mathcal{R} : H_Z(M_k) \oplus H_Z(M_l) = N_k \oplus N_l\right\}.$$

Since $|\mathcal{R}| \leq 2\mu$ and H is δ-almost XOR universal, we have $\sum_{Z \in \mathcal{K}_h} |\mathcal{I}'_Z| \leq 2\mu q\delta |\mathcal{K}_h|$ and $\sum_{Z \in \mathcal{K}_h} |\mathcal{J}'_Z| \leq 2\mu\delta |\mathcal{K}_h|$. Then the probability that the l-th query completes a trail of length 4 satisfying $T_i \oplus T_j \oplus T_k \oplus T_l = \mathbf{0}$ is upper bounded by

$$\sum_{Z \in \mathcal{K}_h} \Pr\left[K_h = Z\right] \cdot \min\left\{\frac{|\mathcal{I}_Z'||\mathcal{J}_Z'|}{2^n}, 1\right\} \leq \frac{1}{|\mathcal{K}_h|} \sum_{Z \in \mathcal{K}_h} \sqrt{\frac{|\mathcal{I}_Z'||\mathcal{J}_Z'|}{2^n}}$$

$$\leq \frac{1}{|\mathcal{K}_h|} \sqrt{\left(\sum_{Z \in \mathcal{K}_h} \frac{|\mathcal{I}_Z'|}{2^n}\right)\left(\sum_{Z \in \mathcal{K}_h} |\mathcal{J}_Z'|\right)} \leq \sqrt{\frac{4\mu^2 q \delta^2}{2^n}}.$$

Therefore this case happens with probability at most

$$q\sqrt{\frac{4\mu^2 q \delta^2}{2^n}}. \tag{2}$$

By symmetry, (1) and (2) cover the other cases (i.e., $i > \max\{j, k, l\}$ and $j > \max\{i, k, l\}$). Therefore we have

$$\Pr\left[\mathsf{bad}_{2e}\right] \leq \mu\sqrt{\frac{q^3 \delta^2}{2^n}} + q\sqrt{\frac{4\mu^2 q \delta^2}{2^n}} = \frac{3\mu q^{\frac{3n}{2}} \delta}{2^{\frac{n}{2}}}.$$

7. When an adversary makes a verification query (N_j', M_j', T_j'), there is at most one MAC query (N_i, M_i, T_i) such that $N_i = N_j'$ and $T_i = T_j'$ without bad_{2b}, since there would not be a pair of MAC queries whose nonces and tags are all the same.[2] For this pair of indices, the probability that $X_i = X_j'$ is upper bounded by $v\delta$. Therefore, we have

$$\Pr[\mathsf{bad}_{3a} \mid \neg\mathsf{bad}_{2b}] \leq v\delta.$$

8. Suppose that an adversary makes a verification query (N_l', M_l', T_l'), assuming $\mathsf{bad}_1 \vee \mathsf{aux}$ did not happen. In order for this verification query to complete a cycle of length 4 containing it, there should be only a single MAC query, say (N_i, M_i, T_i), such that $N_i = N_l'$ since otherwise we have bad_1. Let $T = T_i \oplus T_l'$. Then it should be the case that either $X_j = X_i$ or $X_j = X_l'$ for some $j \in I_T$, which happens with probability at most $2L_3\delta$. Therefore, we have

$$\Pr\left[\mathsf{bad}_{3b} \wedge \neg\mathsf{bad}_1 \wedge \neg\mathsf{aux}\right] \leq 2L_3 v\delta.$$

9. The number of possible choices for j is at most 2μ since the j-th query uses a repeated nonce. For a fixed $i \in [q]$, the probability that $X_i = X_j$ is at most δ. By Markov inequality, we have

$$\Pr\left[\mathsf{bad}_4\right] \leq \frac{2\mu q \delta}{L_1}.$$

10. By Markov inequality, we have

$$\Pr\left[\mathsf{bad}_5\right] \leq \frac{q^2 \delta}{L_2}.$$

---

[2] For simplicity of analysis, one can assume that an adversary begins making verification queries after it makes all the MAC queries.

All in all, we have

$$\Pr[\mathsf{T}_{\mathsf{id}} \in \Gamma_{\mathsf{bad}}] \leq \Pr[\mathsf{bad}_1 \vee \mathsf{bad}_2 \vee \mathsf{bad}_3 \vee \mathsf{bad}_4 \vee \mathsf{bad}_5]$$

$$\leq \Pr[\mathsf{aux}] + \Pr[\mathsf{bad}_1] + \sum_{x \in \{a,b,c,d,e\}} \Pr[\mathsf{bad}_{2x}]$$

$$+ \Pr[\mathsf{bad}_{3a} \mid \neg\mathsf{bad}_{2b}] + \Pr[\mathsf{bad}_{3b} \wedge \neg\mathsf{bad}_1 \wedge \neg\mathsf{aux}]$$

$$+ \Pr[\mathsf{bad}_4] + \Pr[\mathsf{bad}_5]$$

$$\leq \frac{2\mu q \delta}{L_1} + \frac{q}{2^n} + \frac{q^2 \delta}{L_2} + \frac{q^2 \delta}{2^n} + 4\mu^2 \delta + \frac{\mu^2}{2^n} + \frac{3\mu q^{\frac{3n}{2}} \delta}{2^{\frac{n}{2}}}$$

$$+ \frac{4\mu^2 q \delta}{2^n} + (2L_3 + 1)v\delta + 2^n \left(\frac{e\mu^2}{L_3 2^n}\right)^{L_3}.$$

$\square$

4.3 Concluding the Proof Using Mirror Theory

For any good transcript τ, let $\mathcal{G}_\tau^=$ denote the graph obtained by deleting all $\neq$-labeled edges from $\mathcal{G}_\tau$. We can decompose $\mathcal{G}_\tau^=$ into four subgraphs in the same way as we did in Sect. 3, namely,

$$\mathcal{G}_\tau^= = \mathcal{G}_3^= \sqcup \mathcal{G}_2^= \sqcup \mathcal{G}_1^= \sqcup \mathcal{G}_0^=,$$

where $\mathcal{G}_3^=$ is the union of the components containing at least one trail of length three, $\mathcal{G}_2^=$ is the union of "stars", $\mathcal{G}_1^=$ is the set of isolated edges, and $\mathcal{G}_0^=$ is the set of isolated vertices. We also decompose $\mathcal{G}_3^=$ and $\mathcal{G}_2^=$ into connected components as follows.

$$\mathcal{G}_3^= = (\mathcal{V}_3, \mathcal{E}_3^=) = \mathcal{C}_1' \sqcup \cdots \sqcup \mathcal{C}_{k'}',$$
$$\mathcal{G}_2^= = (\mathcal{V}_2, \mathcal{E}_2^=) = \mathcal{C}_1 \sqcup \cdots \sqcup \mathcal{C}_k,$$

for some k and k'. Let $c_i = |\mathcal{C}_i|$ for $i = 1, \dots, k$. We will also write $c = |\mathcal{G}_2^=|$ ($= \sum_{i=1}^k c_i$) and $c' = |\mathcal{G}_3^=|$.

The probability of obtaining τ in the real world is computed over the randomness of π. By Theorem 1, the number of possible ways of evaluating π at the unknowns in $\mathcal{V}$ (i.e., $h^*(\mathcal{G}_\tau)$) is lower bounded by

$$\frac{(2^n)_{|\mathcal{V}|}}{2^{nq}} (1 - \varepsilon_1(\tau))$$

where

$$\varepsilon_1(\tau) \stackrel{\text{def}}{=} \frac{c'^4}{2^{2n}} + \frac{(c+c')^2}{2^{2n}} \sum_{i=1}^k c_i^2 + \frac{8(c+c')q^2}{2^{2n}} + \frac{18q^2}{2^{2n}} + \frac{16q^4}{2^{3n}} + \frac{2v}{2^n} + \frac{16qv}{2^{2n}}. \quad (3)$$

Since the probability that π realizes each assignment is exactly $1/(2^n)_{|\mathcal{V}|}$, and

$$\Pr[\mathsf{T}_{\mathsf{id}} = \tau] = \frac{1}{|\mathcal{K}_h| \cdot 2^{nq}},$$

we have

$$\frac{\Pr\left[\mathsf{T_{re}} = \tau\right]}{\Pr\left[\mathsf{T_{id}} = \tau\right]} \geq 1 - \varepsilon_1(\tau). \tag{4}$$

UPPER BOUNDING c AND c'. Each component $\mathcal{C}_i'$ has a trail of length 3, so without bad_1, $\mathcal{V}_3 \cap \mathcal{P}$ should contain at least one vertex of degree one (i.e., a leaf of $\mathcal{C}_i'$). We fix such a vertex, denoted P_i^*, and its unique neighbor, denoted Q_i^*, for every $i = 1, \dots, k'$. Again, without bad_1, every vertex of $\mathcal{C}_i'$ except P_i^* and Q_i^* should be connected with Q_i^* by a trail of length 1, 2, or 3. Without bad_4, the number of vertices in $\mathcal{V}_3 \cap \mathcal{P}$ that are connected with some Q_i^* by a trail of length 3 is at most L_1. The number of vertices in $\mathcal{V}_3 \cap \mathcal{Q}$ that are connected with some Q_i^* by a trail of length 2 is at most μ. Since $k' \leq L_1$, we have

$$c' \leq 2k' + L_1 + \mu \leq 3L_1 + \mu. \tag{5}$$

On the other hand, we observe that each edge of $\mathcal{E}_2^{=} \sqcup \mathcal{E}_3^{=}$ corresponds to either a repeated nonce or a collision on X. Therefore, we have

$$c + c' = k + k' + |\mathcal{E}_2^{=} \sqcup \mathcal{E}_3^{=}| \leq k + k' + 2\mu + L_2 \leq 2L_2 + 3\mu \tag{6}$$

since $k + k' \leq \mu + L_2$.

TAKING THE EXPECTATION OF $\varepsilon_1(\tau)$. Connected components $\mathcal{C}_i$ of $\mathcal{G}_2^{=}$ can be classified into two types; a vertex $P \in \mathcal{P}$ and its adjacent vertices in $\mathcal{Q}$, called a P-star, and a vertex $Q \in \mathcal{Q}$ and its adjacent vertices in $\mathcal{P}$, called a Q-star. By renaming the components, let $\mathcal{D}_1, \dots, \mathcal{D}_r$ denote the Q-stars in $\mathcal{G}_2^{=}$, and let $\mathcal{D}_1', \dots, \mathcal{D}_s'$ denote the P-stars in $\mathcal{G}_2^{=}$ for some r and s. Let $d_i = |\mathcal{D}_i|$ for $i = 1, \dots, r$ and let $d_i' = |\mathcal{D}_i'|$ for $i = 1, \dots, s$. When a single nonce is repeatedly used $d+1$ times for any $d \geq 1$, the d faulty nonces will make a P-star containing $d + 2$ vertices. Therefore we have

$$\sum_{i=1}^{s}(d_i' - 2) \leq \mu$$

and

$$\sum_{i=1}^{s} d_i'^2 \leq \sum_{i=1}^{s}(d_i' - 2)^2 + 4\sum_{i=1}^{s}(d_i' - 1) \leq \mu^2 + 4\mu.$$

Each Q-star $\mathcal{D}_i$ corresponds to an equivalent class of size $d_i - 1$ (defined in Lemma 1). Therefore we have

$$\begin{aligned}
\frac{(c + c')^2}{2^{2n}} \sum_{i=1}^{k} c_i{}^2 &\leq \frac{(2L_2 + 3\mu)^2}{2^{2n}} \sum_{i=1}^{k} c_i{}^2 \\
&= \frac{(2L_2 + 3\mu)^2}{2^{2n}} \left(\sum_{i=1}^{r} d_i{}^2 + \sum_{i=1}^{s} d_i'^2\right) \\
&\leq \frac{(2L_2 + 3\mu)^2}{2^{2n}} \left(\sum_{i=1}^{r} d_i{}^2 + \mu^2 + 4\mu\right)
\end{aligned} \tag{7}$$

Furthermore, by using Lemma 1 with $p_i = d_i - 1$ and a δ-AXU hash function $(N, M) \mapsto N \oplus H_{K_h}(M)$, and since $d_i \geq 3$ for every $i = 1, \ldots, r$, we have

$$\mathsf{Ex}\left[\sum_{i=1}^{r} d_i^2\right] \leq \mathsf{Ex}\left[\sum_{i=1}^{r}(d_i - 1)^2 + \sum_{i=1}^{r} 2d_i\right] \leq \mathsf{Ex}\left[\sum_{i=1}^{r} 3(d_i - 1)^2\right] \leq 6q^2\delta. \quad (8)$$

By (3), (5), (6), (7) and (8), we have

$$\mathsf{Ex}\left[\varepsilon_1(\tau)\right] \leq \frac{(3L_1 + \mu)^4}{2^{2n}} + \frac{(2L_2 + 3\mu)^2(6q^2\delta + \mu^2 + 4\mu)}{2^{2n}}$$
$$+ \frac{8(2L_2 + 3\mu)q^2}{2^{2n}} + \frac{18q^2}{2^{2n}} + \frac{16q^4}{2^{3n}} + \frac{2v}{2^n} + \frac{16qv}{2^{2n}}. \quad (9)$$

By (4), (9), Lemma 2 and Lemma 6, and by setting $L_1 = \frac{\mu}{3}$ and $L_2 = 2^{n-1}\delta^{\frac{1}{2}}$, we obtain Theorem 2.

5   Security of nEHtM Based on a Pseudorandom Function

In this section, we consider nEHtM$[H, F]$ based on an $(n-1)$-bit δ-AXU hash function H and an n-to-s bit keyed function F, where $1 \leq s \leq n$. Up to the PRF-security of F, we will replace F by a truly random function ρ, and prove the security of nEHtM$[H, \rho]$.

GRAPH REPRESENTATION OF TRANSCRIPTS. Suppose that an adversary $\mathcal{A}$ makes q MAC queries using at most μ faulty nonces, and makes v verification queries, obtaining

$$\tau_m = (N_i, M_i, T_i)_{1 \leq i \leq q},$$
$$\tau_v = \left(N'_j, M'_j, T'_j, b'_j\right)_{1 \leq j \leq v}.$$

as well as K_h for free at the end of the attack. Once K_h is fixed, we can also fix $X_i = H_{K_h}(M_i) \oplus N_i$ for $i = 1, \ldots, q$, and $X'_j = H_{K_h}(M'_j) \oplus N'_j$ for $j = 1, \ldots, v$. Then, exactly in the same way as we did in Sect. 4, we can define the transcript graph of τ, denoted $\mathcal{G}_\tau$, and the graph obtained by deleting all $\neq$-labeled edges from $\mathcal{G}_\tau$, denoted $\mathcal{G}_\tau^=$.

BAD TRANSCRIPTS. A transcript $\tau = (K_h, \tau_m, \tau_v)$ is defined as *bad* if one of the following conditions holds.

- bad$_1$ $\Leftrightarrow$ there exists $(i, j) \in [q]^{*2}$ such that $N_i = N_k$ for some $k(\neq i)$, $N_j = N_{k'}$ for some $k'(\neq j)$, and $X_i = X_j$.[3]
- bad$_2$ $\Leftrightarrow$ there exist $i \in [q]$ and $j \in [v]$ such that $N_i = N'_j$, $X_i = X'_j$, and $T_i = T'_j$.
- bad$_3$ $\Leftrightarrow$ there exist $(i, j, k) \in [q]^{*3}$ and $l \in [v]$ such that $X_i = X_j$, $N_j = N_k$, $X_k = X'_l$, $N'_l = N_i$, and $T_i \oplus T_j \oplus T_k \oplus T'_l = \mathbf{0}$.

---

[3] It is possible that $k = j$ and $k' = i$.

If a transcript τ is not bad, then it will be called a *good* transcript. For a good transcript τ, we observe that

1. $\mathcal{G}_\tau^=$, being a bipartite graph, contains no cycle without bad_1;
2. if two vertices are connected by a λ-labeled trail in $\mathcal{G}^=$, then they cannot be connected with a $(\lambda, \neq)$-labeled edge without $\mathsf{bad}_1 \vee \mathsf{bad}_2 \vee \mathsf{bad}_3$.

For a good transcript τ, the transcript graph $\mathcal{G}_\tau^=$ is decomposed into trees. Due to the second property above, any $\neq$-labeled edge connects two different trees.

UPPER BOUNDING THE PROBABILITY OF BAD EVENTS. In order to upper bound the probability of each bad event (in the ideal world), we fix a positive number L, let

$$I_T \overset{\text{def}}{=} \{i \in [q] : N_i = N_j \text{ and } T_i \oplus T_j = T \text{ for some } j \text{ such that } j < i\}$$

for $T \in \{0, 1\}^s$, and then define the following two auxiliary events.

– $\mathsf{aux}_1 \Leftrightarrow$ there exists $(i, j) \in [q]^{*2}$ such that $N_i = N_j$ and $T_i = T_j$.
– $\mathsf{aux}_2 \Leftrightarrow$ there exists $T^* \in \{0, 1\}^s$ such that $|I_{T^*}| > L$.

Events aux_1, aux_2, bad_1, bad_2 and bad_3 are similar to bad_{2b}, aux, bad_1, bad_{3a} and bad_{3b} defined in Sect. 4, respectively (except that the tag size is s bits). So we have

$$\Pr[\mathsf{aux}_1] \le \frac{\mu^2}{2^s}, \qquad \Pr[\mathsf{aux}_2] \le 2^s \left(\frac{e\mu^2}{L2^s}\right)^L, \qquad \Pr[\mathsf{bad}_1] \le 4\mu^2\delta,$$

$$\Pr[\mathsf{bad}_2 \wedge \neg\mathsf{aux}_1] \le v\delta, \qquad \Pr[\mathsf{bad}_3 \wedge \neg\mathsf{bad}_1 \wedge \neg\mathsf{aux}_2] \le 2Lv\delta,$$

and hence,

$$\Pr[\mathsf{T}_{\mathsf{id}} \in \varGamma_{\mathsf{bad}}] \le \Pr[\mathsf{aux}_1 \vee \mathsf{aux}_2 \vee \mathsf{bad}_1 \vee \mathsf{bad}_2 \vee \mathsf{bad}_3]$$

$$\le \frac{\mu^2}{2^s} + 4\mu^2\delta + (2L + 1)v\delta + 2^s \left(\frac{e\mu^2}{L2^s}\right)^L. \tag{10}$$

CONCLUDING THE PROOF. For any good transcript τ, let $\mathcal{V}$ denote the vertex set of $\mathcal{G}_\tau^=$. Then the number of components of $\mathcal{G}_\tau^=$ is $|\mathcal{V}| - q$, so the number of solutions to the set of all equations in $\mathcal{G}_\tau^=$ is exactly $2^{s(|\mathcal{V}|-q)}$. When a single $\neq$-labeled edge is replaced by a $=$-labeled edge, the resulting graph has $|\mathcal{V}| - q - 1$ components. This means that there are exactly $2^{s(|\mathcal{V}|-q-1)}$ solutions to $\mathcal{G}_\tau^=$ that violate a single non-equation. Since there are v non-equations, we conclude that the number of solutions to $\mathcal{G}_\tau$ is at least

$$2^{s(|\mathcal{V}|-q)} - v2^{s(|\mathcal{V}|-q-1)}.$$

Since the probability that ρ realizes each assignment (in the real world) is exactly $1/2^{s|\mathcal{V}|}$, we have

$$\Pr[\mathsf{T}_{\mathsf{re}} = \tau] \ge \frac{1}{|\mathcal{K}_h|} \left(\frac{1}{2^{sq}} - \frac{v}{2^{s(q+1)}}\right).$$

Since

$$\Pr\left[\mathsf{T_{id}} = \tau\right] = \frac{1}{|\mathcal{K}_h| \cdot 2^{sq}},$$

we have

$$\frac{\Pr\left[\mathsf{T_{re}} = \tau\right]}{\Pr\left[\mathsf{T_{id}} = \tau\right]} \geq 1 - \frac{v}{2^s}. \tag{11}$$

By (10), (11) and Lemma 2, we obtain following theorem.

Theorem 3. *Let $\delta > 0$, and let $H : \mathcal{K} \times \mathcal{M} \to \{0,1\}^n$ be a δ-almost universal hash function. For positive integers μ, q, v, and for any $L > 0$, we have*

$$\mathsf{Adv}^{\mathrm{mac}}_{\mathsf{nEHtM}[H,\rho]}(\mu, q, v) \leq \frac{\mu^2}{2^s} + 4\mu^2\delta + \frac{v}{2^s} + (2L+1)v\delta + 2^s \left(\frac{e\mu^2}{L2^s}\right)^L.$$

When $L = \mu + 1$, we have $\Pr\left[\mathsf{aux}_2\right] = 0$ since $|I_T| \leq \mu$. Then, by Theorem 3, we have

$$\mathsf{Adv}^{\mathrm{mac}}_{\mathsf{nEHtM}[H,\rho]}(\mu, q, v) \leq \frac{\mu^2}{2^s} + 4\mu^2\delta + \frac{v}{2^s} + (2\mu+3)v\delta. \tag{12}$$

When $1 \leq s \leq \frac{1}{\delta 2^s}$, let $L = \frac{1}{\delta 2^s}$. Assuming $2e\mu^2\delta \leq 1$, we have

$$2^s \left(e\mu^2\delta\right)^{\frac{1}{\delta 2^s}} \leq 2^s \left(e\mu^2\delta\right)^s \leq 2e\mu^2\delta,$$

and hence,

$$\mathsf{Adv}^{\mathrm{mac}}_{\mathsf{nEHtM}[H,\rho]}(\mu, q, v) \leq \frac{\mu^2}{2^s} + (2e+4)\mu^2\delta + \frac{3v}{2^s} + v\delta. \tag{13}$$

ALTERNATIVE BOUND. Interestingly, we can obtain an alternative bound by slightly modifying the bad events. A transcript τ is defined as *bad* if it satisfies bad_1 (as defined above), bad'_2 or bad'_3, where

- $\mathsf{bad}'_2 \Leftrightarrow$ there exist $i \in [q]$ and $j \in [v]$ such that $N_i = N'_j$ and $X_i = X'_j$.
- $\mathsf{bad}'_3 \Leftrightarrow$ there exist $i \in [q]$ and $j \in [v]$ such that $N_i = N_k$ for some $k(\neq i)$ and $X_i = X'_j$.

If two vertices are connected by a λ-labeled trail in $\mathcal{G}^=$, then they cannot be connected with a $(\lambda, \neq)$-labeled edge without $\mathsf{bad}'_2 \vee \mathsf{bad}'_3$.

1. When an adversary makes a verification query (N'_j, M'_j, T'_j), there are at most $\mu + 1$ MAC queries (N_i, M_i, T_i) such that $N_i = N'_j$. For each such pair, the probability that $X_i = X'_j$ is upper bounded by δ. Therefore, we have

$$\Pr[\mathsf{bad}'_2] \leq (\mu+1)v\delta.$$

2. For a verification query (N'_j, M'_j, T'_j) and a query (N_i, M_i, T_i) using any repeated nonce, the probability that $X_i = X'_j$ is at most δ. Therefore, we have

$$\Pr[\mathsf{bad}'_3] \leq 2\mu v\delta.$$

With this type of bad transcripts, we have the following theorem.

Theorem 4. *Let $\delta > 0$, and let $H : \mathcal{K} \times \mathcal{M} \to \{0,1\}^n$ be a δ-almost universal hash function. For positive integers μ, q, v, we have*

$$\mathsf{Adv}^{mac}_{\mathsf{nEHtM}[H,\rho]}(\mu, q, v) \leq 4\mu^2\delta + \frac{v}{2^s} + (3\mu + 1)v\delta.$$

The main difference of Theorem 4 from Theorem 3 is that the tag size s does not affect the number of faulty queries μ, while this bound contains the term $\mu v\delta$ (which is not in Theorem 3), so μ possibly limits the number of verification queries v.

INTERPRETATION. Given that $\mathsf{nEHtM}[H, \rho]$ is secure up to any number of MAC queries and 2^s verification queries, one might wonder how many faulty queries can be allowed. Assuming $\delta \approx \frac{1}{2^n}$, we observe the following:

1. When $\frac{n}{2} < s \leq \frac{1}{\delta 2^s}$, $\mathsf{nEHtM}[H,\rho]$ is secure as long as $\mu < \max\{2^{\frac{s}{2}}, 2^{n-s}\}$ by (13) and Theorem 4.
2. When $s \leq \frac{n}{2}$, $\mathsf{nEHtM}[H,\rho]$ is secure as long as $\mu < 2^{\frac{n}{2}}$ by Theorem 4.

When $s = n$, we have

$$\mathsf{Adv}^{mac}_{\mathsf{nEHtM}[H,\rho]}(\mu, q, v) \leq 4\mu^2\delta + \frac{\mu^2}{2^n} + \frac{2e\mu^2}{n2^n} + (2n + 1)v\delta + \frac{v}{2^n}$$

by Theorem 3 with $L = n(= s)$, which means that $\mathsf{nEHtM}[H, \rho]$ is secure when $\mu < 2^{\frac{n}{2}}$ and $v < \frac{2^n}{n}$.

6 Security of Truncated nEHtM

In this section, we analyze how tag truncation affects the security of nEHtM when nEHtM is based on a block cipher E (which is modeled as a truly random permutation π). We can take two different approaches.

First, we can use Theorem 5 in [8]; let $F : \mathcal{K} \times \mathcal{N} \times \mathcal{M} \to \{0,1\}^n$ be a nonce-based MAC with key space $\mathcal{K}$, nonce space $\mathcal{N}$, message space $\mathcal{M}$ and tag space $\mathcal{T} = \{0,1\}^n$. For any $1 \leq s \leq n-1$, let $\mathsf{Tr}_s : \{0,1\}^n \to \{0,1\}^s$ be a function that takes s bits of the input in any way (e.g., the leftmost s bits of an n-bit input). Let

$$F_s \overset{\text{def}}{=} \mathsf{Tr}_s \circ F$$

denote a truncated variant of F that returns only s bits of the original tag. Cogliati et al. [8] proved that

$$\mathsf{Adv}^{mac}_{F_s}(\mu, q, v, t) \leq \mathsf{Adv}^{mac}_F(\mu, q, 2^{n-s}v, t). \tag{14}$$

We can combine (14) with Theorem 2. However, the threshold number of MAC queries would not go beyond $2^{\frac{3n}{4}}$ anyway.

An alternative approach is to use Theorem 3 and 4 by seeing a truncated permutation as a pseudorandom function. In [13,30], it has been proved that

$$\mathsf{Adv}^{\mathsf{prf}}_{\mathsf{Tr}_s \circ \pi}(q) \leq \frac{q}{2^{n-\frac{s}{2}}}$$

for a random permutation π. Since a (μ, q, v)-forging adversary makes at most $2(q + v)$ calls to the underlying (truncated) block cipher, we have the following theorem.

Theorem 5. *Let $\delta > 0$, and let $H : \mathcal{K} \times \mathcal{M} \to \{0,1\}^n$ be a δ-almost universal hash function. For positive integers μ, q, v, and for any $L > 0$, we have*

$$\mathsf{Adv}^{\mathsf{mac}}_{\mathsf{nEHtM}[H,\pi]_s}(\mu, q, v) \leq \min\{A, B\},$$

where

$$A = \frac{\mu^2}{2^s} + 4\mu^2\delta + \frac{v}{2^s} + (2L + 1)v\delta + 2^s \left(\frac{e\mu^2}{L2^s}\right)^L + \frac{q + v}{2^{n-\frac{s}{2}-1}},$$

$$B = 4\mu^2\delta + \frac{v}{2^s} + (3\mu + 1)v\delta + \frac{q + v}{2^{n-\frac{s}{2}-1}}.$$

INTERPRETATION. When $s \leq \frac{2n}{3}$, $\mathsf{nEHtM}[H, \pi]_s$ is secure up to $2^{n-\frac{s}{2}}$ MAC queries and 2^s verification queries as long as $\mu < \min\{2^{\frac{s}{2}}, 2^{n-s}\}$ by Theorem 5 (using B). In particular, we observe that

1. when $s = \frac{n}{2}$, $\mathsf{nEHtM}[H, \pi]_s$ is secure up to $2^{\frac{3n}{4}}$ MAC queries, 2^s verification queries, and $2^{\frac{n}{2}}$ faulty queries;
2. when $s = \frac{n}{4}$, $\mathsf{nEHtM}[H, \pi]_s$ is secure up to $2^{\frac{7n}{8}}$ MAC queries, 2^s verification queries, and $2^{\frac{n}{2}}$ faulty queries.

A   Proof of Theorem 1

Proof. For $i = 1, 2, 3$, let $q_i = |\mathcal{E}_i^{=}|$ and let $v_i = |\mathcal{E}_i^{\neq}|$. Then we have $q = q_1 + q_2 + q_3$ (with $q_0 = 0$) and $v = v_0 + v_1 + v_2 + v_3$. Note that we interchangeably write $|\mathcal{G}_i|$, $|\mathcal{G}_i^{=}|$ and $|\mathcal{V}_i|$ for $i = 1, 2, 3$.

Suppose that $\mathcal{G}_3^{=}$ is decomposed into k' components $\mathcal{C}_1', \ldots, \mathcal{C}_{k'}'$ for some k'. Then by Lemma 3, the number of solutions to $\mathcal{G}_3$, denoted $h(\mathcal{G}_3)$, satisfies

$$\frac{h(\mathcal{G}_3)N^{q_3}}{(N)_{|\mathcal{V}_3|}} \geq 1 - \frac{|\mathcal{V}_3|^2}{N^2} \sum_{i=1}^{k'} |\mathcal{C}_i'|^2 - \frac{2v_3}{N} \geq 1 - \frac{|\mathcal{V}_3|^4}{N^2} - \frac{2v_3}{N}. \quad (15)$$

Again, by Lemma 3, for a fixed solution to $\mathcal{G}_3$, the number of solutions to $\mathcal{G}_2$, denoted $h(\mathcal{G}_2)$, satisfies

$$\frac{h(\mathcal{G}_2)N^{q_2}}{(N - |\mathcal{V}_3|)_{|\mathcal{V}_2|}} \geq 1 - \frac{(|\mathcal{V}_3| + |\mathcal{V}_2|)^2}{N^2} \sum_{i=1}^{k} |\mathcal{C}_i|^2 - \frac{2v_2}{N}. \quad (16)$$

By Lemma 4, for a fixed solution to $\mathcal{G}_2$, the number of solutions to $\mathcal{G}_1$, denoted $h(\mathcal{G}_1)$, satisfies

$$
\frac{h(\mathcal{G}_1)N^{q_1}}{(N - |\mathcal{V}_3| - |\mathcal{V}_2|)_{|\mathcal{V}_1|}} \geq 1 - \frac{4(|\mathcal{V}_3| + |\mathcal{V}_2|)^2 q_1}{N^2} - \frac{4(|\mathcal{V}_3| + |\mathcal{V}_2|)q_1^2}{N^2}
$$

$$
- \frac{18q_1^2}{N^2} - \frac{32(|\mathcal{V}_3| + |\mathcal{V}_2|)q_1^3}{3N^3} - \frac{16q_1^4}{N^3} - \frac{2v_1}{N} - \frac{16q_1 v_1}{N^2}
$$

$$
\geq 1 - \frac{8(|\mathcal{V}_3| + |\mathcal{V}_2|)q^2}{N^2} - \frac{18q^2}{N^2} - \frac{64q^4}{3N^3} - \frac{2v_1}{N} - \frac{16qv}{N^2}
\tag{17}
$$

since $|\mathcal{V}_3| + |\mathcal{V}_2| + 2q_1 \leq 2q \leq N/4$. By Lemma 5, for a fixed solution to $\mathcal{G}_1$, the number of solutions to $\mathcal{G}_0$, denoted $h(\mathcal{G}_0)$, satisfies

$$
\frac{h(\mathcal{G}_0)}{(N - |\mathcal{V}_3| - |\mathcal{V}_2| - |\mathcal{V}_1|)_{|\mathcal{V}_0|}} \geq 1 - \frac{2v_0}{N}.
\tag{18}
$$

By (15), (16), (17), (18), we have

$$
\frac{h^*(\mathcal{G})N^q}{(N)_{|\mathcal{V}|}} = \frac{h(\mathcal{G}_3)N^{q_3}}{(N)_{|\mathcal{V}_3|}} \cdot \frac{h(\mathcal{G}_2)N^{q_2}}{(N - |\mathcal{V}_3|)_{|\mathcal{V}_2|}}
$$

$$
\times \frac{h(\mathcal{G}_1)N^{q_1}}{(N - |\mathcal{V}_3| - |\mathcal{V}_2|)_{|\mathcal{V}_1|}} \cdot \frac{h(\mathcal{G}_0)}{(N - |\mathcal{V}_3| - |\mathcal{V}_2| - |\mathcal{V}_1|)_{|\mathcal{V}_0|}}
$$

$$
\geq 1 - \frac{|\mathcal{V}_3|^4}{N^2} - \frac{(|\mathcal{V}_3| + |\mathcal{V}_2|)^2}{N^2} \sum_{i=1}^{k} |\mathcal{C}_i|^2 - \frac{8(|\mathcal{V}_3| + |\mathcal{V}_2|)q^2}{N^2}
$$

$$
- \frac{18q^2}{N^2} - \frac{64q^4}{3N^3} - \frac{2v_3}{N} - \frac{2v_2}{N} - \frac{2v_1}{N} - \frac{2v_0}{N} - \frac{16qv}{N^2}
$$

$$
\geq 1 - \frac{|\mathcal{V}_3|^4}{N^2} - \frac{(|\mathcal{V}_3| + |\mathcal{V}_2|)^2}{N^2} \sum_{i=1}^{k} |\mathcal{C}_i|^2 - \frac{8(|\mathcal{V}_3| + |\mathcal{V}_2|)q^2}{N^2}
$$

$$
- \frac{18q^2}{N^2} - \frac{64q^4}{3N^3} - \frac{2v}{N} - \frac{16qv}{N^2}.
$$

$\square$

References

1. Banik, S., Pandey, S.K., Peyrin, T., Sasaki, Yu., Sim, S.M., Todo, Y.: GIFT: a small present. In: Fischer, W., Homma, N. (eds.) CHES 2017. LNCS, vol. 10529, pp. 321–345. Springer, Cham (2017). https://doi.org/10.1007/978-3-319-66787-4_16
2. Bellare, M., Canetti, R., Krawczyk, H.: Keying hash functions for message authentication. In: Koblitz, N. (ed.) CRYPTO 1996. LNCS, vol. 1109, pp. 1–15. Springer, Heidelberg (1996). https://doi.org/10.1007/3-540-68697-5_1
3. Bellare, M., Goldreich, O., Krawczyk, H.: Stateless evaluation of pseudorandom functions: security beyond the birthday barrier. In: Wiener, M. (ed.) CRYPTO 1999. LNCS, vol. 1666, pp. 270–287. Springer, Heidelberg (1999). https://doi.org/10.1007/3-540-48405-1_17

4. Bellare, M., Kilian, J., Rogaway, P.: The security of the cipher block chaining message authentication code. J. Comput. Syst. Sci. **61**(3), 362–399 (2000)
5. Bernstein, D.J.: Stronger security bounds for wegman-carter-shoup authenticators. In: Cramer, R. (ed.) EUROCRYPT 2005. LNCS, vol. 3494, pp. 164–180. Springer, Heidelberg (2005). https://doi.org/10.1007/11426639_10
6. Black, J., Rogaway, P.: A block-cipher mode of operation for parallelizable message authentication. In: Knudsen, L.R. (ed.) EUROCRYPT 2002. LNCS, vol. 2332, pp. 384–397. Springer, Heidelberg (2002). https://doi.org/10.1007/3-540-46035-7_25
7. Bogdanov, A., et al.: PRESENT: an ultra-lightweight block cipher. In: Paillier, P., Verbauwhede, I. (eds.) CHES 2007. LNCS, vol. 4727, pp. 450–466. Springer, Heidelberg (2007). https://doi.org/10.1007/978-3-540-74735-2_31
8. Cogliati, B., Lee, J., Seurin, Y.: New constructions of macs from (tweakable) block ciphers. IACR Trans. Symmetric Cryptol. **2**, 27–58 (2017)
9. Cogliati, B., Seurin, Y.: EWCDM: an efficient, beyond-birthday secure, nonce-misuse resistant MAC. In: Robshaw, M., Katz, J. (eds.) CRYPTO 2016. LNCS, vol. 9814, pp. 121–149. Springer, Heidelberg (2016). https://doi.org/10.1007/978-3-662-53018-4_5
10. Datta, N., Dutta, A., Nandi, M., Yasuda, K.: Encrypt or decrypt? to make a single-key beyond birthday secure nonce-based MAC. In: Shacham, H., Boldyreva, A. (eds.) CRYPTO 2018. LNCS, vol. 10991, pp. 631–661. Springer, Cham (2018). https://doi.org/10.1007/978-3-319-96884-1_21
11. Dutta, A., Jha, A., Nandi, M.: Tight Security Analysis of EHtM MAC. IACR Trans. Symmetric Cryptol. **3**, 130–150 (2017)
12. Dutta, A., Nandi, M., Talnikar, S.: Beyond birthday bound secure mac in faulty nonce model. In: Ishai, Y., Rijmen, V. (eds.) EUROCRYPT 2019. LNCS, vol. 11476, pp. 437–466. Springer, Cham (2019). https://doi.org/10.1007/978-3-030-17653-2_15
13. Gilboa, S., Gueron, S., Morris, B.: How many queries are needed to distinguish a truncated random permutation from a random function? J. Cryptol. **31**(1), 162–171 (2017). https://doi.org/10.1007/s00145-017-9253-0
14. Guo, J., Peyrin, T., Poschmann, A., Robshaw, M.: The LED block cipher. In: Preneel, B., Takagi, T. (eds.) CHES 2011. LNCS, vol. 6917, pp. 326–341. Springer, Heidelberg (2011). https://doi.org/10.1007/978-3-642-23951-9_22
15. Hoang, V.T., Tessaro, S.: Key-alternating ciphers and key-length extension: exact bounds and multi-user security. In: Robshaw, M., Katz, J. (eds.) CRYPTO 2016. LNCS, vol. 9814, pp. 3–32. Springer, Heidelberg (2016). https://doi.org/10.1007/978-3-662-53018-4_1
16. Iwata, T., Kurosawa, K.: OMAC: one-key CBC MAC. In: Johansson, T. (ed.) FSE 2003. LNCS, vol. 2887, pp. 129–153. Springer, Heidelberg (2003). https://doi.org/10.1007/978-3-540-39887-5_11
17. Jaulmes, É., Joux, A., Valette, F.: On the security of randomized CBC-MAC beyond the birthday paradox limit a new construction. In: Daemen, J., Rijmen, V. (eds.) FSE 2002. LNCS, vol. 2365, pp. 237–251. Springer, Heidelberg (2002). https://doi.org/10.1007/3-540-45661-9_19
18. Jaulmes, É., Lercie, R.: FRMAC, a fast randomized message authentication code. IACR Cryptology ePrint Archive, Report 2004/166 (2004). http://eprint.iacr.org/2004/166
19. Jha, A., Nandi, M.: Tight Security of Cascaded LRW2. Journal of Cryptology, pages 1–46, 2020

20. Joux, A.: Authentication failures in NIST Version of GCM. Comments submitted to NIST Modes of Operation Process (2006). http://csrc.nist.gov/groups/ST/toolkit/BCM/documents/comments/800-38_Series-Drafts/GCM/Joux_comments.pdf

21. Kim, S., Lee, B., Lee, J.: Tight security bounds for double-block hash-then-sum MACs. In: Canteaut, A., Ishai, Y. (eds.) EUROCRYPT 2020. LNCS, vol. 12105, pp. 435–465. Springer, Cham (2020). https://doi.org/10.1007/978-3-030-45721-1_16

22. Leurent, G., Nandi, M., Sibleyras, F.: Generic attacks against beyond-birthday-bound MACs. In: Shacham, H., Boldyreva, A. (eds.) CRYPTO 2018. LNCS, vol. 10991, pp. 306–336. Springer, Cham (2018). https://doi.org/10.1007/978-3-319-96884-1_11

23. Mennink, B., Neves, S.: Encrypted davies-meyer and its dual: towards optimal security using mirror theory. In: Katz, J., Shacham, H. (eds.) CRYPTO 2017. LNCS, vol. 10403, pp. 556–583. Springer, Cham (2017). https://doi.org/10.1007/978-3-319-63697-9_19

24. Minematsu, K.: How to thwart birthday attacks against MACs via small randomness. In: Hong, S., Iwata, T. (eds.) FSE 2010. LNCS, vol. 6147, pp. 230–249. Springer, Heidelberg (2010). https://doi.org/10.1007/978-3-642-13858-4_13

25. Naito, Y.: Blockcipher-based MACs: beyond the birthday bound without message length. In: Takagi, T., Peyrin, T. (eds.) ASIACRYPT 2017. LNCS, vol. 10626, pp. 446–470. Springer, Cham (2017). https://doi.org/10.1007/978-3-319-70700-6_16

26. Nandi, M.: Mind the composition: birthday bound attacks on EWCDMD and SoKAC21. In: Canteaut, A., Ishai, Y. (eds.) EUROCRYPT 2020. LNCS, vol. 12105, pp. 203–220. Springer, Cham (2020). https://doi.org/10.1007/978-3-030-45721-1_8

27. Patarin, J.: Introduction to mirror theory: analysis of systems of linear equalities and linear non equalities for cryptography. IACR Cryptology ePrint Archive, Report 2010/287 (2010). http://eprint.iacr.org/2010/287

28. Patarin, J.: Mirror theory and cryptography. IACR Cryptology ePrint Archive, Report 2016/702 (2016). http://eprint.iacr.org/2016/702

29. Shoup, V.: On fast and provably secure message authentication based on universal hashing. In: Koblitz, N. (ed.) CRYPTO 1996. LNCS, vol. 1109, pp. 313–328. Springer, Heidelberg (1996). https://doi.org/10.1007/3-540-68697-5_24

30. Stam, A.J.: Distance between sampling with and without replacement. Stat. Neerl. **32**(2), 81–91 (1978)

31. Wegman, M.N., Carter, J.L.: New hash functions and their use in authentication and set equality. J. Comput. Syst. Sci. **22**(3), 265–279 (1981)

32. Yasuda, K.: The sum of CBC MACs is a secure PRF: In: Pieprzyk, J. (ed.) CT-RSA 2010. LNCS, vol. 5985, pp. 366–381. Springer, Heidelberg (2010). https://doi.org/10.1007/978-3-642-11925-5_25

33. Yasuda, K.: A new variant of PMAC: beyond the birthday bound. In: Rogaway, P. (ed.) CRYPTO 2011. LNCS, vol. 6841, pp. 596–609. Springer, Heidelberg (2011). https://doi.org/10.1007/978-3-642-22792-9_34

34. Zhang, L., Wu, W., Sui, H., Wang, P.: 3kf9: enhancing 3GPP-MAC beyond the birthday bound. In: Wang, X., Sako, K. (eds.) ASIACRYPT 2012. LNCS, vol. 7658, pp. 296–312. Springer, Heidelberg (2012). https://doi.org/10.1007/978-3-642-34961-4_19

On the Adaptive Security of MACs and PRFs

Andrew Morgan[1]($\boxtimes$), Rafael Pass[2], and Elaine Shi[1]

[1] Cornell University, Ithaca, USA
asmorgan@cs.cornell.edu, runting@gmail.com
[2] Cornell Tech, New York City, USA
rafael@cornell.edu

Abstract. We consider the security of two of the most commonly used cryptographic primitives—message authentication codes (MACs) and pseudorandom functions (PRFs)—in a *multi-user setting with adaptive corruption*. Whereas is it well known that any secure MAC or PRF is also multi-user secure under adaptive corruption, the trivial reduction induces a security loss that is linear in the number of users.

Our main result shows that black-box reductions from "standard" assumptions cannot be used to provide a tight, or even a linear-preserving, security reduction for adaptive multi-user secure deterministic stateless MACs and thus also PRFs. In other words, a security loss that grows with the number of users is necessary for any such black-box reduction.

1 Introduction

Message authentication codes (MACs) are one of the most fundamental cryptographic primitives. MACs are secret-key primitives that enable a party to produce a "tag" for messages in such a way that, while anyone possessing the secret key can verify the validity of the tag, an adversary without access to the key is unable to forge a correct tag for a message. This allows the participating parties to use the tags to confirm that a tagged message is *authentic*—that is, that it originated from a trusted sender and was delivered without modification. A *pseudorandom function* (PRF) is a related primitive which can easily be used

---

Supported in part by NSF Award SATC-1704788, NSF Award RI-1703846, NSF Award CNS-1561209, AFOSR Award FA9550-18-1-0267, DARPA SIEVE award HR00110C0086, and a JP Morgan Faculty Award. This research is based upon work supported in part by the Office of the Director of National Intelligence (ODNI), Intelligence Advanced Research Projects Activity (IARPA), via 2019-19-020700006. The views and conclusions contained herein are those of the authors and should not be interpreted as necessarily representing the official policies, either expressed or implied, of ODNI, IARPA, or the U.S. Government. The U.S. Government is authorized to reproduce and distribute reprints for governmental purposes notwithstanding any copyright annotation therein.

S. Moriai and H. Wang (Eds.): ASIACRYPT 2020, LNCS 12491, pp. 724–753, 2020.
https://doi.org/10.1007/978-3-030-64837-4_24

to construct a MAC; in addition to being unforgeable by an adversary, the output ("tag") from a PRF is also pseudorandom (i.e., indistinguishable from true randomness to the adversary).

Multi-user Security and Adaptive Corruptions. MACs and PRFs are also some of the most commonly used cryptographic primitives in practice; as such, they are often deployed in contexts with huge numbers of users. For instance, MACs are used in protocols for secure key exchange (as first formalized in [21]), including the well-known and widely employed TLS protocol [18–20], which is used today by major websites with billions of daily active users. A natural question, then, is to what extent the *multi-user setting* in which MACs or PRFs are practically employed affects the security of these primitives. In particular, in a multi-user setting it is natural to consider an *adaptive* adversary who may decide to corrupt a subset of the users (and as a result of the corruption receive their secret keys); given such an adversary, we would like to guarantee that uncorrupted users' instances remain secure. Indeed, various forms of multi-user security have been considered since the work of Bellare et al. [9] (see also e.g., [7,8,10,36, 39]). In recent work, Bader et al. [3] explicitly consider a notion of adaptive multi-user security for signature schemes and MACs. They remark that a simple "guessing" reduction, originally proposed in [9] for multi-user security of PRFs without corruption, shows that any single-user secure MAC is adaptively multi-user secure. Specifically, given a multi-user adversary that runs, say, ℓ instances of a MAC, one can construct a single-user adversary that, given an instance of the MAC, simulates the game for the multi-user adversary by embedding its own instance into a random one of the multi-user instances and generating $\ell - 1$ keys to simulate the rest of the instances (including returning the respective keys for corruption queries). If the multi-user adversary picks the correct instance to break by forging a tag, then the single-user adversary can use the forgery it returns to win its own game.

Security Loss and Linear-Preserving Reductions. The above argument shows that any "single-user" secure MAC also is multi-user secure under adaptive corruption; a similar argument holds also for PRFs [2]. However, security is only "polynomially" preserved; in a concrete sense, the reduction incurs a significant *security loss* [32], as one might note that the single-user adversary we describe is far less efficient than the multi-user adversary on which it is based. In particular, in a setting where we have a large number ℓ of instances available to the adversary, the single-user adversary's probability of success is indeed reduced by a proportionate factor of ℓ. As discussed in works such as [36,39], this has considerable implications on the concrete security of such a primitive in a setting where a large number of instances might be in use at once. More formally, the *security loss* is defined as the "work", or *expected running time*, required by the reduction to break the underlying assumption (in the above example, single-user security) using a particular adversary against a primitive (adaptive multi-user security) as an oracle, divided by the work required by the adversary to break the primitive. Intuitively, the "best possible" type of reduction is one with a constant security loss, or a *tight* [32] reduction, which guarantees that the primitive will inherit roughly the same level of concrete security as the underlying assumption. A reduction with a security loss equal to a fixed polynomial $p(n)$ in the security parameter, also known as a *linear-preserving* reduction, is still intuitively desirable. The "guessing" reduction above, however, has a security loss of ℓ, or the number of instances in the multi-user security game, and so it is neither tight nor linear-preserving. A natural question, then, is whether we can do better than this trivial reduction and construct a provably secure MAC with a linear-preserving reduction.

In fact, the work of [3] shows how to overcome the security loss of this "trivial" guessing reduction: as a key building block towards an "almost-tightly secure" authenticated key exchange protocol, the authors present an elegant construction of an adaptively multi-user secure *digital signature scheme* with a linear-preserving reduction. In particular, the security loss of their constructions is linear in the security parameter n, and *independent* of the number of users!

On the Importance of Determinstic Tagging. However, the signature construction given in [3] requires introducing *randomness* into the signing algorithm. While this scheme can indeed be interpreted as a MAC, the fact that the signing algorithm is randomized means that the resulting MAC also becomes *randomized*. While some theoretical textbooks (see e.g., [25]) allow the tagging mechanism in the definition of a MAC to be randomized, practical texts (e.g., the Handbook of Applied Cryptography [34]), as well as NIST standardizations [6], require the tagging algorithm to be *deterministic*. As far as we know, all constructions used in practice, as well as all standardized constructions of MACs, are deterministic; indeed, there are several good reasons for sticking to deterministic constructions. First, reliable randomness is hard to generate, and thus randomized constructions are avoided in practice for time-critical primitives that are used repeatedly and on a large scale, as is the case for MACs. Furthermore, any PRF, when viewed as a MAC, is by definition deterministic, and additionally is internally *stateless*; in fact, we remark that almost all practical MAC constructions are also stateless, a notable exception being GMAC [22].[1] Obtaining a tightly secure PRF in a multi-user setting requires, at a minimum, a tightly secure deterministic and stateless MAC.

As such, the current state of affairs leaves open the important problem of determining the concrete multi-user security of the MACs and PRFs used in practice today. In particular, focusing on the case of stateless MACs, we consider the question of whether either deterministic MACs or PRFs can, in an adaptive multi-user setting, have a security loss that is independent of the number of users:

Can there exist tight or linear-preserving reductions for proving the adaptive multi-user security of any deterministic (and stateless) MAC or any PRF based on some "standard assumption"?

---

[1] GMAC is deterministic but stateful; it keeps an internal counter to use as an additional non-reusable input, or *nonce*. Stateful MACs such as GMAC are not subject to the results we prove here.

At first glance, it may seem that answering this question is trivial, since any randomized MAC can be made deterministic. Indeed, as shown in [25] for signature schemes, one may simply fix the randomness to be the result of applying a PRF to the input message. This construction, however, only preserves the tightness of the reduction if the underlying PRF itself is tightly secure in the adaptive multi-user setting—however, since any such PRF is already trivially a (deterministic) MAC, we end up precisely where we started.

1.1   Our Results

Our main result, in fact, provides a strong *negative* answer to the above question. We demonstrate that there exists no linear-preserving (or, hence, tight) black-box reduction for basing adaptive multi-user security of any deterministic MAC, and thus also any PRF, on any secure "standard" assumption. By a "standard" assumption, we here refer to any assumption that can be modeled as a game, or an interaction between a challenger C and a polynomial-time adversary A, that proceeds in an *a priori* bounded number of rounds—following [38], we refer to this class of assumptions as *bounded-round assumptions*.

Theorem 1 (Informal). *If there exists a linear-preserving black-box reduction R for basing adaptive multi-user security of a deterministic MAC on some bounded-round assumption C, then C can be broken in polynomial time.*

In particular, we show that any such black-box reduction (to a secure bounded-round assumption) requires a security loss of $\Omega(\sqrt{\ell})$, where ℓ is the number of users. We remark that since any PRF or deterministic digital signature scheme trivially implies a deterministic MAC (via a tight security reduction), our theorem also directly rules out linear-preserving black-box reductions for basing adaptive multi-user security of PRFs or deterministic signatures on standard assumptions.

Related Results. A few prior works have in fact dealt with this question for other types of primitives. Non-adaptive multi-user security was originally introduced by Bellare, Canetti, and Krawczyk [9] for pseudorandom function families; the authors also introduced the original version of the classical "guessing" reduction from multi-user to single-user security in that context. As mentioned above, [3] introduced adaptive multi-user security in the context of signatures and MACs (and presented applications for secure key exchange), and [2] considered it in the context of PRFs. Recently, there has been a wealth of positive results demonstrating the achievability of tight reductions from multi-user to single-user security of authenticated encryption protocols and block cipher-based schemes (see, e.g., [3,13,27,28,33]); some of these results, as we have noted, consider the case of *randomized* or *stateful* (nonce-based) MACs such as GMAC, which are not subject to our security bound.

Concerning negative results, several prior works have ruled out certain *restricted* classes of linear-preserving reductions from multi-user security of various primitives. Bellare et al. [8] first introduced the (non-adaptive) notion of multi-user security for public-key encryption and demonstrated that there does not exist an efficient *generic* reduction from multi-user to single-user security which works for *every* encryption scheme. But one may still hope to circumvent this by constructing a specific encryption scheme for which such a reduction exists, or by directly basing multi-user security on some other (standard) assumption; indeed, [8] does demonstrate certain schemes for which security loss can be avoided. A later work by Jager et al. [30] proves a negative result for *authenticated encryption*, showing that certain *restricted* types of black-box reductions—in particular, "straight-line" (i.e., non-rewinding) reductions—from *adaptive* multi-user security to single-user security of *any* authenticated encryption scheme possessing a strong "key uniqueness" property (i.e., that any two keys which produce the same ciphertexts for some polynomial number of inputs must agree on *all* inputs) must inherit a similarly large security loss.

Most relevantly to our work, Chatterjee et al. [15] show a negative result for the case of *generic* reductions from adaptive multi-user to single-user security of MACs. Specifically, the authors propose a "collision-finding" attack on multi-user MAC security whose success probability increases by a factor of roughly ℓ (the number of instances) in a multi-user setting as compared to its single-user analogue against an *idealized* MAC. Similarly to [8], this elegantly demonstrates that a security loss is inherent in *generic* reductions from multi-user to single-user security; however, their results still leave open the question of whether the same holds true for a reduction to a specific MAC (where, as [8] shows for public-key encryption, there may be more effective single-user attacks), let alone whether it holds for directly reducing multi-user security to an underlying assumption without relying on single-user security.

In contrast to the above results, the bound we show here applies to *any* (i.e., not a restricted class of) black-box reduction and to any "standard" (bounded-round) assumption; additionally, it applies to any construction of the primitives we consider (i.e., deterministic MACs and PRFs).

Our work builds on a line of research on using "meta-reductions" [12] to prove impossibility results for black-box reductions, and in particular to study the inherent security loss of (single-user) secure digital signatures. Most recently, expanding upon earlier results [4,16,29,31] which dealt with restricted reductions, [35] provides a security loss bound ruling out linear-preserving reductions for single-user security of a primitive called *unique signature schemes*. While we rely on a significant amount of insight from these prior results (and in particular from [35]), adapting their techniques to our setting is quite non-trivial (as we shall explain below). Indeed, as far as we are aware, all known black-box separations using the meta-reduction paradigm only apply to primitives that embody some form of uniqueness or rerandomizability (which in turn can be viewed as a "distributional uniqueness") property—we will return to what this uniqueness property means shortly (and how it is used). In contrast, our impossibility result does not (explicitly) refer to or require a primitive that embodies such a property.

Summarizing the above discussion, as far as we know, our results not only constitute the first "complete" black-box lower bound (in the sense that we consider "unrestricted" reductions) on the security loss of any primitive in the multi-user setting, but also address the security of two of the most fundamental primitives—MACs and PRFs—used practically in a multi-user setting. Additionally, we present the first usage of the meta-reduction paradigm to rule out reductions from a primitive that does not itself embody a uniqueness (or rerandomizability) property.

1.2   Overview

The Meta-reduction Paradigm. We prove our security loss bound using an adaptation of the "meta-reduction" paradigm, originally devised in [12] (see also [1,5,11,14,23,24,26,38] for related work concerning meta-reductions). The paradigm was originally used to show black-box *impossibility* results, but Coron in [16] pioneered the usage of meta-reductions to instead show *lower bounds on security loss*; this line of work was continued in [4,31,35]. Meta-reductions were first used in relation to multi-user security in [30], which dealt with multi-user to single-user reductions for authenticated encryption (satisfying a key-uniqueness property).

At a high level, the meta-reduction paradigm proves the impossibility of any black-box reduction from a primitive Π to a *secure* assumption C.[2] To illustrate this approach for the case of an impossibility result, consider attempting to prove the impossibility of such a reduction $\mathcal{R}$ that breaks the assumption C by using black-box access to some "ideal adversary" $\mathcal{A}$ (which in turn breaks security of the constructed primitive). By definition, if $\mathcal{A}$ breaks the primitive with probability 1, then $\mathcal{R}^{\mathcal{A}}$ should break C with non-negligible probability, even if we construct $\mathcal{A}$ to be inefficient (e.g., win by brute force).

It remains then to show that, if such an $\mathcal{R}$ exists, then C can be broken *efficiently*, contradicting the assumption of C's security. While $\mathcal{R}^{\mathcal{A}}$ itself clearly will not break C efficiently if $\mathcal{A}$ uses brute force, one can instead create an efficient *meta-reduction* $\mathcal{B}$ that efficiently "emulates" $\mathcal{A}$ while running $\mathcal{R}$. If one can show that the meta-reduction $\mathcal{B}$ always succeeds in emulating the real interaction $\mathcal{R}^{\mathcal{A}}$, then the meta-reduction breaks C with non-negligible probability.

On the other hand, it might be impossible to create a meta-reduction that emulates $\mathcal{R}^{\mathcal{A}}$ perfectly; instead, it might be the case that we can construct $\mathcal{B}$ that emulates $\mathcal{R}^{\mathcal{A}}$ with probability at least $1 - p(n)$ for some inverse polynomial $p(\cdot)$. In this case, if $\mathcal{R}^{\mathcal{A}}$ breaks C with probability non-negligibly greater than $p(n)$, then $\mathcal{B}$, being identically distributed to $\mathcal{R}^{\mathcal{A}}$ except with probability $p(n)$, will in fact still break C with non-negligible probability, thus ruling out any such $\mathcal{R}$. By bounding $\mathcal{R}$'s success probability in terms of its running time, this observation

---

[2] Consider C to be the "challenger" for the security game; an efficient adversary "breaks" C by forcing it to output Accept with probability non-negligibly better than a certain threshold t.

can be used to derive a *security loss bound* for any reduction $\mathcal{R}$ in cases where such reductions may not be fully impossible.

Rewinding Techniques. Of course, a useful meta-reduction requires two important constructions: (1) the ideal and inefficient adversary $\mathcal{A}$, and (2) the meta-reduction $\mathcal{B}$. Most importantly, while it would be simple to construct an adversary $\mathcal{A}$ that breaks $\mathcal{C}$ by brute force, $\mathcal{B}$ must also be able to gain enough information by simulating and receiving responses to $\mathcal{A}$'s messages in order to determine, with high probability, the secret information necessary to break $\mathcal{C}$ without brute force.

Coron's original meta-reduction presents an effective way of accomplishing this in the setting where $\mathcal{A}$ breaks the unforgeability of unique signatures, or, more generally, any "one-more" style security game where an adversary, after making some number of queries, must then guess the result of querying a new input. Specifically, if we assume $\mathcal{A}$ makes a significant number of queries $\ell(n)$ with inputs $x_1, \ldots, x_{\ell(n)}$ before brute-forcing its guess (and, importantly, will return $\perp$ instead if the answers to its queries are incorrect), $\mathcal{B}$ can make the same set of queries and, rather than brute-forcing a guess, may instead pick the new input x^* and *rewind* the reduction $\mathcal{R}$ up to $\ell(n)$ different times[3], each time replacing a different one of the messages with x^* in the hopes that $\mathcal{R}$ will provide a valid response that $\mathcal{B}$ can use in the main execution.

This rewinding technique in fact can be shown to emulate $\mathcal{A}$ except with probability $O(1/\ell(n))$; intuitively, this is because, if $\mathcal{B}$ is *unable* to extract a correct response in some rewinding, that rewinding corresponds to a sequence of randomness where, if it occurs in the non-rewound execution, $\mathcal{A}$ receives an incorrect response to one of its queries and hence does not need to return a forgery. Hence, at a very high level, for each sequence of messages $x_1, \ldots, x_{\ell(n)}$ where $\mathcal{B}$ fails to extract a forgery, $\mathcal{B}$ must receive an incorrect response to x^* in each of the $\ell(n)$ rewindings, and so there are $\ell(n)$ sequences where $\mathcal{B}$ can successfully emulate $\mathcal{A}$ (as both can return $\perp$).

It is important to note where *uniqueness* of the signature scheme comes in: to ensure that $\mathcal{B}$ is correctly simulating the *distribution* of $\mathcal{A}$'s messages, we need to make sure that the forgery extracted by $\mathcal{B}$ from $\mathcal{R}$ is the same as the forgery that $\mathcal{A}$ would have generated. In the case of a unique signature, we know there can only be a single valid forgery; as such, $\mathcal{B}$ indeed generates the right distribution if it manages to extract a forgery from $\mathcal{R}$.

The Case of Adaptive Multi-user Unforgeability. Coron's meta-reduction was tailored to the specific case of unique signatures; however, in our case, adaptive multi-user unforgeability—that is, the security of a MAC—can also be thought of as a type of "one-more" assumption. Specifically, an adversary against ℓ instances of a MAC can make $\ell - 1$ key-opening queries and subsequently guess the last key in order to break the security of the respective unopened instance (i.e., by guessing the MAC on an unqueried input); a natural approach to creating

---

[3] In fact, in Coron's theorem, it was sufficient to pick a random *one* of these rewindings, but this is not sufficient for our result.

a meta-reduction for this case, then, would be to have $\mathcal{B}$ rewind these key-opening queries and try opening the final instance in the rewindings, similar to Coron's treatment of queries for unique signatures. However, there are several complications with this approach that, for various reasons, did not need to be considered in [16]; we next present a high-level overview of these issues and how we approach them in this work.

"Effective" Key Uniqueness. First, recall that $\mathcal{R}$ does not necessarily need to act as an honest challenger, and so $\mathcal{B}$ must have a way to verify that $\mathcal{R}$'s responses to its queries (in this case, key-opening queries) are correct. As mentioned above, this is why Coron's results (and those following) only applied to *unique* signatures, and why, for the case of adaptive multi-user security, [30] considered only schemes with a key uniqueness property.

We do not want to require any sort of inherent "key uniqueness" for the class of MACs we rule out; hence, we instead move to considering a more elaborate "ideal" adversary $\mathcal{A}$. In particular, we let $\mathcal{A}$ first make a large number of random tag queries to each instance of the MAC; then, upon receiving a response to a key-opening query, $\mathcal{A}$ will verify that all of the responses to the tag queries are consistent with the returned key. Towards analyzing this technique, we present an information-theoretic lemma showing that if the number of queries $q(n)$ is sufficiently larger than the length of the key n, then, with high probability, any pair of keys that are consistent with one another on the $q(n)$ tag queries is such that the keys will also agree on another random input (i.e., the input for which we produce the forgery to break security of the MAC).

In essence, then, our approach makes keys "effectively" unique in the sense that, with high probability, they operate indistinguishably on random inputs with respect to our particular ideal adversary $\mathcal{A}$. As far as we know, this stands in contrast to all prior impossibility results following the meta-reduction paradigm, which explicitly worked only with primitives where the adversary's responses to the queries to be rewound are unique or "distributionally unique" (i.e., rerandomizable).

Reductions with Concurrency and Rewinding. Furthermore, Coron's result in [16], as well as many subsequent security loss bounds proven using meta-reductions (e.g., [4,30,31]) only apply to *restricted* reductions that are *"straight-line"* in the sense that $\mathcal{R}$ will never attempt to rewind $\mathcal{A}$ and $\mathcal{R}$ will always finish executing a single instance of $\mathcal{A}$ before starting another one. In general, reductions may run multiple instances of the adversary concurrently, which can be highly problematic for rewinding-based meta-reductions, as $\mathcal{B}$ may have to rewind a "nested" instance of its adversary to produce a correctly-distributed output while already in the middle of rewinding another instance. If many instances need to be rewound concurrently, the running time of $\mathcal{B}$ can potentially be super-polynomial, which fails to uphold the requirement that $\mathcal{B}$ break $\mathcal{C}$ efficiently.

Luckily, some recent works have presented meta-reductions that deal with concurrent interactions, primarily by using techniques from concurrent zero-knowledge (see [35,38]). We build on the technique established in the generalization of Coron's bound given in [35], which shows that $\mathcal{B}$ can safely ignore any rewindings which would require any sort of nested rewinding. At a high level, if $\mathcal{R}$ runs few instances of $\mathcal{A}$, then other instances rarely interfere with rewinding during $\mathcal{B}$, resulting in virtually no change to the failure probability; on the other hand, if $\mathcal{R}$ runs many instances, then the time taken by $\mathcal{R}$ compared to $\mathcal{A}$ will be the dominant factor in the security loss, so the increase in failure probability caused by potentially having many ignored rewindings has very limited relevance in the analysis.

This approach nonetheless requires non-trivial modification to work in our case, due to the additional caveat that $\mathcal{R}$ may attempt to rewind instances of $\mathcal{A}$. While [35] relied on a "rewinding-proof" construction of $\mathcal{A}$ and $\mathcal{B}$ where the randomness was determined at the start, so that the uniqueness property would guarantee only a single possible accepting transcript (thus making rewinding pointless), recall that we no longer have a guaranteed uniqueness property, but instead one that holds "most of the time". Furthermore, we can no longer construct $\mathcal{A}$ to be fully resilient to rewinding, due to the additional complexity of having both tag queries and key-opening queries; instead, we construct $\mathcal{A}$ to be resilient to *most* rewinding—particularly, all rewinding except from the key-opening query phase to the tag query phase—and prove our bound in terms of how often "meaningful" rewinding (i.e., rewinding that does affect the result) can occur in addition to the number of instances of $\mathcal{A}$.

This requires some additional care, however: while $\mathcal{A}$ can easily be made rewinding-proof (with the exception of the "meaningful" rewinding), we in fact can only show that $\mathcal{B}$ is resilient to rewinding as long as key uniqueness holds; otherwise, while $\mathcal{A}$ can always pick a determinstic one of the brute-forced keys for a forgery, $\mathcal{B}$ cannot necessarily do this efficiently just from the responses to rewound queries, and so $\mathcal{R}$ could theoretically rewind $\mathcal{B}$ to try and get multiple different forgeries to correspond to multiple different keys. We thus require a hybrid argument with an unconditionally rewinding-proof but inefficient hybrid $\mathcal{B}'$ (which acts identically to $\mathcal{B}$ when uniqueness holds and to $\mathcal{A}$ when it does not) for the majority of our analysis, subsequently showing that $\mathcal{B}'$ is identically distributed to $\mathcal{B}$ except in the rare case when uniqueness fails.

Interactive Assumptions. Lastly, many of the preceding works were restricted to ruling out reductions to *non-interactive*, or two-round, assumptions, since $\mathcal{B}$ rewinding the reduction $\mathcal{R}$ might require additional, or different, queries to be made to the challenger $\mathcal{C}$ for the underlying assumption, which cannot be rewound and whose output may be dependent on the number, order, or content of queries made. However, as demonstrated in earlier rewinding-based meta-reductions such as [35,38], we may once again safely ignore rewindings that contain such external communication as long as the number of rounds of external communication is bounded by some polynomial $r(\cdot)$ in the security parameter— that is, as long as the underlying assumption is a *bounded-round* assumption.

2   Preliminaries and Definitions

We note that the definitions we provide in Sects. 2.2 through 2.4 are adapted from [35].

2.1   Multi-user Secure MACs Under Adaptive Corruption

First, we define the notion of a *message authentication code*.

Definition 1. *We refer to a tuple of efficient (poly(n)-time) algorithms $\Pi =$ (Gen, Tag, Ver), where:*

- *Gen$(1^n) \to k$ takes as input a security parameter n and outputs a secret key $k \in \{0,1\}^n$,*
- *Tag$_k(m) \to \sigma$ takes as input a secret key k and a message m from some message space $\mathcal{M}_n$ of size super-polynomial in n, and outputs a tag σ for the message, and*
- *Ver$_k(m, \sigma) \to$ {Accept, Reject} takes as input a secret key k, a message m, and a tag σ, and outputs Accept or Reject denoting whether the tag σ is valid for the message m, specifically in such a manner that $\Pr[k \leftarrow$ Gen(1^n); Ver$_k(m, Tag_k(m)) \to$ Accept$] = 1$ for any valid message $m \in \mathcal{M}_n$,*

*as a **message authentication code** (MAC). If, in addition, the following hold:*

- *Tag$_k(m)$ is a deterministic function, and*
- *Ver$_k(m, \sigma) \to$ Accept if and only if Tag$_k(m) = \sigma$,*

*then we refer to Π as a **deterministic MAC**.*

Note that we focus here on MACs having both an input (message) and output (tag) space superpolynomial in the length of a key (the security parameter n), a property which is satisfied by virtually all standard definitions and constructions.

The traditional notion of security for a MAC states that, given some instance of a MAC (i.e., a secret key $k \leftarrow$ Gen(1^n)), an efficient adversary given an oracle for the Tag algorithm is unable to forge a valid tag for a new message (i.e., return a pair (m, σ) where Ver$_k(m, \sigma) \to$ Accept) without having queried a tag for that message using the oracle. Our definition of multi-user security with adaptive corruption expands this to a polynomial number $\ell(n)$ of instances of the MAC, and allows the adversary to make *key-opening* queries (i.e., to "corrupt" an instance and recover its key) in addition to tag queries; the adversary wins if they produce a valid forgery (m, σ) for some instance without having either queried the tag for m on that instance or corrupted the instance itself. Formally:

Definition 2. *A MAC $\Pi =$ (Gen, Tag, Ver) is an $\ell(n)$-**key unforgeable MAC under adaptive corruption** (or **adaptively $\ell(n)$-key unforgeable**) if, for any interactive oracle-aided non-uniform probabilistic polynomial-time algorithm $\mathcal{A}$, there is a negligible function $\epsilon(\cdot)$ such that, for all $n \in \mathbb{N}$,*

$$Pr\left[\langle \mathcal{A}, \mathcal{C}_\Pi^{\ell(n)} \rangle (1^n) = \text{Accept}\right] \leq \epsilon(n)$$

where $C_\Pi^{\ell(n)}$ *is the interactive challenger that does as follows on input* 1^n:

- *Let* $(k_1, \ldots, k_{\ell(n)}) \leftarrow \mathsf{Gen}(1^n)$. *Initialize empty transcript* τ.
- *Upon receiving a tag query* (Query, i, m) *for* $i \in [\ell(n)]$, *append* $((\mathsf{Query}, i, m), \mathsf{Tag}_{k_i}(m))$ *to* τ *and send* τ.
- *Upon receiving a* key-opening *query* (Open, i) *for* $i \in [\ell(n)]$, *append the tuple* $((\mathsf{Open}, i), k_i)$ *to* τ *and send* τ.
- *Upon receiving a forgery* (m^*, σ^*, i^*) *from* $\mathcal{A}$, *output* Reject *if one of the following three conditions is true:*
  - τ *contains a key opening query* (Open, i^*).
  - τ *contains an oracle query* $(\mathsf{Query}, i^*, m^*)$.
  - $\mathsf{Ver}_{k_{i^*}}(m^*, \sigma^*) \to$ Reject.
- *Otherwise, output* Accept.

We call a MAC Π an **adaptively multi-key unforgeable MAC** *if it is adaptively* $\ell(n)$-*key unforgeable for every polynomial* $\ell(\cdot)$.

For syntactic clarity, we will assume that a machine interacting with a multi-key MAC adversary will begin interaction with a new instance of the adversary by sending a special message (Init, s), where s is the "identifier" for the instance, and communicate with the adversary by sending a partial transcript and receiving a next message as described above for oracle interaction.

2.2 Intractability Assumptions

We define a notion of "game-based security assumptions" as in [37,38]. Informally, an assumption can be thought of as a pair of a challenger and a threshold function, where an adversary is able to "break" the assumption by causing the challenger to accept an interaction with probability non-negligibly greater than the given threshold.

Definition 3. *For polynomial* $r(\cdot)$, *we call a pair* $(\mathcal{C}, t(\cdot))$ *an* $r(\cdot)$-**round intractability assumption** *if* $t(\cdot) \in [0, 1]$ *is a function and* $\mathcal{C}$ *is a (possibly randomized) interactive algorithm taking input* 1^n *and outputting either* Accept *or* Reject *after at most* $r(n)$ *rounds of external communication.*

Given a probabilistic interactive algorithm $\mathcal{A}$ *which interacts with* $\mathcal{C}$, *we say that* $\mathcal{A}$ **breaks** *the assumption* $(\mathcal{C}, t(\cdot))$ *with some non-negligible probability* $p(\cdot)$ *if, for infinitely many* $n \in \mathbb{N}$: $Pr[\langle \mathcal{A}, \mathcal{C} \rangle(1^n) = \mathsf{Accept}] \geq t(n) + p(n)$.

Conversely, we refer to $\mathcal{C}$ *as* **secure** *if there exists no* $\mathcal{A}$ *which breaks* $\mathcal{C}$ *with non-negligible probability.*

Lastly, we call an assumption $(\mathcal{C}, t(\cdot))$ *a* **bounded-round intractability assumption** *if there exists some polynomial* $r(\cdot)$ *such that* $(\mathcal{C}, t(\cdot))$ *is an* $r(\cdot)$-*round intractability assumption.*

The general notion of an intractability assumption captures any standard cryptographic assumption, including our earlier definition of adaptive multi-key unforgeability. Specifically, this would be the *unbounded-round* assumption

$(\mathcal{C}_\Pi^{\ell(n)}, 0)$ (using the challenger defined in Definition 2). Clearly, we cannot hope to rule out tight reductions from, say, adaptive multi-key unforgeability to itself; as such, we focus on ruling out only reductions to bounded-round assumptions, but we note that virtually all "standard" cryptographic assumptions fall into this category.[4]

2.3 Black-Box Reductions

We next formalize what it means to "base the security of one assumption $(\mathcal{C}_1)$ on another assumption $(\mathcal{C}_2)$". Intuitively, this requires a proof that, if there exists an adversary breaking $\mathcal{C}_1$, then there likewise must exist an adversary breaking $\mathcal{C}_2$, which implies the desired result by contrapositive.

In practice, virtually all reductions are "black-box" reductions, where the adversary breaking $\mathcal{C}_2$ is given by an efficient oracle-aided machine $\mathcal{R}$ which interacts in a "black-box" manner with an adversary which breaks $\mathcal{C}_1$ and uses the view of the interaction to break $\mathcal{C}_2$. Formally:

Definition 4. *Given a probabilistic polynomial-time oracle-aided algorithm $\mathcal{R}$, we say that $\mathcal{R}$ is a **black-box reduction for basing the hardness of assumption** $(\mathcal{C}_1, t_1(\cdot))$ **on that of** $(\mathcal{C}_2, t_2(\cdot))$ if, given any deterministic algorithm $\mathcal{A}$ that breaks $(\mathcal{C}_1, t_1(\cdot))$ with non-negligible probability $p_1(\cdot)$, $\mathcal{R}^{\mathcal{A}}$ breaks $(\mathcal{C}_2, t_2(\cdot))$ with non-negligible probability $p_2(\cdot)$.*

*Furthermore, if on common input 1^n $\mathcal{R}^{\mathcal{A}}$ queries $\mathcal{A}$ only on input 1^n, we refer to $\mathcal{R}$ as **fixed-parameter**.*

We notably allow reductions to rewind their oracles (by sending a transcript from earlier in the interaction) and even run multiple, potentially interleaved, instances of their oracle.

The restriction to deterministic oracles $\mathcal{A}$ may seem strange at first, but we stress that we can (and will) in fact simply model a randomized oracle by a family of deterministic oracles (where each deterministic oracle represents some fixed setting of the randomness). Using deterministic oracles enables us to reason about cases where the reduction $\mathcal{R}$ can rewind or restart the oracle. We also will restrict to fixed-parameter reductions: this is a restriction inherent to the meta-reduction paradigm, yet it is a natural one (since, as far as we know, all reductions in practice are indeed fixed-parameter).

Of course, we can apply the definition of a reduction to adaptive unforgeability as defined above, using the natural formulation as an intractability assumption:

Definition 5. *We shall refer to a probabilistic polynomial-time oracle-aided algorithm $\mathcal{R}$ as a **fixed-parameter black-box reduction for basing adaptive $\ell(n)$-key unforgeability of a MAC Π on the hardness of an assumption***

---

[4] An example of a "non-standard" assumption that does not fit this definition would be a non-falsifiable assumption, e.g., a "knowledge of exponent" assumption (see, e.g., [17]).

$(\mathcal{C}, t(\cdot))$ *if it is a fixed-parameter black-box reduction for basing the hardness of assumption* $(\mathcal{C}_{\Pi}^{\ell(n)}, 0)$ *on that of* $(\mathcal{C}, t(\cdot))$, *where* $\mathcal{C}_{\Pi}^{\ell(n)}$ *is as given in Definition 2.*

We refer to a probabilistic polynomial-time oracle-aided algorithm $\mathcal{R}$ as a **fixed-parameter black-box reduction for basing adaptively secure unforgeability of a MAC Π on the hardness of an assumption** $(\mathcal{C}, t(\cdot))$ *if there exists polynomial* $\ell(\cdot)$ *for which* $\mathcal{R}$ *is a fixed-parameter black-box reduction for basing adaptively secure* $\ell(n)$-*key unforgeability of* Π *on the hardness of* $(\mathcal{C}, t(\cdot))$.

2.4   Security Loss

Finally, we define a notion of the "inherent efficiency" of a reduction, or the *security loss*, intuitively representing a worst-case ratio between the "work" (expected time) needed to break the assumption $\mathcal{C}_2$ (i.e., the underlying assumption) and the "primitive" $\mathcal{C}_1$ (in our case, adaptive multi-key unforgeability). If the primitive is significantly easier to break than the underlying assumption, this indicates that the reduction is intuitively "less powerful" at guaranteeing security for the primitive, which corresponds to a higher security loss.

Definition 6. *Let* $\mathcal{R}$ *be a black-box reduction for basing the hardness of assumption* $(\mathcal{C}_1, t_1(\cdot))$ *on that of* $(\mathcal{C}_2, t_2(\cdot))$. *Given any deterministic* $\mathcal{A}$, *we define the following, where* $\tau_{\mathcal{M}}(x)$ *denotes the time taken by an algorithm* $\mathcal{M}$ *in experiment* x, $r_{\mathcal{A}}$ *denotes all random coins used by* $\mathcal{A}$ *and* $\mathcal{C}_1$ *in the experiment* $\langle \mathcal{A}, \mathcal{C}_1 \rangle$, *and* $r_{\mathcal{R}}$ *denotes all random coins used by* $\mathcal{A}$, $\mathcal{C}_2$, *and* $\mathcal{R}$ *in the experiment* $\langle \mathcal{R}^{\mathcal{A}}, \mathcal{C}_2 \rangle$:

- $\mathsf{Success}_{\mathcal{A}}(n) = \Pr_{r_{\mathcal{A}}}[\langle \mathcal{A}, \mathcal{C}_1 \rangle_{r_{\mathcal{A}}}(1^n) = \mathsf{Accept}] - t_1(n)$
- $\mathsf{Success}_{\mathcal{R}^{\mathcal{A}}}(n) = \Pr_{r_{\mathcal{R}}}[\langle \mathcal{R}^{\mathcal{A}}, \mathcal{C}_2 \rangle_{r_{\mathcal{R}}}(1^n) = \mathsf{Accept}] - t_2(n)$
- $\mathsf{Time}_{\mathcal{A}}(n) = max_{r_{\mathcal{A}}}(\tau_{\mathcal{A}}([\mathcal{A} \leftrightarrow \mathcal{C}_1]_{r_{\mathcal{A}}}(1^n)))$
- $\mathsf{Time}_{\mathcal{R}^{\mathcal{A}}}(n) = max_{r_{\mathcal{R}}}(\tau_{\mathcal{R}^{\mathcal{A}}}([\mathcal{R}^{\mathcal{A}} \leftrightarrow \mathcal{C}_2]_{r_{\mathcal{R}}}(1^n)))$.

*Then the **security loss** [32] of* $\mathcal{R}$ *is defined as:*

$$\lambda_{\mathcal{R}}(n) = max_{\mathcal{A}} \left(\frac{\mathsf{Success}_{\mathcal{A}}(n)}{\mathsf{Success}_{\mathcal{R}^{\mathcal{A}}}(n)} \frac{\mathsf{Time}_{\mathcal{R}^{\mathcal{A}}}(n)}{\mathsf{Time}_{\mathcal{A}}(n)} \right)$$

If there exists polynomial $p(\cdot)$ *for which* $\lambda_{\mathcal{R}}(n) \le p(n)$ *given sufficiently large* $n \in \mathbb{N}$, *we call* $\mathcal{R}$ **linear-preserving**. *If there exists a constant* c *for which* $\lambda_{\mathcal{R}}(n) \le c$ *given sufficiently large* $n \in \mathbb{N}$, *we call* $\mathcal{R}$ **tight**.

3   Main Theorem

We present our main result, which rules out the possibility of basing the provable security of a deterministic MAC on any "standard" (bounded-round) assumption with a linear-preserving reduction:

Theorem 2. *Let* Π *be a deterministic MAC. If there exists a fixed-parameter black-box reduction* $\mathcal{R}$ *for basing adaptive multi-key unforgeability of* Π *on some* $r(\cdot)$-*round intractability assumption* $(\mathcal{C}, t(\cdot))$ *(for polynomial* $r(\cdot)$), *then either:*

(1) $\mathcal{R}$ is not a linear-preserving reduction, or
(2) there exists a polynomial-time adversary $\mathcal{B}$ breaking the assumption $(\mathcal{C}, t(\cdot))$.

As we mentioned in the introduction, Theorem 2 can be generalized fairly directly to apply as written to several other primitives besides simply deterministic MACs; however, as we focus on the case of MACs in this paper, we present our result for deterministic MACs in full here and opt to refer the interested reader to the full version of our paper for detailed discussion of its applications to other primitives. Specifically, in the full version, we show that we can rule out linear-preserving reductions from adaptively multi-key unforgeable deterministic *digital signature schemes* to bounded-round assumptions, and that we can rule out linear-preserving reductions from adaptive multi-key *pseudorandomness* of a family of functions (i.e., adaptive multi-key PRFs) to bounded-round assumptions.

To prove Theorem 2, we first present the following crucial lemma, which we prove in full in Sect. 4:

Lemma 1. *Let Π be a deterministic MAC, and let $(\mathcal{C}, t(\cdot))$ be some $r(\cdot)$ -round intractability assumption for polynomial $r(\cdot)$. If for some polynomial $\ell(\cdot)$ there exists a fixed-parameter black-box reduction $\mathcal{R}$ for basing adaptive $\ell(n)$ -key unforgeability of Π on the hardness of $(\mathcal{C}, t(\cdot))$, then either $\mathcal{R}$'s security loss is at least*

$$\lambda_{\mathcal{R}}(n) \geq \left(1 - \frac{1}{2\ell(n)^2}\right)\left(\sqrt{\ell(n)} - (r(n) + 2)\right)$$

for all sufficiently large $n \in \mathbb{N}$, or there exists a polynomial-time adversary $\mathcal{B}$ that breaks the assumption $(\mathcal{C}, t(\cdot))$.

Because $p(\cdot)$ in the definition of a linear-preserving reduction is an *a priori* fixed polynomial, and in particular cannot depend on $\ell(n)$, this lemma will prove Theorem 2, as follows:

Proof. Let $\mathcal{R}$ be a reduction from adaptive multi-key unforgeability of Π to the hardness of $(\mathcal{C}, t(\cdot))$. Assume for the sake of contradiction that Lemma 1 is true, yet $\mathcal{R}$ is linear-preserving and $(\mathcal{C}, t(\cdot))$ is secure. Because $\mathcal{R}$ is linear-preserving, there is some polynomial $p(\cdot)$ such that $\lambda_{\mathcal{R}}(n) \leq p(n)$ for sufficiently large n . Furthermore, $\mathcal{R}$ is by definition a reduction from adaptive $\ell(n)$ -key unforgeability for *every* polynomial $\ell(n)$, including, say, $\ell(n) = (2p(n) + r(n) + 3)^2$, so by Lemma 1 we have:

$$\lambda_{\mathcal{R}}(n) \geq \left(1 - \frac{1}{2\ell(n)^2}\right)\left(\sqrt{\ell(n)} - (r(n) + 2)\right) \geq \frac{1}{2}(2p(n) + 1) > p(n)$$

which is a clear contradiction. $\square$

3.1   Technical Overview

Next, we shall explain the methodology for the proof of Lemma 1 at a high level.

The Ideal Adversary. We begin by constructing and investigating an "ideal" adversary $\mathcal{A}$. To summarize, $\mathcal{A}$ will first make $q(n)$ random tag queries (where $q(n)$ is a polynomial to be determined later) to each of the $\ell(n)$ instances of the MAC Π, continue by opening all but one of the keys in a random order (while also verifying that the challenger or $\mathcal{R}$ answered its queries consistently with the opened keys), and lastly, if it received correct responses for the opened instances, use the information gained from the queries for the remaining instance to attempt to brute-force a forgery for that instance. (On the other hand, if verification fails, $\mathcal{A}$ will "reject", returning $\perp$ instead of a forgery.)

In virtually all meta-reductions to date, the ideal adversary is able to perfectly brute-force the challenger's secret information and break the primitive with probability 1. Here, however, that is not the case; $\mathcal{A}$ is limited to a polynomial number of tag queries (which is necessary for simulatability) and furthermore has no way to publicly verify whether a certain key or forgery is correct. The most $\mathcal{A}$ can do, in fact, is brute-force the set of all keys consistent with the tag queries it makes for the unopened instance, pick one of those keys, and use it to generate a forgery in the hopes that it will match with the key the challenger has selected.

This is where the "key uniqueness" property discussed in the introduction will first factor in. We show that, since the key picked by the adversary agrees with the key picked by the challenger on all $q(n)$ tag queries, then it must with overwhelming probability also agree on a large fraction $(1 - 2n/q(n))$ of possible messages. Hence, $\mathcal{A}$ will have a $1 - 2n/q(n)$ chance of producing a correct forgery when it evaluates the Tag function using the key it extracts on a random message m^* (i.e., the message it eventually will randomly select for its forgery)—that is, $\mathsf{Success}_{\mathcal{A}}(n) \geq 1 - 2n/q(n)$.

Before proceeding to discuss the meta-reduction, we need to address one final technical issue with the ideal adversary. Namely, since $\mathcal{A}$ works by returning the "next-message" function given a transcript of the interaction thus far, we need to ensure that $\mathcal{R}$ must actually complete the full interaction with $\mathcal{A}$ in order to cause $\mathcal{A}$ to accept and return a forgery, rather than potentially guessing a "fake" accepting transcript for a later point in the interaction to "skip" or avoid responding to certain queries from $\mathcal{A}$. In particular, a reduction $\mathcal{R}$ that skips key-opening queries would be extremely problematic in our analysis of the meta-reduction later on, since the meta-reduction will rely on $\mathcal{R}$'s responses to these queries to properly emulate the ideal adversary $\mathcal{A}$.

Unfortunately, it turns out that $\mathcal{A}$'s key-opening queries, since they convey no information besides the instance to open, have low entropy and thus are easy to predict (and skip) by $\mathcal{R}$. To fix this, we introduce additional "dummy" queries—specifically, random tag queries to instances whose keys have not yet been opened—made after each of the key-opening queries. These serve the purpose of increasing the entropy present in the key-opening phase of the transcript—which guarantees that $\mathcal{R}$ must answer all $\ell(n) - 1$ of $\mathcal{A}$'s key-opening queries to successfully complete the interaction (unless it can correctly guess the random input for the dummy query)—but are otherwise ignored.

The Meta-reduction. In our discussion of $\mathcal{A}$, we were able to bound $\mathsf{Success}_{\mathcal{A}}(n)$; thus, we turn next to investigating $\mathsf{Success}_{\mathcal{R}^{\mathcal{A}}}(n)$. To do this, we construct a *meta-reduction* $\mathcal{B}$ which runs $\mathcal{R}$ while attempting to efficiently emulate the interaction between $\mathcal{R}$ and $\mathcal{A}$. $\mathcal{B}$ will simulate instances of $\mathcal{A}$ by, exactly as before, making $q(n)$ random tag queries to each instance, opening the key for all but one instance (in a random order and with the interleaved tag queries as above), and checking $\mathcal{R}$'s responses for consistency.

The key difference, of course, is that $\mathcal{B}$ cannot brute-force a forgery; instead, for the unopened instance, $\mathcal{B}$ will attempt to extract a correct key from $\mathcal{R}$ by rewinding the interaction to the key-opening queries and substituting the unopened instance for each other instance in turn. If $\mathcal{R}$ responds to any of the valid queries with a key that matches with the tag queries for that instance, then $\mathcal{B}$ will apply that key to a random message m^* to generate a forgery. If $\mathcal{B}$ does not receive a valid key in this fashion, then it will abort, returning Fail.

Notably, $\mathcal{B}$ will also have to ignore rewindings where, before returning its response to the key-opening query, either $\mathcal{R}$ attempts to communicate externally with $\mathcal{C}$ (which could change the state of the challenger if forwarded), $\mathcal{R}$ requests a forgery from another instance of $\mathcal{A}$ (as this would require additional "nested" rewinding which could grow exponentially), or $\mathcal{R}$ would rewind $\mathcal{A}$ (which precludes $\mathcal{R}$ returning a key); this will factor into the analysis of the failure probability later.

The main task in proving our lemma, then, reduces to that of bounding $\Pr[\langle \mathcal{R}^{\mathcal{A}}, \mathcal{C} \rangle \to \mathsf{Accept}] - \Pr[\langle \mathcal{B}, \mathcal{C} \rangle \to \mathsf{Accept}]$. Intuitively, if we come up with such a bound (call it $p(n)$), then, if $\mathsf{Success}_{\mathcal{R}^{\mathcal{A}}}$ is non-negligibly higher than $p(n)$—that is, $\langle \mathcal{R}^{\mathcal{A}}, \mathcal{C} \rangle$ accepts with such a probability—then $\langle \mathcal{B}, \mathcal{C} \rangle$ will accept with non-negligible probability, hence breaking $\mathcal{C}$. Bounding this probability $p(n)$ is in fact quite non-trivial, as one cannot, say, naïvely apply earlier techniques for meta-reduction analysis to the meta-reduction $\mathcal{B}$. Intuitively, this is because we no longer have a strong "uniqueness" property characteristic of meta-reductions to date—that is, there is no longer a *unique* possible valid forgery $\mathcal{B}$ can extract from its rewinding. Not only does this make it difficult to guarantee that $\mathcal{A}$ and $\mathcal{B}$ produce close distributions of forgeries, but, in conjunction with $\mathcal{B}$'s rewinding strategy, this makes analyzing the failure probability problematic for more complex reasons. For example, consider a reduction $\mathcal{R}$ which might try to rewind $\mathcal{A}$ and change its responses to queries in order to attempt to change the forgery generated; it is straightforward to see that proof techniques such as that of [35] immediately fail (due to a potentially unbounded number of nested forgery requests) if $\mathcal{R}$ can theoretically expect to receive many different forgeries by repeatedly rewinding the same instance.

A "Hybrid" Meta-reduction. We present a way to effectively separate dealing with the issues of uniqueness and rewinding, namely by defining a "hybrid" meta-reduction $\mathcal{B}'$ which, while inefficient, is easy to compare to either $\mathcal{A}$ or $\mathcal{B}$.

At a high level, we construct $\mathcal{B}'$ so that it behaves identically to $\mathcal{B}$ as long as there is only a single possible forgery to return, and so that it behaves identically to $\mathcal{A}$ whenever rewinding succeeds. More specifically, it acts identically to $\mathcal{B}$ until after rewinding finishes, then, if it obtains a forgery, brute-forces one in the same manner as $\mathcal{A}$. Clearly, $\mathcal{B}'$ can only diverge from $\mathcal{B}$ if the forgery $\mathcal{B}$ extracts is different from the one $\mathcal{B}'$ brute-forces. A straightforward application of our earlier "key uniqueness" lemma shows that this happens with at most $2n/q(n)$ probability per forgery returned by $\mathcal{B}'$.

On the other hand, $\mathcal{B}'$ will always return the same forgery as $\mathcal{A}$ *if* it returns a forgery, but we still need to determine the probability with which $\mathcal{B}'$ fails to return a forgery due to unsuccessful rewinding. Luckily, since $\mathcal{B}'$ now *does* have the uniqueness property, we can proceed along the same lines as in [35] and bound the rewinding failure probability by effectively bounding the probability that a randomly chosen ordering of key-opening queries can result in rewinding failure (while assuming that the rest of the randomness in the interaction is fixed arbitrarily, as, if the bound applies to arbitrarily fixed randomness, it must likewise apply when taken over all possible assignments of the same randomness).

The intuition behind the argument is that, if we assume a bound of $W(n)$ on the number of times $\mathcal{R}$ will rewind past when $\mathcal{B}'$ generates the ordering π of the key-opening queries (and note that, due to uniqueness and careful construction, $W(n)$ will also be a bound on the number of distinct forgery requests $\mathcal{R}$ can make, as we show that any others will be internally simulatable and thus "pointless"), every sequence π that causes $\mathcal{B}'$ to fail must do so because all of its rewindings fail, and the rewindings specifically correspond to other sequences π that can occur. Furthermore, if a rewinding fails due to $\mathcal{R}$ responding to a query incorrectly (as opposed to, e.g., external communication or a nested forgery request), then this rewinding corresponds to a "good" sequence where $\mathcal{A}$ and $\mathcal{B}'$ return $\perp$ (and emulation is successful). So, if some sequence π contains more than $W(n) + r(n) + 1$ queries at which rewindings of other sequences fail, then, since we can have at most $W(n)$ (unique) forgery requests and $r(n)$ rounds of external communication, at least one query must fail due to an incorrect response, which shows that π is a "good" sequence. A counting argument then allows us to achieve a bound of $(W(n) + r(n) + 1)/\ell(n)$ on the failure probability of $\mathcal{B}'$ each time it performs rewinding, or $W(n)(W(n) + r(n) + 1)/\ell(n)$ overall failure probability.

Bounding Security Loss. Combining all of the facts so far, we know that the above quantity is equivalent to the probability with which $\mathcal{A}$ and $\mathcal{B}'$ diverge, while the probability with which $\mathcal{B}'$ and $\mathcal{B}$ diverge is $2nW(n)/q(n)$ (i.e., the probability that uniqueness fails for at least one of the $W(n)$ forgeries). Thus, $\mathsf{Success}_{\mathcal{R}^{\mathcal{A}}}(n)$, as we have argued, is bounded above by the sum of these, which (taking $q(n)$ sufficiently large) is at most $W(n)(W(n) + r(n) + 2)/\ell(n)$. Furthermore, $\mathsf{Time}_{\mathcal{R}^{\mathcal{A}}}(n)/\mathsf{Time}_{\mathcal{A}}(n) \geq W(n)$ by our assumption that in the worst case $\mathcal{R}$ runs $W(n)$ instances of $\mathcal{A}$. Lastly, $\mathsf{Success}_{\mathcal{A}}(n) \geq 1 - 2n/q(n)$ as we noted earlier.

Hence, either $(\mathcal{C}, t(\cdot))$ is insecure (and our bound for $\mathsf{Success}_{\mathcal{R}^{\mathcal{A}}}(n)$ does not apply), or, by the above facts and case analysis (to deal with the possibility that $W(n)$ might be arbitrarily large), we obtain the result:

$$\lambda_{\mathcal{R}}(n) \geq \left(1 - \frac{1}{2\ell(n)^2}\right)\left(\sqrt{\ell(n)} - (r(n) + 2)\right)$$

4   Proof of Lemma 1

We continue by formally proving Lemma 1. Assume a deterministic MAC Π, a reduction $\mathcal{R}$, and an assumption $(\mathcal{C}, t(\cdot))$ as defined in the statement of Lemma 1. Consider an ideal but inefficient adversary $\mathcal{A}$, which technically is given by a random selection from a *family* of inefficient adversaries $\mathcal{A} \leftarrow \{\mathcal{A}^{\mathcal{O}}\}$ (where $\mathcal{O}$ is a uniformly chosen random function) defined as in Figs. 1 and 2; also consider an efficient meta-reduction $\mathcal{B}$ defined as in Figs. 3 and 4.

Before analyzing the properties of $\mathcal{A}$ and $\mathcal{B}$, we verify that $\mathcal{B}$ runs efficiently through the following claim, proven in the full version:

Claim 1. $\mathcal{B}(1^n)$ *runs in time polynomial in* n.

4.1   Analyzing the Ideal Adversary

In order to establish a bound to the security loss $\lambda_{\mathcal{R}}(n)$, we shall determine bounds for $\mathsf{Success}_{\mathcal{A}}(n)$ and $\mathsf{Success}_{\mathcal{R}^{\mathcal{A}}}(n)$; time analysis will follow naturally.

We begin by analyzing the probability $\mathsf{Success}_{\mathcal{A}}(n)$. This is fairly straightforward, following from the critical "key uniqueness" lemma which states that two keys agreeing on all of the $q(n)$ tag queries made by $\mathcal{A}$ are overwhelmingly likely to agree on "most" messages m. Hence, the key chosen by $\mathcal{A}$, even if not the same as that chosen by the challenger, is by definition consistent with it on all of the tag queries and thus should agree on a large fraction of the possible forgery inputs m^*. Formally:

Claim 2. *There exists a negligible function* $\nu(\cdot)$ *such that:*

$$\mathsf{Success}_{\mathcal{A}}(n) \geq 1 - \frac{2n}{q(n)} - \nu(n)$$

Proof. The claim follows readily from the following lemma (and the fact that there is only a negligible chance that $\mathcal{A}$ generates an invalid m^*):

Lemma 2. *There exists negligible* $\nu(\cdot)$ *such that, for any family of functions* $\mathcal{U} = \{f_k : \mathcal{X}_n \to \mathcal{Y}_n\}_{k \in \{0,1\}^n, n \in \mathbb{N}}$, *except with probability* $\nu(n)$ *over* $q(n)$ *uniformly random queries* $(x_{1,j^*}, \ldots, x_{q(n),j^*}) \leftarrow (\mathcal{X}_n)^{q(n)}$, *for any* $k_1, k_2 \in (\{0,1\}^n)^2$ *such that* $f_{k_1}(x_{i,j^*}) = f_{k_2}(x_{i,j^*})$ *for all* $i \in [q(n)]$, *it is true that:*

$$Pr[x^* \leftarrow \mathcal{X}_n : f_{k_1}(x^*) = f_{k_2}(x^*)] \geq 1 - \frac{2n}{q(n)} \tag{1}$$

– On receiving an initialization message (Init, s), let $m_{1,1}$ denote a uniformly random message in $\mathcal{M}_n$ generated by random coins resulting from applying the oracle $\mathcal{O}$ to the input $(s, 1, 1, 1)$, and send $(\mathsf{Query}, 1, m_{1,1})$.
– On receiving a transcript of the form

$$\tau = (q_{1,1}, q_{1,2}, \ldots, q_{1,\ell(n)}, q_{2,1}, \ldots, q_{i,j})$$

where either $i < q(n)$ or $i = q(n)$ and $j < \ell(n)$, such that each $q_{u,v}$ is of the form $((\mathsf{Query}, v, m_{u,v}), \sigma_{u,v})$, do the following:
  • Let $j' = (j \bmod \ell(n)) + 1$.
  • Let $i' = i + 1$ if $j' = 1$ and $i' = i$ otherwise.
  • Let $m_{i',j'}$ be a uniformly random message in $\mathcal{M}_n$ generated by random coins resulting from applying the oracle $\mathcal{O}$ to the input $(s, i', j', 1)$.
  • Return $(\mathsf{Query}, j', m_{i',j'})$.
– On receiving a transcript of the form $\tau = \tau_1 \| \tau_2$, where

$$\tau_1 = (q_{1,1}, q_{1,2}, \ldots, q_{1,\ell(n)}, q_{2,1}, \ldots, q_{q(n),\ell(n)})$$

and where each $q_{u,v}$ is of the form $((\mathsf{Query}, v, m_{u,v}), \sigma_{u,v})$, do the following:
  • Let c be the number of Open queries that have so far appeared in τ_2.
  • Let $\pi = (\pi_1, \ldots, \pi_{\ell(n)})$ be a uniformly random permutation of $[\ell(n)]$, generated by random coins resulting from applying $\mathcal{O}$ to the input τ_1.
  • If τ_2 is empty or ends with messages of the form $((\mathsf{Open}, j), k_j)$, then:
    ∗ Generate ω_{c+1} as a uniformly random message in $\mathcal{M}_n$ generated by random coins resulting from applying the oracle $\mathcal{O}$ to the input $\tau_1 \| (s, q(n) + 1, c + 1, \mathsf{Valid}(\mathcal{O}, \tau^*, s))$ and return $(\mathsf{Query}, q, \omega_{c+1})$, where q is the lexicographically first instance for which τ_2 does not contain an Open query.
  • Otherwise, if $c < \ell(n) - 1$ and the last part of τ_2 contains messages of the form $((\mathsf{Query}, q, \omega_{c+1}), \cdot)$, then return $(\mathsf{Open}, \pi_{c+1})$.
  • Lastly, if τ_2 ends with $((\mathsf{Query}, q, \omega_{\ell(n)}), \cdot)$ and $c = \ell(n) - 1$, return a forgery as follows:
    ∗ If $\mathsf{Valid}(\mathcal{O}, \tau, s) = 0$, return $\perp$.
    ∗ Otherwise, use exhaustive search to find the set K^* of all keys k^* such that, given $j^* = \pi_{\ell(n)}$ as determined above, and for each $i \in [q(n)]$, $\mathsf{Ver}_{k^*}(m_{i,j^*}, \sigma_{i,j^*}) = \mathsf{Accept}$. If K^* is empty then return $\perp$.
    ∗ Lastly, using random coins generated by applying $\mathcal{O}$ to a new input $\tau_1 \| (s, q(n) + 2, 0, 1)$, generate a uniformly random message m^* (which will be distinct from all m_{i,j^*} with all-but-negligible probability) and take the *lexicographically first* element k^* of K^*. Return the forgery $(m^*, \mathsf{Tag}_{k^*}(m^*), j^*)$.

Fig. 1. Formal description of the "ideal" adversary $\mathcal{A}^{\mathcal{O}}$ (1).

Proof. For any key pair (k_1, k_2), let

$$S_{k_1,k_2} \triangleq \{x^* \in \mathcal{X}_n : f_{k_1}(x^*) = f_{k_2}(x^*)\}$$

Let the predicate $\mathsf{Valid}(\mathcal{O}, \tau, s)$ be defined as follows:

- Parse τ as $\tau_1 \| \tau_2$, where

$$\tau_1 = (q_{1,1}, q_{1,2}, \ldots, q_{1,\ell(n)}, q_{2,1}, \ldots, q_{q(n),\ell(n)})$$

such that each $q_{u,v}$ is of the form $((\mathsf{Query}, v, m_{u,v}), \sigma_{u,v})$. If τ cannot be parsed as such, return 0.

- Let $\pi = (\pi_1, \ldots, \pi_{\ell(n)})$ be a permutation of $[\ell(n)]$ generated in the same manner as in $\mathcal{A}$, using random coins generated by applying $\mathcal{O}$ to the input τ_1.

- Parse

$$\tau_2 = (q_1^*, q_2^*, \ldots, q_c^*[, q_{c+1}^*])$$

such that each q_i^* is of the form $((\mathsf{Query}, q_i, \omega_i), \cdot, (\mathsf{Open}, \pi_i), k_{\pi_i})$ and q_{c+1}^*, if present, is of the form $((\mathsf{Query}, q_i, \omega_{c+1}), \cdot)$. If τ_2 cannot be parsed as such, or if $c > \ell(n) - 1$, return 0.

- Verify that each q_i in τ_2 is equal to the lexicographically first instance $q \in [\ell(n)]$ such that q does not appear in an Open query earlier in τ_2. If not true, return 0.

- Verify that, for all $i \in [q(n)]$ and all $j \in \{\pi_1, \ldots, \pi_c\}$, $\mathsf{Ver}_{k_j}(m_{i,j}, \sigma_{i,j}) = \mathsf{Accept}$. (Do not verify the responses to queries ω_i in τ_2.) If not true, return 0.

- Verify that every $m_{i,j}$ parsed from the transcript is correctly generated by random coins resulting from applying $\mathcal{O}$ to the input $(s, i, j, 1)$ (for $i \in [q(n)]$) and that each ω_j is correctly generated by random coins resulting from applying $\mathcal{O}$ to the input $\tau_1 \| (s, q(n) + 1, j, 1)$. If not true, return 0.

- Otherwise, return 1.

Fig. 2. Formal description of the "ideal" adversary $\mathcal{A}^{\mathcal{O}}$ (2).

be the set of inputs where the two keys' outputs are identical.

So, if (1) is false for some pair (k_1, k_2), i.e., $|S_{k_1,k_2}| \leq |\mathcal{X}_n| \left(1 - \frac{2n}{q(n)}\right)$; then the probability over $\{x_{i,j^*}\}$ that both keys agree in all $q(n)$ queries to f made by $\mathcal{A}$, or equivalently the probability that $q(n)$ uniformly random queries $\{x_{i,j^*}\}$ lie in S_{k_1,k_2}, is bounded above by:

$$\left(1 - \frac{2n}{q(n)}\right)^{q(n)} = \left(\left(1 - \frac{2n}{q(n)}\right)^{q(n)/2n}\right)^{2n} < \left(\frac{1}{e}\right)^{2n} = \exp(-2n)$$

There exist no more than $(2^n)^2 = 2^{2n}$ possible key pairs $(k_1, k_2) \in (\{0,1\}^n)^2$, each of which by the above must either have the property (1) or be such that

$$\Pr\left[(x_{1,j^*}, \ldots, x_{q(n),j^*}) \leftarrow (\mathcal{X}_n)^{q(n)} : f_{k_1}(x_{i,j^*}) = f_{k_2}(x_{i,j^*}) \forall i \in [q(n)]\right]$$

$$= \Pr\left[(x_{1,j^*}, \ldots, x_{q(n),j^*}) \leftarrow (\mathcal{X}_n)^{q(n)} : x_{i,j^*} \in S_{k_1,k_2} \forall i \in [q(n)]\right]$$

$$\leq \exp(-2n)$$

Then the probability over $\{x_{i,j^*}\}$ that *some* key pair exists which does not have property (1) yet does have $f_{k_1}(x_{i,j^*}) = f_{k_2}(x_{i,j^*})$ for all x_{i,j^*} is, by a union bound, at most:

$$\Pr\left[(x_{1,j^*}, \ldots, x_{q(n),j^*}) \leftarrow (\mathcal{X}_n)^{q(n)} : \exists (k_1, k_2) \in (\{0,1\}^n)^2 : \right.$$

$$\left. x_{i,j^*} \in S_{k_1,k_2} \forall i \in [q(n)] \text{ and } |S_{k_1,k_2}| \leq |\mathcal{X}_n| \left(1 - \frac{2n}{q(n)}\right)\right]$$

$$\leq \sum_{(k_1,k_2)\in(\{0,1\}^n)^2} \mathbb{1}_{|S_{k_1,k_2}| \leq |\mathcal{X}_n|(1-2n/q(n))} \Pr\left[(x_{1,j^*}, \ldots, x_{q(n),j^*}) \leftarrow (\mathcal{X}_n)^{q(n)} : \right.$$

$$\left. x_{i,j^*} \in S_{k_1,k_2} \forall i \in [q(n)]\right]$$

$$< 2^{2n} e^{-2n} = (2/e)^{2n}$$

which is clearly negligible in n.   □

To prove the claim, we consider the above lemma, letting f_k be the deterministic function Tag_k. When interacting with an honest challenger, the responses to tag queries for each instance will always be consistent with the respective keys, and so $\mathcal{A}$ will never return $\bot$ due to the Valid predicate failing or K^* being empty. Furthermore, for the instance $\pi_{\ell(n)}$ for which $\mathcal{A}$ outputs a forgery, it is overwhelmingly likely (with probability $1 - \nu(n)$), by Lemma 2, that all keys in the set K^* recovered by $\mathcal{A}$ will agree with the *correct* (challenger's) key k' for that instance on a large $(1 - 2n/q(n))$ fraction of random messages m^*. Specifically, this means that, given any choice of key k^* from K^*, $\mathcal{A}$ will produce a correct forgery (m^*, σ^*) (i.e., such that $\sigma^* = \mathsf{Tag}_{k'}(m^*)$, or equivalently $\mathsf{Ver}_{k'}(m^*, \sigma^*) = \mathsf{Accept}$) given random m^* with probability at least $1 - 2n/q(n)$.

Thus, $\mathcal{A}$ succeeds in the interaction in the event that Lemma 2 does not fail (i.e., property (1) holds for every key pair) and that $\mathcal{A}$ chooses a "good" m^* (i.e., one which does not repeat a previous query and produces the same tag under k^* as under the challenger's key k') given its choice of $k^* \leftarrow K^*$; the claim follows from the union bound over these events.   □

We require one additional claim concerning the adversary, which states that the reduction $\mathcal{R}$ must have actually responded to all $\ell(n) - 1$ key-opening queries to have a non-negligible chance of receiving a forgery. This will be important later, to ensure that $\mathcal{R}$ cannot "cheat" by sending a fake transcript while interacting with $\mathcal{B}$.

Claim 3. *There exists a negligible function $\nu(\cdot)$ such that, for all $n \in \mathbb{N}$, the probability, over all randomness in the experiment $[\mathcal{R}^{\mathcal{A}^{\mathcal{O}}} \leftrightarrow \mathcal{C}](1^n)$, that some instance of $\mathcal{A}$ returns a forgery (i.e., something besides $\bot$) to $\mathcal{R}$ without having received responses to all $\ell(n) - 1$ (Open, i) (key-opening) queries from $\mathcal{R}$, is less than $\nu(n)$.*

Proof. We demonstrate that, if $\mathcal{A}$ returns a forgery (i.e., not $\perp$) to $\mathcal{R}$ after $\mathcal{R}$ responds to strictly fewer than $\ell(n) - 1$ distinct key-opening queries from $\mathcal{A}$, then this requires $\mathcal{R}$ to guess a uniformly random message generated using the output of $\mathcal{A}$'s random oracle $\mathcal{O}$ on a new input, which can happen with at most probability $p(n)/|\mathcal{M}_n|$ for some polynomial $p(\cdot)$ due to $\mathcal{O}$ being uniformly random.

Assume that $\mathcal{R}$ responds to fewer than $\ell(n) - 1$ key-opening queries. Then there exists some $i \in [\ell(n) - 1]$ for which $\mathcal{R}$ does not send $\mathcal{A}$ a partial transcript ending with $((\mathsf{Open}, \pi_i), k_{\pi_i})$ (i.e., a response to $\mathcal{A}$'s i^{th} key-opening query). By the definition of the Valid predicate, in order for $\mathcal{R}$ to receive a final message from $\mathcal{A}$ that contains a forgery (and not $\perp$), $\mathcal{R}$ must send to $\mathcal{A}$ a complete transcript

$$\tau = \tau_1 || (\ldots, (\mathsf{Open}, \pi_i), k_{\pi_i}, (\mathsf{Query}, q, \omega_{i+1}), \ldots)$$

where ω_{i+1} is a uniformly random message generated by random coins resulting from applying $\mathcal{O}$ to $\tau_1 || (s, q(n) + 1, i + 1, 1)$.

By construction of $\mathcal{A}$ and the assumption that $\mathcal{R}$ does not send $\mathcal{A}$ a partial transcript ending with $((\mathsf{Open}, \pi_i), k_{\pi_i})$, however, $\mathcal{R}$ can never have received either ω_{i+1} or any message depending on the correct input $\tau_1 || (s, q(n) + 1, i + 1, 1)$ to $\mathcal{O}$. Hence, since ω_{i+1} is uniformly distributed and independent of any other message, we can conclude that $\mathcal{R}$ will send the correct ω_{i+1} in its final transcript with at most probability $1/|\mathcal{M}_n|$ (i.e., by guessing a random message correctly). While $\mathcal{R}$ can attempt to retrieve a forgery multiple times, it is restricted to polynomial time, so the probability with which it can guess ω_{i+1} (which is necessary to receive a forgery from $\mathcal{A}$) is bounded above by $\nu(n) = p(n)/|\mathcal{M}_n|$ for polynomial $p(\cdot)$, which is negligible because we assume the message space to be super-polynomial (asymptotically greater than any polynomial) in n. $\qquad\square$

4.2 Analyzing the Meta-reduction

The remaining part of the proof is devoted to analyzing the success probability $\mathsf{Success}_{\mathcal{R}^{\mathcal{A}}}(n)$. This, as previously discussed, involves investigating the probability with which the meta-reduction $\mathcal{B}$ and the ideal adversary $\mathcal{R}^{\mathcal{A}}$ diverge while interacting with $\mathcal{C}$. We formalize this with the following claim:

Claim 4. *If $(\mathcal{C}, t(\cdot))$ is a secure assumption and we can bound*

$$\Pr[\langle \mathcal{R}^{\mathcal{A}}, \mathcal{C} \rangle \to \mathsf{Accept}] - \Pr[\langle \mathcal{B}, \mathcal{C} \rangle \to \mathsf{Accept}] \leq p(n)$$

then there is a negligible $\epsilon(\cdot)$ such that $\mathsf{Success}_{\mathcal{R}^{\mathcal{A}}}(n) \leq p(n) + \epsilon(n)$.

Proof. Since $\mathcal{B}$ is efficient and $(\mathcal{C}, t(\cdot))$ is secure, there is a negligible $\epsilon(\cdot)$ such that $\Pr[\langle \mathcal{B}, \mathcal{C} \rangle \to \mathsf{Accept}] \leq t(n) + \epsilon(n)$.

So, given $\Pr[\langle \mathcal{R}^{\mathcal{A}}, \mathcal{C} \rangle \to \mathsf{Accept}] - \Pr[\langle \mathcal{B}, \mathcal{C} \rangle \to \mathsf{Accept}] \leq p(n)$, then we conclude that $\Pr[\langle \mathcal{R}^{\mathcal{A}}, \mathcal{C} \rangle \to \mathsf{Accept}] \leq t(n) + p(n) + \epsilon(n)$, and thus:

$$\mathsf{Success}_{\mathcal{R}^{\mathcal{A}}}(n) = \Pr[\langle \mathcal{R}^{\mathcal{A}}, \mathcal{C} \rangle \to \mathsf{Accept}] - t(n) \leq p(n) + \epsilon(n)$$

$\qquad\square$

- Set initial view $v \leftarrow \perp$ and set $J \leftarrow 1$. Execute $\mathcal{R}$, updating the current view v according to the following rules.
- When $\mathcal{R}$ begins a new instance of $\mathcal{A}$ with some message (Init, s), label this instance as instance J. Generate and store $\ell(n)q(n)$ uniformly random queries $\boldsymbol{m}_J^1 = (m_{J,1,1}^1, \dots, m_{J,q(n),\ell(n)}^1)$. Also initialize a variable $k_J \leftarrow \{\}$. Lastly, respond with $\tau_J^* = (\mathsf{Query}, 1, m_{J,1,1}^1)$ and increment J.
- When $\mathcal{R}$ attempts to communicate externally with $\mathcal{C}$, forward the message, return $\mathcal{C}$'s response to $\mathcal{R}$, and update v accordingly.
- For any $i \in [q(n)]$, when $\mathcal{R}$ sends to some instance I of $\mathcal{A}$ a transcript of the form

$$\tau = (q_{1,1}, q_{1,2}, \dots, q_{1,\ell(n)}, q_{2,1}, \dots, q_{i,j})$$

where either $i < q(n)$ or $i = q(n)$ and $j < \ell(n)$, such that each $q_{u,v}$ is of the form $((\mathsf{Query}, v, m_{u,v}), \sigma_{u,v})$, do the following:
  - Let $j' = (j \bmod \ell(n)) + 1$.
  - Let $i' = i + 1$ if $j' = 1$ and $i' = i$ otherwise.
  - Return the response $(\mathsf{Query}, j', m_{I,i',j'}^1)$.
- When $\mathcal{R}$ sends to some instance I of $\mathcal{A}$ a transcript of the form $\tau = \tau_1 || \tau_2$, where

$$\tau_1 = (q_{1,1}, q_{1,2}, \dots, q_{1,\ell(n)}, q_{2,1}, \dots, q_{q(n),\ell(n)})$$

and where each $q_{u,v}$ is of the form $((\mathsf{Query}, v, m_{u,v}), \sigma_{u,v})$, do the following:
  - Let c be the number of Open messages appearing in τ_2 so far.
  - If there is some tuple $(\tau_1, I, \pi, \boldsymbol{\omega}, m^*)$ stored, let π, $\boldsymbol{\omega}$, and m^* be as stored in the tuple. Otherwise, let $\pi = (\pi_1, \dots, \pi_{\ell(n)})$ be a uniformly random permutation of $[\ell(n)]$, generate $2\ell(n)$ additional messages $\boldsymbol{\omega} = (\omega_1^0, \dots, \omega_{\ell(n)}^0, \omega_1^1, \dots, \omega_{\ell(n)}^1)$ and a target forgery m^*, and store the tuple $(\tau_1, I, \pi, \boldsymbol{\omega}, m^*)$.
  - Consider the suffix transcript τ_2. If τ_2 is empty or ends with messages of the form $((\mathsf{Open}, j), k_j)$, then return $(\mathsf{Query}, q, \omega_{c+1}^{\mathsf{Valid}(\tau, I)})$, where q is the lexicographically first instance for which τ_2 does not contain an Open query.
  - Otherwise, if $c < \ell(n) - 1$ and τ_2 ends with messages of the form $((\mathsf{Query}, q, \omega_{c+1}), \cdot)$, then return $(\mathsf{Open}, \pi_{c+1})$.
  - Otherwise, if τ_2 ends with $((\mathsf{Query}, q, \omega_{\ell(n)}), \cdot)$ and $c = \ell(n) - 1$, generate a forgery as follows:
    * If $\mathsf{Valid}(\tau, I) = 0$, then return $\perp$.
    * Otherwise, run the procedure Rewind below for the instance I.
    * If, after running Rewind, there is a stored key k_I, then return the forgery $(m^*, \mathsf{Tag}_{k_I}(m^*), \pi_{\ell(n)})$ and continue executing $\mathcal{R}$ as above. Otherwise, abort the entire execution of $\mathcal{B}$ and return Fail.

Let the predicate $\mathsf{Valid}(\tau, I)$ be defined as follows:

- Parse τ as $\tau_1 || \tau_2$, where $\tau_1 = (q_{1,0}, q_{1,1}, \dots, q_{1,\ell(n)-1}, q_{2,0}, \dots, q_{q(n),\ell(n)})$ such that each $q_{u,v}$ is of the form $((\mathsf{Query}, v, m_{u,v}), \sigma_{u,v})$. If τ cannot be parsed as such, return 0.

Fig. 3. Formal description of the meta-reduction $\mathcal{B}$ (1).

- If there is a stored tuple $(\tau_1, I, \pi, \boldsymbol{\omega}, m^*)$ then set $\pi = (\pi_1, \ldots, \pi_{\ell(n)})$ equal to the third element of this tuple and set $\boldsymbol{\omega} = (\omega_1^0, \ldots, \omega_{\ell(n)}^0, \omega_1^1, \ldots, \omega_{\ell(n)}^1)$ equal to the fourth element. If there is no such tuple then return 0.
- Parse $\tau_2 = (q_1^*, q_2^*, \ldots, q_c^*[, q_{c+1}^*])$ such that each q_i^* is of the form $((\mathsf{Query}, q_i, \omega_i), \cdot, (\mathsf{Open}, \pi_i), k_{\pi_i})$ and q_{c+1}^*, if present, is of the form $((\mathsf{Query}, q_i, \omega_{c+1}), \cdot)$. If τ_2 cannot be parsed as such, or if $c > \ell(n) - 1$, return 0.
- Verify that each q_i in τ_2 is equal to the lexicographically first instance $q \in [\ell(n)]$ such that q does not appear in an Open query earlier in τ_2. If not true, return 0.
- Verify that, for all $i \in [q(n)]$ and all $j \in \{\pi_1, \ldots, \pi_c\}$, $\mathsf{Ver}_{k_j}(m_{i,j}, \sigma_{i,j}) = \mathsf{Accept}$. (Do not verify the responses to queries ω_i in τ_2.) If not true, return 0.
- Verify that every $m_{i,j}$ parsed from the transcript τ_1 is equal to the stored $m_{I,i,j}^1$, and that every ω_j parsed from τ_2 is equal to the respective ω_j^1. If not, then return 0. Otherwise, return 1.

Rewind procedure:

- Given instance I, for $j \in [\ell(n)]$ let V^j denote the view immediately before the query $(\omega_{\pi_j}, (\mathsf{Open}, \pi_j))$ for instance I (i.e., the query corresponding to the opening of the jth instance after the order of instances π to open is randomized).
- For $j \in [\ell(n)]$, "rewind" the view to V^j as follows: Let $J' \leftarrow J$, let π' be identical to π except with $\pi_{\ell(n)}$ and π_j swapped (i.e., $\pi_j' = \pi_{\ell(n)}$ and $\pi'_{\ell(n)} = \pi_j$), and begin executing $\mathcal{R}$ from the view $V' \leftarrow V^j$ as in the main routine, with the following exceptions:
  - Replace any instances of π with π' (including in Valid).
  - When $\mathcal{R}$ begins a new instance of $\mathcal{A}$, label this instance as instance J' and increment J'.
  - When $\mathcal{R}$ attempts to communicate externally with $\mathcal{C}$ or "rewind" the current instance of $\mathcal{A}$ by sending a message corresponding to a point in the interaction before V^j, abort the rewinding and continue to the next repetition.
  - When $\mathcal{R}$ sends an end message for a valid instance $I' \neq I$ of $\mathcal{A}$ (i.e., a transcript τ such that $\mathcal{A}$'s next message would be a forgery (m^*, σ^*) for instance I'), abort the rewinding and continue to the next repetition. (If instead $\mathcal{A}$'s next message would be $\bot$ because $\mathsf{Valid}(\tau, I) = 0$, return $\bot$.)
  - If v' ever contains a message whose transcript contains a response k_I to any query for $(\mathsf{Open}, \pi_{\ell(n)})$ (i.e., (Open, π'_k)), then, if it is the case that $\mathsf{Ver}_{k_I}(m_{I,i,\pi_{\ell(n)}}, \sigma_{I,i,\pi_{\ell(n)}}) = \mathsf{Accept}$ for every $i \in [q(n)]$ (letting m and σ variables be defined as in the Valid predicate), store k_I and end the Rewind procedure (i.e., return to the outer execution); if k_I is not a correct key, store nothing to k_I and continue to the next repetition.

Fig. 4. Formal description of the meta-reduction $\mathcal{B}$ (2).

So it suffices to bound $\Pr[\langle \mathcal{R}^{\mathcal{A}}, \mathcal{C} \rangle \rightarrow \mathsf{Accept}] - \Pr[\langle \mathcal{B}, \mathcal{C} \rangle \rightarrow \mathsf{Accept}]$. In order to do so, we begin by defining an *inefficient* "hybrid" meta-reduction $\mathcal{B}'$ which acts identically to $\mathcal{B}$, with the sole exception that, during the Rewind procedure, if $\mathcal{B}'$ encounters a response k_I to a query for $(\mathsf{Open}, \pi_{\ell(n)})$ (i.e., a key for the instance for which $\mathcal{B}'$ must produce a forgery), and if the recovered k_I is valid (i.e., $\mathsf{Ver}_{k_I}(m_{I,i,\pi_{\ell(n)}}, \sigma_{I,i,\pi_{\ell(n)}}) = \mathsf{Accept}$ for every $i \in [q(n)]$), then $\mathcal{B}'$ will first determine, using brute force, whether there are any other keys k' such that $\mathsf{Ver}_{k'}(m_{I,i,\pi_{\ell(n)}}, \sigma_{I,i,\pi_{\ell(n)}}) = \mathsf{Accept}$ for every $i \in [q(n)]$ but $\mathsf{Tag}_{k'}(m_I^*) \neq \mathsf{Tag}_{k_I}(m_I^*)$. If not (i.e., either k_I is the only such key or there is a unique correct forgery (m_I^*, σ_I^*)), then $\mathcal{B}'$ stores k_I, identically to $\mathcal{B}$; otherwise, $\mathcal{B}'$ stores the *lexicographically first* such key k' and uses that key instead of k_I to produce the forgery (identically to $\mathcal{A}$).

For ease of notation, let us further define some experiments and variables:

- Let $\mathsf{Real}(1^n)$ denote the experiment $[\mathcal{B} \leftrightarrow \mathcal{C}](1^n)$, and $\mathsf{Output}[\mathsf{Real}(1^n)]$ the output distribution $\langle \mathcal{B}, \mathcal{C} \rangle(1^n)$. Let $\mathsf{Hyb}(1^n)$ and $\mathsf{Output}[\mathsf{Hyb}(1^n)]$ be defined analogously for the "hybrid" experiment $[\mathcal{B}' \leftrightarrow \mathcal{C}](1^n)$, and lastly $\mathsf{Ideal}(1^n)$ and $\mathsf{Output}[\mathsf{Ideal}(1^n)]$ for the "ideal" experiment $[\mathcal{R}^{\mathcal{A}} \leftrightarrow \mathcal{C}](1^n)$.
- For any such experiment, let $\{m_I, \pi_I\}$ define the randomness used to generate, respectively, all query variables ($m_{(.)}$ or $\omega_{(.)}$) and the permutation π for an instance I (real or simulated) of $\mathcal{A}$ (including the case where a query or permutation might be regenerated after, e.g., rewinding). Let $\mathcal{O}_{ext}$ denote all other randomness. Furthermore, let $M(n)$ be an upper bound to the number of instances of $\mathcal{A}$ started by $\mathcal{R}$.
- For instance, an experiment $\mathsf{Real}_{\{m_I, \pi_I\}_{I \in [M(n)] \setminus J}, \mathcal{O}_{ext}}(1^n)$ (which we henceforth abbreviate as $\mathsf{Real}_{\{m_I, \pi_I\}_{-J}, \mathcal{O}_{ext}}(1^n)$) would indicate the interaction between $\mathcal{B}$ and $\mathcal{C}$ with all randomness fixed *except* for the variables m and π for a particular instance J of $\mathcal{A}$ (simulated by $\mathcal{B}$).
- Naturally, an experiment denoted by, e.g., $\mathsf{Real}_{\{m_I, \pi_I\}_{I \in [M(n)]}, \mathcal{O}_{ext}}(1^n)$, has all randomness fixed and hence is deterministic.

Let $\mathsf{Unique}(\{m_I, \pi_I\}_{I \in [M(n)]}, \mathcal{O}_{ext})$ be the "key-uniqueness" predicate on the randomness of Real (or Ideal) which is true if, during execution of the experiment $\mathsf{Real}_{\{m_I, \pi_I\}_{I \in [M(n)]}, \mathcal{O}_{ext}}(1^n)$, whenever $\mathcal{B}$ returns a forgery (m^*, σ^*), it is the case that $\sigma^* = \mathsf{Tag}_{k^*}(m^*)$, where k^* is the lexicographically first key k such that $\mathsf{Ver}_k(m_{I,i,\pi_{I,j}}, \sigma_{I,i,\pi_{I,j}}) = \mathsf{Accept}$ for all $i \in [q(n)]$. That is, Unique is true whenever, given the randomness of an experiment, $\mathcal{B}$ (if rewinding succeeds) returns the same forgery as $\mathcal{A}$ would in the Ideal experiment. The occurrence of Unique is hence fully determined by the randomness ($\{m_I, \pi_I\}_{I \in [M(n)]}$ and $\mathcal{O}_{ext}$) that fully determines the execution of Real or Ideal.

We must also deal with the fact that $\mathcal{R}$ may rewind $\mathcal{A}$. Let $W(n)$ be a polynomial upper bound to the number of times that $\mathcal{R}$ causes $\mathcal{A}$ to generate a permutation π (including by rewinding) in the experiment $\mathsf{Ideal}(1^n)$, and note that, trivially, $W(n) \geq M(n)$.

Now, with setup completed, we can proceed in two major steps. Our goal is to bound

$$|\Pr[\mathsf{Output}[\mathsf{Real}(1^n)] = \mathsf{Accept}] - \Pr[\mathsf{Output}[\mathsf{Ideal}(1^n)] = \mathsf{Accept}]|$$

which we can do by bounding

$$|\Pr[\mathsf{Output}[\mathsf{Real}(1^n)] = \mathsf{Accept}] - \Pr[\mathsf{Output}[\mathsf{Hyb}(1^n)] = \mathsf{Accept}]|$$

and

$$|\Pr[\mathsf{Output}[\mathsf{Hyb}(1^n)] = \mathsf{Accept}] - \Pr[\mathsf{Output}[\mathsf{Ideal}(1^n)] = \mathsf{Accept}]|$$

4.3   Comparing the Real and Hybrid Experiments

We begin with the first of these quantities, which is relatively straightforward to bound. Informally, whenever Unique holds (the probability of which is dictated by Lemma 2), $\mathcal{B}$ and $\mathcal{B}'$ behave identically by construction. The complete proof is given in the full version.

Claim 5. *There exists negligible $\nu(\cdot)$ such that, for all $n \in \mathbb{N}$:*

$$|\Pr[\mathsf{Output}[\mathsf{Real}(1^n)] = \mathsf{Accept}] - \Pr[\mathsf{Output}[\mathsf{Hyb}(1^n)] = \mathsf{Accept}]|$$

$$< \frac{2nW(n)}{q(n)} + \nu(n)$$

taken over the randomness of $\{m_I, \pi_I\}_{I \in [M(n)]}$ and $\mathcal{O}_{ext}$.

4.4   Comparing the Hybrid and Ideal Experiments

To relate the hybrid $\mathcal{B}'$ to the "ideal" interaction with $\mathcal{R}^{\mathcal{A}}$, we next present the following claim, which informally holds because, by construction, $\mathcal{B}'$ behaves identically to $\mathcal{A}$ as long as rewinding does not fail (in which case it would return Fail). The complete proof is again given in the full version.

Claim 6

$$|\Pr[\mathsf{Output}[\mathsf{Hyb}(1^n)] = \mathsf{Accept}] - \Pr[\mathsf{Output}[\mathsf{Ideal}(1^n)] = \mathsf{Accept}]|$$

$$\leq \Pr[\mathsf{Output}[\mathsf{Hyb}(1^n)] = \mathsf{Fail}]$$

taken over the randomness of $\{m_I, \pi_I\}_{I \in [M(n)]}$ and $\mathcal{O}_{ext}$.

4.5   Bounding the Hybrid's Failure Probability

So all that remains is to investigate the probability of Hyb outputting Fail; to do this we can make a critical observation about rewinding in the context of our construction. Formally, we prove the following:

Proposition 1. *There exists a negligible function $\epsilon(\cdot)$ such that, for all $n \in \mathbb{N}$, taken over the randomness of $\{m_I, \pi_I\}_{I \in [M(n)]}$ and $\mathcal{O}_{ext}$:*

$$\Pr[\mathsf{Output}[\mathsf{Hyb}(1^n)] = \mathsf{Fail}] \leq W(n) \left(\frac{W(n) + r(n) + 1}{\ell(n)} \right) + \epsilon(n)$$

Proof. First, we show that without loss of generality $\mathcal{R}$ can never rewind *except* from a point after π is generated to a point before π is generated; intuitively, this is because all of $\mathcal{A}$'s queries to $\mathcal{R}$ are dependent only on (1) the permutation π and (2) the validity of $\mathcal{R}$'s responses, and as such any rewinding that does not result in π being regenerated can in fact be internally simulated by $\mathcal{R}$. Formally, we state the following claim, which we prove in the full version:

Claim 7. *Given any $\mathcal{R}$ that rewinds any instance of $\mathcal{A}$ either (1) from a point before π is generated or (2) to a point after π is generated, there exists an $\mathcal{R}'$ with identical success probability that does not perform such rewinding.*

Hence, we assume without loss of generality that $\mathcal{R}$ sends at most $W(n)$ "end messages" (i.e., forgery requests) requiring rewinding, as π is by assumption generated no more than $W(n)$ times and the responses to any further end messages are effectively simulatable by $\mathcal{R}$. We disregard end messages sent for instances for which $\mathcal{R}$ has not answered all $\ell(n) - 1$ key opening queries, since, with all-but-negligible probability, $\mathcal{A}$ or $\mathcal{B}'$ can directly respond to these with $\perp$ (as Valid will evaluate to 0 unless $\mathcal{R}$ guesses a random and unknown ω_i correctly).

At this point, we have shown that our hybrid experiment gives us a setting with minimal rewinding and guaranteed key uniqueness, much like the setting discussed in [35] for the case of unique signatures. Hence, we can leverage this observation to prove the following claim, analogous to the key "rewinding lemma" therein. Consider the following for any possible execution $\mathsf{Hyb}_{\{m_I,\pi_I\}_{-J},m_J,\mathcal{O}_{ext}}(1^n)$ (i.e., for any fixed setting of all randomness aside from π_J), and notice that, since it applies to arbitrarily fixed randomness, it must thus apply over all possible randomness of the experiment $\mathsf{Hyb}(1^n)$:

Claim 8. *Given any experiment $\mathsf{Hyb}_{\{m_I,\pi_I\}_{-J},m_J,\mathcal{O}_{ext}}(1^n)$, the probability, over the uniformly chosen permutation π_J, that the simulated instance J will return* Fail *when rewinding any end message, is, for all $n \in \mathbb{N}$, at most*

$$\frac{W(n) + r(n) + 1}{\ell(n)}$$

The claim is nearly identical to its analogue in [35], but for completeness we provide a proof in the full version of our paper. We can conclude as desired that the probability of any forgery request causing $\mathcal{B}'$ to return Fail in the experiment Hyb is at most

$$W(n) \left(\frac{W(n) + r(n) + 1}{\ell(n)} \right) + \epsilon(n)$$

by combining Claim 8 (taken over all possible assignments of the fixed randomness) with the union bound over our bound of $W(n)$ possible (unique) forgery requests for which $\mathcal{R}$ has answered all key-opening queries. For any requests for which this is *not* the case, we know by Claim 3 that the probability of such requests causing $\mathcal{B}'$ to return anything besides $\perp$ is negligible, so, since $\mathcal{R}$ is polynomial-time, these requests add at most a negligible $\epsilon(n)$ to the probability of Hyb returning Fail. $\square$

4.6 Bounding the Security Loss

Finally, we must translate this bound on the failure probability of $\mathcal{B}'$ into a bound on the security loss of the reduction $\mathcal{R}$. As the argument is fairly similar to that of [35], we defer the complete argument to the full version of our paper; to conclude, we derive that, if $(\mathcal{C}, t(\cdot))$ is secure, then:

$$\lambda_{\mathcal{R}}(n) \geq \left(1 - \frac{1}{2\ell(n)^2}\right)\left(\sqrt{\ell(n)} - (r(n) + 2)\right)$$

which finishes the proof of Lemma 1.

References

1. Abe, M., Groth, J., Ohkubo, M.: Separating short structure-preserving signatures from non-interactive assumptions. In: Lee, D.H., Wang, X. (eds.) ASIACRYPT 2011. LNCS, vol. 7073, pp. 628–646. Springer, Heidelberg (2011). https://doi.org/10.1007/978-3-642-25385-0_34
2. Abraham, I., Chan, T.H.H., Dolev, D., Nayak, K., Pass, R., Ren, L., Shi, E.: Communication complexity of byzantine agreement, revisited. In: Robinson, P., Ellen, F. (eds.) 38th ACM PODC, pp. 317–326. ACM, July/August 2019. https://doi.org/10.1145/3293611.3331629
3. Bader, C., Hofheinz, D., Jager, T., Kiltz, E., Li, Y.: Tightly-secure authenticated key exchange. In: Dodis, Y., Nielsen, J.B. (eds.) TCC 2015. LNCS, vol. 9014, pp. 629–658. Springer, Heidelberg (2015). https://doi.org/10.1007/978-3-662-46494-6_26
4. Bader, C., Jager, T., Li, Y., Schäge, S.: On the impossibility of tight cryptographic reductions. In: Fischlin, M., Coron, J.-S. (eds.) EUROCRYPT 2016. LNCS, vol. 9666, pp. 273–304. Springer, Heidelberg (2016). https://doi.org/10.1007/978-3-662-49896-5_10
5. Baecher, P., Brzuska, C., Fischlin, M.: Notions of black-box reductions, revisited. In: Sako, K., Sarkar, P. (eds.) ASIACRYPT 2013. LNCS, vol. 8269, pp. 296–315. Springer, Heidelberg (2013). https://doi.org/10.1007/978-3-642-42033-7_16
6. Barker, E.: Guideline for Using Cryptographic Standards in the Federal Government: Cryptographic Mechanisms. NIST Special Publication 800–175B (2016)
7. Baudron, O., Pointcheval, D., Stern, J.: Extended notions of security for multicast public key cryptosystems. In: Montanari, U., Rolim, J.D.P., Welzl, E. (eds.) ICALP 2000. LNCS, vol. 1853, pp. 499–511. Springer, Heidelberg (2000). https://doi.org/10.1007/3-540-45022-X_42
8. Bellare, M., Boldyreva, A., Micali, S.: Public-key encryption in a multi-user setting: security proofs and improvements. In: Preneel, B. (ed.) EUROCRYPT 2000. LNCS, vol. 1807, pp. 259–274. Springer, Heidelberg (2000). https://doi.org/10.1007/3-540-45539-6_18
9. Bellare, M., Canetti, R., Krawczyk, H.: Pseudorandom functions revisited: the cascade construction and its concrete security. In: 37th FOCS, pp. 514–523. IEEE Computer Society Press, October 1996. https://doi.org/10.1109/SFCS.1996.548510
10. Bellare, M., Ristenpart, T., Tessaro, S.: Multi-instance security and its application to password-based cryptography. In: Safavi-Naini, R., Canetti, R. (eds.) CRYPTO 2012. LNCS, vol. 7417, pp. 312–329. Springer, Heidelberg (2012). https://doi.org/10.1007/978-3-642-32009-5_19

11. Bernhard, D., Fischlin, M., Warinschi, B.: On the hardness of proving CCA-security of signed ElGamal. In: Cheng, C.-M., Chung, K.-M., Persiano, G., Yang, B.-Y. (eds.) PKC 2016. LNCS, vol. 9614, pp. 47–69. Springer, Heidelberg (2016). https://doi.org/10.1007/978-3-662-49384-7_3

12. Boneh, D., Venkatesan, R.: Breaking RSA may not be equivalent to factoring. In: Nyberg, K. (ed.) EUROCRYPT 1998. LNCS, vol. 1403, pp. 59–71. Springer, Heidelberg (1998). https://doi.org/10.1007/BFb0054117

13. Bose, P., Hoang, V.T., Tessaro, S.: Revisiting AES-GCM-SIV: multi-user security, faster key derivation, and better bounds. In: Nielsen, J.B., Rijmen, V. (eds.) EUROCRYPT 2018. LNCS, vol. 10820, pp. 468–499. Springer, Cham (2018). https://doi.org/10.1007/978-3-319-78381-9_18

14. Bresson, E., Monnerat, J., Vergnaud, D.: Separation results on the "one-more" computational problems. In: Malkin, T. (ed.) CT-RSA 2008. LNCS, vol. 4964, pp. 71–87. Springer, Heidelberg (2008). https://doi.org/10.1007/978-3-540-79263-5_5

15. Chatterjee, S., Menezes, A., Sarkar, P.: Another look at tightness. In: Miri, A., Vaudenay, S. (eds.) SAC 2011. LNCS, vol. 7118, pp. 293–319. Springer, Heidelberg (2012). https://doi.org/10.1007/978-3-642-28496-0_18

16. Coron, J.-S.: Optimal security proofs for PSS and other signature schemes. In: Knudsen, L.R. (ed.) EUROCRYPT 2002. LNCS, vol. 2332, pp. 272–287. Springer, Heidelberg (2002). https://doi.org/10.1007/3-540-46035-7_18

17. Damgård, I.: Towards practical public key systems secure against chosen ciphertext attacks. In: Feigenbaum, J. (ed.) CRYPTO 1991. LNCS, vol. 576, pp. 445–456. Springer, Heidelberg (1992). https://doi.org/10.1007/3-540-46766-1_36

18. Dierks, T., Allen, C.: The TLS Protocol Version 1.0. RFC 2246, January 1999. https://doi.org/10.17487/RFC2246. https://rfc-editor.org/rfc/rfc2246.txt

19. Dierks, T., Rescorla, E.: The Transport Layer Security (TLS) Protocol Version 1.1. RFC 4346, April 2006. https://doi.org/10.17487/RFC4346. https://rfc-editor.org/rfc/rfc4346.txt

20. Dierks, T., Rescorla, E.: The Transport Layer Security (TLS) Protocol Version 1.2. RFC 5246, August 2008. https://doi.org/10.17487/RFC5246. https://rfc-editor.org/rfc/rfc5246.txt

21. Diffie, W., Hellman, M.: New directions in cryptography. IEEE Trans. Inf. Theory **22**(6), 644–654 (1976). https://doi.org/10.1109/TIT.1976.1055638. http://dx.doi.org/10.1109/TIT.1976.1055638

22. Dworkin, M.: Recommendation for Block Cipher Modes of Operation: Galois/Counter Mode (GCM) and GMAC. NIST Special Publication 800–38D (2007)

23. Fischlin, M., Schröder, D.: On the impossibility of three-move blind signature schemes. In: Gilbert, H. (ed.) EUROCRYPT 2010. LNCS, vol. 6110, pp. 197–215. Springer, Heidelberg (2010). https://doi.org/10.1007/978-3-642-13190-5_10

24. Gentry, C., Wichs, D.: Separating succinct non-interactive arguments from all falsifiable assumptions. In: Fortnow, L., Vadhan, S.P. (eds.) 43rd ACM STOC, pp. 99–108. ACM Press, June 2011. https://doi.org/10.1145/1993636.1993651

25. Goldreich, O.: Foundations of Cryptography. Basic Applications, vol. 2, 1st edn. Cambridge University Press, New York (2009)

26. Haitner, I., Rosen, A., Shaltiel, R.: On the (im)possibility of Arthur-Merlin witness hiding protocols. In: Reingold, O. (ed.) TCC 2009. LNCS, vol. 5444, pp. 220–237. Springer, Heidelberg (2009). https://doi.org/10.1007/978-3-642-00457-5_14

27. Hoang, V.T., Tessaro, S.: Key-alternating ciphers and key-length extension: exact bounds and multi-user security. In: Robshaw, M., Katz, J. (eds.) CRYPTO 2016. LNCS, vol. 9814, pp. 3–32. Springer, Heidelberg (2016). https://doi.org/10.1007/978-3-662-53018-4_1

28. Hoang, V.T., Tessaro, S., Thiruvengadam, A.: The multi-user security of GCM, revisited: tight bounds for nonce randomization. In: Lie, D., Mannan, M., Backes, M., Wang, X. (eds.) ACM CCS 2018, pp. 1429–1440. ACM Press, October 2018. https://doi.org/10.1145/3243734.3243816

29. Hofheinz, D., Jager, T., Knapp, E.: Waters signatures with optimal security reduction. In: Fischlin, M., Buchmann, J., Manulis, M. (eds.) PKC 2012. LNCS, vol. 7293, pp. 66–83. Springer, Heidelberg (2012). https://doi.org/10.1007/978-3-642-30057-8_5

30. Jager, T., Stam, M., Stanley-Oakes, R., Warinschi, B.: Multi-key authenticated encryption with corruptions: reductions are lossy. In: Kalai, Y., Reyzin, L. (eds.) TCC 2017. LNCS, vol. 10677, pp. 409–441. Springer, Cham (2017). https://doi.org/10.1007/978-3-319-70500-2_14

31. Kakvi, S.A., Kiltz, E.: Optimal security proofs for full domain hash, revisited. In: Pointcheval, D., Johansson, T. (eds.) EUROCRYPT 2012. LNCS, vol. 7237, pp. 537–553. Springer, Heidelberg (2012). https://doi.org/10.1007/978-3-642-29011-4_32

32. Luby, M.: Pseudorandomness and Cryptographic Applications. Princeton University Press, January 1996. https://doi.org/10.2307/j.ctvs32rpn

33. Luykx, A., Mennink, B., Paterson, K.G.: Analyzing multi-key security degradation. In: Takagi, T., Peyrin, T. (eds.) ASIACRYPT 2017. LNCS, vol. 10625, pp. 575–605. Springer, Cham (2017). https://doi.org/10.1007/978-3-319-70697-9_20

34. Menezes, A.J., Vanstone, S.A., Oorschot, P.C.V.: Handbook of Applied Cryptography, 1st edn. CRC Press Inc., Boca Raton (1996)

35. Morgan, A., Pass, R.: On the security loss of unique signatures. In: Beimel, A., Dziembowski, S. (eds.) TCC 2018. LNCS, vol. 11239, pp. 507–536. Springer, Cham (2018). https://doi.org/10.1007/978-3-030-03807-6_19

36. Mouha, N., Luykx, A.: Multi-key security: the Even-Mansour construction revisited. In: Gennaro, R., Robshaw, M. (eds.) CRYPTO 2015. LNCS, vol. 9215, pp. 209–223. Springer, Heidelberg (2015). https://doi.org/10.1007/978-3-662-47989-6_10

37. Naor, M.: On cryptographic assumptions and challenges. In: Boneh, D. (ed.) CRYPTO 2003. LNCS, vol. 2729, pp. 96–109. Springer, Heidelberg (2003). https://doi.org/10.1007/978-3-540-45146-4_6

38. Pass, R.: Limits of provable security from standard assumptions. In: Fortnow, L., Vadhan, S.P. (eds.) 43rd ACM STOC, pp. 109–118. ACM Press, June 2011. https://doi.org/10.1145/1993636.1993652

39. Tessaro, S.: Optimally secure block ciphers from ideal primitives. In: Iwata, T., Cheon, J.H. (eds.) ASIACRYPT 2015. LNCS, vol. 9453, pp. 437–462. Springer, Heidelberg (2015). https://doi.org/10.1007/978-3-662-48800-3_18

How to Build Optimally Secure PRFs Using Block Ciphers

Benoît Cogliati[1], Ashwin Jha[2(✉)], and Mridul Nandi[2]

[1] CISPA Helmholtz Center for Information Security, Saarbrücken, Germany
benoit.cogliati@cispa.saarland
[2] Indian Statistical Institute, Kolkata, India
ashwin.jha1991@gmail.com , mridul.nandi@gmail.com

Abstract. In EUROCRYPT '96, Aiello and Venkatesan proposed two candidates for $2n$-bit to $2n$-bit pseudorandom functions (PRFs), called Benes and modified Benes (or mBenes), based on n-bit to n-bit PRFs. While Benes is known to be secure up to 2^n queries (Patarin, AFRICA-CRYPT '08), the security of mBenes has only been proved up to $2^{n(1-\epsilon)}$ queries for all $\epsilon > 0$ by Patarin and Montreuil in ICISC '05. In this work, we show that the composition of a $2n$-bit hash function with mBenes is a secure variable input length (VIL) PRF up to 2^{n-2} queries (given appropriate hash function bounds). We extend our analysis with block ciphers as the underlying primitive and obtain two optimally secure VIL PRFs using block ciphers. The first of these candidates requires 6 calls to the block cipher. The second candidate requires just 4 calls to the block cipher, but here the proof is based on Patarin's mirror theory. Further, we instantiate the hash function with a PMAC+/LightMAC+ like hash, to get six candidates for deterministic message authentication codes with optimal security.

Keywords: PRF · MAC · Benes · Modified Benes · PMAC+ · LightMAC+

1 Introduction

PSEUDORANDOM FUNCTIONS (PRF) over variable length inputs are keyed functions that take as input a bit string of arbitrary length and output a fixed length bit string that should be indistinguishable from uniformly random bits. This primitive is useful in practice as it can serve as a Message Authentication Code (MAC) in order to provide integrity and authenticity of messages. Moreover, when adequately combined with an encryption scheme (e.g. using the generic SIV structure [1]), it can also provide authenticated encryption. Unfortunately, barring a few examples like SURF [2], SipHash [3] and AES-PRF [4], building a concrete secure PRF from scratch has remained elusive.

BLOCK CIPHER-BASED PRF: Given the ubiquity of block ciphers (BC), building a provably secure PRF from block ciphers has been a widely studied problem

© International Association for Cryptologic Research 2020
S. Moriai and H. Wang (Eds.): ASIACRYPT 2020, LNCS 12491, pp. 754–784, 2020.
https://doi.org/10.1007/978-3-030-64837-4_25

in symmetric cryptography. As far as fixed input length (FIL) is concerned, the problem is essentially solved as several highly secure constructions already exist. For example, given two n-bit permutations Π_1 and Π_2, the following PRP-to-PRF constructions offer security up to (roughly) 2^n adversarial queries:

- the sum $x \mapsto \Pi_1(x) \oplus \Pi_2(x)$ of both permutations and its single-keyed variant the TWIN construction $x \mapsto \Pi_1(0||x) \oplus \Pi_1(1||x)$: after their introduction by Bellare et al. [5], their security has been the subject of a long line of research [5–7], culminating with [8,9] and [10] where optimal security has been proven;
- the Encrypted Davies-Meyer (EDM) construction $x \mapsto \Pi_2(\Pi_1(x) \oplus x)$ and its dual (EDMD) $x \mapsto \Pi_2(\Pi_1(x)) \oplus \Pi_1(x)$: EDM has been introduced in [11], and security up to roughly $2^n/n$ queries has been proven in [12], while EDMD has been designed and proven optimally secure in [12].

However, for the case of variable input length (VIL), very few constructions actually provide security beyond the birthday bound. The most notable exceptions are, the SUM-ECBC construction [13], the PMAC+ construction [14] and its single-key variant 1k-PMAC+ [15], 3kf9 [16] and LightMAC+ [17] since they offer beyond the birthday bound (but still suboptimal) security. Those modes of operations use the relatively new Double-block Hash-then-Sum or DbHtS paradigm [18], which applies n-bit block cipher calls to the two n-bit halves of a $2n$-bit hash function and then sums the encrypted output. Although the DbHtS paradigm is known to achieve very high security [19,20], it is not yet known whether it can achieve optimal security. A more traditional approach towards PRF construction is the classical Hash-then-PRF paradigm [21], that relies on an n-bit block cipher along with two other components:

- a hash function with $2n$-bit output; and
- a $2n$-bit to n-bit PRF.

Designing the latter primitive is deeply linked to the problem of domain extension for PRFs, which has also been the subject of a long line of research. Since we focus on the problem of designing an optimally secure construction from a block cipher, this restricts the set of possible finalization constructions to the Benes construction and its variants [22], and Feistel networks with at least four rounds [23][1]. Unfortunately, optimal security for Feistel networks when round functions are instantiated with PRPs still remains to be proven. Hence, using Feistel networks as a finalization function would require implementing the round PRFs as the xor of two permutations, thus increasing the number of block cipher calls to 8. As we will see, considering other structures will allow the design of more efficient schemes.

BENES AND MODIFIED BENES: In [22], Aiello and Venkatesan introduced the Benes and modified Benes (or mBenes) constructions that build a $2n$-bit to n-bit

---

[1] The actual Feistel networks are from $2n$-bit to $2n$-bit. In that case, 5 rounds are required for optimal security. Since we only require n-bit outputs, the final round can actually be dropped.

PRF[2] from respectively 6 and 4 independent n-bit PRFs, where each underlying PRF is called once for each call to the construction. Patarin showed that Benes transformation is n-bit secure [24]. For mBenes, although Aiello and Venkatesan conjecture n-bit security, until now only a high level proof idea is shown [24, 25] for security up to (roughly) $2^{n(1-\epsilon)}$ queries for all $\epsilon > 0$. In order to use PRPs as the underlying primitive in Benes and mBenes while keeping optimal security, the most obvious solution would be to rely on an optimally secure PRP-to-PRF conversion method. However, this would increase the number of PRP calls of the construction to 12 for the Benes construction, and 8 for the mBenes construction. Current proof techniques unfortunately are not sufficient to prove optimal security for PRP-based Benes and mBenes constructions using a smaller number of permutation calls. Indeed, the current best result by Jha and Nandi shows that mBenes using 4 block ciphers is secure up to $2^{3n/4}$ queries [19].

1.1 Our Contributions

Table 1. Summary of beyond-the-birthday bound secure variable input length pseudorandom functions. Here ℓ denotes the length of the input message after padding.

Scheme	Primitive		Security	
	Type	No. of calls	Bound	Restriction
3kf9 [16]	PRP	$\ell+2$	$O\left(\frac{\ell^2 q^{4/3}}{2^n}\right)$ [20]	–
PMAC+ [14]	PRP	$\ell+2$	$O\left(\frac{q^{4/3}\ell^{2/3}+\ell^2 q}{2^n}\right)$ [20]	$\ell \ll 2^{n/2}$ [20]
1k-PMAC+ [15]	PRP	$\ell+2$	$O\left(\frac{q\sigma^2}{2^{2n}}\right)$	–
LightMAC+[a] [17]	PRP	$2\ell+2$	$O\left(\frac{q^{4/3}}{2^n}\right)$ [20]	–
LightMac+2[a] [17]	PRP	$2\ell+2+t$	$O\left(\frac{q^{t+1}}{2^t}\right)$	$t \leq 7; \ell = O\left(2^{n/2}\right)$
mPMAC+-f	PRF/PRP	$\ell+3$	$O\left(\frac{\sigma}{2^n}\right)$	$\ell = O\left(2^{n/2}\right)$
mPMAC+-p1	PRP	$\ell+5$	$O\left(\frac{\sigma}{2^n}\right)$	$\ell = O\left(2^{n/2}\right)$
mPMAC+-p2	PRP	$\ell+3$	$O\left(\frac{\sigma}{2^n}\right)$	$\ell = O\left(2^{n/2}\right)$
mLightMAC+-f[a]	PRF/PRP	$2\ell+3$	$O\left(\frac{q}{2^n}\right)$	$\ell = O\left(2^{n/2}\right)$
mLightMAC+-p1[a]	PRP	$2\ell+5$	$O\left(\frac{q}{2^n}\right)$	$\ell = O\left(2^{n/2}\right)$
mLightMAC+-p2[a]	PRP	$2\ell+3$	$O\left(\frac{q}{2^n}\right)$	$\ell = O\left(2^{n/2}\right)$

[a]In order to simplify the comparison, we focus on the case $m = n/2$ for LightMAC+-based constructions

Our contribution is twofold. First, we introduce a novel construction dubbed HtmB for Hash-then-modified-Benes. This construction captures the design of a VIL-PRF based on a FIL primitive where the input is first hashed, then given as input to mBenes. This hashing step is what allows us to avoid the main difficulties that are encountered when one tries to prove optimal security for the mBenes

---

[2] The actual Benes and mBenes constructions are from $2n$-bit to $2n$-bit, requiring 8 and 6 calls respectively (see Sect. 3 for details). For now, just n-bit output suffices.

construction. In more details, we introduce a new statistical property for hash functions with $2n$-bit outputs: Diblock Almost q-Collision-free Universality or $DbACU_q$ (see Sect. 2.2). We then show that the composition of a $DbACU_q$ hash function and the mBenes construction is n-bit secure (see Sect. 4), and propose several extensions:

- HtmB-f: the standard HtmB construction based on 4 functions;
- HtmB-p1: the HtmB construction where two functions are replaced with permutations, and the remaining ones are replaced with the sum of two permutations
- HtmB-p2: the standard HtmB based on 4 permutations.

It is worth noting that the security proofs for the first two constructions are straightforward and rely on the same technique as Patarin's classical proofs for Benes [24]. The security proof for the last construction relies on the fundamental result of Mirror Theory [9, Theorem 6]. Note that $DbACU_q$ can be easily achieved by concatenation of two independent almost universal (AU) hash functions. Moreover, we will show two instances where this property is also achieved for concatenation of dependent AU hash functions.

Second, we define two families of block cipher modes of operation dubbed mLightMAC+ and mPMAC+ (see Sect. 5). Both are concrete instantiations of HtmB where the hashing algorithm is based respectively on the LightMAC+ and PMAC+ algorithms. In more details, both schemes are provably secure PRFs with n-bit output and have the following properties:

- mPMAC+ processes n bits of (padded) input per block cipher call during the hashing phase and is secure as long as the number of (padded) queried blocks is small in front of 2^n and no query is longer than $2^{n/2}$ blocks;
- for any fixed integer $m \in \{1, \ldots, n-1\}$, mLightMAC+ processes $n - m$ bits of input per block cipher call during the hashing phase and is secure as long as the number of adversarial queries is small in front of 2^{n3} and no query is longer than 2^m blocks.

Table 1 summarizes this information and compares our modes with the original LightMAC+ and PMAC+ constructions, while Fig. 1 highlights the changes between mPMAC+-p2, our mPMAC+ instantiation based on HtmB-p2, and the original PMAC+ construction.

In [26], Naito proposed a PMAC variant based on PMAC+ like masking and claimed length-independent bounds on the collision probability of the underlying hash layer. However, the proof is incorrect owing to a flaw identified in [27], and apparently it cannot be fixed within the proof setup developed in [26] (see [27] for further details). Consequently, in Sect. 6.2, we first discuss this flaw and then derive a slightly worse bound which is still sufficient to prove optimal security of mPMAC+.

The key sizes in HtmB could be an issue in some memory-constrained environments. In Sect. 7, we address this problem and present some variants of HtmB

---

[3] Note that this is true regardless of the total length of all adversarial queries.

that require lesser key material. Finally, we conclude in Sect. 8 with some open problems.

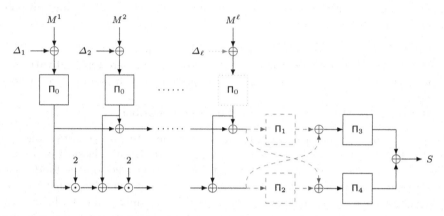

Fig. 1. Schematic of mPMAC+-p2, operating over a padded message of length ℓn bits. $\Pi_0, \ldots, \Pi_4$ are independent random permutations, and $\Delta_i = 2^i \odot \Pi_0(0) \oplus 2^{2i} \odot \Pi_0(1)$, where $\odot$ denotes the multiplication operator of $GF(2^n)$. Components drawn in blue dashed lines represent the addition over the original PMAC+ construction. Components drawn in red dotted lines represent the deletion over the original PMAC+ construction. Note that the modified hash layer saves one block cipher call as compared to the one in PMAC+. (Color figure online)

2 Preliminaries

NOTATIONAL SETUP: For $n \in \mathbb{N}$, $[n]$ denotes the set $\{1, 2, \ldots, n\}$, and $\{0,1\}^n$ denotes the set of bit strings of length n. Let $GF(2^n)$ be the field of order 2^n. We identify bit string and finite field element of $GF(2^n)$ by representing the string $a = a_{n-1} \ldots a_0 \in \{0,1\}^n$ as polynomial $a(x) = a_{n-1}x^{n-1} + \ldots + a_0 \in GF(2^n)$ and vice versa. As usual, we define field addition $\oplus$ as polynomial addition, and multiplication $\odot$ as polynomial multiplication modulo the irreducible polynomial $f(x)$ used to represent $GF(2^n)$. Therefore, we can view $\{0,1\}^n$ as the finite field $GF(2^n)$ with $\oplus$ as field addition and $\odot$ as field multiplication. When the context is clear, we will denote by 2 the primitive element of $GF(2^n)$. The set of all bit strings (including the empty string) is denoted $\{0,1\}^*$, and $|X|$ denotes the number of bits in $X \in \{0,1\}^*$. For any integer m, $\{0,1\}^{\leq m}$ denotes the set of all bit strings of bit length at most m. For $n \in \mathbb{N}$ and any two bit strings M and M', we denote by $M\|M'$ the concatenation of M and M', and we define $\mathsf{pad}(M)$ as $M\|10\cdots0$, such that $|\mathsf{pad}(M)|$ is the smallest multiple of n that is greater than $|M|$. For $i, m \in \mathbb{N}$ such that $i < 2^m$, we define $<i>_m$ as the m-bit little endian encoding of the integer i. For $n, r \in \mathbb{N}$, such that $0 \leq r \leq n$, we define the falling factorial $(n)_r := n!/(n-r)! = n(n-1)\cdots(n-r+1)$. The set of all functions from $\mathcal{X}$ to $\mathcal{Y}$ is denoted $\mathcal{F}(\mathcal{X}, \mathcal{Y})$, and the set of all permutations of $\mathcal{X}$

is denoted $\mathcal{P}(\mathcal{X})$. We simply write $\mathcal{F}(a,b)$ and $\mathcal{P}(a)$, whenever $\mathcal{X} = \{0,1\}^a$ and $\mathcal{Y} = \{0,1\}^b$. For a finite set $\mathcal{X}$, $X \leftarrow_\$ \mathcal{X}$ denotes the uniform at random sampling of X from $\mathcal{X}$. For any property P of some random variable X, $\Pr[P[X]]$ denotes the probability that $P[X]$ is satisfied.

For $q \in \mathbb{N}$, X^q denotes the q-tuple $(X_1, X_2, \ldots, X_q)$. By an abuse of notation we also use X^q to denote the multiset $\{X_i : i \in [q]\}$. For $q \in \mathbb{N}$, for any set $\mathcal{X}$, $(\mathcal{X})_q$ denotes the set of all q-tuples with distinct elements from $\mathcal{X}$. For a pair of tuples X^q and Y^q, (X^q, Y^q) denotes the 2-ary q-tuple $((X_1, Y_1), \ldots, (X_q, Y_q))$. An n-ary q-tuple is defined analogously. For any tuple $X^q \in \mathcal{X}^q$, and for any function $f : \mathcal{X} \to \mathcal{Y}$, $f(X^q)$ denotes the tuple $(f(X_1), \ldots, f(X_q))$.

2.1   Keyed Functions and Block Ciphers

KEYED FUNCTION: A $(\mathcal{K}, \mathcal{X}, \mathcal{Y})$-*keyed function* F with key space $\mathcal{K}$, domain $\mathcal{X}$, and range $\mathcal{Y}$ is a function $F : \mathcal{K} \times \mathcal{X} \to \mathcal{Y}$. We write $F_K(X)$ for $F(K, X)$.

BLOCK CIPHER: A $(\mathcal{K}, \{0,1\}^n)$-*block cipher* E with key space $\mathcal{K}$ and block space $\{0,1\}^n$ is a $(\mathcal{K}, \{0,1\}^n, \{0,1\}^n)$-keyed function, such that for any key $K \in \mathcal{K}$, $X \mapsto E(K, X)$ is a permutation of $\{0,1\}^n$. We write $E_K(X)$ for $E(K, X)$.

Security Definitions: A (q, t)-distinguisher is an interactive algorithm with access to an oracle, that makes at most q oracle queries, runs in time at most t, and outputs a single bit. By convention, $t = \infty$ denotes computationally unbounded (information-theoretic) and deterministic distinguishers. In this paper, we assume that the distinguisher never makes a duplicate query.

PSEUDORANDOM FUNCTION: The pseudorandom function or PRF advantage of any distinguisher $\mathscr{A}$ against a $(\mathcal{K}, \mathcal{X}, \mathcal{Y})$-keyed function F is defined as

$$\mathbf{Adv}_F^{\mathsf{prf}}(\mathscr{A}) = \mathbf{Adv}_{F;\Gamma}(\mathscr{A}) := \left| \Pr_{K \leftarrow_\$ \mathcal{K}}\left[\mathscr{A}^{F_K} = 1\right] - \Pr_{\Gamma \leftarrow_\$ \mathcal{F}(\mathcal{X},\mathcal{Y})}\left[\mathscr{A}^{\Gamma} = 1\right] \right|. \quad (1)$$

Deterministic message authentication codes (or MAC) are keyed functions which provide both integrity and authenticity of data. It is a well-known fact [28] that a secure PRF is a good candidate of deterministic MAC.

PSEUDORANDOM PERMUTATION: The *pseudorandom permutation* or PRP advantage of any distinguisher $\mathscr{A}$ against a $(\mathcal{K}, \{0,1\}^n)$-block cipher E is defined as

$$\mathbf{Adv}_E^{\mathsf{prp}}(\mathscr{A}) = \mathbf{Adv}_{E;\Pi}(\mathscr{A}) := \left| \Pr_{K \leftarrow_\$ \mathcal{K}}\left[\mathscr{A}^{E_K} = 1\right] - \Pr_{\Pi \leftarrow_\$ \mathcal{P}(n)}\left[\mathscr{A}^{\Pi} = 1\right] \right|. \quad (2)$$

Remark 2.1. All our results will be given in the information-theoretic setting, and their computational counterparts can be easily obtained via a boilerplate hybrid argument. In other words, instead of first starting with block ciphers (or PRFs), we will directly work with random permutations (or functions) as the underlying primitives.

SUM OF PERMUTATIONS: In 1998, two independent works [5,29] on building PRFs from PRPs proposed the Sum of Permutation (SoP) construction. For two independent random permutations $\Pi_1, \Pi_2 \leftarrow_\$ \mathcal{P}(n)$, the SoP, denoted $\Pi_1 \oplus \Pi_2$, is defined as the mapping $X \mapsto \Pi_1(X) \oplus \Pi_2(X)$. After several attempts [6,7,9], Dai et al. [10] finally showed that SoP is a secure PRF up to 2^n queries. In Proposition 2.1, we restate the well-known and celebrated result of [10]. A proof of Proposition 2.1 is available in [10].

Proposition 2.1. *For $n \geq 4$, $q \leq 2^{n-4}$, and all (q, ∞)-distinguisher $\mathscr{A}$ we have*

$$\mathbf{Adv}^{\mathsf{prf}}_{\Pi_1 \oplus \Pi_2}(\mathscr{A}) \leq \frac{q^{1.5}}{2^{1.5n}}.$$

2.2   Universal Hash Functions

We recall the usual definition of universal hash function. A $(\mathcal{K}, \mathcal{X}, \mathcal{Y})$-keyed function H is said to be ϵ-*almost universal (AU) hash function* if for any distinct $X, X' \in \mathcal{X}$, we have

$$\Pr_{\mathsf{K} \leftarrow_\$ \mathcal{K}} [H_\mathsf{K}(X) = H_\mathsf{K}(X')] \leq \epsilon. \tag{3}$$

Let us fix a non-empty set $\mathcal{X} \subset \{0,1\}^*$. In this article, we are going to consider a slightly more general notion of universality. Namely, let H be a $(\mathcal{K}, \mathcal{X}, \mathcal{Y})$-keyed function that processes its inputs in n-bit blocks. H is said to be (q, σ, ϵ)-*Almost θ-Collision-free Universal* (or ACU_θ) if, for every $X^q \in (\mathcal{X})_q$ such that X^q contains at most σ blocks, one has $\Pr[C \geq \theta] \leq \epsilon$, where

$$C := |\{(i,j) : 1 \leq i < j \leq q, H_K(X_i) = H_K(X_j)\}|.$$

In the case of a (q, σ, ϵ)-ACU_1 hash function H, we simply say that H is (q, σ, ϵ)-AU. Note that if $q = 2$, we recover the standard AU notion. Moreover, the following proposition is a simple application of Markov's inequality.

Proposition 2.2. *For $q, \theta \in \mathbb{N}$ and $0 \leq \epsilon \leq 1$, let H be an ϵ-AU hash function. Then H is $(q, \infty, \frac{q^2 \epsilon}{\theta}) - ACU_\theta$.*

The proof of Proposition 2.2 follows from Markov's inequality and is thus skipped here.

We also define a new combined notion for the concatenation of two hash function. Namely, we say that a pair $H = (H_1, H_2)$ of two $(\mathcal{K}, \mathcal{X}, \mathcal{Y})$-keyed hash functions H_1, H_2 is $(q, \sigma, \epsilon_2, \epsilon_1)$-*Diblock* ACU_q (or DbACU_q) if H is (q, σ, ϵ_2)-AU and H_1, H_2 are (q, σ, ϵ_1)-ACU_q. A simple example of DbACU_q hash function is the concatenation of two independent AU hash functions. In section 5, we present two other DbACU_q hash functions LightHash and PHash based respectively on the LightMAC+ and PMAC+ constructions.

THE CONCATENATION OF TWO INDEPENDENT AU HASH FUNCTIONS: Let H_1 and H_2 be two ϵ-AU hash functions with key space $\mathcal{K}$, message space $\mathcal{X}$ and range $\mathcal{Y}$. We define the concatenation $H = (H_1, H_2)$ of H_1 and H_2 as a $(\mathcal{K}^2, \mathcal{X}, \mathcal{Y}^2)$-keyed function defined as $H_{(K_1, K_2)}(X) = (H_{1,K_1}(X), H_{2,K_2}(X))$ for every $X \in \mathcal{X}$, $(K_1, K_2) \in \mathcal{K}^2$. The following result holds.

Proposition 2.3. *Let H_1, H_2 be two ϵ-AU hash functions keyed independently and $H = (H_1, H_2)$. For $q, \sigma \in \mathbb{N}$, H is $(q, \sigma, q^2\epsilon^2, q\epsilon)$-DbACU$_q$.*

A proof of Proposition 2.3 relies on the independence of both components and on Proposition 2.2.

2.3 Coefficient-H Technique

The coefficient-H technique by Patarin [30,31] is a tool to upper bound the distinguishing advantage of any deterministic and computationally unbounded distinguisher $\mathscr{A}$ in distinguishing the real oracle $\mathcal{R}$ from the ideal oracle $\mathcal{I}$. The collection of all queries and responses that $\mathscr{A}$ made and received to and from the oracle, is called the transcript of $\mathscr{A}$, denoted as τ.

Let $\mathbb{T}_{re}$ and $\mathbb{T}_{id}$ denote the transcript random variable induced by $\mathscr{A}$'s interaction with $\mathcal{R}$ and $\mathcal{I}$, respectively. Let $\mathcal{T}$ be the set of all transcripts. A transcript $\tau \in \mathcal{T}$ is said to be *attainable* if $\Pr[\mathbb{T}_{id} = \tau] > 0$, i.e., it can be realized by $\mathscr{A}$'s interaction with $\mathcal{I}$. Following these notations, we state the main result of coefficient-H technique in Theorem 2.1. A proof of this theorem is available in [4,32], among others.

Theorem 2.1. *For $\epsilon_1, \epsilon_2 \geq 0$, suppose there is a set $\mathcal{T}_{bad} \subseteq \mathcal{T}$, that we call the set of bad transcripts, such that the following conditions hold:*

- $\Pr[\mathbb{T}_{id} \in \mathcal{T}_{bad}] \leq \epsilon_1$; and
- *For any $\tau \notin \mathcal{T}_{bad}$, τ is attainable and $\dfrac{\Pr[\mathbb{T}_{re} = \tau]}{\Pr[\mathbb{T}_{id} = \tau]} \geq 1 - \epsilon_2$.*

Then, for any computationally unbounded and deterministic distinguisher $\mathscr{A}$, we have

$$\mathbf{Adv}_{\mathcal{R};\mathcal{I}}(\mathscr{A}) \leq \epsilon_1 + \epsilon_2.$$

3 Benes and mBenes Transformations

BUTTERFLY TRANSFORMATION: Given four functions $f_1, \ldots, f_4 \in \mathcal{F}(n, n)$, the Butterfly transformation (illustrated in Fig. 2) is a function from $\{0, 1\}^{2n}$ to $\{0, 1\}^{2n}$, which is defined as Butterfly$[f_1, \ldots, f_4](L, R) := (X, Y)$, where

$$X := f_1(L) \oplus f_2(R) \text{ and } Y := f_3(L) \oplus f_4(R).$$

BENES TRANSFORMATION: Given eight functions $f_1, \ldots, f_8 \in \mathcal{F}(n, n)$, the Benes transformation (illustrated in Fig. 2) is a function from $\{0, 1\}^{2n}$ to $\{0, 1\}^{2n}$, which is defined as the composition of two Butterfly transformations, i.e. Benes$[f_1, \ldots, f_8](L, R) := (S, T)$, where

$$S := f_5(f_1(L) \oplus f_2(R)) \oplus f_6(f_3(L) \oplus f_4(R)) = f_5(X) \oplus f_6(Y),$$
$$T := f_7(f_1(L) \oplus f_2(R)) \oplus f_8(f_3(L) \oplus f_4(R)) = f_7(X) \oplus f_8(Y).$$

MODIFIED BENES TRANSFORMATION: The modified Benes or mBenes transformation (illustrated in Fig. 2) is a simplification of the Benes transformation,
where f_2 and f_3 are identity functions. So, we have $X = f_1(L) \oplus R$, $Y = f_4(R) \oplus L$,
and $(S, T) = \text{mBenes}[f_1, f_4, f_5, \dots, f_8](L, R)$, such that $S = f_5(X) \oplus f_6(Y)$ and
$T = f_7(X) \oplus f_8(Y)$.

For brevity we drop the parameters $f_1, \dots, f_8$, whenever they are understood
from the context.

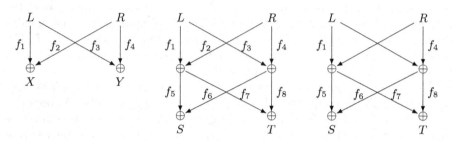

Fig. 2. Left to right: Butterfly, Benes and mBenes transformations. An edge (u, v) with
label g denotes the mapping $v = g(u)$. Unlabelled edges are identity mapping.

3.1   Revisiting the Security Analysis of Benes and mBenes

Let (L^q, R^q) denote a q-tuple of inputs. Given $f_1, \dots, f_4 \in \mathcal{F}(n, n)$, we can define
(X^q, Y^q) by the definition of Benes or mBenes, as applicable.

DEPENDENCY GRAPH: To (L^q, R^q) and any $f_1, \dots, f_4 \in \mathcal{F}(n, n)$, we associate
the dependency graph $\mathcal{G}[L^q, R^q; f_{1,\dots,4}] = ([q], \mathcal{E})$, over the set of all query indices
$[q]$, where $\{i, j\} \in \mathcal{E}$ if and only if $X_i = X_j$ (the edge is colored red) or $Y_i = Y_j$
(the edge is colored blue). $\mathcal{G}[L^q, R^q; f_{1,\dots,4}]$ may contain parallel edges, but their
coloring will be different. Figure 3 is a possible dependency graph for $q = 12$.

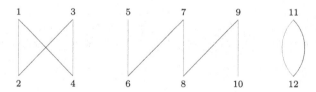

Fig. 3. A possible dependency graph for some 12-tuple of inputs. (Color figure online)

Definition 3.1 (Alternating cycle). *An alternating cycle or circle of length
$k \geq 2$, k even, is simply a cycle denoted by a sequence of $k + 1$ indices, $v^{k+1} =
(v_1, \dots, v_k, v_{k+1})$ such that*

- $v_{k+1} = v_1$,
- $\{v_i, v_{i+1}\} \in \mathcal{E}$ *for all* $i \in [k]$,

- $\{v_1, v_2\}$ *is colored red, and*
- $\{v_i, v_{i+1}\}$ *and* $\{v_{i+1}, v_{i+2}\}$ *do not share the same color, for all* $i \in [k-1]$.

Example 3.1. Any parallel edge is an example of alternating cycle. In Fig. 3, $(1, 2, 3, 4, 1)$ and $(11, 12, 11)$ are two possible alternating cycles.

Let $\mathsf{AC}[L^q, R^q; f_{1,...,4}]$ denote the property that $\mathcal{G}[L^q, R^q; f_{1,...,4}]$ contains an alternating cycle. We will drop the parameters $(L^q, R^q; f_{1,...,4})$, whenever they are understood from the context.

For $f_1, \ldots, f_8 \leftarrow_\$ \mathcal{F}(n, n)$, Aiello and Venkatesan [22] showed that PRF advantage of any distinguisher against Benes and mBenes is at most the probability that AC is satisfied. Similar results were later also shown in [24,25]. Theorem 3.1 is a reformulation of [22, Lemma 2] (also [25, Theorem 5.2] and [24, Theorem 1]) in our notations.

Theorem 3.1. *For* $\Gamma_1 \ldots, \Gamma_8 \leftarrow_\$ \mathcal{F}(n, n)$, $F \in \{Benes, mBenes\}$, *and any* (q, ∞)-*distinguisher* $\mathscr{A}$, *we have*

$$\mathbf{Adv}^{\mathsf{prf}}_{F[\Gamma_1,...,\Gamma_8]}(\mathscr{A}) \leq \mathrm{ACP}(q) := \max_{(L^q, R^q)} \Pr_{\Gamma_1,...,\Gamma_4} [\mathsf{AC}[L^q, R^q; \Gamma_{1,...,4}]].$$

A proof of Theorem 3.1 is available in [25] among others. For the sake of completeness, we reproduce it in the full version of this paper.

Aiello and Venkatesan [22] claimed that $\mathrm{ACP}(q) \leq q^2/2^{2n}$. Later, Patarin and Montreuil [25] showed that the initial analysis of $\mathrm{ACP}(q)$ by Aiello and Venkatesan was overly optimistic, and subsequently gave a non-tight estimate for Benes. The main idea of their analysis was to consider each equation in the alternating cycle, one-by-one, distinguishing whether the equation is dependent over the previous equations or not. If the i-th equation is independent then they freely choose the new index[4], i.e., $(i+1)$-th index in $q - i$ ways. However, when the equation is dependent, then there exist $j, j' < i$ such that $L_i = L_j$ and $R_i = R_{j'}$, hence we only have $i(i-1)$ ways to choose the $(i+1)$-th index. By continuing in this way and making some algebraic simplifications, they derive the upper bound

$$\mathrm{ACP}(q) \leq d(k)\frac{q^2}{2^{2n+1}} + \frac{q^4}{2^{4n+2}} + \frac{q^{k+1}}{2^{nk}},$$

for all $k \geq 1$, where $d(k) = 6.5 + \sum_{j=6}^{k} j^{2j} + k^{2k}$. So, for any k and sufficiently large n, we can claim security up to $q \leq \min\{2^{nk/k+1}, \sqrt{2^{2n}/d(k)}\}$. However, the bound becomes increasingly moot as we increase the value of k. Suppose we aim for security up to $2^{kn/k+1}$ queries. Then, for $k = 6$ we need $n > 112$, for $k = 7$ we need $n > 161$, and for $k = 9$ we need $n > 290$, where n denotes the output size of the underlying functions. Clearly, very high security (close to $0.9n$) is only possible for large output size ($n > 290$). In practice, with such a large output size, even a birthday bound security guarantee might suffice.

---

[4] Each equation (except the last one) gives a new index.

Patarin and Montreuil also claimed similar security bounds for mBenes [25]. However, they only gave a very high level and terse sketch of the proof. We refer the readers to [25] for details.

First Dependency and Tight Bound for Benes: Patarin [24] devised an elegant way to derive a more tighter estimate for $\mathrm{ACP}(q)$ in case of Benes.

Definition 3.2 (Alternating trail). *An alternating trail or line of length $k \geq 2$ is simply a trail denoted by a sequence of $k + 1$ vertices, $v^{k+1} = (v_1, \ldots, v_k, v_{k+1})$ such that*

- *$\{v_i, v_{i+1}\} \in \mathcal{E}$, for all $i \in [k]$.*
- *$\{v_i, v_{i+1}\}$ and $\{v_{i+1}, v_{i+2}\}$ do not share the same color, for all $i \in [k-1]$.*

In addition, we say that v^{k+1} is a red (res. blue) trail if $\{v_1, v_2\}$ is colored red (res. blue).

Example 3.2. An alternating cycle is in fact a special type of alternating red trail with even length. In Fig. 3, $(1, 2, 3, 4, 1)$, $(5, 6, 7, 8, 9, 10)$, and $(11, 12, 11)$ are some of the possible alternating trails. Note that all these trails are red trails. On the other hand, $(2, 3, 4, 1, 2)$ is a blue trail.

ASSOCIATED SYSTEM OF EQUATIONS: By definition, each edge in the dependency graph $\mathcal{G}$ corresponds to an equation. For example, say we have an edge $\{u, v\}$ with red color, then the associated equation is $X_u = X_v$. By extension, each connected component corresponds to a system of equations. In particular, any alternating trail (or cycle) v^{k+1} can be uniquely associated with a system of k equations. For example, suppose v^{k+1} is an alternating red trail of even length. Then, the associated system of equation is $X_{v_1} = X_{v_2}, \ldots, Y_{v_k} = Y_{v_{k+1}}$.

Example 3.3. In Fig. 3, we can have the following associated system of equations:

- For alternating cycle $(1, 2, 3, 4, 1)$: $X_1 = X_2$, $Y_2 = Y_3$, $X_3 = X_4$, $Y_4 = Y_1$.
- For alternating trail $(5, 6, 7, 8, 9, 10)$: $X_5 = X_6$, $Y_6 = Y_7$, $X_7 = X_8$, $Y_8 = Y_9$, $X_9 = X_{10}$.
- For parallel edge $(11, 12, 11)$: $X_{11} = X_{12}$, $Y_{12} = Y_{11}$.

Definition 3.3 (First dependency [24]). *An alternating trail of length $k \geq 2$ is said to have first dependency if all the equations in the associated system of equations, except the last one are independent of others, and the last equation is a consequence of the previous equations.*

An alternating cycle of length $k \geq 2$ is said to have first dependency if all the equations in the associated system of equations, except one are independent of others, and exactly one is a consequence of the other equations.

Example 3.4. In Fig. 3, suppose $L_5 = L_9$, $L_6 = L_{10}$, $R_5 = R_6$, $R_9 = R_{10}$. Then, $X_5 = X_6$ holds if $f_1(L_5) = f_1(L_6)$ (as $R_5 = R_6$). Similarly, $X_9 = X_{10}$ holds if $f_1(L_9) = f_1(L_{10})$ (as $R_9 = R_{10}$). But, $L_9 = L_5$ and $L_{10} = L_6$. Thus, $X_9 = X_{10}$ is a consequence of $X_5 = X_6$. Hence, $X_5 = X_6$, $Y_6 = Y_7$, $X_7 = X_8$, $Y_8 = Y_9$, $X_9 = X_{10}$ is an alternating trail of length 5 with first dependency.

Any alternating cycle of length k must have one of the following:

1. All the equations in the associated system of equations are independent.
2. The cycle has first dependency, i.e., all equations are independent except one.
3. The cycle contains an alternating trail of length $< k$ which has first dependency.

The first case is easy to bound as we have to choose k indices and we have k independent equations, which gives $O(q^k/2^{nk})$ bound. The second case is similar to the last one, which is more general. Patarin argued that whenever an alternating trail has first dependency, then among the $k + 1$ indices at least two are fixed once the other $k - 1$ indices are chosen. Indices 6 and 9, for instance, are fixed once we choose indices 5 and 10 in Example 3.4. This observation immediately gives a bound of the form $O(q^{k-1}/2^{n(k-1)})$, since the first $k - 1$ equations are independent. On combining the three cases, Patarin obtained the following bound on $\mathrm{ACP}(q)$ in case of Benes.

$$\mathrm{ACP}(q) \leq \frac{8590q^2}{2^{2n}} \tag{4}$$

Notice the large constant in the bound, which compels large n to get appreciable security in practice. The main component of this constant is an infinite sum $\sum_{k=3}^{\infty} \left(\frac{k^5}{2^{k-3}} \right)$. For large k, we observed that this sum can be approximated to 8588. In the same paper, Patarin also gave another improved bound [24, Theorem 9] using a more involved analysis which can be approximated to $26q^2/2^{2n} + 200076q^3/2^{4n}$ for large k.

First Dependency in mBenes: While the first dependency idea is quite useful for deriving tight security bound of Benes, Patarin noted that the same is not true in case of mBenes. In fact, a crucial argument—*among the $k + 1$ indices 2 indices are fixed once we fix $k-1$ indices*—fails in case of mBenes. For example, suppose $X_1 = X_2$, $Y_2 = Y_3$, $X_3 = X_4$ is an alternating trail with first dependency, such that $L_1 = L_3$, $L_2 = L_4$, and $R_1 \oplus R_2 \oplus R_3 \oplus R_4 = 0$. It is clear to see that here only one index is fixed given the other three ($L_4 = L_2$ and $R_4 = R_1 \oplus R_2 \oplus R_3$). Consequently, Patarin speculates:

Therefore, a proof of security in $O(2^n)$ for the Modified Benes will be different, and probably more complex than our proof of security on $O(2^n)$ for the regular Benes.

4   HtmB: Hash Then Modified Benes

Section 3 gives a clear indication that the exact security of mBenes is a difficult problem. The main difficulty in the analysis is a simple fact that the distinguisher has complete control over the inputs to mBenes. However, in practice PRFs are mostly required to work over arbitrary domains, which requires an additional preprocessing phase before the application of fixed input length PRF.

This preprocessing is often done via a universal hash function—the so-called Hash-then-PRF paradigm [21]. This added layer of preprocessing somewhat curtails the distinguisher's ability to control the inputs to mBenes. Indeed, now we show that the composition of a universal hash function with mBenes leads to optimal security, with domain extension as byproduct.

HASH-THEN-MODIFIED-BENES: Let $\mathcal{M} \subseteq \{0,1\}^*$. Given a pair $H = (H_1, H_2)$ of two $(\mathcal{K}, \mathcal{M}, \{0,1\}^n)$-keyed hash functions ($H_1$ and H_2 may share the same key), and $f_1, \ldots, f_4 \in \mathcal{F}(n,n)$, the Hash-then-modified-Benes or HtmB transformation is a function from $\mathcal{M}$ to $\{0,1\}^n$, which is defined as $\mathsf{HtmB}[H, f_1, \ldots, f_4](M) := S$, where

$$(L, R) := H_K(M) \quad X := f_1(L) \oplus R \quad Y := f_2(R) \oplus L \quad S = f_3(X) \oplus f_4(Y). \quad (5)$$

Remark 4.1. Note that, we reduced the output length of HtmB from $2n$ bits to n bits. This is mainly due to the fact that n bits of the output of a VIL PRF is sufficient to achieve 2^n query deterministic MAC security (a major inspiration for this work). In any case, another n-bit block can be easily generated by setting $T = f_5(X) \oplus f_6(Y)$ for some $f_5, f_6 \in \mathcal{F}(n,n)$.

We extend the dependency graph of Sect. 3.1 to incorporate the hash function H. To any input $M^q \in (\mathcal{M})_q$, $K \in \mathcal{K}$, and $f_1, f_2 \in \mathcal{F}(n,n)$, we associate the dependency graph $\mathcal{G}[M^q; K, f_{1,2}] = ([q], \mathcal{E})$, where $\mathcal{E}$ is defined as before. Thus, $\mathcal{G}$ is again a bichromatic graph. We define $\mathsf{AC}[M^q; K, f_{1,2}]$, $\mathsf{ACP}(q)$, alternating trails, cycles, and the first dependency property analogously as in Sect. 3.1.

In the following subsections we present three security results on HtmB based on the choice of $f_1, \ldots, f_4$.

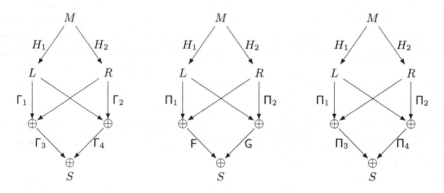

Fig. 4. The three instantiations of Hash-then-modified-Benes or HtmB transformation. $H = (H_1, H_2)$ is a DbACU_q hash function. From left to right: $\mathsf{HtmB\text{-}f}[H, \Gamma_1, \ldots, \Gamma_4] = \mathsf{HtmB}[H, \Gamma_1, \ldots, \Gamma_4]$ based on $\Gamma_1, \ldots, \Gamma_4 \leftarrow_\$ \mathcal{F}(n,n)$; $\mathsf{HtmB\text{-}p1}[H, \Pi_1, \ldots, \Pi_6] = \mathsf{HtmB}[H, \Pi_1, \Pi_2, \mathsf{F}, \mathsf{G}]$ based on $\Pi_1, \ldots, \Pi_6 \leftarrow_\$ \mathcal{P}(n)$, where $\mathsf{F}(X) = \Pi_3(X) \oplus \Pi_4(X)$ and $\mathsf{G}(Y) = \Pi_5(Y) \oplus \Pi_6(Y)$; and $\mathsf{HtmB\text{-}p2}[H, \Pi_1, \ldots, \Pi_4] = \mathsf{HtmB}[H, \Pi_1, \ldots, \Pi_4]$ based on $\Pi_1, \ldots, \Pi_4 \leftarrow_\$ \mathcal{P}(n)$. An edge (u, v) with label g denotes the mapping $v = g(u)$. Unlabelled edges are identity mapping.

4.1 HtmB-f: Random Function Based Construction

Given $\Gamma_1, \ldots, \Gamma_4 \leftarrow_\$ \mathcal{F}(n, n)$, we obtain the hash-then-PRF instance where the PRF is instantiated with $\mathsf{mBenes}[\Gamma_1, \ldots, \Gamma_4]$ (truncated to first n-bit). Formally, we define $\mathsf{HtmB\text{-}f}[H, \Gamma_1, \ldots, \Gamma_4]$ (see Fig. 4) as $\mathsf{HtmB}[H, \Gamma_1, \ldots, \Gamma_4]$.

Recall that $\mathrm{ACP}(q)$ denotes the maximum probability of getting an alternating cycle in the dependency graph $\mathcal{G}$, where the probability is maximized over all choices of message tuple M^q. Lemma 4.1 gives a bound on $\mathrm{ACP}(q)$.

Lemma 4.1. *For $\epsilon_1, \epsilon_2, \sigma \geq 0$, $q \leq 2^{n-1}$, $(q, \sigma, \epsilon_2, \epsilon_1)$-DbACU$_q$ hash function H_K instantiated with $K \leftarrow_\$ \mathcal{K}$, and $\Gamma_1, \Gamma_2 \leftarrow_\$ \mathcal{F}(n, n)$, we have*

$$\mathrm{ACP}(q) \leq \frac{4q^2}{2^{2n}} + \frac{2q^2}{2^{3n}} + \epsilon_2 + 2\epsilon_1.$$

Proof. Fix a q-tuple $M^q \in (\mathcal{M})_q$ that maximizes $\mathrm{ACP}(q)$. Recall that $(L^q, R^q) = H_K(M^q)$, $X_q = \Gamma_1(L^q) \oplus R^q$ and $Y^q = \Gamma_2(R^q) \oplus L^q$. We bound the probability of $\mathsf{AC}[M^q; K, \Gamma_{1,2}]$ conditioned on the following events:

- **Fresh:** $\forall\, i, j \in [q]$, $(L_i, R_i) \neq (L_j, R_j)$.
- **Lpairs:** $|\{(i, j) : 1 \leq i < j \leq q, L_i = L_j\}| < q$.
- **Rpairs:** $|\{(i, j) : 1 \leq i < j \leq q, R_i = R_j\}| < q$.

Let $\mathtt{Triv} = \neg(\mathtt{Fresh} \cap \mathtt{Lpairs} \cap \mathtt{Rpairs})$.

First, consider the probability of getting an alternating cycle of length 2 (parallel edge). Suppose the alternating cycle is $X_{i_1} = X_{i_2}$, $Y_{i_1} = Y_{i_2}$, which can be rewritten as

$$\Gamma_1(L_{i_1}) \oplus R_{i_1} = \Gamma_1(L_{i_2}) \oplus R_{i_2}$$
$$\Gamma_2(R_{i_1}) \oplus L_{i_1} = \Gamma_2(R_{i_2}) \oplus L_{i_2}.$$

Suppose $L_{i_1} = L_{i_2}$. Then, since $\mathtt{Fresh}$ holds, $R_{i_1} \neq R_{i_2}$, whence the first equation is not satisfied. Therefore, $L_{i_1} \neq L_{i_2}$. A similar argument implies $R_{i_1} \neq R_{i_2}$. Then, the system of equations must have full rank, i.e. rank 2. Using the randomness of Γ_1 and Γ_2, we get $q^2/2^{2n}$.

For even $k > 2$, let $X_{i_1} = X_{i_2}$, $Y_{i_2} = Y_{i_3}$, $\cdots$, $Y_{i_k} = Y_{i_1}$ be an alternating cycle of length k. Then, we can rewrite it as

$$\Gamma_1(L_{i_1}) \oplus R_{i_1} = \Gamma_1(L_{i_2}) \oplus R_{i_2}$$
$$\Gamma_2(R_{i_2}) \oplus L_{i_2} = \Gamma_2(R_{i_3}) \oplus L_{i_3}$$

$$\vdots$$

$$\Gamma_2(R_{i_k}) \oplus L_{i_k} = \Gamma_2(R_{i_1}) \oplus L_{i_1}.$$

Now, we must have one of the following three cases:

1. *Independent cycle:* All k equations are independent, i.e., rank is k. Then, we can bound the probability to $q^k/2^{kn}$.

2. *Strict sub-trail with first dependency:* The cycle contains an alternating sub-trail of length $k' < k$, which has first dependency. Therefore, all the equations are independent except the last equation which is a consequence of previous equations. Without loss of generality, we assume that k' is odd. Then, we must have an associated system of equations

$$\Gamma_1(L_{i_1}) \oplus R_{i_1} = \Gamma_1(L_{i_2}) \oplus R_{i_2}$$
$$\Gamma_2(R_{i_2}) \oplus L_{i_2} = \Gamma_2(R_{i_3}) \oplus L_{i_3}$$
$$\vdots$$
$$\Gamma_1(L_{i_{k'}}) \oplus R_{i_{k'}} = \Gamma_1(L_{i_{k'+1}}) \oplus R_{i_{k'+1}}.$$

Since the last equation is a consequence of previous equations, we must have some $i_j, i_{j'} < i_{k'}$, such that $L_{i_{k'}} = L_{i_j}$ and $L_{i_{k'+1}} = L_{i_{j'}}$. Using the fact that Lpairs holds, we can have at most q choices for $(i_{k'}, i_j)$ and at most q choices for $(i_{k'+1}, i_{j'})$. Similarly, we can use Rpairs when k' is even. The remaining $k' - 3$ indices can be chosen in at most $q^{k'-3}$ ways. Finally, we bound the probability to at most $q^{k'-1}/2^{(k'-1)n}$ (as exactly $k' - 1$ equations are independent).

3. *Circle has first dependency:* All the equations are independent except for the last one. This case can be handled in a similar manner as case 2. In fact, we get $q^{k-2}/2^{(k-1)n}$ which is a better bound as compared to case 2.

Combining the three cases we have

$$\Pr[\mathsf{AC}|\neg\mathsf{Triv}] \leq \sum_{i=2}^{\infty} \frac{q^i}{2^{in}} + \sum_{j=4}^{\infty} \frac{q^{j-2}}{2^{(j-1)n}} + \sum_{k=3}^{\infty} \frac{q^{k-1}}{2^{(k-1)n}}$$

$$\leq \frac{1}{1 - \frac{q}{2^n}} \times \left(\frac{2q^2}{2^{2n}} + \frac{q^2}{2^{3n}} \right)$$

$$\leq \frac{4q^2}{2^{2n}} + \frac{2q^2}{2^{3n}}, \tag{6}$$

where the last inequality follows from $q \leq 2^{n-1}$. Finally, we have

$$\Pr[\mathsf{AC}] \leq \Pr[\mathsf{AC}|\neg\mathsf{Triv}] + \Pr[\neg\mathsf{Fresh}] + \Pr[\neg\mathsf{Lpairs}] + \Pr[\neg\mathsf{Rpairs}]$$

$$\leq \frac{4q^2}{2^{2n}} + \frac{2q^2}{2^{3n}} + \epsilon_2 + 2\epsilon_1.$$

At the last inequality, the third term on the right hand side follows from the (q, σ, ϵ_2)-AU property of H, and the fourth term follows from the (q, σ, ϵ_1)-ACU$_q$ property of H_1 and H_2. $\square$

Remark 4.2. The utility of universal hash layer lies in the analysis of case 2 (and 3) in the proof. Specifically, we use the (q, σ, ϵ_1)-ACU$_q$ property of H_1 and H_2 to reduce the count of pairs with same L (or R) value from q^2 to q, which in turn helps us in reducing the overall choices for the $k' + 1$ indices to $k' - 1$.

Remark 4.3. This pair idea is not applicable to mBenes as the distinguisher has full control over the inputs (L_i, R_i). For instance, the distinguisher can fix a single L value across all q queries, so that we have exactly $q(q-1)$ pairs.

By now, it should be clear that Lemma 4.1 resolves the main hurdle in a proof of security up to $O(2^n)$ queries for HtmB-f. Theorem 4.1 quantifies the PRF security of HtmB-f.

Theorem 4.1. *For* $\epsilon_1, \epsilon_2, \sigma \geq 0$, $q \leq 2^{n-1}$, $\Gamma_1 \ldots, \Gamma_4 \leftarrow_\$ \mathcal{F}(n, n)$, *and* $(q, \sigma, \epsilon_2, \epsilon_1)$-*DbACU$_q$ hash function* H_K *instantiated with* $K \leftarrow_\$ \mathcal{K}$, *the PRF advantage of any* (q, ∞)-*distinguisher* $\mathscr{A}$ *against* HtmB-f$[H, \Gamma_1, \ldots, \Gamma_4]$ *is given by*

$$\mathbf{Adv}^{\text{prf}}_{\text{HtmB-f}[H, \Gamma_1, \ldots, \Gamma_4]}(\mathscr{A}) \leq \frac{4q^2}{2^{2n}} + \frac{2q^2}{2^{3n}} + \epsilon_2 + 2\epsilon_1.$$

Proof. A proof of this theorem can be derived using similar arguments as in case of Theorem 3.1 after substituting the bound of ACP(q) from Lemma 4.1.

4.2 HtmB-p1: Random Permutation Based Construction

In this subsection, we aim to give a random permutation based instantiation of HtmB, called HtmB-p1. The obvious inspiration behind this is the wide availability of block ciphers which can be used to instantiate HtmB-p1.

A trivial way to achieve this is to replace the random functions with sum of independent random permutations. But this will cost 8 random permutation calls (2 calls for each f_i, $i \in [4]$). Instead, we observe that f_1 and f_2 can each be instantiated with single random permutation without any appreciable drop in security. This reduces the number of random permutation calls to 6.

Given $\Pi_1, \ldots, \Pi_6 \leftarrow_\$ \mathcal{P}(n)$, we define the mappings, $\mathsf{F}, \mathsf{G} \in \mathcal{F}(n, n)$ as

$$\mathsf{F}(X) = \Pi_3(X) \oplus \Pi_4(X) \text{ and } \mathsf{G}(Y) = \Pi_5(Y) \oplus \Pi_6(Y),$$

and HtmB-p1$[H, \Pi_1, \ldots, \Pi_6]$ (see Fig. 4) is defined as HtmB$[H, \Pi_1, \Pi_2, \mathsf{F}, \mathsf{G}]$. Theorem 4.2 gives the PRF security of HtmB-p1.

Theorem 4.2. *For* $n \geq 4$, $\epsilon_1, \epsilon_2, \sigma \geq 0$, $q \leq 2^{n-4}$, $\Pi_1, \ldots, \Pi_6 \leftarrow_\$ \mathcal{P}(n)$, *and* $(q, \sigma, \epsilon_2, \epsilon_1)$-*DbACU$_q$ hash function* H_K *instantiated with key* $K \leftarrow_\$ \mathcal{K}$, *the PRF advantage of any* (q, ∞)-*distinguisher* $\mathscr{A}$ *against* HtmB-p1$[H, \Pi_1, \ldots, \Pi_6]$ *is given by*

$$\mathbf{Adv}^{\text{prf}}_{\text{HtmB-p1}[H, \Pi_1, \ldots, \Pi_6]}(\mathscr{A}) \leq \frac{2q^{1.5}}{2^{1.5n}} + \frac{16q^2}{2^{2n}} + \frac{16q^2}{2^{3n}} + \epsilon_2 + 2\epsilon_1.$$

Proof. Using hybrid argument, we replace F and G functions in the lower layer with independent random functions $\Gamma_3, \Gamma_4 \leftarrow_\$ \mathcal{F}(n, n)$. This incurs a cost of $2q^{1.5}/2^{1.5n}$ (using Proposition 2.1). We denote the resulting construction by HtmB*. Then we must have a (q, ∞)-distinguisher $\mathscr{B}$ against HtmB*, such that

$$\mathbf{Adv}^{\text{prf}}_{\text{HtmB-p1}[H, \Pi_1, \ldots, \Pi_6]}(\mathscr{A}) \leq \mathbf{Adv}^{\text{prf}}_{\text{HtmB}^\star}(\mathscr{B}) + \frac{2q^{1.5}}{2^{1.5n}}. \tag{7}$$

Now, using a similar line of argument as used in Theorem 3.1, one can show that

$$\mathbf{Adv}^{\mathsf{prf}}_{\mathsf{HtmB}^*}(\mathscr{B}) \leq \mathrm{ACP}(q). \tag{8}$$

Lemma 4.2 bounds $\mathrm{ACP}(q)$ to $\frac{16q^2}{2^{2n}} + \frac{16q^2}{2^{3n}} + \epsilon_2 + 2\epsilon_1$, which in combination with Eq. (7) and (8) gives the result. $\square$

Lemma 4.2. *For* $q \leq 2^{n-2}$, $K \leftarrow_\$ \mathcal{K}$, *and* $\Pi_1, \Pi_2 \leftarrow_\$ \mathcal{P}(n)$, *we have*

$$\mathrm{ACP}(q) \leq \frac{16q^2}{2^{2n}} + \frac{16q^2}{2^{3n}} + \epsilon_2 + 2\epsilon_1.$$

Proof. The proof idea is similar to the proof of Lemma 4.1 given in the previous subsection. So, we reuse the same set of notations and definitions.

Fix a q-tuple $M^q \in (\mathcal{M})_q$ that maximizes $\mathrm{ACP}(q)$. We bound the probability of $\mathsf{AC}[M^q; K, \Pi_{1,2}]$ conditioned on the following events:

- Fresh: $\forall\ i, j \in [q]$, $(L_i, R_i) \neq (L_j, R_j)$.
- Lpairs: $|\{(i,j) : 1 \leq i < j \leq q, L_i = L_j\}| < q$.
- Rpairs: $|\{(i,j) : 1 \leq i < j \leq q, R_i = R_j\}| < q$.

The proof follows in exactly the same manner, except a minor change in the probability bound, due to a distributional change in the underlying randomness (random function to random permutation). It is easy to see that a system of k independent equations holds with probability less than $1/(2^n - k)^k$, when Π_1 and Π_2 are random permutations. We further simplify it to $2^k/2^{kn}$ using $k < q < 2^{n-1}$.

Using the above mentioned probability bound, along with the argumentation used in the proof of Lemma 4.1, we get

$$\Pr[\mathsf{AC}|\mathtt{Fresh} \cap \mathtt{Lpairs} \cap \mathtt{Rpairs}] \leq \sum_{i=2}^{\infty} \frac{2^i q^i}{2^{in}} + \sum_{j=4}^{\infty} \frac{2^{j-1} q^{j-2}}{2^{(j-1)n}} + \sum_{k=3}^{\infty} \frac{2^{k-1} q^{k-1}}{2^{(k-1)n}}$$

$$\leq \frac{1}{1 - \frac{q}{2^{n-1}}} \times \left(\frac{8q^2}{2^{2n}} + \frac{8q^2}{2^{3n}} \right)$$

$$\leq \frac{16q^2}{2^{2n}} + \frac{16q^2}{2^{3n}}, \tag{9}$$

where the last inequality follows from $q \leq 2^{n-2}$. Finally, we have

$$\mathrm{ACP}(q) \leq \frac{16q^2}{2^{2n}} + \frac{16q^2}{2^{3n}} + \epsilon_2 + 2\epsilon_1.$$

$\square$

4.3   HtmB-p2: An Improvement over HtmB-p1

One can further reduce the number of permutation calls in HtmB-p1, if the generalized version of Mirror Theory [9, 33, 34] is correct. Specifically, we simply replace F and G in the definition of HtmB-p1 with the permutations Π_3 and Π_4 to get HtmB-p2. Formally, given $\Pi_1, \ldots, \Pi_4$ we define HtmB-p2$[H, \Pi_1, \ldots, \Pi_4]$ (see Fig. 4) as HtmB$[H, \Pi_1, \ldots, \Pi_4]$.

For any $M^q \in (\mathcal{M})_q$, $K \in \mathcal{K}$, and $\pi_1, \pi_2 \in \mathcal{P}(n)$, X^q, Y^q, and S^q are well-defined. In addition to AC$[M^q; K, \pi_{1,2}]$, we define two more properties on $\mathcal{G}[M^q; K, \pi_{1,2}]$:

- LC$[M^q; K, \pi_{1,2}](\xi)$: The largest component in $\mathcal{G}[M^q; K, \pi_{1,2}]$ contains at least $\xi + 1$ vertices.
- DG$[M^q; K, \pi_{1,2}]$: $\mathcal{G}[M^q; K, \pi_{1,2}]$ contains an alternating trail v^{k+1}, k odd, such that $\bigoplus_{j=1}^{k+1} S_{v_j} = 0$.

Patarin's Mirror Theory: Mirror theory [9,33,34] is a tool to obtain lower bound on the number of solutions of a system of equalities and non-equalities in finite groups. We restrict ourselves to the binary field GF(2^n) with $\oplus$ as the group operation. We use Mennink and Neves interpretation [12,19,35] of mirror theory, tailored to our needs and notational setup.

From X^q and Y^q, we define the mappings $\phi, \psi \in \mathcal{F}([q], [q])$ as $\phi(i) = \min\{j : X_j = X_i\}$ and $\psi(i) = \min\{k : Y_k = Y_i\}$. Let $\phi([q])$ and $\psi([q])$ denote the range of ϕ and ψ, respectively. Consider the set of equations $\mathcal{L} := \{U_{\phi(i)} \oplus V_{\psi(i)} = S_i : i \in [q]\}$, where U_j and V_k denote the unknowns for all $j \in \phi([q])$ and $k \in \psi([q])$. We define three properties on $\mathcal{L}$:

- *Circle-free*: $\mathcal{L}$ is called circle-free if AC$[M^q; K, \pi_{1,2}]$ is false.
- *Non-degenerate*: $\mathcal{L}$ is called non-degenerate if DG$[M^q; K, \pi_{1,2}]$ is false.
- *ξ-block-maximal*: $\mathcal{L}$ is called ξ-block-maximal if LC$[M^q; K, \pi_{1,2}](\xi)$ is false.

Whenever $\mathcal{L}$ is circle-free, non-degenerate, and ξ-block-maximal, then we say that $\mathcal{L}$ is *mirror theory compatible till ξ*. The fundamental result of mirror theory [9, Theorem 6] is given in Theorem 4.3.

Theorem 4.3. (Theorem 3 in[12]). *Suppose $\mathcal{L}$, as defined above, is mirror theory compatible till ξ. Then, as long as $\xi^2 \cdot \max\{|\phi([q])|, |\psi([q])|\} \leq 2^n/67$, the number of solutions for $\mathcal{L}$, such that $U_i \neq U_j$ for distinct $i, j \in \phi([q])$ and $V_k \neq V_\ell$ for distinct $k, \ell \in \psi([q])$, is at least*

$$\frac{(2^n)_{|\phi([q])|}(2^n)_{|\psi([q])|}}{2^{nq}}.$$

In [9], Patarin gave a very high level sketch of the proof. Later, in [34] Nachef, Patarin and Volte gave a proof that works till $q < 2^{n-3}$. In [12], Mennink and Neves gave a detailed exposition on mirror theory, and utilized the theory to get close to n-bit security bounds for EDM (and EWCDM [11], in nonce-respecting[5] setting). Jha and Nandi [19] developed a variant of mirror theory to derive tight security bounds for CLRW2 [36] and DbHtS. Independently, Kim et al. [20] used the theory to derive tight security bounds for several DbHtS MACs, including PMAC+ and LightMAC+. We use Theorem 4.3 in the security proof of HtmB-p2.

---

[5] Each query requires a distinct nonce input.

Theorem 4.4. *For $\epsilon_1, \epsilon_2, \sigma \geq 0$, $q \leq \min\{2^{n-2}, 2^n/67n^2\}$, $\Pi_1, \ldots, \Pi_4 \leftarrow\!\!{}_\$ \mathcal{P}(n)$, and $(q, \sigma, \epsilon_2, \epsilon_1)$-DbACU$_q$ hash function H instantiated with key $K \leftarrow\!\!{}_\$ \mathcal{K}$, the PRF advantage of any (q, ∞)-distinguisher $\mathscr{A}$ against HtmB-p2$[H, \Pi_1, \ldots, \Pi_4]$ is given by*

$$\mathbf{Adv}^{\mathrm{prf}}_{\mathsf{HtmB\text{-}p2}[H,\Pi_1\ldots,\Pi_4]}(\mathscr{A}) \leq \frac{16q^2}{2^{3n}} + \frac{36q^2}{2^{2n}} + \frac{4q}{2^n} + \epsilon_2 + 2\epsilon_1.$$

PROOF APPROACH: The idea is quite similar to the proof of HtmB-f. However, just avoiding AC in $\mathcal{G}$ is not enough. This is due to the switch from random functions to random permutations. For example, the system of equations $\Pi_3(X^q) \oplus \Pi_4(Y^q) = S^q$ should be non-degenerate. Otherwise, we might get a case where $\Pi_3(X_i) = \Pi_3(X_j)$ for $X_i \neq X_j$, which is clearly not possible. We show that the system is mirror theory compatible till n, except with very negligible probability as long as $q \leq 2^{n-2}$. Then, we apply the fundamental result of mirror theory to get the proof of security using coefficient-H technique.

Proof. $\mathscr{A}$ tries to distinguish the real oracle $\mathcal{R} := (\mathsf{HtmB\text{-}p2}[H, \Pi_1, \ldots, \Pi_4])$ from the ideal oracle $\mathcal{I} := (\Gamma')$ for $\Gamma' \leftarrow\!\!{}_\$ \mathcal{F}(\mathcal{M}, \{0,1\}^n)$. Let $[q]$ denote the set of all query indices, and (M^q, S^q) denote $\mathscr{A}$'s transcript, where M^q is the q-tuple of inputs and S^q is the q-tuple of outputs.

Consider a variant distinguishing game, where the oracle releases L^q, R^q, X^q, and Y^q, once the distinguisher has made all q queries. Note that this can only increase $\mathscr{A}$'s advantage, and not diminish it. In $\mathcal{R}$, this is quite straightforward, as L^q, R^q, X^q, and Y^q, are already computed during the query phase. The ideal oracle $\mathcal{I}$, samples dummy $K \leftarrow\!\!{}_\$ \mathcal{K}$ and $\Pi_1, \Pi_2 \leftarrow\!\!{}_\$ \mathcal{P}(n)$, and sets $(L^q, R^q) = H_K(M^q)$, $X^q = \Pi_1(L^q) \oplus R^q$ and $Y^q = \Pi_2(R^q) \oplus L^q$.

BAD TRANSCRIPT: Let $\mathcal{T}$ denote the set of all transcripts. Let Bad denote the event that the system of equations $\mathcal{L} := \{U_{\phi(i)} \oplus V_{\psi(i)} = S_i : i \in [q]\}$ is not mirror theory compatible till n, and good otherwise. So Bad holds if at least one of AC, LC(n), or DG is satisfied. We say that a transcript $(M^q, L^q, R^q, X^q, Y^q, S^q)$ is bad if Bad happens, and good otherwise. Let $\mathcal{T}_{\mathrm{bad}} \subset \mathcal{T}$ denote the set of all bad transcripts. Then, we have $\Pr[\mathbb{T}_{\mathrm{id}} \in \mathcal{T}_{\mathrm{bad}}] = \Pr[\mathsf{Bad}]$.

We bound the probability of Bad conditioned on the following events:

- Fresh: $\forall\, i, j \in [q]$, $(L_i, R_i) \neq (L_j, R_j)$.
- Lpairs: $|\{(i,j)\ :\ 1 \leq i < j \leq q, L_i = L_j\}| < q$.
- Rpairs: $|\{(i,j)\ :\ 1 \leq i < j \leq q, R_i = R_j\}| < q$.

Let Triv $= \neg(\mathsf{Fresh} \cap \mathsf{Lpairs} \cap \mathsf{Rpairs})$. Then, we have

$$\Pr[\mathsf{Bad}] \leq \Pr[\mathsf{Bad}|\neg\mathsf{Triv}] + \Pr[\mathsf{Triv}]$$

$$\overset{(*)}{\leq} \Pr[\mathsf{LC}(n)|\neg\mathsf{Triv}] + \Pr[\mathsf{DG}|\neg\mathsf{Triv}] + \Pr[\mathsf{AC}|\neg\mathsf{Triv}] + \Pr[\mathsf{Triv}]$$

$$\overset{(**)}{\leq} \Pr[\mathsf{LC}(n)|\neg\mathsf{Triv}] + \Pr[\mathsf{DG}|\neg\mathsf{Triv}] + \frac{16q^2}{2^{2n}} + \frac{16q^2}{2^{3n}} + \epsilon_2 + 2\epsilon_1, \quad (10)$$

where inequality $(*)$ follows from the definition of Bad, and inequality $(**)$ follows from Lemma 4.2. Lemma 4.3 bounds the probability of $LC(n)$ and Lemma 4.4 bounds the probability of DG conditioned on $\neg$Triv.

GOOD TRANSCRIPT: Fix a good transcript $(M^q, L^q, R^q, X^q, Y^q, S^q)$. Since the ideal oracle faithfully (identical to the real oracle) simulates the computation of L^q, R^q, X^q, and Y^q, it is sufficient to concentrate on the ratio of the probabilities that (X^q, Y^q) maps to S^q in the real oracle and M^q maps to S^q in the ideal oracle.

$$\frac{\Pr\left[\mathbb{T}_{\mathsf{re}} = (M^q, L^q, R^q, X^q, Y^q, S^q)\right]}{\Pr\left[\mathbb{T}_{\mathsf{id}} = (M^q, L^q, R^q, X^q, Y^q, S^q)\right]} = \frac{\Pr\left[\Pi_3(X^q) \oplus \Pi_4(Y^q) = S^q\right]}{\Pr\left[\Gamma'(M^q) = S^q\right]}$$

$$\overset{(*)}{=} 2^{nq} \times \frac{h_q}{(2^n)_{|\phi([q])|}(2^n)_{|\psi([q])|}}$$

$$\overset{(**)}{\geq} 1. \tag{11}$$

where h_q denotes the number of solutions of the system of equations $\Pi_3(X^q) \oplus \Pi_4(Y^q) = S^q$, such that $\Pi_3(X_i) \neq \Pi_3(X_j)$ and $\Pi_4(Y_k) \neq \Pi_4(Y_\ell)$ for all $X_i \neq X_j$ and $Y_k \neq Y_\ell$. Further, each solution holds with exactly $1/(2^n)_{|\phi([q])|}(2^n)_{|\psi([q])|}$ probability, since Π_3 and Π_4 are invoked on exactly $|\phi([q])|$ and $|\psi([q])|$, respectively, distinct points. This justifies equality $(*)$. Let $U_{\phi(i)} = \Pi_3(X_i)$ and $V_{\psi(i)} = \Pi_4(Y_i)$ for all $i \in [q]$. Since the transcript is good, $\mathcal{L} := \{U_{\phi(i)} \oplus V_{\psi(i)} = S_i : i \in [q]\}$ is mirror theory compatible till n. Hence, using Theorem 4.3, we have

$$h_q \geq \frac{(2^n)_{|\phi([q])|}(2^n)_{|\psi([q])|}}{2^{nq}}. \tag{12}$$

This justifies the inequality $(**)$. The result follows from Eq. (10), Lemmata 4.3 and 4.4, and Theorem 2.1. $\square$

Remark 4.4. In Eq. (11) we have substituted h_q with the lower bound claimed in the fundamental result of mirror theory (see Theorem 4.3). However, as reported in multiple works [10,19,35,37], a concrete proof of this result is still not available. Here, we discuss the impact of a weaker mirror theory result on Theorem 4.4. Suppose, in future we get a mirror theory proof that holds for some $\xi < n$ and the lower bound is

$$(1 - \delta) \times \frac{(2^n)_{|\phi([q])|}(2^n)_{|\psi([q])|}}{2^{nq}},$$

for some $\delta > 0$. Here δ can be viewed as the degree of deviation from the perfect bound. Then, the bound in Theorem 4.4 is revised asymptotically to

$$\mathbf{Adv}^{\mathsf{prf}}_{\mathsf{HtmB\text{-}p2}[H, \Pi_1 ..., \Pi_4]}(\mathscr{A}) = O\left(\frac{q^2}{2^{2n}}\right) + O\left(\frac{q^{\xi+1}}{2^{n\xi}}\right) + \delta + \epsilon_2 + 2\epsilon_1,$$

where the red colored terms are due to the degradation in mirror theory bound. Specifically, $O(q^{\xi+1}/2^{n\xi})$ arises in the bound of $LC(\xi)|\neg$Triv, and δ appears on the right hand side of Eq. (11) by substituting the weaker bound for h_q.

Lemma 4.3. *For $q \leq 2^{n-2}$, $K \leftarrow_\$ \mathcal{K}$, and $\Pi_1, \Pi_2 \leftarrow_\$ \mathcal{P}(n)$, we have*

$$\Pr\left[\mathtt{LC}(n)|\neg\mathtt{Triv}\right] \leq \frac{8q^2}{2^{2n}} + \frac{4q}{2^n}.$$

Lemma 4.4. *For $q \leq 2^{n-2}$, $K \leftarrow_\$ \mathcal{K}$, $\Pi_1, \Pi_2 \leftarrow_\$ \mathcal{P}(n)$, and $\Gamma' \leftarrow_\$ \mathcal{F}(\mathcal{M}, \{0,1\}^n)$, we have*

$$\Pr\left[\mathtt{DG}|\neg\mathtt{Triv}\right] \leq \frac{12q^2}{2^{2n}}.$$

Given the similarity of the proofs of Lemmata 4.3 and 4.4 with the proof of Lemma 4.2, they are deferred to the full version of this paper.

5   mLightMAC+ and mPMAC+

In this section, we define two families mLightMAC+ and mPMAC+ of deterministic MAC candidates based on block ciphers. Both families are constructed as the HtmB construction, where the DbACU_q hash functions (see Sect. 2) are instantiated with the LightHash and PHash hash functions. In particular, our schemes have the following properties:

- they are secure VIL PRFs as long as the number of queried blocks are small in front of 2^n, where n denotes the block size;
- the calls to the underlying permutation can be computed in parallel.

5.1   mLightMAC+

In this section, we define the mLightMAC+ construction and prove its security. We are going to proceed in two steps: first, we define the LightHash family of permutation-based hash functions and upper bound the probability to get colliding outputs in Lemma 5.1, and then we use Theorems 4.1–4.4 to prove the actual security bound on mLightMAC+ in Corollary 5.1.

THE LightHash UNIVERSAL HASH FUNCTION: Given a permutation $\pi \in \mathcal{P}(n)$ and a positive integer $m \in [n-2]$, the LightHash universal hash function is a function from $\{0,1\}^{\leq (n-m)2^m-1}$ to $\{0,1\}^{2n}$ defined as follows. For all messages $M \in \{0,1\}^{\leq (n-m)2^m-1}$, we let $M' = \mathsf{pad}(M)$, $l = |M'|/(n-m)$ and $M' = M^1||\cdots||M^l$, where $|M^i| = n-m$ for all $i \in [l]$. The hash of the message M is defined as $\mathsf{LightHash}[\pi,m](M) = (\mathsf{LightHash}_1[\pi,m](M), \mathsf{LightHash}_2[\pi,m](M))$, where

$$\mathsf{LightHash}_1[\pi,m](M) = (\langle l \rangle_m || M^l) \oplus \bigoplus_{i=1}^{l-1} \pi\left(\langle i \rangle_m || M^i\right),$$

$$\mathsf{LightHash}_2[\pi,m](M) = (\langle l \rangle_m || M^l) \oplus \bigoplus_{i=1}^{l-1} 2^{l-i}\pi\left(<i>_m || M^i\right).$$

Note that LightHash requires 1 less block cipher call as compared to the hash layer in LightMAC+. The probability that two distinct messages generate colliding outputs in both components of LightHash can be upper bounded as follows.

Lemma 5.1. *Let* $n \in \mathbb{N}$, $m \in [n-2]$. *For any two distinct messages* M_1, M_2 *in* $\{0,1\}^{\leq(n-m)2^m-1}$ *and* $\Pi \leftarrow_\$ \mathcal{P}(n)$, *one has*

$$\Pr\left[\text{LightHash}[\Pi,m](M_1) = \text{LightHash}[\Pi,m](M_2)\right] \leq \frac{4}{2^{2n}},$$

$$\Pr\left[\text{LightHash}_b[\Pi,m](M_1) = \text{LightHash}_b[\Pi,m](M_2)\right] \leq \frac{2}{2^n},$$

for $b \in \{0,1\}$. *In particular* LightHash *is* $(q, \infty, \frac{2q^2}{2^{2n}}, \frac{q}{2^n})$-*DbACU$_q$*.

The proof of this Lemma can be found in Sect. 6.1.

THE mLightMAC+ FAMILY OF PRFs: Given $\pi_0, \ldots, \pi_6 \in \mathcal{P}(n)$, $f_1, \ldots, f_4 \in \mathcal{F}(n,n)$ and an integer $m \in [n-2]$, the functions of the mLightMAC+ family are functions from $\{0,1\}^{\leq(n-m)2^m-1}$ to $\{0,1\}^n$ that are formally defined as

$$\text{mLightMAC+-f}[\pi_0, f_1 \ldots, f_4, m] := \text{HtmB-f}\left[\text{LightHash}[\pi_0, m], f_1, \ldots, f_4\right],$$

$$\text{mLightMAC+-p1}[\pi_0, \pi_1 \ldots, \pi_6, m] := \text{HtmB-p1}\left[\text{LightHash}[\pi_0, m], \pi_1, \ldots, \pi_6\right],$$

$$\text{mLightMAC+-p2}[\pi_0, \pi_1 \ldots, \pi_4, m] := \text{HtmB-p2}\left[\text{LightHash}[\pi_0, m], \pi_1, \ldots, \pi_4\right].$$

Corollary 5.1 gives the PRF security of mLightMAC+.

Corollary 5.1. *For* $q < 2^{n-4}$, $m \leq n-2$, *and* $\Pi_0, \ldots, \Pi_6 \leftarrow_\$ \mathcal{P}(n)$, $\Gamma_1, \ldots,$ $\Gamma_4 \leftarrow_\$ \mathcal{F}(n,n)$, *the PRF advantage of any* (q, ∞)-*distinguisher* $\mathcal{A}$ *against* mLight-MAC+ *is given by*

$$\mathbf{Adv}^{\text{prf}}_{mLightMAC+\text{-}f[\Pi_0,\Gamma_1,\ldots,\Gamma_4,m]}(\mathcal{A}) \leq \frac{6q^2}{2^{2n}} + \frac{2q^2}{2^{3n}} + \frac{2q}{2^n},$$

$$\mathbf{Adv}^{\text{prf}}_{mLightMAC+\text{-}p1[\Pi_0,\ldots,\Pi_6,m]}(\mathcal{A}) \leq \frac{2q^{1.5}}{2^{1.5n}} + \frac{18q^2}{2^{2n}} + \frac{16q^2}{2^{3n}} + \frac{2q}{2^n},$$

$$\mathbf{Adv}^{\text{prf}}_{mLightMAC+\text{-}p2[\Pi_0,\ldots,\Pi_4,m]}(\mathcal{A}) \leq \frac{16q^2}{2^{3n}} + \frac{38q^2}{2^{2n}} + \frac{6q}{2^n}.$$

For the second and third inequalities, we also assume $n \geq 4$ and $q \leq 2^n/67n^2$, respectively.

Proof. This result is a direct combination of Lemma 5.1 and Theorems 4.1, 4.2 and 4.4. □

5.2 mPMAC+

As in the previous section, we define the mPMAC+ construction and prove its security. We first define the PHash family of permutation-based hash functions and upper bound the probability to get colliding outputs in Lemma 5.2, and then we use Theorems 4.1–4.4 to prove the actual security bound on mPMAC+ in Corollary 5.2.

THE PHash UNIVERSAL HASH FUNCTION: Given a permutation $\pi \in \mathcal{P}(n)$, the PHash universal hash function is a function from $\{0,1\}^{\leq n2^{n/2}-1}$ to $\{0,1\}^{2n}$

defined as follows. For all messages $M \in \{0,1\}^{\leq n2^{n/2}-1}$, we let $M' = \mathrm{pad}(M)$, $l = |M'|/n$ and $M' = M^1|| \cdots ||M^l$, where $|M^i| = n$ for all $i \in [l]$. The hash of the message M is then defined as $\mathsf{PHash}[\pi](M) = (\mathsf{PHash}_1[\pi](M), \mathsf{PHash}_2[\pi](M))$, where

$$
\mathsf{PHash}_1[\pi](M) = M^l \oplus \bigoplus_{i=1}^{l-1} \pi \left(M^i \oplus 2^i \pi(0^n) \oplus 2^{2i} \pi(10^{n-1}) \right),
$$

$$
\mathsf{PHash}_2[\pi](M) = M^l \oplus \bigoplus_{i=1}^{l} 2^{l-i} \pi \left(M^i \oplus 2^i \pi(0^n) \oplus 2^{2i} \pi(10^{n-1}) \right).
$$

Again note that PHash requires 1 less block cipher call as compared to the hash layer in PMAC+. One has the following result on the DbACU_q bound of PHash.

Lemma 5.2. *Let* $n \geq 6$. *For* $\Pi \twoheadleftarrow \$ \mathcal{P}(n)$, $\sigma \in \mathbb{N}$, *PHash*$[\Pi]$ *is* $(q, \sigma, \epsilon_2, \epsilon_1)$-*DbACU$_q$ where*

$$
\epsilon_2 \leq \frac{2\sigma^2 + 28q\sigma + 28q^2}{2^{2n}} + \frac{3q}{2^n - 2} + 3\frac{\sigma + q}{2^n - 1} \quad and \quad \epsilon_1 \leq \frac{4\sigma + 9q}{2^n}.
$$

The proof of this Lemma can be found in Sect. 6.2.

THE mPMAC+ FAMILY OF PRFs: Given $\pi_0, \ldots, \pi_6 \in \mathcal{P}(n)$ and $f_1, \ldots, f_4 \in \mathcal{F}(n,n)$, the functions of the mPMAC+ family are functions from $\{0,1\}^{n2^{n/2}-1}$ to $\{0,1\}^n$ that are formally defined as

$$
\mathsf{mPMAC+}\text{-}\mathsf{f}[\pi_0, f_1, \ldots, f_4] := \mathsf{HtmB\text{-}f}\left[\mathsf{PHash}[\pi_0], f_1, \ldots, f_4]\right],
$$

$$
\mathsf{mPMAC+}\text{-}\mathsf{p1}[\pi_0, \pi_1, \ldots, \pi_6] := \mathsf{HtmB\text{-}p1}\left[\mathsf{PHash}[\pi_0], \pi_1, \ldots, \pi_6]\right],
$$

$$
\mathsf{mPMAC+}\text{-}\mathsf{p2}[\pi_0, \pi_1, \ldots, \pi_4] := \mathsf{HtmB\text{-}p2}\left[\mathsf{PHash}[\pi_0], \pi_1, \ldots, \pi_4]\right]
$$

Corollary 5.2 gives the PRF security of mPMAC+.

Corollary 5.2. *Let* $n \geq 6$. *For* $q < 2^{n-4}$ *and* $\Pi_0, \ldots, \Pi_6 \twoheadleftarrow \$ \mathcal{P}(n)$, *and* $\Gamma_1, \ldots, \Gamma_4 \twoheadleftarrow \$ \mathcal{F}(n,n)$, *the PRF advantage of any* (q, ∞)-*distinguisher* $\mathscr{A}$ *against mPMAC+ is given by*

$$
\mathbf{Adv}^{\mathsf{prf}}_{mPMAC+\text{-}f[\Pi_0, \Gamma_1, \ldots, \Gamma_4]}(\mathscr{A}) \leq \frac{2q^2}{2^{3n}} + \frac{2\sigma^2 + 28q\sigma + 32q^2}{2^{2n}} + \frac{11\sigma + 15q}{2^n - 2},
$$

$$
\mathbf{Adv}^{\mathsf{prf}}_{mPMAC+\text{-}p1[\Pi_0, \ldots, \Pi_6]}(\mathscr{A}) \leq \frac{2q^{1.5}}{2^{1.5n}} + \frac{16q^2}{2^{3n}} + \frac{2\sigma^2 + 28q\sigma + 44q^2}{2^{2n}} + \frac{11\sigma + 15q}{2^n - 2},
$$

$$
\mathbf{Adv}^{\mathsf{prf}}_{mPMAC+\text{-}p2[\Pi_0, \ldots, \Pi_4]}(\mathscr{A}) \leq \frac{16q^2}{2^{3n}} + \frac{2\sigma^2 + 28q\sigma + 64q^2}{2^{2n}} + \frac{11\sigma + 19q}{2^n - 2},
$$

where σ *denotes an upper bound on the total number of n-bit blocks queried by* $\mathscr{A}$. *For the last inequality, we also assume* $q \leq 2^n/67n^2$.

Proof. This result is a direct combination of Lemma 5.2 and Theorem 4.1, 4.2 and 4.4. □

6 Proofs Related to **LightHash** and **PHash**

6.1 Proof of Lemma 5.1

Let $q \in \mathbb{N}$, $m \in [n-2]$, $M^q \in \left(\{0,1\}^{(n-m)2^m-1}\right)_q$.

Let us now fix two distinct integers $i_1, i_2 \in [q]$, and let $M_1 = M_{i_1}$, $M_2 = M_{i_2}$.

The proof for the first inequality closely follows the proof of [17, Lemma 1] for the original LightHash construction, with slight changes to handle our variant. It is thus deferred to the full version of this paper for reasons of space.

We now consider the second inequality we have to prove, and denote by l_1 (resp. l_2) the length of $\mathsf{pad}(M_1)$ (resp. $\mathsf{pad}(M_2)$) in $(n-m)$-bit blocks. Note that $1 \leq l_1, l_2 \leq 2^m \leq 2^{n-2}$. Then the event

$$\mathsf{LightHash}_1[\Pi, m](M_1) = \mathsf{LightHash}_1[\Pi, m](M_2)$$

is equivalent to:

$$\left(\langle l_1 \rangle_m || M_1^{l_1}\right) \oplus \bigoplus_{i=1}^{l_1-1} \Pi\left(\langle i \rangle_m || M_1^i\right) = \left(\langle l_2 \rangle_m || M_2^{l_2}\right) \oplus \bigoplus_{i=1}^{l_2-1} \Pi\left(\langle i \rangle_m || M_2^i\right). \quad (13)$$

We consider two different cases: $l_1 \neq l_2$ and $l_1 = l_2$. Consider the first case. Let us assume that $1 \leq l_1 < l_2$. Thus, thanks to domain separation of the inputs and since at most $l_1 + l_2 \leq 2^{n-1}$ outputs appear in Eq. (13), fixing all the other outputs will provide a unique solution for $\Pi(\langle l_2 \rangle_m || M_2^{l_2})$. Hence, the probability that (13) is satisfied is at most $1/(2^n - l_1 - l_2 + 3)$. Now consider the second case. Since the adversary cannot repeat queries and our padding is injective, $\mathsf{pad}(M_1)$ and $\mathsf{pad}(M_2)$ must differ in at least one block. Let $i_0 \geq 1$ be the first such index. Then, even when eliminating the colliding outputs from Eq. (13), at least the outputs with index i_0 will remain. If $i_0 \leq l_1 - 1$, fixing all the other outputs will provide a unique solution for $\Pi(\langle i_0 \rangle_m || M_1^{i_0})$, and the probability that Eq. (13) is satisfied is also at most $1/(2^n - l_1 - l_2 + 3)$. Otherwise, if $i_0 = l_1$, Eq. (13) is reduced to $M_1^{l_1} = M_2^{l_2}$, which cannot hold by definition of i_0.

Overall, since $l_1 + l_2 \leq 2^{n-1}$, one has

$$\Pr\left[\mathsf{LightHash}_1[\Pi, m](M_1) = \mathsf{LightHash}_1[\Pi, m](M_2)\right] \leq \frac{2}{2^n}.$$

Similarly, one has

$$\Pr\left[\mathsf{LightHash}_2[\Pi, m](M_1) = \mathsf{LightHash}_2[\Pi, m](M_2)\right] \leq \frac{2}{2^n}.$$

We conclude the proof of the second part of Lemma 5.1 by summing over the $q(q-1)/2$ pairs of queries and using Markov's inequality.

6.2 Proof of Lemma 5.2

A FLAW IN [26]: The probability of observing a full collision in PHash has already been considered in [26]. However, Chakraborty et al. [27] identified a flaw in the argument. In more details, when considering what is referred to as Type-5 collisions, the author tries to upper bound the probability, over the random choice of two n-bit masks L_1 and L_2, that the following system is satisfied:

$$(2^{i_1} \oplus 2^{i_2})L_1 \oplus (2^{3i_1} \oplus 2^{3i_2})L_2 = X_1$$
$$(2^{i_3} \oplus 2^{i_4})L_1 \oplus (2^{3i_3} \oplus 2^{3i_4})L_2 = X_2$$

for some n-bit values X_1, X_2 and four integers i_1, i_2, i_3, i_4 such that at least three of them are distinct. It is then argued that either the system is of rank two, and has exactly one solution, or both equations are equal. In the second case, the author shows that $2^{i_1} \oplus 2^{i_2} = 2^{i_3} \oplus 2^{i_4}$ and $2^{3i_1} \oplus 2^{3i_2} = 2^{3i_3} \oplus 2^{3i_4}$ imply $i_1 = i_2 = i_3 = i_4$ which is impossible. However, it seems that another case is possible: the second equation can be a multiple of the first one. In that case, there exists a non-zero value α such that $\alpha(2^{i_1} \oplus 2^{i_2}) = 2^{i_3} \oplus 2^{i_4}$, $\alpha(2^{3i_1} \oplus 2^{3i_2}) = 2^{3i_3} \oplus 2^{3i_4}$ and $\alpha X_1 = X_2$, and the previous impossibility argument does not apply anymore. With a more complex analysis, it may still be possible to prove a bound that is independent from the length of the queries. Another approach could be to use a different masking, as demonstrated in [27,38], that avoids the above mentioned case. In our work, we leave this question as an interesting open problem and we use a slightly worse bound that depends on the number of queried message blocks, but is still sufficient to provide optimal security.

PROOF OF LEMMA 5.2. Let $n \geq 6$, $q \leq 2^n$ be two integers and let us fix a q-tuple of messages $M^q \in \left(\{0,1\}^{n2^{n/2}-1}\right)_q$ whose total block length is σ. We parse $\mathsf{pad}(M_i)$ as $M_i^1 || \cdots || M_i^{l_i}$, where $i \in [q]$, $|M_i^j| = n$ for every $i \in [l_i]$, and $l_i \leq 2^{n/2}$. Note that, because of our padding, $\sum_{i=1}^q l_i \leq \sigma + q$. We are going to introduce several new random variables that depend on the uniformly random draw of Π:

- $L_1 = \Pi(0^n)$ and $L_2 = \Pi(10^{n-1})$;
- for all $i \in [q]$ and all $j \in [l_i - 1]$, $X_i^j = M_i^j \oplus 2^j L_1 \oplus 2^{2j} L_2$ and $Y_i^j = \Pi(X_i^j)$;
- for $i \in [q]$,

$$\Sigma_i = \mathsf{PHash}_1[\Pi](M_i) = M^{l_i} \oplus \bigoplus_{j=1}^{l_i-1} Y_i^j \text{ and}$$

$$\Theta_i = \mathsf{PHash}_2[\Pi](M_i) = M^{l_i} \oplus \bigoplus_{j=1}^{l_i-1} 2^{l_i-j} Y_i^j.$$

Let us fix two distinct integers i_1, i_2 in $[q]$, and assume w.l.o.g. that $l_{i_1} \geq l_{i_2}$. The first step of our proof is to upper bound the probability to create a collision in the output of PHash_1. More precisely, we want to upper bound the probability that $\Sigma_{i_1} = \Sigma_{i_2}$.

Claim 6.1. *One has*

$$\Pr\left[\Sigma_{i_1} = \Sigma_{i_2}\right] \le 2\frac{l_{i_1} + l_{i_2} + 4}{2^n},$$

$$\Pr\left[\Theta_{i_1} = \Theta_{i_2}\right] \le 2\frac{l_{i_1} + l_{i_2} + 4}{2^n}.$$

The proof of this claim is deferred to the full version of this paper for reasons of space.

Let C_1 (resp. C_2) be the number of Σ (resp. Θ) collisions. Summing over every pair of queries yields

$$\mathsf{Ex}\left[C_1\right] \le \sum_{i_1 < i_2} 2\frac{l_{i_1} + l_{i_2} + 4}{2^n} \le \frac{4q(\sigma + q) + 4q^2}{2^n} \le \frac{4q\sigma + 9q^2}{2^n}.$$

Similarly, one has $\mathsf{Ex}\left[C_2\right] \le \frac{4q\sigma + 9q^2}{2^n}$. Using Markov's inequality ends the first part of the proof of this lemma.

Our goal is now to upper bound the probability of the following event (dubbed Coll in the following): there exist two distinct indices i_1 and i_2 such that

$$\mathsf{PHash}[\Pi](M_{i_1}) = \mathsf{PHash}[\Pi](M_{i_2}).$$

We are going to break this event into several different events that will be easier to handle:

- Coll0: there exist $i \in [q]$ and $j \in [l_i - 1]$ such that $X_i^j = 0^n$;
- Coll1: there exist $i \in [q]$ and $j \in [l_i - 1]$ such that $X_i^j = 10^{n-1}$;
- 3Coll: there exist $i \in [q]$ and three pairwise distinct integers $j_1, j_2, j_3 \in [l_i - 1]$ such that $X_i^{j_1} = X_i^{j_2} = X_i^{j_3}$;
- CleanColl: this event corresponds to Coll $\wedge \neg$Coll0 $\wedge \neg$Coll1 $\wedge \neg$3Coll.

Clearly, one has

$$\Pr\left[\mathsf{Coll}\right] \le \Pr\left[\mathsf{Coll0}\right] + \Pr\left[\mathsf{Coll1}\right] + \Pr\left[\mathsf{3Coll}\right] + \Pr\left[\mathsf{CleanColl}\right]. \tag{14}$$

It is also easy to see that

$$\Pr\left[\mathsf{Coll0}\right] \le \frac{\sigma + q}{2^n - 1} \quad \text{and} \quad \Pr\left[\mathsf{Coll1}\right] \le \frac{\sigma + q}{2^n - 1}. \tag{15}$$

Let us now consider the event 3Coll. Fix any $i \in [q]$ and any pairwise distinct $j_1, j_2, j_3 \in [l_i - 1]$. The system (S) of equations $X_i^{j_1} = X_i^{j_2} = X_i^{j_3}$ can be rewritten as

$$(2^{j_1} \oplus 2^{j_2})L_1 \oplus (2^{2j_1} \oplus 2^{2j_2})L_2 = M_i^{j_1} \oplus M_i^{j_2}$$

$$(2^{j_1} \oplus 2^{j_3})L_1 \oplus (2^{2j_1} \oplus 2^{2j_3})L_2 = M_i^{j_1} \oplus M_i^{j_3}$$

Since j_1, j_2, j_3 are pairwise distinct and smaller than $2^n - 1$, the values $2^{j_1}, 2^{j_2}, 2^{j_3}$ are pairwise distinct and (S) is equivalent to

$$L_1 \oplus (2^{j_1} \oplus 2^{j_2})L_2 = (M_i^{j_1} \oplus M_i^{j_2})/(2^{j_1} \oplus 2^{j_2})$$
$$L_1 \oplus (2^{j_1} \oplus 2^{j_3})L_2 = (M_i^{j_1} \oplus M_i^{j_3})/(2^{j_1} \oplus 2^{j_3}).$$

Since $2^{j_2} \neq 2^{j_3}$, the system has a unique solution, and is verified with probability at most $1/2^n(2^n - 1)$.

Summing over every possible choice of i, j_1, j_2, j_3 yields

$$\Pr\left[\texttt{3Coll}\right] \leq \sum_{i=1}^{q} \frac{l_i^3}{2^n(2^n - 1)} \overset{(*)}{\leq} \sum_{i=1}^{q} \frac{l_i}{2^n - 1} \leq \frac{\sigma + q}{2^n - 1}, \tag{16}$$

where inequality $(*)$ comes from the fact that $l_i \leq 2^{n/2}$ for every $i \in [q]$.

We now have to handle the event $\texttt{CleanColl}$. We make the following claim.

Claim 6.2

$$\Pr\left[\texttt{CleanColl}\right] \leq \frac{2\sigma^2 + 28q\sigma + 28q^2}{2^{2n}} + \frac{3q}{2^n - 2}.$$

The proof this claim is deferred to the full version of this paper for reasons of space.

Combining Eqs. (14), (15), (16) and Claim 6.2 yields

$$\Pr\left[\texttt{Coll}\right] \leq \frac{2\sigma^2 + 28q\sigma + 28q^2}{2^{2n}} + \frac{3q}{2^n - 2} + \frac{3(\sigma + q)}{2^n - 1},$$

which ends the proof.

7   Reducing the Number of Keys

HtmB-f, HtmB-p1, and HtmB-p2 need 4, 6, and 4 keys, respectively, apart from the hash key. This could be an issue in certain memory-restricted scenarios. In this section, we present some simple variants of these constructions that require less key material, albeit with a slight loss of security.

For any function $F \in \mathcal{F}$ and $b \in \{0,1\}^{<n}$, we define two mappings:

$$\widehat{F}^b := \lfloor F(b\|\cdot) \rfloor_{n-|b|} \qquad \widetilde{F}^b(X) := F(b\|\cdot),$$

where $\lfloor Y \rfloor_{n-d}$ denotes the $(n-d)$-least significant bits of Y for all $Y \in \{0,1\}^n$ and $d < n$. In the following discussion $\mathcal{M} \subseteq \{0,1\}^*$.

SINGLE-KEY VARIANT OF HtmB-f: Given $\Gamma \leftarrow_\$ \mathcal{F}(n,n)$ and a pair $H = (H_1, H_2)$ of two $(\mathcal{K}, \mathcal{M}, \{0,1\}^{n-2})$-keyed hash functions, we define the single-key variant of HtmB-f, denoted 1k-HtmB-f, as:

$$\text{1k-HtmB-f}[H, \Gamma] := \text{HtmB-f}[H, \widehat{\Gamma}^{00}, \widehat{\Gamma}^{01}, \widetilde{\Gamma}^{10}, \widetilde{\Gamma}^{11}].$$

Theorem 7.1. *For $\epsilon_1, \epsilon_2, \sigma \geq 0$, $q \leq 2^{n-3}$, $\Gamma \leftarrow_\$ \mathcal{F}(n,n)$, and $(q, \sigma, \epsilon_2, \epsilon_1)$-DbACU$_q$ hash function H_K instantiated with $K \leftarrow_\$ \mathcal{K}$, the PRF advantage of any (q, ∞)-distinguisher $\mathscr{A}$ against 1k-HtmB-f$[H, \Gamma]$ is given by*

$$\mathbf{Adv}^{\mathsf{prf}}_{\textsf{1k-HtmB-f}[H,\Gamma]}(\mathscr{A}) \leq \frac{64q^2}{2^{2n}} + \frac{128q^2}{2^{3n}} + \epsilon_2 + 2\epsilon_1.$$

THREE-KEY VARIANT OF HtmB-p1: Given $\Pi_1, \Pi_2, \Pi_3 \leftarrow_\$ \mathcal{P}(n)$ and a pair $H = (H_1, H_2)$ of two $(\mathcal{K}, \mathcal{M}, \{0,1\}^{n-1})$-keyed hash functions, we define the three-key variant of HtmB-p1, denoted 3k-HtmB-p1, as:

$$\textsf{3k-HtmB-p1}[H, \Pi_1, \Pi_2, \Pi_3] := \textsf{HtmB-p1}[H, \widehat{\Pi}_1^0, \widehat{\Pi}_1^1, \widetilde{\Pi}_2^0, \widetilde{\Pi}_2^1, \widetilde{\Pi}_3^0, \widetilde{\Pi}_3^1].$$

Theorem 7.2. *For $n \geq 8$, $\epsilon_1, \epsilon_2, \sigma \geq 0$, $q \leq 2^{n-5}$, $\Pi_1, \Pi_2, \Pi_3 \leftarrow_\$ \mathcal{P}(n)$, and $(q, \sigma, \epsilon_2, \epsilon_1)$-DbACU$_q$ hash function H_K instantiated with key $K \leftarrow_\$ \mathcal{K}$, the PRF advantage of any (q, ∞)-distinguisher $\mathscr{A}$ against 3k-HtmB-p1$[H, \Pi_1, \Pi_2, \Pi_3]$ is given by*

$$\mathbf{Adv}^{\mathsf{prf}}_{\textsf{3k-HtmB-p1}[H,\Pi_1,\Pi_2,\Pi_3]}(\mathscr{A}) \leq \frac{2q}{2^n} + \frac{6q^{1.5}}{2^{1.5n}} + \frac{64q^2}{2^{2n}} + \frac{128q^2}{2^{3n}} + \epsilon_2 + 2\epsilon_1.$$

TWO-KEY VARIANT OF HtmB-p2: Given $\Pi_1, \Pi_2 \leftarrow_\$ \mathcal{P}(n)$ and a pair $H = (H_1, H_2)$ of two $(\mathcal{K}, \mathcal{M}, \{0,1\}^{n-1})$-keyed hash functions, we define the two-key variant of HtmB-p2, denoted 2k-HtmB-p2, as:

$$\textsf{2k-HtmB-p2}[H, \Pi_1, \Pi_2] := \textsf{HtmB-p2}[H, \widehat{\Pi}_1^0, \widehat{\Pi}_1^1, \widetilde{\Pi}_2^0, \widetilde{\Pi}_2^1].$$

Theorem 7.3. *For $\epsilon_1, \epsilon_2, \sigma \geq 0$, $q \leq \min\{2^{n-3}, 2^n/67n^2\}$, $\Pi_1, \Pi_2 \leftarrow_\$ \mathcal{P}(n)$, and $(q, \sigma, \epsilon_2, \epsilon_1)$-DbACU$_q$ hash function H instantiated with key $K \leftarrow_\$ \mathcal{K}$, the PRF advantage of any (q, ∞)-distinguisher $\mathscr{A}$ against 2k-HtmB-p2$[H, \Pi_1, \Pi_2]$ is given by*

$$\mathbf{Adv}^{\mathsf{prf}}_{\textsf{2k-HtmB-p2}[H,\Pi_1,\Pi_2]}(\mathscr{A}) \leq \frac{128q^2}{2^{3n}} + \frac{136q^2}{2^{2n}} + \frac{8q}{2^n} + \epsilon_2 + 2\epsilon_1.$$

The proofs of Theorem 7.1, 7.2, and 7.3 follow very similar strategies as used in the proofs of Theorem 4.1, 4.2, and 4.4, respectively. So, we skip formal proofs for economical reasons. For the sake of verification, we provide proof sketches in the full version of this paper.

8 Conclusion

In this paper, we proposed a novel method of constructing VIL PRFs, dubbed as the Hash-then-modified-Benes or HtmB transformation. Based on the type of internal primitive, we gave three instances of HtmB, viz. HtmB-f, HtmB-p1, and HtmB-p2. We showed that all three instances retain security for close to 2^n queries. We instantiate the three VIL PRFs using LightMAC+ and PMAC+ based hash functions, called LightHash and PHash, respectively. We explicitly derived relevant collision probability bounds for LightHash and PHash that, in combination with the bounds for HtmB instances, implies almost 2^n blocks security. Lastly, we proposed some reduced-key variants of HtmB-f, HtmB-p1, and HtmB-p2.

8.1   Further Discussion

ON SINGLE-KEY VARIANTS FOR HTMB-P1 AND HTMB-P2:   There is a scope
of further reducing the key size in case of HtmB-p1 and HtmB-p2 by using 2 and
1 extra bit(s), respectively, for domain separation. However, there is an obstacle
in proving the security of resulting constructions. This obstacle stems from the
fact that the permutation calls in the lower level are no longer independent of
the permutation calls in the upper layer. As a result, the existing bounds on the
sum of permutations [8,10] (in case of HtmB-p1) and mirror theory [9,33,34]
(in case of HtmB-p2) are no longer applicable. It seems that we need a stronger
result like sum of permutations under some added input/output restrictions. A
partial positive result in this direction has been shown in [15], where the authors
show similar result for queries up to $2^{2n/3}$. We leave it as an open problem to
extend the result to close to 2^n queries under appropriate conditions.

ON HASH FUNCTION REQUIREMENT: The reduced-key variants of HtmB need
hash functions with unusual output sizes like $2n - 2$ and $2n - 4$ bits. However,
one can easily generate such hash outputs by chopping appropriate bits of an ϵ-
Almost XOR Universal (AXU) hash function, i.e. a hash function H_K such that for
distinct inputs x, y and any difference δ, $\Pr_K [H_K(x) \oplus H_K(y) = \delta] \leq \epsilon$. Suppose
we have a pair of n-bit hash functions $H = (H_1, H_2)$ that satisfies two properties:

- H_b are ϵ_1-AXU hash functions for $b \in [2]$, and
- H is an ϵ_2-AXU hash function.

Then, if we chop $d < n$ bits from each of H_1 and H_2, the resulting hash function
can be shown to be $(q, \sigma, q^2 2^{2d} \epsilon_2, q 2^d \epsilon_1)$-DbACU$_q$.

Unfortunately, LightHash and PHash of Sect. 5 do not satisfy the AXU condition. Note that, we saved one block cipher call in LightHash and PHash as
compared to the hash layer in LightMAC+ and PMAC+, by absorbing the last
data block directly. It would be interesting to see whether the original hash
layer in LightMAC+ and PMAC+ can be used as appropriate replacements for
LightHash and PHash, respectively, in the reduced-key variants.

References

1. Rogaway, P., Shrimpton, T.: A provable-security treatment of the key-wrap problem. In: Vaudenay, S. (ed.) EUROCRYPT 2006. LNCS, vol. 4004, pp. 373–390.
   Springer, Heidelberg (2006). https://doi.org/10.1007/11761679_23
2. Bernstein, D.J.: SURF: simple unpredictable random function (1997)
3. Aumasson, J.-P., Bernstein, D.J.: SipHash: a fast short-input PRF. In: Galbraith,
   S., Nandi, M. (eds.) INDOCRYPT 2012. LNCS, vol. 7668, pp. 489–508. Springer,
   Heidelberg (2012). https://doi.org/10.1007/978-3-642-34931-7_28
4. Mennink, B., Neves, S.: Optimal PRFs from blockcipher designs. IACR Trans.
   Symmetric Cryptol. **2017**(3), 228–252 (2017)
5. Bellare, M., Krovetz, T., Rogaway, P.: Luby-Rackoff backwards: increasing security
   by making block ciphers non-invertible. In: Nyberg, K. (ed.) EUROCRYPT 1998.
   LNCS, vol. 1403, pp. 266–280. Springer, Heidelberg (1998). https://doi.org/10.
   1007/BFb0054132

6. Bellare, M., Impagliazzo, R.: A tool for obtaining tighter security analyses of pseudorandom function based constructions, with applications to PRP to PRF conversion. IACR Cryptology ePrint Archive **1999**, 24 (1999)
7. Lucks, S.: The sum of PRPs is a secure PRF. In: Preneel, B. (ed.) EUROCRYPT 2000. LNCS, vol. 1807, pp. 470–484. Springer, Heidelberg (2000). https://doi.org/10.1007/3-540-45539-6_34
8. Patarin, J.: A proof of security in O(2n) for the Xor of two random permutations. In: Proceedings of the Third International Conference on Information Theoretic Security, ICITS 2008, pp. 232–248 (2008)
9. Patarin, J.: Introduction to mirror theory: analysis of systems of linear equalities and linear non equalities for cryptography. IACR Cryptology ePrint Archive **2010**, 287 (2010)
10. Dai, W., Hoang, V.T., Tessaro, S.: Information-theoretic indistinguishability via the Chi-squared method. In: Katz, J., Shacham, H. (eds.) CRYPTO 2017, Part III. LNCS, vol. 10403, pp. 497–523. Springer, Cham (2017). https://doi.org/10.1007/978-3-319-63697-9_17
11. Cogliati, B., Seurin, Y.: EWCDM: an efficient, beyond-birthday secure, noncemisuse resistant MAC. In: Robshaw, M., Katz, J. (eds.) CRYPTO 2016, Part I. LNCS, vol. 9814, pp. 121–149. Springer, Heidelberg (2016). https://doi.org/10.1007/978-3-662-53018-4_5
12. Mennink, B., Neves, S.: Encrypted Davies-Meyer and its dual: towards optimal security using mirror theory. In: Katz, J., Shacham, H. (eds.) CRYPTO 2017, Part III. LNCS, vol. 10403, pp. 556–583. Springer, Cham (2017). https://doi.org/10.1007/978-3-319-63697-9_19
13. Yasuda, K.: The sum of CBC MACs is a secure PRF. In: Pieprzyk, J. (ed.) CT-RSA 2010. LNCS, vol. 5985, pp. 366–381. Springer, Heidelberg (2010). https://doi.org/10.1007/978-3-642-11925-5_25
14. Yasuda, K.: A new variant of PMAC: beyond the birthday bound. In: Rogaway, P. (ed.) CRYPTO 2011. LNCS, vol. 6841, pp. 596–609. Springer, Heidelberg (2011). https://doi.org/10.1007/978-3-642-22792-9_34
15. Datta, N., Dutta, A., Nandi, M., Paul, G., Zhang, L.: Single key variant of PMAC_plus. IACR Trans. Symmetric Cryptol. **2017**(4), 268–305 (2017)
16. Zhang, L., Wu, W., Sui, H., Wang, P.: 3kf9: enhancing 3GPP-MAC beyond the birthday bound. In: Wang, X., Sako, K. (eds.) ASIACRYPT 2012. LNCS, vol. 7658, pp. 296–312. Springer, Heidelberg (2012). https://doi.org/10.1007/978-3-642-34961-4_19
17. Naito, Y.: Blockcipher-based MACs: beyond the birthday bound without message length. In: Takagi, T., Peyrin, T. (eds.) ASIACRYPT 2017, Part III. LNCS, vol. 10626, pp. 446–470. Springer, Cham (2017). https://doi.org/10.1007/978-3-319-70700-6_16
18. Datta, N., Dutta, A., Nandi, M., Paul, G.: Double-block hash-then-sum: a paradigm for constructing BBB secure PRF. IACR Trans. Symmetric Cryptol. **2018**(3), 36–92 (2018)
19. Jha, A., Nandi, M.: Tight security of cascaded LRW2. J. Cryptol. **33**(3), 1272–1317 (2020)
20. Kim, S., Lee, B., Lee, J.: Tight security bounds for double-block hash-then-sum MACs. In: Canteaut, A., Ishai, Y. (eds.) EUROCRYPT 2020, Part I. LNCS, vol. 12105, pp. 435–465. Springer, Cham (2020). https://doi.org/10.1007/978-3-030-45721-1_16
21. Shoup, V.: Sequences of games: a tool for taming complexity in security proofs. IACR Cryptology ePrint Archive **2004**, 332 (2004)

22. Aiello, W., Venkatesan, R.: Foiling birthday attacks in length-doubling transformations. In: Maurer, U. (ed.) EUROCRYPT 1996. LNCS, vol. 1070, pp. 307–320. Springer, Heidelberg (1996). https://doi.org/10.1007/3-540-68339-9_27

23. Patarin, J.: Security of balanced and unbalanced Feistel schemes with linear non equalities. IACR Cryptology ePrint Archive **2010**, 293 (2010)

24. Patarin, J.: A proof of security in $O(2^n)$ for the benes scheme. In: Vaudenay, S. (ed.) AFRICACRYPT 2008. LNCS, vol. 5023, pp. 209–220. Springer, Heidelberg (2008). https://doi.org/10.1007/978-3-540-68164-9_14

25. Patarin, J., Montreuil, A.: Benes and butterfly schemes revisited. In: Won, D.H., Kim, S. (eds.) ICISC 2005. LNCS, vol. 3935, pp. 92–116. Springer, Heidelberg (2006). https://doi.org/10.1007/11734727_10

26. Naito, Y.: The exact security of PMAC with two powering-up masks. IACR Trans. Symmetric Cryptol. **2019**(2), 125–145 (2019)

27. Chakraborty, B., Chattopadhyay, S., Jha, A., Nandi, M.: On length independent security bounds for the PMAC family. IACR Cryptol. ePrint Arch. **2020**, 656 (2020)

28. Bellare, M., Goldreich, O., Mityagin, A.: The power of verification queries in message authentication and authenticated encryption. IACR Cryptology ePrint Archive **2004**, 309 (2004)

29. Hall, C., Wagner, D., Kelsey, J., Schneier, B.: Building PRFs from PRPs. In: Krawczyk, H. (ed.) CRYPTO 1998. LNCS, vol. 1462, pp. 370–389. Springer, Heidelberg (1998). https://doi.org/10.1007/BFb0055742

30. Patarin, J.: Etude des Générateurs de Permutations Pseudo-aléatoires Basés sur le Schéma du DES. Ph.D. thesis, Université de Paris (1991)

31. Patarin, J.: The "coefficients H" technique. In: Avanzi, R.M., Keliher, L., Sica, F. (eds.) SAC 2008. LNCS, vol. 5381, pp. 328–345. Springer, Heidelberg (2009). https://doi.org/10.1007/978-3-642-04159-4_21

32. Chen, S., Steinberger, J.: Tight security bounds for key-alternating ciphers. In: Nguyen, P.Q., Oswald, E. (eds.) EUROCRYPT 2014. LNCS, vol. 8441, pp. 327–350. Springer, Heidelberg (2014). https://doi.org/10.1007/978-3-642-55220-5_19

33. Patarin, J.: Mirror theory and cryptography. Appl. Algebra Eng. Commun. Comput. **28**(4), 321–338 (2017). https://doi.org/10.1007/s00200-017-0326-y

34. Nachef, V., Patarin, J., Volte, E.: Feistel Ciphers - Security Proofs and Cryptanalysis. Springer, Cham (2017). https://doi.org/10.1007/978-3-319-49530-9

35. Mennink, B.: Towards tight security of cascaded LRW2. In: Beimel, A., Dziembowski, S. (eds.) TCC 2018, Part II. LNCS, vol. 11240, pp. 192–222. Springer, Cham (2018). https://doi.org/10.1007/978-3-030-03810-6_8

36. Landecker, W., Shrimpton, T., Terashima, R.S.: Tweakable blockciphers with beyond birthday-bound security. In: Safavi-Naini, R., Canetti, R. (eds.) CRYPTO 2012. LNCS, vol. 7417, pp. 14–30. Springer, Heidelberg (2012). https://doi.org/10.1007/978-3-642-32009-5_2

37. Datta, N., Dutta, A., Nandi, M., Yasuda, K.: Encrypt or decrypt? To make a single-key beyond birthday secure nonce-based MAC. In: Shacham, H., Boldyreva, A. (eds.) CRYPTO 2018, Part I. LNCS, vol. 10991, pp. 631–661. Springer, Cham (2018). https://doi.org/10.1007/978-3-319-96884-1_21

38. Naito, Y.: The exact security of PMAC with three powering-up masks. IACR Cryptol. ePrint Arch. **2020**, 731 (2020)

Side-Channel Analysis

SILVER – Statistical Independence and Leakage Verification

David Knichel$^{(\boxtimes)}$ ⓘ, Pascal Sasdrich ⓘ, and Amir Moradi ⓘ

Ruhr University Bochum, Horst Görtz Institute for IT Security, Bochum, Germany
{david.knichel,pascal.sasdrich,amir.moradi}@rub.de

Abstract. Implementing cryptographic functions securely in the presence of physical adversaries is still a challenge although a lion's share of research in the physical security domain has been put in development of countermeasures. Among several protection schemes, *masking* has absorbed the most attention of research in both academic and industrial communities, due to its theoretical foundation allowing to provide proofs or model the achieved security level. In return, masking schemes are difficult to implement as the implementation process often is manual, complex, and error-prone. This motivated the need for formal verification tools that allow the designers and engineers to analyze and verify the designs before manufacturing.

In this work, we present a new framework to analyze and verify masked implementations against various security notions using different security models as reference. In particular, our framework – which directly processes the resulting gate-level netlist of a hardware synthesis – particularly relies on Reduced Ordered Binary Decision Diagrams (ROBDDs) and the concept of statistical independence of probability distributions. Compared to existing tools, our framework captivates due to its simplicity, accuracy, and functionality while still having a reasonable efficiency for many applications and common use-cases.

Keywords: Verification · Side-Channel Analysis · Probing security · Reduced Ordered Binary Decision Diagram · Statistical independence · Probability distribution

1 Introduction

Even after two decades of research since the seminal description of Side-Channel Analysis (SCA) as a threat to cryptographic implementations [32,33], secure implementation of cryptographically strong algorithms is still a challenging and open problem. In particular, those decades of research have shown that SCA on cryptographic implementations can be performed by observing various physical sources and effects, such as timing [32], power consumption [33], electromagnetic (EM) emanations [27], or temperature and heat dissipation [30]. Eventually,

---

D. Knichel and P. Sasdrich—These authors contributed equally to the work.

© International Association for Cryptologic Research 2020
S. Moriai and H. Wang (Eds.): ASIACRYPT 2020, LNCS 12491, pp. 787–816, 2020.
https://doi.org/10.1007/978-3-030-64837-4_26

observing the physical characteristics of an electronic device during security-critical cryptographic operations can reveal secret and sensitive information to any observer and adversary. As a consequence, a wide range of protection mechanisms and countermeasures have been proposed to prevent or mitigate any side-channel leakage.

Among all candidates, *masking* (based on the concepts of *secret sharing*) is one of the most promising countermeasures against SCA due to its formal and sound security foundation [18]. As a consequence, many different schemes and variants have been introduced and proposed over the years [28,29,31,39,42,43] to address different implementation and security requirements. Unfortunately, not a few of those schemes have been shown to be insecure due to design flaws or inaccurate models or assumptions [36]. As a result, all these examples confirm that design and implementation of protection mechanisms and countermeasures against SCA is a mostly manual, complex, and error-prone process which requires good understanding of the execution environment and careful consideration of physical and security models.

To this end, an entirely new branch of research started to focus on the development of formal models for adversaries and physical execution environments to simplify and assist in formal verification [5,23,26,31]. Ideally, strong theoretical foundations in security models can assist and help to simplify the design, implementation, and verification of cryptographic implementations and appropriate security mechanisms. In the context of *masking*, formal verification often is conducted in the simple and abstract Ishai-Sahai-Wagner (ISW) d-probing security model [31] (under some basic assumptions on noise and independence of inputs), which allows an adversary to probe (observe) up to d intermediate values during the processing of sensitive information.

Due to its conceptual simplicity and level of abstraction, the d-probing model was rapidly and widely adopted for formal verification [2–4,6,11,20,24,38,44]. Indeed, the introduction of this simple but effective security model propelled the automation of formal verification, allowing to reduce the combinatorial complexity of security proofs for masking schemes and their implementations. In fact, development of automated formal verification tools also – in return – stimulated the research and progress on masking schemes, e.g., reducing the cost in terms of randomness [9] or solving the problem of secure composition of masked circuits and gadgets [3,4,17].

However, in its basic manifestation, the d-probing model does not consider specific physical defaults, such as *glitches*, *transitions*, or *couplings* [26], that may occur during the processing of sensitive information on a physical device. In fact, many schemes proven to be secure in the d-probing model, eventually fail in security analyzes when concretely implemented. That is mainly due to undesired and unintentional physical defaults that particularly violate the assumption on the independence of inputs. In particular for hardware implementations, *glitches* are well-known to be an issue and concern for masking schemes [39], wherefore Bloem *et al.* [11] and Faust *et al.* [26] independently proposed an extension of the basic ISW d-probing model considering glitches for hardware implementations of masking schemes.

In addition, Bloem *et al.* used the concept of Fourier coefficient estimation to implement an automated tool formally verifying the security of masking schemes and their implementations against the basic and glitch-extended d-probing model. However, due to computational limitations based on the estimation of Fourier coefficients, this tool primarily applies to the security analysis of the first-order setting without consideration of advanced notions such as Non-Interference (NI), Strong Non-Interference (SNI), and Probe-Isolating Non-Interference (PINI). In contrast to this, Barthe *et al.* [2] recently presented a language-based formal verification tool called maskVerif which uses the probabilistic information flow to assess the security of masking schemes and their implementations. In particular, using conservative heuristics and an optimistic sampling method, maskVerif executes more efficiently than the tool by Bloem *et al.*, while minimizing but still accepting false negatives for non-linear cases.

Contributions. In this work, we present and introduce an efficient methodology to analyze and verify the security of masked circuits and implementations under various security notions. Due to a symbolic and exhaustive analysis of probability distributions and statistical independence of joint distributions, we can avoid false negatives and overly conservative decisions. In particular, by means of ROBDDs, a well-known concept and methodology for Integrated Circuit (IC) testing and verification, we formally analyze and verify masked circuits in the ISW d-probing model even in the presence of *glitches* as physical defaults.

In addition, based on the seminal work of De Meyer *et al.* [21], we reformulate the security notions of d-probing security, d-Non-Interference, d-Strong Non-Interference, and, for the first time, d-Probe-Isolating Non-Interference based on statistical independence which can be efficiently checked and verified by our tool. Hence, for the first time, state-of-the-art security notions for masked circuits can be analyzed exhaustively without false negatives. Eventually, this contribution is even extended further by efficient verification methods to check and verify the uniformity for output sharings of arbitrary masked circuits.

Outline. While Sect. 2 briefly summarizes our notations and introduces preliminary concepts and notions, including ROBDDs, our circuit model, and security notions, Sect. 3 is dedicated to a conception and discussion of our verification approach. Besides, Sect. 3 outlines our leakage models and discusses the main ideas of our verification concept, particularly sketching the application of ROBDDs to check and verify security notions. In Sect. 4, we then provide formal proofs for all security notions and our leakage verification concept based on statistical independence checks. Before we present details on practical evaluations and experiments in Sect. 6, we briefly discuss and compare our approach and concept to essential related work in Sect. 5. Eventually, we conclude our work in Sect. 7.

2   Background

2.1   Notation

We use upper-case characters to denote random variables, bold ones for sets of random variables, and subscripts for elements within a set of variables. Further, let us denote $\mathbf{X}_{\bar{i}}$ as the set of variables $\mathbf{X} \setminus X_i$. Accordingly, we use lower-case characters to denote values a random variable can take, bold ones for sets of values, and subscripts for elements within the set of values. Again, let us denote $\mathbf{x}_{\bar{i}}$ as the set of values $\mathbf{x} \setminus x_i$. In addition, we use $Pr[X = x]$ for the probability that a random variable X takes a value x, while $Pr[\mathbf{X} = \mathbf{x}]$ denotes the joint probability that each $X_i \in \mathbf{X}$ takes the value $x_i \in \mathbf{x}$. Accordingly, the conditional probability for $X = x$ given $Y = y$ is written as $Pr[X = x|Y = y]$. Hence, $Pr[\mathbf{X} = \mathbf{x}|\mathbf{Y} = \mathbf{y}]$ denotes the conditional probability that each $X_i \in \mathbf{X}$ takes the value $x_i \in \mathbf{x}$, if each $Y_i \in \mathbf{Y}$ takes the value $y_i \in \mathbf{y}$. Moreover, the joint distribution over the set $\mathbf{X}$ is denoted as $Pr[\mathbf{X}]$, while $Pr[\mathbf{X}|\mathbf{Y}] = Pr[\mathbf{X}]$ is simply equivalent to $Pr[\mathbf{X} = \mathbf{x}|\mathbf{Y} = \mathbf{y}] = Pr[\mathbf{X} = \mathbf{x}]$ for all possible combination of $\mathbf{x}$ and $\mathbf{y}$. Extending this notation, $Pr[\mathbf{X}|\mathbf{Y}] = Pr[\mathbf{X}|\mathbf{Z}]$ is the same as $Pr[\mathbf{X} = \mathbf{x}|\mathbf{Y} = \mathbf{y}] = Pr[\mathbf{X} = \mathbf{x}|\mathbf{Z} = \mathbf{z}]$ for all possible combination of $\mathbf{x}$,$\mathbf{y}$, and $\mathbf{z}$.

Further, functions are denoted using sans-serif fonts. Handling masked functions, we denote the s-th share of the a variable as X^s. Hence, the set of all unshared inputs of a function f is denoted as $\mathbf{X} = (X_0, \ldots, X_{n-1})$ while the set containing all t shares of each variable in $\mathbf{X}$ is denoted as $Sh(\mathbf{X}) = (X_0^0, X_0^1, \ldots, X_0^{t-1}, X_1^0, \ldots, X_{n-1}^0, \ldots, X_{n-1}^{t-1})$. Similarly, the set containing all shares of $X_i \in \mathbf{X}$ is denoted as $Sh(X_i)$. Eventually, for a set of indices $\mathbf{I} \subseteq [0, \ldots, t-1]$, $Sh(\mathbf{X})^{\mathbf{I}}$ denotes the set containing all shares X_i^s with $0 \leq i < n$ and $s \in \mathbf{I}$.

2.2   Reduced Ordered Binary Decision Diagrams (ROBDDs)

Binary Decision Diagrams (BDDs) are a basic structure in discrete mathematics and computer science introduced by Akers [1] and refined by Bryant (introducing variable ordering) [15]. In particular, many applications in computer-aided IC design and verification make use of (reduced, ordered) BDDs.

In general, BDDs are concise and unique (i.e., canonical) graph-based representations of Boolean functions $\mathbb{F}_2^n \rightarrow \mathbb{F}_2$ with a single root node and two terminal nodes (leaves) $\{\mathbf{T}, \mathbf{F}\}$. The formal definition of ROBDDs, given in the following paragraphs, is divided into a purely *syntactical* definition, describing the structure based on (DAGs), before providing a *semantical* definition, clarifying the representation of Boolean functions as ROBDDs.

Syntactical Definition of ROBDDs. Before providing a syntactical definition for ROBDDs, we first recall the (syntactical) definition of Ordered Binary Decision Diagrams (OBDDs).

Definition 1 (OBDD Syntax). *An* Ordered Binary Decision Diagram *is a pair* $(\pi, \mathcal{G})$, *where* π *denotes the variable ordering of the OBDD and* $\mathcal{G} = (\mathcal{V}, \mathcal{E})$ *is a finite DAG with vertices* $\mathcal{V}$, *edges* $\mathcal{E}$, *and the following properties:*

(1) There is a single root node and each node $v \in \mathcal{V}$ *is either a non-terminal node or one of two terminal nodes* $\{\mathbf{T}, \mathbf{F}\}$.

(2) Each non-terminal node v *is labeled with a variable in* $\mathbf{X}$, *with* $|\mathbf{X}| = n$, *denoted as* $\mathsf{var}(v)$, *and has exactly two child nodes in* $\mathcal{V}$ *which are denoted as* $\mathsf{then}(v)$ *and* $\mathsf{else}(v)$.

(3) For each path from the root node to a terminal node, the variables in $\mathbf{X}$ *are encountered at most once and in the same order defined by the variable ordering* π. *More precisely, the variable ordering* π *of an OBDD is a bijection* $\pi : \{1, 2, \ldots, n\} \to \mathbf{X}$.

Furthermore, assuming the following two restrictions ensures a concise and canonical representation (under a given variable ordering π), defined as ROBDD.

Definition 2 (ROBDD Syntax). *An OBDD is called* Reduced Ordered Binary Decision Diagram, *if and only if there is no node* $v \in \mathcal{V}$ *such that* $\mathsf{then}(v) = \mathsf{else}(v)$ *and there are no duplicate nodes, i.e., two nodes* $\{v, v'\} \in \mathcal{V}$ *such that* $\mathsf{var}(v) = \mathsf{var}(v')$, $\mathsf{then}(v) = \mathsf{then}(v')$, *and* $\mathsf{else}(v) = \mathsf{else}(v')$.

Semantical Definition of ROBDDs. Each ROBDD with root $v \in \mathcal{V}$ recursively defines a Boolean function $\mathsf{f} : \mathbb{F}_2^n \to \mathbb{F}_2$ according to the following definition.

Definition 3 (ROBDD Semantics). *An ROBDD over* $\mathbf{X}$ *represents a Boolean function* f *recursively carried out at each node and defined as follows:*

(1) If v *is the terminal node* $\mathbf{F}$, *then* $\mathsf{f}_v|_x = 0$, *otherwise, if* v *is the terminal node* $\mathbf{T}$, *then* $\mathsf{f}_v|_x = 1$.

(2) If v *is a non-terminal node and* $\mathsf{var}(v) = x_i$, *then* f_v *is defined by the Shannon decomposition* $\mathsf{f}_v = x_i \cdot \mathsf{f}_{\mathsf{then}(v)}|_{x_i=1} + \overline{x_i} \cdot \mathsf{f}_{\mathsf{else}(v)}|_{x_i=0}$.

Boolean Operations over ROBDDs. Given the syntactical and semantical definitions for ROBDDs, we now can define arbitrary Boolean operations over Boolean functions f_{v_1} and f_{v_2} represented by two ROBDDs with root nodes v_1 and v_2. In particular, let $\mathsf{f} = \mathsf{f}_{v_1} \circ \mathsf{f}_{v_2}$ where $\circ$ denotes any binary Boolean operation, then the ROBDD for f can be derived and composed recursively as:

$$
\begin{aligned}
\mathsf{f} &= x_i \cdot \mathsf{f}|_{x_i=1} + \overline{x_i} \cdot \mathsf{f}|_{x_i=0} \\
&= x_i \cdot (\mathsf{f}_{v_1} \circ \mathsf{f}_{v_2})|_{x_i=1} + \overline{x_i} \cdot (\mathsf{f}_{v_1} \circ \mathsf{f}_{v_2})|_{x_i=0} \\
&= x_i \cdot (\mathsf{f}_{v_1}|_{x_i=1} \circ \mathsf{f}_{v_2}|_{x_i=1}) + \overline{x_i} \cdot (\mathsf{f}_{v_1}|_{x_i=0} \circ \mathsf{f}_{v_2}|_{x_i=0})
\end{aligned}
\tag{1}
$$

2.3 Circuit Model

For the remainder of this work, we consider and model a deterministic circuit C as a DAG, where the vertices are combinational gates and edges are wires carrying elements from the finite field $\mathbb{F}_2$.

Physical Model. Without loss of generality, the physical structure of a deterministic circuit C at gate level is modeled using the set of combinational gates {not, and, nand, or, nor, xor, xnor} (with fan-in at most 2) while all sequential memory gates reg model a clock-dependent synchronization point. Further, each Boolean input variable is associated with a single in gate (with fan-in 0), while the output and result of a Boolean function is associated with a single out gate (with fan-out 0). Eventually, ref are special-purpose gates with fan-in 0 that introduce a *independently and identically distributed* (i.i.d) random element from the finite field $\mathbb{F}_2$.

Functional Model. Each deterministic circuit C realizes an $n \times m$ vectorial Boolean function $F : \mathbb{F}_2^n \to \mathbb{F}_2^m$ given its *coordinate functions* $f_1, \ldots, f_m$ defined over $\mathbf{X} \in \mathbb{F}_2^n$. In particular, each $X_i \in \mathbf{X}$ is assumed to be *independently and identically distributed* (i.i.d) and associated with a single in gate, while each f_i is associated with a single out gate.

Further, the function of each gate within the circuit model C is derived recursively over the functions of its fan-in gates by means of Boolean operations over ROBDDs. Hence, each gate in the circuit model itself can be considered as a Boolean function over (a subset of) the inputs $\mathbf{X} \in \mathbb{F}_2^n$ and we can introduce a functional abstraction layer to the physical circuit model using ROBDDs to canonically represent and store the derived Boolean functions.

Security Model. Eventually, security critical circuits handling a sensitive secret X are associated with a security order d and protected (masked) based on Boolean sharing. This means, each security critical and sensitive secret X is shared with at least $d+1$ shares such that $X = \bigoplus_0^d X^i$. Similarly, sensitive and security critical outputs of a masked circuit are shared using Boolean sharing, such that $F(\mathbf{X}) = \bigoplus_0^d F^i(\mathbf{X})$.

2.4 Security Notions

Before introducing our verification approach and methodology to analyze an arbitrary circuit under various security notions, we first introduce the definitions of all necessary security notions. In particular, our security definitions are based on the work in [21] while we reformulate the definitions in order to provide generalizations from circuits with $d+1$ input shares to circuits with an arbitrary number of shares when examining dth-order security. In addition, we extend the definitions from single sensitive and secret variable to a set of arbitrary number of secret variables.

Probing Security. Probing security is defined as the probes being statistically independent of any sensitive input. More precisely, the joint distribution of the considered set of probes has to be independent of the joint distribution of all sensitive inputs. This can be formally defined as:

Definition 4 (d-Probing Security.). *A circuit* C *with secret input set* $\mathbf{X} \in \mathbb{F}_2^n$ *is d-probing secure, if and only if for any observation set* $\mathbf{Q}$ *containing* d *wires,* $\mathbf{X}$ *is statistically independent of the observation set, i.e., the following condition holds:*

$$Pr[\mathbf{Q}|\mathbf{X}] = Pr[\mathbf{Q}] \tag{2}$$

Non-Interference. The notion of *Non-Interference* allows partial information on the sensitive inputs becoming available to the adversary through probing the circuit. In particular, if the observed circuit is d-NI, the adversary is not able to successfully distinguish the circuit result from a simulator working on partial information knowing, i.e., using at most d shares of each input.

More formally, each adversarial probe set should be perfectly simulatable knowing only a subset of all shares of each input. Let $\mathbf{S}$ be a set over arbitrary input shares X_i^j, i.e., $\mathbf{S} \subset Sh(\mathbf{X})$, and $|\mathbf{S}|_i$ denote the number of shares in $\mathbf{S}$ that correspond to input X_i. In order to guarantee d-NI, there exist a simulation set $\mathbf{S}$ with $|\mathbf{S}|_{\forall i} \leq d$ for which a probe in $\mathbf{Q}$ is perfectly simulatable, i.e., an attacker is not able to distinguish between a simulation of C using only elements in $\mathbf{S}$ from the observations of C even when knowing all input shares. This can be directly translated into the condition that there has to exist a simulation set $\mathbf{S}$ with $|\mathbf{S}|_{\forall i} \leq d$, for which the distributions $Pr[\mathbf{Q}|\mathbf{S}]$ and $Pr[\mathbf{Q}|Sh(\mathbf{X})]$ are equal.

Definition 5 (d-Non-Interference). *A circuit* C *with secret input set* $\mathbf{X} \in \mathbb{F}_2^n$ *provides d-Non-Interference if and only if for any observation set of* $t \leq d$ *wires* $\mathbf{Q}$ *there exists a set* $\mathbf{S}$ *of input shares with* $|\mathbf{S}|_{\forall i} \leq t$ *such that*

$$Pr[\mathbf{Q}|\mathbf{S}] = Pr[\mathbf{Q}|Sh(\mathbf{X})]. \tag{3}$$

Strong Non-Interference. The notion of SNI has been introduced as extension to NI correcting deficiencies in terms of composability of secure gadgets within a circuit. In contrast to NI, any probe on a circuit output (also, through composition, considered as input to a subsequent gadget) is not allowed to give information about any share in the input. This means, each probe on an output wire must be perfectly simulatable without knowledge of any input shares in order to stop the flow of sensitive information between composed gadgets.

More formally, each adversarial probe set again should be perfectly simulatable knowing only a subset of all shares of each input. However, for a set $\mathbf{Q}$ of d probes with t_1 probes on internal wires and t_2 probes on output wires while $t_1 + t_2 \leq d$, the size of the set $\mathbf{S}$ is bounded by the internal probes only, i.e., $|\mathbf{S}|_{\forall i} \leq t_1$. This directly translates into the following definition and condition.

Definition 6 (d-Strong Non-Interference). *A circuit* C *with secret input set* $\mathbf{X} \in \mathbb{F}_2^n$ *provides d-Strong Non-Interference if and only if for any observation set of* $t = t_1 + t_2 \leq d$ *wires* $\mathbf{Q}$ *of which* t_1 *are internal wires and* t_2 *are output wires, there exists a simulation set* $\mathbf{S}$ *of input shares with* $|\mathbf{S}|_{\forall i} \leq t_1$ *such that Eq. (3) holds.*

Probe-Isolating Non-Interference. Unfortunately, the security notion of SNI in practice is often very conservative and inefficient as it introduces more area and randomness than necessary to achieve certain security goals. To address this issue, Cassiers *et al.* introduced the notion of Probe-Isolating Non- Inter-ferencePINI [17] which offers trivial composition of any gadgets inspired by the trivial composition of linear functions and the concept of sharing domain separations as introduced in [29]. As the original SNI definition limits composability to single-output gadgets, Cassiers *et al.* also introduced a generalization of SNI to gadgets with multiple inputs and multiple outputs (Multiple-Input- Multiple-Output SNI (MIMO-SNI)). This is a very strong notion which in fact already implies security under the PINI notion, i.e., every gadget that provides d-MIMO-SNI also provides d-PINI. As PINI already guarantees trivial composition, we do not consider MIMO-SNI any further in this work.

In the context of PINI, each circuit input and output is assigned a unique circuit share index (i.e., a share domain) and any probe set on these wires should be perfectly simulatable knowing only the set of inputs that are assigned to the same circuit share index. Further, any additional probe on internal wires gives the adversary access to at most one additional circuit share, i.e., must be perfectly simulatable knowing only the according set of inputs assigned to these circuit shares. Eventually, this translates to the following definition.

Definition 7 (d-Probe-Isolating Non-Interference). *Let* $\mathbf{P}$ *be the set of internal probes with* $|\mathbf{P}| = t_1$*. Let further* $\mathbf{I_O}$ *be the index set assigned to the probed output wires* $\mathbf{O}$ *with* $|\mathbf{I_O}| = t_2$*.*

A circuit C *with secret input set* $\mathbf{X} \in \mathbb{F}_2^n$ *provides* d-*Probe-Isolating Non-Interference if and only if for every* $\mathbf{P}$ *and* $\mathbf{O}$ *with* $t_1 + t_2 \leq d$ *there exists a set* $\mathbf{I_I}$ *of circuit indices with* $|\mathbf{I_I}| \leq t_1$ *such that* $\mathbf{Q} = \mathbf{P} \cup \mathbf{O}$ *can be perfectly simulated by* $\mathbf{S} = Sh(\mathbf{X})^{\mathbf{I_I} \cup \mathbf{I_O}}$*, i.e., Eq. (3) holds.*

Uniformity. The security of (Boolean) masking schemes relies on a fundamental assumption: *uniform sharing*. For that, the initial sharing of any secret variable X using $d + 1$ shares, such that $X = \bigoplus_0^d X^i$, can be done by assigning random values to $X^0, \dots, X^{d-1}$ and deriving $X^d = X \oplus \bigoplus_0^{d-1} X^i$. Such a sharing then is uniform if all random variables $X^0, \dots, X^{d-1}$ are independent of each other and have a uniform distribution over $\mathbb{F}_2$.

In practice, the uniformity of the output sharing of gadgets has been defined as a fundamental requirement for (TIs), particularly for secure composition of gadgets [39]. Otherwise, a non-uniform output sharing of a gadget becomes the non-uniform input sharing of another gadget, hence violating the essential assumption of uniformity for (Boolean) masking schemes. Note, however, that a gadget can be probing secure, but it is not necessarily uniform. Likewise, a uniform gadget does not automatically lead to a probing-secure construction. This has been handled specifically in NI and SNI gadgets, e.g., by injecting fresh randomness at the output thereby refreshing the output sharing, i.e., achieving uniformity.

Definition 8 formalizes the notion of a uniform sharing as it states that for every unshared value, each valid sharing has to occur with the same probability.

Definition 8 (Uniform Sharing). *Let* $\mathbf{Y}$ *be a set of binary random variable and* $Sh(\mathbf{Y})$ *its corresponding Boolean sharing. Then* $Sh(\mathbf{Y})$ *is said to be a uniform sharing iff for some constant* p

$$Pr\left[Sh(\mathbf{Y}) = \mathbf{y}^* | \mathbf{Y} = \mathbf{y}\right] = \begin{cases} p & \textit{if } \mathbf{y}^* \textit{ is a valid sharing for } \mathbf{y} \\ 0 & \textit{else} \end{cases}. \qquad (4)$$

3 Verification Concept

This section briefly elaborates our main idea and concept for our verification model and approach.

3.1 Leakage Models

For verification, we additionally consider each security notion under two different leakage models denoted *standard* respectively *robust* leakage model.

Standard Leakage Model. For our standard leakage model following the concept of the traditional ISW d-probing model [31], we assume an ideal circuit without any physical defaults such as *glitches* or *transitions*. In practice, this leakage model relates to a software scenario where each result of an operation (i.e., a gate in a circuit C) is stored in a register before it is used by subsequent operations (gates). Note that in this model, the implementation platform's specific effects like pipelines are entirely ignored. In this model, an adversarial probe provides access to the field element carried on the probed wire. More precisely, the adversary gains full access to the Boolean function represented by the driving gate in order to derive the field element.

Robust Leakage Model. In contrast to our standard leakage model, for our robust model following the leakage model in [26], we also take physical default in terms of glitches into consideration, hence, in practice this model relates to a hardware scenario. Since only circuit inputs and memory elements are assumed to switch synchronous to a circuit clock, glitches will propagate through all combinational gates between two synchronization points. Therefore, by probing a wire, the adversary not only gains access to the field element of the driving gate but also can access all stable field elements of the last synchronization points which drive the probed gate (having a path to the driving gate in the circuit graph). More precisely, the adversary gains full access to the set of these field elements (and any subset) through so called *glitch-extended* probes.

3.2   Verification Approach

Based on some fundamental observation, this section outlines our basic concept and explains our main approach to verify different security notions starting from a circuit model given as gate-level netlist.

Random Variables with Binary Events. According to our circuit model, each edge in the circuit graph models a wire and carries an element from the field $\mathbb{F}_2$ with two elements. Thus, we first observe each wire, and its associated field element can be modeled as a binary random variable defined over the sample space $\Omega = \{0, 1\}$ of two basic events given the assumption that all primary circuit inputs are independent and identically distributed (i.i.d.). Based on this observation, we can use the probability distributions of all random variables in order to analyze and verify a circuit model against the security notions defined in Sect. 2.4.

Probability Distribution and Satisfiability. In general, the probability of an event is defined by the sum of the probabilities of all *outcomes* that satisfy the event. In the context of our circuit model, an *outcome* can be considered as a variable assignment to the primary circuit inputs that leads to the desired element of the sample space at the observed random variable. For this, computing the probability density function of a random variable associated with a circuit wire reduces to enumerating and counting the primary input variable assignments that satisfy the corresponding basic events for the observed random variable.

Symbolic Simulation Using ROBDDs. As the naive approach of exhaustive and literal simulation of the circuit model expeditiously becomes infeasible with increasing circuit complexity and number of primary circuit inputs, symbolic simulation and analysis is necessary to maintain the generation of all probability distributions practicable even for large and complex circuit models. More precisely, each gate in the circuit model represents a sub-circuit and is associated with a Boolean function given as ROBDD that computes the gate output over the set of primary circuit inputs. Since ROBDDs are concise and canonical representations of Boolean functions, counting the number of *cubes*, i.e., the satisfying variable assignments, for each basic binary event can be done efficiently using symbolic analysis. Knowing the total number of possible variable assignments, computing the probability distribution for each random variable remains feasible even for large and complex circuits.

Standard and Glitch-Extended Probes. Considering our two different leakage models, we also have to differentiate the capabilities and knowledge of the adversary. Firstly, for the standard model we thus assume that an adversarial probe gives access to the probability distribution of a field element carried on an arbitrary wire observed by the adversarial probe. More precisely, the adversary in this case learns the Boolean sub-function associated with the driving gate in order to compute the field element and its probability distribution as function of the primary circuit inputs. Secondly, in contrast to the standard model, a robust or *glitch-extended* probe extends the capabilities and knowledge of the adversary as it also provides access to the joint distribution of all hindmost contributing synchronization points (memory elements or primary inputs). Hence, in order to model physical defaults and in particular glitches, the adversary also learns the Boolean sub-functions associated with the corresponding synchronization elements.

Statistical Independence and Security Checks. Eventually, depending on the targeted security order d, an adversarial *observation* can consist of up to d independently placed adversarial probes and the adversary is allowed to combine the information and knowledge of all probes to learn details of the secret. In order to verify security under the given security notions as defined in Sect. 2.4, we perform an exhaustive exploration and check of all possible adversarial observations $\mathbf{Q}$ combining up to d probes. For this, the following section is dedicated to a detail description and verification of our performed security checks.

4   Statistical Independence and Security Checks

Before formally analysis and verification of the correctness of our security checks, we briefly recap the definitions of (joint) probability mass functions and statistical independence for sets of random variables.

4.1   Statistical Independence

The probability mass function provides the probability of all possible values for a set of discrete random variables based on their probability distribution.

Definition 9 (Probability Mass Function). *Let* $\mathbf{X}$ *be a set of discrete random variables. The* probability mass function $p_{\mathbf{X}}(\mathbf{x})$ *is defined as:*

$$p_{\mathbf{X}}(\mathbf{x}) = Pr[\mathbf{X} = \mathbf{x}].$$

Based on this, given two arbitrary sets of discrete random variables, the joint probability mass function between these two variable sets then is defined as follows.

Definition 10 (Joint Probability Mass Function). *Let* $\mathbf{X}, \mathbf{Y}$ *be two sets of discrete random variables. The* joint probability mass function $p_{\mathbf{X},\mathbf{Y}}(\mathbf{x}, \mathbf{y})$ *is defined as:*

$$p_{\mathbf{X},\mathbf{Y}}(\mathbf{x}, \mathbf{y}) = Pr[\mathbf{X} = \mathbf{x} \ and \ \mathbf{Y} = \mathbf{y}].$$

Using the definitions of probability mass function and joint probability mass function, we can express the notion of statistical independence of two sets of discrete random variables according to the following definition.

Definition 11 (Statistical Independence). *Let* $\mathbf{X}, \mathbf{Y}$ *be two sets of discrete random variables.* $\mathbf{X}, \mathbf{Y}$ *are statistically independent if and only if the joint probability mass function for* $\forall \mathbf{x}$ *and* $\forall \mathbf{y}$ *satisfies*

$$p_{\mathbf{X},\mathbf{Y}}(\mathbf{x}, \mathbf{y}) = p_{\mathbf{X}}(\mathbf{x}) \cdot p_{\mathbf{Y}}(\mathbf{y}).$$

Statistical Independence of Binary Random Variables. In the context of our security notions, we are mainly interested in statistical independence of *binary random variables*. As any binary random variable can only take two different events, Theorem 1 states that checking statistical independence for one event implies statistical independence for both events, even extending to the case of sets of binary random variables.

Theorem 1. *Let* $\mathbf{X}, \mathbf{Y}$ *be two sets of binary random variables. Then* $\mathbf{X}$ *and* $\mathbf{Y}$ *are statistically independent, if and only if* $p_{\mathbf{X}',\mathbf{Y}'}(\mathbf{a}, \mathbf{b}) = p_{\mathbf{X}'}(\mathbf{a}) \cdot p_{\mathbf{Y}'}(\mathbf{b})$ *for any fixed values* $\mathbf{a}$ *and* $\mathbf{b}$ *and every possible combination of* $\mathbf{X}' \subseteq \mathbf{X}$ *and* $\mathbf{Y}' \subseteq \mathbf{Y}$.

In order to proof correctness of Theorem 1, we start with the basic case of two binary random variables (i.e., sets of cardinality one).

Lemma 1. *Let* $X, Y \in \mathbb{F}_2$ *be two binary random variables. Then, a necessary and sufficient condition for* X *to be statistically independent of* Y *is that, for any fixed values* $a, b \in \{0, 1\}$, *it holds*

$$p_{X,Y}(a, b) = p_X(a) \cdot p_Y(b).$$

Proof. According to Definition 11, the necessity of this proposition is obvious, hence, the proof focuses on the sufficiency. Without loss of generality, we now assume Theorem 1 is true for $a = b = 1$, i.e., $p_{X,Y}(1,1) = p_X(1) \cdot p_Y(1)$. Since $X = 0$ and $X = 1$ are counter events for binary variables, both the fact $p_X(0) + p_X(1) = 1$ and the fact $p_{X,Y}(0,1) + p_{X,Y}(1,1) = p_Y(1)$ hold, and we have

$$
\begin{aligned}
& p_{X,Y}(0,1) + p_{X,Y}(1,1) = p_Y(1) \\
\Leftrightarrow\ & p_{X,Y}(0,1) + p_X(1) \cdot p_Y(1) = p_Y(1) \\
\Leftrightarrow\ & p_{X,Y}(0,1) = (1 - p_X(1)) \cdot p_Y(1) \\
\Leftrightarrow\ & p_{X,Y}(0,1) = p_X(0) \cdot p_Y(1)
\end{aligned}
$$

Proving the cases for $a = 1, b = 0$ and $a = b = 0$ is trivial as it follows the same approach, hence is left out for brevity. $\qquad\square$

In a next step, we extend the basic case through mathematical induction in order to prove statistical independence between a single random binary variable and a set of random binary variables.

Lemma 2. *Let X be a binary random variable and $\mathbf{Y}$ a set of n random binary variables. Further, let X be statistically independent of the joint distribution of $\mathbf{Y}$. Now, the joint distribution $\mathbf{Y}^+$, with $\mathbf{Y} \subset \mathbf{Y}^+$ and $|\mathbf{Y}^+| = n+1$ is statistically independent of X, if and only if $p_{X,\mathbf{Y}^+}(a, \mathbf{b}^+) = p_X(a) \cdot p_{\mathbf{Y}^+}(\mathbf{b}^+)$ for any fixed values $a, \mathbf{b}^+$.*

Proof. We now give a formal proof using mathematical induction on n.

<u>Base case:</u> We first show that Lemma 2 holds for $n = 0$.

Clearly, if $n = 0$, $\mathbf{Y}$ is the empty set while $\mathbf{Y}^+$ is a single binary random variable. Then, according to Lemma 1, X and $\mathbf{Y}^+$ are statistically independent if and only if for any fixed values a, b it holds that $p_{X,\mathbf{Y}^+}(a, b) = p_X(a) \cdot p_{\mathbf{Y}^+}(b)$.
□

<u>Induction:</u> If Lemma 2 holds for $n = k$, it also holds for $n = k + 1$ with $k \geq 0$.

For this, we first show that, without loss of generality, for $X, \mathbf{Y}^+$ the following fact $p_{X,\mathbf{Y}^+}(a, \mathbf{b}_{\bar{i}}^+) = p_X(a) \cdot p_{\mathbf{Y}^+}(\mathbf{b}_{\bar{i}}^+)$ with $\mathbf{b}_{\bar{i}}^+ = \{y_0, y_1, \ldots, \overline{y_i}, \ldots, y_k, y_{k+1}\}$ holds, if:

(i) $p_{X,\mathbf{Y}}(a, \mathbf{b}) = p_X(a) \cdot p_{\mathbf{Y}}(\mathbf{b})$ with $\mathbf{b} = \{y_0, y_1, \ldots, y_{i-1}, y_{i+1}, \ldots, y_k, y_{k+1}\}$,

(ii) $p_{X,\mathbf{Y}^+}(a, \mathbf{b}^+) = p_X(a) \cdot p_{\mathbf{Y}^+}(\mathbf{b}^+)$ with $\mathbf{b}^+ = \{y_0, y_1, \ldots, y_i, \ldots, y_k, y_{k+1}\}$

Further, we note that for binary random variables it always holds that:

$$p_{X,\mathbf{Y}}(a, \mathbf{b}) = p_{X,\mathbf{Y}^+}(a, \mathbf{b}^+) + p_{X,\mathbf{Y}^+}(a, \mathbf{b}_{\bar{i}}^+)$$

Given that (i), (ii) are conditions for Lemma 2, we can state the following:

$$p_{X,\mathbf{Y}}(a, \mathbf{b}) = p_X(a) \cdot p_{\mathbf{Y}}(\mathbf{b})$$
$$\Leftrightarrow \ p_{X,\mathbf{Y}^+}(a, \mathbf{b}^+) + p_{X,\mathbf{Y}^+}(a, \mathbf{b}_{\bar{i}}^+) = p_X(a) \cdot p_{\mathbf{Y}}(\mathbf{b})$$
$$\Leftrightarrow \ p_X(a) \cdot p_{\mathbf{Y}^+}(\mathbf{b}^+) + p_{X,\mathbf{Y}^+}(a, \mathbf{b}_{\bar{i}}^+) = p_X(a) \cdot p_{\mathbf{Y}}(\mathbf{b})$$
$$\Leftrightarrow \ p_{X,\mathbf{Y}^+}(a, \mathbf{b}_{\bar{i}}^+) = p_X(a) \cdot p_{\mathbf{Y}}(\mathbf{b}) - p_X(a) \cdot p_{\mathbf{Y}^+}(\mathbf{b}^+)$$
$$\Leftrightarrow \ p_{X,\mathbf{Y}^+}(a, \mathbf{b}_{\bar{i}}^+) = p_X(a) \cdot [p_{\mathbf{Y}}(\mathbf{b}) - p_{\mathbf{Y}^+}(\mathbf{b}^+)]$$
$$\Leftrightarrow \ p_{X,\mathbf{Y}^+}(a, \mathbf{b}_{\bar{i}}^+) = p_X(a) \cdot p_{\mathbf{Y}^+}(\mathbf{b}_{\bar{i}}^+)$$

As the sorting of variables in $\mathbf{Y}^+$ is not fixed, this approach also extends to inversion of any other event and therefore can easily be extended to show statistical independence for every combination of events.
□

Eventually, this also proves Theorem 1. In particular, knowing that $\mathbf{X}, \mathbf{Y}$ are statistically independent, we can argue that $\mathbf{X}^+, \mathbf{Y}$ with $\mathbf{X} \subset \mathbf{X}^+$, $|\mathbf{X}| = n$, and $|\mathbf{X}^+| = n + 1$ must be statistically independent, if and only if $p_{\mathbf{X}^+,\mathbf{Y}}(\mathbf{a}^+, \mathbf{b}) = p_{\mathbf{X}^+}(\mathbf{a}^+) \cdot p_{\mathbf{Y}}(\mathbf{b})$ using the same approach as for Lemma 2.

Algorithm 1: Explore d-Probing Security.

    Input   : **X** – Set of n secret variables.
    Output: **Q** – Set of $d + 1$ successful probes.

1 $d \leftarrow 1$
2 **while** *true* **do**
3 | **foreach** *probing set* **Q** *with* $|\mathbf{Q}| = d$ **do**
4 | | **for** $t = 1$ *to* n **do**
5 | | | **foreach** $\mathbf{X}' \subseteq \mathbf{X}$ *with* $\mathbf{X}' = t$ **do**
6 | | | | **if** $p_{\mathbf{Q},\mathbf{X}'}(1, 1) \neq p_{\mathbf{Q}}(1) \cdot p_{\mathbf{X}'}(1)$ **then**
7 | | | | | **return Q**
8 | | | | **end**
9 | | | **end**
10 | | **end**
11 | **end**
12 | $d \leftarrow d + 1$
13 **end**

4.2 d-Probing Security

Checking d-probing security according to Definition 4 requires to verify statistical independence of the set of secret variables and any observation of at most d probes. This section presents an exploration algorithm that allows to find and verify the maximum security order of a given circuit with secret variables **X**. Eventually, the algorithm will return the first set of $d + 1$ probes that is not statistically independent of the secret variables.

Algorithmic Verification Approach. Algorithm 1 presents our algorithmic approach to explore and verify d-probing security of a (CUT). In general, the algorithm is initialized with $d = 1$, i.e., starts to explore and verify first-order security before extending verification to higher orders. Since for $|\mathbf{Q}| = 1$ each observation set contains only a single binary variable (observed by a single probe placed on a wire within the circuit C), according to Theorem 1 it is sufficient to verify:

$$p_{\mathbf{Q},\mathbf{X}'}(1, 1) \overset{?}{=} p_{\mathbf{Q}}(1) \cdot p_{\mathbf{X}'}(1) \tag{5}$$

for all possible combinations of secret variables $\mathbf{X}' \subseteq \mathbf{X}$. If any of those checks fails, the current observation is not statistically independent of the secret variables and Algorithm 1 terminates with returning the current set of observation indicating the security of the CUT to be at most $d = |\mathbf{Q}| - 1$.

    If probing security is verified for all joint distributions of d probes, the algorithm continues with all combinations of $d + 1$ probes. However, for independence of the current set of probes **Q**, it is still sufficient to check Eq. (5) for all combinations of secret variables (but only the current combination of probes), since any subset of probes has already been verified during previous iterations (for smaller d).

Algorithm 2: Explore d-Non-Interference Security.

 Input : $Sh(\mathbf{X})$ – Set of all shares of n secret variables $\mathbf{X}$.
 Output: $\mathbf{Q}$ – Set of $d+1$ successful probes.

1 $d \leftarrow 1$
2 **while** *true* **do**
3 **foreach** *probing set* $\mathbf{Q}$ *with* $|\mathbf{Q}| = d$ **do**
4   *simulatable* $\leftarrow$ *true*
5   **for** $t = 0$ *to* d **do**
6   **foreach** $\mathbf{S} \subseteq Sh(\mathbf{X})$ *with* $|\mathbf{S}|_{\forall i} = t$ **do**
7   **if** $p_{\mathbf{Q},Sh(\mathbf{X})}(\mathbf{1},\mathbf{1}) \neq p_{\mathbf{Q},\mathbf{S}}(\mathbf{1},\mathbf{1}) \cdot p_{\overline{\mathbf{S}}}(\mathbf{1})$ **then**
8   *simulatable* $\leftarrow$ *false*
9   **end**
10   **end**
11   **end**
12   **if** *not simulatable* **then**
13   **return** $\mathbf{Q}$
14   **end**
15 **end**
16 $d \leftarrow d + 1$
17 **end**

Eventually, all verification and statistical independence checks are performed based on ROBDDs in order to generate all (joint) probability mass functions $p_{\mathbf{Q}}$, $p_{\mathbf{X}}$, and $p_{\mathbf{Q},\mathbf{X}}$. In particular, evaluation of the probability mass functions for $\mathbf{1}$ is very efficient for ROBDD-based representations, usually implemented as *satisfiability-check*.

4.3 d-Non-Interference

Checking d-NI security using Definition 5 requires to verify Eq. (3) that every set of at most d probes $\mathbf{Q}$ on a circuit C has to be perfectly simulatable using only a subset $\mathbf{S}$ of all shares of the secret variables $\mathbf{X}$. Using the concept of statistical independence of two sets of random binary variables, we can express NI using the following theorem.

Theorem 2. *Let* $\overline{\mathbf{S}} := Sh(\mathbf{X}) \setminus \mathbf{S}$. *Since all input shares are i.i.d., Eq. (3) simplifies to:*

$$p_{\mathbf{Q},Sh(\mathbf{X})}(\mathbf{q},\mathbf{x}) = p_{\mathbf{Q},\mathbf{S}}(\mathbf{q},\mathbf{s}) \cdot p_{\overline{\mathbf{S}}}(\overline{\mathbf{s}}). \tag{6}$$

In particular, since $Sh(\mathbf{X}) = \mathbf{S} \cup \overline{\mathbf{S}}$*, we can simply verify statistical independence of* $\mathbf{Q} \cup \mathbf{S}$ *and* $\overline{\mathbf{S}}$ *(with* $\mathbf{x} = \mathbf{s} \cup \overline{\mathbf{s}}$*).*

Algorithm 3: Explore d-Probe-Isolating Non-Interference Security.

    Input   : $Sh(\mathbf{X})$ – Set of all shares of n secret variables $\mathbf{X}$.
    Output: $\mathbf{Q}$ – Set of $d+1$ successful probes.

1 $d \leftarrow 1$
2 **while** *true* **do**
3 | **foreach** *probing set* $\mathbf{Q}$ *with* $|\mathbf{Q}| = t_1 + t_2 \le d$ *(t_1 internal, t_2 output probes)* **do**
4 | | *simulatable* $\leftarrow$ *true*
5 | | **for** $t = 0$ *to* t_1 **do**
6 | | | **foreach** $\mathbf{S} \subseteq Sh(\mathbf{X})$ *with* $|\mathbf{S}|_{\forall i} = t$ **do**
7 | | | | **if** $p_{\mathbf{Q},Sh(\mathbf{X})}(\mathbf{1},\mathbf{1}) \ne p_{\mathbf{Q},\mathbf{S}}(\mathbf{1},\mathbf{1}) \cdot p_{\overline{\mathbf{S}}}(\mathbf{1})$ **then**
8 | | | | | *simulatable* $\leftarrow$ *false*
9 | | | | **end**
10 | | | **end**
11 | | **end**
12 | | **if** *not simulatable* **then**
13 | | | **return Q**
14 | | **end**
15 | **end**
16 | $d \leftarrow d + 1$
17 **end**

Proof.

$$Pr[\mathbf{Q}|\mathbf{S}] = Pr[\mathbf{Q}|Sh(\mathbf{X})]$$
$$\Leftrightarrow Pr[\mathbf{Q},\mathbf{S}] \cdot Pr[Sh(\mathbf{X})] = Pr[\mathbf{Q}, Sh(\mathbf{X})] \cdot Pr[\mathbf{S}]$$
$$\overset{\text{i.i.d.} Sh(\mathbf{X})}{\Leftrightarrow} Pr[\mathbf{Q},\mathbf{S}] \cdot Pr[\overline{\mathbf{S}}] = Pr[\mathbf{Q}, Sh(\mathbf{X})]$$
$$\Leftrightarrow p_{\mathbf{Q},\mathbf{S}}(\mathbf{q},\mathbf{s}) \cdot p_{\overline{\mathbf{S}}}(\overline{\mathbf{s}}) = p_{\mathbf{Q},Sh(\mathbf{X})}(\mathbf{q},\mathbf{x})$$

$\square$

Algorithmic Verification Approach. Algorithm 2 explores and verifies d-NI for increasing d and all possible observations $\mathbf{Q}$ of at most d probes. In particular, the algorithm proceeds as soon as a successful simulation set $\mathbf{S}$ of input shares is found for the current set of probes $\mathbf{Q}$, such that $\mathbf{Q}$ is perfectly simulatable using $\mathbf{S}$. However, if the algorithm encounters a set of probes $\mathbf{Q}$ with $|\mathbf{Q}| = d+1$ which is not simulatable for set of input shares (according to the definition of NI), the algorithm terminates and returns the current set of probes indicating d-NI with $d = |\mathbf{Q}| - 1$.

4.4 d-Strong Non-Interference

Checking d-SNI is very similar to checking d-NI, except for stronger constraints on the simulation set $\mathbf{S}$ due to stronger distinction between internal and output probes.

Algorithm 4: Explore d-Probe-Isolating Non-Interference Security.

    Input   : $Sh(\mathbf{X})$ – Set of all shares of n secret variables $\mathbf{X}$.
    Output: $\mathbf{Q}$ – Set of $d+1$ successful probes.

 1 $d \leftarrow 1$
 2 **while** *true* **do**
 3   **foreach** *probing set* $\mathbf{Q}$ *with* $|\mathbf{Q}| = d$ **do**
 4        $simulatable \leftarrow true$
 5   **foreach** $\mathbf{S} \subseteq Sh(\mathbf{X})^{\mathbf{I}_O \cup \mathbf{I}_I}$ **do**
 6   **if** $p_{\mathbf{Q},Sh(\mathbf{X})}(\mathbf{1},\mathbf{1}) \neq p_{\mathbf{Q},\mathbf{S}}(\mathbf{1},\mathbf{1}) \cdot p_{\overline{\mathbf{S}}}(\mathbf{1})$ **then**
 7 | $simulatable \leftarrow false$
 8   **end**
 9   **end**
10   **if** *not simulatable* **then**
11   **return** $\mathbf{Q}$
12   **end**
13   **end**
14     $d \leftarrow d+1$
15 **end**

Algorithmic Verification Approach. In contrast to NI, for SNI the number of shares per input in each simulation set is bounded by the number of internal probes (instead of the number of all probes). Hence, except for minor difference, the algorithmic verification approach given in Algorithm 3 (notation matching the one given in Definition 6) has the same structure as the approach for NI, but enforcing stronger constraints on the selection of shares (lines 5 and 6) for the simulation set $\mathbf{S}$.

4.5 d-Probe-Isolating Non-Interference

For the notion of PINI, the index of any input or output wires correspond to the associated circuit share. In contrast to NI and SNI, the concept of PINI constrains the simulation set not by the number of (internal) probes, but according to the associated circuit shares.

Verification Approach. The algorithmic verification approach in order to explore and verify the security notion of PINI for increasing security order d is given in Algorithm 4. Again, the algorithm is based on the concept of perfect simulatability of every $\mathbf{Q}$ with a set $\mathbf{S}$, in conformity with the notions in Definition 7.

4.6 Uniformity

In order to examine the uniformity of the output sharing of a gadget, we start with the following observation.

Lemma 3. *Assume the function* f *with single output* $Y \in \mathbb{F}_2$ *whose shared version is realized by a gadget with* $d+1$ *output shares* $Sh(Y) = (Y^0, \ldots, Y^d)$. *The gadget's output sharing is uniform iff any selection of* d *output shares make a balanced function.*

Proof. We start with $d = 1$, i.e., 2 output shares. Let us denote the joint probability of the output shares by $\rho_{0,0} = Pr[Y^0 = 0, Y^1 = 0]$, $\rho_{0,1} = Pr[Y^0 = 0, Y^1 = 1]$, $\rho_{1,0} = Pr[Y^0 = 1, Y^1 = 0]$, and $\rho_{1,1} = Pr[Y^0 = 1, Y^1 = 1]$, assuming that the gadget's input is uniformly distributed, which is true since the gadget's input sharing should be uniform (essential assumption of Boolean masking, see Sect. 2.4). Hence, the probability of the output shares can be written as

$$Pr[Y^0 = 0] = \rho_{0,0} + \rho_{0,1}, \qquad Pr[Y^0 = 1] = \rho_{1,0} + \rho_{1,1},$$
$$Pr[Y^1 = 0] = \rho_{0,0} + \rho_{1,0}, \qquad Pr[Y^1 = 1] = \rho_{0,1} + \rho_{1,1}.$$

1) If $Sh(Y)$ is uniform, $(Y^0 = 0, Y^1 = 0)$ and $(Y^0 = 1, Y^1 = 1)$ are equally likely to occur, i.e., $\rho_{0,0} = \rho_{1,1}$. The same holds for $(Y^0 = 0, Y^1 = 1)$ and $(Y^0 = 1, Y^1 = 0)$, i.e., $\rho_{0,1} = \rho_{1,0}$. Therefore, $Pr[Y^0 = 0] = \rho_{0,0} + \rho_{0,1} = \rho_{1,1} + \rho_{1,0} = Pr[Y^0 = 1]$, i.e., the gadget's coordinate function f^0 with output Y^0 is balanced. The same trivially holds for Y^1. Hence, individual balancedness of each output share is essential for uniformity.

2) If the coordinate functions of Y^0 and Y^1 are balanced, we can write

$$Pr[Y^0 = 0] = Pr[Y^0 = 1] \qquad \Longleftrightarrow \qquad \rho_{0,0} + \rho_{0,1} = \rho_{1,0} + \rho_{1,1},$$
$$Pr[Y^1 = 0] = Pr[Y^1 = 1] \qquad \Longleftrightarrow \qquad \rho_{0,0} + \rho_{1,0} = \rho_{0,1} + \rho_{1,1}.$$

These two equations directly translate into $\rho_{0,0} = \rho_{1,1}$ and $\rho_{0,1} = \rho_{1,0}$. This means that $(Y^0 = 0, Y^1 = 0)$ and $(Y^0 = 1, Y^1 = 1)$ are equally likely to occur. The same holds for $(Y^0 = 0, Y^1 = 1)$ and $(Y^0 = 1, Y^1 = 0)$, i.e., $Sh(Y)$ is a uniform sharing. Hence, individual balancedness of each output share is also a sufficient condition for uniformity.

For $d = 2$, we have $Sh(Y) = (Y^0, Y^1, Y^2)$. Assuming a uniform sharing for the gadget's input, similar to the above case for $d = 1$, we denote the joint probability of the output shares by $\rho_{y^0, y^1, y^2} = Pr[Y^0 = y^0, Y^1 = y^1, Y^2 = y^2]$, e.g., $\rho_{1,0,1} = Pr[Y^0 = 1, Y^1 = 0, Y^2 = 1]$. Exemplary, the joint probability of two output shares (Y^0, Y^1) can be derived as

$$Pr[Y^0 = 0, Y^1 = 0] = \rho_{0,0,0} + \rho_{0,0,1}, \quad Pr[Y^0 = 0, Y^1 = 1] = \rho_{0,1,0} + \rho_{0,1,1}, \tag{7}$$
$$Pr[Y^0 = 1, Y^1 = 0] = \rho_{1,0,0} + \rho_{1,0,1}, \quad Pr[Y^0 = 1, Y^1 = 1] = \rho_{1,1,0} + \rho_{1,1,1}.$$

1) In case $Sh(Y)$ is uniform, we have

$$\rho_{0,0,0} = \rho_{0,1,1} = \rho_{1,0,1} = \rho_{1,1,0}, \qquad \rho_{0,0,1} = \rho_{0,1,0} = \rho_{1,0,0} = \rho_{1,1,1}. \tag{8}$$

Hence, it can be trivially seen that

$$Pr[Y^0 = 0, Y^1 = 0] = Pr[Y^0 = 0, Y^1 = 1] = Pr[Y^0 = 1, Y^1 = 0] = Pr[Y^0 = 1, Y^1 = 1],$$

meaning that (Y^0, Y^1) are jointly balanced. The same holds for other output shares (Y^0, Y^2) and (Y^1, Y^2).

2) If (Y^0, Y^1) are jointly balanced, all probabilities given in Eq. (7) are the same, i.e.,

$$p_{0,0,0} + p_{0,0,1} = p_{0,1,0} + p_{0,1,1} = p_{1,0,0} + p_{1,0,1} = p_{1,1,0} + p_{1,1,1}.$$

The same can be written for (Y^0, Y^2) and (Y^1, Y^2) as

$$p_{0,0,0} + p_{0,1,0} = p_{0,0,1} + p_{0,1,1} = p_{1,0,0} + p_{1,1,0} = p_{1,0,1} + p_{1,1,1},$$
$$p_{0,0,0} + p_{1,0,0} = p_{0,0,1} + p_{1,0,1} = p_{0,1,0} + p_{1,1,0} = p_{0,1,1} + p_{1,1,1}.$$

Combination of these equations leads to the expressions given in Eq. (8), indicating the uniformity of $Sh(Y)$.

The same procedure can be followed to trivially verify Lemma 3 for $d > 2$. □

Lemma 4. *Assume the function* f *with n-bit output* $\mathbf{Y} = (Y_0, \ldots, Y_{n-1}) \in \mathbb{F}_2^n$ *whose shared version is realized by a gadget with* $d + 1$ *output shares* $Sh(\mathbf{Y}) = (\mathbf{Y}^0, \ldots, \mathbf{Y}^d)$. *The gadget's output sharing is uniform iff any selection of up to* $n \cdot d$ *output shares is balanced excluding the cases where all* $d + 1$ *shares of the same output are involved in the selection.*

Proof. For $n = 1$ it is the same as Lemma 3. Hence, we start with $n = 2$ and minimum number of output shares, $d + 1 = 2$. Assuming a uniform sharing for the gadget's input, we denote the joint probability of the output shares by $p_{(y_0^0, y_0^1),(y_1^0, y_1^1)} = Pr[Y_0^0 = y_0^0, Y_0^1 = y_0^1, Y_1^0 = y_1^0, Y_1^1 = y_1^1]$, e.g., $p_{(1,0),(1,1)} = Pr[Y_0^0 = 1, Y_0^1 = 0, Y_1^0 = 1, Y_1^1 = 1]$.

Exemplary, the joint probability of two output shares (Y_0^0, Y_1^1) is written as

$$
\begin{aligned}
Pr[Y_0^0 = 0, Y_1^1 = 0] &= p_{(0,0),(0,0)} + p_{(0,0),(1,0)} + p_{(0,1),(0,0)} + p_{(0,1),(1,0)}, \\
Pr[Y_0^0 = 0, Y_1^1 = 1] &= p_{(0,0),(0,1)} + p_{(0,0),(1,1)} + p_{(0,1),(0,1)} + p_{(0,1),(1,1)}, \\
Pr[Y_0^0 = 1, Y_1^1 = 0] &= p_{(1,0),(0,0)} + p_{(1,0),(1,0)} + p_{(1,1),(0,0)} + p_{(1,1),(1,0)}, \\
Pr[Y_0^0 = 1, Y_1^1 = 1] &= p_{(1,0),(0,1)} + p_{(1,0),(1,1)} + p_{(1,1),(0,1)} + p_{(1,1),(1,1)}.
\end{aligned}
\tag{9}
$$

1) If $Sh(\mathbf{Y})$ is uniform, we have

$$
\begin{aligned}
p_{(0,0),(0,0)} &= p_{(0,0),(1,1)} = p_{(1,1),(0,0)} = p_{(1,1),(1,1)}, \\
p_{(0,0),(0,1)} &= p_{(0,0),(1,0)} = p_{(1,1),(0,1)} = p_{(1,1),(1,0)}, \\
p_{(0,1),(0,0)} &= p_{(0,1),(1,1)} = p_{(1,0),(0,0)} = p_{(1,0),(1,1)}, \\
p_{(0,1),(0,1)} &= p_{(0,1),(1,0)} = p_{(1,0),(0,1)} = p_{(1,0),(1,0)}.
\end{aligned}
$$

This results in equal probabilities for all probabilities given in Eq. (9), such that

$$Pr[Y_0^0 = 0, Y_1^1 = 0] = Pr[Y_0^0 = 0, Y_1^1 = 1] = Pr[Y_0^0 = 1, Y_1^1 = 0] = Pr[Y_0^0 = 1, Y_1^1 = 1],$$

i.e., the two output shares (Y_0^0, Y_1^1) are jointly balanced. The same can be similarly verified all other combinations (Y_0^0, Y_1^0), (Y_0^1, Y_1^0), and (Y_0^1, Y_1^1).

2) If (Y_0^0, Y_1^1) are jointly balanced, based on Eq. (9) we have

$$
\begin{aligned}
&P_{(0,0),(0,0)} + P_{(0,0),(1,0)} + P_{(0,1),(0,0)} + P_{(0,1),(1,0)} \\
&= P_{(0,0),(0,1)} + P_{(0,0),(1,1)} + P_{(0,1),(0,1)} + P_{(0,1),(1,1)} \\
&= P_{(1,0),(0,0)} + P_{(1,0),(1,0)} + P_{(1,1),(0,0)} + P_{(1,1),(1,0)} \\
&= P_{(1,0),(0,1)} + P_{(1,0),(1,1)} + P_{(1,1),(0,1)} + P_{(1,1),(1,1)} = 1/4.
\end{aligned}
\tag{10}
$$

This leads to

$$
\begin{aligned}
&P_{(0,0),(0,0)} + P_{(0,0),(1,0)} + P_{(0,1),(0,0)} + P_{(0,1),(1,0)} \\
&\quad + P_{(0,0),(0,1)} + P_{(0,0),(1,1)} + P_{(0,1),(0,1)} + P_{(0,1),(1,1)} \\
&= P_{(1,0),(0,0)} + P_{(1,0),(1,0)} + P_{(1,1),(0,0)} + P_{(1,1),(1,0)} \\
&\quad + P_{(1,0),(0,1)} + P_{(1,0),(1,1)} + P_{(1,1),(0,1)} + P_{(1,1),(1,1)} = 1/2,
\end{aligned}
\tag{11}
$$

meaning that $Pr[Y_0^0 = 0] = Pr[Y_0^0 = 1]$, i.e., it is balanced. The same can be written for $Pr[Y_1^1 = 0] = Pr[Y_1^1 = 1]$, and similarly for (Y_0^0, Y_1^0), (Y_0^1, Y_1^0), and (Y_0^1, Y_1^1). In short, every single output bit is balanced, hence, according to Lemma 3, the sharing of every output is individually uniform. Note that, in general when a function with d output bits is balanced, any combination of $d' < d$ output bits also makes a balanced function [34, §12.1.2].

According to Eqs. (9) and (10), we exemplary write

$$
Pr[Y_0^0 = 0, Y_1^1 = 0] = 1/4.
$$

On the other hand, according to Eq. (11) we have

$$
Pr[Y_0^0 = 0] = 1/2, \qquad\qquad Pr[Y_1^1 = 0] = 1/2,
$$

which implies $Pr[Y_0^0 = 0, Y_1^1 = 0] = Pr[Y_0^0 = 0] \cdot Pr[Y_1^1 = 0]$. The same can similarly be seen for $(Y_0^0, Y_1^1) = (0,1)$, $(1,0)$ and $(1,1)$, meaning that

$$
Pr[Y_0^0, Y_1^1] = Pr[Y_0^0] \cdot Pr[Y_1^1].
\tag{12}
$$

In other words, Y_0^0 and Y_1^1 are statistically independent. In a similar way, statistical independence of (Y_0^0, Y_1^0), (Y_0^1, Y_1^0), and (Y_0^1, Y_1^1) can be shown.

Now, let us denote conditional probability $Pr[Y_0^0 = y_0^0, Y_0^1 = y_0^1, Y_1^0 = y_1^0, Y_1^1 = y_1^1 | Y_0 = y_0, Y_1 = y_1]$ by $P_{(y_0^0, y_0^1),(y_1^0, y_1^1)|(y_0, y_1)}$. For the sharing $Sh(\mathbf{Y})$ to be uniform, according to Eq. (4) and exemplary for $\mathbf{Y} = (0,0)$ we should have

$$
P_{(0,0),(0,0)|(0,0)} = P_{(0,0),(1,1)|(0,0)} = P_{(1,1),(0,0)|(0,0)} = P_{(1,1),(1,1)|(0,0)} = 1/4.
\tag{13}
$$

The same should hold for other values of $\mathbf{Y} = (0,1)$, $(1,0)$, and $(1,1)$. Considering the statistical independence of (Y_0^1, Y_1^0) explained above, We can write

$$
\begin{aligned}
P_{(0,0),(0,0)|(0,0)} &= Pr\left[Y_0^0 = 0, Y_0^1 = 0, Y_1^0 = 0, Y_1^1 = 0 \,\middle|\, Y_0 = 0, Y_1 = 0\right] \\
&= Pr\left[Y_0^0 = 0, Y_1^1 = 0 \,\middle|\, Y_0^1 = 0, Y_1^0 = 0, Y_0 = 0, Y_1 = 0\right] \cdot Pr\left[Y_0^1 = 0, Y_1^0 = 0 \,\middle|\, Y_0 = 0, Y_1 = 0\right] \\
&= 1 \cdot Pr\left[Y_0^1 = 0 \,\middle|\, Y_0 = 0, Y_1 = 0\right] \cdot Pr\left[Y_1^0 = 0 \,\middle|\, Y_0 = 0, Y_1 = 0\right]
\end{aligned}
$$

Due to the balancedness of every individual output, we have

$$Pr\left[Y_0^1 = 0 \middle| Y_0 = 0, Y_1 = 0\right] = Pr\left[Y_0^1 = 0 \middle| Y_0 = 0, Y_1 = 0\right] = 1/2.$$

This leads to $\rho_{(0,0),(0,0)|(0,0)} = 1/4$. The same can be shown for $\rho_{(0,0),(1,1)|(0,0)}$, $\rho_{(1,1),(0,0)|(0,0)}$, and $\rho_{(1,1),(1,1)|(0,0)}$, satisfying Eq. (13). The same can be similarly verified for $\mathbf{Y} = (0,1)$, $(1,0)$, and $(1,1)$, hence the uniformity of $Sh(\mathbf{Y})$.

The same procedure can be followed to verify Lemma 4 for $n > 2$ and $d > 2$. □

Indeed, for a given circuit netlist we efficiently perform balancedness checks directly based on the ROBDDs of the circuit.

5   Related Work

For formal verification of masked implementations, both in software and hardware, several tools and frameworks have been proposed, each following a different methodology and verification approach.

Formal Verification of Software Implementations. For automated masking of software implementations, the work of Moss *et al.* [38] was first to consider a type-based methodology for security annotation while dynamically repairing the masked implementation based on heuristics if leakage was detected at some point in the program flow. As any type-based approach inevitably results in an overly conservative verification, logic-based methods have been proposed as an alternative approach. Here, the work by Byrak *et al.* Byrak [6] translates verification to a set of Boolean satisfiability problems which can then be solved by a SAT solver. Nonetheless, both approaches only consider verification of masking against first-order attacks.

Later, an SMT-solver-based method for formally verifying even higher-order security has been introduced in [24]. As for [6], this verification method is also based on the notion of *perfect masking* as presented in [13]. Similarly, in [44] another method for verifying perfect masking was introduced, this time aiming to optimize the trade-off between accuracy (as offered by logic-based approaches) and efficiency (as given in type-based verification). Eventually, a composition-based verification approach in direct conformity with d-probing security (i.e., without any false negatives) is given by Belaïd *et al.* in [9].

Formal Verification of Hardware Implementations. Considering hardware designs, the work of Bloem *et al.* [11,12] resulted in a seminal tool enabling formal verification even in the presence of glitches, but with restriction to verification of probing security only. Most recently, the work of Cassiers *et al.* [16] proposes a composition-based approach of verifying probing security of a concrete implementation composed of so-called *Hardware Private Circuits*.

Besides, the latest version of `maskVerif` – as presented in [2] – supports efficient verification of d-probing security, d-NI, and d-SNI for arbitrary orders for both software and hardware designs, even in the presence of glitches. Currently, `maskVerif` is the state-of-the-art tool offering the widest-ranging verification features which is not composition-based, hence, in the following we provide a more detailed discussion and comparison to our developed tool.

5.1 Comparison to `maskVerif`

In general, `maskVerif` offers an efficient approach to verify security of masked software and hardware implementations. In contrast to our approach, `maskVerif` utilizes a symbolic representation of leakage defined by a given syntax and semantic. For verifying security, the tool first assigns a symbolic leakage set to every instruction. Depending on the security order, each combination of symbolic leakage sets, i.e., each possible observation, is exploited afterwards and tested for the absence of secret dependency through performing a syntactical check and applying semantic-preserving transformation on the sets.

Due to its language-based verification approach, security checks in `maskVerif` follow a very conservative approach for particular designs. More precisely, it may falsely reject some secure designs because the checks are not based on explicit statistical properties in conformity with the actual definition of the security notions. Due to these limitations of a purely syntactical verification, it more likely fails to provide correct verification of probing security if an output of a masked circuit is not non-complete (as used for TIs) but also does not rely on fresh randomness. In other words, its computation is a result of all input shares of at least one input without using any fresh randomness for blinding purposes. In particular, a computation using all input shares not necessarily implies statistical dependency on the corresponding input (e.g., due to blinding with shares of different inputs). Nonetheless, since the verification approach of `maskVerif` is mainly based on syntactical checks, it may falsely categorize the design as not being probing secure although it is (i.e., resulting in false negative).

Examples for False Negatives in `maskVerif`. One small example is a shared version of the 4-bit bijection quadratic class $\mathcal{Q}_{12}^4$ (based on the classification given in [10]), utilizing two shares per input, as presented in Appendix of [42]. Using `maskVerif`, this design is falsely categorized as not being first-order probing secure although all possible probes are statistically independent of the secrets. Hence, according to `maskVerif`, in order to gain successful verification, one possible solution would be to introduce additional randomness $r \in \mathbb{F}_2$ into the design, such that:

$$x_1 = F_1(\mathbf{a}, \mathbf{b}, \mathbf{c}, \mathbf{d}) = a_1$$
$$x_2 = F_2(\mathbf{a}, \mathbf{b}, \mathbf{c}, \mathbf{d}) = a_2$$
$$y_1 = G_1(\mathbf{a}, \mathbf{b}, \mathbf{c}, \mathbf{d}) = a_1 c_1 \oplus b_1 \oplus r \qquad\qquad \bar{x}_1 = x_1$$

$$y_2 = G_2(\mathbf{a}, \mathbf{b}, \mathbf{c}, \mathbf{d}) = a_1 c_2 \qquad\qquad \bar{x}_2 = x_2$$

$$y_3 = G_3(\mathbf{a}, \mathbf{b}, \mathbf{c}, \mathbf{d}) = a_2 c_1 \oplus b_2 \oplus r \qquad\qquad \bar{y}_1 = y_1 \oplus y_2$$

$$y_4 = G_4(\mathbf{a}, \mathbf{b}, \mathbf{c}, \mathbf{d}) = a_2 c_2 \qquad\qquad \bar{y}_2 = y_3 \oplus y_4$$

$$z_1 = H_1(\mathbf{a}, \mathbf{b}, \mathbf{c}, \mathbf{d}) = a_1 b_1 \oplus a_1 c_1 \oplus c_1 \qquad\qquad \bar{z}_1 = z_1 \oplus z_2$$

$$z_2 = H_2(\mathbf{a}, \mathbf{b}, \mathbf{c}, \mathbf{d}) = a_1 b_2 \oplus a_1 c_2 \oplus r \qquad\qquad \bar{z}_2 = z_3 \oplus z_4$$

$$z_3 = H_3(\mathbf{a}, \mathbf{b}, \mathbf{c}, \mathbf{d}) = a_2 b_1 \oplus a_2 c_1 \oplus r \qquad\qquad \bar{t}_1 = t_1$$

$$z_4 = H_4(\mathbf{a}, \mathbf{b}, \mathbf{c}, \mathbf{d}) = a_2 b_2 \oplus a_2 c_2 \oplus c_2 \qquad\qquad \bar{t}_2 = t_2$$

$$t_1 = K_1(\mathbf{a}, \mathbf{b}, \mathbf{c}, \mathbf{d}) = d_1$$

$$t_2 = K_2(\mathbf{a}, \mathbf{b}, \mathbf{c}, \mathbf{d}) = d_2$$

This new realization of $\mathcal{Q}_{12}^4$ is now correctly verified by `maskVerif` as being first-order probing secure. However, introducing randomness is costly and not necessary to gain independence of the secret input, i.e., fulfilling first-order probing security.

However, this given example based on $\mathcal{Q}_{12}^4$ is only a small design. For larger and more complex circuits, this inaccurate determination of the security level will lead to significantly more overhead being introduced during the design process. An example for a more complex design, which is falsely classified as not begin first-order probing secure, is the PRESENT S-box realized as a TI utilizing three shares for every output and input bit as presented in [40].

In fact, in order to achieve a sufficient security level while only introducing marginal overhead into the design, it is thus necessary to be in conformity with the security notions. As our verification is based on actual statistical properties between probes and inputs, i.e., in accordance with the formal definitions of the security notions, we actually meet this need and completely avoid false negatives. This eventually is expected to result in less overhead in terms of area and randomness when designing and implementing masked implementations. Moreover, and in addition to features in `maskVerif`, our tool is extended to verify dth-order PINI and the output uniformity of a given design while also returning the first probe combination found which is not in conformity with the respective security notion.

Hence, despite being slower and slightly less efficient for larger design compared to a type-based approach, as used for instance in `maskVerif`, our tool is assumed to close the gap between accuracy and efficiency by providing a complete and sound verification framework for the security and composability of both software and hardware designs.

6 Experiments and Evaluations

This section presents implementation, evaluation, and performance results of our proposed tool[1] for formal verification of masked circuits.

---

[1] https://github.com/chair-for-security-engineering/silver.

Implementation. For a practical evaluation of our proposed concepts and methodologies, we opted to implement a formal verification tool using `Sylvan` [22], a state-of-the-art BDD high-performance, multi-core decision diagram package implemented in C/C++. Further, we also customized and extended the native instructions of `Sylvan` in order to provide and support dedicated operations computing $p_{\mathbf{X}}(1)$ and $p_{\mathbf{X},\mathbf{Y}}(1,1)$ based on [35], i.e., without formal construction of new BDDs each time these operations are executed. Eventually, our framework implements all verification algorithms presented in Sect. 4 for both, standard and robust probing model, and is running in a 64-bit Linux Operating System (OS) environment on an Intel Xeon E5-1660v4 CPU with a clock frequency of 3.20 GHz and 128 GB of (RAM).

Our tool process a netlist file as the specification of the CUT. The user can either make such a netlist manually, e.g., for software applications or a sequence of operations, or can provide a verilog file as the result of a hardware synthesis, e.g., Design Compiler or Yosys,[2] using a restricted library (defined in Sect. 2.3). It is beneficial to directly evaluate the circuit's netlist as any user-originated mistakes or flaws (e.g., not keeping design hierarchy, hence violating non-completeness [39]) can be detected.

Experiments and Benchmarks. In Table 1, we summarize verification and performance results for our tool using various different examples as a benchmark. For this, the number d indicates the masking order of the circuit design (i.e., the number of input shares given as $d + 1$), while the number next to the tick indicates the maximum security order found by our tool during security check and verification (i.e., the number of probes that did not lead to a failing check). For all designs, we provide analysis results for the security notions of d-probing, NI, SNI, PINI, and uniformity of the output sharing. Except for uniformity, all security checks are performed for the standard (i.e., without physical defaults in terms of *glitches*) and robust (i.e., with *glitches*) leakage models as presented in Sect. 3. Eventually, along with the number of potential probe positions, i.e., the number of distinct wires determined by the number of gates in the circuit, the security parameter d yields the verification complexity in terms of possible observations $\mathcal{O} = \sum_{i=1}^{d} \binom{pos}{i}$.

Examples. In Table 1, we list verification results for three different categories of masked circuits. In the first category, denoted as **Gadgets**, we analyze different variants to implement a masked field multiplication for $\mathbb{F}_2$. Note, that for the SNI variant of Domain-Oriented Masking (DOM) multiplier [29], we simply added additional registers at the output to achieve an SNI-secure circuit. Interestingly, PARA1 [5] and PARA2 gadgets are up to d-SNI secure in both models, but higher-order variants cannot achieve full security, and need design modifications instead (although still SNI for smaller d). We should stress that `maskVerif` reports PARA3 to be not SNI, while it is up to 2-SNI, which is correctly reported

---

[2] http://www.clifford.at/yosys/.

Table 1. Verification of various masked circuits and security notions.

Scheme	Pos.†	d	Probing		NI		SNI		PINI		Unif.
			std.	rob.	std.	rob.	std.	rob.	std.	rob.	
Gadgets											
DOM [29]	19	1	✓[0 ms]	✓[0 ms]	✓[0 ms]	✓[0 ms]	✓[0 ms]	^{1}✗[0 ms]	^{1}✗[0 ms]	^{1}✗[0 ms]	✓[0 ms]
DOM [29]	42	2	^{2}✓[3 ms]	^{2}✓[4 ms]	^{2}✓[6 ms]	^{2}✓[19 ms]	^{2}✓[8 ms]	^{1}✗[0 ms]	^{1}✗[0 ms]	^{1}✗[0 ms]	✓[0 ms]
DOM [29]	74	3	^{3}✓[98 ms]	^{3}✓[1.2 s]	^{3}✓[2.2 s]	^{3}✓[23.7 s]	^{3}✓[3.2 s]	^{1}✗[0 ms]	^{1}✗[0 ms]	^{1}✗[0 ms]	✓[0 ms]
DOM SNI [26]	21	1	✓[0 ms]	✓[0 ms]	✓[0 ms]	✓[0 ms]	✓[0 ms]	✓[0 ms]	^{1}✗[0 ms]	^{1}✗[0 ms]	✓[0 ms]
DOM SNI [26]	45	2	^{2}✓[3 ms]	^{2}✓[5 ms]	^{2}✓[6 ms]	^{2}✓[30 ms]	^{2}✓[7 ms]	^{2}✓[29 ms]	^{1}✗[0 ms]	^{1}✗[0 ms]	✓[0 ms]
DOM SNI [26]	78	3	^{3}✓[0.1 s]	^{3}✓[1.5 s]	^{3}✓[2.4 s]	^{3}✓[39.4 s]	^{3}✓[3.7 s]	^{3}✓[39.4 s]	^{1}✗[0.0 s]	^{1}✗[0.0 s]	✓[0.0 s]
PARA1 [5]	22	1	✓[0 ms]	✓[0 ms]	✓[0 ms]	✓[0 ms]	✓[0 ms]	✓[0 ms]	^{1}✗[0 ms]	^{1}✗[0 ms]	✓[0 ms]
PARA2 [5]	45	2	^{2}✓[3 ms]	^{2}✓[6 ms]	^{2}✓[5 ms]	^{2}✓[32 ms]	^{2}✓[8 ms]	^{2}✓[37 ms]	^{1}✗[0 ms]	^{1}✗[0 ms]	✓[0 ms]
PARA3 [5]	68	3	^{3}✓[61 ms]	^{3}✓[0.5 s]	^{3}✓[1.2 s]	^{3}✓[12.1 s]	^{3}✗/✓[0.6 s]		^{1}✗[0 ms]	^{1}✗[0 ms]	✓[0 ms]
PARA3 SNI [5]	82	3	^{3}✓[0.2 s]	^{3}✓[1.4 s]	^{3}✓[2.8 s]	^{3}✓[35.5 s]	^{3}✓[4.1 s]	^{3}✓[40.4 s]	^{1}✗[0 ms]	^{1}✗[0 ms]	✓[0 ms]
PINI1 [17]	21	1	✓[0 ms]	^{1}✗[0 ms]	✓[0 ms]	^{1}✗[0 ms]	✓[0 ms]	^{1}✗[0 ms]	✓[0 ms]	^{1}✗[0 ms]	✓[0 ms]
PINI2 [17]	51	2	^{2}✓[7 ms]	^{1}✗[0 ms]	^{2}✓[10 ms]	^{1}✗[0 ms]	^{2}✓[12 ms]	^{1}✗[0 ms]	^{2}✓[22 ms]	^{1}✗[0 ms]	✓[0 ms]
HPC1 [16]	22	1	✓[0 ms]	✓[0 ms]	✓[0 ms]	✓[0 ms]	✓[0 ms]	^{1}✗[0 ms]	✓[0 ms]	^{1}✗[0 ms]	✓[0 ms]
HPC1 [16]	52	2	^{2}✓[5 ms]	^{2}✓[7 ms]	^{2}✓[7 ms]	^{2}✓[23 ms]	^{2}✓[9 ms]	^{1}✗[0 ms]	^{2}✓[16 ms]	^{2}✓[46 ms]	✓[0 ms]
HPC2 [16]	32	1	✓[0 ms]	✓[0 ms]	✓[0 ms]	✓[0 ms]	✓[0 ms]	^{1}✗[0 ms]	✓[0 ms]	✓[0 ms]	✓[0 ms]
HPC2 [16]	75	2	^{2}✓[6 ms]	^{2}✓[12 ms]	^{2}✓[11 ms]	^{2}✓[37 ms]	^{2}✓[13 ms]	^{1}✗[0 ms]	^{2}✓[19 ms]	^{2}✓[61 ms]	✓[0 ms]
ISW SNI REF [26]	26	1	✓[0 ms]	✓[0 ms]	✓[0 ms]	✓[0 ms]	✓[0 ms]	✓[0 ms]	✓[0 ms]	✓[0 ms]	✓[0 ms]
ISW SNI REF [26]	65	2	^{2}✓[5 ms]	^{2}✓[8 ms]	^{2}✓[7 ms]	^{2}✓[36 ms]	^{2}✓[9 ms]	^{2}✓[34 ms]	^{2}✓[16 ms]	^{2}✓[59 ms]	✓[0 ms]
CMS3 [36]	104	3	^{3}✗/✓[0.1 s]	^{3}✗/✓[0.3 s]	^{3}✗/✓[0.8 s]	^{3}✗/✓[2.6 s]	^{3}✗/✓[1.3 s]	^{3}✗/✓[4.4 s]	^{1}✗[0 ms]	^{1}✗[0 ms]	✓[0 ms]
UMA2 [36]	81	2	^{2}✗/✓[2 ms]	^{2}✗/✓[0 ms]	^{2}✗/✓[7 ms]	^{2}✗/✓[4 ms]	^{2}✗/✓[6 ms]	^{2}✗/✓[3 ms]	^{1}✗[0 ms]	^{1}✗[0 ms]	✓[0 ms]
DOM2 DEP‡ [36]	56	2	^{2}✓[4 ms]	^{2}✗/✓[8 ms]	^{2}✓[3 ms]	^{2}✗/✓[20 ms]	^{2}✓[4 ms]	^{1}✗[0 ms]	^{2}✓[4 ms]	^{2}✗/✓[21 ms]	✓[0 ms]
S-boxes											
PRESENT$_{TI}$ [40]	177	2	✓[4 ms]	✓[8 ms]	^{1}✗[4 ms]	^{1}✗[0 ms]	^{1}✗[3 ms]	^{1}✗[0 ms]	^{1}✗[0 ms]	^{1}✗[0 ms]	✓[2 ms]
PRESENT$_{TI}$ [25]	377	2	✓[15 ms]	✓[6 ms]	^{1}✗[2 ms]	^{1}✗[0 ms]	^{1}✗[2 ms]	^{1}✗[0 ms]	^{1}✗[1 ms]	^{1}✗[0 ms]	✓[0 ms]
PRESENT$_{TI}$ [25]	161	2	^{1}✗[3 ms]	^{1}✗[4 ms]	^{1}✗[32 ms]	^{1}✗[0 ms]	^{1}✗[26 ms]	^{1}✗[0 ms]	^{1}✗[2 ms]	^{1}✗[0 ms]	✗[0 ms]
PRINCE$_{TI}$ [37]	150	2	✓[2 ms]	✓[10 ms]	^{1}✗[2 ms]	^{1}✗[0 ms]	^{1}✗[2 ms]	^{1}✗[0 ms]	^{1}✗[0 ms]	^{1}✗[0 ms]	✓[0 ms]
PRINCE$_{CMS}$ [14]	261	1	✓[3 ms]	✓[97 ms]	✓[7 ms]	✓[2.8 s]	✓[9 ms]	^{1}✗[1 ms]	^{1}✗[0 ms]	^{1}✗[0 ms]	✓[0 ms]
SKINNY8$_{TI}$ [7]	240	2	✓[51.2 s]	✓[2 min]	^{1}✗[2 min]	^{1}✗[2.0 s]	^{1}✗[2 min]	^{1}✗[2.0 s]	^{1}✗[77 ms]	^{1}✗[1.3 s]	✓[29.6 s]
SKINNY8$_{CMS}$ [8]	192	1	✓[20 ms]	✓[0.3 s]	^{1}✗[0.3 s]	^{1}✗[17 ms]	^{1}✗[0.3 s]	^{1}✗[15 ms]	^{1}✗[1 ms]	^{1}✗[1 ms]	✓[1 ms]
AES$_{DOM}$ [29]	884	1	✓[3.3 s]	✓[21 min]	^{1}✗[0.8 s]	^{1}✗[0.4 s]	^{1}✗[0.8 s]	^{1}✗[0.4 s]	^{1}✗[0.2 s]	^{1}✗[40 ms]	✓[0.1 s]
AES$_{CMS}$ [19]	938	1	✓[9.4 s]	✓[2.9 h]	^{1}✗[0.9 s]	^{1}✗[0.5 s]	^{1}✗[0.9 s]	^{1}✗[0.5 s]	^{1}✗[0.2 s]	^{1}✗[42 ms]	✓[1.8 s]
Functions											
A$_{in}$ [37]	18	1	✓[0 ms]	✓[0 ms]	✓[0 ms]	✓[0 ms]	^{1}✗[0 ms]	^{1}✗[0 ms]	✓[0 ms]	✓[0 ms]	✓[0 ms]
A$_m$ [37]	20	1	✓[0 ms]	✓[0 ms]	✓[0 ms]	✓[0 ms]	^{1}✗[0 ms]	^{1}✗[0 ms]	✓[0 ms]	✓[0 ms]	✓[0 ms]
A$_{out}$ [37]	20	1	✓[0 ms]	✓[0 ms]	✓[0 ms]	✓[0 ms]	^{1}✗[0 ms]	^{1}✗[0 ms]	✓[0 ms]	✓[0 ms]	✓[0 ms]
$\mathcal{Q}^4_{12}$ [42]	48	1	✓[0 ms]	✓[0 ms]	^{1}✗[0 ms]	^{1}✗[0 ms]	^{1}✗[0 ms]	^{1}✗[0 ms]	^{1}✗[0 ms]	^{1}✗[0 ms]	✓[0 ms]

† Number of possible probe positions, i.e., output wires of gates. ‡ Assuming identical inputs, i.e., $a = b$.

by our tool. Also, our tool could identify and report all flaws described in [36] including the probes as identified by the authors. Our second category lists different masked **S-boxes** of lightweight and standard block ciphers implemented following the concepts of (CMS) [42], TI [39], or DOM [29]. Eventually, our last category **Functions** lists arbitrary masked functions with linear or quadratic algebraic complexity.

Interestingly, besides the linear functions, only the Hardware Private Circuit (HPC) gadgets [16] and the ISW-SNI gadget [26] extended by an additional refresh of one input are secure in the robust, glitch-extended probing model under the notion of PINI. Since PINI gadgets [17] are not robust probing secure, they are mainly useful in software applications (i.e., standard probing model). Indeed, since all HPC gadgets are secure under the PINI notion (for both probing models) and can be composed trivially, security under the SNI notion is no longer compulsory (as confirmed by our evaluation results for the robust, glitch-extended probing model). Also, besides $\mathcal{Q}_{12}^4$ we also analyzed other quadratic functions provided in [42] and our tool revealed that the implementation of $\mathcal{Q}_{300}^4$ as given by the authors is not uniform.

Verification Complexity. In contrast to the language-based verification approach of maskVerif, our framework heavily relies on statistical independence verification of probability distributions in order to avoid false negatives. Therefore, the overall run time of our verification approach is mainly governed by construction of intermediate ROBDDs representing the logical conjunctions as part of the statistical independence checks for the security notions. As already shown in [41], the complexity of constructing ROBDDs increases mainly by the number of product terms occurring in the minimal Disjunctive Normal Form (DNF) of the represented Boolean function.

Generally speaking, when considering higher-order security verification, we have to test for statistical independence of larger sets of random variables with possible non-linear dependence on many of the inputs. As our test of statistical independence is based on logical conjunctions of sets of random variables (and every possible subset), this leads to a high number of product terms occurring in the resulting DNF, and hence to an increased complexity of the constructed ROBDDs. As a result, verification speed of our framework is mainly influenced by the complexity, i.e., input dependencies of wires, and the maximum security order of the CUT.

Further, with increasing security order, the combinatorial complexity $\mathcal{O}$ of constructing all possible observations grows exponentially. However, as we opted for accurate security verification without relying on heuristics, reducing the number of probe combinations is not trivial, but instead we have to check and verify all of them. Although some joint distributions might be similar for different probe combinations,[3] we still have to analyze most combinations which is rather time consuming for higher security orders and larger circuits. It is worth to mention that if any of the combinations leads to a negative statistical independence, the tool stops and reports the found leaking probes. Hence, the maximum run time is taken only if the CUT passes all desired security checks.

7 Conclusion

In this work, we developed and presented a sound and accurate framework to verify the security and composability of masked gate-level netlists and circuits

---

[3] This case is caught by the internal caching scheme of the SylvanBDD package which first checks if the current operation has been performed and cached recently before executing the actual operation in case no cache entry was found.

directly resulting from hardware logic synthesis processes. In particular, our approach enables formal verification of all pertinent security notions in the domain of physical security and is applicable to both, software and hardware designs, even considering physical defaults in terms of *glitches*. More concretely, it supports sound, accurate, and immediate verification whether a masked implementation provides probing security, Non-Interference, Strong Non-Interference, and Probe-Isolating Non-Interference even for higher security orders. In addition, we proposed and integrated a novel methodology of verifying uniformity of the output sharing of a masked gadget. Eventually, if verification fails, it reports the failing set of probes being in non-conformity with the corresponding security notion.

In contrast to common type-based methods, our approach is based on formal verification of statistical properties in direct conformity with the fundamental definitions of the security notions. As a result, our approach completely avoids overly conservative decisions when falsely declaring designs as not being secure (false negatives), ultimately leading to a reduction in design overhead as otherwise introduced by additional (and expensive) fresh randomness. For this, all verification checks of statistical properties are executed efficiently by reducing statistical independence checks on joint distributions over multiple binary random variables to checks of distributions over single binary random variables, which can be efficiently done utilizing the concepts of ROBDDs. Eventually, this results in a framework exceeding comparable tools in accuracy and functionality while still being reasonable efficient for most applications and common use cases.

The current version of our tool is mainly beneficial to evaluate gadgets, particularly at higher orders, although we have given its capability to examine the entire S-boxes (see Table 1). For future work, we will focus on extending capabilities and improving efficiency of our tool, mainly with respect to larger and more complex circuits and implementations and higher security orders. For this, distinguishing univariate and multivariate leakages would be interesting, as it would allow *divide-and-conquer* approaches based on partitioning complex circuits along register stages while security analysis then would be performed an smaller circuits automatically. Certainly, verification then can be performed more efficiently, even for large and complex designs and higher-orders as long as the design is not entirely combinational but contains register stages. The future version of our tool should receive the netlist of a complete cipher implementation, unroll the loops, divide it into separate gadgets, and conduct security evaluation respectively.

Acknowledgments. The work described in this paper has been supported in part by the German Research Foundation (DFG) under Germany's Excellence Strategy - EXC 2092 CASA - 390781972, and through the project 393207943 "Security for Internet of Things with Low Energy and Low Power Consumption (GreenSec).

References

1. Akers, S.B.: Binary decision diagrams. IEEE Trans. Comput. **C-27**, 509–516 (1978)
2. Barthe, G., Belaïd, S., Cassiers, G., Fouque, P.-A., Grégoire, B., Standaert, F.-X.: maskVerif: automated verification of higher-order masking in presence of physical defaults. In: Sako, K., Schneider, S., Ryan, P.Y.A. (eds.) ESORICS 2019. LNCS, vol. 11735, pp. 300–318. Springer, Cham (2019). https://doi.org/10.1007/978-3-030-29959-0_15
3. Barthe, G., Belaïd, S., Dupressoir, F., Fouque, P.-A., Grégoire, B., Strub, P.-Y.: Verified proofs of higher-order masking. In: Oswald, E., Fischlin, M. (eds.) EURO-CRYPT 2015. LNCS, vol. 9056, pp. 457–485. Springer, Heidelberg (2015). https://doi.org/10.1007/978-3-662-46800-5_18
4. Barthe, G., et al.: Strong non-interference and type-directed higher-order masking. In: Proceedings of the 2016 ACM SIGSAC Conference on Computer and Communications Security, pp. 116–129. ACM (2016)
5. Barthe, G., Dupressoir, F., Faust, S., Grégoire, B., Standaert, F.-X., Strub, P.-Y.: Parallel implementations of masking schemes and the bounded moment leakage model. In: Coron, J.-S., Nielsen, J.B. (eds.) EUROCRYPT 2017. LNCS, vol. 10210, pp. 535–566. Springer, Cham (2017). https://doi.org/10.1007/978-3-319-56620-7_19
6. Bayrak, A.G., Regazzoni, F., Novo, D., Ienne, P.: Sleuth: automated verification of software power analysis countermeasures. In: Bertoni, G., Coron, J.-S. (eds.) CHES 2013. LNCS, vol. 8086, pp. 293–310. Springer, Heidelberg (2013). https://doi.org/10.1007/978-3-642-40349-1_17
7. Beierle, C., et al.: The SKINNY family of block ciphers and its low-latency variant MANTIS. In: Robshaw, M., Katz, J. (eds.) CRYPTO 2016. LNCS, vol. 9815, pp. 123–153. Springer, Heidelberg (2016). https://doi.org/10.1007/978-3-662-53008-5_5
8. Beierle, C., et al.: SKINNY-AEAD and SKINNY-Hash. IACR Trans. Symmetric Cryptol. (2020)
9. Belaïd, S., Goudarzi, D., Rivain, M.: Tight private circuits: achieving probing security with the least refreshing. In: Peyrin, T., Galbraith, S. (eds.) ASIACRYPT 2018. LNCS, vol. 11273, pp. 343–372. Springer, Cham (2018). https://doi.org/10.1007/978-3-030-03329-3_12
10. Bilgin, B., Nikova, S., Nikov, V., Rijmen, V., Tokareva, N.N., Vitkup, V.: Threshold implementations of small S-boxes. Cryptogr. Commun. **7**, 3–33 (2015)
11. Bloem, R., Gross, H., Iusupov, R., Könighofer, B., Mangard, S., Winter, J.: Formal verification of masked hardware implementations in the presence of glitches. In: Nielsen, J.B., Rijmen, V. (eds.) EUROCRYPT 2018. LNCS, vol. 10821, pp. 321–353. Springer, Cham (2018). https://doi.org/10.1007/978-3-319-78375-8_11
12. Bloem, R., Groß, H., Iusupov, R., Krenn, M., Mangard, S.: Sharing independence & relabeling: efficient formal verification of higher-order masking. IACR Cryptology ePrint Archive (2018)
13. Blömer, J., Guajardo, J., Krummel, V.: Provably secure masking of AES. IACR Cryptology ePrint Archive (2004)
14. Božilov, D., Knežević, M., Nikov, V.: Optimized threshold implementations: minimizing the latency of secure cryptographic accelerators. In: Belaïd, S., Güneysu, T. (eds.) CARDIS 2019. LNCS, vol. 11833, pp. 20–39. Springer, Cham (2020). https://doi.org/10.1007/978-3-030-42068-0_2

15. Bryant, R.E.: Graph-based algorithms for boolean function manipulation. IEEE Trans. Comput. **C-35**, 677–691 (1986)
16. Cassiers, G., Grégoire, B., Levi, I., Standaert, F.: Hardware private circuits: from trivial composition to full verification. IACR Cryptology ePrint Archive (2020)
17. Cassiers, G., Standaert, F.: Trivially and efficiently composing masked gadgets with probe isolating non-interference. IEEE Trans. Inf. Forensics Secur. **15**, 2542–2555 (2020)
18. Chari, S., Jutla, C.S., Rao, J.R., Rohatgi, P.: Towards sound approaches to counteract power-analysis attacks. In: Wiener, M. (ed.) CRYPTO 1999. LNCS, vol. 1666, pp. 398–412. Springer, Heidelberg (1999). https://doi.org/10.1007/3-540-48405-1_26
19. De Cnudde, T., Reparaz, O., Bilgin, B., Nikova, S., Nikov, V., Rijmen, V.: Masking AES with $d+1$ shares in hardware. In: Gierlichs, B., Poschmann, A.Y. (eds.) CHES 2016. LNCS, vol. 9813, pp. 194–212. Springer, Heidelberg (2016). https://doi.org/10.1007/978-3-662-53140-2_10
20. Coron, J.-S.: Formal verification of side-channel countermeasures via elementary circuit transformations. In: Preneel, B., Vercauteren, F. (eds.) ACNS 2018. LNCS, vol. 10892, pp. 65–82. Springer, Cham (2018). https://doi.org/10.1007/978-3-319-93387-0_4
21. De Meyer, L., Bilgin, B., Reparaz, O.: Consolidating security notions in hardware masking. IACR Trans. Cryptogr. Hardw. Embed. Syst. (2019)
22. van Dijk, T.: Sylvan: multi-core decision diagrams. Ph.D. thesis, University of Twente, Enschede, Netherlands (2016)
23. Duc, A., Dziembowski, S., Faust, S.: Unifying leakage models: from probing attacks to noisy leakage. In: Nguyen, P.Q., Oswald, E. (eds.) EUROCRYPT 2014. LNCS, vol. 8441, pp. 423–440. Springer, Heidelberg (2014). https://doi.org/10.1007/978-3-642-55220-5_24
24. Eldib, H., Wang, C., Schaumont, P.: Formal verification of software countermeasures against side-channel attacks. ACM Trans. Softw. Eng. Methodol. (2014)
25. Ender, M., Ghandali, S., Moradi, A., Paar, C.: The first thorough side-channel hardware Trojan. In: Takagi, T., Peyrin, T. (eds.) ASIACRYPT 2017. LNCS, vol. 10624, pp. 755–780. Springer, Cham (2017). https://doi.org/10.1007/978-3-319-70694-8_26
26. Faust, S., Grosso, V., Pozo, S.M.D., Paglialonga, C., Standaert, F.: Composable masking schemes in the presence of physical defaults & the robust probing model. IACR Trans. Cryptogr. Hardw. Embed. Syst. (2018)
27. Gandolfi, K., Mourtel, C., Olivier, F.: Electromagnetic analysis: concrete results. In: Koç, Ç.K., Naccache, D., Paar, C. (eds.) CHES 2001. LNCS, vol. 2162, pp. 251–261. Springer, Heidelberg (2001). https://doi.org/10.1007/3-540-44709-1_21
28. Groß, H., Mangard, S.: A unified masking approach. J. Cryptogr. Eng. **8**, 109–124 (2018)
29. Gross, H., Mangard, S., Korak, T.: An efficient side-channel protected AES implementation with arbitrary protection order. In: Handschuh, H. (ed.) CT-RSA 2017. LNCS, vol. 10159, pp. 95–112. Springer, Cham (2017). https://doi.org/10.1007/978-3-319-52153-4_6
30. Hutter, M., Schmidt, J.-M.: The temperature side channel and heating fault attacks. In: Francillon, A., Rohatgi, P. (eds.) CARDIS 2013. LNCS, vol. 8419, pp. 219–235. Springer, Cham (2014). https://doi.org/10.1007/978-3-319-08302-5_15
31. Ishai, Y., Sahai, A., Wagner, D.: Private circuits: securing hardware against probing attacks. In: Boneh, D. (ed.) CRYPTO 2003. LNCS, vol. 2729, pp. 463–481. Springer, Heidelberg (2003). https://doi.org/10.1007/978-3-540-45146-4_27

32. Kocher, P.C.: Timing attacks on implementations of Diffie-Hellman, RSA, DSS, and other systems. In: Koblitz, N. (ed.) CRYPTO 1996. LNCS, vol. 1109, pp. 104–113. Springer, Heidelberg (1996). https://doi.org/10.1007/3-540-68697-5_9

33. Kocher, P., Jaffe, J., Jun, B.: Differential power analysis. In: Wiener, M. (ed.) CRYPTO 1999. LNCS, vol. 1666, pp. 388–397. Springer, Heidelberg (1999). https://doi.org/10.1007/3-540-48405-1_25

34. Mesnager, S.: Bent Functions - Fundamentals and Results. Springer, Cham (2016). https://doi.org/10.1007/978-3-319-32595-8

35. Miller, D.M.: An improved method for computing a generalized spectral coefficient. IEEE Trans. CAD Integr. Circuits Syst. **17**, 233–238 (1998)

36. Moos, T., Moradi, A., Schneider, T., Standaert, F.: Glitch-resistant masking revisited or why proofs in the robust probing model are needed. IACR Trans. Cryptogr. Hardw. Embed. Syst. (2019)

37. Moradi, A., Schneider, T.: Side-channel analysis protection and low-latency in action. In: Cheon, J.H., Takagi, T. (eds.) ASIACRYPT 2016. LNCS, vol. 10031, pp. 517–547. Springer, Heidelberg (2016). https://doi.org/10.1007/978-3-662-53887-6_19

38. Moss, A., Oswald, E., Page, D., Tunstall, M.: Compiler assisted masking. In: Prouff, E., Schaumont, P. (eds.) CHES 2012. LNCS, vol. 7428, pp. 58–75. Springer, Heidelberg (2012). https://doi.org/10.1007/978-3-642-33027-8_4

39. Nikova, S., Rijmen, V., Schläffer, M.: Secure hardware implementation of nonlinear functions in the presence of glitches. J. Cryptol. **24**(2), 292–321 (2010)

40. Poschmann, A., Moradi, A., Khoo, K., Lim, C., Wang, H., Ling, S.: Side-channel resistant crypto for less than 2, 300 GE. J. Cryptol. **24**(2), 322–345 (2011)

41. Raseen, M., Prasad, P.W.C., Assi, A.: An efficient estimation of the ROBDD's complexity. Integr. (2006)

42. Reparaz, O., Bilgin, B., Nikova, S., Gierlichs, B., Verbauwhede, I.: Consolidating masking schemes. In: Gennaro, R., Robshaw, M. (eds.) CRYPTO 2015. LNCS, vol. 9215, pp. 764–783. Springer, Heidelberg (2015). https://doi.org/10.1007/978-3-662-47989-6_37

43. Trichina, E.: Combinational Logic Design for AES SubByte Transformation on Masked Data. IACR Cryptology ePrint Archive (2003)

44. Zhang, J., Gao, P., Song, F., Wang, C.: SCInfer: refinement-based verification of software countermeasures against side-channel attacks. In: Chockler, H., Weissenbacher, G. (eds.) CAV 2018. LNCS, vol. 10982, pp. 157–177. Springer, Cham (2018). https://doi.org/10.1007/978-3-319-96142-2_12

Cryptanalysis of Masked Ciphers: A Not So Random Idea

Tim Beyne$^{(\boxtimes)}$, Siemen Dhooghe$^{(\boxtimes)}$, and Zhenda Zhang$^{(\boxtimes)}$

imec-COSIC, ESAT, KU Leuven, Leuven, Belgium
{tim.beyne,siemen.dhooghe,zhenda.zhang}@esat.kuleuven.be

Abstract. A new approach to the security analysis of hardware-oriented masked ciphers against second-order side-channel attacks is developed. By relying on techniques from symmetric-key cryptanalysis, concrete security bounds are obtained in a variant of the probing model that allows the adversary to make only a bounded, but possibly very large, number of measurements. Specifically, it is formally shown how a bounded-query variant of robust probing security can be reduced to the linear cryptanalysis of masked ciphers. As a result, the compositional issues of higher-order threshold implementations can be overcome without relying on fresh randomness. From a practical point of view, the aforementioned approach makes it possible to transfer many of the desirable properties of first-order threshold implementations, such as their low randomness usage, to the second-order setting. For example, a straightforward application to the block cipher LED results in a masking using less than 700 random bits including the initial sharing. In addition, the cryptanalytic approach introduced in this paper provides additional insight into the design of masked ciphers and allows for a quantifiable trade-off between security and performance.

Keywords: Linear cryptanalysis · Masking · Probing security · Side-channel analysis · Threshold implementations

1 Introduction

Side-channel attacks such as differential power analysis [29] are an important concern for the security of implementations of cryptographic primitives in hardware and software. Accordingly, several adversarial models and side-channel countermeasures have been developed during the past two decades. Many of these countermeasures attempt to achieve security in the probing model of Ishai, Sahai and Wagner [28], or slight variants thereof.

A common theme among different countermeasures is that they rely on splitting all secret variables in the circuit into $d + 1$ or more random shares. As demonstrated by Ishai *et al.* [28], this approach can be used to achieve probing security against adversaries who can observe the values of up to d wires in the circuit. However, the probing security model is not quite sufficient for

© International Association for Cryptologic Research 2020
S. Moriai and H. Wang (Eds.): ASIACRYPT 2020, LNCS 12491, pp. 817–850, 2020.
https://doi.org/10.1007/978-3-030-64837-4_27

hardware-oriented countermeasures. Indeed, glitches may allow the adversary to obtain more than one wire value from a single probe. To counter this, Nikova, Rechberger, and Rijmen [35] introduced the threshold implementation approach. From a formal point of view, the security of hardware-oriented countermeasures should be analyzed in a glitch-extended or *robust probing model* as formalized by Faust *et al.* [23] and it can be shown that threshold implementations achieve such first-order robust probing security [21].

Unsurprisingly, achieving probing security often comes at a cost with respect to area usage, latency, energy consumption, and so on. This paper is primarily concerned with another important cost factor, namely the reliance of many countermeasures on the availability of a large number of random bits. Creating these bits can be quite expensive, especially since their generation should also be gray-box secure. In this regard, first-order threshold implementations provide an efficient countermeasure. In particular, if one ensures that each circuit layer satisfies the so-called *uniformity property*, glitch-extended first-order probing security can be achieved without using any randomness beyond what is necessary to share the state. If instead good randomness is readily available, threshold implementations allow trading this off for reduced area [7]. At ASIACRYPT 2014, Bilgin *et al.* [6] proposed a higher-order variant of threshold implementations. However, Reparaz [36] later demonstrated that it succumbs to multivariate attacks. In further work at CRYPTO 2015, Reparaz *et al.* [37] propose to use remasking with fresh randomness to address this issue. However, as pointed out by Moos *et al.* [32], this and other schemes still lack a formal security analysis in the robust probing model.

As proposed by Faust *et al.* [23], an alternative approach is to design sharings based on a robust variant of the strong non-interference framework of Barthe *et al.* [2]. This has the benefit of allowing formal security proofs, which rely on establishing the composability of different gadgets in the shared circuit. However, ensuring composability unfortunately comes at an inherent randomness cost. Amortizing this cost is possible to some extend, but remains nontrivial – see for instance the work of Faust, Paglialonga, and Schneider [24] in the context of software-oriented masking. In addition, as for example pointed out by De Meyer, Wegener, and Moradi [20], it is often desirable to mask Boolean functions directly as opposed to falling back to a gate-level approach. Although verifying larger gadgets directly is possible within the strong non-interference framework, it requires nontrivial tools such as *maskVerif* due to Barthe *et al.* [1]. Of course, this does not directly address how to design efficient sharings. Also, one might hope to quantify to what extend verification fails; in the words of Barthe *et al.*: "It would be interesting to extend our work beyond purely qualitative security definitions, and to consider quantitative definitions that upper bound how much leakage reveals about secrets – using total variation distance or more recent metrics that directly or indirectly relate to noisy leakage security" [1, §7].

Contribution. This paper overcomes the composability problem for second-order threshold implementations without relying on fresh randomness. As a result, second-order probing secure masked ciphers that require no or almost no randomness beyond what is necessary to share the input are obtained. In order to achieve these results, we introduce a variant of the probing model in which the adversary can make only a bounded number of queries. Our approach is based on a completely formal reduction from this model to the security of the masked cipher against linear cryptanalysis and leads to concrete upper bounds on the advantage (*i.e.* total variation distance) of such bounded-query adversaries.

From a practical point of view, our methods provide a means to reason about and to correct potential flaws in the higher-order threshold implementations of Bilgin *et al.* [6]. Importantly, the additional requirements imposed by our analysis are relatively easy to satisfy when the underlying cipher has been designed with linear cryptanalysis in mind. As a result, one can benefit from the desirable properties of first-order threshold implementations – in particular their low randomness requirements – while simultaneously maintaining demonstrable security in the second-order probing model with glitches.

From a theoretical point of view, this paper introduces a radically different approach to the security-evaluation of masked ciphers. Rather than attempting to show perfect probing security against adversaries making an arbitrary number of queries, we allow for a limited amount of leakage but show that it can not be exploited unless the adversary makes an infeasibly large number of measurements. In this approach, the concrete security bound of a masked cipher directly depends on the maximum absolute correlation of certain linear approximations over parts of the design. To estimate correlation upper bounds, standard techniques from linear cryptanalysis can be used. In particular, one can use the piling-up approximation. Although the latter is only a heuristic, it is an integral part of the security argument of essentially all modern symmetric-key primitives and is widely accepted to result in meaningful estimates if properly used. In a sense, the piling-up lemma acts as a substitute for the strong composability requirements that are typically imposed. An important advantage of this approach is that it provides additional insight into the design of masked ciphers, and allows for a quantifiable trade-off between performance and security. In addition, one can benefit from the large literature on the theory and practice of linear cryptanalysis.

After introducing a number of preliminaries in Sect. 2, a bounded-query variant of the glitch-extended probing model is formalized in Sect. 3. The reduction to linear cryptanalysis is spread over Sects. 4 and 5. To limit the scope of the paper, only second-order probing adversaries are considered. The possibility of further extensions to higher orders is discussed in Sect. 9.

Section 6 presents a high-level overview of the properties the masked cipher needs to satisfy and the cryptanalytic process that should be followed to obtain concrete security bounds. Roughly speaking, for probes that are separated by a small number of rounds of the cipher, zero-correlation linear approximations can be exploited. If the adversary places its probes further apart, the analysis relies on upper bounds for the absolute correlation of linear approximations.

In Sect. 7, the framework developed in Sects. 4 to 6 is illustrated by the design and analysis of a second-order masking of the block cipher LED [27].

The implementation requires a total 664 bits of randomness, *i.e.* 24 bits more than what is needed to share the plaintext and key, but no serious attempt was made to optimize this number. Note that the choice for LED was mainly motivated by didactical reasons: LED is a classical wide-trail design with 4-bit S-boxes, which results in a very transparent security analysis. A software-based simulation, which allows experimenting with our security claims, is found on GitLab [40].

The broader applicability of our approach is illustrated in Sect. 8. Finally, Sect. 9 summarizes several directions for future work and concludes the paper.

2   Preliminaries

This section introduces key concepts related to linear cryptanalysis and threshold implementations. The reader is assumed to have some, but not necessarily extensive, familiarity with these concepts. For convenience, all random variables in this paper are denoted in boldface. All other nonstandard notation will be introduced as necessary.

2.1   Fourier Analysis

The relation between linear cryptanalysis and the Fourier transformation on vector spaces over $\mathbb{F}_2$ is well-established [5,11,17]. This section introduces the necessary notation for two important concepts that will be used throughout this work. The first is the Fourier transformation of a probability distribution, or more generally any complex-valued function, on a vector space V over $\mathbb{F}_2$. The second is the notion of the correlation matrix of a function $F : V \to V$, the coordinates of which coincide with the correlations of linear approximations over F.

The definitions below are formulated for functions on an arbitrary subspace $V \subseteq \mathbb{F}_2^n$, as opposed to functions on $\mathbb{F}_2^n$ itself – as is commonly the case. Since any vector space over $\mathbb{F}_2$ is isomorphic to $\mathbb{F}_2^n$ for some n, this generalization is mostly a matter of notation. Nevertheless, this extended notation will be very beneficial later on in this work.

Recall that the orthogonal complement of a subspace V of $\mathbb{F}_2^n$ is the vector space $V^\perp = \{x \in \mathbb{F}_2^n \mid \forall v \in V : v^\top x = 0\}$. The quotient space $\mathbb{F}_2^n/V^\perp$ is by definition the vector space of cosets of $V^\perp$. For convenience, an element $x + V^\perp \in \mathbb{F}_2^n/V^\perp$ will simply be denoted by x. For $x \in \mathbb{F}_2^n/V^\perp$ and $v \in V$, the expression $x^\top v$ is well-defined. Consequently, the following definition is proper.

Definition 1. *Let $V \subseteq \mathbb{F}_2^n$ be a vector space and $f : V \to \mathbb{C}$ be a complex-valued function on V. The Fourier transformation of f is a function $\widehat{f} : \mathbb{F}_2^n/V^\perp \to \mathbb{C}$ defined by*

$$\widehat{f}(u) = \sum_{x \in V}(-1)^{u^\top x}f(x),$$

where we write u for $u + V^\perp$. Equivalently, $\widehat{f}$ is the representation of f in the basis of functions $x \mapsto (-1)^{u^\top x}$ for $u \in \mathbb{F}_2^n/V^\perp$.

Remark 1. Unlike in standard treatments of the Fourier transformation on finite abelian groups [22,38], Definition 1 introduces $\widehat{f}$ as a function on $\mathbb{F}_2^n/V^\perp$ rather than on the Pontryagin dual group $\widehat{V}$. Throughout this document, the isomorphism $\widehat{V} \cong \mathbb{F}_2^n/V^\perp$ is used to simplify notation. Other choices are possible, but this one is the most convenient.

As one often encounters transformations of random variables, it is convenient to encode the action of a function $F : V \to V$ on probability distributions as a linear operator. The coordinate representation of this operator with respect to the standard basis $\{\delta_x\}_{x \in V}$ may be called the *transition matrix* of F. Following [4,5], the correlation matrix of F is then the same operator expressed with respect to the Fourier basis. Note that correlation matrices were first introduced by Daemen *et al.* [17], where their definition is given in terms of concepts from linear cryptanalysis.

Definition 2 (Transition matrix). *Let V be a set and $F : V \to V$ a function. The transition matrix T^F of F is a real $|V| \times |V|$ matrix such that, in the standard basis, if $\mathbf{x}$ has probability mass function $p_{\mathbf{x}} : V \to [0, 1]$, then $F(\mathbf{x})$ has probability mass function $T^F p_{\mathbf{x}}$. Equivalently, indexing the coordinates of T^F by elements of V, we have $T^F_{y,x} = \delta_{y,F(x)}$.*

Definition 3 (Correlation matrix). *Let $V \subseteq \mathbb{F}_2^n$ be an $\mathbb{F}_2$-vector space and $F : V \to V$ a function. The correlation matrix C^F of F is the coordinate representation of the linear map defined by T^F with respect to the basis of character functions $x \mapsto (-1)^{u^\top x}$ for $u \in \mathbb{F}_2^n/V^\perp$. Equivalently, indexing the coordinates of C^F by elements of $\mathbb{F}_2^n/V^\perp$, we have*

$$C^F_{v,u} = \frac{1}{|V|} \sum_{x \in V} (-1)^{u^\top x + v^\top F(x)}.$$

The relation between Definition 3 and linear cryptanalysis is as follows: the coordinate $C^F_{v,u}$ is equal to the correlation of a linear approximation over F with input mask u and output mask v. That is, $C^F_{v,u} = 2 \Pr[v^\top F(\mathbf{x}) = u^\top \mathbf{x}] - 1$ for $\mathbf{x}$ uniform random on V.

2.2 Boolean Masking and Threshold Implementations

Boolean masking was independently introduced by Goubin and Patarin [25] and Chari *et al.* [12]. It serves as a sound and widely-deployed countermeasure against side-channel attacks. The technique is based on splitting each secret variable x in the circuit into shares $\bar{x} = (x^1, x^2, \ldots, x^{s_x})$ such that $x = \sum_{i=1}^{s_x} x^i$ over a finite field K. If the field K is binary, this masking approach is referred to as Boolean masking. A random Boolean masking of a fixed secret is uniform if all sharings of that secret are equally likely.

There are many ways to modify a given circuit in order to ensure that it operates on shared inputs and intermediates. For example, this can be done at the level of individual gates, or at a higher level involving generic Boolean functions. However, care must be taken to ensure that the sharing of the circuit is not only correct but also secure. This is especially challenging in hardware implementations due to the presence of glitches. Nikova *et al.* [35] introduced threshold implementations as a particular approach to share circuits. This approach achieves first-order glitch-extended probing security in the sense defined in Sect. 3 below. Later Bilgin *et al.* [6] generalized the threshold implementation approach in order to achieve higher-order univariate security. In the following, the main properties of threshold implementations are reviewed.

A threshold implementation consists of several layers of Boolean functions, as shown in Fig. 1. As for any masked implementation, a black-box encoder function generates a uniform random sharing of the input before it enters the shared circuit and the output shares are recombined by a decoder function. At the end of each layer, synchronization is ensured by means of registers.

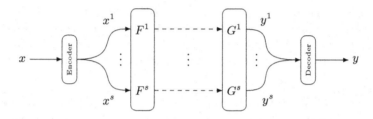

Fig. 1. Schematic illustration of a threshold implementation assuming an equal number of input and output shares.

Let $\bar{F}$ be a layer in the threshold implementation corresponding to a part of the circuit $F : \mathbb{F}_2^n \to \mathbb{F}_2^m$. For example, F might be the linear layer of a block cipher. The function $\bar{F} : \mathbb{F}_2^{n s_x} \to \mathbb{F}_2^{m s_y}$, where we assume s_x shares per input bit and s_y shares per output bit, will be called a *sharing* of F. Sharings can have a number of properties that are relevant in the security argument for a threshold implementation; these properties are summarized in Definition 4.

Definition 4 (Properties of sharings [6,35]). *Let* $F : \mathbb{F}_2^n \to \mathbb{F}_2^m$ *be a function and* $\bar{F} : \mathbb{F}_2^{n s_x} \to \mathbb{F}_2^{m s_y}$ *a sharing of* F. *The sharing* $\bar{F}$ *is said to be*

1. *correct if* $\sum_{i=1}^{s_y} F^i(x^1, \ldots, x^{s_x}) = F(x)$ *for all* $x \in \mathbb{F}_2^n$ *and for all shares* $x^1, \ldots, x^{s_x} \in \mathbb{F}_2^n$ *such that* $\sum_{i=1}^{s_x} x^i = x$,
2. d^{th}-*order non-complete if any function in* d *or fewer component functions* $\bar{F}_i$ *depends on at most* $s_x - 1$ *input shares,*
3. *uniform if* $\bar{F}$ *maps a uniform random sharing of any* $x \in \mathbb{F}_2^n$ *to a uniform random sharing of* $F(x) \in \mathbb{F}_2^m$.

The correctness property from Definition 4 is an absolute minimum requirement to obtain a meaningful implementation. Furthermore, if all layers of a threshold implementation are first-order non-complete and uniform, the resulting shared circuit can be proven secure in the first-order probing model considering glitches [21]. In the higher-order setting, the situation is more complicated.

Using higher-order non-completeness and uniformity, one can secure a threshold implementation against higher-order univariate attacks. Nevertheless, perfect multivariate security can not be guaranteed using uniform sharings alone [36]. Instead, the threshold implementation approach was generalized to use fresh randomness [37]. However, even this last work has been shown to exhibit flaws against higher-order attacks [32].

In Sect. 3, a variant of the probing model – which we call the *bounded-query probing model* – will be introduced. In the main body of this work, we will then show that the issues surrounding higher-order threshold implementations can be overcome if the bounded-query probing model is adopted.

3   A Bounded-Query Probing Model

Section 3.1 introduces a variant of the threshold probing model of Ishai *et al.* [28] in which the adversary can make only a bounded number of queries. In addition, Sect. 3.2 discusses a further extension of this model in order to account for the effect of glitches.

3.1   Threshold Probing

Let $\ell \geq t$ be positive integers. A *t-threshold-probing adversary on* $\mathbb{F}_2^\ell$ is an algorithm $\mathcal{A}$ that interacts as follows with an oracle that holds an arbitrary sequence $(x_1, ..., x_\ell) \in \mathbb{F}_2^\ell$:

1. $\mathcal{A}$ may specify a set $\mathcal{I} = \{i_1, ..., i_{|\mathcal{I}|}\} \subset \{1, ..., \ell\}$ of cardinality at most t,
2. $\mathcal{A}$ then receives $(x_{i_1}, \ldots, x_{i_{|\mathcal{I}|}})$.

Note in particular that the adversary $\mathcal{A}$ is computationally unbounded, and must specify the location of the probes before querying the oracle. However, the adversary can change the location of the probes over multiple queries.

Ishai *et al.* [28] define a randomized stateless circuit C to be t-probing secure if it can be simulated from scratch such that no t-threshold probing adversary can distinguish $\mathsf{Dec} \circ C \circ \mathsf{Enc}$ from the simulation. Importantly, the adversary's interaction with the circuit or simulator is mediated through the encoder and decoder algorithms Enc and Dec, neither of which can be probed.

In this work, the security of a circuit C with input k against a t-threshold-probing adversary will be quantified by means of a left-or-right security game as depicted in Fig. 2. The challenger picks a random bit b and provides the oracle $\mathcal{O}^b$, to which adversary $\mathcal{A}$ is given query access. The adversary queries the oracle by choosing up to t wires to probe, we denote this set by $\mathcal{P}$, and sends it to the oracle along with the inputs k_0 and k_1. Note that we consider the input of the circuit to consist of both the plaintext and the key. The oracle responds by giving back the probed wire values of $C(k_b)$. After a total of q queries, the adversary responds to the challenger with a guess for b. For $b \in \{0, 1\}$, denote the result of the adversary after interacting with the oracle $\mathcal{O}^b$ using q queries by $\mathcal{A}^{\mathcal{O}^b}$. For left-or-right security, the advantage of the adversary $\mathcal{A}$ is then as defined as

$$\mathrm{Adv}_{t\text{-thr}}(\mathcal{A}) = |\Pr[\mathcal{A}^{\mathcal{O}^0} = 1] - \Pr[\mathcal{A}^{\mathcal{O}^1} = 1]|.$$

We refer to this security notion as the *bounded-query probing model*.

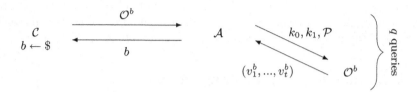

Fig. 2. The privacy model for t-threshold-probing security consisting of a challenger $\mathcal{C}$, an adversary $\mathcal{A}$, a left-right oracle $\mathcal{O}^b$, two inputs k_0, k_1, a set of probes $\mathcal{P}$, and a set of probed wire values $(v_1^b, ..., v_t^b)$ of the circuit $C(k_b)$.

If an arbitrary number of queries is allowed, the above security definition is equivalent to the simulation-based definition of Ishai *et al.* [28] for stateless circuits. Indeed, if the simulator simply evaluates the circuit for an arbitrary choice of the secret inputs, no adversary can distinguish the simulation from the real circuit with advantage higher than $\mathrm{Adv}_{t\text{-thr}}(\mathcal{A})$. We opt for the left-or-right formulation as this leads to a slightly more direct proof of Theorem 1 in Sect. 4. However, note that there exist stronger notions of security such as the *strong non-interference model* of Barthe *et al.* [2]. In the latter model, the adversary controls not only the unshared input of the circuit but also some of its shares. This is useful since probing security does not necessarily allow composition, as illustrated by Coron *et al.* [14]. As the approach developed in Sects. 4 and 5 considers the circuit in its entirety, security under composition need not be considered. In fact, as our approach allows for secure sharings that do not use any randomness beyond what is necessary to encode the circuit input, it is clear that arbitrary composability cannot be achieved.

3.2 Modeling Glitches

It has been shown that hardware glitches can result in significant leakage that is not accounted for by the probing model, see for example the attacks of Mangard *et al.* on several masked AES implementations [31]. Consequently, it is necessary to extend the capabilities of threshold probing adversaries in order to capture the physical effect of glitches on a hardware platform. In this work, we take a conservative approach to the modeling of glitches by bundling groups of wires over which a glitch could carry information from one wire to another. Whereas one of the adversary's probes normally results in the value of a single wire, a glitch-extended probe allows obtaining the values of all wires in a bundle.

This extension of the probing model has been discussed in the work of Reparaz *et al.* [37] and formalized by Faust *et al.* [23]. The formulation of the latter work is as follows: "For any ϵ-input circuit gadget G, combinatorial recombinations (aka glitches) can be modeled with specifically ϵ-extended probes so that probing any output of the function allows the adversary to observe all its ϵ inputs."

In the setting of threshold implementations, the above extension can be simplified. Recall that each layer of a threshold implementation consists of Boolean functions $\bar{F}_i$, for which the synchronization of the inputs is ensured by means of registers. Thus, a glitch-extended probe placed in the circuit for $\bar{F}_i$ yields at most all of the input bits on which $\bar{F}_i$ depends – but no more, since the layers of a threshold implementation are separated by registers.

Note that, apart from the glitch extension of the probing model, other effects such as transition leakage can be considered. More information on other leakage effects can be found in the work of Faust *et al.* [23]. The scope of this work is limited to the modeling of the effects that are traditionally considered in threshold implementations, thus we only consider hardware implementations in the presence of glitches.

4   Bound on the Advantage

This section connects the bounded-query probing model from Sect. 3 to the cryptanalytic approach that will be developed in Sects. 5 and 6. The link is established by means of Theorem 1 below, which provides an upper bound on the advantage of threshold probing adversaries in terms of the nontrivial Fourier coefficients of certain probability distributions associated with probed wire values. As a first step towards this result, the following lemma gives an upper bound on the entropy of a probability distribution in terms of its Fourier transform as defined in Definition 1 from Sect. 2.

Lemma 1. *Let* $\mathbf{x}$ *be a random variable on* $\mathbb{F}_2^m$ *with probability distribution* $p_{\mathbf{x}}$. *It holds that*

$$m - \mathsf{H}(\mathbf{x}) \leq \|\widehat{p}_{\mathbf{x}} - \delta_0\|_2^2 / \log 2,$$

where $\mathsf{H}(\mathbf{x})$ *denotes the information entropy of* $\mathbf{x}$ *with respect to the binary logarithm.*

Proof. By definition, the binary information entropy of $\mathbf{x}$ is the quantity

$$\mathsf{H}(\mathbf{x}) = -\mathbb{E}\log_2 p_{\mathbf{x}}(\mathbf{x}) \leq m.$$

The goal is to upper bound the quantity $m - \mathsf{H}(\mathbf{x})$ in terms of the *correlations* of $\mathbf{x}$, or equivalently the coordinates of the Fourier transformation of $p_{\mathbf{x}}$. It holds that

$$\mathsf{H}(\mathbf{x}) \geq -\log_2 \mathbb{E}\, p_{\mathbf{x}}(\mathbf{x}) = -\log_2 \|p_{\mathbf{x}}\|_2^2,$$

due to Jensen's inequality. Note that the right-hand side is equal to the Rényi entropy of $\mathbf{x}$. Let $\widehat{p}_{\mathbf{x}}$ denote the Fourier transformation of $p_{\mathbf{x}}$, then

$$\mathsf{H}(\mathbf{x}) \geq m - \log_2 \|\widehat{p}_{\mathbf{x}}\|_2^2.$$

Remark that $\widehat{p}_{\mathbf{x}}(0) = 1$, since $p_{\mathbf{x}}$ is a probability mass function. Isolating this coefficient, one obtains

$$m - \mathsf{H}(\mathbf{x}) \leq \log_2 \left(1 + \|\widehat{p}_{\mathbf{x}} - \delta_0\|_2^2\right) \leq \|\widehat{p}_{\mathbf{x}} - \delta_0\|_2^2 / \log 2.$$

$\square$

Note that the inequality in Lemma 1 is rather sharp since $\|\widehat{p}_{\mathbf{x}} - \delta_0\|_2^2 \ll 1$ for the purposes of this work. Indeed $\widehat{p}_{\mathbf{x}}$ will typically have a small support, thereby enabling the use of Fourier-analytic methods.

Before turning to the proof of Theorem 1, we briefly consider the content of its statement. The theorem essentially shows that for a bounded-query probing secure circuit, all probed wire values either closely resemble uniform randomness or reveal nothing about the secret input. The usefulness of the result comes from the fact that it allows 'bad' probe values. These are values that might leak information about the secret, but which nevertheless cannot be distinguished from uniform random values unless a very large number of probing queries is made. In practice, the 'bad' values will be shares of the state resulting from probes placed far apart (*i.e.* separated by many rounds). The 'good' values then correspond to probes that are placed in nearby locations, such as within an S-box. As will be clarified in Sects. 6 and 7, the 'good' values can also play an important role in the analysis of the key-schedule of a masked cipher.

Theorem 1. *Let $\mathcal{A}$ be a t-threshold-probing adversary for a circuit C. Assume that for every query made by $\mathcal{A}$ on the oracle $\mathcal{O}^b$, there exists a partitioning (depending only on the probe positions) of the resulting wire values into two random variables $\mathbf{x}$ ('good') and $\mathbf{y}$ ('bad') such that*

1. *The conditional probability distribution $p_{\mathbf{y}|\mathbf{x}}$ satisfies $\mathbb{E}_{\mathbf{x}}\|\widehat{p}_{\mathbf{y}|\mathbf{x}} - \delta_0\|_2^2 \leq \varepsilon,$*
2. *Any t-threshold-probing adversary for the same circuit C and making the same oracle queries as $\mathcal{A}$, but which only receives the 'good' wire values (i.e. corresponding to $\mathbf{x}$) for each query, has advantage zero.*

The advantage of $\mathcal{A}$ can be upper bounded as

$$\mathrm{Adv}_{t\text{-thr}}(\mathcal{A}) \leq \sqrt{\frac{2q\,\varepsilon}{\log 2}},$$

where q is the number of queries to the oracle $\mathcal{O}^b$.

Proof. The first part of the proof consists of a standard game-hopping argument. Consider the following two additional games:

1. Game 't-thr-good' is a modification of the t-threshold probing game in which the oracle $\mathcal{O}^b$ replaces the 'bad' values in each query by uniform random values. In this game, $\mathcal{A}$ essentially only receives information about 'good' wire values.

2. In the game 'Δ-bad', the adversary chooses a secret input k and is given access to an oracle with the same t-threshold-probing interface as $\mathcal{O}^b$. This oracle is either a t-threshold-probing oracle for the real circuit with input k, or a modification thereof in which the 'bad' values in each query are replaced by uniform random bits. The goal is to distinguish between these two cases.

We construct an adversary $\mathcal{B}$ for the game 'Δ-bad' by running $\mathcal{A}$. Specifically, $\mathcal{B}$ picks a uniform random bit b and forwards the corresponding secret k_b chosen by $\mathcal{A}$ to its challenger. Adversary $\mathcal{B}$ reports the oracle as real if and only if $\mathcal{A}$ correctly recovers b. Hence,

$$\text{Adv}_{t\text{-thr}}(\mathcal{A}) \leq \text{Adv}_{t\text{-thr-good}}(\mathcal{A}) + 2\text{Adv}_{\Delta\text{-bad}}(\mathcal{B}).$$

The factor two in front of $\text{Adv}_{\Delta\text{-bad}}(\mathcal{B})$ is due to our definition of 'advantage', *i.e.* the absolute difference between the winning and failure probabilities of $\mathcal{B}$. It is given that $\text{Adv}_{t\text{-thr-good}}(\mathcal{A}) = 0$, so it suffices to upper bound $\text{Adv}_{\Delta\text{-bad}}(\mathcal{B})$.

Since $\mathcal{B}$ makes exactly the same queries to its oracle as $\mathcal{A}$, the result of query i made by $\mathcal{B}$ can also be partitioned into 'good' and 'bad' wire values. Denote these values by $\mathbf{x}_i$ and $\mathbf{y}_i$ respectively when $\mathcal{B}$ is interacting with the real threshold probing oracle, and by $\mathbf{x}_i'$ and $\mathbf{y}_i'$ when $\mathcal{B}$ interacts with the (partially) randomized oracle.

Let $\delta_{\text{TV}}(\cdot, \cdot)$ denote the total variation distance and $\otimes$ the tensor product. The distinguishing advantage of the adversary $\mathcal{B}$ is then upper bounded by

$$\text{Adv}_{\Delta\text{-bad}}(\mathcal{B}) \leq \delta_{\text{TV}}\Big(\bigotimes_{i=1}^q p_{\mathbf{x}_i,\mathbf{y}_i}, \bigotimes_{i=1}^q p_{\mathbf{x}_i',\mathbf{y}_i'} \Big)$$
$$\leq \sqrt{\frac{1}{2} D_{\text{KL}}\Big(\bigotimes_{i=1}^q p_{\mathbf{x}_i,\mathbf{y}_i} \,\|\, \bigotimes_{i=1}^q p_{\mathbf{x}_i',\mathbf{y}_i'} \Big)}$$
$$\leq \sqrt{\frac{q}{2} \max_{1 \leq i \leq q} D_{\text{KL}}\big(p_{\mathbf{x}_i,\mathbf{y}_i} \,\|\, p_{\mathbf{x}_i',\mathbf{y}_i'} \big)},$$

where D_{KL} denotes the Kullback-Leibler divergence and the second inequality is due to Pinsker. By definition of 'Δ-bad', the random variables $\mathbf{x}_i$ and $\mathbf{x}_i'$ have the same probability distribution. Consequently,

$$D_{\text{KL}}\big(p_{\mathbf{x}_i,\mathbf{y}_i} \,\|\, p_{\mathbf{x}_i',\mathbf{y}_i'} \big) = \mathbb{E}_{\mathbf{t}} D_{\text{KL}}\big(p_{\mathbf{y}_i|\mathbf{x}_i=\mathbf{t}} \,\|\, p_{\mathbf{y}_i'|\mathbf{x}_i'=\mathbf{t}} \big).$$

Finally, remark that $\mathbf{y}_i'$ is uniformly distributed and independent of $\mathbf{x}_i$. If the number of bits of $\mathbf{y}_i$ is denoted by m_i, then

$$D_{\text{KL}}\big(p_{\mathbf{y}_i|\mathbf{x}_i=\mathbf{t}} \,\|\, p_{\mathbf{y}_i'|\mathbf{x}_i'=\mathbf{t}} \big) = m_i - \text{H}(\mathbf{y}_i|\mathbf{x}_i) \leq \|\widehat{p}_{\mathbf{y}_i|\mathbf{x}_i} - \delta_0\|_2^2 / \log 2.$$

The inequality above follows from Lemma 1. Since it is given that, for all i, $\mathbb{E}_{\mathbf{x}_i}\|\widehat{p}_{\mathbf{y}_i|\mathbf{x}_i} - \delta_0\|_2^2 \leq \varepsilon$, we have

$$\text{Adv}_{\Delta\text{-bad}}(\mathcal{B}) \leq \sqrt{\frac{q\varepsilon}{2\log 2}}.$$

Hence, we conclude that

$$\mathrm{Adv}_{t\text{-thr}}(\mathcal{A}) \le 2\mathrm{Adv}_{\Delta\text{-bad}}(\mathcal{B}) \le \sqrt{\frac{2q\,\varepsilon}{\log 2}}.$$

$\square$

5   Fourier Analysis of Shared Functions

Theorem 1 provides an upper bound on the advantage of t-threshold probing adversaries in terms of the Fourier coefficients of the probability distribution of observed wire values. This section clarifies why it is beneficial to express the advantage upper bound in this particular form. Specifically, it will be shown that this reveals a strong link with the linear cryptanalysis of shared functions.

5.1   Restrictions of Shared Functions

Remark that all probability distributions referred to in Theorem 1 are with respect to a fixed value of the secret inputs. Consequently, it is clear that the relevant Fourier coefficients can not be directly related to the Walsh-Hadamard coefficients (or equivalently, the correlation matrix) of the shared function itself. Instead, the relevant properties are those of restrictions of the shared function to sets of all valid sharings of a specific secret. Below, we argue that these restrictions are indeed well-defined and that they come with a natural notion of linear cryptanalysis.

Recall from Sect. 2 that Boolean masking and threshold implementations are based on linear secret sharing. In general, any $\mathbb{F}_2$-linear secret sharing scheme can be thought of as an algorithm that maps a secret $x \in \mathbb{F}_2^n$ to a random element of a corresponding coset of a vector space $\mathbb{V} \subset \mathbb{F}_2^\ell$. The vector space $\mathbb{V}$ consists of all possible sharings of $0 \in \mathbb{F}_2^n$. Let $\rho : \mathbb{F}_2^n \to \mathbb{F}_2^\ell$ be a map that sends secrets to their corresponding coset representative.

Example. In Boolean masking, a secret $x \in \mathbb{F}_2$ is shared as $(x^1, \ldots, x^\ell)$ where $x^1, \ldots, x^{\ell-1}$ is sampled uniformly at random and $x^\ell = x + \sum_{i=1}^{\ell-1} x^i$. In this case, $\mathbb{V}$ corresponds to the parity bit code

$$\mathbb{V} = \{(x^1, \ldots, x^\ell) \in \mathbb{F}_2^\ell \mid \textstyle\sum_{i=1}^\ell x^i = 0\}.$$

Furthermore, one possible choice of ρ is $\rho(x) = (x, 0, \ldots, 0)$.   ▷

Let $F : \mathbb{F}_2^n \to \mathbb{F}_2^n$ be any function. A function $\bar{F} : \mathbb{F}_2^\ell \to \mathbb{F}_2^\ell$ is said to be a correct sharing of F if, for all $x \in \mathbb{F}_2^n$,

$$\bar{F}(\rho(x) + \mathbb{V}) \subseteq \rho(F(x)) + \mathbb{V}. \tag{1}$$

If $\bar{F}$ is a uniform sharing, then the above inclusion is in fact an equality. For convenience, let $\mathbb{V}_a = a + \mathbb{V}$. Due to (1), the restriction of $\bar{F}$ to $\mathbb{V}_a$ is a well-defined function $\mathbb{V}_a \to \mathbb{V}_b$ whenever $a = \rho(x)$ and $b = \rho(F(x))$ for some $x \in \mathbb{F}_2^n$.

By slight abuse of notation, the same notation will be used for $\bar{F}$ and for its restrictions.

Any random variable $\mathbf{x}$ on $\mathbb{V}_a$ has a corresponding probability mass function $p_{\mathbf{x}} : \mathbb{V}_a \rightarrow [0, 1]$. Since $\mathbb{V}$ is a vector space, the Fourier transformation $\widehat{p}_{a+\mathbf{x}}$ of $p_{a+\mathbf{x}}$ is well-defined (see Definition 1). In addition, for any restriction $\bar{F} : \mathbb{V}_a \rightarrow \mathbb{V}_b$, the correlation matrix of $x \mapsto \bar{F}(a+x)+b$ is well defined by Definition 3. For convenience, we introduce the following definition. Note that it does not depend on the choice of the coset representatives a and b.

Definition 5. *For $\mathbb{V} \subseteq \mathbb{F}_2^\ell$, let $\bar{F} : \mathbb{V}_a \rightarrow \mathbb{V}_b$ be a well-defined restriction of a shared function. Let $\bar{F}'(x) = \bar{F}(x+a)+b$. The correlation matrix of $\bar{F}$ is defined as the matrix with coordinates*

$$C_{u,v}^{\bar{F}} = (-1)^{u^\top a + v^\top b} C_{u,v}^{\bar{F}'},$$

for $u, v \in \mathbb{F}_2^\ell / \mathbb{V}^\perp$.

5.2   Correlations Between Probed Values

As shown in Sect. 4, the advantage of a probing adversary against the circuit can be upper bounded in terms of $\|\widehat{p}_{\mathbf{z}} - \delta_0\|_2$ where $p_{\mathbf{z}}$ is the probability distribution of any measured set of 'bad' wire values, possibly conditioned on several 'good' wire values. Note that the conditioning on 'good' values simply corresponds to fixing some variables in the circuit to constants before applying the results below. This section provides the essential link between $\widehat{p}_{\mathbf{z}}$ and the linear cryptanalysis of the shared circuit that will enable us to upper bound the quantity $\|\widehat{p}_{\mathbf{z}} - \delta_0\|_2$ for a concrete masked cipher in Sect. 7.

For simplicity, from this point on, we only consider second-order probing adversaries. For a brief outlook on how these results could be extended to third-order security and higher, the reader is referred to Sect. 9. To obtain the desired link with linear cryptanalysis, it will be shown that the coordinates of $\widehat{p}_{\mathbf{z}}$ are entries of the correlation matrix of the state-transformation between the specified probe locations. This is illustrated in Fig. 3.

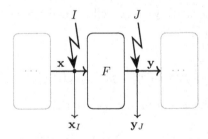

Fig. 3. Two probes giving the observation $\mathbf{z} = (\mathbf{x}_I, \mathbf{y}_J)$.

The main result is stated in Theorem 2. To obtain it, the following property of correlation matrices will be used.

Lemma 2. *Let* $\mathbb{V} \subset \mathbb{F}_2^{\ell}$ *be a set of correct sharings and* $L : \mathbb{V} \to \mathbb{F}_2^m$ *a linear map. If* $\mathbf{x}$ *is a random variable with probability distribution* $p_{\mathbf{x}}$, *then it holds that*

$$\widehat{p}_{L\mathbf{x}}(u) = \widehat{p}_{\mathbf{x}}(L^{\top}u),$$

where we write $L^{\top}u = L^{\top}u + \mathbb{V}^{\perp}$ *as usual.*

Proof. The result is a well-known property, see [5, Theorem 3.5] for the general case. For completeness, we provide a short derivation. Remark that $p_{L\mathbf{x}}(z) = \sum_{x \in \mathbb{V}} p_{\mathbf{x}}(x) \delta_{Lx}(z)$. Hence, by the definition of the Fourier transformation, it holds that

$$\widehat{p}_{L\mathbf{x}}(u) = \sum_{z \in \mathbb{F}_2^m} (-1)^{u^{\top}z} p_{L\mathbf{x}}(z) = \sum_{x \in \mathbb{V}} p_{\mathbf{x}}(x) \left(\sum_{z \in \mathbb{F}_2^m} (-1)^{u^{\top}z} \delta_{Lx}(z) \right).$$

This simplifies to

$$\widehat{p}_{L\mathbf{x}}(u) = \sum_{x \in \mathbb{V}} (-1)^{u^{\top}Lx} p_{\mathbf{x}}(x) = \widehat{p}_{\mathbf{x}}(L^{\top}u).$$

$\square$

For an index set $I = \{i_1, \ldots, i_m\}$, we denote the restriction of $x \in \mathbb{V}$ to I by $x_I = (x_{i_1}, \ldots, x_{i_m}) \in \mathbb{F}_2^{|I|}$. Note that the maps $x \mapsto x_I$ and its restriction to $\mathbb{V}$ are linear.

Theorem 2. *Let* $F : \mathbb{V}_a \to \mathbb{V}_b$ *be a function with* $\mathbb{V} \subset \mathbb{F}_2^{\ell}$ *and* $I, J \subset \{1, \ldots, \ell\}$. *For* $\mathbf{x}$ *uniform random on* $\mathbb{V}_a$ *and* $\mathbf{y} = F(\mathbf{x})$, *let* $\mathbf{z} = (\mathbf{x}_I, \mathbf{y}_J)$. *The Fourier transformation of the probability mass function of* $\mathbf{z}$ *then satisfies*

$$\widehat{p}_{\mathbf{z}}(u, v) = C^F_{\widetilde{v}, \widetilde{u}},$$

where $\widetilde{u}, \widetilde{v} \in \mathbb{F}_2^{\ell}/\mathbb{V}^{\perp}$ *are such that* $\widetilde{u}_I = u$, $\widetilde{u}_{[\ell] \backslash I} = 0$, $\widetilde{v}_J = v$ *and* $\widetilde{v}_{[\ell] \backslash J} = 0$.

Proof. Note that $(a + \mathbf{x}, b + \mathbf{y})$ is a well-defined random variable on $\mathbb{V}^2$. Let $\mathbf{z}' = (a_I, b_J) + \mathbf{z}$, then $\widehat{p}_{\mathbf{z}}(u, v) = (-1)^{u^{\top}a_I + v^{\top}b_J} \widehat{p}_{\mathbf{z}'}(u, v)$. Due to Lemma 2, the distribution of $\mathbf{z}'$ satisfies

$$\widehat{p}_{\mathbf{z}'}(u, v) = \widehat{p}_{a+\mathbf{x}, b+\mathbf{y}}(\widetilde{u}, \widetilde{v}).$$

The probability distribution of $(a + \mathbf{x}, b + \mathbf{y})$ satisfies

$$p_{a+\mathbf{x}, b+\mathbf{y}} = (I \otimes T^G) p_{a+\mathbf{x}, a+\mathbf{x}},$$

where $G(x) = F(x + a) + b$. Taking the Fourier transformation, one obtains

$$\widehat{p}_{a+\mathbf{x}, b+\mathbf{y}} = (I \otimes C^G) \widehat{p}_{a+\mathbf{x}, a+\mathbf{x}}.$$

Note that, by the definition of C^F, it holds that $C^F_{\widetilde{u},\widetilde{v}} = (-1)^{\widetilde{u}^\top a + \widetilde{v}^\top b} C^G_{\widetilde{u},\widetilde{v}}$. Combining the results above, one obtains

$$\widehat{p}_{\mathbf{z}}(u,v) = \sum_{u',v' \in \mathbb{F}_2^\ell / \mathbb{V}^\perp} \delta_{\widetilde{u},u'} \, C^F_{\widetilde{v},v'} \, \widehat{p}_{a+\mathbf{x},a+\mathbf{x}}(u',v')$$

$$= \sum_{v' \in \mathbb{F}_2^\ell / \mathbb{V}^\perp} C^F_{\widetilde{v},v'} \, \widehat{p}_{a+\mathbf{x},a+\mathbf{x}}(\widetilde{u},v')$$

$$= \sum_{v' \in \mathbb{F}_2^\ell / \mathbb{V}^\perp} C^F_{\widetilde{v},v'} \, \widehat{p}_{a+\mathbf{x}}(\widetilde{u}+v').$$

Since $p_{a+\mathbf{x}}$ is the uniform distribution on $\mathbb{V}$, it holds that $\widehat{p}_{a+\mathbf{x}} = \delta_0$. It follows that all terms except $v' = \widetilde{u}$ in the sum above vanish, whence $\widehat{p}_{\mathbf{z}}(u,v) = C^F_{\widetilde{v},\widetilde{u}}$. □

Theorem 2 relates the linear approximations of F to $\widehat{p}_{\mathbf{z}}(u)$ and hence provides a method to upper bound $\|\widehat{p}_{\mathbf{z}} - \delta_0\|_2$ based on linear cryptanalysis. However, it should be noted that the result relates to linear cryptanalysis with respect to $\mathbb{V}$ rather than $\mathbb{F}_2^\ell$. The differences are mostly minor, but there is a subtle difference in relation to the important notion of 'activity'. In standard linear cryptanalysis, an S-box is said to be active if its output mask is nonzero. The same definition applies for linear cryptanalysis with respect to $\mathbb{V}$, but one must take into account that the mask is now an element of the quotient space $\mathbb{F}_2^\ell / \mathbb{V}^\perp$. In particular, if the mask corresponding to the shares of a particular bit can be represented by an all-one vector $(1,1,\ldots,1)^\top$, it may be equivalently represented by the zero vector. It is still true that a valid linear approximation for a permutation must have either both input masks equivalent to zero or neither equivalent to zero. More generally, this condition is ensured by any uniform sharing.

Finally, note that Theorem 2 assumes that all intermediate states of the shared implementation are uniformly distributed on a coset of $\mathbb{V}$. This condition is guaranteed by the uniformity property of threshold implementations. In fact, it corresponds to the fact that the approximation with – up to equivalence – an all-zero input mask, must also have an all-zero output mask in order to have nonzero correlation. In particular, this is achieved if all shared functions are permutations. Accounting for a non-uniform distribution would require similar modifications to Theorem 2 as would be necessary to achieve higher than second-order security. In addition, if non-uniform sharings are used, the standard wide-trail argument [18] that will be used in later sections breaks down. For these reasons, our masking of LED in Sect. 7 relies on uniform sharings. A complete assessment of the consequences of non-uniformity on first and second order security is left as future work. Regarding this, we note that an analysis of the security degradation for non-uniform mappings has been made by Daemen [15] and has been tested in practice by Wegener et al. [39]. An interesting direction for future work would be to combine our methods in order to further increase the efficiency of shared implementations.

6   Cryptanalysis of Masked Ciphers

Theorems 1 and 2 provide the basic tools by which the security analysis of a masked cipher can be reduced to its linear cryptanalysis. This section provides a high-level overview of the analytic process. In addition, for each component of a typical masked cipher, the cryptanalytical properties that play a prominent role in the security analysis are discussed. This discussion can be useful not only to determine an appropriate masking of a cipher, but also as a factor in the design strategy of the cipher itself.

Our analysis of a masked cipher begins by partitioning the set of possible probe positions into three parts. This is closely related to the labeling of wire values as 'good' or 'bad' as required by Theorem 1. Each part corresponds to a different level of 'locality' and is analyzed by different methods. Specifically, the following cases can be distinguished:

S-box level. If both probes are placed within an S-box, we ensure perfect probing security and consequently such wire values are labeled 'good' in the proof. Hence, the S-box must be shared such that it is higher-order probing secure. Based on this, one can verify the probing security of one cipher round.

Nearby rounds. If the probes are separated by a small number of rounds, we rely on zero-correlation linear cryptanalysis. If the probe positions lead to zero-correlation approximations, then the probed values are uniformly distributed. In this case, from the point of view of Theorem 1, it does not matter if the values are marked as 'good' or 'bad'. Indeed, since the distribution of the values is perfectly uniform in this case, one also has perfect probing security. This part of the analysis strongly depends on the linear layer of the cipher.

Distant rounds. When the probes are separated by many rounds, we rely on Theorem 2 and upper bound the absolute correlations of linear approximations. This is done using traditional techniques from linear cryptanalysis, in particular the piling-up principle. As discussed in more detail in Sect. 7.5, this is where we truly leave the realm of information-theoretical arguments and enter the domain of statistical cryptanalysis. Needless to say, all such wire values must be labeled as 'bad' from the point of view of Theorem 1.

For the key-schedule, the situation is slightly more complicated. If the key-schedule is sufficiently simple, as in the case of LED, one can label all key bits as 'good'. It then suffices – but is not necessary – to perform the analysis above for a fixed key. Several reasons for using this simplified approach are mentioned below. For more complicated key-schedules, a similar analysis as above for the key-schedule is likely to be necessary.

A detailed example of the design of a secure sharing and its complete security evaluation is given in Sect. 7 for the block cipher LED. The remainder of this section briefly discusses how the analysis above translates to each of the components of a masked cipher.

S-Box Sharing and Static Randomness. The S-box should be shared following the threshold implementation approach. For efficiency reasons, the S-box is often

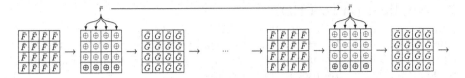

Fig. 4. The addition of *static randomness* with the S-box decomposed as $\bar{S} = \bar{G} \circ \bar{F}$.

decomposed into several lower degree functions. The sharing of these functions should satisfy the uniformity property without using randomness, and be second-order non-complete. If the S-box is decomposed, the security of the composition must also be ensured. A simple way to achieve this is to add randomness between the decomposed functions. This randomness can be re-used in every S-box. We call this *static randomness* as it is generated by the black-box encoder and is used throughout the masked cipher. This is illustrated in Fig. 4.

As discussed in Sect. 5.2, due to the uniformity of the shared S-box, the wide-trail strategy can be applied. In order to lower the potential advantage of the adversary, the sharing of the S-box is required to have strong nonlinear properties.

Linear Layer. The linear layer of the cipher affects the security of the masked cipher for two reasons. The first is the diffusion between shares, resulting in zero-correlation trails. The second is that the layer ensures a minimum number of active S-boxes when probing distant rounds, resulting in correlation upper bounds.

Key Schedule. In our analysis, we opt for simplicity by analyzing the key-schedule and state-transformation separately. This comes at a potential loss in the upper bounds, since many linear approximations will have correlation zero when averaged over some of the unknown key-bits. Nevertheless, there are several good reasons for making such a simplification:

- It allows us to stick as closely as possible to the basic wide-trail approach. Indeed, conventional linear cryptanalysis of block ciphers does not usually consider the combined effect of the key-schedule and state-transformation.
- Although many trails have average correlation zero for a random sharing of the key, this can be quite difficult to analyze as it depends not only on which key-bits the adversary can measure but also on the details of the key-schedule (the key-dependence of the sign of trail correlations can cancel out).
- No additional arguments are required for cryptographic permutations. In particular, the masked cipher can be used with a fixed key in order to obtain a secure implementation of a cryptographically strong permutation – provided of course that the cipher allows for such usage.

7   Application to LED

This section applies the techniques developed in Sect. 4 to Sect. 5 to the block cipher LED. This results in a masking requiring less than 700 bits of randomness while attaining second-order probing security.

7.1   Description of LED

LED is a 64-bit block cipher designed by Guo *et al.* [27]. The cipher's state is divided into 16 four-bit cells. The variant considered here has a 128-bit master key, from which subkeys are derived using a nibble-wise permutation. The cipher consists of 12 steps, each comprising four rounds. The step function is shown in Fig. 5. For further details, we refer the reader to the work of Guo *et al.* [27].

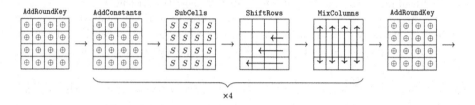

×4

Fig. 5. The step function of LED.

7.2   Sharing Second-Order LED

Following the principles outlined in Sect. 6, this section constructs a sharing of the LED cipher. Figure 6 gives an overview of the shared round function.

Masking State and Key. For the sharing of LED we use classical Boolean masking. The 64-bit state is shared using seven shares per bit, requiring 384 random bits. The 128-bit key is shared using three shares, which costs 256 random bits.

Sharing Affine Components. The masking of LED's linear components such as ShiftRows, MixColumns, and the key schedule are simply done share-wise. Constants are added to the first share of the concerning variable. The key addition is done by adding the key shares to the first three shares of the state.

Sharing the S-Box. LED uses the PRESENT S-box. Following the decomposition given by Kutzner *et al.* [30], this S-box can be decomposed into two quadratic maps $S_1 = G \circ C$ and $S_2 = B \circ G$ where B and C are affine. Further details on this decomposition are given in Appendix A.1. The sharing of the S-box is constructed from the sharing of G which we detail in Appendix A.2 and has been verified to be uniform and second-order non-complete. In between the two

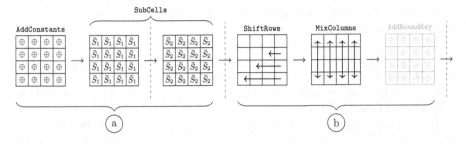

Fig. 6. One round of masked LED. The locations of the registers are indicated by dashed lines. The round key addition is depicted in gray to show that it only happens every four rounds.

G functions, a layer of *static randomness* consisting of zero sharings is added[1]. This randomness is re-used in every S-box call and consists of 24 bits.

Alternative Sharings. The S-box could be shared using fewer shares. For example, the work of Moradi *et al.* [34] constructs a uniform sharing using five input shares. Additionally, a uniform three-sharing is presented in Appendix A.3. However, both sharings achieve second-order probing security by first expanding their inputs and then re-compressing the cross products. Due to this expansion phase, there is an intermediate layer which is not uniform. As discussed in Sect. 5.2, the use of non-uniform functions would require a more thorough security analysis.

The sharing of the S-box can also be adapted to give better linear properties improving the security bounds. One such option based on composing with a nontrivial sharing of the identity function, is explored in Appendix A.4.

Security. In Sects. 7.3 to 7.6 below, the following concrete security claim will be established.

Security Claim 1. *For the masked LED described in this section, the following bound on the advantage of the adversary (assuming piling-up) in the probing model is claimed:*

$$\mathrm{Adv}_{\text{2-thr}}(\mathcal{A}) \leq \sqrt{\frac{q}{2^{120}}}.$$

7.3 Probing Security of One Round

This section establishes the second-order probing security of one round of masked LED, such that all wire values corresponding to such probing queries can be labeled as 'good'. Recall that, since each layer of the masked cipher is uniformly shared, the input distribution to the round is uniform. To establish the probing-security claim, it suffices to consider all possible probe positions. If both probes

---

[1] The randomness can be avoided by using a second-order sharing of the entire S-box. However, as this would increase the number of shares, we did not pursue this option.

are placed in the same layer, the claim follows directly from the second-order non-completeness of each function.

When both probes are placed in part (a) in Fig. 6, the only nontrivial new case corresponds to placing one probe in $\bar{S}_1$ and one in $\bar{S}_2$. Due to the refreshing layer $\bar{R}$, the input to $\bar{S}_2$ is uniformly random even if $\bar{S}_1$ is probed. Since $\bar{S}_2$ is second-order non-complete, placing the second probe in $\bar{S}_2$ then reveals no information about the secret.

If one probe is placed in part (a) and another in part (b), then the second probe reveals at most a single share (the same) of each variable by the linearity of part (b). Due to a consistent choice of the covering scheme used for non-completeness, the previous arguments are not limited to the bit-level. Consequently, the analysis is the same as for the case with two probes in part (a).

Every four rounds, a round key is also added to the state. The effect of the key-schedule and key addition is discussed in Sect. 7.6.

7.4 Probing Nearby Rounds: Zero Correlation

This section shows the distribution of any pair of measurements from probes which are at most three rounds apart almost always conforms to one of two cases: either the observations are uniformly distributed, or they do not reveal anything about the secret. To prove the uniformity claim of our observations, we rely on techniques from zero-correlation linear cryptanalysis. The latter case, *i.e.* independence of the secret for possibly non-uniform observations, was discussed in the previous section. For these cases, the advantage of the adversary is zero as specified in the proof of Theorem 1. All other cases will be considered in Sect. 7.5.

The argument consists of an analysis of all possible probe placements. As noted above, the analysis in this section is restricted to probes that are at most three rounds apart. This results in the following cases:

Rounds i and $i+1$. If the adversary probes in part (a) of round i, then the MDS matrix ensures that a full column of the state will be active at the input of round $i+1$. A measurement in part (a) of round $i+1$ can activate shares from at most one cell of the state such that the corresponding approximations have correlation zero. Similarly, due to the shift rows operation, by probing in part (b) of round $i+1$, the adversary can never activate all cells of a single column at the input of round $i+1$. Hence, approximations with nonzero correlation can only be obtained by probing in part (b) of round i. However, in this case only a single share of each bit is learned, such that a second probe in part (a) or (b) of round $i+1$ reveals nothing about the secret by the same argument for the case where both probes are placed in round i.

Rounds i and $i+2$. If either part (a) or (b) of round i are probed, this results (up to symmetry) in one of the four activity patterns shown in Fig. 7 for rounds $i+1$ and on. By probing anywhere in round $i+2$, the adversary can clearly activate at most four cells at the input of this round. In cases (1)–(3) in Fig. 7, at least eight S-boxes are active at the input of round $i+2$ such that the correlation of such approximations is zero. In the remaining case, *i.e.*

activity pattern (4), only a single column of the state is active at the input of round $i + 2$. However, by probing in part (a) of round $i + 2$, only a single cell can be activated. Probing part (b) allows activating four cells but never from the same column due to the shift rows step.

Rounds i and $i + 3$. It is easy to see that activity patterns (2)-(4) in Fig. 7 lead to correlation zero since at least eight S-boxes are then active at the input of round $i + 3$. Indeed, if the second probe is placed anywhere in round $i + 3$, at most four cells of the state can be activated. For pattern (1) in Fig. 7, the correlation may be nonzero and will be bounded in Sect. 7.5.

The above case analysis shows that, when the probes are placed in nearby rounds, perfect security is obtained. The only remaining cases are probes in rounds i and $i + r$ for $r > 4$ and the activity pattern (1) in Fig. 7 when probes are placed in rounds i and $i + 3$. These cases are analyzed in Sect. 7.5.

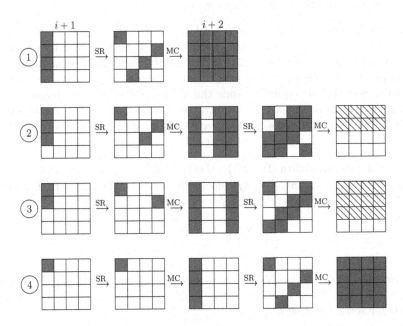

Fig. 7. Activity patterns for masked LED, corresponding (up to symmetry) the four possible patterns created by a probe placed in round i. SR is short for ShiftRows and MC for MixColumns. White cells are inactive, cells in gray are active, and hatched cells correspond to an example trail with a minimum number of active cells.

7.5 Five Rounds or More: Low Correlation

As discussed in Sect. 7.4, if the probes are placed in rounds that are far apart, the observed values are usually not uniformly distributed. Nevertheless, it is possible to show that they will be nearly uniform in the sense that all nontrivial coordinates of the Fourier transform of their probability distribution are small. To show this, we rely on standard techniques from linear cryptanalysis: we bound the correlation of all linear trails whose activity pattern is compatible with the probe positions.

Remark 2. The analysis in this section relies on the piling-up approximation, *i.e.* we use upper bounds on the correlation of trails as an approximation for upper bounds on the correlation of linear approximations. This heuristic is widely used in symmetric-key cryptanalysis, and is an integral part of the security argument of essentially all contemporary symmetric-key primitives. In addition, as detailed in Sect. 7.6, our correlation upper bounds need not hold for all key and refreshing variables but only in the average over the unobserved variables. Finally, any adversary that can distinguish the probed wire values from uniform randomness gives rise to a linear distinguisher. Consequently, we believe it is reasonable to apply the piling-up heuristic in this setting.

To upper bound absolute trail correlations, we rely on the standard wide-trail argument [18]. Specifically, the fact that any linear trail over four rounds of (shared) LED activates at least 25 S-boxes will be used. Additionally, an upper bound on the correlation of the best linear approximations over the shared S-box from Sect. 7.2 is required. Since the shared S-box is quite large, a direct calculation of its nonlinearity is nontrivial. Instead, the following lemma for quadratic Boolean functions can be used. A slight restatement of this result can be found in the book chapter by Carlet [11].

Lemma 3 (Proposition 16 [11]). *Let $f : \mathbb{F}_2^n \to \mathbb{F}_2$ be a quadratic Boolean function. Denote the rank of its symplectic form by r. That is, $r = \operatorname{rank}(S)$ where $S \in \mathbb{F}_2^{n \times n}$ is the symmetric matrix for which $y^\top S x = f(x + y) + f(x) + f(y)$. Then*

$$\frac{1}{2^n} \left| \sum_{x \in \mathbb{F}_2^n} (-1)^{f(x)} \right| \leq 2^{-r/2}.$$

Lemma 4. *Let $\bar{G} : \mathbb{V}_a \to \mathbb{V}_b$ be any restriction of the sharing of G defined in Sect. 7.2. Denote its correlation matrix by $C^{\bar{G}}$. For any $u, v \in \mathbb{F}_2^\ell / \mathbb{V}^\perp$ such that $u_i^j \neq 0$ for some $i \neq 3$, it holds that $|C_{u,v}^{\bar{G}}| \leq 2^{-3}$.*

Proof. Since $\bar{G}$ is a function of 28 variables, bounding all of its correlations is nontrivial. However, one can use the fact that $\bar{G}$ is a quadratic function. Indeed, if $B \in \mathbb{F}_2^{\ell \times d}$ is a basis matrix for $\mathbb{V}$, then

$$|C_{u,v}^{\bar{G}}| \leq \max_{w \in \mathbb{F}_2^\ell / \mathbb{V}^\perp} \frac{1}{|\mathbb{V}|} \left| \sum_{x \in \mathbb{V}} (-1)^{u^\top \bar{G}(x+a) + w^\top x} \right|$$

$$\leq \max_{w \in \mathbb{F}_2^\ell / \mathbb{V}^\perp} \frac{1}{2^d} \left| \sum_{x \in \mathbb{F}_2^d} (-1)^{u^\top \bar{G}(Bx+a) + w^\top Bx} \right|.$$

Since $u^{\top}\bar{G}(Bx+a)+w^{\top}Bx$ is a quadratic Boolean function, Lemma 3 is applicable. Let $S_{i,j}$ denote the symplectic form matrix of $G_i^j(Bx+a)$. Since $S_{3,j}=0$ for $j=1,\ldots,7$, we must require that u_i^j is nonzero for some $i\neq 3$ to obtain a nonzero minimum rank. Specifically, it suffices to verify that for all nonzero $u\in\mathbb{F}_2^\ell/\mathbb{V}^\perp$ with $u_3^j=0$ for $j=1,\ldots,7$,

$$\mathrm{rank}\left(\sum_{i=1}^{4}\sum_{j=1}^{7}u_i^j\,S_{i,j}\right)\geq 6.$$

Lower bounding the left-hand side above reduces to the MinRank problem. For our purposes, a brute force search over all representative choices of u is feasible. The verification code can be found on GitLab [40]. $\qquad\square$

Theorem 3. *Let $\bar{S}=\bar{S}_2\circ\bar{S}_1:\mathbb{V}_{a_1}\to\mathbb{V}_{a_3}$ be the sharing of $S=S_2\circ S_1$ defined in Sect. 7.2. Denote the correlation matrix of $\bar{S}_i:\mathbb{V}_{a_i}\to\mathbb{V}_{a_{i+1}}$ by $C^{\bar{S}_i}$. For any $u,v\in\mathbb{F}_2^\ell/\mathbb{V}^\perp$ not both equal to zero and for all $w\in\mathbb{F}_2^\ell/\mathbb{V}^\perp$, it holds that $|C_{u,w}^{\bar{S}_2}C_{w,v}^{\bar{S}_1}|\leq 2^{-3}$.*

Proof. Since $\bar{S}$ is affine equivalent to $\bar{G}\circ\bar{G}$, it suffices to analyze the latter function. By Lemma 4, it holds that $|C_{u,w}^{\bar{G}}|\leq 2^{-3}$ unless $u_i^j=0$ for $j=1,\ldots,7$ and for all $i\neq 3$. However, for such u, $|C_{u,w}^{\bar{G}}|=0$ whenever w also satisfies $w_i^j=0$ for $j=1,\ldots,7$ and for all $i\neq 3$. Indeed, the ith-share of the third bit $\bar{G}_3^i$ does not depend on any shares from the third input variable. It follows that $|C_{u,w}^{\bar{G}}C_{w,v}^{\bar{G}}|\leq 2^{-3}$. $\qquad\square$

Remark 3. Experimentally, we find that the piling-up approximation gives the correct upper bound 2^{-3} for the maximum absolute correlation of the shared S-box. Due to resource constraints, the experiment was limited to the verification for one choice of static randomness.

For probes placed in rounds i and $i+r$ with $r\geq 4$, the relevant linear trails all have at least 25 active S-boxes. This is a consequence of the wide-trail design strategy and can be derived in exactly the same way as for the AES [18]. Hence, by Theorem 3, the correlations of these trails are bounded by 2^{-75}. By Theorem 2, it then follows that the 2-norm of the nontrivial Fourier coefficients of the observed bits $\mathbf{z}$ can be upper bounded by

$$\varepsilon:=\|\widehat{p}_{\mathbf{z}}-\delta_0\|_2^2\leq|\mathrm{supp}\,\widehat{p}_{\mathbf{z}}|\,\|\widehat{p}_{\mathbf{z}}-\delta_0\|_\infty^2\leq 2^{22}\,2^{-150}=2^{-128},$$

where we have used the inequality $|\mathrm{supp}\,\widehat{p}_{\mathbf{z}}|\leq 2^{22}$, which follows from the fact that the observed value $\mathbf{z}$ consists of at most 22 bits in the glitch-extended probing model: if an output coordinate of $\bar{G}$ is read, at most 10 shares are learned; if an output of the shared linear layer is probed, at most 11 shares are observed. The latter number of shares is due to the fact that LED's MDS matrix has at least five zeros per row when viewed over $\mathbb{F}_2$. Note that, in practice, the upper bound above is not likely to be tight, because it is unlikely that a glitch will reveal the exact value of all 11 bits in a single measurement.

The only remaining case is when the adversary probes in rounds i and $i + 3$, assuming the activity pattern in case ① from Fig. 7. In this case, only 24 S-boxes are active. Furthermore, we again have $|\text{supp } \widehat{p}_z| \leq 2^{22}$. Hence,

$$\varepsilon := \|\widehat{p}_z - \delta_0\|_2^2 \leq 2^{22} \, 2^{-144} = 2^{-122}.$$

Note that a more careful analysis results in slightly improved bounds. Nevertheless, since we believe the bound on ε is sufficiently small for all practical purposes, we avoid such an analysis and opt for simplicity instead.

7.6 Influence of the Key-Schedule

The arguments in Sects. 7.4 and 7.5 directly establish the security of our proposed masked LED design against an adversary which does not look at shares of the key or the bits which are added in the refreshing layer. Indeed, for such an adversary, we may mark all wire values for queries with probe positions considered in Sect. 7.4 as 'good' and all others (considered in Sect. 7.5) as 'bad'. Theorem 1 then provides the desired upper bound. However, showing the conventional security where all wires in the circuit can be probed requires a slightly more careful choice of 'good' and 'bad' wire values.

Fortunately, the LED key-schedule consists only of bit-permutations. Hence, its sharing is perfectly secure against second-order threshold-probing adversaries. The same holds for the random bits used in the refreshing layer. Hence, Theorem 1 can be applied with the following labeling of wire values:

Probes discussed in Sect. 7.3–7.4. For all these probe positions, all wire values can be considered as 'good'. This includes any key bits (and additional randomness in the refreshing layer) that might be observed by the adversary. Indeed, even with glitch-extended probes, the adversary can observe at most two shares of each key bit.

Probes discussed in Sect. 7.5. For all these probe For these probe positions, all wire values corresponding to state shares should be marked as 'bad'; shares of the key (or additional randomness used in the refreshing layer) are labeled 'good'. The arguments in Sect. 7.5 then apply directly.

At least one probe in the key-schedule. In this case, all wire values may be considered 'good'. Indeed, recall that any non-complete subset of state bits at a particular layer is uniformly distributed and the adversary observes at most two shares of each key bit.

For the upper bound ε, the values derived in Sect. 7.5 may be used directly – as the analysis of the trails there is valid for any choice of the key. Note that the latter assumption is stronger than necessary; it suffices to assume that the bounds derived in Sect. 7.5 are valid in the average over all unobserved randomness and key variables.

7.7   Simulation-Based Verification

This section verifies the assumptions of Theorem 1 using a software simulation of the masked LED. Measurements of wire values are taken and their entropy is estimated. In case a serious vulnerability would be present, there would be probing positions where the estimated entropy would deviate from the number of observed bits. For some choices of probe positions, the results are shown in Fig. 8. The confidence intervals clearly converge to the number of observed bits in each case. This software is found on GitLab [40]. More information on our estimators and software can be found in Appendix C.

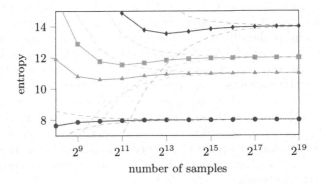

Fig. 8. The solid lines show the entropy estimates, the dashed lines represent a 95% confidence interval. The bottom curve corresponds to probing the first bit of `MixColumns` in rounds i and $i + 3$. For the blue curve (squares), the third bits of `MixColumns` from rounds i and $i + 4$ are observed. For the yellow curve (triangles) a linear layer in round i and an S-box in round $i + 4$ were probed. For the top curve, probes are in an S-box in round i and the linear layer of round $i + 4$.

8   Application to Other Primitives

The approach developed in Sect. 3 to 6 of this paper was illustrated in Sect. 7 by applying it to the block cipher LED. This section briefly discusses the broader applicability of our techniques to various other block ciphers and cryptographic permutations. In fact, as will be shown in Sect. 8.1 below, the analysis for LED from Sect. 7 carries over to several other ciphers with only minor changes. However, for different ciphers, the arguments need to be adapted more significantly or there are obstacles which prevent a direct application of our techniques. In Sect. 8.2, the main difficulties for a number of relevant ciphers are identified. This section may also be of relevance from the point-of-view of the design of block ciphers and permutations.

8.1   Immediate Applications

As discussed above, the security analysis and masking choice of LED can be directly adapted to several other primitives. In general, our approach is often directly applicable to primitives following the wide-trail design strategy. Two illustrative examples, one permutation and one block cipher, are given below.

Photon. PHOTON is a family of lightweight sponge-based hash functions introduced by Guo *et al.* [26] at CRYPTO 2011. The state of the PHOTON permutation corresponds to a $d \times d$ array of four or eight bit cells. The design of the permutation follows the wide-trail strategy: the linear layer consists of the parallel application of d MDS matrices and a ShiftRows operation. For four bit cells, the PRESENT S-box is used. Using the S-box sharing introduced in Sect. 7.2 and a straightforward splitting of the linear layer, a second-order probing secure sharing of the PHOTON permutation is obtained. The security analysis is essentially the same as for LED, subject to the simplification that there is no key-schedule. By verifying that at least $(d + 1)^2 - 1$ S-boxes must be active in any relevant trail with non-zero correlation, one directly obtains the bound $\varepsilon \leq 2^{4d - 6[(d+1)^2 - 1]}$. Note that the latter result assumes that each output bit of the linear layer depends on at most $4d$ input bits – this is a rough bound which can easily be improved. Accordingly, a rough upper bound on the advantage of a second-order threshold probing adversary model making at most q queries is $2\sqrt{q}/2^{d(3d+4)}$. The sharing uses only 24 bits of randomness beyond what is necessary to share the state.

Prince. PRINCE is a low-latency block cipher introduced by Borghoff *et al.* [10]. The PRINCE S-box can be decomposed into three quadratic functions in the affine equivalence class $\mathcal{Q}_{294}$ [8]. In Appendix B, a uniform seven-sharing for this class is given. By using similar techniques as in Sect. 7.5, it can be verified that the sharing for this class has a maximal correlation of 2^{-3}. Using the piling-up principle, the same upper bound is obtained for linear trails through the shared PRINCE S-box.

Contrary to LED and PHOTON, the linear layer of PRINCE is based on quasi-MDS matrices rather than an MDS matrix. However, the zero-correlation argument still works for up to three rounds in most cases. For all other cases, the wide-trail approach taken by PRINCE guarantees that at least 15 S-boxes are active. Thus, a direct application of our approach would result in an advantage of $\sqrt{q/2^{64}}$ which for a large number of queries admits a lower advantage than the security achieved by the cipher in most modes of operation. The state sharing would need a total of 408 random bits, including the initial sharing and static randomness. In case more security is desired, techniques such as the one presented in Appendix A.4 can be applied in order to improve the properties of the S-box sharing.

8.2   Applications Requiring Additional Techniques

Some ciphers do not follow the wide-trail strategy. Consequently, their linear cryptanalysis will look somewhat different compared to the analysis in Sects. 7.5

and 7.4 for LED. For example, automated tools might be necessary to find good bounds on the minimum number of active S-boxes. As mentioned above, there are also a number of ciphers that present some obstacles to a direct application of our techniques. Two examples are given below.

Present. Since LED uses the same S-box as PRESENT, an application to the PRESENT cipher by Bogdanov *et al.* [9] seems like the natural next step. However, due to the cipher's linear layer and well-known weaknesses with respect to linear cryptanalysis [13], it becomes challenging to design a sharing with reduced randomness cost. Since the output bits of the PRESENT S-box layer are piped directly into the next layer using a bit-permutation, the zero-correlation argument covers fewer rounds. Furthermore, the linear layer of PRESENT guarantees only 10 active S-boxes over five rounds [9]. In order to securely reduce randomness costs, one would need to significantly improve the linear properties of its S-box sharing. Alternatively, one could attempt to improve the diffusion of the shared cipher without affecting correctness.

AES. Another natural application is the AES, due to Daemen and Rijmen [19]. Since AES is a wide-trail design, the security analysis would be very similar to the analysis for LED in Sect. 7. However, currently we are not aware of any uniform sharing of the AES S-box. Note that a direct application of the *changing of the guards* method by Daemen [16] would alter the diffusion of the shared cipher and consequently demand a more detailed security analysis. We thus wish to re-highlight the merit of finding a uniform sharing of the AES S-box.

9 Conclusion and Future Work

This paper has tilted the security paradigm for side-channel countermeasures from perfect security arguments in a simulation-based model to a bounded-query cryptanalytic framework. It was shown that bounded-query probing security can be reduced to the linear cryptanalysis of masked ciphers. As the security analysis presented in our work is new, it allows for several directions for future work.

While the scope of this paper was limited to second-order protection, we believe the theoretical framework for higher-order security would remain largely the same. However, as the adversary gains the ability to place more probes, it will be able to exploit non-zero correlations even over a small number of rounds. Thus, to achieve adequate levels of security, a more detailed analysis of the trails in the masked cipher will typically be required.

In addition to generalizing to higher-orders, it would be worthwhile to apply our techniques to other ciphers. In Sect. 8 potential difficulties with AES and PRESENT were discussed. Overcoming these would require innovations in the design and analysis of masked ciphers. One such technique involves finding sharings with high non-linearity.

Finally, in our example of LED, we have carefully analyzed possible trails to derive an upper bound on the advantage of the adversary. However, a more holistic approach would involve the practical verification of this bound on hardware and the real-world security level.

Acknowledgment. We thank Joan Daemen for pointing us to his paper [15], which renewed our interest in working on this problem and eventually led us to a random idea. Dusan Bozilov kindly answered our questions about sharing PRINCE's S-box. Finally, we acknowledge Svetla Nikova and Vincent Rijmen for helpful comments. Tim Beyne and Siemen Dhooghe are supported by a PhD Fellowship from the Research Foundation – Flanders (FWO).

A   Sharings of the Present S-Box

This appendix gives a decomposition of the PRESENT S-box and two possible sharings. One uses seven shares and is detailed in the main text, the other uses three shares and verifying its security would require more analysis. Appendix A.3 gives a construction to improve the non-linearity of the shared S-box.

Concerning the PRESENT S-box, (x, y, z, w) denotes the input nibble from most significant to least significant bit. Similarly, $(G_1, ..., G_4)$ denotes the output from most significant to least significant bit.

A.1   Decomposition

The PRESENT S-box S can be decomposed as follows

$$S(x, y, z, w) = B'(G(G(C'(x, y, z, w) + d)) + e).$$

In the above, the nonlinear function $G(x, y, z, w)$ is given as

$$G_1 = x + yz + yw \qquad G_2 = w + xy \qquad G_3 = y \qquad G_4 = z + yw,$$

the linear transformations as

$$B' = \begin{bmatrix} 1&0&1&0 \\ 0&1&0&0 \\ 1&0&0&0 \\ 1&0&1&1 \end{bmatrix}, C' = \begin{bmatrix} 1&1&0&0 \\ 0&1&1&0 \\ 0&0&1&0 \\ 0&1&0&1 \end{bmatrix},$$

and the constants as

$$d = \begin{bmatrix} 0&0&0&1 \end{bmatrix}, e = \begin{bmatrix} 0&1&0&1 \end{bmatrix}.$$

A.2   Seven-Sharing of $G(x, y, z, w)$

For each share $i \in \{1, ..., 7\}$, the permutation $G(x, y, z, w)$ is shared as

$$\begin{aligned}
G_1^i &= x^i + y^i z^i + y^i z^{i+1} + y^{i+1} z^i + y^i z^{i+3} + y^{i+3} z^i + y^{i+1} z^{i+3} + y^{i+3} z^{i+1} \\
&\quad + y^i w^i + y^i w^{i+1} + y^{i+1} w^i + y^i w^{i+3} + y^{i+3} w^i + y^{i+1} w^{i+3} + y^{i+3} w^{i+1}, \\
G_2^i &= w^i + x^i y^i + x^i y^{i+1} + x^{i+1} y^i + x^i y^{i+3} + x^{i+3} y^i + x^{i+1} y^{i+3} + x^{i+3} y^{i+1}, \\
G_3^i &= y^i, \\
G_4^i &= z^i + y^i w^i + y^i w^{i+1} + y^{i+1} w^i + y^i w^{i+3} + y^{i+3} w^i + y^{i+1} w^{i+3} + y^{i+3} w^{i+1},
\end{aligned}$$

where the convention is used that superscripts wrap around at seven.

A.3 Three-Sharing of $G(x, y, z, w)$

For each share $i \in \{1, 2, 3\}$, the permutation $G(x, y, z, w)$ is shared as

$$G_1^i = x^i + y^i z^i + y^i z^{i+1} + y^{i+1} z^i + y^i w^i + y^i w^{i+1} + y^{i+1} w^i,$$
$$G_2^i = w^i + x^i y^i + x^i y^{i+1} + x^{i+1} y^i,$$
$$G_3^i = y^i,$$
$$G_4^i = z^i + y^i w^i + y^i w^{i+1} + y^{i+1} w^i,$$

where the convention is used that superscripts wrap around at three. Whereas the above sharing is verified to be uniform, it is not second-order non-complete. Instead one can achieve second-order probing security by calculating each cross product separately, XORing them with randomness, and finally registering the result. Afterwards, one then re-compresses the cross products back to 3 output shares. In case one uses static randomness, further analyses should be performed to ensure the security of the construction.

The above sharing was verified to have a maximal absolute correlation of 2^{-2}. In case randomness is used to make the sharing second-order probing secure, one should re-verify this correlation for all possible choices of the static randomness.

A.4 Improved Linear Properties

The following method can be used to improve the linear properties of the shared S-box from Appendix A.2. A sharing $\bar{P}$ of the identity function is composed with the S-box such that $\bar{S}_2 \circ \bar{P} \circ \bar{S}_1$ is still a sharing of the PRESENT S-box. One can choose any permutation $\bar{P}$ and verify the linear properties of $\bar{S}_2 \circ \bar{P} \circ \bar{S}_1$. As an example, we consider a function which adds the first shared output bit of $\bar{S}_1$ to the second and third bits. The addition of the shares is done such that correctness still holds. More specifically, for each share $i \in \{1, ..., 7\}$, the permutation $\bar{P}(\bar{x}, \bar{y}, \bar{z}, \bar{w})$ is

$$P_1^i = x^i \qquad P_2^i = y^i + x^i + x^{i+1} \qquad P_3^i = z^i + x^i + x^{i+1} \qquad P_4^i = w^i,$$

where the convention is used that superscripts wrap around at seven.

Since $\bar{P}$ is a permutation, it is clearly uniform. Additionally, $\bar{P}$ is second-order non-complete. This choice of $\bar{P}$ ensures that one can not find an optimal trail with 2^{-3} through the shared S-box. From experiments, we conclude that the maximum absolute correlation of $\bar{S}_2 \circ \bar{P} \circ \bar{S}_1$ is $2^{-4.3}$. Again, due to resource constraints, the experiment was limited to the verification for one choice of static randomness.

Whereas the addition of $\bar{P}$ significantly increases our security margin, it requires an extra register stage as $\bar{P} \circ \bar{S}_1$ nor $\bar{S}_2 \circ \bar{P}$ is second-order non-complete. A more thorough search for a better permutation could result in a further increase in security as well as potential performance improvements.

B   Seven-Sharing of the Prince S-Box

Moradi and Schneider [33] show that the inverse PRINCE S-box can be decomposed as

$$S^{-1} = D \circ \mathcal{Q}_{294} \circ C \circ \mathcal{Q}_{294} \circ B \circ \mathcal{Q}_{294} \circ A,$$

with A, B, C, D affine layers and $\mathcal{Q}_{294}$ a representative of a particular affine equivalence class. The affine layers with input (x, y, z, w) are given as follows

$$
\begin{array}{llll}
A_1 = y & A_2 = x & A_3 = z & A_4 = 1 + x + w, \\
B_1 = w & B_2 = z & B_3 = 1 + y & B_4 = 1 + x, \\
C_1 = z & C_2 = z + w & C_3 = y & C_4 = x + y, \\
D_1 = x + y & D_2 = 1 + x + z & D_3 = y + w & D_4 = z.
\end{array}
$$

We can write $S = E \circ S^{-1} \circ E$ with E,

$$E_1 = 1 + x + y + w \qquad E_2 = 1 + x \qquad E_3 = z \qquad E_4 = 1 + z.$$

The above affine layers are straightforwardly shares by applying the functions to each share separately. The algebraic normal form of $\mathcal{Q}_{294}(x, y, z, w)$ is given by

$$Q_1 = x \qquad Q_2 = y \qquad Q_3 = xy + z \qquad Q_4 = xz + w.$$

This function is shared into 7 shares by

$$
\begin{aligned}
Q_1^i &= x^i, \\
Q_2^i &= y^i, \\
Q_3^i &= z^i + x^i y^i + x^i y^{i+1} + x^{i+1} y^i + x^i y^{i+3} + x^{i+3} y^i + x^{i+1} y^{i+3} + x^{i+3} y^{i+1}, \\
Q_4^i &= w^i + x^i z^i + x^i z^{i+1} + x^{i+1} z^i + x^i z^{i+3} + x^{i+3} z^i + x^{i+1} z^{i+3} + x^{i+3} z^{i+1},
\end{aligned}
$$

for the shares $i \in \{1, ..., 7\}$, where the convention is used that superscripts wrap around at seven. The above sharing is verified to be second-order non-complete and uniform.

The sharing is made second-order probing secure by adding two layers of static randomness between the nonlinear functions.

C   Entropy Estimators and Software Details

On GitLab one can find software to measure the entropy of probed values in a C simulation of the masked LED from Sect. 7 [40]. The software accepts six arguments specifying which round, operation, and share each probe targets. The best probing location, giving the most advantage to the adversary, is found by searching for the best trails in the masked cipher. For example, the bottom curve of Fig. 8 is related to the first activity pattern of Fig. 7. As discussed in Sect. 7.5, this activity pattern would constitute a promising trail.

Further-on, the entropy estimator used in the simulation is discussed. Since the variance of the estimator scales exponentially with the number of observed bits, significantly more samples are needed to get a narrow confidence interval if more bits are observed. Note that in our experiments, we used 2^{19} samples. However, given sufficient computational power, this number is easily increased.

The reader is encouraged to verify our results using the C simulation for their own choice of probe locations and sample size.

C.1 Entropy Estimation and Confidence Intervals

To estimate the entropy of an m-bit random variable given N samples with replacement, we use the straightforward 'plug-in' estimator with first-order bias correction. One first estimates the probability $\mathbf{q}(x)$ of each observation $x \in \mathbb{F}_2^m$ by counting the number of occurrences of each x in the sample. Note that $\mathbb{E}\,\mathbf{q} = p$ where p is the true probability distribution. The entropy can then be estimated as

$$\hat{\mathbf{H}} = - \sum_{x \in \mathbb{F}_2^m} \mathbf{q}(x) \log_2 \mathbf{q}(x).$$

Unfortunately, this results in a negatively biased estimator with bias $\Omega(1/N)$. Specifically, taking a Taylor series expansion, one gets

$$\mathbb{E}\,\hat{\mathbf{H}} = H - \frac{1}{2N} \sum_{x \in \mathbb{F}_2^m} \frac{\mathrm{Var}\,[\mathbf{q}(x)]}{p(x)} + \mathcal{O}(1/N^2).$$

Since $\mathrm{Var}\,[\mathbf{q}(x)] = p(x)(p(x)+1)$, we obtain

$$\mathbb{E}\,\hat{\mathbf{H}} = H - \frac{2^m + 1}{2N} + \mathcal{O}(1/N^2).$$

For the variance, a similar but more technical argument [3] shows that

$$\mathrm{Var}\,\hat{\mathbf{H}} = -\frac{H^2}{N} + \frac{1}{N} \sum_{x \in \mathbb{F}_2^m} p(x) \log_2^2 p(x) + \mathcal{O}(1/N^2).$$

For the bias-corrected estimator, the variance is thus

$$\sigma^2 = \frac{(2^m + 1)^2}{4N^2} - \frac{H^2}{N} + \frac{1}{N} \sum_{x \in \mathbb{F}_2^m} p(x) \log_2^2 p(x) + \mathcal{O}(1/N^2).$$

Assuming asymptotic normality, an asymptotic two-sized 95% confidence interval can be estimated obtained by adding $\pm 1.96\sigma$ to the estimate.

References

1. Barthe, G., Belaïd, S., Cassiers, G., Fouque, P.-A., Grégoire, B., Standaert, F.-X.: maskVerif: automated verification of higher-order masking in presence of physical defaults. In: Sako, K., Schneider, S., Ryan, P.Y.A. (eds.) ESORICS 2019, Part I. LNCS, vol. 11735, pp. 300–318. Springer, Cham (2019). https://doi.org/10.1007/978-3-030-29959-0_15

2. Barthe, G., Belaïd, S., Dupressoir, F., Fouque, P.-A., Grégoire, B., Strub, P.-Y.: Verified proofs of higher-order masking. In: Oswald, E., Fischlin, M. (eds.) EURO-CRYPT 2015, Part I. LNCS, vol. 9056, pp. 457–485. Springer, Heidelberg (2015). https://doi.org/10.1007/978-3-662-46800-5_18

3. Basharin, G.P.: On a statistical estimate for the entropy of a sequence of independent random variables. Theory Probab. Appl. **4**(3), 333–336 (1959)

4. Beyne, T.: Block cipher invariants as eigenvectors of correlation matrices. In: Peyrin, T., Galbraith, S. (eds.) ASIACRYPT 2018, Part I. LNCS, vol. 11272, pp. 3–31. Springer, Cham (2018). https://doi.org/10.1007/978-3-030-03326-2_1

5. Beyne, T.: Linear cryptanalysis in the weak key model (2019). https://homes.esat.kuleuven.be/~tbeyne/masterthesis/thesis.pdf

6. Bilgin, B., Gierlichs, B., Nikova, S., Nikov, V., Rijmen, V.: Higher-order threshold implementations. In: Sarkar, P., Iwata, T. (eds.) ASIACRYPT 2014, Part II. LNCS, vol. 8874, pp. 326–343. Springer, Heidelberg (2014). https://doi.org/10.1007/978-3-662-45608-8_18

7. Bilgin, B., Gierlichs, B., Nikova, S., Nikov, V., Rijmen, V.: Trade-offs for threshold implementations illustrated on AES. IEEE Trans. CAD Integr. Circuits Syst. **34**(7), 1188–1200 (2015)

8. Bilgin, B., Nikova, S., Nikov, V., Rijmen, V., Stütz, G.: Threshold implementations of All 3 ×3 and 4 ×4 S-boxes. In: Prouff, E., Schaumont, P. (eds.) CHES 2012. LNCS, vol. 7428, pp. 76–91. Springer, Heidelberg (2012). https://doi.org/10.1007/978-3-642-33027-8_5

9. Bogdanov, A., et al.: PRESENT: an ultra-lightweight block cipher. In: Paillier, P., Verbauwhede, I. (eds.) CHES 2007. LNCS, vol. 4727, pp. 450–466. Springer, Heidelberg (2007). https://doi.org/10.1007/978-3-540-74735-2_31

10. Borghoff, J., et al.: PRINCE – a low-latency block cipher for pervasive computing applications. In: Wang, X., Sako, K. (eds.) ASIACRYPT 2012. LNCS, vol. 7658, pp. 208–225. Springer, Heidelberg (2012). https://doi.org/10.1007/978-3-642-34961-4_14

11. Carlet, C., Crama, Y., Hammer, P.L.: Boolean functions for cryptography and error correcting codes. Boolean Model. Methods Math. Comput. Sci. Eng. **2**, 257–397 (2010)

12. Chari, S., Jutla, C.S., Rao, J.R., Rohatgi, P.: Towards sound approaches to counteract power-analysis attacks. In: Wiener, M. (ed.) CRYPTO 1999. LNCS, vol. 1666, pp. 398–412. Springer, Heidelberg (1999). https://doi.org/10.1007/3-540-48405-1_26

13. Cho, J.Y.: Linear cryptanalysis of reduced-round PRESENT. In: Pieprzyk, J. (ed.) CT-RSA 2010. LNCS, vol. 5985, pp. 302–317. Springer, Heidelberg (2010). https://doi.org/10.1007/978-3-642-11925-5_21

14. Coron, J.-S., Prouff, E., Rivain, M., Roche, T.: Higher-order side channel security and mask refreshing. In: Moriai, S. (ed.) FSE 2013. LNCS, vol. 8424, pp. 410–424. Springer, Heidelberg (2014). https://doi.org/10.1007/978-3-662-43933-3_21

15. Daemen, J.: Spectral characterization of iterating lossy mappings. In: Carlet, C., Hasan, M.A., Saraswat, V. (eds.) SPACE 2016. LNCS, vol. 10076, pp. 159–178. Springer, Cham (2016). https://doi.org/10.1007/978-3-319-49445-6_9

16. Daemen, J.: Changing of the guards: a simple and efficient method for achieving uniformity in threshold sharing. In: Fischer, W., Homma, N. (eds.) CHES 2017. LNCS, vol. 10529, pp. 137–153. Springer, Cham (2017). https://doi.org/10.1007/978-3-319-66787-4_7

17. Daemen, J., Govaerts, R., Vandewalle, J.: Correlation matrices. In: Preneel, B. (ed.) FSE 1994. LNCS, vol. 1008, pp. 275–285. Springer, Heidelberg (1995). https://doi.org/10.1007/3-540-60590-8_21

18. Daemen, J., Rijmen, V.: The wide trail design strategy. In: Honary, B. (ed.) Cryptography and Coding 2001. LNCS, vol. 2260, pp. 222–238. Springer, Heidelberg (2001). https://doi.org/10.1007/3-540-45325-3_20

19. Daemen, J., Rijmen, V.: Advanced Encryption Standard (AES). National Institute of Standards and Technology (NIST), FIPS PUB 197, U.S. Department of Commerce, November 2001

20. De Meyer, L., Wegener, F., Moradi, A.: A note on masking generic Boolean functions. Cryptology ePrint Archive, Report 2019/1247 (2019). https://eprint.iacr.org/2019/1247

21. Dhooghe, S., Nikova, S., Rijmen, V.: Threshold implementations in the robust probing model. In: Bilgin, B., Petkova-Nikova, S., Rijmen, V. (eds.) Proceedings of ACM Workshop on Theory of Implementation Security Workshop, TIS@CCS 2019, London, UK, 11 November 2019, pp. 30–37. ACM (2019). https://doi.org/10.1145/3338467.3358949

22. Diaconis, P.: Group Representations in Probability and Statistics. Lecture Notes-Monograph Series, vol. 11. Institute of Mathematical Statistics, Hayward, CA (1988). https://doi.org/10.1214/lnms/1215467418

23. Faust, S., Grosso, V., Pozo, S.M.D., Paglialonga, C., Standaert, F.X.: Composable masking schemes in the presence of physical defaults & the robust probing model. IACR TCHES **2018**(3), 89–120 (2018). https://doi.org/10.13154/tches.v2018.i3.89-120. https://tches.iacr.org/index.php/TCHES/article/view/7270

24. Faust, S., Paglialonga, C., Schneider, T.: Amortizing randomness complexity in private circuits. In: Takagi, T., Peyrin, T. (eds.) ASIACRYPT 2017, Part I. LNCS, vol. 10624, pp. 781–810. Springer, Cham (2017). https://doi.org/10.1007/978-3-319-70694-8_27

25. Goubin, L., Patarin, J.: DES and differential power analysis the "duplication" method. In: Koç, Ç.K., Paar, C. (eds.) CHES 1999. LNCS, vol. 1717, pp. 158–172. Springer, Heidelberg (1999). https://doi.org/10.1007/3-540-48059-5_15

26. Guo, J., Peyrin, T., Poschmann, A.: The PHOTON family of lightweight hash functions. In: Rogaway, P. (ed.) CRYPTO 2011. LNCS, vol. 6841, pp. 222–239. Springer, Heidelberg (2011). https://doi.org/10.1007/978-3-642-22792-9_13

27. Guo, J., Peyrin, T., Poschmann, A., Robshaw, M.: The LED block cipher. In: Preneel, B., Takagi, T. (eds.) CHES 2011. LNCS, vol. 6917, pp. 326–341. Springer, Heidelberg (2011). https://doi.org/10.1007/978-3-642-23951-9_22

28. Ishai, Y., Sahai, A., Wagner, D.: Private circuits: securing hardware against probing attacks. In: Boneh, D. (ed.) CRYPTO 2003. LNCS, vol. 2729, pp. 463–481. Springer, Heidelberg (2003). https://doi.org/10.1007/978-3-540-45146-4_27

29. Kocher, P., Jaffe, J., Jun, B.: Differential power analysis. In: Wiener, M. (ed.) CRYPTO 1999. LNCS, vol. 1666, pp. 388–397. Springer, Heidelberg (1999). https://doi.org/10.1007/3-540-48405-1_25

30. Kutzner, S., Nguyen, P.H., Poschmann, A., Wang, H.: On 3-share threshold implementations for 4-bit s-boxes. In: Prouff, E. (ed.) COSADE 2013. LNCS, vol. 7864, pp. 99–113. Springer, Heidelberg (2013). https://doi.org/10.1007/978-3-642-40026-1_7

31. Mangard, S., Pramstaller, N., Oswald, E.: Successfully attacking masked AES hardware implementations. In: Rao, J.R., Sunar, B. (eds.) CHES 2005. LNCS, vol. 3659, pp. 157–171. Springer, Heidelberg (2005). https://doi.org/10.1007/11545262_12

32. Moos, T., Moradi, A., Schneider, T., Standaert, F.X.: Glitch-resistant masking revisited. IACR TCHES **2019**(2), 256–292 (2019). https://doi.org/10.13154/tches. v2019.i2.256-292. https://tches.iacr.org/index.php/TCHES/article/view/7392

33. Moradi, A., Schneider, T.: Side-channel analysis protection and low-latency in action. In: Cheon, J.H., Takagi, T. (eds.) ASIACRYPT 2016, Part I. LNCS, vol. 10031, pp. 517–547. Springer, Heidelberg (2016). https://doi.org/10.1007/978-3-662-53887-6_19

34. Moradi, A., Wild, A.: Assessment of hiding the higher-order leakages in hardware - what are the achievements versus overheads? In: Güneysu, T., Handschuh, H. (eds.) CHES 2015. LNCS, vol. 9293, pp. 453–474. Springer, Heidelberg (2015). https://doi.org/10.1007/978-3-662-48324-4_23

35. Nikova, S., Rechberger, C., Rijmen, V.: Threshold implementations against side-channel attacks and glitches. In: Ning, P., Qing, S., Li, N. (eds.) ICICS 2006. LNCS, vol. 4307, pp. 529–545. Springer, Heidelberg (2006). https://doi.org/10.1007/11935308_38

36. Reparaz, O.: A note on the security of higher-order threshold implementations. Cryptology ePrint Archive, Report 2015/001 (2015). http://eprint.iacr.org/2015/001

37. Reparaz, O., Bilgin, B., Nikova, S., Gierlichs, B., Verbauwhede, I.: Consolidating masking schemes. In: Gennaro, R., Robshaw, M. (eds.) CRYPTO 2015, Part I. LNCS, vol. 9215, pp. 764–783. Springer, Heidelberg (2015). https://doi.org/10.1007/978-3-662-47989-6_37

38. Serre, J.-P.: Linear Representations of Finite Groups. GTM, vol. 42. Springer, New York (1977). https://doi.org/10.1007/978-1-4684-9458-7

39. Wegener, F., Baiker, C., Moradi, A.: Shuffle and mix: on the diffusion of randomness in threshold implementations of KECCAK. In: Polian, I., Stöttinger, M. (eds.) COSADE 2019. LNCS, vol. 11421, pp. 270–284. Springer, Cham (2019). https://doi.org/10.1007/978-3-030-16350-1_15

40. Zhang, Z.: LED_SHARING (2020). https://gitlab.esat.kuleuven.be/Zhenda. Zhang/LED_SHARING

Packed Multiplication: How to Amortize the Cost of Side-Channel Masking?

Weijia Wang[1,2,3], Chun Guo[1,2,3(✉)], François-Xavier Standaert[4], Yu Yu[5,6(✉)], and Gaëtan Cassiers[4]

[1] School of Cyber Science and Technology, Shandong University,
Qingdao 266237, China
{wjwang,chun.guo}@sdu.edu.cn
[2] Key Laboratory of Cryptologic Technology and Information Security of Ministry
of Education, Shandong University, Qingdao 266237, China
[3] State Key Laboratory of Information Security (Institute of Information
Engineering), Chinese Academy of Sciences, Beijing 100093, China
[4] Institute of Information and Communication Technologies, Electronics and Applied
Mathematics (ICTEAM), UCLouvain, 1348 Louvain-la-Neuve, Belgium
{francois-xavier.standaert,gaetan.cassiers}@uclouvain.be
[5] Department of Computer Science and Engineering, Shanghai Jiao Tong University,
Shanghai 200240, China
yuyu@yuyu.hk
[6] Shanghai Qizhi Institute, Shanghai 200232, China

Abstract. Higher-order masking countermeasures provide strong provable security against side-channel attacks at the cost of incurring significant overheads, which largely hinders its applicability. Previous works towards remedying cost mostly concentrated on "local" calculations, i.e., optimizing the cost of computation units such as a single AND gate or a field multiplication. This paper explores a complementary "global" approach, i.e., considering multiple operations in the masked domain as a batch and reducing randomness and computational cost via amortization. In particular, we focus on the amortization of ℓ parallel field multiplications for appropriate integer $\ell > 1$, and design a kit named *packed multiplication* for implementing such a batch. For $\ell + d \leq 2^m$, when ℓ parallel multiplications over $\mathbb{F}_{2^m}$ with d-th order probing security are implemented, packed multiplication consumes $d^2 + 2\ell d + \ell$ bilinear multiplications and $2d^2 + d(d+1)/2$ random field variables, outperforming the state-of-the-art results with $O(\ell d^2)$ multiplications and $\ell \lfloor d^2/4 \rfloor + \ell d$ randomness. To prove d-probing security for packed multiplications, we introduce some weaker security notions for multiple-inputs-multiple-outputs gadgets and use them as intermediate steps, which may be of independent interest. As parallel field multiplications exist almost everywhere in symmetric cryptography, lifting optimizations from "local" to "global" substantially enlarges the space of improvements. To demonstrate, we showcase the method on the AES Subbytes step, GCM and TET (a popular disk encryption). Notably, when $d = 8$, our implementation of AES Subbytes in ARM Cortex M architecture achieves a gain

© International Association for Cryptologic Research 2020
S. Moriai and H. Wang (Eds.): ASIACRYPT 2020, LNCS 12491, pp. 851–880, 2020.
https://doi.org/10.1007/978-3-030-64837-4_28

of up to 33% in total speeds and saves up to 68% random bits than the state-of-the-art bitsliced implementation reported at ASIACRYPT 2018.

1   Introduction

Side-channel attacks that exploit leakage emitting from devices pose an important threat for cryptographic implementations. Masking [14,26] is one of the most investigated protection techniques. The core idea is to randomly split each secret-dependent variable into a vector of $d+1$ shares called *sharing*, and then implements the cryptographic algorithm over sharings instead of the raw secrets. This ensures that the initial secret cannot be rebuilt from any less than d intermediate variables in the implementation, which is called *d-private security* (a.k.a. *d-probing security*).[1]

To have secure functionalities over sharings, a masking scheme, or a *private circuit*, firstly constructs *gadgets* for various elementary calculations over sharings, and then compose the gadgets to reach the desired functionality. Obviously, to improve efficiency, it is crucial to have better gadgets (particularly for multiplications). This has motivated plenty of works concentrating on e.g., reducing the randomness complexity [5,6,12,28], and securing processing dependent inputs [12,20].

Recently proposed masking schemes are typically accomplished by *formal proofs* of the aforementioned *d-private security* notion. To establish this notion, the naive method is to show that the possible tuples of intermediate variables are all independent of the secret by enumeration. Though, such an enumeration becomes intricate as the size of function grows, and it is only feasible for small circuits such as a single multiplication gadget. This naturally motivates the composition approach, i.e., proving that under certain conditions, a large circuit built upon *d*-private gadgets is *d*-private. In this respect, several composable security notions have been introduced, such as the notions of *d*-Non-Inference (NI) and *d*-Strong Non-Inference (SNI) [2]. Thanks to those security notions, a composition of gadgets with some refreshing added in-between, can be proved to be globally *d*-private secure.

Besides the above foundational advances, the past two decades have also witnessed the rapid efficiency improvement of masking schemes. Despite these, higher-order masking with many shares remains of limited use due to the overhead, especially in the resource-constraint environment [19,27]. *It is still compelling and challenging to decrease the complexity of masking schemes.*

Local Versus Global Efficiency Optimization. As discussed before, the community has devoted to designing better gadgets [5,6,12,28] due to their fundamental influences on the high-level circuits. In fact, to our knowledge, modulo a few exceptions that will be discussed later, most of the prior works only concentrated

---

[1] While the leakages of all the $d+1$ shares enable reconstruction of information theoretically, the intrinsic noise in the leakages renders secret recovery infeasible in practice [14,17,21,33].

on "local" optimizations, i.e., on reducing the complexity of individual elementary calculation such as an S-box or even a single AND gate. This "local" approach considerably simplifies the situation and enables pushing the limits of gadgets. At the same time, by the aforementioned composition framework, this naturally results in high-level circuits with better performance and provable security.

On the other hand, note that cryptographic algorithms typically consist of executing a basic function for many times in parallel. For example, the AES (more generally, virtually all the block ciphers except for the so-called ARX designs) evaluates an S-box for 16 times within each round. And, at a higher level, many modes of operations are explicitly designed to support running several primitives in parallel. For instance, the Counter (CTR) mode encrypts several blocks in parallel, and the Galois/Counter Mode (GCM) combines the CTR mode with a structure consisting of several field multiplications in parallel.

Facing this situation, this paper takes a complementary "global" view, considers multiple such parallel functions as a batch, and seeks for optimizations within such batches. This switch enables many possibilities of improvements that used to be excluded in the classical "local" optimizations. In particular, the presence of multiple calculations naturally motivates using the *amortization* technique, which aims at *reducing the averaged complexity for the masking of several operations*.

While the idea of "global" optimization via amortizing appears natural, the technique of security proof is quite non-trivial. Particularly, due to amortization, various operations in the same batch now share randomness or intermediate variables, and thus cannot be analyzed independently. To cope with this difficulty, in our security analysis, we will treat parallel operations in the same batch as a whole, and consider the corresponding *gadgets with multiple input and output sharings (shorted as MIMO gadgets in the rest of the paper)*. This shift of viewpoint clearly excludes NI/SNI as the security goal. Informally speaking, any composition of d-NI and d-SNI gadgets is still d-SNI if each sharing is used at most once as input of any d-NI gadget and the input sharings of a gadget come from different gadgets. Designing secure circuits under this condition may requires many refresh gadgets, which are expensive. Therefore, new security notions for MIMO gadgets are required.

1.1   Our Contributions

We investigate global optimizations within batches of several field multiplications.[2] The concrete technique is to amortize the randomness and computational costs of several parallel masked multiplications. As a result, we propose a new construction named *packed multiplication*, which computes ℓ masked multiplications in parallel for any integer $\ell \geq 1$. Then, in order to prove security for our scheme, we introduce a new set of security notions for MIMO gadgets. We finally demonstrate potential applications and showcase the packed multiplication method on AES, Galois/Counter Mode (GCM) [30], and a popular disk

---

[2] Note that the AND gate can be viewed as the field multiplication in $\mathbb{F}_2$.

encryption scheme TET (which is short for linear-Transformation; ECB; linear-Transformation) [23]. We details these contributions below.

Packed Multiplication. To maximize the efficiency of linear gadgets, this paper concentrates on Boolean sharings (a.k.a. additive sharings) over the finite field $\mathbb{F}_q$ of characteristic 2, meaning that the XOR of the shares equals the initial secret. In this setting, a packed multiplication scheme takes two vectors of ℓ Boolean sharings as inputs, which encode the 2ℓ inputs of the ℓ field multiplications, and gives ℓ Boolean sharings as outputs encoding the ℓ multiplication results, as depicted in Fig. 1 (right). Packed multiplication proceeds in two steps. First, each input vector is (re)encoded as a "packed" sharing using a randomized linear code. When the field size $q \geq \ell+d$, each resulted "packed" sharing consists of only $\ell+d$ shares in total, meaning that the size of data is compressed from $\ell(d+1)$ to $\ell+d$. Second, a multiplication over the packed sharings is calculated, resulting in Boolean sharings (the number of result shares is $\ell(d+1)$). This step can be seen as a batch of ℓ masked local multiplications *sharing* some randomness and intermediate results. Besides, our scheme is compatible even when the field size $q \leq \ell+d$, at the cost of raising the number of shares, say n, to $n > d+1$ with security order d, as long as the linear codes of length $\ell+n-1$ with dual distance $d+1$ exist.

In contrast, following the classical "local" approach, the two input vectors are viewed as ℓ pairs of sharings, and each of the ℓ pairs is processed independently, as shown in Fig. 1 (left). As mentioned before, such independence simplifies security analysis at the expense of limiting optimizations to local. For a more complete comparison, we consider the setting of masking ℓ parallel multiplications, and list the complexities of packed multiplication and some other popular schemes in Table 1, where the complexity of our scheme is typical estimated when the field size $q \geq \ell+d$. In the comparison, we regard the number of bilinear multiplications (i.e., of general multiplications of two non-constant variables in the finite field) and the number of random elements as the metrics for computational [6] and randomness complexities respectively.

Towards Provable Security. Packed multiplication schemes produce MIMO gadgets. For their provable security, Cassiers el al. introduced a stronger variant of SNI named Multiple-Inputs/Multiple-Outputs Strong Non-Inference (MIMO-SNI) [13]. They also introduced Probe Isolating Non-Interference (PINI) [13] notion that enables the building of more efficient gadgets. Unfortunately, both MIMO-SNI and PINI are too strong and could not be achieved by ours. To rescue, we identify a set of intermediate composable security notions for MIMO gadgets that interpolates between the stronger MIMO-SNI and the weaker (S)NI. In addition, ours are orthogonal to PINI. We refer to Fig. 2 for an illustration. With the new notions, our gadgets can be securely composed with each other, either by satisfying our specialized composition theorem, or through direct proof in the probe propagation framework introduced in [5,11].

Applications. As parall multiplications exist almost everywhere in symmetric cryptography, our packed multiplication has potentially broad applicability and deep impact. To demonstrate, we showcase the method on the *AES Subbytes step* and *the polynomial-evaluation hash*.

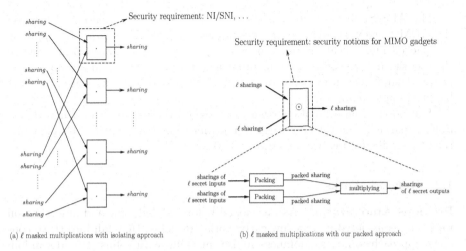

(a) ℓ masked multiplications with isolating approach

(b) ℓ masked multiplications with our packed approach

Fig. 1. Packed multiplication in general (right) and the comparison with classical isolating approach (left).

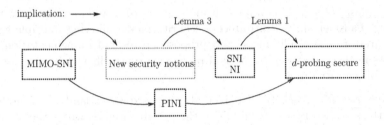

Fig. 2. Relations among different security notions.

Table 1. Complexities of ℓ parallel multiplications with security order d

		Computational complexity	Randomness complexity
Our scheme	**Packing**	**0**	d^2
	Multiplying	$d^2 + 2\ell d + \ell$	$d(d+1)/2$
	Total	$d^2 + 2\ell d + \ell$	$2d^2 + d(d+1)/2$
Tight private circuits [26]		$\ell d^2 + 2\ell d + \ell$	$\ell d(d+1)/2$
Masking with reduced randomness [5]		$\ell d^2 + 2\ell d + \ell$	$\ell(d + \lfloor d^2/4 \rfloor)$
Multiplication over finite fields[a]	[6, Algorithm 4]	$2\ell d + \ell$	$\ell(2d^2 + d(d+1)/2)$
	[6, Algorithm 5]	$\ell d^2 + 2\ell d + \ell$	ℓd
Code-based masking [38]		$d^2 + 2\ell d + \ell^2$	$2d(d + \ell)$

[a] Despite the small instantiations for $d \leq 4$ [28], it requires large enough finite fields, e.g., the field size $q > d(d+1)\Delta(12d)^d$ [6, Theorem 5.4]

The AES Subbytes step consists of parallel S-boxes evaluations. Based on the ARM Cortex M architecture, we implement 16 AES S-boxes by applying the packed multiplication and report the performance results. Notably, when the security order is of $d = 8$, our implementation achieves a gain of up to 33% in speeds and saves up to 68% random bits compared with the state-of-the-art bitsliced implementation [9].

The polynomial-evaluation hash involves a structure of several multiplications in parallel, and thus our packed multiplication is well suited. This benefits the SCA resilience for two scenarios: GCM and TET.

1.2 Related Works

Previous Amortization. As mentioned before, global view and amortization were only considered in very few early works. Roughly, they fall into three concrete approaches, i.e., randomness re-use, masking with robust Pseudorandom Generator (PRG) and the code-based masking. The former two approaches aim at amortization of randomness rather than reducing computational cost, while the last addresses both.

Randomness Re-use. This approach aims at re-using random bits in different gadgets. Faust et al. [18] introduce a security model allowing multiple gadgets to securely re-use randomness, and proposed threshold implementation-based gadgets in their model. This method provides a quite efficient scheme for small values of security order.

Masking with Robust PRGs. Ishai et al. proposed to expand the randomness using the so-called robust PRG [25] in the private circuits, where the number of True Random Number Generator (TRNG) calls for seeds is independent of the circuit size. A recent work of Coron et al. describes a quite practical construction in this direction [15], where the number of random bits is only $\tilde{O}(t^2)$ for security against t probes. This strategy can be regarded as a certain form of amortization (of TRNG calls), but it is a bit of orthogonal to ours. In contrast, we consider the amortization of both randomness and computational costs.

Code-Based Masking. It was recently shown by Wang et al. [38] that the general type of masking called code-based masking is able to encode multiple secrets together into one codeword and calculate parallel operations over these secrets together in the masked domain. Admittedly, the packed multiplication proposed in this paper shares some ideas with the code-based masking. But we give a practical and much more efficient scheme. Notably, our scheme generally works with Boolean sharings, which enables more efficient masked linear operations. In contrast, the code-based masking proposed in [38] was a generic scheme, whose further specification and optimization were left as an open problem. We give a complexity comparison in Table 1 to highlight the improvement of our scheme.

Polynomial masking with packed secret sharing technique [22] can be regarded as a variant of the code-based masking, and its multiplications are performed based on the MPC protocol of Damgård et al. [16]. This scheme however requires a heavy random generation process that becomes an efficiency bottleneck.

Security Notions for MIMO Gadgets. Cassiers el al. introduced a stronger variant of SNI named Multiple-Inputs/Multiple-Outputs Strong Non-Inference (MIMO-SNI) [13].[3] Though, MIMO-SNI gadget comes at a higher complexity compared to the SNI ones. They also introduced the Probe Isolating Non-Interference (PINI) [13] notion that enables the building of more efficient gadgets. Informally speaking, a composition of multiple gadgets is d-PINI (resp., d-MIMO-SNI) if every gadget is d-PINI (resp., d-MIMO-SNI). In addition, d-PINI (resp., d-MIMO-SNI) alone implies the d-private security. Unfortunately, these two notions are both too strong for our new multiplication gadget. For this reason, we will propose in Sect. 3 a set of new security notions that bridge our new gadgets to the probing security.

1.3 Organization

In the remainder of this paper, we present notations and necessary notions in Sect. 2. We then introduce our new security notions in Sect. 3. We propose the packed multiplication in Sect. 4, and in Sect. 5 propose a construction of the linear operations that complies with the new security notions. Sect. 7 illustrates the applications.

2 Preliminary

2.1 Notations

In the following, we denote by $\mathbb{F}_q$ a characteristic 2 finite field, where $q = 2^m$ for any $m \geq 1$, and denote field elements by lower-case letters. We use $\oplus$ to denote plus over the finite field. For simplicity, we use $\sum$ for the summation over any fields or rings. For a natural number n we denote by $[n]$ the set of integers from 1 to n both included. Let calligraphies (e.g., $\mathcal{I}$) be sets, and $|\mathcal{I}|$ denote the length of the set $\mathcal{I}$. Let bold lower cases (e.g., $\mathbf{x}$) be the vectors over $\mathbb{F}_q^{|\mathbf{x}|}$, where $|\mathbf{x}|$ denotes the length of the vector, $\mathbf{x}[i]$ denotes the ith element of vector $\mathbf{x}$, and $\mathbf{x}[i:j]$ denotes the vector made up of ith to j^{th} elements of vector $\mathbf{x}$. Unless otherwise noted, we assume the vectors are row vectors in this paper, and the column vectors are denoted as $\mathbf{x}^{\text{T}}$.

Let bold capital letters (e.g., $\mathbf{A}$) be the matrices in $\mathbb{F}_q^{r \times c}$ (or $r \times c$ matrix), for row and column counts being r and c respectively. $\mathbf{A}[i,j]$ denotes the element of $\mathbf{A}$ at i^{th} row and j^{th} column, $\mathbf{A}[i,]$ (resp., $\mathbf{A}[,i]$) denotes the ith row (resp., column) of matrix $\mathbf{A}$, and $\mathbf{A}[i:j,]$ denotes the matrix made up of ith to j^{th} rows of $\mathbf{A}$. Let $\mathbf{A}^{\text{T}}$ denote the transpose of the matrix $\mathbf{A}$. For a $r \times c$ matrix $\mathbf{A}$ and

---

[3] The notion of MIMO gadgets shall be distinguished from MIMO-SNI: the former are gadgets with multiple input and output sharings, while the latter is a security model for MIMO gadgets.

a set $\mathcal{I} \subseteq [r]$ (resp., $\mathcal{J} \subseteq [c]$), $\mathbf{A}[\mathcal{I},]$ (resp., $\mathbf{A}[,\mathcal{J}]$) denotes the submatrix of $\mathbf{A}$ made up of the rows (resp., columns) indexed by $\mathcal{I}$ (resp., $\mathcal{J}$). For matrices $\mathbf{A}$ and $\mathbf{B}$, we denote their product as $\mathbf{A} \times \mathbf{B}$, or in short $\mathbf{AB}$ in non-ambiguous cases. Specifically, we use $\mathbf{O}^{r \times c}$ to denote the zero matrix in $\mathbb{F}_q^{r \times c}$ and $\mathbf{I}^n$ the identity matrix in $\mathbb{F}_q^{n \times n}$; to ease understanding, when there is no ambiguity, their superscripts will be omitted. For two matrices $\mathbf{A}$ and $\mathbf{B}$, $[\mathbf{A}, \mathbf{B}]$ is the concatenation of $\mathbf{A}$ and $\mathbf{B}$ by columns, and $[\mathbf{A}; \mathbf{B}]$ is the concatenation of $\mathbf{A}$ and $\mathbf{B}$ by rows. A set of n variables can be represented as $\{x_i\}_{i=1}^n \overset{\text{def}}{=} \{x_1, \ldots, x_n\}$, and this representation can be adopted for a set of vectors or matrices.

2.2   Private Circuits

We view a circuit C as a directed acyclic graph with gates and wires being vertices and edges respectively. We assume that the wires carry variables in $\mathbb{F}_q$ and the gates are elementary calculations over $\mathbb{F}_q$. A randomized circuit is a circuit augmented with random gates. A random gate is a gate that puts a random variable in its output wire. Variables carried in the wires of a circuit C are called intermediate variables of C. A probe to a circuit is an intermediate variable whose value is assumed to be revealed to the adversary. For a circuit C with input $\mathbf{x} \in \mathbb{F}_q^\ell$, $\mathsf{C}(\mathbf{x})$ produces the output $\mathbf{y} \in \mathbb{F}_q^{\ell'}$ that we denote $\mathsf{C}(\mathbf{x}) \overset{\text{def}}{=} \mathbf{y}$. And for a set $\mathcal{P}$ of probes, $\mathsf{C}_{\mathcal{P}}(\mathbf{x})$ returns the values of the probes by feeding $\mathbf{x}$ as the input of C. We call a set (or vector) of variables (say, $\mathbf{x}$) over $\mathbb{F}_q$ independent of the other vector of variables $\mathbf{y}$ if $\Pr(\mathbf{x} = \alpha \mid \mathbf{y} = \beta) = \Pr(\mathbf{x} = \alpha)$ for any value α of $\mathbf{x}$ and any value β of $\mathbf{y}$, where the probability is taken over the random coins used to generate these vectors.

We begin by recalling the notion of sharings, the basis of masking. We also provide our new notion of *packed sharing*. It should be noted that, for the notion of sharing, we let the number of shares be n (rather than $d+1$) for compatibility (of any field sizes) reason. As mentioned in the introduction, our scheme is also compatible with a small field size (i.e., $q < \ell + d$ with ℓ parallel multiplications), at the cost of raising the number of shares in a sharing to $n > d+1$ with security order d.

Definition 1 (Sharing and packed sharing). *For a variable $x \in \mathbb{F}_q$, we say $\hat{\mathbf{x}} \in \mathbb{F}_q^n$ is a sharing of x if there exists an encoder $\mathsf{Enc} : (\mathbb{F}_q, \mathbb{F}_q^{n-1}) \to \mathbb{F}_q^n$, a decoder $\mathsf{Dec} : \mathbb{F}_q^n \to \mathbb{F}_q$ and $\mathbf{r} \in \mathbb{F}_q^{n-1}$ such that $\hat{\mathbf{x}} = \mathsf{Enc}(x, \mathbf{r})$ and $x = \mathsf{Dec}(\hat{\mathbf{x}})$. Particularly, a sharing $\hat{\mathbf{x}}$ of x is called a Boolean sharing, if $x = \mathsf{Dec}(\hat{\mathbf{x}}) = \sum_{i=1}^n \hat{\mathbf{x}}[i]$.*

For $\ell > 1$ and a vector of variables $\mathbf{x} \in \mathbb{F}_q^\ell$, we say $(\tilde{\mathbf{x}}, \hat{\mathbf{u}}) \in (\mathbb{F}_q^\ell, \mathbb{F}_q^{n-1})$ is a packed sharing of $\mathbf{x}$ if there exists an encoder $\mathsf{Enc} : (\mathbb{F}_q^\ell, \mathbb{F}_q^{n-1}) \to (\mathbb{F}_q^\ell, \mathbb{F}_q^{n-1})$, a decoder $\mathsf{Dec} : (\mathbb{F}_q^\ell, \mathbb{F}_q^{n-1}) \to \mathbb{F}_q^\ell$ and $\mathbf{r} \in \mathbb{F}_q^{n-1}$ such that $(\tilde{\mathbf{x}}, \hat{\mathbf{u}}) = \mathsf{Enc}(\mathbf{x}, \mathbf{r})$ and $\mathbf{x} = \mathsf{Dec}(\tilde{\mathbf{x}}, \hat{\mathbf{u}})$. Moreover, an element of a packed sharing $(\tilde{\mathbf{x}}, \hat{\mathbf{u}})$ is an element of either $\tilde{\mathbf{x}}$ or $\hat{\mathbf{u}}$.

Elements of a sharing or packed sharing are called shares.

In the rest of the paper, unless explicitly stated, all sharings are Boolean sharings. We next recall the notion of private circuit compiler [26] as follows.

Definition 2 (Private circuit compiler [26]). *A private circuit compiler for a circuit C with input in $\mathbb{F}_q^\ell$ and output in $\mathbb{F}_q^{\ell'}$ is defined by a triple $(\mathsf{I}, \mathsf{T}, \mathsf{O})$ where*

- $\mathsf{I} : \mathbb{F}_q \to \mathbb{F}_q^n$, *is an encoder that randomly maps each input $x \in \mathbb{F}_q$ to a sharing.*
- T *is a circuit transformation whose input is circuit C, and output is a randomized circuit C' with ℓ sharings as the input, and ℓ' sharings as the output.*
- $\mathsf{O} : \mathbb{F}_q^n \to \mathbb{F}_q$ *is a decoder that maps each output sharing $\hat{\mathbf{z}} \in \mathbb{F}_q^n$ to the corresponding output $z \in \mathbb{F}_q$.*

We say that $(\mathsf{I}, \mathsf{T}, \mathsf{O})$ is a private circuit compiler and C' is a d-private circuit (or d-probing secure) if the following requirements hold:

- *Correctness: for any input $\mathbf{x} \in \mathbb{F}_q^\ell$, $\Pr\left(\mathsf{O}^\circ\big(C'(\mathsf{I}^\circ(\mathbf{x}))\big) = C(\mathbf{x})\right) = 1$, where I° (resp., O°) is a canonical encoder (resp., decoder) that encodes (resp., decodes) each element of input secrets $\mathbf{x}$ (resp., each sharing of output sharings) by repeatedly calling I (resp., O).*
- *Privacy: for any input $\mathbf{x} \in \mathbb{F}_q^\ell$ and any set of probes $\mathcal{P}$ such that $|\mathcal{P}| \leq d$, $C'_{\mathcal{P}}(\mathsf{I}(\mathbf{x}))$ are independent of the input $\mathbf{x}$, where d is called the security order.*

We consider the circuit transformation T realized by the composition of gadgets. An *gadget* is a randomized circuit whose inputs (resp., outputs) are either sharings or packed sharings. We say that a gadget G implements a function $f : \mathbb{F}_q^\ell \to \mathbb{F}_q^{\ell'}$, if and only if $\mathsf{O}^\circ\big(G(\mathsf{I}^\circ(\mathbf{x}))\big) = f(\mathbf{x})$ for any $\mathbf{x} \in \mathbb{F}_q^\ell$, where I° (resp., O°) encodes (resp., decodes) each input (resp., output). Gadget composition builds bigger circuits from a number of gadgets, by connecting the output wires of some gadgets to the input wires of the others. To cleanly pinpoint the "pattern" of a composition, we appeal to an acyclic graph C. I.e., the resulted bigger circuit is obtained by replacing the vertices of C with the gadgets. In such a graph, the involved gadgets are called *sub-gadgets*, and the edges carry sharings or packed sharings. An *MIMO gadget* is a gadget with multiple input sharings or output sharings. Note that the composed gadget C' is a gadget, and thus a recursive composition of gadgets is also a gadget.

2.3 Composable Security Notions

While the notion of d-private security nicely protects against side-channel attacks, it is not trivial to prove that large circuits such the AES fulfill it. The difficulty stems from enumerating the probes within the circuit, the complexity of which increases exponentially with the circuit size. The natural solution is to use the composition method, so that one can focus on each individual gadget, while the global d-private security is ensured by composition. Barthe et al. introduced first composable security notions [2] for (small) gadgets that are sufficient to result in provable probing security.

Simulatability. We first recall the definition of simulatability introduced in [5]:

Definition 3 (Simulatability [5]). *Let $\mathcal{P} = \{p_1, ..., p_d\}$ be a set of d probes of a gadget G with input shares $\mathcal{X}$. Let $\mathcal{S} \subseteq \mathcal{X}$ be a subset of input shares. A simulator is a randomized function $S \colon \mathbb{F}_q^{|\mathcal{X}|} \to \mathbb{F}_q^d$. A distinguisher is a randomized function $D \colon (\mathbb{F}_q^d, \mathbb{F}_q^{|\mathcal{X}|}) \to \{0, 1\}$. The set of probes $\mathcal{P}$ can be simulated with shares in $\mathcal{S}$ if and only if there exists a simulator S such that for any distinguisher D and any inputs shares $\mathcal{X}$, we have:*

$$\Pr\left[D\big(G_{\mathcal{P}}(\mathcal{X}), \mathcal{X}\big) = 1\right] = \Pr\left[D\big(S(\mathcal{S}), \mathcal{X}\big) = 1\right] ,$$

where the probability is over the random coins in G, S and D.

(Strong) Non-inference. We then recall the first set of composable security notions introduced in [2]. The probes of a gadget are separated as follows:

- Output probes: output variables.
- Internal probes: variables except for the output probes.

Definition 4 (d-(Strong) Non-inference ($(S)NI$) [2]). *Let G be a gadget with sharings as inputs and outputs. G is d-NI (resp., d-SNI), if any probes consisting of t_{int} internal probes and t_{out} outputs probes with $t_{int} + t_{out} \leq d$ can be simulated with $t_{int} + t_{out}$ (resp., t_{int}) shares of each input sharing.*

As shown in Lemma 1, both d-NI and d-SNI imply the d-private security.

Lemma 1 (NI/SNI implies probing security [2]). *If a gadget G is d-SNI or d-NI, then G is a d-private circuit if any d shares in each input sharing are independent of the secrets and all input sharings are independently encoded.*

More importantly, in the proof of probing security, NI and SNI can reduce the elaboration from trying all tuples of probes of a full circuit to only verifying each small gadget. Informally speaking, any composition of d-NI and d-SNI gadgets is still d-NI if each sharing is used at most once as input of any d-NI gadget and the input sharings of a gadget come from different gadgets.

2.4 Different Types of Gadgets

As gadgets can be used as building blocks of private circuits, it is necessary to specify types of gadgets that are required for protecting cryptographic algorithms.

The first type of gadgets is linear gadgets that implement linear functions. As the encoder is usually homomorphic (for example, the encoder of the Boolean sharing) over linear functions, linear gadgets can be correctly constructed by applying linear functions on the shares of the same index, which we will denote as *the trivial implementation of a linear function*. It becomes more difficult for (nonlinear) gadgets implementing nonlinear functions such as multiplication, since the encoder is usually not homomorphic over nonlinear functions. The last type of gadgets is the refresh gadget (a.k.a, the refreshing) that re-randomizes a sharing, which is usually needed for the composition of gadgets. Existing works (e.g., [1,3,4]) have provided different refresh gadgets that are asymptotically more efficient than multiplication gadgets. In the rest of the paper, we mainly focus on a typical nonlinear gadget: multiplication gadget that implements the multiplication over $\mathbb{F}_q$ in the masked domain.

3   New Security Notions for MIMO gadgets

To motivate, this section begins by recalling the limitation of NI/SNI with MIMO gadgets. Then, to ease understanding, we serve intuition for our new security notions in Subsect. 3.2. The core concept will be the notion of t-chunk that describes a set of shares from the input or output sharings of a gadget. The formal definitions are finally given in Subsect. 3.3.

3.1   Limitation of NI/SNI with MIMO Gadgets

The notions of NI and SNI are not perfectly suitable for MIMO gadgets. To see this, let's consider, for example, the compositions of two gadgets, as illustrated in Fig. 3. In Fig. 3-(a), the composition of G_1 and G_2 subjects to the rule in Lemma 1, and thus is 3-SNI. Figure 3-(b) shows an improper composition, where two probes (one internal and one output) of G_2 requires 4 input variables to simulate, which cannot be further simulate with the input of G_1 since G_1 is 3-SNI. Figure 3-(c) fixes the issue of Fig. 3-(b) by adding SNI refreshings, which however comes at huge overheads. Note that a similar illustration can be found in [13, Figure 5], where the authors considered a linear operation between two outputs of a nonlinear gadget.

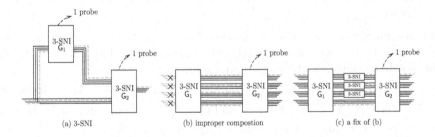

(a) 3-SNI   (b) improper compostion   (c) a fix of (b)

Fig. 3. Limitation of (S)NI.

In the rest of this section, we investigate more suitable security notions for gadgets with multiple input and output. However, for example, the packed multiplication that we will introduce in Sect. 4 is neither d-MIMO-SNI nor d-PINI, but is d-SNI. It indicates that there should exist some security notions between MIMO-SNI and SNI (stronger than SNI and weaker than MIMO-SNI) and more suitable to the packed multiplication. In this respect, we put forward a set of new security notions.

3.2 Intuition Behind the New Security Notions

The notion of simulatability captures that a set of output shares and t_{int} internal shares can be simulated with some input shares called *propagated shares*. In this respect, how to define the output shares and the propagated shares is critical in different security notions. Let $\hat{\mathbf{x}}_1, \ldots, \hat{\mathbf{x}}_\ell$ be ℓ sharings that can be either input sharings or output sharings of a gadget. For an integer t, we define the types of set $\mathcal{X}$ consisting of some shares in $\hat{\mathbf{x}}_1, \ldots, \hat{\mathbf{x}}_\ell$ as follows:

  i. $|\mathcal{X}| = t$, i.e., $\mathcal{X}$ consists of t shares in $\hat{\mathbf{x}}_1, \ldots, \hat{\mathbf{x}}_\ell$.
  ii. $|\mathcal{X}| = \ell t$, and $\mathcal{X}$ consists of t shares in each sharing of $\hat{\mathbf{x}}_1, \ldots, \hat{\mathbf{x}}_\ell$.

It can be seen that, in (S)NI, output and propagated shares relate to types *i* and *ii* respectively. The only difference between SNI and NI is the values of the parameters t for output and propagated shares. And in MIMO-SNI, output and propagated shares relate to types *ii* and *i* respectively, which makes it a stronger property than (S)NI. It is because, compared with (S)NI, MIMO-SNI allows that a larger set of output shares can be simulated with a smaller set of propagated shares. Examples can be found in Fig. 5-(a) (b) and (c).

For our new security notions, we introduce a new type of set $\mathcal{X}$ as follows:

  iii. $\mathcal{X}$ consists of a *t-chunk* of $\hat{\mathbf{x}}_1, \ldots, \hat{\mathbf{x}}_\ell$, where the *t-chunk* is defined below, and we also depict an example in Fig. 4.

Definition 5. *A t-chunk of sharings $\hat{\mathbf{x}}_1, \ldots, \hat{\mathbf{x}}_\ell \in \mathbb{F}_q^n, \ldots, \mathbb{F}_q^n$ is a subset of a set made up of the following two parts:*

1. *(α part) $\{\hat{\mathbf{x}}_k[i] \mid k \in \mathcal{K}, i \in \mathcal{I}\}$ for $\mathcal{K} \subseteq [\ell]$, $\mathcal{I} \subseteq [n]$ and $|\mathcal{K}| + |\mathcal{I}| = t_\alpha$.*
2. *(β part) t_β shares from $\hat{\mathbf{x}}_1, \ldots, \hat{\mathbf{x}}_\ell$.*

such that $t \geq t_\alpha + t_\beta$.

It should be noted that the t-chunk is only defined with sharings, rather than the packed sharings.

The Rationale of the t-Chunk Definition. The t-chunk is defined in accordance with the formalism of packed multiplication given latter in Sect. 4. We will mostly consider an abstract computation that takes sharings $\hat{\mathbf{x}}_1, \ldots, \hat{\mathbf{x}}_\ell \in \mathbb{F}_q^n, \ldots, \mathbb{F}_q^n$ as inputs and sums (XOR) the rows of $\mathbf{X} \stackrel{\text{def}}{=} \hat{\mathbf{X}} \oplus \hat{\mathbf{Q}}$, resulting in $\tilde{\mathbf{x}} \in \mathbb{F}_q^\ell$, where $\hat{\mathbf{X}}[, k] \stackrel{\text{def}}{=} \hat{\mathbf{x}}_k$ for $k \in [\ell]$ and $\hat{\mathbf{Q}} \in \mathbb{F}_q^{n \times \ell}$ is a random matrix. During the process, there also exist variables $f(\hat{\mathbf{Q}}[i,])$ for any function $f : \mathbb{F}_q^\ell \to \mathbb{F}_q$ and any $i \in [n]$. A specification of such abstract algorithm is the packing in Gadget 1-P, and an example will be depicted in Fig. 6. In this case, a certain amount of probes to $f(\hat{\mathbf{Q}}[i,])$, $\hat{\mathbf{X}}$, $\mathbf{X}$ and $\tilde{\mathbf{x}}$ can be simulated with a t-chunk of $\hat{\mathbf{x}}_1, \ldots, \hat{\mathbf{x}}_\ell$ for some $t \geq 0$. More concretely (but informally),

  – Let $\mathcal{I} \subseteq [n]$ and $\mathcal{K} \subseteq [\ell]$, the probes to $f(\hat{\mathbf{Q}}[i,])$ for $i \in \mathcal{I}$ can be simulated by sampling the corresponding random distribution, and probes to $\tilde{\mathbf{x}}[k]$ for $k \in \mathcal{K}$ can be simulated with the α part of $\hat{\mathbf{x}}_1, \ldots, \hat{\mathbf{x}}_\ell$ corresponding to $\mathcal{I}$ and $\mathcal{K}$. In the example of Fig. 4, the probes of this type relate to $\mathcal{I} = \{2, 3, 4\}$ and $\mathcal{K} = \{5, 6\}$.

$$\beta \text{ part, } t_\beta = 3 \qquad \alpha \text{ part, } t_\alpha = 5$$

$$\hat{\mathbf{x}}_1[1], \hat{\mathbf{x}}_2[1], \hat{\mathbf{x}}_3[1], \hat{\mathbf{x}}_4[1], \hat{\mathbf{x}}_5[1], \hat{\mathbf{x}}_6[1], \hat{\mathbf{x}}_7[1], \hat{\mathbf{x}}_8[1], \hat{\mathbf{x}}_9[1]$$
$$\hat{\mathbf{x}}_1[2], \hat{\mathbf{x}}_2[2], \boxed{\hat{\mathbf{x}}_3[2]}, \hat{\mathbf{x}}_4[2], \hat{\mathbf{x}}_5[2], \hat{\mathbf{x}}_6[2], \hat{\mathbf{x}}_7[2], \hat{\mathbf{x}}_8[2], \hat{\mathbf{x}}_9[2]$$
$$\hat{\mathbf{x}}_1[3], \hat{\mathbf{x}}_2[3], \hat{\mathbf{x}}_3[3], \hat{\mathbf{x}}_4[3], \hat{\mathbf{x}}_5[3], \hat{\mathbf{x}}_6[3], \hat{\mathbf{x}}_7[3], \hat{\mathbf{x}}_8[3], \hat{\mathbf{x}}_9[3]$$
$$\hat{\mathbf{x}}_1[4], \boxed{\hat{\mathbf{x}}_2[4]}, \hat{\mathbf{x}}_3[4], \hat{\mathbf{x}}_4[4], \boxed{\hat{\mathbf{x}}_5[4]}, \boxed{\hat{\mathbf{x}}_6[4]}, \hat{\mathbf{x}}_7[4], \hat{\mathbf{x}}_8[4], \hat{\mathbf{x}}_9[4]$$
$$\hat{\mathbf{x}}_1[5], \hat{\mathbf{x}}_2[5], \hat{\mathbf{x}}_3[5], \hat{\mathbf{x}}_4[5], \hat{\mathbf{x}}_5[5], \hat{\mathbf{x}}_6[5], \hat{\mathbf{x}}_7[5], \hat{\mathbf{x}}_8[5], \hat{\mathbf{x}}_9[5]$$
$$\hat{\mathbf{x}}_1[6], \hat{\mathbf{x}}_2[6], \boxed{\hat{\mathbf{x}}_3[6]}, \hat{\mathbf{x}}_4[6], \hat{\mathbf{x}}_5[6], \hat{\mathbf{x}}_6[6], \hat{\mathbf{x}}_7[6], \hat{\mathbf{x}}_8[6], \hat{\mathbf{x}}_9[6]$$
$$\hat{\mathbf{x}}_1[7], \hat{\mathbf{x}}_2[7], \hat{\mathbf{x}}_3[7], \hat{\mathbf{x}}_4[7], \hat{\mathbf{x}}_5[7], \hat{\mathbf{x}}_6[7], \hat{\mathbf{x}}_7[7], \hat{\mathbf{x}}_8[7], \hat{\mathbf{x}}_9[7]$$

Fig. 4. An examples of an 8-chunk of sharings $\hat{\mathbf{x}}_1, \ldots, \hat{\mathbf{x}}_7$, where $t_\alpha = 5$ and $t_\beta = 3$. Each column of the matrix corresponds to a distinct sharing.

- The probes to $\hat{\mathbf{X}}$ can be simulated with the β part of sharings $\hat{\mathbf{x}}_1, \ldots, \hat{\mathbf{x}}_\ell$. In the example of Fig. 4, the probes of this type are $\hat{\mathbf{X}}[3,2]$, $\hat{\mathbf{X}}[2,4]$ and $\hat{\mathbf{X}}[3,6]$.

Below in Lemma 2, we show that the union of two t-chunks is a $2t$-chunk. Its proof is in the full version. This property enables merging several t-chunk probes.

Lemma 2 (Closure of t-chunk under union). *If S_1 and S_2 are t_1-chunk and t_2-chunk of sharings $\hat{\mathbf{x}}_1, \ldots, \hat{\mathbf{x}}_\ell$ respectively, then $S_1 \cup S_2$ is a $(t_1 + t_2)$-chunk of $\hat{\mathbf{x}}_1, \ldots, \hat{\mathbf{x}}_\ell$.*

Cautionary Note. By definition, a subset of a t-chunk is also a t-chunk. Thus, a t-chunk should also be a t'-chunk for any $t' > t$. Moreover, the partition of S (into α and β parts) is not unique. For example, the set of share highlighted in Fig. 4 can also be 9-chunk, if it is partitioned in a way that β part contains all the highlighted shares and α part is empty. Also note that, there always exists a minimum value of t for any set of shares. For example, the set of share highlighted in Fig. 4 can not be t-chunk for any $t < 8$.

3.3 New Security Notion for MIMO Gadgets

In this sub-section, we formally introduce the new security notions. We begin with the first one:

1. d-Chunk Strong Non-Inference and d-Chunk Non-Inference, abbreviated as d-*CNI* and d-*CSNI* respectively.

They share a similar structure with NI/SNI, but output and propagated shares are replaced with a t-chunk of the output and input sharings respectively, making them to be positioned in-between d-(S)NI and d-MIMO-SNI. The formal definition of d-C(S)NI is as follows.

Definition 6 (*d-C(S)NI*). *Let* G *be a gadget with sharings as inputs and outputs.* G *is d-CNI (resp., d-CSNI), if any probes consisting of t_{int} internal probes and a t_{out}-chunk of output sharings with $t_{int} + t_{out} \leq d$ can be simulated with a $(t_{int} + t_{out})$-chunk (resp., t_{int}-chunk) of input sharings.*

In Fig. 5-(a)(b)(c)(d), we give examples to illustrate the differences of the *d*-C(S)NI, (S)NI and MIMO-SNI. Also note that type *iii* shares cover type *i* shares with the same value of *t*, and thus, as shown in Lemma 3, *d*-C(S)NI implies the (S)NI security. The proof is given in the full version.

Lemma 3. *d-CNI* $\Rightarrow$ *d-NI, d-CSNI* $\Rightarrow$ *d-SNI and d-CSNI* $\Rightarrow$ *d-CNI.*

3.4   New Security Notion for Gadgets with Packed sharings

While the *d*-C(S)NI meets the minimal requirement for protecting any cryptographic algorithm, it is (by definition) only for gadgets with sharings as inputs and outputs, and thus incompatible with packed sharings. Such compatibility has the (obvious) advantage of enabling extension to any gadgets that are composed of packing, multiplying and linear gadgets. For example the masked AES S-box that we will present latter in Fig. 9, Sect. 6. The security proof of such composition can be much simplified if there exist secure notions particularly for packing and multiplying gadgets, more generally, for gadgets with packed sharings as inputs or outputs.

Therefore, to facilitate the compositions for gadgets with packed sharings, two other new notions are necessary:

2. For the gadgets with input sharings and output packed sharings, we propose *d*-Input-Chunk Non-Inference and *d*-Input-Chunk Strong Non-Inference, abbreviated as *d*-ICNI and *d*-ICSNI respectively.
3. For the gadgets with input packed sharings and output sharings, we propose *d*-Output-Chunk Non-Inference and *d*-Output-Chunk Strong Non-Inference, abbreviated as *d*-OCNI and *d*-OCSNI respectively

The formal definitions are in Definitions 7 and 8. Also see Fig. 5-(e)(f) for the corresponding illustrations.

Definition 7 (*d-IC(S)NI*). *Let* G *be a gadget with sharings as inputs and packed sharings as outputs.* G *is d-ICNI (resp., d-ICSNI), if any probes consisting of t_{int} internal probes and t_{out} shares from output packed sharings with $t_{int} + t_{out} \leq d$ can be simulated with a $(t_{int} + t_{out})$-chunk (resp., t_{int}-chunk) of input sharings.*

Definition 8 (*d-OC(S)NI*). *Let* G *be a gadget with packed sharings as inputs and sharings as outputs.* G *is d-OCNI (resp., d-OCSNI), if any probes consisting of d_{int} internal probes and a d_{out}-chunk of output sharings with $t_{int} + t_{out} \leq d$ can be simulated with $t_{int} + t_{out}$ (resp., t_{int}) shares of each input packed sharing.*

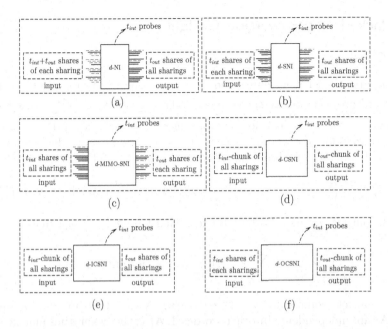

Fig. 5. Difference between the security notions. (a) d-NI: t_{out} output probes and t_{int} internal probes can be simulated with propagated shares that consist of $t_{int} + t_{out}$ shares of each input sharing. (b) d-SNI: output probes are the same as d-NI case, and the propagated shares consist of t_{int} shares of each input sharing. (c) d-MIMO-SNI: the output probes consist of t_{out} shares of each output sharing, and the propagated share is only t_{int} input share of all input sharings. (d) d-CSNI: output probes consists of a t_{out}-chunk of output sharings, and the propagated shares consist of a t_{int}-chunk of output sharings. (e) d-ICSNI: output probes are shares from packed sharings, and the propagated shares are the same as d-CSNI case. (f) d-OCSNI: output probes are the same as d-CSNI case, and the propagated shares are shares from packed sharings.

In Sects. 4 and 5, we will propose constructions for d-CSNI and d-CNI packed gadgets that we will use in tailored analyzes of some relevant circuits in Sects. 6 and 7.1. We leave the proposition and proof of more generic composition rules as an important goal for further research and present in the full version of the paper first steps in this direction.

Composability of all the new notions (i.e., d-C(S)NI, d-IC(S)NI and d-OC(S)NI) can be proved by using the probe propagation framework introduced in [3,11] (see a description in the full version).

4   Packed Multiplication Gadget

4.1   Construction

We consider the element-wise product (a.k.a., the entrywise product or the Hadamard product) of two secret vectors. That is, for $\mathbf{x} \stackrel{\text{def}}{=} (\mathbf{x}[1], \ldots, \mathbf{x}[\ell])$ and $\mathbf{y} \stackrel{\text{def}}{=} (\mathbf{y}[1], \ldots, \mathbf{y}[\ell])$, we consider computing $\mathbf{z} = \mathbf{x} \odot \mathbf{y} \stackrel{\text{def}}{=} (\mathbf{x}[1]\mathbf{y}[1], \ldots, \mathbf{x}[\ell]\mathbf{y}[\ell])$ in the masked domain, where $\odot$ denotes the element-wise multiplication over $\mathbb{F}_q^{\ell}$. The inputs of the packed multiplication gadget are $\ell \times 2$ Boolean sharings:

$$\{\hat{\mathbf{x}}_i\}_{i=1}^{\ell} \stackrel{\text{def}}{=} \big\{ (\hat{\mathbf{x}}_i[1], \ldots, \hat{\mathbf{x}}_i[n]) \big\}_{i=1}^{\ell} \quad \text{and} \quad \{\hat{\mathbf{y}}_i\}_{i=1}^{\ell} \stackrel{\text{def}}{=} \big\{ (\hat{\mathbf{y}}_i[1], \ldots, \hat{\mathbf{y}}_i[n]) \big\}_{i=1}^{\ell}$$

And the outputs should also be ℓ Boolean sharings $\{\hat{\mathbf{z}}_i\}_{i=1}^{\ell}$ such that:

$$\sum_{i=1}^{n} \hat{\mathbf{z}}_k[i] = \big(\sum_{i=1}^{n} \hat{\mathbf{x}}_k[i] \big) \big(\sum_{i=1}^{n} \hat{\mathbf{y}}_k[i] \big), \text{ for any } k \in [\ell].$$

The gadget requires an $(n-1) \times \ell$ matrix $\mathbf{A}$ such that any $d < n$ columns of $[\mathbf{I}, \mathbf{A}]$ are independent. In other words, $[\mathbf{I}, \mathbf{A}]$ is the generating matrix (with the size $(n-1) \times (\ell+n-1)$) of a liner code with dual distance $d+1$. A typical example of $\mathbf{A}$ is an $(n-1) \times \ell$ MDS matrix, and in this case, $d = n-1$.

The packed multiplication can be divided into two sub-gadgets: *Packing* and *Multiplying*. Generally speaking, the first gadget manipulates $\{\hat{\mathbf{x}}_i\}_{i=1}^{\ell}$ and $\{\hat{\mathbf{y}}_i\}_{i=1}^{\ell}$ separately to compute the packed sharings $(\tilde{\mathbf{x}}, \hat{\mathbf{u}}) \in (\mathbb{F}_q^{\ell}, \mathbb{F}_q^{n-1})$ and $(\tilde{\mathbf{y}}, \hat{\mathbf{v}}) \in (\mathbb{F}_q^{\ell}, \mathbb{F}_q^{n-1})$, and the second gadget computes the result from the packed sharings. More details are elaborated as follows:

- Packing: This sub-gadget packs the sharings $\{\hat{\mathbf{x}}_i\}_{i=1}^{\ell}$ into a packed sharing that is a tuple $(\tilde{\mathbf{x}}, \hat{\mathbf{u}}) \in (\mathbb{F}_q^{\ell}, \mathbb{F}_q^{n-1})$, such that for any $k \in [\ell]$, x_k can be reconstructed from $\tilde{\mathbf{x}}[k]$ and $\hat{\mathbf{u}}$ via $x_k = \tilde{\mathbf{x}}[k] \oplus \hat{\mathbf{u}}\mathbf{A}[, k]$. The packed sharings should also meet the requirement of security, that is, any d elements of $(\tilde{\mathbf{x}}, \hat{\mathbf{u}})$ are independent of the secret variables $\mathbf{x}$.
Similarly, $\{\hat{\mathbf{y}}_i\}_{i=1}^{\ell}$ are also packed into a packed sharings $(\tilde{\mathbf{y}}, \hat{\mathbf{v}})$ in the same vein.
- Multiplying: This sub-gadget computes the sharings of $\mathbf{x} \odot \mathbf{y}$ from the packed sharings $(\tilde{\mathbf{x}}, \hat{\mathbf{u}})$ and $(\tilde{\mathbf{y}}, \hat{\mathbf{v}})$. At a high level, for each $k \in [\ell]$, this sub-gadget perform a calculation with two-stages that first calculates outer product of the input shares $(\tilde{\mathbf{x}}[k], \hat{\mathbf{v}})^{\mathrm{T}} \times (\tilde{\mathbf{y}}[k], \hat{\mathbf{u}})$, and then compresses the results with some randomness. More importantly, the random matrix $\mathbf{R}$ and the calculation of $\mathbf{S}$ are shared (amortized) for different values of k.

We give the packed multiplication gadget in Gadget 1, which is made up of Gadget 1-P and Gadget 1-M for packing and multiplying respectively. We also present examples of Gadget 1-P and Gadget 1-M in Figs. 6 and 7 respectively.

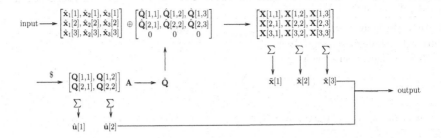

Fig. 6. Illustration of Gadget 1-P for $n = 3$ and $\ell = 3$

$\mathbf{a}_k^{\mathrm{T}} = \mathbf{A}[, k]$ for $k \in [\ell]$

$\mathbf{R}$ is a 2×2 symmatric random matrix

$\mathbf{R}_{\mathrm{diag}}$ is the diagonal matrix of $\mathbf{R}$

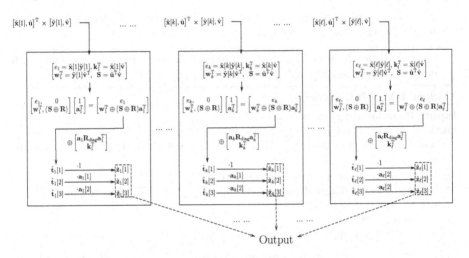

Fig. 7. Illustration of Gadget 1-M for $n = 3$

Gadget 1. Packed Multiplication

Input: Boolean sharings $\{\hat{\mathbf{x}}_i\}_{i=1}^{\ell} \in (\mathbb{F}_q^n, \ldots, \mathbb{F}_q^n)$ and $\{\hat{\mathbf{y}}_i\}_{i=1}^{\ell} \in (\mathbb{F}_q^n, \ldots, \mathbb{F}_q^n)$.
Output: Boolean sharings $\{\hat{\mathbf{z}}_i\}_{i=1}^{\ell} \in (\mathbb{F}_q^n, \ldots, \mathbb{F}_q^n)$.
1: The gadget ensures that:

$$\hat{\mathbf{z}}_k[1] \oplus \ldots \oplus \hat{\mathbf{z}}_k[n] = \Big(\sum_{i=1}^{n} \hat{\mathbf{x}}_k[i]\Big)\Big(\sum_{i=1}^{n} \hat{\mathbf{y}}_k[i]\Big), \text{ for any } k \in [\ell].$$

2: $\mathbf{A}$ is an $(n-1) \times \ell$ matrix over $\mathbb{F}_q$ such that any d columns of $[\mathbf{I}, \mathbf{A}]$ are independent.

Gadget 1-P: Packing

Input: Boolean sharings $\{\hat{\mathbf{x}}_i\}_{i=1}^{\ell}$
Output: Packed sharings $(\tilde{\mathbf{x}}, \hat{\mathbf{u}}) \in (\mathbb{F}_q^{\ell}, \mathbb{F}_q^{n-1})$
    The gadget ensures that: $\mathbf{x}_k = \tilde{\mathbf{x}}[k] \oplus \hat{\mathbf{u}}\mathbf{A}[, k]$, for any $k \in [\ell]$.
1: Randomly generate a matrix $\mathbf{Q} \in \mathbb{F}_q^{(n-1) \times (n-1)}$
                                        ▷ Amortization: The size of $\mathbf{Q}$ is independent of ℓ
2: $\hat{\mathbf{Q}} := \mathbf{Q}\mathbf{A}$
3: $\mathbf{X} := [\hat{\mathbf{x}}_1^{\mathrm{T}}, \ldots, \hat{\mathbf{x}}_{\ell}^{\mathrm{T}}] \oplus [\hat{\mathbf{Q}}; \mathbf{0}^{\ell}]$ ▷ $\mathbf{0}^{\ell}$ denotes an ℓ-length zero vector.
4: $\hat{\mathbf{u}} := \sum_{i=1}^{n-1} \mathbf{Q}[i,]$ and $\tilde{\mathbf{x}} := \sum_{i=1}^{n} \mathbf{X}[i,]$

For the packing from $\{\hat{\mathbf{y}}_i\}_{i=1}^{\ell}$ to $(\hat{\mathbf{v}}, \tilde{\mathbf{y}})$: Repeat Gadget 1-P with input $\{\hat{\mathbf{y}}_i\}_{i=1}^{\ell}$. It ensures that: $\mathbf{y}_k = \tilde{\mathbf{y}}[k] \oplus \hat{\mathbf{v}}\mathbf{A}[, k]$, for any $k \in [\ell]$.

Gadget 1-M: Multiplying

Input: Packed sharings $(\tilde{\mathbf{x}}, \hat{\mathbf{u}})$ and $(\tilde{\mathbf{y}}, \hat{\mathbf{v}})$.
Output: Boolean sharings $\{\hat{\mathbf{z}}_k\}_{k=1}^{\ell}$.
    The gadget ensures that $\sum_{i=1}^{n} \hat{\mathbf{z}}_k[i] = (\tilde{\mathbf{x}}[k] \oplus \hat{\mathbf{u}}\mathbf{A}[, k])(\tilde{\mathbf{x}}[k] \oplus \hat{\mathbf{v}}\mathbf{A}[, k])$, for any $k \in [\ell]$.
1: Randomly generate a symmetric matrix $\mathbf{R} \in \mathbb{F}_q^{(n-1) \times (n-1)}$
2: Let $\mathbf{R}_{\text{diag}}$ be the diagonal matrix such that $\mathbf{R}_{\text{diag}}[i,i] = \mathbf{R}[i,i]$ for $i \in [n-1]$
3: **for** $k = 1; k \leq \ell; k{+}{+}$ **do**
4:     Let $\mathbf{a}_k^{\mathrm{T}} = \mathbf{A}[, k]$
5:     $e_k := \tilde{\mathbf{x}}[k]\tilde{\mathbf{y}}[k], \mathbf{k}_k := \tilde{\mathbf{x}}[k]\hat{\mathbf{v}}, \mathbf{w}_k^{\mathrm{T}} := \hat{\mathbf{u}}^{\mathrm{T}}\tilde{\mathbf{y}}[k], \mathbf{S} := \hat{\mathbf{u}}^{\mathrm{T}}\hat{\mathbf{v}}$
        ▷ Compute the outer product: $\begin{bmatrix} e_k, & \mathbf{k}_k \\ \mathbf{w}_k^{\mathrm{T}}, & \mathbf{S} \end{bmatrix} = [\tilde{\mathbf{x}}[k], \hat{\mathbf{u}}]^{\mathrm{T}} \times [\tilde{\mathbf{y}}[k], \hat{\mathbf{v}}]$
        ▷ Amortization: $\mathbf{S}$ only need to be computed once for different values of k
6:     $\hat{\mathbf{t}}_k^{\mathrm{T}} := \begin{bmatrix} e_k, & 0 \\ \mathbf{w}_k^{\mathrm{T}}, & (\mathbf{S} \oplus \mathbf{R}) \end{bmatrix}\begin{bmatrix} 1 \\ \mathbf{a}_k^{\mathrm{T}} \end{bmatrix} \oplus \begin{bmatrix} \mathbf{a}_k\mathbf{R}_{\text{diag}}\mathbf{a}_k^{\mathrm{T}} \\ \mathbf{k}_k^{\mathrm{T}} \end{bmatrix}$
        ▷ Amortization: $\mathbf{R}$ and $\mathbf{R}_{\text{diag}}$ are re-used for different values of k
7:     $\hat{\mathbf{z}}_k := \hat{\mathbf{t}}_k \odot [1, \mathbf{a}_k]$
8: **end for**

4.2 Correctness of Gadget 1

In the following, we claim the correctness of Gadget 1, and the proof is given in the full version.

Theorem 1. *The correctness of Gadget 1-P and Gadget 1-M are ensured, i.e., for any $k \in [\ell]$, $\mathbf{x}_k = \tilde{\mathbf{x}}[k] \oplus \hat{\mathbf{u}}\mathbf{A}[,k]$, $\mathbf{y}_k = \tilde{\mathbf{y}}[k] \oplus \hat{\mathbf{v}}\mathbf{A}[,k]$, and $\sum_{i=1}^{n} \hat{\mathbf{z}}_k[i] = \left(\tilde{\mathbf{x}}[k] \oplus \hat{\mathbf{u}}\mathbf{A}[,k]\right)\left(\tilde{\mathbf{x}}[k] \oplus \hat{\mathbf{v}}\mathbf{A}[,k]\right)$.*

4.3 Security of Gadget 1

We first describe some intuitions behind the construction with respect to the security. Then, we give the security claim of Gadget 1 in Theorem 2, where the proof will be given in the full version.

Gadget 1-P first generates a uniformly distributed matrix $\mathbf{Q}$, which is then multiplied by $\mathbf{A}$. And, the result is used to mask the input sharings, resulting in $\mathbf{X}$. As any d columns of $[\mathbf{I}, \mathbf{A}]$ are independent, any d columns of $[\mathbf{Q}, \mathbf{QA}]$ are uniformly distributed. We can see that all probes (at most d) to Gadget 1-P should relate to no more than d columns of $[\mathbf{Q}, \mathbf{QA}]$. To ease the analysis, we can consider a simple case that the entries of $\mathbf{Q}$ are unknown (and there is no probe to the calculation of $\mathbf{QA}$), the process of summing the rows of $[\mathbf{Q}, \mathbf{X}]$ should be randomized by uniform random elements, preventing the leaks of inputs. Then, regarding the case that $\mathbf{Q}$ leaks, one can refer to the rationale of the t-chunk definition in Sect. 3.2.

The intuition behind the construction of Gadget 1-M is similar, but analysis will be more scrupulous, since the random matrix $\mathbf{R}$ is symmetric.

Theorem 2. *Gadget 1-P is d-ICSNI, Gadget 1-M is d-OCNI, and Gadget 1 is d-CSNI.*

5 Linear Gadgets

In this section, we discuss how to implement a linear transformation $\mathsf{L} : \mathbb{F}_q^\ell \to \mathbb{F}_q^{\ell'}$ with sharings. First, Subsect. 5.1 shows that the trivial implementation of a linear function is d-NI. Though, such a trivial implementation suffers from limitations in the composition with d-CSNI gadgets (e.g., the packed multiplication), which is shown in Subsect. 5.2. This motivates the construction of a more secure d-CNI linear gadget in Subsect. 5.3.

5.1 Trivial Implementation

Gadget 2 shows the trivial implementation of a linear operation with Boolean sharings $\{\hat{\mathbf{x}}_i\}_{i=1}^\ell$. The gadget manipulates shares with different indices separately. Each internal probe relates to at most one index of $\{\hat{\mathbf{x}}_i\}_{i=1}^\ell$, and any t_{out} shares of $\{\hat{\mathbf{z}}_i\}_{i=1}^\ell$ relates to at most t_{out} indices of $\{\hat{\mathbf{x}}_i\}_{i=1}^\ell$, and in total any t_{int} internal probes and t_{out} shares of $\{\hat{\mathbf{z}}_i\}_{i=1}^\ell$ can be simulated with at most $(t_{int} + t_{out})$ shares of $\{\hat{\mathbf{x}}_i\}_{i=1}^\ell$. Thus, Gadget 2 is d-NI for any $d \le n$.

However, Gadget 2 is not d-CNI. For example, if $\mathsf{L}(\{\hat{\mathbf{x}}_k[i]\}_{k=1}^\ell) = \sum_{k=1}^\ell \hat{\mathbf{x}}_k[i]$ for $i \in [n]$, then for $t \le d$, any t shares of $\hat{\mathbf{z}}$ depend on t shares of each of $\hat{\mathbf{x}}_k[i]$ for $i \in [n]$, rather than a t-chunk of input sharings. An exception is when shares

Gadget 2. Trivial linear operation

Input: Boolean sharings $\{\hat{\mathbf{x}}_i\}_{i=1}^{\ell} \in (\mathbb{F}_q^n, \ldots, \mathbb{F}_q^n)$
Output: Boolean sharings $\{\hat{\mathbf{z}}\}_{i=1}^{\ell'} \in (\mathbb{F}_q^n, \ldots, \mathbb{F}_q^n)$
1: **for** $i = 1$; $i \leq n$; $i{+}{+}$ **do**
2:     $\hat{\mathbf{z}}_1[i], \ldots, \hat{\mathbf{z}}_{\ell'}[i] = \mathsf{L}(\hat{\mathbf{x}}_1[i], \ldots, \hat{\mathbf{x}}_\ell[i])$
3: **end for**

---

of input sharings are operated separately, which is shown in Lemma 4, and the proof is given in the full version.

Lemma 4. *Any gadget that manipulates the shares of input sharings separately (i.e., there is no single variable related to more than one input shares), is d-CNI for any $d \geq 0$.*

5.2 Why a d-CNI Linear Gadget Is Necessary?

While trivially implemented linear gadgets are quite efficient, its composition with the d-CSNI packed multiplication gadget (described in Sect. 4) is not. Below we elaborate with an example.

Figure 8-(a) shows an improper composition: G_1 and G_2 are 3-CSNI and 3-NI respectively, and one probe of G_2 can be simulated with one share of each G_2's input sharing, which however cannot be simulated with the input of G_2. To fix this issue, one can rely on the strategy of adding refreshings between the two gadgets in the same way as Fig. 3-(c) in Sect. 2.3. Note that a d-SNI refresh gadget for one sharing of size n asymptotically requires up to $O(n \log n)$ random elements [1,4], and with all the sharings, it leads to an inefficient composition. Figure 3-(b) shows a more efficient solution, where G_2 is changed with a 3-CNI gadget to make the composition work. The latter solution (of Fig. 3-(b)) raises the following question:

> Can a d-CNI linear gadget be more efficient than the strategy of combining a trivial linear gadget with d-SNI refreshings?

5.3 New Construction of Linear Operation

We answer the question affirmatively. In Gadget 3, we give a new construction of linear operation for Boolean sharings. It first refreshes each input sharing by using the so-called locality refreshing [15,25], which requires $n - 1$ random elements. Then, it performs the linear operation on the refreshed sharings. In total, Gadget 3 uses $\ell(n-1)$ random elements for ℓ input sharings. In Theorem 3, we claim the security of Gadget 3, and the proof is given in the full version.

Theorem 3. *Gadget 3 is d-CNI for any d such that $d \leq n$.*

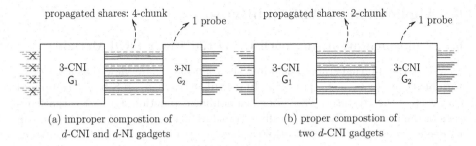

(a) improper compostion of
d-CNI and d-NI gadgets

(b) proper compostion of
two d-CNI gadgets

Fig. 8. An example to show the necessity of d-CNI linear gadget

---

Gadget 3. d-CNI Linear operation

Input: Boolean sharings $\{\hat{\mathbf{x}}_i\}_{i=1}^{\ell} \in (\mathbb{F}_q^n, \ldots, \mathbb{F}_q^n)$
Output: Boolean sharings $\{\hat{\mathbf{z}}_i\}_{i=1}^{\ell'} \in (\mathbb{F}_q^n, \ldots, \mathbb{F}_q^n)$
1: **for** $k = 1$; $k \le \ell$; $k{+}{+}$ **do**
2:　　Generate a uniformly distributed vector $\mathbf{r}_k \in \mathbb{F}_q^{n-1}$
3:　　$\hat{\mathbf{y}}_k[1{:}n-1] = \hat{\mathbf{x}}_k[1{:}n-1] \oplus \mathbf{r}_k$
4:　　$\hat{\mathbf{y}}_k[n] = \hat{\mathbf{x}}_k[n] \oplus \sum_{i=1}^{n-1} \mathbf{r}_k[i]$
5: **end for**
6: Call Gadget 2 with input sharings $\{\hat{\mathbf{y}}_i\}_{i=1}^{\ell}$ and output sharings $\{\hat{\mathbf{z}}_i\}_{i=1}^{\ell'}$

5.4 Linear Gadgets for Packed sharings

The linear gadget investigated above only considers (Boolean) sharings, which is already sufficient to protect the cryptographic algorithms. For the packed sharings, the linear gadget are more complicated and may come at high overhead. The main reason is that, the trivial implementation of linear transformation gadget is based on the premise that Boolean sharings encode each secret independently, which however is not standing for the packed sharings. Besides, the code-based masking also face this issue, and a similar reasoning can be found in [38, Sect. 5.2].

An exception is that the addition over packed sharings can be trivially implemented by manipulating shares with different indices separately. That is, for input packed sharings $(\tilde{\mathbf{x}}, \hat{\mathbf{u}})$ and $(\tilde{\mathbf{y}}, \hat{\mathbf{v}})$, the trivial addition is $(\tilde{\mathbf{x}} \oplus \tilde{\mathbf{y}}, \hat{\mathbf{u}} \oplus \hat{\mathbf{v}})$. In Lemma 5, we give the security of this trivial addition, which can be regarded as a variant of d-NI for the packed sharings (note that the d-NI is defined only for gadgets with input and output sharings). The proof will be given in the full version.

Lemma 5. *For a trivial addition gadget with two input packed sharings, any t_{out} shares of output packed sharings and t_{int} internal probes can be simulated with $t_{int} + t_{out}$ shares of each of input packed sharings.*

6   Application to AES SubBytes

6.1   Implementation Approach Using the Tower Field Method

AES-128, the internal states, including the round keys, are viewed as a set of 16 variables (say, $\{x_1, \ldots, x_{16}\}$) in $\mathbb{F}_{2^8}$. In its SubBytes step, an S-box is computed over each of the 16 states. The S-box is a nonlinear function $\mathbb{F}_{2^8} \to \mathbb{F}_{2^8}$ that consists of the inverse in $\mathbb{F}_{2^8}$ and an affine transformation. In the field inversion can be decomposed into several multiplications in $\mathbb{F}_{2^4}$ (that can be fully tabulated) and linear operations using the tower field method [29]:

1. $(a_h, a_l) := \delta(x) \in (\mathbb{F}_{2^4}, \mathbb{F}_{2^4})$ 2. $a := \lambda a_h^2 \oplus a_l(a_h \oplus a_l) \in \mathbb{F}_{2^4}$
3. $a' := (a^2 a)^4 a^2 \in \mathbb{F}_{2^4}$ 4. $a'_h := a' a_h \in \mathbb{F}_{2^4}$
5. $a'_l := a'(a_h + a_l) \in \mathbb{F}_{2^4}$ 6. $\mathsf{S}(x) := \mathrm{Aff}\Big(\delta^{-1}\big((a'_h, a'_l)\big)\Big) \in \mathbb{F}_{2^8}$

In detail, the input $x \in \mathbb{F}_{2^8}$ is mapped to $a_h, a_l \in \mathbb{F}_{2^4}$ using a linear isomorphism mapping $\delta : \mathbb{F}_{2^8} \to (\mathbb{F}_{2^4}, \mathbb{F}_{2^4})$, and λ is a constant in $\mathbb{F}_{2^4}$. After computations over $\mathbb{F}_{2^4}$ in steps 2 to 5, the inverse isomorphism mapping $\delta^{-1} : (\mathbb{F}_{2^4}, \mathbb{F}_{2^4}) \to \mathbb{F}_{2^8}$ maps (a'_h, a'_l) back to an element in field $\mathbb{F}_{2^8}$, and finally an affine transformation $\mathrm{Aff} : \mathbb{F}_{2^8} \to \mathbb{F}_{2^8}$ yields the S-box output.

We use MDS matrices from the Reed-Solomon code [34], and thus $n = d + 1$. By the MDS conjecture [36], $d \times \ell$ MDS matrix over $\mathbb{F}_{2^4}$ shall satisfy $\ell + d \leq |\mathbb{F}_{2^4}| = 16$. Thus, we set $\ell = 8$ and implement 8 S-boxes together by using the packed multiplication (16 S-boxes can be achieved by invoking this implementation twice). The input and output of masked S-boxes are 8 sharings. The implementation is optimized by separating the packing and multiplying gadgets to reduce the number of calls to packing, as well as to re-use the packed sharings to the largest extent. The process is shown in Fig. 9, in which P and M denote the packing and multiplying of Gadget 1-P and Gadget 1-M with $\ell = 8$ respectively. The $()^2$, $()^4$, δ, λa^2 and $\oplus$ are trivial implementations of the corresponding linear operations, and the last gadget that is a combination of inverse isomorphism and affine is implemented by Gadget 3.

In the security analysis, to be strictly consistent with the definition of circuits, where all variables are in the same finite field, we map each variables (say a) in $\mathbb{F}_{2^4}$ to a variable (say b) in $\mathbb{F}_{2^8}$, such that the most significant 4 bits of b are identical to the 4 bits of a, and the least significant 4 bits of b are zeros. Then, each function over $\mathbb{F}_{2^4}$ is isomorphically mapped to a gate over $\mathbb{F}_{2^8}$ by which the function is performed only over the most significant 4 bits of the variables. The function $\delta : \mathbb{F}_{2^8} \to (\mathbb{F}_{2^4}, \mathbb{F}_{2^4})$ (resp., $\delta^{-1} : (\mathbb{F}_{2^4}, \mathbb{F}_{2^4}) \to \mathbb{F}_{2^8}$) is isomorphically mapped to a gate $\mathbb{F}_{2^8} \to (\mathbb{F}_{2^8}, \mathbb{F}_{2^8})$ (resp., $\mathbb{F}_{2^8} \to (\mathbb{F}_{2^8}, \mathbb{F}_{2^8})$) by which each output (resp., input) is mapped to a variable in $\mathbb{F}_{2^8}$ by the same vein as before. Note that these mappings are only for the security analysis and do not impact the efficiency of the implementation.

Proposition 1 (The SubBytes implementation is d-CSNI). *The composed gadget in Fig. 9 is d-CSNI.*

The full proof is given in the full version.

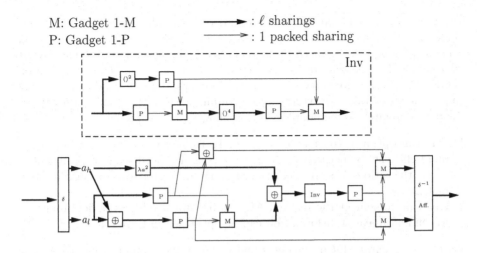

Fig. 9. Masked AES S-box with packed multiplication.

Though we adopt the tower field method [29] and separate the packing and multiplying gadgets for the sake of reducing the cost to the utmost. We believe a simpler implementation using the multiplication chain [35] in a larger field $\mathbb{F}_{2^8}$ will be interesting as well. In this respect, we describe such a masked AES implementation in the full version.

6.2 Implementation Results

It can be seen that, the implementation of 8 S-boxes contains 6 instances of Gadget 1-P and 5 instances of Gadget 1-M. The random requirements of Gadget 1-P and Gadget 1-M are d^2 and $d(d+1)/2$ 4-bit variables respectively. The δ^{-1} and affine operation are implemented together by Gadget 3, which requires $8d\ell$ bytes of randomness. At last, the total random bits for 16 AES S-boxes is

$$\left(\left(d^2 \times 6 + (d(d+1)/2) \times 5 \right) \times 4 + d\ell \times 8 \right) \times 2 = 68d^2 + 20d + 16d\ell.$$

For $\ell = 8$, the above result is $68d^2 + 148d$.

The S-boxes are implemented with security orders $d = 4, 8$ based on the ARM Cortex M architecture. The multiplication by matrix **A** at line 2 of Gadget 1-P and line 6 of Gadget 1-M are tabulated, which in total requires $16d\ell$ bytes of memory. For the consistency with the state-of-the-art results, the randomness in our implementations can be obtained from a constrained TRNG that outputs 32-bit of fresh randomness every 80 clock cycles, which is also used in [9] and recommended in [27]. For the comparison with the state-of-the-art implementations, we consider the implementations of bitslice AES S-boxes reported in [9,19] as the benchmarks.

The performance results are summarized in Table 2. Compared with the work of [9], our implementation saves 55% and 68% cycles for the generation of randomness for $d = 4$ and 8 respectively. The code sizes of our implementations are larger, which is due to the loop unrolling of our implementation. Indeed, our implementations are slightly slower than the bitsliced methods in computation, which is because that bitsliced methods perfectly fit the bitwise AND and XOR instructions. By contrast, our implementations are based on the multiplication in $GF(2^4)$, which is not directly supported in microprocessors and can only rely on pre-computed tables. Nevertheless, we emphasize that this computational loss could be mitigated or eliminated via the following two approaches:

1. One can optimize the matrix **A** to make the corresponding multiplication more efficient. Sometimes an MDS matrix is not needed: even though $d < n - 1$, the ratio of cost to security order may be better (than using the MDS matrix).
2. One can implement the masked AES on hardware, where the field multiplication and linear transformation can be optimized in bit-level.

We refer to them as future works. Finally, despite the computational loss, our implementation still achieves a gain of up to 33% in total speed when $d = 8$.

Regarding computational cost, the issue of field multiplication in software indicates that bitsliced implementations may be more efficient. However, the bitsliced consumes more randomness. With same value of security order d and the number of parallel multiplications (say, ℓ), larger field (say, $\mathbb{F}_{2^4}$ or $\mathbb{F}_{2^8}$) may give a smaller number of shares n for a packed sharing. Generally, if $\ell + d \leq |\mathbb{F}_q|$, we can choose **A** in Gadget 1 an MDS matrix, and then we have $n = \ell + d$. But for bitsliced case, $|\mathbb{F}_q| = 2$, and thus $n > \ell + d$. Therefore, the situation of combining bitsliced implementation with the packed multiplication is more complicated: operation can be more efficient (with the bitwise AND instruction) at the cost of more randomness bits. We refer to this investigation as a future work.

Last but not least, we make the source codes of our AES-Sboxes implementation available on https://github.com/wjwangcrypto/Packed_mul.

Table 2. Summary of performances for 16 AES S-boxes

	Cycles for Computation	Cycles for Generating Randomness	Total Cycles	Code size	RAM size
[19, R.-P. method], $d = 4$	19 232	34 944	54 176	4 KB	Unreported
[19, Bitsliced method], $d = 4$	11 502	17 472	28 974	3.1 KB	Unreported
[9, Bitsliced method], $d = 4$	9 222	9 282	18 504	Unreported	Unreported
Our work, $d = 4$	15 998	4 200	**20198**	9.8 KB	10.9 KB
[19, R.-P. method], $d = 8$	70 840	163,072	233 912	4 KB	Unreported
[19, Bitsliced method], $d = 8$	34 798	81 536	116 334	3.1 KB	Unreported
[9, Bitsliced method], $d = 8$	27 028	43 316	70 344	Unreported	Unreported
Our work, $d = 8$	33 142	13 840	**46982**	17 KB	11.8 KB

7 Application to GHASH, AES-GCM, and More

7.1 A Brief Description of GHASH and AES-GCM

Authenticated encryption aims at ensuring both confidentiality and integrity simultaneously [10], and has became the de facto standard for secure data transferring. The authenticated encryption algorithm AES-GCM was proposed by McGrew and Viega in [30] and standardized by NIST since 2007. It combines an encryption based on the widely used AES algorithm in counter mode and an authenticator based on the GHASH function involving multiplications in $F_{2^{128}}$. The authenticator mixes ciphertexts, potential associated data and a secret parameter derived from the encryption key to produce a tag.

It is compulsory to seek for side-channel secure implementations for such a standard. A crucial step is to secure the GHASH function, which is essentially a *polynomial-evaluation hash*. Its takes $\iota + 1$ variables $s_0, \ldots, s_\iota$ in $F_{2^{128}}$ as well as an authentication key $h \in F_{2^{128}}$ as inputs, and evaluates Eq. 2 below.

$$\text{tag} = h^\iota s_0 \oplus h^{\iota-1} s_1 \oplus \ldots \oplus h s_\iota . \tag{1}$$

A sequential calculation of the polynomial-evaluation hash can be built by the Horner's rule [24]:

$$x_i = \begin{cases} 0 & \text{for } i = 0 \\ (x_{i-1} \oplus s_i) h & \text{for } i = 1, \ldots, \iota \end{cases}, \tag{2}$$

where the output $\text{tag} = x_\iota$.

For the underlying block cipher AES, the implementation approach has been discussed in Sect. 6. Here we concentrate on the other main indigent GHASH. Note that various SCAs against GHASH have been reported in e.g., [7,8], which enable recovering the key h and creating forgeries. It is thus unsurprising that masking GHASH has received quite a lot attention, see e.g., [32,37]. However, existing masked implementations of GHASH only considered protecting against known SCAs, leaving out *provable security*. Here we will fill in the gap. In detail, we study the case that h and $s_0, \ldots, s_\iota$ are encoded into sharings: $\hat{h}$ and $\hat{s}_0, \ldots, \hat{s}_\iota$, and the masked GHASH outputs the sharing of the tag. The crux is to masking the polynomial-evaluation hash (Eq. 2), on which we will elaborate in the next sub-section.

7.2 Provably Secure Masked Implementation of Polynomial-Evaluation Hash

To mask the polynomial-evaluation hash, the most straightforward approach is to apply ISW multiplication (more concretely, the generalized version for finite field in [35]) in the sequential calculation of Eq. 2. This approach consumes $\iota + 1$ ISW multiplications, each of which consists of $(d+1)^2$ bilinear multiplications and requires $64(d+1)d$ random bits. Based on the above, the cost of this approach is estimated and summarized in Table 3.

Note that the computation of polynomial-evaluation hash can be parallelized. In detail, assuming $\ell \mid \iota$, the parallelized version computes $\{x_1^{(i)}, \ldots, x_\ell^{(i)}\}$ from $i = 0$ to $i = \frac{\iota}{\ell}$ as follows:

$$x_k^{(i)} = \begin{cases} s_k h^k & \text{for } i = 0 \\ (x_k^{(i-1)} \oplus s_{k+ik}) h^k & \text{for } i = 1, \ldots, \frac{\iota}{\ell} \end{cases} , \text{ for } k \in [\ell] \qquad (3)$$

Finally, the summation $\sum_{k=1}^{\ell} x_k^{(\frac{\iota}{\ell})}$ is taken as the tag. The computation of $\{x_1^{(i)}, \ldots, x_\ell^{(i)}\}$ for $i \in [\frac{\iota}{\ell}]$ can be parallelized and thus fits our packed multiplication of Gadget 1. In Fig. 10, we present our new approach based on packed multiplication.

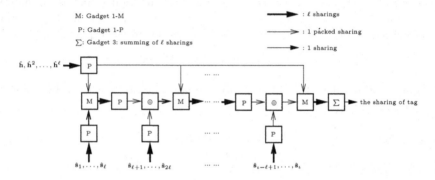

Fig. 10. Masked polynomial-evaluation hash with packed multiplication.

Based on the probing propagation framework, it is easy to see that the composed gadget in Fig. 10 is d-CSNI. To estimate the cost, we use the MDS matrix from the Reed-Solomon code for the matrix $\mathbf{A}$ of our packed multiplication gadgets, and thus $n = d + 1$. By the MDS conjecture [36], ℓ and d can be arbitrarily large as long as $\ell + d \leq |\mathbb{F}_{2^{128}}| = 2^{128}$. The estimated cost of this approach is also given in Table 3. It can be seen that, asymptotically, the new scheme with packed multiplication achieves a gain of cost up to ℓ times from the straightforward approach.

Table 3. Estimated costs of the masked polynomial-evaluation hash over $\mathbb{F}_{2^{128}}$

	Sequential implementation with ISW multiplication	Figure 10 with packed multiplication
Randomness complexity (in bits)	$64(\iota + 1)d(d + 1)$	$\frac{64(\iota+1)d(d+1)+128(\iota+1)d^2}{\ell}$
Computational complexity[a]	$(\iota + 1)(d + 1)^2$	$\frac{(\iota+1)(d+1)^2}{\ell}$

[a]Metric: the number of bilinear multiplications

7.3 More Applications of the Masked Polynomial-Evaluation Hash

Besides the GCM, polynomial-evaluation hashes have wide applications, see [31, 39]. We thus believe our approach have a great impact. To demonstrate, we take disk encryption as another example. For this purpose, Halevi proposed a mode named TET (short for linear-Transformation; ECB; linear-Transformation) [23]. The mode can be seen as the ECB encryption sandwiched between two layers of "blockwise-universal hash". An instance of such hashes proposed in [23] was named Blockwise Polynomial-Evaluation (BPE). With inputs $x_1, \ldots, x_\tau \in \mathbb{F}_{2^p}$ and key $(\beta, \tau) \in (\mathbb{F}_{2^p}, \mathbb{F}_{2^p})$, BPE firstly computes

$$s = x_1 \tau \oplus x_2 \tau^2 \oplus \ldots \oplus x_\iota \tau^\iota. \tag{4}$$

Then, the result is obtained by

$$y_i = x_i \oplus s \oplus \alpha^{i-1} \beta, \text{ for } i \in [\iota],$$

where $\alpha \in \mathbb{F}_{2^p}$ is a constant. It is clear that BPE is essentially a polynomial-evaluation hash following Eq. 1, and thus it can also be parallelized and implemented in the same vein as that of Fig. 10.

Acknowledgments. We would like to thank the anonymous reviewers of Asiacrypt 2020. Weijia Wang was partly supported by the Program of Qilu Young Scholars (Grant No. 61580082063088) of Shandong University. Chun Guo was partly supported by the Program of Qilu Young Scholars (Grant No. 6158008996-3177) of Shandong University & National Key Research and Development Project under Grant No.2018YFA0704702 & Major Scientific and Technological Innovation Project of Shandong Province, China under Grant No.2019JZZY010133 & Major Scientific and Technological Innovation Project of Shandong Province, China under Grant No.2017CXGC0704. Gaëtan Cassiers and François-Xavier Standaert are resp. Research Fellow and Senior Associate Researcher of the Belgian Fund for Scientific Research (FNRS-F.R.S.). This work has been funded in parts by the European Union through the ERC project SWORD (724725) and the European Union and Walloon Region FEDER USERMedia project 501907379156. Yu Yu was supported by the National Key Research and Development Program of China (Grant No. 2018YFA0704701), National Natural Science Foundation of China (Grant No. 61872236 and 61971192), and the National Cryptography Development Fund (Grant No. MMJJ20170209).

References

1. Barthe, G., et al.: Improved parallel mask refreshing algorithms: generic solutions with parametrized non-interference and automated optimizations. J. Crypt. Eng. **10**(1), 17–26 (2019). https://doi.org/10.1007/s13389-018-00202-2
2. Barthe, G., et al.: Strong non-interference and type-directed higher-order masking. In: Weippl, E.R., Katzenbeisser, S., Kruegel, C., Myers, A.C., Halevi, S. (eds.) CCS 2016, pp. 116–129. ACM (2016). https://doi.org/10.1145/2976749.2978427
3. Barthe, G., Dupressoir, F., Faust, S., Grégoire, B., Standaert, F.-X., Strub, P.-Y.: Parallel implementations of masking schemes and the bounded moment leakage model. In: Coron, J.-S., Nielsen, J.B. (eds.) EUROCRYPT 2017. LNCS, vol. 10210, pp. 535–566. Springer, Cham (2017). https://doi.org/10.1007/978-3-319-56620-7_19

4. Battistello, A., Coron, J.-S., Prouff, E., Zeitoun, R.: Horizontal side-channel attacks and countermeasures on the ISW masking scheme. In: Gierlichs, B., Poschmann, A.Y. (eds.) CHES 2016. LNCS, vol. 9813, pp. 23–39. Springer, Heidelberg (2016). https://doi.org/10.1007/978-3-662-53140-2_2

5. Belaïd, S., Benhamouda, F., Passelègue, A., Prouff, E., Thillard, A., Vergnaud, D.: Randomness complexity of private circuits for multiplication. In: Fischlin, M., Coron, J.-S. (eds.) EUROCRYPT 2016. LNCS, vol. 9666, pp. 616–648. Springer, Heidelberg (2016). https://doi.org/10.1007/978-3-662-49896-5_22

6. Belaïd, S., Benhamouda, F., Passelègue, A., Prouff, E., Thillard, A., Vergnaud, D.: Private multiplication over finite fields. In: Katz, J., Shacham, H. (eds.) CRYPTO 2017. LNCS, vol. 10403, pp. 397–426. Springer, Cham (2017). https://doi.org/10.1007/978-3-319-63697-9_14

7. Belaïd, S., Coron, J.-S., Fouque, P.-A., Gérard, B., Kammerer, J.-G., Prouff, E.: Improved side-channel analysis of finite-field multiplication. In: Güneysu, T., Handschuh, H. (eds.) CHES 2015. LNCS, vol. 9293, pp. 395–415. Springer, Heidelberg (2015). https://doi.org/10.1007/978-3-662-48324-4_20

8. Belaïd, S., Fouque, P.-A., Gérard, B.: Side-channel analysis of multiplications in GF(2^{128}). In: Sarkar, P., Iwata, T. (eds.) ASIACRYPT 2014. LNCS, vol. 8874, pp. 306–325. Springer, Heidelberg (2014). https://doi.org/10.1007/978-3-662-45608-8_17

9. Belaïd, S., Goudarzi, D., Rivain, M.: Tight private circuits: achieving probing security with the least refreshing. In: Peyrin, T., Galbraith, S. (eds.) ASIACRYPT 2018. LNCS, vol. 11273, pp. 343–372. Springer, Cham (2018). https://doi.org/10.1007/978-3-030-03329-3_12

10. Bellare, M., Namprempre, C.: Authenticated encryption: relations among notions and analysis of the generic composition paradigm. J. Crypt. **21**(4), 469–491 (2008). https://doi.org/10.1007/s00145-008-9026-x

11. Cassiers, G., Standaert, F.: Improved bitslice masking: from optimized non-interference to probe isolation. IACR Crypt. ePrint Arch. **2018**, 438 (2018)

12. Cassiers, G., Standaert, F.: Towards globally optimized masking: From low randomness to low noise rate or probe isolating multiplications with reduced randomness and security against horizontal attacks. IACR Trans. Cryptogr. Hardw. Embed. Syst. **2019**(2), 162–198 (2019). https://doi.org/10.13154/tches.v2019.i2.162-198

13. Cassiers, G., Standaert, F.: Trivially and efficiently composing masked gadgets with probe isolating non-interference. IEEE Trans. Inf. Forensics Secur. **15**, 2542–2555 (2020). https://doi.org/10.1109/TIFS.2020.2971153

14. Chari, S., Jutla, C.S., Rao, J.R., Rohatgi, P.: Towards sound approaches to counteract power-analysis attacks. In: Wiener, M. (ed.) CRYPTO 1999. LNCS, vol. 1666, pp. 398–412. Springer, Heidelberg (1999). https://doi.org/10.1007/3-540-48405-1_26

15. Coron, J.-S., Greuet, A., Zeitoun, R.: Side-channel masking with pseudo-random generator. In: Canteaut, A., Ishai, Y. (eds.) EUROCRYPT 2020. LNCS, vol. 12107, pp. 342–375. Springer, Cham (2020). https://doi.org/10.1007/978-3-030-45727-3_12

16. Damgård, I., Ishai, Y., Krøigaard, M.: Perfectly secure multiparty computation and the computational overhead of cryptography. In: Gilbert, H. (ed.) EUROCRYPT 2010. LNCS, vol. 6110, pp. 445–465. Springer, Heidelberg (2010). https://doi.org/10.1007/978-3-642-13190-5_23

17. Duc, A., Dziembowski, S., Faust, S.: Unifying leakage models: from probing attacks to noisy leakage. In: Nguyen, P.Q., Oswald, E. (eds.) EUROCRYPT 2014. LNCS, vol. 8441, pp. 423–440. Springer, Heidelberg (2014). https://doi.org/10.1007/978-3-642-55220-5_24

18. Faust, S., Paglialonga, C., Schneider, T.: Amortizing randomness complexity in private circuits. In: Takagi, T., Peyrin, T. (eds.) ASIACRYPT 2017. LNCS, vol. 10624, pp. 781–810. Springer, Cham (2017). https://doi.org/10.1007/978-3-319-70694-8_27

19. Goudarzi, D., Rivain, M.: How fast can higher-order masking be in software? In: Coron, J.-S., Nielsen, J.B. (eds.) EUROCRYPT 2017. LNCS, vol. 10210, pp. 567–597. Springer, Cham (2017). https://doi.org/10.1007/978-3-319-56620-7_20

20. Groß, H., Mangard, S., Korak, T.: Domain-oriented masking: compact masked hardware implementations with arbitrary protection order. In: Bilgin, B., Nikova, S., Rijmen, V. (eds.) ACM 2016, p. 3. ACM (2016). https://doi.org/10.1145/2996366.2996426

21. Grosso, V., Standaert, F.-X.: Masking proofs are tight and how to exploit it in security evaluations. In: Nielsen, J.B., Rijmen, V. (eds.) EUROCRYPT 2018. LNCS, vol. 10821, pp. 385–412. Springer, Cham (2018). https://doi.org/10.1007/978-3-319-78375-8_13

22. Grosso, V., Standaert, F.-X., Faust, S.: Masking vs. multiparty computation: how large is the gap for AES? In: Bertoni, G., Coron, J.-S. (eds.) CHES 2013. LNCS, vol. 8086, pp. 400–416. Springer, Heidelberg (2013). https://doi.org/10.1007/978-3-642-40349-1_23

23. Halevi, S.: Invertible universal hashing and the TET encryption mode. In: Menezes, A. (ed.) CRYPTO 2007. LNCS, vol. 4622, pp. 412–429. Springer, Heidelberg (2007). https://doi.org/10.1007/978-3-540-74143-5_23

24. Horner, W.G.: XXI. a new method of solving numerical equations of all orders, by continuous approximation. Philos. Trans. Roy. Soc. Lond. **109**, 308–335 (1819)

25. Ishai, Y., et al.: Robust pseudorandom generators. In: Fomin, F.V., Freivalds, R., Kwiatkowska, M., Peleg, D. (eds.) ICALP 2013. LNCS, vol. 7965, pp. 576–588. Springer, Heidelberg (2013). https://doi.org/10.1007/978-3-642-39206-1_49

26. Ishai, Y., Sahai, A., Wagner, D.: Private circuits: securing hardware against probing attacks. In: Boneh, D. (ed.) CRYPTO 2003. LNCS, vol. 2729, pp. 463–481. Springer, Heidelberg (2003). https://doi.org/10.1007/978-3-540-45146-4_27

27. Journault, A., Standaert, F.-X.: Very high order masking: efficient implementation and security evaluation. In: Fischer, W., Homma, N. (eds.) CHES 2017. LNCS, vol. 10529, pp. 623–643. Springer, Cham (2017). https://doi.org/10.1007/978-3-319-66787-4_30

28. Karpman, P., Roche, D.S.: New instantiations of the CRYPTO 2017 masking schemes. In: Peyrin, T., Galbraith, S. (eds.) ASIACRYPT 2018. LNCS, vol. 11273, pp. 285–314. Springer, Cham (2018). https://doi.org/10.1007/978-3-030-03329-3_10

29. Kim, H.S., Hong, S., Lim, J.: A fast and provably secure higher-order masking of AES S-Box. In: Preneel, B., Takagi, T. (eds.) CHES 2011. LNCS, vol. 6917, pp. 95–107. Springer, Heidelberg (2011). https://doi.org/10.1007/978-3-642-23951-9_7

30. McGrew, D.A., Viega, J.: The Galois/Counter mode of operation (GCM). http://luca-giuzzi.unibs.it/corsi/Support/papers-cryptography/gcm-spec.pdf

31. Naor, M., Reingold, O.: A pseudo-random encryption mode

32. Oshida, H., Ueno, R., Homma, N., Aoki, T.: On masked galois-field multiplication for authenticated encryption resistant to side channel analysis. In: Fan, J., Gierlichs, B. (eds.) COSADE 2018. LNCS, vol. 10815, pp. 44–57. Springer, Cham (2018). https://doi.org/10.1007/978-3-319-89641-0_3

33. Prouff, E., Rivain, M.: Masking against side-channel attacks: a formal security proof. In: Johansson, T., Nguyen, P.Q. (eds.) EUROCRYPT 2013. LNCS, vol. 7881, pp. 142–159. Springer, Heidelberg (2013). https://doi.org/10.1007/978-3-642-38348-9_9

34. Reed, I.S., Solomon, G.: Polynomial codes over certain finite fields. J. Soc. Ind. Appl. Math. **8**(2), 300–304 (1960)

35. Rivain, M., Prouff, E.: Provably secure higher-order masking of AES. In: Mangard, S., Standaert, F.-X. (eds.) CHES 2010. LNCS, vol. 6225, pp. 413–427. Springer, Heidelberg (2010). https://doi.org/10.1007/978-3-642-15031-9_28

36. Segre, B.: Curve razionali normali ek-archi negli spazi finiti. Annali di Matematica Pura ed Applicata **39**(1), 357–379 (1955)

37. Seo, S.C., Kim, H.: SCA-resistant GCM implementation on 8-bit AVR microcontrollers. IEEE Access **7**, 103961–103978 (2019). https://doi.org/10.1109/ACCESS.2019.2930986

38. Wang, W., Méaux, P., Cassiers, G., Standaert, F.: Efficient and private computations with code-based masking. IACR Trans. Cryptogr. Hardw. Embed. Syst. **2020**(2), 128–171 (2020). https://doi.org/10.13154/tches.v2020.i2.128-171

39. Wegman, M.N., Carter, L.: New hash functions and their use in authentication and set equality. J. Comput. Syst. Sci. **22**(3), 265–279 (1981). https://doi.org/10.1016/0022-0000(81)90033-7

Side Channel Information Set Decoding Using Iterative Chunking

Plaintext Recovery from the "Classic McEliece" Hardware Reference Implementation

Norman Lahr[1]([✉]), Ruben Niederhagen[1], Richard Petri[1], and Simona Samardjiska[2]

[1] Fraunhofer SIT, Darmstadt, Germany
norman@lahr.email, ruben@polycephaly.org, rp@rpls.de
[2] Radboud Universiteit, Nijmegen, The Netherlands
simonas@cs.ru.nl

Abstract. This paper presents an attack based on side-channel information and (ISD) on the code-based Niederreiter cryptosystem and an evaluation of the practicality of the attack using an electromagnetic side channel. We start by directly adapting the timing side-channel plaintext-recovery attack by Shoufan et al. from 2010 to the constant-time implementation of the Niederreiter cryptosystem as used in the official FPGA-implementation of the NIST finalist "Classic McEliece". We then enhance our attack using ISD and a new technique that we call *iterative chunking* to further significantly reduce the number of required side-channel measurements. We theoretically show that our attack improvements have a significant impact on reducing the number of required side-channel measurements. For example, for the 256-bit security parameter set `kem/mceliece6960119` of "Classic McEliece", we improve the basic attack that requires 5415 measurements to less than 562 measurements on average to mount a successful plaintext-recovery attack. Further reductions can be achieved at the price of increasing the cost of the ISD computations. We confirm our findings by practically mounting the attack on the official FPGA-implementation of "Classic McEliece" for all proposed parameter sets.

Keywords: ISD · Reaction attack · Iterative chunking · SCA · FPGA · PQC · Niederreiter · Classic McEliece

1 Introduction

Many fields of research and industry are having high hopes on the power of quantum computing, e.g., for artificial intelligence, drug design, traffic control,

This work has been funded by the German Federal Ministry of Education and Research and the Hessen State Ministry for Higher Education, Research and the Arts within their joint support of the National Research Center for Applied Cybersecurity ATHENE and by the European Commission through the ERC Starting Grant 805031 (EPOQUE).

S. Moriai and H. Wang (Eds.): ASIACRYPT 2020, LNCS 12491, pp. 881–910, 2020.
https://doi.org/10.1007/978-3-030-64837-4_29

and weather forecast [24]. This growing interest in quantum computing has led to a rapid development of quantum computers in the last decade. At the Consumer Electronics Show (CES) in 2019, IBM announced their first commercial quantum computer with 20 qubits [29]. Even larger experimental quantum computers are operating in the labs of Google, IBM, and Microsoft. However, besides the high hopes on a new area of quantum computing, quantum computers pose a severe threat on today's IT security: A sufficiently large and stable quantum computer can solve the integer factorization and discrete logarithm problems in polynomial time using Shor's quantum-computer algorithm [35], thus completely breaking most of the current asymmetric cryptography like RSA, DSA, and DH as well as ECC schemes like ECDSA and ECDH.

As an answer to this threat on asymmetric cryptography, the research field of post-quantum cryptography (PQC) has emerged in the last two decades, developing and revisiting alternative cryptographic schemes that are able to withstand attacks by quantum computers. The most popular approaches are multivariate, hash-, lattice-, code-, and isogeny-based cryptography. For details on the basic ideas behind these approaches, we refer the reader to, e.g., [5,15]. Code-based cryptography is often regarded as the most mature and reliable, but with a major drawback of being much less efficient than, e.g., lattice-based cryptosystems. The McEliece [27] and the Niederreiter [30] cryptosystems using binary Goppa codes are typically considered as conservative but safe post-quantum solutions.

The National Institute of Standards and Technology (NIST) started a public process for the standardization of PQC schemes [12] in November 2017; schemes from all classes mentioned above have been submitted. Very recently, the standardization process entered its third and final phase. The "Classic McEliece" cryptosystem [8] was chosen as one of the four finalists for the standardization of key-encapsulation mechanisms (KEMs) [1]. It is highly expected by the community that "Classic McEliece" will become part of a NIST standard of PQC.

An important question in the standardization process besides the definition of secure schemes and the choice of secure parameters is the impact of the implementation of a scheme on its security. A general requirement on the implementation of a scheme is that the runtime of the operations, e.g., key generation, signing, or decryption, does not vary based on secret information like the private key or the plaintext, i.e., that the scheme has a constant-time implementation. (Constant time in regard to public input data like the public key or the ciphertext is not required for this property.) However, there are more side channels besides timing that might enable an attacker to get access to private information like power consumption and electromagnetic, photonic, or acoustic emissions. For many PQC schemes, it is still unknown what side-channel attacks are practically feasible and how to protect against them. A general overview of the state of attacks on the implementation of PQC schemes is presented in [40].

In this work, we focus on the "Classic McEliece" cryptosystem, the well understood and trusted KEM finalist in the NIST standardization process, and describe a plaintext-recovery attack on its decryption algorithm using side-channel information. The "Classic McEliece" cryptosystem—though honouring

Robert J. McEliece, the pioneer of code-based cryptography, with its name—is using the equivalent approach proposed by Harald Niederreiter as described in Sect. 2.3.

Our Contributions. We start by directly adapting the side-channel attack from Shoufan et al. [36] for plaintext recovery on the McEliece cryptosystem to a side-channel attack on the Niederreiter cryptosystem. There are some important differences that we overcome in this adaptation: The attack of Shoufan et al. is aiming at a timing side channel present due to the non-constant time Patterson's decoder; in contrast, we attack the constant-time hardware reference implementation [41] of "Classic McEliece" that uses a constant-time implementation of the Berlekamp-Massey (BM) decoder. Therefore, a timing side channel does not exist any more—instead we perform an electromagnetic (EM) side-channel attack.

Our attack is a reaction-based attack that makes use of decoding failures: Adding more errors to the ciphertext leads to a failed decoding of the BM decoder and the output error-locator polynomial has very few roots. This can be detected over the EM side channel and used to learn the value of the error position.

Our main contribution is the optimization of the number of required side-channel queries in our reaction-based attack:

1. We introduce a new technique that we call *iterative chunking* which enables us to iteratively increase the number of learned error positions (chunks) in one (cumulative) query. We analyze our approach and theoretically derive an estimate for the optimal chunk size for an attack based on the system parameters. Our technique provides huge improvement in the number of required queries of up to 90% for the "Classic McEliece" parameters [9].
2. We further improve our attack by introducing the possibility of a trade-off between required queries and computational power. We do this by performing a certain amount of queries, reducing the problem to a smaller one, and applying known information set decoding algorithms on the remaining problem. The trade-off strongly depends on the computational capabilities of the attacker, but even for relatively small computational effort of 2^{40} operations, we can further reduce the necessary queries by around 15%.

We implement and demonstrate a practical attack on the official hardware implementation [41] of "Classic McEliece" [9]. The practically achieved improvements almost perfectly match our theoretical analysis.

Related Work. In [36] Shoufan et al. present a timing attack on the McEliece cryptosystem that recovers the plaintext of a given ciphertext using a decryption oracle (see Sect. 2.4). In this attack, a bit-flip error is added to the ciphertext, which results in a shorter timing during decryption if the flipped bit was set in the original error vector. Fault attacks on the variables used during encryption by McEliece and Niederreiter schemes are examined in [10]. A differential power analysis (DPA) attack is presented in [11] that recovers the secret key of a QC-MDPC McEliece FPGA implementation by measuring the leakage of the carry occurring during the key rotation operation. A similar attack on a software implementation is presented in [15], using the detection of counter overflows. An attack described in [33] uses information gained by DPA about the positions of set bits to recover the secret key in a cryptanalytic attack.

The attack in [36] by Shoufan et al. can be considered as a reaction-based side channel attack. In a different scenario, reaction attacks have been successfully applied to several code-based cryptosystems [2,17,18,34]. In these attacks, the attacker (typically) sends carefully chosen encrypted messages to a decryption oracle and observes whether these cause decryption failures. Based only on observing whether there was a failure, these attacks can extract the secret key.

Information set decoding is a well known decoding technique that is dating back to the work of Prange [31] in the 1960's. The basic approach has been improved throughout the years by the works of Lee and Brickell [21], Leon [22], Stern [39] (and concurrently Dumer [14]) who first proposed to use *collision decoding* (actually the term was introduced later [7]). All subsequent improvements build on top of Stern's algorithm by exploring more refined techniques for collision search. The list is extensive and includes: [3,7,16,25,26].

We are not aware of a previous work that combines information set decoding with side-channel analysis and cumulative reactions.

Structure of This Paper. Section 2 provides some background information on information set decoding and on the code-based McEliece and Niederreiter cryptosystems and gives a brief introduction to the side-channel attack from Shoufan et al. [36]. Section 3 follows up with a description of our adaption of Shoufan et al.'s attack to Niederreiter and our improvements for reducing the number of queries with iterative chunking. Here, we mathematically estimate the optimal parameter for our chunking strategy, describe an implementation using an ideal decryption oracle, and discuss the first evaluation results. In Sect. 4, we provide a leakage analysis of the FPGA implementation from [41] using EM leakage, present a construction of a practical decryption oracle, and evaluate the entire approach practically. We discuss the applicability of the iterative chunking approach in Sect. 5 and conclude the paper in Sect. 6.

Notation. In the following, $\mathrm{GF}(q)$ denotes the Galois field of order q. Capital bold letters like $\mathbf{H}$ denote matrices and small bold letters denote column vectors over a Galois field, e.g., plaintext message $\mathbf{m}$, ciphertext $\mathbf{c}$, and error vector $\mathbf{e}$. The corresponding rows vectors are denoted as $\mathbf{m}^\top$. The i-th column vector of a matrix $\mathbf{H}$ is denoted as $\mathbf{H}_i$ and the j-th coordinate in a vector $\mathbf{m}$ as $\mathbf{m}_j$. The function $\mathrm{w}(\mathbf{v})$ returns the Hamming weight (HW) of an input vector $\mathbf{v}$.

2   Background

In this section, we briefly introduce information set decoding, the McEliece cryptosystem, and its dual variant, the Niederreiter cryptosystem, which will be the object of our attack, as well as the timing attack from Shoufan et al. [36].

2.1 Information Set Decoding

Suppose we are given a parity check matrix $\mathbf{H} \in \mathrm{GF}(2)^{(n-k)\times n}$ of a binary $[n, k]$ code of dimension k and length n, and a syndrome $\mathbf{s} \in \mathrm{GF}(2)^{n-k}$. An information set decoding (ISD) algorithm solves the decoding problem:

$$\text{Find } \mathbf{e} \in \mathrm{GF}(2)^n, \mathrm{w}(\mathbf{e}) = w \text{ such that } \mathbf{H} \cdot \mathbf{e} = \mathbf{s}. \tag{1}$$

Basically, the algorithm guesses the error vector on k coordinates, and then uses this information to obtain the remaining error coordinates. The set of k coordinates is called *information set*, since it carries enough information to recover the entire error vector. The decoding problem gives rise to a linear system with the error coordinates $\mathbf{e}_1, \ldots, \mathbf{e}_n$ as unknowns. If k coordinates are correctly guessed, the system can be uniquely solved. We check the correctness of the solution by measuring the weight of the error. If the guess was wrong, we guess again.

ISD was proposed by Prange [31]. In this simplest form, we assume an error-free information set. The probability that we guess k error-free coordinates is $\binom{n-k}{w}/\binom{n}{w}$. Stern's variant [39] first introduced collision decoding that makes use of the birthday paradox. In essence, we allow some errors in the information set which increases the probability of success. The information set is split into sets with equal amount of errors p. Then the algorithm searches for collisions on these two sets, such that the sum of p columns restricted to ℓ coordinates matches the appropriate coordinates of the syndrome. It is the birthday decoding idea that improves asymptotically with respect to the previous variants. This idea was further generalized in the May-Meurer-Thomae (MMT) [25] and the Becker-Joux-May-Meurer (BJMM) [3] variants that use the more elaborate generalized birthday problem. Here instead of looking for collisions between two lists, the collision search is between 4 or 8 lists in multiple layers. May and Ozerov [26] noticed that Stern's approach can be improved by using more sophisticated algorithms for approximate matching. Their approach is general enough to be applied to other variants such as BJMM.

2.2 McEliece Cryptosystem

In 1978, McEliece proposed a cryptosystem using error correcting codes [27]. The basic idea of this cryptosystem is to use an error correcting code with an efficient error correction algorithm that can correct up to t errors as secret key and an obfuscated generator matrix of the corresponding code as public key. With code length n and code dimension k, the public key is a $k \times n$ generator matrix $\mathbf{G}$. Encryption works by computing a code word for the plaintext $\mathbf{m}$ using the generator matrix and by adding an error $\mathbf{e}$ with $\mathrm{w}(\mathbf{e}) \leq t$ that is small enough so that the error correction algorithm is able to correct the error. The ciphertext $\mathbf{c}$ is therefore computed as $\mathbf{c}^\top = \mathbf{m}^\top \mathbf{G} + \mathbf{e}^\top$. The receiver simply corrects the error by applying his secret error correction algorithm and recovers the plaintext from the code word. The security of the system is based on the hardness of decoding a general linear code, a problem known to be NP-hard [4], and the difficulty to recover the secret structure of the code from the public generator matrix.

2.3 Niederreiter Cryptosystem

In 1986, Niederreiter proposed a dual variant of the McEliece cryptosystem using a $(n - k) \times n$ parity-check matrix $\mathbf{H}$ instead of a generator matrix as public key [30]. In this case, an error vector $\mathbf{e}$ of weight $\mathrm{w}(\mathbf{e}) = t$ is the plaintext; the syndrome $\mathbf{s} = \mathbf{He}$ of the error vector is the ciphertext. Here, an efficient syndrome decoding algorithm is used for decryption. Due to the format requirements on the plaintext of having a certain length and weight, this scheme is usually used as a hybrid scheme with a random error vector that is used with a key derivation function to obtain a symmetric key for the encryption of the actual message.

In general, any error correcting code can be used for the McEliece and Niederreiter cryptosystems; however, in order to obtain an efficient and secure system, the code must be efficient to decode with possession of the secret key and hard to decode given only the public key and a ciphertext. McEliece proposed to use binary Goppa codes, which is still considered secure, while Niederreiter originally proposed to use Reed-Solomon codes, which turned out to be insecure [37]. Today, there are many variants of the McEliece and Niederreiter systems using different codes with different properties. However, using binary Goppa codes (for both McEliece and Niederreiter) is generally the most conservative choice. A drawback of using binary Goppa codes is the large size of the public key of around 1 MB for 256-bit security.

In the following, we will focus on the Niederreiter cryptosystem with binary Goppa codes with parameters as defined in the NIST submission "Classic McEliece" for Round 1 [8] and Round 2 [9] (see also [6]). We have summarized the notation that we will use in Table 1.

Key generation of the Niederreiter cryptosystem using binary Goppa codes works as follows (see [41]): Choose a random irreducible polynomial $g(x)$ over $\mathrm{GF}(2^m)$ of degree t and a list $(\alpha_0, \alpha_1, \ldots \alpha_{n-1}) \in \mathrm{GF}(2^m)^n$ of distinct elements of $\mathrm{GF}(2^m)$ (the support). From $g(x)$ and $(\alpha_0, \alpha_1, \ldots \alpha_{n-1})$, compute the $t \times n$ matrix $\tilde{\mathbf{H}}$ over $\mathrm{GF}(2^m)$. Transform $\tilde{\mathbf{H}}$ into a $mt \times n$ binary matrix $\mathbf{H}$ by replacing each $\mathrm{GF}(2^m)$-entry by a m-bit column. Finally, compute the systematic form $\mathbf{H}' = [\mathbf{I}_{mt}|\mathbf{K}]$ of $\mathbf{H}$ (where $\mathbf{I}_{mt} \in \mathrm{GF}(2)^{mt \times mt}$ denotes the identity matrix) and return $g(x)$ and $(\alpha_0, \alpha_1, \ldots \alpha_{n-1})$ as private key and $\mathbf{K}$ as public key. The last step of computing the systematic form $\mathbf{H}'$ of the parity-check matrix $\mathbf{H}$ compresses the size of the public key from mtn bits to $mt(n - mt)$ bits, because the preceding identity matrix $\mathbf{I}_{mt}$ does not need to be stored or communicated.

Encryption works as follows: The sender constructs the $mt \times n$ binary parity-check matrix $\mathbf{H}' = [\mathbf{I}_{mt}|\mathbf{K}]$ by appending $\mathbf{K}$ to the identity matrix $\mathbf{I}_{mt}$ and encrypts the error vector $\mathbf{e} \in \mathrm{GF}(2)^n$ (i.e., the plaintext) with $\mathrm{w}(\mathbf{e}) = t$ to the syndrome $\mathbf{s} \in \mathrm{GF}(2)^{mt}$ as $\mathbf{s} = \mathbf{H}'\mathbf{e}$ (i.e., the ciphertext).

Decryption of the syndrome depends on the error-correcting algorithm used. Examples are Patterson's algorithm and the BM algorithm. Using the BM algorithm as in [6,41], decryption works as follows: First, use the idea attributed to Sendrier in [19] and compute the double-size $2t \times n$ matrix $\tilde{\mathbf{H}}^{(2)}$ over $\mathrm{GF}(2^m)$.

Table 1. Symbols for "Classic McEliece" (Niederreiter) [9,41].

Symbol	Description
$m \in \mathbb{N}$	Size of the binary field
$t \in \mathbb{N}$	Correctable errors
$n \in \mathbb{N}$	Code length
$k \in \mathbb{N}$	Code dimension $(k = n - mt)$
$g(x)$	Goppa polynomial over $GF(2^m)$ of degree t
$(\alpha_0, \alpha_1, \ldots \alpha_{n-1}) \in GF(2^m)^n$	Support of n distinct elements of $GF(2^m)$
$\mathbf{H} \in GF(2)^{mt \times n}$	Parity-check matrix
$\mathbf{H}' = [\mathbf{I}_{mt}|\mathbf{K}] \in GF(2)^{mt \times n}$	Parity-check matrix in systematic form
$\mathbf{K} \in GF(2)^{mt \times (n-mt)}$	Public key
$\mathbf{e} \in GF(2)^n$	Error vector (plaintext)
$\mathbf{s} \in GF(2)^{mt}$	Syndrome (ciphertext)
$\sigma(x)$	Error-locator polynomial over $GF(2^m)$ of degree t

Table 2. Parameter sets of "Classic McEliece" [9].

	kem/mceliece-				
	348864	460896	6688128	6960119	8192128
m	12	13	13	13	13
t	64	96	128	119	128
n	3488	4608	6688	6960	8192
$k = n - mt$	2720	3360	5024	5413	6528

Compute the double-size syndrome $\mathbf{s}^{(2)} = \tilde{\mathbf{H}}^{(2)} \cdot (\mathbf{s}|0)$ by appending $n - mt$ zeros to the syndrome $\mathbf{s}$. Now, we can use the BM algorithm to compute the error-locator polynomial $\sigma(x)$ of $\mathbf{s}^{(2)}$. The roots of $\sigma(x)$ correspond to the error-positions. Therefore, the error-vector bits can be determined by evaluating $\sigma(x)$ at all points in $(\alpha_0, \alpha_1, \ldots \alpha_{n-1})$. If $\sigma(\alpha_i) = 0$, $0 \leq i < n$, the i-th bit of the error vector $\mathbf{e}_i = 1$, otherwise $\mathbf{e}_i = 0$.

A KEM is constructed in "Classic McEliece" from the basic encryption/decryption primitives using a standard transformation. Table 2 shows the parameters proposed by [9].

2.4   Timing Side-Channel Attack on McEliece

Shoufan et al. in [36] describe a plaintext-recovery attack on the McEliece cryptosystem that is based on distinguishing the number of added error bits during the decoding step: The idea of the attack is to add (xor) an additional error bit to a given ciphertext at a certain position. If previously there had not been an error added to the code word on that position, in total, there is now one more error in the code word. If previously there had already been an error at that position, the error is extinguished and there is now one error less. If the attacker is able to distinguish these two cases based on some side channel, he is able to mount the following attack: By iteratively adding an error to each position of the ciphertext and determining via the side channel if in total the number of errors has increased or decreased, the attacker is able to determine the position of all error bits, to correct the errors, and to decode the ciphertext.

Patterson's algorithm is a popular decoding algorithm for binary Goppa codes. However, the runtime of Patterson's algorithm depends on the number of errors that have been added to the code word. Shoufan et al. are using these timing variations in Patterson's algorithm as side-channel information to mount their attack: If an error is added to a previously error-free position, Patterson's algorithm has a slightly longer runtime; if an error is extinguished by the additional error bit, the runtime of Patterson's algorithm is slightly shorter. Precisely measuring and categorizing the runtime of Patterson's algorithm gives the required information to recover the error positions.

3   Reaction-based Side-Channel Analysis

In this section, we describe our reaction-based plaintext-recovery attack on the Niederreiter cryptosystem. In Sect. 3.1, we explain how to adapt the timing attack by Shoufan et al. [36] introduced in Sect. 2.4 on the McEliece cryptosystem to an EM side-channel attack on the Niederreiter cryptosystem. We describe how to reduce the number of queries required for a side-channel attack when using ISD in Sect. 3.2 and we improve our basic attack in Sect. 3.3 using the *iterative chunking* technique. Further, we mathematically estimate the optimal parameter for our query strategy and evaluate its implementation with a simulation using an ideal decryption oracle. Finally, we explain how to combine the ISD techniques with our improved attack in Sect. 3.4.

3.1   Side-Channel Attack on Niederreiter

In the attack by Shoufan et al. in [36] on the McEliece cryptosystem, the number of errors in the ciphertext is modified simply by adding one more error on varying positions to the original ciphertext. However, the Niederreiter cryptosystem is not operating with erroneous code words as ciphertext but with syndromes. Here, the equivalent of adding an error to a code word in McEliece, is to add a column of the parity-check matrix (i.e., the public key) to the syndrome (i.e., the ciphertext). Therefore, the attack from [36] can trivially be adapted to the Niederreiter cryptosystem by systematically adding columns of the public key one by one to the original syndrome. If the bit corresponding to the column was not set in the original error vector (i.e., the plaintext), the number of errors in the modified syndrome is increased. Accordingly, if the corresponding bit was set, an error in the original error vector is effectively removed from the syndrome, reducing the number of errors. If an attacker can find a side channel that enables

---

Algorithm 1: Iterative Reaction-based SCA

---

input : "Classic McEliece" parameters $n, m, t \in \mathbb{N}^{+}$,
parity-check matrix $\mathbf{H}' = [\mathbf{I}_{mt}|\mathbf{K}] \in \mathrm{GF}(2)^{mt \times n}$,
syndrome $\mathbf{s} \in \mathrm{GF}(2)^{mt}$.
output: Error vector $\mathbf{e} \in \mathrm{GF}(2)^{n}$.
1 $\mathbf{e} \leftarrow (0, \ldots, 0)$;
2 **for** $i \in E = \{1, \ldots, n\}$ **do**
3 $\quad$ $\mathbf{s}' \leftarrow \mathbf{s} \oplus \mathbf{H}'_i$;
4 $\quad$ **if** $\mathtt{Oracle}(\mathbf{s}') = true$ **then** $\mathbf{e}_i \leftarrow 1$;
5 **end**
6 **return** $\mathbf{e}$;

---

him to distinguish these two cases, he is able to mount an attack. Algorithm 1 shows the general approach for this attack. In order to distinguish the cases with a reduced number of errors from the cases with an increased number of errors, a query to an oracle is required (line 4 in Algorithm 1) that returns *true* if the number is reduced and thus an error position has been found.

This decryption oracle can practically be achieved by having the victim decrypt the manipulated ciphertext and by measuring the side channel during the decryption. Therefore, when a non-constant time decoding algorithm like Patterson's algorithm is used, a timing side-channel attack as in [36] can be mounted on Niederreiter as well.

Attacking Constant-Time Implementations. Modern implementations typically avoid timing side channels by providing a constant-time implementation of critical algorithms. Thus, in this case another side channel is required to mount the attack. In Sect. 4, we investigate the EM side channel in the reference hardware implementation by Wang et al. [41] using a constant-time implementation of the BM algorithm to demonstrate a practical attack. Another side channel could for example be a response in a communication protocol if adding an error results in a decoding failure and if this failure is reported over the network.

For a side-channel attack based on EM, the attacker needs to be in possession of the device under attack, e.g., a smart card or a security token, that has physical measures protecting secret information such as private and secret keys, but no explicit countermeasures prohibiting the exploitation of the side channel. Furthermore, the attacker needs to be in possession of a ciphertext that he intends to decrypt, e.g., intercepted on a communication channel. Under these requirements, the attacker can perform a series of measurements of EM emissions of the device under attack while decrypting manipulated ciphertexts.

The number of side-channel measurements that is needed for this basic iterative attack algorithm is the number of columns n in the parity check matrix, which ranges from 3488 to 8192 queries for the NIST parameters of "Classic McEliece" (cf. Sect. 2.3). However, depending on the attack scenario, the attacker might only be able to take a limited amount of measurements, e.g., due to the

---

Algorithm 2: ISD-supported Iterative Reaction-based SCA

---

    input : Same as Algorithm 1
    output: Same as Algorithm 1

1 $\widehat{E} \subset E = \{1, \ldots, n\}, |\widehat{E}| \leqslant k;$

2 Same as Algorithm 1 lines **1-5** with $\widehat{E}$ instead of E

3 $\tilde{\mathbf{s}} \leftarrow \mathbf{s} - \mathbf{H}' \cdot \mathbf{e};$

4 $\tilde{\mathbf{e}} := (\mathbf{e}_i)_{i \in E \setminus \widehat{E}}; \quad \hat{\mathbf{e}} := (\mathbf{e}_i)_{i \in \widehat{E}};$

5 $\tilde{\mathbf{H}}' := (\mathbf{H}'_i)_{i \in E \setminus \widehat{E}};$

6 $\tilde{\mathbf{e}} \leftarrow \mathtt{ISD}(n - |\widehat{E}|, k - |\widehat{E}|, w - \mathrm{w}(\hat{\mathbf{e}}), \tilde{\mathbf{H}}', \tilde{\mathbf{s}});$

7 $\mathbf{e} \leftarrow \mathtt{Reconstruct}(\hat{\mathbf{e}}, \tilde{\mathbf{e}});$

8 **return** e;

---

cost of each measurement, limited access to the device, or additional counter-measures on the device. In the next sections, we describe improvements to this basic algorithm that allow the attacker to significantly reduce the number of decoding operations that he needs to query from the device under attack.

3.2 Reducing the Number of Queries with Information Set Decoding

In the reaction attack described in Algorithm 1, we clearly do not have to reconstruct the entire error vector (all error coordinates) using side-channel information. We can recover an information set of size $k < n$, instead, and use basic linear algebra to recover the rest of the error vector (cf. Sect. 2.1). We can do even better if the attacker is in a position to trade-off queries for computational power—first collect a number of queries *less* than k, use them to reduce the problem to a smaller one, and then solve the smaller problem using some of the ISD algorithms described in Sect. 2.1.

In more detail, let $\mathrm{ISD}(n, k, w, \mathbf{H}, \mathbf{s})$ be any ISD algorithm, such as Stern's or Ball Collision decoding, that on input of a parity check matrix $\mathbf{H} \in \mathrm{GF}(2)^{(n-k) \times n}$ and syndrome $\mathbf{s} \in \mathrm{GF}(2)^{n-k}$ outputs an error vector $\mathbf{e} \in \mathrm{GF}(2)^n$ with $\mathrm{w}(\mathbf{e}) = w$—a solution to the decoding problem (1).

Suppose we are given an oracle as in Algorithm 1 that we can use to learn the value of a coordinate $\mathbf{e}_i$ of the error vector. Using the oracle, we learn a subset of error indices $\widehat{E} \subset E = \{1, \ldots, n\}$ where $|\widehat{E}| \leqslant k$. We denote the corresponding subvector of $\mathbf{e}$ by $\hat{\mathbf{e}} = (\mathbf{e}_i)_{i \in \widehat{E}}$ and its complement by $\tilde{\mathbf{e}} = (\mathbf{e}_i)_{i \in E \setminus \widehat{E}}$. Similarly $\widehat{\mathbf{H}} = (\mathbf{H}'_i)_{i \in \widehat{E}}$ and $\tilde{\mathbf{H}}' = (\mathbf{H}'_i)_{i \in E \setminus \widehat{E}}$. From the obtained information, setting $\tilde{\mathbf{s}} = \mathbf{s} - \widehat{\mathbf{H}} \cdot \hat{\mathbf{e}}$, the decoding problem (1) transforms to:

$$\tilde{\mathbf{H}}' \cdot \tilde{\mathbf{e}} = \tilde{\mathbf{s}}. \tag{2}$$

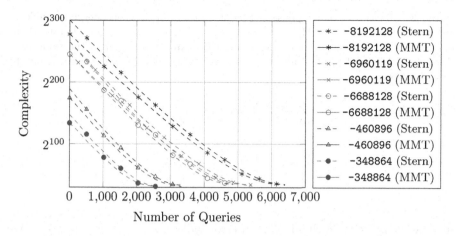

Fig. 1. Time-queries trade-off when using ISD decoding algorithms.

So, we have reduced our initial problem to a smaller decoding problem with parameters $k' = k - |\widehat{E}|$, $n' = n - |\widehat{E}|$, $w' = w - \mathrm{w}(\hat{\mathbf{e}})$. We solve this problem by calling the available ISD algorithm $\mathrm{ISD}(n', k', w', \tilde{\mathbf{H}}', \tilde{\mathbf{s}})$. If $|\widehat{E}| = k$, we have recovered an entire information set and we only need to solve a linear system using Gaussian elimination. Thus, for convention, we assume $\mathrm{ISD}(n, 0, w, \mathbf{H}, \mathbf{s})$ simply performs Gaussian elimination. Algorithm 2 details the whole procedure.

The performance of Algorithm 2 depends directly on the size of the set $\widehat{E}$, i.e., on the number of queries to the oracle. There is a clear trade-off between the running time and the queries to the oracle, which is depicted in Fig. 1. Basically, the attacker is free to choose the number of queries that he performs based on his computational resources. In our depiction of the trade-off, for simplicity, we used only two ISD algorithms—Stern's and MMT. We did not use the state of the art BJMM variant, because there is no compact representation of the concrete complexity of this algorithm.

3.3 Reducing the Number of Queries with Iterative Chunking

For the approach that we describe here, we need to slightly change the oracle from the previous section. In particular, we assume the oracle returns *true* if the number of errors has not increased (instead of reduced as in Sect. 3.1) and *false* otherwise. Note that the real oracle that we construct in Sect. 4.2 actually captures both cases.

To get some intuition on how our *iterative chunking* works, we first present a simpler variant that already reduces the number of needed queries by more than 35%.

Iterative Chunking with Chunks of Size $\beta = 2$. Suppose that instead of a single error index, we query two error indices (a chunk of size $\beta = 2$) at once. We

Table 3. All cases of the response of the decryption oracle when querying chunks of size two at once ($s' = s \oplus H_i' \oplus H_j'$). The first column shows the initial state of the queried chunk, the second shows the state of the pair after 'flipping' the values, the third shows the total number of errors in the new state, and the last column shows the oracle's answer.

(e_i, e_j)	(e_i', e_j')	$w(e')$	Oracle
$(0,0)$	$(1,1)$	$w+2$	false
$(0,1)$	$(1,0)$	w	true
$(1,0)$	$(0,1)$	w	true
$(1,1)$	$(0,0)$	$w-2$	true

first randomly select a chunk (i,j) of error indices, $i,j \in \{1,\ldots,n\}, i \neq j$. We add both columns H_i' and H_j' to the syndrome s to obtain the new syndrome s'. We give the input s' to the decryption oracle. Note that the decryption oracle will output *false* only in the case when the values at the corresponding error indices in the error vector were $(e_i, e_j) = (0,0)$ (which we call a 'low' chunk). In all the other cases (we refer to them as 'high' chunks, to indicate that there is at least one '1' in the chunk) the decryption oracle will output *true*. Indeed, if $(e_i, e_j) = (0,0)$, after adding the pair of columns (H_i', H_j') to the syndrome, we obtain $(e_i', e_j') = (1,1)$, and in total $w+2$ errors. Hence, the number of errors has increased beyond w and the decryption oracle will output *false*. If $(e_i, e_j) = (0,1)$ or $(e_i, e_j) = (1,0)$, we get $(e_i', e_j') = (1,0)$ and $(e_i', e_j') = (0,1)$ respectively, and in this case the number of errors does not change (it remains w) so the decryption oracle returns *true*. In the last case, $(e_i, e_j) = (1,1)$, after adding the columns we obtain $(e_i', e_j') = (0,0)$. So in this case, the number of errors reduces to $w-2$, and the decryption oracle returns *true* as well. Table 3 summarizes the above.

What we can conclude from the previous is that if *false* is returned, we can be sure that the corresponding error positions in the error vector were $(e_i, e_j) = (0,0)$. We perform the procedure for new random pairs of positions (i,j) until we find $k/2$ pairs whose initial state was $(0,0)$, i.e., until we encounter $k/2$ *false* oracle answers. Note that after a pair has been queried, we need to undo the changes made, i.e., return the pair to its initial state.

The improvement using chunks of two is easy to see: Since the length of the error vector is much bigger than its Hamming weight, most of the time the randomly chosen chunk will be $(e_i, e_j) = (0,0)$, and we can confirm these values by *only one* query, instead of two as in the approach from the previous section.

Iterative Chunking for $\beta > 2$. This simple strategy for $\beta = 2$ is already significantly better than the naïve approach from the previous section, but we can do much better by extending this idea to chunks $(e_{i_1}, \ldots, e_{i_\beta})$ of size β. We keep the convention of calling the all-zero chunk $(0,\ldots,0)$ 'low' chunk and all other chunks containing 1s 'high' chunks.

Table 4. Overview of the oracle answers for $\beta = 3$ when the number of errors in the syndrome $\mathbf{s}$ are reduced to $w(\mathbf{e}') - 1$ ($\mathbf{s}' = \mathbf{s} \oplus \mathbf{H}'_i$) with the knowledge of an error position i in the original error vector $\mathbf{e}$.

		$\mathbf{s}$		$\mathbf{s}' = \mathbf{s} \oplus \mathbf{H}'_i$	
$(\mathbf{e}_i, \mathbf{e}_j, \mathbf{e}_k)$	$(\mathbf{e}'_i, \mathbf{e}'_j, \mathbf{e}'_k)$	$w(\mathbf{e}')$	Oracle	$w(\mathbf{e}') - 1$	Oracle
$(0,0,0)$	$(1,1,1)$	$w+3$	false	$w+2$	false
$(0,0,1)$	$(1,1,0)$	$w+1$	false	w	true
$(0,1,0)$	$(1,0,1)$	$w+1$	false	w	true
$(1,0,0)$	$(0,1,1)$	$w+1$	false	w	true
$(1,1,0)$	$(0,0,1)$	$w-1$	true	$w-2$	true
$(1,0,1)$	$(0,1,0)$	$w-1$	true	$w-2$	true
$(0,1,1)$	$(1,0,0)$	$w-1$	true	$w-2$	true
$(1,1,1)$	$(0,0,0)$	$w-3$	true	$w-4$	true

First, note that we cannot directly use the same approach for chunks of size $\beta > 2$. For example for $\beta = 3$ we have Table 4 analogous to Table 3. Table 4 shows (columns 3 and 4) that there is ambiguity in the oracle answers, so if the oracle answers *false* we cannot distinguish whether the chunk was $(0, 0, 0)$, $(0, 0, 1)$, $(0, 1, 0)$, or $(1, 0, 0)$. However, we can remedy this situation if we reduce the initial number of errors from w to $w - 1$ as columns 5 and 6 from Table 4 show. This requires knowledge about the position of one 1 in the error vector. Adding the corresponding column of the matrix $\mathbf{H}'$ to the syndrome reduces the number of errors to $w - 1$. So how can we find the position of one 1? Well, this can easily be done by first querying chunks of size $\beta = 2$ until a 'high' chunk is found. Querying both positions within the 'high' chunk of size $\beta = 2$ reveals the position of one 1. The same reasoning extends to any chunk size β: If the number of errors before we start querying β size chunks is $w - (\beta - 2)$, the oracle answers *false* only for low chunks, and we can use this information to distinguish low chunks. To summarize, the procedure informally goes as follows:

Part I: For a chunk size β, starting at $\beta = 2$:

1. Query random chunks of size β without replacement until the oracle returns *true* which indicates a 'high' chunk.
2. Inspect the positions within the 'high' chunk and locate the 1 s.
3. Use these 1s to increase the size of the chunks that we query: by adding to the syndrome a column $\mathbf{H}'_i$ of the matrix $\mathbf{H}'$ corresponding to a 1 at position i in the error vector we reduce the number of errors by one.
4. Increase the chunk size to $\beta + 1$ and repeat from step 1 until $\beta = \beta_T$.

Part II: When a threshold β_T is reached, change the procedure to:

1. Query random chunks of size β_T without replacement. If the oracle returns *true* save the 'high' chunk in a bucket of capacity $n - k$.
2. End the whole procedure when k error positions have been learned.

The threshold β_T is an optimization parameter—the optimal value for the chunk size β at which we need to stop increasing. We determine its value so that the number of necessary queries to recover an information set is minimized.

Note that, in Part II, we only care about finding enough 'low' chunks so that we recover an information set. So in principle, we can throw away the 'high' chunks, unless there are too few chunks remaining—not enough to recover an information set. This is why we save them in a bucket. After the bucket has been filled, we start inspecting 'high' chunks as well, because we will not be able to recover an information set otherwise.

Remark 1. Typically there will be only one 1 in a 'high' chunk, so to simplify our analysis, in Part I we will always increase the size of the queried chunks only by one, although in theory, it is also possible to increase by more than one, precisely by the weight of the 'high' chunk.

Remark 2. We could continue Part I, i.e., increase the size of the queried chunks, until we have learned k error positions—enough to recover an information set. However, the increase only makes sense as long as there is a good probability that the queried chunk is 'low'—in which case one can learn β zeros in the error vector in only one query. In contrast, if the chunk size is 'high', since we want to increase the chunk size further, a more expensive inspection with additional queries is required (around $\mathcal{O}(\log \beta)$ queries using a divide-and-conquer strategy). Thus, if the chunk is 'high' with big probability, the advantage from the increased chunk size quickly diminishes.

The details of the procedure are given in Algorithm 3. The algorithm for inspecting the 'high' chunks is given in Algorithm 4. It uses a divide-and-conquer strategy to reduce the number of needed queries.

Finding the Optimal β_T. We next analyze the approach in order to determine the best threshold value and estimate the number of queries needed for the attack. First let us make some simple but important observations.

The process of querying chunks of size β can be modeled as a sequence of independent and identical Bernoulli trials in which success means querying a 'high' chunk. Indeed, since we assume uniform distribution of the error vectors, the success probability of all the trials is the same, and depends only on the number of 1s in the error vector and the size of the queried chunks. As a result, the number of queries needed to find a 'high' chunk follows the geometric distribution. Based on these observations, we have the following results.

Proposition 1. *Suppose we query chunks of size β without replacement, until we find a 'high' chunk.*

a. *The probability that a queried chunk is high is $p_\beta = 1 - \dfrac{\binom{n-w}{\beta}}{\binom{n}{\beta}}$.*

Algorithm 3: Iterative Chunking with $\beta \geq 2$

---

input : "Classic McEliece" parameters $n, m, t \in \mathbb{N}^{+}$,
binary parity-check matrix $\mathbf{H}' = [\mathbf{I}_{mt}|\mathbf{K}] \in \mathrm{GF}(2)^{mt \times n}$,
syndrome $\mathbf{s} \in \mathrm{GF}(2)^{mt}$,
threshold β_T.

output: Partial error vector $\mathbf{e}' \in \mathrm{GF}(2)^n$,
bucket of chunks containing an error position,
list of remaining column indices.

```
1  e' ← [0, ..., 0] ;                                    // initialize with zero vector
2  β ← 2 ;                                               // start with chunk size 2
3  s'[1] ← s; s'[β] ← s ;      // list of syndromes s'[i] for each chunk size 0 < i ≤ βT
4  indices ← [n, ..., 0] ;                               // column indices in reverse order
5  bucket ← [];
6  while Len(indices) > β do
7  │   chunk ← Pop(indices, β) ;                          // pop β-many indices
8  │   s'' ← s'[β] + Sum([H'[i] for i in chunk]) ;        // add columns in chunk to s'
9  │   if Oracle(s'') = true then                         // a 'high' chunk is found
10 │   │   if β < βT or |bucket| > n − k then              // conditions for inspecting
11 │   │   │   e_id ← FindErrorPositions(chunk, s', H');    // inspect 'high' chunk
12 │   │   │   for i in e_id do
13 │   │   │   │   e_i ← 1 ;             // update e' with found errors from 'high' chunk
14 │   │   │   │   if β < βT then
15 │   │   │   │   │   s'[β + 1] ← s'[β] − H'[i] ;          // remove found errors from s'
16 │   │   │   │   │   β ← β + 1 ;                          // increase chunk size, up to βT
17 │   │   │   end
18 │   │   else
19 │   │   │   bucket ← bucket + chunk ;   // collect chunks with remaining errors
20 end
21 return e', bucket, indices;
```

---

b. *The probability that the weight of the chunk is j under the condition that it is a 'high' chunk is given by*

$$Pr(w(\beta) = j | High) = \frac{\binom{w}{j}\binom{n-w}{\beta-j}}{\binom{n}{\beta} - \binom{n-w}{\beta}}. \tag{3}$$

c. *The expected number of queries until we find a 'high' chunk of size β is*

$$E(\beta) = \frac{1}{p_\beta}. \tag{4}$$

d. *The expected weight of a 'high' chunk of size β is*

$$E(w(\beta)) = \frac{w\binom{n-1}{\beta-1}}{\binom{n}{\beta} - \binom{n-w}{\beta}}. \tag{5}$$

Algorithm 4: FindErrorPositions

---

input : $chunk \in \mathbb{N}^i$,
        list of temporary syndromes $\mathbf{s}'$ with $\mathbf{s}[i] \in GF(2)^{mt}$,
        binary parity-check matrix $\mathbf{H}' = [\mathbf{I}_{mt}|\mathbf{K}] \in GF(2)^{mt \times n}$.
output: List with error indices.

1   $stack \leftarrow [\text{Left}(chunk), \text{Right}(chunk)]$;
2   $e_{id} \leftarrow []$;
3   **while** $stack$ *not empty* **do**
4      $chunk \leftarrow \text{Pop}(stack)$;
5      $s'' \leftarrow s'[\text{Len}(chunk)] + \text{Sum}([\mathbf{H}'[i] \text{ for } i \text{ in } chunk])$;
6   **if** $\text{Oracle}(s'') = true$ **then** $next \leftarrow chunk$;   // **there is an error position**
7   **else** $next \leftarrow \text{Pop}(stack)$;   // **continue search in the stack head**
8   **if** $\text{Len}(next) = 1$ **then**   // **found an error position**
9          $\text{Push}(e_{id}, next[0])$;
10         $stack \leftarrow [\text{Flatten}(stack)]$;   // **inspect entire stack**
11   **else**   // **split the next chunk directly**
12         $\text{Push}(stack, \text{Left}(next))$;
13         $\text{Push}(stack, \text{Right}(next))$;
14 **end**
15 **return** e_{id};

Proof. a. Directly, since the probability of hitting a low chunk is

$$\Pr(Low) = \frac{\binom{n-w}{\beta}}{\binom{n}{\beta}}.$$

b. Let $\Pr(w(\beta) = j | High)$ denote the probability that the weight of the chunk is j under the condition that it is a high chunk. Then,

$$\Pr(w(\beta) = j | High) = \frac{\Pr(w(\beta) = j)}{p_\beta}.$$

Since $\Pr(w(\beta) = j) = \frac{\binom{w}{j}\binom{n-w}{\beta-j}}{\binom{n}{\beta}}$ we obtain (3).

c. Since the querying of chunks of size β follows the geometric distribution, we immediately obtain the claim.

d. From a. we can directly calculate

$$E(w(\beta)) = \sum_{j=1}^{\beta} j \cdot \Pr(w(\beta) = j | High) = \frac{1}{\binom{n}{\beta} - \binom{n-w}{\beta}} \sum_{j=1}^{\beta} j \cdot \binom{w}{j}\binom{n-w}{\beta-j}$$

$$= \frac{1}{\binom{n}{\beta} - \binom{n-w}{\beta}} \sum_{j=1}^{\beta} w \cdot \binom{w-1}{j-1}\binom{n-w}{\beta-j} = \frac{w \cdot \binom{n-1}{\beta-1}}{\binom{n}{\beta} - \binom{n-w}{\beta}}.$$

$\square$

Now that we know the expected weight $E(w(\beta))$ of a 'high' chunk from Proposition 1, we should also estimate the number of queries to inspect a 'high' chunk, i.e., to determine all error positions within the 'high' chunk. Various strategies can be applied for this task. The simplest one is to just query all positions, which requires β queries, but this would make sense only if many 1s are expected within the chunk. In our problem we typically have a 'high' chunk of weight only 1, so a divide-and-conquer approach is more suitable: We split the chunk in half and query the left half depth first. When one 1 is identified, we collect all remaining unknown positions (denoted as "Flatten(*stack*)" in Algorithm 4), and query them at once as one chunk. The probability is high that this chunk will be 'low', so we do not need any more queries. If it happens that the chunk is high, we repeat the same procedure for this smaller chunk. The details are given in Algorithm 4. Proposition 2 estimates the number of queries needed to inspect a 'high' chunk using this algorithm.

Proposition 2. *Suppose we inspect a 'high' chunk of size β. Then, the expected number of queries to learn all positions within the 'high' chunk of size β using Algorithm 4 is bounded from above by*

$$E_{High}(\beta) \leqslant \sum_{j=1}^{\beta} (\frac{\binom{w}{j}\binom{n-w}{\beta-j}}{\binom{n}{\beta} - \binom{n-w}{\beta}}) \cdot (j - \frac{j}{\beta} + \sum_{i=0}^{j-1} \log_2(\beta - i)). \qquad (6)$$

Proof. To estimate $E_{High}(\beta)$, we will first write it as

$$E_{High}(\beta) = \sum_{j=1}^{\beta} \Pr(w(\beta) = j | High) \cdot E_{High}(\beta | w(\beta) = j),$$

where $E_{High}(\beta | w(\beta) = j)$ denotes the expected number of queries to learn all positions within a high chunk of size β under the condition that there are exactly j 1s in the chunk.

We consider first $E_{High}(\beta | w(\beta) = 1)$. Note that we need $\log_2 \beta$ queries to locate the 1, and on average $1 - 1/\beta$ additional queries for the remaining unqueried positions. Here, $-1/\beta$ comes from the case where the 1 is on the last β-th position of the chunk. Hence $E_{High}(\beta | w(\beta) = 1) = \log_2 \beta + 1 - 1/\beta$. Next,

$$E_{High}(\beta | w(\beta) = 2) =$$

$$= \frac{1}{\binom{\beta}{2}} \sum_{\substack{1 \leqslant i,j \leqslant \beta \\ j \neq \beta}} (\log_2 \beta + \log_2(\beta - i) + 2) + \frac{1}{\binom{\beta}{2}} \sum_{\substack{1 \leqslant i,j \leqslant \beta \\ j = \beta}} (\log_2 \beta + \log_2(\beta - i) + 1)$$

$$= \frac{1}{\binom{\beta}{2}} \sum_{1 \leqslant i,j \leqslant \beta} (\log_2 \beta + \log_2(\beta - i)) + 2 - \frac{\binom{\beta-1}{1}}{\binom{\beta}{2}}$$

$$\leqslant \frac{1}{\binom{\beta}{2}} \sum_{1 \leqslant i,j \leqslant \beta} (\log_2 \beta + \log_2(\beta - 1)) + 2 - \frac{2}{\beta} = \log_2 \beta + \log_2(\beta - 1) + 2 - \frac{2}{\beta}$$

where the second sum in the first row comes from the fact that if the second 1 is on the last position, we need one less query. We bound $E_{High}(\beta|w(\beta) = 2)$ from above, instead of calculating it exactly, in order to simplify the expression and the analysis. It is a rather tight bound, which can be confirmed by the simulation and experiments we have performed (see Table 5).

Using induction it is easy to show that

$$E_{High}(\beta|w(\beta) = j) = \sum_{i=0}^{j-1} \log_2 (\beta - i) + j - \frac{j}{\beta} .$$

Finally, $\Pr(w(\beta) = j|High)$ can be easily calculated from Proposition 1, which gives the final expression.   □

Using Propositions 1 and 2 we can now estimate the number of queries required in Algorithm 3.

Proposition 3. *The number of queries required to recover k error positions using Algorithm 3 is given by*

$$Q(\beta_T) = \sum_{i=2}^{\beta_T-1} (E(i) + E_{High}(i)) + N_1 \cdot E(\beta_T) + N_2 \cdot (E(\beta_T) + E_{High}(\beta_T)), \quad (7)$$

where N_1 and N_2 are given by

$$N_1 = min\{\frac{n - k}{\beta_T}, \frac{k- \sum_{i=2}^{\beta_T-1} i \cdot E(i)}{\beta_T \cdot (E(\beta_T)-1)}\}, \quad N_2 = \frac{k - \sum_{i=2}^{\beta_T-1} i \cdot E(i)+N_1 \cdot \beta_T}{\beta_T \cdot E(\beta_T)} - N_1. \quad (8)$$

The optimal β_T is then the one that minimizes the number of queries $Q(\beta_T)$.

Proof. With the notation introduced so far, the number of error positions $I_1(\beta_T)$ that we learn before we reach the threshold β_T and the required queries $Q_1(\beta_T)$ in the process is

$$I_1(\beta_T) = \sum_{i=2}^{\beta_T-1} i \cdot E(i), \quad \text{and} \quad Q_1(\beta_T) = \sum_{i=2}^{\beta_T-1} (E(i) + E_{High}(i)). \quad (9)$$

When we reach the threshold value β_T, we change the strategy and continue to query only chunks of size β_T. Recall that we do not inspect 'high' chunks, but save them in a bucket of capacity $n - k$ and only start inspecting them if the bucket is full and we have not yet recovered k error positions. Suppose we query $N_1 \cdot E(\beta_T)$ chunks while the bucket is sill not full and $N_2 \cdot E(\beta_T)$ chunks after the bucket is full, for some unknown N_1, N_2. The number of learned error positions $I_2(\beta_T)$ and the required number of queries $Q_2(\beta_T)$ is

$$\begin{aligned} I_2(\beta_T) &= N_1 \cdot \beta_T \cdot (E(\beta_T) - 1) + N_2 \cdot \beta_T \cdot E(\beta_T), \\ Q_2(\beta_T) &= N_1 \cdot E(\beta_T) + N_2 \cdot (E(\beta_T) + E_{High}(\beta_T)). \end{aligned} \quad (10)$$

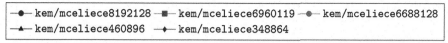

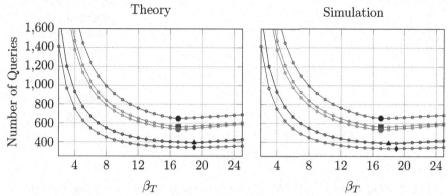

Fig. 2. The expected number of queries needed for threshold values from 2 to 25 both for the theoretical prediction and averaged simulations. The minima are marked.

The algorithm stops when k error positions have been learned, i.e., when the condition

$$I_1(\beta_T) + I_2(\beta_T) \geqslant k \tag{11}$$

is satisfied. Since the bucket has capacity $n - k$, we also have the condition

$$N_1 \cdot \beta_T \leqslant n - k. \tag{12}$$

From (11) and (12) we find the expressions in (8) for N_1 and N_2. Now, (7) follows by combining (9) and (10).   □

Evaluation. Using the estimate from Proposition 3 we get the expected number of queries for $\beta_T \in \{2, \ldots, 25\}$ for all the parameter sets `kem/mceliece348864`, `kem/mceliece460896`, `kem/mceliece6688128`, `kem/mceliece6960119`, as well as `kem/mceliece8192128` of "Classic McEliece" (see Table 2).

In order to evaluate our findings, we implemented the described iterative chunking strategy using Python and SageMath[1] and ran the implementation as a simulation with an ideal oracle that always returns the correct response. The simulation was applied to ten different key pairs using ten different plaintext/ciphertext pairs for each key pair (100 in total) per parameter set and β_T value. We generated the key pairs as well as the plain- and ciphertext pairs using the SageMath scripts that are enclosed with the publicly available FPGA implementation of the Niederreiter cryptosystem from Wang et al.

The optimal threshold values for the parameter sets together with the number of needed queries are given in Table 5 and depicted in Fig. 2. The results of

---

[1] http://www.sagemath.org/.

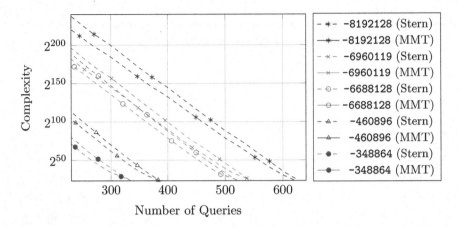

Fig. 3. Time-queries trade-off when using optimal iterative chunking and ISD.

the simulation and the later experiments in Sect. 4.3 show that the estimate matches very well (see Fig. 2). For the parameter set kem/mceliece460896, in the simulation $\beta_T = 18$ turned out to be slightly more efficient than the expected $\beta_T = 19$. However, we believe that this is only because the number of queries for $\beta_T = 18$ and $\beta_T = 19$ in the theoretical estimate are very close to each other.

Compared to recovering the information set without iterative chunking (the case of aquiring k traces from the oracle in Algorithm 2) the number of traces is decreased by approximately 87.7% for kem/mceliece348864 and 90% for kem/mceliece8192128.

3.4   Combining Iterative Chunking with Information Set Decoding

The number of needed queries can be further decreased by combining iterative chunking with some non-trivial ISD algorithm. Instead of recovering an entire information set from queries, we can stop early, when we have learned only $\delta < k$ error coordinates. Assume at this point we have n' columns remaining, the weight of the error vector on these coordinates is w' and we need to recover $k' = k - \delta$ more elements from the information set.

Then we are left with the decoding problem with parameters (n', k', w') which we can solve using any ISD algorithm. Of course this comes at a price, since ISD algorithms are exponential in time. Finding the right trade-off depends on the computational power (CPU hours) the attacker has at hand. Figure 3 gives the trade-off when using Stern's or MMT algorithm.

In order to express the trade-off more accurately, but at the same time avoid complicated expressions due to in-between or corner cases, we will discretize the possible values for the number of performed queries and learned error positions. This discretization is quite natural, since it follows exactly the steps of our algorithm. Using the notation from the proof of Proposition 3 we consider the partial sums of the number of performed queries $Q(\beta_T)$ defined as

$$Q_i(\beta_T) = \begin{cases} Q_{i-1}(\beta_T) + E(i) + E_{High}(i), & i \in \{2, \ldots, \beta_T - 1\} \\ Q_{i-1}(\beta_T) + E(\beta_T) + b \cdot E_{High}(\beta_T), & i \in \{\beta_T, \ldots, \beta_T + N_1 + N_2 - 1\} \end{cases}$$

with $Q_1(\beta_T) = 0$ and $b = 0$ if $i < \beta_T + N_1$ and $b = 1$ otherwise.

Similarly, we define the partial sums of the learned error positions $I(\beta_T)$ as

$$I_i(\beta_T) = \begin{cases} I_{i-1}(\beta_T) + iE(i), & i \in \{2, \ldots, \beta_T - 1\} \\ I_{i-1}(\beta_T) + \beta_T(E(\beta_T) - (1 - b)), & i \in \{\beta_T, \ldots, \beta_T + N_1 + N_2 - 1\} \end{cases}$$

with $I_1(\beta_T) = 0$ and $b = 0$ if $i < \beta_T + N_1$ and $b = 1$ otherwise. Let $I_i'(\beta_T)$ be the same as $I_i(\beta_T)$ except $b = 1$ for all $i \in \{\beta_T, \ldots, N_1 + N_2 - 1\}$. Finally, let $w_1 = 0$ and $w_i = w_{i-1} + E(i)$ for $i \in \{2, \ldots, \beta_T + N_1 + N_2 - 1\}$.

Now it is not difficult to verify that the trade-off between performed queries and computational power is given by the following proposition.

Proposition 4. *An attacker performing $Q_i(\beta_T)$ queries to the decryption oracle can recover the secret message by solving the $ISD(n - I_i'(\beta_T), k - I_i(\beta_T), w - w_i)$ problem. The case of $i = 1$ corresponds to the case of no side-channel information, and the case of $i = \beta_T + N_1 + N_2 - 1$ corresponds to recovering an entire information set using side-channel information.*

4   Attack Evaluation

For the practical attack evaluation we adapted the implementation presented in [41] for field programmable gate arrays (FPGAs). In Sect. 4.1 we describe our approach for a preliminary leakage analysis of the decryption module design and in Sect. 4.2 we construct a practical decryption oracle. Finally, in Sect. 4.3 we evaluate the practical attack.

4.1   Leakage Analysis

To construct a decryption oracle for our attack approach we investigated the implementation by Wang et al. from [41] in detail to find a proper point of interest at which we can find significant leakage. The selected implementation uses a constant-time implementation of the BM algorithm for the error correction. The BM algorithm returns an error-locator polynomial that has roots at the points that correspond to an error position. Thus, if there are $t' \leq t$ errors, t' input points to the error-locator polynomial evaluate to zero. If the number of errors is larger than t, a random polynomial is returned by the BM algorithm, which most likely has a very small number of roots. Thus, in order to distinguish whether the number of errors has increased or decreased, we need to distinguish cases where the reconstructed error vector has a low HW (for cases with an increased error number where error correction failed) and where it has a high HW (for cases with a decreased error number where error correction succeeded).

The FPGA implementation of the decryption module in [41] consists of five major steps: First, an additive (FFT) evaluates the secret Goppa polynomial.

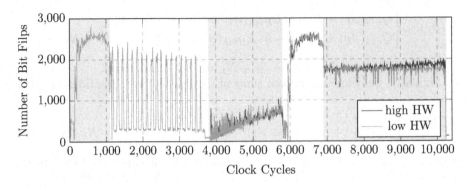

Fig. 4. Simulated power consumption based on a Hamming-distance model for success-ful decoding (high HW in the resulting error vector) and unsuccessful decoding (low HW) using a small parameter set with $m = 12$, $t = 66$, and $n = 3307$. The different parts of the algorithm can clearly be seen (marked with alternating blue background color). In the first block, an additive FFT is performed for evaluating the secret Goppa polynomial. In the second block, the double syndrome is computed. In the third block, BM is performed. In the fourth block, another additive FFT is performed in order to evaluate the error-locator polynomial. Finally, the error vector is constructed. A clear difference in the simulation is visible in the last step for the low and high HW results. (Color figure online)

Then the double syndrome is computed. Afterwards the BM algorithm is per-formed and another additive FFT is applied to evaluate the error-locator poly-nomial. In the final step, the error vector is constructed.

In addition to the analysis of the source code we simulated the implemen-tation for a preliminary leakage analysis in order to find possible leakage in a noise-free simulated environment. We wrote a Python script that computes a simulated power trace from a VCD-file (value change dump) of an Icarus Verilog (iverilog) simulation using a simple Hamming-distance model. This results in a simulated power trace with cycle accuracy. Figure 4 shows the resulting graphs of the simulation for two different simulated power traces, one for a successful decoding (high HW error vector) and one for an unsuccessful decoding (low HW error vector). The five steps of the decryption are highlighted.

The first point at which side-channel information may be leaked is at the last round of the second additive FFT operation that evaluates the error-locator polynomial returned from the BM decoder. The result of this evaluation equals to zero if there is a root and results in other values if not. Thus, it should be distinguishable in general. However, because the implementation of the additive FFT uses several multiplicator instances in parallel, the logical noise added to the exploitable leakage is quite high.

The second point of possible leakage is at the last step, the error vector construction. Here, the graph of the high HW error vector (blue) increases during the construction in contrast to the low HW error vector (red) such that there is a growing distance between them. The reason for the increasing number of bit flips at this stage is that the result of the error vector construction is shifted

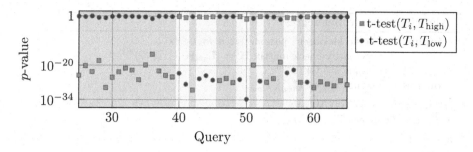

Fig. 5. Example p-values of the t-tests of consecutive oracle queries. For each query a trace T_i is compared to a known faulty (T_{low}) and a known decodable trace (T_{high}). If a trace is similar to the faulty trace (i.e., due to a higher p-value), a decoding failure is detected (light blue background). In the opposite case (light red background) the syndrome could be decoded. (Color figure online)

into a large flip-flop shift-register step by step. To lower the effort compared to the analysis of the second FFT we exploit the significant leakage of the iterative reconstruction at the end of the decryption process. Therewith, the side-channel information enables the construction of a decryption oracle.

4.2 Building an Oracle in Practice

We decided to use the (EMR) leakage emanated by the FPGA during the decryption and developed a (DEMA). Power leakage could be exploited in the same way.

In order to get a response for individual queried syndromes, we apply Welch's t-test [42] to compare the means of the traces from the error-vector construction range against two known reference traces. The reference traces stem from deciphering the original syndrome for which we know that it is decodable, and from a faulty syndrome that includes more than t errors so that it cannot be decoded. This has the disadvantage that it adds an overhead of two traces to the total number of required traces. Alternatively, we could statistically determine a threshold to compare it to the result of a t-test with just one of the reference traces, which would save one trace. However, we decided to spend one additional trace and avoid the statistical computation. The faulty syndrome is constructed by adding five columns randomly chosen from the public key matrix $\mathbf{H}'$. The probability that this results in a syndrome with more errors than can be corrected is high; nevertheless, we use a t-test comparison to the trace of the original syndrome to ensure this requirement. Algorithm 5 details the preparation procedure. Now, we compute the difference p_Δ of the p-values of the t-tests comparing a trace T_i against the original syndrome trace T_{high} and against the faulty syndrome trace T_{low} as

$$p_\Delta = \text{t-test}(T_i, T_{high}) - \text{t-test}(T_i, T_{low}). \tag{13}$$

Thus, if the difference of the p-values p_Δ is positive, the acquired trace is similar to the original syndrome trace and interpreted as decodable. Otherwise, if p_Δ

Algorithm 5: GetReferences

---

    input : "Classic McEliece" parameters $n, m, t \in \mathbb{N}^{+}$,
                binary parity-check matrix $\mathbf{H}' = [\mathbf{I}_{mt}|\mathbf{K}] \in \mathrm{GF}(2)^{mt \times n}$,
                syndrome $\mathbf{s} \in \mathrm{GF}(2)^{mt}$.
    output: Reference traces T'_{high}, T'_{low}.

1 Decrypt(s) $\rightsquigarrow T_{high}, Clk_{high}$;
2 $T'_{high} \leftarrow$ Compress(T_{high}, Clk_{high});

3 $\mathbf{s}^{*} \leftarrow \mathbf{s}$;
4 **repeat**
5   **for** $i \leftarrow 1$ **to** 5 **do** $\mathbf{s}^{*} \leftarrow \mathbf{s}^{*} \oplus \mathbf{H}'_{j}, \ j \in^{R} \{0 \ldots n-1\}$;
6   Decrypt($\mathbf{s}^{*}$) $\rightsquigarrow T_{low}, Clk_{low}$;
7      $T'_{low} \leftarrow$ Compress(T_{low}, Clk_{low});
8 **until** t-test(T'_{high}, T'_{low}) ≈ 0;

9 **return** T'_{high}, T'_{low};

Algorithm 6: DEMA-based Oracle

---

    input : Manipulated syndrome $\mathbf{s}' \in \mathrm{GF}(2)^{mt}$, reference traces T'_{high}, T'_{low}.
    output: Oracle response.

1 Decrypt($\mathbf{s}'$) $\rightsquigarrow T_{j}, Clk_{j}$;
2 $T'_{j} \leftarrow$ Compress(T_{j}, Clk_{j});
3 $p_{\Delta} \leftarrow$ t-test(T'_{j}, T'_{high}) $-$ t-test(T'_{j}, T'_{low});

4 **return** $\begin{cases} true & if \ p_{\Delta} > 0 \\ false & otherwise \end{cases}$;

---

becomes negative it is interpreted as not decodable. Figure 5 gives an example section of p-values of consecutive oracle queries. The response when used as decryption oracle therefore is

$$response = \begin{cases} true \ (decodable), & if \ p_{\Delta} > 0 \\ false \ (not \ decodable), & otherwise \end{cases}. \tag{14}$$

Algorithm 6 shows a query process. This approach requires just a single trace per query plus two traces for the reference traces at the beginning. In detail, we cannot apply the t-test to the raw traces directly because of misalignment between the signals. To handle this, we apply a trace compression similar as described in [23]. We reduce the raw signal to the maximum peak-to-peak difference of the amplitudes of the EM signal in each first clock half-wave and take it as the new value for the entire clock cycle. We just need to know the clock frequency to identify the clock cycle ranges in the raw signal.

Optimization. The quality metric of the side-channel oracle is the difference of the p-values p_{Δ}. The greater the absolute value is the better is the differentiability of the 'low' and the 'high' case. The more errors are removed from the syndrome during the iterative chunking process the less 1s are in the resulting error vector and its weight decreases. Since we are using the Hamming weight of the error-vector construction as the exploitable leakage, $|p_\Delta|$ decreases during the attack as well. Therefore, we optimized our side-channel oracle by updating the reference trace T_{high} by the trace which is recorded if a single 1 is recovered.

4.3 Practical Evaluation

To evaluate the attack in practice, we ported the FPGA design of [41] to a Xilinx Kintex-7 (XC7K160T) on a SAKURA-X[2] board running at 24MHz clock frequency. We added a UART communication interface, a control unit that handles the storage of the secret key parts $(g(x), (\alpha_0, \alpha_1, \ldots \alpha_{n-1}))$, and a trigger signal to one of the output ports that indicates the start and the end of a decryption operation. We acquired the EMR profiles and the trigger signal using a PicoScope 5244D MSO oscilloscope at 500MSamples/s and a near-field probe from Langer (RF-U 5-2). We added a 10 MHz high-pass filter to remove noise in the lower frequency range and used a customized Python script for an automatic acquisition and analysis process. The ISD-support was implemented using the GF(2) arithmetic of SageMath.

We analyzed the design of the Niederreiter decryption for all parameter sets proposed for "Classic McEliece" in the second round of the NIST PQC competition (see Table 2). Corresponding to the simulated trace in Fig. 4, the five individual parts of the decryption process were identifiable.

We evaluated the ISD-supported iterative approach (Sect. 3.2) and the chunk-based approach (Sect. 3.3) using the oracle described in Algorithm 6 for all parameter sets. We are using plain ISD (Prange) as ISD algorithm, replacing the "guessing" with queries to our oracle, effectively implementing the ISD as Gaussian elimination on $n - k$ columns that are collected in the bucket. If an attacker is able to invest additional computing power, he is able to reduce the number of traces even further, trading in a higher complexity of the ISD.

We are using the same implementation of the iterative chunking as the simulation described in Sect. 3.3—however, we substituted the ideal oracle with the real side-channel oracle described in Algorithm 6. We examined the same data sets as used for the simulation, i.e., ten different key pairs using ten different plaintext/ciphertext pairs for each key pair (100 in total) per parameter set. To demonstrate the feasibility of the side-channel-based oracle, we ran the practical evaluation of the plaintext-recovery attack for the optimal chunk size threshold (β_T) that was determined from the simulation (see Table 5).

For each "Classic McEliece" parameter set we were able to recover the entire plaintexts with our iterative chunking approach. Since the responses of the side-channel oracle and the ideal oracle in the simulation are equal, we get the same average number of traces for the same value of β_T in the simulation as well as the experiments.

---

[2] http://satoh.cs.uec.ac.jp/SAKURA/hardware/SAKURA-X.html.

Table 5. Statistical data for the required number of queries for a successful recovery of an entire error vector. The data for the simulation and the experiments was gathered from the same sets of ten different key pairs and ten different plaintext/ciphertexts per key pair (100 in total) for each parameter set. We also give the theoretical prediction and the number of required queries for applying ISD at a cost of around 2^{40} operations. For comparison, we also give the number of traces when no chunking is used, i.e., $\beta = 1$ for all queries.

kem/ mceliece-	Approach	Simulation			Theory		Experiment
		min.	avg.	max.	plain	cost $\approx 2^{40}$	
348864	$\beta = 1$	–	2722 $(k+2)$	–			
	$\beta_T = 17$	281	335.89	483	346.17	—	—
	$\beta_T = 18$	275	334.51	481	345.16	—	—
	$\boldsymbol{\beta_T = 19}$	273	**334.16**	481	**345.06**	**287.26**	**334.16**
	$\beta_T = 20$	279	337.36	494	345.74	—	—
	$\beta_T = 21$	282	337.92	482	347.09	—	—
460896	$\beta = 1$	–	3362 $(k+2)$	–			
	$\beta_T = 16$	353	397.01	523	404.41	—	—
	$\beta_T = 17$	343	391.72	513	400.00	—	—
	$\boldsymbol{\beta_T = 18}$	337	**389.33**	514	396.95	—	**389.33**
	$\boldsymbol{\beta_T = 19}$	333	390.33	515	**395.06**	**337.66**	—
	$\beta_T = 20$	329	392.14	517	396.62	—	—
	$\beta_T = 21$	326	399.59	532	403.45	—	—
6688128	$\beta = 1$	–	5026 $(k+2)$	–			
	$\beta_T = 15$	505	553.56	608	556.73	—	—
	$\beta_T = 16$	480	540.10	598	544.22	—	—
	$\boldsymbol{\beta_T = 17}$	468	**532.11**	595	**534.14**	**470.91**	**532.11**
	$\beta_T = 18$	456	534.30	604	535.31	—	—
	$\beta_T = 19$	448	540.46	617	543.39	—	—
6960119	$\beta = 1$	–	5415 $(k+2)$	–			
	$\beta_T = 15$	529	584.15	708	585.21	—	—
	$\beta_T = 16$	518	569.93	692	571.24	—	—
	$\boldsymbol{\beta_T = 17}$	505	**561.29**	680	**559.87**	**493.90**	**561.29**
	$\beta_T = 18$	508	562.15	679	561.61	—	—
	$\beta_T = 19$	499	567.68	685	567.58	—	—
8192128	$\beta = 1$	–	6530 $(k+2)$	–			
	$\beta_T = 15$	618	679.41	788	676.59	—	—
	$\beta_T = 16$	596	661.87	771	658.28	—	—
	$\boldsymbol{\beta_T = 17}$	587	**653.97**	760	**648.66**	**576.96**	**653.97**
	$\beta_T = 18$	571	654.86	760	652.85	—	—
	$\beta_T = 19$	586	658.33	778	657.53	—	—

5   Application Perspectives of Iterative Chunking

In general, our iterative chunking approach requires a) a controllable decryption failure using public information (the public key) to manipulate the syndrome and b) a reliable decryption oracle for the feedback. The feedback can be, e.g., some side-channel information or an explicit protocol response. Thus, any decryption implementation, hardware or software, with these two characteristics is vulnerable to our iterative chunking approach if a reliable feedback can be established.

As presented in this work, the Berlekamp-Massey decoding algorithm exhibits the first required property. If also the second property, i.e., a side channel as feedback exists, then the following implementations of "Classic McEliece" are vulnerable to our attack: The NIST reference C implementation [9] which is based on the work of "McBits revisited" [13] and the implementation found in the project PQClean [20] which is included in several projects, e.g., the library from the Open Quantum Safe project [38]. The code-based scheme HQC [28] also uses the Berlekamp-Massey decoder and is attackable as well if a detectable difference is revealed when the decoding fails.

Furthermore, the attack of Shoufan et al. in [36] can be improved using iterative chunking when exploiting the distinguishable behavior of the deployed Patterson's decoder since it shows a timing side-channel information when the syndrome exceeds its decoding capacity.

Further open research questions are whether iterative chunking is applicable to rank-based schemes or if it can improve reaction attacks revealing the private key, as for example shown for CCA-secure lattice-based KEM schemes in [32].

6   Conclusion

In this paper, we showed that side-channel attacks on code-based cryptosystems can significantly be improved using our new iterative chunking approach and that the cost of an ISD attack can be significantly reduced when it is combined with this improved side-channel attack, revealing the plaintext of a given message.

If "Classic McEliece" is used as a basis for a KEM scheme in a key exchange, the plaintext is used to derive a session key even if the long-term decryption key is protected. Therefore, we suggest to research proper countermeasures against decryption leakage.

References

1. Alagic, G., et al.: NISTIR 8309: Status report on the second round of the NIST post-quantum cryptography standardization process. Technical report, National Institute of Standards and Technology (2020)
2. Aragon, N., Gaborit, P.: A key recovery attack against LRPC using decryption failures. In: International Workshop on Coding and Cryptography - WCC 2019 (2019)

3. Becker, A., Joux, A., May, A., Meurer, A.: Decoding random binary linear codes in $2^{n/20}$: how $1 + 1 = 0$ improves information set decoding. In: Pointcheval, D., Johansson, T. (eds.) EUROCRYPT 2012. LNCS, vol. 7237, pp. 520–536. Springer, Heidelberg (2012). https://doi.org/10.1007/978-3-642-29011-4_31
4. Berlekamp, E.R., McEliece, R.J., van Tilborg, H.C.A.: On the inherent intractability of certain coding problems (corresp.). IEEE Trans. Inf. Theory **24**(3), 384–386 (1978)
5. Bernstein, D.J., Buchmann, J., Dahmen, E. (eds.): Post-Quantum Cryptography. Springer, Heidelberg (2009). https://doi.org/10.1007/978-3-540-88702-7. ISBN 978-3-540-88702-7
6. Bernstein, D.J., Chou, T., Schwabe, P.: McBits: fast constant-time code-based cryptography. In: Bertoni, G., Coron, J.-S. (eds.) CHES 2013. LNCS, vol. 8086, pp. 250–272. Springer, Heidelberg (2013). https://doi.org/10.1007/978-3-642-40349-1_15
7. Bernstein, D.J., Lange, T., Peters, C.: Smaller Decoding exponents: ball-collision decoding. In: Rogaway, P. (ed.) CRYPTO 2011. LNCS, vol. 6841, pp. 743–760. Springer, Heidelberg (2011). https://doi.org/10.1007/978-3-642-22792-9_42
8. Bernstein, D.J., et al.: Classic McEliece: conservative code-based cryptography – round 1, November 2017. https://classic.mceliece.org/nist/mceliece-20171129.pdf
9. Bernstein, D.J., et al.: Classic McEliece: conservative code-based cryptography – round 2, March 2019. https://classic.mceliece.org/nist/mceliece-20190331.pdf
10. Cayrel, P.-L., Dusart, P.: McEliece/Niederreiter PKC: sensitivity to fault injection. In: 5th International Conference on Future Information Technology, pp. 1–6. IEEE (2010)
11. Chen, C., Eisenbarth, T., von Maurich, I., Steinwandt, R.: Horizontal and vertical side channel analysis of a McEliece cryptosystem. IEEE Trans. Inform. Forensics Secur. **11**(6), 1093–1105 (2016)
12. Chen, L., Moody, D., Liu, Y.-K.: Post-quantum cryptography. NIST. https://csrc.nist.gov/Projects/post-quantum-cryptography
13. Chou, T.: McBits revisited. In: Fischer, W., Homma, N. (eds.) CHES 2017. LNCS, vol. 10529, pp. 213–231. Springer, Cham (2017). https://doi.org/10.1007/978-3-319-66787-4_11
14. Dumer, I.I.: Two decoding algorithms for linear codes. Probl. Peredachi Inf. **25**, 24–32 (1989)
15. De Feo, L., Jao, D., Plût, J.: Towards quantum-resistant cryptosystems from supersingular elliptic curve isogenies. J. Math. Cryptol. **8**(3), 209–247 (2014)
16. Finiasz, M., Sendrier, N.: Security bounds for the design of code-based cryptosystems. In: Matsui, M. (ed.) ASIACRYPT 2009. LNCS, vol. 5912, pp. 88–105. Springer, Heidelberg (2009). https://doi.org/10.1007/978-3-642-10366-7_6
17. Guo, Q., Johansson, T., Stankovski, P.: A key recovery attack on MDPC with CCA security using decoding errors. In: Cheon, J.H., Takagi, T. (eds.) ASIACRYPT 2016. LNCS, vol. 10031, pp. 789–815. Springer, Heidelberg (2016). https://doi.org/10.1007/978-3-662-53887-6_29
18. Hall, C., Goldberg, I., Schneier, B.: Reaction attacks against several public-key cryptosystem. In: Varadharajan, V., Mu, Y. (eds.) ICICS 1999. LNCS, vol. 1726, pp. 2–12. Springer, Heidelberg (1999). https://doi.org/10.1007/978-3-540-47942-0_2
19. Heyse, S., Güneysu, T.: Code-based cryptography on reconfigurable hardware: tweaking Niederreiter encryption for performance. JCEN **3**(1), 29–43 (2013)
20. Kannwischer, M.J., Rijneveld, J., Schwabe, P., Stebila, D., Wiggers, T.: The PQClean Project, August 2020. https://github.com/PQClean/PQClean

21. Lee, P.J., Brickell, E.F.: An observation on the security of McEliece's public-key cryptosystem. In: Barstow, D., et al. (eds.) EUROCRYPT 1988. LNCS, vol. 330, pp. 275–280. Springer, Heidelberg (1988). https://doi.org/10.1007/3-540-45961-8_25

22. Leon, J.S.: A probabilistic algorithm for computing minimum weights of large error-correcting codes. IEEE Trans. Inf. Theory **34**(5), 1354–1359 (1988)

23. Mangard, S., Oswald, E., Popp, T.: Power Analysis Attacks: Revealing the Secrets of Smart Cards. Advances in Information Security. Springer, Heidelberg (2007). ISBN 978-0-387-30857-9

24. Marr, B.: 6 practical examples of how quantum computing will change our world (2017). Forbes. https://www.forbes.com/sites/bernardmarr/2017/07/10/6-practical-examples-of-how-quantum-computing-will-change-our-world/

25. May, A., Meurer, A., Thomae, E.: Decoding random linear codes in $\tilde{\mathcal{O}}(2^{0.054n})$. In: Lee, D.H., Wang, X. (eds.) ASIACRYPT 2011. LNCS, vol. 7073, pp. 107–124. Springer, Heidelberg (2011). https://doi.org/10.1007/978-3-642-25385-0_6

26. May, A., Ozerov, I.: On Computing Nearest Neighbors with Applications to Decoding of Binary Linear Codes. In: Oswald, E., Fischlin, M. (eds.) EUROCRYPT 2015. LNCS, vol. 9056, pp. 203–228. Springer, Heidelberg (2015). https://doi.org/10.1007/978-3-662-46800-5_9

27. McEliece, R.J.: A public-key cryptosystem based on algebraic coding theory. In: DSN Progress Report 42–44, pp. 114–116 (1978)

28. Melchor, C.A., et al.: Hamming Quasi-Cyclic (HQC)—second round version, May 2020. http://pqc-hqc.org/doc/hqc-specification_2020-05-29.pdf

29. Nay, C.: IBM unveils world's first integrated quantum computing system for commercial use. IBM News Roomm (2019). https://newsroom.ibm.com/2019-01-08-IBM-Unveils-Worlds-First-Integrated-Quantum-Computing-System-for-Commercial-Use

30. Niederreiter, H.: Knapsack-type cryptosystems and algebraic coding theory. Probl. Control Inform. **15**, 19–34 (1986)

31. Prange, E.: The use of information sets in decoding cyclic codes. IRE Trans. Inf. Theory **8**(5), 5–9 (1962)

32. Ravi, P., Roy, S.S., Chattopadhyay, A., Bhasin, S.: Generic side-channel attacks on CCA-secure lattice-based PKE and KEMS. IACR Trans. Cryptogr. Hardware Embed. Syst. - TCHES **2020**(3), 307–335 (2020)

33. Rossi, M., Hamburg, M., Hutter, M., Marson, M.E.: A side-channel assisted cryptanalytic attack against QcBits. In: Fischer, W., Homma, N. (eds.) CHES 2017. LNCS, vol. 10529, pp. 3–23. Springer, Cham (2017). https://doi.org/10.1007/978-3-319-66787-4_1

34. Samardjiska, S., Santini, P., Persichetti, E., Banegas, G.: A reaction attack against cryptosystems based on LRPC codes. In: Schwabe, P., Thériault, N. (eds.) LATINCRYPT 2019. LNCS, vol. 11774, pp. 197–216. Springer, Cham (2019). https://doi.org/10.1007/978-3-030-30530-7_10

35. Shor, P.W.: Polynomial-time algorithms for prime factorization and discrete logarithms on a quantum computer. SIAM Rev. **41**(2), 303–332 (1999)

36. Shoufan, A., Strenzke, F., Molter, H.G., Stöttinger, M.: A timing attack against patterson algorithm in the McEliece PKC. In: Lee, D., Hong, S. (eds.) ICISC 2009. LNCS, vol. 5984, pp. 161–175. Springer, Heidelberg (2010). https://doi.org/10.1007/978-3-642-14423-3_12

37. Sidelnikov, V.M., Shestakov, S.O.: On insecurity of cryptosystems based on generalized Reed-Solomon codes. Discrete Math. Appl. **2**(4), 439–444 (1992)

38. Stebila, D., Mosca, M.: Open Quantum Safe Project, August 2020. https://github. com/open-quantum-safe/liboqs
39. Stern, J.: A method for finding codewords of small weight. In: Cohen, G., Wolfmann, J. (eds.) Coding Theory 1988. LNCS, vol. 388, pp. 106–113. Springer, Heidelberg (1989). https://doi.org/10.1007/BFb0019850
40. Taha, M., Eisenbarth, T.: Implementation attacks on post-quantum cryptographic schemes. Cryptology ePrint Archive, Report 2015/1083
41. Wang, W., Szefer, J., Niederhagen, R.: FPGA-based Niederreiter cryptosystem using binary Goppa codes. In: Lange, T., Steinwandt, R. (eds.) PQCrypto 2018. LNCS, vol. 10786, pp. 77–98. Springer, Cham (2018). https://doi.org/10.1007/978-3-319-79063-3_4
42. Welch, B.L.: The generalization of 'Student's' problem when several different population variances are involved. Biometrika **34**(1/2), 28–35 (1947)

Author Index

914   Author Index

Printed in the United States
By Bookmasters